The Handbook of Attitudes

THE HANDBOOK OF ATTITUDES

Edited by

Dolores Albarracín
University of Florida

Blair T. Johnson
University of Connecticut

Mark P. Zanna
University of Waterloo

 LAWRENCE ERLBAUM ASSOCIATES, PUBLISHERS
2005   Mahwah, New Jersey   London

Senior Editor:	Debra Riegert
Editorial Assistant:	Kerry Breen
Cover Design:	Kathryn Houghtaling Lacey
Textbook Production Manager:	Paul Smolenski
Full-Service Compositor:	TechBooks
Text and Cover Printer:	Hamilton Printing Company

This book was typeset in 10/12 pt. Times, Italic, Bold, Bold Italic.
The heads were typeset in Americana Bold, Americana Italic, and Americana Bold.

Lawrence Erlbaum Associates, Inc., Publishers
10 Industrial Avenue
Mahwah, New Jersey 07430
www.erlbaum.com

Library of Congress Cataloging-in-Publication Data

The handbook of attitudes / edited by Dolores Albarracin, Blair T. Johnson,
   Mark P. Zanna.
      p.   cm.
   Includes bibliographical references and index.
     ISBN 0-8058-4492-9 (case : alk. paper) – ISBN 0-8058-4493-7 (pbk. : alk. paper)
     1. Attitude (Psychology)   I. Albarracin, Dolores, 1965-   II. Johnson, Blair T.
   III. Zanna, Mark P.

   BF327.H36   2005
   152.4—dc22   2005001804

Printed in the United States of America
10 9 8 7 6 5 4 3 2 1

Contents

Preface   vii
List of Contributors   xi

I: INTRODUCTION AND MEASURES

1 Attitudes: Introduction and Scope   3
       Dolores Albarracín, Blair T. Johnson, Mark P. Zanna, & G. Tarcan Kumkale
2 The Measurement of Attitudes   21
       Jon A. Krosnick, Charles M. Judd, & Bernd Wittenbrink

II: THE MATRIX OF ATTITUDE-RELEVANT INFLUENCES

3   The Structure of Attitudes   79
        Leandre R. Fabrigar, Tara K. MacDonald, & Duane T. Wegener
4   The Origins and Structure of Behavior: Conceptualizing Behavior
        in Attitude Research   125
        James Jaccard & Hart Blanton
5   The Influence of Attitudes on Behavior   173
        Icek Ajzen & Martin Fishbein
6   The Influence of Behavior on Attitudes   223
        James M. Olson & Jeff Stone
7   Belief Formation, Organization, and Change: Cognitive and
        Motivational Influences   273
        Robert S. Wyer, Jr. & Dolores Albarracín
8   The Influence of Beliefs and Goals on Attitudes: Issues of Structure,
        Function, and Dynamics   323
        Arie W. Kruglanski & Wolfgang Stroebe
9   The Influence of Attitudes on Beliefs: Formation and Change   369
        Kerry L. Marsh & Harry M. Wallace
10 The Structure of Affect   397
        Ulrich Schimmack & Stephen L. Crites, Jr.
11 The Influence of Affect on Attitude   437
        Gerald L. Clore & Simone Schnall

III: INTEGRATIVE VIEWS ON ATTITUDES

12 Cognitive Processes in Attitude Formation and Change   493
        Duane T. Wegener & Donal E. Carlston
13 Implicit and Explicit Attitudes: Research, Challenges, and Theory   543
        John N. Bassili & Rick D. Brown

14   Individual Differences in Attitude Change   575
         Pablo Briñol & Richard E. Petty
15   Communication and Attitude Change: Causes, Processes, and Effects   617
         Blair T. Johnson, Gregory R. Maio, & Aaron Smith-McLallen
16   Social Influence in Attitudes and Attitude Change   671
         Radmila Prislin & Wendy Wood
17   Attitude Theory and Research: Intradisciplinary and
         Interdisciplinary Connections   707
         Victor Ottati, John Edwards, & Nathaniel D. Krumdick
18   Attitude Research in the 21st Century: The Current State of Knowledge   743
         Alice H. Eagly & Shelly Chaiken

Author Index   769
Subject Index   807

Preface

A recent search for the term *attitude* in the American Psychological Association's comprehensive index to psychological and related literature (PsycINFO) yielded 180,910 references. This impressive number certainly suggests that attitude research has come a long way since 1918, when Thomas and Snaniecki defined social psychology as the study of attitudes. William J. McGuire's 1985 chapter in the third edition of the *Handbook of Social Psychology* nicely documented the impressive growth of the psychology of attitudes and simultaneously stimulated many graduate students with its insightful framework of the cognitive processes that may interplay as people evaluate aspects of their worlds. Nearly 10 years later, in 1993, Alice H. Eagly and Shelly Chaiken published *The Psychology of Attitudes*, which represented the most detailed and comprehensive account ever written in this area. In the decade since then, and in part stimulated by Eagly and Chaiken's seminal volume, research concerning attitudes continued to appear at a considerable pace.

In light of the great productivity of attitude researchers, we were struck by the fact that there was no handbook for the field, despite the fact that over the last 2 decades valuable handbooks have appeared for nearly every other subdivision of social psychology, from social cognition to motivation to affect. Thus, the time seemed more than ripe for a comprehensive attempt at summarizing the tradition and for relying on the joint expertise of the researchers who study attitudes and attitude-related phenomena. The result is the current volume, the first handbook on the subject.

A plan emerged in March of 2001, after various conference calls, e-mails, and a meeting over coffee in Gainesville, Florida. The book would entail a detailed analysis of attitudes in relation to other important psychological constructs—particularly affect, beliefs, and behavior—as well as a more integrative section focused on processes, individual differences that relate to attitudes, communication, and social influence. We authored a prospectus and solicited reactions from Icek Ajzen, Alice H. Eagly, Martin Fishbein, Russell H. Fazio, Richard E. Petty, Jon A. Krosnick, Robert S. Wyer, Jr., and Wendy Wood; each provided feedback that refined the original plan. Feedback from numerous anonymous reviewers of the prospectus also enriched the plan for this book.

That fall, we sent invitations to authors, and obtained an overwhelmingly positive response. Not only did we find a group of top specialists who represent various countries and diverse theoretical backgrounds, but also had authors who agreed to collaborate with researchers with whom they had never worked in the past or with whom they had not worked in quite some time (Johnson, Maio, & Smith-McLallen; Kruglanski & Stroebe; Marsh & Wallace; Olson & Stone; Ottati, Edwards, & Krumdick; Prislin & Wood; Wegener & Carlston). To put it mildly, these factors made the editing process extremely interesting! Once we had the authors' commitments, we reviewed detailed outlines in preparation for an extraordinary meeting that took place prior to the 2002 meeting of the Society for Experimental Social Psychology in Columbus, Ohio, during which the contributors presented their plans and exchanged ideas. After 6 months the chapters arrived in a steady stream; we editors provided feedback and obtained outside reviews whenever possible. Now that we are at the end of this project, we realize that each of us has read each of these 18 chapters at least two times and that each of us has read some of these chapters three, four, or five times, which totals some 12 months of almost nonstop reading in the hope of producing the best possible book.

The book surveys classic and contemporary knowledge in the area of attitudes. It entails a process analysis of the phenomena of interest in the field and had the objective of presenting the material in a coherent fashion so as to allow students and researchers to appreciate what is known as well as the gaps that need to be filled. As the first chapter details, the organization involves three parts: one on definitions and methods, another on the relations of attitudes with beliefs, behavior, and affect, and a final one that integrates these relations into the broader areas of cognitive processes, communication and persuasion, social influence, and applications.

The structure of the book was designed to serve pedagogical objectives, thus allowing the book to be used for advanced courses on attitudes within the context of general psychology programs as well as marketing, political psychology, health behavior, communication, and other applied disciplines. In particular, we hope that the book will excite future students to conduct research in this fascinating area, providing them with a heuristic to learn and remember the field in a way that other books do not. We have learned a great deal about the field in the process of editing this volume and believe that readers will gain similar insights for many years to come.

We have organized the book in order to guide the reader through the complex relations involving attitudes, beliefs, behavior, and affect. There are chapters on the influence of beliefs on attitudes as well as of attitudes on beliefs. There are also chapters on the influence of attitudes on behavior and of behavior on attitudes, as well as of attitudes on affect. These chapters are preceded by a detailed analysis of the structure and formation of attitudes, beliefs, behavior, and affect. To our knowledge, these topics have never been thoroughly surveyed within the same volume before.

We could not be more appreciative of the writers' contributions to the book. Each set of authors faced the challenge of covering broad territory, which often extended well beyond their current interests. In order to produce a book that would have a long-lasting and significant impact, we encouraged every writer to avoid dwelling on the latest controversies in the field and to work from as unbiased a perspective as possible. We identified handbooks and handbook chapters with intellectual breadth and depth as our gold standard. It is our sincere hope that exercising this philosophy has created a book with which many different people can identify. In all cases, we have tried to instill an overarching point of view, and to some extent a contextualist standpoint (in McGuire's sense) that recognizes and respects the validity of various different approaches.

In an era when publishers routinely expect scholarly volumes to go to press far after the deadlines set in contract, the current volume nearly made it on time. We can only thank our contributors, whose love for attitude theory and research is nearly boundless. Indeed, the execution of this project has been remarkably smooth and even bumps in the road quickly become opportunities. In one case, an originally envisioned chapter on the influence of attitudes on affect creatively became an inquisitive chapter on implicit attitudes. Moreover, despite a few pessimistic predictions, all of our originally solicited authors completed their charges; none withdrew from the book. We owe them all a debt of gratitude for patiently and graciously suffering our feedback through multiple iterations—a feedback process that was far more thorough than is the norm for book chapters and perhaps even for other handbook chapters.

Finally, we would like to thank our associates at the University of Florida and the University of Connecticut, who provided invaluable feedback on the plan for this book, including Laura R. Glasman, G. Tarcan Kumkale, Kerry L. Marsh, Penny S. McNatt, Amy L. Mitchell,

Aaron Smith-McLallen, Harry M. Wallace, the participants in the Florida graduate seminar on attitudes and social cognition during the spring semesters of 2002 and 2004, and participants in the Connecticut graduate seminar on attitude organization and change in fall, 2002. We thank Gregory R. Maio, William R. McGuire, and David O. Sears, who graciously reviewed the prospectus for the publisher. Finally, we thank Debra Riegert and Larry Erlbaum for their efforts in publishing this book, Kristin Schatmeyer for managing the webpage through which we all interacted, Erica Pittman for editorial assistance, Pamela Lavallee, Cindy McLean, and Allecia Reid for clerical assistance, and Alice H. Eagly and Shelly Chaiken for the precious time they devoted to reading and reflecting on every chapter in this volume.

List of Contributors

Icek Ajzen
University of Massachusetts
  at Amherst

Dolores Albarracín
University of Florida

John N. Bassili
University of Toronto at Scarborough

Hart Blanton
University of North Carolina at
  Chapel Hill

Pablo Briñol
Universidad Autónoma de Madrid

Rick D. Brown
University of Florida

Donal E. Carlston
Purdue University

Shelly Chaiken
New York University

Gerald L. Clore
University of Virginia

Stephen L. Crites, Jr.
University of Texas, El Paso

Alice H. Eagly
Northwestern University

John Edwards
Loyola University, Chicago

Leandre R. Fabrigar
Queen's University

Martin Fishbein
University of Pennsylvania

James Jaccard
Florida International University

Blair T. Johnson
University of Connecticut

Charles M. Judd
University of Colorado

Jon A. Krosnick
Stanford University

Arie W. Kruglanski
University of Maryland

Nathaniel D. Krumdick
Loyola University, Chicago

G. Tarcan Kumkale
University of Florida

Tara K. MacDonald
Queen's University

Gregory R. Maio
Cardiff University

Kerry L. Marsh
University of Connecticut

James M. Olson
University of Western Ontario

Victor Ottati
Loyola University, Chicago

Richard E. Petty
Ohio State University

Radmila Prislin
San Diego State University

Ulrich Schimmack
University of Toronto at Mississauga

Simone Schnall
University of Virginia

Aaron Smith-McLallen
University of Connecticut

Jeff Stone
University of Arizona

Wolfgang Stroebe
University of Utrecht

Harry M. Wallace
Trinity University

Duane T. Wegener
Purdue University

Bernd Wittenbrink
University of Chicago

Wendy Wood
Duke University

Robert S. Wyer, Jr.
Hong Kong University of Science
    and Technology

Mark P. Zanna
University of Waterloo

The Handbook of Attitudes

I

Introduction and Measures

1

Attitudes: Introduction and Scope

Dolores Albarracín
University of Florida

Mark P. Zanna
University of Waterloo

Blair T. Johnson
University of Connecticut

G. Tarcan Kumkale
University of Florida

ATTITUDES: DEFINITIONS, PROCESSES, AND THEORIES

Human beings react to their environments in an evaluative fashion. They love and protect their kin and strive to maintain positive evaluations of themselves as well as those around them. They evaluate others' attractiveness. They also evaluate and select leaders, decide how to spend their resources, and plan for the futures they envision. Such covert and overt actions often involve judgments about whether objects, events, oneself, and others are favorable or unfavorable, likeable or unlikeable, good or bad. Scholars who study attitudes investigate factors involved in these evaluations: how they are formed, changed, represented in memory, and translated into cognitions, motivations, and actions.

In this introductory chapter, we first discuss the nature of attitudes and then the organization of this handbook. Scholars have investigated many different constructs related to attitudes using many different theoretical frameworks and methods. The constructs that investigators have studied often concern affect, beliefs, and (overt) behaviors. *Affect* entails the feelings that people experience and may or may not concern a particular object or event (Berkowitz, 2000). *Beliefs* are cognitions about the probability that an object or event is associated with a given attribute (Fishbein & Ajzen, 1975). *Behaviors* are typically defined as the overt actions of an individual. Each of these individual phenomena is central to the dynamic forces that form and transform existing attitudes. Similarly, attitudes have a reciprocal impact on affects, beliefs, and behaviors. It is this matrix of reciprocal attitudinal forces that constitutes a major portion of this handbook.

Before providing a more extensive introduction to the matrix of reciprocal attitudinal relations and the rationale for its use, we first discuss definitions of the attitude concept itself and distinguish attitudes from affects, beliefs, and behaviors. We continue by explaining why attitudes are not necessarily stable entities. We then discuss the rationale for the volume's organization and introduce each chapter. The organization of the volume is centered around basic phenomena that attitudes scholars consider conventional relations rather than on a particular singular theoretical viewpoint. Nonetheless, theories play a central role within each chapter of this volume.

THE NATURE OF ATTITUDES

Defining Attitude

A handbook is a collective enterprise. Consequently, reaching definitions that satisfy all contributors and readers is as difficult as it is indispensable. It is difficult because hundreds of definitions exist. It is indispensable because, to develop a handbook of attitudes, contributors must know the range of phenomena they might cover and precisely conceptualize the processes at stake. Eagly and Chaiken (1993) provided what may be the most conventional contemporary definition; specifically, an *"attitude is a psychological tendency that is expressed by evaluating a particular entity with some degree of favor or disfavor"* (p. 1, emphasis in original). The contributors to the current volume have embraced evaluative aspects as central to the topic, as have prominent other treatises on the subject (e.g., Eagly & Chaiken, 1998; Zanna & Rempel, 1988). Although definitions may have varied somewhat across time, if one inspects how scholars have operationalized the concept of attitude across the field's history, evaluative aspects have always played a prominent role (e.g., Bogardus, 1931; Fishbein & Ajzen, 1975; Hovland, Janis, & Kelley, 1953; Katz, 1960; Osgood, Suci, & Tannenbaum, 1957; Petty & Cacioppo, 1981, 1986; Petty & Wegener, 1998; Sherif & Hovland, 1961; Thurstone, 1928).

The study of attitudes includes both the judgments that individuals form online (Schwarz & Bohner, 2001) as well as the evaluative representations in memory (Fazio, 1986). If the term *attitude* were reserved only to refer to stable structures in memory, excluded would be all the work in which researchers verify only temporary changes on an attitude scale, as well as an impressive amount of research on context effects in the study of attitudes. Moreover, conceptualizing attitudes as *memories* but not *judgments* could possibly exclude the literature on attitude formation and change, because these literatures concern the observation of judgmental outcomes much more often than they involve measures of memory. Thus, attitudes can be judgments, memories, or both.

A good definition of a construct must not only be general but also sufficiently discriminating. After all, there are multiple levels of generality and almost all definitions could be represented at an even more abstract level. Consider the definition of beliefs as the perceived likelihood that an attribute is associated with an object (e.g., Fishbein, 1963). For instance, I may believe that Coca-Cola is sweet or that my country is now in a state of military alert. An examination of the deep structure of attitudes makes it clear that one could also define attitudes as beliefs (see Kruglanski & Stroebe, this volume; Wyer & Albarracín, this volume). Thus, a favorable attitude toward social psychology might be defined as the perceived probability that the object *social psychology* is positive or negative (Wyer, 1974).

Because attitudes and beliefs are at some level both categorizations, one could argue that treating them as indistinct would make for a more compact definition. Indeed, compactness was one of our explicit objectives in initiating this handbook. Nonetheless, we also had the conflicting objective to reach sufficiently discriminating definitions so that one could distinguish between categories that have different properties and, often, different outcomes. In this fashion, the concepts may appear to differ phenomenologically with some consensus. For instance, although a *belief* and an *attitude* are both categorizations, and all categorizations can be conceptualized as a probability assignment, Eagly and Chaiken (1993) noted that at least some beliefs can be verified or falsified with external, objective criteria, whereas attitudes have more difficulty facing such criteria. For instance, the belief that water freezes at 0 degrees Celsius can be verified by agreement among different individuals. Sampling individuals from different groups should have little influence on the extent to which this belief is verified in light of external evidence. Yet few attitudes could withstand the same intersubjective validation. Most social attitudes, such as political, aesthetic, or consumer preferences, are largely variable across judges. A prominent exception is people's judgments of targets' physical attractiveness, which typically show very high reliability across judges (e.g., Bersheid & Walster, 1974). Hence, some attitudes will exhibit a high degree of social consensus, which some might interpret as representing social reality. It is important to note that even among the most agreed-upon attitudes we would find notable exceptions. To take another example, although most human beings are afraid of snakes or apprehensive about heights, people who have pet snakes enjoy them as much as skydivers are fond of heights.

Similarly, attitudes can be distinguished from affective reactions in that affective reactions are not necessarily tied to a particular entity. Of course, it is common to equate how one feels about an object with one's evaluation of it. Yet, there are several reasons to distinguish attitudes from affect per se. Perhaps the most important one is that affect is often a powerful basis for attitudes (see Wyer & Srull, 1989). Defining these two concepts as identical thus creates logical complications that we and the other contributors hoped to avoid (see Schimmack & Crites, this volume). In addition, it appears that affect and evaluation are distinct in their actual phenomenology. For example, one might experience a pleasant sensory affect (see Schimmack & Crites, this volume) if one walks by a bakery while on a diet, yet still feel apprehensive toward cookies because of their unfortunate fattening side effects. This example, and many similar ones that attitudinal ambivalence scholars have long studied (see Fabrigar, MacDonald, & Wegener, this volume) would be difficult to conceptualize if one equated attitudes and affect.

Similarly, several positions have emerged that explicate the components of attitudes. Most notably, scholars have classified different types of attitude responses as well as different types of information that can serve as bases for attitudes. For instance, Katz and Stotland (1959) proposed that attitudes encompass cognitive, affective, and behavioral components. Eagly and Chaiken's (1993, 1998) more contemporary analyses of this literature concluded that these components best represent the types of responses that allow researchers to diagnose attitudes. Moreover, people form attitudes on the basis of their cognitive, affective, and behavioral responses to an entity (Eagly & Chaiken, 1993, 1998; Zanna & Rempel, 1988). Regardless of the origins of attitudes, the term *attitudes* is reserved for evaluative tendencies, which can both be inferred from and have an influence on beliefs, affect, and overt behavior. Treating attitudes in a similar fashion, the contributors to this volume have analyzed the mutual relations of these evaluations with beliefs, affect, and behavior. Thus, affect, beliefs, and behaviors are seen as interacting with attitudes rather than as being their parts.

Psychologically Positioning Attitudes: Why Attitudes Need Not Be Stable

There is another important distinction in defining attitudinal phenomena that concerns the level or psychological location of the mental representation of the attitude. Specifically, attitudes can be represented in permanent memory or manifest themselves as more temporary states of consciousness. For instance, one may retrieve a well-defined memory of liking strawberry ice cream whenever ice cream becomes relevant. Yet, the judgment that one likes ice cream at one particular point is not identical to the representation stored in one's memory. Instead, the judgment represents the translation or instantiation of the memory into a conscious evaluation of ice cream at that particular point. Although the current judgment may derive directly from one's

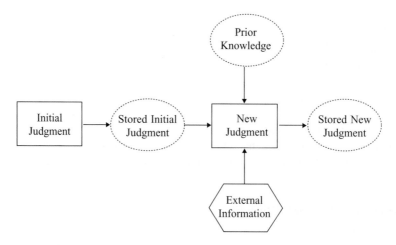

FIG 1.1.   Attitudes depicted as judgments influenced by external information, the memory of past judgments, prior knowledge, and stored new judgments.

memory of a prior judgment, people often form judgments on the basis of information that is temporarily available to them because the information is externally salient and/or momentarily accessible in memory (see, e.g., Higgins, 1996). To this extent, people's evaluations of an object can be represented in permanent memory or as judgments that individuals compute in an online fashion at the time the evaluation becomes relevant. Therefore, although we differentiate attitudes from affect, beliefs, and behavior, our definition of attitudes is inclusive enough to encompass both stable, memory-based evaluations, and online, temporarily constructed ones.

Figure 1.1 depicts the possibility that people's initial judgment about an object may be stored for later use. The representation of that evaluative judgment in permanent memory, however, is distinct from the initial judgment performed online and from later judgments that one can possibly form after recalling the initial judgment. One kind of representation exists in a latent, stored fashion (see dotted contours), even when people are currently unaware of it (see Krosnick, Judd, & Wittenbrink, this volume). The other type of representation, the judgment, only exists in consciousness or working memory (solid contours), either after retrieving an old judgment or computing a new one on the basis of a prior judgment or other information that is accessible in memory or externally supplied.

ORGANIZATION OF THE HANDBOOK OF ATTITUDES

The chapters in this handbook clearly show that the attitudes field is vast and diverse on both methodological and conceptual grounds, accumulating over 80-plus years. The field is concerned with a variety of phenomena that occur as a result of the interaction between individuals and the society in which they live. These phenomena take place in the hearts and minds of the individual members of a society, but also across interpersonal communications and in the context of cultural and social representations that transcend the individual. For example, people's attitudes are generally the result both of relatively long-term processes such as socialization and of relatively short-term exposures to information in the environment. Some attitudes may even be inherited (e.g., Tesser, 1993). These inputs undergo sequential transformations that give way to individual and social affective reactions, beliefs, attitudes, and overt actions. These cognitions and behaviors acquire a life of their own and interact dynamically, generating and receiving influences in a mutual, ever-changing cycle. This dynamic has different degrees of consciousness, going from largely deliberate processes to subtle mechanisms of control that may lie completely outside of awareness.

Theories remain important in contemporary studies of attitude, perhaps even more important than they have been in the past. Yet because the numerous attitudes theories do not necessarily make the same predictions about attitudinal phenomena nor even concern the same phenomena and because there is no one theory with hegemony over the field, it would be misleading to use any single theoretical approach to organize all knowledge about the topic. Instead, the contributors to the current volume have kept as a distinct philosophy a fair treatment of the theoretical diversity relevant to the attitudinal phenomenon under consideration.

Methodological Considerations

Regardless of which theories scholars use to explore attitudinal phenomena, central to the endeavor is the use of scientific methods to provide observations that may be confirmed and extended by other scholars. Where relevant, each of the chapters in this volume considers methods of import. Most centered on methodological aspects is Jon Krosnick, Charles Judd, and Bernd Wittenbrink's chapter, which thoroughly reviews classic and contemporary measurement methods in the area of attitudes, including an insightful analysis of the advantages and disadvantages of each procedure. The chapter is unique in its concentration on the processes by which attitudes are expressed. Exemplifying this focus is their framework describing the cognitive processes that generate an attitudinal evaluation as well as other response tendencies. Krosnick and colleagues use this framework to derive various important recommendations for the optimal measurement of attitudes. Following this chapter are a series of chapters analyzing reciprocal causal relations of attitudes with affects, beliefs, and behaviors, and the structural features of each of these four phenomena. We introduce these chapters next, before introducing the concluding series of chapters that systematically describe ways in which the phenomena in earlier chapters can be integrated.

Chapters on Individual Attitudinal Phenomena—A *Matrix* of Attitude Relations

A central organizing principle of the handbook is the matrix depicted in Table 1.1, which includes general *causes* and *effects* relevant to attitudes. Similar to a correlation matrix, the cells off the diagonal are heterocorrelations and on the diagonal are autocorrelations. Thus, the different cells in Table 1.1 depict possible causal influences of (a) attitudes on affective reactions, beliefs, and behavior, (b) behavior on affective reactions, beliefs, and attitudes, (c) beliefs on affective reactions, attitudes, and behavior, and (d) affective reactions on beliefs, attitudes, and behavior. The upper and lower triangles of the matrix are mirror images of each other, reversing the direction of the causal relation. Most of these influences are described in the body of this handbook; others receive indirect coverage. In addition, the diagonal of the matrix comprises the structure of affective reactions, beliefs, attitudes, and behavior, or in other words, the way in which each psychological component is organized. These chapters on structure correspond to the diagonal cells in the matrix and address the way each psychological component is organized as well as the factors that influence the entire group of components. Table 1.1 also summarizes topics relevant to the matrix cells.

The heart of the handbook is a series of chapters that focus sequentially on the processes involving the reciprocal relations of affect, beliefs, and behaviors with attitudes, and the structure of each component. Goals are often considered simultaneously with beliefs, consistent with

TABLE 1.1

A Matrix of Psychological Attitude-Relevant Influences; Entries on the Diagonal Consider the Structure of the Variable in the Headings

	Variable			
	Attitudes	*Behavior*	*Beliefs*	*Affect (feelings)*
Attitudes	Chapter 3 *The Structure of Attitudes* – Relations among attitude structure, strength, and function – Types of attitude-structure (intra-attitudinal vs. inter-attitudinal structure and ideology) – Properties of attitude structure and their impact on attitude stability, resistance to change, attitude-behavior consistency, and information processing – Processes underlying the role of structure in judgment making and attitude stability	Chapter 5 *The Influence of Attitudes on Behavior* – Attitude-behavior relationship and its moderators – Selective attention and exposure – Distal and immediate predictors of behavior – Multidimensionality of attitudes and evaluative inconsistence – Prediction of behavior from implicit and explicit attitudes – Attitude-behavior theories – Past behavior and habit – Changing behavior through persuasion	Chapter 9 *The Influence of Attitudes on Beliefs* – Expectancy-value models – Social-judgment theory – Motivated reasoning – Wishful thinking – Thought introspection and attitude polarization – Inferring beliefs from attitudes (congruency) – Attitude-belief effects – Biased perception, processing, retrieval, and attitude-induced distortion in beliefs – Cognitive consistency, emergence of thought systems	*The Influence of Attitudes on Affect*
Behavior	Chapter 6 *The Influence of Behavior on Attitudes* – Cognitive dissonance, biased scanning, role-playing, self-perception, reactance, impression management, self-affirmation, selective exposure, automaticity, reasoned and automatic influences – The role of individual difference (e.g., preference for consistency, attributional complexity) – Paradigms and theories of cognitive dissonance	Chapter 4 *The Origins and Structure of Behavior* – Types and structure of behavior – Relationship between past behavior (habit), current behavior, and future behavior – Prediction vs. postdiction of behavior – Methodological and data-analytic issues in research on behavior – Distal and proximal determinants of behavior	*The Influence of Behavior on Beliefs*	*The Influence of Behavior on Affect*

	Attitudes	Behavior	Beliefs	Affect
Beliefs	Chapter 8 *The Influence of Beliefs on Attitudes* – Relations among attitudes, beliefs, and goals in the context of attitude structure, functions, and dynamics – Attitudes, goals, and beliefs as knowledge structures – Belief-based models of attitudes – Ambivalence, dimensionality, mere exposure, conditioning, conformity – Current theorizing on persuasion – Majority and minority influence – Motivated reasoning	*The Influence of Beliefs on Behavior*	Chapter 7 *The Structure of Beliefs* – Definition, structure, acquisition, and change of beliefs – Theories of belief organization and change – Computation and motivational processes from which beliefs emerge – Inference, comprehension, and memory processes in belief formation and change – Heuristic and motivational bases of belief formation and change	*The Influence of Beliefs on Affect*
Affect (feelings)	Chapter 11 *The Influence of Affect on Attitudes* – The role of affect in attitude formation and persuasion – Dimensions of affective experience (valence and arousal) and attitudes – Mood effects on judgment, affect-as-information, affect-as-evidence – Role of emotion and mood in styles of thinking or processing – Unconscious affective influences on attitudes – Affect and the use of category information (stereotyping) – Affect and evolutionary perspectives	*The Influence of Affect on Behavior*	*The Influence of Affect on Beliefs*	Chapter 10 *The Structure of Affect* – Operationalization and conceptualization of affect in attitude research – Unconscious and conscious affective experiences – Types of affective experiences and their origins and implications for attitudes – Frequency, intensity, and duration of affective experiences – Conditioning, mere-exposure, mood-as-information – Representation of affect in memory – Recent findings in affective neuroscience

Note: Each cell off the diagonal refers to a causal combination of the attitudes, behavior, beliefs, and affect (feelings) variables. Shaded cells indicate phenomena with only indirect coverage in this handbook.

trends in recent research. As relevant, each set of authors discuss theories for their attitudinal phenomena. The dimensions that organize the handbook and the specific interactions they generate have charted some new territory. For example, as we describe in the following sections, attitude researchers have conceptualized the interrelations among beliefs, affect, attitudes, and behavior. Yet researchers have rarely considered the degree to which an extant attitude biases subsequent affective reactions. Therefore, the challenge of the handbook was sometimes to identify research outside of the writers' domain, extrapolate findings, generate a relatively complete line of facts and hypotheses about the issues at stake, and encourage future research (see, e.g., Marsh & Wallace, this volume). Research conducted in other fields (e.g., political behavior, intergroup relationships, mental health) and research not surveyed in prior books of attitudes was also useful in achieving this synthesis (see, e.g., Ottati, Edwards, & Krumdick, this volume).

Chapter 3. The Structure of Attitudes (Fabrigar, MacDonald, & Wegener). As we previously discussed, attitudes impute some degree of favor or disfavor to an entity (Eagly & Chaiken, 1993). They are sometimes relatively isolated from other representations and other times tightly connected with other attitudes forming an ideology. There are already wonderful reviews of attitude structure in the literature (see Eagly & Chaiken, 1993, 1998), but Leandre Fabrigar, Tara MacDonald, and Duane Wegener's chapter concentrates on the specific structure of attitudes (Fazio, 1986; Judd & Kulik, 1980; Kerlinger, 1984; Ostrom, 1989; Sherif & Hovland, 1961) and its properties, including strength, accessibility, importance, and confidence. Finally, this chapter addresses attitude complexity, general principles of change in attitude structure, and awareness of attitude structure.

Chapter 4. The Origins and Structure of Behavior: Conceptualizing Behavior in Attitude Research (Jaccard & Blanton). As James Jaccard and Hart Blanton review, the field of attitudes is particularly fascinating in recent years because it attempts to understand behavior outside of awareness as well as conscious and goal-directed behavior (see, e.g., Bargh, 1997; Vallacher & Wegner, 1985; Wegner, 1994). Despite the current interest in behavior, there are still limitations to our understanding of behavioral processes. For example, how many behaviors compose the act of smoking? What is the structure of behaviors, and how do the perception and recall of behaviors operate (see, e.g., Nisbett & Borgida, 1975; Schank & Abelson, 1977)? How do people determine that they consistently engage in a behavior? When people determine that they have performed a behavior, do they use habitual behavior as information, or do they simply use past behaviors that are salient at a given time?

Chapter 5. The Influence of Attitudes on Behavior (Ajzen & Fishbein). It seems obvious that people's attitudes are likely to orient their behavior in the future (Allport, 1935; but see LaPiere, 1934; Wicker, 1969). If one likes a given brand of coffee, one should then be more likely to select that brand over others. The issues surrounding the relation between attitudes and behavior are, however, more complex. As Icek Ajzen and Martin Fishbein review, over the years, researchers have identified numerous factors that moderate the size of the attitude–behavior association, including such factors as prior experience, confidence, accessibility, and attitude change. In addition, an effort to further theorize the mechanisms involved in the attitudinal control of behavior seems desirable. Finally, the attitude–behavior relation includes attention and exposure to information, such as search strategies that may sometimes be directed by people's preferences (Frey, 1986).

The field has known for some time that people's attitudes and intentions serve as a basis for the behaviors they manifest (see Dulany, 1968; Fishbein & Ajzen, 1975). In addition, unconscious attitudes may have the same effects depending on the circumstances in which they are activated (Bargh, 1997; Wilson, Lindsey, & Schooler, 2000). Both conscious and nonconscious attitudes are likely to guide behavior provided external factors allow for implementation of those actions. Self-efficacy and control beliefs may have similar effects, both because of their motivational effects and as reflections of environmental obstacles and facilitators (Ajzen, 1991). In addition, people's self-serving goals are important. For example, people's goals may create a barrier between their attitudes and behaviors, as when individuals privately disagree with a given advocacy but publicly comply in order to save face (see, e.g., Kelman, 1961; Nail, 1986).

Chapter 6. The Influence of Behavior on Attitudes (Olson & Stone).   How do people form attitudes about their past or imagined behaviors? Are these attitudes formed by associations, as Ajzen and Fishbein (2000) maintained? Or are they the result of more reasoned observations about the effects of their actions (see e.g., Zanna & Cooper, 1974)? As James Olson and Jeff Stone's chapter reveals, there is extensive research on how the actions that people take influence their rationalizations of these attitudes. For example, the theory of cognitive dissonance (Festinger, 1957) maintains that people who become aware that they have behaved in a way that conflicts with their beliefs rationalize their behavior by generating attitudes in support of the behavior. In addition, the attitudes that individuals generate on the basis of their past behavior may sometimes be the result of more passive mechanisms. Thus, Janis and King (1954) postulated that people who engage in a behavior can use that behavior as a basis for a memory search. Consequently, they are likely to retrieve prior beliefs that are consistent with their behavior, and these beliefs influence the attitudes (Albarracín & Wyer, 2000).

Furthermore, self-perception theory (Bem, 1965, 1972) postulates that when individuals need to report an attitude, they often infer it from the implications of a past behavior that happens to be salient to them at the time. Yet, people may not reach this conclusion if they feel that they were forced to perform the behavior (Brehm, 1966). Other possible effects of past behavior are worth considering. For example, attention to a past behavior may increase the accessibility of a strongly held attitude with which this behavior is associated (see Fazio, 1986, 1990). Thus, both reasoned and automatic mechanisms may underlie the influence of behavior on attitudes.

Chapter 7. Beliefs Formation, Organization, and Change: Cognitive and Motivational Influences (Wyer & Albarracín).   Beliefs are cognitions about the probability that an object or event is associated with an attribute (Fishbein & Ajzen, 1975). As Robert Wyer and Dolores Albarracín review in their chapter, the structure and formation of beliefs have been addressed over the course of several decades by various researchers, including Asch (1952, 1956), Kelley (1967), McGuire (1968) and Sherif (1935). Other theories have analyzed the organization of knowledge and beliefs in memory, although the storage of beliefs as such may be more rare than it seems (Wyer & Radvansky, 1999). Abelson (1959) and McGuire (1964) have analyzed how conflict among beliefs can be reconciled and how conflict sometimes induces the persistence of one's beliefs over time. Of course, this chapter addresses various other questions as well, such as: What is the narrative structure of beliefs and implicit theories? How do beliefs change? (see, e.g., Heider, 1946)? What is the role of statistical reasoning and biases in belief formation (see Nisbett, Krantz, Jepson, & Kunda, 1983; Ross, Greene, & House, 1977; Tversky & Kahneman, 1973)? And, how do goals and motivational processes influence beliefs?

Chapter 8. The Influence of Beliefs and Goals on Attitudes: Issues of Structure, Function, and Dynamics (Kruglanski & Stroebe).   Following other expectancy-value analyses (e.g., Carlson, 1956; Peak, 1955), Fishbein and Ajzen's (1975; see also Anderson, 1981) theory of reasoned action asserts that the attitude toward the behavior is a function of subjectively weighting the evaluative implications of each possible outcome i of the behavior ($e_i, i = 1, \ldots, n$) by the belief that this outcome i will occur ($b_i, i = 1, \ldots, n$), and then summing these weighted evaluations. Similarly, extrapolating Greenwald's (1968) cognitive-response framework, Petty and Cacioppo (1986) also argued that thoughts about an issue can influence people's attitudes, provided that they have the ability and motivation to think about the issues being considered. Other theories have elaborated on the way in which different kinds of beliefs influence attitudes. For example, Deutsch and Gerard (1955) argued that people may form positive attitudes about an issue because they are convinced that there is evidence in support of the issue or as a result of changes in normative beliefs.

In this chapter, Arie Kruglanski and Wolfgang Stroebe use attitude *structure*, *function*, and *dynamics* to examine social psychological research on the influences of beliefs and goals on attitudes. According to Kruglanski and Stroebe, attitude structure, functions, and dynamics have typically been treated as separate and as though they are concerned with rather different issues. Given that attitudes, goals, and beliefs are to some extent knowledge structures, their functions and dynamics are also isomorphic. In this context, the authors review such diverse past and contemporary work as expectancy–value models, information integration theory, probabilogical models, mere exposure and conditioning phenomena, the elaboration likelihood model, and the unimodel.

Chapter 9. The Influence of Attitudes on Beliefs: Formation and Change (Marsh & Wallace).   Expectancy–value models assert that beliefs and the evaluations that are associated with them are the informational basis for attitudes (Carlson, 1956). Yet, plenty of other work highlights the reciprocal influences of attitudes on beliefs, as Kerry Marsh and Harry Wallace review in this chapter. For example, McGuire (1960, 1990) has long argued that people often believe that positive events are likely to happen and negative events are unlikely to take place, and Rosenberg (1956) demonstrated that changing the value of an event can alter the subjective probability of that event. There is also fascinating evidence of the effects of justifying attitudes on the generation of beliefs. For instance, Wilson and his colleagues (see e.g., Wilson, Dunn, Kraft & Lisle, 1989) argued that, when people are first asked to think about reasons for liking or disliking an object, they generate criteria that seem plausible and easy to articulate and then change their attitudes to make them consistent with these reasons. Similarly, Tesser (1978) has reported that thinking about an issue generally yields a polarization of attitudes toward that issue. Nonetheless, after the passage of some time, people may return to the original basis for their attitudes and regret decisions guided by their reason-based attitudes (Wilson & Hodges, 1992; Wilson & Schooler, 1991).

Traditionally, attitudinal models focused on the effects of beliefs on attitudes (see Kruglanski & Stroebe, this volume). Consequently, much less is known about the causal relation linking attitudes to beliefs. Nonetheless, Marsh and Wallace convincingly demonstrate that this part of the equation deserves more attention. In general, attitudes exert biasing effects on beliefs, such that people accept or revise their beliefs about attributes of the attitudinal object to make them congenial with their attitudes. These biases are pervasive and obey both cognitive and motivational principles. Marsh and Wallace close their chapter with speculation about the conditions that strengthen or weaken attitude–belief congruence effects.

Chapter 10. The Structure of Affect (Schimmack & Crites).   Without a doubt, people experience affect and this experience guides their cognitions, attitudes, and behavior, as Ulrich Schimmack and Stephen Crites review in their chapter. *Affect* concerns the feelings that people experience and may or may not concern a particular object or event (Berkowitz, 2000). Affect is presumably organized along dimensions of arousal and valence (Watson &

Tellegen, 1985), although this conceptualization is not without controversy. For example, an important question in relation to the structure of affect is whether positive and negative affect are two poles of the same construct or, instead, orthogonal dimensions. Furthermore, to what extent is it necessary to distinguish among different emotions to understand attitudes? How is affect represented in memory? How does affect change over time? How can we induce affective change over time? How and when do people become aware of their affective experience?

Chapter 11. The Influence of Affect on Attitudes (Clore & Schnall). People's responses to the affect they experience are both reflex-like and voluntary, as Gerald Clore and Simone Schnall examine in this chapter. For example, sensory inputs like taste or exposure to heights can trigger visceral reactions, and these reactions can automatically induce avoidance. Many of these hard-wired responses are the result of evolutionary influences. In addition, affect arising from any reaction to the environment, including mere exposure to an attitude object (Zajonc, 1968), can influence attitudes. In this regard, Schwarz and Clore (1983) postulated that people are inclined to misattribute their mood states to the object they are asked to judge. As a consequence of this misattribution, people rely on a how-do-I-feel-about-it heuristic to infer their attitudes toward the other persons, things, and events they encounter. There are, however, other mechanisms that may underlie the influences of one's affective reactions on one's attitudes (see, e.g., Festinger, 1957; Forgas, 1995; Hovland et al., 1953; Kaplan & Anderson, 1973). For example, Hildum and Brown (1956; see also Insko, 1965) were able to condition people to form positive attitudes toward an issue when the interviewer's nonverbal reactions were positive, and negative attitudes when the interviewer's subtle feedback was negative. Research on the potential mechanisms of this effect has accumulated over the years, suggesting that at least some of these influences do occur outside of awareness. As the chapter describes, however, the role of awareness in this domain remains controversial. Individuals may scrutinize information more carefully when they experience negative affect than when they experience positive affect (Schwarz & Clore, 1996; Worth & Mackie, 1987), an issue that this chapter also examines.

Integrative Chapters on Attitudinal Phenomena

The matrix chapters examine with great detail a particular attitudinal phenomenon. However, many theories of attitudes address general principles that apply to a variety of pairs of variables at a time and thus may appear in a variety of cells within the matrix. For example, self-perception (Bem, 1965, 1972) and affect-as-information (Schwarz & Clore, 1983, 1996) mechanisms were initially linked to attitudes but also apply to beliefs. Similarly, Wyer and Srull (1989) or Fazio (1986) have used associative network models to represent the structure of beliefs *and* attitudes. Similar conceptualizations could be used to understand more complex arrays of affect, beliefs, attitudes, and behavior.

Other such principles include conditioning, cognitive consistency, drive reduction, and incentives. These ideas cut across most cells of the matrix as they are relevant to all issues of structure and relations involving affect, beliefs, attitudes, and behavior (see Johnson, Maio, & Smith-McLallen, this volume; Ottati et al., this volume; Wegener & Carlston, this volume). More recent ideas about parallel distributed processing (Carlston & Smith, 1996; Smith, 1996, 1998) may also explicate a variety of the relations represented in the matrix. To this extent, Bassili and Brown's chapter in this volume serves to highlight the degree to which these distributed perspectives can contribute to our understanding of implicit phenomena and attitude stability or instability. Similarly, the theories of reasoned action and planned behavior (Ajzen & Fishbein, 1980; Ajzen, 1991) postulate influences that are relevant to various associations among beliefs, attitudes, and behavior and also to various domains (see Johnson et al., this volume; Kruglanski & Stroebe, this volume; Ottati et al., this volume; Prislin & Wood, this volume). Other such models include McGuire and McGuire's (1991) theory of thought systems, which describes the complex relations among probability and desirability judgments, as well as the elaboration likelihood (Petty & Cacioppo, 1986) and the heuristic systematic models (Chaiken, 1980; Chaiken, Liberman, & Eagly, 1989), which describe effects of beliefs on attitudes (e.g., *central route*; systematic and heuristic processing) and of affect or behavior on attitudes (*peripheral route*; see Briñol & Petty, this volume; Fabrigar et al., this volume). In a similar vein, Fazio (1990) maintained that either elaborative or nonelaborative processes may trigger behavior depending on the extent to which people think about their behavior at a given time and the degree of behavior automaticity (see also Ouellette & Wood, 1998, and Jaccard & Blanton, this volume). This line of theorizing has been extremely influential in recent decades, as the chapter by Wegener and Carlston reveals across several domains. Finally, various conceptualizations that have emerged in the last decade (Albarracín, 2002; Albarracín, Wallace, & Glasman, 2004; Kruglanski & Thompson, 1999; Petty, Briñol, & Tormala, 2002) promise to illuminate topics that cut across this book.

Chapter 12: Cognitive Processes in Attitude Formation and Change (Wegener & Carlston). An understanding of cognitive processes underlies theorizing about attitudes. Duane Wegener and Donal Carlston discuss these following the notion of *elaboration continuum*, which serves to organize contemporary models of persuasion including: the elaboration likelihood model (Petty & Cacioppo, 1986), heuristic-systematic model (Chaiken, Liberman, & Eagly, 1989), and the unimodel (Kruglanski & Thompson, 1999). The chapter also reviews recent developments regarding longstanding questions such as "how do people make attitudinal judgments?" and "how are evaluative judgments represented in memory?"

Chapter 13: Implicit and Explicit Attitudes: Research, Challenges, and Theory (Bassili & Brown). Most research on attitudes has addressed people's explicit attitudes, defined as self-reports. Recent research, however, has revealed that people's thoughts and behaviors depend on implicit psychological processes (for a review, see Greenwald & Banaji, 1995). Implicit attitudes are typically defined as automatically activated evaluations with unknown origins (Wilson, Lindsey, & Schooler, 2000). In their chapter, John Bassili and Rick Brown identify a need for theoretical reconciliation between implicit and explicit modes of attitude experience and expression. In response to this challenge, they first examine current theories of attitudes and then introduce a potentiated recruitment model as an integrative framework to reconcile prior empirical discrepancies.

Chapter 14: Individual Differences in Attitude Change (Briñol & Petty). No matter how much attitude and attitude components interrelate (Table 1.1), there are still many other individual differences that may influence attitudes. For example, the need for cognition (Cacioppo, Petty, Feinstein, & Jarvis, 1996; Cacioppo, Petty, Kao, & Rodriguez, 1986) determines the extent to which individuals analyze information in an effortful fashion. People who score high in this trait form attitudes on the basis of their beliefs about the information validity to a greater extent than individuals with low need-for-cognition scores. Similarly, Jarvis and Petty (1996) found that people's chronic tendencies to evaluate information predict attitude strength. The need to evaluate as well as dogmatism (Rokeach, 1954) and the need for closure (Webster & Kruglanski, 1994) may influence other structural properties of attitudes as well. For example, dogmatism concerns the extent to which people make clear-cut distinctions between beliefs and disbeliefs, which in turn refers to the polarization and complexity of the attitude structure. In any event, Pablo Briñol and Richard Petty's chapter considers personality, cognitive style, and demographic factors that fall under the motives of knowledge seeking, consistency, self-worth, and social approval. These four motives cut across almost all domains of social psychology, including the study of the self, identity, and social cognition. Briñol and Petty first describe these core motives and then discuss the relationship between motives and attitude change processes and, in conclusion, their implications for attitude strength.

Chapter 15: Communication and Attitude Change: Causes, Processes, and Effects (Johnson, Maio, & Smith-McLallen).   For many decades, researchers of persuasion have amassed a great deal of knowledge about the impact of persuasive communications on the attitudes of recipients. To the extent that communication has been one of the main paradigms in the study of attitude change, this research is covered in the context of chapters 3 to 11. In chapter 15, Blair Johnson, Greg Maio, and Aaron Smith-McLallen depict main points cutting across the different cells of the matrix and describe current and historical trends in communication and persuasion research. In line with the major theme of the handbook—the interrelations of key attitudinally relevant variables—the chapter examines: (a) the *causes* of communication-induced attitude change, including factors that relate to change at message exposure and to change following message exposure; (b) the *effects* of communication-induced attitude change on other variables like behavior; and (c) the *processes* by which communication-induced attitude change occurs and affects other variables. In each section, relevant theories and evidence are reviewed, followed by suggestions for future research.

Chapter 16: Social Influence in Attitudes and Attitude Change (Prislin & Wood).   Attitudes are formed and persist in a cultural and social niche. In this chapter, Radmila Prislin and Wendy Wood review such issues in relation to the matrix in Table 1.1 and other factors. For example, normative beliefs are important determinants of attitudes as well as behavior. Such norms most likely reflect the cultural structure of the social environment and the interactions it contains (Eagly & Chaiken, 1993). Thus, individuals' attitudes, affect, beliefs, and behavior have social correlates, both because they often derive from socially shared information, and because they collectively influence social representations, rules, and actions. Therefore, in addition to reviewing classic topics of social influence (e.g., minority and majority influence, conformity), Prislin and Wood's chapter integrates social scientific knowledge that is relevant to the handbook matrix.

Chapter 17: Attitude Theory and Research: Intradisciplinary and Interdisciplinary Connections (Ottati, Edwards, & Krumdick).   In their chapter, Victor Ottati, John Edwards, and Nathaniel Krumdick argue that many areas of study within and outside of social psychology *are infused with and connected to* attitudinal concepts and processes. In exploring intradisciplinary connections between the attitude literature and other areas of social psychology, the chapter focuses on intrapersonal processes (e.g., impression formation), interpersonal processes (e.g., close relationships), intragroup processes (e.g., group decision making), and intergroup processes (e.g., intergroup prejudice and discrimination). Within each of these four domains, Ottati and colleagues also consider interdisciplinary connections to areas falling outside of social psychology (e.g., political cognition, marital interaction, organizational behavior, and stigma). Thus, the chapter proposes that attitudes are an integrative theme for understanding human behavior.

Chapter 18: Attitude Research in the 21st Century: The Current State of Knowledge (Eagly & Chaiken).   The main objective of the handbook is to review a tradition of established knowledge in the area of attitudes and attitude change. In this final chapter, Alice Eagly and Shelly Chaiken summarize this tradition, draw conclusions about the state of the attitude literature, and point to areas that need further development.

CONCLUSION

This handbook attests to the mass of scientific knowledge that has accrued about attitudes: Here is what is now known and may be learned about seemingly all nuances of the attitudinal phenomena. Yet the chapters also point to areas in which understanding can be improved through enhancements of method and theory, which can benefit future studies of attitudes. By casting an attitudes spotlight on human affect, cognition, and behavior, the chapters in this handbook collectively show that attitudes remain and will continue to be an indispensable construct with which to understand the human condition.

ACKNOWLEDGMENT

The writing of this chapter was supported in part by grants K01-MH01861, R01-NR08325, and R01-MH58563 from the National Institutes of Health.

REFERENCES

Abelson, R. P. (1959). Modes of resolution of belief dilemmas. *Conflict Resolution, 3*, 343–352.

Ajzen, I. (1991). The theory of planned behavior. *Organizational Behavior and Human Decision Processes, 50*, 179–211.

Ajzen, I., & Fishbein, M. (1980). *Understanding attitudes and predicting social behavior.* Englewood Cliffs, NJ: Prentice-Hall.

Ajzen, I., & Fishbein, M. (2000). Attitudes and the attitude-behavior relation: Reasoned and automatic processes. In W. Stroebe & M. Hewstone (Eds.), *European review of social psychology* (pp. 1–33). Chichester, UK: Wiley.

Albarracín, D. (2002). Cognition in persuasion: An analysis of information processing in response to persuasive communications. In M. P. Zanna (Ed.), *Advances in experimental social psychology* (pp. 61–130). San Diego, CA: Academic Press.

Albarracín, D., Wallace, H. M., & Glasman, L. R. (2004). Survival and change of attitudes and other social judgments: A model of activation and comparison. In M. P. Zanna (Ed.), *Advances in experimental social psychology* (Vol. 36, pp. 252–315). San Diego, CA: Academic Press.

Albarracín, D., & Wyer, R. S., Jr. (2000). The cognitive impact of past behavior: Influences on beliefs, attitudes, and future behavioral decisions. *Journal of Personality and Social Psychology, 79*, 5–22.

Allport, G. W. (1935). Attitudes. In C. Murchison (Ed.), *Handbook of social psychology* (pp. 798–884). Worchester, MA: Clark University Press.

Anderson, N. H. (1981). *Foundations of information integration theory.* San Diego, CA: Academic Press.

Asch, S. E. (1952). *Social psychology.* Englewood Cliffs, NJ: Prentice-Hall.

Asch, S. E. (1956). Studies of independence and conformity: A minority of one against a unanimous majority. *Psychological Monographs, 70*(9, Whole No. 416).

Bargh, J. A. (1997). The automaticity of everyday life. In R. S. Wyer (Ed.), *Advances in social cognition* (pp. 1–61). Mahwah, NJ: Lawrence Erlbaum Associates.

Bem, D. J. (1965). An experimental analysis of self-persuasion. *Journal of Personality and Social Psychology, 1*, 199–218.

Bem, D. J. (1972). Self perception theory. In L. Berkowitz (Ed.), *Advances in experimental social psychology* (Vol. 6, pp. 1–62). New York: Academic Press.

Berkowitz, L. (2000). *Causes and consequences of feelings.* New York: Cambridge University Press.

Bersheid, E., & Walster, E. (1974). Physical attractiveness. In M. P. Zanna (Ed.), *Advances in experimental social psychology* (Vol. 8, pp. 157–215). New York: Academic Press.

Bogardus, E. S. (1931). *Fundamentals of social psychology.* New York: Century Press.

Brehm, J. W. (1966). *A theory of psychological reactance.* San Diego, CA: Academic Press.

Cacioppo, J. T., Petty, R. E., Feinstein, J. A., & Jarvis, W. B. G. (1996). Dispositional differences in cognitive motivation: The life and times of individuals varying in need for cognition. *Psychological Bulletin, 119*, 197–253.

Cacioppo, J. T., Petty, R. E., Kao, C. F., & Rodriquez, R. (1986). Central and peripheral routes to persuasion: An individual difference perspective. *Journal of Personality and Social Psychology, 51*, 1032–1043.

Carlson, E. R. (1956). Attitude change through modification of attitude structure. *Journal of Abnormal and Social Psychology, 52*, 256–261.

Carlston, D. E., & Smith, E. R. (1996). Principles of mental representation. In E. T. Higgins & A. W. Kruglanski (Eds.), *Social psychology: Handbook of basic principles* (pp. 184–210). New York: Guilford.

Chaiken, S. (1980). Heuristic versus systematic information processing and the use of source versus message cues in persuasion. *Journal of Personality and Social Psychology, 39*, 752–766.

Chaiken, S., Liberman, A., & Eagly, A. H. (1989). Heuristic and systematic processing within and beyond the persuasion context. In J. S. Uleman & J. A. Bargh (Eds.), *Unintended thought* (pp. 212–252). New York: Guilford.

Deutsch, M., & Gerard, H. B. (1955). A study of normative and informational social influences upon individual judgment. *Journal of Abnormal and Social Psychology, 51*, 629–636.

Dulany, D. E. (1968). Awareness, rules, and propositional control: A confrontation with S-R behavior theory. In T. Dixon & D. Horton (Eds.), *Verbal behavior and behavior theory* (pp. 340–387). New York: Prentice-Hall.

Eagly, A. H., & Chaiken, S. (1993). *The psychology of attitudes*. Orlando, FL: Harcourt Brace Jovanovich.

Eagly, A. H., & Chaiken, S. (1998). Attitude structure and function. In D. Gilbert, S. T. Fiske, & G. Lindsey (Eds.), *Handbook of social psychology* (Vol. 2, pp. 269–322). Boston: McGraw-Hill.

Fazio, R. H. (1986). How do attitudes guide behavior? In R. M. Sorrentino & E. T. Higgins (Eds.), *Handbook of motivation and cognition* (pp. 204–243). New York: Guilford.

Fazio, R. H. (1990). Multiple processes by which attitudes guide behavior: The MODE model as an integrative framework. In M. P. Zanna (Ed.), *Advances in experimental psychology* (Vol. 23, pp. 75–109). San Diego, CA: Academic Press.

Festinger, L. (1957). *A theory of cognitive dissonance*. Evanston, IL: Row, Peterson.

Fishbein, M. (1963). An investigation of the relationships between beliefs about an object and the attitude toward that object. *Human Relations, 16*, 233–240.

Fishbein, M., & Ajzen, I. (1975). *Belief, attitude, intention, and behavior: An introduction to theory and research.* Reading, MA: Addison-Wesley.

Forgas, J. P. (1995). Mood and judgment: The affect infusion model. *Psychological Bulletin, 117*, 39–66.

Frey, D. (1986). Recent research on selective exposure to information. In L. Berkowitz (Ed.), *Advances in experimental social psychology* (Vol. 19, pp. 41–80). San Diego, CA: Academic Press.

Greenwald, A. G. (1968). Cognitive learning, cognitive response persuasion, and attitude change. In A. G. Greenwald, T. C. Brock, & T. M. Ostrom (Eds.), *Psychological foundations of attitudes* (pp. 147–170). New York: Academic Press.

Greenwald, A. G., & Banaji, M. R. (1995). Implicit social cognition: Attitudes, self-esteem, and stereotypes. *Psychological Review, 102*, 4–27.

Heider, F. (1946). Attitudes and cognitive organization. *Journal of Psychology, 21*, 107–112.

Higgins, E. T. (1996). Knowledge activation: Accessibility, applicability, and salience. In E. T. Higgins & A. W. Kruglanski (Eds.), *Social psychology: Handbook of basic principles* (pp. 133–168). New York: Guilford.

Hildum, D. C., & Brown, R. W. (1956). Verbal reinforcement and interviewer bias. *Journal of Abnormal and Social Psychology, 53*, 108–111.

Hovland, C. I., Janis, I. L., & Kelley, H. H. (1953). *Communication and persuasion: Psychological studies of opinion change.* New Haven, CT: Yale University.

Insko, C. A. (1965). Verbal reinforcement of attitude. *Journal of Personality and Social Psychology, 2*, 621–623.

Janis, I. L., & King, B. T. (1954). The influence of role-playing on opinion change. *Journal of Abnormal and Social Psychology, 49*, 211–218.

Jarvis, W. B. G., & Petty, R. E. (1996). The need to evaluate. *Journal of Personality and Social Psychology, 70*, 172–194.

Judd, C. M., & Kulik, J. A. (1980). Schematic effects of social attitudes on information processing and recall. *Journal of Personality & Social Psychology, 38*, 569–578.

Kaplan, M. F., & Anderson, N. H. (1973). Information integration theory and reinforcement theory as approaches to interpersonal attraction. *Journal of Personality and Social Psychology, 28*, 301–312.

Katz, D. (1960). The functional approach to the study of attitudes. *Public Opinion Quarterly, 24*, 163–204.

Katz, D., & Stotland, E. (1959). A preliminary statement to a theory of attitude structure and change. In S. Koch (Ed.), *Psychology: A study of a science* (pp. 423–475). New York: McGraw-Hill.

Kelley, H. H. (1967). Attribution theory in social psychology. In D. Levine (Ed.), *Nebraska symposium on motivation* (Vol. 15, pp. 192–238). Lincoln: University of Nebraska Press.

Kelman, H. C. (1961). Processes of attitude change. *Public Opinion Quarterly, 25*, 57–78.

Kerlinger, F. N. (1984). *Liberalism and conservatism: The nature and structure of social attitudes.* Hillsdale, NJ: Lawrence Erlbaum Associates.

Kruglanski, A. W., & Thompson, E. P. (1999). Persuasion by a single route: A view from the unimodel. *Psychological Inquiry, 10*, 83–109.

LaPiere, R. T. (1934). Attitudes vs. actions. *Social Forces, 13*, 230–237.

McGuire, W. (1960). A syllogistic analysis of cognitive relationships. In M. Rosenberg, C. Hovland, W. McGuire, R. Abelson, & J. Brehm (Eds.), *Attitude organization and change* (pp. 65–111). New Haven, CT: Yale University Press.

McGuire, W. J. (1964). Inducing resistance to persuasion: Some contemporary approaches. In L. Berkowitz (Ed.), *Advances in experimental social psychology* (Vol. 1, pp. 191–229). New York: Academic Press.

McGuire, W. J. (1968). Personality and attitude change: An information-processing theory. In A. G. Greenwald, T. C. Brock, & T. M. Ostrom (Eds.), *Psychological foundations of attitudes* (pp. 171–196). San Diego, CA: Academic Press.

McGuire, W. J. (1990). Dynamic operations of thought systems. *American Psychologist, 45*, 504–512.

McGuire, W. J., & McGuire, C. V. (1991). The content, structure, and operation of thought systems. In R. S. Wyer & T. Srull (Eds.), *Advances in social cognition* (pp. 1–78). Hillsdale, NJ: Lawrence Erlbaum Associates.

Nail, P. R. (1986). Toward an integration of some models and theories of social response. *Psychological Bulletin, 100*, 190–206.

Nisbett, R. E., & Borgida, E. (1975). Attribution and the psychology of prediction. *Journal of Personality and Social Psychology, 32*, 932–943.

Nisbett, R. E., Krantz, D. H., Jepson, C., & Kunda, Z. (1983). The use of statistical heuristics in everyday inductive reasoning. *Psychological Review, 90*, 339–363.

Osgood, C. E., Suci, G. J., & Tannenbaum, P. H. (1957). *The measurement of meaning.* Urbana, IL: University of Illinois Press.

Ostrom, T. M. (1989). Interdependence of attitude theory and measurement. In A. R. Pratkanis, S. J. Breckler, & A. G. Greenwald (Eds.), *Attitude structure and function* (pp. 11–36). Mahwah, NJ: Lawrence Erlbaum Associates.

Ouellette, J. A., & Wood, W. (1998). Habit and intention in everyday life: The multiple processes by which past behavior predicts future behavior. *Psychological Bulletin, 124*, 54–74.

Peak, H. (1955). Attitude and motivation. In M. R. Jones (Ed.), *Nebraska symposium on motivation* (Vol. 3, pp. 149–188). Lincoln: University of Nebraska Press.

Petty, R. E., Briñol, P., & Tormala, Z. L. (2002). Thought confidence as a determinant of persuasion: The self-validation hypothesis. *Journal of Personality and Social Psychology, 82*, 722–741.

Petty, R. E., & Cacioppo, J. T. (1981). *Attitudes and persuasion: Classic and contemporary approaches.* Dubuque, IA: Brown.

Petty, R. E., & Cacioppo, J. T. (1986). *Communication and persuasion: Central and peripheral routes to attitude change.* New York: Springer-Verlag.

Petty, R. E., & Wegener, D. T. (1998). Attitude change: Multiple roles for persuasion variables. In D. Gilbert, S. Fiske, & G. Lindzey (Eds.), *Handbook of social psychology* (pp. 323–390). New York: McGraw-Hill.

Rokeach, M. (1954). The nature and meaning of dogmatism. *Psychological Review, 61*, 194–204.

Rosenberg, M. J. (1956). Cognitive structure and attitudinal affect. *Journal of Abnormal and Social Psychology, 53*, 367–372.

Ross, L., Greene, D., & House, P. (1977). The "false consensus effect": An egocentric bias in social perception and attribution processes. *Journal of Experimental Social Psychology, 13*, 279–301.

Schank, R., & Abelson, R. (1977). *Scripts, plans, goals, and understanding.* Hillsdale, NJ: Lawrence Erlbaum Associates.

Schwarz, N., & Bohner, G. (2001). The construction of attitudes. In A. Tesser & N. Schwarz (Eds.), *Blackwell handbook of social psychology: Intrapersonal processes* (pp. 436–457). Oxford, UK: Blackwell.

Schwarz, N., & Clore, G. L. (1983). Mood, misattribution, and judgments of well-being: Informative and directive functions of affective states. *Journal of Personality and Social Psychology, 45*, 513–523.

Schwarz, N., & Clore, G. L. (1996). Feelings and phenomenal experiences. In E. T. Higgins & A. W. Kruglanski (Eds.), *Social psychology: Handbook of basic principles* (pp. 433–465). New York: Guilford.

Sherif, M. (1935). A study of some social factors in perception. *Archives of Psychology, 27*, 1–60.

Sherif, M., & Hovland, C. I. (1961). *Social judgment: Assimilation and contrast effects in communication and attitude change.* New Haven, CT: Yale University Press.

Smith, E. R. (1996). What do connectionism and social psychology offer each other? *Journal of Personality and Social Psychology, 70*, 893–912.

Smith, E. R. (1998). Mental representation and memory. In D. Gilbert, S. T. Fiske, & G. Lindsey (Eds.), *Handbook of social psychology* (pp. 391–445). Boston: McGraw-Hill.

Tesser, A. (1978). Self-generated attitude change. In L. Berkowitz (Ed.), Advances in experimental social psychology (Vol. 11, pp. 289–338). New York: Academic Press.

Thurstone, L. L. (1928). Attitudes can be measured. *American Journal of Sociology, 33*, 529–544.

Tversky, A., & Kahneman, D. (1973). Availability: A heuristic for judging frequency and probability. *Cognitive Psychology, 5*, 207–232.

Vallacher, R. R., & Wegner, D. M. (1985). *A theory of action identification.* Hillsdale, NJ: Lawrence Erlbaum Associates.

Watson, D., & Tellegen, A. (1985). Toward a consensual structure of mood. *Psychological Bulletin, 98,* 219–235.

Webster, D. M., & Kruglanski, A. W. (1994). Individual differences in need for cognitive closure. *Journal of Personality and Social Psychology, 67,* 1049–1062.

Wegner, D. M. (1994). Ironic processes of mental control. *Psychological Review, 101,* 34–52.

Wicker, A. W. (1969). Attitudes versus actions: The relationship between verbal and overt behavioral responses to attitude objects. *Journal of Social Issues, 25,* 41–78.

Wilson, T. D., Dunn, D. S., Kraft, D., & Lisle, D. J. (1989). Introspection, attitude change, and attitude–behavior consistency: The disruptive effects of explaining why we feel the way we do. In L. Berkowitz (Ed.), *Advances in experimental social psychology* (Vol. 22, pp. 287–343). Orlando, FL: Academic Press.

Wilson, T. D., & Hodges, S. D. (1992). Attitudes as temporary constructions. In L. Martin & A. Tesser (Eds.), *The construction of social judgment* (pp. 37–65). Hillsdale, NJ: Lawrence Erlbaum Associates.

Wilson, T. D., Lindsey, S., & Schooler, T. Y. (2000). A model of dual attitudes. *Psychological Review, 107,* 101–126.

Wilson, T. D., & Schooler, J. W. (1991). Thinking too much: Introspection can reduce the quality of preferences and decisions. *Journal of Personality and Social Psychology, 60,* 181–192.

Worth, L. T., & Mackie, D. M. (1987). Cognitive mediation of positive affect in persuasion. *Social Cognition, 5,* 76–94.

Wyer, R. S. (1974). *Cognitive organization and change: An information-processing approach.* Hillsdale, NJ: Lawrence Erlbaum Associates.

Wyer, R. S., & Radvansky, G. A. (1999). The comprehension and validation of social information. *Psychological Review, 106,* 89–118.

Wyer, R. S., & Srull, T. K. (1989). *Memory and cognition in its social context.* Hillsdale, NJ: Lawrence Erlbaum Associates.

Zajonc, R. (1968). Attitudinal effects of mere exposure. *Journal of Personality and Social Psychology Monographs, 9*(2, pt. 2), 1–27.

Zanna, M. P., & Cooper, J. (1974). Dissonance and the pill: An attribution approach to studying the arousal properties of dissonance. *Journal of Personality and Social Psychology, 29,* 703–709.

Zanna, M. P., & Rempel, J. K. (1988). Attitudes: A new look at an old concept. In D. Bar-Tal & A. W. Kruglanski (Eds.), *The social psychology of knowledge* (pp. 315–334). Cambridge, UK: Cambridge University Press.

2

The Measurement of Attitudes

Jon A. Krosnick
Stanford University

Charles M. Judd
University of Colorado

Bernd Wittenbrink
University of Chicago

Attitude measurement is pervasive. Social psychologists routinely measure attitudes when studying their causes (e.g., Fishbein & Ajzen, 1975; Tesser, Whitaker, Martin, & Ward, 1998; Zajonc, 1968), how they change (e.g., Festinger, 1957; Hovland, Janis, & Kelley, 1953; Petty & Cacioppo, 1986) and their impact on cognition and behavior (e.g., Lord, Ross, & Lepper, 1979). Attitude measurement is also frequently done by political scientists, sociologists, economists, and other academics. Commercial market researchers are constantly engaged in measuring attitudes toward real and imagined consumer products and services. Beginning in the 1990s, all agencies of the U.S. federal government initiated surveys to measure attitudes toward the services they provided. And the news media regularly conduct and report surveys assessing public attitudes toward a wide range of objects. One of the most consequential examples is the routine measurement of Americans' approval of their president.

To gauge people's attitudes, researchers have used a wide variety of measurement techniques. These techniques have varied across history, and they vary across professions today. This variation is due both to varying philosophies of optimal measurement and varying availability of resources that limit assessment procedures. When attitude measurement was first formalized, the pioneering scholars presumed that an attitude could be accurately assessed only using a large set of questions that were selected via an elaborate procedure (e.g., Likert, 1932; Thurstone, 1928). But today, attitudes are most often assessed using single questions with relatively simple wordings and structures, and the variability of the approaches is striking, suggesting that there is not necessarily one optimal way to achieve the goal of accurate measurement.

Recently, however, scholars have begun to recognize that the accumulating literature points to clear advantages and disadvantages of various assessment approaches, so there may in fact be ways to optimize measurement by making good choices among the available tools. Furthermore, some challenging puzzles have appeared in the literature on attitude measurement that are stimulating a reevaluation of widely shared presumptions. This makes the present a particularly exciting time for reconsidering the full range of issues relevant to attitude measurement.

In this chapter, we offer a review of issues and literatures of use to researchers interested in assessing attitudes. We begin by considering the definition of attitudes, because no measurement procedure can be designed until the construct of interest has been specified. We review a range of different definitions that have been adopted throughout the history of social psychology but settle in on one that we believe captures the core essence of the notion of attitudes and that we use to shape our discussions throughout.

Because attitudes, like all psychological constructs, are latent, we cannot observe them directly. So all attitude measurement depends on those attitudes being revealed in overt responses, either verbal or nonverbal. We, therefore, turn next to outlining the processes by which we believe attitudes are expressed, so we can harness those processes to accurately gauge the construct. Finally, we outline the criteria for optimal measurement that we use throughout the rest of the chapter: reliability, validity, and generalizability.

Having thus set the stage, we turn to describing and evaluating various techniques for measuring attitudes, beginning with direct self-reports (which overtly ask participants to describe their attitudes). We outline many ways by which a researcher can design direct self-report measures well and less well. Next, we acknowledge the limits of such direct self-reports. A range of alternative assessment techniques, some old and others very new, have been developed to deal with these limitations, and we review those techniques next.

DEFINING THE CONSTRUCT

Attitudes have been central to social psychology since its inception. In the first edition of the *Handbook of Social Psychology* (1935), Gordon Allport started his highly influential chapter on the topic with the following observation:

> The concept of attitude is probably the most distinctive and indispensable concept in contemporary social psychology.... This useful, one might almost say peaceful concept has been so widely adopted that it has virtually established itself as the keystone in the edifice of American social psychology. In fact several writers (cf. Bogardus, 1931; Thomas and Znaniecki, 1918; Folsom, 1931) *define* social psychology as the scientific study of attitudes. (p. 784; emphasis in original)

Given this centrality, one might expect to find great consistency over years and consensus across scholars in the discipline on a definition of attitudes. But such is certainly not the case. Early on, attitudes were very broadly defined. As Allport (1935) put it, "An attitude is a mental and neural state of readiness, organized through experience, exerting a directive or dynamic influence upon the individual's response to all objects and situations with which it is related" (p. 784). Given this definition, it is hardly surprising that attitudes were seen as the central construct of social psychology, for they were whatever internal sets or predispositions motivated social behavior.

Since Allport, the definition of attitudes has evolved considerably, focusing much more on approach and avoidance behaviors and defining attitudes as the evaluative predispositions that lead to these. Thus, for instance, Eagly and Chaiken (1993) defined the construct as "a psychological tendency that is expressed by evaluating a particular entity with some degree of favor or disfavor (p. 1)." Accordingly, an attitude is focused on a particular entity or object, rather than all objects and situations with which it is related. Additionally, an attitude is a predisposition to like or dislike that entity, presumably with approach or avoidance consequences.

Although the evolution of the definition of attitudes in the discipline has many causes, it is interesting to note that measurement considerations were at least partly responsible. The early definitions, as sets or predispositions that motivated social behavior, were so broad that early measurement attempts were necessarily forced to simplify and place limits on the construct.

Indeed Thurstone (1931), among the first to systematically address attitude measurement, noted that:

> An attitude is a complex affair which cannot be wholly described by any single numerical index. For the problem of measurement this statement is analogous to the observation that an ordinary table is a complex affair which cannot be wholly described by any single numerical index. So is a man [*sic*] such a complexity which cannot be wholly represented by a single index. Nevertheless we do not hesitate to say that we measure the table. (p. 255)

He then more narrowly defined what he proposed to measure: "Attitude is here used to describe potential action toward the object with regard only to the question whether the potential action will be favorable or unfavorable toward the object (p. 255)." The demands of measurement meant that the construct was limited only to evaluative predispositions and that it was narrowed to predispositions toward a single attitude object, in a very similar manner to Eagly and Chaiken's recent definition.

The need for measurement not only mandated the narrowing of the construct; it also led to the important recognition that manifestations of attitudes, as assessed by any measurement procedure, are not the same as the attitude itself. Measurement permits one to assign values to individuals in a theoretically meaningful manner, such that differences in those values are thought to reflect differences in the underlying construct that is being measured (Dawes & Smith, 1985; Judd & McClelland, 1998). However, measurement is imperfect: The numerical values that are assigned contain both random errors and systematic errors, with the latter reflecting differences in underlying constructs other than the attitude that one intended to measure. All measurement procedures are necessarily errorful in both of these ways. Accordingly, the attitude is a *latent* evaluation of an object, manifested imperfectly both by our measurement procedures and by other observable behaviors that it in part motivates.

To say that an attitude is a latent evaluation of an object is not to say that it necessarily exists as a single entity in the mind of the attitude holder. It may, of course; and in that case, it seems reasonable to think of an attitude as a single evaluative association with the attitude object, capable of being reported (albeit with error) in any given measurement scenario. However, there are alternatives.

Perhaps a person has many stored associations with a particular attitude object, and these stored associations each have evaluative implications. However, for whatever reason, these evaluative implications have never been integrated or crystallized into a single evaluative summary stored in memory. For instance, perhaps when you think about your neighbor, you think about the fact that his yard is messy, that he accumulates rusting cars in his driveway, and that he has a couple of dogs that are nuisances. Each of these attributes that you associate with your neighbor tend to have negative evaluative overtones: You generally don't like messy yards, rusting cars, and nuisance dogs. But, somehow, you have never integrated these evaluative implications into a net evaluation of your neighbor. In this case, when there is no summary evaluation of the object (i.e., the neighbor), can we really speak of an attitude? We believe that we can, although the latent evaluation is doubly latent. Not only is it not observable by someone who wishes to measure it, but it also never exists as a discrete stored association. Rather, it becomes crystallized only under circumstances that demand a summary evaluation, such as when an overall attitude is demanded by a behavioral encounter (e.g., when you are asked "So, do you like your neighbor?").

When a single evaluative association does not exist, attitude reports may vary depending on the particular context in which those attitudes are reported, because different contexts may invoke different integration rules. For instance, if you are asked how much you like your neighbor when he has just acquired a new puppy, then the negative implications of the nuisance dogs might be perceptually overshadowed by the cuteness of the new arrival. An integrated overall evaluation constructed at that point in time might be slightly less negative as a result. If time were to pass and the salience of the new puppy were to decrease, the overall evaluation of your neighbor might become increasingly negative again.

Because of this context-driven variability in attitude reports, some theorists have suggested that there is in fact no single attitude stored in memory for anyone (for reviews, see Bassili & Brown and Kruglanski & Stroebe, both this volume). Instead, these scholars argue that attitudes are constructions, fleeting by their very nature and subject to the direction in which the proverbial wind is blowing at the moment the construction is built. The construction vanishes shortly thereafter, to be replaced by another construction, built largely independently sometime later. Indeed, some speak of individuals as having multiple attitudes toward an object instead of just one (Schwarz & Strack, 1991; Tourangeau & Rasinski, 1988; Wilson, Lindsey, & Schooler, 2000). However, we see great theoretical and practical value in resisting this extreme formulation and prefer still to hypothesize that a single attitude exists in a person's mind: the net evaluation associated with the object. The observable report of the attitude, representing the integration of evaluative implications at a given point in time, may vary as a function of the specific context in which that integration takes place, but the underlying ingredients from which that report is built (and which constitute the attitude in our formulation) are relatively stable over time.

Because an attitude is a latent construct, either existing in a relatively crystallized form or yet to be integrated into a summary representation, it is important to recognize that the attitude is *not* the numerical summary or the behavioral response that our measurement procedure produces as a product. Nevertheless, the process of attitude measurement is one of attempting to work backwards, going from the response back to the latent construct that is the attitude. To understand this process, it behooves us to better understand the cognitive processes that intervene between the latent attitude and particular responses that are manifested when attitude measurement is attempted. As we will see, understanding these processes, from the latent evaluation to manifest responses, will help us define some of the differences between what we will call *direct* measurement procedures (where we take literally the verbal self-reports of attitudes as indicative of latent attitudes) and *indirect* procedures (where we infer attitudes without asking people directly to report them).

A PROCESSING FRAMEWORK FOR ATTITUTE REPORTS

In this section, we outline a framework for the cognitive processes by which an attitudinal evaluation is generated and by which this evaluation then subsequently shapes response tendencies. The past 20 or so years of attitude research have seen a variety of such processing accounts (e.g., Bassili & Brown, this volume, Chaiken, 1987; Fazio, 1990; Petty & Cacioppo, 1986; Strack & Martin, 1987; Wegener & Petty, 1997; Wilson, Lindsey, & Schooler, 2000). The specific framework that we present here is largely based on these accounts and distinguishes between three stages of the evaluation process: (a) an initial spontaneous activation of memory contents, (b) a deliberation phase, and (b) a response phase.

Automatic Activation Phase

During the initial stage of evaluative processing, an attitude object or its symbolic representation (e.g., a lexical or verbal reference) may elicit evaluations automatically, without intent, effort, or even conscious awareness. Supplementing early demonstrations (e.g., Fazio, Sanbonmatsu, Powell, & Kardes, 1986; Kunst-Wilson & Zajonc, 1980), many studies now document such spontaneous evaluations, which are commonly thought to result from an automatic activation of associated contents in long-term memory (e.g., Bargh, Chaiken, Govender, & Pratto, 1992; De Houwer, Hermans, & Eelen, 1998; Giner-Sorolla, Garcia, & Bargh, 1999; Greenwald, Klinger, & Liu, 1989; Wittenbrink, Judd, & Park, 2001a), although they may also arise from nondeclarative processes such as those underlying fluency effects (Bornstein & D'Agostino, 1994; Murphy & Zajonc, 1993; Reber, Winkielman, & Schwarz, 1998) or physiological feedback effects (Laird, 1974; Strack, Martin, & Stepper, 1988).

Memory activation occurs fast, within a few hundred milliseconds after encountering the attitude object (Fazio et al., 1986; Klauer, Rossnagel, & Musch, 1997). This initial activation requires only very limited cognitive resources and does not emanate from an active search for relevant memory contents. Instead, it is the result of a passive process that runs its course automatically following exposure to the attitude object (Roskos-Ewoldsen & Fazio, 1992; Shiffrin & Schneider, 1977). Because of the passive nature of this initial activation, a person does not have to be aware of the attitude object or of the activation (e.g., Devine, 1989; Greenwald et al., 1989; Wittenbrink, Judd, & Park, 1997)—a fact that can have important consequences for subsequent stages of the evaluation process.

Automatic processes are thought to develop from frequent, repetitive experiences with a given stimulus (Shiffrin & Schneider, 1977). As a result, the particular memory contents that can be triggered automatically by an attitude object depend on the strength of their association with the object. If, as a result of past experiences, an overall evaluation of the attitude object has already been formed and strongly associated with the object, the evaluation itself may be spontaneously activated (e.g., spinach—"yuck!"). At the same time, other associations that have been strongly linked to the object can be activated as well. To the extent that they have evaluative implications, these evaluations may also shape subsequent evaluative responses (e.g., spinach—"bitter taste").

Because automatic activation depends on the accessibility of evaluative information, not all attitudes are equally likely to be activated automatically. Instead, automatic activation should occur especially for strong attitudes, which are more accessible and more consistent in their evaluative implications (see Petty & Krosnick, 1995). Empirical findings generally support the notion that attitude accessibility and consistency moderate automatic activation (Fazio et al., 1986), although in some instances, automatic activation has been observed for evaluatively consistent but inaccessible attitudes (Bargh et al., 1992; De Houwer et al., 1998).

Deliberation Phase

To the extent that a person has the opportunity and is sufficiently motivated, the initial activation phase is followed by a deliberation stage. During this second stage of evaluative processing, a controlled search for relevant information takes place. Both stored evaluations ("I liked the spinach at dinner last week") and other relevant associations ("spinach—it's healthy") might be retrieved from memory. Whether a particular piece of information will be retrieved at this point depends on its temporary accessibility (Salancik & Conway, 1975; Tourangeau, Rasinski, Bradburn, & D'Andrade, 1989), which in turn is influenced by a variety of factors.

First, memory contents vary in their chronic accessibility. Certain beliefs and experiences come to mind more easily than others, and certain memory contents are more closely linked to the attitude object than others. Second, as numerous studies have shown, this chronic accessibility may be moderated by the context in which the attitude object is encountered (for reviews, see Sudman, Bradburn, & Schwarz, 1996; Tesser, 1978; Wilson & Hodges, 1992). For example, the order of questions in a questionnaire may impact the deliberation phase by influencing the temporary accessibility of certain memory contents (e.g., Tourangeau et al., 1989). Likewise, the wording of a question or the particular exemplar of an attitude object that is encountered may highlight specific aspects of the object and thereby raise the temporary accessibility of certain pieces of information (e.g., Bodenhausen, Schwarz, Bless, & Wänke, 1995; Kinder & Sanders, 1990). Moreover, the search strategy that a person uses for retrieval can affect what information comes to mind during deliberation (e.g., Lord, Lepper, & Preston, 1984; Zajonc, 1960).

The deliberation phase requires motivation and opportunity because it involves effortful and willful processes. If these prerequisites are not met, input from the initial automatic activation stage will instead have a direct impact on a person's evaluative response. Motivation to spend time and effort on this process is the first critical determinant of the extent to which an attitude report will be deliberated. Having the opportunity to do so is the second.

There are many reasons why a person may be motivated to carefully reflect on his or her attitude before reporting it. Circumstances in the reporting situation may induce such motivation. That is, situational cues that highlight the positive consequences of being accurate and/or increase the perceived costliness of making a judgmental error are likely to increase a person's motivation to deliberate. For example, situations in which people feel accountable for their evaluations (e.g., because people expect to have to explain their attitudes to others) tend to foster deliberation (e.g., Kruglanski & Freund, 1983; Tetlock, 1983). Likewise, salient cues in a situation that highlight the normative implications of stating one's attitude also lead to more systematic deliberation of evaluations (e.g., Chen, Shechter, & Chaiken, 1996).

Aside from situational cues, motivation to deliberate can also be induced by internal factors. For example, some individuals have a higher overall need for accuracy (e.g., Kruglanski, 1989) or enjoy thinking (Cacioppo & Petty, 1982) and are therefore more motivated to exert mental effort in reaching an evaluation. Others are especially inclined to consider their own opinions and thus are more likely to introspect and deliberate about an issue (e.g., Snyder, 1979).

Assuming that a person is motivated to deliberate about an attitude, the opportunity to do so must also exist. This second prerequisite for deliberation is constrained first by a person's awareness of the attitude object. As long as the object remains outside of conscious awareness, no deliberation can take place. Although this precondition is probably met in very few situations in everyday life, this possibility is important for attitude measurement. Techniques that prevent the attitude object from reaching participants' conscious awareness (e.g., short exposure times) allow the assessment of evaluation effects free of further deliberation (Greenwald et al., 1989; Wittenbrink et al., 1997).

A second constraint on the opportunity to deliberate is the availability of cognitive resources. Many situations in everyday life place significant cognitive demands on people, as when multiple tasks occur simultaneously or when judgments must be made under time pressure (Bargh, 1997; Gilbert, 1989). As a result, a person's capacity for deliberation may often be limited, or, in extreme cases, entirely lacking (e.g., Kruglanski & Freund, 1983; Sanbonmatsu & Fazio, 1990). In these cases, the input from the initial automatic activation stage will be the primary determinant of a person's evaluative response, even though the person may be quite motivated to reflect on the evaluation in a more controlled fashion.

Response Phase

The evaluations generated either automatically or deliberately then shape overt responses. These influences can be either explicit, with the person aware of the connection between attitude and response, or they can be implicit, with the person remaining unaware of the link (Greenwald & Banaji, 1995). In the case of explicit influence, the response follows from a deliberate consideration of the input generated during the previous two processing stages. For this response to occur, the information has to be integrated, creating the crystallized form of the attitude in working memory, and then it is linked to the available response alternatives.

Of particular interest for understanding attitude measurement is the role that metacognitions play in the integration of inputs to yield a final response (e.g., Metcalfe & Shimamura, 1994). For example, a person may reflect on his or her subjective experience of the deliberation process itself. Specifically, the ease with which information comes to mind during deliberation may be regarded as diagnostic for one's evaluation. That is, having a difficult time generating reasons for why one might like an object has been found to negatively affect one's evaluation of the object (e.g., Wänke, Bohner, & Jurkowitsch, 1997).

Likewise, metacognitions about the appropriateness of information shaping a particular response may also influence this final step of evaluative processing. That is, people hold naïve theories about how a particular situation might bias their judgments and how to correct for the bias. Thus, if a person's theories suggest that an evaluation is the result of inappropriate information, he or she may attempt to correct the final evaluation accordingly (Martin, 1986; Schwarz & Bless, 1992; Strack, 1992; Wegener & Petty, 1997). For example, in evaluating an ordinary target person, a judge may adjust for the fact that he or she just saw a picture of Adolf Hitler, possibly making the target person seem more appealing and therefore justifying a downward correction in evaluations of him or her (Wegener & Petty, 1995). Correction strategies of this kind are closely related to the control mechanisms that operate during the deliberation stage and that guide the controlled search of information. However, correction during the response stage may simply consist of an adjustment of one's reported evaluation, without any further information search.

Finally, the result of integration has to be mapped onto the available response alternatives. To the extent that the alternatives are clearly prescribed by the situation, as they are in standard self-report measures of attitudes, this step requires that the response be formatted in accordance with the specified options, according to inferences made about the intended meaning of response alternatives (Strack & Martin, 1987).

So far, our description of the response phase has focused on explicit influences of the prior evaluation process on overt responses. These explicit influences require an effortful review of how the available information should be used. In other situations, the evaluation process may influence overt responses implicitly. First, when the attitude object remains outside of aware-ness, information generated during the evaluation process may impact responses implicitly. When an attitude object triggers an automatic activation, it may influence responses as long as it remains activated. Subliminal priming techniques assess implicit evaluation effects of this kind (e.g., Wittenbrink et al., 1997). Second, the attitude object itself may be noticed, but the evaluation it triggers may remain outside of conscious awareness and influence subsequent responses. Various response latency procedures for attitude measurement assess such implicit evaluation effects (e.g., Fazio, Jackson, Dunton, & Williams, 1995). Finally, a third way by which evaluations may implicitly affect responses is through misattribution of the evaluation. That is, a person may deliberately recall or construct an evaluation, and this evaluation may subsequently influence a response, but the person does not recognize the link between evalu-ation and response. This kind of implicit evaluative influence is illustrated by the impact that answering one question can have on answers to later questions in a questionnaire (e.g., Strack, Martin, & Schwarz, 1988).

Conclusion

The cognitive processes by which evaluations of objects are generated are multifaceted, com-plex, and variable over time and across situations and individuals in systematic ways. Therefore, there is no reason to believe that a single person will always report the same attitude toward an object when asked about it on multiple occasions in different contexts. Yet, this variability does not mean that the person lacks an attitude or that the attitude concept should be revised to remove notions of stability or consistency. The goal of attitude measurement is to gauge the stable construct underlying responses. Accordingly, the variability in the processes that generate those responses must be understood.

CRITERIA FOR ATTITUDE MEASUREMENT

The fundamental question in attitude measurement is whether the obtained response appropriately indexes the latent attitude construct. Because that construct itself is not directly observable, any attempt to measure it will necessarily do so only inadequately and incompletely. Consequently, it is important to index that inadequacy; in other words, to index the degree to which our measurement procedures capture the latent construct that we seek to measure.

In the history of attitude measurement, there have been two rather different approaches for addressing the issue of measurement adequacy: the axiomatic or representational approach, and the psychometric approach. The first of these has its origins in some of the earliest work on attitude measurement (e.g., Thurstone, 1927) and has since been developed in mathematically rigorous and even elegant detail (e.g., Luce, Krantz, Suppes, & Tversky, 1990). Nevertheless, the second of these approaches currently dominates the field of attitude measurement. There are a variety of reasons for its dominance (see Cliff, 1992; Dawes, 1994), not the least of which is that it was never clear that the representational approach, for all its mathematical rigor, really did a better job than the much more straightforward psychometric approach. Accordingly, in what follows, we focus exclusively on the psychometric approach (for comprehensive treatments of the other tradition, see Dawes & Smith, 1985; Judd & McClelland, 1998).

The fundamental issue in psychometrics is the issue of construct validity (Cronbach, 1984; Messick, 1989): To what extent do the variables we measure adequately represent or capture the psychological construct that is of interest? And the fundamental approach to answering this question is to examine patterns of covariances or correlations between alternative measures. Initially, the focus of such work was on the assessment of the reliability of a measure. Subsequently, issues of convergent and discriminant validity were addressed as a part of the larger issue of construct validity.

Reliability

Initial psychometric formulations assumed that any measured variable had two underlying components: true score and random error (the i subscript refers to individuals):

$$\mathbf{X_i} = \mathbf{T_i} + \mathbf{E_i}$$

Errors were assumed to be exclusively random perturbations, so they were assumed to be uncorrelated with true scores (and all other variables). The variance in the measured variable was therefore presumed to equal the sum of the variance in the true scores and the variance of the random errors of measurement:

$$\sigma_X^2 = \sigma_T^2 + \sigma_E^2$$

From this equation followed the definition of reliability: The proportion of the variance in a measured variable that was true score:

$$\rho_{XX} = \frac{\sigma_T^2}{\sigma_X^2} = \frac{\sigma_T^2}{\sigma_T^2 + \sigma_E^2}$$

This provides only a definition of reliability. To estimate it, a researcher must have at least two measures of a construct, sometimes referred to as *parallel forms*, sharing the true score to the same extent and having random errors of the same magnitude. It can be shown that the correlation between the two measures equals the reliability of each:

$$r_{X_1 X_2} = \rho_{X_1 X_1} = \rho_{X_2 X_2}$$

In practice, the reliability of a measure could be estimated by correlating two (almost) perfectly equivalent measures of the same construct. Alternative ways of doing this acquired different names: Split-half reliability involved parallel forms based on two randomly selected subsets of a battery of questions; test–retest reliability assumed that measurements at different time points were parallel.

With multiple questions in a battery, all of which are assumed to measure the same under- lying construct, the random measurement errors in responses to any one question will cancel each other out when a composite score (sum or average) is computed across all the questions. The degree to which this is true is given by the Spearman-Brown Prophecy formula for the reliability of the sum (or average) of k parallel items:

$$\rho_{\text{sum}} = \frac{k r_{ij}}{1 + (k-1) r_{ij}}$$

where r_{ij} is the correlation between every pair of items (assumed to be constant across all pairs, because of the parallel forms assumption).

The generalization of Spearman-Brown, allowing unequal true score variances across dif- ferent questions, is coefficient alpha, the reliability of a sum (or average) of a set of items, all presumed to measure the same construct, albeit with unequal item reliabilities:

$$\alpha = \left(\frac{k}{k-1} \right) \left(1 - \frac{\sum \sigma_i^2}{\sigma_{\text{sum}}^2} \right)$$

where $\sum \sigma_i^2$ is the sum of the variances of the individual items and σ_{sum}^2 is the variance of their sum.

Both of these formulas assume that responses have been coded so that they are all positively correlated. Before items are combined and the reliability of their sum (or average) is estimated, a principal components analysis can be conducted to verify that all questions load highly on the first unrotated component. Most computer programs that compute coefficient alpha will also report item-total correlations, as well as coefficient alpha values omitting each item in turn from the sum. According to this perspective, items that do not load highly on the first principal component or that do not correlate highly with the sum should be omitted because they may assess other constructs than the one shared by the other items. Doing so will generally increase coefficient alpha computed on the remaining items.

Convergent and Discriminant Validity

The classic psychometric model that we have just reviewed is theoretically inadequate because it presumes that all nonrandom variation in an attitude measure is due to the construct that we wish to measure, in other words, to the true score. All measures, however, have in them multiple sources of systematic nonrandom variance. Therefore, a more adequate theoretical model for any measure is that it likely taps three classes of phenomena, to varying extents:

1. The construct of theoretical interest.
2. Other constructs that are not of theoretical interest.
3. Random errors of measurement.

The broad issue of construct validity concerns the extent to which all three of these contribute to the variance of responses to an item. An item with high construct validity is one in which the construct of interest contributes a great deal to the item's variance, while other constructs and random error contribute very little. How reliable an item is (i.e., the relative absence of random errors of measurement) is accordingly one component of construct validity: It indexes the relative contribution of random errors without differentiating between the two systematic components of item variance. The reliability of an item therefore sets only an upper limit on the extent to which the item validly measures the construct of interest.

The other two components of construct validity, beyond reliability, concern convergent validity and discriminant validity (Campbell & Fiske, 1959). The former represents the extent to which variance in the item is attributable uniquely to the construct of theoretical interest. The more it does so, the higher the convergent validity. The latter represents the extent to which other constructs, those that are not of theoretical interest, contribute systematic error variance to an item's overall variance. The more an item contains unwanted systematic error variance because of other constructs, the lower its discriminant validity. In sum, then, the overall construct validity of an item depends on three sources of variation in scores:

1. The more the variation is attributable to the latent construct of interest, the higher the convergent validity.
2. The less the variation is attributable to other constructs, i.e., sources of systematic error, the higher the discriminant validity.
3. The less the variation is attributable to random error, the higher the reliability.

Campbell and Fiske (1959) were the first to explore ways in which convergent and discriminant validity could be estimated from the patterns of correlations (or covariances) among different measured variables. The tool they used was the multitrait–multimethod matrix, which can be built when a number of different constructs of theoretical interest are measured, each using a number of different assessment procedures. For instance, a researcher might measure attitudes toward three different attitude objects (e.g., three different minority ethnic groups) using each of three different assessment procedures. From these nine items (three attitude objects crossed with three assessment methods), one can construct a 9 × 9 correlation matrix. As Campbell and Fiske argued, the pattern of these correlations can be used to infer the extent to which there is convergent validity (measures of the same attitude using different methods all correlate highly), there is discriminant validity between the three attitudes (correlations between measures of different attitudes are relatively low), and there is discriminant validity between the measurement methods (correlations between different attitudes measured with the same method are no higher than correlations between different attitudes measured with different methods).

Campbell and Fiske's (1959) approach to the multitrait–multimethod matrix relies on a fundamental tenant of the psychometric approach to construct validity: To the extent that measures covary, it is because they share systematic variance, either because of the construct(s) of interest or because of other constructs that are not of interest (systematic error variance). In general, to argue for discriminant validity, a researcher must show relatively low correlations between items that are thought to measure different constructs, with the caveat of course that those different constructs may themselves be correlated. To argue for convergent validity, a researcher must show large correlations between different items that are all believed to measure the construct of interest. To rule out other shared systematic sources of error variation as responsible for such high correlations, the different items all thought to measure the construct of interest must be maximally dissimilar in other ways (so that the other constructs they measure are maximally dissimilar). In general, the quest for construct validity mandates what might be called a *multi-operationalization* approach: The adequacy of measurement can only be assessed by examining patterns of covariation between alternative measures of the same and different constructs.

Lee Cronbach and colleagues extended notions underlying the multitrait–multimethod matrix to more generalized research designs permitting comprehensive assessments of construct validity (Cronbach, Gleser, Nanda, & Rajaratnam, 1972; Shavelson & Webb, 1991). One can think about the multitrait–multimethod matrix as a two-factor design, crossing traits (i.e., attitudes) with methods and measuring participants under all levels of both factors. Given this conception, a researcher can conduct an analysis of variance with the resulting data, devoting primary attention to the variance components due to participants, traits, and methods (and their interactions) rather than to the F tests typically reported. These variance components and their ratios (which are intraclass correlations, Shrout & Fleiss, 1979) provide information about the construct validity and reliability of the measured variables. For instance, if the different traits (or attitudes) show discriminant validity, then the variance component due to traits should be large relative to the variance components due to participants and due to the participant by trait interaction (Kenny, 1994).

Cronbach generalized this variance components approach into what became known as *generalizability theory*, in which additional factors are added to the analysis of variance design, with factors representing, for instance, occasions, experimenters, locations, etc. In essence, this generalization amounts to an extension of the multitrait–multimethod matrix to incorporate additional factors so that one could examine whether those additional factors systematically affect the variance in responses. From the resulting variance components estimation, a researcher can estimate convergent and discriminant validity for the various factors that were used in the research design. For instance, if multiple attitudes were measured using multiple methods on multiple occasions, one could assess whether different methods yield the same answer (discriminant validity against method variance) and whether different occasions yield the same answer (discriminant validity against time variance—indicating stability of responses).

Although generalizability theory offers a comprehensive approach for examining issues of construct validity, the recommended fully crossed designs are certainly cumbersome. Ideally, researchers would like to estimate the contributions of various factors (i.e., constructs both of interest and those not of interest) to variance in responses with data matrices on which analysis of variance decompositions are not possible. Doing so is possible in some cases through the use of confirmatory factor analysis (CFA) procedures (see Judd & McClelland, 1998; Kenny & Kashy, 1992; Kline, 1998). In essence, a researcher constructs a theoretical measurement model of the latent constructs thought to be responsible for the variances of and covariances between a set of measured variables. Assuming that the model is identified (i.e., there are fewer parameters in the model to estimate than the number of independent bits of information in the observed variance–covariance matrix), then one can estimate the model's parameters, providing direct estimates of convergent validity, discriminant validity, and reliability. The development of such CFA procedures represents a significant recent contribution to the set of tools researchers have available to them for examining issues of construct validity. In fully crossed designs, such as the multitrait–multimethod matrix or the more elaborate designs of generalizability theory, parameter estimates resulting from confirmatory factor analytic estimation provide equivalent information to that which derives from the analysis of variance approach (Judd & McClelland, 1998).

TRADITIONAL DIRECT SELF-REPORT METHODS

With this perspective on measurement theory established, we can now turn to the procedures available for measuring attitudes. We begin with a focus on direct self-reports that involve asking participants explicitly to describe their own attitudes. Our discussion starts with a review of the relatively cumbersome measurement techniques proposed by the pioneers of attitude measurement nearly 70 years ago. Although widely appreciated, these techniques are rarely implemented these days, in favor of simpler practices. We, therefore, review a range of guidelines for optimally building such simpler measures and identify sources of random and systematic measurement error in responses to them.

Classic Self-Report Measurement Methods

The origins of elaborate attitude measurement via direct self-reports lie in the work of Louis Thurstone (1928), Rensis Likert (1932), and Charles Osgood (Osgood, Suci, & Tannenbaum (1957). Each of these scholars developed a unique technique for measuring attitudes with multiple self-report items that have strong face validity. To put common practices in use today into context, we outline these techniques first.

Thurstone's Equal-Appearing Intervals Method

The title of Thurstone's landmark 1928 publication was "Attitudes Can Be Measured," a phrase that seemed as if it should end with an exclamation point. The method of attitude measurement he proposed involved seven steps of materials preparation (!). The first stage entailed gathering or generating between 100 and 150 statements of favorable or unfavorable evaluations of an object. Next, this set is edited down to a set of 80 to 100 statements that seem to have the most potential to perform effectively in later stages. Then, between 200 and 300 judges place each statement into one of 11 piles, with the piles defined as representing equally spaced points along the evaluative continuum running from extremely negative to extremely positive. Next, each statement is assigned a numeric value from 1 to 11, representing the place at which each participant placed it, and then the mean and variance of the numbers assigned to each statement are calculated. Statements with large variances are interpreted in different ways by different judges, so they are dropped from consideration. Then, two or three statements with means very close to each point along the continuum are selected, thus yielding a final battery with sets of statements that are equally spaced from one another. At this point, the measure is ready for administration. Participants are asked to read all of the selected statements and to indicate those with which they agree. Each participant is assigned an attitude score by averaging the mean scale values of the statements that he or she endorses. Ideally, each participant agrees with just 2 or 3 statements, pinpointing his or her place along the continuum.

Likert's Method of Summated Ratings

Rensis Likert's (1932) summated rating method is less labor intensive during the materials preparation phase. First, the researcher prepares about 100 statements that express positions either strongly favorable or unfavorable toward an object. In contrast to Thurstone's method, statements expressing neutrality are not included here. A set of pretest participants are then given a set of five response options (strongly disagree, disagree, undecided, agree, or strongly agree) and are asked to choose one response to express their view of each statement. For statements expressing favorable views of the object, responses are coded 1, 2, 3, 4, and 5, respectively. For statements expressing unfavorable views of the object, responses are coded 5, 4, 3, 2, and 1, respectively.

Each pretest participant is then assigned a total score by summing his or her scores on all of the items. Finally, for each item, each person's score is correlated with his or her total score, and items with low item-to-total correlations are dropped. Approximately 20 items with the strongest correlations are retained for use in the final battery. When this final battery is later administered to other samples, participants express their extent of agreement or disagreement with each statement, and total scores are generated accordingly for each participant. This procedure shares some of the spirit of Thurstone's but involves a unique feature: assessment of the validity of each item via the item-to-total correlation.

Osgood, Suci, and Tannenbaum's Semantic Differential

The semantic differential is the simplest and easiest to administer of the landmark attitude measurement techniques. Through extensive developmental research, Osgood and his colleagues identified a set of adjective pairs that represent the evaluative dimension, including good–bad, valuable–worthless, wise–foolish, pleasant–unpleasant, and others. Each pair anchors the ends of a 7-point rating scale, and participants select the point on each scale to indicate their evaluation of the object.

Osgood, Suci, and Tannenbaum's (1957, pp. 29, 83) response scale consisted of a long horizontal line, intersected by six short vertical lines dividing the horizontal line into seven sections. At the two ends of each horizontal line were two antonyms, such as good and bad. Participants were instructed to mark a spot on the horizontal line to evaluate the goodness or badness of an object. In addition, Osgood et al. (1957) provided extensive instructions explaining the meanings of all the points on the rating scale. For example, for a rating scale anchored on the ends by *good* and *bad*, participants were told that the end point labeled good meant extremely good, the next point over meant quite good, the next point meant slightly good, the midpoint meant neither good nor bad/equally good and bad, the next point meant slightly bad, and so on. The semantic differential is the foundational technique used most often in research today, but it is typically administered *not* following Osgood et al.'s (1957) procedure. Instead, the horizontal line is presented with no labels on any points except the end points, and these end points are not labeled extremely (good instead of extremely good and bad instead of extremely bad). Typically the scale points are scored 1, 2, 3, 4, 5, 6, and 7, running from the most negative response to the most positive response, and the participant's attitude score is the average of the scores he or she receives on each item in the battery.

Advantages and Disadvantages of These Methods

All three of these foundational methods involve the administration of a large set of questions to measure a single attitude. Therefore, these approaches are time consuming and demanding for participants. In addition, the Thurstone and Likert procedures entail a great deal of preparatory work up front, prior to the administration of the battery to one's focal sample of participants. However, these methods have at least two key advantages. First, administering many items yields a final score that contains less random measurement error (Allison, 1975). Second, these procedures have the advantage of being built using empirical evidence of convergence of interpretations across people and of correlational validity of the statements.

Unfortunately, the time pressures typical of most data collection efforts these days mean that researchers find it difficult to justify expending the resources necessary to build and then administer full-blown Thurstone, Likert, or Osgood rating batteries to measure a single attitude. Therefore, most researchers measure attitudes using a very small number of questions that have not been selected based on extensive pretesting and development work. This practice means that there is a strong incentive to design these few items to yield maximally reliable and valid assessments. We turn next to the literature on such item design.

Designing Direct Self-Report Attitude Measures Optimally

Designing any question to ask people directly for descriptions of their attitudes requires that researchers make a series of decisions about structure and wording. These decisions were made differently by the three principal founders of attitude measurement, and such heterogeneity continues to this day. This might seem to suggest that there is no optimal measurement approach and that all of the many direct attitude measures are equally reliable and valid.

However, a huge literature has accumulated during the last 100 years throughout the social sciences challenging this conclusion. When taken together, this literature recommends best practices for designing attitude measures, so we turn now to review some of the highpoint of this literature (for a more comprehensive review, see Krosnick & Fabrigar, forthcoming).

We begin by addressing the issue of whether direct attitude measures should be open-ended or closed-ended. Then, we consider a series of design decisions required when building closed-ended questions with rating scales: how many points to put on the rating scales, how to label the scale points, in what order to present the points, and whether or not to offer don't know response options.

Open Versus Closed Questions

One of the first decisions a researcher must make when designing an attitude measure is whether to make it an open-ended question (permitting the participant to answer in his or her own words) or a closed-ended question (requiring the participant to select an answer from a set of choices). By a wide margin, closed-ended questions dominate attitude measurement. But open-ended questions can certainly be used to measure attitudes (see, e.g., Holbrook, Krosnick, Visser, Gardner, & Cacioppo, 2001), and the accumulated literature suggests that these may well be worthwhile under some circumstances.

No doubt, a major reason for the widespread use of closed-ended questions is the complexity entailed in the coding of answers to open-ended questions. If a questionnaire is administered to 300 people, nearly 300 different answers will be given to a question asking people what they like and dislike about the president of the United States (for example), if the answers are considered word-for-word. But in order to analyze these answers, a coding scheme must be developed for each open-ended question; multiple people must read and code the answers into categories; the level of agreement between the coders must be ascertained; and the procedure must be refined and repeated if agreement is too low. The time and financial costs of such a procedure no doubt have led many researchers to favor closed-ended questions, which in essence ask participants to code themselves directly into categories that the researcher provides.

Unfortunately, closed-ended questions can have distinct disadvantages. The precise formulation of an attitude rating scale in terms of the number of points on the scale, the extent of verbal labeling of those points, the particular verbal phrases selected to label the points, the order in which the points are presented to participants, and offering *don't know* response options can all be done suboptimally. As a result, reliability and validity can be compromised. Because open-ended questions do not present answer choices to participants, these sources of researcher-induced measurement error do not distort responses in principle. And in practice, past studies show that open-ended questions have higher reliabilities and validities than closed-ended questions (e.g., Hurd, 1932; Remmers, Marschat, Brown, & Chapman, 1923).

One might hesitate before using open-ended questions because such questions may themselves be susceptible to unique problems. For example, some scholars feared that open-ended questions might not work well for participants who are not especially articulate, because they might have special difficulty explaining their feelings. However, this fear seems unfounded in most cases (England, 1948; Geer, 1988). Second, some scholars feared that participants would be especially likely to answer open-ended questions by mentioning the most salient possible responses, not those that are truly most appropriate. But this, too, seems not to be the case (e.g., Schuman, Ludwig, & Krosnick, 1986). Thus, open-ended questions may be worth the trouble they take to ask and the complexities inherent in the analysis of their answers.

Number of Points on Rating Scales

The predominant response format for direct self-report attitude measures these days is the rating scale. When designing a rating scale, a researcher must specify the number of points on the scale. Rating scale lengths vary a great deal in the work of academic social scientists, commercial practitioners, and government researchers. This variation is evident even in the pioneers' attitude measures: Classic Likert (1932) scaling uses 5-point scales; Osgood, Suci, and Tannenbaum's (1957) semantic differential uses 7-point scales; and Thurstone's (1928) equal-appearing interval method uses 11-point scales. Rating scales used to measure public approval of the U.S. president's job performance also vary considerably across commercial survey houses, from 2-point scales to 5-point scales (Morin, 1993; Sussman, 1978). For the last 60 years, the National Election Study surveys have measured Americans' political attitudes using 2-, 3-, 4-, 5-, 7-, and 101-point scales (Miller, 1982). Robinson, Shaver, and Wrightsman's (1999) recent catalog of popular rating scales for measuring a range of social psychological constructs and political attitudes describes 37 using 2-point scales, 7 using 3-point scales, 10 using 4-point scales, 27 using 5-point scales, 6 using 6-point scales, 21 using 7-point scales, 2 using 9-point scales, and 1 using a 10-point scale.

Thus, there appears to be no standard for the number of points to be used on rating scales, and common practice varies widely. Nonetheless, the accumulated literature suggests that some rating scale lengths may be preferable to maximize reliability and validity. To review this literature, we begin with a discussion of theoretical issues and then catalogue the findings of relevant empirical studies.

Theoretical Issues

When a participant is confronted with a rating scale, his or her job is to execute a matching or mapping process. First, the participant must assess his or her own attitude in conceptual terms (e.g., "I like it a lot") and then find the point on the rating scale that most closely matches that attitude (see Ostrom & Gannon, 1996). Given this perspective, a number of general conditions must be met in order for a rating scale to work effectively. First, the points offered should cover the entire measurement continuum, leaving out no regions. Second, these points must appear to be ordinal, progressing from one end of a continuum to the other, and the meanings of adjacent points should overlap with one another minimally if at all. Third, each participant must have a relatively precise and stable understanding of the meaning of each point on the scale. Fourth, most or all participants must agree in their interpretations of the meanings of each scale point, and a researcher must know what those interpretations are.

If some or all of these conditions are not met, data quality is likely to suffer. For example, if a participant falls in a particular region of an underlying evaluative dimension (e.g., *like somewhat*) but no response options are offered in this region (e.g., a scale comprised only of *dislike* and *like*), the participant will be unable to rate himself or herself accurately. If a participant interprets the points on a scale one way today and differently next month, then he or she may respond differently at the second time point, even if his or her underlying attitude has not changed. If two or more points on a scale appear to have the same meaning to a participant, he or she may be puzzled about which one to select, leaving him or her open to making an arbitrary choice. If two participants differ in their interpretations of the points on a scale, they may give different responses even though they may have identical underlying attitudes. If participants interpret scale point meanings differently than researchers do, the researchers may assign numbers to the scale points for statistical analysis that misrepresent the messages participants attempted to send via their ratings.

Translation Ease.   The length of scales can influence the process by which participants map their attitudes onto the provided response alternatives. The ease of this mapping or translation process varies, partly depending on the underlying attitude. For instance, if a participant has an extremely positive or negative attitude toward an object, a dichotomous scale (e.g., *like, dislike*) easily permits reporting that attitude. Yet, for a participant with a neutral attitude, a dichotomous scale not offering a midpoint would be suboptimal, because it would not offer the point most obviously needed to permit accurate mapping.

A trichotomous scale (e.g., *like, neutral, dislike*) may be problematic for another person who has a moderately positive or negative attitude, equally far from the scale midpoint and from the extreme end on the underlying continuum. Adding a moderate point on the negative side (e.g., *dislike somewhat*) and one on the positive side of the scale (e.g., *like somewhat*) seems to be a good way to solve this problem. Thus, individuals who want to report neutral, moderate, or extreme attitudes would all have opportunities for accurate mapping.

The value of adding even more points to a rating scale may depend on how refined people's mental representations of the construct are. Perhaps a 5-point scale is adequate, but perhaps people routinely make more fine-grained distinctions. For example, most people may be able to differentiate feeling slightly favorable, moderately favorable, and extremely favorable toward objects, in which case a 7-point scale would be more desirable than a 5-point scale.

If people do make such fine distinctions, potential information gain increases as the number of scale points increases, because of greater differentiation in the judgments made (for a review, see Alwin, 1992). This will be true, however, only if two conditions are met. First, participants must make use of the full scale. It is conceivable that when confronted with long scales, participants simply ignore large portions of the scale. Second, no additional information is gained if the number of scale points exceeds the degree to which participants differentiate between levels of an attribute in their minds. If people's psychological representations differentiate into no more than 7 categories, for example, then additional scale points gain no more information for a researcher.

The ease of mapping a judgment onto a response scale is likely to be determined in part by how close the judgment is to the conceptual divisions between adjacent points on the scale. For example, when a person with an extremely negative attitude is asked, "Is your opinion of the president very negative, slightly negative, neutral, slightly positive, or very positive?", he or she can easily answer "very negative", because his or her attitude is far from the conceptual division between *very negative* and *slightly negative*. However, for a person who is moderately negative, his or her true attitude is close to the conceptual division between *very negative* and *slightly negative*, so this person may face a greater challenge in using this 5-point rating scale. The *nearness* of the participant's true judgment to the nearest conceptual division between adjacent scale points is associated with unreliability of responses—participants with greater nearness are more likely to pick one option on one occasion and another option on a different occasion (Kuncel, 1973, 1977).

Clarity of Scale Point Meanings.   In order for ratings to be reliable, participants must have a clear understanding of the meanings of the points on the rating scale. If the meaning of scale points is ambiguous, then both reliability and validity of measurement may be compromised.

A priori, it seems that dichotomous response option pairs are very clear in meaning, that is, there is likely to be considerable consensus on the meaning of options such as *favor* and *oppose* or *agree* and *disagree*. Clarity may be compromised when a dichotomous scale becomes longer, because each point that is added on the rating scale is one more point that must be interpreted. And the more such interpretations a person must make, the more chance there is for inconsistency over time or across participants. That is, it is presumably easier for a participant to decide precisely where the conceptual divisions are between favoring, opposing, and being neutral on a trichotomous item than in the case of a 7-point scale, where six conceptual divisions must be specified.

For rating scales up to 7 points long, it may be easy to specify intended meanings of points with words, as with *like a great deal*, *like a moderate amount*, *like a little*, *neither like nor dislike*, *dislike a little*, *dislike a moderate amount*, and *dislike a great deal*. But once the scale point number increases beyond that length, point meanings may become considerably less clear. For example, on 101-point scales measuring attitudes, what exactly do 76, 77, and 78 mean conceptually? Even for 11- or 13-point scales, participants may be hard pressed to define the meaning of the scale points.

Uniformity of Scale Point Meaning.   The number of scale points used is inherently confounded with the extent of verbal labeling possible, and this confounding may affect uniformity of interpretations of scale point meanings across people. Every dichotomous and trichotomous scale must, of necessity, include verbal labels on all scale points, thus enhancing their clarity. But when scales have 4 or more points, it is possible to label only the end points with words. In such cases, comparisons with dichotomous or trichotomous scales reflect the impact of both number of scale points and verbal labeling. It may be possible to provide an effective verbal label for each point on a scale containing, say, 11 or fewer scale points, but doing so becomes quite difficult as the number of scale points increases beyond that length.

One could argue that the participant's task is made that much more difficult when presented with numerical rather than verbal labels. To make sense of a numerically labeled rating scale, a participant must first generate a verbal definition for each point and then match these definitions against his or her mental representation of the attitude of interest. Verbal labels might therefore be advantageous, because they may clarify the meanings of the scale points while at the same time reducing participant burden by removing one step from the cognitive processes entailed in answering a rating question.

Satisficing.   Finally, the optimal number of rating scale points may depend on participants' cognitive skills and motivation to provide accurate reports. Unfortunately, when answering questionnaires, some individuals do not expend the effort necessary to provide optimal answers. Instead, they look for cues in questions pointing to reasonable answer choices that are easy to select with little thought, a behavior termed *questionnaire satisficing* (Krosnick, 1991, 1999). Such satisficing is thought to be more common among individuals with more limited cognitive skills and less motivation to provide accurate answers.

Offering a midpoint on a scale may constitute a satisficing cue to such participants, especially if its meaning is clearly either *neutral/no preference* or *status quo*—keep things as they are now. If pressed to explain these answers, satisficing participants would have little difficulty defending such replies. Consequently, offering a midpoint may encourage satisficing by providing a clear cue offering an avenue for doing so.

However, there is a potential cost to eliminating midpoints. Some participants may truly belong at the scale midpoint and may wish to select such an option to communicate their genuine neutrality or endorsement of the status quo. If many people have neutral attitudes to report, eliminating the midpoint will force them to pick a point either on the positive side or on the negative side of the scale, resulting in an inaccurate measurement of their attitudes.

The number of points on a rating scale can also impact satisficing via a different route: task difficulty. High task difficulty is thought to inspire some participants to satisfice instead of optimizing (Krosnick, 1991). The number of scale points offered on a rating scale may be a determinant of task difficulty. Two-point scales simply require a decision of direction (e.g., pro vs. con), whereas longer scales require decisions of both direction and extremity. Very long scales require participants to choose between many options, so these scales may be especially difficult in terms of scale point meaning interpretation and mapping. Yet providing too few scale points may contribute to difficulty by making impossible the expression of moderate positions. Consequently, task difficulty (and satisficing as well) may be at a minimum for moderately long rating scales, resulting in more accurate responses.

Existing Evidence on the Optimal Number of Scale Points

During the last 40 years, many research investigations have produced evidence useful for inferring the optimal number of points on rating scales. Some of this work has systematically varied the number of scale points offered while holding constant all other aspects of questions, examining effects on reliability and validity. Other work has attempted to discern people's natural discrimination tendencies in using rating scales. We review this work next. It is important to note that some of the studies we review did not explicitly set out to compare reliability or validity of measurement across scale lengths but instead reported data that permit us to make such comparisons post hoc.

Reliability.   Lissitz and Green (1975) explored the relation of number of scale points to reliability using simulations. These investigators generated sets of true attitudes and random errors for groups of hypothetical participants and then added these components to generate hypothetical responses to attitude questions on different-length scales in two hypothetical waves of data. Cross-sectional and test–retest reliability increased from 2- to 3- to 5-point scales but were equivalent thereafter for 7-, 9-, and 14-point scales. Similar results were obtained in simulations by Jenkins and Taber (1977), Martin (1978), and Srinivasan and Basu (1989).

Some studies have found the number of scale points to be unrelated to cross-sectional reliability. Bendig (1954) found that ratings using either 2-, 3-, 5-, 7-, or 9-point scales were equivalently reliable. Similar results have been reported for scales ranging from 2 to 7-points (Komorita & Graham, 1965; Masters, 1974) and for longer scales ranging from 2 to 19 points (Birkett, 1986; Jacoby & Matell, 1971; Matell & Jacoby, 1971). Other studies have yielded differences that are consistent with the notion that scales of intermediate lengths are optimal (Birkett, 1986; Givon & Shapira, 1984; Masters, 1974). For example, Givon and Shapira (1984) found pronounced improvements in item reliability when moving from 2-point scales toward 7-point scales. Reliability continued to increase up to lengths of 11 points, but the increases beyond 7 points were quite minimal for single items. Matell and Jacoby (1971; Jacoby & Matell, 1971) reported lower reliabilities for scales with 19 points as compared to scales with 7 to 8 points.

Another way to assess optimal scale length is to collect data on a scale with many points and recode it into a scale with fewer points. If longer scales contain more random measurement error, then recoding should improve reliability. But if longer scales contain valid information that is lost in the recoding process, then recoding should reduce data quality. Consistent with this hypothesis, Komorita (1963) found that cross-sectional reliability for 6-point scales was .83, but was only .71 when the items were first recoded to be dichotomous. Thus, it appears that more reliable information was contained in the full 6-point ratings than in the dichotomies. Similar findings were reported by Matell and Jacoby (1971), indicating that collapsing scales longer than 3-points threw away reliable information.

Although there is some variation in the patterns yielded by these various studies, they can be viewed as supporting the notion that reliability is higher for scales with many points than for scales with only 2 or 3. Furthermore, one might argue that scales with too many points compromise reliability as well.

Validity.   Research on the effect of the number of scale points on validity has relied on various gauges of validity, including simulations, concurrent and predictive validity, interrater agreement, and susceptibility to question order effects and interviewer effects.

Studies estimating correlations between true attitude scores and observed ratings on scales of different lengths using simulated data have found that validity increases as scales increase from 2 points to longer lengths; however as the scales grow longer, the gains in validity become correspondingly smaller (Green & Rao, 1970; Lehmann & Hulbert, 1972; Lissitz & Green, 1975; Martin, 1973; Martin, 1978; Ramsay, 1973). Besides simulation, several other techniques have been used to assess the validity of scales of different lengths: correlating responses obtained from two different ratings of the same construct (e.g., Matell & Jacoby, 1971; Smith, 1994a; Smith & Peterson, 1985; Warr, Barter, & Brownridge, 1983; Watson, 1988), correlating attitude measures obtained using scales of different lengths with other attitudes (e.g., Schuman & Presser, 1981, pp. 175–176), and using the ratings obtained using different scale lengths to predict other attitudes (Rosenstone, Hansen, & Kinder, 1986; Smith & Peterson, 1985). Studies have typically found concurrent validity to increase with increasing scale length (Matell & Jacoby, 1971; Rosenstone, Hansen, & Kinder, 1986; Schuman & Presser, 1981; Smith, 1994a, 1994b; Smith & Peterson, 1985; Warr, Barter, & Brownridge, 1983; Watson, 1988).

Participants' answers to attitude measures are often influenced by prior questions that precede a measure in a questionnaire. One such effect is a *contrast effect*, which can occur when a given stimulus is evaluated partly in comparison with stimuli presented previously. Another source of invalidity in ratings is interviewers' opinions in face-to-face or telephone surveys. Presumably partly because of how interviewers ask questions, participants sometimes express opinions that are distorted toward those of the individuals who interview them (see Groves, 1989). These sources of systematic measurement error are apparently related to scale length in ways that suggest more and less optimal lengths.

Several studies suggest that longer scales are less susceptible to question-order effects (Wedell & Parducci, 1988; Wedell, Parducci, & Geiselman, 1987; Wedell, Parducci, & Lane, 1990). However, one study indicates that scales that are especially long might be more susceptible to context effects than those of moderate length (Schwarz & Wyer, 1985). Stember and Hyman (1949/1950) found that answers to dichotomous questions were influenced by interviewer opinions, but this influence disappeared among individuals who were also offered a middle alternative, yielding a trichotomous question.

There is again some variation in the patterns yielded by these studies, but they can be viewed as supporting the notion that validity is higher for scales with a moderate number of points than for scales with fewer, and that validity is compromised by especially long scales.

Discerning Natural Scale Differentiation.   In a study by Champney and Marshall (1939), judges provided ratings on various scales by placing "x"s on 9-centimeter-long lines. Five, six, or seven points along the lines were labeled with sentences to establish the meanings of the parts of the scale. The continuous measurement procedure allowed Champney and Marshall (1939) to divide the lines into as many equally sized categories as they wished and then assess the cross-sectional reliability of the various divisions for two items that were both designed to measure sociability. Cross-sectional reliability increased dramatically from a 2-point scale ($r = .56$) to a 9-point scale ($r = .70$), and a further significant increase appeared when moving to 18 scale points ($r = .74$). Reliabilities, however, were essentially the same for 22 ($r = .75$), 30 ($r = .76$), 45 points ($r = .77$), and 90 points ($r = .76$). The judges returned 3 weeks later to re-rate the objects on a total of 12 scales, which allowed the computation of test–retest reliability of ratings, and results were consistent with the cross-sectional findings.

McKelvie (1978) had participants rate various objects by marking points on lines with no discrete category divisions. Participants also indicated their *confidence interval* around each judgment. By dividing the total line length by the average magnitude of the confidence interval, McKelvie (1978) could estimate the number of scale points participants were naturally employing, which turned out to be 5.

Another study along these lines examined the number of scale points that participants used on scales of increasing length. Matell and Jacoby (1972) had participants provide a series of ratings on scales of lengths ranging from 2 points to 19 points. Nearly all participants used both points on the dichotomous items, and most participants used all 3 points on the trichotomous items. For longer scales, participants used about half the points offered, regardless of length. That is, the more scale points that were offered up to 19, the more points participants used, up to about 9.

Rundquist and Sletto (1936) had participants complete a set of ratings either by marking points on lines or by using 5- or 7-point category scales. When the line marks were coded according to a 7-point division, the distribution of ratings was identical to that obtained from the 7-point scale. But when the line marks were coded according to a 5-point division, the distribution was significantly different from the 5-point scale, with fewer extreme and midpoint ratings being made for the latter than for the former. This finding, again, supports the use of 7-point scales.

Middle Alternatives and Satisficing.   The validity of the satisficing perspective regarding middle alternatives can be gauged by determining whether attraction to them is greatest under the conditions that are thought to foster satisficing, two of which are low cognitive skills and low attitude strength (see Krosnick, 1991). However, Kalton, Roberts, and Holt (1980), Schuman and Presser (1981), O'Muircheartaigh, Krosnick, and Helic (1999), and Narayan and Krosnick (1996) concluded that attraction to middle alternatives was unrelated to participants' education (a proxy measure for cognitive skills). Krosnick and Schuman (1988) and Bishop (1990) found more attraction among those for whom the issue was less important and whose attitudes were less intense, and O'Muircheartaigh et al. (1999) found that attraction to middle alternatives was greater among people with less interest in the topic. But Stember and Hyman (1949/1950) found attraction to middle alternatives on a specific foreign policy issue was unrelated to general interest in foreign policy, and O'Muircheartaigh et al. (1999) found no relation of attraction to middle alternatives with volume of knowledge about the object. Thus, at best, the available evidence on this point is mixed with regard to predictors of attraction to middle alternatives.

More important, O'Muircheartaigh and colleagues (1999) found that adding midpoints to rating scales improved the reliability and validity of ratings. Structural equation modeling of error structures revealed that omitting the middle alternative led participants to randomly select one of the moderate scale points closest to where a midpoint would appear. This suggests that offering midpoints is desirable.[1]

Labeling of Rating Scale Points

Once the length of a rating scale has been specified, a researcher must decide how to label the points on the scale. Various studies suggest that the reliability of attitude rating scales is higher when all scale points are labeled with words than when only some are (e.g., Krosnick & Berent, 1993). Furthermore, participants are more satisfied when more rating scale points are verbally labeled (e.g., Dickinson & Zellinger, 1980). When selecting labels, researchers can maximize reliability and validity by selecting ones with meanings that divide up the continuum into approximately equal units (e.g., Klockars & Yamagishi, 1988; for a summary, see Krosnick & Fabrigar, in press). For example, "very good, good, and poor" is a combination that should be avoided, because the terms do not divide the evaluative continuum equally.

Many closed-ended attitude measures are modeled after Likert's technique, offering statements to participants and asking them to indicate whether they agree or disagree with each or to indicate their level of agreement or disagreement on a scale. Other attitude measures offer assertions and ask participants to report the extent to which the assertions are true or false, and some attitude measures ask people yes/no questions (e.g., "Do you favor limiting imports of foreign steel?").

These sorts of item formats are very appealing from a practical standpoint, because such items are easy to write. If one wants to identify people who have positive attitudes toward bananas, for example, one simply needs to write a statement expressing an attitude (e.g., "I like bananas") and ask people whether they agree or disagree with it or whether it is true or false. Also, these formats can be used to measure a wide range of different constructs efficiently. Instead of having to change the response options from one question to the next as one moves from measuring liking to perceived goodness or badness, the same set of response options can be used. The popularity of agree/disagree, true/false, and yes/no questions is therefore no surprise.

Despite this popularity, there has been a great deal of concern expressed over the years that these question formats may be seriously problematic. The concern expressed is that some participants may sometimes say "agree," "true," or "yes" regardless of the question being asked of them. So, for example, a person might agree with a statement that the U.S. should forbid speeches against democracy and might also agree with a statement that the U.S. should allow such speeches. This behavior, labeled *acquiescence*, can be defined as endorsement of an assertion made in a question, regardless of the content of the assertion. In theory, this behavior could result from a desire to be polite rather than confrontational in interpersonal interactions (Leech, 1983), from a desire of individuals of lower social status to defer to individuals of higher social status (Lenski & Leggett, 1960), or from an inclination to satisfice rather than optimize when answering questionnaires (Krosnick, 1991).

The evidence documenting acquiescence is now voluminous and consistently compelling, based on a range of different demonstration methods (for a review, see Krosnick & Fabrigar, forthcoming). For example, consider first just agree/disagree questions. When people are given such answer choices, are not told any questions, and are asked to guess what answers an experimenter is imagining, people guess "agree" much more often than "disagree" (e.g., Berg & Rapaport, 1954). In other studies, pairs of statements were constructed stating mutually exclusive views (e.g., "I enjoy socializing" vs. "I don't enjoy socializing"), and people were asked to agree or disagree with both. Although answers to such pairs should be strongly negatively correlated, 41 studies yielded an average correlation of only −.22. This correlation may be far from −1.0 partly because of random measurement error, but it may also be because of acquiescence.

Consistent with this claim, combining across 10 studies, an average of 52% of people agreed with an assertion, whereas an average of only 42% of people disagreed with the opposite assertion. Thus, people are apparently inclined toward agreeing rather than disagreeing, manifesting what might be considered an acquiescence effect of 10 percentage points. Another set of 8 studies compared answers to agree/disagree questions with answers to forced choice questions where the order of the views expressed by the response alternatives was the same as in the agree/disagree questions. On average, 14% more people agreed with an assertion than expressed the same view in the corresponding forced choice question. Averaging across 7 studies, 22% of people on average agreed with both a statement and its reversal, whereas only 10% of people disagreed with both. Thus, all of these methods suggest an average acquiescence effect of about 10%.

Other evidence indicates that the tendency to acquiesce is a general inclination of some individuals across questions. For example, the average cross-sectional reliability of the tendency to agree with assertions is .65 across 29 studies. Furthermore, the over-time consistency of the tendency to acquiesce is about .75 over 1 month, .67 over 4 months, and .35 over 4 years (e.g., Couch & Keniston, 1960; Hoffman, 1960; Newcomb, 1943).

These same sorts of results (regarding correlations between opposite assertions, endorsement rates of items, their reversals, forced choice versions, and so on) have been produced in studies of true/false questions and of yes/no questions, suggesting that acquiescence is present in responses to these items as well. There is other such evidence regarding these response alternatives. For example, people are much more likely to answer yes/no factual questions correctly when the correct answer is "yes" than when it is "no" (e.g., Larkins & Shaver, 1967; Rothenberg, 1969), presumably because people are biased toward saying "yes." Similarly, factual reports are more likely to disagree with informants' answers when a yes/no question is answered "yes" than when it is answered "no," again presumably because of a bias toward "yes" answers (Sigelman & Budd, 1986). When people say they are guessing the answer to a true/false question, 71% of answers are "true," and only 29% are "false."

Acquiescence is most common among participants of lower social status (e.g., Gove & Geerken, 1977; Lenski & Leggett, 1960), with less formal education (e.g., Ayidiya & McClendon, 1990; Narayan & Krosnick, 1996), of lower intelligence (e.g., Forehand, 1962; Hanley, 1959; Krosnick, Narayan, & Smith, 1996), of lower cognitive energy (Jackson, 1959), who don't like to think (Messick & Frederiksen, 1958), and of lower bias toward conveying a socially desirable image of themselves (e.g., Goldsmith, 1987; Shaffer, 1963). Also, acquiescence is most common when a question is difficult to answer (Gage, Leavitt, & Stone, 1957; Hanley, 1962; Trott & Jackson, 1967), after participants have become fatigued by answering many prior questions (e.g., Clancy & Wachsler, 1971), and during telephone interviews as opposed to face-to-face interviews (e.g., Calsyn, Roades, & Calsyn, 1992; Holbrook, Green, & Krosnick, 2003). Although some of these results are consistent with the notion that acquiescence results from politeness or deferral to people of higher social status, all of the results are consistent with the satisficing explanation.

If this interpretation is correct, then acquiescence might be reduced by assuring (through pretesting) that questions are easy for participants to comprehend and answer and by taking steps to maximize participant motivation to answer carefully and thoughtfully. However, no evidence is yet available testing whether acquiescence can be reduced in these ways. Therefore, a better approach to eliminate acquiescence is avoiding the use of agree/disagree, true/false, and yes/no questions altogether. This is especially sensible because answers to these sorts of questions are less valid and less reliable than answers to the same questions expressed in a format that offers all competing points of view and asks participants to choose among them (e.g., Eurich, 1931; Isard, 1956; Watson & Crawford, 1930).

One alternative approach to controlling for acquiescence is derived from the presumption that certain people have acquiescent personalities and are likely to do all of the acquiescing. According to this view, a researcher needs to identify those people and statistically adjust their answers to correct for this tendency (e.g., Couch & Keniston, 1960). To this end, many batteries of items have been developed to measure a person's tendency to acquiesce, and people who offer lots of "agree," "true," or "yes" answers across a large set of items can then be spotlighted as likely acquiescers. However, the evidence on moderation previously reviewed suggests that acquiescence is not simply the result of having an acquiescent personality; rather, it is mainly influenced by circumstantial factors. Because this "correction" approach does not take that into account, the corrections performed are not likely to fully and precisely account for acquiescence.

It might seem that acquiescence can be controlled by measuring a construct with a large set of agree/disagree or true/false items, half of them making assertions opposite to the other half (called "item reversals;" see Paulhus, 1991). This approach is designed to place acquiescers in the middle of the final dimension but will do so only if the assertions made in the reversals are equally extreme as the statements in the original items. Furthermore, it is difficult to write large sets of item reversals without using the word "not" or other such negations, and evaluating assertions that include negations is cognitively burdensome and error-laden for participants, thus adding measurement error and increasing participant fatigue (e.g., Eifermann, 1961; Wason, 1961). Even if one is able to construct appropriately reversed items, acquiescers presumably end up at a point on the measurement dimension where most probably do not belong on substantive grounds. That is, if these individuals were induced not to acquiesce but to answer the items thoughtfully, their final scores would presumably be more valid than placing them at or near the midpoint of the dimension.

Most important, answering an agree/disagree, true/false, or yes/no question always requires a participant to answer a comparable rating question with construct-specific response options in his or her mind first. For example, if a person is asked to agree or disagree with the assertion "I do not like bananas," he or she must first decide how much bananas are liked (perhaps concluding "I love bananas") and then translate that conclusion into the appropriate selection in order to answer the question one was asked ("disagree" to the original item). Researchers who use such questions presume that the arraying of participants along the agree/disagree dimension corresponds monotonically to the arraying of those individuals along the underlying substantive dimension of interest. That is, the more a person agrees with the assertion "I do not like bananas," the more negative his or her true attitude toward bananas is.

Yet consider the following scenario. Our hypothetical banana-lover encounters the following item: "I sort of like bananas." He or she may respond "disagree" because "sort of like" does not express the extremity of his or her liking. Thus, people who disagree with this question would include those who genuinely dislike bananas, as well as those whose positive regard vastly exceeds the phrase "sort of like," which clearly violates the monotonic equivalence of the response dimension and the underlying attitude construct of interest.

As this example makes clear, it would be simpler to ask participants directly how much they like or dislike objects. Every agree/disagree, true/false, or yes/no question implicitly requires the participant to make a rating of an object along a continuous dimension in his or her mind, so asking about that dimension directly is bound to be less burdensome. Not surprisingly, then, the reliability and validity of rating scale questions that array the full attitude dimension explicitly (e.g., from *extremely bad* to *extremely good*, or from *dislike a great deal* to *like a great deal*) are higher than those of agree/disagree, true/false, and yes/no questions that focus on only a single point of view (e.g., Ebel, 1982; Mirowsky & Ross, 1991; Ruch & DeGraff, 1926; Saris & Krosnick, 2000; Wesman, 1946). Consequently, it seems best to avoid agree/disagree, true/false, and yes/no formats altogether and instead ask questions using rating scales that explicitly display the evaluative dimension.

The Order of Response Alternatives

Many studies have shown that the order in which response alternatives are presented to participants can affect their selection among the alternatives, but until recently, it has not been clear when such effects occur, what their direction will be, and why they occur. Some past studies identified primacy effects (in which response choices presented early were most likely to be selected); other studies found recency effects (in which response choices presented last were more likely to be selected), and still other studies found no order effects at all. Fortunately, this apparently disorderly set of evidence can be explained by the theory of questionnaire satisficing (Krosnick, 1991).

Because the vast majority of attitude measurement involves the use of rating scales that ask participants to choose a descriptor from among a set that represents some sort of dimension or continuum (e.g., from *dislike a great deal* to *like a great deal*), our greatest interest is with such scales. But to understand the satisficing explanation of response order effects, it is helpful to begin with an explanation of how response choice order effects occur when answering categorical questions, which ask people to make a choice among a set of objects that do not represent a continuum (e.g., "Which do you like more, peas or carrots?").

Response order effects in categorical questions appear to be attributable to *weak satisficing*, which entails executing all the steps of optimal answering (interpreting a question, retrieving information from memory, integrating the information into a judgment, and reporting the judgment), but in a superficial, biased, and shortcut fashion (see Krosnick, 1991; Krosnick & Alwin, 1987). When confronted with categorical questions, optimal answering would entail carefully assessing the appropriateness of each of the offered response alternatives before selecting one. In contrast, a weak satisficer could simply choose the first response alternative he or she considers that appears to constitute a reasonable answer. Exactly which alternative is most likely to be chosen depends in part on whether the response options are presented visually or orally to participants.

When response alternatives are presented visually, either on a show-card in a face-to-face interview or in a self-administered questionnaire, weak satisficing is likely to bias participants toward selecting choices displayed early in a list. Participants are likely to begin at the top of the list and consider each response alternative individually, and their thoughts are likely to be biased in a confirmatory direction (Klayman & Ha, 1984; Koriat, Lichtenstein, & Fischhoff, 1980; Yzerbyt & Leyens, 1991). Given that researchers typically include in questions response choices that are reasonable answers, this confirmation-biased thinking is likely to generate at least a reason or two in favor of selecting almost any alternative a participant thinks about.

After considering one or two response alternatives, the potential for fatigue becomes significant, because participants' minds become cluttered with thoughts about initial alternatives. Also, fatigue may result from proactive interference, whereby thoughts about the initial alternatives interfere with and confuse thinking about later, competing alternatives (Miller & Campbell, 1959). Weak satisficers can cope by thinking only superficially about later response alternatives; the confirmatory bias would thereby give the earlier items an advantage. Alternatively, weak satisficers can simply terminate their evaluation process altogether once they come upon a response alternative that seems to be a reasonable answer to the question. And again, because most answers are likely to seem reasonable, these participants are likely to end up choosing alternatives near the beginning of a list. Thus, weak satisficing seems likely to produce primacy effects under conditions of visual presentation.

When response alternatives are presented orally, as in face-to-face or telephone interviews, the effects of weak satisficing are more difficult to anticipate. This is so because response order effects reflect not only evaluations of each option, but also the limits of memory. When response alternatives are read aloud, participants are not given the opportunity to process the first alternative extensively. Presentation of the second alternative terminates processing of the first one, usually relatively quickly. Therefore, participants are able to devote the most processing time to the final items read; these items remain in short-term memory after interviewers pause to let participants answer.

It is conceivable that some participants listen to a short list of response alternatives without evaluating any of them. Once the list is completed, these individuals may recall the first alternative, think about it, and then progress through the list forward from there. Given that fatigue should instigate weak satisficing relatively quickly, a primacy effect would be expected. However, because this process requires more effort than simply considering the final items in the list first, weak satisficers are unlikely to do this very often. Therefore, considering only the allocation of processing, we would anticipate both primacy and recency effects, though the latter should be more common than the former.

These effects of deeper processing are likely to be reinforced by the effects of memory. Items presented early in a list are most likely to enter long-term memory (e.g., Atkinson & Shiffrin, 1968), and items presented at the end of a list are most likely to be in short-term memory immediately after the list is heard (e.g., Atkinson & Shiffrin, 1968). Furthermore, items presented late are more likely to be recalled (Baddeley & Hitch, 1977). So items presented at the beginning and end of a list are more likely to be recalled after the question is read, particularly if the list is long. Therefore, given that a response alternative must be remembered in order for a participant to select it, both early and late items should be more available for selection, especially among weak satisficers. Typically, short-term memory dominates long-term memory immediately after acquiring a list of information (Baddeley & Hitch, 1977), so memory factors should promote recency effects more than primacy effects. Thus, in response to orally presented questions, recency effects would be mostly expected, though some primacy effects might occur as well.

Schwarz and Hippler (1991; Schwarz, Hippler, & Noelle-Neumann, 1992) pointed out two additional factors that may govern response-order effects: the plausibility of the response alternatives presented and perceptual contrast effects. If deep processing is accorded to a response alternative that seems highly implausible, even participants with a confirmatory bias in reasoning may fail to generate any reasons to select it. Thus, deeper processing of some alternatives may make them especially *un*likely to be selected.

Although the results of past studies of response order effects in categorical questions seem to offer a confusing pattern of results when considered as a group, coherence appears when the studies are separated into those involving visual and oral presentation. Whenever a visual presentation has been used, primacy effects have been found (Ayidiya & McClendon, 1990; Becker, 1954; Bishop, Hippler, Schwarz, & Strack, 1988; Campbell & Mohr, 1950; Israel & Taylor, 1990; Krosnick & Alwin, 1987; Schwarz, Hippler, & Noelle-Neumann, 1992). In studies involving oral presentation, nearly all response order effects have been shown to be recency effects (Berg & Rapaport, 1954; Bishop, 1987; Bishop et al., 1988; Cronbach, 1950; Krosnick, 1992; Krosnick & Schuman, 1988; Mathews, 1927; McClendon, 1986, 1991; Rubin, 1940; Schuman & Presser, 1981; Schwarz, Hippler, & Noelle-Neumann, 1992; Visser, Krosnick, Marquette, & Curtin, 2000).

If the response order effects demonstrated in these studies are due to weak satisficing, then these effects should be stronger under conditions where satisficing is most likely. And indeed, these effects were stronger when participants had relatively limited cognitive skills (Krosnick, 1990; Krosnick & Alwin, 1987; Krosnick, Narayan, & Smith, 1996; McClendon, 1986, 1991; Narayan & Krosnick, 1996). Mathews (1927) also found stronger primacy effects as questions became more and more difficult and as participants became more fatigued. Although McClendon (1986) found no relation between the number of words in a question and the magnitude of response order effects, Payne (1949/1950) found more response-order effects in questions involving more words and words that were more difficult to comprehend. Also, Schwarz et al. (1992) showed that a strong recency effect was eliminated when prior questions on the same topic were asked, which presumably made participants' knowledge of the topic more accessible and thereby made optimizing easier for them.

Much of the logic previously articulated regarding categorical questions seems applicable to rating scales, but in a different way than for categorical questions. Many people's attitudes are probably not perceived as precise points on an underlying evaluative dimension but rather are seen as ranges or "latitudes of acceptance" (M. Sherif & Hovland, 1961; C. W. Sherif, Sherif, & Nebergall, 1965). If a satisficing participant considers the options on a rating scale sequentially, then he or she may select the first one that falls in his or her latitude of acceptance, yielding a primacy effect under both visual and oral presentation.

Nearly all of the studies of response order effects in rating scales involved visual presentation, and when order effects appeared, they were nearly uniformly primacy effects (Carp, 1974; Chan, 1991; Holmes, 1974; Johnson, 1981; Payne, 1971; Quinn & Belson, 1969). Furthermore, two oral presentation studies of rating scales found primacy effects as well (Kalton, Collins, & Brook, 1978; Mingay & Greenwell, 1989). Consistent with the satisficing notion, Mingay and Greenwell (1989) found that their primacy effect was stronger for people with more limited cognitive skills. However, these investigators found no relation of the magnitude of the primacy effect to the speed at which interviewers read questions to participants, despite the fact that a fast pace presumably increased task difficulty. Also, response-order effects were found to be no stronger when questions were placed later in a questionnaire (Carp, 1974). Thus, the moderators of rating scale response order effects may be different from the moderators of such effects in categorical questions, though more research is clearly needed to fully address this question.

How should researchers handle these response choice order effects when designing attitude measures? One possibility would be to ignore them, in the hope that they are relatively rare and, when they do occur, rarely displace variables' distributions by large degrees. Unfortunately, this approach seems overly optimistic. Even if a researcher is interested primarily in associations between variables (rather than univariate distributions), tests of the form-resistant correlation hypothesis suggest that the conclusions of correlational analysis can be significantly altered by response order effects (see Krosnick & Fabrigar, forthcoming). It therefore seems wiser to take some steps to address these effects in the design phase of a research project.

One seemingly effective way to do so is to counterbalance the order in which response choices are presented to participants. Counterbalancing is relatively simple to accomplish with dichotomous questions; half of a set of participants can be given one order, and the other half can be given the reverse order. When the number of response choices increases, the counterbalancing task can become more complex. However, it would make no sense to completely randomize the order in which rating scale points are presented, because that would eliminate the sensible progressive ordering of them from positive to negative, negative to positive, most to least, least to most, or whatever. Therefore, for rating scales, only two orders would presumably be used, regardless of how many points are on the scale.

Unfortunately, counterbalancing order across participants creates a new problem: variance in responses because of systematic measurement error. Once response alternative orders have been varied across participants, their answers will probably differ from one another partly because different people received different orders. One might view this new variance as *random* error variance, the effect of which would be to attenuate observed relations among variables and leave marginal distributions of variables unaltered. However, given the theoretical explanations for response order effects previously proposed, this error seems unlikely to be random.

We therefore suggest considering an alternative approach to solving this problem. In addition to counterbalancing presentation order, it seems potentially valuable to take steps to prevent the effects from ever occurring in the first place. The most effective method for doing so presumably depends on the cognitive mechanism producing the effect. If primacy effects in rating scale questions are due to satisficing, then steps that reduce satisficing should reduce the effects. For example, with regard to motivation, questionnaires can be kept short, and accountability can be induced by occasionally asking participants to justify their answers. And with regard to task difficulty, the wording of questions and answer choices can be made as simple as possible.

No-Opinion Filters and Attitude Strength

When we ask participants to report their attitudes, we presume that their answers reflect information or opinions that they previously had stored in memory. If a person does not have a preexisting opinion about the object of interest, the question itself presumably prompts him or her to draw on relevant beliefs or attitudes in order to concoct a reasonable, albeit new, evaluation (see, e.g., Zaller & Feldman, 1992). Consequently, whether based on a preexisting judgment or a newly formulated one, responses presumably reflect the individual's orientation toward the object.

What happens when people are asked about an object regarding which they have no knowledge and no opinion? Ideally they will say that they have no opinion or aren't familiar with the object or don't know how they feel about it (we refer to all such responses as no opinion or NO responses). But when participants are asked a question in such a way as to suggest that they ought to have opinions of the object, they may wish not to appear foolishly uninformed and may therefore give arbitrary answers (Converse, 1964). In order to reduce the likelihood of such behavior, some questionnaire design experts have recommended that no-opinion options routinely be included in questions (e.g., Bogart, 1972; Converse & Presser, 1986; Payne, 1950; Vaillancourt, 1973). In essence, such options tell participants that it is acceptable to say they have no attitude toward an object.

Do no-opinion filters work? Do they successfully encourage people without meaningful opinions to admit it? That is, is the overall quality of data obtained by a filtered question better than the overall quality of data obtained by an unfiltered question? Might filters go too far and discourage people who have meaningful opinions from expressing them? These important issues can be explored by drawing on a large body of existing research, and this work suggests clearly that no-opinion filters are a bad idea.

Support for this conclusion comes from a series of studies that explored whether the substantive responses provided by people who would have said "don't know" if that had been offered to them are in fact meaningless. In one nonexperimental study, Gilljam and Granberg (1993) asked participants three questions tapping attitudes toward building nuclear power plants. The first of these questions offered a NO option, and 15% of participants selected it. The other two questions, asked later in the interview, did not offer NO options, and only 3% and 4% of participants, respectively, failed to offer substantive responses to them. Thus, the majority of participants who initially said NO offered opinions on the later two questions. However, these later responses mostly reflected meaningful opinions, because the two attitude reports correlated moderately with one another and predicted participants' later voting behavior.

Other studies examined the predictive validity and reliability of attitude reports and reached similar conclusions. Bishop, Oldendick, Tuchfarber, and Bennett (1979) found slightly stronger associations of attitudes with other criterion items when NO options were offered than when they were not, but Schuman and Presser (1981) rarely found such differences. In addition, Alwin and Krosnick (1991), McClendon and Alwin (1993), Krosnick and Berent (1990), Krosnick et al. (2002), and Poe, Seeman, McLaughlin, Mehl, and Dietz (1988) found no greater reliability of self-reports when NO filters were included in questions than when they were not.

Krosnick et al. (2002) found that offering NO options did not enhance the degree to which people's answers were responsive to question manipulations that should have affected them. Specifically, participants in their study were told about a program that would prevent future oil spills and were asked whether they would be willing to pay a specified amount for it in additional taxes. Different participants were told different prices, on the presumption that fewer people would be willing to pay for the program as the price escalated. In fact, this is what happened. If pressing NO responses into substantive ones creates meaningless answers, then sensitivity to the price of the program would be less among people pressed to offer substantive opinions than among people offered a NO option. But in fact, sensitivity to price was the same in both groups. Finally, Visser, Krosnick, Marquette, and Curtin (2000) found that pre-election polls predict election outcomes more accurately when participants who initially say they don't know are pressed to identify the candidate toward whom they lean.

Taken together, the literature on how filters affect data quality suggests that NO filters do not remove only people without meaningful opinions. Thus, we see here reason to hesitate regarding the use of such filters. In order to make sense of this surprising evidence, it is useful to turn to studies by cognitive psychologists of the process by which people decide that they do not know something. Norman (1973) proposed a two-step model that seems to account for observed data quite well. If asked a question such as "Do you favor or oppose U.S. government aid to Nicaragua?", a participant's first step would be to search long-term memory for any information relevant to the objects mentioned: U.S. foreign aid and Nicaragua. If no information about either is recalled, the individual can quickly respond by saying he or she has no opinion. But if some information is located about either object, the person must then retrieve that information and decide whether it can be used to formulate a reasonable opinion. If not, he or she presumably replies "don't know," but the required search time make this a relative slow response. Glucksberg and McCloskey (1981) reported a series of studies demonstrating that "don't know" responses can indeed occur either quickly or slowly, the difference resulting from whether or not any relevant information can be retrieved in memory.

This distinction between first-stage and second-stage NO responses suggests different reasons for them. According to the proponents of NO filters, the reason presumed to be most common is that the participant lacks the necessary information and/or experience with which to form an attitude. Such circumstances would presumably yield quick, first-stage NO responses. In contrast, second-stage NO responses could occur, for example, because of ambivalence. That is, some participants may know a great deal about an object and/or have strong feelings toward it, but their thoughts and/or feelings may be highly contradictory, making it difficult to select a single response.

It also seems possible that NO responses can result at what might be considered a third stage, the point at which participants attempt to translate their retrieved judgments onto the response choices offered by a question. For example, a participant may know approximately where he or she falls on an attitude scale (e.g., around 6 or 7 on a 1–7 scale), but because of ambiguity in the meaning of the scale points or of his or her internal attitudinal cues, he or she may be unsure of exactly which point to choose, yielding a NO response. A participant who has some information about an object, has a neutral overall orientation toward it, and is asked a question without a neutral response option might say NO because the answer he or she would like to give has not been conferred legitimacy. Or a participant may be concerned that he or she does not know enough about the object to defend an opinion toward it, so that opinion may be withheld rather than reported.

Finally, it seems possible that some NO responses occur at a pre-first stage, before participants have even begun to attempt to retrieve relevant information. For example, if a participant does not understand the question being asked and is unwilling to answer until its meaning is clarified, he or she might respond "I don't know" (see, e.g., Fonda, 1951).

There is, in fact, evidence that some NO responses occur for all of these reasons, but when people are asked directly why they give NO responses, people rarely attribute such responses to a complete lack of information or a lack of opinion, and they most often occur for the other reasons as previously outlined (Coombs & Coombs, 1976; Faulkenberry & Mason, 1978; Klopfer & Madden, 1980; Schaeffer & Bradburn, 1989).

Another explanation for the fact that NO filters do not consistently improve data quality is satisficing (Krosnick, 1991). According to this perspective, people have many latent attitudes that they are not immediately aware of holding. Because the bases of those opinions reside in memory, people can retrieve those bases and integrate them to yield an overall attitude, but doing so requires significant cognitive effort (*optimizing*). When people are disposed not to do this work and instead prefer to shortcut the effort they devote in generating answers, they will attempt to satisfice by looking for cues in a question that point to an answer that will appear to be acceptable and sensible but that requires little effort to select. A NO option constitutes just such a cue and may therefore encourage satisficing, whereas omission of the NO option would instead inspire participants to do the cognitive work necessary to retrieve relevant information from memory.

This perspective suggests that NO options should be especially likely to attract participants under the conditions thought to foster satisficing: low ability to optimize, low motivation to do so, or high task difficulty. Consistent with this reasoning, NO filters attract participants with more limited cognitive skills, as well as participants with relatively little knowledge and exposure to information about the attitude object (for a review, see Krosnick, 1999). In addition, NO responses are especially common among people for whom an object is low in personal importance, is of little interest, and arouses little affective involvement, and this may be because of lowered motivation to optimize under these conditions. Furthermore, people are especially likely to say NO when they feel they lack the ability to formulate informed opinions (i.e., subjective competence), and when they feel there is little value in formulating such opinions (i.e., demand for opinionation). These associations may arise at the time of attitude measurement: low motivation inhibits a person from drawing on knowledge available in memory to formulate and carefully report a substantive opinion of an object.

NO responses are also more likely when questions appear later in a questionnaire, at which point participant motivation to optimize is presumably waning (Culpepper, Smith, & Krosnick, 1992; Dickinson & Kirzner, 1985; Ferber, 1966; Krosnick et al., 2002; Ying, 1989). Also, NO responses become increasingly common as questions become more difficult to understand (Converse, 1976; Klare, 1950). Additionally, Houston and Nevin (1977) found experimentally that describing a research study as being conducted by a prestigious sponsor for a purpose consistent with its identity (a university seeking to advance knowledge) decreased NO responses, presumably via enhanced participant motivation to optimize.

Hippler and Schwarz (1989) proposed another reason why NO filters discourage reporting of real attitudes: Strongly worded NO filters might suggest to participants that a great deal of knowledge is required to answer an attitude question and thereby intimidate people who feel they might not be able to adequately justify their opinions. Consistent with this reasoning, Hippler and Schwarz found that participants inferred from the presence and strength of a NO filter that follow-up questioning would be more extensive, would require more knowledge, and would be more difficult. If participants were motivated to avoid extensive questioning or were concerned that they couldn't defend whatever opinions they might offer, then they might be biased toward a NO response.

Another reason why people might prefer to select NO options rather than offer meaningful opinions is the desire not to present a socially undesirable or unflattering image of themselves. Consistent with this claim, many studies found that people who offered NO responses frequently would have provided socially undesirable responses (Cronbach, 1950, p. 15; Fonda, 1951; Johanson, Gips, & Rich, 1993; Kahn & Hadley, 1949; Rosenberg, Izard, & Hollander, 1955).

Taken together, these studies suggest that NO responses often result not from genuine lack of attitudes but rather from ambivalence, question ambiguity, satisficing, intimidation, and self-protection. In each of these cases, there is something meaningful to be learned from pressing participants to report their opinions, but NO response options discourage people from doing so. As a result, data quality does not improve when such options are explicitly included in questions.

A better way to accomplish the goal of differentiating "real" opinions from "non-attitudes" is to measure the strength of an attitude using one or more follow-up questions. Krosnick and Petty (1995) proposed that strong attitudes can be defined as those that are resistant to change, are stable over time, and have powerful impact on cognition and action. Many empirical investigations have confirmed that attitudes vary in strength, and the participants' presumed task when confronting a "don't know" response option is to decide whether his or her attitude is sufficiently weak to be best described by selecting that option. However, because the appropriate cut point along the strength dimension seems exceedingly hard to specify and unlikely to be specified uniformly by participants, it seems preferable to ask people to describe where their attitudes fall along the strength continuum.

Many different attitude attributes are correlated with attitude strength, and these attributes are all somewhat independent of each other (see, e.g., Krosnick, Boninger, Chuang, Berent, & Carnot, 1993). For example, people can be asked how important the object is to them personally or how much they have thought about it or how certain they are of their opinion or how knowledgeable they feel about it (for details on measuring these and many other dimensions, see Wegener, Downing, Krosnick, & Petty, 1995). Measuring each of these dimensions can help to differentiate attitudes that are crystallized and consequential from those that are not.

Summary

All of these studies and many others suggest optimal and less optimal ways to produce reliable and valid measurements of attitudes via direct self-reports (see Krosnick & Fabrigar, forthcoming). Each of the sources of error outlined (e.g., the number of points on a rating scale, the verbal labeling, and order of response choices) may have a relatively small effect, but when a set of compromises are conglomerated, the net measurement error induced may be quite considerable. If researchers wish to make accurate assessments of people's attitudes and to have the greatest chance of finding statistically significant correlations between variables and statistically significant effects of manipulations on attitudes, then following the guidelines outlined to minimize measurement error seems well-advised.

ALTERNATIVES TO DIRECT SELF-REPORTS

Given that direct self-reports will only be valid if participants are willing to describe themselves accurately, it is understandable that researchers have wondered whether motivational forces might sometimes lead participants to abandon this goal and to misrepresent themselves, creating a different sort of measurement error. A great deal of research has addressed this issue, and we turn to that work next.

The Notion of Social Desirability Response Bias

The idea that research participants might lie to researchers is not an implausible proposition, to be sure. For example, DePaulo, Kashy, Kirkendol, Wyer, and Epstein (1996) had people complete daily diaries in which they recorded any lies that they told during a 7-day period. On average, people reported telling one lie per day, with some people telling many more, and 91% of the lies involved misrepresenting oneself in some way. This evidence is in line with theoretical accounts from sociology (Goffman, 1959) and psychology (Schlenker & Weigold, 1989) asserting that an inherent element of social interaction is constructing an image of oneself in the eyes of others in pursuit of relevant goals. The fact that being viewed more favorably by others is more likely to bring rewards and minimize punishments may motivate people to construct favorable self-images, sometimes via deceit. If such behavior is common in daily life, why wouldn't people lie when answering questionnaires as well?

There are, in fact, a number of reasons to believe that the motivation to lie when answering questionnaires might be minimal. First, when filling out an anonymous questionnaire, no rewards or punishments can possibly be at stake. And second, in most surveys and laboratory experiments, the participants' relationships with a researcher are so short-lived and superficial that very little of consequence is at stake as well. Certainly, a small frown of disapproval from a total stranger can cause a bit of discomfort, but little more than that. The cognitive task of figuring out which response to each question one is asked will garner the most respect from a researcher is likely to be demanding enough to be worth doing only when the stakes are significant. So perhaps there isn't so much danger here after all.

Unfortunately, however, there is another potential source of systematic distortion in responses to even self-administered anonymous questionnaires: self-deception. Not only do people want to maintain favorable images of themselves in the eyes of others, but they also want to have such images in their own eyes as well. According to many psychological analyses, the pursuit of self-esteem is a basic human motive (see, e.g., Sedikides & Strube, 1997), and it is driven partly by such inevitable realities as the prospect of death (e.g., Greenberg, Solomon, & Pyszczynski, 1997). So people may be motivated to convince themselves that they are respectable, good people, and doing so may at times entail misconstrual of facts (see Paulhus, 1984, 1986, 1991). If people fool themselves in this way, then of course such misconstrual will find its way into questionnaire responses, even when participants want to accurately report their attitudes to an interviewer and/or researcher. Obviously, it is tricky business to fool oneself, because part of the mind would need to know that it's fooling another part. However, such self-deception can be so automatic that people may not be aware of it at all.

Documenting the Extent of Self-Presentational Social Desirability Response Bias

The evidence documenting systematic and intentional misrepresentation in questionnaire responses is now quite voluminous and very convincing, partly because the same conclusion has been supported by studies using many different methods. One such method is the "bogus pipeline technique," which involves telling participants that the researcher can otherwise determine the correct answer to a question they will be asked, so they might as well answer it accurately (see, e.g., Roese & Jamieson, 1993). Under these conditions, people are more willing to report substance use than they would be if asked directly (Evans, Hansen, & Mittlemark, 1977; Murray & Perry, 1987). Likewise, White participants are more willing to ascribe undesirable personality characteristics to African Americans (Sigall & Page, 1971; Pavlos, 1972, 1973) and are more willing to report disliking African Americans (e.g., Allen, 1975) under bogus pipeline conditions. Women are less likely to report supporting the women's movement under bogus pipeline conditions than under normal reporting conditions (Hough & Allen, 1975). Similarly, people are more likely to admit having been given secret information under bogus pipeline conditions (Quigley-Fernandez & Tedeschi, 1978).

Another approach to documenting such distortion is to compare responses given when people believe their answers will have significant consequences for them to responses given when no such consequences exist. For example, in one study, participants who believed that they had already been admitted to an apprenticeship program admitted to having less respectable personality characteristics than did comparable participants who believed they were being evaluated for possible admission to the program (Michaelis & Eysenck, 1971).

Yet another approach to this problem involves the "randomized response technique" (Warner, 1965). Here, participants answer one of various different questions, depending on what a randomizing device instructs. The researcher does not know exactly which question each person is answering, so participants can presumably feel freer to be honest. In one such study, Himmelfarb and Lickteig (1982) had participants secretly toss three coins before answering a yes/no question. Participants were instructed to say "yes" if all three coins came up heads, "no" if all three coins came up tails, and to answer the yes/no question truthfully if any combination of heads and tails came up. People answering in this fashion admitted to falsifying their income tax reports and enjoying soft-core pornography more than did participants who were asked these questions directly.

Still another approach to assessing the impact of social desirability is by studying interviewer effects. The presumption here is that the observable characteristics of an interviewer may suggest to a participant which answers are considered most respectable. So if answers vary in a way that corresponds with interviewer characteristics, it suggests that participants tailored their answers accordingly. For example, various studies have found that African Americans report more favorable attitudes toward Whites when their interviewer is White than when the interviewer is African American (Anderson, Silver, & Abramson, 1988; Campbell, 1981; Schuman & Converse, 1971). Likewise, White participants express more favorable attitudes toward African Americans to African American interviewers than to White interviewers (Campbell, 1981; Cotter, Cohen, & Coulter, 1982; Finkel, Guterbock, & Borg, 1991). These effects have occurred both in face-to-face interviews and in telephone interviews as well (Cotter et al., 1982; Finkel et al., 1991). Similarly, in another study, people expressed more positive attitudes toward firefighters when they thought their interviewer was a firefighter than when they did not hold this belief (Atkin & Chaffee, 1972/1973).

Another approach to this issue involves comparisons of different modes of data collection. In general, pressure to appear socially desirable is presumably greatest when a participant is being interviewed by another person, either face-to-face or over the telephone. This pressure is presumably lessened when participants are completing written questionnaires. Consistent with this reasoning, Catholics in one study were more likely to report favoring legalized abortion and birth control when completing a self-administered questionnaire than when being interviewed by telephone or face-to-face (Wiseman, 1972). Additionally, people report being happier with their lives in interviews than on self-administered questionnaires (Cheng, 1988).

Anonymity of self-administered questionnaires further reduces social pressure, so it, too, offers an empirical handle for addressing this issue. In one study, Gordon (1987) asked participants about dental hygiene on questionnaires; half the participants (selected randomly) were asked to write their names on the questionnaires, whereas the other half were not. Dental checkups, brushing, and flossing were all reported to have been done more often when people wrote their names on the questionnaires than when they did not. Thus, socially desirable responses were apparently more common under conditions of high identifiability. Similarly, people reported having more desirable personality characteristics when they wrote their names, addresses, and telephone numbers on questionnaires than when they did not (Paulhus, 1984).

Taken together, these studies all suggest that some people sometimes distort their answers to questionnaire items in order to present themselves as having more socially desirable or respectable characteristics or behavioral histories. These studies also validate a series of methods that can be used to detect social desirability bias in responses. That is, if a researcher is worried that answers to a particular question might be distorted by intentional misrepresentation, an experiment can be conducted employing a technique such as randomized response to see whether different results are obtained.

It is important to note that only relatively small distortions in results have been documented in all of the social desirability studies reviewed. But the social desirability-driven distortions previously documented represent only those involving other-deception. Therefore, there may be significant amounts of self-deception going on as well, and when combined with other-deception, social desirability-driven error may be substantial.

Implicit Measurement Techniques

To overcome the problems with intentional and unintentional distortion of direct attitude reports, much research has explored using measurement techniques that keep self-presentational concerns from entering a person's deliberation of his or her evaluation in the first place. Such techniques have a long history in attitude research, but have, in recent years, become more popular because of the availability of increasingly sophisticated technologies. We discuss three kinds of implicit measures in this section: unobtrusive behavioral observation, response latency measures, and physiological measures.

Unobtrusive Behavioral Observation

Originally, measures designed to limit self-presentational concerns relied primarily on unobtrusive assessments of overt behaviors. These assessments disguise what is being measured and/or conceal the measurement itself. For example, Milgram's classic *lost-letter technique* involves the placement of ostensibly lost letters in public places (Milgram, Mann, & Harter, 1965). The address on the envelopes is manipulated (and in some cases the sender information: Benson, Karabenick, & Lerner, 1976). Based on the assumption that individuals with more positive attitudes toward the addressee will be more likely to pick up the envelope and put it in a mailbox, the rate and speed of return for these letters is recorded as an indicator of attitudes toward the addressee (e.g., "Friends of the Nazi party" in Milgram et al., 1965).

Other examples of unobtrusive observation techniques focus on responses that are more closely linked to the assessed attitude but are rather incidental behaviors that people are unlikely to suspect are monitored by researchers. For instance, in Westie's (1953) seating task, participants are asked to take a seat in a waiting room where an outgroup target person is already waiting. The critical measure is how closely the participant sits to the target when given a choice of seats that vary in physical proximity. Presumably, the more negative a person's attitude toward the outgroup, the farther away he or she will choose to sit from the target.

Yet another strategy for unobtrusive observation is to disguise what attitude is actually being studied. For example, studies on intergroup attitudes have considered helping behavior in interpersonal contexts as a measure of racial attitudes. These studies have assessed how a person responds when given the opportunity to aid another individual who is either an ingroup or outgroup member (e.g., Gaertner & Dovidio, 1977). Likewise, studies by Donnerstein and colleagues used the same approach for assessing the flip side of pro-social behavior. They provided participants with a legitimate opportunity to aggress toward another individual in the context of a learning experiment, varying the individual's group membership (e.g., Donnerstein & Donnerstein, 1975). Although the participants in these helping and aggression studies were in all likelihood cognizant of the fact that their behavior was being recorded, they may nevertheless have been unaware that their attitudes toward a particular social group were the focus of the measurement effort.

Of course, the expressed goal of these kinds of measurement techniques is to reduce the impact of normative concerns on a person's responses and thereby eliminate strategic misrepresentation. The effectiveness of these techniques is often assumed to be based on the fact that normative concerns will not come to mind during the assessment and are not used for the targeted response. Therefore, the assessment context is designed to curtail the presence of cues that could trigger deliberation about the social acceptability of one's attitude, so responses are ostensibly unmonitored. However, there may be another reason why these types of measures can be effective in limiting self-presentational bias. They may simply assess responses under conditions in which people fail to recognize the impact of their attitudes and thus ignore not only normative implications but all aspects of those attitudes. This possibility is most apparent in the case of techniques designed to disguise the purpose of the assessment. Such strategies may not simply render the normative implications of an attitude less salient for people, but they may also make it more difficult for people to recognize the attitude in question as a potential determinant of their behavior. Thus, when deliberating whether or not to assist another person in need of help, or when choosing a chair in the waiting room, participants may remain unaware of the implicit influences that the target's race has on their decision. Even unobtrusive obser-vation techniques that draw attention to the critical attitude, like the lost-letter technique, may have a similar effect on evaluative processing, as they assess behaviors under circumstances in which the motivation to deliberate is likely to be rather limited. In the absence of much controlled deliberation of one's attitude, its impact on responses may easily go unnoticed. In short, aside from controlling the salience and relevance of normative considerations during as-sessment, self-presentational bias in attitude measurement can be limited by assessing implicit evaluative influences on behavior.

Measures of nonverbal communication make up a final set of traditional unobtrusive ob-servation techniques intended to capture implicit evaluations even in circumstances in which people are motivated to monitor the appropriateness of their behavior. In the past, various non-verbal behaviors, including body posture, eye contact, and fidgeting have been used to assess intergroup attitudes (e.g., McConnell & Leibold, 2001; Word, Zanna, & Cooper, 1974). The general idea behind the use of such measures is that nonverbal channels of communication are more difficult to control than are most aspects of verbal behavior (Dovidio, Kawakami, & Gaertner, 2002). Nonverbal channels therefore allow researchers to assess implicit evalua-tive influences on interpersonal behavior even when people are deliberately trying to control such influences. For example, in an interracial interaction, people may be more successful at keeping negative racial attitudes from influencing their verbal statements than suppressing their impact on nonverbal expressions. Thus, measures of nonverbal behavior would reveal evaluative biases that could be hidden in other, more deliberate, channels of communication.

Of course, none of these measures offer precise control over the exact nature of the evaluative processing that takes place during the assessment. Nor do the measures necessarily guarantee that the attitude in question will be a particularly prominent influence on the assessed response. After all, behavior is generally influenced by a multitude of factors, a person's attitude being just one among many (Jaccard & Blanton, this volume). As a result, measures based on behavioral observation may be particularly noisy. These are just some of the reasons why these measures are not especially popular today.

Several recent implicit assessment techniques are intended to overcome these problems. Instead of capturing complex behaviors, these new implicit measures assess the activation of an evaluation independent of processes that take place during the deliberation and response phases of evaluative processing. We discuss them in the following sections.

Response Latency Measures

Among the new kinds of implicit measures that have received the most attention are those based on response latencies. Such measures try to determine attitude activation from the impact that an attitude object has on the speed with which a person can make certain judgments. These mea-sures fall into two general classes: (a) measures based on sequential priming procedures, and (b) measures using response competition tasks, such as the Implicit Association Test (IAT).[2]

Priming Measures.   Priming measures that have been used to assess attitude activation are all variants of a classic paradigm from research on spreading activation in long-term memory, first introduced by Meyer and Schvaneveldt (1971). In this paradigm, participants are shown letter strings (e.g., BUTTER) and are asked to decide whether or not the target string forms a word. In addition, the letter string is paired with a prime, another word that in the common implementation of this paradigm precedes the target—hence, the term *sequential* priming. The classic finding, replicated in numerous experiments, is that participants are faster in making such lexical decisions when prime and target string are semantically associated, when for example the string BUTTER is preceded by the prime BREAD (for a review, see

Neely, 1991). One explanation for the effect holds that the prime automatically activates other semantically related concepts in long-term memory, which subsequently reduces the time that is required for the activation of related targets to reach recognition threshold (Neely, 1977; Posner & Snyder, 1975).

The paradigm has been adapted for the assessment of attitude activation by using attitude objects as primes and by systematically varying the targets that are paired with this prime. The magnitude of facilitation observed for a given prime/target combination can then serve as an indicator of the degree to which a prime triggers activation of a particular target (e.g., spinach—pleasant versus spinach—awful). Two particular variants of this general paradigm have been used for attitude measurement: evaluative priming and concept priming. Both variants take steps to limit priming effects to automatic activation and to preclude effects that could result from deliberate processing of the attitude prime. For example, priming measures may present primes below the threshold of conscious recognition (e.g., Wittenbrink et al., 1997). Alternatively, a researcher may manipulate the time interval between prime and target onset so that the target appears before any controlled processing of the prime can take place (usually within a few hundred milliseconds, e.g., Fazio et al., 1986). In this latter case, the attitude primes are clearly visible for participants. The procedure therefore requires some kind of cover story that instructs participants to respond to the target items, while at the same time justifying the presentation of primes. For example, the primes may be introduced as being part of a secondary memory task meant to make the actual target response task more difficult. Aside from these commonalities, the two types of measures systematically differ in terms of the nature of the target items that they use and the task that participants perform.

The most common priming procedure used for attitude measurement was introduced by Fazio and his colleagues and termed *evaluative priming* (Fazio et al., 1986). In this paradigm, participants judge target strings for their evaluative connotation. Participants indicate as quickly as possible whether the meaning of the target implies either *good* or *bad* by pressing the appropriately labeled response key. Thus, participants are first presented with an attitude prime (e.g., spinach), followed by a target (e.g., pleasant), and participants press a key marked either *good* or *bad*. Of interest is whether, across several trials with different targets, the attitude prime facilitates responses to positively valenced targets and/or responses to negatively valenced targets. The magnitude of such facilitation serves as a measure of automatic activation of a positive and/or negative evaluation.

Evaluative priming has been used to study attitudes toward a variety of different kinds of objects, ranging from commonplace items such as cake to politically important objects such as war and racial minority groups (for a review, see Fazio, 2001). This priming technique aims to assess an overall evaluation of an attitude object. That is, given the nature of the evaluative discrimination task, evaluative priming uses target words of polarized valence (e.g., pleasant, awful). Aside from their evaluative implications, the target items are otherwise unrelated to the object in question. Thus, the evaluative priming procedure aims to assess the extent to which an attitude object may automatically trigger an evaluation, and not whether it may activate other declarative memory contents with evaluative implications (e.g., spinach—healthy).

In contrast, the activation of such declarative memory contents may be assessed by what we will call *concept priming* procedures. Also based on the original Meyer and Schvaneveldt procedure and therefore in many respects similar to evaluative priming, concept priming includes target items that are descriptive of the attitude object. To the extent that these attributes have evaluative implications (e.g., healthy), their activation can influence the evaluative response. For example, Wittenbrink et al. (1997) used concept priming for the assessment of group attitudes. In this procedure, African American and White group primes are paired with trait attributes contained in the cultural stereotype for either of the two groups (*athletic, intelligent*). In addition, half of the items for each stereotype are positive in valence, and half are negative.

The facilitation observed for the various combinations of primes and types of target items then offers separate estimates for the degree to which a group prime yields automatic stereotype activation, the extent to which this automatic stereotype activation is evaluatively biased (i.e., whether primarily negative or positive traits are activated), and the capacity for a group prime to trigger an overall evaluation (i.e., to facilitate any item of particular valence, independent of the stereotype).

Also different from evaluative priming, concept priming procedures usually use Meyer and Schvaneveldt's original lexical decision task, instead of an evaluative discrimination task (e.g., Gaertner & McLaughlin, 1983; Wittenbrink et al., 1997). As a result, participants are likely to focus on different features of primes and target items in these two kinds of priming procedures. Specifically, Wittenbrink, Judd, and Park (2001b) argued that the evaluative discrimination task focuses participants on the evaluative implications of the encountered stimuli, whereas a lexical decision task induces concept identification and thus focuses participants on conceptual attributes of the stimuli.

Consistent with this argument, Wittenbrink et al. (2001b) observed different patterns of activation as a result of manipulating the task instructions in a priming measure of racial attitudes. In the context of a lexical decision task, group primes showed facilitation for trait attributes associated with the respective group stereotype. Moreover, outgroup primes yielded disproportionately strong facilitation for negative stereotypic attributes compared to ingroup primes. However, when the same priming procedure was administered with an evaluative decision task, the stereotypicality of the target items did not matter for the observed priming effect. Outgroup primes produced overall stronger facilitation for any negatively valenced attribute. Parallel effects of task instructions have also been reported by Klauer and Musch (2002). Moreover, Livingston and Brewer (2002) demonstrated that the nature of the priming stimulus also affects what kind of activation a priming measure captures. In their studies, using image primes (African American and White faces) instead of lexical group primes produced a general evaluative response but no activation of the group concept (i.e., stereotype).

The experiments by Livingston and Brewer (2002) point to another important way in which priming measures may vary. Depending on the nature of the prime and the instructions for processing them, priming measures can assess evaluative responses to specific attitude objects or to classes of objects. That is, primes can be category referents such as flowers or African American or exemplars like tulip or a portrait of an African American male. If the exemplars vary in how representative they are of their respective categories, exemplars may activate somewhat different evaluations than category references. In fact, in the Livingston and Brewer research, prototypical African American faces produced stronger facilitation for negatively valenced target items than did less prototypical African American faces in evaluative priming. Only when participants were explicitly instructed to attend to the race of the faces did this effect of prototypicality disappear.

The considerable differences in priming effects that can be observed as a result of procedural variations point to a more general issue. The fact that automatic processes, the results of which these measures aim to assess, are unintended and uncontrollable does not mean that the processes are insensitive to variations in the situation that trigger them. Just as with other types of attitude measures, the nature of the assessment context matters for what a given procedure will capture.

Response Competition Measures.   The second set of response latency measures is based on procedures that capture effects on latencies of judgments by overtly pitting two alternative categorizations of a stimulus target against one another. The most popular measure of this kind is the IAT proposed by Greenwald, Banaji, and their colleagues (Greenwald, McGhee, & Schwartz, 1998). In this task, participants classify two sets of target items along two dimensions of judgment. For example, one set of items may be targets of polarized valence (e.g., poison, love), for which participants perform an evaluative discrimination task using two response keys. A second set of target items may include exemplars of two contrasting categories of attitude objects (e.g., flowers: tulip, rose versus insects: spider, ant). The task for this second set of items is to classify them according to their category membership.

During a set of trials, both judgment tasks are combined, and the targets from the two sets of valence and attitude items appear in random order. Both judgment tasks are performed using the same two response keys. Two separate assessment blocks vary the mapping of categories on the response keys, so that each attitude object is paired once with the positive response key and once with the negative key (e.g., flower/pleasant and insect/unpleasant versus flower/unpleasant and insect/pleasant). The critical measure assesses which of these two blocks produces more fluent, faster responses. For example, relatively faster responses when flower is paired with pleasant and insect is paired with unpleasant would indicate that flowers automatically activate a more positive evaluation than insects. The size of this difference estimates the degree to which these spontaneous evaluations differ (for a detailed review of experimental procedure and data analysis, see Greenwald, Nosek, & Banaji, 2003).

As indicated by its name, the IAT is generally thought to measure associative strength between each target concept and a particular attribute, which for the purpose of attitude measurement may be its evaluation. To the extent that concept and attribute are associated, an exemplar will trigger activation of both concept and attribute. In such cases, responses to the IAT trials should be facilitated when concept and attribute are assigned to the same key, because activation from both feeds the same key response. However, responses should be slowed when concept and attribute are assigned to different keys because, in this case, they trigger competing key presses. If no association exists, only the concept will be activated, and no response facilitation or interference will occur.

Aside from this association-based process, other cognitive mechanisms have been suggested to explain IAT effects as well (for an overview, see Mierke & Klauer, 2001). The debate about the particular cognitive processes contributing to the IAT effect is still ongoing, but there seems to be increasing agreement that IAT effects are largely attributable to the target category (e.g., flowers) and are less sensitive to the specific exemplars chosen to represent these categories (e.g., tulip). For example, in an IAT comparing attitudes toward the British and toward foreigners, De Houwer (2001) found that British participants showed pro-British bias in their responses irrespective of whether the ingroup exemplars were positive (e.g., Princess Diana) or negative (e.g., Rosemary West, a convicted mass murderer) or whether the outgroup exemplars were positive (e.g., Albert Einstein) or negative (e.g., Adolf Hitler). Thus, the evaluations associated with specific exemplars did not affect IAT responses, even when they contradicted the evaluation of the overall target category.

The IAT has recently been criticized because to some extent it may tap widely shared evaluative associations that may not be personally endorsed (Karpinski & Hilton, 2001; Olson & Fazio, 2004). To illustrate, consider the example of *peanuts* suggested by Olson and Fazio. In our society there probably are shared positive sentiments toward peanuts known by all, even someone who is violently allergic toward them. Olson and Fazio have shown that these widely shared evaluations may contribute to IAT scores over and above personally experienced evaluations. Some simple changes in the IAT, for instance using response labels such as *I like* and *I dislike* versus the more traditional *pleasant* and *unpleasant* labels, seem to reduce the impact of these widely shared, but perhaps not personally endorsed evaluations.

The IAT has become the most widely used implicit attitude measure. It has been used for investigating attitudes in a broad variety of domains, including attitudes toward race and gender groups (e.g., McConnell & Leibold, 2001; Nosek, Banaji, & Greenwald, 2002), violence among criminal offenders (Gray, MacCulloch, Smith, Morris, & Snowden, 2003), the use of contraception during intercourse (Marsh, Johnson, & Scott-Sheldon, 2001), and alcohol consumption (Jajodia & Earleywine, 2003). Several IAT-based attitude measures are available via a demonstration Web site on the Internet, which collected data from 1.2 million volunteer participants during less than 5 years (Greenwald, Nosek, & Banaji, 2003). The IAT is popular partly because it produces relatively large effect sizes—substantially larger than those observed with other response latency measures (Greenwald et al., 1998)—with relatively limited technical effort. Whereas other response latency measures rely on precise stimulus timing and therefore require significant procedural control in order to produce useful estimates of attitude activation, the IAT is much less constrained in this regard. As a result, the measure is relatively easy to implement and can be administered outside of laboratory settings.[3]

In addition to the original IAT, two closely related variants of the procedure have been proposed: the Go/No-go Association Task (GNAT; Nosek & Banaji, 2001) and the Extrinsic Affective Simon Task (De Houwer, 2003). Both procedures are meant to address problems associated with the fact that the IAT assesses attitudes not in absolute terms but only in relation to a second contrasting category. In many cases, the contrasting category is not an obviously mutually exclusive category and instead is selected from among many plausible alternatives (e.g., spinach vs. [for instance] broccoli, corn, peas, beans, asparagus, salmon, hamburger, French fries). The choice of a contrasting category is likely to influence what features of the target category become salient (Tversky, 1977). For example, an IAT is likely to yield different results for the attitude toward spinach when it is paired with carrot than when it appears in contrast to French fries. Moreover, even for naturally dichotomous categories (e.g., male, female) or for objects that imply an obvious contrast category (e.g., republicans vs. democrats), the relativity of the attitude estimate yielded by the IAT may pose problems. It is often of interest to assess the attitude toward each target separately. For example, a relatively positive IAT score for a given political candidate may result from very positive evaluations associated with that particular politician or from very negative attitudes toward the opponent. Obviously, the two interpretations paint very different portraits of attitudes toward the individual candidates. Likewise, in assessing attitudes toward social groups, it is often of interest to differentiate positive evaluations of an ingroup (ingroup favoritism) from negative attitudes toward an outgroup (outgroup derogation, see Brewer, 2001). An IAT with an ingroup and an outgroup as target categories (e.g., African American/White) cannot distinguish ingroup liking and outgroup disliking.

To address this issue, the GNAT includes only a single target attitude. As in the IAT, presentation of exemplars of this target attitude alternates in random order with stimuli that vary on a particular dimension (pleasant/unpleasant). Unlike the IAT, however, participants have to give a response only when a stimulus fits one of two categories. That is, participants may be shown names of flowers, positive words, and negative words (in some versions of the task, unrelated distractors as well). On some trials, participants press a key whenever the name of a flower or a positive word appears. On other trials, participants respond to flowers and negative words. Relatively faster responses to the first set of trials indicate a positive attitude toward flowers.

A second modification of the IAT was recently proposed by De Houwer (2003), termed the Extrinsic Affective Simon Task (EAST) to stress its similarity to the Simon paradigm in which feature overlap between response and target stimuli influences response latencies (Simon, 1990). Essentially, the EAST works by adding color to an IAT with lexical stimuli. As in the IAT, participants classify two separate sets of stimuli, one related to an attribute dimension (e.g., good/bad) and the other made up of object exemplars (e.g., tulip). Different from the IAT, the EAST uses only a single classification task, which is based on the attribute dimension (e.g., good/bad). The object exemplars are presented in one of two font colors, and participants are instructed to press the *good* key whenever a word appears in, say, green, and to press the *bad* key for words in blue. Attribute stimuli are presented in white and have to be classified based on their valence. Because the font color of object stimuli can be varied across trials, each object stimulus can be paired once with the *good* and once with the *bad* response key. Faster responses on trials when the object target is paired with the *good* key indicate a more positive attitude toward the target. In principle, the EAST should also work with other irrelevant features besides font color.

Finally, the Stroop task is another response competition paradigm that has been used to measure automatic evaluation effects. In this paradigm, participants quickly identify the color of words. In general, responses take longer when the meaning of the word conflicts with the response implied by the font color—when, for example, the word green appears in red color (MacLeod, 1991). Pratto and John (1991) adopted the task to assess automatic evaluative responses by varying the valence of the target stimuli. Reasoning that negative stimuli would more easily divert attention during stimulus processing, they expected negative words to show more interference on the color-naming task. Results from several studies are consistent with this argument, showing increased response latencies for negative words, whereas positive or neutral words did not affect the color-naming task. Use of this procedure for attitude assessment may be complicated by the fact that highly accessible attitudes have generally been found to direct attention, not just when they are negative (Smith, Fazio, & Cejka, 1996). As a result, valence effects are potentially confounded with effects of accessibility in this type of measure.

Physiological Measures

Physiological attitude measures seek to capture the physiological correlates of evaluative responses. Because people generally have no control over physiological responses, researchers early on considered the assessment of these kinds of responses to be a way of overcoming intentional misrepresentation in direct attitude self-reports. Physiological measures operate implicitly because, in most cases, people have no introspective access to their response and its connection with a specific evaluation.

Early attempts to use physiological responses for attitude measurement focused on non-invasive measures of autonomic responses such as galvanic skin conductance and pupillary responses. Rankin and Campbell (1955) were among the first to use galvanic skin response (GSR), a measure of the ability of skin to conduct electricity, in attitude research. In their experiment, White participants showed an elevated GSR during interactions with an African American experimenter compared to a condition with a White experimenter. Subsequent research, however, indicated that GSR is primarily sensitive to arousal and cannot differentiate whether this arousal is triggered by a positively evaluated stimulus or a negatively evaluated stimulus or by a novel stimulus (Cacioppo & Sandman, 1981).

The use of pupillary responses for attitude measurement has not fared much better. In principle, this measure, first proposed by Hess (1965), was thought to differentiate between positive evaluations, which are believed to yield a dilation of the pupil, and negative evaluations, which are supposed to trigger pupil constriction. However, like the GSR, pupillary responses are influenced by the novelty of a stimulus (Petty & Cacioppo, 1983). In addition, empirical evidence testing whether negatively evaluated stimuli trigger pupil constriction is mixed at best (see Himmelfarb, 1993).

A more effective measurement approach assesses subtle muscle activity in specific areas of the face, commonly over the brow (frowning) and the cheek (smiling). For example, Cacioppo, Petty, Losch, and Kim (1986) found that electromyographic (EMG) activity in these areas showed distinct patterns following exposure to either positive or negative stimuli. Observing judges failed to detect any overt expressions of positive or negative emotions, thus documenting the subtlety of the responses (see also Fridlund, Schwartz, & Fowler, 1984).

Facial EMG measures are generally based on multiple recordings of activity over a short period of time, during which participants think about the stimulus. The measure is, therefore, not well-suited for the assessment of automatic evaluative responses free of deliberation. In addition, this measure is open to misrepresentation. People can fake or intentionally distort their facial expressions (Cacioppo et al., 1986). However, extra precautions to disguise the purpose of the assessment—for example, the placement of additional dummy electrodes in places other than the face—can make facial EMG an effective measure of socially sensitive attitudes (McHugo & Lanzetta, 1983; Vanman, Paul, Ito, & Miller, 1997).

Another attitude measure based on facial EMG activity assesses the modulation of eyeblink reflexes during exposure to an object. For this procedure, a startle probe (e.g., a short blast of acoustic noise or a visual flash) is used to elicit a reflexive eyeblink while participants watch images of an object. Startle eyeblink reflexes are modulated as a function of affective valence of the target stimulus. Exposure to positively evaluated stimuli is associated with eyeblink inhibition, whereas negatively evaluated stimuli elicit amplification of the reflex (Lang, Bradley, & Cuthbert, 1990). Some evidence suggests that affective modulation of the eyeblink reflex occurs only for highly arousing stimuli, which would limit its use to the assessment of attitudes involving strong evaluations (Cuthbert, Bradley, & Lang, 1996). Moreover, affective modulation is observable only after considerable exposure to the target stimulus. Early startle eyeblink responses, within 800 ms of stimulus onset, remain insensitive to the valence of the target stimulus (Bradley, Cuthbert, & Lang, 1993). Thus, although this measure captures responses that remain outside of participants' voluntary control, the nature of the responses can be determined by both automatic reactions to the target and by controlled deliberation of it.

A final set of physiological attitude measures is based on the assessment of brain activity. Most recently, these measure have begun to employ newly emerging brain imaging techniques, like positron emission tomography (PET) and functional magnetic resonance imagery (fMRI). These brain imaging techniques determine neural activity based on changes in blood flow in the brain and can be used to identify the brain regions that operate in the processing of a given stimulus.

Initial steps have been taken to link evaluative processing to activity in specific areas of the brain. For, example, activity in the amygdala, a neural structure that is part of the limbic system and is located in the anterior part of the temporal lobes, is linked to the processing of negatively evaluated stimuli (e.g., Adolphs, Tranel, & Damasio, 1998; LeDoux, 1996). Based on these findings, a recent study by Phelps et al. (2000) explored the role of amygdala activity in more complex social attitudes. Using fMRI, this study recorded amygdala activity for White participants while they were shown images of African American and White faces and found it to be correlated with two other implicit racial attitude measures, an IAT and a startle eyeblink measure. Similarly, Hart et al. (2000) found increased amygdala activity in response to outgroup faces for both African American and White participants. This effect was observed, however, only on later trials, which the authors interpreted as evidence that participants more quickly habituated to ingroup faces. Once this area of research has developed a sufficient account for the localization of psychological processes in the brain, imaging techniques will play an important role in the assessment of the neural substrates of attitudes.

Another technique for the use of brain activity in attitude measurement is a procedure based on event-related brain potentials (ERP) proposed by Cacioppo and his colleagues (Cacioppo, Crites, Berntson, & Coles, 1993; Cacioppo, Crites, Gardner, & Berntson, 1994). For an ERP, neural electric activity is recorded via electrodes placed on the scalp, and changes in this activity following a critical event (e.g., the presentation of an attitude object) are recorded. The procedure is based on a particular component of the ERP waveform, known as the P300: a relative increase in neural activity that occurs relatively late in the ERP, approximately 300 ms after event onset.

This component is sensitive to the meaning of an event for the overall task that is performed during an ERP. For example, when participants are asked to classify stimuli according to a certain dimension (high tones vs. low tones), oddball stimuli that are inconsistent with prior stimuli (e.g., a low tone that follows a series of high tones) evoke a larger P300 in a specific location of the scalp (e.g., Fabiani, Gratton, Karis, & Donchin, 1987). The Cacioppo et al. measure, termed *late positive potential* (LPP), employs such an oddball paradigm with an evaluative classification task, whereby a target stimulus is embedded into a sequence of stimuli of known valence. Ideally, attitude assessments would be derived from this measure by comparing trials in which the target is embedded in a sequence of positive stimuli with trials in which it is paired with negative stimuli. However, reliable ERP waveforms can only be obtained across several presentations of the same stimulus sequence. In order to limit the repetitiveness of the procedure, LPP measures typically use only one valence context (Crites, Cacioppo, Gardner, & Berntson, 1995). The LPP amplitude, averaged across several presentations of the target stimulus, can be used as an indicator of the degree of evaluative mismatch between target and context stimuli.

The LPP measure offers precise control over the timing of evaluative processing. It is also unaffected by attempts to deliberately falsify evaluations during the classification task (Crites et al., 1995). Thus, it appears to be an effective measure of automatic evaluative responses free of controlled deliberation.

Other Implicit Measures

A variety of other implicit assessment techniques do not fit squarely into the above categories. For example, the latency and intensity of approach and avoidance motor movements have been used as indicators of evaluations. In a study by Solarz (1960), participants responded to positive and negative words (e.g., smart, stupid) by operating a lever in one of two ways: by pulling it toward them, an arm movement consistent with approach behavior, or by pushing it away from them, an arm movement associated with avoiding an object. Half of the participants were instructed to pull the lever for words that they liked and to push the lever if they saw a word they did not like. The other participants were told to do the opposite. Participants responded significantly faster when the word's valence was consistent with the evaluation implied by the motor movement: They pulled the lever more quickly in response to a positive word and pushed it more quickly in response to a negative one. Chen and Bargh (1999) replicated Solarz's findings and showed that the effect persisted even when participants were not explicitly instructed to evaluate the target stimuli. Moreover, several recent studies have used the strength of arm extension and flexion as indicators of the motivation to approach or avoid a valenced stimulus (see Förster, Higgins, & Idson, 1998).

Paper-and-pencil measures also offer simple means of implicit measurement. For example, a relatively easy way to assess attitude accessibility is by means of a word-fragment completion task. Participants complete letter strings to form complete words (e.g., POL_E— POLITE). Construct accessibility influences participants' choices of how to complete a given word fragment (Bassili & Smith, 1986; Tulving, Schacter, & Stark, 1982). If a letter string can be completed with either attitude-related or unrelated words, the task can be used as a quick indicator of attitude accessibility. Likewise, if the possible completions include both positive and negative alternatives, it may be used to assess attitude valence as well (e.g., B_D—BAD vs. BUD, see Dovidio, Kawakami, Johnson, Johnson, & Howard, 1997).

A slightly more complicated implicit paper-and-pencil measure has been used in research on intergroup attitudes. Proposed by von Hippel and his colleagues (von Hippel, Sekaquaptewa, & Vargas, 1997), this measure is based on evidence that people tend to describe behavior in more abstract terms when the behavior is consistent with expectations (Maass, Salvi, Arcuri, &

Semin, 1989). Participants are presented with several ostensible news clippings that describe stereotypic and counterstereotypic events involving either ingroup or outgroup targets. The events systematically vary in terms of the valence of the described behavior. Participants then rate a set of possible headlines for how well they capture the described event. The headlines vary in the level of linguistic abstraction (e.g., "Johnson performs 360-degree slam-dunk" vs. "Johnson is athletic"). Of interest is the degree to which participants show a bias in favor of abstract headlines when they describe negative events as opposed to positive behaviors for the outgroup target.

Limitations of Implicit Measures

Implicit attitude measures have received significant attention in recent years. Their most obvious appeal is that they promise to capture attitudes in circumstances where people are unwilling to report them accurately in response to direct questions. Implicit measures also assess attitudes without the need for participants to introspect about their feelings and beliefs. The measures therefore offer the opportunity to capture attitudes that people are unable to report directly because they are unaware of holding the attitudes. Because of limitations in people's willingness and ability to report attitudes, implicit measures offer the promise of improving our ability to accurately capture attitudes.

Implicit measures operate by limiting participants' control over the evaluation process. They do so by precluding participants from deliberating about the evaluation (e.g., response latency measures and the LPP) or by curtailing opportunities to bring responses in line with deliberate evaluation (e.g., unobtrusive behavioral observation techniques and various physiological measures). Attitude measures' ability to predict a person's behavioral responses to an object depends on whether the measures properly capture the evaluative processing as it occurs during an encounter with the attitude object (see Ajzen & Fishbein, this volume). If controlled deliberation during assessment gives rise to self-presentational concerns, whereas those concerns are irrelevant in behavioral situations, measures that preclude control during the assessment may be more accurate predictors. Likewise, measures that preclude control over one's response may be more effective predictors in situations in which such control is not possible. Thus, just as with any other attitude measure, the effectiveness of implicit measures in predicting behaviors depends in large part on what exactly it is that they are supposed to predict.

Furthermore, despite a few results to the contrary (e.g., Cunningham, Preacher, & Banaji, 1999; Phelps et al., 2000), implicit measures are remarkably weakly correlated with one another (Cameron, Alvarez, & Bargh, 2000; Marsh et al., 2001; Olson & Fazio, 2003; Sherman, Rose, Presson, & Chassin, 2003). The same implicit measure can produce quite different results when implemented in different contexts, even though the measure may target automatic activation of the same attitude. For example, Wittenbrink et al. (2001a) obtained different estimates of racial attitudes using an IAT when participants had previously watched a brief video about African Americans at a family barbeque than when they had seen a video involving African American gang members.

Thus, irrespective of whether a measure is implicit or explicit, a careful analysis of the assessment situation is necessary in order to understand what a given attitude measure really measures—as Klauer and Musch (2002) argued:

> Paying more attention to the processes mediating effects of automatic attitude activation can help social cognition researchers in interpreting their findings. Just as conventional explicit measures of attitudes are sensitive to output norms and self-presentation concerns, to mood states and motivational needs, the processes driving measures of automatic attitude activation may be differently responsive to situational, attentional, and even motivational factors. (p. 813)

All this makes it clear that although our repertoire of implicit measures is large and growing, we still have much to learn about the meaning of the assessments thus obtained and the cognitive and affective processes that give rise to them.

CONCLUSION

Attitude researchers have many techniques available to them for assessing the constructs they study, and these various techniques all offer useful handles for empirical study. The future of attitude measurement research will no doubt be very interesting, as the relations among implicit measures become better understood and as their relations to direct self-reports of attitudes become better understood as well. In the meantime, we see value in the classic approach to measurement: Any study of a construct is more likely to be informative if multiple measures of that construct are used instead of just one. Only then can issues of construct validity be successfully addressed.

Although implicit measures of attitudes offer great promise, in terms of their ability to assess attitudes freed of participants' self-presentational concerns, at present their claims to validity rest largely on intuitive appeals. It seems crucial that researchers in attitude measurement establish that such measures, in fact, predict socially significant criterion behaviors.

Additionally, as we claimed in the beginning of this chapter, attitudes are not simple productions that emerge intact, ripe for measurement. Rather they manifest themselves in many different shapes, as a result of complex cognitive processes. Our measures need to be sensitive to the ways in which they may be produced. In some situations, assessments of automatically formed evaluations may be most important in predicting behaviors. In others, more deliberative and potentially critically monitored evaluative responses may be what we want to measure. Just because a participant is unaware that his or her attitude is being assessed, that does not mean that the attitude in question has been measured with greater construct validity.

Without doubt both traditional self-report and more indirect attitude measures will continue to be used. The goal is not to come up with a single "best" attitude measure, but rather to measure attitudes in all their complexity and all their manifestations.

ACKNOWLEDGMENT

Preparation of this chapter was partially supported by NIMH grant R01 MH45049 to the second author. Jon Krosnick is University Fellow at Resources for the Future.

ENDNOTES

[1] Almost all studies reviewed involved experimental designs varying the number of rating scale points, holding constant all other aspects of questions. Some additional studies have explored the impact of number of scale points using a different approach: meta-analysis. These studies have taken large sets of questions asked in preexisting surveys, estimated their reliability and/or validity, and meta-analyzed the results to see whether data quality varies with scale point number (e.g., Alwin, 1992, 1997; Alwin & Krosnick, 1991; Andrews, 1984, 1990; Scherpenzeel, 1995). However, these meta-analyses sometimes mixed together measures of subjective judgments with measurements of objective constructs such as numeric behavior frequencies (e.g., number of days) and routinely involved strong confounds between number of scale points and other item characteristics, only some of which were measured and controlled for statistically. Consequently, it is not surprising that these studies yielded inconsistent findings. For example, Andrews (1984) found that validity and reliability were worst for 3-point scales, better for 2-point and 4-point scales, and even better as scale length increased from 5 points to 19 points. In contrast, Alwin and Krosnick (1991) found that 3-point scales had the *lowest* reliability, found no difference in the reliabilities of 2-, 4-, 5-, and

7-point scales, and found 9-point scales to have maximum reliability (though these latter scales actually offered 101 response alternatives to participants). And Scherpenzeel (1995) found the highest reliability for 4/5-point scales, lower reliability for 10 points, and even lower for 100 points. We therefore view these studies as less informative than experiments manipulating rating scale length.

[2]We use this distinction between priming measures and response competition measures merely for descriptive purposes, to facilitate the review of a growing number of different implicit measurement techniques. The distinction is meant to capture how a measurement procedure presents itself to the participant. It is not meant to capture distinctions in the underlying mechanism on which they operate. In fact, although participants may not experience a priming procedure as triggering competing responses, response competition may nevertheless be an important determinant for priming effects (see Klauer & Musch, 2003; Wentura & Rothermund, 2003).

[3]Dabbs, Bassett, & Dyomina (2003) recently introduced a version of the IAT that can be administered using small, hand-held devices such as a Palm organizer.

REFERENCES

Adolphs, R., Tranel, D., & Damsio, A. R. (1998). The human amygdala in social judgment. *Nature, 393*, 470–474.

Ajzen, I., & Sexton, J. (1999). Depth of processing, belief congruence, and attitude-behavior correspondence. In S. Chaiken & Y. Trope (Eds.), *Dual-process theories in social psychology* (pp. 117–138). New York: Guilford.

Allen, B. P. (1975). Social distance and admiration reactions of "unprejudiced" Whites. *Journal of Personality, 43*, 709–726.

Allison, P. D. (1975). A simple proof of the Spearman-Brown formula for continuous length tests. *Psychometrika, 40*, 135–136.

Allport, G. W. (1935). Attitudes. In C. Murchison (Ed.), *Handbook of social psychology* (pp. 798–884). Worcester, MA: Clark University Press.

Alwin, D. F. (1992). Information transmission in the survey interview: Number of response categories and the reliability of attitude measurement. *Sociological Methodology, 22*, 83–118.

Alwin, D. F. (1997). Feeling thermometers versus 7-point scales: Which are better? *Sociological Methods and Research, 25*, 318–340.

Alwin, D. F., & Krosnick, J. A. (1991). The reliability of survey attitude measurement: The influence of question and respondent attributes. *Sociological Methods and Research, 20*, 139–181.

Anderson, B. A., Silver, B. D., & Abramson, P. R. (1988). The effects of race of the interviewer on measures of electoral participation by Blacks in SRC national election studies. *Public Opinion Quarterly, 52*, 53–83.

Andrews, F. M. (1984). Construct validity and error components of survey measures: A structural modeling approach. *Public Opinion Quarterly, 48*, 409–442.

Andrews, F. M. (1990). Some observations on meta-analysis of MTMM studies. In W. E. Saris & A. van Meurs (Eds.), *Evaluation of measurement instruments by meta-analysis of multitrait multimethod studies* (pp. —). Amsterdam, The Netherlands: Royal Netherlands Academy of Arts and Sciences.

Atkin, C. K., & Chaffee, S. H. (1972–1973). Instrumental response strategies in opinion interview. *Public Opinion Quarterly, 36*, 69–79.

Atkinson, R. C., & Shiffrin, R. M. (1968). Human memory: A proposed system and its control processes. In K. W. Spence & J. T. Spence (Eds.), *The psychology of learning and motivation: Advances in research and theory* (Vol. 2, pp. 89–195). New York: Academic Press.

Ayidiya, S. A., & McClendon, M. J. (1990). Response effects in mail surveys. *Public Opinion Quarterly, 54*, 229–247.

Baddeley, A. D., & Hitch, G. J. (1977). Recency reexamined. In S. Dornic (Ed.), *Attention and performance*. Hillsdale, NJ: Lawrence Erlbaum Associates.

Bargh, J. A. (1997). The automaticity of everyday life. In R. S. Wyer (Ed.), *Advances in social cognition, X: The automaticity of everyday life* (Vol. 10, pp. 1–61). Mahwah, NJ: Lawrence Erlbaum Associates.

Bargh, J. A., Chaiken, S., Govender, R., & Pratto, F. (1992). The generality of the automatic attitude activation effect. *Journal of Personality and Social Psychology, 62*, 893–912.

Bassili, J. N., & Smith, M. C. (1986). On the spontaneity of trait attribution: Converging evidence for the role of cognitive strategy. *Journal of Personality & Social Psychology, 50*, 239–245.

Becker, S. L. (1954). Why an order effect. *Public Opinion Quarterly, 18*, 271–278.

Bendig, A. W. (1954). Reliability and the number of rating scale categories. *Journal of Applied Psychology, 38*, 38–40.

Benson, P. L., Karabenick, S. A., & Lerner, R. M. (1976). Pretty pleases: The effects of physical attractiveness, race, and sex on receiving help. *Journal of Experimental Social Psychology, 12*, 409–415.

Berg, I. A., & Rapaport, G. M. (1954). Response bias in an unstructured questionnaire. *Journal of Psychology, 38*, 475–481.

Birkett, N. J. (1986). Selecting the number of response categories for a Likert-type scale. *Proceedings of the American Statistical Association*, 488–492.

Bishop, G. F. (1987). Experiments with the middle response alternative in survey questions. *Public Opinion Quarterly, 51*, 220–232.

Bishop, G. F. (1990). Issue involvement and response effects in public opinion surveys. *Public Opinion Quarterly, 54*, 209–218.

Bishop, G. F., Hippler, H. J., Schwarz, N., & Strack, F. (1988). A comparison of response effects in self-administered and telephone surveys. In R. M. Groves, P. P. Biemer, L. E. Lyberg, J. T. Massedy, W. L. Nicholls, & J. Waksberg (Eds.), *Telephone survey methodology* (pp. 321–334). New York: Wiley.

Bishop, G. F., Oldendick, R. W., Tuchfarber, A. J., & Bennett, S. E. (1979). Effects of opinion filtering and opinion floating: Evidence from a secondary analysis. *Political Methodology, 6*, 293–309.

Bodenhausen, G. V., Schwarz, N., Bless, H., & Wänke, M. (1995). Effects of atypical exemplars on racial beliefs: Enlightened racism or generalized appraisals? *Journal of Experimental Social Psychology, 31*, 48–63.

Bogardus, E. S. (1931). Attitudes and the Mexican immigrant. In K. Young (Ed.) *Social attitudes* (pp. 291–327). New York: Henry Holt.

Bogart, L. (1972). *Silent politics: Polls and the awareness of public opinion*. New York: Wiley–Interscience.

Boote, A. S. (1981). Markets segmentation by personal and salient product attributes. *Journal of Advertising Research, 21*, 29–35.

Bornstein, R. F., & D'Agostino, P. R. (1994). The attribution and discounting of perceptual fluency: Preliminary tests of a perceptual fluency/attributional model of the mere exposure effect. *Social Cognition, 12*, 103–128.

Bradley, M. M., Cuthbert, B. N., & Lang, P. J. (1993). Pictures as prepulse: Attention and emotion in startle modification. *Psychophysiology, 30*, 541–545.

Brewer, M. B. (2001). Ingroup identification and intergroup conflict: When does ingroup love become outgroup hate? In R. D. Ashmore, L. Jussim & D. Wilder (Eds.), *Social identity, intergroup conflict, and conflict reduction. Rutgers series on self and social identity* (Vol. 3, pp. 17–41). Oxford: Oxford University Press.

Cacioppo, J. T., Crites, S. L., Berntson, G. G., & Coles, M. G. (1993). If attitudes affect how stimuli are processed, should they not affect the event-related brain potential? *Psychological Science, 4*, 108–112.

Cacioppo, J. T., Crites, S. L., Gardner, W. L., & Berntson, G. G. (1994). Bioelectrical echoes from evaluative categorizations: I. A late positive brain potential that varies as a function of trait negativity and extremity. *Journal of Personality and Social Psychology, 67*, 115–125.

Cacioppo, J. T., & Petty, R. E. (1982). The need for cognition. *Journal of Personality and Social Psychology, 42*, 116–131.

Cacioppo, J. T., Petty, R. E., Losch, M. E., & Kim, H. S. (1986). Electromyographic activity over facial muscle regions can differentiate the valence and intensity of affective reactions. *Journal of Personality and Social Psychology, 50*, 260–268.

Cacioppo, J. T., & Sandman, C. A. (1981). Psychophysiological functioning, cognitive responding, and attitudes. In R. E. Petty, T. M. Ostrom, & T. C. Brock (Eds.), *Cognitive responses in persuasion* (pp. 81–103). Hillsdale, NJ: Lawrence Erlbaum Associates.

Calsyn, R. J., Roades, L. A., & Calsyn, D. S. (1992). Acquiescence in needs assessment studies of the elderly. *The Gerontologist, 32*, 246–252.

Cameron, J. A., Alvarez, J. M., & Bargh, J. A. (2000, February). *Examining the validity of implicit measures of prejudice*. Paper presented at the first meeting of the Society for Personality and Social Psychology, Nashville, TN.

Campbell, B. A. (1981). Race-of-interviewer effects among southern adolescents. *Public Opinion Quarterly, 45*, 231–244.

Campbell, D. T., & Fiske, D. W. (1959). Convergent and discriminant validation by the multitrait–multimethod matrix. *Psychological Bulletin, 56*, 81–105.

Campbell, D. T., & Mohr, P. J. (1950). The effect of ordinal position upon responses to items in a checklist. *Journal of Applied Psychology, 34*, 62–67.

Carp, F. M. (1974). Position effects on interview responses. *Journal of Gerontology, 29*, 581–587.

Chaiken, S. (1987). The heuristic model of persuasion. In M. P. Zanna & J. M. Olson (Eds.), *Social influence: The Ontario symposium* (Vol. 5, pp. 3–39). Hillsdale, NJ: Lawrence Erlbaum Associates.

Champney, H., & Marshall, H. (1939). Optimal refinement of the rating scale. *Journal of Applied Psychology, 23*, 323–337.

Chan, J. C. (1991). Response-order effects in Likert-type scales. *Educational and Psychological Measurement, 51*, 531–540.

Chen, M., & Bargh, J. A. (1999). Consequences of automatic evaluation: Immediate behavioral predispositions to approach or avoid the stimulus. *Personality and Social Psychology Bulletin, 25*, 215–224.

Chen, S., Shechter, D., & Chaiken, S. (1996). Getting at the truth or getting along: Accuracy versus impression-motivated heuristic and systematic processing. *Journal of Personality and Social Psychology, 71,* 262–275.

Cheng, S. (1988). Subjective quality of life in the planning and evaluation of programs. *Evaluation and Program Planning, 11,* 123–134.

Clancy, K. J., & Wachsler, R. A. (1971). Positional effects in shared-cost surveys. *Public Opinion Quarterly, 35,* 258–265.

Cliff, N. (1992). Abstract measurement theory and the revolution that never happened. *Psychological Science, 3,* 186–190.

Converse, J. M. (1976). Predicting no opinion in the polls. *Public Opinion Quarterly, 40,* 515–530.

Converse, J. M., & Presser, S. (1986). *Survey questions: Handcrafting the standardized questionnaire.* Beverly Hills, CA: Sage.

Converse, P. E. (1964). The nature of belief systems in the mass public. In D. E. Apter (Ed.), *Ideology and discontent* (pp. 206–261). New York: Free Press.

Coombs, C. H., & Coombs, L. C. (1976). "Don't know": Item ambiguity or respondent uncertainty? *Public Opinion Quarterly, 40,* 497–514.

Cotter, P., Cohen, J., & Coulter, P. B. (1982). Race of interviewer effects in telephone interviews. *Public Opinion Quarterly, 46,* 278–294.

Couch, A., & Keniston, K. (1960). Yeasayers and naysayers: Agreeing response set as a personality variable. *Journal of Abnormal and Social Psychology, 60,* 151–174.

Crites, S. L., Cacioppo, J. T., Gardner, W. L., & Berntson, G. G. (1995). Bioelectrical echoes from evaluative categorization: II. A late positive brain potential that varies as a function of attitude registration rather than attitude report. *Journal of Personality and Social Psychology, 68,* 997–1013.

Cronbach, L. J. (1950). Further evidence on response sets and test design. *Educational and Psychological Measurement, 10,* 3–31.

Cronbach, L. J. (1984). *Essentials of psychological testing.* New York: Harper & Row.

Cronbach, L. J., Gleser, G. C., Nanda, H., & Rajaratnam, N. (1972). *The dependability of behavioral measurements: Multifacet studies of generalizability.* New York: Wiley.

Culpepper, I. J., Smith, W. R., & Krosnick, J. A. (1992, May). *The impact of question order on satisficing in surveys.* Paper presented at the Midwestern Psychological Association Annual Meeting, Chicago, IL.

Cunningham, W. A., Preacher, K. J., & Banaji, M. R. (1999). Implicit attitude measures: Consistency, stability, and convergent validity. *Psychological Science, 121,* 163–170.

Cuthbert, B. N., Bradley, M. M., & Lang, P. J. (1996). Probing picture perception: Activation and emotion. *Psychophysiology, 33,* 103–111.

Dabbs, J. M., Jr., Bassett, J. F., & Dyomina, N. V. (2003). The Palm IAT: A portable version of the Implicit Association Test. *Behavior Research Methods, Instruments, and Computers, 35,* 90–95.

Dawes, R. M. (1994). *House of cards: Psychology and psychotherapy build on myth.* New York: The Free Press.

Dawes, R. M. (1998). Behavioral decision making and judgment. In D. T. Gilbert, S. T. Fiske, & G. Lindzey (Eds.), *The handbook of social psychology* (4th ed., Vol. 1, pp. 497–548). Boston, MA: McGraw-Hill.

Dawes, R. M., & Smith, T. L. (1985). Attitude and opinion measurement. In G. Lindzey & E. Aronson (Eds.), *The handbook of social psychology* (Vol. 1, pp. 509–566). Hillsdale, NJ: Lawrence Erlbaum Associates.

De Houwer, J. (2001). A structural and process analysis of the Implicit Association Test. *Journal of Experimental Social Psychology, 37,* 443–451.

De Houwer, J. (2003). The extrinsic affective Simon task. *Experimental Psychology, 50,* 77–85.

De Houwer, J., Hermans, D., & Eelen, P. (1998). Affective Simon effects using facial expressions as affective stimuli. *Zeitschrift Fuer Experimentelle Psychologie, 45,* 88–98.

DePaulo, B. M., Kashy, D. A., Kirkendol, S. E., Wyer, M. M., & Epstein, J. A. (1996). Lying in everyday life. *Journal of Personality and Social Psychology, 70,* 979–995.

Devine, P. G. (1989). Stereotypes and prejudice: Their automatic and controlled components. *Journal of Personality and Social Psychology, 56,* 5–18.

Dickinson, J. R., & Kirzner, E. (1985). Questionnaire item omission as a function of within-group question position. *J. Business Research, 13,* 71–75.

Dickinson, T. L., & Zellinger, P. M. (1980). A comparison of the behaviorally anchored rating mixed standard scale formats. *Journal of Applied Psychology, 65,* 147–154.

Donnerstein, E., & Donnerstein, M. (1975). The effect of attitudinal similarity on interracial aggression. *Journal of Personality, 43,* 485–502.

Dovidio, J. F., Kawakami, K., & Gaertner, S. L. (2002). Implicit and explicit prejudice and interracial interaction. *Journal of Personality and Social Psychology, 82,* 62–68.

Dovidio, J. F., Kawakami, K., Johnson, C., Johnson, B., & Howard, A. (1997). On the nature of prejudice: Automatic and controlled processes. *Journal of Experimental Social Psychology, 33,* 510–540.

Eagly, A. H., & Chaiken, S. (1993). *The psychology of attitudes*. Fort Worth, TX: Harcourt Brace Jovanovich.

Ebel, R. L. (1982). Proposed solutions to two problems of test construction. *Journal of Educational Measurement, 19*, 267–278.

Eifermann, R. R. (1961). Negation: A linguistic variable. *Acta Psychologica, 18*, 258–273.

England, L. R. (1948). Capital punishment and open-end questions. *Public Opinion Quarterly, 12*, 412–416.

Eurich, A. C. (1931). Four types of examinations compared and evaluated. *Journal of Educational Psychology, 22*, 268–278.

Evans, R. I., Hansen, W. B., & Mittlemark, M. B. (1977). Increasing the validity of self-reports of smoking behavior in children. *Journal of Applied Psychology, 62*, 521–523.

Fabiani, M., Gratton, G., Karis, D., & Donchin, E. (1987). Definition, identification, and reliability of measurement the P300 component of the event-related brain potential. In P. K. Ackles, J. R. Jennings, & M. G. Coles (Eds.), *Advances in psychophysiology* (Vol. 2, pp. 1–78). Greenwich, CT: JAI Press.

Faulkenberry, G. D., & Mason, R. (1978). Characteristics of nonopinion and no opinion response groups. *Public Opinion Quarterly, 42*, 533–543.

Fazio, R. H. (1990). Multiple processes by which attitudes guide behavior: The MODE model as an integrative framework. In M. Zanna (Ed.), *Advances in experimental social psychology* (Vol. 23, pp. 75–109). San Diego: Academic Press.

Fazio, R. H. (2001). On the automatic activation of associated evaluations: An overview. *Cognition and Emotion, 15*, 115–141.

Fazio, R. H., Jackson, J. R., Dunton, B. C., & Williams, C. J. (1995). Variability in automatic activation as an unobtrusive measure of racial attitudes: A bona fide pipeline? *Journal of Personality and Social Psychology, 69*, 1013–1027.

Fazio, R. H., & Olson, M. A. (2003). Implicit measures in social cognition research: Their meaning and uses. *Annual Review of Psychology, 54*, 297–327.

Fazio, R. H., Sanbonmatsu, D. M., Powell, M. C., & Kardes, F. R. (1986). On the automatic activation of attitudes. *Journal of Personality and Social Psychology, 50*, 229–238.

Ferber, R. (1966). Item nonresponse in a consumer survey. *Public Opinion Quarterly, 30*, 399–415.

Festinger, L. (1957). *A theory of cognitive dissonance*. Evanston, IL: Row Peterson & Co.

Finkel, S. E., Guterbock, T. M., & Borg, M. J. (1991). Race-of-interviewer effects in a preelection poll: Virginia 1989. *Public Opinion Quarterly, 55*, 313–330.

Fishbein, M., & Ajzen, I. (1975). *Belief, attitude, intention, and behavior: An introduction to theory and research*. Reading, MA: Addison-Wesley.

Förster, J., Higgins, E., & Idson, L. C. (1998). Approach and avoidance strength during goal attainment: Regulatory focus and the "goal looms larger" effect. *Journal of Personality and Social Psychology, 75*, 1115–1131.

Folsom, J. K. (1931). *Social psychology*. New York: Harper.

Fonda, C. P. (1951). The nature and meaning of the Rorschach white space response. *Journal of Abnormal and Social Psychology, 46*, 367–377.

Forehand, G. A. (1962). Relationships among response sets and cognitive behaviors. *Educational and Psychological Measurement, 22*, 287–302.

Fridlund, A. J., Schwartz, G. E., & Fowler, S. C. (1984). Pattern recognition of self-reported emotional state from multiple-site facial EMG activity during affective imagery. *Psychophysiology, 21*, 622–637.

Gaertner, S. L., & Dovidio, J. F. (1977). The subtlety of White racism, arousal, and helping behavior. *Journal of Personality and Social Psychology, 35*, 691–707.

Gaertner, S. L., & McLaughlin, J. P. (1983). Racial stereotypes: Associations and ascriptions of positive and negative characteristics. *Social Psychology Quarterly, 46*, 23–30.

Gage, N. L., Leavitt, G. S., & Stone, G. C. (1957). The psychological meaning of acquiescence set for authoritarianism. *Journal of Abnormal and Social Psychology, 55*, 98–103.

Geer, J. G. (1988). What do open-ended questions measure? *Public Opinion Quarterly, 52*, 365–371.

Gilbert, D. T. (1989). Thinking lightly about others: Automatic components of the social inference process. In J. S. Uleman & J. A. Bargh (Eds.), *Unintended thought* (pp. 189–211). New York: Guilford.

Gilljam, M., & Granberg, D. (1993). Should we take don't know for an answer? *Public Opinion Quarterly, 57*, 348–357.

Giner-Sorolla, R., Garcia, M. T., & Bargh, J. A. (1999). The automatic evaluation of pictures. *Social Cognition, 17*, 76–96.

Givon, M. M., & Shapira, Z. B. (1984). Response to rating scales: A theoretical model and its application to the number of categories problem. *Journal of Marketing Research, 21*, 410–419.

Glucksberg, S., & McCloskey, M. (1981). Decisions about ignorance: Knowing that you don't know. *Journal of Experimental Psychology: Human Learning and Memory, 7*, 311–325.

Goffman, E. (1959). *The presentation of self in everyday life*. Garden City, NY: Doubleday/Anchor.

Goldsmith, R. E. (1987). Two studies of yeasaying. *Psychological Reports, 60*, 239–244.

Gordon, R. A. (1987). Social desirability bias: A demonstration and technique for its reduction. *Teaching of Psychology, 14*, 40–42.

Gove, W. R., & Geerken, M. R. (1977). Response bias in surveys of mental health: An empirical investigation. *American Journal of Sociology, 82*, 1289–1317.

Gray, N. S., MacCulloch, M. J., Smith, J., Morris, M., & Snowden, R. J. (2003). Violence viewed by psychopathic murderers: Adapting a revealing test may expose those psychopaths who are most likely to kill. *Nature, 423*, 497–498.

Green, P. E., & Rao, V. R. (1970). Rating scales and information recovery—How many scales and response categories to use? *Journal of Marketing, 34*, 33–39.

Greenberg, J., Solomon, S., & Pyszczynski, T. (1997). Terror management theory of self-esteem and cultural worldviews: Empirical assessments and conceptual refinements. In M. P. Zanna (Ed.), *Advances in experimental social psychology* (Vol. 29, pp. 61–139). New York: Academic Press.

Greenwald, A. G., & Banaji, M. R. (1995). Implicit social cognition: Attitudes, self-esteem, and stereotypes. *Psychological Review, 102*, 4–27.

Greenwald, A. G., Klinger, M. R., & Liu, T. J. (1989). Unconscious processing of dichoptically masked words. *Memory and Cognition, 17*, 35–47.

Greenwald, A. G., McGhee, D. E., & Schwartz, J. L. K. (1998). Measuring individual differences in implicit cognition: The implicit association test. *Journal of Personality and Social Psychology, 74*, 1464–1480.

Greenwald, A. G., Nosek, B. A., & Banaji, M. R. (2003). Understanding and using the Implicit Association Test: I. An improved scoring algorithm. *Journal of Personality and Social Psychology, 85*, 197–216.

Groves, R. M. (1989). *Survey errors and survey costs.* New York: Wiley.

Hanley C. (1959). Responses to the wording of personality test items. *Journal of Consulting Psychology, 23*, 261–265.

Hanley, C. (1962). The "difficulty" of a personality inventory item. *Educational and Psychological Measurement, 22*, 577–584.

Hart, A. J., Whalen, P. J., Shin, L. M., McInerney, S. C., Fischer, H., & Rauch, S. L. (2000). Differential response in the human amygdala to racial outgroup vs. ingroup face stimuli. *Neuroreport, 11*, 2351–2355.

Hess, E. H. (1965). Attitude and pupil size. *Scientific American, 212*, 46–54.

Himmelfarb, S. (1993). The measurement of attitudes. In A. H. Eagly & S. Chaiken (Eds.), *The psychology of attitudes* (pp. 23–87). Fort Worth, TX: Harcourt Brace Jovanovich.

Himmelfarb, S., & Lickteig, C. (1982). Social desirability and the randomized response technique. *Journal of Personality and Social Psychology, 43*, 710–717.

Hippler, H. J., & Schwarz, N. (1989). "No-opinion" filters: A cognitive perspective. *International Journal of Public Opinion Research, 1*, 77–87.

Hoffman, P. J. (1960). Social acquiescence and "education." *Educational and Psychological Measurement, 20*, 769–776.

Holbrook, A. L., Green, M. C., & Krosnick, J. A. (2003). Telephone vs. face-to-face interviewing of national probability samples with long questionnaires: Comparisons of respondent satisficing and social desirability response bias. *Public Opinion Quarterly, 67*, 79–125.

Holbrook, A. L., Krosnick, J. A., Visser, P. S., Gardner, W. L., & Cacioppo, J. T. (2001). Attitudes toward presidential candidates and political parties: Initial optimism, inertial first impressions, and a focus on flaws. *American Journal of Political Science, 45*, 930–950.

Holmes, C. (1974). A statistical evaluation of rating scales. *Journal of the Market Research Society, 16*, 86–108.

Hough, K. S., & Allen, B. P. (1975). Is the "women's movement" erasing the mark of oppression from the female psyche? *Journal of Psychology, 89*, 249–258.

Houston, M. J., & Nevin, J. R. (1977). The effects of source and appeal on mail survey response patterns. *Journal of Marketing Research, 14*, 374–378.

Hovland, C. I., Janis, I. L., & Kelley, J. J. (1953). *Communication and persuasion.* New Haven, CT: Yale University Press.

Hurd, A. W. (1932). Comparisons of short answer and multiple choice tests covering identical subject content. *Journal of Educational Psychology, 26*, 28–30.

Isard, E. S. (1956). The relationship between item ambiguity and discriminating power in a forced-choice scale. *Journal of Applied Psychology, 40*, 266–268.

Israel, G. D., & Taylor, C. L. (1990). Can response order bias evaluations? *Evaluation and Program Planning, 13*, 365–371.

Jackman, M. R. (1973). Education and prejudice or education and response-set? *American Sociological Review, 38*, 327–339.

Jackson, D. N. (1959). Cognitive energy level, acquiescence, and authoritarianism. *Journal of Social Psychology, 49*, 65–69.

Jacoby, J., & Matell, M. S. (1971). Three-point Likert scales are good enough. *Journal of Marketing Research, 7*, 495–500.

Jajodia, A., & Earleywine, M. (2003). Measuring alcohol expectancies with the implicit association test. *Psychology of Addictive Behaviors, 17*, 126–133.

Jenkins, G. D., & Taber, T. D. (1977). A Monte Carlo study of factors affecting three indices of composite scale reliability. *Journal of Applied Psychology, 62*, 392–398.

Johanson, G. A., Gips, C. J., & Rich, C. E. (1993). If you can't say something nice—A variation on the social desirability response set. *Evaluation Review, 17*, 116–122.

Johnson, J. D. (1981). Effects of the order of presentation of evaluative dimensions for bipolar scales in four societies. *Journal of Social Psychology, 113*, 21–27.

Judd, C. M., & McClelland, G. H. (1998). Measurement. In D. Gilbert, S. Fiske, & G. Lindzey (Eds.), *The handbook of social psychology* (4th ed, Vol. 1, pp. 180–232). New York, NY: McGraw-Hill.

Kahn, D. F., & Hadley, J. M. (1949). Factors related to life insurance selling. *Journal of Applied Psychology, 33*, 132–140.

Kalton, G., Collins, M., & Brook, L. (1978). Experiments in wording opinion questions. *Applied Statistics, 27*, 149–161.

Kalton, G., Roberts, J., & Holt, D. (1980). The effects of offering a middle response option with opinion questions. *The Statistician, 29*, 65–79.

Karpinski, A., & Hilton, J. L. (2001). Attitudes and the Implicit Association Test. *Journal of Personality and Social Psychology, 81*, 774–788.

Kenny, D. A. (1994). *Interpersonal perception: A social relations analysis*. New York: Guilford.

Kenny, D. A., & Kashy, D. A. (1992). The analysis of the multitrait–multimethod matrix by confirmatory factor analysis. *Psychological Bulletin, 112*, 165–172.

Kinder, D. R., & Sanders, L. M. (1990). Mimicking political debate with survey questions: The case of White opinion on affirmative action for Blacks. *Social Cognition, 8*, 73–103.

Klare, G. R. (1950). Understandability and indefinite answers to public opinion questions. *International Journal of Opinion and Attitude Research, 4*, 91–96.

Klauer, K. C., & Musch, J. (2002). Goal-dependent and goal-independent effects of irrelevant evaluations. *Personality and Social Psychology Bulletin, 28*, 802–814.

Klauer, K. C., & Musch, J. (2003). Affective priming: Findings and theories. In J. Musch & K. C. Klauer (Eds.), *The psychology of evaluation: Affective processes in cognition and emotion* (pp. 7–50). Mahwah, NJ: Lawrence Erlbaum Associates.

Klauer, K. C., Rossnagel, C., & Musch, J. (1997). List-context effects in evaluative priming. *Journal of Experimental Psychology: Learning, Memory, and Cognition, 23*, 246–255.

Klayman, J., & Ha, Y. (1984). *Confirmation, disconfirmation, and information in hypothesis-testing*. Unpublished manuscript. Graduate School of Business, Center for Decision Research, University of Chicago, IL.

Kline, R. B. (1998). *Principles and practice of structural equation modeling*. New York: Guilford.

Klockars, A. J., & Yamagishi, M. (1988). The influence of labels and positions in rating scales. *Journal of Educational Measurement, 25*, 85–96.

Klopfer, F. J., & Madden, T. M. (1980). The middlemost choice on attitude items: Ambivalence, neutrality, or uncertainty. *Personality and Social Psychology Bulletin, 6*, 97–101.

Komorita, S. S. (1963). Attitude context, intensity, and the neutral point on a Likert scale. *Journal of Social Psychology, 61*, 327–334.

Komorita, S. S., & Graham, W. K. (1965). Number of scale points and the reliability of scales. *Educational and Psychological Measurement, 25*, 987–995.

Koriat, A., Lichtenstein, S., & Fischhoff, B. (1980). Reasons for confidence. *Journal Experimental Psychology: Human Learning and Memory, 6*, 107–118.

Krosnick, J. A. (1990). Americans' perceptions of presidential candidates: A test of the projection hypothesis. *Journal of Social Issues, 46*, 159–182.

Krosnick, J. A. (1991). Response strategies for coping with the cognitive demands of attitude measures in surveys. *Applied Cognitive Psychology, 5*, 213–236.

Krosnick, J. A. (1992). The impact of cognitive sophistication and attitude importance on response order effects and question order effects. In N. Schwarz & S. Sudman (Eds.), *Order effects in social and psychological research* (pp. 203–18). New York: Springer.

Krosnick, J. A. (1999). Survey methodology. *Annual Review of Psychology, 50*, 537–567.

Krosnick, J. A., & Alwin, D. F. (1987). An evaluation of a cognitive theory of response-order effects in survey measurement. *Public Opinion Quarterly, 51*, 201–219.

Krosnick, J. A., & Berent, M. K. (1990, May). *The impact of verbal labeling of response alternatives and branching on attitude measurement reliability in surveys*. Paper presented at the American Association for Public Opinion Research Annual Meeting, Lancaster, PA.

Krosnick, J. A., & Berent, M. K. (1993). Comparisons of party identification and policy preferences: The impact of survey question format. *American Journal of Political Science, 37*, 941–964.

Krosnick, J. A., Boninger, D. S., Chuang, Y. C., Berent, M. K., & Carnot, C. G. (1993). Attitude strength: One construct or many related constructs? *Journal of Personality and Social Psychology, 65*, 1132–1151.

Krosnick, J. A., & Fabrigar, L. R. (forthcoming). *Handbook of questionnaire design*. New York: Oxford University Press.

Krosnick, J. A., Holbrook, A. L., Berent, M. K., Carson, R. T., Hanemann, W. M., Kopp, R. J., Mitchell, R. C., Presser, S., Ruud, P. A., Smith, V. K., Moody, W. R., Green, M. C., & Conaway, M. (2002). The impact of no opinion response options on data quality: Non-attitude reduction or an invitation to satisfice? *Public Opinion Quarterly, 66*, 371–403.

Krosnick, J. A., Narayan, S., & Smith, W. R. (1996). Satisficing in surveys: Initial evidence. *New Directions for Evaluation, 70*, 29–44.

Krosnick, J. A., & Petty, R. E. (1995). Attitude strength: An overview. In R. E. Petty and J. A. Krosnick (Eds.), *Attitude strength: Antecedents and consequences*. Hillsdale, NJ: Lawrence Erlbaum Associates.

Krosnick, J. A., & Schuman, H. (1988). Attitude intensity, importance, and certainty and susceptibility to response effects. *Journal of Personality and Social Psychology, 54*, 940–952.

Kruglanski, A. W. (1989). The psychology of being "right": The problem of accuracy in social perception and cognition. *Psychological Bulletin, 106*, 395–409.

Kruglanski, A. W., & Freund, T. (1983). The freezing and unfreezing of lay-inferences: Effects of impressional primacy, ethnic stereotyping, and numerical anchoring. *Journal of Experimental Social Psychology, 19*, 448–468.

Kuncel, R. B. (1973). Response processes and relative location of subject and item. *Educational and Psychological Measurement, 33*, 545–563.

Kuncel, R. B. (1977). Ordering items by endorsement value and its effect upon text validity. *Educational and Psychological Measurement, 37*, 897–905.

Kunst-Wilson, W. R., & Zajonc, R. (1980). Affective discrimination of stimuli that cannot be recognized. *Science, 207*, 557–558.

Laird, J. D. (1974). Self-attribution of emotion: The effects of expressive behavior on the quality of emotional experience. *Journal of Personality and Social Psychology, 29*, 475–486.

Lang, P. J., Bradley, M. M., & Cuthbert, B. N. (1990). Emotion, attention, and the startle reflex. *Psychological Review, 97*, 377–395.

Larkins, A. G., & Shaver, J. P. (1967). Matched-pair scoring technique used on a first-grade yes–no type economics achievement test. *Utah Academy of Science, Art, and Letters: Proceedings, 44-I*, 229–242.

LeDoux, J. E. (1996). *The emotional brain: The mysterious underpinnings of emotional life*. New York: Simon & Schuster.

Leech, G. N. (1983). *Principles of pragmatics*. London: Longman.

Lehmann, D. R., & Hulbert, J. (1972). Are three-point scales always good enough? *Journal of Marketing Research, 9*, 444–446.

Lenski, G. E., & Leggett, J. C. (1960). Caste, class, and deference in the research interview. *American Journal of Sociology, 65*, 463–467.

Likert, R. (1932). A technique for measurement of attitudes. *Archives of Psychology, 140*, 1–55.

Lissitz, R. W., & Green, S. B. (1975). Effect of the number of scale points on reliability: A Monte Carlo approach. *Journal of Applied Psychology, 60*, 10–13.

Livingston, R. W., & Brewer, M. B. (2002). What are we really priming? Cue-based versus category-based processing of facial stimuli. *Journal of Personality and Social Psychology, 82*, 5–18.

Lord, C. G., Lepper, M. R., & Preston, E. (1984). Considering the opposite: A corrective strategy for social judgment. *Journal of Personality and Social Psychology, 47*, 1231–1243.

Lord, C. G., Ross, L., & Lepper, M. R. (1979). Biased assimilation and attitude polarization: The effects of prior theories on subsequently considered evidence. *Journal of Personality and Social Psychology, 37*, 2098–2109.

Luce, R. D., Krantz, D. H., Suppes, P., & Tversky, A. (1990). *Foundations of measurement: Vol. 3. Representation, axiomatization, and invariance*. San Diego, CA: Academic Press.

Maass, A., Salvi, D., Arcuri, L., & Semin, G. R. (1989). Language use in intergroup contexts: The linguistic intergroup bias. *Journal of Personality and Social Psychology, 57*, 981–993.

MacLeod, C. M. (1991). Half a century of research on the Stroop effect: An integrative review. *Psychological Bulletin, 109*, 163–203.

Marsh, K. L., Johnson, B. T., & Scott-Sheldon, L. A. (2001). Heart versus reason in condom use: Implicit versus explicit attitudinal predictors of sexual behavior. *Zeitschrift Fuer Experimentelle Psychologie, 48*, 161–175.

Martin, L. L. (1986). Set/reset: Use and disuse of concepts in impression formation. *Journal of Personality and Social Psychology, 51*, 493–504.

Martin, W. S. (1973). The effects of scaling on the correlation coefficient: A test of validity. *Journal of Marketing Research, 10*, 316–318.

Martin, W. S. (1978). Effects of scaling on the correlation coefficient: Additional considerations. *Journal of Marketing Research, 15*, 304–308.

Masters, J. R. (1974). The relationship between number of response categories and reliability of Likert-type questionnaires. *Journal of Educational Measurement, 11*, 49–53.

Matell, M. S., & Jacoby, J. (1971). Is there an optimal number of alternatives for Likert scale items? Study I: Reliability and validity. *Educational and Psychological Measurement, 31*, 657–674.

Matell, M. S., & Jacoby, J. (1972). Is there an optimal number of alternatives for Likert-scale items? Effects of testing time and scale properties. *Journal of Applied Psychology, 56*, 506–509.

Mathews, C. O. (1927). The effect of position of printed response words upon children's answers to questions in two-response types of tests. *Journal of Educational Psychology, 18*, 445–457.

McClendon, M. J. (1986). Response-order effects for dichotomous questions. *Social Science Quarterly, 67*, 205–211.

McClendon, M. J. (1991). Acquiescence and recency response-order effects in interview surveys. *Sociological Methods and Research, 20*, 60–103.

McClendon, M. J., & Alwin, D. F. (1993). No-opinion filters and attitude measurement reliability. *Sociological Methods and Research, 21*, 438–464.

McConnell, A. R., & Leibold, J. M. (2001). Relations among the Implicit Association Test, discriminatory behavior, and explicit measures of racial attitudes. *Journal of Experimental Social Psychology, 37*, 435–442.

McHugo, G., & Lanzetta, J. T. (1983). Methodological decisions in social psychophysiology. In J. T. Cacioppo & R. E. Petty (Eds.), *Social psychophysiology: A sourcebook* (pp. 630–665). New York: Guliford.

McKelvie, S. J. (1978). Graphic rating scales—How many categories? *British Journal of Psychology, 69*, 185–202.

Messick, S. (1989). Validity. In R. L. Linn (Ed.), *Educational measurement* (3rd ed., pp. 13–103). New York: Macmillan.

Messick, S., & Frederiksen, N. (1958). Ability, acquiescence, and "authoritarianism." *Psychological Reports, 4*, 687–697.

Metcalfe, J., & Shimamura, A. P. (Eds.). (1994). *Metacognition: Knowing about knowing.* Cambridge, MA: MIT Press.

Meyer, D. E., & Schvaneveldt, R. W. (1971). Facilitation in recognizing pairs of words: Evidence of a dependence between retrieval operations. *Journal of Experimental Psychology, 90*, 227–234.

Michaelis, W., & Eysenck, H. J. (1971). The determination of personality inventory factor patterns and intercorrelations by changes in real-life motivation. *Journal of Genetic Psychology, 118*, 223–234.

Mierke, J., & Klauer, K. C. (2001). Implicit association measurement with the IAT: Evidence for effects of executive control porcesses. *Zeitschrift Fuer Experimentelle Psychologie, 48*, 107–122.

Milgram, S., Mann, L., & Harter, S. (1965). The lost-letter technique: A tool of social research. *Public Opinion Quarterly, 29*, 437–438.

Miller, N., & Campbell, D. T. (1959). Recency and primacy in persuasion as a function of the timing of speeches and measurement. *Journal of Abnormal and Social Psychology, 59*, 1–9.

Miller, W. E. (1982). *American national election study, 1980: Pre and post election surveys.* Ann Arbor, MI: Inter-University Consortium for Political and Social Research.

Mingay, D. J., & Greenwell, M. T. (1989). Memory bias and response-order effects. *Journal of Official Statistics, 5*, 253–263.

Mirowsky, J., & Ross, C. E. (1991). Eliminating defense and agreement bias from measures of the sense of control: A 2 × 2 index. *Social Psychology Quarterly, 54*, 127–145.

Morin, R. (1993, December 6–12). Ask and you might deceive: The wording of presidential approval questions might be producing skewed results. *The Washington Post National Weekly Edition*, p. 37.

Murphy, S. T., & Zajonc, R. B. (1993). Affect, cognition, and awareness: Affective priming with optimal and suboptimal stimulus exposures. *Journal of Personality and Social Psychology, 64*, 723–739.

Murray, D. M., & Perry, C. L. (1987). The measurement of substance use among adolescents: When is the bogus pipeline method needed? *Addictive Behaviors, 12*, 225–233.

Narayan, S., & Krosnick, J. A. (1996). Education moderates some response effects in attitude measurement. *Public Opinion Quarterly, 60*, 58–88.

Neely, J. H. (1977). Semantic priming and retrieval from lexical memory: Roles of inhibitionless spreading activation and limited-capacity attention. *Journal of Experimental Psychology—General, 106*, 226–254.

Neely, J. H. (1991). Semantic priming effects in visual word recognition: A selective review of current findings and theories. In D. Besner & G. W. Humphreys (Eds.), *Basic processes in reading: Visual word recognition* (pp. 264–336). Hillsdale, NJ: Lawrence Erlbaum Associates.

Newcomb, T. E. (1943). *Personality and social change.* New York: Dryden Press.

Norman, D. A. (1973). Memory, knowledge, and the answering of questions. In R. L. Solso (Ed.), *Contemporary issues in cognitive psychology: The Loyola Symposium.* Washington, DC: Winston.

Nosek, B. A., & Banaji, M. R. (2001). The Go/No-go Association Task. *Social Cognition, 19*, 625–666.

Nosek, B. A., Banaji, M. R., & Greenwald, A. G. (2002). Math = male, me = female, therefore math not = me. *Journal of Personality and Social Psychology, 83*, 44–59.

Olson, M. A., & Fazio, R. H. (2003). Relations between implicit measures of prejudice: What are we measuring? *Psychological Science, 14*, 636–639.

Olson, M. A., & Fazio, R. H. (2004). Reducing the influence of extrapersonal associations on the Implicit Association Test: Personalizing the IAT. *Journal of Personality and Social Psychology, 86*, 653–667.

O'Muircheartaigh, C., Krosnick, J. A., & Helic, A. (1999, May). *Middle alternatives, acquiescence, and the quality of questionnaire data*. Paper presented at the American Association for Public Opinion Research Annual Meeting, St. Petersburg, FL.

Osgood, C. E., Suci, G. J., & Tannenbaum, P. H. (1957). *The measurement of meaning*. Urbana, IL: University of Illinois Press.

Ostrom, T. M., & Gannon, K. M. (1996). Exemplar generation: Assessing how respondents give meaning to rating scales. In N. Schwarz & S. Sudman (Eds.), *Answering questions: Methodology for determining cognitive and communicative processes in survey research* (pp. 293–441). San Francisco: Jossey-Bass.

Paulhus, D. L. (1984). Two-component models of socially desirable responding. *Journal of Personality and Social Psychology, 46*, 598–609.

Paulhus, D. L. (1986). Self-deception and impression management in test responses. In A. Angleitner & J. Wiggins (Eds.), *Personality assessment via questionnaires: Current issues in theory and measurement* (pp. 143–165). New York: Springer-Verlag.

Paulhus, D. L. (1991). Measurement and control of response bias. In J. P. Robinson, P. R. Shaver, & L. S. Wrightman (Eds.), *Measures of personality and social psychological attitudes. Volume 1 in Measures of Social Psychological Attitudes Series*. San Diego, CA: Academic Press.

Pavlos, A. J. (1972). Racial attitude and stereotype change with bogus pipeline paradigm. *Proceedings of the 80th Annual Convention of the American Psychological Association, 7*, 292–292.

Pavlos, A. J. (1973). Acute self-esteem effects on racial attitudes measured by rating scale and bogus pipeline. *Proceedings of the 81st Annual Convention of the American Psychological Association, 8*, 165–166.

Payne, J. D. (1971). The effects of reversing the order of verbal rating scales in a postal survey. *Journal of the Marketing Research Society, 14*, 30–44.

Payne, S. L. (1949–1950). Case study in question complexity. *Public Opinion Quarterly, 13*, 653–658.

Payne, S. L. (1950). Thoughts about meaningless questions. *Public Opinion Quarterly, 14*, 687–696.

Petty, R. E., & Cacioppo, J. T. (1983). The role of bodily responses in attitude measurement and change. In J. T. Cacioppo & R. E. Petty (Eds.), *Social psychophysiology: A sourcebook* (pp. 51–101). New York: Guilford.

Petty, R. E., & Cacioppo, J. T. (1986). The elaboration-likelihood model of persuasion. In L. Berkowitz (Ed.), *Advances in experimental social psychology* (Vol. 19, pp. 123–205). Orlando, FL: Academic Press.

Petty, R. E., & Krosnick, J. A. (Eds.) (1995). *Attitude strength: Antecedents and consequences*. Mahwah, NJ: Lawrence Erlbaum Associates.

Phelps, E. A., O'Connor, K. J., Cunningham, W. A., Funayama, E., Gatenby, J., Gore, J. C., et al. (2000). Performance on indirect measures of race evaluation predicts amygdala activation. *Journal of Cognitive Neuroscience, 12*, 729–738.

Poe, G. S., Seeman, I., McLaughlin, J., Mehl, E., & Dietz, M. (1988). Don't know boxes in factual questions in a mail questionnaire. *Public Opinion Quarterly, 52*, 212–222.

Posner, M. I., & Snyder, C. R. R. (1975). Attention and cognitive control. In R. L. Solso (Ed.), *Information processing and cognition* (pp. 55–85). Hillsdale, NJ: Lawrence Erlbaum Associates.

Pratto, F., & John, O. P. (1991). Automatic vigilance: The attention-grabbing power of negative social information. *Journal of Personality and Social Psychology, 61*, 380–391.

Quigley-Fernandez, B., & Tedeschi, J. T. (1978). The bogus pipeline as lie detector: Two validity studies. *Journal of Personality and Social Psychology, 36*, 247–256.

Quinn, S. B., & Belson, W. A. (1969). *The effects of reversing the order of presentation of verbal rating scales in survey interviews*. London: Survey Research Centre.

Ramsay, J. O. (1973). The effect of number of categories in rating scales on precision of estimation of scale values. *Psychometrika, 38*, 513–532.

Rankin, R. E., & Campbell, D. T. (1955). Galvanic skin response to Negro and White experimenters. *Journal of Abnormal & Social Psychology, 51*, 30–33.

Reber, R., Winkielman, P., & Schwarz, N. (1998). Effects of perceptual fluency on affective judgments. *Psychological Science, 9*, 45–48.

Remmers, H. H., Marschat, L. E., Brown, A., & Chapman, I. (1923). An experimental study of the relative difficulty of true–false, multiple-choice, and incomplete-sentence types of examination questions. *Journal of Educational Psychology, 14*, 367–372.

Robinson, J. P., Shaver, P. R., & Wrightsman, L. S. (1999). *Measures of political attitudes*. San Diego, CA: Academic Press.

Roese, N. J., & Jamieson, D. W. (1993). Twenty years of bogus pipeline research: A critical review and meta-analysis. *Psychological Bulletin, 114*, 363–375.

Rosenberg, N., Izard, C. E., & Hollander, E. P. (1955). Middle category response: Reliability and relationship to personality and intelligence variables. *Educational and Psychological Measurement, 15*, 281–290.

Rosenstone, S. J., Hansen, J. M., & Kinder, D. R. (1986). Measuring change in personal economic well-being. *Public Opinion Quarterly, 50*, 176–192.

Roskos-Ewoldsen, D. R., & Fazio, R. H. (1992). On the orienting value of attitudes: Attitude accessibility as a determinant of an object's attraction of visual attention. *Journal of Personality and Social Psychology, 63*, 198–211.

Rothenberg, B. B. (1969). Conservation of number among four- and five-year-old children: Some methodological considerations. *Child Development, 40*, 383–406.

Rubin, H. K. (1940). *A constant error in the Seashore test of pitch discrimination*. Unpublished master's thesis. University of Wisconsin, Madison.

Ruch, G. M., & DeGraff, M. H. (1926). Corrections for chance and "guess" vs. "do not guess" instructions in multiple-response tests. *Journal of Educational Psychology, 17*, 368–375.

Rugg, D., & Cantril, H. (1944). The wording of questions. In H. Cantril (Ed.), *Gauging public opinion* (pp. 23–50). Princeton, NJ: Princeton University Press.

Rundquist, E. A., & Sletto, R. F. (1936). *Personality in the depression*. Minneapolis: University of Minnesota Press.

Salancik, G. R., & Conway, M. (1975). Attitude inferences from salient and relevant cognitive content about behavior. *Journal of Personality and Social Psychology, 32*, 829–840.

Sanbonmatsu, D. M., & Fazio, R. H. (1990). The role of attitudes in memory-based decision making. *Journal of Personality and Social Psychology, 59*, 614–622.

Saris, W., & Krosnick, J. A. (2000, May). *The damaging effect of acquiescence response bias on answers to agree/disagree questions*. Paper presented at the American Association for Public Opinion Research Annual Meeting, Portland, OR.

Schaeffer, N. C., & Bradburn, N. M. (1989). Respondent behavior in magnitude estimation. *Journal of the American Statistical Association, 84*, 402–413.

Scherpenzeel, A. (1995). Meta-analysis of a European comparative study. In W. Saris & A. Munnich (Eds.), *The multitrait–multimethod approach to evaluate measurement instruments*. Budapest, Hungary: Eotvos University Press.

Schlenker, B. R., & Weigold, M. F. (1989). Goals and the self-identification proces: Constructing desired identities. In L. A. Pervin (Ed.), *Goal concepts in personality and social psychology* (pp. 243–290). Hillsdale, NJ: Lawrence Erlbaum Associates.

Schuman, H., & Converse, J. M. (1971). The effect of Black and White interviewers on Black responses. *Public Opinion Quarterly, 35*, 44–68.

Schuman, H., Ludwig, J., & Krosnick, J. A. (1986). The perceived threat of nuclear war, salience, and open questions. *Public Opinion Quarterly, 50*, 519–536.

Schuman, H., & Presser, S. (1981). *Questions and answers in attitude surveys*. New York: Academic Press.

Schwarz, N., & Bless, H. (1992). Constructing reality and its alternatives: An inclusion/exclusion model of assimilation and contrast effects in social judgment. In L. L. Martin & A. Tesser (Eds.), *The construction of social judgment* (pp. 217–245). Hillsdale, NJ: Lawrence Erlbaum Associates.

Schwarz, N., & Clore, G. L. (1996). Feelings and phenomenal experiences. In E. T. Higgins & A. W. Kruglanski (Eds.), *Social psychology: Handbook of basic principles* (pp. 433–465). New York: Guilford.

Schwarz, N., & Hippler, H. J. (1991). Response alternatives: The impact of their choice and presentation order. In P. Biemer, R. M. Groves, L. E. Lyberg, N. A. Mathiowetz, & S. Sudman (Eds.), *Measurement error in surveys* (pp. 41–56). New York: Wiley.

Schwarz, N., Hippler, H. J., & Noelle-Neumann, E. (1992). A cognitive model of response-order effects in survey measurement. In N. Schwarz & S. Sudman (Eds.), *Context effects in social and psychological research* (pp. 187–201). New York: Springer-Verlag.

Schwarz, N., & Strack, F. (1991). Context effects in attitude surveys: Applying cognitive theory to social research. *European Review of Social Psychology, 2*, 31–50.

Schwarz, N., & Wyer, R. S. (1985). Effects of rank ordering stimuli on magnitude ratings of these and other stimuli. *Journal of Experimental Social Psychology, 21*, 30–46.

Sedikides, C., & Strube, M. J. (1997). Self-evaluation: To thine own self be good, to thine own self be sure, to thine own self be true, and to thine own self be better. In M. P. Zanna (Ed.), *Advances in experimental social psychology* (Vol. 29, pp. 209–269). New York, NY: Academic Press.

Shaffer, J. W. (1963). A new acquiescence scale for the MMPI. *Journal of Clinical Psychology, 19*, 412–415.

Shavelson, R., & Webb, N. (1991). *Generalizability theory: A primer*. Newbury Park, CA: Sage.

Sherif, C. W., Sherif, M., & Nebergall, R. E. (1965). *Attitude and attitude change*. Philadelphia: Saunders.

Sherif, M., & Hovland, C. I. (1961). *Social judgment: Assimilation and contrast effects in communication and attitude change*. New Haven, CT: Yale University Press.

Sherman, S. J., Rose, J. S., Koch, K., Presson, C. C., & Chassin, L. (2003). Implicit and explicit attitudes toward cigarette smoking: The effects of context and motivation. *Journal of Social and Clinical Psychology, 22*, 13–39.

Shiffrin, R. M., & Schneider, W. (1977). Controlled and automatic human information processing: II. Perceptual learning, automatic attending, and a general theory. *Psychological Review, 84*, 127–190.

Shrout, P. E., & Fleiss, J. L. (1979). Intraclass correlations: Uses in assessing rater reliability. *Psychological Bulletin, 86*, 420–428.

Sigall, H., & Page, R. (1971). Current stereotypes: A little fading, a little faking. *Journal of Personality and Social Psychology, 18*, 247–255.

Sigelman, C. K., & Budd, E. C. (1986). Pictures as an aid in questioning mentally retarded persons. *Rehabilitation Counseling Bulletin, 29*, 173–181.

Simon, J. (1990). The effects of an irrelevant directional cue on human information processing. In R. W. Proctor & T. G. Reeve (Eds.), *Stimulus–response compatibility: An integrated perspective. Advances in psychology* (Vol. 65, pp. 31–86). Amsterdam: North-Holland.

Smith, T. W. (1994a). *A comparison of two confidence scales*. GSS Methodological Report No. 80, National Opinion Research Center, Chicago, IL.

Smith, T. W. (1994b). *A comparison of two governmental spending scales*. GSS Methodological Report No. 81, National Opinion Research Center, Chicago, IL.

Smith, T. W., & Peterson, B. L. (1985, August). *The impact of number of response categories on inter-item associations: Experimental and simulated results*. Paper presented at the American Sociological Association Meeting, Washington, DC.

Smith, E. R., Fazio, R. H., & Cejka, M. A. (1996). Accessible attitudes influence categorization of multiply categorizable objects. *Journal of Personality and Social Psychology, 71*, 888–898.

Snyder, M. (1979). Self-monitoring processes. In L. Berkowitz (Ed.), *Advances in experimental social psychology* (Vol. 12, pp. 86–128). New York: Academic Press.

Solarz, A. K. (1960). Latency of instrumental responses as a function of compatibility with the meaning of eliciting verbal signs. *Journal of Experimental Psychology, 59*, 239–245.

Srinivasan, V., & Basu, A. K. (1989). The metric quality of ordered categorical data. *Marketing Science, 8*, 205–230.

Stember, H., & Hyman, H. (1949–1950). How interviewer effects operate through question form. *International Journal of Opinion and Attitude Research, 3*, 493–512.

Strack, F. (1992). The different routes to social judgments: Experiential versus informational strategies. In L. L. Martin & A. Tesser (Eds.), *The construction of social judgments* (pp. 249–275). Hillsdale, NJ: Lawrence Erlbaum Associates.

Strack, F., & Martin, L. (1987). Thinking, judging, and communicating: A process account of context effects in attitude surveys. In H. J. Hippler, N. Schwarz, & S. Sudman (Eds.), *Social information processing and survey methodology* (pp. 123–148). New York: Springer-Verlag.

Strack, F., Martin, L. L., & Schwarz, N. (1988). Priming and communication: Social determinants of information use in judgments of life satisfaction. *European Journal of Social Psychology, 18*, 429–442.

Strack, F., Martin, L. L., & Stepper, S. (1988). Inhibiting and facilitating conditions of the human smile: A nonobtrusive test of the facial feedback hypothesis. *Journal of Personality and Social Psychology, 54*, 768–777.

Sudman, S., Bradburn, N. M., & Schwarz, N. (1996). *Thinking about answers: The application of cognitive processes to survey methodology*. San Francisco: Jossey-Bass.

Sussman, B. (1978). President's popularity in the polls is distorted by rating questions. *The Washington Post*, pp.

Tamulonis, V. (1947). *The effects of question variations in public opinion surveys*, Unpublished masters thesis. University of Denver, CO.

Tesser, A. (1978). Self-generated attitude change. In L. Berkowitz (Ed.), *Advances in experimental social psychology* (Vol. 11, pp. 289–338). New York: Academic Press.

Tesser, A., Whitaker, D., Martin, L., & Ward, D. (1998). Attitude heritability, attitude change and physiological responsivity. *Personality and Individual Differences, 24*, 89–96.

Tetlock, P. E. (1983). Accountability and the complexity of thought. *Journal of Personality and Social Psychology, 45*, 74–83.

Thomas, W. I., & Znaniecki, R. (1918). *The Polish peasant in Europe and America: Monograph of an immigrant group*. Boston: Badger.

Thurstone, L. L. (1927). A law of comparative judgment. *Psychological Review, 34*, 251–259.

Thurstone, L. L. (1928). Attitudes can be measured. *American Journal of Sociology, 33*, 529–554.

Thurstone, L. L. (1931). Measurement of social attitudes. *Journal of Abnormal and Social Psychology, 26*, 249–269.

Tourangeau, R., & Rasinski, K. A. (1988). Cognitive processes underlying context effects in attitude measurement. *Psychological Bulletin, 103*, 299–314.

Tourangeau, R., Rasinski, K. A., Bradburn, N., & D'Andrade, R. (1989). Carryover effects in attitude surveys. *Public Opinion Quarterly, 53*, 495–524.

Trott, D. M., & Jackson, D. N. (1967). An experimental analysis of acquiescence. *Journal of Experimental Research in Personality, 2*, 278–288.

Tulving, E., Schacter, D. L., & Stark, H. A. (1982). Priming effects in word-fragment completion are independent of recognition memory. *Journal of Experimental Psychology: Learning, Memory, and Cognition, 8*, 336–342.

Tversky, A. (1977). Features of similarity. *Psychological Review, 84*, 327–352.

Vaillancourt, P. M. (1973). Stability of children's survey responses. *Public Opinion Quarterly, 37*, 373–387.

Vanman, E. J., Paul, B. Y., Ito, T. A., & Miller, N. (1997). The modern face of prejudice and structural features that moderate the effect of cooperation on affect. *Journal of Personality and Social Psychology, 71*, 941–959.

Visser, P. S., Krosnick, J. A., Marquette, J. F., & Curtin, M. F. (2000). Improving election forecasting: Allocation of undecided respondents, identification of likely voters, and response order effects. In P. L. Lavrakas & M. Traugott (Eds.), *Election polls, the news media, and democracy* (pp. 224–260). New York: Chatham House.

von Hippel, W., Sekaquaptewa, D., & Vargas, P. (1997). The linguistic intergroup bias as an implicit indicator of prejudice. *Journal of Experimental Social Psychology, 33*, 490–509.

Wänke, M., Bohner, G., & Jurkowitsch, A. (1997). There are many reasons to drive a BMW: Does imagined ease of argument generation influence attitudes? *Journal of Consumer Research, 24*, 170–177.

Warner, S. L. (1965). Randomized response: A survey technique for eliminating evasive answer bias. *Journal of the American Statistical Association, 60*, 63–69.

Warr, P., Barter, J., & Brownridge, G. (1983). On the interdependence of positive and negative affect. *Journal of Personality and Social Psychology, 44*, 644–651.

Wason, P. C. (1961). Response to affirmative and negative binary statements. *British Journal of Psychology, 52*, 133–142.

Watson, D. (1988). The vicissitudes of mood measurement: Effects of varying descriptors, time frames, and response formats on measures of positive and negative affect. *Journal of Personality and Social Psychology, 55*, 128–141.

Watson, D. R., & Crawford, C. C. (1930). Four types of tests. *The High School Teacher, 6*, 282–283.

Wedell, D. H., & Parducci, A. (1988). The category effect in social judgment: Experimental ratings of happiness. *Journal of Personality and Social Psychology, 55*, 341–356.

Wedell, D. H., Parducci, A., & Geiselman, R. E. (1987). A formal analysis of ratings of physical attractiveness: Successive contrast and simultaneous assimilation. *Journal of Experimental Social Psychology, 23*, 230–249.

Wedell, D. H., Parducci, A., & Lane, M. (1990). Reducing the dependence of clinical judgment on the immediate context: Effects of number of categories and type of anchors. *Journal of Personality and Social Psychology, 58*, 319–329.

Wegener, D. T., Downing, J., Krosnick, J. A., & Petty, R. E. (1995). Measures and manipulations of strength-related properties of attitudes: Current practice and future directions. In R. E. Petty and J. A. Krosnick (Eds.), *Attitude strength: Antecedents and consequences.* Hillsdale, NJ: Lawrence Erlbaum.

Wegener, D. T., & Petty, R. E. (1995). Flexible correction processes in social judgment: The role of naive theories in corrections for perceived bias. *Journal of Personality and Social Psychology, 68*, 36–51.

Wegener, D. T., & Petty, R. E. (1997). The flexible correction model: The role of naive theories of bias in bias correction. In M. P. Zanna (Ed.), *Advances in experimental social psychology* (Vol. 29, pp. 141–208). San Diegeo, CA: Academic Press.

Wentura, D., & Rothermund, K. (2003). The "meddling-in" of affective information: A general model of automatic evaluation effects. In J. Musch & K. C. Klauer (Eds.), *The psychology of evaluation: Affective processes in cognition and emotion* (pp. 51–86). Mahwah, NJ: Lawrence Erlbaum Associates.

Wesman, A. G. (1946). The usefulness of correctly spelled words in a spelling test. *Journal of Educational Psychology, 37*, 242–246.

Westie, F. R. (1953). A technique for the measurement of race attitudes. *American Sociological Review, 18*, 73–78.

Wilson, T. D., & Hodges, S. D. (1992). Attitudes as temporary constructions. In L. L. Martin & A. Tesser (Eds.), *The construction of social judgment* (pp. 37–66). Hillsdale, NJ: Lawrence Erlbaum Associates.

Wilson, T. D., Lindsey, S., & Schooler, T. Y. (2000). A model of dual attitudes. *Psychological Review, 107*, 101–126.

Winkler, J. D., Kanouse, D. E., & Ware, J. E. (1982). Controlling for acquiescence response set in scale development. *Journal of Applied Psychology, 67*, 555–561.

Wiseman, F. (1972). Methodological bias in public opinion surveys. *Public Opinion Quarterly, 36*, 105–108.

Wittenbrink, B., Judd, C. M., & Park, B. (1997). Evidence for racial prejudice at the implicit level and its relationship with questionnaire measures. *Journal of Personality and Social Psychology, 72*, 262–274.

Wittenbrink, B., Judd, C. M., & Park, B. (2001a). Evaluative versus conceptual judgments in automatic stereotyping and prejudice. *Journal of Experimental Social Psychology, 37*, 244–252.

Wittenbrink, B., Judd, C. M., & Park, B. (2001b). Spontaneous prejudice in context: Variability in automatically activated attitudes. *Journal of Personality and Social Psychology, 81*, 815–827.

Word, C. O., Zanna, M. P., & Cooper, J. (1974). The nonverbal mediation of self-fulfilling prophecies in interracial interaction. *Journal of Experimental Social Psychology, 10*, 109–120.

Ying, Y. (1989). Nonresponse on the center for epidemiological studies—Depression scale in Chinese Americans. *International Journal of Social Psychiatry, 35*, 156–163.

Yzerbyt, V. Y., & Leyens, J. (1991). Requesting information to form an impression: The influence of valence and confirmatory status. *Journal of Experimental Social Psychology, 27*, 337–356.

Zajonc, R. B. (1960). The process of cognitive tuning and communication. *Journal of Applied Social Psychology, 61*, 159–167.

Zajonc, R. B. (1968). Attitude effects of mere exposure. *Journal of Personality and Social Psychology, 9*, 1–27.

Zaller, J., & Feldman, S. (1992). A simple theory of the survey response: Answering questions versus revealing preferences. *American Journal of Political Science, 36*, 579–616.

II

The Matrix of Attitude-Relevant Influences

3

The Structure of Attitudes

Leandre R. Fabrigar
Tara K. MacDonald
Queen's University

Duane T. Wegener
Purdue University

Throughout its history in social psychology, the attitude construct has been defined in myriad ways. Core to most definitions has been that attitudes reflect evaluations of objects on a dimension ranging from positive to negative. Thus, researchers have characterized attitudes in terms of their valence and extremity. In practice, attitudes have been routinely represented by a single numerical index reflecting the position of an attitude object on an evaluative continuum. However, social scientists have long recognized that characterizing attitudes solely in terms of valence and extremity is insufficient to fully capture all relevant properties of an attitude. For example, in his seminal article on attitude measurement, Thurstone (1928) noted that attitudes are multifaceted and that attempting to describe them with a single numerical index is analogous to attempting to describe an object like a kitchen table with a single numerical index. Other early attitude researchers also noted a variety of relevant attitudinal properties. For example, early advocates of the tripartite perspective proposed that evaluative responses could be classified into the categories of affect, behavior, and cognition (e.g., Katz & Stotland, 1959; Rosenberg & Hovland, 1960; Smith, 1947). Other scholars distinguished among the underlying functions a global evaluation might serve (e.g., Katz, 1960; Katz & Stotland, 1959; Smith, Bruner, & White, 1956). And still others noted that evaluations might vary in the amount of information on which they were based (e.g., Rosenberg & Abelson, 1960) and the extent to which they were linked to other attitudes (e.g., Converse, 1964). Thus, social scientists have long recognized the importance of attitude structure. In this chapter, our first goal is to acquaint readers with the major theories and empirical findings that have emerged in over 60 years of attitude structure research. We also hope to highlight important unresolved issues, suggest some new ways of organizing and interpreting past results, and provide possible directions for future research.

CORE DEFINITIONS AND CONCEPTS

What Is Attitude Structure?

Although the term *attitude structure* is ubiquitous in the literature, precise definitions are less common. The concept of structure must begin with one's conceptualization of attitude. For an attitude per se to exist, it makes sense to view the attitude as a type of knowledge structure stored in memory or created at the time of judgment. Some attitude theorists (e.g., Fazio, 1989, 1995) have proposed that attitudes be thought of as object–evaluation associations. That is, an attitude can be viewed as a simple two-node semantic network, with one node representing the object, the second node the global evaluation of the object, and the link between the two nodes the strength of the association.[1]

Although attitudes can be characterized as simple object-evaluation associations, attitudes may be part of larger sets of knowledge structures (e.g., see Eagly & Chaiken, 1993, 1998; Petty & Krosnick, 1995; Pratkanis, Breckler, & Greenwald, 1989). For example, one might associate specific attributes with the representation of the object and each of these attributes might in turn be associated with an evaluation (Fishbein & Ajzen, 1975). Likewise, one might associate specific emotional responses with an object and each of these affective states might be associated with an evaluation (e.g., see Zanna & Rempel, 1988). From this perspective, the structure of an attitude can be represented as an object-evaluation association and the knowledge structures linked to it. The term attitude structure refers to the content and the number of knowledge structures, the strength of the associative links making up the attitude and its related knowledge structures, and the pattern of associative links among the attitude and its related knowledge structures (see also Eagly & Chaiken, 1998; Wegener & Gregg, 2000).

Some researchers have distinguished between two general types of attitude structure (Eagly & Chaiken, 1993, 1995, 1998; McGuire, 1989). *Intra-attitudinal structure* refers to the structure of a single attitude. *Inter-attitudinal structure* refers to structures involving more than one attitude (also referred to as *attitude systems,* e.g., Judd, Drake, Downing, & Krosnick, 1991; McGuire, 1989; or *belief systems,* e.g., Converse, 1964). As noted earlier, an overall attitude toward an object might be influenced by evaluations of many specific attributes of the object or emotions associated with the object. Therefore, one could technically refer to many situations as involving inter-attitudinal structure even when only one object is considered. In our discussions, however, we retain the previous labels of intra-attitudinal when a single object is considered and inter-attitudinal when two or more objects are involved (usually at roughly the same level of abstraction).

Attitudes: Stored Knowledge Structures or Temporary Constructions?

The traditional and most prevalent conceptualization of attitudes is that attitudes are global evaluations that people can access from memory when called on to do so. However, some researchers have suggested that it may be useful to conceptualize attitudes as temporary constructions, created at the time people are asked to make attitudinal judgments (e.g., Bem, 1972; Schwarz & Bohner, 2001; Wilson & Hodges, 1992). According to this perspective, people often lack preconsolidated general evaluations. When asked to report attitudes, people consider readily available information and integrate this information into an overall attitudinal judgment.

From a structural perspective, the *constructionist* view suggests that people may often have representations of objects that are associated with various knowledge structures that are evaluative in nature (e.g., beliefs about the object's attributes or emotional reactions associated with the object). However, the object representation may have no global evaluation associated with it. Thus, people construct a summary evaluation based on linked knowledge structures that are either strongly associated with the object representation or are temporarily accessible at the time of judgment. Presuming the newly formed global evaluation does not become strongly associated with the object representation, this global evaluation should decay over time. Thus, at a later time, the construction process might once again need to be undertaken.

It should be noted that the strongest version of a constructionist view (i.e., that no attitudes are stored in memory, see also Wyer & Albarracín, this volume) would not allow for stored evaluations of attributes or emotions any more than for global evaluations of objects, because an attribute for one attitude object could also be its own attitude object. Information would have to be stored in a *nonevaluative* form, waiting to take on evaluative meaning in a particular context. But one would have to possess a concept of evaluation in order to interpret those contexts. Because of the functionality of overall evaluations preparing people for approach or avoidance, it simply seems odd to assume that all assessments of goodness or badness must be constructed anew when encountering familiar objects (see Fazio & Olson, 2003a). This is not to say that all attitudes must be stored and that construction never occurs. Rather, it seems likely that for any given attitude object, some people may have clearly formed global evaluations that are strongly linked to the attitude object representation. For these people, construction may often be unlikely. However, other people may lack well-developed global evaluations, and construction may be more likely (Priester, Nayakankuppum, Fleming, & Godek, 2004). Similarly, some attitudes may be a mixture of these conceptualizations (i.e., a global evaluation may exist, but may be only weakly associated with the object representation). Thus, both traditional and temporary construction perspectives may simply describe attitudes with different structural properties. We will touch on this issue throughout the chapter.

REVIEW OF ATTITUDE STRUCTURE PROPERTIES

Attitude Accessibility

Perhaps the most basic structural property of attitudes is that of attitude accessibility. Accessibility can be viewed as the strength of the associative link between object and evaluation, such that for highly accessible attitudes, the evaluation of an object is automatically activated from memory when that object is encountered (Fazio, Sanbonmatsu, Powell, & Kardes, 1986). Alternatively, accessibility could be conceptualized as represented in the connection weights within a connectionist model. In this model, accessibility would correspond to the ability of partial stimulus input to *quickly* and accurately produce the entire pattern of activation for the attitude (e.g., see Smith & DeCoster, 1998; Smith, Fazio, & Cejka, 1996; see also Bassili & Brown, this volume). Consistent with either conceptualization, attitude accessibility is usually assessed using an adjective connotation task, in which participants are presented with an attitude object on a computer screen, and then are asked to make an evaluation (e.g., good or bad) in response to that object. Response latencies are recorded, and it is inferred that quick reaction times indicate high accessibility, whereas slow reaction times indicate low accessibility.

Accessibility is determined in part by the frequency with which the attitude is activated, such that repeated expressions strengthen the associations between objects and evaluations, thereby increasing the ease of retrieval of the evaluation from memory (Fazio, Chen, McDonel, & Sherman, 1982; Powell & Fazio, 1984). Attitudes can also be particularly accessible when based on information the person considers as highly diagnostic (i.e., credible evaluative information). Fazio (1995) posits that sensory information about the object, emotional reactions engendered by the object, past behavior toward the object, and direct experience with the object are classes of information that are commonly viewed as highly diagnostic.

Types of Attitude-Relevant Information

Affective/Cognitive/Behavioral Bases

The tripartite theory, or the notion that attitudes have three components—affect, cognition, and behavior—has enjoyed a long history (e.g., Katz & Stotland, 1959; Rosenberg & Hovland, 1960; Smith, 1947). Traditionally, affect has been used to describe the positive and negative feelings that one holds toward an attitude object (Rosenberg & Hovland, 1960). Cognition has been used to refer to beliefs that one holds about the attitude object, and behavior has been used to describe overt actions and responses to the attitude object. In its original form, the tripartite theory held that attitudes were comprised of these three components, which subsequent researchers demonstrated are distinguishable from each other (Breckler, 1984; Kothandapani, 1971; Ostrom, 1969).

Although acknowledging these early contributions, more contemporary attitude researchers have modified the tripartite theory (e.g., Cacioppo, Petty, & Geen, 1989; Petty & Cacioppo, 1986; Zanna & Rempel, 1988). These theorists have argued that affect can best be described as consisting of specific and distinct emotional states (see also Schimmack & Crites, this volume), in contrast to the more generally evaluative "approval or disapproval" (Smith, 1947, p. 509) or "attribution of good or bad qualities" (Katz & Stotland, 1959, p. 430). Moreover, the traditional tripartite theorists tended to imply that all three components were constituents that were the "anatomy" of an attitude (Smith, 1947, p. 508) or were three types of possible responses to a stimulus (e.g., Rosenberg & Hovland, 1960). In contrast, the contemporary view holds that an attitude is an entity distinguishable from the classes of affect, behavior, and cognition. An attitude, therefore, does not consist of these elements, but is instead a general evaluative summary of the information derived from these bases (Cacioppo et al., 1989; Crites, Fabrigar, & Petty, 1994; Zanna & Rempel, 1988).

With this shift to considering attitude as conceptually separable from the bases of the attitude, research has addressed the potential differences across attitudes primarily based on affect, cognition, or behavior. A fair amount of research has addressed attitudes based primarily on affect or cognition (including studies that have experimentally created such attitudes in the absence of past behavior), but less attention has been given to attitudes with purely behavioral bases. Consistent with Bem's (1972) self-perception theory, social perceivers might sometimes directly infer an attitude from past behaviors. Yet, because these past behaviors could also have influenced beliefs or emotional responses, it is also plausible for effects of past behavior to be mediated by these classes of responses. Although some research has attempted to control for behavioral effects on beliefs (e.g., Albarracín & Wyer, 2000), investigations controlling for both beliefs and affect have yet to be conducted.

Functional Nature of Attitudes

Researchers have long speculated about the motivations for forming and holding attitudes (e.g., Katz & Stotland, 1959; Kelman, 1961; Smith, Bruner, & White, 1956; for reviews, see Kruglanski & Stroebe, this volume; Shavitt, 1989). For instance, Katz (1960) proposed that there are four classes of attitude functions. The knowledge function posits that attitudes facilitate the management and simplification of information processing by providing a schema with which to integrate existing and new information. The utilitarian (or instrumental) function posits that attitudes help individuals to achieve desired goals and avoid negative outcomes. The ego-defensive function, derived from psychoanalytic principles, pertains to the maintenance or promotion of self-esteem. Finally, the value-expressive function states that individuals use attitudes to convey information about their values and self-concepts. Smith et al. (1956) also proposed the social-adjustive function, which posits that attitudes facilitate the maintenance of relationships with others who are liked. None of the proposed taxonomies are necessarily exhaustive nor are they necessarily mutually exclusive.

Although seldom described as such, functions may be linked to structural properties of attitudes (e.g., see Fabrigar, Smith, & Brannon, 1999). Specifically, whether an attitude serves a particular function may, to some extent, be a result of the content of the knowledge structures associated with that attitude. For example, attitudes based on information linked to core values could result in an attitude that serves a value-expressive function. Likewise, an attitude based on information directly relevant to self worth could produce an ego-defensive attitude, and so on. Functions themselves would also likely have implications for knowledge content, such that a value-expressive function, for example, would encourage attention to, and memory for, value-relevant information. Thus, in certain respects, taxonomies of attitude functions can be thought of as systems for categorizing attitude-relevant information.

Amount and Breadth of Attitude-Relevant Information

Working Knowledge

Working knowledge is defined as the number of attitude-relevant thoughts and experiences that spontaneously come to mind when encountering an object (Wood, Rhodes, & Biek, 1995).[2] As such, working knowledge is likely a subset of all the knowledge available in memory, with thoughts and experiences strongly associated with the attitude object most likely to be included as working knowledge (Wood, 1982). In this way, knowledge pertains directly to core aspects of attitude structure such as the number of knowledge structures associated with the attitude and the strength of the associations among the structures and the attitude.

One common measure of working knowledge is to ask participants to generate lists of all the thoughts and experiences that they believe are relevant to an attitude object (e.g., Biek, Wood, & Chaiken, 1996; Davidson, Yantis, Norwood, & Montano, 1985; Wood, 1982). Other measures ask participants for their subjective impressions of how knowledgeable they are about an attitude object (e.g., Wood, 1982; Davidson et al., 1985; Wilson, Kraft, & Dunn, 1989). It is notable that the knowledge-listing technique and subjective reports of knowledge are modestly correlated (see Krosnick, Boninger, Chuang, Berent, & Carnot, 1993; see also Wood, 1982; Wood et al., 1995).[3]

When asked to list thoughts and experiences, some individuals generate factually correct information, whereas others generate erroneous information. Indeed, working knowledge is not always highly correlated with factual accuracy (see Scott, 1969; Wood et al., 1995). Wood et al. (1995) contend that knowledge-listing is the most representative index of the thoughts, feelings, and behavioral information that a person uses when evaluating an attitude object, and so may be generally more useful than factual accuracy. In some cases, however, accuracy of information may be diagnostic of attitude outcomes (e.g., see Davidson, 1995).

To be considered part of working knowledge, attitude-relevant thoughts and experiences must be accessible in response to an attitude object. It follows, then, that working knowledge will be determined in part by factors that increase the ease with which thoughts or experiences are brought to mind. Frequent exposure to the attitude object and high levels of cognitive elaboration about the attitude object are among the variables that could increase the likelihood that many thoughts or experiences are recalled when an attitude object is encountered.

Complexity

Complexity of knowledge refers to the extent to which attitude-relevant information represents a number of distinct underlying dimensions (i.e., the extent to which information can be classified as pertaining to multiple categories; Scott, 1969; Tetlock, 1989). For example, two people could be equally positive in their evaluation of an attitude object and demonstrate the same amount of working knowledge. Despite these similarities, they could differ greatly in terms of complexity. A person whose knowledge represents multiple underlying dimensions or perspectives (high differentiation) would be higher in complexity than a person whose knowledge corresponds to a single dimension or perspective (i.e., low differentiation). Some researchers have also distinguished between two different types of complex attitudes: those based on multiple orthogonal dimensions (i.e., attitudes high in differentiation and low in integration) and those based on multiple related dimensions (i.e., attitudes high in differentiation and integration; e.g., Judd & Lusk, 1984; Scott, 1969; Tesser, Martin, & Mendolia, 1995).

Indeed, evaluating the relations among the dimensions that underlie beliefs is a defining feature of some classifications of complexity. *Integrative complexity* (Tetlock, 1989) pertains not only to the number of distinct dimensions underlying an attitude, but also the extent to which these dimensions are linked or conceptually related to one another. Attitudes that are high in integrative complexity are characterized by a high number of underlying dimensions that are highly connected to each other. In contrast, attitudes low in integrative complexity are characterized by underlying dimensions that are relatively isolated and diffuse.

Integrative complexity is typically assessed through content analysis (e.g., Baker-Brown, Ballard, Bluck, deVries, Suedfeld, & Tetlock, 1992; Tetlock & Suedfeld, 1988). Raters assign a value of 1 (representing no differentiation or integration) to 7 (representing both high differentiation and integration) to text. In this coding system, differentiation refers not only to mention of multiple dimensions, but there must also be some conflict or tension implied among dimensions. Scores on this scale are routinely low (e.g., means of around 2 for undergraduates and around 4 for U.S. Supreme Court Justices; Baker-Brown et al., 1992), representing some differentiation, but no integration. Because scores for most people simply reflect the presence or absence of conflicting dimensions, one might argue that research on integrative complexity differs from traditional complexity, and may be reconceptualized as pertaining to ambivalence.

Although the structural properties of working knowledge and complexity are theoretically distinct, these two constructs may often be positively correlated. The more information a person generates in response to an attitude object, the greater the possibility that these responses will tap into a high number of distinct underlying dimensions (see Linville, 1982). Of course, this relation is not necessarily true (e.g., a person could generate 2 or 42 beliefs representing a single dimension), but in general, the greater the amount of working knowledge, the greater the potential for high complexity. Cognitive elaboration is also a likely determinant of complexity. Individuals who elaborate may be likely to generate a greater number of dimensions underlying their attitude and recognize increasing and more intricate bonds among those dimensions (e.g., see work on accountability by Tetlock, 1983a; Tetlock & Kim, 1987).

Evaluative Consistency of Attitude-Relevant Information: Ambivalence

Attitudinal Ambivalence

Attitudinal ambivalence occurs when there is evaluative tension associated with one's attitude because the summary includes both positive and negative evaluations (Kaplan, 1972; Scott, 1969; Thompson, Zanna, & Griffin, 1995). Direct measures of the experience of ambivalence include measures of the person feeling *mixed* or *torn* about the attitude object (Jamieson, 1988, 1993; Priester & Petty, 1996; Tourangeau, Rasinski, Bradburn, & D'Andrade, 1989), whereas potential ambivalence is typically assessed by combining the positive and negative evaluations using one of a number mathematical models (Kaplan, 1972; Priester & Petty, 1996; Thompson et al., 1995). Correlations between potential and experienced ambivalence tend to be moderate

(Priester & Petty, 1996; 2001; Thompson et al., 1995). The relation is particularly strong when the conflicting evaluations are simultaneously accessible, especially among people high in preference for consistency (Newby-Clark, McGregor, & Zanna, 2002). Priester and Petty (2001) have also demonstrated that individuals experience ambivalence when their attitudes are discrepant from those of others who are liked (e.g., parents, high-status peers).

Types of Ambivalence

Attitudinal ambivalence can result from different types of evaluative inconsistency. Within-dimension ambivalence occurs when one's evaluations within a dimension conflict (e.g., both positive and negative beliefs or both positive and negative emotions related to an attitude object). Between-dimension ambivalence is experienced when there is a conflict between two dimensions, such as affective-cognitive inconsistency (i.e., when emotions and beliefs are not congruent), evaluative-affective inconsistency (i.e., when overall attitude conflicts with the feelings or emotions associated with the object, see Chaiken, Pomerantz, & Giner-Sorolla, 1995) or evaluative-cognitive inconsistency (i.e., when overall attitude conflicts with the knowledge or beliefs associated with the object, Chaiken et al., 1995).[4]

Most research on between-dimension and within-dimension ambivalence uses the dimensions of affect and cognition; however, the study of ambivalence need not be limited to these dimensions. Ambivalence can occur when any dimensions of attitude structure are inconsistent, whether these dimensions are the bases described by the tripartite model, functions associated with an attitude object, or other dimensions relevant to an attitude object.

Few researchers assessing ambivalence have attempted to classify or label the type of ambivalence under investigation. However, the consequences of holding ambivalent attitudes may vary according to the specific type of ambivalence that is experienced. It may therefore be instructive for researchers to make distinctions among types of ambivalence to more effectively compare findings across studies and to work toward the development of a coherent framework that can explain how the specific types of inconsistencies operate to affect attitudes and behavior.

Inter-Attitudinal Structure

Research in attitude structure has typically focused on the intra-attitudinal properties previously described. However, it is also possible to view attitudes as units that are linked together in cognitive structures (e.g., Converse, 1964; Eagly & Chaiken, 1995; Judd, Drake, Downing, & Krosnick, 1991; Judd & Krosnick, 1989; McGuire, 1985). Thus, one can characterize structure in terms of the relations among attitudes toward different but related attitude objects. Similarly, researchers have recently discussed structure in terms of two or more attitudes toward the same object (e.g., *dual attitudes*, Wilson, Lindsey, & Schooler, 2000).

Attitude Systems

Initial work assessing consistency among related attitudes generated influential cognitive consistency theories (Abelson & Rosenberg, 1958; Festinger, 1957; Heider, 1958; see also Cartwright & Harary, 1956). These theories posited that individuals experience tension when they recognize attitudinal inconsistency and are motivated to maintain inter-attitudinal congruity (see Abelson et al., 1968; for reviews, see Olson & Stone, this volume; Wyer & Albarracín, this volume). More recently, researchers have studied specific properties of inter-attitudinal structure, including the extent to which attitudes are associated in long-term memory, and the consistency and strength of those links (Judd et al., 1991; Judd & Krosnick, 1989; Lavine, Thomsen, & Gonzales, 1997).

Applying associative network principles of spreading activation (Anderson, 1983), Judd and his colleagues (Judd et al., 1991; Judd & Krosnick, 1989) theorized that attitudes are linked together in cognitive structures in such a way that, if one attitude is called to mind, other attitudes linked in memory will also be activated. Links are formed when attitude objects are considered simultaneously, which happens when a person "comes to believe that one object implies, favors, contradicts, or opposes the other object" (Judd & Krosnick, 1989, p. 109). In this model, attitudes are the nodes. Links among the nodes are characterized by implicational relations (consistent or inconsistent) and strength (the probability that the nodes will activate each other).

Attitudes can be linked and organized in cognitive frameworks according to general ideologies such as liberalism or conservatism (Converse, 1964), or because they influence a common set of consequences such as value-expression (Lavine et al., 1997). Attitudes that are organized within such schemas are more likely to be consistent with one another than are attitudes with fewer and weaker associative links (Judd & Krosnick, 1989). In this way, individuals are likely to have attitudes that are consistent in valence when they know about relevant attitude objects (i.e., have a high number of nodes), and recognize connections among those attitudes (i.e., have a high number of links per node). For example, Judd and Krosnick (1989) hypothesized that these criteria would be fulfilled by political experts, who should be able to invoke ideologies when thinking about attitude objects and thus recognize links to other attitude objects. Similarly, when individuals view an attitude as important, they should spend more time thinking about the attitude object and develop stronger links to related attitude objects. Indeed, Judd and Krosnick demonstrated that individuals who were experts in the domain of politics (who held extensive knowledge about, and interest in, politics) were more likely to demonstrate evaluative consistency. Judd and Downing (1990) established that the relation between political expertise and evaluative consistency was mediated by the propensity of experts, relative to nonexperts, to organize their attitudes in cognitive frameworks such as ideologies. Although nonexperts may not organize attitudes according to elaborate schemas such as ideologies, they can recognize other links among attitudes (e.g., in terms of value goal attainment), and so can also achieve attitudinal consistency (Lavine et al., 1997).

Dual-Attitude Structure

The inter-attitudinal structures discussed refer to links among evaluations of separate attitude objects. It is possible, however, to hold two (or more) attitudes toward the same attitude object, as has been proposed in the dual attitude model (Wilson et al., 2000) and the past attitudes still there (PAST) model (Petty, Tormala, Briñol & Jarvis, 2005).

In the dual attitude model, Wilson and colleagues assert that when an attitude changes, the old attitude is not necessarily discarded. Instead, older attitudes may be retained alongside the new attitude. They argue that individuals can hold dual attitudes because one attitude is expressed at a conscious level (i.e., explicit) whereas the other is often outside awareness (i.e., implicit, see Greenwald & Banaji, 1995). In this view, either the implicit or the explicit attitude can be activated. Implicit attitudes are the default attitudes that are activated automatically, whereas explicit attitudes are expressed only when an individual has sufficient capacity and motivation to override the implicit attitude and retrieve the explicit attitude.

The PAST model also holds that after attitude change occurs, the older attitude still exists. This model assumes that when an individual changes his or her attitude, that person will *tag* the original attitude as *false* or as being associated with low confidence. Both the new attitude and the old attitude are still linked to the attitude object in memory, and so either (or both) can be activated. According to the PAST model, the original attitude will be activated when the original attitude has not been tagged, when that tag cannot be retrieved in memory, or when that attitude cannot be inhibited.

At first glance, dual-attitude structures may seem akin to the intra-attitudinal property of ambivalence. Wilson and his colleagues, however, draw a number of distinctions between these two concepts. They note that when ambivalence occurs, tension results as a consequence of two conflicting evaluations that are both in awareness. They maintain that with dual attitudes, there is no psychological tension to resolve when an individual is not consciously aware of the implicit attitude, and so only acknowledges the explicit attitude. Interestingly, Petty and colleagues have recently conducted research suggesting that inconsistency between self-report and implicit association test measures of attitudes (indexing implicit ambivalence) can have similar processing consequences to those observed using traditional explicit measures of ambivalence (Briñol, Petty & Wheeler, 2005). Even so, the PAST model differs from the dual-attitude approach because, in some circumstances (e.g., when individuals do not successfully access the false tag), both the old and new attitude can be simultaneously activated and open to awareness. In such instances, individuals can experience a state similar to explicit ambivalence.

Although most of the research on dual attitudes focuses on implicit–explicit dual attitude structures, it is theoretically possible to hold implicit–implicit dual attitudes, or explicit–explicit dual attitudes. Implicit–implicit dual attitudes could occur when both attitudes are formed at a level below awareness (e.g., via mere exposure or conditioning, see Olson & Fazio, 2001, 2002; Walther, 2002). Explicit–explicit dual attitudes could occur when attitude change occurs, but the individual recalls both the original attitude and the new attitude (Petty et al., 2003). In fact, some researchers (e.g., Fazio & Olson, 2003b) have questioned whether it has been demonstrated that implicit attitudes are actually below awareness at all. Furthermore, much of the research on dual-attitude structures implies that the two attitudes are evaluatively inconsistent (see Wilson et al., 2000). It could be, however, that the attitudes would be similarly valenced. In domains such as prejudice, attitudes assessed via implicit measures exhibit low correlations with attitudes assessed via explicit measures. Yet, with more mundane objects, the correlations tend to be higher (Fazio & Olson, 2003b). In future research, it will be instructive to assess the possible combinations of dual-attitude structures. As with ambivalence, the consequences of dual attitudes may vary as a function of the type of dual attitude held.

ASSOCIATIONS AMONG STRUCTURAL PROPERTIES AND WITH OTHER CONSTRUCTS

As the previous section illustrates, theorists have proposed a host of structural properties of attitudes. Thus, it is not surprising that one important theme in attitude structure research has been attempting to develop more parsimonious conceptual organizations of structural properties. Because many of the properties are related to the strength of attitudes, it is perhaps reasonable that properties might covary. Researchers have also been interested in examining the extent to which structural properties relate to other attitude strength constructs. Research has identified a number of subjective beliefs about attitudes (e.g., attitude confidence) as well as properties of the attitude itself (e.g., attitude extremity) associated with strength. Hence, researchers have examined whether structural properties of attitudes are related to these beliefs and properties.

Taxonomies of Attitude Structure and Related Constructs

The goal of developing a conceptual organization of structural properties and related constructs is an intuitively compelling objective for both theoretical and practical reasons. Unfortunately, although useful advances have been made, empirical research to date has been far from definitive. Findings have often been inconsistent across studies and no widely accepted taxonomy of structural properties or other strength-related constructs has emerged. For example,

Erber, Hodges, and Wilson (1995) proposed that structural properties and other strength-related constructs could be conceptualized as two factors reflecting the evaluative consistency of the database underlying the attitude and the strength of the evaluation. However, a principal components analysis of 13 strength-related constructs failed to provide evidence of two underlying factors.

Bassili (1996) proposed a taxonomy based on the nature of the measurement procedure used. He distinguished between *meta-attitudinal* measures, which involve reporting subjective beliefs about some aspect of the attitude or attitude object (e.g., subjective reports of certainty), and *operative* measures, which involve objective—rather than subjective—indices of judgmental processes in attitudinal responses (e.g., response latencies of attitudinal responses). Factor analyses provided some evidence of a two-factor structure consistent with the meta-attitudinal/operative distinction. However, attitude certainty (a meta-attitudinal measure) was found to load on both factors. Furthermore, other interpretations of the factor structure are possible. For instance, measures that loaded on the meta-attitudinal factor could also be argued to be measures likely to reflect the amount of information underlying the attitude (e.g., self-reports of knowledge, frequency of thought, and importance). Measures that loaded on the operative factor could be alternatively conceptualized as measures sensitive to the evaluative consistency of information underlying the attitude (e.g., attitude response latencies, ambivalence, extremity). This alternative conceptualization might also explain why certainty loaded on both factors. It is intuitively sensible that certainty regarding attitudes would be related to both the amount and evaluative consistency of information underlying an attitude.

Krosnick et al. (1993) conducted confirmatory factor analyses of structural properties, attitude extremity, and strength-related beliefs. Their analyses rejected a model postulating a single underlying strength factor and supported a model with each strength-related property as a distinct construct. Though this preferred model fit the data well, it was not particularly parsimonious, nor did it provide guidance regarding why structural properties and other strength-related properties are more versus less related to one another.[5]

Limitations of Past Research

Why have results been so inconsistent in research on taxonomies of structure and other strength-related constructs? One possibility may be that somewhat different sets of measures have been used across studies and many studies have incompletely sampled strength-related constructs. Furthermore, the psychometric properties of measures have seldom been explored. Ultimately, the results of any factor analysis are dependent on the extent to which the measures adequately sample the domain of interest and possess sound psychometric properties (e.g., see Fabrigar, Wegener, MacCallum, & Strahan, 1999).

A second limitation has been the lack of fully developed theoretical rationales for proposed taxonomies. The precise mechanisms by which specific constructs are related to one another have seldom been articulated. Consider the Erber et al. (1995) two-factor taxonomy of consistency of database and strength of evaluation. This model implies that various forms of evaluative consistency load on a common factor (i.e., these properties should be highly intercorrelated). However, there seems little reason to expect that because one type of inconsistency exists (e.g., affective-cognitive inconsistency), another type of inconsistency should also exist (e.g., belief inconsistency). Similarly, the Bassili (1996) meta-attitudinal/operative distinction implies that sharing a measurement method is sufficient for two measures to be highly correlated. Based on this logic, a subjective (meta-attitudinal) report of ambivalence should be more highly correlated with a subjective report of knowledge than it is with an *operative* measure of ambivalence. Yet, there seems to be little reason people who subjectively experience low levels of ambivalence should perceive themselves as highly knowledgeable. People are likely to experience little ambivalence when they know very little about an attitude object. Likewise, this perspective cannot account for correlations between subjective reports of ambivalence and operative measures of ambivalence (e.g., see Priester & Petty, 1996, 2001; Thompson et al., 1995) or for stronger relations between these alternative measures of the same construct than between pairs of meta-attitudinal or operative constructs (e.g., Krosnick et al., 1993).[6]

Another potential reason for past inconsistencies is that the studies have failed to examine whether associations among constructs are sometimes nonlinear or moderated by other strength-related constructs. For instance, consider the seemingly obvious prediction that subjective certainty increases as working knowledge increases. This prediction is only sensible if increases in working knowledge involve evaluatively consistent information. When knowledge is inconsistent, there may be no association between working knowledge and certainty. Past research has not generally addressed such possibilities. A final limitation is that most studies of associations among strength-related constructs have been nonexperimental. Thus, it is difficult to know the degree to which third variables have obscured true associations among constructs (see Wegener, Downing, Krosnick, & Petty, 1995).

Exploring Associations Among Structural Properties and Related Constructs

Although no widely accepted taxonomy of attitude structure exists, it is nonetheless important to consider how such properties are related to one another. Here, we review structural properties of attitudes and propose hypotheses regarding their associations with other structural properties and strength-related constructs. Although there are theoretical bases to make hypotheses about virtually all combinations of structural variables, not all of these associations have received empirical attention. In the interest of brevity, we confine our discussion to the pairings for which there are some data, the findings of which are summarized in Table 3.1.

Associations With Attitude Accessibility

Accessibility is perhaps the most widely studied structural property of attitudes. In considering its associations with other constructs, it is important to recognize that associations might be driven by effects of accessibility on the other strength variable or by effects of the strength variable on accessibility. Thus, in our discussion of accessibility (and other structural properties), we consider both possibilities.

Type of Attitude-Relevant Information and Accessibility.   As noted earlier, attitude theorists have distinguished among various types of attitude relevant information. There seems to be little reason to expect that simply strengthening the object–evaluation association should result in an attitude based on a particular type of information. However, it is possible that attitudes derived from different types of information could produce attitudes that differ in accessibility. It has been suggested that the perceived diagnosticity of the informational basis of an attitude may influence the strength of an object–evaluation association and that affective information may be perceived as more diagnostic of attitudes than cognitive information (Fazio, 1995).

In a study examining 20 different attitude objects, analyses revealed a positive correlation between the extent to which attitude objects were described in affective terms and the accessibility of attitudes toward those objects (see Fazio, 1995). Giner-Sorolla (2001) measured the extent to which attitudes were based on affect/cognition and the accessibility of attitudes in two studies. Controlling for attitude extremity, there was no overall effect of attitude basis on accessibility. However, a significant interaction between extremity and attitude basis revealed that for extreme attitudes, affective attitudes were more accessible than cognitive attitudes.

TABLE 3.1
Summary of Associations Among Structural Properties
of Attitudes and Other Strength-Related Properties

	Accessibility		Type of Information		Knowledge	
Type of Information						
	Fazio (1995)	+sig				
	Giner-Sorolla (2001)	non-sig				
Knowledge						
	Erber et al. (1995)-subjective	.16	None			
	Krosnick et al. (1993)-subjective	.25				
	MacDougall et al. (2003)-subjective	non-sig				
	Krosnick et al. (1993)-listing	.11				
Complexity						
	None		None		None	
Ambivalence						
	Erber et al. (1995)-aff/cog	.03	None		Erber et al. (1995)-aff/cog	.01
	Krosnick et al. (1993)-aff/cog	−.24			Krosnick et al (1993)-aff/cog	−.05
	Erber et al. (1995)-belief	.01			Erber et al. (1995)-belief	−.16
	MacDougall et al. (2003)-belief	−sig				
	Bargh et al. (1992)-general	−.24				
Inter-Attitudinal						
	None		None		Bishop et al. (1980)	+sig
					Converse (1964)	+sig
					Judd et al. (1981)	non-sig
					Judd & Downing (1990)	+sig
					Judd & Krosnick (1989)	+sig
					Judd & Milburn (1980)	non-sig
					Lavine et al. (1997)	+sig
Extremity						
	Bargh et al. (1992)-nonexp	.69	None		Erber et al. (1995)-subj	.33
	Erber et al. (1995)-nonexp	.43			Krosnick et al. (1993)-subj	.26/.47/.22/.25
	Fazio et al. (1989)-nonexp	.18			Smith et al. (2003)-actual	non-sig
	Fazio & Williams (1986)-nonexp	.53/.53			Krosnick et al. (1993)-list	.11
	Houston & Fazio (1989)-nonexp	.21				
	Krosnick et al. (1993)-nonexp	.35				
	Powell & Fazio (1984)-nonexp	.30				
	Bizer & Krosnick (2001)-exp	non-sig				
	Brauer et al. (1995)-exp	+sig				
	Downing et al. (1992)-exp	+sig				
	Fabrigar et al. (1998)-exp	non-sig				
	Fazio et al. (1986)-exp	non-sig				
	Fazio et al. (2000)-exp	non-sig				
	Judd et al. (1991)-exp	+sig				
	Powell & Fazio (1984)-exp	non-sig				
	Roskos-Ewoldsen & Fazio (1992)-exp	non-sig				
	Smith et al. (1996)-exp	+sig				
Importance						
	Erber et al. (1995)-nonexp	.14	None		Erber et al. (1995)-subj	.48
	Krosnick (1989)-nonexp	.29/.31/.20			Krosnick et al. (1993)-subj	.47/.56/.64/.19/.44
	Krosnick et al. (1993)-nonexp	.26			Krosnick et al. (1993)-list	.19
	Lavine et al. (1996)-nonexp	+sig				
	Tourangeau et al. (1991)-nonexp	.31/.13			Berent & Krosnick (1993a)	+sig
	Bizer & Krosnick (2001)-exp	non-sig			Berent & Krosnick (1993b)	+sig
	Roese & Olson (1994)-exp	.33				
	MacDougall et al. (2003)-exp	non-sig				
Certainty						
	Krosnick et al. (1993)-nonexp	.26	Edwards (1990)	non-sig/+sig	Smith et al. (2003)	+sig
	MacDougall et al. (2003)-exp	non-sig	Edwards & von Hippel (1995)	+sig/non-sig		

Complexity		Ambivalence		Inter-Attitudinal	
None					
None		None			
Judd & Lusk (1984)	+/-sig	Bargh et al. (1992)-general	−.54	None	
Linville (1982)	−sig	Krosnick et al. (1993)-aff/cog	−.29/−.17/−.38		
Linville & Jones (1980)	−sig	Smith et al. (2003)-belief	−sig		
Millar& Tesser (1986b)	+sig				
Tesser & Leone (1977)	+sig				
None		Krosnick et al. (1993)-aff/cog	.00/−.13/−.14	Judd & Krosnick (1982)	+sig
		Smith et al. (2003)-belief	non-sig	Judd & Krosnick (1989)	+sig
None		Krosnick et al. (1993)-aff/cog	.01/−.09/−.05	None	
		Smith et al. (2003)-belief	−sig		

In contrast, for moderate attitudes, cognitive attitudes were more accessible than affective attitudes.

These studies present a mixed picture, and some additional caveats seem warranted. First, given the correlational nature of the data, it is possible that confounds may have been present in comparisons of affective/cognitive attitudes. Second, the extent to which information of a particular type is seen as diagnostic of attitudes may be moderated by a variety of factors. For example, different types of information may be seen as diagnostic for different classes of attitude objects. The manner in which information is acquired and/or subsequently processed may also influence its perceived diagnosticity. Fazio (1995) has noted that cognitive information may be seen as diagnostic if it is carefully elaborated (e.g., see Chaiken, Liberman, & Eagly, 1989; Petty & Cacioppo, 1986). Given these issues, it is not clear that one should generally expect a simple association between the basis or bases of attitudes and attitude accessibility.

Working Knowledge and Accessibility. Researchers have suggested that accessibility is related to working knowledge (e.g., Davidson et al., 1985; Kallgren & Wood, 1986), though the mechanisms underlying this association have not been explicitly stated. Because increased accessibility is associated with increased frequency of attitude activation (Powell & Fazio, 1984), spreading activation to linked structures should lead to frequent coactivation of these structures, thereby resulting in stronger associative links between the attitude and attitude-relevant information (Judd & Brauer, 1995). As noted earlier, one important determinant of working knowledge is the strength of associative links of information to the attitude. Therefore, repeated activation of the attitude could increase reports of working knowledge. To the extent that increasing accessibility of attitudes increases the sheer amount of working knowledge, attitude accessibility might also increase *working complexity* of that knowledge.

There is also reason to predict that increases in working knowledge/complexity might lead to greater accessibility. First, each time a new link between a piece of information and an attitude is formed, the attitude is likely to be activated. Thus, increasing working knowledge is likely to produce repeated attitude activation. Second, attitudes linked to numerous knowledge structures and/or to knowledge structures reflecting multiple dimensions may be more likely to be activated as a result of situational cues. The more extensive or complex the representation of an attitude object, the more likely that a situation will contain cues relevant to some aspect of the attitude object representation and thus trigger activation of the attitude.

It is interesting to note that only a little empirical research on the working knowledge-accessibility association exists. Research examining the association between subjective reports of knowledge and attitude accessibility (assessed using response latencies) have produced positive, but weak, correlations (Erber et al., 1995; Krosnick et al., 1993)[7] as has research assessing knowledge through a knowledge-listing measure (Krosnick et al., 1993). One experiment using repeated attitude expression to manipulate attitude accessibility did not produce differences in perceived knowledge (MacDougall, Fabrigar, Ackbar, & Smith, 2003). Although past research suggests only a weak association between working knowledge and accessibility, our previously stated limitations of past research apply. For example, one relatively obvious moderator of the working knowledge–accessibility association may be the evaluative consistency of attitude-relevant information. An implicit assumption in our discussions of working knowledge and accessibility has been that attitude-relevant information is evaluatively consistent. However, when ambivalence exists, greater working knowledge should not necessarily lead to enhanced accessibility. Many objects used in past studies were objects likely to elicit ambivalence (e.g., abortion, capital punishment).

Ambivalence and Accessibility. There are numerous reasons why accessibility might be related to ambivalence. As stated earlier, strengthening the object–evaluation association involves repeated attitude activation, which in turn could lead to activation of linked knowledge structures thereby strengthening associations with the attitude. However, attitude activation may differentially influence knowledge structures that are evaluatively consistent versus inconsistent with the attitude (see Judd & Brauer, 1995). When an object representation is activated, features primarily used to initially categorize the object are more likely to be activated than features that did not play a dominant role in the categorization of the object. Given that global evaluation is one important dimension by which objects are categorized (Osgood, Suci, & Tannenbaum, 1957), repeated attitude activation may strengthen associations among evaluatively consistent pieces of information more than evaluatively inconsistent pieces of information. Additionally, research suggests that activation of an attitude tends to facilitate activation of knowledge structures that are evaluatively consistent with the attitude and inhibit activation of knowledge structures that are evaluatively inconsistent with the attitude (Bargh, Chaiken, Govender, & Pratto, 1992; Bargh, Chaiken, & Hymes, 1996; Fazio, 1995; Fazio, Jackson, Dunton, & Williams, 1995; Fazio et al., 1986). Hence, repeated attitude activation should lead to stronger links between the attitude and evaluatively consistent rather than inconsistent information, thus leading to less ambivalence. Considering a reverse causal mechanism, increasing (decreasing) ambivalence could lead to decreased (increased) accessibility for similar reasons. Each time a link is established between an attitude and a knowledge structure that is evaluatively inconsistent, this adds another related knowledge structure whose activation could inhibit activation of the attitude.

It is interesting to note that these processes may not be the same for different types of ambivalence. Within-dimension ambivalence involves highly interrelated information, so coactivation of contradictory information may be likely. Thus, it might be difficult for activation of an attitude to activate information evaluatively consistent with the attitude and not also activate information evaluatively inconsistent with the attitude. In such situations, repeated attitude activation may not decrease ambivalence. However, decreased ambivalence within a dimension should still increase accessibility. In contrast, for between-dimension ambivalence, differential activation of information that is consistent versus inconsistent with the attitude may be more likely because contradictory information is less strongly linked and thus less likely to be coactivated.

Evidence of relations between ambivalence and accessibility is inconsistent. Studies of general ambivalence and accessibility have reported negative associations (Bargh et al., 1992; see also Fazio, 1995). Studies assessing the relation between affective-cognitive ambivalence and accessibility have produced mixed results (Erber et al., 1995; Krosnick et al., 1993). Ambivalence within beliefs has been uncorrelated with accessibility (Erber et al., 1995).

Attitude Extremity and Accessibility.   There has also been interest in examining the relation of accessibility to other strength properties such as attitude extremity. Perhaps the most well-developed model related to the accessibility–extremity association was proposed by Judd and Brauer (1995). They began with the assumption that repeated attitude activation/expression leads to greater attitude accessibility and also stated that repeated attitude activation/expression can alter extremity by influencing stages of the attitudinal response process. According to this model (and discussed earlier), repeated attitude activation/expression strengthens associations with those features that served as the primary basis for the initial evaluation of the object. Thus, if an attitude object was initially evaluated positively, repeated attitude activation will cause positive object features to become more strongly associated with the object than negative features, thereby leading to greater extremity. Similarly, if prompted to recompute an evaluation of an attitude object, this strengthening of associative links can lead people to weight attitude-consistent features more than attitude-inconsistent features, thereby producing greater extremity. Finally, when people are asked to report their attitudes, this task usually involves mapping the evaluation onto a numerical and/or verbal response scale. Repeated expression of an attitude on that scale may enhance the association of a particular response label (e.g., good) with the object, which in turn may lead to more extreme responses.

Nonexperimental research suggests a positive association between extremity and accessibility (Bargh et al., 1992; Erber et al., 1995; Fazio, Powell, & Williams, 1989; Fazio & Williams, 1986; Houston & Fazio, 1989; Krosnick et al., 1993; Powell & Fazio, 1984). Interestingly, experimental tests have produced more mixed results. Although nearly all experiments have indicated that repeated attitude expression increases attitude accessibility, most studies have found no increases in extremity (Bizer & Krosnick, 2001; Fabrigar, Priester, Petty, & Wegener, 1998; Fazio, Ledbetter, & Towles-Schwen, 2000; Fazio et al., 1986; Powell & Fazio, 1984; Roskos-Ewoldsen & Fazio, 1992), although some have shown extremity effects (Brauer, Judd, & Gliner, 1995; Downing, Judd, & Brauer, 1992; Judd et al., 1991; Smith, Fazio, & Cejka, 1996).

Judd and colleagues (Downing et al., 1992; Judd & Brauer, 1995) have suggested that failures to find extremity effects were due to the particular response scales used. They argue that when repeated attitude expressions occur on a response scale, the internal representation of the evaluation takes the form of that response label. Thus, when subsequently reporting attitudes, people provide a response that reflects the particular response label that has become their internal representation of the attitude. However, if people express their attitudes using only the scale endpoints or using an open-ended format, no specific point on the response continuum is internalized and thus greater extremity on a subsequent rating scale occurs.

This interpretation has not gone unchallenged. Fazio (1995) noted that some studies using dichotomous repeated attitude expression manipulations have still failed to produce increased extremity (Fazio et al., 1986; Roskos-Ewoldsen & Fazio, 1992). Furthermore, when such extremity effects occur, they may be driven primarily by people who were initially neutral. Because dichotomous attitude expressions force them to adopt a position on one side of the issue, neutral people may come to see themselves as possessing a positive or negative evaluation. Consistent with this interpretation, Fazio and Powell (1994; as cited in Fazio, 1995) categorized people at varying levels of initial attitude extremity. They found that repeated dichotomous attitude expression only produced greater extremity for people who were initially neutral.[8]

Strength-Related Beliefs and Accessibility.   Attitude strength-related beliefs are subjective beliefs about attitudes or attitude objects that have been found to relate to the underlying strength of an attitude (see Petty & Krosnick, 1995). Although there is substantial evidence that these beliefs are associated with strength-related outcomes (for reviews, see Boninger, Krosnick, Berent, & Fabrigar, 1995; Crano, 1995; Davidson, 1995; Gross, Holtz, & Miller, 1995; Wood et al., 1995), little is known of their origins. Nonetheless, accessibility has often been assumed to be a cause and/or consequence of such beliefs.

The most extensive research on accessibility and strength-related beliefs has focused on the importance–accessibility association. There are numerous reasons for an accessibility–importance relation. First, people may use the ease of retrieving their attitudes as a basis for inferring how important those attitudes are (Roese & Olson, 1994). Second, one function served by attitudes is to help orient a person to attend to consequential objects in their environment (Roskos-Ewoldsen & Fazio, 1992). Attitudes assist people in allocating cognitive resources by signaling that an object has hedonic consequences. Because accessible attitudes are spontaneously activated and thus signal that objects have hedonic consequences, highly accessible attitudes may be seen as more important than less accessible attitudes (Fabrigar et al., 1998). Finally, accessibility and importance could be associated because increased importance causes increases in accessibility. Importance can result in more active seeking of attitude-relevant information and more extensive elaboration of that information, which can lead to greater accessibility (Bizer & Krosnick, 2001; Boninger et al., 1995; Petty, Haugtvedt, & Smith, 1995).

Nonexperimental studies have reported positive associations between importance and accessibility (Erber et al., 1995; Krosnick et al., 1993; Lavine, Sullivan, Borgida, & Thomsen, 1996; Tourangeau, Rasinski, & D'Andrade, 1991). Yet, experimental studies have provided less consistent results. On one hand, Roese and Olson (1994) conducted a repeated attitude expression manipulation and found that this manipulation produced increases in both accessibility and importance. Mediational analyses suggested that repeated expression enhanced accessibility, which in turn led to increased importance. However, other studies manipulating repeated expression have revealed evidence of increased accessibility without corresponding increases in importance (Bizer & Krosnick, 2001; MacDougall et al., 2003). Some evidence also points to importance leading to accessibility. Bizer and Krosnick (2001) reported data suggesting that, when people can seek out and elaborate attitude-relevant information, increases in importance lead to increases in accessibility. Thus, to date, there seems to be substantial theoretical and empirical support for an association between accessibility and importance. However, the causal direction of that association and the precise mechanisms underlying it remain in doubt. It is possible that these mechanisms are not mutually exclusive and may manifest themselves under different conditions. For example, use of ease of retrieval to infer importance may primarily occur when people have not previously formed clear beliefs about the importance of their attitudes and when other salient information is not present to allow them to construct judgments of importance. Importance may lead to enhanced accessibility under conditions when importance can produce greater information seeking and elaboration.

Far less research has occurred on the association of accessibility with other strength-related beliefs. For example, some have proposed that certainty and accessibility should be positively related (Gross et al., 1995). It is intuitively plausible that frequency of attitude activation and ease of attitude retrieval could serve as cues to infer certainty. Although nonexperimental research has supported such a prediction (Krosnick et al., 1993), one experimental study involving a repeated attitude expression manipulation did not find significant increases in certainty, although the effects were in the expected direction (MacDougall et al., 2003).

Associations With Working Knowledge and Complexity

Ambivalence and Working Knowledge.   Although there are reasons to expect a relation between ambivalence and working knowledge, this is unlikely to be a simple relation. Because the total number of contradictory knowledge structures in memory will be greater as working knowledge increases, a number of theoretical perspectives predict that increases in working knowledge are likely to lead to greater evaluative conflict (see Festinger, 1957; Priester & Petty, 1996; Thompson et al., 1995). When knowledge is generally consistent, however, increases in knowledge could leave ambivalence unchanged or even decrease ambivalence. There could be reverse causal effects (i.e., ambivalence leading to greater working knowledge), though the form of this relation is unlikely to be a simple one. Processing of inconsistent information might be difficult and might sometimes lead to greater effort (e.g., Jonas, Diehl, & Bromer, 1997), though, as described later in this chapter, ambivalence might enhance processing of some persuasive messages and not others (e.g., Clark, Wegener, & Fabrigar, 2004). When taken as a whole, it is not surprising that studies find only weak associations between ambivalence and working knowledge (Erber et al., 1995; Krosnick et al., 1993).

Inter-Attitudinal Structure and Amount/Complexity of Knowledge.   There are reasons to expect that both the amount and complexity of working knowledge will be related to inter-attitudinal structure. Inter-attitudinal links often result from perceiving logical relations between attitude objects (e.g., relevance to common values). If attitudes are based on information that is extensive and complex, people are more likely to be able to recognize logical links between attitude objects. Some indirect evidence supports this prediction. Nonexperimental studies have shown that increases in political expertise are related to the strength of associations among political attitudes (e.g., Bishop, Hamilton, & McConahay, 1980; Converse, 1964; Judd & Krosnick, 1989). However, other studies have provided somewhat more mixed evidence (Judd, Krosnick, & Milburn, 1981; Judd & Milburn, 1980). Studies have also shown that manipulating thought about political issues and considering the relations among issues strengthens the associations among political attitudes (Judd & Downing, 1990, Lavine et al., 1997). Interestingly, this effect is stronger for people high rather than low in political expertise.

Extremity, Working Knowledge, and Complexity.   Although it is intuitive to expect that working knowledge and complexity are related to attitude extremity, these relations are not as straightforward as they seem. For example, with working knowledge, this association is likely to depend on the evaluative consistency of information and the manner in which it is combined to form the attitude. If working knowledge is evaluatively consistent and it is combined using a summation strategy (e.g., see Fishbein & Ajzen, 1975), increases in working knowledge might lead to more extreme attitudes. However, if information is evaluatively inconsistent and/or information is combined using an averaging strategy (e.g., see Anderson, 1996), increased working knowledge may not lead to greater extremity.

The few nonexperimental studies examining the relation between self-reports of knowledge and attitude extremity have found positive correlations (Erber et al., 1995; Krosnick et al., 1993). Of course, these properties may have been confounded with other constructs that were responsible for the association. For example, as we later discuss, subjective reports of knowledge may reflect more than working knowledge (e.g., elaboration). Studies examining the association between knowledge listing measures and attitude extremity have failed to produce significant effects (Krosnick et al., 1993; see also Wood et al., 1995). Likewise, in experiments in which working knowledge was manipulated, no effect was found on extremity (Smith, Fabrigar, MacDougall, & Wiesenthal, 2003). Thus, empirical evidence in support of an association between working knowledge and extremity is not especially compelling.

Complexity has also long been assumed to be related to the extremity of attitudes (see Tesser et al., 1995). Some researchers have argued that greater complexity should be associated with increased extremity (Millar & Tesser, 1986a; Tesser & Leone, 1977). This prediction is based on the notion that when people think about an attitude object, a well-developed representation of an object will guide thinking in ways that are consistent with the representation, thereby resulting in greater extremity. Studies assessing complexity using measures of topic expertise have revealed greater increases in extremity as a result of mere thought about the object for people with high topic expertise than with low topic expertise (Millar & Tesser, 1986a; Tesser & Leone, 1977).[9]

In contrast, Linville (1982) has suggested that increased complexity is associated with less extremity because a greater number of distinct dimensions underlying an attitude should increase the likelihood that some inconsistencies will arise. Studies assessing complexity by counting the number of independent dimensions underlying attitudes and then examining the extremity of attitudes have confirmed this prediction (Linville, 1982; Linville & Jones, 1980).

Subsequent researchers (Judd & Lusk, 1984) resolved this apparent contradiction by proposing that the complexity–extremity association is moderated by the extent to which dimensions of knowledge are correlated (i.e., the extent to which knowledge of standing on one dimension has clear implications for standing on the other dimension). When dimensions are correlated (and evaluatively consistent), increased complexity should lead to greater extremity. In contrast, when dimensions are orthogonal (i.e., when knowledge of standing on one dimension does not imply standing on the other dimension), enhanced complexity should lead to less extremity. Judd and Lusk (1984) found support for this moderator both in studies in which correlations among dimensions were measured and in which correlations among dimensions were experimentally manipulated. Likewise, Millar and Tesser (1986a) conducted an induced thought experiment in which complexity and correlations among dimensions were measured. Inducing thought produced a greater increase in extremity for complex correlated-dimension attitudes, but produced a decrease in extremity for complex orthogonal-dimension attitudes.

Strength-Related Beliefs, Working Knowledge, and Complexity. As noted earlier, subjective judgments of knowledge and knowledge listing measures are only modestly correlated. Studies manipulating the amount of working knowledge have found that increases in working knowledge produce increases in perceived knowledge (Fabrigar, Petty, Smith, & Crites, 2003; MacDougall et al., 2003; Smith et al., 2003). In contrast, studies manipulating complexity have found effects of perceived knowledge to be weak or nonsignificant (Fabrigar et al., 2003; Smith et al., 2003).

Researchers have assumed that perceptions of attitude certainty should be a function of working knowledge (Gross et al., 1995). Nonexperimental studies using subjective knowledge ratings have supported this contention (Krosnick et al., 1993). However, a study that examined the correlation between a knowledge listing measure and perceived certainty failed to produce a significant effect (Krosnick et al., 1993). Experimental manipulations of working knowledge have demonstrated significant effects on certainty (Fabrigar et al., 2003; MacDougall et al., 2003; Smith et al., 2003). Experiments exploring the impact of complexity on certainty have revealed very weak or nonsignificant effects (Fabrigar et al., 2003; Smith et al., 2003).

Some researchers have also theorized that perceived importance should be associated with working knowledge (Boninger et al., 1995). Perceiving an attitude as important should motivate people to seek out and think about attitude-relevant information, which should result in greater working knowledge and complexity. Some studies have suggested that people with high importance attitudes are more likely to obtain information about an attitude object when given an opportunity to do so (see Boninger et al., 1995). Studies assessing subjective knowledge and importance have produced sizable correlations (Erber et al., 1995; Krosnick et al., 1993), but one study examining the correlation between a knowledge listing measure and perceived importance produced a much weaker correlation (Krosnick et al., 1993; see also Wood, 1982).

Associations With Ambivalence

Extremity and Ambivalence. It has long been assumed that ambivalence should decrease attitude extremity. Both averaging and summation models of attitude formation predict that extremity should be negatively related to ambivalence (e.g., Anderson, 1996; Fishbein & Ajzen, 1975). Also, ambivalence has been assumed to be most likely with near midpoint responses, requiring means to differentiate between ambivalence and indifference (Kaplan, 1972). Although some research has found no association between certain forms of ambivalence and extremity (Erber et al., 1995), most nonexperimental studies have reported significant negative correlations (Bargh et al., 1992; Krosnick et al., 1993). Manipulations of ambivalence also show that greater ambivalence results in less extremity (Priester & Petty, 1996; Smith et al., 2003).

Strength-Related Beliefs and Ambivalence. As stated earlier, nonexperimental studies have demonstrated that subjective judgments of ambivalence are positively associated with actual levels of evaluative inconsistency (Conner & Sparks, 2002; Lipkus, Green,

Feaganes, & Sedikides, 2002; Priester & Petty, 1996, 2001; Thompson et al., 1995). Experimental studies have confirmed that manipulations of ambivalence influence subjective judgments of ambivalence (Jonas et al., 1997; Priester & Petty, 1996; Smith et al., 2003).

Ambivalence might also influence perceptions of certainty (Gross et al., 1995), but few data exist. Krosnick et al. (1993) found no evidence that affective-cognitive consistency was related to certainty. In contrast, Smith et al. (2003) found that manipulated ambivalence produced lower levels of certainty. Finally, ambivalence has not been related to subjective judgments of importance or knowledge (Krosnick et al., 1993; Smith et al., 2003).

Associations With Inter-Attitudinal Structure

Strength-Related Beliefs and Inter-Attitudinal Structure.   Although little work has explored the relations between strength-related beliefs and inter-attitudinal structure, one exception is attitude importance. Greater importance should produce stronger motivation to maintain consistency among attitudes. Also, people may be more likely to think about important attitudes and, thus, more likely to recognize logical connections among attitudes. Nonexperimental studies have suggested that political attitudes are more strongly linked when these attitudes are rated as highly important rather than unimportant (Judd & Krosnick, 1982, 1989).

THE ROLE OF STRUCTURE IN ATTITUDE CHANGE PROCESSES

Although numerous studies have documented the impact of structural properties on attitude change (e.g., see Eagly & Chaiken, 1993, 1998; Petty & Krosnick, 1995; Pratkanis et al., 1989), much of this research has not explored underlying processes. In this section, we outline a conceptual framework for the impact of structure on attitude change that relies heavily on distinctions among low, moderate, and high levels of elaboration in attitude change (see also, Petty & Wegener, 1998a; Wegener & Carlston, this volume). In using this framework to organize the literature on structural variables in attitude change, we begin each section by discussing how the various structural properties might influence attitude change under low elaboration conditions. We then review potential mechanisms for each structural variable under high elaboration conditions. Finally, we discuss mechanisms for each structural property under moderate elaboration. Although the present framework could potentially be applied to any structural variable, we restrict our discussion to properties for which data currently exist.

A Conceptual Framework for the Role of Structure in Attitude Change

Thoughtfulness and Attitude Change

Mechanisms by which structural properties influence persuasion may vary depending on whether attitude change occurs via relatively thoughtful or nonthoughtful processes. This continuum of thoughtfulness was first advanced in the elaboration likelihood model (ELM; Petty & Cacioppo, 1981, 1986) and the heuristic-systematic model (HSM; Chaiken, 1987; Chaiken, Liberman, & Eagly, 1989) and has since become a broadly accepted premise in many subsequent models of persuasion (e.g., Albarracín, 2002; Kruglanski & Thompson, 1999; see also Johnson, Maio, & Smith-McLallen, this volume). These models generally posit that highly thoughtful attitude change occurs when individuals are willing and able to carefully consider available information about the issue or object. When motivation and ability are high, attitudes are largely determined by a person's assessments of the central merits of the attitude object.

Less thoughtful attitude change occurs when individuals lack the motivation or the capacity to evaluate information carefully and instead rely on heuristics or other peripheral cues as a simple basis to arrive at an attitude. In the discussion that follows, many features of these models would apply to the theoretical framework that we put forward. Because these models employ different terminologies, however, for the sake of simplicity we use terms consistent with the ELM.

Thoughtful versus nonthoughtful attitude change is not simply a dichotomous distinction; elaboration of information lies along a continuum (Petty & Cacioppo, 1986; Petty & Wegener, 1999). According to the ELM, variables can serve multiple roles in persuasion, and the likelihood of each role differs across different levels of elaboration (Petty & Cacioppo, 1986; Petty & Wegener, 1998a, 1999). If elaboration is high, impact of persuasion variables is most likely when the variable acts as a persuasive argument (i.e., when the variable can represent a central merit of the issue or object) or produces a bias in processing of attitude-relevant information. If elaboration is low, impact of variables is most likely when they can function as a simple cue. When elaboration is not constrained to be high nor low (i.e., under more moderate levels), variables can affect the extent of elaboration.[10] Like many other persuasion variables, structural properties associated with initial (pre-message) attitudes should also function in multiple roles across the elaboration continuum (see also Petty & Wegener, 1998a).

The Role of Structure With Low Elaboration Likelihood

When people lack ability or motivation to carefully consider a persuasive appeal, pre-message attitudes can serve as peripheral cues to infer if the appeal should be accepted (Fabrigar, Petty, Wegener, Priester, & Brooksbank, 2002; Wegener, Petty, Smoak, & Fabrigar, 2004). In the absence of effortful processing, a message congruent with the pre-message attitude is likely to be accepted, whereas a message that is incongruent is likely to be rejected (see Sanbonmatsu & Fazio, 1990). This is predicated on the assumption that one's pre-message attitude is activated at the time of the persuasive appeal—if an attitude is not activated, it cannot serve as a cue. Various structural properties might influence the likelihood that pre-message attitudes are activated and become available to serve as a cue to accept or reject a message.

The Role of Structure With High Elaboration Likelihood

When individuals have capacity and motivation to consider the merits of a persuasive appeal, pre-message attitudes can bias evaluation of the arguments in a message (Fabrigar et al., 2002; Wegener et al., 2004). Arguments compatible with one's pre-message attitudes are accepted, whereas arguments incompatible with one's pre-message attitude are undermined (Edwards & Smith, 1996; Kunda, 1990; Lord, Ross, & Lepper, 1979). There are a number of ways that structural variables can moderate the extent to which pre-message attitudes will serve as biasing factors. Attitudes should only bias processing if they are activated at the time of message processing, so highly accessible attitudes should be more likely to bias processing (Houston & Fazio, 1989). However, even if attitudes are accessible and activated, individuals can try to correct for their attitudes when they are perceived as inappropriate influences (Wegener & Petty, 1997). Even if the attitude is judged as applicable and appropriate, the level of bias exerted will vary according to factors affecting one's ability to implement the bias (e.g., informational resources) and one's motivation to implement the bias (e.g., consistency pressures). Thus, as discussed in the following sections, other structural variables (such as the type, the amount, or the consistency of attitude-relevant knowledge) may influence the extent to which pre-message attitudes bias judgments and may determine the magnitude and the evaluative valence of that bias (see also Biek, Wood, & Chaiken, 1996).

The Role of Structure With Moderate Elaboration Likelihood

When no constraints render elaboration high or low, pre-message attitudes may influence the extent to which one processes a persuasive message. Structural properties of attitudes may influence a person's motivation or ability to process information via their impact on such variables as the activation of the attitude, the perceived self-relevance of the message, or the person's ability to scrutinize the message.

Empirical Research on the Role of Structure in Attitude Change

A substantial amount of empirical evidence has accumulated documenting the impact of structural properties on attitude change. However, as implied by our framework, such effects could occur for a number of reasons. In the sections that follow, we begin by briefly reviewing empirical evidence for impact of various structural properties on attitude change and discuss how each of these demonstrated effects could be a result of low elaboration processes. We then review how these effects could be a result of high elaboration processes. Finally, we discuss potential moderate elaboration mechanisms that might account for past effects.

Structure and Attitude Change Under Low Elaboration

Accessibility. The current literature suggests that accessible attitudes are harder to change than less accessible attitudes. Such studies begin with a measurement of accessibility (e.g., Bassili, 1996; Bassili & Fletcher, 1991) or a manipulation of accessibility (Houston & Fazio, 1989), followed by a persuasive message and a reassessment of attitudes after the message. Although there is consistent evidence that accessibility increases resistance to persuasion, the mechanisms underlying this relationship have not been identified. When elaboration is low, accessibility may influence attitude change by moderating the extent to which a person's pre-message attitude will serve as a peripheral cue (see Wegener et al., 2004). Independent of thoughtful scrutiny, a person may be likely to accept an evaluatively consistent persuasive message or reject an evaluatively inconsistent message.

Types of Attitude-Relevant Information. We noted previously that most research has focused on the distinction between attitudes that are primarily cognitive versus affective in nature (see Crites et al., 1994). Researchers have also used this distinction to classify persuasive appeals as being either affective or cognitive (e.g., Becker, 1963; Knepprath & Clevenger, 1965; Ruechelle, 1958). Integrating these two concepts, research has examined whether affective or cognitive communications are more persuasive when they match or mismatch the base of the attitude. Some studies have found greater impact of mismatching appeals (Millar & Millar, 1990), whereas others have found greater impact of matching appeals (Edwards, 1990; Edwards & von Hippel, 1995; Fabrigar & Petty, 1999).

Other work has tested function matching. For example, Snyder and DeBono (1985) posited that high self-monitors' attitudes would largely serve a social-adjustive function, whereas low self-monitors' attitudes would largely serve a value-expressive function. They presented participants with product advertisements that were either social-adjustive in nature (i.e., highlighting image) or value-expressive (i.e., highlighting quality) in nature. High self-monitors rated the social-adjustive ads more positively than the value-expressive ads, whereas low self-monitors rated the value-expressive ads more positively than the social-adjustive ads. Others have provided further support for the function-matching hypothesis (DeBono, 1987; Lavine & Snyder, 1996; Murray, Haddock, & Zanna, 1996; Shavitt, 1990).

Although matching effects have been generally replicable (for exceptions, see Millar & Millar, 1990; Petty & Wegener, 1998b), the cognitive processes responsible for matching (or mismatching) effects have not been clearly specified (see Lavine & Snyder, 1996; 2000). The framework described in this chapter may help resolve inconsistencies in this domain and explain the processes underlying matching and mismatching effects (see also Lavine & Snyder, 2000; Petty & Wegener, 1998b; Petty, Wheeler, & Bizer, 2000). When elaboration likelihood is low, a match between the content of a message and the functional or affective/cognitive base underlying one's attitude may increase the likelihood of attitude activation, thus allowing that attitude to serve as a cue to accept or reject messages. Also, when a message matches the basis of an attitude, the match per se might be taken as a cue that the advocacy has merit.

Working Knowledge and Complexity. Manipulations and measurements of knowledge have shown that attitudes are more resistant to change when the attitudes are associated with high levels of knowledge (e.g., Lewan & Stotland, 1961; Wood, 1982; Wood & Kallgren, 1988; Wood, Kallgren, & Preisler, 1985). This result is consistent with the idea that attitudes with high levels of *horizontal structure* (i.e., many pieces of information leading to the same evaluation) should be more difficult to change (McGuire, 1960). As previously implied, there are reasons to expect working knowledge to be positively related to accessibility. Thus, it is possible that greater likelihood of activation would make the attitude available for use as a cue and thereby account for greater resistance of attitudes based on high versus low levels of knowledge.

Ambivalence. Relatively little research has investigated the relation between ambivalence and attitude change. Some studies show that ambivalent attitudes are more susceptible to persuasive communications (e.g., Armitage & Conner, 2000; Chaiken & Baldwin, 1981) and others have found weak or inconsistent evidence (see Chaiken et al., 1995). Perhaps one reason for this mixed pattern is that the effects of ambivalence on persuasion may depend on the extent to which people elaborate messages. Without the requisite motivation and ability to process a persuasive communication thoroughly, ambivalence may decrease the likelihood that an existing attitude is activated and thus available for use as an acceptance/rejection cue. Because most research addresses counterattitudinal messages, decreased attitude activation (with high ambivalence) would result in less likelihood of the attitude serving as a rejection cue.

Structure and Attitude Change Under High Elaboration

Accessibility. With high levels of elaboration, accessibility may affect the likelihood of pre-message attitudes biasing processing. Accessible attitudes may therefore be more resistant to change because individuals are more likely to use their pre-message attitudes to interpret available information. Consistent with this reasoning, Fazio and his colleagues have found that highly accessible pre-message attitudes were more likely to bias evaluation of presidential debates (Fazio & Williams, 1986) or favorable and unfavorable messages about capital punishment (Houston & Fazio, 1989; Schuette & Fazio, 1995).

Types of Attitude-Relevant Information. Existing attitudes, once activated, may bias how new information is perceived and evaluated (Cacioppo, Petty, & Sidera, 1982; Lord, Ross, & Lepper, 1979). Provided that the argument is relatively strong (or at least ambiguous), arguments based on information that matches the affective/cognitive or functional basis of an attitude may be viewed as more compelling than arguments based on mismatching information. Lavine and Snyder (1996, 2000) tested the biased processing hypothesis that perceptions of message quality mediate the relationship between functional matching and postmessage attitudes. Low and high self-monitors were presented with either value-expressive or social-adjustive messages to encourage voting behavior. Consistent with predictions, functionally relevant messages were associated with greater pro-voting attitudes than were functionally irrelevant messages. Furthermore, perceptions of message quality mediated the relationship between functional matching status and attitudes (see also Lavine et al., 1999). Another possible high-elaboration mechanism is greater likelihood that one will recognize the attitude as applicable to the message if the content of the message matches the affective/cognitive or functional basis of the attitude.

It is possible, however, that the relations among matching status, perceptions of message quality, and attitude change are more complex than previously described. Factors such as argument strength and the consistency with a person's existing attitude may moderate these relations, such that arguments that match rather than mismatch a person's affective/cognitive or functional base may sometimes be evaluated more negatively and may be less persuasive. This could especially occur if they are inconsistent with one's attitude and particularly if the arguments are weak. If elaboration is high, and a dimension is central to a person's attitude, that person may be able and motivated to counterargue opposing messages (see Millar & Millar, 1990). That is, information matching the attitude basis may motivate resistance if viewed as more threatening than information mismatching the attitude basis. Also, the predominant information type in memory may enable people to better find flaws in information that matches that type of information. Thus, when counterattitudinal arguments are weak, matching arguments may actually be less persuasive than arguments mismatching the basis of the attitude.

Working Knowledge and Complexity.   Knowledge can affect the likelihood that an attitude is activated and biases processing. It is also likely that individuals with a wealth of information about an attitude object will be more apt to recognize that their attitude is applicable to the persuasive message. Here, the complexity of knowledge may be more important than the amount of knowledge. Attitudes with high levels of differentiation may be more likely to be judged as applicable to a message than those that are relatively undifferentiated, because there is a greater probability that the arguments contained in the message will pertain to the specific dimensions represented by the attitude. Even when a message is not relevant to the dimensions underlying an attitude, complex attitudes (that are evaluatively consistent) may still be judged as applicable to a given message because one may be willing to extrapolate beyond one's knowledge base and assume that the attitude is generally informative (Fabrigar et al., 2003).

Knowledge may also affect willingness to use one's attitude in processing. Even if an attitude has been deemed applicable to a message, a person with a relatively impoverished or undifferentiated information base may lack confidence in the validity of the attitude and question whether it should be used. In contrast, a person with multidimensional (consistent) knowledge may be more likely to believe that attitude use is legitimate. Finally, knowledge may increase the biasing impact of attitudes by conferring ability to generate effective counterarguments to opposing information and to integrate compatible information into existing schemas.

Wood and her colleagues (e.g., Biek et al., 1996; Wood et al., 1995) have demonstrated that knowledge does not always lead to biased processing of new information. Highly knowledgeable individuals can employ their knowledge in either biased or impartial ways, depending on whether they are motivated to defend their attitude. Wood et al. (1995) hypothesized that when an attitude is associated with intense affect, individuals are motivated to defend their existing attitude because change may be threatening because of its implications for the self, personal outcomes, and cherished values (Biek et al., 1996; Wood et al., 1995). One could think of this approach as knowledge providing the ability to process in a biased manner and affect providing the motivation to do so. When attitudes are not affect-laden, individuals may be less motivated to preserve their existing attitude and high levels of knowledge may be associated with motivation for accuracy. The hypotheses put forward by Wood and colleagues would most likely extend beyond affect intensity as there are other strength-related properties (e.g., importance, certainty) that would also heighten one's motivation to defend one's attitude (see also Petty, Tormala, & Rucker, 2004; Wegener et al., 2004).

Ambivalence. Ambivalence may attenuate the likelihood that an attitude is used in processing, because ambivalent attitudes are less accessible than nonambivalent attitudes. Even if the attitude is activated, it may be that ambivalent attitudes are less likely to be viewed as an appropriate influence on information processing. Individuals may recognize the underlying conflict associated with their attitudes and thus be less certain of their validity. This may lead people to conclude that they should attempt to avoid use of the attitude. Finally, even when the attitude is activated and seen as applicable, ambivalence may decrease ability to effectively counterargue a message (Chaiken & Yates, 1985; Eagly & Chaiken, 1995) because conflicting evaluations underlying an attitude may preclude generating strong and consistent refutations.

We believe that the decreased likelihood that an attitude will bias processing might be particularly marked if the ambivalence is within-dimension, as opposed to cross-dimension. If a person holds within-dimension ambivalence toward an attitude object, any message that applies to that dimension will activate both the positive and the negative aspects of the attitude, thus decreasing the likelihood that a person will view the attitude as a clear guide to message processing. Although cross-dimension ambivalence might allow for more biased processing to occur, the direction of this biased processing might depend on the direction of knowledge activated by the message. A message addressing a dimension on which a person's evaluation is positive should activate positive elements of the attitude, such that favorable information is likely to be bolstered, and unfavorable information is likely to be counterargued. However, a message addressing a negative dimension would activate negative elements of the attitude and lead to a bias such that negative information is favored.

Decreased impact of ambivalent attitudes may not always be the outcome, however. For example, if people seek to resolve inconsistencies in their attitude-relevant knowledge, then processing could be biased in high elaboration settings to favor whichever attitudinal position seems most likely to the message recipient to serve this resolution. This bias could favor the original direction of the overall evaluation (such that pre-message ambivalent attitudes create especially strong biases) or the direction of the message (even if opposing initial attitudes, as long as the message appears capable of providing a consistent rationale and basis for favoring one side of the issue rather than the other).

Structure and Attitude Change Under Moderate Elaboration

Accessibility. Under moderate elaboration conditions, attitude accessibility can influence the amount of elaboration given to a persuasive message. Fabrigar et al. (1998) proposed that high levels of accessibility could lead one to infer that the attitude is important (because of the corresponding ease of retrieval or through associations of accessibility with greater hedonic consequences, e.g., Roskos-Ewoldsen & Fazio, 1992). These increases in perceived importance could elevate motivation to devote cognitive resources to message processing. In two studies, measured and manipulated accessibility have been associated with enhanced message scrutiny (Fabrigar et al., 1998). That is, the quality of arguments influenced post-message attitudes to a greater extent when accessibility was high rather than low. More recently, Clark, Wegener, and Fabrigar (2004) have found that increases in accessibility need not always increase message scrutiny. In particular, when a message is consistent with a person's existing attitude, greater accessibility can be associated with less rather than more message scrutiny, perhaps because the message seems redundant with what the recipient already knows.

Types of Attitude-Relevant Information.   Some researchers have suggested that messages whose content matches the functional or affective/cognitive basis of an attitude are scrutinized more carefully than messages that mismatch the basis of the attitude (Lavine & Snyder, 2000; Petty et al., 2000; Petty & Wegener, 1998b). One hypothesized mediator of the relation between matching messages and increased elaboration is perceived relevance. Indeed, past research has shown that messages matching the functional base of one's attitudes are perceived as more pertinent to the self than are mismatching messages (DeBono, 1987). Such increased self-relevance is associated with more thoughtful information processing (Petty & Cacioppo, 1979, 1986). Moreover, one may be more able to process matching messages, because one may have greater knowledge directly relevant to the information contained in the arguments.

The strongest support for this hypothesis was reported by Petty and Wegener (1998b). Participants received product ads containing strong or weak messages that were functionally matched or mismatched with the basis of participants' attitudes. Argument quality influenced post-message attitudes more when the message matched rather than mismatched the functional base. One implication of these findings is that matching a message with one's attitudinal basis does not necessarily lead to greater persuasion than mismatching messages. Instead, the efficacy of matching and mismatching arguments may vary as a function of argument quality. Although these ideas were assessed in the functional domain, they may also help to resolve inconsistencies in the literature on matching messages to affective/cognitive bases (see Fabrigar & Petty, 1999).

Working Knowledge and Complexity.   Complexity of knowledge might influence the extent of processing because of the increased likelihood of matching the basis of the attitude with the message. If the attitude is activated and individuals are sufficiently motivated to scrutinize a message, knowledge can also increase *ability* to process a persuasive message by enabling individuals to encode, understand, evaluate, and integrate new information. Consistent with these speculations, Wood and colleagues (Wood et al., 1985; Wood & Kallgren, 1988) found that participants highly knowledgeable about environmental preservation were more likely to carefully process arguments related to this issue. Less knowledgeable people were less likely to critically evaluate new information and relied on cues such as message length (Wood et al., 1985) and source characteristics (Wood & Kallgren, 1988). Of course, the issue was not affectively charged for most participants, and, thus, knowledgeable individuals might be less threatened by counterattitudinal messages and might choose to seek out such information (see Wood et al., 1995). Without strong affect, knowledge might signal interest in the issue.

Ambivalence.   Individuals who are ambivalent about an attitude object may be more motivated than nonambivalent individuals to scrutinize a message if they believe that it will help them to resolve the concomitant psychological tension associated with ambivalence. This hypothesis was tested by Maio, Bell, and Esses (1996), who assessed participants' ambivalence, and then presented strong or weak messages. Ambivalent participants were more sensitive to message quality than nonambivalent participants. Moreover, among ambivalent participants, issue-related thoughts mediated the relationship between message strength and attitudes.

However, the impact of ambivalence on processing may be more complex than depicted in past work. If elaboration is supposed to be in the service of decreasing ambivalence, then elaboration might be more likely when available information is proattitudinal (and thinking is likely to resolve or overwhelm inconsistencies by adding "dominant reactions"; Priester & Petty,

1996) rather than counterattitudinal (when, before deliberation can decrease ambivalence, it would add to "conflicting reactions"; Priester & Petty, 1996). Also, motives to process a message in order to decrease ambivalence might be greater among those with within-dimension ambivalence, rather than cross-dimension ambivalence. With within-dimension ambivalence, a persuasive message that applies to the dimension might often exacerbate feelings of uncertainty about the attitude object, which would then heighten the motivation to resolve the ambivalence. In contrast, with cross-dimension ambivalence, a message addressing any single dimension may decrease feelings of uncertainty. This would decrease the likelihood of people recognizing their conflicting evaluations, thereby decreasing motives to alleviate inconsistency-based tension.

THE ROLE OF STRUCTURE IN ATTITUDE-BEHAVIOR CONSISTENCY AND RELATED PROCESSES

A Conceptual Framework for the Role of Structure in Attitude–Behavior Consistency

In the sections that follow, we draw parallels between the previous discussions of attitude change and structural influences on the attitude–behavior relation. In addition, we note the ways in which this approach to prediction of behavior diverges from other current approaches. After outlining this extension of attitude change theories to attitude–behavior consistency, we present effects of the specific structural variables on attitude–behavior relations. Before describing the framework, however, it is useful to summarize the status of the attitude–behavior literature and to note some issues that complicate interpretation of attitude–behavior studies.

Status of the Attitude–Behavior Consistency Literature

A central theme of attitude structure research has been the impact of structural properties on attitude–behavior consistency (e.g., see Kraus, 1995; Petty & Krosnick, 1995; Pratkanis et al., 1989; Raden, 1985).[11] Despite important advances, there are nonetheless notable limitations to our understanding. First, some researchers (e.g., Fazio, 1990) have noted that there has been relatively little theorizing and few empirical investigations of the psychological processes underlying the effects of structure on attitude–behavior consistency. Second, much of the attitude structure literature on attitude–behavior consistency has been nonexperimental in nature.

Distinguishing Between Prediction and Influence

Researchers have typically defined attitude–behavior consistency in terms of prediction. That is, attitude–behavior consistency has been assessed by measuring an attitude, measuring a behavior at a subsequent point in time, and then computing the association between the attitude and the behavior. Moderators (e.g., attitude structure) have then been tested by comparing attitude–behavior associations under differing levels of the proposed moderator. It is important to recognize that the extent to which an attitude *predicts* a behavior is not synonymous with the extent to which an attitude *influences* a behavior. Variations in predictive ability can be a result of different causes. A moderator may regulate how well a measure of attitudes accurately reflects the attitude at the time of behavior. Also, the moderator may determine the extent to which an attitude directly influences a behavior at the time of behavior or directly influences a mediator of the attitude–behavior association. Although most research has not distinguished between these possible causes of differential prediction, such distinctions are important because they imply different processes by which structure might regulate attitude–behavior consistency.

Structure, Attitude Measurement, and Attitude Stability

We focus on two mechanisms by which structure can affect prediction independent of variation in actual influence on behavior. First, structural properties may affect the extent to which measures accurately capture the attitude (see Bassili & Krosnick, 2000; Lavine, Huff, Wagner, & Sweeney, 1998). For instance, if structure inhibits attitude activation when responding to a measure, that response may be shaped by factors external to the actual attitude. If these factors are transitory and/or unlikely to influence the target behavior, the attitude measure will be a poor predictor of behavior. However, this does not necessarily imply that the attitude did not influence the behavior. It could be that the attitude exerted a strong influence, but that the influence was not reflected in the attitude–behavior correlation because responses to the attitude measure were a poor representation of the attitude.

Structure might also moderate the attitude–behavior relation (without changes in actual influence) via attitude stability (e.g., see Davidson et al., 1985; Doll & Ajzen, 1992; Eagly & Chaiken, 1993; Wilson et al., 1989). As discussed in the following, structural properties of attitudes may be associated with attitude stability. Thus, even if an attitude measure accurately captures the attitude at a particular point in time, it is possible the attitude could change during the time interval between attitude measurement and behavior, thereby producing low attitude–behavior correlations. However, such a mechanism does not imply anything about the magnitude of influence being exerted by attitudes at the time of behavior.[12]

Deliberative and Nondeliberative Influences of Attitudes on Behavior

Although some attitude structure effects may be independent of changes in actual influence, there are theoretical reasons to expect that structure can also moderate the influence of attitudes on behavior. In considering this possibility, our framework follows an important distinction made by the MODE model of attitude–behavior consistency (Fazio, 1990; Fazio & Towles-Schwen, 1999) as well as theories of attitude change such as the ELM and HSM. We assume that the impact of attitudes on behaviors may be a result of processes ranging from those that are highly deliberative to those that are relatively nondeliberative. Thus, this framework postulates that the mechanisms by which attitudes influence behavior will depend on the level of deliberativeness of the behavior in question (Fazio, 1990; Fazio & Towles-Schwen, 1999). Furthermore, based on the ELM's postulate that variables can serve multiple roles (Petty & Cacioppo, 1986; Petty & Wegener, 1999), our framework assumes that there are multiple processes by which a structural property can moderate the impact of attitudes on behavior. The specific process involved in a given situation will depend on the extent to which people are deliberative in their behaviors.

The Role of Structure With Low Deliberation Behaviors. When people are constrained to be relatively nondeliberative in the performance of behaviors, attitudes may influence behavior in two ways. First, the attitude may serve as a direct peripheral cue to determine if a behavior relevant to the attitude object is appropriate (see Petty & Cacioppo, 1986; Petty & Wegener, 1999). For example, imagine a case where a person needs to purchase a particular type of product from one of two stores. A person's general attitudes toward those stores could serve as simple cues to select a particular store in the absence of any scrutiny of the relative merits of the services and product selection provided for that category of products. The attitude may also serve as an indirect cue by focusing attention on attitude-congruent features of the attitude object or behavioral context that could themselves serve as cues for behavior (Fazio & Dunton, 1997; Fazio et al., 2000; Smith et al., 1996; see also Fazio, 1990; Fazio & Towles-Schwen, 1999).[13] Of course, in order for the attitude to be a direct or indirect cue, it must be activated at the time of the behavior (Fazio, 1990; 1995; Fazio & Towles-Schwen, 1999). Structural properties of attitudes may moderate the impact of attitudes on behavior under nondeliberative conditions via their influence on attitude activation at the time of behavior.

The Role of Structure With High Deliberation Behaviors.   When people are motiivated and able to be highly deliberative, attitudes may influence behavior by serving as either an argument or a biasing factor (Petty & Cacioppo, 1986; Petty & Wegener, 1999). If the attitude is perceived as directly relevant to the behavior in question, it may serve as a direct argument in favor of or against a course of action (i.e., the attitude may serve as information directly relevant to evaluating the merits of a particular behavior; Fabrigar et al., 2003). For example, the relative liking for two people could be seen as an argument in favor of one person versus the other when deciding which of two competing social invitations to accept. However, even if the attitude is not a direct basis for evaluating the merits of a behavior, it could still influence behavior by biasing the interpretation of information relevant to the behavior (presuming the behavioral context contains information sufficiently ambiguous to allow for bias in interpretation; see Chaiken & Maheswaran, 1994). For example, imagine choosing between cars from two salespeople. Attitudes toward the salespeople, although not directly relevant to evaluating the merits of the cars, might bias how information about the two vehicles is interpreted.

As with nondeliberative behaviors, attitudes will not always influence deliberative behaviors. Attitudes must be activated at the time of the behavior if they are to serve as an argument or biasing factor. Structure may influence the likelihood of attitude activation. However, under high levels of deliberation, there are other mechanisms by which structure may play a role in attitude–behavior consistency. First, activating an attitude may not be sufficient for it to influence behavior. The attitude may also have to be viewed as applicable to the behavior (e.g., see Borgida & Campbell, 1982; Fabrigar et al., 2003; Lord, Lepper, & Mackie, 1984; Snyder & Kendzierski, 1982). If an attitude is judged as an irrelevant or inappropriate guide, it will be disregarded as an argument in favor of or against a particular course of action. Second, people may try to eliminate any inappropriate biasing impact that this attitude might have on their interpretation of information relevant to the behavior (e.g., Dunton & Fazio, 1997; Schuette & Fazio, 1995; Towles-Schwen & Fazio, 2003; see also Wegener & Petty, 1997). Structural properties may influence whether an attitude is seen as applicable to a particular behavior.

It is important to note that this applicability mechanism should play a role primarily when behaviors are highly deliberative. Considering the applicability of an attitude and disregarding it if it is judged inapplicable (or inappropriate) is likely to require substantial cognitive effort. Consistent with this view, it has been demonstrated that corrections for perceived biases in social judgments are relatively effortful processes (Martin, Seta, & Crelia, 1990; see Wegener & Petty, 1997). Similarly, research on attitude–decision consistency has revealed that when people are unable and/or unmotivated to think carefully about decisions, they may rely on attitudes even if they are inappropriate guides (Fabrigar et al., 2003; Sanbonmatsu & Fazio, 1990; Schuette & Fazio, 1995). In contrast, when people are motivated and able to think, they rely less on such attitudes.

Another high deliberation mechanism by which attitude structure might influence attitude–behavior consistency is structure determining the magnitude of bias that an attitude exerts on the processing of information. The structure of an attitude may determine the motivation and ability a person has to process behavior-relevant information in a biased manner.

The Role of Structure With Moderate Deliberation.   When people are neither constrained to be extremely deliberative nor nondeliberative, structure may influence attitude–behavior processes by determining the extent to which a person is deliberative in performing the behavior. The mechanisms by which structure may do so could be due to motivation or ability.

Empirical Research on the Role of Structure in Attitude–Behavior Consistency

Numerous empirical studies have documented the impact of various structural properties on attitude–behavior consistency. However, as with attitude change, these effects could be due to a number of processes. In the sections that follow, we review evidence for impact of structural properties on attitude–behavior consistency and discuss the extent to which these effects could be a result of measurement and/or stability processes. We then discuss potential mechanisms for the influence of structural variables on attitude–behavior consistency under conditions that encourage nondeliberative behaviors and highly deliberative behaviors. Finally, we discuss potential moderate deliberation mechanisms that might account for past effects.

Structure, Measurement, Stability, and Attitude–Behavior Consistency

Accessibility. A number of studies have documented that increased accessibility is associated with greater attitude–behavior consistency. Some studies have measured accessibility via response latencies (Bassili, 1993; 1995; Fazio, Powell, & Williams, 1989; Fazio & Williams, 1986; Kokkinaki & Lunt, 1997), whereas others have manipulated accessibility via repeated attitude expression or attitude object presentation (Fazio et al., 1982; Posavac, Sanbonmatsu, & Fazio, 1997). Although these studies provide evidence of the moderating role of attitude accessibility, the psychological mechanisms responsible for these effects are less clear. The framework we have outlined suggests that the mechanisms by which accessibility influences attitude–behavior consistency are quite varied.

One possibility is that past effects may be due to measurement and/or stability processes. For example, if an attitude is highly accessible, it is likely to be spontaneously activated on presentation of the attitude object (Fazio et al., 1986). This activation should result in the attitude exerting a substantial impact on responses to the attitude measure. In contrast, attitudes low in accessibility may not be activated, and thus individuals will need to construct an attitude in response to the measure (see Tourangeau & Rasinski, 1988; Wilson & Hodges, 1992). This response may be based on attitude-relevant information salient at the time of judgment or factors external to the attitude object. Such responses may fail to reflect people's typical evaluation of the object and thus be poor predictors of behavior (see Wilson, Dunn, Kraft, & Lisle, 1989).

Accessibility could also influence attitude–behavior consistency via its effect on stability (Doll & Ajzen, 1992; Fazio, 1995). To the extent that an evaluation is strongly linked to an object representation, that attitude might persist over time and tend to be spontaneously activated, thereby further strengthening the object–evaluation association. Some research has revealed a positive association between accessibility and stability (Bargh et al., 1992; Grant, Button, & Noseworthy, 1994). However, these studies have not examined whether the accessibility–stability relation might account for the moderating role of accessibility in attitude–behavior consistency. The work most closely related to stability mechanisms was reported by Doll and Ajzen (1992). In this study, direct experience with computer video games was manipulated. Direct experience produced greater attitude–behavior consistency, attitude accessibility, and attitude stability than indirect experience. It is interesting to note that contrary to previous interpretations of direct experience effects (Fazio et al., 1982), analyses revealed that the impact of direct experience was mediated by stability rather than accessibility. Thus, these data might be interpreted as implying that accessibility has no influence on behavior independent of stability. However, the manner in which the responses' latency data were collected and analyzed in this study did not follow standard procedures (see Fazio, 1995). Furthermore, the basic effect of attitude accessibility on attitude–behavior consistency was not obtained. Hence, these data may not provide a clear test of the role of stability in accessibility effects.

Types of Attitude-Relevant Information.   Little work has assessed the role of attitude bases in attitude–behavior consistency. To date, this work has examined whether attitudes that differ in the type of information on which they are based best predict behaviors most relevant to the bases of attitudes. Most notably, Millar and Tesser (1986b) argued that attitudes based on affect best predict consumatory behaviors (i.e., those performed for their intrinsic reward), but attitudes based on cognition best predict instrumental behaviors (i.e., those performed to obtain some goal external to the behavior). Millar and Tesser (1989) showed that these attitude bases-behavior matching effects only emerged when affective and cognitive bases were inconsistent with one another.[14] Recent research by Fabrigar et al. (2003) has suggested that attitude bases-behavior matching effects can also occur for distinct dimensions of cognition. Although attitude bases may moderate the extent to which attitudes predict different types of behavior, little evidence exists regarding the underlying mechanisms. To date, there is no clear evidence to suggest that measurement of attitudes based on a particular type of information or function is more reliable or valid. Likewise, there is no clear evidence that attitudes vary in their stability as a result of being based on different types of information.

Working Knowledge and Complexity.   Although complexity has received little attention in attitude–behavior consistency research, working knowledge has been shown to be positively associated with attitude–behavior consistency (Davidson et al., 1985; Kallgren & Wood, 1986). However, the mechanisms underlying these working knowledge effects are poorly understood (Davidson et al., 1985; Eagly & Chaiken, 1993; Fabrigar et al., 2004a; Kallgren & Wood, 1986). One explanation for the influence of working knowledge and complexity is via their effects on the accuracy of attitude measures. As noted earlier, working knowledge and complexity may both be related to attitude accessibility, which could, in turn, influence the accuracy of attitude reports. It is also possible that attitudes based on greater working knowledge and complexity could be more predictive of behaviors because these attitudes are more stable and resistant to change than are attitudes based on little knowledge (see Davidson et al., 1985; Eagly & Chaiken, 1993; Wilson et al., 1989). Although direct tests have not been conducted, Wilson et al. (1989) reported research consistent with this idea, such that introspection decreased attitude–behavior consistency (see also Wilson, Dunn, Kraft, & Lisle, 1989) only among individuals who were unknowledgeable. Wilson et al. argued that attitude–behavior consistency was unaffected for high knowledge people because their attitudes were less likely to be changed by introspection.

Ambivalence.   Most studies assessing the relation between ambivalence and attitude–behavior consistency have measured some form of ambivalence and have reported decreases in attitude–behavior consistency as attitude ambivalence increases. This pattern occurred using independent ratings of the global positive and global negative evaluations of the object (Conner, Povey, Sparks, James, & Shepherd, 2003; Conner, Sparks, Povey, James, Shepherd, & Armitage, 2002), ratings of felt ambivalence (Priester, 2002; Sparks, Hedderley, & Shepherd, 1992; but see Norman & Smith, 1995), ambivalence among beliefs (Armitage, 2003; Moore, 1973), or inconsistency between evaluations and beliefs (Norman, 1975; but see Fazio & Zanna, 1978).

A few studies have experimentally manipulated the evaluative consistency of information underlying attitudes. Armitage (2003) found that greater ambivalence among beliefs resulted in lower attitude–behavior consistency. In contrast, Jonas et al. (1997) found greater ambivalence in beliefs *increased* attitude–behavior consistency. They argued that this was due to ambivalence prompting people to engage in elaboration of the information in order to resolve inconsistencies. This greater elaboration, in turn, resulted in stronger attitude–behavior relations.

Sengupta and Johar (2002) explored the apparent contradiction between Jonas et al. (1997) and other ambivalence studies. Sengupta and Johar argued that when people engage in elaboration directed toward forming an integrated attitude, ambivalence should lead to greater attitude–behavior consistency (as in Jonas et al., 1997). However, when individuals do not specifically attempt to resolve inconsistencies (e.g., because they do not engage in elaboration or because that elaboration is not directed toward integrating evaluative responses), ambivalence should lead to lower attitude–behavior consistency. Sengupta and Johar (2002) manipulated ambivalence and accessibility of beliefs. Increased ambivalence led to greater attitude–behavior consistency when accessibility of beliefs was high and to lower attitude–behavior consistency when belief accessibility was low. In a second experiment, greater ambivalence led to enhanced attitude–behavior consistency when people were made accountable for their views and to less attitude–behavior consistency when they were not accountable.

Increased inconsistency could be associated with less valid measurement of attitudes. As noted earlier, there are conceptual reasons and some empirical evidence (Bargh et al., 1992; Erber et al., 1995; Fazio, 1995; Krosnick et al., 1993) suggesting ambivalence and attitude accessibility are inversely related. If an attitude is not activated at the time of measurement, extraneous factors rather than the attitude will drive attitudinal responses. Also, contextual factors could temporarily alter the evaluation that is activated at the time of measurement, thereby leading to an attitudinal response that is not representative of the typical evaluation of the object (e.g., see Bell & Esses, 1997; Erber et al., 1995; MacDonald & Zanna, 1998). Susceptibility to such factors may depend on the nature of the underlying ambivalence. For example, cross-dimension ambivalence may result in more extreme shifts in judgment than within-dimension ambivalence because the relative independence of positive and negative evaluative responses for cross-dimensionally ambivalent attitudes may allow for greater likelihood of activating one component and not the other (MacDonald & Grant, 2003). One may also expect increased inconsistency to be associated with less attitude stability. Changes in the measurement context over time are more likely to change attitudes or their reports if the attitudes are ambivalent than if they are unambivalent (see Chaiken et al., 1995; Erber et al., 1995; Norman, 1975).

Structure and Attitude-Behavior Consistency Under Low Deliberation

Accessibility.   With nondeliberative behaviors, attitude accessibility should be a primary determinant of whether an attitude is activated and can thus serve as a direct cue or indirect cue for behavior. Some data are suggestive of this possible role. For example, studies have shown that activation of attitudes can direct attention to features of an object. Smith et al. (1996) manipulated the accessibility of attitudes toward social categories (e.g., Black, White, men, women). Participants were then presented with pictures of people and asked to quickly indicate if they belonged to particular social categories. Increased accessibility of attitudes toward a category was associated with greater speed in judging if people were members of that category, suggesting that attitudes directed people's attention toward features relevant to that category.

Fazio et al. (2000) manipulated the accessibility of attitudes toward photos of people via an attitude expression manipulation. Participants were subsequently presented with the same photos as well as photos that had been morphed to look slightly different. Participants were asked to judge if each photo was a previously seen photo or a different photo. Increased accessibility resulted in slower and less accurate judgments, presumably because perception of features of new photos were assimilated toward the existing attitude.

Taken together, these studies provide good evidence that the more likely an attitude is activated, the more likely that attitude will exert a directive influence on how objects are perceived (i.e., the first step in our proposed causal chain of accessibility moderating attitudes ability to serve as indirect cues). Evidence that selective attention to object features can, in turn, serve as cues to subsequent behavior has yet to be explicitly tested.[15]

Types of Attitude-Relevant Information.   The match of the basis of an attitude to the nature of the behavior could also influence the likelihood of attitude activation. For instance, when a possible behavior is highly affective in nature, the setting or object itself might be more likely to trigger activation of the attitude if the attitude is affectively rather than cognitively based (by virtue of the shared affective content among the setting, behavior, and attitude).

Working Knowledge and Complexity.   Working knowledge and complexity may also influence the likelihood of attitude activation, influencing the likelihood the attitude will serve as a direct or indirect cue. In addition, when the nature of a behavior matches the basis of an attitude, the opportunity for the behavior might activate the attitude. Because complex attitudes are based on more distinct informational dimensions, complex attitudes are more likely to have a basis or bases directly relevant to any given behavior (see Fabrigar et al., 2003).

Ambivalence.   Because ambivalent attitudes are also less likely to be activated at the time of behavior, these attitudes should be less likely to serve as a direct or indirect cue to behavior.

Structure and Attitude-Behavior Consistency Under High Deliberation

Accessibility.   For deliberative behaviors, there are two potential mechanisms by which accessibility might regulate attitude–behavior consistency. First, if an attitude is relevant to the merits of an action, accessibility could determine the likelihood that an attitude is activated and can thus serve as a direct argument for a behavior. Second, even if an attitude is not relevant to the merits of a behavior, accessibility may regulate the likelihood that an attitude is activated and can thus bias elaboration of information relevant to the behavior. The studies on biased processing in attitude change support this possibility, though not explicitly within the context of behavior prediction.[16] Although our framework allows for two additional mechanisms (i.e., perceived applicability to a behavior or the ability and/or motivation of a person to be biased in elaboration of information), once an attitude is activated, there seems little basis to expect that additional accessibility would affect perceptions of the applicability of the attitude to the behavior. To the extent that consistency pressures help to motivate bias in processing, however, accessible attitudes might enhance such pressure compared with nonaccessible attitudes.

Types of Attitude-Relevant Information.   Several high-deliberation mechanisms might account for attitude–behavior matching effects. Similar to low deliberation, the extent to which attitude bases match the nature of the behavior could influence the likelihood of attitude activation. Also, the match of attitude bases to behavior bases could influence whether an attitude serves as a compelling argument for or against a behavior (see Fabrigar et al., 2003). For instance, if a behavior is directly relevant to core values, a value-expressive attitude might be viewed as a compelling argument for or against the behavior. In contrast, if the attitude is based on another function, the attitude might be judged as a less applicable argument. For similar reasons, the match of attitude bases to behavior might influence the extent to which an attitude biases interpretations of behavior-related information. An attitude based on information recognized as irrelevant to the behavior might be ignored or seen as an inappropriate influence.

Attitude bases might also influence motivation or ability biases. People may be more able to identify behavioral information as consistent with an attitude if that information matches the basis of the attitude. In contrast, if the information is unrelated to the basis of the attitude, it may be more difficult for people to interpret the information as consistent with the attitude (an ability bias). People may also be motivated to interpret information as attitudinally consistent if it matches the basis of their attitudes because interpreting the information as inconsistent would more directly challenge their attitudes than inconsistent information related to a different basis.

To date, there is only one set of studies providing clear evidence for any of these mechanisms. Fabrigar et al. (2003) manipulated the cognitive information on which attitudes were based. Participants formed attitudes toward two department stores after receiving information about the camera departments of each store. Participants were then asked to decide which store they would choose if they needed to purchase a camera (matching condition) or jewelry (mismatching condition). Attitudes were better predictors of decisions in the matching condition than in the mismatching condition. These findings are most plausibly interpreted as evidence of an argument applicability effect. Such matching effects were unlikely to be due to differences in attitude activation because these studies deliberately made all attitudes accessible. Likewise, because no new information was presented with the decision task, attitudes should not have biased the processing of information relevant to the behavior.

Working Knowledge and Complexity.   As previously mentioned, amount and complexity of knowledge may moderate attitude–behavior consistency via their association with attitude activation. Both constructs might also influence whether an attitude is seen as an argument directly applicable to the behavior. With respect to working knowledge, individuals might be more confident in using their attitudes as a direct argument for or against a behavior when that attitude is based on extensive rather than little knowledge. In terms of complexity, the more complex the knowledge base, the more likely the attitude will be based on information directly relevant to a given behavior (Fabrigar et al., 2003). Interestingly, complex attitudes might also be judged as applicable to a behavior even when the bases of the attitude are not directly relevant to the behavior. When a person's attitude has multiple bases that are evaluatively consistent with one another, a person may assume that other potential bases for which the person has no information are likely to be evaluatively similar to the bases from which the attitude is derived. Thus, one might conclude that an attitude with multiple consistent bases is an informative guide even when the goal of the behavior has little relevance to the existing bases of the attitude.

Only a few studies have directly tested these possible mechanisms. Fabrigar et al. (2003) crossed manipulations of amount of knowledge, complexity of knowledge, and relevance of information to a decision. Attitudes were excellent predictors of decisions when at least one basis of the attitude was directly relevant to the decision and much poorer predictors when this was not the case. Even more interesting, complex attitudes remained good predictors of decisions even when decisions were not directly relevant to the bases of the attitude, whereas simple attitudes were poor predictors. There was no evidence that amount of working knowledge per se influenced attitude–decision consistency.[17]

Both working knowledge and complexity may influence the extent to which attitudes bias the processing of information relevant to a behavior. Low levels of working knowledge or low complexity (failing to match the nature of the behavior) might cause one to disregard the attitude and/or attempt to correct for any biases the attitude might exert. Both constructs might also play a role in the ability of attitudes to bias processing of behavior-relevant information. The more extensive and diverse the knowledge base underlying an attitude, the greater the informational resources individuals will have to construe new information in attitude-consistent ways.

Ambivalence.   Ambivalence may influence attitude–behavior consistency as a function of attitude activation mechanisms. It may also alter the extent to which an attitude is judged to be applicable as a direct argument or a biasing factor in behavior. For example, increased within-dimension or cross-dimension ambivalence could lead to less overall confidence in the attitude, which could lead people to conclude that the attitude is not a compelling argument for or against a given behavior or that the attitude constitutes a bias that should be actively corrected.

Cross-dimension ambivalence could also affect judgments of applicability in two other ways (Fabrigar, Smith, Petty, & Crites, 2004). First, if a behavior happens to be relevant to a single dimension or a subset of dimensions, cross-dimensional ambivalence could lead to decreased attitude–behavior consistency if the basis (or bases) relevant to the behavior is inconsistent with the overall evaluation. In such situations, individuals may recognize that their global attitudes are uninformative and should not be used as direct arguments for or against a behavior and that their global attitudes should not be allowed to shape their interpretation of information relevant to the behavior. Second, when ambivalence exists across dimensions, people may be unwilling to extrapolate beyond what they know. Thus, when faced with a behavior that is directly relevant to a dimension for which they have no information, people may conclude that their attitudes are uninformative and, thus, should not be used as arguments and should not be permitted to influence their interpretation of information about the behavior. These mechanisms also suggest when cross-dimension ambivalence may not decrease attitude–behavior consistency. When a behavior is relevant to a dimension that is consistent with the overall evaluation or when a behavior is relevant to all of the dimensions on which an attitude is based, the global evaluation might well be judged to be an informative guide to behavior.

Although no studies have tested these principles as they relate to attitudes as biasing factors, some research has addressed possible applicability of attitudes as arguments for or against a behavior. Fabrigar et al. (2004) created simple attitudes about a department store (based on information about sporting goods) and created ambivalence in complex attitudes by making information about one department (sporting goods) inconsistent with the information about the other departments (cameras and garden supplies). Participants then completed one of three decision tasks: purchasing sporting goods (single high-relevant basis), purchasing housewares (single low-relevant basis), and purchasing sporting goods, a camera, and gardening supplies (multiple high-relevant basis).

As predicted, multidimensional ambivalent attitudes were poor predictors of decisions relevant to the contradictory dimension (i.e., purchasing sporting goods). They were also poor predictors of decisions for which participants had no information regarding the relevant behavioral dimension (i.e., purchasing housewares). In both situations, people recognized that the attitude was of questionable merit as a guide to the decision. This was in contrast to the earlier research in which evaluatively consistent multidimensional attitudes were good predictors of decisions relevant to a single basis of the attitude as well as decisions relevant to a dimension for which participants had no information (Fabrigar et al., 2003). But introducing ambivalence did not always harm attitude–decision consistency. When the decision was relevant to all three bases, the attitude was a good predictor. This is because the attitude was an informative guide, given that the decision required balancing the same competing goals as in the overall attitude.

A final way in which ambivalence might influence behavior under high deliberation is by moderating motivation and ability to be biased in processing behavioral information. On one hand, similar to dissonance-based biases in processing, ambivalence may make people prefer interpretations that enable them to reduce the ambivalence. On the other hand, ambivalence may make people less motivated or able to be biased because the ambivalence undermines confidence in use of the attitude as a guide in processing. Also, if amount of information is equal, ambivalence within or across dimensions would mean fewer informational resources supporting the global attitude to use when attempting to interpret information in an attitude-congruent manner.

Structure and Attitude–Behavior Consistency Under Moderate Deliberation

Accessibility.   When background factors do not constrain behavior to be highly deliberative or nondeliberative, attitude accessibility could determine how much effort is expended in thinking about the behavior. Similar to processing of persuasive messages, accessible attitudes may be more likely to alert people to objects that have hedonic consequences (Roskos-Ewoldsen & Fazio, 1992). This might motivate people to allocate more cognitive resources to deliberating about behaviors related to the object. Direct tests have yet to be conducted, but some research suggests that increased accessibility enhances scrutiny of the attitude object or related information (Roskos-Ewoldsen & Fazio, 1992; see also the earlier discussion of accessibility effects on scrutiny of persuasive messages).

Types of Attitude-Relevant Information.   Matching attitude bases to behavior might enhance deliberation because such attitudes are more likely to be activated, so it is more likely that the attitude will signal that an object has hedonic relevance. Additionally, when a behavior matches the basis of the attitude, it may be seen as more self-relevant and, thus, receive greater scrutiny. These notions directly parallel the work on scrutiny of persuasive messages.

Working Knowledge and Complexity.   People may be more able to carefully deliberate about behaviors if they have extensive or complex knowledge. Additionally, because of the enhanced possibility of attitude basis-behavior matching as complexity increases, people may be more likely to see behaviors as self-relevant and, thus, be motivated to deliberate.

Ambivalence.   Ambivalence may play a role in encouraging or discouraging careful deliberation. This could occur for all the same reasons discussed regarding processing of persuasive messages.

CONCLUSIONS

Attitude structure has long been a central topic in the attitudes literature, and many effects of attitude structure have been demonstrated. In many of these cases, however, the mechanisms responsible for these effects are only now beginning to be understood. Many process-oriented questions remain, and we have attempted to point out a number of potentially fruitful directions for future research. Because a number of structural features of attitudes may covary with one another, future research would benefit greatly from greater manipulation of key variables and measurement of key alternative structures. This would often afford greater confidence in the independent effects of structure variables. In addition to treatment of structural variables as alternative explanations, however, consideration of structural variables in combination points to the utility of theorizing about possible interactions among structural properties. Thus, key questions remain about both moderation of structure effects (often by other structure variables) and mediation of those effects. We look forward to continued integration of research on attitude structure and attitude–behavior consistency with the process-oriented models of attitude change. In our view, much is to be gained by such integration.

ACKNOWLEDGMENTS

Preparation of this chapter was supported by grant BCS 0094510 from the National Science Foundation, by grant MOP-64197 from the Canadian Institutes of Health Research, by two grants from the Social Sciences and Humanities Research Council of Canada, and by a Fellowship to the Center for Behavioral and Social Sciences at Purdue University.

ENDNOTES

[1] Though not yet well integrated in the attitude structure literature, some researchers have also treated attitudes as represented within connectionist networks (e.g., Eiser, Fazio, Stafford, & Prescott, 2003; Smith, Fazio, & Cejka, 1996). Although the language of these networks is a bit different, they appear generally compatible with the distinctions and effects originally conceptualized using localist associative networks.

[2] Some may think of knowledge as pertaining primarily to the cognitive base of attitudes. However, measurement of this construct simply asks respondents to list "the characteristics and facts that they believe to be true" about the object (e.g., Wood, 1982; Wood & Kallgren, 1988), which can include emotional reactions or prior behaviors as well as beliefs. Using this operationalization, knowledge refers to the amount of attitude-relevant information that a respondent lists about the attitude object, and no distinction is made among the three bases of attitudes. Accordingly, we use a definition of knowledge that refers not only to the cognitive base of attitudes, but also incorporates affect and behavior.

[3] It is generally assumed that subjective knowledge is a consequence of the actual amount of knowledge rather than a cause of it. In fact, any causal impact of subjective knowledge could be negative. People who perceive themselves as highly knowledgeable may decide that they need not invest cognitive resources seeking out and processing new information. Similar predictions could be made for the relation between perceived certainty and amount of knowledge.

[4] Although structural consistency is often treated separately from ambivalence (and the two are measured differently, see Wegener, Downing, Krosnick, & Petty, 1995), presence of evaluative-cognitive inconsistency, for example, implies some lack of consistency between cognition and the actual basis of the evaluation.

[5] Other articles have also reported studies exploring taxonomies of strength-related constructs (Abelson, 1988; Pomerantz, Chaiken, & Tordesillas, 1995). However, because these studies focused on perceptions of attitudes (e.g., importance, conviction) with few traditional measures of structure per se, we do not discuss the taxonomies in this chapter.

[6] By using factor analytic models to test taxonomies, researchers have clearly implied that attitude properties within the same "factor" tap a common underlying construct and should be highly intercorrelated. However, one might argue that, even if a taxonomy is not supported by a factor analytic model, this does not necessarily invalidate the proposed taxonomy. It could be that constructs within the same category do not co-vary with one another but do produce similar outcomes or exert influence via similar processes. However, such a taxonomy would seem to require clear theoretical rationales regarding common mechanisms and outcomes shared by constructs within the same category. Existing taxonomies have not provided such rationales.

[7] Krosnick et al. (1993) report correlations among latent variables (i.e., correlations after removing the influence of random error). For this reason, the correlations are likely larger than if simple Pearson correlation coefficients had been examined.

[8] Of course, one potential objection to these results may be ceiling effects. That is, the more extreme one initially is, the less room there is for enhanced extremity after repeated expressions. However, even moderate attitudes (which presumably allowed for increased extremity) showed no evidence of extremity effects with repeated expression. Another interesting issue is how to account for open-ended repeated attitude expressions producing enhanced extremity on subsequent rating scales. In theory, such expressions do not force neutral people to state either a positive or negative evaluation. However, subtle wording effects of such questions may create subtle pressures to do so. Some researchers have suggested that it is socially undesirable to report no opinion on issues (e.g., see Krosnick & Fabrigar, 1997; Krosnick & Fabrigar, in press; Schuman & Presser, 1981). Respondents may perceive no opinion or neutral answers to be unhelpful to researchers or to make the respondent appear unknowledgeable about the issue.

[9] Domain expertise seems likely to be a relatively "impure" index of complexity. Although it is quite plausible that domain expertise is associated with greater complexity, expertise is also likely to be strongly related to the mere amount of information on which an attitude is based as well as the extent to which people have previously thought about that information.

[10] For a different perspective on the role of variables in moderate elaboration conditions, see Albarracín (2002), Albarracín and Kumkale (2003) and Albarracín, Wallace, and Glasman (in press).

[11]In this section, we discuss the role of attitude structure in regulating the impact of attitudes on behaviors, intentions, decisions, and judgments. The psychological mechanisms and predictions are largely applicable to understanding attitudinal impact on all of these constructs. Thus, for the sake of simplicity, our use of the term behavior should be construed broadly, to include expression of intentions and making of decisions or judgments (unless otherwise noted).

[12]It is useful to note that attitude stability is typically assessed by examining the correlation between attitude measures at two points in time. However, the correlation between two attitude measures can be influenced by different mechanisms. For example, variations in the validity and/or reliability of measures can produce variations in attitude test–retest correlations. Alternatively, variation in correlations can reflect fluctuations in the actual attitudes. In our discussion, we use the term attitude stability to refer to fluctuations of the actual attitudes.

[13]In the MODE model of attitude–behavior consistency, nondeliberative attitude–behavior consistency is primarily conceptualized as a result of the attitude biasing perception of the attitude object, which, in turn, could influence how a person perceives a particular behavioral context. Such a process is assumed to be relatively automatic and thus involving little cognitive effort. For example, a positive attitude might trigger selective perception of attitudinally congruent features of the attitude object in the absence of any extensive thought about the object. In our discussion of nondeliberative attitude–behavior processes, we deviate slightly from the MODE perspective in two ways. First, we allow for the possibility that an attitude could also sometimes serve as a direct cue for inferring an appropriate behavior independent of any biasing effects on perception. In some cases, information in the behavioral context may be unambiguous and thus unlikely to be distorted (see Chaiken & Maheswaran, 1994). Alternatively, some behavioral or decision contexts may contain relatively little information to be distorted (see Lord & Lepper, 1999). In such cases, one still might expect attitudes to influence behaviors by serving as a direct cue. Second, we use the term *indirect cue* to refer to the sorts of low effort biasing processes discussed in the MODE. We use this term to differentiate this process from *biased elaboration* or *biased processing*, which has typically been used in the ELM to refer to the process by which a given factor biases thoughts about the central merits of an attitude object. Such biasing of effortful thinking is discussed in the MODE model under the rubric of mixed models of attitude–behavior processes (i.e., automatic components within deliberative processes).

[14]A key assumption underlying the Millar and Tesser (1986b, 1989) studies is that asking participants to focus on how they feel creates affective attitudes, whereas asking participants to focus on why they feel the way they do creates cognitive attitudes. However, there is little direct evidence supporting this assumption (see Fabrigar & Petty, 1999). Because such manipulations have produced differences in attitude–behavior consistency, it seems possible that focus instructions do alter the bases of attitudes. Whether the altered bases are purely affective versus cognitive is less than clear, however.

[15]We have discussed these selective attention studies in relation to nondeliberative behavior. We do so because visual features of an object require relatively little effort to process and can thus be easily used as cues in behavioral contexts in which people are either unable or unmotivated to allocate substantial cognitive resources. However, this does not preclude the possibility that such features could also play a role in very deliberative behavior.

[16]Studies examining the influence of accessibility on attitude–judgment relations have often been interpreted as evidence of biased processing of information, perhaps because the studies involved presentation of relatively complex information (e.g., Fazio & Williams, 1986; Houston & Fazio, 1989; Schuette & Fazio, 1995). The presumption is that correlations between attitudes and judgments reflect attitudes biasing the interpretation and evaluation of information and these interpretations and evaluations serving as the basis for subsequent judgments. Thus, we have presented these studies as demonstration of biased processing. However, no direct evidence for this assumption exists in the studies. It is possible that participants might not have based their judgments (e.g., ratings of study quality) on the thoughts they generated in response to the information, but instead simply used their attitudes as cues to directly infer their judgments.

[17]Although this experiment found that amount of knowledge had little impact on attitude–decision consistency, this does not necessarily imply that amount of knowledge never plays a role in perceiving attitudes as valid guides to behavior. Amount of knowledge might have had an effect if conditions with lower levels of knowledge were included.

REFERENCES

Abelson, R. P. (1988). Conviction. *American Psychologist, 43*, 267–275.

Abelson, R. P., Aronson, E., McGuire, W. J., Newcomb, T. M., Rosenberg, M. J., & Tannenbaum, P. H. (Eds.). (1968). *Theories of cognitive consistency: A sourcebook.* Chicago: Rand McNally.

Abelson, R. P., & Rosenberg, M. J. (1958). Symbolic psychologic: A model of attitudinal cognition. *Behavioral Science, 3*, 1–13.

Ajzen, I. (1991). The theory of planned behavior. *Organizational Behavior and Human Decision Processes, 50*, 179–211.

Albarracín, D. (2002). Cognition in persuasion: An analysis of information processing in response to persuasive communications. In M. P. Zanna (Ed.), *Advances in experimental social psychology* (Vol. 34, pp. 61–130). San Diego, CA: Academic Press.

Albarracín, D., & Kumkale, G. T. (2003). Affect as information in persuasion: A model of affect identification and discounting. *Journal of Personality and Social Psychology, 84*, 453–469.

Albarracín, D., Wallace, H. M., & Glasman, L. R. (in press). Survival and change of attitudes and other social judgments: A model of activation and comparison. In M. P. Zanna (Ed.), *Advances in experimental social psychology* (Vol. 36). San Diego, CA: Academic Press.

Albarracín, D., & Wyer, R. S., Jr. (2000). The cognitive impact of past behavior: Influences on beliefs, attitudes, and future behavioral decisions. *Journal of Personality and Social Psychology, 79*, 5–22.

Anderson, J. R. (1983). *The architecture of cognition.* Cambridge, MA: Harvard University Press.

Anderson, N. H. (1996). *A functional theory of cognition.* Mahwah, NJ: Lawrence Erlbaum Associates.

Armitage, C. J. (2003). Beyond attitudinal ambivalence: Effects of belief homogeneity on attitude-intention-behaviour relations. *European Journal of Social Psychology, 33*, 551–563.

Armitage, C. J., & Conner, M. (2000). Attitudinal ambivalence: A test of three key hypotheses. *Personality and Social Psychology Bulletin, 26*, 1421–1432.

Baker-Brown, G., Ballard, E. J., Bluck, S., de Vries, B., Suedfeld, P., & Tetlock, P. E. (1992). The conceptual/integrative complexity scoring manual. In C. P. Smith (Ed.), *Motivation and personality: Handbook of thematic content analysis* (pp. 401–418). New York: Cambridge University Press.

Bargh, J. A., Chaiken, S., Govender, R., & Pratto, F. (1992). The generality of the automatic attitude activation effect. *Journal of Personality and Social Psychology, 62*, 893–912.

Bargh, J. A., Chaiken, S., & Hymes, C. (1996). The automatic evaluation effect: Un-conditional automatic attitude activation with a pronunciation task. *Journal of Experimental Social Psychology, 32,* 104–128.

Bassili, J. N. (1993). Response latency versus certainty as indexes of the strength of voting intentions in a CATI survey. *Public Opinion Quarterly, 57*, 54–61.

Bassili, J. N. (1995). Response latency and the accessibility of voting intentions: What contributes to accessibility and how it affects vote choice. *Personality and Social Psychology Bulletin, 21*, 686–695.

Bassili, J. N. (1996). Meta-judgmental versus operative indexes of psychological attributes: The case of measures of attitude strength. *Journal of Personality and Social Psychology, 71*, 637–653.

Bassili, J. N., & Fletcher, J. (1991). Response-time measurement in survey research. *Public Opinion Quarterly, 55*, 331–346.

Bassili, J. N., & Krosnick, J. A. (2000). Do strength-related attitude properties determine susceptibility to response effects? New evidence from response latency, attitude extremity, and aggregate indices. *Political Psychology, 21*, 107–132.

Becker, S. L. (1963). Research on emotional and logical proofs. *Southern Speech Journal, 28*, 198–207.

Bell, D. W., & Esses, V. M. (1997). Ambivalence and response amplification toward native peoples. *Journal of Applied Social Psychology, 27*, 1063–1084.

Bem, D. J. (1972). Self-perception theory. In L. Berkowitz (Ed.), *Advances in experimental social psychology* (Vol. 6, pp. 1–62). San Diego, CA: Academic Press.

Berent, M. K., & Krosnick, J. A. (1993a). *Attitude importance and selective exposure to attitude-relevant information.* Unpublished manuscript, Ohio State University, Columbus.

Berent, M. K., & Krosnick, J. A. (1993b). *Attitude importance and memory for attitude-relevant information.* Unpublished manuscript, Ohio State University, Columbus.

Biek, M., Wood, W., & Chaiken, S. (1996). Working knowledge, cognitive processing, and attitudes: On the inevitability of bias. *Personality and Social Psychology Bulletin, 22*, 547–556.

Bishop, G. D., Hamilton, D. L., & McConahay, J. B. (1980). Attitudes and non-attitudes in the belief systems of mass publics: A field study. *Journal of Social Psychology, 110*, 53–64.

Bizer, G. Y., & Krosnick, J. A. (2001). Exploring the structure of strength-related attitude features: The relation between attitude importance and attitude accessibility. *Journal of Personality and Social Psychology, 81*, 566–586.

Boninger, D. S., Krosnick, J. A., Berent, M. K., & Fabrigar, L. R. (1995). The causes and consequences of attitude importance. In R. E. Petty & J. A. Krosnick (Eds.), *Attitude strength: Antecedents and consequences* (pp. 159–189). Mahwah, NJ: Lawrence Erlbaum Associates.

Borgida, E., & Campbell, B. (1982). Belief relevance and attitude–behavior consistency: The moderating role of personal experience. *Journal of Personality and Social Psychology, 42*, 239–247.

Brauer, M., Judd, C. M., & Gliner, M. D. (1995). The effects of repeated expressions on attitude polarization during group discussions. *Journal of Personality and Social Psychology, 68*, 1014–1029.

Breckler, S. J. (1984). Empirical validation of affect, behavior, and cognition as distinct components of attitude. *Journal of Personality and Social Psychology, 47*, 1191–1205.

Briñol, P., Petty, R. E., & Wheeler, S. C. (2005). *Discrepancies between explicit and implicit self-concepts: Consequences for information processing*. Unpublished manuscript. Columbus, OH: Ohio State University.

Cacioppo, J. T., Petty, R. E., & Geen, T. R. (1989). Attitude structure and function: From the tripartite to the homeostasis model of attitudes. In A. R. Pratkanis, S. J. Breckler, & A. G. Greenwald (Eds.), *Attitude structure and function* (pp. 275–309). Hillsdale, NJ: Lawrence Erlbaum Associates.

Cacioppo, J. T., Petty, R. E., & Sidera, J. (1982). The effects of a salient self-schema on the evaluation of proattitudinal editorials: Top-down versus bottom-up message processing. *Journal of Experimental Social Psychology, 18*, 324–338.

Cartwright, D., & Harary, F. (1956). Structural balance: A generalization of Heider's theory. *Psychological Review, 63*, 277–293.

Chaiken, S. (1987). The heuristic model of persuasion. In M. P. Zanna, J. M. Olson, & C. P. Herman (Eds.), *Social influence: The Ontario symposium* (Vol. 3, pp. 143–177). Hillsdale, NJ: Lawrence Erlbaum Associates.

Chaiken, S., & Baldwin, M. W. (1981). Affective-cognitive consistency and the effect of salient behavioral information on the self-perception of attitudes. *Journal of Personality and Social Psychology, 41*, 1–12.

Chaiken, S., Liberman, A., & Eagly, A. H. (1989). Heuristic and systematic processing within and beyond the persuasion context. In J. S. Uleman & J. A. Bargh (Eds.), *Unintended thought* (pp. 212–252). New York: Guilford.

Chaiken, S., & Maheswaran, D. (1994). Heuristic processing can bias systematic processing: Effects of source credibility, argument ambiguity, and task importance on attitude judgment. *Journal of Personality and Social Psychology, 66*, 460–473.

Chaiken, S., Pomerantz, E. M., & Giner-Sorolla, R. (1995). Structural consistency and attitude strength. In R. E. Petty & J. A. Krosnick (Eds.), *Attitude strength: Antecedents and consequences* (pp. 387–412). Mahwah, NJ: Lawrence Erlbaum Associates.

Chaiken, S., & Yates, S. M. (1985). Affective-cognitive consistency and thought-induced attitude polarization. *Journal of Personality and Social Psychology, 49*, 1470–1481.

Chen, S., & Chaiken, S. (1999). The heuristic-systematic model in its broader context. In S. Chaiken & Y. Trope (Eds.), *Dual-process theories in social psychology* (pp. 73–96). New York: Guilford.

Clark, J. K., Wegener, D. T., & Fabrigar, L. R. (2004). Raw data. Purdue University.

Conner, M., Povey, R., Sparks, P., James, R., & Shepherd, R. (2003). Moderating role of attitudinal ambivalence within the theory of planned behaviour. *British Journal of Social Psychology, 42*, 75–94.

Conner, M., & Sparks, P. (2002). Ambivalence and attitudes. *European Review of Social Psychology, 12*, 37–70.

Conner, M., Sparks, P., Povey, R., James, R., Shepherd, R., & Armitage, C. J. (2002). Moderator effects of attitudinal ambivalence on attitude–behavior relationships. *European Journal of Social Psychology, 32*, 705–718.

Converse, P. E. (1964). The nature of belief systems in the mass public. In D. E. Apter (Ed.), *Ideology and discontent* (pp. 201–261). New York: Free Press.

Crano, W. D. (1995). Attitude strength and vested interest. In R. E. Petty & J. A. Krosnick (Eds.), *Attitude strength: Antecedents and consequences* (pp. 131–157). Mahwah, NJ: Lawrence Erlbaum Associates.

Crites, S. L., Jr., Fabrigar, L. R., & Petty, R. E. (1994). Measuring the affective and cognitive properties of attitudes: Conceptual and methodological issues. *Personality and Social Psychology Bulletin, 20*, 619–634.

Davidson, A. R. (1995). From attitudes to actions to attitude change: The effects of amount and accuracy of information. In R. E. Petty & J. A. Krosnick (Eds.), *Attitude strength: Antecedents and consequences* (pp. 315–336). Mahwah, NJ: Lawrence Erlbaum Associates.

Davidson, A. R., Yantis, S., Norwood, M., & Montano, D. E. (1985). Amount of information about the attitude object and attitude–behavior consistency. *Journal of Personality and Social Psychology, 49*, 1184–1198.

DeBono, K. G. (1987). Investigating the social-adjustive and value-expressive functions of attitudes: Implications for persuasion processes. *Journal of Personality and Social Psychology, 52*, 279–287.

DeBono, K. G., & Packer, M. (1991). The effects of advertising appeal on perceptions of product quality. *Personality and Social Psychology Bulletin, 17*, 194–200.

Doll, J., & Ajzen, I. (1992). Accessibility and stability of predictors in the theory of planned behavior. *Journal of Personality and Social Psychology, 63*, 754–765.

Downing, J. W., Judd, C. M., & Brauer, M. (1992). Effects of repeated expressions on attitude extremity. *Journal of Personality and Social Psychology, 63*, 17–29.

Dunton, B. C., & Fazio, R. H. (1997). An individual difference measure of motivation to control prejudiced reactions. *Personality and Social Psychology Bulletin, 23*, 316–326.

Eagly, A. H., & Chaiken, S. (1993). *The psychology of attitudes*. Fort Worth, TX: Harcourt Brace Jovanovich.

Eagly, A. H., & Chaiken, S. (1995). Attitude strength, attitude structure, and resistance to change. In R. E. Petty & J. A. Krosnick (Eds.), *Attitude strength: Antecedents and consequences* (pp. 413–432). Mahwah, NJ: Lawrence Erlbaum Associates.

Eagly, A. H., & Chaiken, S. (1998). Attitude structure and function. In D. Gilbert, S. Fiske, & G. Lindzey (Eds.), *Handbook of social psychology* (4th ed., pp. 269–322). New York: McGraw-Hill.

Edwards, K. (1990). The interplay of affect and cognition in attitude formation and change. *Journal of Personality and Social Psychology, 59,* 202–216.

Edwards, K., & von Hippel, W. (1995). Hearts and minds: The priority of affective versus cognitive factors in person perception. *Personality and Social Psychology Bulletin, 21,* 996–1011.

Edwards, K., & Smith, E. E. (1996). A disconfirmation bias in the evaluation of arguments. *Journal of Personality and Social Psychology, 71,* 5–24.

Eiser, J. R., Fazio, R. H., Stafford, T., & Prescott, T. J. (2003). Connectionist simulation of attitude learning: Asymmetries in the acquisition of positive and negative evaluations. *Personality and Social Psychology Bulletin, 29,* 1221–1235.

Erber, M. W., Hodges, S. D., & Wilson, T. D. (1995). Attitude strength, attitude stability, and the effects of analyzing reasons. In R. E. Petty & J. A. Krosnick (Eds.), *Attitude strength: Antecedents and consequences* (pp. 433–454). Mahwah, NJ: Lawrence Erlbaum Associates.

Fabrigar, L. R., & Petty, R. E. (1999). The role of the affective and cognitive bases of attitudes in susceptibility to affectively and cognitively based persuasion. *Personality and Social Psychology Bulletin, 25,* 363–381.

Fabrigar, L. R., Priester, J. R., Petty, R. E., & Wegener, D. T. (1998). The impact of attitude accessibility on elaboration of persuasive messages. *Personality and Social Psychology Bulletin, 24,* 339–352.

Fabrigar, L. R., Petty, R. E., Wegener, D. T., Priester, J., & Brooksbank, L. (2002). Unpublished data. Queen's University, Kingston, Ontario, Canada.

Fabrigar, L. R., Smith, S. M., & Brannon, L. A. (1999). Applications of social cognition: Attitudes as cognitive structures. In F. T. Durso, R. S. Nickerson, R. W. Schvaneveldt, S. T. Dumais, D. S. Lindsay, & M. T. H. Chi (Eds.), *Handbook of applied cognition* (pp. 173–206). Chichester, UK: Wilkey.

Fabrigar, L. R., Petty, R. E., Smith, S. M., & Crites, S. L., Jr. (2003). *Examining the role of amount and complexity of knowledge in attitude-decision consistency.* Unpublished manuscript.

Fabrigar, L. R., Petty, R. E., Smith, S. M., & Crites, S. L., Jr. (2004a). *The role of attitude bases in understanding the impact of attitude-relevant knowledge on attitude–decision consistency.* Unpublished manuscript, Queen's University, Kingston, Ontario, Canada.

Fabrigar, L. R., Petty, R. E., Smith, R. E., & Crites, S. L., Jr. (2004b). *The role of attitude bases in understanding the impact of ambivalence on attitude–decision consistency.* Unpublished manuscript, Queen's University, Kingston, Ontario, Canada.

Fabrigar, L. R., Wegener, D. T., MacCallum, R. C., & Strahan, E. J. (1999). Evaluating the use of exploratory factor analysis in psychological research. *Psychological Methods, 4,* 272–299.

Fazio, R. H. (1989). On the power and functionality of attitudes: The role of attitude accessibility. In A. R. Pratkanis, S. J. Breckler, & A. G. Greenwald (Eds.), *Attitude structure and function* (pp. 153–179). Hillsdale, NJ: Lawrence Erlbaum Associates.

Fazio, R. H. (1990). Multiple processes by which attitudes guide behavior: The MODE model as an integrative framework. In L. Berkowitz (Ed.), *Advances in experimental social psychology* (Vol. 23, pp. 75–109). San Diego, CA: Academic Press.

Fazio, R. H. (1995). Attitudes as object-evaluation associations: Determinants, consequences, and correlates of attitude accessibility. In R. E. Petty & J. A. Krosnick (Eds.), *Attitude strength: Antecedents and consequences* (pp. 247–282). Mahwah, NJ: Lawrence Erlbaum Associates.

Fazio, R. H., Chen, J., McDonel, E. C., & Sherman, S. J. (1982). Attitude accessibility, attitude–behavior consistency, and the strength of the object–evaluation association. *Journal of Experimental Social Psychology, 18,* 339–357.

Fazio, R. H., & Dunton, B. C. (1997). Categorization by race: The impact of automatic and controlled components of racial prejudice. *Journal of Experimental Social Psychology, 33,* 451–470.

Fazio, R. H., Jackson, J. R., Dunton, B. C., & Williams, C. J. (1995). Variability in automatic activation as an unobtrusive measure of racial attitudes: A bona fide pipeline? *Journal of Personality and Social Psychology, 69,* 1013–1027.

Fazio, R. H., Ledbetter, J. E., & Towles-Schwen, T. (2000). On the costs of accessible attitudes: Detecting that the attitude object has changed. *Journal of Personality and Social Psychology, 78,* 197–210.

Fazio, R. H., & Olson, M. A. (2003a). Attitudes: Foundations, functions, and consequences. In M. A. Hogg & J. Cooper (Eds.), *The SAGE handbook of social psychology* (pp. 139–160). Thousand Oaks, CA: Sage.

Fazio, R. H., & Olson, M. A. (2003b). Implicit measures in social cognition research: Their meaning and use. *Annual Review of Psychology, 54,* 297–327.

Fazio, R. H., & Powell, M. C. (1994). *Attitude expression, extremity, and accessibility.* Unpublished manuscript, Indiana University, Bloomington.

Fazio, R. H., Powell, M. C., & Williams, C. J. (1989). The role of attitude accessibility in the attitude-to-behavior process. *Journal of Consumer Research, 16,* 280–288.

Fazio, R. H., Sanbonmatsu, D. M., Powell, M. C., & Kardes, F. R. (1986). On the automatic activation of attitudes. *Journal of Personality and Social Psychology, 50,* 229–238.

Fazio, R. H., & Towles-Schwen, T. (1999). The MODE model of attitude–behavior processes. In S. Chaiken & Y. Trope (Eds.), *Dual-process theories in social psychology* (pp. 97–116). New York: Guilford.

Fazio, R. H., & Williams, C. J. (1986). Attitude accessibility as a moderator of the attitude–perception and attitude–behavior relations: An investigation of the 1984 presidential election. *Journal of Personality and Social Psychology, 51,* 505–514.

Fazio, R. H., & Zanna, M. P. (1978). Attitudinal qualities relating to the strength of the attitude–behavior relationship. *Journal of Experimental Social Psychology, 14,* 398–408.

Festinger, L. (1957). *A theory of cognitive dissonance.* Stanford, CA: Stanford University Press.

Fishbein, M., & Ajzen, I. (1975). *Belief, attitude, intention, and behavior: An introduction to theory and research.* Reading, MA: Addison-Wesley.

Giner-Sorolla, R. (2001). Affective attitudes are not always faster: The moderating role of extremity. *Personality and Social Psychology Bulletin, 27,* 666–677.

Grant, M. J., Button, C. M., & Noseworthy, J. (1994). Predicting attitude stability. *Canadian Journal of Behavioural Science, 26,* 68–84.

Greenwald, A. G., & Banaji, M. R. (1995). Implicit social cognition: Attitudes, self-esteem, and stereotypes. *Psychological Review, 102,* 4–27.

Gross, S. R., Holtz, R., & Miller, N. (1995). Attitude certainty. In R. E. Petty & J. A. Krosnick (Eds.), *Attitude strength: Antecedents and consequences* (pp. 215–245). Mahwah, NJ: Lawrence Erlbaum Associates.

Heider, F. (1958). *The psychology of interpersonal relations.* New York: Wiley.

Houston, D. A., & Fazio, R. H. (1989). Biased processing as a function of attitude accessibility: Making objective judgments subjectively. *Social Cognition, 7,* 51–66.

Jamieson, D. W. (1988, June). *The influence of value conflicts on attitudinal ambivalence.* Paper presented at the Annual Meeting of the Canadian Psychological Association, Montreal, Quebec, Canada.

Jamieson, D. W. (1993, August). *The attitude ambivalence construct: Validity, utility, and measurement.* Paper presented at the 101st Annual Convention of the American Psychological Association, Toronto, Ontario, Canada.

Jonas, K., Diehl, M., & Bromer, P. (1997). Effects of attitudinal ambivalence on information processing and attitude–intention consistency. *Journal of Experimental Social Psychology, 33,* 190–210.

Judd, C. M., Brauer, M. (1995). Repetition and evaluative extremity. In R. E. Petty & J. A. Krosnick (Eds.), *Attitude strength: Antecedents and consequences* (pp. 43–71). Mahwah, NJ: Lawrence Erlbaum Associates.

Judd, C. M., & Downing, J. W. (1990). Political expertise and the development of attitude consistency. *Social Cognition, 8,* 104–124.

Judd, C. M., Drake, R. A., Downing, J. W., & Krosnick, J. A. (1991). Some dynamic properties of attitude structures: Context-induced response facilitation and polarization. *Journal of Personality and Social Psychology, 60,* 193–202.

Judd, C. M., & Krosnick, J. A. (1982). Attitude centrality, organization, and measurement. *Journal of Personality and Social Psychology, 42,* 436–447.

Judd, C. M., & Krosnick, J. A. (1989). The structural bases of consistency among political attitudes: Effects of political expertise and attitude importance. In A. R. Pratkanis, S. J. Breckler, & A. G. Greenwald (Eds.), *Attitude structure and function* (pp. 99–128). Hillsdale, NJ: Lawrence Erlbaum Associates.

Judd, C. M., Krosnick, J. A., & Milburn, M. A. (1981). Political involvement and attitude structure in the general public. *American Sociological Review, 45,* 627–643.

Judd, C. M., & Lusk, C. M. (1984). Knowledge structures and evaluative judgments: Effects of structural variables on judgmental extremity. *Journal of Personality and Social Psychology, 46,* 1193–1207.

Judd, C. M., & Milburn, M. A. (1980). The structure of attitude systems in the general public: Comparison of a structural equation model. *American Sociological Review, 45,* 627–643.

Kallgren, C. A., & Wood, W. (1986). Access to attitude-relevant information in memory as a determinant of attitude–behavior consistency. *Journal of Experimental Social Psychology, 22,* 328–338.

Kaplan, K. J. (1972). On the ambivalence-indifference problem in attitude theory and measurement: A suggested modification of the semantic differential technique. *Psychological Bulletin, 77,* 361–372.

Katz, D. (1960). The functional approach to the study of attitudes. *Public Opinion Quarterly, 24,* 163–204.

Katz, D., & Stotland, E. (1959). A preliminary statement to a theory of attitude structure and change. In S. Koch (Ed.), *Psychology: A study of a science: Vol. 3 Formulations of the person and the social context* (pp. 423–475). New York: McGraw-Hill.

Kelman, H. C. (1961). Processes of opinion change. *Public Opinion Quarterly, 25,* 57–78.

Knepprath, E., & Clevenger, T., Jr. (1965). Reasoned discourse and motive appeals in selected political speeches. *Quarterly Journal of Speech, 51,* 152–156.

Kokkinaki, F., & Lunt, P. (1997). The relationship between involvement, attitude accessibility, and attitude-behaviour consistency. *British Journal of Social Psychology, 36,* 497–509.

Kothandapani, V. (1971). Validation of feeling, belief, and intention to act as three components of attitude and their contribution to prediction of contraceptive behavior. *Journal of Personality and Social Psychology, 19,* 321–333.

Kraus, S. J. (1995). Attitudes and the prediction of behavior: A meta-analysis of the empirical literature. *Personality and Social Psychology Bulletin, 21*, 58–75.

Krosnick, J. A. (1989). Attitude importance and attitude accessibility. *Personality and Social Psychology Bulletin, 15*, 297–308.

Krosnick, J. A., Boninger, D. S., Chuang, Y. C., Berent, M. K., & Carnot, C. G. (1993). Attitude strength: One construct or many related constructs? *Journal of Personality and Social Psychology, 65*, 1132–1151.

Krosnick, J. A., & Fabrigar, L. R. (1997). Designing rating scales for effective measurement in surveys. In L. Lyberg, P. Biemer, M. Collins, L. Decker, E. de Leeuw, C. Dippo, N. Schwarz, & D. Trewin (Eds.), *Survey measurement and process quality* (pp. 141–164). New York: Wiley and Interscience.

Krosnick, J. A., & Fabrigar, L. R. (in press). *Questionnaire design for attitude measurement in social and psychological research*. New York: Oxford University Press.

Kruglanski, A. W., & Thompson, E. P. (1999). Persuasion by a single route: A view from the unimodel. *Psychological Inquiry, 10*, 83–109.

Kunda, Z. (1990). The case for motivated reasoning. *Psychological Bulletin, 108*, 480–498.

Lavine, H., Burgess, D., Snyder, M., Transue, J., Sullivan, J. L., Haney, B., & Wagner, S. H. (1999). Threat, authoritarianism, and voting: An investigation of personality and persuasion. *Personality and Social Psychology Bulletin, 25*, 337–347.

Lavine, H., Huff, J. W., Wagner, S. H., & Sweeney, D. (1998). The moderating influence of attitude strength on the susceptibility to context effects in attitude surveys. *Journal of Personality and Social Psychology, 75*, 359–373.

Lavine, H., & Snyder, M. (1996). Cognitive processing and the functional matching effect in persuasion: The mediating role of subjective perceptions of message quality. *Journal of Experimental Social Psychology, 32*, 580–604.

Lavine, H., & Snyder, M. (2000). Cognitive processes and the functional matching effect in persuasion: Studies of personality and political behavior. In G. R. Maio & J. M. Olson (Eds.), *Why we evaluate: Functions of attitudes* (pp. 97–131). Mahwah, NJ: Lawrence Erlbaum Associates.

Lavine, H., Sullivan, J. L., Borgida, E., & Thomsen, C. J. (1996). The relationship of national and personal issue salience to attitude accessibility on foreign and domestic policy issues. *Political Psychology, 17*, 293–316.

Lavine, H., Thomsen, C. J., & Gonzales, M. H. (1997). The development of inter-attitudinal consistency: The shared-consequences model. *Journal of Personality and Social Psychology, 72*, 735–749.

Lewan, P. C., & Stotland, E. (1961). The effects of prior information on susceptibility to an emotional appeal. *Journal of Abnormal and Social Psychology, 62*, 450–453.

Linville, P. W. (1982). The complexity-extremity effect and age-based stereotyping. *Journal of Personality and Social Psychology, 42*, 193–211.

Linville, P. W., & Jones, E. E. (1980). Polarized appraisals of out-group members. *Journal of Personality and Social Psychology, 38*, 689–703.

Lipkus, I. M., Green, J. D., Feaganes, J. R., & Sedikides, C. (2002). The relationship between attitudinal ambivalence and desire to quit smoking among college smokers. *Journal of Applied Social Psychology, 31*, 113–133.

Lord, C. G., & Lepper, M. R. (1999). Attitude representation theory. In M. P. Zanna (Ed.), *Advances in experimental social psychology* (Vol. 31, pp. 265–343). San Diego, CA: Academic Press.

Lord, C. G., Lepper, M. R., & Mackie, D. (1984). Attitude prototypes as determinants of attitude–behavior consistency. *Journal of Personality and Social Psychology, 46*, 1254–1266.

Lord, C. G., Ross, L., & Lepper, M. R. (1979). Biased assimilation and attitude polarization: The effects of prior theories on subsequently considered evidence. *Journal of Personality and Social Psychology, 37*, 2098–2109.

MacDonald, T. K., & Grant, N. (2003). [Cross-dimension ambivalence, within-dimension ambivalence, and priming]. Unpublished raw data.

MacDonald, T. K., & Zanna, M. P. (1998). Cross-dimension ambivalence toward social groups: Can ambivalence affect intentions to hire feminists? *Personality and Social Psychology Bulletin, 24*, 427–441.

MacDougall, B. L., Fabrigar, L. R., Ackbar, S., & Smith, S. M. (2003). [The impact of attitude accessibility on strength-related beliefs]. Unpublished raw data. Queen's University, Kingston, Ontario, Canada.

Maio, G. R., Bell, D. W., & Esses, V. M. (1996). Ambivalence and persuasion: The processing of messages about immigrant groups. *Journal of Experimental Social Psychology, 32*, 513–536.

Martin, L. L., Seta, J. J., & Crelia, R. A. (1990). Assimilation and contrast as a function of people's willingness and ability to expend effort in forming an impression. *Journal of Personality and Social Psychology, 59*, 27–37.

McGuire, W. J. (1960). A syllogistic analysis of cognitive relationships. In C. I. Hovland & M. J. Rosenberg (Eds.), *Attitude organization and change: An analysis of consistency among attitude components* (pp. 65–111). New Haven, CT: Yale University Press.

McGuire, W. J. (1985). Attitudes and attitude change. In G. Lindzey & E. Aronson (Eds.), *Handbook of social psychology* (3rd ed., Vol. 2, pp. 233–346). New York: Random House.

McGuire, W. J. (1989). The structure of individual attitudes and attitude systems. In A. R. Pratkanis, S. J., Breckler, & A. G. Greenwald (Eds.), *Attitude structure and function* (pp. 37–69). Hillsdale, NJ: Lawrence Erlbaum Associates.

Millar, M. G., & Millar, K. U. (1990). Attitude change as a function of attitude type and argument type. *Journal of Personality and Social Psychology, 59*, 217–228.

Millar, M., & Tesser, A. (1986a). Thought induced attitude change: The effects of schema structure and commitment. *Journal of Personality and Social Psychology, 51*, 259–269.

Millar, M., & Tesser, A. (1986b). Effects of affective and cognitive focus on the attitude–behavior relationship. *Journal of Personality and Social Psychology, 51*, 270–276.

Millar, M., & Tesser, A. (1989). The effects of affective–cognitive consistency and thought on the attitude–behavior relation. *Journal of Experimental Social Psychology, 25*, 189–202.

Moore, M. (1973). Ambivalence in attitude measurement. *Educational and Psychological Measurement, 33*, 481–483.

Murray, S. L., Haddock, G., & Zanna, M. P. (1996). On creating value-expressive attitudes: An experimental approach. In C. Seligman, J. M. Olson, & M. P. Zanna (Eds.) *The psychology of values: The Ontario Symposium* (Vol. 8, pp. 107–133). Mahwah, NJ: Lawrence Erlbaum Associates.

Newby-Clark, I. R., McGregor, I., & Zanna, M. P. (2002). Thinking and caring about cognitive inconsistency: When and for whom does attitudinal ambivalence feel uncomfortable? *Journal of Personality and Social Psychology, 82*, 157–166.

Norman, R. (1975). Affective–cognitive consistency, attitudes, conformity, and behavior. *Journal of Personality and Social Psychology, 32*, 83–91.

Norman, P., & Smith, L. (1995). The theory of planned behavior and exercise: An investigation into the role of prior behaviour, behavioural intentions, and attitude variability. *European Journal of Social Psychology, 25*, 403–415.

Olson, M. A., & Fazio, R. H. (2001). Implicit attitude formation through classical conditioning. *Psychological Science, 12*, 413–417.

Olson, M. A., & Fazio, R. H. (2002). Implicit acquisition and manifestation of classically conditioned attitudes. *Social Cognition, 20*, 89–104.

Osgood, C. E., Suci, G. J., & Tannenbaum, P. H. (1957). *The measurement of meaning.* Urbana: University of Illinois Press.

Ostrom, T. M. (1969). The relationship between the affective, behavioral, and cognitive components of attitude. *Journal of Experimental Social Psychology, 5*, 12–30.

Petty, R. E., & Cacioppo, J. T. (1979). Issue involvement can increase or decrease persuasion by enhancing message relevant cognitive responses. *Journal of Personality and Social Psychology, 37*, 1915–1926.

Petty, R. E., & Cacioppo, J. T. (1981). *Attitudes and persuasion: Classic and contemporary approaches.* Dubuque, IA: Brown.

Petty, R. E., & Cacioppo, J. T. (1986). *Communication and persuasion: Central and peripheral routes to attitude change.* New York: Springer-Verlag.

Petty, R. E., & Krosnick, J. A. (Eds.). (1995). *Attitude strength: Antecedents and consequences.* Mahwah, NJ: Lawrence Erlbaum Associates.

Petty, R. E., Haugtvedt, C. P., & Smith, S. M. (1995). Elaboration as a determinant of attitude strength: Creating attitudes that are persistent, resistant, and predictive of behavior. In R. E. Petty & J. A. Krosnick (Eds.), *Attitude strength: Antecedents and consequences* (pp. 93–130). Mahwah, NJ: Lawrence Erlbaum Associates.

Petty, R. E., Tormala, Z. L., & Rucker, D. (2004). An attitude strength perspective on resistance to persuasion. In M. R. Banaji, J. T. Jost, & D. Prentice (Eds.) *The yin and yang of social cognition: Festschrift for William McGuire* (pp. 37–51). Washington, DC: American Psychological Association.

Petty, R. E., & Wegener, D. T. (1998a). Attitude change: Multiple roles for persuasion variables. In D. Gilbert, S. Fiske, & G. Lindzey (Eds.), *The handbook of social psychology* (4th ed., pp. 323–390). New York: McGraw-Hill.

Petty, R. E., & Wegener, D. T. (1998b). Matching versus mismatching attitude functions: Implications for scrutiny of persuasive messages. *Personality and Social Psychology Bulletin, 24*, 227–240.

Petty, R. E., & Wegener, D. T. (1999). The elaboration likelihood model: Current status and controversies. In S. Chaiken & Y. Trope (Eds.), *Dual-process theories in social psychology* (pp. 41–72). New York: Guilford.

Petty, R. E., Wheeler, S. C., & Bizer, G. Y. (2000). Attitude functions and persuasion: An elaboration likelihood approach to matched versus mismatched messages. In G. R. Maio & J. M. Olson (Eds.), *Why we evaluate: Functions of attitudes* (pp. 133–162). Mahwah, NJ: Lawrence Erlbaum Associates.

Petty, R. E., Tormala, Z. L., Briñol, P., & Jarvis, W. B. G. (2005). *Implicit ambivalence from attitude change: An exploration of the PAST model.* Unpublished manuscript. Columbus, OH: Ohio State University.

Pomerantz, E. M., Chaiken, S., & Tordesillas, R. S. (1995). Attitude strength and resistance processes. *Journal of Personality and Social Psychology, 69*, 408–419.

Posavac, S. S., Sanbonmatsu, D. M., & Fazio, R. H. (1997). Considering the best choice: Effects of the salience and accessibility of alternatives on attitude–decision consistency. *Journal of Personality and Social Psychology, 72*, 253–261.

Powell, M. C., & Fazio, R. H. (1984). Attitude accessibility as a function of repeated attitudinal expression. *Personality and Social Psychology Bulletin, 10*, 139–148.

Pratkanis, A. R., Breckler, S. J., & Greenwald, A. G. (Eds.). (1989). *Attitude structure and function*. Hillsdale, NJ: Lawrence Erlbaum Associates.

Priester, J. R. (2002). Sex, drugs, and attitudinal ambivalence: How feelings of evaluative tension influence alcohol use and safe sex behaviors. In W. D. Crano & M. Burgoon (Eds.), *Mass media and drug prevention: Classic and contemporary theories and research* (pp. 145–162). Mahwah, NJ: Lawrence Erlbaum Associates.

Priester, J. R., Nayakankuppum, D. J., Fleming, M. A., & Godek, (2004). The A-sup-25C-sup-2 model: The influence of attitudes and attitude strength on consideration and choice. *Journal of Consumer Research.*

Priester, J. R., & Petty, R. E. (1996). The gradual threshold model of ambivalence: Relating the positive and negative bases of attitudes to subjective ambivalence. *Journal of Personality and Social Psychology*, *71*, 431–449.

Priester, J. R., & Petty, R. E. (2001). Extending the bases of subjective attitudinal ambivalence: Interpersonal and intrapersonal antecedents of evaluative tension. *Journal of Personality and Social Psychology*, *80*, 19–34.

Raden, D. (1985). Strength-related attitude dimensions. *Social Psychology Quarterly*, *48*, 312–330.

Roese, N. J., & Olson, J. M. (1994). Attitude importance as a function of repeated attitude expression. *Journal of Experimental Social Psychology*, *30*, 39–51.

Rosenberg, M. J., & Abelson, R. P. (1960). An analysis of cognitive balancing. In C. I. Hovland, & M. J. Rosenberg (Eds.), *Attitude organization and change: An analysis of consistency among components* (pp. 112–163). New Haven, CT: Yale University Press.

Rosenberg, M. J., & Hovland, C. I. (1960). Cognitive, affective, and behavioral components of attitudes. In M. Rosenberg, C. Hovland, W. McGuire, R. Abelson, & J. Brehm (Eds.), *Attitude organization and change* (pp. 1–14). New Haven, CT: Yale University Press.

Roskos-Ewoldsen, D. R., & Fazio, R. H. (1992). On the orienting value of attitudes: Attitude accessibility as a determinant of an object's attraction of visual attention. *Journal of Personality and Social Psychology*, *63*, 198–211.

Ruechelle, R. C. (1958). An experimental study of audience recognition of emotional and intellectual appeals in persuasion. *Speech Monographs*, *25*, 49–58.

Sanbonmatsu, D. M., & Fazio, R. H. (1990). The role of attitudes in memory-based decision making. *Journal of Personality and Social Psychology*, *59*, 614–622.

Schuette, R. A., & Fazio, R. H. (1995). Attitude accessibility and motivation as determinants of biased processing: A test of the MODE model. *Personality and Social Psychology Bulletin*, *21*, 704–710.

Schuman, H., & Presser, S. (1981). *Questions and answers in attitude surveys: Experiments on question form, wording, and context*. San Diego, CA: Academic Press.

Scott, W. A. (1969). Structure of natural cognitions. *Journal of Personality and Social Psychology, 12*, 261–278.

Schwarz, N., & Bohner, G. (2001). The construction of attitudes. In A. Tesser & N. Schwarz (Eds.), *Blackwell handbook of social psychology: Intraindividual processes* (pp. 436–457). Malden, MA: Blackwell.

Sengupta, J., & Johar, G. V. (2002). Effects of inconsistent attribute information on the predictive value of product attitudes: Toward a resolution of opposing perspectives. *Journal of Consumer Research*, *29*, 39–56.

Shavitt, S. (1990). The role of attitude objects in attitude functions. *Journal of Experimental Social Psychology, 26*, 124–148.

Shavitt, S. (1989). Operationalizing functional theories of attitude. In A. R. Pratkanis, S. J. Breckler, & A. G. Greenwald (Eds.), *Attitude structure and function* (pp. 311–338). Hillsdale, NJ: Lawrence Erlbaum Associates.

Smith, E. R., & DeCoster, J. (1998). Knowledge acquisition, accessibility, and use in person perception and stereotyping: Simulation with a recurrent connectionist network. *Journal of Personality and Social Psychology*, *74*, 21–35.

Smith, E. R., Fazio, R. H., & Cejka, M. A. (1996). Accessible attitudes influence categorization of multiply categorizable objects. *Journal of Personality and Social Psychology*, *71*, 888–898.

Smith, M. B. (1947). The personal setting of public opinions: A study of attitudes toward Russia. *Public Opinion Quarterly, 11*, 507–523.

Smith, M. B., Bruner, J. S., & White, R. W. (1956). *Opinions and personality*. New York: Wiley.

Smith, S. M., Fabrigar, L. R., MacDougall, B. L., & Wiesenthal, N. L. (2003). *An examination of determinants of attitude strength-related beliefs*. Unpublished manuscript, Queen's University, Kingston, Ontario, Canada.

Snyder, M., & DeBono, K. G. (1985). Appeals to images and claims about quality: Understanding the psychology of advertising. *Journal of Personality and Social Psychology, 49*, 586–597.

Snyder, M., & Kendzierski, D. (1982). Acting on one's attitudes: Procedures for linking attitude and behavior. *Journal of Experimental Social Psychology, 18*, 165–183.

Sparks, P., Hedderley, D., & Shepherd, R. (1992). An investigation into the relationship between perceived control, attitude variability, and the consumption of two common foods. *European Journal of Social Psychology, 22*, 55–71.

Tesser, A., & Leone, C. (1977). Cognitive schemas and thought as determinants of attitude change. *Journal of Experimental Social Psychology, 13*, 340–356.

Tesser, A., Martin, L., & Mendolia, M. (1995). The impact of thought on attitude extremity and attitude–behavior consistency. In R. E. Petty & J. A. Krosnick (Eds.), *Attitude strength: Antecedents and consequences* (pp. 73–92). Mahwah, NJ: Lawrence Erlbaum Associates.

Tetlock, P. E. (1983). Accountability and complexity of thought. *Journal of Personality and Social Psychology, 45,* 74–83.

Tetlock, P. E., & Kim, J. L. (1987). Accountability and judgment processes in a personality prediction task. *Journal of Personality and Social Psychology, 52,* 700–709.

Tetlock, P. E. (1989). Structure and function in political belief systems. In A. R. Pratkanis, S. J. Breckler, & A. G. Greenwald (Eds.), *Attitude structure and function* (pp. 129–151). Hillsdale, NJ: Lawrence Erlbaum Associates.

Tetlock, P. E., & Suedfeld, P. (1988). Integrative complexity coding of verbal behavior. In C. Antaki (Ed.), *Analysing everyday explanation: A casebook of methods* (pp. 43–59). Thousand Oaks, CA: Sage.

Thompson, M. M., & Zanna, M. P. (1995). The conflicted individual: Personality-based and domain-specific antecedents of ambivalent social attitudes. *Journal of Personality, 63,* 259–288.

Thompson, M. M., Zanna, M. P., & Griffin, D. W. (1995). Let's not be indifferent about attitudinal ambivalence. In R. E. Petty & J. A. Krosnick (Eds.), *Attitude strength: Antecedents and consequences* (pp. 361–386). Mahwah, NJ: Lawrence Erlbaum Associates.

Thurstone, L. L. (1928). Attitudes can be measured. *American Journal of Sociology, 33,* 529–554.

Tourangeau, R., & Rasinski, K. A. (1988). Cognitive processes underlying context effects in attitude measurement. *Psychological Bulletin, 103,* 299–314.

Tourangeau, R., Rasinski, K. A., Bradburn, N., & D'Andrade, R. (1989). Belief accessibility and context effects in attitude measurement. *Journal of Experimental Social Psychology, 25,* 401–421.

Tourangeau, R., Rasinski, K. A., & D'Andrade, R. (1991). Attitude structure and belief accessibility. *Journal of Experimental Social Psychology, 27,* 48–75.

Towles-Schwen, T., & Fazio, R. H. (2003). Choosing social situations: The relation between automatically activated racial attitudes and anticipated comfort interacting with African Americans. *Personality and Social Psychology Bulletin, 29,* 170–182.

Walther, E. (2002). Gulty by mere association: Evaluative conditioning and the spreading attitude effect. *Journal of Personality and Social Psychology, 82,* 919–934.

Wegener, D. T., Downing, J., Krosnick, J. A., & Petty, R. E. (1995). Strength-related properties of attitudes: Measures, manipulations, and future directions. In R. E. Petty and J. A. Krosnick (Eds.), *Attitude strength: Antecedents and consequences* (pp. 455–487). Mahwah, NJ: Lawrence Erlbaum Associates.

Wegener, D. T., & Gregg, A. (2000). Attitude structure. In A. E. Kazdin (Ed.), *Encyclopedia of psychology* (Vol. 1, pp. 305–309). New York: APA Press.

Wegener, D. T., & Petty, R. E. (1997). The flexible correction model: The role of naive theories of bias in bias correction. In M. P. Zanna (Ed.), *Advances in experimental social psychology* (Vol. 29, pp. 141–208). San Diego, CA: Academic Press.

Wegener, D. T., Petty, R. E., Smoak, N. D., & Fabrigar, L. R. (2004). Multiple routes to resisting attitude change. In E. S. Knowles & J. A. Linn (Eds.), *Resistance and persuasion* (pp. 13–38). Mahwah, NJ: Lawrence Erlbaum Associates.

Wilson, T. D., Dunn, D. S., Kraft, D., & Lisle, D. J. (1989). Introspection, attitude change, and attitude–behavior consistency: The disruptive effects of explaining why we feel the way we do. In L. Berkowitz (Ed.), *Advances in experimental social psychology* (Vol. 22, pp. 287–343). Orlando, FL: Academic Press.

Wilson, T. D., & Hodges, S. D. (1992). Attitudes as temporary constructions. In L. L. Martin & A. Tesser (Eds.), *The construction of social judgments* (pp. 37–65). Hillsdale, NJ: Lawrence Erlbaum Associates.

Wilson, T. D., Kraft, D., & Dunn, D. S. (1989). The disruptive effects of explaining attitudes: The moderating effect of knowledge about the attitude object. *Journal of Experimental Social Psychology, 25,* 379–400.

Wilson, T. D., Lindsey, S., & Schooler, T. Y. (2000). A model of dual attitudes. *Psychological Review, 107,* 101–126.

Wood, W. (1982). The retrieval of attitude-relevant information from memory: Effects on susceptibility to persuasion and on intrinsic motivation. *Journal of Personality and Social Psychology, 42,* 798–810.

Wood, W., & Kallgren, C. A. (1988). Communicator attributes and persuasion: Attitude-relevant information in memory. *Personality and Social Psychology Bulletin, 14,* 172–182.

Wood, W., Kallgren, C. A., & Preisler, R. M. (1985). Access to attitude-relevant information in memory as a determinant of persuasion: The role of message attributes. *Journal of Experimental Social Psychology, 21,* 73–85.

Wood, W., Rhodes, N., & Biek, M. (1995). Working knowledge and attitude strength: An information-processing analysis. In R. E. Petty & J. A. Krosnick (Eds.), *Attitude strength: Antecedents and consequences* (pp. 283–313). Mahwah, NJ: Lawrence Erlbaum Associates.

Zanna, M. P., & Rempel, J. K. (1988). Attitudes: A new look at an old concept. In D. Bar-Tal & A. W. Kruglanski (Eds.), *The social psychology of knowledge* (pp. 315–334). Cambridge, UK: Cambridge University Press.

4

The Origins and Structure of Behavior: Conceptualizing Behavior in Attitude Research

James Jaccard
Florida International University

Hart Blanton
University of North Carolina at Chapel Hill

"Only in action can you fully realize the forces operative in social behavior."
—Stanley Milgram, *Obedience and Authority*

A married mother of two children quietly walks into a room to await crossing the border. She walks up to three soldiers, presses a concealed button in her hand, and explodes herself and the soldiers. A perfectly healthy "bug chaser" seeks out a sexual partner who is HIV infected so that he can engage in unprotected sex. He says he wants to experience the rush of "joining the brotherhood" of HIV-infected people. A woman becomes a living donor by donating her kidney to a complete stranger. A man drives his car to work on a new route that he has never tried before. A woman opens an umbrella so she does not get wet from the rain that is beginning to fall.

As these examples make clear, human behavior is diverse, ranging from the dramatic to the mundane. Psychologists have long been interested in explaining human behavior, and the behaviors they have focused on have been as diverse as these examples. There have been debates about the best way to understand behavior, as exemplified by controversies between certain schools of behaviorism that disdain the reliance on mental events and psychologists who readily embrace mental constructs, like cognitions, attitudes, and personality. This chapter explores the nature and structure of behaviors as studied by contemporary attitude researchers. Our focus is on behavior itself, in the abstract, with an eye toward characterizing the ways in which attitude theorists have used the construct of behavior in their research and the issues they consider (or should consider) when doing so.

THE CONSTRUCT OF BEHAVIOR IN ATTITUDE THEORY AND RESEARCH

Behavior and behavioral measures have been at the forefront of attitude research since the construct of attitude was first introduced in social psychology. In his seminal review of the attitude literature in 1935, Gordon Allport summarized definitions of attitudes that had been offered by theorists up to that time. Common to all of these definitions is the idea that attitudes are dispositions to behave in certain ways:

- "[An attitude is] readiness for attention or action of a definite sort" (Baldwin, 1901, p. 11).
- "Attitudes are literally mental postures, guides to conduct to which each new experience is referred before a response is made" (Morgan, 1934, p. 34).
- "An attitude is a complex of feelings, desires, fears, convictions, prejudices or other tendencies that have given a set or readiness to act" (Chave, 1928, p. 365).
- "An attitude is a tendency to act toward or against something in the environment which becomes thereby a positive or negative value" (Bogardus, 1931, p. 62).
- "An attitude is a mental disposition of the human individual to act for or against a definite object" (Droba, 1933, p. 309).
- "An attitude, roughly is a residuum of experience by which further activity is conditioned and controlled" (Krueger & Reckless, 1931, p. 238).

More recent influential attitude theorists also have offered varying definitions of attitude, but many have retained a central focus on behavior:

- "An attitude is a disposition to react with characteristic judgments and with characteristics goals across a variety of situations" (Anderson, 1981, p. 93).
- "An attitude is an idea charged with emotion which predisposes a class of actions to a particular class of social situations" (Triandis, 1971, p. 2).
- "An attitude is a learned predisposition to respond to an object in a consistently favorable or unfavorable way" (Fishbein & Ajzen, 1975, p. 6).
- "An attitude is a mediating process grouping a set of objects of thought in a conceptual category that evokes a significant pattern of responses" (McGuire, 1985, p. 239).

In all of these definitions of an attitude, some sort of evaluation or cognitive process representing an attitude is linked explicitly to the concept of behavior. Given this link, it is not surprising that a large amount of research and theorizing has been devoted to the relationship between attitudes and behavior (see Ajzen & Fishbein, this volume). To be sure, some theorists have divorced definitions of attitudes from behavior, arguing that including behavior in the definition is tantamount to building a theory of attitude–behavior relations within a definition of a construct (e.g., Eagly & Chaiken, 1993; Wyer, 1974). Even so, few would argue with the idea that a central source of interest in the attitude construct was and still is its promise in helping us to understand and predict the behavior of individuals.

Although behavior has served as an outcome variable in a wide range of attitude theories and research, it also has taken on an important role in theories of the determinants of attitudes. For example, theories of cognitive dissonance (Festinger, 1962) emphasize how people adjust their beliefs and attitudes in order to be consistent with their past behaviors (see also Bem's classic theory of self perception, which emphasizes self attributions about attitudes based on how people "observe" their own behavior; Bem, 1967; Maass, Colombo, Colombo, & Sherman, 2001; Olson & Stone, this volume). Adolescents who are pressured by peers into using drugs will, under some circumstances, change their beliefs and attitudes about drugs after first use (Guialamo-Ramos, Jaccard, & Dittus, 2004). Classic brainwashing techniques used during the Korean War often induced American prisoners of war to perform counter-attitudinal behaviors with the idea that the prisoners' attitudes eventually would shift to conform to those behaviors that had been performed (Cialdini, 2001).

Behavior also has been used in a third way in attitude research. Rather than as a determinant or outcome of an attitude, behavior has been used as an indicator of attitude, or, stated another way, as a means of measuring attitudes. Because attitudes are hypothetical constructs that are not directly observable, researchers infer a person's attitude based on observable behaviors that the individual performs. Most typically, the behaviors are responses to questions on an attitude survey. Sometimes, the behaviors are those observed in highly structured laboratory settings. Other times, the behaviors are naturally occurring behaviors in the real world, such as when someone makes a blatantly racist remark. And sometimes, the indicators are behavioral traces, as reflected in the classic work on unobtrusive measures of attitude (Stewart, 2000; Webb, Campbell, Schwartz, & Sechrest, 1966; see Krosnick, Judd, & Wittenbrink, this volume). Indeed, one could take the view that any study of attitudes is a study of behavior, whether the theoretical focus is on implicit or explicit attitudes, whether the methods used are obtrusive or unobtrusive, and whether the study takes place in a laboratory or a field setting. One cannot infer an attitude without the presence of at least some observable behavior, and so it cannot be removed from the study of attitudes.

Given the central role that the construct of behavior has in attitude research, it is useful to examine more closely the nature, structure, and measurement of behavior in attitude theory and research. The present chapter does so. In the remainder of this chapter, we first consider behavioral typologies and the wide range of behaviors that attitude researchers have studied. We discuss the ways in which attitude researchers have grouped behaviors and the functions that such groupings serve. The second section considers the structure of behavior, focusing on four core elements of a behavior that researchers need to consider when defining behavioral criteria. We also consider strategies for *scaling* behaviors and how scaling can impact the analysis of the attitude–behavior relationship. Differences between dichotomous behaviors, behavioral counts, and continuous behaviors are highlighted, as are single-act versus multiple-act behavioral criteria and the distinction between behaviors and behavioral outcomes. The third section of the chapter focuses on the relationship between past behavior, current behavior, and future behavior. This section discusses recent literature that uses past behavior to predict future behavior and describes the different ways in which past behavior has been conceptualized in the context of such prediction. We also discuss issues surrounding the use of prospective versus retrospective measures of behavior when studying the attitude–behavior relationship. The next section considers how people recall and report behaviors that they have performed in the past, with particular emphasis on the accuracy of their self-reports of behavior. This section also considers fundamental issues in the measurement of behavior. The sixth section considers data analytic strategies for the analysis of behavioral data, and the final section considers general theoretical frameworks on the origins of behavior. We conclude by highlighting core issues in the use of behavior in attitude research.

BEHAVIORAL TYPOLOGIES

Implicit Versus Explicit Responses

Behaviors take many forms. Anderson (1981) has distinguished between implicit responses and explicit or observable responses. An implicit response is a mental reaction or judgment that an individual makes with respect to a stimulus object. A person might feel positive emotions while listening to an inspiring speech by a politician. While interacting with a person of Arabic descent, an American might form impressions that are colored by the tragic events of September 11, 2001. An observable response is the translation of that implicit response to an observable, clearly demarcated action with respect to the stimulus. An individual may cast a vote for a politician on election day. Or, a person might decide not to help a member of a minority group who has requested assistance. Although all of these responses might be construed as behavior, the focus of the present chapter is on explicit behavior; namely, actions that are, in principle, observable to another person.

Some observable responses are answers to attitudinal questions on a survey or marks on rating scales that are meant to inform a researcher about the nature of an implicit response. In such cases, interest is not in the observable behavior per se, but rather in its ability to permit inferences about an implicit response or to infer a person's attitude about an attitude object. One can, of course, take the perspective that any measure of attitude, be it implicit or explicit, obtrusive or unobtrusive, is an index of behavior. It might be the behavior of circling a number or a descriptor on a survey, or the behavior of pressing a button in response to the presentation of a target stimulus. In this sense, attitude–behavior research can be viewed as behavior–behavior research, but where the focus of one of the behavioral elements is on behavior as an indicator of attitude, whereas the other behavioral element is of interest in its own right. We omit from consideration in this chapter measurement-oriented behaviors (see the chapter by Krosnik et al. in this volume for a discussion of such behaviors) and focus instead on observable behaviors that are of theoretical or conceptual interest in their own right.

A behavior is any denotable overt action that an individual, a group of individuals, or some living system (e.g., a business, a town, a nation) performs. An action has a denotable beginning and a denotable ending and is performed in an environmental context in which the individual or group is embedded. Bakeman and Casey (1995) discussed the importance of identifying *behavioral units* or *events* that occur within an ongoing stream of behavior. Sometimes such events are molar, relatively distinct within the stream of behavior and can be described without regard to context, such as smoking a cigarette or using an illegal drug. Other times, the behavior is meaningful only when positioned within a context. Bakeman and Casey (1995), for example, explained a behavioral taxonomy for describing ongoing reciprocal interactions between dyads discussing a topic of importance to them (see Table 4.1). Such behaviors are only meaningful when viewed in the context of the dyadic interaction that is taking place.

Meaningful Versus Trivial Behaviors

Attitude research has explored an incredibly diverse array of behaviors. Some of these behaviors are of interest because they are of social, personal, or societal significance. These include such behaviors as drug use, sexual risk taking, smoking, performance in school, exercise behavior, and compliance with physician instructions, to name but a few. Other behaviors have no such significance and are of interest primarily because they are convenient for purposes of theory tests that link attitudes or cognitions to behavior. These include such behaviors as how fast someone walks from one experiment to another (Bargh, Chen, & Burrows, 1996); whether someone hangs a poster of abstract art on a wall (Wilson et al., 1993); whether someone signs a bogus petition endorsing a school exam policy (Petty, Cacioppo, & Goldman, 1981); and the duration with which someone squeezes a hand exerciser (Muraven & Baumeister, 2000).

Research that focuses on trivial behaviors such as these can be important in that such studies often serve as an effective means for making significant theoretical advances and insights. However, a theory is that much more powerful if it ultimately can be extended to behaviors that are of consequence. Sometimes, researchers create behavioral outcomes in the laboratory that appear to have some degree of correspondence to real world phenomena, such as when they ask participants to vote on something that matters to them (Haddock, Zanna, & Esses, 1994; Son Hing, Li, & Zanna, 2002) or to chose between different affirmative action programs (e.g., Bobocel, Son Hing, Davey, Stanley, & Zanna, 1998). Too often, however, attitude researchers are content to test their theories with behavioral criteria that are easily assessed in laboratory settings using college student samples. The desire to avoid behavioral self-reports and, instead,

TABLE 4.1

Example of Behavior Taxonomy for Dynamic Interactions

Code	Behavior
AG	Agree
AP	Approve
AR	Accept responsibility
AS	Assent
AT	Attention
CM	Command
CO	Compliance
CP	Complain
CR	Criticize
CS	Compromise
DG	Disagree
DR	Deny Responsibility
EX	Excuse
HM	Humor
IN	Interrupt
MR	Mind read
NC	Noncompliance
NO	Normative
NR	No response
NS	Negative solution
NT	Not response
PD	Problem description
PP	Positive physical contact
PR	Paraphrase, reflection
PS	Positive solution
PU	Put down
QU	Question
SL	Smile, laugh
TA	Talk
TO	Turn off

to use behaviors that can be observed directly leads many to focus on trivial behaviors that are laboratory bound. This practice can lead to an unfortunate devaluing of attitude theory and research by those who directly address problems of social and applied significance. We believe that it is important that theorists make an effort to extend their theoretical innovations to a wide range of meaningful behaviors that extend beyond those that are artificially induced or laboratory based. Indeed, it is in the real world where behaviors typically have their most impact, whether communicated through political action, commercial activities, group activities, or individual actions. It is outside of the laboratory where one person can infect another with a deadly virus, end another's life with violence, or grace another's life with great kindness. Too often, systematic and scientifically valid extensions of a theory to these kinds of behaviors are left unpursued.

Behavioral Groupings and Taxonomies

Theorists have distinguished many types of behavior in attitude research. Some such distinctions are based on the factors that are thought to influence the behavior. For example, goal-directed behaviors are actions that an individual performs to help him or her attain an explicitly stated goal (Aarts & Dijksterhuis, 2000; Austin & Vancouver, 1996). The behavior is goal-related in the sense that it is thought to be influenced by the goals that the individual has. Unconscious or automated behaviors are those that are influenced by features of the environment that operate outside of conscious awareness (Bargh & Chartrand, 1999). Volitional behaviors are those that are thought to be under the volitional control of the individual and influenced by his or her behavioral intentions (Fishbein & Ajzen, 1975). Impulsive behaviors are those that are performed with little thought and that are influenced primarily by one's quick judgments and emotions (Bachorowski & Newman, 1990). Fazio's MODE model distinguishes between conscious, deliberate, and reasoned behaviors versus those that are relatively nonconscious, impulsive, and unplanned, again emphasizing the different determinants of the behavior when making behavioral distinctions (see Fazio & Towles-Schwen, 1999).

Other distinctions focus not on the determinants of the behaviors but rather on the consequences of the behavior. For example, health behaviors are those behaviors that are thought to have implications for the mental or physical health of the individual (Baum, Revenson, & Singer, 2001). AIDS risk behaviors are those behaviors that increase the probability of an individual contracting HIV. Unsafe driving behaviors are those that increase the risk of a motor vehicle accident. Still other behavioral characterizations focus on the content of the behaviors per se rather than the determinants or consequences of behavior. For example, interpersonal or social behaviors are those that deal with interactions between two or more individuals or the social context of behaviors (e.g., extroversion, self-monitoring). Drinking behaviors are those associated with acts of alcohol consumption. Sexual behaviors are those associated with acts of sex between individuals. Diagnostic classifications in clinical psychology often involve the grouping of behavioral syndromes. Finally, distinctions are made in terms of the characteristics of the actors who are performing the behavior. For example, parenting behaviors are those behaviors that a parent performs with respect to raising his or her child. Child behaviors are behaviors performed by the child. Physician behaviors are those behaviors that a medical doctor performs.

Although the labeling of behavior groups sometimes seems to be little more than a means of highlighting one's independent or dependent variables, such groupings can serve important functions. One function is that of theory testing. If a scientist develops a general theory that specifies determinants or consequences of all instances of a behavioral category, then the behavioral category provides guidelines to researchers who wish to test that theory using one or two specific behavioral instances of that category. A clearly defined behavioral category helps researchers choose specific behavioral instances for purposes of performing more focused theory tests.

A second function is that behavioral grouping often calls attention to the range of behaviors that researchers must consider in order to address a conceptual or applied problem in an exhaustive way. For example, to understand fully the spread of HIV, elucidation of all of the behaviors that increase the risk of HIV transmission provides researchers with a map of the core behaviors one must study, understand, and modify to reduce HIV transmission. These include such AIDS risk behaviors as needle sharing among intravenous drug users, unprotected vaginal intercourse, unprotected anal intercourse, and sexual intercourse with a large number of sexual partners, to name a few.

A third function of behavioral labels or groupings is that the grouping can draw attention to common determinants or common consequences of clusters of behavior. A classic example is that of Jessor and Jessor's problem behavior theory (Donovan & Jessor, 1985). This theory specifies a cluster of adolescent risk behaviors (drug use, sexual behavior, drinking, general deviant behavior) that are all thought to be influenced by the same core variables (e.g., parental support and control, religiosity, alienation, self-esteem). Such theories encourage researchers to isolate and study core variables that have broad-based implications for multiple behaviors. Yet, a danger with these approaches is that they can lead investigators to underappreciate the importance of unique determinants of a single behavior (Guialmo-Ramos, Litardo, & Jaccard, 2003).

In some cases, there have been attempts to identify empirically the core dimensions of behavior within a behavioral category. For example, Triandis's (1964) classic research on the behavioral differential attempted to isolate the basic dimensions of interpersonal behavior. Triandis analyzed a cube of data in which one face of the cube consisted of stimulus persons that varied in characteristics such as their race, sex, age, occupation, and religion. The second face of the cube consisted of behaviors that one might perform relative to another person. Triandis identified 700 such behaviors based on a content analysis of 80 randomly selected American novels. The third face of the cube consisted of characteristics of the respondents, who varied in Triandis' study on such characteristics as their gender and their religion. Factor analyses of the cube of data suggested five core dimensions of interpersonal behavior: (a) formal social acceptance with subordination versus rejection with super ordination, (b) marital acceptance versus rejection, (c) friendship acceptance versus rejection, (d) hostile acceptance versus social distance, and (e) interaction between superiors–subordinates. Empirical efforts to identify the scope and core dimensions of a behavioral domain such as this one are relatively rare in attitude research. Application of cluster and factor analytic techniques to multiple behaviors can yield behavioral taxonomies that not only have a conceptual basis but an empirical basis as well.

THE STRUCTURE OF BEHAVIOR

Four Elements of a Behavior

Fishbein and colleagues (e.g., Ajzen & Fishbein, 1977, 1981, this volume; Fishbein & Jaccard, 1973) have argued that many behaviors have four core elements: (a) an action (e.g., talking about drugs), (b) an object or target toward which the action is directed (e.g., to your teenage daughter), (c) a setting (e.g., in your home at the kitchen table), and (d) a time (e.g., on Monday night). When researchers measure a behavior, they implicitly, if not explicitly, commit to treating these behavioral elements at some level of specificity or abstraction. For example, a self-report of how many alcoholic drinks a person has consumed in the past 30 days ignores or collapses across the settings in which the drinking occurs as well as the specific times at which the drinking occurs (although a feature of time is invoked by requiring that the drinking occur in the past 30 days). In addition, the object (alcoholic drinks) represents an abstract category that subsumes multiple instantiations of that category (e.g., beer, wine, hard liquor). Ajzen and Fishbein (1977) have emphasized the importance of making explicit and careful decisions about how the four elements are defined when specifying a behavioral criterion because the relevant predictors and determinants of that behavior can vary depending on how the four elements are treated (see also Jaccard, 1974; Jaccard, King, & Pomazal, 1977). For example, situational variables are more likely to be predictive of behavioral criteria that explicitly include situational contexts in their definition than behavioral criteria that collapse across situational factors.

A fundamental tenet of behavioral prediction is that attitudes will best predict behavior if the measured attitude is correspondent with the behavioral criterion on the four target elements of a behavior (Ajzen & Fishbein, 1977, this volume). For example, if one measures the attitude toward using condoms in general but then uses as a behavioral criterion the use of condoms at one's next instance of sexual intercourse, there is a mismatch in the correspondence of the target elements of the measured attitude (which ignores who the sexual partner is, ignores the context in which the behavior is being performed, and ignores the time at which the behavior is performed) and the target elements of the behavior (which occurs with a specific person, in a specific setting, and at a specific time). Attitudes toward condom use, in general, will be less predictive of behavioral criteria that include specific partners, setting, and times and more predictive of behavioral measures that collapse across partners, settings, and time (as discussed in the following). This example underscores the importance of being explicit about how each target element is treated when choosing a behavior to focus on.

The Scaling of Behaviors

Behaviors, with respect to some attitude objects differ in the extent to which they reflect positive or negative attitudes about that object. For example, behaviors that imply positive attitudes toward energy conservation might include purchasing a car that yields high miles-per-gallon of gasoline, keeping a thermostat at 65 during the winter months, and not using air conditioning during the summer months. Behaviors that imply negative attitudes toward energy conservation might include voting for referendums that implicitly or explicitly encourage energy use, driving a gas guzzling car, and using heat during the winter months to maintain comfort without regard to how much energy is being consumed. Attitude researchers routinely think of behaviors as being positive or negative with respect to an attitude object, and they also tend to assume that the more positive an individual feels about the attitude object, the more likely it is he or she will perform positive behaviors with respect to it (and less likely he or she will perform negative behaviors).

Conceptualizing a behavior as being either positive or negative with respect to an attitude object is analogous to scaling the behavior, in a crude sense, onto the attitudinal dimension for that object. Stated another way, any given behavior can be viewed as having a certain *scale value* on the underlying attitudinal dimension in terms of the degree of favorability or unfavorability that it implies about the attitude object (Anderson, 1981). Viewing behaviors as positive or negative with respect to an attitude object is analogous to assigning scale values of -1 and $+1$ to behaviors on the underlying attitudinal dimension. However, this practice makes no distinction between the *degree* of positivity or the *degree* of negativity implied by the behavior. It seems obvious, however, that some behaviors imply a high degree of favorability toward the attitude object, whereas other behaviors imply only slight favorability toward the attitude object, and still other behaviors imply moderate unfavorability toward the attitude object, and so on.

It is possible to consider the range of scale values that a given behavior can assume when representing the degree of favorability or unfavorability toward an attitude object, X. Rather than using a crude -1 and $+1$ scaling function, researchers can instead adopt a more fine-grained approach that honors the continuous character of the attitudinal dimension. For example, one could estimate the relative or approximate scale value of a behavior on the attitudinal dimension using *objective judges* in the spirit of Thurstone's method of equal appearing intervals (Edwards, 1957). This method might involve having a group of judges rate on a scale from 0 to 10 the degree of favorability or unfavorability that a behavior implies about X (with 5 being a neutral point), with the scale value of the behavior being represented by the median rating assigned by the judges (see Edwards, 1957 and Fishbein & Ajzen, 1975, for a discussion of issues surrounding the use of such judges).

A central construct in psychometrics is that of an item operating characteristic (IOC). In the present context, an IOC involves three concepts: (a) the probability that an individual will perform a given behavior, (b) the scale value of that behavior with respect to the attitude object, X, and (c) the individual's own location on the underlying dimension, or, stated differently, the individual's own attitude toward X (Green, 1954). An IOC specifies the relationship between the person's own attitude toward X and the probability of behavioral performance and how it varies as a function of the scale value of the behavior.

There exist a number of plausible IOCs for any given behavior. One type of IOC derives from the logic of Thurstone's scaling and states that the probability of performing a behavior should be highest for an individual whose attitude toward X matches the scale value of the behavior with respect to X. For example, an individual with a neutral attitude toward X should be most likely to perform neutral behaviors with respect to X, an individual with a moderately positive attitude toward X should be most likely to perform moderately positive behaviors with respect to X, and a person with an extremely unfavorable attitude toward X should be most likely to perform extremely unfavorable behaviors with respect to X. The more discrepant an individual's attitude is from the scale value of the behavior, in either a positive or a negative direction, the less likely the individual should be to perform the behavior.

Figure 4.1 presents the IOCs based on this logic for three behaviors that differ in their scale values (Fishbein & Ajzen, 1975). The scale values, in principle, vary from 0 to 10, with higher scores indicating higher degrees of favorability and 5 representing a neutral point. The first behavior in Fig. 4.1 has an extremely positive scale value, and it can be seen that the IOC for this behavior is linear in form: The more positive the person's attitude, the more likely it is the person will perform the behavior. The second behavior has a scale value of 5, which represents a neutral behavior. In this case, individuals with neutral attitudes are most likely to perform the behavior and the probability of behavioral performance decreases as one's attitude becomes more negative or more positive. This IOC is curvilinear in form and one would expect a low correlation between attitudes and behavior, because a correlation coefficient is primarily sensitive to linear relationships. To capture adequately this IOC, one must use analytic strategies that are sensitive to the curvilinearity. The third behavior has a scale value that is moderately positive and, again, implies a curvilinear relationship between attitudes and behavior.

An alternative conceptualization of the IOC derives from the basic logic of Guttman's scaling (Edwards, 1957). Guttman assumed step-shaped IOCs: If an individual's attitude is less favorable than the degree of favorability implied by the behavior (i.e., its scale value), then the probability of performing the behavior is zero. However, if the individual's attitude is as favorable or more favorable than the scale value of the behavior, the probability of performance is 1.0. Figure 4.2 presents IOCs for the same three behaviors using Guttman's logic (see Edwards, 1957, for elaboration of this rationale). Again, the IOCs require statistics other than correlations to capture adequately the relationship between attitudes and behavior.

Attitude researchers have, by and large, ignored the potential utility of scaling behaviors onto the underlying attitudinal dimension and then using plausible item operating characteristics to describe the relationship between attitudes and behavior. The approach has important implications for the attitude–behavior relationship because the different IOC models suggest that attitudes and behavior can be nonlinearly related depending on the scale value of the behavior. For example, in the Thurstone-based IOC model, only behaviors that are extremely positive or extremely negative should exhibit linear relationships with attitudes. When attitude researchers focus exclusively on correlation coefficients or linear regression to assess the relationship between attitudes and behaviors, they may be using misspecified models that assume linearity when, in fact, nonlinear relationships between attitudes and behavior exist. To be sure, even when a correlation is applied to a misspecified model, a significant and nontrivial correlation can result. For example, if one were to calculate a correlation for data that conform to the IOCs depicted in Figs. 4.1c, 4.2a, 4.2b, and 4.2c, a moderate correlation would result because of the presence of scores that are low on both the attitude and the behavior and scores that are high on both the attitude and behavior (see the extreme ends of the plots). However, it would be incorrect to assume a linear relationship given such correlations, and more fine-grained statistical analyses that respect the possible nonlinearity of the IOCs would be necessary (Myers & Well, 2002).

More research is needed to explore the utility and implications of behavioral scale values. Although we illustrated the idea of behavioral scaling on an evaluative dimension, behaviors

(a) Scale Value of 10

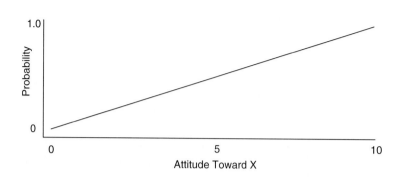

(b) Scale Value of 5

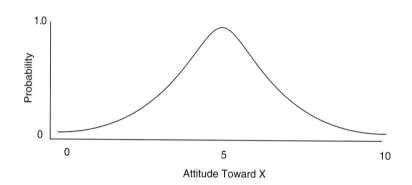

(c) Scale Value of 7

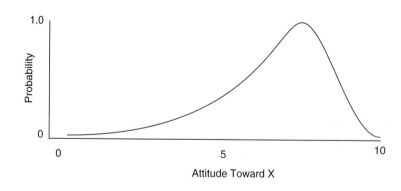

FIG 4.1. Item operating characteristics based on Thurstone scaling.

(a) Scale Value of 10

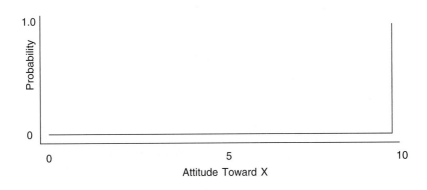

(b) Scale Value of 5

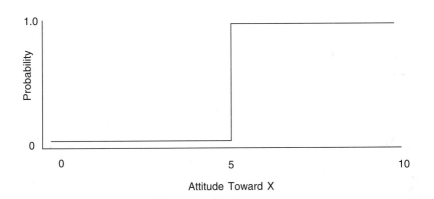

(c) Scale Value of 7

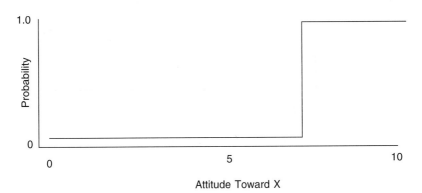

FIG 4.2.   Item operating characteristics based on Guttman scaling.

can, in principle, be scaled on any dimension of interest. For example, the scale value of a behavior in terms of how much aggression it reflects, how much dominance it reflects, or how much sociability it reflects can be determined, and then this scale value can be taken into account in conjunction with different IOCs when predicting behavior from variables that reflect constructs other than attitudes.

Dichotomous Behaviors, Behavioral Counts, and Continuous Behaviors

Some behaviors are dichotomous in character (e.g., whether a person has ever smoked marijuana), others are quantitative, multivalued, and discrete (e.g., how many times in the past 30 days the person has smoked marijuana), and still others are continuous in nature (e.g., the amount of time someone waits for an appointment). Some of the most influential theories of attitudes are well suited to predicting and understanding dichotomous behaviors, but are less readily applicable to the prediction and understanding of behavioral counts or continuous behaviors. For example, the theory of reasoned action can be used effectively to predict whether or not an adolescent engages in sexual intercourse in the next 6 months by measuring the adolescent's intention to engage in sexual intercourse in the next 6 months, the adolescent's attitude toward engaging in sexual intercourse in the next 6 months, and the adolescent's subjective norm about engaging in sexual intercourse in the next 6 months. By contrast, the theory is less well suited to predicting the number of times an individual engages in sexual intercourse during the next 6 months because of ambiguities in specifying the relevant attitudes and subjective norms. The measure of behavioral intent is straightforward (e.g., "how many times do you intend to have sexual intercourse in the next 6 months"), but the framing of the relevant attitude and subjective norm is more difficult. According to the theory, the relevant attitude should be how favorable or unfavorable the individual feels about performing the behavioral criterion. But in this case, there are multiple behaviors that compose the behavioral count, namely not having sexual intercourse at all, having sexual intercourse just once, having sexual intercourse just twice, and so on. Given these multiple behavioral options, there are multiple attitudes involved, namely, how favorable or unfavorable the individual feels about not having sexual intercourse at all, how favorable or unfavorable the individual feels about having sexual intercourse just once, how favorable or unfavorable the individual feels about having sexual intercourse just twice, and so on. Somehow, these multiple attitudes (and subjective norms) need to be incorporated into the analysis.

It is beyond the scope of this chapter to consider ways in which the theory of reasoned action can be adapted to handle behavioral counts. Our main point is that focusing on behavioral counts and continuous behaviors may impact in nontrivial ways the strategies researchers use to understand and predict a behavior, and these strategies often will require nontrivial theoretical adaptations and innovations.[1]

Behavioral counts often are amalgamations of many dichotomous behaviors that have been performed over time. For example, consider the behavioral outcome of the number of children that a couple has in their completed family. A couple who has two children reaches that point after making a series of sequential decisions about whether or not to have a child. After 6 months of being married, the couple may decide to have their first child. Then, 12 months later, the couple may talk about the matter again and decide to have another child. Then, 12 months later, the couple may revisit the issue and decide not to have any additional children (even though, for example, prior to marriage, they had intended to have four children). Every few years subsequent to this decision point, the couple discusses the matter and continues to affirm the decision not to have additional children. The final count, in essence, is an aggregation of a series of dichotomous acts feeding into it. This characterization is also true of other count variables, such as how many times a person has smoked cigarettes in the past 30 days. In this case, the aggregation is across individual instances of smoking a cigarette. Insights into count variables often can be gained by studying the separate dichotomous behaviors that occur over time and that contribute to the count, rather than focusing on the more global count per se. For example, at any given point in time during a couple's marriage, one could study the intention to have a child, the attitude toward having a child, the normative pressures that are being brought to bear to have a child, and so on. Conversely, some count variables might prove to be difficult to study in such a fashion (as in the smoking example previously described). Most count variables have this sequential quality to them, and theorists may benefit from considering whether more fine-grained analysis at specific points within that sequence would prove to be beneficial to gaining insights into the count.

Another important consideration that is sometimes relevant when considering behavioral counts is the opportunity structure surrounding the individual dichotomous behaviors that compose the count. The meaning of a global behavioral count can vary depending on the opportunities for behavioral performance. Suppose, for example, that two adolescents each report that they have engaged in sexual intercourse 3 times over the past month, but that one of the adolescents had 12 opportunities for doing so, whereas the other had only 3 opportunities for doing so. Even though the absolute number of times the two adolescents engaged in sexual intercourse is identical, the fact that one did so every time an opportunity presented itself and the other individual did so for only 25% of the opportunities suggests that the individuals may have different behavioral proclivities. Analyses that take into account opportunity structures may reveal systematic relationships between attitudes and behaviors, whereas those that ignore opportunity structures may find that attitude–behavior relationships are obscured by "noise." Such analyses are further complicated by the fact that some individuals actively try to create behavioral opportunities rather than simply responding to them passively. Recognition of the importance of opportunity structures underlying count variables has generally been ignored by attitude researchers.

Continuous behavioral outcomes usually pose similar problems and challenges to those of count variables, but they do so in a more complex way because there are an infinite number of values that a continuous variable can take on. In addition, some continuous variables are of a decidedly different character than simple counts. For example, a study of changes in eating attitudes over time might use weight loss as an outcome variable. Weight loss is not a simple aggregation of a series of dichotomous acts, and, hence, is different from a behavioral count. However, like behavioral counts, theorists can measure attitudes and perceptions about different target weights (e.g., the attitude toward trying to lose 20 pounds, the attitude toward trying to lose 15 pounds, and so on), and the actual amount of weight loss may be some function of these multiple attitudes and perceptions (see Endnote 1).

Behavioral Alternatives

Many behaviors that are of interest to attitude researchers represent choices between behavioral alternatives. For example, when choosing a method of pregnancy protection, a women chooses between alternatives such as birth control pills, a diaphragm, a patch, and the rhythm method. When an intoxicated individual is faced with getting home from a party, he or she can drive, can call a taxi, or can ask a friend for a ride, among other things. Decision theorists have long emphasized the importance of considering all of the behavioral alternatives available to the individual when trying to predict and understand a given behavior (Jaccard, 1981; Jaccard & Becker, 1985; Jaccard, Radecki, Wilson, & Dittus, 1995). Two individuals may have identical attitudes toward one alternative, but behave very differently with respect to it depending on their attitudes toward the other behavioral alternatives. For example, two women may each have only slightly favorable attitudes toward using birth control pills. One woman might have very negative attitudes toward all other forms of pregnancy protection, so she uses the pill because it is the best choice of the group. The other woman might have a very positive attitude toward using the patch, so she uses it instead of birth control pills because her attitude toward the patch is more positive than her attitude toward birth control pills. Even though the two women have identical attitudes toward using birth control pills, one woman uses them whereas the other woman does not because of the nature of their attitudes toward the behavioral alternatives. When conceptualizing behavior, it often will be useful for researchers to think about the set of behavioral alternatives that an individual might be considering.

In sum, behavioral outcomes can be dichotomous, count-like, or continuous, and they may be just one behavior among a broader set of behavioral alternatives that an individual might perform. The nature of the outcome along these lines can impact the theoretical frameworks and research strategies that researchers invoke to understand those behaviors.

Single-Act Versus Multiple-Act Criteria

Fishbein (1973) has offered an insightful analysis of the structure of behavioral criteria that emphasizes the notion of single-act versus multiple-act criteria. According to Fishbein, there are many different behaviors that one can perform with respect to an attitude object at various points in time. Fishbein presented a behavior X occasion matrix to define different behavioral criteria that attitude researchers can use, which Fig. 4.3 depicts. The rows of the matrix are the different behaviors that an individual might perform with respect to an attitude object. For example, in the case of religious attitudes, the behaviors might include attending church, donating money to one's church, saying prayers at night, and so on. The columns of the matrix are different occasions and/or time periods over which the behavior is performed. For example, each column in Fig. 4.3 might represent a different week, and the cell entry for a behavior might be whether the individual has performed that behavior during the week in question. Cell entries can be dichotomous-scored variables, count-scored variables, or continuous-scored variables.

One type of behavioral criterion is a *single-act, single-observation* criterion, which is represented by a single cell in the matrix (e.g., B_{11}), where the focus is on understanding and predicting one behavior performed on a single occasion. A second type of criterion is a *single-act, repeated-observation* criterion. This criterion is based on a given row marginal in the matrix and involves collapsing, summing, or averaging across multiple occasions ($B_{1.}$). Although the measure of a single-act, repeated-observation criterion typically is an aggregation of the individual measures composing a row of the matrix, it sometimes is possible to obtain direct estimates of the row aggregate. For example, an investigator might be interested

	Occasion 1	Occasion 2	Occasion 3	...	Occasion k	Marginal
Behavior 1	B_{11}	B_{12}	B_{13}	...	B_{1k}	$B_{1.}$
Behavior 2	B_{21}	B_{22}	B_{23}	...	B_{2k}	$B_{2.}$
Behavior 3	B_{31}	B_{32}	B_{33}	...	B_{3k}	$B_{3.}$
.	.	.	.	...	.	
Behavior m	B_{m1}	B_{m2}	B_{m3}	...	B_{mk}	$B_{4.}$
Marginal	$B_{.1}$	$B_{.2}$	$B_{.3}$		$B_{.k}$	$B_{..}$

FIG 4.3. Behavior X occasion matrix.

in condom use over a 6-month period. Measures of reported use are obtained at each (perhaps biweekly) period designated by a column of the matrix, and these scores are then aggregated to yield an overall single act, repeated observation criterion score. Alternatively, the investigator can obtain an independent estimate of the overall marginal score without measuring the individual row cells by simply asking individuals to report the consistency or frequency of condom use over the extended period of time (6 months). Even though only a single measure is obtained, conceptually, the behavioral criterion is a single-act, repeated-observation criterion that represents an (albeit imperfect) aggregation across multiple occasions or sexual encounters.

The idea of aggregating or collapsing across occasions is important because of the implications it has for isolating predictors of behavior. Consider a criterion such as the consistent use of condoms at each act of sexual intercourse over a 6-month period. During any given sexual encounter, there will be at least two classes of factors influencing condom use. One set of factors includes relatively stable, enduring variables (such as the general attitude toward condoms). These bias the individual toward (or away from) condom use in each sexual encounter and so the influence of such variables will be constant (i.e., stable) across occasions. The other set of factors influencing behavior will be more transitory. Some occasions will bias behavior toward condom use (e.g., a partner who is favorable toward using condoms) and some will bias behavior away from condom use (e.g., a partner who is opposed to using condoms). When behavioral scores are aggregated across occasions, the constant influence of the general, stable variables will be reflected in the aggregate index, whereas the more specific situational influences cancel each other, thereby failing to reveal any systematic relationship with the overall score. This emphasis on aggregation is not to say that situational variables are unimportant. Rather, it illustrates that more stable, enduring variables tend to be more highly correlated with single-act, repeated-observation criteria than with single-act, single-observation criteria.

A third type of behavioral criterion is a *multiple-act, single-observation* criterion in which an aggregate score is obtained across a given column of the matrix in Fig. 4.3 ($B_{.1}$). This criterion is focused not on a single behavior but rather on a behavioral pattern with respect to the attitude object. For example, in the research literature on AIDS, the focus might be on a variety of risk behaviors that focus on a relatively narrow time frame and that are used to document an overall pattern of behavioral risk. Individuals with high scores tend to exhibit a pattern of behaviors that is risky, whereas individuals with low scores tend to exhibit a pattern of behaviors that is of low risk. Aggregate scores for multiple-act, single-observation criteria reflect the constant influence of attitudinal and situational variables across behaviors, with behavior-specific influences tending to cancel each other out.

Finally, one can specify a *multiple-act, repeated-observation* criterion ($B_{..}$) in which an overall index of behavior is calculated across behaviors and across occasions or time periods. Examples of this criterion in the AIDS literature are measures of multiple risk behaviors across extended time periods that are aggregated to yield an overall index of behavioral risk taking. Like single-act, repeated-observation criteria and multiple-act, single-observation criteria, the multiple-act, repeated-observation criteria tend to cancel the influence of behavior-specific and transitory influences of behavior. They also are more amenable to revealing relationships with stable, enduring variables that have a constant influence across behaviors and occasions, such as general attitudes or personality traits. Although there are some ambiguities in this analysis, the general sense of the four types of behavioral criteria is important theoretically. This conclusion has been affirmed in numerous studies (e.g., Ajzen & Fishbein, 1977; Epstein, 1979).

Thus far, the emphasis has been on the aggregation of scores across cells, but attitude researchers also can study behavioral trends that characterize patterns of behavior across cells of the matrix. For example, one can apply growth curve models to identify behavioral trajectories over time for single-act, repeated-observation criteria. Instead of predicting an aggregate score based on a marginal mean or marginal sum across columns, an attitude variable might be used

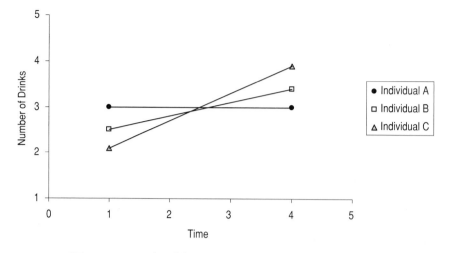

FIG 4.4.   Example of the analysis of behavioral trajectories.

to predict a behavioral trajectory across time. As an example, consider the data for a single act, repeated observation criterion for three individuals in Fig. 4.4, where the outcome variable at a given occasion is a behavioral count, namely, the number of alcoholic drinks consumed in the past week. All three individuals show a linear increase in alcohol consumption over time and occasions and all three individuals have roughly the same marginal scores when cell entries are summed across columns of the matrix. However, the individuals vary in how sharp the increase in alcohol consumption is across weeks, as reflected by the differing slopes of the lines plotting their behavioral trajectories. The individuals with steeper slopes progress toward higher levels of drinking more quickly than the individuals with flatter slopes. Instead of predicting the average drinking score across time from an attitudinal variable, the focus instead might be on predicting the slope of the line for each individual that describes how drinking changes over time. When appropriate, nonlinear models can also be accommodated in such analyses. For a discussion of growth curve modeling methods, see Bryk and Raudenbush (2002).

For multiple-act, single-observation measures, one can explore the extent to which the different behaviors composing the rows of the matrix are interrelated with one another at a given time or occasion by using appropriate cluster or factor analytic methods. Of interest here is identifying either higher order behavioral constructs or identifying clusters of behavior that empirically group together in terms of behavioral performance.

Finally, for multiple-act, multiple-observation data, one can explore even more complex factor structures involving both behaviors and occasions using three-mode factor analysis or three-mode multidimensional scaling (Tucker, 1972). Alternatively, one can compare the similarity of behavioral patterns at one point in time with those at another point in time using Euclidean distance scores (which require that the cell entries for each behavior be on the same metric). Specifically, the (dis)similarity of behavioral patterns at any two points in time for a single individual is indexed by the sum of the squared differences in behaviors at the two time points:

$$D_{jk} = \sum_{i=1}^{m} (X_{ij} - X_{ik})^2$$

where D_{jk} is the dissimilarity between the behavioral pattern at time/occasion j as compared to the behavioral pattern at time/occasion k, m is the number of behaviors, X_{ij} is the cell score for behavior i at time/occasion j and X_{ik} is the cell score for behavior i at time/occasion k. A D_{jk} score of 0 implies complete similarity of the two behavioral patterns for the individual and as scores deviate from 0, greater dissimilarity is implied, everything else being equal. One can explore attitudinal correlates of pattern dissimilarity as well as attitudinal predictors of more fine-grained components of the dissimilarity scores (see Jaccard, Wan, & Wood, 1988, for details).

Behaviors, End-State Behaviors, and Outcomes of Behavior

Ajzen and Fishbein (1981) made an important distinction between behaviors and outcomes of behaviors. Specifically, when researchers use attitude constructs to predict and understand variables like the occurrence of an unintended pregnancy, the contraction of HIV, or weight gain or weight loss, they are not studying behavior directly. Rather, such outcomes are physical states that are the direct result of the performance of one or more behaviors. The loss of weight is not a behavior in the sense of being an overt action that one actively performs. Rather, it is a change from one physical state to another physical state that is the result of performing behaviors like exercising, eating less, and consuming diet pills.

When studying behavior, it is essential that a researcher determine if the criterion that is being predicted and studied is truly a behavior or, if instead, it is a state of being that is the outcome or result of performing one or more behaviors. If the latter is the case, then the theorist usually will find it helpful to specify those behaviors that impact the outcome and then focus analysis on those behavioral mediators. The matter is important because attitudes may show systematic relationships with a behavior but fail to exhibit a relationship with an outcome, if the behavior makes only a minor contribution to it in the particular target population under study. For example, if the primary source of HIV infection in a population is through needle sharing, attitudes toward condoms would not be predictive of HIV status, even though the attitudes contribute to condom use.

Even if the criterion variable is a behavior, it often is useful to consider if there are more immediate behaviors that mediate performance of the terminal or end-state behavior. For example, the behavior of voting for a candidate in a presidential election is dependent on the behaviors of registering to vote, ensuring that one's schedule is free on election day at a time when the person can vote, and making sure that one has transportation to the voting station. Behavioral mediators of physical or behavioral end states are an important part of theoretical networks that try to explain and understand behavior.

In sum, behaviors can differ on four target elements: the action, the object toward which the action is directed, the setting in which the behavior occurs, and the time at which the behavior occurs. When a researcher defines a behavioral criterion, he or she implicitly if not explicitly makes decisions about how these elements are to be treated and the level of abstraction that will be imposed onto them. Any given behavior can be *scaled* in terms of the degree of positivity or negativity it implies about the attitude object. Behavioral scale values can then be taken into account to construct a variety of models about the relationship between attitudes and behavior, using item operating characteristic theories in psychometrics. Behavioral scores can take many forms, but the most common are dichotomous, count-like, and continuous. Some theories of attitudes are more amenable to explaining dichotomous behaviors than count-like or continuous behaviors. When the focus is on count or continuous variables, theories must be adapted to take into account the multiple attitudes that probably underlie the behavior. Also important for count variables is the potential need to incorporate opportunity structures into the theoretical analysis. Behavioral criteria also differ in the extent to which they focus on a single act on a single occasion, a single act on repeated occasions, multiple acts on a single occasion, or multiple acts on multiple occasions. The kinds of explanatory variables one utilizes can differ depending on the structure of the behavior along these lines. Finally, attitude researchers sometimes focus on criteria that are physical states of nature or behavioral end states that are the product of one or more behavioral mediators. In such cases, the careful identification of behavioral mediators is important.

PAST BEHAVIOR, CURRENT BEHAVIOR, AND FUTURE BEHAVIOR

One of the best predictors of future behavior is past behavior. This dictum holds in many areas of research and psychologists recently have turned their attention to identifying the mechanisms that account for this relation. In this section, we consider different models that can explain why past behavior relates to current behavior, including a proxy model, an influenced mediator model, and a habit model.

Behavior as a Proxy

One account for the ability of past behavior to predict future behavior views past behavior as a spurious proxy for the true causal influences on future behavior. According to this view, the causal factors that led to behavior in the past continue to influence behavior later in time, resulting in behavioral consistency across time. Past behavior predicts subsequent behavior, but only because it is a proxy for the factors that truly influence current or future behavior. Consider these dynamics in the context of the theory of planned behavior, an influential theory of attitudes and behavior (Ajzen, 1991). According to the theory, behavior is a function of one's intention to perform that behavior and the intention to perform the behavior is, in turn, a function of the attitudes, subjective norms, and perceived behavioral control associated with the behavior. If one assumes that past attitudes, subjective norms, and perceived behavioral control that influenced behavioral intentions and thus behavior remain stable, then they should continue to control intentions and behavior later in time. Such causal stability is expected when individuals remain in environmental contexts that mostly are unchanged. Developmental changes, historical events, or even the sheer passage of time might intervene to alter the individual's attitudes, norms, and perceptions of control in ways that render past behavior a poor proxy for the causes of future behavior. In such instances, the proxy model is invalidated. Even when the individual's perceptions remain stable, changing environments can yield behavior change if the cognitions that were salient or relevant in an earlier situation are less salient or less relevant in the future.

The proxy model of behavioral consistency imbues past behavior with no psychological significance. Past behavior predicts future behavior simply because it stands in for more meaningful variables. To establish such a proxy explanation, researchers must demonstrate (a) that past behavior loses its ability to predict subsequent behavior when the causal influences on behavior are controlled and (b) that the causal influences remain stable over time. Using the theory of planned behavior, for instance, one could measure the attitudes, subjective norms and control beliefs that influence intentions and behavior and then determine if the resulting behavior predicts subsequent behavior after these variables are controlled. One also would evaluate the stability of these predictors over time. If, contrary to the proxy model, past behavior exerts unique influences on subsequent behavior even when the supposed true causal influences are controlled, then the proxy model appears invalid (or that it is valid and the researcher failed to adequately identify, measure, and control the causal factors that are influencing subsequent behavior).

An important type of behavioral influence in proxy models not represented in the theory of planned behavior are those associated with what Bargh and his associates have called *automatic behaviors* (Bargh, 1989; Bargh & Chartrand, 1999; Wegner & Bargh, 1998). Bargh argues that there are features of the environment that influence behavior outside of the awareness of the individual. To the extent that such environmental influences are stable across time, then past behavior can be correlated with future behavior even when the core components of the theory of planned behavior are controlled. Again, tests of the proxy model require complete specification of the other variables that influence behavior.

Behavior as a Causal Factor: Influenced Mediators

Although the proxy model views past behavior as a spurious indicator of the true causal mechanisms of future behavior, there are several theories that suggest that past behavior will be psychologically significant and exert causal influences on future behavior in ways that are not spurious. These theories suggest that past behavior promotes beliefs and attitudes that are consistent with that behavior, and the extent to which these past behavior-induced cognitions and attitudes influence future behavior, high behavioral consistency across time will be observed. Cognitive dissonance theory predicts, for instance, that people experience psychological discomfort when they freely choose to perform behaviors that lead to foreseeable negative consequences or that challenge cherished views about the self (Aronson, 1969; Cooper & Fazio, 1984; Olson & Stone, this volume; Steele, 1988). One way of reducing this discomfort is to change attitudes so that they are consistent with the past behavior, which creates a justification for the past act and thereby lowers the discomfort associated with past actions. These new attitudes, in turn, reinforce future intentions to act in ways that are consistent with the past behavior.

Dissonance is predicted only in situations in which someone has engaged in actions that cause psychological distress, but this need not occur for behavior to reinforce attitudes that promote behavioral consistency. Self-perception processes also can cause individuals to infer that they have attitudes that are consistent with behavior (Bem, 1967, 1972). Self-perception is likely when situational factors elicit behaviors in a manner that individuals incorrectly attribute to personal attitudes. In such instances, one need not assume that behavior causes discomfort, only that the situational determinants of behavior were subtle enough that the actor failed to realize their effects (Fazio, Zanna, & Cooper, 1977). The inference of a corresponding attitude can then cause the individual to act consistently with past behavior in the future, even in situations without the previous eliciting factors.[2]

Similar kinds of mechanism can operate for normative influences. After performing a behavior, for instance, people may come to overestimate its prevalence (Ross, Greene, & House, 1977; Sherman, Chassin, Presson, & Agostinelli, 1984) or the approval it generates from others (Gerrard, Gibbons, Reis-Bergan, & Russell, 2000). Experience with a behavior might also increase perceptions of control, confidence, and self-efficacy, and it might reduce the perceived psychological barriers to acting (Corrigan, McCracken, Kommana, Edwards, & Simpatico, 1996; McCallum, Wiebe, & Keith, 1988; Meekers & Klein, 2002; Sattler, Kaiser, & Hittner, 2000). Any such changes might result in behavioral consistency over time.

It is possible that both the influenced-mediator model and the proxy model operate across time. For example, at one point in time, it may indeed be the case that behavior influences attitudes, such as when an adolescent starts to smoke cigarettes because of peer pressure and then decides, subsequent to that, that smoking is fun. The resulting positive attitude toward smoking may become asymptotic and stabilize after a period of time, yet continue to guide behavior for the next year or two. Depending on when in this sequence the investigator happens to study the processes by which past behavior influences 5 future behavior, support will be found for either the influenced mediator model (if the research is conducted early in the sequence), the proxy model (if the research is conducted late in the sequence), or both (if research spans the entire sequence and focuses on many time periods). An informed test of the models requires that the researcher (a) knows the true determinants of behavior, (b) knows the function by which these determinants impact behavior (linear or curvilinear), (c) has reliable and valid measures of all involved constructs, (d) has intimate knowledge of the causal lags and causal dynamics that are operating, and (e) studies the process at multiple time points that represent an adequate sampling of the dynamics of the behavioral sequence.

Habit

When past behavior predicts future behavior independent of the supposed behavioral mediators, then this outcome leaves open the question of through what psychological mechanisms the past behavior is influencing future behavior. This situation is common, as studies often reveal direct effects of past behavior over and above presumed behavioral mediators (see Hunt, Matarazzo, Weiss, & Gentry, 1979; Norman & Conner, 1996; Ronis, Yates, & Kirscht, 1989; Sutton, 1994; for relevant meta-analyses, see Albarracín, Johnson, Fishbein, & Muellerleile, 2001; Ouellette & Wood, 1998; see Ajzen, 2002, for the view that such effects are questionable for methodological reasons). One mundane possibility is that direct effects simply reflect methodological limitations. A researcher's inability to find psychological measures that have the appropriate level of correspondence to predict behavior may therefore result in a fair amount of "unexplained" variance in behavior (Ajzen, 2002). It certainly seems reasonable that some of the seeming unmediated effects of past behavior are actually mediated by unmeasured or unmeasureable psychological variables, it is nonetheless compelling to consider reasons why past behavior might have direct effects on future behavior.

Some speculate that the direct effects of behavior result from the fact that behavioral repetition leads to habit formation, which then induces people to act consistently with prior behavior (Triandis, 1977, 1980). A habit model is actually another type of influenced-mediator model, but now the mediator is the psychological construct of *habit*, which guides future behavior. Habit differs from the variables discussed earlier, however, because it can only arise through past behavior. One can develop attitudes, norm perceptions, and control beliefs about a behavior without experiencing the behavior directly, but habit is derived solely from behavioral repetition. In fact, a standard index of habit strength is the frequency with which a behavior has been performed in the past (Triandis, 1977, 1980).

A common view of habit is that, through behavioral repetition, one develops behavioral tendencies that later are engaged automatically with little deliberation or explicit intention to act (Ouellette & Wood, 1998; Triandis, 1977, 1980; see Ajzen, 2002). This conceptualization of habit is consistent with Anderson's (1990, 1996) adaptive character of thought theory, which considers the process of behavioral adaptation as the accrual of simple units of knowledge that are consolidated in memory over time to produce spontaneous responses to the environment. Accordingly, complex responses to the environment can result from the accumulation of many simple responses, each of which becomes associated with one another in memory to produce a seamless stream of behavior.

To test if the effects of past behavior on subsequent behavior are due to habit, one can specify conditions under which habit should or should not exert direct (unmediated) effects of behavior and then test these predictions empirically. Such an approach was pursued by Ouellette and Wood (1998). They proposed that past behavior exerts direct influences only under situations in which people act with little deliberation. When actions are well learned and easy and when the conditions of their occurrence are stable, people may reflexively respond in the future in the ways that they have in the past. In contrast, when actions are not well learned or difficult and when the conditions of their occurrence are unstable, past behavior may exert influences mediated by attitudes and intentions. Ouellette and Wood tested this idea in a meta-analytic review of studies documenting the influence of past behavior on subsequent behavior. They categorized behaviors as either occurring frequently (e.g., seatbelt use, coffee consumption) or infrequently (e.g., getting flu shots, donating blood) and as occurring in either situations that are relatively stable (e.g., attending class in college, clipping coupons) or unstable (e.g., political protests, exercising after childbirth). Consistent with hypotheses, the direct influences of behavior were found to be greatest when the opportunities for behavior were frequent and when the conditions surrounding them were stable (see also Albarracín et al., 2001).

Although this result is consistent with the operation of habit, alternative explanations are plausible. It may be that behavior that occurs frequently and in stable situations reflects the operation of stable third-variable influences or reflects situations that exert greater influence on mediating attitudes and cognitions. Without an independent measure of habit that can be incorporated into empirical tests of models that also include measures of past behavior and future behavior, the invocation of habit as an explanatory construct is on somewhat tenuous scientific grounds. Making this same point, Ajzen (2002; Bamberg, Ajzen, & Schmidt, 2003) has argued that researchers who equate habit with past behavior and its effects on future behavior are using circular logic. If habit strength is defined as the tendency for past behavior to exert unique effects on subsequent behavior, then one cannot empirically demonstrate situations in which someone has a strong habit to act and resists. Habit is as habit does.

Bamberg, Ajzen, and Schmidt (2003) pursued an independent measure of habit by adapting a measurement approach suggested by Verplanken, Aarts, van Knippenberg, & van Knippenberg (1994). Their *fast response measure* presented participants with a series of rapid-fire situations and asked them to choose as quickly as possible from a set of behavioral responses. To measure habitual mode of transportation, for instance, they presented participants with 10 travel destinations and purposes (e.g., going to a movie, taking a summer excursion) and then asked them to answer quickly and without deliberation whether they would travel by car, bus, bicycle, train, or by walking. The logic was that the speed of responding would circumnavigate any explicit evaluations the individual may have regarding the travel situations. Verplanken and Orbell (2003) developed a self-report measure of habit, based on the assumption that people have insight into habit and can thus answer questions about habitual ways of acting. They argued that habit is characterized by four attributes: (a) a history of behavioral repetition, (b) difficulty controlling behavior, (c) lack of awareness of one's action, and (d) a view of behavior as reflective of one's personal identity or style. Their measure assesses these four perceptions for any given behavior one wishes to study.

Though these two approaches to measurement are promising, much work needs to be pursued to establish that independent measures assess habit and not some other constructs. To accomplish this end, researchers first must identify the criterion by which measures of habit are validated. Bamberg, Ajzen, and Schmidt (2003) worked under an assumption that a valid measure of habit will mediate the relationship between past and future behavior whenever habit is operating. In contrast, Verplanken and Orbell (2003) used degree of association with past behavior as an indication of validity. The latter validation method comes perilously close to the circular logic one hopes to avoid by developing an independent measure of habit. Clearly, much work is required to determine how best to conceptualize and validate an independent measure of habit.

Despite the scientific difficulties of studying habit, the construct does make intuitive sense in examples from everyday life. Consider the case of an individual who drives the same route to work every morning. This behavior is such an ingrained part of the individual's work week that it occurs automatically and without conscious monitoring, reflection, or control. The habitual nature of this behavior is revealed when the individual decides to take a new route to work, but finds himself or herself accidentally driving the exact same route as always. Such behavior clearly occurs because the individual is unconsciously following a familiar behavioral routine.

In sum, although past behavior tends to be a good predictor of future behavior, the psychological mechanisms that can account for this relation remain somewhat elusive. We discussed three models that could account for the effects—a proxy model, an influenced-mediator model, and a habit model. In reality, all three models probably operate to some extent. Research is needed to further explicate the dynamics of each model, and this research can benefit tremendously from the development of an independent measure of habit. Greater clarification along these lines could be of tremendous import to applied endeavors.

Applied scientists often are interested in attitude theories because they provide a framework for designing interventions to bring about behavior change. Knowing that past behavior influences future behavior is of little use for these scientists, because it is not possible to change behaviors that have already occurred in the past. To the extent that a behavioral disposition such as habit is the underlying mechanism by which past and future behavior are linked, then there is little that an interventionist can do to change that habit. One solution is not to attempt to change the habit disposition per se, but instead attempt to alter its relative impact on behavior. This end could be accomplished by increasing the importance of other potential influences, such as attitudes, norms, and perceived control. One might, for instance, have individuals engage in thought-listing activities or mentally rehearse implementation strategies that are counter to the habit. Research also is needed on strategies that render the impact of a bad habit moot.

Additional Perspectives on Behavior–Behavior Relationships

Although the research previously discussed has focused on the ability of past behavior to predict future behavior primarily in correlational research, a great deal of research also investigates behavior–behavior relations in which a participant's behavior is manipulated and then the effects of those manipulations on subsequent behavior are assessed. As one example, researchers studying dissonance processes have had participants write counterattitudinal essays in order to gauge subsequent tendencies to act consistent with the positions advocated (Cooper & Fazio, 1984). Similarly, researchers studying social influence have had participants comply with small requests and then examined subsequent tendencies to comply with larger requests (Cialdini, Cacioppo, Bassett, & Miller, 1978). As a final example, researchers studying social stereotypes have had participants answer questions about their race in order to gauge tendencies to act consistent with the stereotypes regarding their race (Steele & Aronson, 1995). In each instance, formal manipulations of behavior are used to isolate a psychological mechanism or mediator that is thought to influence behavior–behavior relations. With a few notable exceptions (e.g., Albarracín & Wyer, 2000), the vast majority of studies exploring behavior–behavior relations that involve a behavioral manipulation have focused on temporary psychological states (e.g., dissonance arousal, psychological commitment, stereotype threat) that are thought to mediate behavior–behavior pathways at the moment (see the chapter by Olson and Stone in this volume for more detailed consideration of this research). In contrast, applied studies have tended to focus on more stable psychological factors (e.g., habit) that can lead to behavioral consistency over time and across situations. Although both emphases are needed to generate a complete understanding of behavioral consistency, it is unclear at this time how a meaningful integration might emerge between these differing research traditions.

PREDICTING VERSUS POSTDICTING BEHAVIOR

Many researchers wish to assert a causal relationship between attitudes and behavior, where attitudes are thought to be the cause of behavior. Research that explores such links uses different types of behavioral criteria. In some studies, an attitude is measured in conjunction with behavior during the recent past and a non-zero correlation between the two is taken to be consistent with the proposition that attitudes cause behavior. For example, a researcher may correlate a measure of attitude toward smoking cigarettes with how much an individual reports having smoked cigarettes in the past 30 days. Or, a researcher may correlate an attitude toward using condoms with whether condoms were used at one's last sexual intercourse. In such studies, attitudes are not predicting behavior: They are postdicting it.

An alternative approach to establishing a causal link is to use longitudinal or prospective designs in which attitudes are measured at one point in time and behavior is measured at a later point in time. To the extent that the attitude measured at Time 1 predicts the behavior measured at Time 2, then this evidence is said to support with the proposition that attitudes cause behavior. For example, at Time 1, a researcher may measure the attitude toward smoking cigarettes and then, 4 weeks later, reinterview the same participants and ask them how much they smoked cigarettes in the past 4 weeks. The Time 1 measure is used to predict the Time 2 measure.

The philosophical issues involved in trying to establish causality are far too complex to be covered here, but one issue deserving attention has direct bearing on the formal design of research studies. This is the issue of time. Owing perhaps to Hume's formal account of the conditions needed to establish causality, researchers appreciate that any causal factor of behavior must precede that behavior in time (see Heise, 1975; Kenny, 1979; Pearl, 2000). This principle suggests to many scholars that analyses of behavioral antecedents should use research designs in which the theorized causal influence precedes the criterion behavior under study. This principle is true particularly in field or survey research, where issues of reverse causality, reciprocal relations, and third variable confounds are greater concerns.

Closer inspection of the underlying issues suggests that this viewpoint is simplistic. Consider a researcher interested in identifying the attitudinal variables that influence the number of packs of cigarettes smoked in a group of adults. A cross-sectional study could be conducted to determine which attitudes are associated with heavier smoking, but concerns for causality might lead the investigator to conduct a longitudinal analysis. The question that becomes central in the longitudinal study is the time duration that should be chosen between the measurement of attitudes and the measurement of behavior. It is unlikely that smoking would change much in 2 days, 2 weeks, or possibly even 2 months. One should not expect, therefore, to obtain any different results in a longitudinal analysis that uses one of these time periods than one that focuses on cross-sectional studies relying on postdicting." Smoking behavior certainly might change in 2 years, but it seems doubtful that these changes would be caused by the attitudes that one measured 2 years prior.

For behaviors that are stable over time, cross-sectional analyses can be just as informative as longitudinal analyses because the behavioral estimate one obtains at the cross-section is likely to be the same as that which one would obtain at the later point in time. Stated another way, for behaviors that are stable, the behavioral scores that individuals yield at one point in time should be equivalent to the behavioral scores they yield at a future point in time (except for random measurement error), so it does not matter at what time the measures are taken (be it prior to the measurement of attitudes, at the same time as the measurement of attitudes, or after the measurement of attitudes). Indeed, cross-sectional studies may even be preferable because they are cheaper to conduct and are not subject to attrition bias, as participants who were interviewed at Time 1 are lost to follow-up at Time 2. In addition, a longitudinal study that uses only a 2-week interval as an index of behavioral smoking patterns (because of the practical constraints of having too long a follow-up period) may ultimately yield less reliable estimates of smoking patterns than a cross-sectional study that can ask about a longer time interval (e.g., 30 days) when it is focused on retrospective accounts of smoking. To be sure, longitudinal studies can be designed to circumvent these problems, but it often is costly to do so.

When behavior is unstable over time, then longitudinal designs that measure both attitudes and behavior at multiple time points can be more informative than simple cross-sectional designs or designs involving postdiction. Such studies, in principle, permit one to determine if changes in attitudes are associated with changes in behavior. But even here, knowledge of causal lags is crucial for meaningful tests of causal models in such data. For example, if it takes considerable time for a change in attitude to produce a change in behavior, but the behavior is measured before this time has transpired, then faulty causal inferences can result. A time lag that is too short is problematic. Similarly, if the time lag is too long, then the changes in behavior that were produced by the changes in attitude may have dissipated, again masking the true causal dynamics that are operating.

At the most basic level, decisions about the choice of a cross-sectional versus a longitudinal design should consider the stability of the behavioral criterion. If behavior is not likely to change over a given time period, little can be gained if one studies behavior across that time period. It could be argued that longitudinal studies with stable behavioral criteria can be informative if changes in attitudes are observed without concomitant change in behavior. Such a result might be interpreted as questioning the causal relevance of attitudes. However, many methodological artifacts can suggest false instability in attitudes (e.g., unreliability of measures, changing scale metrics, regression to the mean), so such designs are suboptimal in the face of stable behavioral criteria (see Shadish, Cook, & Campbell, 2002).

Any number of variables might lead to stability in behavior and so these should be considered in decisions regarding research design. Returning to the discussion of habit (Ouellette & Wood, 1998), we would note that a person in a stable environment who performs a behavior frequently and in similar circumstances probably will not change dramatically over a given time period. For instance, it is doubtful that someone would dramatically change seatbelt use, bathing habits, or flossing behavior in the absence of a notable life transition. One also should consider whether the sample one wishes to study is in a maintenance stage of behavior or in the initiation stage vis-à-vis classic stages of change theory (Prochaska, DiClemente, & Norcross, 1992). Those in the maintenance stage of a behavior may be more strongly identified with a behavior, may have attracted like-minded and like-acting individuals who reinforce behavioral stability, and may have moved from conscious decision and choice to more automated ways of reacting. Individuals in this stage of change would be more likely to show behavioral stability across time than individuals who are still transitioning from one behavioral state to another. As an example, although adolescents or other groups in transition might show changes in the tendency to take up smoking, the amount of smoking in a group of heavy smokers is not likely to change during the time periods researchers typically study.

In sum, testing causal models with correlational data is difficult and fraught with many complexities. It is simplistic to assume that longitudinal designs are, by definition, superior to cross-sectional designs when testing such models. The stability of behavior over time is a major factor influencing whether a researcher might choose to postdict rather than predict. Cross-sectional, postdiction strategies coupled with the use of instrumental variables in multiple indicator structural equation models can, in many cases, be more informative about the underlying causal dynamics than a longitudinal design.

PERCEIVED BEHAVIOR VERSUS ACTUAL BEHAVIOR

Individuals often are asked to recall their behavior for purposes of reporting it to an experimenter. Of interest are the psychological processes that are used when making such judgments. In this section, we consider how individuals recall and report estimates of their past behavior. Because self-reports of behavior are so central to attitude research, we also consider methodological strategies that maximize their validity.

Self-Reports: Recalling or Reconstructing Instances of Past Behavior

A large literature has examined the cognitive processes that people use when making reports of their past behavior (e.g., Blair & Burton, 1987; Bradburn, Rips, & Shevell, 1987; Gigerenzer, 1996; Mathiowetz, 1986; Means, Mingay, Nigam, & Zarrow, 1988; Menon, 1993, 1997; Menon, Raghubir, & Schwarz, 1995; Schwarz, 1996; Strube, 1987). Many processes are involved. For example, answering a question about how frequently one has performed a behavior in the past requires (a) that individuals comprehend the question asking for the behavioral frequency, (b) that they recall or reconstruct from memory relevant instances of the behavior, (c) that they determine if the instances occurred during the time period, if a time frame is given (d) that they infer an answer from these relevant instances, and (d) that they convey the answer to an interviewer or translate it as a mark on a rating scale (see Krosnick, Judd, & Wittenbrink, this volume). Some of these points are methodological in character. Here, we focus on the cognitive processes involved in recall per se.

Episodic Memory.   One might suspect that people use an orderly, systematic *identify and count* strategy when asked to report the frequency with which they have performed a behavior in the past. For example, if asked to report the number of times one has engaged in sexual intercourse over the past 3 months, an individual might think about the relevant time frame and try to recall each occurrence of the event, counting them up as each one is recalled. Individuals could either begin with the most recent event and count backward in time, called a *think-backward* strategy, or they could start at the beginning of the time period and count recalled instances that occur sequentially since the inception date, called a *think-forward* strategy (Loftus & Fathi, 1985). Left to their own, most people adopt think-forward strategies, although think-backward strategies often yield more accurate estimates (Loftus & Fathi, 1985). During the recall process, the memory of one event may blur or interfere with the memory of another event (e.g., Means, Mingay, Nigam, & Zarrow, 1988). Indeed, some researchers have suggested that because of interference, behavioral representations in memory often lack specific time or location indicators (Mathiowetz, 1986; Strube, 1987). Nevertheless, the fundamental nature of the judgment process, as previously described, is episodic in that the individual tries to recall specific episodes of the event in question.

Semantic Memory.   An alternative strategy to making count estimates does not rely on recall of individual episodes. Cognitive psychologists distinguish two types of memories, episodic and semantic (Means & Loftus, 1991; Tulving, 1983). *Episodic memory* refers to the retrieval of information about specific episodes of a behavior, as previously described. In contrast, *semantic memory* refers to generalizations about behavior that are stored in memory. For example, individuals who wash their hair every day may have poor recall of the details of each specific episode of shampooing (hence, poor episodic memory), but they can readily report behavioral frequencies of this behavior because of the stored rule in semantic memory: "I wash my hair every day." When people report behavioral frequencies, sometimes they use episodic memory and other times they rely on rules in semantic memory.

The types of rules stored in semantic memory can vary considerably. Some individuals use a *representative period* heuristic where, for example, a rate of occurrence for a limited period of time is estimated and then multiplied by a time factor to yield the requested judgment. Another strategy is to use one's current behavior adjusted for perceived stability. As Ross (1989) described, individuals may use their current behavioral base rates as a benchmark and then invoke an implicit theory of the self and of the stability of events to infer previous behavior. Another strategy involves using normative expectations (Bradburn et al., 1987). Asked to make a frequency estimate, the individual makes a judgment about what most people do (or should do) and then adjusts this upward or downward to characterize his or her own behavior, based on self-perceptions ("I am not like most people in this regard").

Use of Episodic and Semantic Memory.   Many factors influence whether individuals rely on episodic or semantic memory when making frequency judgments. One factor is the form of the behavioral query. Questions that ask individuals to report an actual number of instances tend to encourage the individual to recall the behavioral events and tally them up, thus invoking episodic memory. By contrast, asking individuals more global characterizations, such as if they do something *never*, *sometimes*, or *very frequently* (as is often done with rating scales) tends to encourage the use of semantic memory, because individuals are less focused on providing the actual number of instances.

The length of the recall period also influences an individual's tendency to use episodic versus semantic memory (Blair & Burton, 1987). For short time intervals (e.g., being asked to recall behavior over the past week), individuals are more likely to try to recall distinct episodes. For longer time periods (e.g., being asked to recall behavior over 3 months), the individual resorts to heuristics stored in semantic memory, because it often is difficult to retrieve information for individual events that occurred so long ago.

Individual difference variables also are relevant. If a person performs a behavior infrequently or only rarely, then he or she will develop a *general behavioral principle* and store it in semantic memory. The memory traces of a rarely occurring episode may be distinct, at least in comparison to behaviors that are performed frequently, where the details of one episode can blur and interfere with the details of another episode. Thus, individuals who engage in the behavior infrequently may tend to rely on episodic memory. In contrast, those who engage in the behavior regularly and frequently are more likely to have stored a *behavioral generalization* rule in semantic memory. Given the difficulty in recalling individual episodes of the behavior, these individuals might naturally turn to semantic memory when providing recall judgments.

Factors Influencing Self-Report Accuracy

Most studies on the accuracy of behavioral reports in adults have tended to study overall accuracy rates per se rather than factors that influence those accuracy rates. Accuracy rates can differ as a function of a complex interaction between the type and content of the target behavior, the setting in which recall takes place, the circumstances under which the behavior was performed, and individual difference variables. As examples, some studies report differences in accuracy as a function of the education levels of the respondent (e.g., Jaccard, McDonald, Wan, & Guilamo-Ramos, in press), although others do not (Jaccard, McDonald, Wan, Dittus, & Quinlan, 2002). Research suggests that the mood an individual has when the behavior is enacted as well as the mood the individual has when behavior is recalled can impact recall accuracy of that behavior (e.g., Raymark, Skowronski, Bevard, & Hamann, 2001). Attitudes also can be a factor, as people find it easier to recall behaviors that are consistent with their attitudes, which can lead to inflated estimates of attitude–behavior consistency (Ross, McFarland, Conway, & Zanna, 1983). There also is evidence that judgments of behavioral frequencies across a specified time period are influenced by recently occurring events as opposed to earlier occurring events. Thus, an individual's statement about what happened over the past 3 months may be influenced too much by what happened in the previous week or two as opposed to what happened in the initial weeks of the 3-month period. The existence of such biases was evident in a study by Jaccard and Wan (1995), who found that the behavior during the final 2 weeks of a recall period correlated .70 with the overall frequency estimate provided by individuals, whereas behavior during the first 2 weeks of the recall period correlated only .34 with the overall frequency estimate.

It is commonly believed that the shorter the time frame that one uses when requesting recall of behaviors, the more accurate recall will be. For example, asking individuals to recall their sexual activity over the past month should yield more accurate estimates than asking individuals to recall their sexual activity over the past 6 months. Although the use of very short time frames can increase accuracy (e.g., recall of sexual activity in the past day or two), this result does not generalize to time frames of all durations. For example, Jaccard et al. (2002) found that recall of sexual behavior over a 3-month interval tended to be more accurate than recall of sexual behavior over a 1-month interval. One reason for this pattern was that the use of the shorter time period encouraged highly sexually active individuals to adopt episodic recall strategies, which were subject to greater distortions than the more efficient (and accurate) rule-based judgments invoked for the longer time frames.

Research on the accuracy of recall of behavioral reports is in its infancy, and there is no adequate, comprehensive theory of behavioral recall that yields highly generalizable statements about factors that influence recall for different behaviors. As research proceeds in this important area of inquiry, greater insights into the ways people make behavior estimates will be gained as well as strategies for improving the accuracy of these estimates.

Methodological Perspectives: Improving the Accuracy of Self-Reports of Behavior

Despite the complexity of the process, there are some strategies that researchers can use that will help to increase the accuracy of behavioral self-reports. We consider three of these: (a) ensuring question comprehension, (b) use of cued recall, and (c) establishing conditions for motivated and truthful reporting.

Ensuring Comprehension of the Question.   It seems rather obvious that in order for an individual to provide an accurate answer to a question about past behavior, the individual must understand the question. Despite its obviousness, researchers often fail to conduct the necessary pilot research to ensure that the concepts and wording used in questions about behavior are properly understood. For example, in research we have conducted with young adolescents, the phrase "oral sex" was taken by some to refer to "having sex while talking." "Having sex" was interpreted by some as having vaginal sexual intercourse, whereas others adopted a more broad-based definition of the term that included touching and oral sex. The phrase "during the past year" was sometimes construed as the last calendar year and sometimes as a year from the present date (sometimes including or excluding the current month).

Cued Recall.   One strategy for improving the accuracy of behavioral recall is to provide cues that help bring events to memory. Different cues have varying impact in this regard. The date of an event usually has been found to be a poor retrieval cue as compared to cues about what happened, where it happened, and who was involved (Wagenaar, 1988). Some researchers have stressed the importance of matching cues in the recall questions to contextual cues that were present when the individual encoded the event in question (Smyth, Morris, Levy, & Ellis, 1987). This principle suggests that accuracy of recall might be improved by conducting careful studies of the contexts surrounding the performance of a behavior and then incorporating cues about these contexts into the structuring of the recall questions.

Recall also tends to improve when respondents have sufficient time to search memory (a problem for survey research in which the time per question is routinely short). Also, the direction of search may be relevant. Because recent experiences are richer in detail and these then serve as retrieval cues for earlier events, Loftus and Fathi (1985) suggested that better recall may result when respondents begin with the most recent occurrence of a behavior and then count backward to the reference point. Nonetheless, most individuals tend to prefer the strategy of forward recall starting with the beginning of the reference period (Loftus & Fathi, 1985). Psychological landmarks also can be used to establish more firmly reference periods for recall (e.g., Loftus & Marburger, 1983). In longitudinal studies, for example, Neter and Waksberg (1964) have suggested that previous interviews can be used as landmarks to facilitate the proper frame of reference.

Truthful Responding.   It is crucial that individuals respond honestly when providing self-reports of their behavior. Of particular concern is socially desirable responding in which the individual purposely misrepresents his or her behavior in order to create a favorable impression. There are several practices that a researcher can do to minimize socially desirable responding. First, one can assure individuals of the confidentiality of their responses and explain how the coding system ultimately guarantees anonymity. Second, one can stress the importance of honest answers for the scientific integrity of the project. Third, one can structure the data collection so that the respondent never has to reveal potentially socially undesirable behaviors in a face-to-face situation. Research using computer-assisted interviewing that reads questions aloud via earphones and where the respondent then records answers directly on a laptop suggests that this mode of assessment may encourage truthful answers (Schroder, Carey, & Vanable, 2003). Fourth, when individuals complete informed consent forms prior to participation, they can be asked to sign a statement that the responses they will be providing in the surveys will be truthful, to the best of their knowledge. This technique engenders a formal, public commitment to honest responding that some survey researchers have found to be effective in reducing socially desirable responses. Finally, researchers can include measures assessing general social desirability tendencies and then examine the relationship of this variable to the various self-reports. Where appropriate, statistical adjustments in parameter estimates can be pursued by using the measure of social desirable response tendencies as a covariate. Classic measures of social desirability response tendency, such as the Marlow-Crowne scale, have been found to be problematic and more psychometrically viable measures are available (e.g., Paulhus, 1984, 1991).

Methodological Perspectives: Metrics

Measures of behaviors can have different metrics. For example, a behavioral count might be assessed by asking an individual to report a direct numerical frequency. In this case, the metric consists of zero and any positive whole number that is greater than zero. Alternatively, the count might be assessed on a rating scale in which the individual rates how frequently he or she engages in a behavior using a set of ordered, labeled categories. One could, for example, ask participants to rate the number of days they have consumed alcohol in the last month on a scale of *none* to *many*, or how often one has had more than five drinks in one sitting on scale from *not at all* to *frequently*. The ordered categories are assigned numbers from 1 to k, where k is the number of categories, and these numbers represent the scale metric. Behavioral counts and frequency-based rating scales have both desirable and undesirable features. Consideration of these features may help researchers determine which type of measure to use for a particular research question.

Frequency-based rating scales require not only that an individual make a cognitive judgment about a behavioral count, but also that the individual translate that count onto a mark on a category of the rating scale. The latter task can be difficult. For instance, a smoker who smokes a half a pack of cigarettes a day may know very well how many he or she smokes yet have trouble reporting whether this amount constitutes *light, moderate* or, *heavy* smoking because the meaning of these terms is unclear and may vary across respondents.

Reported counts, if they are accurate, are more precise than rating scales in the sense that they permit a greater number of discriminations. However, when the counts can be large, many individuals round the reported number to the nearest 5 or 10 (Schroder, Carey, & Vanable, 2003). Thus, the precision is somewhat misleading at higher numbers and the distributions of counts can be unusual because of some individuals choosing to round to the nearest 5 or 10, whereas others do not. Indeed, there is some question as to whether one should treat a respondent who reports a frequency of, say, 63 as having a different behavioral frequency than someone who reports a frequency of 65, because the disparity in scores may simply reflect a tendency to round rather than a true behavioral difference.

Because of calibration issues and accuracy issues, it should not be assumed that a self-reported count has ratio properties even though the true count (if it could be known) does. Reported counts are best treated as having interval properties at best, or, more conservatively, as having only ordinal properties. Frequency-based rating scales also may have either interval-level properties or only ordinal properties. Psychophysics strategies can determine the measurement properties of rating scales in this respect (see Anderson, 1981).

One objection to count data is that such scores fail to capture the psychological meaning of a behavior for the individual actor. For instance, a college student who regularly meets the criterion of binge drinking (five or more drinks in one sitting for men and three or more drinks in one sitting for women) may feel that his or her level of drinking is moderate, whereas a college professor who drinks the same amount may feel that his or her drinking is extreme. The identical behavior will thus have different emotional and motivational relevance for these two individuals, and count data will fail to capture this dimension (see also, Windschitl & Wells, 1996). To assess the meaning of a behavior, many have suggested that scales that tap into comparative evaluations (e.g., drinking more or less than comparable others) are the most appropriate (e.g., Klein, 1997; Klein & Weinstein, 1997). To the extent that people think spontaneously in comparative terms, as many comparison theorists argue, they may find it easier to report behavioral frequencies using comparative rating scales as opposed to behavioral counts.

If a researcher's interest is in characterizing the general behavior patterns of a given population, then count-based approaches probably are best. One might, for instance, want to show that an intervention is effective in reducing the number of days a week a student binge drinks and this dimension is best documented using count measures (assuming such measures are reasonable, valid, and reliable). Similarly, if one is interested in assessing the HIV infection risk of a particular population, one would want to obtain information on the number of instances of unprotected sex, the number of sexual partners, the number of times intravenous needles were shared, and so on.

If interest instead is in constructing theories that focus on individual's interpretations and representations of behavioral frequencies, then frequency-based rating scales probably are best. A woman who feels she has been drinking a lot in recent months and a man who feels that his sexual risk taking has been more frequent than others might be more likely to change behavior, irrespective of the way in which these perceptions correspond to the responses they might make using a raw behavioral count.

Researchers who use frequency-based rating scales need to assess critically the types of evaluative anchors and adverbs that are easiest for participants to use and that best capture the psychological meaning of the target behavior. Interesting research by Schwarz, Strack, Müller, and Chassein (1988) has shown, for example, that response options can influence the meaning of terms used in a question. These researchers found that participants reported different frequencies for *feeling annoyed*, depending on whether they were provided with a rating scale that ranged from *less than once a year* to *more frequently than 3 months* as compared with a rating scale that ranged from *less than 2 times a week* to *several times a day*. The first scale, by virtue of its longer time period, caused participants to interpret the question as referring to major annoyances and, hence, reported mostly infrequent occurrences of annoyance. The second scale caused participants to interpret the question as referring to minor annoyances, and so they mostly reported frequent tendencies to be annoyed. Such effects can even occur with behaviors that seem to have an unambiguous meaning, such as television watching. Schwarz, Hippler, Deutsch, & Strack (1985) found that the number of people reporting that they watched television for more than 2.5 hours was higher if they used a scale that ranged from *up to 2.5 hours* to *more than 4.5 hours*, as opposed to a scale that ranged from *up to ¹/₂ hour* to *more than 2.5 hours*. With the first, high-frequency scale, participants appeared to include in their estimates incidental acts of television watching, such as when they tune in and out while working on a paper. With the second, low-frequency scale, participants appeared only to count time spent actively watching specific television shows. These examples highlight the importance of considering both the formal definitions of behaviors that are given to participants and the informal definitions that are implied by the nature and structure of the question.

Observer Reports

In addition to self-reports of behavior, attitude researchers often are interested in observer reports of behavior. Observer reports of behavior have been analyzed from two vantage points. First, there are methodological perspectives in which the focus is on strategies for training observers to make accurate behavioral characterizations while observing participants in an empirical study. Second, there are studies of how individuals who are themselves actors in a real world setting perceive the behavioral activities of others. For example, parents of adolescents may report to a researcher judgment about whether their adolescent has consumed alcohol in the past 30 days.

There are extensive and excellent discussions of the former perspective and interested readers are referred to the classic treatments by Wiggins (1973; see chapters 7 and 8) and Weick (1968) as well as the more recent treatment by Hoyt (2000). In terms of the perceptions of lay people as observers, social-psychological models tend to emphasize the role of (a) observer attentiveness (or lack of attention) to cues that imply performance or nonperformance of the behavior in question, (b) the use of stereotypes about the kinds of people who do or do not perform the behavior in question, and (c) the affective environment surrounding the observer–actor relationship (Fiske & Taylor, 1991; Jussim, 1990, 1991, 1993). There is a large body of research on eyewitness accounts of criminal activity that also has addressed the ability of individuals to recall or accurately describe the behavior of other individuals (Kassin, Tubb, Hosch, & Memon, 2001; Wells et al., 1998). These analyses emphasize the importance of question formats, characteristics of the actor, characteristics of the observer, characteristics of the behavior, characteristics of the setting in which the action takes place, and the number and nature of cues that facilitate recall or that lead recall astray. The research in this area suggests that the correlation between accuracy of an eyewitness report and the observer's reported confidence in the accuracy of the report varies considerably and often is rather low (Kassin, Rigby, & Castillo, 1991; but see also McCullogh, 2002).

DATA-ANALYTIC PERSPECTIVES
ON BEHAVIORAL CRITERIA

As noted, behavioral outcomes can be dichotomous, count-like, or continuous. The nature of outcomes has implications for the kinds of statistical tools that are brought to bear in their analysis. It is beyond the scope of this chapter to consider the many issues that must be taken

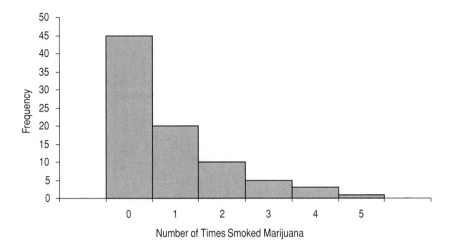

FIG 4.5. Frequency histogram of the number of times adolescents smoked marijuana.

into account when choosing an appropriate analytic method. However, some general guidelines are provided because of the tendency for attitude researchers to use controversial approaches when predicting certain kinds of behavioral criteria.

When the behavioral outcome is dichotomous, many researchers score the outcome variable with 1s and 0s and then conduct traditional multiple regression analysis, predicting the outcome from a set of continuous or dummy coded predictors. For example, if an adolescent has smoked marijuana, he or she may receive a score of 1, otherwise a score of 0 is given. The mean of a dichotomous variable scored with 1s and 0s reflects the proportion of individuals with a score of 1. Stated another way, the mean of such a variable estimates the probability of observing a score of 1, or, in our example, the probability of having smoked marijuana.

The traditional regression analysis of this dichotomous behavioral measure invokes what is often termed a *linear probability model*, because it presumes that probability of performing the behavior in question is a linear function of the predictors. However, applying traditional ordinary least squares (OLS) regression strategies in the context of the linear probability model is problematic. The major problem is that inferential tests in traditional regression analyses assume residuals that are normally distributed and whose variances are homogeneous at any given fixed set of scores of the predictors. Both assumptions are false when dichotomous outcome variables are analyzed. Significance tests are biased, accordingly, and often lead to inappropriate conclusions. The linear probability model can be applied to data, but estimation methods other than traditional OLS must be used in order for the standard errors to be correct (Wilcox, 1997).

An alternative approach for dichotomous outcomes is to use logistic regression. As Long (1997) detailed, this approach yields significance tests that can accommodate a dichotomous behavioral outcome, but it assumes that the probability of the behavior in question is a nonlinear function of the predictors. A crucial issue in the choice of an analytic model is assuring that the relationship between the predictors and the outcome is correctly specified. Although a logistic regression will often be the model of choice for dichotomous behavioral outcomes, if the logistic function fails to capture the true relationship between the predictors and the criterion, then alternative strategies should be pursued instead.

When the behavioral outcome is a count, most attitude theorists again apply traditional multiple regression analysis. This practice is not necessarily problematic as long as the residuals are approximately normally distributed and as long as they exhibit homogeneity of variance, as just described. Yet count data only rarely satisfy these assumptions. A more typical distribution, especially for risk behaviors, appears in Fig. 4.4. In this distribution, a large number of individuals have a count of zero and decreasingly fewer individuals having successively higher scores. In such cases, a better method for analyzing data is one that can accommodate such distributions and that respects the discrete quality of the behavioral outcome. One class of regression models that does so is called Poisson regression and a related class of models is called negative binomial regression. Long (1997) gave a description of these models and their zero-inflated variants.[3]

When the behavioral outcome is continuous, traditional OLS regression is appropriate as long as the fundamental assumptions of the approach are approximately met. Wilcox (1997, 2003) has argued that the assumptions are rarely met and that robust regression analytic methods are preferable. He also made a compelling case for robust methods and provided computer programs that easily implement the analyses.[4]

In sum, when the behavioral outcome is dichotomous, logistic regression typically is applicable; when the behavioral outcome is a count, Poison regression or negative binomial regression typically is applicable; and, when the behavioral outcome is continuous, traditional OLS regression or a robust variant of it typically is applicable.

THE ORIGINS AND BASES OF BEHAVIOR: THE BIGGER PICTURE

Behavior derives from and is influenced by a wide range of factors. Attitude theorists tend to emphasize such constructs as beliefs, goals, attitude, affect, intentions, habits, personality, and automaticity when building models of behavior. By contrast, many social scientists (and some attitude theorists) rely on more distal constructs to explain behavior. These include such factors as genetic influences, biological influences, media influences, family influences, social influences, school influences, gender influences, religious influences, cultural influences, economic influences, policy influences, and developmental influences, to name only a few. It would be presumptuous of us to suggest a comprehensive framework of the origins of behavior given the diverse kinds of explanatory variables and behavioral criteria that have been studied by attitude researchers in particular and social scientists more generally. Instead, we briefly characterize a general system of thought that dominates much of social psychology, namely, causal analysis. We discuss broad categories of variables relative to causal frameworks that are often invoked to explain behavior. We conclude by briefly mentioning other systems of thought that can be applied to the analysis of the origins of behavior but that have received lesser attention by attitude researchers.

Causal Frameworks

Theories of behavior in the attitude area have been heavily influenced by causal analysis and the general system of structural equation modeling. At the simplest level, there are six types of relationships that can occur within a causal model, as illustrated in Fig. 4.6. A *direct* causal relationship is one in which a variable, X, is a direct cause of another variable, Y. It is the immediate determinant of Y within the theoretical system. An *indirect* causal relationship is one in which X exerts a causal impact on Y, but only through its impact on a third variable, Z. A *spurious* relationship is one in which X and Y are related, but only because of a common cause, Z. There is no formal causal link between X and Y. A *bi-directional* or *reciprocal* causal relationship is one in which X has a causal influence on Y, which, in turn, has a causal impact on X. An *unanalyzed* relationship is one in which X and Y are related, but the source

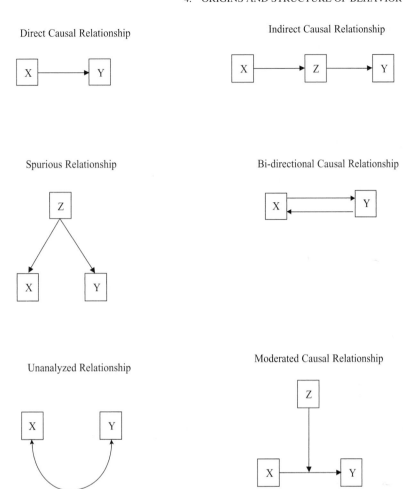

FIG 4.6. Examples of causal relationships.

of the relationship is unspecified. Finally, a *moderated* causal relationship is one in which the relationship between X and Y is moderated by a third variable, Z. In other words, the nature of the relationship between X and Y varies, depending on the value of Z.

All causal models incorporate one or more of these types of relationships. An example of a model that includes most of them is presented in Fig. 4.7 and is based on the theory of

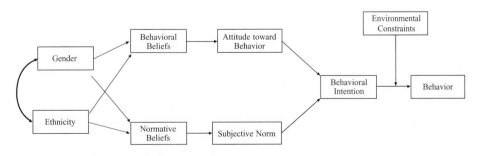

FIG 4.7. A model illustrating multiple causal relationships.

reasoned action (Ajzen & Fishbein, 1981). According to this model, a person's behavior is a function of the individual's intention to perform the behavior; that is, people are assumed to do what they intend to do (hence, behavioral intentions are a direct cause of behavior). However, the relationship between behavioral intention and behavior is moderated by environmental constraints. Even if someone intends to perform a behavior, if the environment is structured such that it is impossible to do so, the behavior will not occur. A person's behavioral intention, in turn, has two immediate determinants: (a) how favorable or unfavorable he or she personally feels about performing the behavior (the attitude toward performing the behavior), and (b) a global perception of the perceived normative pressure from important others to engage in the behavior (the subjective norm). Both of these represent direct causes with respect to behavioral intention (because they influence intentions directly) and indirect causes of behavior (because they influence behavior through their influence on behavioral intentions). Behavioral beliefs are a direct cause of the attitude toward performing the behavior and normative beliefs are a direct cause of the subjective norm. Both of these types of beliefs (behavioral and normative) are influenced by more distal variables, in this case, ethnicity and gender. The fact that gender influences both behavioral beliefs and normative beliefs suggests that these latter two variables are correlated (because they share a common cause). However, the correlation is spurious in the sense that no causal influence between behavioral beliefs and normative beliefs is assumed. The model assumes that gender and ethnicity are related, but the relationship between these variables is unanalyzed.

Attitude theorists who rely on causal models for describing the bases of behavior think in terms of the these types of relationships. The models may include a time dimension on which variables at one point in time are thought to influence variables at a later point in time. The construct of behavior can take any of the roles that Fig. 4.6 describes. It can be an outcome variable that is impacted by other variables. It can be a mediating variable that mediates the impact of one variable on another (as when adolescent attitudes toward school influence performance in school which, in turn, influences avoidance of adolescent problem behaviors). It can be a moderating variable that moderates the impact of one variable on another (as when a person's intention to vote for a candidate translates into actual voting behavior only when that person is given a ride to the voting station by another individual). It can be the source of spuriousness between two variables if it is a common cause of them. It can bear a reciprocal relationship with a variable (such as when attitudes lead someone to use drugs but the use of drugs alters that person's attitude toward using drugs).

Although causal models of the form of Fig. 4.7 often are associated with correlational or observational data, they apply with equal vigor to experimental data. Thinking about causal relationships between variables is not tied to a mode of data collection. Rather, it is a way of thinking about theoretical mechanisms. Most experiments can be represented by path diagrams just as field studies can. For example, a researcher might experimentally manipulate the expertise of the source of a persuasive message by attributing it to a college professor in one condition and a college student in the other condition. The researcher crosses this factor with a manipulation of topic involvement. The outcome variable is attitude change. Figure 4.8 presents the path diagram for this experiment. The hypothesis is that expertise will have an effect on attitude change but that the effects of expertise are qualified by topic involvement, with the effects of expertise being lower when individuals have high-topic involvement than when they have low involvement. For a greater discussion of moderator-like hypotheses in experimental designs, see Jaccard (1998).

The types of causal relationships in a theoretical system always are relative to that system. What is a direct causal relationship in one's person theory might be an indirect causal relationship in another person's theory. For example, in one theoretical system, gender might be represented as a direct cause of attitudes toward choosing a career in the sciences. In another

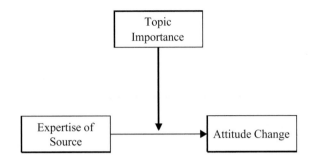

FIG 4.8. Path diagram of a factorial design with an interaction effect.

theoretical system, gender might be thought to influence the kinds of encouragement that teachers and parents give to children to choose a career in the sciences and that this differential encouragement, in turn, influences attitudes toward choosing a career in the sciences. In the second case, the theorist has turned a direct cause into an indirect cause by specifying the mechanism by which the *independent variable* (gender) influences the *dependent variable* (attitudes toward choosing a career in science). One always has the option of making a direct relationship into an indirect one by specifying a more immediate determinant (or mechanism) through which the influencing variable operates. However, at some point, the theorist chooses not to pursue increasingly specific levels of explanation and instead closes the theoretical system to additional variables.

Although exceptions exist, there is a tendency for attitude theorists to explain behavior by focusing on micro-level variables such as beliefs, attitudes, and intentions and to ignore more macro-level variables such as gender, ethnicity, and social class. This focus is understandable given the desires to keep one's theory manageable and to explore a limited number of phe-nomena in depth. However, there also is something to be said for broadening one's focus and pursuing integrative theories that include both macro-level variables as well as micro-level variables. In so doing, the micro-level mediators can be used to provide insights into why the macro-level variables influence behavior by elucidating the underlying mechanisms. At the same time, the macro-level variables can provide a richer understanding of the bases and origins of the micro-level variables and the boundary conditions under which the micro-level variables may impact behavior.

We now briefly characterize broad classes of variables that have been used in attitude research to explain why people do what they do and that can be invoked in one form or another to explain the bases of a behavior. We recognize that there are many different ways of classifying such variables and that we necessarily must omit some classes of variables that are near and dear to some theorists. Our intent merely is to make salient the diverse types of variables impinging on behavior that are reflected in the kinds of constructs that attitude researchers have explored in their theories and research.

Biological and Physiological Influences

Many theorists think of the most immediate determinants of behavior as the different neuro-logical pathways by which the brain is stimulated as organisms interact with their physical and psychological environments. There is a growing body of literature in social neuroscience that relates many attitudinal phenomena to brain functioning and that has the potential for trac-ing the neurological mechanisms by which such constructs influence behavior (Bernston & Cacioppo, 2003; Cacioppo et al., 2003). At the same time, biological variables also have taken the role of more distal determinants of attitudes, such as when the hormonal changes that an adolescent experiences as he or she approaches sexual maturity influences the kinds of moods and emotions that an adolescent experiences (Bancroft & Reinisch, 1990). Olson, Vernon, Harris, and Jang (2001) report data consistent with the idea that certain social attitudes have a genetic base, suggesting that genetic mechanisms can serve as distal determinants of attitudes and behavior. Research integrating biological and neurological variables into more traditional theoretical systems linking behavior and attitudes represents an interesting and important area of activity in behavioral analysis.

Knowledge, Beliefs, Values, Cognitions, Goals, Attitudes, Intentions

Theories of the impact of constructs like knowledge, beliefs, attitudes, values, goals, and intentions on behavior abound in the attitude literature and, indeed, many chapters in the present volume are directly concerned with how such variables relate to behavior. We refer the reader to these chapters to gain a sense of the range of theories that have been invoked. Most of these theories are abstract in character in the sense that they are thought to reflect general processes that apply across multiple content areas and domains of application. By contrast, applied researchers often are interested in content-bound constructs to understand and predict behavior, such as religious beliefs to understand religious behavior, educational aspirations to predict school performance, and sexual attitudes to predict sexual risk behavior.

Personality and Aptitudes

Social scientists have relied on hundreds of personality variables in the quest to describe the bases of a behavior. For example, the Web site http://ipip.ori.org provides measures for over 170 personality concepts that have been studied empirically as determinants of behavior of one form or another. There have been attempts to describe higher order personality dimensions from which many of these personality constructs might emanate. For example, Costa and McCrae (1992) used factor-analytic approaches to isolate what they call *the big five* or five core dimensions of personality: extraversion, agreeableness, conscientiousness, emotional stability, and intellect/imagination. Research that pursues the identification of such general factors invariably is subject to controversy about the number of factors thought to underlie personality, the labeling of those factors, and the obscuring of unique variance associated with individual personality traits (e.g., Goldberg, 1999; Matthews & Oddy, 1993; McKenzie, 1998). Personality variables are used in different theoretical systems as mediators, moderators, causes of spuriousness, and direct or reciprocal influences when linked to behavior. Ajzen (1988) has presented a thoughtful analysis of links between research on attitudes and research on personality.

In addition to personality, psychologists interested in individual differences have focused on a wide range of aptitudes as the bases of behavior. These include such constructs as intelligence, critical thinking, scholastic aptitudes, creativity, problem-solving skills, and spatial and perceptual skills, to name just a few.

Emotions and Affect

Emotions and other affect-oriented concepts have been linked to behavior in numerous studies and constitute an important area of inquiry in attitude research. The chapter by Schimmack and Crites in this volume reviews many emotion- and affect-related constructs and presents a taxonomy of affective experiences based on the type of experience (emotions, moods, affective sensation), the qualities of the experience (distinct emotions, pleasure, displeasure), and the aspects of the experience (frequency, intensity, duration). The chapter in this volume by Clore and Schnall also provides useful perspectives on affect and emotions. Ekman and Davidson (1994) present an integrative analysis of fundamental questions about the nature of emotions from diverse theoretical perspectives. Emotion and affective concepts have been used in causal models as mediators, moderators, and as having direct and reciprocal effects on behavior.

Social Influences

Attitude researchers have given considerable attention to social influences on behavior. Much of this work has focused on the social bases of beliefs and attitudes, which, in turn, are thought to impact behavior. This work has included such research as the two-step flow of communication (McGuire, 1985), the effects of social group membership on attitudes (e.g., Martin, Hewstone, & Martin, 2003), and how the beliefs and attitudes of people shift as a function of the social context in which they find themselves (e.g., Bem, 1970; Gibbons, Lane, Gerrard, Pomery, & Lautrup, 2002; see Prislin & Wood, this volume, for a review).

Normative influences on behavior have been used by attitude theorists to explain attitude–behavior discrepancies. The idea is that to the extent that a behavior is primarily determined by normative considerations, then attitudes may have little predictive utility for that behavior (Ajzen & Fishbein, 1981). Two types of social norms have received research attention, *injunctive norms* and *descriptive norms* (Cialdini, 2003). Injunctive norms refer to perceptions of whether important others approve or disapprove of the individual performing the behavior. Descriptive norms refer to perceptions of base rates, such as how many of one's peers are performing the behavior (Borsari & Carey, 2003). A useful theory for understanding the impact of base rates on behavior is deviance regulation theory (Blanton & Christie, 2003). Social influences are not restricted to peer groups. Behavior is influenced by a wide range of others, including parents, siblings, other relatives, coworkers, neighbors, and community leaders, to name a few.

Automatic, Implicit, and Unconscious Factors

There has been a great deal of recent research on automaticity, namely, the nonconscious effects on behavior of features of the environment (Bargh & Chartrand, 1999). Bargh and Chartrand (1999) argue for a two-stage process of behavioral influence in which features of the environment cause certain perceptions to be activated outside of conscious awareness and then these perceptions create behavioral tendencies to act in ways that are consistent with those perceptions. Bargh and Chartrand review a number of studies on diverse phenomena that are consistent with this viewpoint. Implicit attitudes also are receiving a great deal of attention as possible determinants of behavior (see Bassili & Brown, this volume). Implicit attitudes are typically measured using response latencies and are thought to represent attitudinal preferences that are not directly accessible in declarative memory. Theoretical networks that stress such attitudes are described in Greenwald and Banaji (1995) and Fazio, Jackson, Dunton and Williams (1995). Although most studies linking implicit attitudes and automatic processing to behavior have been limited in that the behavioral criteria are typically somewhat mundane, it seems evident that such processes are operative for many behaviors of interest to psychologists.

Demographic Variables

Demographic variables typically include such constructs as gender, race, ethnicity, age, education, income, social class, and religion. There are large empirical literatures on demographic correlates of behavior (e.g., Adler & Snibbe, 2003; the special section of American Psychologist, 2003; Eagly, Johannesen-Schmidt, & van Engen, 2003). Attitude theorists have tended to treat demographic variables as distal constructs whose effects on behavior are mediated by cognitions, attitudes, personality, and other more immediate behavioral determinants. Theorists also have created psychological constructs of group identification that are closely tied to demographic constructs, such as ethnic identity, gender identity, religious identity, and age-group identity, all of which are assumed to impact behavior in one way or another.

Environmental Contexts

It is widely recognized that contextual factors have an important role in influencing the behavior of individuals. School contexts, work contexts, family contexts, neighborhood contexts, and community contexts all have been shown to be relevant to behavioral prediction (e.g., Duncan, Duncan, Okut, Strycker, & Small, 2003; Guialamo-Ramos, Turrisi, Jaccard, Wood, & Gonzales, 2004; Hoffmann, 2003). The dimensions and variables used to describe contexts are diverse, and in some ways, are as plentiful as variables used to describe individual-level characteristics. For example, it is possible to characterize the ethnicity of a given individual, the ethnic composition of a school that individuals attend, the ethnic composition of the neighborhood in which schools are located, the ethnic composition of the city in which neighborhoods are located, and the ethnic composition of the state within which cities are located. One then can examine how these multiple levels of context characterized in terms of ethnicity influence the behavior of individuals. As another example, one can measure a person's attitude toward smoking cigarettes, the mean attitude toward smoking cigarettes of students in the school that a given student attends, the mean attitude toward smoking cigarettes of people in the neighborhood where the schools are located, the mean attitude toward smoking cigarettes of people in the city where the neighborhoods are located, the mean attitude toward smoking of people in the state where the cities are located. One can then examine how these multiple levels of context influence the behavior of individuals. Such contextual analyses require that an adequate number of higher level units of analysis be included in the study (e.g., schools, neighborhoods). For example, to study how variations in school ethnicity influence behavior, one must include multiple schools in the analysis such that ethnic composition varies across the schools. Major advances in statistical methods for analyzing multilevel data have been made in recent years and can be gainfully used by attitude theorists trying to explain behavior (e.g., Bryk & Raudenbush, 2002; Duncan et al., 2003).

Child psychologists also have emphasized the importance of environmental contexts and have described frameworks for conceptualizing environmental influences. For example, Bronfenbrenner's (1986) ecological model described four levels of the environment—microsystems, mesosystems, exosystems, and macrosystems. The microsystem is the immediate behavioral setting; the mesosytem is the connections or relations between the multiple microsystems an individual acts within; the exosystem is the settings that, though not directly encountered by the actor, indirectly affect the actor (e.g., the behavior of a child is indirectly affected by the work environment of a parent because that work environment may affect the way the parent acts toward the child when the parent comes home after work); and the macrosystem refers to consistencies and relationships across all systems within a society or culture. Organizational psychologists emphasize the importance of organizational culture and climate as environmental contexts that influence behavior (Glisson, 2002). Environmental and contextual variables also can be measured from the perspective of the individuals whose behaviors are being explained. Thus, rather than characterizing the actual family environment within which an individual resides, the focus might be on measuring how an individual *perceives* the family environment on selected dimensions. For a useful set of articles on environmental influences and the different forms they take, see the special issue in the *American Journal of Community Psychology* (1996).

Media Influences

There are large research literatures on the effects of the mass media on behavior (e.g., Bushman & Anderson, 2001; Crano & Burgoon, 2002; Fishbein, Jamieson, Zimmer, vonHaeften, & Robin, 2002; McGuire, 1985). Media sources include television, movies, videos, radio, magazines, books, newspapers, and other audio, visual, and print media used to educate or entertain the public. It is increasingly clear that the mass media has a nontrivial impact on a wide array of attitudes and behavior of the public. Important media-related variables for behavioral analysis include how often someone is exposed to a message, the content of the message, the timing of message exposure, the source of the message, the way in which the message is conveyed, and the characteristics of the person processing the message. Not only has research examined how the media influences the behavior of individuals, but research also has explored how interventionists and policymakers can use the media to influence the behavior of individuals. For example, there is a great deal of research on the use of public service announcements (PSAs) and their relative effectiveness in changing unhealthy behaviors of the public (Crano & Burgoon, 2002). Also of recent interest has been direct-to-consumer advertising of prescription drugs and how it affects physician prescribing practices (Paul, Handlin, & Stanton, 2002).

Developmental Perspectives

Many behaviors are influenced heavily by the way we are socialized by our parents and other authority figures. From birth until death, individuals mature and experience a host of significant events as they pass from one life stage to another. Formal distinctions often are made between different stages of development, with noteworthy differences in behavior distinguishing those in different periods of transition. For example, within the period known as adolescence, developmentalists distinguish between early adolescence, middle adolescence, and late adolescence. There are documented differences between these groups in terms of physical development, cognitive development, emotional development, social development, and moral development. These differences have important influences on behavior. More generally, the variables that influence behavior and/or the dynamics by which variables manifest their influence on behavior can vary from one point in time to another point in time, so time-based variables are important facets of causal-based theories of behavior.

The Multivariate Bases of Behavior

This brief characterization of categories of behavioral influences makes evident that the bases of behavior can be extremely complex. The categories are not exhaustive and others could be enumerated (e.g., categories for self-concept, categories for self-regulation processes). Variables within and across categories can be arrayed into a dizzying number of mediated, moderated, spurious, direct, and reciprocal causal relationships. As we think about behavior and the somewhat narrow theories of it that we build as social scientists, it sometimes is instructive (and sobering) to step back and consider the broader context of behavioral influences. For instance, consider the case of binge drinking in high school students. When thinking about the bases and origins of this behavior, all of the categories of variables previously discussed have been suggested in the empirical literature to be of relevance. For example, there is evidence for a genetic base to alcohol use. In addition, certain levels of hormones in adolescence have been found to be associated with binge drinking tendencies. Drinking behavior has been shown to be related to knowledge about alcohol, beliefs and expectancies about alcohol, and a wide range of values, goals, attitudes, and intentions with respect to alcohol use. Personality variables have been implicated in binge drinking, including such traits as sensation sinking, risk taking, and sociability. Both intelligence as measured by IQ tests and aspects of academic performance have been linked to alcohol use in high school youth. Mood and affect have been shown to predict binge drinking, and there are a large number of studies that suggest the importance of social influences as well. In the alcohol literature, both injunctive and descriptive norms have been predictive of binge drinking, as have a variety of other social relationships (e.g., relationships with one's parents). There are notable demographic correlates of binge drinking. For example, males are more likely to binge drink than females and European Americans and Latinos are more likely to binge drink than African Americans and Asian Americans. It is widely recognized that environmental contexts influence binge drinking, such as school climate and the availability of alcohol in the broader community in which adolescents reside. Advertising of beer on television has been linked to increased beer consumption in youth. Developmentally, adolescents are more likely to binge drink as they progress through high school. Binge drinking in high school is predictive of binge drinking in college. Given such complexity and the myriad of ways in which the different categories of variables can influence binge drinking, isolating one or two variables that account for 2% to 3% of the variance in binge drinking is an impressive feat. Many social scientists think of such effects as being trivial in magnitude, but when one appreciates the complexity of the phenomenon, effect sizes of 2% to 3% explained variance are rather impressive. The multitude of factors influencing behavior also helps us to appreciate the difficulty and challenges of designing effective social interventions to bring about meaningful and sustained behavior change.

Our analysis has considered just one vantage point for thinking about the bases of behavior, namely, that of causal models and the variables that compose them. However, there are different systems of thought that emphasize alternative ways of thinking about the bases of behavior. For example, evolutionary perspectives emphasize processes of variation, selection, and retention when thinking about the bases of behavior (Colarelli, 1998). In evolutionary analyses, individuals are thought to adapt to the world in such ways that certain behaviors are selected and retained. The emphasis is on identifying the functions of behavior, so that one can understand why a given behavior has evolved. Given that evolutionary processes occur over time, evolutionary perspectives emphasize the historical contexts of behavior (Campbell, 1965). As another example, neural network models attempt to explain behavior through analogies to mechanisms by which neural systems operate in the human brain (Abdi, Valentin, & Edelman, 1999). Variables (called *units*) are linked to behavior and to each other through a set of weighted connections. The units are organized in layers, called input layers, hidden layers (also called intermediate layers), and output layers. Intermediate layers are analogous roughly to mediating variables in causal models. A given unit (variable) is activated vis-à-vis interaction with the environment and as a result of the activation, it sends an impulse to one or more other units for further processing. The process of activation of units continues until the last layer is reached (behavior). Connection weights between units are dynamic and can change as individuals engage in learning. Impulses sent from one unit to another can be either excitatory or inhibitory in character (thereby increasing the likelihood or decreasing the likelihood of behavior). Stepping outside of traditional causal thinking and drawing on alternative systems of thought leads one to different ways of thinking about the bases of behavior.

CONCLUDING COMMENTS

We began this chapter with a quotation from Stanley Milgram's classic book *Obedience and Authority*: "Only in action can you fully realize the forces operative in social behavior." The present chapter illustrates that even a construct as seemingly simple as an action has layers of complexity that often are unappreciated. The meaning and connotations of an action can vary as a function of the time and context in which it is performed as well as the object to which it is directed. Actions can be dichotomous, continuous, or discrete and can be represented as either single-act or multiple-act predictors or criteria, either at one point in time or over extended periods of time. Actions also can be characterized differently depending on the person who is observing and recording the action, be it the individual actor or a trained scientist, and actions can have varied determinants that often are not apparent from these observations. It is only when behavioral observations are organized under a meaningful theoretical, methodological, and analytic framework can one begin to "realize the forces operative in social behavior."

ENDNOTES

[1]One strategy for adapting the theory of reasoned action for a count-like variable is to focus on one number from among the count that is of particular theoretical or applied significance. For example, when predicting condom use, Reinecke, Schmidt & Ajzen (1996) measured the attitude and subjective norm about "using condoms every time you have sexual intercourse." This strategy will be viable for some behaviors but not others. Another approach is to group the counts into a smaller number of categories and then measure the attitude toward performing each category. For example, one might measure an adolescent's attitude toward not engaging in sex at all in the next month, the attitude toward engaging in sex a few times (defined as once or twice) in the next month, the attitude toward engaging in sex a moderate amount of time in the next month (defined as three to six times), an attitude toward engaging in sex frequently in the next month (defined as seven to ten times), and an attitude toward engaging in sex a great deal during the next month (defined as more than ten times). One would then predict behavior from each of these five attitudes, perhaps in accord with an optimizing rule from decision theory (see Jaccard, 1981; Jaccard & Becker, 1985). This approach requires that the grouping of instances (i.e., the defining of behavioral categories) be theoretically guided and meaningful to the respondent.

[2]It is important to note, however, that self-perception processes also can operate in ways that reduce behavioral consistency. When strong situational factors elicit a behavior regardless of attitudes or intent, individuals may infer that the behaviors were situationally driven and that behaviors are not consistent with their attitudes (Cioffi, 1995; Lepper, Greene, & Nisbett, 1973).

[3]Sometimes count-like variables are operationalized using rating scales rather than the actual count itself. In these cases, ordinal regression models often are the most viable methods for analysis (see Long, 1997). When count data are subject to rounding bias when reported by respondents (Schroder, Carey, & Vanable, 2003), adjustments need to be made to effectively apply the Poisson and negative binomial models.

[4]For a computer program that seamlessly interfaces the Wilcox programs with SPSS for Windows, see the Web site www.zumastat.com

REFERENCES

Aarts, H., & Dijksterhuis, A. (2000). Habits as knowledge structures: Automaticity in goal-directed behavior. *Journal of Personality and Social Psychology, 78*, 53–63.

Abdi, H., Valentin, D., & Edelman, B. (1999). *Neural networks.* Thousand Oaks, CA: Sage.

Adler, N., & Snibbe, A. C. (2003). The role of psychosocial processes in explaining the gradient between socioeconomic status and health. *Current Directions in Psychological Science, 12*, 119–123.

Ajzen, I. (1988). *Attitudes, personality, and behavior.* Homewood, IL: Dorsey Press.

Ajzen, I. (1991). The theory of planned behavior. *Organizational Behavior and Human Decision Processes, 50*, 179–211.

Ajzen, I. (2002). Residual effects of past on later behavior: Habituation and reasoned action perspectives. *Personality and Social Psychology Review, 6*, 107–122.

Ajzen, I., & Fishbein, M. (1977). Attitude–behavior relations: A theoretical analysis and review of empirical research. *Psychological Bulletin, 84*, 888–918.

Ajzen, I., & Fishbein, M. (1981). *Understanding attitudes and predicting social behavior.* Englewood Cliffs, NJ: Prentice-Hall.

Albarracín, D., Johnson, B. T., Fishbein, M., & Muellerleile, P. A. (2001). Theories of reasoned action and planned behavior as models of condom use: A meta-analysis. *Psychological Bulletin, 127*(1), 142–161.

Albarracín, D., & Wyer, R. S., Jr. (2000). The cognitive impact of past behavior: Influence on beliefs, attitudes, and future behavioral decisions. *Journal of Personality and Social Psychology, 79*, 5–22.

Allport, G. (1935). Attitudes. In C. Murchison (Ed.), *Handbook of social psychology* (pp. 798–884). Worcester, MA: Clark University Press.

American Journal of Community Psychology. (1996). Special section on environmental influences. *American Journal of Community Psychology, 24,* 1–207.

American Psychologist. (2003). Special section on spirituality, religion and health. *American Psychologist, 58,* 24–74.

Anderson, J. R. (1990). *The adaptive character of thought.* Hillsdale, NJ: Lawrence Erlbaum Associates.

Anderson, J. R. (1996). A simple theory of complex cognition. *American Psychologist, 51,* 355–365.

Anderson, N. H. (1981). *Foundations of information integration theory.* New York: Academic Press.

Aronson, E. (1969). The theory of cognitive dissonance: A current perspective. In L. Berkowitz (Ed.), *Advances in experimental social psychology* (Vol. 4, pp. 1–34). San Diego, CA: Academic Press.

Austin, J. T., & Vancouver, J. B. (1996). Goal constructs in psychology: Structure, process, and content. *Psychological Bulletin, 120,* 338–375.

Bachorowski, J., & Newman, J. P. (1990). Impulsive motor behavior: Effects of personality and goal salience. *Journal of Personality and Social Psychology, 58,* 512–518.

Bakeman, R., & Casey, R. L. (1995). Analyzing family interaction: Taking time into account. *Journal of Family Psychology, 9,* 131–143.

Baldwin, J., M. (1901). *Dictionary of philosophy and psychology.* New York: Macmillan.

Bamberg, S., Ajzen, I., & Schmidt, P. (2003). Choices of travel mode in the theory of planned behavior: The roles of past behavior, habit and reasoned action. *Basic and Applied Social Psychology, 25,* 175–187.

Bancroft, J., & Reinisch, J. (1990). *Adolescence and puberty.* New York: Oxford University Press.

Bargh, J. A. (1989). Conditional automaticity: Varieties of automatic influence in social perception and cognition. In J. S. Uleman & J. A. Bargh (Eds.), *Unintended thought* (pp. 3–51). New York: Guilford.

Bargh, J. A., & Chartrand, T. L. (1999). The unbearable automaticity of being. *American Psychologist, 54,* 462–479.

Bargh, J. A., Chen, M., & Burrows, L. (1996). Automaticity of social behavior: Direct effects of trait construct and stereotype priming on action. *Journal of Personality and Social Psychology, 71,* 230–244.

Baum, A., Revenson, T. A., & Singer, J. E. (2001). *The handbook of health psychology.* Mahwah, NJ: Lawrence Erlbaum Associates.

Bem, D. J. (1967). Self-perception: An alternative interpretation of cognitive dissonance phenomena. *Psychological Review, 74,* 183–200.

Bem, D. J. (1970). *Beliefs, attitudes, and human affairs.* Belmont, CA: Brooks/Cole.

Bem, D. J. (1972). Self-perception theory. In L. Berkowitz (Ed.), *Advances in experimental social psychology* (Vol. 6, pp. 1–62). San Diego, CA: Academic Press.

Bernston, G. G., & Cacioppo, J. T. (2003). A contemporary perspective on multilevel analyses and social neuroscience. In F. Kessel and P. Rosenfield (Eds.), *Expanding the boundaries of health and social science: Case studies in interdisciplinary innovation* (pp. 18–40). London, Oxford University Press.

Blair, E., & Burton, S. (1987). Cognitive processes used by survey respondents to answer behavioral frequency questions. *Journal of Consumer Research, 14,* 280–288.

Blanton, H., & Christie, C. (2003). Deviance: A theory of action and identity. *Review of General Psychology, 7,* 115–149.

Bobocel, D. R., Son Hing, L. S., Davey, L. M., Stanley, D. J., & Zanna, M. P. (1998). Justice-based opposition to social policies: Is it genuine? *Journal of Personality and Social Psychology, 75*(3), 653–669.

Bobocel, D. R., Son Hing, L. S., Holmvall, C. M., & Zanna, M. P. (2002). Policies to redress social injustice: Is the concern for justice a cause both of support and of opposition? In M. Ross & D. T. Miller (Eds.), *The justice motive in everyday life* (pp. 204–225). New York: Cambridge University Press.

Bogardus, E. S. (1931). *Fundamentals of social psychology.* New York: Century.

Borsari, B., & Carey, K. B. (2003). Descriptive and injunctive norms in college drinking: A meta-analytic integration. *Journal of Studies in Alcohol, 64,* 331–341.

Bradburn, N. M., Rips, L. J., & Shevell, S. K. (1987). Answering autobiographical questions: The impact of memory and inference on surveys. *Science, 236,* 157–161.

Bronfenbrenner, U. (1986). Ecology of the family as a context for human development: Research perspectives. *Developmental Psychology, 22,* 723–742.

Bryk, A., & Raudenbush, S. (2002). *Hierarchical linear models.* Newbury Park, CA: Sage.

Bushman, B. J., & Anderson, C. (2001). Media violence and the American public: Scientific facts versus media misinformation. *American Psychologist, 56,* 477–489.

Cacioppo, J. T., Berntson, G. G., Lorig, T. S., Norris, C. J., Rickett, E., & Nusbaum, H. (2003). Just because you're imaging the brain doesn't mean you can stop using your head: A primer and set of first principles. *Journal of Personality and Social Psychology, 85,* 650–661.

Campbell, D. T. (1965). Variation and selective retention in socio-cultural evolution. In J. Baum & J. Singh (Eds.), *Social change in developing areas* (pp. 19–49). Cambridge, MA: Schenkman.

Chave, E. J. (1928). A new type of scale for measuring attitudes. *Religious Education, 23*, 364–369.

Cialdini, R. (2001). *Influence: Science and practice*. Boston: Allyn & Bacon.

Cialdini, R. (2003). Crafting normative messages to protect the environment. *Current Directions in Psychological Science, 12*, 105–109.

Cialdini, R. B., Cacioppo, J. T., Bassett, R., & Miller, J. A. (1978). Low-ball procedure for producing compliance: Commitment then cost. *Journal of Personality and Social Psychology, 36*, 463–476.

Cioffi, D. (1995). Who's opinion is this anyway? Self inferential effects of representing one's social group. *Social Cognition, 13*, 341–363.

Colarelli, S. M. (1998). Psychological interventions in organizations: An evolutionary perspective. *American Psychologist, 53*(9), 1044–1056.

Cooper, J., & Fazio, R. H. (1984). A new look at dissonance theory. In L. Berkowitz (Ed.), *Advances in experimental social psychology* (Vol. 17, pp. 229–266). New York: Academic Press.

Costa, P. T., Jr., & McCrae, R. R. (1992). *Revised NEO Personality Inventory (Neo-PI-R) and NEO Five-Factor Inventory (NEO-FFI): Professional manual*. Odessa, FL: Psychological Assessment Resources.

Corrigan, P. W., McCracken, S. G., Kommana, S., Edwards, M., & Simpatico, T. (1996). Staff perceptions about barriers to innovative behavioral rehabilitation programs. *Cognitive Therapy and Research, 20*, 541–551.

Crano, W., & Burgoon, M. (2002). *Mass media and drug prevention: Classic and contemporary theories and research*. Mahwah, NJ: Lawrence Erlbaum Associates.

Donovan, J., & Jessor, R. (1985). Structure of problem behavior in adolescence and young adulthood. *Journal of Consulting and Clinical Psychology, 53*, 890–904.

Droba, D. D. (1933). Methods for measuring attitudes. *Psychological Bulletin, 29*, 309–325.

Duncan, T. E., Duncan, S. C., Okut, H., Strycker, A. H., & Small, H. (2003). A multilevel contextual model of neighborhood collective efficacy. *American Journal of Community Psychology, 32*, 245–252.

Eagly, A., & Chaiken, S. (1993). *Psychology of attitudes*. New York: Harcourt Brace Jovanovich.

Eagly, A. H., Johannesen-Schmidt, M., & van Engen, M. (2003). Transformational, transactional, and laissez-faire leadership styles: A meta-analysis comparing women and men. *Psychological Bulletin, 129*, 569–591.

Edwards, A. (1957). *Techniques of attitude scale construction*. New York: Appleton-Century-Crofts.

Ekman, P., & Davidson, R. J. (1994). *The nature of emotion: Fundamental questions*. New York: Oxford University Press.

Epstein, S. (1979). The stability of behavior I: On predicting most of the people much of the time. *Journal of Personality and Social Psychology, 37*, 1097–1126.

Fazio, R. H., Jackson, J. R., Dunton, B. C., & Williams, C. (1995). Variability in automatic activation as an unobtrusive measure of racial attitudes: A bona fide pipeline? *Journal of Personality and Social Psychology, 69*, 1013–1027.

Fazio, R. H., & Towles-Schwen, T. (1999). The MODE model of attitude–behavior processes. In C. Shelly & Y. Trope (Eds.), *Dual-process theories in social psychology* (pp. 97–116). New York: Guilford.

Fazio, R. H., Zanna, M. P., & Cooper, J. (1977). Dissonance and self-perception: An integrative view of each theory's proper domain of application. *Journal of Experimental Social Psychology, 13*, 464–479.

Festinger, L. (1962). *A theory of cognitive dissonance*. Oxford, UK: Stanford University Press.

Fishbein, M. (1973). The prediction of behavior from attitudinal variables. In C. D. Mortensen and K. Soreno (Eds.), *Advances in communication research* (pp. 3–31). New York: Harper & Row.

Fishbein, M., & Ajzen, I. (1975). *Beliefs, attitudes, intentions and behavior*. Reading, MA: Addison-Wesley.

Fishbein, M., & Jaccard, J. (1973). Theoretical and methodological considerations in the prediction of family planning intentions and behavior. *Representative Research in Social Psychology, 4*, 37–52.

Fishbein, M., Jamieson, K., Zimmer, E., vonHaeften, I. & Robin, N. (2002). Avoiding the boomerang: Testing the relative effectiveness of anti-drug public service announcements before a national campaign. *American Journal of Public Health, 92*, 238–245.

Fiske, S. T., & Taylor, S. E. (1991). *Social cognition*. Reading, MA: Addison-Wesley.

Gerrard, M., Gibbons, F. X., Reis-Bergan, M., & Russell, D. W. (2000). Self-esteem, self-serving cognitions, and health risk behavior. *Journal of Personality, 68*, 1177–1201.

Gibbons, F., Lane, D. J., Gerrard, M., Pomery, E., & Lautrup, C. (2002). Drinking and driving: A prospective assessment of the relation between risk cognitions and risk behavior. *Risk Decision and Policy, 7*, 267–283.

Gigerenzer, G. (1996). On narrow norms and vague heuristics: A reply to Kahneman and Tversky. *Psychological Review, 103*, 592–596.

Glisson, C. (2002). The organizational context of children's mental health services. *Clinical Child and Family Psychology Review, 5*, 233–253.

Goldberg, L. (1999). A broad-bandwidth, public-domain, personality inventory measuring the lower-level facets of several five-factor models. In I. Mervielde, I. Deary, F. De Fruyt, & F. Ostendorf (Eds.), *Personality psychology in Europe* (Vol. 7, pp. 7–28). Tilburg, The Netherlands: Tilburg University Press.

Green, B. F. (1954). Attitude measurement. In G. Lindzey (Ed.), *The handbook of social psychology* (pp. 335–369). Reading, MA: Addison-Wesley.

Greenwald, A. G., & Banaji, M. (1995). Implicit social cognition: Attitudes, self esteem, and stereotypes. *Psychological Review, 102,* 4–27.

Guialamo-Ramos, V., Jaccard, J., & Dittus, P. (2004). *The Linking Lives program for the reduction of adolescent risk behavior.* New York: School of Social Work, Columbia University.

Guialamo-Ramos, V., Jaccard, J., & Dittus, P. (in press). Parental and school correlates of binge drinking in middle school. *American Journal of Public Health.*

Guialamo-Ramos, V., Turrisi, R., Jaccard, J., Wood, E., Gonzales, B. (2004). Progressing from light experimentation to heavy episodic drinking in early and middle adolescence. *Journal of Studies on Alcohol, 65*(4), 494–500.

Guilamo, V., Litardo, H., & Jaccard, J. (2003). Prevention programs for reducing adolescent problem behaviors: Implications of the co-occurrence of problem behaviors in adolescence. *Journal of Adolescent Health.*

Haddock, G., Zanna, M. P., & Esses, V. M. (1994). The (limited) role of trait-laden stereotypes in predicting attitudes toward Native peoples. *British Journal of Social Psychology, 33,* 83–106.

Heise, D. (1975). *Causal analysis.* New York: Wiley.

Hoffmann, J. P. (2003). A contextual analysis of differential association, social control, and strain theories of delinquency. *Social Forces, 81,* 753–785.

Hoyt, W. T. (2000). Rater bias I psychological research: When is it a problem and what can we do about it? *Psychological Methods, 5,* 64–86.

Hunt, W. A., Matarazzo, J. D., Weiss, S. M., & Gentry, W. D. (1979). Associative learning, habit, and health behavior. *Journal of Behavioral Medicine, 2,* 111–124.

Jaccard, J. (1974). Predicting social behavior from personality traits. *Journal of Research in Personality, 7,* 358–367.

Jaccard, J. (1981). Attitudes and behavior: Implications of attitudes towards behavioral alternatives. *Journal of Experimental Social Psychology, 17,* 286–307.

Jaccard, J. (1998). *Interaction effects in factorial analysis of variance.* Newbury Park, CA: Sage.

Jaccard, J., & Becker, M. (1985). Attitudes and behavior: An information integration perspective. *Journal of Experimental Social Psychology, 21,* 440–465.

Jaccard, J., King, G. W., & Pomazal, R. P. (1977). Attitudes and behavior: An analysis of specificity of attitudinal predictors. *Human Relations, 30,* 817–824.

Jaccard, J., McDonald, R., Wan, C., Dittus, P., & Quinlan, S. (2002). The accuracy of self reports of condom use and sexual behavior. *Journal of Applied Social Psychology, 32,* 1863–1905.

Jaccard, J., McDonald, R., Wan, C., & Guilamo-Ramos, V. (in press). Recalling sexual partners: The accuracy of self reports. *Journal of Health Psychology.*

Jaccard, J., Radecki, C., Wilson, T., & Dittus, P. (1995). Methods for identifying consequential beliefs: Implications for understanding attitude strength. In R. Petty and J. Krosnick (Eds.), *Attitude strength: Antecedents and consequences.* Hillsdale, NJ: Lawrence Erlbaum Associates.

Jaccard, J., & Wan, C. (1995). A paradigm for studying the accuracy of self reports of risk behavior relevant to AIDS: Empirical perspectives on stability, recall bias and transitory influences. *Journal of Applied Social Psychology, 25,* 1831–1858.

Jaccard, J., Wan, C., & Wood, G. (1988). Idiothetic methods for the analysis of behavioral decision making: Computer applications. In J. Mancuso & M. Shaw (Eds.), *Cognition and personal structure: Computer access and analysis* (pp. 137–168). New York: Praeger.

Jaccard, J., & Wilson, T. (1991). Personality factors influencing risk behavior. In J. Wasserheit, S. Aral, & K. Holmes (Eds.), *Research in human behavior and sexually transmitted diseases in the AIDS era* (pp. 243–257). Washington, DC: American Society for Microbiology.

Jussim, L. (1990). Social reality and social problems: The role of expectancies. *Journal of Social Issues, 46,* 9–34.

Jussim, L. (1991). Social perception and social reality: A reflection-construction model. *Psychological Review, 98,* 54–73.

Jussim, L. (1993). Accuracy in interpersonal expectations: A reflection-construction analysis of current and classic research. *Journal of Personality, 61,* 637–668.

Kassin, S., Rigby, S., & Castillo, S. (1991). The accuracy–confidence correlation in eyewitness testimony: Limits and extensions of the retrospective awareness effect. *Journal of Personality and Social Psychology, 61,* 698–707.

Kassin, S., Tubb, V. A., Hosch, H. M., & Memon, A. (2001). On the "general acceptance" of eyewitness testimony research. *American Psychologist, 56,* 405–416.

Kenny, D. (1979). *Correlation and causality.* New York: Wiley.

Klein, W. M. (1997). Objective standards are not enough: Affective, self-evaluative, and behavioral responses to social comparison information. *Journal of Personality and Social Psychology, 72,* 763–774.

Klein, W. M., & Weinstein, N. D. (1997). Social comparison and unrealistic optimism about personal risk. In B. P. Buunk & F. X. Gibbons (Eds.), *Health, coping, and well-being: Perspectives from social comparison theory* (pp. 25–61). Hillsdale, NJ: Lawrence Erlbaum Associates.

Krueger, E. T., & Reckless, W. (1931). *Social psychology*. New York: Longman and Green.

Lepper, M. R., Greene, D., & Nisbett, R. E. (1973). Undermining children's intrinsic interest with extrinsic reward: A test of the "overjustification" hypothesis. *Journal of Personality and Social Psychology, 28*, 129–137.

Loftus, E., & Fathi, D. C. (1985). Retrieving multiple autobiographical memories. *Social Cognition, 3*, 280–295.

Loftus, E. F., & Marburger, W. (1983). Since the eruption of Mt. St. Helens, has anyone beaten you up? *Social Cognition, 11*, 114–120.

Long, S. (1997). *Regression models for categorical and limited dependent variables*. Newbury Park, CA: Sage.

Maass, A., Colombo, A., Colombo, A., & Sherman, S. J. (2001). Inferring traits from behaviors versus behaviors from traits: The induction–deduction asymmetry. *Journal of Personality and Social Psychology, 81*, 391–404.

Martin, R., Hewstone, M., & Martin, P. (2003). Resistance to persuasive messages as a function of majority and minority source status. *Journal of Experimental Social Psychology, 39*, 585–593.

Matthews, G., & Oddy, K. (1993). Recovery of major personality dimensions from trait adjective data. *Personality and Individual Differences, 15*, 419–431.

Mathiowetz, N. A. (1986, August). *Epsiodic recall and estimation: Applicability of cognitive theories to survey data*. Paper presented at the Social Science Research Council Seminar on Retrospective Data, New York.

McCallum, D. M., Wiebe, D. J., & Keith, B. R. (1988). Effects of previous medication experience and health beliefs on intended compliance to an imagined regimen. *Journal of Compliance in Health Care, 3*, 125–134.

McCullogh, M. L. (2002). Do not discount lay opinion. *American Psychologist, 57*, 376–377.

McGuire, W. J. (1985). Attitudes and attitude change. In G. Lindzey & E. Aronson (Eds.), *Handbook of social psychology* (3rd ed., Vol. II, pp. 233–346). New York: Random House.

McKenzie, J. (1998). Fundamental flaws in the five factor model: A re-analysis of the seminal correlation matrix from which the "openness-to-experience" factor was extracted. *Personality and Individual Differences, 24*, 475–480.

Means, B., Mingay, D. J., Nigam, A., & Zarrow, M. (1988). A cognitive approach to enhancing health survey reports of medical visits. In M. M. Gruneberg, P. E. Morris, & R. N. Sykes (Eds.), *Practical aspects of memory: Current research and issues* (Vol. 1, pp. 537–542). New York: Wiley.

Means, B., & Loftus, E. (1991). When personal history repeats itself: Decomposing memories for recurring events. *Applied Cognitive Psychology, 5*, 201–222.

Meekers, D., & Klein, M. (2002). Understanding gender differences in condom use self efficacy among youth in urban Cameroon. *AIDS Education and Prevention, 14*, 62–72.

Menon, G. (1993). The effects of accessibility of information in memory on judgments of behavioral frequencies. *Journal of Consumer Research, 20*, 431–440.

Menon, G. (1997). Are the parts better than the whole? The effects of decompositional questions on judgments of frequent behaviors. *Journal of Marketing Research, 34*, 335–346.

Menon, G., Raghubir, P., & Schwarz, N. (1995). Behavioral frequency judgments: An accessibility-diagnosticity framework. *Journal of Consumer Research, 22*, 212–228.

Milgram, S. (1974). *Obedience to authority*. New York: Harper & Row.

Morgan, J. J. (1934). *Keeping a sound mind*. New York: MacMillan.

Muraven, M., & Baumeister, R. F. (2000). Self-regulation and depletion of limited resources: Does self-control resemble a muscle? *Psychological Bulletin, 126*, 247–259.

Myers, J., & Well, A. D. (2002). *Research design and analysis*. Mahwah, NJ: Lawrence Erlbaum Associates.

Neter, J., & Waksberg, J. (1964). A study of response errors in expenditure data from household interviews. *Journal of the American Statistical Association, 59*, 18–55.

Norman, P., & Conner, M. (1996). The role of social cognition models in predicting health behaviors: Future directions. In M. Conner & P. Norman (Eds.), *Predicting health behavior: Research and practice with social cognition models* (pp. 197–224). Buckingham, UK: Open University Press.

Olson, J. M., Vernon, P. A., Harris, J., & Jang, K. L. (2001). The heritability of attitudes: A study of twins. *Journal of Personality and Social Psychology, 80*, 845–860.

Ouellette, J. A., & Wood, W. (1998). Habit and intention in everyday life: The multiple processes by which past behavior predicts future behavior. *Psychological Bulletin, 124*, 56–74.

Page, S. (2000). The lost art of unobtrusive methods. *Journal of Applied Social Psychology, 10*, 2126–2136.

Paul, D., Handlin, A., & Stanton, A. D. (2002). Primary care physicians' attitudes toward direct-to-consumer advertising of prescription drugs: Still crazy after all these years. *Journal of Consumer Marketing, 19*, 564–574.

Paulhus, D. L. (1984). Two-component models of social desirable responding. *Journal of Personality and Social Psychology, 46*, 598–609.

Paulhus, D. L. (1991). *BIDR Reference Manual: Version 6*. Vancouver, Canada: University of British Columbia.

Pearl, J. (2000). *Causality: Models, reasoning and inference*. Cambridge, UK: Cambridge University Press.

Petty, R. E., Cacioppo, J. T., & Goldman, R. (1981). Personal involvement as a determinant of argument based persuasion. *Journal of Personality and Social Psychology, 41*, 847–855.

Prochaska, J. O., DiClemente, C. C., & Norcross, J. C. (1992). In search of how people change: Applications to addictive behaviors. *American Psychologist, 47*, 1102–1114.

Raymark, P., Skowronski, J. J., Bevard, L., & Hamann, S. (2001). Influence of recorder affect on the content of behavioral diaries and the recall of behaviors. *Applied Cognitive Psychology, 15*, 373–393.

Reinecke, J., Schmidt, P., & Ajzen, I. (1996). Application of the theory of planned behavior to adolescent's condom use: A panel study. *Journal of Applied Social Psychology, 26*, 749–772.

Ronis, D. L., Yates, J. F., & Kirscht, J. P. (1989). Attitudes, decisions, and habits as determinants of repeated behavior. In A. R. Pratkanis, S. J. Breckler, & A. G. Greenwald (Eds.), *Attitude structure and function* (pp. 213–239). Hillsdale, NJ: Lawrence Erlbaum Associates.

Ross, L., Greene, D., & House, P. (1977). The false consensus phenomenon: An attributional bias in self perception and social perception processes. *Journal of Experimental Social Psychology, 13*, 279–301.

Ross, M. (1989). The relation of implicit theories to the construction of personal histories. *Psychological Review, 96*, 341–357.

Ross, M., McFarland, C., Conway, M., & Zanna, M. P. (1983). Reciprocal relation between attitudes and behavior recall: Committing people to newly formed attitudes. *Journal of Personality and Social Psychology, 45*, 257–267.

Sattler, D. N., Kaiser, C. F., & Hittner, J. B. (2000). Disaster preparedness: Relationships among prior experience, personal characteristics, and distress. *Journal of Applied Social Psychology, 30*, 1396–1420.

Schroder, K., Carey, M. P., & Vanable, P. (2003). Methodological challenges in research on sexual risk behaviors: Accuracy of self reports. *Annals of Behavioral Medicine, 26*, 104–123.

Schwarz, N. (1996). *Cognition and communication: Judgmental biases, research methods and the logic of conversation*. Hillsdale, NJ: Lawrence Erlbaum Associates.

Schwarz, N., Hippler, H. J., Deutsch, B., & Strack, F. (1985). Response scales: Effects of category range on reported behavior and comparative judgments. *Public Opinion Quarterly, 49*, 388–395.

Schwarz, N., Strack, F., Müller, G., & Chassein, B. (1988). The range of response alternatives may determine the meaning of the question: Further evidence on informative functions of response alternatives. *Social Cognition, 6*, 107–117.

Shadish, W. R., Cook, T. D., & Campbell, D. T. (2002). *Experimental and quasi-experimental designs for generalized causal inference*. Boston: Houghton Mifflin.

Sherman, S. J., Chassin, L., Presson, C. C., & Agostinelli, G. (1984). The role of the evaluation and similarity principles in the false consensus effect. *Journal of Personality and Social Psychology, 47*, 1244–1262.

Smyth, M., Morris, P., Levy, P., & Ellis, A. (1987). *Cognition in action*. Hillsdale, NJ: Lawrence Erlbaum Associates.

Son Hing, L. S., Li, W., & Zanna, M. P. (2002). Inducing hypocrisy to reduce prejudicial responses among aversive racists. *Journal of Experimental Social Psychology, 38*, 71–78.

Steele, C. M. (1988). The psychology of self-affirmation: Sustaining the integrity of the self. In L. Berkowitz (Ed.), *Advances in experimental social psychology* (Vol. 21, pp. 261–302). San Diego, CA: Academic Press.

Steele, C. M., & Aronson, J. (1995). Stereotype threat and the intellectual test performance of African Americans. *Journal of Personality and Social Psychology, 69*, 797–811.

Stewart, P. (2000). Community research: The lost art of unobtrusive methods. *Journal of Applied Social Psychology, 30*(10), 2126–2136.

Strube, G. (1987). Answering survey questions: The role of memory. In H. J. Hippler, N. Schwartz, & S. Sudman (Eds.), *Social information processing and survey methodology* (pp. 86–101). New York: Springer-Verlag.

Sutton, S. (1994). The past predicts the future: Interpreting behavior—behavior relationships in social psychological models of health behavior. In D. R. Rutter & L. Quine (Eds.), *Social psychology and health: European perspectives* (pp. 71–88). Aldershot, UK: Avebury Press.

Triandis, H. C. (1964). Exploratory factor analyses of the behavioral component of social attitudes. *Journal of Abnormal and Social Psychology, 68*, 420–439.

Triandis, H. C. (1971). *Attitude and attitude change*. New York: Wiley.

Triandis, H. C. (1977). *Interpersonal behavior*. Monterey, CA: Brooks/Cole.

Triandis, H. C. (1980). Values, attitudes, and interpersonal behavior. In H. E. Howe, Jr., & M. M Page (Eds.), *Nebraska symposium on motivation, 1979* (Vol. 27, pp. 195–259). Lincoln: University of Nebraska Press.

Tucker, L. (1972). Relations between multidimensional scaling and three mode factor analysis. *Psychometrika, 37*, 3–27.

Tulving, E. (1983). *Elements of episodic memory*. Oxford, UK: Oxford University Press.

Van Overewalle, F., & Jordens, K. (2002). An adaptist connectionist model of cognitive dissonance. *Personality and Social Psychology Review, 6*, 204–231.

Verplanken, B., Aarts, H., van Knippenberg, A., & van Knippenberg, C. (1994). Attitude versus general habit: Antecedents of travel mode choice. *Journal of Applied Social Psychology, 24*, 285–300.

Verplanken, B., & Orbell, S. (2003). Reflections on past behavior: A self-report index of habit strength. *Journal of Applied Social Psychology, 33*, 1313–1330.

Wagenaar, W. A. (1988). People and places in my memory: A study on cue specificity and retrieval from autobiographical memory. In M. M. Gruneberg, P. E. Morris, & R. N. Sykes (Eds.), *Practical aspects of memory: Current research and issues* (Vol. 1, pp. 228–232). New York: Wiley.

Webb, E. J., Campbell, D., Schwartz, R., & Sechrest, L. (1966). *Unobtrusive measures: Nonreactive research in the social sciences.* Oxford, UK: Rand McNally.

Wegner, D. M., & Bargh, J. A. (1998). Control and automaticity in social life. In D. Gilbert, S. T. Fiske, & G. Lindzey (Eds.), *Handbook of social psychology* (Vol. 25, pp. 193–225). San Diego, CA: Academic Press.

Weick, K. (1968). Systematic observational methods. In G. Lindzey & E. Aronson (Eds.), *Handbook of social psychology* (Vol. 2, pp. 357–451). Reading, MA: Addison-Wesley.

Wells, G., Small, M., Penrod, S., Malpass, R., Fulero, S., & Brirnacombe, C. (1998). Eyewitness identification procedures: Recommendations for lineups and photospreads. *Law and Human Behavior, 22*, 603–648.

Wiggins, J. S. (1973). *Personality and prediction: Principles of personality assessment.* Reading, MA: Addison-Wesley.

Wilcox, R. R. (1997). *Introduction to robust estimation and hypothesis testing.* San Diego, CA: Academic Press.

Wilcox, R. R. (2003). *Applying contemporary statistical techniques.* San Diego, CA: Academic Press.

Wilson, T. D., Lisle, D. J., Schooler, J. W., Hodges, S. D., Klaaren, K. J., & LaFleur, S. J. (1993). Introspecting about reasons can reduce post-choice satisfaction. *Personality and Social Psychology Bulletin, 19*, 331–339.

Windschitl, P. D., & Wells, G. L. (1996). Measuring psychological uncertainty: Verbal versus numeric methods. *Journal of Experimental Psychology: Applied, 2*, 343–364.

Wyer, R. S. (1974). *Cognitive organization and change: An information processing approach.* Lawrence Erlbaum: Oxford, England.

5

The Influence of Attitudes on Behavior

Icek Ajzen
University of Massachusetts at Amherst

Martin Fishbein
University of Pennsylvania

On September 11, 2001, a group of terrorists commandeered four airliners filled with passengers and fuel in a coordinated attack on the United States. Two airplanes were flown into the World Trade Center towers in New York City, one into the Pentagon, and the fourth crashed in Pennsylvania when passengers resisted the hijackers. Not only did the attack result in the collapse of the twin towers and in severe damage to the Pentagon—prominent symbols of American financial and military might—but thousands of people lost their lives, including several hundred police officers and firefighters who came to the aid of the victims. The response of the American people was inspiring. A wave of patriotism and national pride washed across the country. Public discussion turned from issues of little substance to serious matters of life and death. The increased solidarity was not limited to words; it found expression in a multitude of private and public deeds. The American flag was prominently displayed on homes, offices, and cars; police officers were cheered in the streets of New York; monetary donations flowed into relief funds; blood banks that had faced dwindling supplies were overwhelmed by volunteer donors; and even otherwise cynical politicians joined in a spontaneous singing of God Bless America on the steps of the Capitol in Washington, DC.

Clearly, the dramatic events of September 11 had a profound impact on people's beliefs and attitudes, and the enhanced pride in country, increased solidarity with fellow citizens, and heightened sense of purpose found expression in a variety of behavioral domains. In light of such evidence, few would question the proposition that people act in accordance with their attitudes. If further evidence were needed, one only need to consider the actions of the terrorists who were prepared to sacrifice their lives for their fundamentalist religious beliefs and extremist political ideology. Yet there was a time when many social psychologists were ready to abandon the attitude construct because they had become convinced that people's attitudes had little to do with their actual behavior.

In this chapter we discuss the role of attitudes in human social behavior. We will show that, in order to understand the influence of attitudes on behavior, we must distinguish between two types of attitude. The first type are general attitudes toward physical objects (Yosemite National Park, the Empire State Building); racial, ethnic, or other groups (African Americans, Jews, gays); institutions (Congress, the Catholic Church); policies (gun control, tax cuts); events (September 11, the World Series); or other general targets. The second type are attitudes toward performing specific behaviors with respect to an object or target (visiting Yosemite National Park, hiring an African American, etc.). These attitudes will be referred to as *attitudes toward a behavior.* A parallel distinction will be made between broad behavioral categories or multiple-act aggregates and single behaviors. We first consider the problems and issues involved in relating general and behavior-specific attitudes to multiple-act aggregates and to single behaviors. Our discussion of the determinants of specific behaviors is guided largely by a reasoned action approach that assumes that people's behavior follows reasonably from their beliefs, attitudes, and intentions. We focus on this causal analysis because a great deal of contemporary research concerning the influence of attitudes on behavior is conducted within this conceptual framework. We recognize the possibility that influence can also flow from attitudes and behaviors to beliefs, but these topics are covered in other chapters of this volume. Similarly, the effect of attitude change on changes in behavior is not a major focus because it is discussed elsewhere in this volume.

BRIEF HISTORICAL OVERVIEW
OF ATTITUDE–BEHAVIOR RESEARCH

In the early days of attitude research, most investigators accepted as a given that human behavior is guided by social attitudes. In fact, the field of social psychology was originally defined as the scientific study of attitudes (Thomas & Znaniecki, 1918; Watson, 1925) because it was assumed that attitude was the key to understanding human behavior. Early work with the attitude construct gave no reason to doubt this assumption. Applying newly developed methods to assess attitudes, divinity students were found to hold more favorable attitudes toward the church than other college students (Thurstone & Chave, 1929); military training groups, veterans, and conservative political groups had more favorable attitudes toward war than labor groups and professional men (Stagner, 1942); business men were found to be more opposed to prohibition of alcohol than were Methodists (Smith, 1932), and so forth (see Bird, 1940).

Yet some investigators challenged the view that verbal reactions to symbolic stimuli (i.e., attitudes) provide insight into how people behave in the real world. To demonstrate that people might say one thing and do another, LaPiere (1934) accompanied a young Chinese couple in their travels across the United States and recorded whether they received service in restaurants and overnight accommodation in motels, hotels, and inns. Following their travel, LaPiere mailed a letter to each establishment they had visited, asking whether it would accept members of the Chinese race as guests. As LaPiere had expected, there was no consistency between the symbolic attitudes (responses to the letter) and actual behavior. The Chinese couple received courteous service in virtually every establishment, but responses to the letter were almost universally negative.

Whereas this first systematic investigation of the attitude–behavior relation started with the assumption that behavior has little to do with attitudes, the second study to examine this issue accepted the proposition that attitudes guide behavior and tried to use a measure of attitude toward cheating to predict actual cheating in the classroom (Corey, 1937). Corey assessed college students' attitudes at the beginning of the semester and provided multiple opportunities to cheat by allowing them to score their own tests. To his dismay, there was virtually no correlation between the students' attitudes and their cheating behavior.

In subsequent years, studies on the attitude–behavior relation started to appear with increasing frequency. By the late 1960s, at least 45 separate studies had been reported in which investigators assessed verbal attitudes and observed actual behavior that they expected to be related to the attitudes. Investigators attempted to predict job performance, absenteeism, and turnover from job satisfaction attitudes (e.g., Bernberg, 1952; Vroom, 1964); they looked at attitudes toward African Americans in relation to conformity with the judgments made by African Americans (Himelstein & Moore, 1963), or in relation to willingness to have a picture taken with an African American (De Fleur & Westie, 1958; Linn, 1965); they used attitudes toward cheating in attempts to predict cheating behavior (Corey, 1937; Freeman & Ataoev, 1960), attitudes toward labor unions to predict attendance at labor union meetings (Dean, 1958), attitudes toward participating as a subject in psychological research to predict actual participation (Wicker & Pomazal, 1971), and so forth.

For anyone inclined to rely on attitudes to predict and explain human behavior, the results of these studies were extremely discouraging: Attitudes were usually found to be very poor predictors of actual behavior, and many social psychologists began to worry about the utility of the attitude construct (e.g., Blumer, 1955; Campbell, 1963; Deutscher, 1966; Festinger, 1964). In a provocative and highly influential review of this literature, Wicker (1969) called attention to the inconsistency between attitudes and behavior and essentially called for abandoning the attitude construct. After conducting his review of relevant studies, he reached the following conclusion regarding the strength of the attitude–behavior relation:

> Taken as a whole, these studies suggest that it is considerably more likely that attitudes will be unrelated or only slightly related to overt behaviors than that attitudes will be closely related to actions. Product-moment correlation coefficients relating the two kinds of responses are rarely above .30, and often are near zero. (p. 65)

Based on this empirical evidence, he questioned the existence of attitudes, or at least the relevance of attitudes to behavior:

> The present review provides little evidence to support the postulated existence of stable, underlying attitudes within the individual which influence both his verbal expressions and his actions. (p. 75)

Wicker's pessimistic conclusions fell on fertile ground in a discipline that in the late 1960s and early 1970s was mired in a crisis of confidence and was searching for new directions.

Reactions to Attitude–Behavior Inconsistency

The development of reliable measurement techniques in the 1920s and 1930s allowed investigators to commence with the scientific study of attitudes. Concern with validation of attitude measures quickly gave way to interest in attitude formation and change. Spurred in part by research on the effectiveness of the Army's wide use of films and other mass communication media during World War II (Hovland, Lumsdaine, & Sheffield, 1949), the major focus in the postwar years turned to questions of communication and persuasion (Hovland, Janis, & Kelley, 1953). The relation between attitudes and behavior was taken for granted, with the implication that changes in attitudes would influence behavior, an assumption that was rarely questioned (but see Festinger, 1964). Wicker's (1969) review challenged this assumption by drawing attention to the mounting evidence for inconsistency between attitudes and behavior.

Wicker's conclusions did not come as a surprise to sociologists who had questioned the importance of personal dispositions and had emphasized instead social context and norms as determinants of human action (De Fleur & Westie, 1958; Deutscher, 1969; LaPiere, 1934). It did, however, shatter the complacency of many psychologists who, like Gordon Allport (1968), considered attitude to be "the most distinctive and indispensable concept in contemporary American social psychology" (p. 59). Maintaining their faith in the predictive validity of attitudes, they reacted to Wicker's conclusions by offering possible explanations for the observed inconsistencies. A few investigators came to the defense of the attitude construct by questioning the relevance of some of the most frequently cited experiments or the representativeness of the sample of studies included in Wicker's review. For example, Dillehay (1973) pointed out that LaPiere's (1934) study on acceptance of a Chinese couple and other similar studies (e.g., Kutner, Wilkins, & Yarrow, 1952) failed to properly address the attitude–behavior relation because the person performing the behavior may not have been the same person who provided the verbal attitude measure. In a different vein, Kelman (1974) argued that Wicker's review focused on experimental studies and neglected survey data that provided much stronger evidence for attitude–behavior consistency.

For the most part, however, social psychologists acknowledged that the field was faced with a serious problem. Negative evidence regarding the attitude–behavior relation had been published sporadically over many years, but it was relatively easy to dismiss each study by pointing to methodological flaws. When the disparate studies were brought together in an integrated review, it became clear that this issue could no longer be ignored, and it forced the field to reexamine the assumption that attitudes can help understand and predict behavior. Several possible explanations for observed attitude–behavior inconsistencies were proposed.

Response Biases

Long before it became evident that attitudes are poor predictors of behavior, investigators were concerned with the validity of verbal attitude measures. It was argued that such measures may be systematically distorted or biased and, thus, may not reflect a person's true attitude (e.g., Campbell, 1950; Cook & Selltiz, 1964; Guilford, 1954). The earliest and most frequently cited response bias is the tendency to give socially desirable responses on attitude and personality inventories (Bernreuter, 1933; Lenski & Leggett, 1960; Vernon, 1934). This possibility provided a ready explanation for the reported failure of attitudes to predict behavior, and it suggested the need to use attitude measures that are less subject to systematic biases. The methods available to avoid social desirability bias were of two types. Disguised procedures of a verbal nature, such as Hammond's (1948) error-choice technique or Waly and Cook's (1965) plausibility technique, were based on the assumption that when the purpose of the instrument is not apparent, respondents are less likely to distort or falsify their answers to attitudinal inquiries (for a recent version of the plausibility technique, see Saucier & Miller, 2003). Alternatively, physiological reactions (e.g., galvanic skin response, heart rate, palmar sweat, or pupillary dilation and constriction) were assumed to prevent bias by assessing involuntary responses over which the individual has little or no control (for a review, see Kidder & Campbell, 1970).

It was expected that disguised and physiological measures would prove superior to the undisguised measures of attitude in terms of behavioral prediction, but few attempts were made to submit this expectation to empirical test. Nor did this situation change with the development of additional indirect assessment methods designed to overcome response bias, such as the bogus pipeline (Jones & Sigall, 1971) or the facial electromyogram (Petty & Cacioppo, 1983). Some of the disguised techniques (e.g., the thematic apperception test, the Rorschach test, doll play) proved to be too unreliable; many physiological indices appeared to assess arousal rather than attitude; and the few studies that tested predictive validity found that undisguised measures performed better than disguised measures (Kidder & Campbell, 1970). There was, thus, no evidence that the indirect assessment approach produced more valid measures of a person's true attitude than did the direct approach, nor could it be used to account for the failure of directly assessed attitudes to predict behavior.

Multi-Dimensionality of Attitudes

Another long-standing concern had to do with the fact that most attitude measurement techniques resulted in a single score representing the respondent's overall positive or negative reaction to the attitude object. Many theorists believed that this focus on a single, evaluative dimension did not do justice to the complexity of the attitude construct (Allport, 1935), a view that offered another basis for explaining the failure of attitudes to predict behavior. At the time of Wicker's (1969) review, the most popular conceptions of attitude incorporated the ancient trilogy of thinking, feeling, and doing. In contemporary language, attitude was defined as a complex, multidimensional construct comprised of cognitive, affective, and conative components (Krech, Crutchfield, & Ballachey, 1962; McGuire, 1969; Rosenberg & Hovland, 1960). From this perspective it was evident that a single evaluative score (although it may assess the affective component) cannot adequately represent the attitude construct in all its complexity. A ready explanation for observed attitude–behavior inconsistencies, then, was to argue that the obtained attitude measures assessed only one of the three components (i.e., affect), and the wrong one at that. It would seem that, if the goal is to predict behavior, we have to assess the conative or behavioral component rather than the affective component (Katz & Stotland, 1959; Kothandapani, 1971; Ostrom, 1969; Triandis, 1964).

An early indication that the tripartite approach might not solve the problem of attitude–behavior inconsistency can be found in Thurstone's (1931) writings in which he observed that various overt behaviors could be scaled "in a manner analogous to the procedure for (scaling) the statements of opinion. It is quite probable that these two types of scale, the opinion scale and the situation (overt action) scale, will be highly correlated" (p. 264). Thurstone's insight that measures of attitude based on different types of responses should be highly correlated was later confirmed in a number of empirical studies. For example, developing a scale to assess attitudes toward African Americans, Woodmansee and Cook (1967) started with a large set of items representative of the three components. Contrary to expectations, the results of a factor analysis "did not produce components identifiable as cognitive, affective, and conative. Instead, a larger number of format-free, content-defined dimensions were found," (p. 240), such as ease in interracial contacts, acceptance in close personal relationships, and integration–segregation policy.

Other investigators approached the problem by applying Thurstone, Likert, and Guttman scaling techniques separately to sets of cognitive, affective, and conative items regarding the church (Ostrom, 1969) and birth control (Kothandapani, 1971). For example, Kothandapani used items such as "Birth control will help me postpone childbirth as long as I want" to assess the cognitive components of attitude; items such as "The very thought of birth control disgusts me" to measure the affective component; and items such as "I would volunteer to speak about the merits of birth control" to assess the conative component. In this fashion, separate Thurstone, Likert, and Guttman scales were developed for the cognitive, the affective, and the behavioral components. Convergent and discriminant validities were evaluated by looking at the correlations among these measures in a multitrait–multimethod matrix (Campbell & Fiske, 1959). A careful secondary analysis of the correlations among components of attitude toward the church reported by Ostrom (1969) revealed virtually no evidence for discriminant validity (Widaman, 1985); all measures were strongly intercorrelated. Also, when the measures of the different components were used to predict such religion-relevant behaviors as church attendance, monetary contributions to the church, or time spent in meditation, the correlations were generally low (median $r = .19$), and there was little support for the postulated superiority of the behavioral component measures. As in the case of Woodmansee and Cook (1967), this study, thus, again indicated that the three-component approach could not account for attitude–behavior inconsistencies.

Statistically significant evidence for convergent and discriminant validity of cognition, affect, and conation measures was obtained in a secondary analysis of Kothandapani's (1971) data regarding attitudes toward use of birth control (Widaman, 1985), and there was some indication that the conative measures were somewhat better predictors of behavior than were the cognitive and affective measures.[1] However, these findings had no bearing on the prediction of behavior from attitudes because in this study, attitudes did predict behavior: All cognitive, affective, and conative measures of attitude toward birth control correlated highly with contraceptive use (median $r = .68$). As we will see in the following discussion, it is likely that attitudes predicted behavior better in the Kothandapani study than in the Ostrom study because Kothandapani assessed attitudes toward the behavior of interest, i.e., using birth control, whereas Ostrom assessed general attitudes toward the church to predict specific behaviors, such as donating money, attending church, and studying for the ministry.

PREDICTIVE VALIDITY OF GENERAL ATTITUDES

Our discussion thus far has shown that the problem of inconsistency between verbal attitudes and overt actions was not resolved by attempts to improve the measures of attitude. To further our understanding of the attitude–behavior relation, it is important to realize that investigators have been concerned with two different types of inconsistency (Schuman & Johnson, 1976). One type is exemplified by LaPiere's (1934) study and involves a contradiction between intentions and action, that is, between what people say they would do and what they actually do. Although LaPiere thought of his study as dealing with *attitudes* versus actions, his measure of willingness to "accept members of the Chinese race as guests" is best viewed as a measure of behavioral intention (Fishbein & Ajzen, 1975). In this type of inconsistency, participants fail to carry out their stated intentions to perform or not to perform a behavior of interest to the investigator. The predictor and criterion are identical, both dealing with the same specific action. Failure to act in accordance with behavioral intentions will therefore be termed *literal inconsistency*.

In a second type of inconsistency, participants do not explicitly indicate whether they intend to engage in the behavior of interest to the investigator. Instead, their general (evaluative) attitudes toward the object of the behavior are assessed in a survey or questionnaire. It is assumed that favorable attitudes predispose positive responses to the object and unfavorable attitudes predispose negative responses. Inconsistency is evidenced when the general attitude fails to correlate with the specific behavior under investigation. This type of inconsistency is illustrated in the study by De Fleur and Westie (1958) who found that attitudes toward African Americans failed to predict willingness to have one's picture taken with an African American of the opposite sex. Because it involves a lack of correspondence in evaluation expressed in verbal attitudes and in actual behavior, it will be termed *evaluative inconsistency*. We will discuss this type of inconsistency first and turn to literal inconsistency later in this chapter.

Evaluative Inconsistency: Broad Attitudes Versus Single Behaviors

Moderating Variables Explanation

Most attitude–behavior inconsistencies reviewed by Wicker (1969) represent instances of evaluative inconsistency, that is, a failure of general attitudes to predict a given behavior with respect to the object of the attitude (e.g., Himelstein & Moore, 1963; Rokeach & Mezei, 1966; Warner & DeFleur, 1969). It is an article of faith in psychology that human behavior is complex and, therefore, very difficult to explain and predict. In line with this reasoning, investigators proposed that general attitudes can have a strong impact on behavior, but that this is to be expected only under certain conditions or for certain types of individuals (see Ajzen, 1988; Sherman & Fazio, 1983). In other words, the degree of attitude–behavior consistency was assumed to be moderated by factors related to the person performing the behavior, the situation in which it is performed, or to characteristics of the attitude itself.

Among the individual difference variables considered as moderators were such factors as self-monitoring tendency, self-consciousness or self-awareness, and need for cognition. For example, individuals high in self-monitoring are assumed to be "highly sensitive to social and interpersonal cues of situationally appropriate performances" whereas individuals low in this tendency are thought to "display expressive behavior that truly reflects their own attitudes, traits, feelings, and other current inner states" (Gangestad & Snyder, 1985, p. 322). Several studies examined the hypothesis that attitudes are better predictors of behavior for people low as opposed to people high in the tendency to monitor their behavior (e.g., Kline, 1987; Snyder & Kendzierski, 1982a; Zanna, Olson, & Fazio, 1980; Zuckerman & Reis, 1978). Similarly, it was suggested that people who have a vested interest in a topic (Regan & Fazio, 1977; Sivacek & Crano, 1982), who hold their attitudes with great confidence (Fazio & Zanna, 1978b; Sample & Warland, 1973), and for whom the attitude object is important, relevant, or involving (Fazio & Zanna, 1978b; Franc, 1999; Krosnick, 1988), are likely to act in accordance with their general attitudes.

Among the situational moderators of the attitude–behavior relation that were examined are time pressure (Jamieson & Zanna, 1989; Kruglanski & Freund, 1983) and presence or absence of a mirror in the behavioral situation (Carver, 1975). Time pressure is assumed to heighten the need for cognitive structure (Kruglanski, 1989), and introduction of a mirror is used to produce a high level of self-awareness (Wicklund, 1975). As a result of these hypothesized effects, general attitudes were expected to predict behavior better under time pressure and in the presence of a mirror.

Regarding qualities of the attitude itself that may moderate the strength of the attitude–behavior relation, investigators examined degree of consistency between the cognitive and affective components of the attitude (Fazio & Zanna, 1978a; Norman, 1975), whether attitudes are formed through direct experience as opposed to second-hand information (Fazio & Zanna, 1981), and whether they are formed as a result of central or peripheral processing (Johnson, Maio, & Smith-McLallen, this volume).

Empirical Evidence.   It has been difficult to demonstrate consistent moderating effects with respect to many of the variables considered, and the amount of research on some of the proposed moderators has been rather limited. Nevertheless, there is good evidence that vested interest or involvement and direct experience with the attitude object tend to improve prediction of specific behavior from general attitudes (see Ajzen, 1988, for a review). For example, in a study on the effect of involvement (Sivacek & Crano, 1982), college students completed a scale designed to assess their attitudes toward instituting a comprehensive exam at their university as a prerequisite for graduation. Vested interest in the topic was operationalized in terms of the extent to which such an exam would affect the participant personally. The behavior recorded was whether or not participants signed a petition opposing the proposed exam, whether or not they volunteered to help distribute petitions, write letters to newspapers, etc., and the number of hours of help they pledged. In addition, an aggregate measure of behavior was obtained by constructing a scale on the basis of these three actions. For the total sample of participants, attitude–behavior correlations ranged from .34 to .43 for the three individual actions, whereas a correlation of .60 was obtained in the prediction of the behavioral aggregate. This demonstrates the importance of aggregation to achieve strong attitude–behavior correlations, an issue we will examine later. As to the effect of vested interest, the correlations between attitudes and single actions ranged from .24 to .42 for participants who fell in the lowest third of the vested interest distribution and from .60 to .74 for participants in the highest third. Using the behavioral aggregate score, the comparable correlations were .53 and .82, respectively.

In addition to vested interest, direct experience with the attitude object is also found to have a consistent moderating effect on the attitude–behavior relation. Specifically, attitudes based on direct experience are more predictive of subsequent behavior than are attitudes based on second-hand information (Fazio & Zanna, 1981). To illustrate, in one of a series of studies in this research program (Regan and Fazio, 1977), the relation between attitudes and behavior was examined with respect to five types of intellectual puzzles. In the second-hand information condition of the experiment, participants were given a description of each puzzle type and were shown previously solved examples of the puzzles. By way of contrast, in the direct experience condition, participants were given an opportunity to work on the same puzzles. Expressed interest in each puzzle type served as a measure of attitude, and behavior (order and proportion of each puzzle type attempted) was assessed during a 15minute freeplay period. Correlations between attitudes and the two measures of behavior were .51 and .54 in the direct experience condition and .22 and .20 in the indirect experience condition.

Even when we can successfully identify moderating variables, however, it must be realized that this success is a mixed blessing. On one hand, work on moderating variables provides information about the processes whereby attitudes guide behavior, and it may thus help us design interventions to increase the likelihood that people will act in accordance with their attitudes. For example, we may be able to strengthen attitude–behavior relations by highlighting the personal relevance of an issue or by encouraging individuals to obtain direct experience with the attitude object or to think carefully about it. On the other hand, when we discover moderating variables, we also identify subsets of individuals and situations for whom attitudes are at best poor predictors of behavior. This problem is compounded by the fact that the moderating effects of many variables depend on yet other variables in higher order interactions (e.g., Snyder & Kendzierski, 1982b; Zanna, Olson, & Fazio, 1980), further limiting the predictive utility of the attitude construct. For example, self-monitoring tendency was found to moderate the strength of the attitude–behavior relation when individuals were asked to think about their attitudes, but it had no significant moderating effect in the absence of reflection (Snyder & Kendzierski, 1982a).

Evaluative Inconsistency Reconsidered: Thurstone's Explanation

That the various attempts to explain inconsistency between general attitudes and specific behaviors have met with only limited success should not come as a surprise. When Thurstone developed his attitude scaling technique he wrote:

> It is quite conceivable that two men may have the same degree or intensity of affect favorable toward a psychological object and that their attitudes would be described in this sense as identical but ... that their overt actions would take quite different forms which have one thing in common, namely, that they are about equally favorable toward the object. (Thurstone, 1931, p. 261–262)

Thus, people who hold the same general attitude can behave in different ways. Consider, for example, two individuals with equally favorable attitudes toward the church. One may express this favorableness by giving money to the church, the other by contributing time. Conversely, starting from the behavioral side of the equation, one person may be observed to donate money to the church and another not, yet they may hold the same attitude toward the church. It is simply that the second expresses his or her attitude differently, perhaps by organizing a church picnic.

The Principle of Aggregation.   In short, we cannot expect strong relations between general attitudes toward an object and any given behavior directed at that object. On close examination, what appear to be inconsistencies at the evaluative level, inconsistencies between general attitudes and specific behaviors with respect to the attitude object, turn out to be more apparent than real. In the early studies reviewed by Wicker (1969), investigators were, by and large, concerned with broad social issues such as racial integration and discrimination, aggression, conformity, authoritarianism, religiosity, labor-management relations, and so forth. They felt that behaviors in these domains were reflections of broad underlying attitudes. Thus, racial discrimination was assumed to reflect prejudicial attitudes toward racial or ethnic minorities, that altruistic behavior could be explained by reference to positive attitudes toward helping others, and that adherence to religious traditions was a reflection of favorable attitudes toward religion and the church. The first step, typically, was to develop an instrument, or select an existing instrument, that would assess attitudes presumed to be relevant to the domain of interest. Our discussion suggests that the next step should be to identify a set of behaviors broadly representative of the same behavioral domain. Instead, investigators tended to select a single behavior that they could readily observe and that they believed would be indicative of behavior in the domain of interest. In retrospect, there is reason to doubt that the particular behaviors selected (or for that matter any single behavior) could be representative of the broad behavioral domains under investigation. For example, in studies on racial prejudice and discrimination, investigators often measured attitudes of White participants toward African Americans and then assumed that these general attitudes would predict whether the participants would sign a petition to extend library hours after watching a Black or White confederate sign or refuse to sign the petition (Himelstein & Moore, 1963); whether, when given a choice between two White and two Black individuals, prejudiced participants would prefer Whites over Blacks (Rokeach & Mezei, 1966); or whether participants would agree to have their pictures taken with a Black person of the opposite sex and to release these picture for a variety of purposes (De Fleur & Westie, 1958; Linn, 1965). Given the idiosyncratic and nonrepresentative nature of the behavioral criteria, it is hardly surprising that investigations of this kind obtained virtually no evidence for a relation between attitudes and behavior. It would be far-fetched to conclude, however, that the negative findings can tell us anything about the predictive validity of attitudes in general.

In fact, when the behavioral criterion is broadly representative of the behavioral domain, rather than a single, arbitrarily selected action, strong relations between attitudes and behavior are observed. For example, in a study of religiosity (Fishbein & Ajzen, 1974) several instruments were used to assess attitudes toward religion, and participants were asked to indicate whether they did or did not perform each of a set of 100 behaviors in this domain. Whereas the general attitudes were typically poor predictors of individual behaviors, they showed strong correlations (ranging from .61 to .71) with an aggregate measure across all 100 behaviors, a measure designed to reflect the general pattern of religiosity. Similar results were reported for abortion activism (Werner, 1978) and for protection of the environment (Weigel & Newman, 1976).

Findings of this kind have done much to dispel the concern that general attitudes toward objects are unrelated to overt action. We now understand that such attitudes can predict behavior, but only if the measure of behavior is broadly representative of the attitude domain. Individual behaviors performed in a particular context tend to be influenced not only by general attitudes but by a wide range of additional factors. By incorporating in our criterion measure a large number of behaviors relevant to the domain of interest, the influence of these additional factors is essentially eliminated, leaving a relatively pure index of the evaluative behavioral disposition. Described in this manner, it may appear that the advantage of aggregation is simply to increase the reliability of the behavioral measure. However, identifying of set of behaviors that have evaluative implications and are broadly representative of the domain under investigation not only increases the measure's reliability but also ensures that the behavioral criterion has construct validity. For example, to obtain a measure of discrimination against a group of people such as the mentally ill, any single behavior (even if reliably assessed) cannot capture the broad meaning of discrimination. To obtain a measure of discrimination against the mentally ill that is not only reliable but also valid, we must observe a variety of behaviors each of which reflects some degree of favorableness or unfavorableness with respect to the mentally ill.

Conclusion: Evaluative Inconsistency

To summarize briefly, we have examined several attempts to explain evaluative inconsistency, attempts designed to understand why general attitudes fail to predict a given behavior with respect to the object of the attitude. Initial reactions focused on the validity of the attitude measure, suggesting either that responses to standard attitude scales were contaminated by social desirability bias and, hence, failed to capture true attitudes or that these measures provided an incomplete assessment of the attitude construct. The development of various indirect assessment techniques in response to the first concern failed to improve predictive validity, and assessment of multiple components of attitude also failed to improve prediction of behavior. Later approaches took the position that variables in addition to attitude must be taken into consideration, suggesting that attitudes play a very limited role because they are important predictors of behavior only for certain individuals and in certain situations.

The inconsistencies between general attitudes and specific actions that emerged in early research led investigators to question the utility and, indeed, the existence of broad behavioral dispositions or attitudes. Contrary to this pessimistic view, our discussion of the principle of aggregation has shown that it is very useful to think of broad behavioral dispositions and that these dispositions are reflected equally well in verbal responses and overt actions. It is for this reason that we obtain very high correlations between attitudes toward objects and multiple-act criteria.

PREDICTING SINGLE BEHAVIORS

The principle of aggregation just described is but a special case of a more general rule dealing with the compatibility between measures of attitude and behavior. When we aggregate behaviors with respect to a given object we ensure compatibility with a measure of attitude toward that object. However, investigators are often interested not in a broad multiple-act index of behavior but with predicting and understanding performance of particular behaviors, perhaps hiring a member of a minority group or renting an apartment to the mentally ill. Many examples are found in the health domain where investigators have a substantive interest in understanding and influencing such behaviors as using condoms to prevent AIDS and other sexually transmitted diseases, cigarette smoking, and breast self-examination; or categories of behavior, such as exercising or eating a low-fat diet. Similarly, in the domain of environmental protection, investigators are concerned with such behaviors as recycling of glass, plastic, and paper; or categories of behavior such as conserving water or reducing the consumption of energy.

The Principle of Compatibility

Just as aggregating behaviors produces a criterion that is compatible with general attitudes toward the object, it is possible to obtain compatibility for a single behavior by assessing attitudes toward the behavior in question. A single behavior can be viewed as involving an *action* directed at a *target*, performed in a given *context*, at a certain point in *time* (Ajzen & Fishbein, 1977, 1980; Fishbein & Ajzen, 1975). For example, we may be interested in understanding why people do or do not enroll (action) in a continuing education course (target) at a local community college (context) the next time it is offered (time). In this example, the four elements are explicitly specified. Alternatively, we may not care where people enroll in a continuing education course but only whether they do so sometime in the next 12 months. In this case, the target and action elements are clearly specified as before, the time element has been expanded, and the context is undefined.

The principle of compatibility (Ajzen, 1988; Ajzen & Fishbein, 1977) requires that measures of attitude and behavior involve exactly the same action, target, context, and time elements, whether defined at a very specific or at a more general level. In this example, we would have to assess attitude to enroll in a continuing education course at a local community college the next time it is offered or, in the more general case, to enroll in a continuing education course in the next 12 months. To the extent that the indicators used to assess attitude and behavior comply with the principle of compatibility, they should correlate highly with each other.

Empirical research has shown that specific behaviors can be predicted quite well from compatible measures of attitude toward the behaviors in question. Earlier, in our discussion of the three-component model of attitudes, we noted that attitudes toward using birth control were found to be good predictors of reported contraceptive use (Kothandapani, 1971). Many other investigations have produced similar results. For example, Manstead, Proffitt, and Smart (1983) reported a study on infant feeding practices. Toward the end of their pregnancies, women completed a questionnaire that assessed, among other things, their attitudes toward breast feeding (as opposed to bottle feeding) their babies. Six weeks following delivery, a questionnaire sent to each woman ascertained their actual feeding practices during the preceding 6 weeks. Attitudes toward the behavior of interest were found to have a correlation of .67 with the feeding method employed. In the domain of illicit drug use, attitudes toward using LSD, amphetamines, cannabis, and ecstasy over the next 6 months were used to predict self-reported frequency of actual use of these drugs during the period in question (McMillan & Conner, 2003). Attitude–behavior correlations across the four drugs ranged from .35 to .58 (all statistically significant). Many studies have examined the relation between attitudes and behavior in the domain of physical exercise. For example, Terry and O'Leary (1995) obtained a measure of attitude toward exercising for at least 20 minutes, three times a week for the next fortnight and 2 weeks later, participants indicated whether they had exercised for at least 20 minutes, three times per week during the past fortnight. The attitude–behavior correlation was .53. In another study (Godin, Valois, Shephard, & Desharnais, 1987), attitudes toward participating in vigorous physical activities were found to have a correlation of .45 with self-reports of the frequency with which participants engaged in such activities.[2]

These findings contrast with the low and often nonsignificant correlations between general measures of attitude toward an object and single behaviors with respect to the object. Thus, just as behavioral aggregation made it possible to demonstrate strong attitude–behavior correlations at a global level, the shift from general attitudes toward objects to attitudes toward behaviors enables us to apply the attitude construct to the prediction of single behaviors.

A narrative review of attitude–behavior research (Ajzen & Fishbein, 1977) provided support for the principle of compatibility by showing that correlations between attitudes and behavior were substantial only when these variables were assessed at compatible levels of specificity or generality; when the measures were incompatible, the correlations were very low and usually not significant. The correlation across studies between degree of compatibility and the magnitude of the attitude–behavior relation was found to be .83. However, the most compelling support for the importance of compatibility comes from studies that have directly compared the predictive validity of attitudes that were compatible (i.e., attitudes toward behaviors) or incompatible (i.e., attitudes toward objects) with a single-act criterion. In a meta-analysis of eight studies that manipulated level of compatibility while holding all other variables constant (Kraus, 1995), the prediction of behavior from attitude toward the behavior resulted in a correlation of .54, whereas the correlation between general attitudes and the single behaviors was only .13 (see also Ajzen, 1971; Ajzen & Fishbein, 1970; Fishbein, Thomas, & Jaccard, 1976).

From Attitudes Toward Objects to Specific Behaviors:
The MODE Model

We have seen that general attitudes toward physical objects, institutions, ethnic or religious groups, and so on are good predictors of behavioral patterns or multiple-act criteria, and that attitudes toward behaviors are good predictors of single actions. Furthermore, if there is one clear conclusion to be derived from work on the attitude–behavior relation it is that general attitudes will usually not provide a good basis for predicting and explaining single behaviors with respect to the attitude object; correlations of single behaviors with general attitudes tend to be modest at best. Nevertheless, many investigators continue to be interested in broad attitudinal dispositions and their possible effects on specific behaviors (Eagly & Chaiken, 1993).

The most direct and sophisticated attempt to deal with the processes whereby general attitudes may influence performance of specific behaviors can be found in Fazio's (1986, 1990a, 1995; Fazio & Towles-Schwen, 1999) MODE model. A schematic representation of the model is shown in Fig. 5.1. Building on past work concerning the effects of attitudes on perceptions and judgments (see Eagly & Chaiken, 1998, for a review), the model assumes that general attitudes can influence or bias perception and judgments of information relevant to the attitude object, a bias that is congruent with the valence of the attitude. However, for this bias to occur, the attitude must first be *activated*. Consistent with the logic of other dual-mode processing theories (see Chaiken & Trope, 1999), the MODE model posits that attitudes can be activated in one of two ways: in a controlled or deliberative fashion and in an automatic or spontaneous fashion. The acronym MODE is used to suggest that "motivation and opportunity

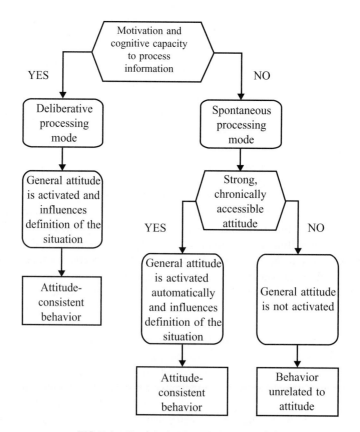

FIG 5.1.   Fazio's (1990a) MODE model.

act as determinants of spontaneous versus deliberative attitude-to-behavior processes" (Fazio, 1995, p. 257). When people are sufficiently motivated and have the cognitive capacity to do so, they can retrieve or construct their attitudes toward an object in an effortful manner. When motivation or cognitive capacity is low, attitudes can become available only if they are automatically activated.

According to the MODE model, such automatic or spontaneous activation is reserved for strong attitudes. Specifically, attitude is defined as a learned association in memory between an object and a positive or negative evaluation of that object, and attitude strength is equivalent to the strength of this association (Fazio, 1990a). Thus, automatic attitude activation occurs when a strong link has been established in memory between the attitude object and a positive or negative evaluation. The stronger the attitude, the more likely it is that it will be automatically activated and, hence, be chronically accessible from memory. The degree of accessibility (i.e., attitude strength) is usually operationalized by measuring the latency of responses to attitudinal questions: the faster the response, the more accessible the attitude is assumed to be (e.g., Fazio & Williams, 1986; see also Fazio, 1990b; Fazio, Sanbonmatsu, Powell, & Kardes, 1986).

Fazio (1990a) has also suggested that by biasing perception and interpretation of new information, strong attitudes are more likely to be resistant to change than are weak attitudes. This is consistent with the general view that strong attitudes involve issues of personal relevance and are held with great conviction or certainty (see Petty & Krosnick, 1995; Raden, 1985). As a result, they are assumed to be persistent over time and be resistant to attack, to influence perceptions and judgments, and to guide overt behavior (Krosnick & Petty, 1995).

Processes that take place in the immediate behavioral situation vary as a function of deliberative versus spontaneous processing mode. When motivation and cognitive capacity to carefully process information are high, attitudes do not have to be chronically accessible because they can be effortfully retrieved. Whether activated automatically or retrieved effortfully, the general attitude is available and can bias deliberations. Individuals who hold favorable attitudes are likely to notice, attend to, and process primarily the object's positive attributes, whereas individuals with unfavorable attitudes toward the object are likely to direct attention to its negative qualities. These perceptions of the object (and relevant contextual elements, such as social norms) influence the person's *definition of the event*, possibly directing attention to positive or negative consequences of performing the behavior in line with the positive or negative evaluation of the object. Consistent with an expectancy-value model of attitude (see Kruglanski & Stroebe in this volume), this process is expected to influence the person's attitude toward the behavior and, thus, guide behavior in accordance with the valence of the general attitude. Although in the deliberative processing mode " . . . the degree to which the individual's attitude toward the object is capable of automatic activation from memory becomes irrelevant to the behavioral decision process" (Fazio, 1990a, p. 93), once activated (whether spontaneously or deliberatively) the attitude can automatically bias information processing and judgments; and this is more likely to be the case for strong, highly accessible attitudes than for weak attitudes. As a result, readily accessible attitudes are more likely than relatively inaccessible attitudes to bias the definition of the event, to influence attitudes toward possible behaviors in the situation, and, hence, to guide performance of specific behaviors with respect to the attitude object.[3]

Attitude activation is more problematic when motivation or cognitive capacity is low. Under these conditions, attitudes are not likely to be retrieved or constructed in an effortful manner; they can become available, however, if they are automatically activated. As previously noted, this is likely to occur only if the attitude is readily accessible in memory. In the spontaneous processing mode, weak attitudes will not be activated and will, thus, not be available to bias the definition of the event or guide behavior. Instead, behavior will be determined by salient cues associated with the attitude object or the behavioral situation.

Empirical Support for the MODE Model

The MODE model has obvious implications for the prediction of specific behaviors from general attitudes. Whether a person operates in the deliberative or spontaneous processing mode, attitudes toward objects should be good predictors of specific behaviors so long as they are readily accessible from memory. As a general rule, therefore, attitudes that are readily accessible from memory should be better predictors of specific behaviors than less accessible attitudes, and the difference should be particularly pronounced in the spontaneous processing mode where people lack the motivation or cognitive capacity to effortfully retrieve their attitudes.

Some of the findings regarding moderating variables reviewed earlier can now be reinterpreted in terms of attitude accessibility. Thus, there is evidence that vested interest and involvement, as well as direct experience of interacting with the attitude object, tend to produce relatively strong attitudes, as indicated by low latency of responses to attitudinal questions (see Fazio, 1995). We saw earlier that, consistent with the MODE model, high-vested interest and direct experience do indeed produce stronger attitude–behavior relations than low-vested interest or second-hand information.

Studies that were designed to directly test the MODE model's predictions concerning the attitude-to-behavior process (Berger & Mitchell, 1989; Fazio, Chen, McDonel, & Sherman, 1982; Fazio, Powell, & Williams, 1989; Fazio & Williams, 1986; Kokkinaki & Lunt, 1997) have focused on behavior in a deliberative processing mode. The results of these studies are also generally consistent with the model. For example, Fazio and Williams (1986) predicted voting choice in the 1984 presidential election from attitudes toward the two major candidates (Reagan and Mondale) assessed several months earlier. In addition to attitude valence, the investigators also assessed the accessibility of these attitudes by asking participants to respond as quickly as possible to the attitude questions and by recording response latencies. As hypothesized, prediction of voting choice was significantly better for participants with relatively accessible (low latency) attitudes toward the candidates than for participants with relatively inaccessible attitudes. Similar results were obtained for the prediction of choice among intellectual puzzles from attitudes toward the puzzles (Fazio et al., 1982, Experiment 4), and selection of a product from attitudes toward the product (Berger & Mitchell, 1989; Fazio, Powell, & Williams, 1989; Kokkinaki & Lunt, 1997).

Issues Related to the MODE Model

The MODE model provides an elegant account of the processes and conditions under which general attitudes toward objects will or will not influence the performance of specific behaviors. Nevertheless, several important issues have been raised in regard to this approach. First, the assumption that only strong attitudes are activated automatically by mere observation of the attitude object has been challenged in priming research where it was found that all attitudes are activated automatically, irrespective of their strength or accessibility (Bargh, Chaiken, Govender, & Pratto, 1992; Bargh, Chaiken, Raymond, & Hymes, 1996).[4] In his rebuttal, Fazio (1993, 2001) reexamined the priming results and concluded that they are not inconsistent with the idea that highly accessible attitudes are more likely to be automatically activated. The MODE model's implications for attitude–behavior consistency, however, do not depend on the assumption that only strong attitudes are automatically activated. All we need to assume is that readily accessible or strong attitudes are more likely than less accessible attitudes to bias perceptions and judgments.

Related to this issue, it has been suggested that the magnitude of the attitude–behavior relation may be moderated not by attitude accessibility but by other correlated factors such as certainty, amount of knowledge, or the attitude's temporal stability (see Eagly & Chaiken, 1993). Support for the superior predictive validity of stable attitudes was provided by Doll and

Ajzen (1992). Compared to secondhand information, direct experience with different video games was found to raise the accessibility of attitudes toward playing those games and to increase the temporal stability of the attitudes. The superior predictive validity of the attitude measures following direct as opposed to indirect experience could be explained better by their greater stability than by their higher level of accessibility.

Another issue has to do with the conditions under which the MODE model's predictions have been tested. As noted, the moderating effect of attitude accessibility has been studied primarily in the context of deliberative behavior. The model would predict that this effect will be stronger under low motivation or cognitive capacity to process behavior-relevant information, that is, in the spontaneous mode. To the best of our knowledge, this prediction has as yet not been submitted to an explicit test. One study (Schuette & Fazio, 1995) has provided suggestive evidence by showing that the moderating effect of attitude accessibility on the attitude–judgment relation depends on motivation. The moderating effect of accessibility was observed only under low motivation to process the information carefully, that is, only in a spontaneous processing mode.

Any model dealing with the influence of general attitudes on specific behaviors should be able to account for the typically low attitude–behavior relations reported in the literature. As we noted earlier, investigators have tried unsuccessfully to use measures of general attitudes to predict such behaviors as job absence and turnover, various types of interaction with African Americans, participation in civil rights activities, attendance of labor union meetings, and so forth (see Wicker, 1969). According to the MODE model, the observed low attitude–behavior correlations imply that participants in these studies held relatively weak attitudes, too weak to influence their definition of the event and, thus, guide their behavior—even if these attitudes were activated. Without further evidence, this supposition cannot be completely discounted, but it seems reasonable to assume that people hold fairly strong attitudes toward their jobs, their labor unions, members of minority groups, and civil rights. Strong attitudes of this kind should be chronically accessible and, thus, available to guide behavior. However, in actuality, even under these ideal conditions from the MODE model perspective, the observed correlations between general attitudes and specific behaviors are found to be disappointing.

Finally, as Eagly and Chaiken (1993) noted, the processes linking general attitudes to specific behaviors in the MODE model are not spelled out in any detail for the spontaneous processing mode. Fazio (1990a) merely suggested that "the activated attitude can . . . color individuals' immediate perceptions and as a result influence their behavior toward the attitude object" (p. 94). The MODE model provides more detailed information about the way in which general attitudes guide behavior in the deliberative processing mode. Here it is assumed that general attitudes, if they are sufficiently strong, color the perceived consequences of the behavior, and, thus, influence attitudes toward the behavior. It is for this reason that general attitudes are re-lated to performance of the behavior itself. It may be argued that similar processes occur under conditions of low motivation or low cognitive capacity. Although Fazio (1990a) assumed that in a spontaneous processing mode "individuals will not be sufficiently motivated to deliberate and construct an attitude toward the behavior" (p. 93), it has been suggested that such processes can occur spontaneously without much cognitive effort (see Ajzen & Fishbein, 2000). The effect of general attitudes on specific behaviors, in deliberative as well as spontaneous processing contexts, may, therefore, be mediated by attitudes toward the behavior. In line with this proposition, we saw earlier that attitudes toward a behavior are consistently found to have greater predictive validity than attitudes toward the object at which the behavior is directed.

Intentions as Predictors of Behavior

The previous discussion indicates that, consistent with the principle of compatibility, perfor-mance of specific behaviors can perhaps be best explained by considering the proximal attitude toward the behavior rather the more distal attitude toward the object at which the behavior is directed. Carrying this idea further, a number of theorists have proposed that the intention to perform a behavior, rather than attitude, is the closest cognitive antecedent of actual behavioral performance (e.g., Fishbein & Ajzen, 1975; Fisher & Fisher, 1992; Gollwitzer, 1993; Triandis, 1977). This implies that we should be able to predict specific behaviors with considerable accuracy from intentions to engage in the behaviors under consideration. Many studies have substantiated the predictive validity of behavioral intentions. When appropriately measured, behavioral intentions account for an appreciable proportion of variance in actual behavior. Meta-analyses covering diverse behavioral domains have reported mean intention–behavior correlations of .47 (Armitage & Conner, 2001; Notani, 1998), .53 (Shepherd, Hartwick, & Warshaw, 1988), .45 (Randall & Wolff, 1994), and .62 (van den Putte, 1993). Studies in specific behavioral domains, such as condom use and exercise, have produced similar results, with intention-behavior correlations ranging from .44 to .56 (Albarracín, Johnson, Fishbein, & Muellerleile, 2001; Godin & Kok, 1996; Hausenblas, Carron, & Mack, 1997; Sheeran & Orbell, 1998). In a meta-analysis of these and other meta-analyses, Sheeran (2002) reported an overall correlation of .53 between intention and behavior.

Low Intention–Behavior Relations

However, notwithstanding these encouraging findings, there is also considerable variability in the magnitude of observed correlations, and relatively low intention–behavior correlations are sometimes obtained. Several factors may be responsible for low relations between intentions and behavior. Clearly, if there is little or no variance either in intention or in behavior, strong correlations cannot be expected. For example, at a very young age few, if any, children intend to use illicit drugs (Hornik et al., 2001), and a measure of their intentions can, therefore, not provide a basis for prediction of future drug use.

Stability of Intentions.   Perhaps more important, if intentions change after they are assessed, they will tend to be poor predictors of later behavior. The time interval between measurement of intention and assessment of behavior is often taken as a proxy for stability because it is assumed that with the passage of time, an increasing number of events may cause intentions to change. Meta-analyses of intention–behavior correlations show the expected pattern over time, although the effect is not always significant. For example, in the area of condom use, prediction of behavior from intention was found to become significantly less accurate with the passage of time (see Albarracín et al., 2001; Sheeran & Orbell, 1998). The correlation between effect size and amount of time in weeks between assessment of intention and behavior was −.59 in the Sheeran and Orbell (1998) analysis. In an review covering a broader range of behaviors (Randall & Wolff, 1994), intention–behavior correlations declined from .65 to .40 for intervals of less than a day to 1 or more years, although this effect reached statistical significance only when objective rather than self-report measures of behavior were obtained.

Instead of relying on time interval as an indication of stability, some studies have assessed stability of intentions directly, and these studies have consistently found that the intention–behavior correlation declines substantially when intentions are unstable. In one of these investigations (Sheeran, Orbell, & Trafimow, 1999), undergraduate college students twice indicated their intentions to study over the winter vacation, 5 weeks apart. After returning from the winter vacation, they reported on how many days a week they had actually studied. For participants whose intentions remained relatively stable during the 5-week period prior to the vacation, the intention–behavior correlation was .58, whereas for participants with relatively unstable intentions, it was .08. Similar results were reported with respect to attending a health screening appointment and eating a low-fat diet (Conner, Sheeran, Norman, & Armitage, 2000).

Intention–Behavior Compatibility.   Beyond the impact of low variance and temporal instability on the predictive validity of intentions, lack of compatibility between measures of intention and behavior may also be responsible for some of the weak correlations reported in the literature. The importance of maintaining compatibility is readily apparent in the case of evaluative inconsistency. General attitudes arguably fail to predict specific behaviors because of a lack of compatibility in the action, context, and time elements. That is, general attitudes identify only the target element, whereas a specific behavior involves a particular action directed at the target in a given context and point in time.

Lack of compatibility is usually not a serious problem when it comes to predicting behavior from intentions because the measures of intention deal not with a general target but with the behavior of interest. In fact, as we saw earlier, meta-analyses of the intention–behavior relation have revealed generally high correlations. Nevertheless, incompatibility can arise even when dealing with the prediction of behavior from intention. For example, in a study of managers who were enrolled in a physical exercise program for health reasons (Kerner & Grossman, 1998), the frequency with which participants performed a specific prescribed exercise behavior (e.g., climbing stairs or lifting weights) over a 5-month period was only weakly ($r = .21$) related to their intentions to exercise in the next 12 months. Just as general attitudes are poor predictors of specific behaviors, intentions with respect to a behavioral category such as exercise cannot be expected to be good predictors of a single instance of the category. A more compatible measure of intentions in this study would have asked participants to indicate the extent to which they intended to engage in the particular prescribed exercise behavior.[5]

Literal Inconsistency: Intentions Versus Actions

Even when measures of intention and behavior have sufficient variance, are relatively stable, and meet the criterion of compatibility, we find that some people do not act on their stated intentions. The gap between intentions and behavior in this case is an instance of literal inconsistency: People say they will do one thing yet do something else. Generally speaking, the pattern of literal inconsistency is asymmetric such that people who do not intend to engage in a socially desirable behavior tend to act in accordance with their negative intentions, but people who intend to perform the behavior may or may not do so. For example, in a study of the intention–behavior relation (Linn, 1965), female students were asked to indicate whether they would be willing to release photos of themselves with an African American male for a variety of purposes related to improving race relations. Almost without exception, those who were unwilling to do so later signed very few releases. Among the participants who indicated a high level of willingness to release their photographs, however, only about one-half actually followed through on their intentions. Similarly, research in the health domain has found that participants who do not intend to use condoms, to undergo a cancer screening, or to exercise rarely if ever do so, but of those who intend to engage in these health-protective behaviors, between 26% and 57% fail to carry out their intentions (Sheeran, 2002).

Pseudo-Inconsistency: An Explanation of Literal Inconsistency.   Perhaps the most ingenious explanation for literal inconsistency was offered by Donald Campbell (1963) who suggested that observed discrepancies between words and deeds may often be more apparent than real. He argued that verbal and overt responses to an attitude object are both indicators of an underlying hypothetical disposition and that one of these responses may be more difficult to perform than the other. Using the LaPiere (1934) study as an example, Campbell assumed that rejecting the Chinese couple in the face-to-face situation (overt behavior) was more difficult than rejecting a symbolic representation of members of the Chinese race in response to a written inquiry. Individuals strongly prejudiced toward the Chinese would

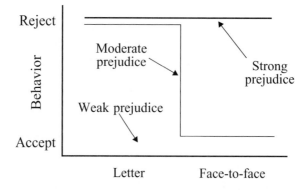

FIG 5.2.   Pseudo-inconsistency (after Campbell, 1963).

be expected to give a negative response in both situations, whereas individuals who are not at all prejudiced should provide a positive response in both. The apparent inconsistency in the LaPiere study reflects, according to Campbell, a moderate degree of prejudice toward the Chinese, sufficiently strong to produce the relatively easy verbal rejection in a letter (negative intention) but not strong enough to generate the more difficult overt rejection in a face-to-face encounter (overt behavior).

Campbell (1963; see Fig. 5.2) argued that literal inconsistency arises because people with moderate dispositions tend to display behaviors consistent with the disposition when the behaviors are easy to perform (e.g., express willingness to perform a behavior) but not when they are difficult to perform (e.g., actually carry out the intention). Although this argument is intuitively compelling, it has rarely been put to empirical test (Ajzen, Brown, & Carvajal, 2004; Sheeran, 2002). Contrary to Campbell's thesis, recent research has found that participants who display literal inconsistency do not necessarily hold the expected moderate dispositions. In one experiment (Ajzen, Brown, & Carvajal, 2004), participants could agree to contribute money to a scholarship fund under hypothetical as well as under real payment conditions. Literal inconsistency was shown by participants who agreed to make a contribution when the question was hypothetical but chose not to make a contribution in the real payment situation. The attitudes of these participants toward making a contribution were found to be no less favorable than those of participants who agreed to make a contribution under both payment conditions. Similar results were reported by Sheeran (2002) in a reanalysis of data from an earlier study (Sheeran & Orbell, 2000) on the prediction of physical exercise. Thus, despite its elegance, the jury is still out on Campbell's pseudo-inconsistency hypothesis. It is clear, however, that this hypothesis cannot explain all cases of literal inconsistency.[6]

Implementation Intentions

Evidence for literal inconsistency challenges us to explain why some people fail to carry out the intentions they have formed.[7] When asked to explain why they failed to act on their intentions, people often mention that they simply forgot or that it slipped their minds (Orbell, Hodgkins, & Sheeran, 1997; Sheeran & Orbell, 1999b). In those instances, a very effective means for closing the intention–behavior gap is to prompt people to form an implementation intention (Gollwitzer, 1999). Simply asking people when, where, and how they will carry out their intentions greatly increases the likelihood that they will do so. The beneficial effects of implementation intentions have been found with respect to such normal, everyday activities as completing a project during Christmas vacation (Gollwitzer & Brandstätter, 1997), taking a daily vitamin C pill (Sheeran & Orbell, 1999b), and eating healthy food (Verplanken & Faes,

1999); as well as for disagreeable tasks, such as performing a breast self-examination (Orbell, Hodgkins, & Sheeran, 1997) and resuming functional activities following surgery (Orbell & Sheeran, 2000). Formulating an implementation intention has been found of particular benefit for individuals with severe cognitive deficits, such as drug addicts undergoing withdrawal and schizophrenic patients (Gollwitzer & Brandstätter, 1997).

According to Gollwitzer (1999; Gollwitzer & Schaal, 1998), implementation intentions are effective because they allow people to delegate control of their goal-directed behaviors to the stimulus situation.[8] Formulation of an implementation intention is assumed to activate the mental representation of a specified situation and make it chronically accessible. Consistent with this assumption, implementation intentions are found to enhance vigilance for relevant situational cues that are well remembered and easily detected (Aarts, Dijksterhuis, & Midden, 1999; Gollwitzer, 1996; Orbell, Hodgkins, & Sheeran, 1997). As a result, when the situational cues are encountered, initiation of the goal-directed action is expected to be swift, efficient, and to require no conscious intent, the hallmarks of automaticity (Bargh, 1996).

Perhaps consistent with this account, implementation intentions may be effective because they improve memory for the behavioral intention. By specifying where, when, and how the behavior will be performed, implementation intentions provide a number of specific cues that can enhance recall of the intention and, hence, make it more likely that the intention will be carried out. Alternatively, it is possible to attribute the effectiveness of implementation intentions to a sense of commitment they engender. When people state explicitly—and publicly—that they will perform a behavior in a certain situation and at a certain point in time, they arguably make a commitment to carry out their intentions. And there is considerable evidence that making a commitment can greatly increase the likelihood that people will perform the behavior to which they have committed themselves (Braver, 1996; Cialdini, 2001; Kiesler, 1971). Consistent with this interpretation, asking people to make an explicit commitment to return a brief survey concerning TV newscasts was found to be just as effective in helping them carry out their intentions as was asking them to form an implementation intention (Ajzen, Czasch, & Flood, 2002). In fact, making a commitment was sufficient to produce a high rate of return, and adding an implementation intention did not further increase intention-consistent behavior. Thus, although there is strong evidence for the power of implementation intentions, more research is needed to determine the mechanism whereby such an intervention achieves is effectiveness.

Behaviors Versus Goals: The Question of Volitional Control

A number of investigators have made a distinction between performing a behavior, such as weight lifting, and attaining a goal, such as losing weight (Ajzen & Fishbein, 1980; Bagozzi & Warshaw, 1990; Bandura, 1997). This distinction has heuristic value, directing our attention to the possibility that intentions are immediate antecedents of behavioral performance but not of goal attainment. Generally speaking, attainment of a goal depends not only on the person's behavior but also on other factors. Thus, to lose weight, a person may reduce food intake and work out at the gym, but actual weight loss may also depend on physiological and other factors not under the person's control. Factors of this kind are less likely to play a role in the performance of a behavior. In other words, people usually have greater volitional control over performing a behavior than over achieving a goal. On closer examination, however, it becomes clear that what at first glance appears to be a volitional behavior can also be subject to incomplete volitional control. In fact, it is sometimes difficult to tell whether a given criterion should be considered a behavior or a goal. Despite their best efforts, people may be unable to donate blood if, for any reason, they are judged to be ineligible. Similarly, driving a car is a behavior whose performance requires possession of a valid driver's license and skills that may turn out to be unavailable. Thus, goals as well as behaviors can involve varying degrees of volitional control, but behaviors typically fall toward the volitional end of the continuum, whereas goals fall toward the nonvolitional end. Clearly, a measure of intention is expected to predict performance of a behavior or attainment of a goal only to the extent that these criteria are under volitional control. Some of the low correlations between intentions and behavior reported in the literature may occur when investigators try to predict a criterion over which people have relatively little volitional control.

This discussion implies that we should be able to improve prediction of behavior if we consider not only intention but also the degree to which an individual actually has control over performing the behavior. Volitional control is expected to moderate the intention–behavior relation such that the effect of intention on behavior is stronger when actual control is high rather than low. In fact, when most people actually have control over performance of a behavior, intention by itself should permit good prediction. It is only when people vary in the degree to which they have control, can we expect that taking control into account will improve behavioral prediction (Ajzen, 1985).

Unfortunately, it is not at all clear what constitutes actual control over a behavior or how to assess it. Although we may be able to measure some aspects of actual control, in most instances we lack sufficient information about all the relevant factors that may facilitate or impede performance of the behavior. However, it is possible that people's *perceptions* of the extent to which they have control over a behavior accurately reflect their actual control. To the extent that perceived behavioral control is indeed veridical, it can serve as a proxy for actual control and be used to improve prediction of behavior.

Numerous studies conducted over the past 10 years have shown that taking into account perceived behavioral control can improve prediction of behavior. Although, conceptually, perceived control is expected to *moderate* the intention–behavior relation, in practice most investigators have looked at the additive effects of intention and perceptions of control.[9] Meta-analyses that have examined the contribution of perceived behavioral control for a wide variety of behaviors have found that, on average, perceived behavioral control explains approximately an additional 2% of the variance in behavior (Armitage & Conner, 2001; Cheung & Chan, 2000), a small though significant increase. Of course, as noted earlier, we would not expect perceived behavioral control to be an important predictor for every type of behavior. When volitional control is high, intentions are good predictors of behavior and including a measure of perceived behavioral control accounts for little if any additional variance. When behavior is not under complete volitional control, however, measuring perceptions of control can make a valuable contribution (Madden, Ellen, & Ajzen, 1992). Consistent with this argument, it is found that the amount of variance in behavior explained by perceived behavioral control varies significantly across behavioral domains (Cheung & Chan, 2000; Notani, 1998). For example, in the case of regularly attending an exercise class (Courneya & McAuley, 1995), the mean level of perceived behavioral control was relatively high, and it explained only 1% of additional variance in behavior beyond a measure of intention. In contrast, in a sample of smokers who, on average, perceived that they had relatively little control over not smoking, the measure of perceived behavioral control accounted for an additional 12% of the variance in smoking behavior (Godin, Valois, Lepage, & Desharnais, 1992; see also Madden et al., 1992).

To summarize briefly, our discussion of research on the prediction of behavior from intentions has shown that, as a general rule, when people have control over performance of a behavior, they tend to act in accordance with their intentions. When the behavior is not under complete volitional control and objective measures of actual control are unavailable, assessing perceptions of behavioral control can help improve prediction. Additionally, it is important to ensure compatibility between measures of intention and behavior and to take into account the intention's stability over time because changes in intentions tend to lower their predictive validity.

PREDICTING INTENTIONS: MODELS OF REASONED ACTION

Because intentions are found to be good predictors of specific behaviors, they have become a critical part of many contemporary theories of human social behavior [social cognitive theory (Bandura, 1997, 1998),[10] the health belief model (Rosenstock, Strecher, & Becker, 1994; Strecher, Champion, & Rosenstock, 1997), the information–motivation–behavioral skills model (Fisher & Fisher, 1992), the theory of interpersonal relations and subjective culture (Triandis, 1977), the theory of trying (Bagozzi & Warshaw, 1990), the prototype/willingness model (Gibbons, Gerrard, Blanton, & Russell, 1998)]. To go beyond prediction and provide an explanation of behavior, these theories also deal with the factors that lead to the formation of intentions. Although the theories differ in detail, there is growing convergence on a small number of variables that account for much of the variance in behavioral intentions (Bandura, 1998; Fishbein, 2000; Fishbein, Triandis, et al., 2001; Petraitis, Flay, & Miller, 1995). These variables can be viewed as representing three major kinds of considerations that influence the decision to engage in a given behavior: the likely positive or negative consequences of the behavior, the approval or disapproval of the behavior by respected individuals or groups, and the factors that may facilitate or impede performance of the behavior.

Considerations of the likely consequences of a behavior have been called behavioral beliefs (Ajzen & Fishbein, 1980; Fishbein & Ajzen, 1975), outcome expectancies (Bandura, 1977), or costs and benefits (Becker, 1974). In the aggregate, these beliefs and their associated evaluations are assumed to produce an overall positive or negative evaluation or attitude toward performing the behavior in question. Specifically, if the perceived advantages of performing the behavior outweigh its perceived disadvantages, people are likely to form a favorable attitude toward the behavior. Conversely, if, on balance, the perceived disadvantages outweigh the perceived advantages, a negative attitude is likely to be formed. (For a detailed discussion of the process whereby beliefs lead to the formation of attitudes, see Kruglanski & Stroebe, in this volume.)

Considerations that deal with the likely approval or disapproval of a behavior by friends, family members, coworkers, and so forth are usually termed normative beliefs and, in their totality, they are assumed to lead to perceived social pressure or subjective norm to engage or not engage in the behavior (Ajzen & Fishbein, 1980; Fishbein & Ajzen, 1975). When people believe that most respected others would expect them to perform the behavior or are themselves performing the behavior, the subjective norm will exert pressure to engage in the behavior. Conversely, when most normative beliefs are antagonistic, the perceived social norm will exert pressure not to perform the behavior.

Finally, beliefs concerning the presence or absence of factors that make performance of a behavior easier or more difficult have been termed control beliefs. In their totality, these control beliefs lead to the perception that one has or does not have the capacity to carry out the behavior, referred to variously as self-efficacy and personal agency (Bandura, 1977) or perceived behavioral control (Ajzen, 1991). People who believe that they have the skills and other resources needed to perform the behavior or overcome barriers are likely to develop a strong sense of self-efficacy or perceived behavioral control, whereas people who believe that they lack some of the requisite resources are likely to have a much weaker sense of personal agency.

The Reasoned Action Approach

The process described whereby people arrive at their intentions represents a *reasoned action* approach to the explanation and prediction of social behavior in the sense that people's behavioral intentions are assumed to follow reasonably from their beliefs about performing the behavior. These beliefs need not be veridical; they may be inaccurate, biased, or even irrational. However, once a set of beliefs is formed, it provides the cognitive foundation from which

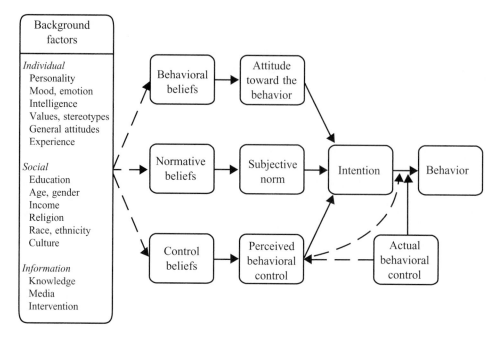

FIG 5.3.   The theories of reasoned action and planned behavior.

attitudes, perceived social norms, and perceptions of control—and ultimately intentions—are assumed to follow in a reasonable and consistent fashion.

It is important to realize that the behavioral, normative, and control beliefs people hold about performance of a given behavior are influenced by a wide variety of cultural, personal, and situational factors. Thus, we may find differences in beliefs between men and women, young and old, Black and White, educated and uneducated, rich and poor, dominant and submissive, shy and outgoing, and between individuals who have an individualistic and those who have a collectivistic orientation. In addition, they may be affected by the physical environment, the social environment, exposure to information, as well as such broad dispositions as values and prejudices.

Figure 5.3 depicts one way in which the antecedents of intentions and behavior can be represented (Ajzen, 1991; Fishbein, 2000). Implicit in this model are several fundamental assumptions:

1. Intention is the immediate antecedent of actual behavior.
2. Intention, in turn, is determined by attitude toward the behavior, subjective norm, and perceived behavioral control.
3. These determinants are themselves a function, respectively, of underlying behavioral, normative, and control beliefs.
4. Behavioral, normative, and control beliefs can vary as a function of a wide range of background factors.

In Fig. 5.3, the solid arrow pointing from actual control to the intention–behavior link indicates that volitional control is expected to moderate the intention–behavior relation such that the effect of intention on behavior is stronger when actual control is high rather than low. Also, as noted earlier, to the extent that perceived behavioral control is veridical, it can serve as a proxy for actual control and be used to improve prediction of behavior. This possibility is shown by the dotted arrows that connect actual control to perceived control and perceived control to the intention–behavior link.

For the sake of simplicity, several important relations are not shown in the Fig. 5.3 diagram. First, performance of a behavior can provide new information about the likely outcomes of the behavior, about expectations of others, and about issues of control. These feedback loops are of course likely to influence future intentions and behavior, and they are partly captured by including past behavior among the background factors that influence beliefs.

Second, once formed, attitudes toward a behavior can work backwards to influence the formation of new behavioral beliefs (see Marsh & Wallace, in this volume). That is, existing attitudes can bias perception and interpretation of new information—sometimes through a process of wishful thinking or rationalization—and, thus, influence the formation of new behavioral beliefs (see McGuire & McGuire, 1991). The same may be true for subjective norms feeding back on normative beliefs, and for existing perceptions of control influencing formation of new control beliefs.

Third, attitudes, subjective norms, and perceptions of control, although conceptually in-dependent, can correlate with each other because they may be based in part on the same information. For example, if a behavior is thought to produce favorable health outcomes, peo-ple may form a positive attitude toward the behavior, and they may also infer that their spouses or other relevant referents would want them to perform it. Similarly, people who believe that they lack the skills required to perform a behavior may anticipate failure and, thus, may develop a negative attitude toward the behavior.

Fourth, the diagram fails to show the relative weights or importance of attitude, subjective norm, and perceived control in the prediction of intention. It is assumed that these weights vary as a function of the particular behavior and the population under consideration. Thus, one behavior may be influenced primarily by attitudinal considerations, whereas another be-havior may be primarily under the influence of normative or control factors. In fact, in some applications, one or another of the three predictors may be irrelevant and make no significant contribution to the prediction of intention. Similar effects may be observed as we move from one population to another. When this happens, it merely indicates that for the particular behav-ior or population under investigation, the factor in question is not an important consideration in the formation of intentions. Such a finding should not be considered evidence inconsistent with a reasoned action approach.

Note also that at the core of the model depicted in Fig. 5.3 is a causal chain of effects starting with the formation of behavioral, normative, and control beliefs. These beliefs are assumed to influence attitudes, subjective norms, and perceived behavioral control which, in turn, produce intentions and behavior. Behavior, thus, rests ultimately on the information people have relevant to the behavior, and it is in this sense that behavior is reasoned. However, this should not be taken to mean that people consciously review every step in the chain each time they engage in a behavior. Once formed, attitudes, norms, perceptions of control, and intentions can be highly accessible and readily available to guide performance of the behavior. That is, people do not have to review their behavioral, normative, or control beliefs for these constructs to be activated. For example, a previously formed attitude toward lifting weights is automatically activated and can be readily available in the future without having to consider all the likely advantages and disadvantages of this behavior (see Ajzen & Fishbein, 2000 for a discussion of automatic processes in reasoned action).

Empirical Evidence

Research conducted over the past 35 years has provided strong support for the utility of the reasoned action approach. In this period of time, literally thousands of studies have attempted to predict behavior in various domains from one or more of the core constructs previously described. We have already seen that intentions are found to be good predictors of behavior, particularly when the behavior is under volitional control. In addition, a great number of studies conducted in the context of Bandura's (1977) social cognitive theory have documented that self-efficacy is a good predictor of behavior (e.g., Garcia & King, 1991; Longo, Lent, & Brown, 1922; Sadri & Robertson, 1993). Further, measures of perceived behavioral control or self-efficacy are often found to improve prediction over and above intention (Armitage & Conner, 2001; Cheung & Chan, 2000), and this is particularly true when the behavior is not under complete volitional control (Madden, Ellen, & Ajzen, 1992). We now turn to research dealing with prediction of intentions.

Prediction of Intentions

Because much of the research on the determinants of behavioral intentions has been conducted in the context of the theories of reasoned action (Ajzen & Fishbein, 1980; Fishbein, 1967; Fishbein & Ajzen, 1975) and planned behavior (Ajzen, 1985, 1991), most of the relevant data comes from tests of these theories. Several meta-analyses of the empirical literature have provided evidence to show that intentions can be predicted with considerable accuracy from measures of attitudes toward the behavior, subjective norms, and perceived behavioral control or self-efficacy (Albarracín et al., 2001; Armitage & Conner, 2001; Godin & Kok, 1996; Hagger, Chatzisarantis, & Biddle, 2002b; Sheeran & Taylor, 1999; Shepherd, Hartwick, & Warshaw, 1988; van den Putte, 1993). For a wide range of behaviors, attitudes are found to correlate well with intentions; across the different meta-analyses, the mean correlations range from .45 to .60. For the prediction of intentions from subjective norms, these correlations range from .34 to .42, and for the prediction of intention from perceived behavioral control, the range is .35 to .46. In the original theory of reasoned action, prior to the introduction of perceived behavioral control, the multiple correlations for predicting intentions from attitudes and subjective norms ranged from .66 to .70. With the addition of perceived behavioral control, the multiple correlations were found to range from .63 to .71. Although these results appear to indicate no improvement by the addition of perceived behavioral control, it must be recognized that the findings come from different data sets. When all variables were measured in the same study, perceived behavioral control accounted, on average, for an additional 6% of the variance in intentions (Armitage & Conner, 2001).[11]

Relative Importance of Attitudes, Norms, and Control as Predictors of Intention. The model previously described suggests that the relative contributions of attitudes, subjective norms, and perceptions of control (or self-efficacy) to the prediction of intentions can vary as a function of the behavior and the population under investigation. For example, we saw that, across a variety of different behaviors, perceived behavioral control contributes significant variance to the prediction of intentions. On closer inspection, however, it is found that the additional variance explained depends greatly on the type of behavior under consideration. Generally speaking, perceived behavioral control takes on greater importance when issues of actual control are associated with performance of the behavior. Thus, control is found to contribute relatively little to the prediction of intentions to consume common foods (Sparks, Hedderley, & Shepherd, 1992) but to be an important predictor of intentions to lose weight (Netemeyer, Burton, & Johnston, 1991).[12]

Turning to the relative contributions of attitudes and subjective norms to the prediction of intentions, one of the first tests of the reasoned action approach (Ajzen & Fishbein, 1970) experimentally induced cooperative or competitive orientations in the context of a prisoner's dilemma game. Intentions to choose the cooperative alternative were controlled primarily by subjective norms in the cooperative condition and by attitudes in the competitive condition.

Similarly, after priming the accessibility of either the private or the collective self, intentions to use condoms during sexual intercourse were found to be more under the control of attitudes in the former condition and more under the control of subjective norms in the latter (Ybarra & Trafimow, 1998).

There is also some evidence that individuals differ consistently in the amount of weight they place on attitudinal and normative considerations. Within-subjects multiple regression analyses across 30 different behaviors (Trafimow & Finlay, 1996; see also Finlay, Trafimow, & Moroi, 1999) showed that for some individuals, attitudes were better predictors of intentions than were subjective norms, whereas for other individuals, subjective norms were better predictors than attitudes.

The Role of Background Factors.   According to a reasoned action approach, the major predictors of intentions and behavior follow reasonably from—and can be understood in terms of—behavioral, normative, and control beliefs. This approach, however, does not address the origins of these beliefs. Clearly, a multitude of variables could potentially influence the beliefs people hold: age, gender, ethnicity, socioeconomic status, education, nationality, religious affiliation, personality, mood, emotion, general attitudes and values, intelligence, group membership, past experiences, exposure to information, social support, coping skills, and so forth. In our discussion of the MODE model earlier in this chapter, we noted that general attitudes toward objects can influence performance of a specific behavior by biasing perception of the behavior's likely consequences and, hence, affecting the attitude toward the behavior. In a similar fashion, such general attitudes may also sometimes be found to exert an effect on normative or control beliefs and, thus, again influence behavior indirectly by changing subjective norms or perceptions of behavioral control.

As was illustrated in Fig. 5.3, a reasoned action approach recognizes the potential importance of various kinds of background factors. However, the dotted arrows in the diagram indicate that, although a given background factor may, in fact, influence behavioral, normative, or control beliefs, there is no necessary connection between background factors and beliefs. Whether a given belief is or is not affected by a particular background factor is an empirical question. In light of the vast number of potentially relevant background factors, it is difficult to know which should be considered without a theory to guide selection in the behavioral domain of interest. Theories of this kind are not part of a reasoned action approach but can complement this approach by identifying relevant background factors and thereby deepen our understanding of a behavior's determinants (see Petraitis, Flay, & Miller 1995).

This discussion implies that background factors influence intentions and behavior indirectly by their effects on behavioral, normative, or control beliefs and, through these beliefs, on attitudes, subjective norms, or perceptions of control. Many studies have obtained patterns of results consistent with this expectation. Although investigators occasionally report significant direct effects of certain background factors after controlling for the reasoned action variables, for the most part the influence of background factors can be traced to their impact on the proximal determinants of intentions. For example, based on self-determination theory (Deci & Ryan, 1985), Hagger, Chatzisarantis, and Biddle (2002a) examined the effects of controlling (i.e., extrinsic) versus autonomous (i.e., intrinsic) motives on adolescents' intentions to engage in physical activity. When considered simultaneously, only the autonomous motive was found to be significantly related to intention. More important, consistent with expectation, the effect of the autonomous motive on intentions was completely mediated by its impacts on attitudes and perceived behavioral control. In another study (Conner & Flesch, 2001), it was found that compared to women, men had significantly stronger intentions to have casual sex, but after controlling for the predictors in the theory of planned behavior, the effect of gender was no longer significant. In an investigation of adolescents' intentions to use marijuana

(Fishbein et al., 2002), a number of background factors were assessed, including time spent with friends who tend to get into trouble, sensation seeking, and parental supervision. As might be expected, intentions to smoke marijuana increased with the amount of time spent in the company of friends who tend to get in trouble and with sensation seeking, and decreased with amount of parental supervision. Consistent with a reasoned action approach, however, the effects of these variables on intentions could be traced to their influence on one or more of the proximal determinants of intentions (i.e., attitudes, subjective norms, and perceived behavioral control). When these determinants were statistically controlled, the background factors no longer correlated significantly with intentions.

Issues Related to the Reasoned Action Approach

Perhaps because it provides a useful framework for understanding and predicting a wide variety of behaviors, the reasoned action approach has stimulated a great deal of interest and research. Many investigators (e.g., Eagly & Chaiken, 1993; Kiesler, 1981; Petraitis, Flay, & Miller, 1995) have noted that the theories of reasoned action and planned behavior have produced very encouraging results, providing "the most complete informational analysis of attitudes and, of equal importance . . . a coherent and highly useful model of the relationships among beliefs, attitudes, and behaviors" (Petty & Cacioppo, 1981, p. 204).

Questions Regarding the Causal Model and Its Major Concepts

Causality.   Despite or perhaps because of its success, investigators have raised a number of important conceptual as well as empirical concerns (see Eagly & Chaiken, 1993, for a discussion). One general issue has to do with the validity of the assumed causal chain that links beliefs to behavior. Most research on the theories of reasoned action and planned behavior, whether cross-sectional or prospective, is correlational in nature and does not provide direct evidence for causal effects. Evidence regarding causality is, however, available in several recent theory-based behavior change interventions (e.g., Bamberg, Ajzen, & Schmidt, 2003; Brubaker & Fowler, 1990; Fishbein, Ajzen, & McArdle, 1980; Fishbein, Hennessy, et al., 2001; Jemmott, Jemmott, Fong, & McCaffree, 1999; Sanderson & Jemmott, 1996; Van Ryn & Vinokur, 1992). In most interventions of this kind, information relevant to one or more of the theory's predictors is provided, and its effect on behavior is traced through the theoretical antecedents. For example, Brubaker and Fowler (1990) exposed male college students to a theory-based tape-recorded message designed to encourage testicular self-examination (TSE) and compared the effects of this intervention to an information-only condition and a no-intervention control group. As expected, the theory-based intervention produced significantly higher rates of TSE than either of the other two conditions. A structural equation analysis showed that, consistent with the assumption of a causal chain of effects, the intervention significantly affected beliefs, which in turn influenced attitudes toward TSE, subjective norms, and perceived behavioral control. Changes in these determinants led to changes in intentions and finally to a significant increase in the proportion of participants who performed TSE.

Meaningfulness of Attitude Toward a Behavior.   Some investigators have been uneasy about the shift in focus from broad behavioral dispositions to attitudes toward a behavior. As we noted in our discussion of the attitude–behavior relation, early work was centered on general attitudes toward institutions, policies, ethnic groups, and so on. We saw that such broad attitudes correlate well with equally broad, aggregated measures of behavior but, unfortunately, they tend to be rather poor predictors of specific behaviors. It is for this reason that in the context of reasoned action models attention turned to behavior-focused attitudes that are compatible with the behavioral criterion in terms of target, action, context, and time elements. Some investigators bemoan this move, fearing that attitudes toward a behavior are too specific to have much psychological significance.

This concern reflects, in large part, a misunderstanding of the principle of compatibility. This principle is sometimes mistakenly interpreted to mean that accurate prediction requires extremely specific behavioral criteria in terms of target, action, context, and time elements, and that the measure of attitude must be equally specific. In reality, the principle of compatibility merely stipulates that predictors and behavioral criteria must be defined at the same level of generality or specificity. The investigator's operationalization of the behavioral criterion determines how specific or general the measure of attitude must be. Thus, an investigator studying energy conservation should construct an aggregate index of this type of behavior as the criterion and then assess attitudes toward the general construct of energy conservation. However, if the behavioral criterion is operationalized as recycling paper every week, then the compatible attitude would be the more specific attitude toward this behavior, that is, attitude toward recycling paper every week. It is up to the investigator to decide at what level of generality or specificity to operate.

The Nature of Attitude, Subjective Norm, and Perceived Behavioral Control. Issues have also been raised with respect to the structure of the theory's three major determinants of intentions: attitude, subjective norm, and perceived behavioral control. It is now generally recognized that attitude toward a behavior contains instrumental (e.g., *desirable–undesirable, valuable–worthless*) as well as experiential (e.g., *pleasant–unpleasant, interesting–boring*) aspects (Ajzen & Driver, 1992; Crites, Fabrigar, & Petty, 1994), and that attitude measures should contain items representing these two sub-components. Similarly, investigators have distinguished between two types of norms: injunctive (i.e., perceptions of what others think one should do) and descriptive or behavioral (i.e, perceptions of what others are doing) (Cialdini, 2003; Heath & Gifford, 2002; Kashima & Gallois, 1993). Items designed to tap both types of norms are needed in order to obtain a complete measure of subjective norm.

More controversial is the nature and measurement of perceived behavioral control. Here too, there appear to be two identifiable factors. Items concerned with the ease or difficulty of performing a behavior, or confidence in one's ability to perform it, tend to load on one factor, whereas items that address control over the behavior, or the extent to which its performance is up to the actor, load on the other (e.g., Armitage & Conner, 1999; Manstead & van Eekelen, 1998; Terry & O'Leary, 1995). Some investigators concluded that the first factor reflects beliefs about internal control issues, whereas the second deals with external control issues. However, there is no reason to assume that an item asking whether performance of a behavior is difficult (first factor) refers to internal control, nor that an item asking whether you feel in complete control over performing the behavior (second factor) refers to external control.

A second, parallel interpretation is sometimes given to the two control factors in which the first factor is said to represent self-efficacy beliefs and the second represents control beliefs (Armitage, Conner, Loach, & Willetts, 1999; Manstead & van Eekelen, 1998). This interpretation, too, is problematic. The proposed inclusion of items assessing ease or difficulty as indicators of self-efficacy is inconsistent with Bandura's (1997) conceptualization of this construct. According to Bandura, " . . . highly self-efficacious individuals may view certain undertakings as inherently difficult but believe firmly that they can succeed through ingenuity and perseverant effort" (p. 127).

Although the nature of the two empirically identified factors remains unclear, items representing the two control factors are found to be correlated, and measures that combine both types of items often reveal high internal consistency (Sparks, Guthrie' & Shepherd 1997; see Ajzen,

2002a for a review). Thus, similar to the measurement of attitudes and subjective norms, a comprehensive measure of perceived control is obtained by including items representing both factors.[13]

The Question of Sufficiency

The concerns discussed thus far have dealt with issues related to the causal structure of the theories of reasoned action and planned behavior, and to the nature of the constructs composing these theories. We now turn to the argument that these constructs may not be sufficient to fully explain people's intentions and actions (see Conner & Armitage, 1998). Indeed, one of the most frequently addressed questions in tests of these theories has to do with the prospect of increasing the amount of explained variance in intentions or behavior by adding one or more predictors.

In many studies, investigators have considered background factors such as demographic variables or personality traits in addition to the predictors in the theories of reasoned action and planned behavior. We noted earlier that factors of this kind can further our understanding of the behavior by providing insight into the origins of underlying beliefs, but their effects on intentions and behavior tend to be indirect. Indeed, even when a background factor is found to explain additional variance in intentions or behavior, the amount of variance accounted for is usually very small, and rarely have investigators proposed that personality or demographic variables be considered proximal determinants of intentions and actions.

A number of other variables, however, have been proposed as additions to the theory's basic predictors. Like the basic components of the theory, the proposed additions are defined at a level compatible with the behavior under investigation. In earlier treatments of the theories of reasoned action and planned behavior (Ajzen, 1991; Ajzen & Fishbein, 1980), this possibility was explicitly left open. In fact, the theory of planned behavior was developed in this fashion by adding perceived behavioral control to the original theory of reasoned action.

Some of the proposed additional predictors essentially focus on one aspect of a component already contained in the theory. For example, several investigators (Corby, Jamner, & Wolitski, 1996; Jamner, Wolitski, Corby, & Fishbein, 1998; Nucifora, Kashima, & Gallois, 1993) interested in HIV prevention have assigned a special role to the normative expectations of one's partner (partner norm), separate from other normative beliefs or measures of subjective norm. In other areas of research, investigators have isolated anticipated regret, independent of other outcome expectancies (Parker, Manstead, & Stradling, 1995; Richard, de Vries, & van der Pligt, 1998; Richard, van der Pligt, & de Vries, 1996; Sheeran & Orbell, 1999a). In his model of interpersonal relations, Triandis (1977; see also Richard, van der Pligt, & de Vries, 1995) included expected emotional responses or affect in his attempt to predict behavioral intention. Like anticipated regret, these anticipated emotions can be considered a subset of behavioral beliefs (Bandura, 1977; Conner, Black, & Stratton, 1998).

Whereas, with respect to normative considerations, some theorists have focused on partner norms, others have proposed to add the concept of moral norm (e.g., Beck & Ajzen, 1991; Gorsuch & Ortberg, 1983; Harrison, 1995; Manstead, 2000; Warburton & Terry, 2000; Zuckerman & Reis, 1978) and, again, doing so tends to increase the proportion of explained variance. Note, however, that partner norms as well as moral norms are applicable only to certain classes of behavior, that is, to behaviors that involve a sex partner in the case of partner norms and behaviors that have a moral component in the case of moral norms. Indeed, to the best of our knowledge, partner norms have been given the status of a separate component only in STD/HIV research, and most of the studies that have shown a residual effect for moral norms have dealt with behaviors that have a clear moral dimension: shoplifting, cheating, and lying (Beck & Ajzen, 1991); returning an erroneous tax refund to the IRS or, for seminary students, to take a job that requires working on Sundays (Gorsuch & Ortberg, 1983); volunteering to work in a homeless shelter (Harrison, 1995) or to provide other community services (Warburton & Terry, 2000); and donating blood (Zuckerman & Reis, 1978).

Other proposed additions to the theories of reasoned action and planned behavior can perhaps best be viewed as alternative measures of existing constructs. Closely related to intentions are measures designed to capture such constructs as behavioral expectations (Warshaw & Davis, 1985), willingness to perform a behavior (Gibbons, Gerrard, Blanton, & Russell, 1998), personal norm with respect to the behavior (Bamberg & Schmidt, 2003; Parker, Manstead, & Stradling, 1995; Vermette & Godin, 1996), and identification with the behavior, that is, self-identity (e.g., Armitage & Conner, 1999; Conner, Warren, Close, & Sparks, 1999; Fekadu & Kraft, 2001; Sparks & Guthrie, 1998). Measures of these constructs tend to correlate highly with behavioral intention, and, consequently, they are found to account for little additional variance in the prediction of behavior. For example, it has been hypothesized that behavioral expectations are better predictors of behavior than are behavioral intentions because the former are more likely to take into account possible impediments to performance of the behavior (Shepherd, Hartwick, & Warshaw, 1988; Warshaw & Davis, 1985). In this research, such items as *I intend to . . . , I will try to . . . ,* and *I plan to . . .* have been used to assess intentions, whereas such items as *I expect to . . .* and *I will . . .* have been used to assess behavioral expectations (Warshaw & Davis, 1985). Recent meta-analyses have failed to provide support for the superiority of behavioral expectation measures over measures of behavioral intention. In studies concerned with the prediction of condom use, Sheeran and Orbell (1998) found no difference in the mean amount of variance accounted for by behavioral expectation (18%) and by behavioral intention (19%). A meta-analysis of a much broader set of behaviors (Armitage & Conner, 2001) also found no difference in the predictive validity of expectations and intentions, and adding a measure of behavioral expectation failed to improve prediction of behavior.

In short, it is possible to consider the addition of various behavior-specific constructs to the theories of reasoned action and planned behavior. Often, these additions are found to slightly improve the prediction of intentions over and above the level obtained by considering attitude, subjective norm, and perceived behavioral control; and in some cases, the proposed additions explain variance in behavior beyond intention and perception of control. However, for the sake of parsimony, additional predictors should be proposed and added to the theory with caution, and only after careful deliberation and empirical exploration.

Past Behavior and Habit

One other issue related to the question of sufficiency is worth discussing. It is well known that past behavior can be a good predictor of later action. Of greater importance, the relation between prior and later behavior is often not fully mediated by the predictors in the theories of reasoned action or planned behavior (Ajzen, 1991; Albarracín, et al., 2001; Bagozzi, 1981; Bentler & Speckart, 1979; Fredricks & Dossett, 1983; for reviews, see Conner & Armitage, 1998; Ouellette & Wood, 1998). For example, in a study of exercise behavior (Norman & Smith, 1995), undergraduate college students completed a theory of planned behavior questionnaire on two occasions, 6 months apart. Without past exercise, the theory of planned behavior variables accounted for 41% of the variance in later exercise behavior. Adding past exercise behavior to the prediction equation raised the proportion of explained variance to 54%, a highly significant increase.

Based on findings of this kind, some investigators have suggested that past behavior be added to the theories of reasoned action and planned behavior. It should be clear, however, that past behavior does not have the same status as the other predictors. Unlike attitude, subjective norm, perceived behavioral control, and intention, frequency of past behavior cannot be used to explain performance of later action. To argue that we behave the way we do now because we performed the behavior in the past begs the question as to why we previously behaved that way. In fact, investigators who have proposed the addition of past behavior have usually done so under the assumption that the frequency with which a behavior has been performed in the past can be used as an indicator of habit strength. With repeated performance, behavior is said to habituate, and it is habit strength—rather than past performance frequency as such—that is assumed to influence later action (see Aarts, Verplanken, & van Knippenberg, 1998; Ouellette & Wood, 1998; Triandis, 1977). Specifically, with repeated performance, behavior is assumed to come under the control of stimulus cues, bypassing intentions and perceptions of behavioral control.

There are, however, a number of problems with this analysis of the role of habit in the context of reasoned action models (see Ajzen, 2002b for a discussion). First, the fact that a behavior has been performed many times is no guarantee that it has habituated. To substantiate this claim, we would need an independent measure of habit strength (Eagly & Chaiken, 1993, p. 181). Work is currently under way to develop valid measures of habit strength that are independent of past performance frequency (see Verplanken & Orbell, 2003). Second, even if habituation occurred, we could not be sure how habit strength is related to the frequency of past performance because low frequency of past performance, just as high frequency, may also be an indication of a strong habit. For example, consistent failure to wear a seatbelt may be indicative of a strong habitual pattern of behavior, not of the absence of habit (see Mittal, 1988).

At least two reasons may be suggested for the unmediated, residual impact of past on later behavior in the context of reasoned action models (see Ajzen, 2002b). The first is methodological, having to do with our measures of intention and behavior. Whereas past and later behavior are typically assessed in terms of frequency of performance over some period of time, measures of intention usually rely on expressions of perceived performance likelihood or subjective strength of the intention. There is, thus, greater scale compatibility between measures of past and later behavior than between measures of intention and behavior (Courneya & McAuley, 1993). The greater shared method variance between measures of past and later behavior may be at least in part responsible for the residual effect of past behavior.

Some evidence for this argument can be found in a study on the prediction of physical activity conducted in the framework of the theory of planned behavior (Courneya & McAuley, 1994). In this study, participants reported the number of times they had engaged in physical activity in the past 4 weeks, and did so again 4 weeks later. At the first interview, they also indicated their intentions to engage in physical activity during the next 4 weeks. These intentions were assessed on a likelihood scale (7-point *extremely unlikely–extremely likely*) and on a numerical scale (the number of times respondents intended to exercise in the next 4 weeks). Clearly, the numerical scale was more compatible with the measure of behavior than was the likelihood scale. Consistent with expectations, the numerical intention scale correlated more highly with later behavior ($r = .60$) than did the likelihood scale ($r = .44$). More important, in a mediational analysis, the strong correlation between prior and later behavior ($r = .62$) was reduced only slightly (to .55) when the likelihood measure was held constant, but much more so and significantly (to .34) when the numerical measure was held constant.

Beyond scale compatibility, the residual effect of past on later behavior may also be due to the possibility that intentions undergo change as people try to implement an intended action. When people encounter unanticipated consequences or difficulties, they may revert to their original pattern of behavior, thus lending predictive validity to prior behavior (see Ajzen, 2002b, for a discussion). Consider, for example, a person who has not exercised regularly in the past, but who forms the intention to do so in the future. Initial attempts to carry out the intention may reveal this behavior to be more difficult or less beneficial than anticipated. As a result, the person may abandon the plan, no longer intending to exercise. The measured intention would fail to predict the person's actual behavior, but a measure of prior behavior would afford accurate prediction. If a sufficient number of participants in a study changed their intentions in this manner, the relation between past and later behavior would not be fully mediated by the original intention.

The Assumption That Action Is Reasoned

The issues and concerns discussed thus far had to do with some of the details of a reasoned action approach: the nature of the theory's predictors and the question of their sufficiency. Some investigators, however, have challenged this approach more broadly, questioning the basic assumption that human behavior can be described as reasoned. According to this critique, the theories of reasoned action and planned behavior are too rational, failing to take into account emotions, compulsions, and other noncognitive or irrational determinants of human behavior (e.g., Armitage, Conner, & Norman, 1999; Gibbons, Gerrard, Blanton, & Russell, 1998; Ingham, 1994; Morojele & Stephenson, 1994; van der Pligt & de Vries, 1998).

It is true that much of the research conducted in the framework of the theories of reasoned action and planned behavior has devoted little attention to the role of emotion in the prediction of intentions and actions. This is not to say, however, that emotions have no place in theories of this kind. On the contrary, within these theories emotions can have a strong impact on intentions and behaviors, but like other background factors, this influence is assumed to be indirect. It is well known that general moods and emotions can have systematic effects on beliefs and evaluations: People in a positive mood tend to evaluate events more favorably and to judge favorable events as more likely than people in a negative mood (e.g., Forgas, Bower, & Krantz, 1984; Johnson & Tversky, 1983; Schaller & Cialdini, 1990, see also Clore & Schrall, in this volume). In a reasoned action approach, such effects would be expected to influence attitudes and intentions and, thus, to have an impact on behavior.

The presence of strong emotions may also help explain why people sometimes seem to act irrationally in the sense that they fail to carry out an intended behavior that is in their best interest. For example, people may realize the benefits of staying calm in the face of provocation yet, in the heat of a confrontation, lash out verbally or physically. To understand how emotions may help account for such apparently irrational behavior, it is important to make a distinction between contemplating performance of a behavior (e.g., when filling out a theory of planned behavior questionnaire) and its actual performance in a real-life context. For one, the beliefs that are activated while filling out a questionnaire may differ from the beliefs that are accessible during behavioral performance (Ajzen & Sexton, 1999; Gold, 1993). As a result, the attitudes and intentions that are assessed by the questionnaire may turn out to be poor representations of the attitudes and intentions that exist in the behavioral situation and, thus, to be poor predictors of actual behavior. More serious still, when filling out a questionnaire, people may find it virtually impossible to correctly anticipate the strong drives and emotions that may compel their behavior in real life. Thus, new army recruits may believe that they will be able to perform well under fire and intend to go fearlessly into battle, but their actual conduct may differ greatly from this imagined scenario when bombs begin to explode. It is for this reason that the military conducts training exercises with live ammunition. If sufficiently true to life, such exercises will not only help soldiers adapt to battlefield conditions, but also lead to the formation of more realistic behavioral expectations.

The potential discrepancy between responses provided on a questionnaire and responses in a behavioral context can be viewed as largely a question of proper measurement. If, when filling out a questionnaire about behavioral performance, respondents could be induced to be realistic in their expectations, the beliefs, attitudes, and intentions assessed should permit prediction of actual behavior in the performance context (Millar & Tesser, 1986; Shavitt & Fazio, 1991). The effectiveness of asking participants to form implementation intentions (Gollwitzer, 1999) or to engage in process simulation (Taylor & Pham, 1998) may be due in part to increased realism.

Not all intention–behavior discrepancies, however, can be eliminated. Even though we may be able to anticipate some of the strong forces that are likely to influence our behavior in a real-life context, there is sometimes little we can do about it. For example, it has been argued that a reasoned action approach cannot account for people's frequent failure to use condoms with casual partners. Confronted with a decision to engage or not to engage in sexual intercourse when a condom is unavailable, individuals may in the heat of passion be unable to resist the impulse despite their ability to anticipate this eventuality and their intentions to the contrary expressed on a questionnaire. Although there is undoubtedly some truth to this argument, the empirical evidence is actually quite supportive of a reasoned action approach even in this case. For example, in a longitudinal study of condom use in such high-risk populations as drug users and commercial sex workers (von Haeften, Fishbein, Kaspryzk, & Montano, 2000), 72.5% of participants who intended to always use condoms with their casual partners (or clients) reported actually doing so. This compares to a 37.5% consistent condom use among participants who did not intend to always take this protective measure. With regard to condom use across diverse populations, a meta-analytic review of 96 data sets (Albarracín et al., 2001) found a respectable correlation of .45 between intended and actual behavior.

Another factor that can produce a discrepancy between measured intentions and actual behavior is the influence of alcohol or drugs. Whereas beliefs, attitudes, and intentions are generally assessed when participants are sober, such behaviors as driving or unprotected sex may be performed under the influence of alcohol or drugs. Indeed, alcohol consumption has been shown to decrease the likelihood of condom use during casual sex (MacDonald, Zanna, & Fong, 1996), a finding interpreted as consistent with alcohol myopia (Steele & Josephs, 1990)—the tendency for alcohol intoxication to decrease cognitive capacity so that people are likely to attend only to the most salient situational cues. It is interesting to note that, alcohol intoxication was also found to increase measured *intentions* to engage in unprotected sex (MacDonald et al., 1996) and measured *intentions* to drink and drive a short distance (MacDonald, Zanna, & Fong, 1995). Nevertheless, because we usually assess attitudes and intentions when respondents are sober, our measures may not permit very accurate prediction of behavior performed while intoxicated.

EXPLICIT VERSUS IMPLICIT ATTITUDES

Our review of the literature up to this point has shown that work on the attitude–behavior relation conducted over the past 4 decades has restored faith in the utility and predictive validity of the attitude construct. However, in recent years a renewed challenge to the postulated relation between attitudes and behavior can be discerned, particularly in the domain of prejudice and discrimination (Fiske, 1998). Work in this field has led investigators to argue that expressions of stereotypical beliefs and prejudicial attitudes have declined markedly over the past decades (e.g., Dovidio, 2001; Schuman, Steeh, Bobo, & Krysan, 1997), yet discrimination against historically disadvantaged racial and ethnic groups continues to be evident in employment, education, housing, healthcare, and criminal justice (e.g., Bushway & Piehl, 2001; Crosby, Bromley, & Saxe, 1980; Daniels, 2001; Hacker, 1995; Landrine, Klonoff, & Alcaraz, 1997; Myers & Chan, 1995).[14]

Although widely accepted, evidence for the disparity between a decline in broad societal patterns of prejudicial attitudes accompanied by continued discriminatory behaviors is indirect and mostly circumstantial. To the best of our knowledge, only one study (Dovidio & Gaertner, 2000) has examined this issue directly. In this study, conducted at a Northeastern liberal arts college, prejudicial attitudes toward African Americans were found to decline slightly, but significantly, from the 1988–1989 to the 1998–1999 academic year. In contrast, hiring recommendations regarding Black and White job candidates with ambiguous qualifications favored the White candidate over the Black candidate to the same extent in both time periods. Note, however, that it is impossible to assess changes in overall discrimination by examining a single judgmental bias. Had the investigators selected a different indicator of discrimination, perhaps voting to elect a Black versus White candidate to student office, the results might have been very different.[15] To make a convincing case that, over the years, prejudice has declined more than discrimination, we would have to construct broad measures of these constructs, standardize them, and observe changes in average values over time. If we did this, we might find that discriminatory behavior has declined just as much—or perhaps even more—than expressed prejudice.

Despite the lack of firm empirical support, many investigators accept the proposition that prejudice has declined much more than discrimination. As in the 1950s, the immediate reaction to the apparent inconsistency between racial attitudes and behavior was to question the validity of our attitude measures (e.g., Crosby, Bromley, & Saxe, 1980; McConahay, Hardee, & Batts, 1981): Because of self-presentational concerns, people were presumably reluctant to express their true (negative) feelings. There was also an assumption, however, that the nature of racial prejudice had changed to become more subtle and nuanced, milder than the blatant racism of the past (McConahay, 1986). Also, prejudice might be expressed indirectly and symbolically, for example, as opposition to preferential treatment for minorities (Sears, 1988). Other theorists proposed that racial attitudes had become ambiguous or aversive, containing explicit egalitarian elements as well as more subtle and unacknowledged negative beliefs and feelings (Gaertner & Dovidio, 1986).

This revised view of the nature of contemporary prejudice provided a ready explanation for the apparent gap between low professed prejudice and high levels of discrimination. The high levels of discrimination suggested that prejudice was still very much present, but that because it had become very subtle, standard attitude scales—which measure *explicit* stereotypes and prejudice—were incapable of capturing these *implicit* dispositions. The contrast between implicit and explicit levels of prejudice plays an important role in Devine's (1989; Devine, Monteith, Zuwerink, & Elliot, 1991) dissociation model. According to this model, prejudiced and nonprejudiced individuals are equally familiar with prevailing cultural stereotypes, and these implicit stereotypes are activated automatically in the actual or symbolic presence of stereotyped group members. Nonprejudiced individuals are assumed to differ from prejudiced individuals in their explicit rejection of the cultural stereotypes and their greater motivation to inhibit the influence of automatically activated stereotypes on judgments, feelings, and actions. A similar line of reasoning underlies application of the MODE model to the relation between prejudice and discrimination (Fazio & Dunton, 1997; Fazio & Towles-Schwen, 1999). Whereas in Devine's dissociation model what is automatically activated are culturally shared stereotypes, in the MODE model the individual's own stereotype is automatically activated. As in Devine's model, however, whether or not this implicit stereotype affects judgments and behavior depends on the individual's motivation to control seemingly prejudiced reactions (Dunton & Fazio, 1997; see also Devine & Monteith, 1999).[16]

These models of prejudice are consistent with the proposition that people can hold two attitudes at the same time, one implicit and often unrecognized, the other explicit and under conscious control (Wilson, Lindsey, & Schooler, 2000). The implicit attitude is assumed to be automatically activated, whereas activation of the explicit attitude is said to require cognitive effort. Prejudicial attitudes, according to this view, may be held implicitly and be activated automatically but, given sufficient motivation and cognitive resources, the more favorable, egalitarian attitude may be retrieved and can override the effect of the implicit prejudicial attitude.

The concern with implicit attitudes in research on prejudice and discrimination is consistent with other theorizing in attitudes and social cognition that emphasizes automatic, unconscious processes assumed to function in parallel with, or in place of, deliberative action (e.g. Bargh, 1989; Bargh & Chartrand, 1999; Fazio, 1990a; Greenwald & Banaji, 1995; Langer, 1978; Wegner & Wheatley, 1999). Research on subtle aspects of prejudice received a further boost with the development of new measurement techniques that rely on reaction times to probe for implicit attitudes, most notably the implicit association test (Greenwald, McGhee, & Schwartz, 1998) and evaluative priming (Dovidio, Evans, & Tyler, 1986; Fazio, Jackson, Dunton, & Williams, 1995; see Fazio & Olson, 2003, for a review). It now became possible to compare implicit and explicit attitude measures and to examine their ability to predict actual behavior.

Predicting Behavior From Implicit and Explicit Attitudes

Although contemporary models of stereotyping and prejudice differ in detail, they agree in their overall expectations regarding the predictive validity of explicit and implicit attitude measures. Generally speaking, implicit attitudes—being automatically activated—are assumed to guide behavior by default unless they are overridden by controlled processes. Because prejudicial attitudes and behavior with respect to racial and ethnic minorities are frowned on in contemporary American society, many people try to inhibit their expression. It follows that implicit prejudicial attitudes should predict primarily behaviors that are not consciously monitored or that are difficult to control (e.g., facial expressions, eye contact, blushing, and other nonverbal behaviors), as well as behaviors that people do not view as indicative of prejudice and, thus, are not motivated to control. In contrast, behaviors that are under volitional control and whose implications for prejudice are apparent should be better predicted from explicit than from implicit measures of prejudice (see Dovidio, Brigham, Johnson, & Gaertner, 1996).

Thus far, only a small number of studies have directly tested these hypotheses, but the results have been generally consistent with predictions (see Fazio & Olson, 2003, for a review). First, as would be expected if we are dealing with two relatively independent attitudes, several studies have reported low or at best modest correlations between explicit and implicit measures of prejudice (e.g., Cunningham, Preacher, & Banaji, 2001; Dovidio, Kawakami, Johnson, Johnson, & Howard, 1997; Fazio, Jackson et al., 1995; Greenwald, McGhee, & Schwartz, 1998; Karpinski & Hilton, 2001; Wittenbrink, Judd, & Park, 1997). Second, and more important, implicit measures of prejudice have been found superior to explicit measures for the prediction of such nonverbal behaviors as blinking and eye contact (Dovidio, Kawakami et al., 1997), the number of times Whites handed a pen to a Black person as opposed to placing it on the table (Wilson, Lindsey, & Schooler, 2000), as well as the friendliness of White participants in their interactions with a Black person, judged by the Black person on the basis of the White person's nonverbal behavior (smiling, eye contact, spatial distance, and body language; Fazio, Jackson et al., 1995). A similar effect was obtained in a recent study (Sekaquaptewa, Espinoza, Thompson, Vargas, & von Hippel, 2003) dealing with behavior whose implications for prejudice was ambiguous. The critical behavior in this study was White males' choice of stereotype-consistent or inconsistent questions in a mock job interview with a Black female applicant. In this situation, an implicit measure of prejudice toward African Americans predicted choice of stereotype-consistent questions better than did an explicit measure. Note, however, that implicit attitude measures tend to have relatively low correlations even with nonverbal behaviors that are not consciously monitored; for the studies reviewed here, the correlations between implicit attitudes and nonverbal behaviors ranged from .25 to .48. This should not come as a surprise, of course, given the lack of compatibility between the general measures of prejudice and the specific behavioral criteria employed in these studies.

Evidence for the superiority of explicit over implicit measures in the prediction of well-controlled behaviors is less persuasive in that most studies have dealt with judgments rather than actual behaviors. Still, the results are consistent with expectations. Thus, it has been found that, in comparison to implicit measures of prejudice, explicit measures are better predictors of judgments concerning the verdict in the Rodney King trial involving police brutality and in attractiveness ratings of facial photographs of Black and White individuals (Fazio, Jackson et al., 1995), as well as ratings of the guilt of African American defendants in a simulated jury trial (Dovidio, Kawakami et al., 1997). In a domain unrelated to prejudice, a behavior under clear volitional control (choice of a candy bar versus an apple) was predicted from explicit but not from implicit measures of attitude toward these products (Karpinski & Hilton, 2001). The correlations between explicit attitudes and judgments or behavior in these studies were modest, ranging from .24 to .54, a finding that may again be attributable to low compatibility between the measures of attitude and behavior.

Implicit Attitudes and the Prediction of Behavior: Conclusions

Research on implicit attitudes was initially stimulated in part by an apparent discrepancy between declining levels of expressed prejudice and continuing patterns of discrimination against racial, ethnic, and other historically disadvantaged groups. Two major findings support the idea that people may express unprejudiced attitudes yet, at an implicit level, continue to harbor negative feeling toward these groups. First, measures of explicit and implicit attitudes are found to correlate weakly with each other, and, second, implicit attitudes tend to predict subtle expressions of prejudice, such as nonverbal behaviors, better than explicit attitudes. It has been suggested that, in interracial contexts, such nonverbal behaviors as nervousness, tone of voice, facial expressions, and seating distance are indicative of affective reactions to the interaction partners (Butler & Geis, 1990; Dovidio, Brigham, et al., 1996; Weitz, 1972; Word, Zanna, & Cooper, 1974). If implicit measures of prejudice can be assumed to reflect the degree of discomfort people experience in relation to African Americans, gays, or other minority groups, this would explain their ability to predict nonverbal behaviors better than explicit measures.

Although interesting and suggestive, findings regarding implicit attitudes must be interpreted with caution. In contrast to the failure of earlier disguised measures, such as physiological responses or projective tests, many investigators assume that assessment techniques based on response times provide valid attitude measures that can overcome self-presentation biases and elicit a person's true underlying attitude. Although sequential evaluative priming and the implicit association test represent promising new developments in the search for valid attitude assessment, the jury is still out on their ability to live up to their promise.[17] Not unlike projective tests and some other indirect assessment techniques (see Kidder & Campbell, 1970), reaction time measures of attitude tend to suffer from relatively low reliability (Cunningham, Preacher, & Banaji, 2001; Kawakami & Dovidio, 2001), and it is perhaps for this reason that tests of convergent validity have also been disappointing (Brauer, Wasel, & Niedenthal, 2000; Fazio & Olson, 2003). Only when corrections are made for their unreliability are different types of implicit measures shown to correlate with each other (Cunningham, Preacher, & Banaji, 2001). These findings are disconcerting from a pragmatic perspective because they suggest that implicit attitude measures can be expected to have only modest predictive validity even in relation to subtle behaviors over which people do not exercise conscious control. The limited research findings available thus far tend to bear out this pessimistic expectation.

DISCUSSION AND CONCLUSIONS

The field of social psychology has, over the years, witnessed marked shifts in the types of issues and problems addressed by investigators: conformity and group cohesion, prejudice and discrimination, communication and persuasion, causal attribution, group decision making, interpersonal attraction and intimate relationships, conflict resolution, cognitive consistency, judgmental biases and errors, and so forth. Throughout these changes the attitude construct has remained a central and vital element in theoretical as well as applied work, based in large measure on the assumption that attitudes can explain and predict social behavior in all of these domains. When empirical evidence concerning the attitude–behavior relation appeared to challenge this assumption, some investigators came to the defense of the attitude construct by questioning the validity of the instruments used to assess attitudes. Other investigators either resigned themselves to the conclusion that attitudes are poor predictors of behavior or suggested that their impact on behavior is moderated by situational factors, by personality traits, or by characteristics of the attitude itself.

The problem of low attitude–behavior correlations was resolved in part when it was realized that, although general attitudes are poor predictors of single behaviors, they correlate strongly with multiple-act criteria or behavioral aggregates. In a parallel fashion, it was shown that single behaviors can be predicted quite well from compatible measures of attitude, that is, attitude toward the behavior. Investigators reacted in one of two ways to these developments. Perhaps influenced by Allport's (1935) argument that general attitudes exert " . . . a directive or dynamic influence upon the individual's response to all objects and situations with which it is related" (p. 820), one line of research examined the processes whereby general attitudes can influence or guide performance of a specific behavior. The most sophisticated account of these processes can be found in Fazio's (1986; 1990a; Fazio & Towles-Schwen, 1999) MODE model. This approach has been highly influential, directing attention to the roles of biased information processing, attitude accessibility, and spontaneous versus deliberative processing modes as important elements linking global attitudes to specific behaviors. We saw, however, that more work is required at a conceptual level to explain the effects of general attitudes on specific behaviors when motivation or ability to process information is low, and to test the moderating effect of attitude accessibility under these conditions.

A second line of research took the single, specific behavior as its starting point and tried to identify the determinants of such a behavior. This work has been guided in large part by a reasoned action approach, in particular the theories of reasoned action and planned behavior (Ajzen, 1991; Ajzen & Fishbein, 1980; Fishbein & Ajzen, 1975). For investigators interested in predicting, understanding, and changing specific behaviors, this line of research has provided a useful conceptual framework and a workable methodology. It has directed attention to the roles of beliefs, attitudes, norms, perceived behavioral control, and intentions as important antecedents of specific behaviors. We also noted, however, that a reasoned action approach has its limits. Lack of volitional control can prevent people from carrying out an intended behavior; inaccurate information can produce unrealistic beliefs, attitudes, and intentions; unanticipated events can lead to changes in intentions; and strong emotions in a behavioral context can activate beliefs and attitudes that were not anticipated while completing a questionnaire.

The principles of aggregation and compatibility, the work linking general attitudes to specific actions, and the reasoned action approach to the prediction of specific behaviors have advanced our understanding of the attitude–behavior relation and have demonstrated the importance of attitudes as determinants of behavior. Recently, however, investigators have reopened this issue by suggesting that there is a disparity in contemporary society between high levels of discriminatory behavior and low levels of explicit prejudice. Now as in the past, a major line of defense is to question the validity of our attitude measures. Contemporary investigators again assume that if we could only measure prejudicial attitudes free of social desirability bias and other self-presentational concerns, we would be able to predict discriminatory behavior. The added twist in current theorizing is the idea that people may not be aware of their true attitudes and may, thus, be unable to explicitly report them even if they wanted to.

Contemporary research on the effects of prejudice on behavior, like early work on the attitude–behavior relation, focuses on general attitudes, primarily on prejudice with respect to ethnic or racial groups, elderly people, gays, etc. In contrast to research in most other behavioral domains, where investigators have found it useful to assess behavior-specific dispositions, in the area of discrimination, researchers continue to concentrate almost exclusively on broad prejudicial attitudes. It is not clear that a focus on general prejudice is the only or most fruitful approach to dealing with problems of discrimination. Instead, we might identify a few particularly problematic discriminatory behaviors, such as biases in hiring or access to health care, and assess dispositions relevant for the behaviors in question. Investigators in other behavioral domains have employed a reasoned action approach to examine such behaviors as using condoms, getting a mammogram, voting, using illicit drugs, adhering to a medical regimen, and so forth. Taking this kind of approach does not preclude consideration of broad dispositions and their effects on the behavior of interest. An investigator studying discriminatory hiring decisions would first assess the proximal determinants of that decision, that is, beliefs, attitudes, subjective norms, perceived control, and intentions with respect to hiring members of a minority group. The investigator could then examine how a measure of general prejudice toward members of the group in question influences these proximal determinants of the discriminatory behavior. Prejudice, thus, is treated as a background factor that can influence hiring decisions indirectly.

To be sure, current research on prejudice and discrimination has produced interesting ideas concerning the nature of prejudicial attitudes, a distinction between implicit and explicit prejudice, as well as methods for the assessment of implicit attitudes. We have seen in this chapter that general attitudes can provide useful information to predict and explain broad patterns of discriminatory behavior. However, as in earlier research, investigators in this domain have tried to relate these general attitudes not to broad patterns of discrimination but rather to single behaviors or judgments in a particular context. Theory and research regarding the attitude–behavior relation suggest that such an approach is bound to produce disappointing results. Indeed, theorists have again had to invoke moderating variables, suggesting that the effect of broad implicit attitudes on specific behaviors depends on the nature of the behavior (spontaneous or deliberative) and on such individual differences as motivation to control prejudiced reactions. It is only when the behavior is not consciously monitored or when motivation to control prejudiced reactions is relatively low that implicit attitudes are expected to predict behavior. It follows that for a wide range of behaviors, and for many individuals, broad implicit attitudes will lack predictive validity. Indeed, *implicit* measures of general attitudes are likely to encounter the same problems as *explicit* measures when it comes to the prediction of specific behaviors. Our understanding of the attitude–behavior relation could perhaps be advanced if researchers used the progress made in social cognition to focus on such proximal determinants of specific actions as attitudes toward the behavior and behavioral intentions rather than on general attitudes toward an object.

ENDNOTES

[1] Breckler (1984) obtained evidence for discriminant validity between the affective component of attitudes toward snakes on one hand and the cognitive and conative components of these attitudes on the other. However, this was the case only in the presence of a live snake, not when the snake was merely imagined. Moreover, no attempt was made in this study to predict actual behavior toward snakes.

[2] The variability in the magnitude of the reported attitude–behavior correlations in different studies may, at least in part, be due to the degree of compatibility between the obtained measures of attitude and behavior. For example, attitudes are usually assessed by asking participants how good or bad it is to perform a given behavior, whereas the measure of behavior often involves the frequency with which it was performed. Respondents who hold very positive attitudes should be very likely to perform the behavior, but there is no expectation that they will necessarily perform the behavior more frequently than respondents who hold less positive attitudes.

[3]In his more recent theorizing, Fazio (e.g., Fazio & Dunton, 1997; Fazio & Towles-Schwen, 1999) has suggested that deliberation permits other motives such as fear of invalidity or motivation to control seemingly prejudiced reactions to override the expression of even strong, chronically accessible attitudes, thus depressing the observed attitude–behavior relation. We will return to this issues in our discussion of implicit versus explicit attitudes.

[4]Similarly, work with the semantic differential on the measurement of meaning (Osgood, Suci, & Tannenbaum, 1957) has shown that attitude or evaluation is the most important aspect of any concept's connotative meaning, and just as the denotative meaning of a concept with which a person is familiar is activated automatically, so too is its evaluative meaning.

[5]Note also that, because all participants in this study were enrolled in an exercise program, the measures of exercise intentions and behavior were likely to have suffered from restriction of range.

[6]Unpublished data (Fishbein, personal communication) from a study on prediction of marijuana use provided some support for Campbell's hypothesis. Attitudes of participants who intended not to use marijuana but actually did fell in between those of participants who acted in accordance with their intentions to use marijuana and those who acted in accordance with their intentions not to use marijuana.

[7]Our discussion focuses on the failure to carry out a positive intention. It should be clear, however, that literal inconsistency is also observed when people who do not intend to perform a behavior are found to do so. For example, many people who intend not to start smoking, later take up the behavior, and some people who do not intend to eat chocolate or ice cream, nevertheless engage in these behaviors.

[8]According to Gollwitzer (personal communication), implementation intentions can also transfer control over a behavior to internal cues, such as moods or emotions.

[9]The reason for this practice is that empirically, even when an interaction is present in the data, statistical regression analyses reveal only main effects. To obtain a statistically significant interaction requires that intention and perceived control scores cover the full range of the measurement scale. For most behaviors, however, a majority of respondents fall on one or the other side of these continua.

[10]Bandura refers to intentions as proximal goals.

[11]Beyond the scope of the present chapter, there is also good evidence to support the effects of beliefs on attitudes, norms, and perceived control, as shown in Fig. 3. Some relevant discussions can be found in other chapters of this volume dealing with the effects of beliefs on attitudes (Chapter 8) and on behavior (Chapter 15).

[12]As we noted earlier, volitional control is expected to be relatively lower for attaining a goal such as losing weight than for performing a behavior such as eating a common food.

[13]Another issue related to the measurement of perceived behavioral control is use of an easy–difficult item. This item should be used with caution because it is sometimes more highly related to evaluative judgments than to perceived behavioral control (Leach, Fishbein, & Hennessy, 2001; Yzer, Hennessy & Fishbein, in press).

[14]Similar arguments have also been made in relation to discrimination based on gender and sexual preference (e.g., Ellis & Riggle, 1996; Herek, 2000; Herek & Capitanio, 1999; Huddy, Neely, & Lafay, 2000; Ridgeway, 1997).

[15]Moreover, it is difficult to derive any clear conclusions from the data in this study. In addition to declines in expressed prejudice, all other responses (e.g., judged qualification of each candidate, hiring recommendations with respect to each candidate) in all conditions of the experiment were, on the average, lower in the 1998–1999 sample than in the 1988–1989 sample. Rather than representing a decline in prejudice, the observed changes over time may simply reflect differences between the two samples.

[16]Dunton and Fazio (1997) have developed an instrument to assess individual differences in motivation to control seemingly prejudiced reactions. A second instrument was developed by Plant and Devine (1998; Devine, Plant, Amodio, Harmon-Jones, & Vance, 2002) to distinguish between internal (personal) and external (normative) motivation to respond without prejudice. With the development of these scales, it has become possible to test some of these hypotheses.

[17]Indeed, questions are currently being raised about the validity of the implicit association test (Blanton, Jaccard, & Gonzales, 2003).

REFERENCES

Aarts, H., Dijksterhuis, A., & Midden, C. (1999). To plan or not to plan? Goal achievement of interrupting the performance of mundane behaviors. *European Journal of Social Psychology, 29*, 971–979.

Aarts, H., Verplanken, B., & van Knippenberg, A. (1998). Predicting behavior from actions in the past: Repeated decision making or a matter of habit? *Journal of Applied Social Psychology, 28*, 1355–1374.

Ajzen, I. (1971). Attitudinal vs. normative messages: An investigation of the differential effects of persuasive communications on behavior. *Sociometry, 34*, 263–280.

Ajzen, I. (1985). From intentions to actions: A theory of planned behavior. In J. Kuhl & J. Beckman (Eds.), *Action-control: From cognition to behavior* (pp. 11–39). Heidelberg, Germany: Springer.

Ajzen, I. (1988). *Attitudes, personality, and behavior.* Chicago: Dorsey.

Ajzen, I. (1991). The theory of planned behavior. *Organizational Behavior and Human Decision Processes, 50,* 179–211.

Ajzen, I. (2002a). Perceived behavioral control, self-efficacy, locus of control, and the theory of planned behavior. *Journal of Applied Social Psychology, 32,* 665–683.

Ajzen, I. (2002b). Residual effects of past on later behavior: Habituation and reasoned action perspectives. *Personality and Social Psychology Review, 6,* 107–122.

Ajzen, I., Brown, T. C., & Carvajal, F. (2004). Explaining the discrepancy between intentions and actions: The case of hypothetical bias in contingent valuation. *Personality and Social Psychology Bulletin, 30,* 1108–1121.

Ajzen, I., Czasch, C., & Flood, M. G. (2002). *From intentions to behavior: Implementation intention, commitment, and conscientiousness.* Manuscript submitted for publication.

Ajzen, I., & Driver, B. L. (1992). Application of the theory of planned behavior to leisure choice. *Journal of Leisure Research, 24,* 207–224.

Ajzen, I., & Fishbein, M. (1970). The prediction of behavior from attitudinal and normative variables. *Journal of Experimental Social Psychology, 6,* 466–487.

Ajzen, I., & Fishbein, M. (1977). Attitude–behavior relations: A theoretical analysis and review of empirical research. *Psychological Bulletin, 84,* 888–918.

Ajzen, I., & Fishbein, M. (1980). *Understanding attitudes and predicting social behavior.* Englewood-Cliffs, NJ: Prentice-Hall.

Ajzen, I., & Fishbein, M. (2000). Attitudes and the attitude–behavior relation: Reasoned and automatic processes. In W. Stroebe & M. Hewstone (Eds.), *European review of social psychology* (Vol. 11, pp. 1–33). Chichester, UK: Wiley.

Ajzen, I., & Sexton, J. (1999). Depth of processing, belief congruence, and attitude–behavior correspondence. In S. Chaiken & Y. Trope (Eds.), *Dual-process theories in social psychology* (pp. 117–138). New York: Guilford.

Albarracín, D., Johnson, B. T., Fishbein, M., & Muellerleile, P. A. (2001). Theories of reasoned action and planned behavior as models of condom use: A meta-analysis. *Psychological Bulletin, 127,* 142–161.

Allport, G. W. (1935). Attitudes. In C. Murchison (Ed.), *Handbood of social psychology* (pp. 798–844). Worcester, MA: Clark University Press.

Allport, G. W. (1968). The historical background of modern social psychology. In G. Lindzey & E. Aronson (Eds.), *Handbook of social psychology* (Vol. 1, pp. 1–80). Reading, MA: Addison-Wesley.

Armitage, C. J., & Conner, M. (1999). Distinguishing perceptions of control from self-efficacy: Predicting consumption of a low-fat diet using the theory of planned behavior. *Journal of Applied Social Psychology, 29,* 72–90.

Armitage, C. J., & Conner, M. (2001). Efficacy of the theory of planned behavior: A meta-analytic review. *British Journal of Social Psychology, 40,* 471–499.

Armitage, C. J., Conner, M., Loach, J., & Willetts, D. (1999). Different perceptions of control: Applying an extended theory of planned behavior to legal and illegal drug use. *Basic and Applied Social Psychology, 21,* 301–316.

Armitage, C. J., Conner, M., & Norman, P. (1999). Differential effects of mood on information processing: Evidence from the theories of reasoned action and planned behaviour. *European Journal of Social Psychology, 29,* 419–433.

Bagozzi, R. P. (1981). An examination of the validity of two models of attitude. *Multivariate Behavioral Research, 16,* 323–359.

Bagozzi, R. P., & Warshaw, P. R. (1990). Trying to consume. *Journal of Consumer Research, 17,* 127–140.

Bamberg, S., Ajzen, I., & Schmidt, P. (2003). Choice of travel mode in the theory of planned behavior: The roles of past behavior, habit, and reasoned action. *Basic and Applied Social Psychology, 25,* 175–188.

Bamberg, S., & Schmidt, P. (2003). Incentive, morality or habit? Predicting students' car use for university routes with the models of Ajzen, Schwartz, and Triandis. *Environment & Behavior, 35,* 1–22.

Bandura, A. (1977). Self-efficacy: Toward a unifying theory of behavioral change. *Psychological Review, 84,* 191–215.

Bandura, A. (1997). *Self-efficacy: The exercise of control.* New York: Freeman.

Bandura, A. (1998). Health promotion from the perspective of social cognitive theory. *Psychology and Health, 13,* 623–649.

Bargh, J. A. (1989). Conditional automaticity: Varieties of automatic influence in social perception and cognition. In J. S. Uleman & J. A. Bargh (Eds.), *Unintended thought* (pp. 3–51). New York: Guilford.

Bargh, J. A. (1996). Automaticity in social psychology. In E. T. Higgins & A. W. Kruglanski (Eds.), *Social psychology: Handbook of basic principles* (pp. 169–183). New York: Guilford.

Bargh, J. A., Chaiken, S., Govender, R., & Pratto, F. (1992). The generality of the automatic attitude activation effect. *Journal of Personality and Social Psychology, 62,* 893–912.

Bargh, J. A., Chaiken, S., Raymond, P., & Hymes, C. (1996). The automatic evaluation effect: Unconditional automatic attitude activation with a pronunciation task. *Journal of Experimental Social Psychology, 32*, 104–128.

Bargh, J. A., & Chartrand, T. L. (1999). The unbearable automaticity of being. *American Psychologist, 54*, 462–479.

Beck, L., & Ajzen, I. (1991). Predicting dishonest actions using the theory of planned behavior. *Journal of Research in Personality, 25*, 285–301.

Becker, M. H. (1974). The health belief model and personal health behavior. *Health Education Monographs, 2*, 324–508.

Bentler, P. M., & Speckart, G. (1979). Models of attitude–behavior relations. *Psychological Review, 86*, 452–464.

Berger, I. E., & Mitchell, A. A. (1989). The effect of advertising on attitude accessibility, attitude confidence, and the Attitude–behavior relationship. *Journal of Consumer Research, 16*, 269–279.

Bernberg, R. E. (1952). Socio-psychological factors in industrial morale: I. The prediction of specific indicators. *Journal of Social Psychology, 36*, 73–82.

Bernreuter, R. (1933). Validity of the personality inventory. *Personnel Journal, 11*, 383–386.

Bird, C. (1940). *Social psychology.* Englewood Cliffs, NJ: Prentice-Hall.

Blanton, H., Jaccard, J. J., & Gonzales, P. M. (2003). *Decoding the implicit association test: Perspectives on criterion prediction.* Manuscript submitted for publication.

Blumer, H. (1955). Attitudes and the social act. *Social Problems, 3*, 59–65.

Brauer, M., Wasel, W., & Niedenthal, P. (2000). Implicit and explicit components of prejudice. *Review of General Psychology, 4*, 79–101.

Braver, S. (1996). Social contracts and the provision of public goods. In D. Schroeder (Ed.), *Social dilemmas: Perspectives on individuals and groups* (pp. 69–86). Westport, CT: Praeger.

Breckler, S. J. (1984). Empirical validation of affect, behavior, and cognition as distinct components of attitude. *Journal of Personality and Social Psychology, 47*, 1191–1205.

Brubaker, R. G., & Fowler, C. (1990). Encouraging college males to perform testicular self-examination: Evaluation of a persuasive message based on the revised theory of reasoned action. *Journal of Applied Social Psychology, 20*, 1411–1422.

Bushway, S. D., & Piehl, A. M. (2001). Judging judicial discretion: Legal factors and racial discrimination in sentencing. *Law & Society Review, 35*, 733–764.

Butler, D., & Geis, F. L. (1990). Nonverbal affect responses to male and female leaders: Implications for leadership evaluations. *Journal of Personality & Social Psychology, 58*, 48–59.

Campbell, D. T. (1950). The indirect assessment of social attitudes. *Psychological Bulletin, 47*, 15–38.

Campbell, D. T. (1963). Social attitudes and other acquired behavioral dispositions. In S. Koch (Ed.), *Psychology: A study of a science* (Vol. 6, pp. 94–172). New York: McGraw-Hill.

Campbell, D. T., & Fiske, D. W. (1959). Convergent and discriminant validation by the multitrait-multimethod matrix. *Psychological Bulletin, 56*, 81–105.

Carver, C. S. (1975). Physical aggression as a function of objective self-awareness and attitudes toward punishment. *Journal of Experimental Social Psychology, 11*, 510–519.

Chaiken, S., & Trope, Y. (Eds.). (1999). *Dual-process theories in social psychology.* New York: Guilford.

Cheung, S.-F., & Chan, D. K.-S. (2000). *The role of perceived behavioral control in predicting human behavior: A meta-analytic review of studies on the theory of planned behavior.* Unpublished manuscript, Chinese University of Hong Kong.

Cialdini, R. B. (2001). *Influence: Science and practice* (4th ed.). Boston, MA: Allyn & Bacon.

Cialdini, R. B. (2003). Crafting normative messages to protect the environment. *Current Directions in Psychological Science, 12*, 105–109.

Conner, M., & Armitage, C. J. (1998). Extending the theory of planned behavior: A review and avenues for further research. *Journal of Applied Social Psychology, 28*, 1429–1464.

Conner, M., Black, K., & Stratton, P. (1998). Understanding drug compliance in a psychiatric population: An application of the theory of planned behaviour. *Psychology, Health and Medicine, 3*, 337–344.

Conner, M., & Flesch, D. (2001). Having casual sex: Additive and interactive effects of alcohol and condom availability on the determinants of intentions. *Journal of Applied Social Psychology, 31*, 89–112.

Conner, M., Sheeran, P., Norman, P., & Armitage, C. J. (2000). Temporal stability as a moderator of relationships in the theory of planned behaviour. *British Journal of Social Psychology, 39*, 469–493.

Conner, M., Warren, R., Close, S., & Sparks, P. (1999). Alcohol consumption and the theory of planned behavior: An examination of the cognitive mediation of past behavior. *Journal of Applied Social Psychology, 29*, 1676–1704.

Cook, S. W., & Selltiz, C. (1964). A multiple-indicator approach to attitude measurement. *Psychological Bulletin, 62*, 36–55.

Corby, N. H., Jamner, M. S., & Wolitski, R. J. (1996). Using the theory of planned behavior to predict intention to use condoms among male and female injecting drug users. *Journal of Applied Social Psychology, 26*, 52–75.

Corey, S. M. (1937). Professed attitudes and actual behavior. *Journal of Educational Psychology, 28*, 271–280.

Courneya, K. S., & McAuley, E. (1993). Predicting physical activity from intention: Conceptual and methodological issues. *Journal of Sport and Exercise Psychology, 15*, 50–62.

Courneya, K. S., & McAuley, E. (1994). Factors affecting the intention–physical activity relationship: Intention versus expectation and scale correspondence. *Research Quarterly for Exercise and Sport, 65*, 280–285.

Courneya, K. S., & McAuley, E. (1995). Cognitive mediators of the social influence-exercise adherence relationship: A test of the theory of planned behavior. *Journal of Behavioral Medicine, 18*, 499–515.

Crites, S. L., Fabrigar, L. R., & Petty, R. E. (1994). Measuring the affective and cognitive properties of attitudes: Conceptual and methodological issues. *Personality & Social Psychology Bulletin, 20*, 619–634.

Crosby, F., Bromley, S., & Saxe, L. (1980). Recent unobtrusive studies of Black and White discrimination and prejudice: A literature review. *Psychological Bulletin, 87*, 546–563.

Cunningham, W. A., Preacher, K. J., & Banaji, M. R. (2001). Implicit attitude measures: Consistency, stability, and convergent validity. *Psychological Science, 121*, 163–170.

Daniels, L. A. (2001). *State of Black America 2000*. New York: National Urban League.

De Fleur, M. L., & Westie, F. R. (1958). Verbal attitudes and overt acts: An experiment on the salience of attitudes. *American Sociological Review, 23*, 667–673.

Dean, L. R. (1958). Interaction, reported and observed: The case of one local union. *Human Organiztion, 17*, 36–44.

Deci, E. L., & Ryan, R. M. (1985). The general causality orientations scale: Self-determination in personality. *Journal of Research in Personality, 19*, 109–134.

Deutscher, I. (1966). Words and deeds: Social science and social policy. *Social Problems, 13*, 235–254.

Deutscher, I. (1969). Looking backward: Case studies on the progress of methodology in sociological research. *American Sociologist, 4*, 35–41.

Devine, P. G. (1989). Stereotypes and prejudice: Their automatic and controlled components. *Journal of Personality & Social Psychology, 56*, 5–18.

Devine, P. G., & Monteith, M. J. (1999). Automaticity and control in stereotyping. In S. Chaiken & Y. Trope (Eds.), *Dual-process theories in social psychology* (pp. 339–360). New York: Guilford.

Devine, P. G., Monteith, M. J., Zuwerink, J. R., & Elliot, A. J. (1991). Prejudice with and without compunction. *Journal of Personality & Social Psychology, 60*, 817–830.

Devine, P. G., Plant, E. A., Amodio, D. M., Harmon-Jones, E., & Vance, S. L. (2002). The regulation of explicit and implicit race bias: The role of motivations to respond without prejudice. *Journal of Personality & Social Psychology, 82*, 835–848.

Dillehay, R. C. (1973). On the irrelevance of the classical negative evidence concerning the effect of attitudes on behavior. *American Psychologist, 28*, 887–891.

Doll, J., & Ajzen, I. (1992). Accessibility and stability of predictors in the theory of planned behavior. *Journal of Personality and Social Psychology, 63*, 754–765.

Dovidio, J. F. (2001). On the nature of contemporary prejudice: The third wave. *Journal of Social Issues, 57*, 829–849.

Dovidio, J. F., Brigham, J. C., Johnson, B. T., & Gaertner, S. L. (1996). Stereotyping, prejudice, and discrimination: Another look. In N. Macrae, C. Stangor, & M. Hewstone (Eds.), *Stereotypes and stereotyping* (pp. 276–319). New York: Guilford.

Dovidio, J. F., Evans, N., & Tyler, R. B. (1986). Racial stereotypes: The contents of their cognitive representations. *Journal of Experimental Social Psychology, 22*, 22–37.

Dovidio, J. F., & Gaertner, S. L. (2000). Aversive racism and selection decisions: 1989 and 1999. *Psychological Science, 11*, 315–319.

Dovidio, J. F., Kawakami, K., Johnson, C., Johnson, B., & Howard, A. (1997). On the nature of prejudice: Automatic and controlled processes. *Journal of Experimental Social Psychology, 33*, 510–540.

Dunton, B. C., & Fazio, R. H. (1997). An individual difference measure of motivation to control prejudiced reactions. *Personality & Social Psychology Bulletin, 23*, 316–326.

Eagly, A. H., & Chaiken, S. (1993). *The psychology of attitudes*. Fort Worth, TX: Harcourt Brace.

Eagly, A. H., & Chaiken, S. (1998). Attitude structure and function. In D. T. Gilbert S. T. Fiske, & G. Lindzey (Eds.), *The handbook of social psychology, Vol. 2* (4th ed., pp. 269–322). Boston, MA: McGraw-Hill.

Ellis, A. L., & Riggle, E. D. B. (1996). *Sexual identity on the job: Issues and services*. New York: Haworth Press.

Fazio, R. H. (1986). How do attitudes guide behavior? In R. M. H. Sorrentino and E. T. Higgins (Eds.), *Handbook of motivation and cognition: Foundations of social behavior* (pp. 204–243). New York: Guilford.

Fazio, R. H. (1990a). Multiple processes by which attitudes guide behavior: The MODE model as an integrative framework. In M. P. Zanna (Ed.), *Advances in experimental social psychology* (Vol. 23, pp. 75–109). San Diego, CA: Academic Press.

Fazio, R. H. (1990b). A practical guide to the use of response latency in social psychological research. In C. Hendrick & M. S. Clark (Eds.), *Research methods in personality and social psychology. Review of personality and social psychology, Vol. 11* (pp. 74–97). Newbury Park, CA: Sage.

Fazio, R. H. (1993). Variability in the likelihood of automatic attitude activation: Data reanalysis and commentary on Bargh, Chaiken, Govender, and Pratto (1992). *Journal of Personality & Social Psychology, 64*, 753–758.

Fazio, R. H. (1995). Attitudes as object–evaluation associations: Determinants, consequences, and correlates of attitude accessibility. In R. E. Petty & J. A. Krosnick (Eds.), *Attitude strength: Antecedents and consequences* (pp. 247–282). Mahwah, NJ: Lawrence Erlbaum Associates.

Fazio, R. H. (2001). On the automatic activation of associated evaluations: An overview [Special Issue: Automatic Affective Processing]. *Cognition & Emotion, 15*, 115–141.

Fazio, R. H., Chen, J., McDonel, E. C., & Sherman, S. J. (1982). Attitude accessibility, Attitude–behavior consistency, and the strength of the object–evaluation association. *Journal of Experimantal Social Psychology, 18*, 339–357.

Fazio, R. H., & Dunton, B. C. (1997). Categorization by race: The impact of automatic and controlled components of racial prejudice. *Journal of Experimental Social Psychology, 33*, 451–470.

Fazio, R. H., Jackson, J. R., Dunton, B. C., & Williams, C. J. (1995). Variability in automatic activation as an unobstrusive measure of racial attitudes: A bona fide pipeline? *Journal of Personality and Social Psychology, 69*, 1013–1027.

Fazio, R. H., & Olson, M. A. (2003). Implicit measures in social cognition research: Their meaning and uses. *Annual Review of Psychology, 54*, 297–327.

Fazio, R. H., Powell, M. C., & Williams, C. J. (1989). The role of attitude accessibility in the attitude-to-behavior process. *Journal of Consumer Research, 16*, 280–288.

Fazio, R. H., Sanbonmatsu, D. M., Powell, M. C., & Kardes, F. R. (1986). On the automatic activation of attitudes. *Journal of Personality & Social Psychology, 50*, 229–238.

Fazio, R. H., & Towles-Schwen, T. (1999). The MODE model of attitude–behavior processes. In S. Chaiken & Y. Trope (Eds.), *Dual-process theories in social psychology* (pp. 97–116). New York: Guilford.

Fazio, R. H., & Williams, C. J. (1986). Attitude accessibility as a moderator of the attitude–perception and attitude–behavior relations: An investigation of the 1984 presidential election. *Journal of Personality and Social Psychology, 51*, 505–514.

Fazio, R. H., & Zanna, M. P. (1978a). Attitudinal qualities relating to the strength of the attitude–behavior relationship. *Journal of Experimental Social Psychology, 14*, 398–408.

Fazio, R. H., & Zanna, M. P. (1978b). On the predictive validity of attitudes: The roles of direct experience and confidence. *Journal of Personality, 46*, 228–243.

Fazio, R. H., & Zanna, M. P. (1981). Direct experience and attitude–behavior consistency. In L. Berkowitz (Ed.), *Advances in experimental social psychology* (Vol. 14, pp. 161–202). New York: Academic Press.

Fekadu, Z., & Kraft, P. (2001). Self-identity in planned behavior perspective: Past behavior and its moderating effects on self-identity–intention relations. *Social Behavior & Personality, 29*, 671–685.

Festinger, L. (1964). Behavioral support for opinion change. *The Public Opinion Quarterly, 28*, 404–417.

Finlay, K. A., Trafimow, D., & Moroi, E. (1999). The importance of subjective norms on intentions to perform health behaviors. *Journal of Applied Social Psychology, 29*, 2381–2393.

Fishbein, M. (1967). Attitude and the prediction of behavior. In M. Fisbein (Ed.), *Readings in attitude theory and measurement* (pp. 477–492). New York: Wiley.

Fishbein, M. (2000). The role of theory in HIV prevention. [*Special Issue: AIDS Impact: 4th International Conference on the Biopsychosocial Aspects of HIV Infection*]. *AIDS Care. 12*, 273–278.

Fishbein, M., & Ajzen, I. (1974). Attitudes towards objects as predictors of single and multiple behavioral criteria. *Psychological Review, 81*, 59–74.

Fishbein, M., & Ajzen, I. (1975). *Belief, attitude, intention, and behavior: An introduction to theory and research.* Reading, MA: Addison-Wesley.

Fishbein, M., Ajzen, I., & McArdle, J. (1980). Changing the behavior of alcoholics: Effects of persuasive communication. In I. Ajzen & M. Fishbein (Eds.), *Understanding attitudes and predicting social behavior* (pp. 217–242). Englewood Cliffs, NJ: Prentice-Hall.

Fishbein, M., Cappella, J., Hornik, R., Sayeed, S., Yzer, M., & Ahern, R. K. (2002). The role of theory in developing effective antidrug public service announcements. In W. D. Crano & M. Burgoon (Eds.), *Mass media and drug prevention: Classic and contemporary theories and research* (pp. 89–117). Mahwah, NJ: Lawrence Erlbaum Associates.

Fishbein, M., Hennessy, M., Kamb, M., Bolan, G. A., Hoxworth, T., Iatesta, M., Rhodes, F., Zenilman, J. M., & Group, P. R. S. (2001). Using intervention theory to model factors influencing behavior change: Project RESPECT. *Evaluation & the Health Professions, 24*, 363–384.

Fishbein, M., Thomas, K., & Jaccard, J. J. (1976). *Voting behavior in Britain: An attitudinal analysis.* London: SSRC Survey Unit.

Fishbein, M., Triandis, H. C., Kanfer, F. H., Becker, M., Middlestadt, S. E., & Eichler, A. (2001). Factors influencing behavior and behavior change. In A. Baum & T. A. Revenson (Eds.), *Handbook of health psychology.* Mahwah, NJ: Lawrence Erlbaum Associates.

Fisher, J. D., & Fisher, W. A. (1992). Changing AIDS-risk behavior. *Psychological Bulletin, 111*, 455–474.

Fiske, S. T. (1998). Stereotyping, prejudice, and discrimination. In D. T. Gilbert, S. T. Fiske, & L. Gardner (Eds.), *The handbook of social psychology*, Vol. 2 (4th ed., pp. 357–411). Boston, MA: McGraw-Hill.

Forgas, J. P., Bower, G. H., & Krantz, S. E. (1984). The influence of mood on perceptions of social interactions. *Journal of Experimental Social Psychology, 20*, 497–513.

Franc, R. (1999). Attitude strength and the attitude–behavior domain: Magnitude and independence of moderating effects of different strength indices. *Journal of Social Behavior and Personality, 14*, 177–195.

Fredricks, A. J., & Dossett, D. L. (1983). Attitude–behavior relations: A comparison of the Fishbein–Ajzen and the Bentler–Speckart models. *Journal of Personality and Social Psychology, 45*, 501–512.

Freeman, L. C., & Ataoev, T. (1960). Invalidity of indirect and direct measures of attitude toward cheating. *Journal of Personality, 28*, 443–447.

Gaertner, S. L., & Dovidio, J. F. (1986). The aversive form of racism. In J. F. Dovidio & S. L. Gaertner (Eds.), *Prejudice, discrimination, and racism*. (pp. 61–89). Orlando, FL: Academic press.

Gangestad, S., & Snyder, M. (1985). "To carve nature at its joints": On the existence of discrete classes in personality. *Psychological Review, 92*, 317–349.

Garcia, A. W., & King, A. C. (1991). Predicting long-term adherence to aerobic exercise: A comparison of two models. *Journal of Sport & Exercise Psychology, 13*, 394–410.

Gibbons, F. X., Gerrard, M., Blanton, H., & Russell, D. W. (1998). Reasoned action and social reaction: Willingness and intention as independent predictors of health risk. *Journal of Personality and Social Psychology, 74*, 1164–1180.

Godin, G., & Kok, G. (1996). The theory of planned behavior: A review of its applications to health-related behaviors. *American Journal of Health Promotion, 11*, 87–98.

Godin, G., Valois, P., Lepage, L., & Desharnais, R. (1992). Predictors of smoking behaviour: An application of Ajzen's theory of planned behaviour. *British Journal of Addiction, 87*, 1335–1343.

Godin, G., Valois, P., Shephard, R. J., & Desharnais, R. (1987). Prediction of leisure-time exercise behavior: A path analysis (LISREL V) model. *Journal of Behavioral Medicine, 10*, 145–158.

Gold, R. S. (1993). On the need to mind the gap: On-line versus off-line cognitions underlying sexual risk taking. In D. J. Terry, C. Gallois, & M. McCamish (Eds.), *The theory of reasoned action: Its application to AIDS-preventive behavior* (pp. 227–252). Oxford, UK: Pergamon Press.

Gollwitzer, P. M. (1993). Goal achievement: The role of intentions. In W. Stroebe & M. Hewstone (Eds.), *European review of social psychology*, Vol. 4 (pp. 141–185). Chichester, UK: Wiley.

Gollwitzer, P. M. (1996). The volitional benefits of planning. In P. M. Gollwitzer & J. A. Bargh (Eds.), *The psychology of action: Linking cognition and motivation to behavior* (pp. 287–312). New York: Guilford.

Gollwitzer, P. M. (1999). Implementation intentions: Strong effects of simple plans. *American Psychologist, 54*, 493–503.

Gollwitzer, P. M., & Brandstätter, V. (1997). Implementation intentions and effective goal pursuit. *Journal of Personality and Social Psychology, 73*, 186–199.

Gollwitzer, P. M., & Schaal, B. (1998). Metacognition in action: The importance of implementation intentions. *Personality and Social Psychology Review, 2*, 124–136.

Gorsuch, R. L., & Ortberg, J. (1983). Moral obligation and attitudes: Their relation to behavioral intentions. *Journal of Personality and Social Psychology, 44*, 1025–1028.

Greenwald, A. G., & Banaji, M. R. (1995). Implicit social cognition: Attitudes, self-esteem, and stereotypes. *Psychological Review, 102*, 4–27.

Greenwald, A. G., McGhee, D. E., & Schwartz, J. L. K. (1998). Measuring individual differences in implicit cognition: The implicit association test. *Journal of Personality and Social Psychology, 74*, 1464–1480.

Guilford, J. P. (1954). *Psychometric methods* (2nd ed.). New York: McGraw-Hill.

Hacker, A. (1995). *Two nations: Black and White, separate, hostile, unequal*. New York: Ballentine.

Hagger, M. S., Chatzisarantis, N. L. D., & Biddle, S. J. H. (2002a). The influence of autonomous and controlling motives on physical activity intentions within the theory of planned behaviour. *British Journal of Health Psychology, 7*, 283–297.

Hagger, M. S., Chatzisarantis, N. L. D., & Biddle, S. J. H. (2002b). A meta-analytic review of the theories of reasoned action and planned behavior in physical activity: Predictive validity and the contribution of additional variables. *Journal of Sport and Exercise Psychology, 24*, 3–32.

Hammond, K. R. (1948). Measuring attitudes by error-choice: An indirect method. *Journal of Abnormal and Social Psychology, 43*, 38–48.

Harrison, D. A. (1995). Volunteer motivation and attendance decisions: Competitive theory testing in multiple samples from a homeless shelter. *Journal of Applied Psychology, 80*, 371–385.

Hausenblas, H. A., Carron, A. V., & Mack, D. E. (1997). Application of the theories of reasoned action and planned behavior to exercise behavior: A meta-analysis. *Journal of Sport and Exercise Psychology, 19*, 36–51.

Heath, Y., & Gifford, R. (2002). Extending the theory of planned behavior: Predicting the use of public transportation. *Journal of Applied Social Psychology, 32*, 2154–2189.

Herek, G. M. (2000). Sexual prejudice and gender: Do heterosexuals' attitudes toward lesbians and gay men differ? Special Issue: Women's sexualities: New perspectives on sexual orientation and gender. *Journal of Social Issues, 56*, 251–266.

Herek, G. M., & Capitanio, J. P. (1999). Sex differences in how heterosexuals think about lesbians and gay men: Evidence from survey context effects. *Journal of Sex Research, 36*, 348–360.

Himelstein, P., & Moore, J. (1963). Racial attitudes and the action of Negro and White background figures as factors in petition-signing. *Journal of Social Psychology, 61*, 267–272.

Hornik, R., Maklin, D., Judkins, D., Cadell, D., Yanevitzky, I., Zador, P., Southwell, B., Mack, K., Das, B., Prado, A., Barmada, C., Jacobsohn, L., Morin, C., Steele, D., Baskin, R., & Zanutto, E. (2001). *Evaluation of the national youth anti-drug media campaign: Second semi-annual report of findings.* Philadelphia: The Annenberg School for Communication.

Hovland, C. I., Janis, I. L., & Kelley, H. H. (1953). *Communication and persuasion; psychological studies of opinion change*: New Haven, CT: Yale University Press.

Hovland, C. I., Lumsdaine, A. A., & Sheffield, F. D. (1949). *Experiments on mass communication. Studies in social psychology in World War II, Vol. 3.* Princeton, NJ: Princeton University Press.

Huddy, L., Neely, F., & Lafay, M. R. (2000). The polls—trends: Support for the women's movement. *Public Opinion Quarterly, 64*, 309–350.

Ingham, R. (1994). Some speculations on the concept of rationality. *Advances in Medical Sociology, 4*, 89–111.

Jamieson, D. W., & Zanna, M. P. (1989). Need for structure in attitude formation and expression. In A. R. B. Pratkanis & S. J. Breckler (Eds.), *Attitude structure and function* (pp. 383–406). Hillsdale, NJ: Lawrence Erlbaum Associates.

Jamner, M. S., Wolitski, R. J., Corby, N. H., & Fishbein, M. (1998). Using the theory of planned behavior to predict intention to use condoms among female sex workers. *Psychology and Health, 13*, 187–205.

Jemmott, J. B. I., Jemmott, L. S., Fong, G. T., & McCaffree, K. (1999). Reducing HIV risk-associated sexual behavior among African American adolescents: Testing the generality of intervention effects. *American Journal of Community Psychology, 27*, 161–187.

Johnson, E. J., & Tversky, A. (1983). Affect, generalization, and the perception of risk. *Journal of Personality & Social Psychology, 45*, 20–31.

Jones, E. E., & Sigall, H. (1971). The bogus pipeline: A new paradigm for measuring affect and attitude. *Psychological Bulletin, 76*, 349–364.

Karpinski, A., & Hilton, J. L. (2001). Attitudes and the Implicit Association Test. *Journal of Personality & Social Psychology, 81*, 774–788.

Kashima, Y., & Gallois, C. (1993). The theory of reasoned action and problem-focused research. In D. J. Terry, C. Gallois, & M. McCamish (Eds.), *The theory of reasoned action: Its application to AIDS-preventive behavior* (pp. 207–226). Oxford, UK: Pergamon.

Katz, D., & Stotland, E. (1959). A preliminary statement to a theory of attitude structure and change. In S. Koch (Ed.), *Psychology: A study of a science. Vol 3. Formulations of the person and the social context* (pp. 423–475). New York: McGraw-Hill.

Kawakami, K., & Dovidio, J. F. (2001). The reliability of implicit stereotyping. *Personality and Social Psychology Bulletin, 27*, 212–225.

Kelman, H. C. (1974). Attitudes are alive and well and gainfully employed in the sphere of action. *American Psychologist, 29*, 310–324.

Kerner, M. S., & Grossman, A. H. (1998). Attitudinal, social, and practical correlates to fitness behavior: A test of the theory of planned behavior. *Perceptual and Motor Skills, 87*, 1139–1154.

Kidder, L. H., & Campbell, D. T. (1970). The indirect testing of attitudes. In G. F. Summers (Ed.), *Attitude measurement* (pp. 333–385). Chicago: Rand McNally.

Kiesler, C. A. (1971). *The psychology of commitment: Experiments linking behavior to belief.* San Diego, CA: Academic Press.

Kiesler, C. A. (1981). Intentional applications. *Contemporary Psychology, 26*, 253–255.

Kline, S. L. (1987). Self-monitoring and attitude–behavior correspondence in cable television subscription. *Journal of Social Psychology, 127*, 605–609.

Kokkinaki, F., & Lunt, P. (1997). The relationship between involvement, attitude accessibility and attitude–behaviour consistency. *British Journal of Social Psychology, 36*, 497–509.

Kothandapani, V. (1971). Validation of feeling, belief, and intention to act as three components of attitude and their contribution to prediction of contraceptive behavior. *Journal of Personality and Social Psychology, 19*, 321–333.

Kraus, S. J. (1995). Attitudes and the prediction of behavior: A meta-analysis of the empirical literature. *Personality and Social Psychology Bulletin, 21*, 58–75.

Krech, D., Crutchfield, R. S., & Ballachey, E. L. (1962). *Individual in society: A textbook of social psychology*. New York: McGraw-Hill.

Krosnick, J. A. (1988). The role of attitude importance in social evaluation: A study of policy preferences, presidential candidate evaluations, and voting behavior. *Journal of Personality and Social Psychology, 55*, 196–210.

Krosnick, J. A., & Petty, R. E. (1995). Attitude strength: An overview. In R. E. Petty & J. A. Krosnick (Eds.), *Attitude strength: Antecedents and consequences* (pp. 1–24). Mahwah, NJ: Lawrence Erlbaum Associates.

Kruglanski, A. W. (1989). *Lay epistemics and human knowledge: Cognitive and motivational bases*. New York: Plenum.

Kruglanski, A. W., & Freund, T. (1983). The freezing and unfreezing of lay-inferences: Effects on impressional primacy, ethnic stereotyping, and numerical anchoring. *Journal of Experimental Social Psychology, 19*, 448–468.

Kutner, B., Wilkins, C., & Yarrow, P. R. (1952). Verbal attitudes and overt behavior involving racial prejudice. *Journal of Abnormal and Social Psychology, 47*, 649–652.

Landrine, H., Klonoff, E. A., & Alcaraz, R. (1997). Racial discrimination in minor's access to tobacco. *Journal of Black Psychology, 23*, 135–147.

Langer, E. J. (1978). Rethinking the role of thought in social interaction. In J. H. Harvey, W. Ickes, & R. F. Kidd (Eds.), *New directions in attribution research*, Vol. 2 (pp. 35–58). Hillsdale, NJ: Lawrence Erlbaum Associates.

LaPiere, R. T. (1934). Attitudes vs. actions. *Social Forces, 13*, 230–237.

Leach, M., Fishbein, M., & Hennessy, M. (2001). Perceptions of easy–difficult: Attitude or self-efficacy? *Journal of Applied Social Psychology, 31*, 1–20.

Lenski, G. E., & Leggett, J. C. (1960). Caste, class, and deference in the research interview. *American Journal of Sociology, 65*, 463–467.

Linn, L. S. (1965). Verbal attitudes and overt behavior: A study of racial discrimination. *Social Forces, 43*, 353–364.

Longo, D. A., Lent, R. W., & Brown, S. D. (1922). Social cognitive variables in the prediction of client motivation and attrition. *Journal of Counseling Psychology, 39*, 447–452.

MacDonald, T. K., Zanna, M. P., & Fong, G. T. (1995). Decision making in altered states: Effects of alcohol on attitudes toward drinking and driving. *Journal of Personality and Social Psychology, 68*, 973–985.

MacDonald, T. K., Zanna, M. P., & Fong, G. T. (1996). Why common sense goes out the window: Effects of alcohol on intentions to use condoms. *Personality and Social Psychology Bulletin, 22*, 763–775.

Madden, T. J., Ellen, P. S., & Ajzen, I. (1992). A comparison of the theory of planned behavior and the theory of reasoned action. *Personality and Social Psychology Bulletin, 18*, 3–9.

Manstead, A. S. R. (2000). The role of moral norm in the attitude–behavior relation. In D. J. Terry & M. A. Hogg (Eds.), *Attitudes, behavior, and social context: The role of norms and group membership. Applied social research* (pp. 11–30). Mahwah, NJ: Lawrence Erlbaum Associates.

Manstead, A. S. R., Proffitt, C., & Smart, J. (1983). Predicting and understanding mothers' infant-feeding intentions and behavior: Testing the theory of reasoned action. *Journal of Personality and Social Psychology, 44*, 657–671.

Manstead, A. S. R., & van Eekelen, S. A. M. (1998). Distinguishing between perceived behavioral control and self-efficacy in the domain of academic intentions and behaviors. *Journal of Applied Social Psychology, 28*, 1375–1392.

McConahay, J. B. (1986). Modern racism, ambivalence, and the Modern Racism Scale. In J. F. Dovidio & S. L. Gaertner (Eds.), *Prejudice, discrimination, and racism* (pp. 91–125). San Diego, CA: Academic Press.

McConahay, J. B., Hardee, B. B., & Batts, V. (1981). Has racism declined in America? It depends on who is asking and what is asked. *Journal of Conflict Resolution, 25*, 563–579.

McGuire, W. J. (1969). The nature of attitudes and attitude change. In G. Lindzey & E. Aronson (Eds.), *The handbook of social psychology* (Vol. 3, pp. 136–314). Reading, MA: Addison-Wesley.

McGuire, W. J., & McGuire, C. V. (1991). The content, structure, and operation of thought systems. In R. S. Wyer, Jr. & T. K. Srull (Eds.), *The content, structure, and operation of thought systems* (pp. 1–78). Hillsdale, NJ: Lawrence Erlbaum Associates.

McMillan, B., & Conner, M. (2003). Applying an extended version of the theory of planned behavior to illicit drug use among students. *Journal of Applied Social Psychology, 33*, 1662–1683.

Millar, M. G., & Tesser, A. (1986). Effects of affective and cognitive focus on the attitude–behavior relation. *Journal of Personality & Social Psychology, 51*, 270–276.

Mittal, B. (1988). Achieving higher seat belt usage: The role of habit in bridging the attitude–behavior gap. *Journal of Applied Social Psychology, 18*, 993–1016.

Morojele, N. K., & Stephenson, G. M. (1994). Addictive behaviours: Predictors of abstinence intentions and expectations in the theory of planned behaviour. In D. R. Rutter & L. Quine (Eds.), *Social psychology and health: European perspectives* (pp. 47–70). Aldershot, UK: Avebury/Ashgate.

Myers, S. L., & Chan, T. (1995). Racial discrimination in housing markets: Accounting for credit risk. *Social Science Quarterly, 76*, 543–561.

Netemeyer, R. G., Burton, S., & Johnston, M. (1991). A comparison of two models for the prediction of vo-litional and goal-directed behaviors: A confirmatory analysis approach. *Social Psychology Quarterly, 54,* 87–100.

Norman, P., & Smith, L. (1995). The theory of planned behaviour and exercise: An investigation into the role of prior behaviour, behavioural intentions and attitude variability. *European Journal of Social Psychology, 12,* 403–415.

Norman, R. (1975). Affective-cognitive consistency, attitudes, conformity, and behavior. *Journal of Personality and Social Psychology, 32,* 83–91.

Notani, A. S. (1998). Moderators of perceived behavioral control's predictiveness in the theory of planned behavior: A meta-analysis. *Journal of Consumer Psychology, 7,* 247–271.

Nucifora, J., Kashima, Y., & Gallois, C. (1993). Influences on condom use among undergraduates: Testing the theories of reasoned action and planned behaviour. In D. J. Terry & C. Gallois (Eds.), *The theory of reasoned action: Its application to AIDS-preventive behaviour. International series in experimental social psychology,* Vol. 28 (pp. 47–64). Oxford, UK: Pergamon.

Orbell, S., Hodgkins, S., & Sheeran, P. (1997). Implementation intentions and the theory of planned behavior. *Personality and Social Psychology Bulletin, 23,* 945–954.

Orbell, S., & Sheeran, P. (2000). Motivational and volitional processes in action initiation: A field study of the role of implementation intentions. *Journal of Applied Social Psychology, 30,* 780–797.

Osgood, C. E., Suci, G. J., & Tannenbaum, P. H. (1957). *The measurement of meaning.* Urbana, IL: University of Illinois Press.

Ostrom, T. M. (1969). The relationship between the affective, behavioral, and cognitive components of attitude. *Journal of Experimental Social Psychology, 5,* 12–30.

Ouellette, J. A., & Wood, W. (1998). Habit and intention in everyday life: The multiple processes by which past behavior predicts future behavior. *Psychological Bulletin, 124,* 54–74.

Parker, D., Manstead, A. S. R., & Stradling, S. G. (1995). Extending the theory of planned behaviour: The role of personal norm. *British Journal of Social Psychology, 34,* 127–137.

Petraitis, J., Flay, B. R., & Miller, T. Q. (1995). Reviewing theories of adolescent substance use: Organizing pieces in the puzzle. *Psychological Bulletin, 117,* 67–86.

Petty, R. E., & Cacioppo, J. T. (1981). *Attitudes and persuasion: Classic and contemporary approaches.* Dubuque, IA: Brown.

Petty, R. E., & Cacioppo, J. T. (1983). The role of bodily responses in attitude measurement and change. In J. T. Cacioppo & R. E. Petty (Eds.), *Social psychophysiology: A sourcebook* (pp. 51–101). New York: Guilford.

Petty, R. E., & Cacioppo, J. T. (1986). *Communication and persuasion: Central and peripheral routes to attitude change.* New York: Springer-Verlag.

Petty, R. E., & Krosnick, J. A. (Eds.). (1995). *Attitude strength: Antecedents and consequences.* Mahwah, NJ: Lawrence Erlbaum Associates.

Plant, E. A., & Devine, P. G. (1998). Internal and external motivation to respond without prejudice. *Journal of Personality & Social Psychology, 75,* 811–832.

Raden, D. (1985). Strength-related attitude dimensions. *Social Psychology Quarterly, 48,* 312–330.

Randall, D. M., & Wolff, J. A. (1994). The time interval in the intention–behaviour relationship: Meta-analysis. *British Journal of Social Psychology, 33,* 405–418.

Regan, D. T., & Fazio, R. H. (1977). On the consistency between attitudes and behavior: Look to the method of attitude formation. *Journal of Experimental Social Psychology, 13,* 28–45.

Richard, R., de Vries, N. K., & van der Pligt, J. (1998). Anticipated regret and precautionary sexual behavior. *Journal of Applied Social Psychology, 28,* 1411–1428.

Richard, R., van der Pligt, J., & de Vries, N. (1995). The impact of anticipated affect on (risky) sexual behaviour. *British Journal of Social Psychology, 34,* 9–21.

Richard, R., van der Pligt, J., & de Vries, N. (1996). Anticipated affect and behavioral choice. *Basic and Applied Social Psychology, 18,* 111–129.

Ridgeway, C. L. (1997). Interaction and the conservation of gender inequality: Considering employment. *American Sociological Review, 62,* 218–235.

Rokeach, M., & Mezei, L. (1966). Race and shared belief as factors in social choice. *Science, 151,* 167–172.

Rosenberg, M. J., & Hovland, C. I. (1960). Cognitive, affective, and behavioral components of attitudes. In C. I. Hovland & M. J. Rosenberg (Eds.), *Attitude organization and change: An analysis of consistency among attitude components* (pp. 1–14). New Haven, CT: Yale University Press.

Rosenstock, I. M., Strecher, V. J., & Becker, M. H. (1994). The health belief model and HIV risk behavior change. In R. J. DiClemente & J. L. Peterson (Eds.), *Preventing AIDS: Theories and methods of behavioral interventions. AIDS prevention and mental health* (pp. 5–24). New York: Plenum.

Sadri, G., & Robertson, I. T. (1993). Self-efficacy and work-related behavior: A review and meta-analysis. *Applied Psychology, 42,* 139–152.

Sample, J., & Warland, R. (1973). Attitude and prediction of behavior. *Social Forces, 51*, 292–304.

Sanderson, C. A., & Jemmott, J. B. I. (1996). Moderation and mediation of HIV-prevention interventions: Relationship status, intentions, and condom use among college students. *Journal of Applied Social Psychology, 26*, 2076–2099.

Saucier, D. A., & Miller, C. T. (2003). The persuasiveness of racial arguments as a subtle measure of racism. *Personality and Social Psychology Bulletin, 29*, 1303–1315.

Schaller, M., & Cialdini, R. B. (1990). Happiness, sadness, and helping: A motivational integration. In E. T. Higgins & R. M. Sorrentino (Eds.), *Handbook of motivation and cognition: Foundations of social behavior* (Vol. 2, pp. 265–296). New York: Guilford.

Schuette, R. A., & Fazio, R. H. (1995). Attitude accessibility and motivation as determinants of biased processing: A test of the MODE model. *Personality & Social Psychology Bulletin, 21*, 704–710.

Schuman, H., & Johnson, M. P. (1976). Attitudes and behavior. *Annual Review of Sociology, 2*, 161–207.

Schuman, H., Steeh, C., Bobo, L., & Krysan, M. (1997). *Racial attitudes in America: Trends and interpretations* (Rev. ed.) Cambridge, MA: Harvard University Press.

Sears, D. O. (1988). Symbolic racism. In P. A. Katz & D. A. Taylor (Eds.), *Eliminating racism: Profiles in controversy. Perspectives in social psychology* (pp. 53–84). New York: Plenum.

Sekaquaptewa, D., Espinoza, P., Thompson, M., Vargas, P., & von Hippel, W. (2003). Stereotypic explanatory bias: Implicit stereotyping as a predictor of discrimination. *Journal of Experimental Social Psychology, 39*, 75–82.

Shavitt, S., & Fazio, R. H. (1991). Effects of attribute salience on the consistency between attitudes and behavior predictions. *Personality and Social Psychology Bulletin, 17*, 507–516.

Sheeran, P. (2002). Intention–behavior relations: A conceptual and empirical review. In W. Stroebe & M. Hewstone (Eds.), *European review of social psychology* (Vol. 12, pp. 1–36). Chichester, UK: Wiley.

Sheeran, P., & Orbell, S. (1998). Do intentions predict condom use? Meta-analysis and examination of six moderator variables. *British Journal of Social Psychology, 37*, 231–250.

Sheeran, P., & Orbell, S. (1999a). Augmenting the theory of planned behavior: Roles for anticipated regret and descriptive norms. *Journal of Applied Social Psychology, 29*, 2107–2142.

Sheeran, P., & Orbell, S. (1999b). Implementation intentions and repeated behaviour: Augmenting the predictive validity of the theory of planned behaviour. *European Journal of Social Psychology, 29*, 349–369.

Sheeran, P., & Orbell, S. (2000). Self-schemas and the theory of planned behaviour. *European Journal of Social Psychology, 30*, 533–550.

Sheeran, P., Orbell, S., & Trafimow, D. (1999). Does the temporal stability of behavioral intentions moderate intention–behavior and past behavior–future behavior relations? *Personality and Social Psychology Bulletin, 25*, 721–730.

Sheeran, P., & Taylor, S. (1999). Predicting intentions to use condoms: A meta-analysis and comparison of the theories of reasoned action and planned behavior. *Journal of Applied Social Psychology, 29*, 1624–1675.

Shepherd, B. H., Hartwick, J., & Warshaw, P. R. (1988). The theory of reasoned action: A meta-analysis of past research with recommendations for modifications and future research. *Journal of Consumer Research, 15*, 325–342.

Sherman, S. J., & Fazio, R. H. (1983). Parallels between attitudes and traits as predictors of behavior. *Journal of Personality, 51*, 308–345.

Sivacek, J., & Crano, W. D. (1982). Vested interest as a moderator of attitude–behavior consistency. *Journal of Personality and Social Psychology, 43*, 210–221.

Smith, H. N. (1932). A scale for measuring attitudes about prohibition. *Journal of Abnormal & Social Psychology, 26*, 429–437.

Snyder, M., & Kendzierski, D. (1982a). Acting on one's attitudes: Procedures for linking attitude and behavior. *Journal of Experimantal Social Psychology, 18*, 165–183.

Snyder, M., & Kendzierski, D. (1982b). Choosing social situations: Investigating the origins of correspondence between attitudes and behavior. *Journal of Personality, 50*, 280–295.

Sparks, P., & Guthrie, C. A. (1998). Self-identity and the theory of planned behavior: A useful addition or an unhelpful artifice? *Journal of Applied Social Psychology, 28*, 1393–1410.

Sparks, P., Guthrie, C. A., & Shepherd, R. (1997). The dimensional structure of the perceived behavioral control construct. *Journal of Applied Social Psychology, 27*, 418–438.

Sparks, P., Hedderley, D., & Shepherd, R. (1992). An investigation into the relationship between perceived control, attitude variability and the consumption of two common foods. *European Journal of Social Psychology, 22*, 55–71.

Stagner, R. (1942). Some factors related to attitude toward war, 1938. *Journal of Social Psychology, 16*, 131–142.

Steele, C. M., & Josephs, R. A. (1990). Alcohol myopia: Its prized and dangerous effects. *American Psychologist, 45*, 921–933.

Strecher, V. J., Champion, V. L., & Rosenstock, I. M. (1997). The health belief model and health behavior. In D. S. Gochman (Ed.), *Handbook of health behavior research 1: Personal and social determinants* (pp. 71–91). New York: Plenum.

Taylor, S. E., & Pham, L. B. (1998). The effect of mental simulation on goal-directed performance. *Imagination, Cognition and Personality, 18*, 253–268.

Terry, D. J., & O'Leary, J. E. (1995). The theory of planned behaviour: The effects of perceived behavioural control and self-efficacy. *British Journal of Social Psychology, 34,* 199–220.

Thomas, W. I., & Znaniecki, F. (1918). *The Polish peasant in Europe and America* (Vol. 1). Boston: Badger.

Thurstone, L. L. (1931). The measurement of social attitudes. *Journal of Abnormal and Social Psychology, 26,* 249–269.

Thurstone, L. L., & Chave, E. J. (1929). *The measurement of attitude: A psychophysical method and some experiments with a scale for measuring attitude toward the church.* Chicago: University of Chicago Press.

Trafimow, D., & Finlay, K. A. (1996). The importance of subjective norms for a minority of people: Between-subjects and within-subjects analyses. *Personality and Social Psychology Bulletin, 22,* 820–828.

Triandis, H. C. (1964). Exploratory factor analyses of the behavioral component of social attitudes. *Journal of Abnormal and Social Psychology, 68,* 420–430.

Triandis, H. C. (1977). *Interpersonal behavior.* Monterey, CA: Brooks/Cole.

van den Putte, B. (1993). *On the theory of reasoned action.* Unpublished doctoral dissertation, University of Amsterdam, The Netherlands.

van der Pligt, J., & de Vries, N. K. (1998). Expectancy-value models of health behavior: The role of salience and anticipated regret. *Psychology and Health, 13,* 289–305.

Van Ryn, M., & Vinokur, A. D. (1992). How did it work? An examination of the mechanisms through which an intervention for the unemployed promoted job-search behavior. *American Journal of Community Psychology, 20,* 577–597.

Vermette, L., & Godin, G. (1996). Nurses' intentions to provide home care: The impact of AIDS and homosexuality. *AIDS Care, 8,* 479–488.

Vernon, P. (1934). The attitude of the subject in personality testing. *Journal of Applied Psychology, 18,* 165–177.

Verplanken, B., & Faes, S. (1999). Good intentions, bad habits, and effects of forming implementation intentions on healthy eating. *European Journal of Social Psychology, 29,* 591–604.

Verplanken, B., & Orbell, S. (2003). Reflections on past behavior: A self-report index of habit strength. *Journal of Applied Social Psychology, 33,* 1313–1330.

von Haeften, I., Fishbein, M., Kaspryzk, D., & Montano, D. (2000). Acting on one's intention: Variations in condom use intentions and behaviors as a function of type of partner, gender, ethnicity, and risk. *Psychology, Health & Medicine, 5,* 163–171.

Vroom, V. H. (1964). *Work and motivation.* New York: Wiley.

Waly, P., & Cook, S. W. (1965). Effect of attitude on judgments of plausibility. *Journal of Personality and Social Psychology, 2,* 745–749.

Warburton, J., & Terry, D. J. (2000). Volunteer decision making by older people: A test of a revised theory of planned behavior. *Basic and Applied Social Psychology, 22,* 245–257.

Warner, L. G., & DeFleur, M. L. (1969). Attitude as an interactional concept: Social constraint and social distance as intervening variables between attitudes and action. *American Sociological Review, 34,* 153–169.

Warshaw, P. R., & Davis, F. D. (1985). Disentangling behavioral intention and behavioral expectation. *Journal of Experimental Social Psychology, 21,* 213–228.

Watson, J. B. (1925). *Behaviorism.* New York: Norton.

Wegner, D. M., & Wheatley, T. (1999). Apparent mental causation: Sources of the experience of will. *American Psychologist, 54,* 480–492.

Weigel, R. H., & Newman, L. S. (1976). Increasing attitude–behavior correspondence by broadening the scope of the behavioral measure. *Journal of Personality and Social Psychology, 33,* 793–802.

Weitz, S. (1972). Attitude, voice, and behavior: A repressed affect model of interracial interaction. *Journal of Personality and Social Psychology, 24,* 14–21.

Werner, P. D. (1978). Personality and attitude-activism correspondence. *Journal of Personality and Social Psychology, 36,* 1375–1390.

Wicker, A. W. (1969). Attitudes versus actions: The relationship of verbal and overt behavioral responses to attitude objects. *Journal of Social Issues, 25,* 41–78.

Wicker, A. W., & Pomazal, R. J. (1971). The relationship between attitudes and behavior as a function of specificity of attitude object and presence of a significant person during assessment conditions. *Representative Research in Social Psychology, 2,* 26–31.

Wicklund, R. A. (1975). Objective self awareness. In L. Berkowitz (Ed.), *Advances in experimental social psychology* (Vol. 8, pp. 233–275). San Diego, CA: Academic Press.

Widaman, K. F. (1985). Hierarchically nested covariance structure models for multitrait–multimethod data. *Applied Psychological Measurement, 9,* 1–26.

Wilson, T. D., Lindsey, S., & Schooler, T. Y. (2000). A model of dual attitudes. *Psychological Review, 107,* 101–126.

Wittenbrink, B., Judd, C. M., & Park, B. (1997). Evidence for racial prejudice at the implicit level and its relationship with questionnaire measures. *Journal of Personality & Social Psychology, 72,* 262–274.

Woodmansee, J. J., & Cook, S. W. (1967). Dimensions of verbal racial attitudes: Their identification and measurement. *Journal of Personality and Social Psychology, 7,* 240–250.

Word, C. O., Zanna, M. P., & Cooper, J. (1974). The nonverbal mediation of self-fulfilling prophecies in interracial interaction. *Journal of Experimental Social Psychology, 10,* 109–120.

Ybarra, O., & Trafimow, D. (1998). How priming the private self or collective self affects the relative weights of attitudes and subjective norms. *Personality and Social Psychology Bulletin, 24,* 362–370.

Yzer, M. C., Hennessy, M., & Fishbein, M. (2004). The usefulness of perceived difficulty for health research. *Psychology, Health and Medicine, 9,* 273–285.

Zanna, M. P., Olson, J. M., & Fazio, R. H. (1980). Attitude–behavior consistency: An individual difference perspective. *Journal of Personality and Social Psychology, 38,* 149–162.

Zuckerman, M., & Reis, H. T. (1978). Comparison of three models for predicting altruistic behavior. *Journal of Personality and Social Psychology, 36,* 498–510.

6

The Influence of Behavior on Attitudes

James M. Olson
University of Western Ontario

Jeff Stone
University of Arizona

In most laypersons' implicit theories of the causes of everyday events, attitudes influence behaviour: People's actions are guided by their internal attitudes. Although social psychologists have certainly investigated this relation (as illustrated most directly by the work described in the preceding chapter), they have given just as much attention to the reverse relation: the influence of behavior on attitudes. This topic has stimulated some of the best known and most-tested theories in social psychology and has elicited significant public interest because it turns laypersons' implicit theories upside down and generates counterintuitive predictions (which have been confirmed). Our goal in this chapter is to review and evaluate this research literature.

There are many ways that individuals' behavior could influence their attitudes. For instance, behavior might induce a selective search of memory or a biased analysis of an issue. By bringing particular information to mind, the behavior might alter individuals' attitudes. A second way that behavior might influence attitudes derives from the fact that actions can serve to commit individuals psychologically to an attitude position. Actors usually feel responsible for the consequences of their volitional behavior and also believe that they should act in accordance with their attitudes. Hence, they may be motivated to change their attitudes to be consistent with their actions. Third, individuals might sometimes treat their behavior as a piece of information that is relevant to judgments about their own attitudes. Given that actions are assumed in the implicit theories noted earlier to reflect attitudes, perceivers might infer an attitude that is consistent with their actions.

Although there are other ways that behavior can influence attitudes, these three processes each have been elaborated in a distinct theoretical model that we review in this chapter: biased scanning, dissonance theory, and self-perception theory. Our review is organized by theoretical framework and by the evolution of the theoretical and empirical development of each framework. After reviewing the literature, we identify dimensions that can be used to classify the various theories, as well as general principles that cut across the different approaches. Finally, we outline some directions for future research in this area.

We should note at the outset that we restrict ourselves in this chapter to *experimental* research on the impact of behavior on attitudes. In the studies we review, participants were induced to behave in a particular way, and the consequences of that action on participants' attitudes were tested. Many other researchers have examined correlations between past behavior and attitudes, sometimes using longitudinal designs that are interesting and informative. But for reasons of space and theoretical focus, we limit ourselves to the experimental approach to understanding how behavior guides attitudes.

BIASED SCANNING

Some of the earliest social psychology experiments to systematically explore the effects of behavior on attitudes were directed at understanding the impact of role playing (for reviews, see Elms, 1967; Janis, 1968; Kelman, 1974). In these studies, participants were instructed to argue in favor of an attitude-discrepant position. It was hypothesized that such role playing would lead to the selective generation and consideration of arguments supporting one side of the issue (namely, the side being advocated), a process labelled *biased scanning*. As a result of biased scanning, role players were expected to convince themselves that the advocated position had merit, which would change their attitudes in the direction of their advocacy.

In one of the first experiments on role playing, Janis and King (1954) required students to improvise a talk advocating an attitude-discrepant position to two listeners on one of three topics. For instance, one topic related to the number of movie theatres that would survive now that televisions became more widely available. All participants had given estimates of this number in a preliminary survey 4 weeks earlier; the experimenter instructed participants to argue for a number that was significantly lower than that provided on the pretest. The student delivering the talk was given an outline prepared by the experimenters, which stated the number to be advocated and summarized several arguments that could be presented. The student read this outline for 3 minutes and then gave an informal talk to the listeners. An important control was that the listeners spent the same 3 minutes looking over the identical outline, allegedly so they could evaluate the talk. After the talk, the speaker and listeners gave their current estimates of how many theatres would survive for 3 years. Results on two of the three topics showed that participants exhibited greater change from their pretest attitude when they actively argued for a position than when they simply listened to another person argue for it (see also Greenwald & Albert, 1968; Watts, 1967).

Joint Effects of Biased Scanning and Incentives

Janis and Gilmore (1965) integrated the concept of biased scanning with an incentive theory perspective that was consistent with the work being done at Yale University by Carl Hovland and his colleagues (e.g., Hovland, Janis, & Kelley, 1953). This incentive theory perspective emphasized that attitude change occurs when the incentives in a situation favor a new attitude; these incentives can derive from information related to the issue (e.g., information indicating that the position is valid) or from external factors in the persuasion setting (e.g., implied social approval or extrinsic reward for a new attitude). To test this integrative perspective, the researchers visited university students in a dormitory and asked them to write an essay arguing the attitude-discrepant idea that all students should be required to take additional courses in science and math. Half of the students were led to believe that the study was funded by a public welfare organization that was developing materials for a nationwide educational survey (the positive inducement condition). The remaining students were told that a private commercial company hoping to sell more science textbooks funded the study (the negative inducement condition). Further, half of the participants actually wrote the essay before completing the dependent measures, whereas the remaining participants completed the dependent measures after simply agreeing to write the essay. This variable was expected to influence whether participants actually engaged in biased scanning of arguments related to the topic. Results showed that participants changed their attitudes in the direction of the essay topic only when they actually wrote the essay *and* the study was sponsored by a public welfare organization. The authors concluded that both biased scanning and positive inducements are necessary for role playing to change attitudes (see also Elms & Janis, 1965).

Kelman (1962; 1974) also combined information processing and incentives in a dynamic, reciprocal model of the relation between actions and attitudes. Kelman argued that role playing an attitude-discrepant position can bring to mind new information about the issue and lead to a new attitude, especially when people are highly motivated to role play effectively. Kelman (1953) offered children extrinsic prizes to write an essay that went counter to their attitudes about comic book characters. Some children were told that everyone who wrote an essay would receive a free movie ticket, whereas others were told that only five would be chosen to receive a movie ticket. Kelman hypothesized that the latter condition would motivate the children to engage in a deeper analysis of supportive information (i.e., more biased scanning), because only the best essays would earn a ticket. As predicted, children who thought they were competing for scarce tickets exhibited more attitude change in the direction advocated in their essay.

Further Analysis of Biased Scanning

In another approach, Greenwald (1969, 1970) hypothesized that role playing leads participants to be more open-minded than usual, and this open-mindedness produces an unbiased evaluation of information opposing their own position, whether self-generated or externally provided. Greenwald (1969) measured participants' opinions on an issue and told them that they would be writing an essay supporting either their own side or the opposing side of the issue. All participants then examined a set of arguments for each side of the issue, rated the validity of each argument, and again reported their own view. Greenwald found that when participants expected to defend their own view, they rated arguments supporting their own side as more valid than arguments supporting the other side and exhibited little change in their own attitude. But when participants expected to argue for the opposite side of the issue, they rated arguments on each side of the issue as equally valid and exhibited substantial attitude change toward the view they expected to advocate. Greenwald concluded that the effect of role playing on attitudes is at least partly attributable to its tendency to make people more receptive to the predominant output of biased scanning—namely, information that opposes their position.

More recently, Albarracín and Wyer (2000) examined the role of biased scanning in the behavior–attitude relation using a novel procedure. Participants were led to believe (falsely) that their responses on a task revealed positive or negative attitudes toward instituting comprehensive examinations at their university. This belief was created by telling participants that questions would be presented to them on a computer screen so quickly that they would not be able to read the questions consciously, but their subconscious would nevertheless perceive and understand the questions. They were asked to make *yes* or *no* responses to each question by following their intuition. In fact, no questions were posed at all, so participants' responses did not reveal their attitudes, but participants were told that their answers consistently supported or consistently opposed the institution of comprehensive exams. Results showed that when participants were later asked to report their attitude toward comprehensive exams, they reported more positive attitudes when they believed they had responded positively to the subliminal questions than when they believed they had responded negatively. Based on some additional measures, Albarracín and Wyer concluded that a biased scanning interpretation of the effects of behavior on attitude was most plausible: The belief that they had acted in a particular way led participants to generate outcome-specific cognitions that influenced their attitude toward the issue.

The biased scanning literature has provided important insights about the impact of behavior on attitudes. The early work presaged the *cognitive response approach* to understanding the effects of persuasive messages (e.g., Eagly & Chaiken, 1984). Role-playing research also provided a foundation for subsequent studies of the effects of self-presentation on the self-concept (e.g., Schlenker & Trudeau, 1990): Under certain conditions, strategically presenting oneself in a biased way can alter the actor's self-concept. Despite these contributions, the early role-playing research was soon overshadowed by a motivational theory that seemed applicable to a broader range of behaviors: dissonance theory, to which we turn next.

DISSONANCE THEORY

Leon Festinger published his book, *A Theory of Cognitive Dissonance*, in 1957. Cognitive dissonance theory adopted a *consistency* perspective, similar to several earlier models of attitude formation and change, including balance formulations (Heider, 1946; Newcomb, 1953) and congruity theory (Osgood & Tannenbaum, 1955). These consistency approaches assumed that people prefer logical, harmonious, or coherent associations among their attitudes, values, and interpersonal relationships. Dissonance theory expanded the scope of consistency, however, to encompass the relations among all *cognitive elements* in an individual's memory, including knowledge about his or her attitudes, beliefs, values, and behavior. Propelled by several dramatic experimental confirmations of the theory's predictions (e.g., Aronson & Mills, 1959; Festinger & Carlsmith, 1959), dissonance theory quickly captured the attention of many social psychologists and became the focus of a great deal of research. In this section, we begin with a brief summary of the original theory and the first 2 decades of research that established the importance of dissonance theory for understanding how behavior can influence attitudes. We then describe the second generation of theoretical refinement and research on dissonance, highlighting the influence of new perspectives on the necessary conditions and motives underlying dissonance-induced attitude change. We then present a number of new developments from the third generation of research on cognitive dissonance processes, including new applications of the theory, new models of dissonance-related processes, and cultural differences in dissonance.

The Original Version of Dissonance Theory

Festinger (1957) observed that there are many inconsistencies in everyday life. His classic example was the plight of the smoker: How can smokers know that smoking is bad for them but continue to smoke? Festinger believed this was possible because smokers often convinced themselves that (a) smoking was enjoyable, (b) the chances of ill health were very low, (c) one cannot avoid all possible dangerous contingencies, and/or (d) weight gain would occur if they stopped smoking. As long as the smoker could recruit cognitions (defined as any knowledge, opinion, or belief about the environment, oneself, or one's behavior) consistent with smoking behavior, Festinger proposed that smoking would not be seen as an inconsistency.

In the presence of an inconsistency between cognitions, or dissonance, Festinger (1957) proposed that people would experience psychological discomfort, which he conceptualized as a drive state similar to hunger or frustration. The discomfort generated by dissonance would motivate persons to reduce the inconsistency and also to avoid situations and information that would likely increase their dissonance. Festinger defined dissonance by stating that "Two elements are in a dissonant relation if, considering these two alone, the obverse of one element would follow from another. To state it a bit more formally, x and y are dissonant if not-x follows from y" (p. 13). He noted that motivations could influence whether or not two elements are dissonant with each other. For example, losing money at a card table could be inconsistent with the knowledge that one player is cheating, unless one has a strong desire to lose his or her money.

The level of discomfort generated by dissonance between relevant cognitions is a function of the magnitude of the dissonance, which depends on two factors. The first factor is the importance of the cognitive elements: "If two elements are dissonant with one another, the magnitude of the dissonance will be a function of the importance of the elements" (1957, p. 16). But dissonant elements are almost always relevant to other elements, so the magnitude of dissonance will also depend on the *total context* in which the inconsistency occurs. If the majority of relevant cognitions are consistent with each other, then the magnitude of dissonance will be relatively low, but if the majority of relevant cognitions are inconsistent with each other, then the magnitude will be relatively high. This reasoning implies that the levels of discomfort people can feel when inconsistencies are present range along a continuum.

According to Festinger, there are a variety of events that can elicit dissonance, including decision making, encountering new information, and observing an unexpected outcome. Dissonance can result from the perception of logical inconsistency between beliefs, or from inconsistency between one's current behavior and cultural mores or past experience. The first chapter of the 1957 book is peppered with examples to support these and other assertions about when dissonance is likely to occur. But the examples offered by Festinger provided only a broad framework for understanding when dissonance would arise. He did not specify a formal model of what cognitions were necessary for cognitive dissonance to unfold. This ambiguity in the original theory was a source of consternation for both his students and other scholars who attempted to test the parameters of the theory (Aronson, 1992; Wicklund & Brehm, 1976).

Dissonance Reduction

If dissonance exists, it can be eliminated by changing one cognitive element: "There are various possible ways in which this can be accomplished, depending upon the type of cognitive elements involved and upon the total cognitive context" (Festinger, 1957, p. 19). Festinger described three general ways in which a person could reduce cognitive dissonance, but he also noted that to predict change, it is important to consider how resistant the cognition is to alteration. He believed that "The first and foremost source of resistance to change for *any* cognitive element is the responsiveness of such elements to reality" (p. 24).

Festinger believed that the simplest way to reduce dissonance was to change behavior. He also thought this was the most frequently used option because "Our behavior and feelings are frequently modified in accordance with new information.... There are persons who do stop smoking if and when they discover it is bad for their health" (p. 20). But Festinger also observed that behavior change may not occur because it is either too difficult or the change would induce other dissonances. For example, behavior change may be painful or involve loss, or the behavior may be otherwise satisfying. The behavior might also be irrevocable, or the requisite change might be outside the person's *behavior repertory* or knowledge about how to act. Thus, despite the *primacy* of behavior change for dissonance reduction, Festinger identified conditions under which a person would have to find another route for reducing the discomfort.

When behavior cannot be changed, individuals can reduce dissonance by changing other relevant cognitions. Festinger said that this could be accomplished by actually changing the behavioral context: "a person who is habitually very hostile toward other people may surround himself with persons who provoke hostility" (Festinger, 1957, p. 20). However, a person can also reduce dissonance by changing the perception of the behavioral context. For this to succeed, the person might have to find others who support the new perception. The astute reader may recognize the connection between this idea and Festinger's experience with how a doomsday cult responded to their failed prophesy (see Festinger, Riecken, & Schachter, 1956).

When it is not possible to change either of the dissonant cognitions, adding new cognitive elements to bolster either cognitive element that is in a state of dissonance can diminish the magnitude of dissonance. One might, for example, look for new information that would justify a difficult decision while avoiding information that would call the decision into question. Alternatively, a person could recruit information that makes the magnitude of the current inconsistency pale in comparison. Festinger illustrated the dissonant smoker who accumulates knowledge about automobile accident rates to conclude that the risk from smoking is nothing compared to the risk from driving a car. "Here, the total dissonance is reduced by reducing the *importance* of the existing dissonance" (Festinger, 1957, p. 22, emphasis added).

A third mechanism can eliminate inconsistency by reconciling the two elements that are dissonant. This requires adding a cognitive element that is consistent with both dissonant cognitions. Festinger gives an example where the prevailing cultural belief is that all people are good, but that children go through a period where they are very aggressive and destructive. Instead of changing either cognition, the culture added the belief that the children were possessed by malevolent ghosts. Thus, dissonance was reduced by adding information that placed the inconsistency into a greater context of consonance.

Finally, Festinger noted that it is not always possible to reduce dissonance. Sometimes a person will not be able to generate new cognitions or will not be able to find social support for the new cognitions. He also noted that the reduction process itself might backfire and lead to more dissonance and psychological discomfort.

Avoidance of Dissonance

Festinger described both the avoidance of *increases* in dissonance and the avoidance of the *occurrence* of dissonance. Avoiding increases in dissonance will be part of the normal dissonance reduction process. An individual might seek out people who support new cognitive elements and avoid people who do not, and also expose him or herself to new information supporting the changes while avoiding information that did not support the new changes.

Where no dissonance exists, there will typically be no selective approach or avoidance of information. Festinger suggested one important exception: when past experience leads individuals to fear, and hence avoid, the initial occurrence of dissonance. The fear of dissonance may also cause people to avoid behavioral commitment. For instance, individuals might delay the decision to commit, or, when the decision or action has occurred, they might cognitively negate the action (e.g., they might announce that they did the wrong thing, that the action was foolish). Festinger noted, "The operational problem would be to independently identify situations and persons where this kind of a priori self-protective behavior occurs" (1957, p. 31).

As should be clear from this brief overview, dissonance theory is a comprehensive framework that describes when, how, and why behavior can influence attitudes. The original book inspired new directions in research that shaped the field of social psychology. We turn now to some of the early research paradigms that were developed to test Festinger's suppositions.

The First Generation: Early Empirical Tests of Dissonance Theory

Decisions and the Free-Choice Paradigm

Festinger (1957) observed that all decisions cause at least some level of dissonance. By definition, decisions involve selecting one option from among two or more alternatives. The choice will necessarily be inconsistent with any unique positive features of the rejected alternative(s) and any unique negative features of the chosen alternative. For instance, choosing Car A over Car B causes dissonance when Car B has positive features that are not present in Car A and Car

A has negative features that are not present in Car B. The magnitude of dissonance following a decision depends on the importance of the decision and the difficulty of the choice between alternatives. Once a final decision has been made, people are motivated to reduce dissonance either by revoking the decision, creating cognitive overlap between the alternatives, or focusing on the consonant aspects of the decision, such as the positive features of the chosen alternative and the negative features of the rejected alternative. Focus on the consonant elements leads to a *spreading of alternatives*, whereby people change their evaluations such that the chosen alternative is rated more favorably and the rejected alternative is rated less favorably than before the decision. Thus, dissonance theory predicts that making a difficult and important decision can cause a person to change his or her attitudes toward the alternatives.

Brehm (1956) published the first empirical test of attitude change from postdecisional dissonance using a procedure that became known as the *free-choice paradigm*. University women were asked to evaluate a number of consumer items such as a toaster and an electric coffeepot. Participants were then given a choice between two items as a gift for completing the study. For some participants, the decision was difficult because they had rated the alternatives as very similar in attractiveness. For other participants, the decision was relatively easy because one alternative had been rated as much more attractive than the other. After making their decision, participants evaluated all of the items again. As predicted, participants who made a difficult choice increased their favorability toward the chosen alternative and decreased their favorability toward the rejected alternative, whereas participants who made a simple decision showed little change in their ratings of the alternatives (see also Gerard & White, 1983; Olson & Zanna, 1982).

The use of the free-choice paradigm has been extended to investigate postdecisional attitude change following many different kinds of decisions, including collective decisions made by small groups (e.g., Zanna & Sande, 1987) and individual choices between jobs in the military (Walster, 1964), between partners in close relationships (e.g., Johnson & Rusbult, 1989), and between types of research participation (Stone, 1999). Festinger (1964) published a book that reported the results of several studies designed to distinguish predecisional conflict from postdecisional dissonance, to establish the timing of postdecisional processes, and to investigate postdecision regret. For example, Walster (1964) showed that immediately after a difficult choice, people typically experience a moment of postdecision regret, during which they view the unchosen alternative more favorably than the chosen alternative. However, the postdecision spreading of the alternatives begins to emerge within minutes (Janis, 1968; Stone, 1999).

Forced Compliance Paradigm

Dissonance theory led to predictions regarding how other types of behavior could influence attitudes. Perhaps the most influential demonstration was conducted by Festinger and Carlsmith (1959). The impact of this study was so great, at least in part, because it revealed a *reverse incentive effect*, such that larger rewards were associated with less positive attitudes, in apparent contradiction to positive incentive effects documented by reinforcement theorists (e.g., Skinner, 1953) and attitudes researchers working in the Yale tradition (e.g., Hovland et al., 1953). The experiment introduced what became known as the *forced compliance paradigm*, in that participants were induced to comply with a request for counter-attitudinal behavior.

In the Festinger and Carlsmith (1959) study, male participants worked for 1 hour on two, very boring tasks (e.g., turning spools on a board). After the hour had passed, participants were told that the experimenter was investigating the effects of expectancies on performance, and they were in a control condition that did not receive any information before beginning the tasks. Participants were told that individuals in another condition, however, were receiving positive information about the tasks prior to performing them. These positive expectancies were created by having a confederate of the experimenter pretend to be someone who just finished the study and tell the waiting student that he really enjoyed the tasks. Participants were then told that another student, who was assigned to the positive expectancies condition, was currently ready to begin but the individual who usually served as the confederate had not yet shown up. Would the participant be willing to tell the waiting student that the tasks were very enjoyable? The critical manipulation was introduced at the same time as the request: Participants were offered either $1 or $20 for giving the waiting student a positive evaluation of the task.

After delivering the positive information to the waiting student (who was actually a confederate), participants were asked by a different researcher to complete a survey for the psychology department, asking how interesting and enjoyable the tasks had been in the respondent's just-completed experiment. Those participants who were paid only $1 for describing the experiment as enjoyable rated the tasks as more enjoyable than did participants who were paid $20 for the same dissimulation (who rated the tasks similarly to control participants, whose ratings presumably reflected the actual enjoyability of the tasks).

Festinger and Carlsmith (1959) argued that participants who lied to the confederate experienced dissonance created by the cognitions "The tasks were boring" and "I told someone the tasks were enjoyable." Those in the $20 condition, however, also had an important consonant cognition for their behavior, namely, "I was paid a lot of money to tell someone the tasks were enjoyable," which reduced the magnitude of their dissonance. Why did participants in the $1 condition change their evaluation of the tasks? Clearly, their behavior was irrevocable and therefore resistant to cognitive distortion. Perceptions of the tasks' enjoyability, however, were more ambiguous and fluid, which made their attitudes toward the task the least resistant cognition to change. Thus, participants in the $1 condition reduced their dissonance by evaluating the task more favorably.

Effort Justification Paradigm

Dissonance-induced attitude change can also occur when people suspect that they have exerted high effort for little purpose. The cognitive elements "I worked hard to achieve this goal" and "This goal is useless" are dissonant. Given that the former cognition concerns recent behavior, it may be resistant to change. A less resistant path to dissonance reduction may be to alter one's perception of the goal by deciding that it has some benefits and was worth the effort.

Aronson and Mills (1959) developed the *effort justification paradigm* to test the dissonance that can follow from wasted effort. Female university students were recruited for a sexual discussion group. Participants were told that they would have to go through a screening test to ensure that they would be comfortable with the material. Some participants were given an embarrassing, unpleasant test where they had to read aloud a list of obscene words (e.g., erection) and detailed descriptions of sexual activities to the male experimenter. Other participants were given a milder test where they read sexually related works that were less graphic (e.g., petting). Participants were then told they could join the group next week, but first they would listen to a tape recording of a previous group discussion. Participants listened to an excruciatingly boring discussion of secondary sex behavior among lower animals, after which they rated how interesting they found the discussion and the group members. Participants who went through the severe screening test rated the group and members as more interesting than did participants who went through the mild screening test or who simply listened to the boring discussion tape. Subsequent replications of the effect indicated that it was the effort, and not other features of the task, that caused participants to alter their attitudes (see also Axsom & Cooper, 1985; Cooper, 1980).

Insufficient Punishment

Dissonance theory also challenged learning theory assumptions about the effects of punishment on behavior and attitudes. Learning principles imply that one way to get someone to avoid a forbidden behavior is by threatening them with a harsh punishment. The more severe the punishment, the more likely a person will be to avoid the act. Dissonance theory, in contrast, predicts that someone can be more likely to avoid a forbidden behavior if first threatened with a *mild* punishment. This prediction was tested by Aronson and Carlsmith (1963) in what became known as the *forbidden toy paradigm*. Aronson and Carlsmith allowed preschool children to play with and evaluate some toys. One of the most attractive toys was then put on a table, and the experimenter told the child that he or she was not allowed to play with the toy while he was gone. Some children were given a strong incentive to obey this order: The adult said that he would be very angry and would take all of the toys away if the child played with the forbidden toy. Other children were given a weaker incentive to obey the order: The adult said that he would be a little unhappy if the child played with the toy. The experimenter then left the room for 10 minutes, during which time none of the children played with the forbidden toy. The adult returned to the room and allowed the children to play with and then evaluate all of the toys again. Children who were threatened with mild consequences evaluated the toy more negatively than did children who were threatened with severe consequences. The authors argued that the severe threat served as a consonant cognition that reduced dissonance between the cognitive elements "I like this toy" and "I did not play with this toy." Once again, dissonance researchers documented a reverse incentive effect: The condition that involved more negative incentive (severe threat) resulted in less attitude change (see also Freedman, 1965).

Selective Exposure Hypothesis

Festinger's (1957, 1964) speculations about the avoidance of dissonance led to the *selective exposure hypothesis*—people selectively approach consonant information and selectively avoid dissonant information. In one study, Mills (1965b) had college women participate in a free-choice task, in which the difficulty of the decision was manipulated by offering a choice between alternatives that were similar or dissimilar in attractiveness. All participants then rated their interest in reading some advertisements for the two products (which would presumably present favorable information). Participants who made a difficult choice expressed more interest in reading advertisements for their chosen product (consonant information) than did participants who made an easy choice. The two groups did not differ in their rated interest in reading advertisements for their nonchosen product (dissonant information).

Although the notion of selective exposure has intuitive appeal, early empirical attempts to document it yielded mixed results (see Freedman & Sears, 1965). These early studies, however, often had methodological problems that clouded their findings. For example, selective avoidance of dissonant information is unlikely if the information will be *useful* for the individual: Deciding to buy Car A is unlikely to cause avoidance of information suggesting that Car A has safety problems because this information is useful (although painful). Other factors affecting the approach and avoidance of information were gradually clarified, and evidence supporting the selective exposure hypothesis accumulated (e.g., Lowin, 1967; Mills, 1965a, 1965b; Olson & Zanna, 1979). At present, selective approach of consonant information has been documented more clearly than selective avoidance of dissonant information (see Frey, 1986; Wicklund & Brehm, 1976, chapter 12).

Counterattitudinal Essay Writing

The methodology that has been used more than any other for experimentally investigating dissonance theory has been to ask participants to write an essay that supports a position inconsistent with their own. The earliest experiments using this methodology varied the monetary incentive participants were offered. For example, Cohen (1962) asked students at Yale University to write an essay concerning a disturbance on campus, where the New Haven police had acted aggressively. Yale students almost uniformly condemned the police actions, but Cohen asked students whether they would be willing to write an essay entitled "Why the New Haven police actions were justified." The critical manipulation was the payment participants were offered: $0.50, $1, $5, or $10. After writing the essay, participants' attitudes toward the police actions were measured, and the reverse incentive effect again emerged: The more money students received for the essay, the more negative they were toward the police actions (i.e., the less influenced they were by their own arguments). Presumably, larger payments provided increasingly consonant cognitions with participants' behavior. The counter-attitudinal essay paradigm quickly caught favor with dissonance researchers, in part because it provided a less cumbersome procedure for testing the effects of inconsistent behavior on attitudes, and in part because it produced conflicting findings that fuelled debate among theorists about the necessary and sufficient conditions for dissonance processes to operate.

The Second Generation: Setting The Parameters of Cognitive Dissonance Theory

Almost immediately after the book's publication in 1957, researchers noted that ambiguities in the original theory limited its ability to predict the conditions under which most people would experience dissonance (see Abelson et al., 1968; Brehm & Cohen, 1962). This led to several empirical and theoretical advances directed at specifying the cognitions necessary for dissonance to be aroused and then reduced through attitude change in the classic paradigms.

Role of Commitment

Brehm and Cohen (1962) noted that, as formally stated, dissonance theory did not allow clear predictions for which cognitions were dissonant or consonant in a given situation, nor for which cognitions would change when dissonance was present. Brehm and Cohen observed that most empirical demonstrations involving attitude change, such as those from the forced compliance and free-choice paradigms, induced psychological commitment to the behavioral cognition. For example, when participants convinced the waiting confederate that the task was enjoyable, or when they made a difficult choice between two alternatives, they could not undo their behavior, making it impossible to change or deny what they had done. Thus, dissonance led to attitude change because the relevant attitudes were less resistant to change. By specifying the role of commitment, Brehm and Cohen provided a way for researchers to determine which cognitions were consonant or dissonant and to predict with more certainty how dissonance was most likely to be reduced in the classic dissonance paradigms (see Keisler, 1971).

Role of Choice

Another important refinement to the theory of cognitive dissonance grew from an early debate over alternative interpretations of the reverse incentive effect found in the Festinger and Carlsmith research (1959). Some theorists argued that the $20 payment was so large that it created incredulity, confusion, or other negative emotions (e.g., the feeling that one was being manipulated), which had a negative impact that eliminated any positive incentive effect of the money (e.g., Chapanis & Chapanis, 1964; Elms, 1967; Janis & Gilmore, 1965). Rosenberg (1965) proposed that the high-incentive condition caused *evaluation apprehension*—concern that the experimenter was evaluating their honesty and autonomy. Rosenberg suggested that if participants changed their attitudes after complying for $20, they would appear to have no self-respect and to be willing to do anything for money, whereas the $1 condition did not elicit this concern. If evaluation apprehension were removed from the situation, there should be more attitude change when incentives are high compared to low. Using Cohen's

(1962) counterattitudinal essay procedures, Rosenberg (1965) found that when different experimenters collected the essay and attitude measure, participants who were paid $5 for their essay reported more attitude change than participants who were paid $0.50. This and other studies that failed to replicate the reverse incentive effect caused a spirited exchange about the proper interpretation of dissonance effects.

Linder, Cooper, and Jones (1967) partially reconciled these viewpoints by noting that the reverse incentive effect may depend on how much choice participants have to write the counterattitudinal essay. Linder et al. (1967) proposed that in experiments that produced the reverse incentive effect, participants were given an explicit opportunity to decline the request before they took any other action. In other experiments, however, the opportunity to decline the request was less clear, either because the procedures induced commitment to the act before a choice was offered or because the incentive was offered after participants agreed to participate. In a clever set of experiments, Linder et al. varied both incentive and choice to decline the request to commit a counterattitudinal act. Results showed that, as predicted by dissonance, participants changed their attitudes more under low compared to high incentive when choice to make the counterattitudinal statement was high. In contrast and in support of Rosenberg's findings, participants changed their attitudes more under high than low incentive when decision freedom was low. By documenting the necessity of choice, this study further refined the use of the counterattitudinal essay task for investigating attitude change following a discrepant behavior.

Role of Arousal

Dissonance theory predicts that engaging in counterattitudinal behavior causes an unpleasant state of arousal or tension, which motivates attitude change or some other form of dissonance reduction. Early research tested this tenet by investigating whether counterattitudinal behavior causes unpleasant arousal. Evidence in support of the hypothesis came from studies showing that, like other arousal states, dissonance manipulations increased performance on simple tasks but impaired performance on complex tasks (e.g., Pallak & Pittman, 1972; Waterman, 1969).

The next step was to investigate whether unpleasant arousal is necessary for attitude change to occur. In perhaps the best known study, Zanna and Cooper (1974) proposed that, consistent with the two-factor theory of emotion (Schachter & Singer, 1962), dissonance might cause a state of arousal that is ambiguous because the source is unknown. If so, dissonance arousal might be misattributed to a source other than one's behavior, which would attenuate the motivation to reduce the arousal via attitude change. If the arousal were correctly attributed to the behavior, however, attitude change would occur. In an ingenious test of this hypothesis, participants were asked to ingest a placebo pill, allegedly to investigate the effect of the drug on memory later in the session. Some participants were told that this pill would have the side effect of making them feel tense and aroused; other participants were told that the pill would make them feel relaxed; a third group was told that the pill would have no noticeable side effects. While they waited for the pill to be absorbed, participants were asked to participate in an unrelated study, which involved writing a counterattitudinal essay under high- or low-choice conditions and reporting their own attitude on the issue. In the condition where participants did not expect any side effects from the drug, those in the high-choice condition reported more favorable attitudes toward the essay than did those in the low-choice condition. When high-choice participants expected the pill to create unpleasant arousal, however, no attitude change occurred: Participants were opposed to the essay topic irrespective of whether they were in the high- or low-choice conditions. Thus, leading participants to attribute the unpleasant arousal to the pill eliminated dissonance reduction via attitude change. These findings strongly imply that attitude change following counterattitudinal behavior is designed to reduce a negative affective state. When participants expected the pill to make them feel relaxed, attitude change in the high-choice condition was magnified: These participants reported the strongest support for the essay topic. Presumably, participants inferred that they would be feeling even more aroused if not for the pill, which heightened their motivation to reduce dissonance. Zanna and Cooper (1974) concluded that dissonance is a phenomenologically aversive state of arousal (see also Higgins, Rhodewalt, & Zanna, 1979; Zanna, Higgins, & Taves, 1976).

Other investigators used different methods to show that dissonance manipulations create a state of negative arousal. For example, counterattitudinal behavior has been shown to produce a state of autonomic arousal as indicated by physiological measures (e.g., Elkin & Leippe, 1986; Losch & Cacioppo, 1990). Giving participants an active drug that pharmacologically reduces physiological arousal (but not telling them it will do so) also reduces attitude change following counterattitudinal behavior, whereas giving participants an active drug that pharmacologically increases physiological arousal (but not telling them it will do so) increases attitude change in a dissonance paradigm (e.g., Cooper, Zanna, & Taves, 1978; Steele, Southwick, & Critchlow, 1981). It has also been shown that people can interpret the arousal state as positive when humor or other cues associated with pleasant states are present (e.g., Rhodewalt & Comer, 1979). Cooper (1998) recently showed that once people have misattributed their dissonance to an external source, the same discrepant act does not arouse dissonance if committed again. Cooper suggested that this indicates people can "unlearn" dissonance. Taken together, these findings show that counterattitudinal behavior must create a state of arousal that is labeled negatively for the act to motivate attitude change. Whether attitude change actually reduces arousal, however, has yet to be empirically documented (see Elkin & Leippe, 1986; Losch & Cacioppo, 1990).

Second Generation Revisions to the Motivational Engine of Dissonance Processes

Other researchers proposed revisions to dissonance theory that shifted the motivational emphasis from psychological consistency to other needs and goals. Like other attempts to refine the theory, these models altered the parameters of dissonance by specifying the cognitions that are necessary for a discrepant behavior to influence attitudes. But these revisions also introduced new perspectives on what people are trying to accomplish via attitude change.

Self-Consistency Theory

Aronson (1968) proposed that most examples of dissonance phenomena were held together by a common thread—the settings challenged people's expectancies or beliefs about themselves. To predict when dissonance would occur, Aronson proposed that theorists needed to consider the expectations people hold for themselves and their behavior. For example, Aronson (1968) argued that the dissonance aroused in Festinger and Carlsmith's (1959) study was not due to inconsistency between the thoughts, "I believe the tasks were boring" and "I told someone the tasks were interesting." Instead, Aronson proposed that dissonance was aroused by inconsistency between cognitions about the self (e.g., "I am a decent and truthful human being") and cognitions about the behavior (e.g., "I have misled a person and conned him into believing something that just isn't true"). Aronson concluded, "at the very heart of dissonance theory, where it makes its clearest and neatest prediction, we are not dealing with just any two cognitions; rather we are usually dealing with the self-concept and cognitions about some behavior. If dissonance exists it is because the individual's behavior is inconsistent with his self-concept" (1968, p. 23).

Aronson's emphasis on the self-concept shifted the motivational nature of dissonance from one of general psychological consistency to a more specific motive for self-consistency. Because beliefs about the self are highly resistant to change, he predicted that dissonance would motivate people to maintain their self-concept by changing their attitudes or beliefs. Aronson also observed that many of the successful dissonance experiments tacitly assumed that subjects held positive expectations for their behavior. Would misleading someone about the dullness of a task or advocating a counterattitudinal position cause dissonance in people who held negative expectancies for their behavior? Aronson proposed that it would not; people with negative self-concepts (i.e., negative expectancies) should not experience dissonance under the same conditions as people with positive self-concepts (i.e., positive expectancies). Aronson (1968) surmised, "... if a person conceives of himself as a 'schnook,' he will expect to behave like a schnook; consequently, wise, reasonable, successful, un-schnooky behavior on his part should arouse dissonance" (p. 24). Thus, the self-consistency perspective provided specific predictions regarding self-concept differences in dissonance phenomena (Thibodeau & Aronson, 1992).

Empirical support for the self-consistency model was provided by studies that manipulated or measured self-concept differences as moderators of dissonance processes. For example, Aronson and Carlsmith (1962) hypothesized that when an important expectancy about the self was disconfirmed by performance on a task, inconsistency between the self-expectancy and performance would invoke dissonance arousal. If given the opportunity, the discomfort could be reduced by changing performance, thereby bringing behavior back in line with the self-expectancy. Thus, a poor performance should cause high-expectancy subjects to try harder to succeed on future trials. However, the critical test of self-consistency was for low-expectancy subjects. If consistency was at stake, a good performance would lead low-expectancy subjects to try harder to *fail* on subsequent trials. The data clearly supported the self-consistency hypothesis: Low-expectancy participants who received positive performance feedback sabotaged their subsequent performances, whereas low-expectancy subjects who received negative performance feedback did not. Other researchers also reported data supporting the prediction that people with negative self-expectancies (Brockner, Wiesenfeld, & Raskas, 1993; Mettee, 1971), low self-esteem (Glass, 1964; Maracek & Mettee, 1972), or mild depression (Rhodewalt & Agustsdottir, 1986) show less attitude change following a discrepant act, compared to people with more positive expectancies, high self-esteem, or neutral moods.

The notion that dissonance is created when behavior threatens important aspects of the self-concept provided a parsimonious explanation for dissonance phenomena. Not everyone accepted self-consistency as the best interpretation of the dissonance literature, however. One problem for the self-consistency view has been a history of equivocal support for its predictions about how the self-concept moderates dissonance (for reviews, see Jones, 1973; Shrauger, 1975). For example, several attempts to replicate and extend the performance findings of Aronson and Carlsmith (1962) met with mixed success (e.g., Ward & Sandvold, 1963), and some attempts to extend the self-consistency analysis found that self-esteem was less important than other factors in dissonance processes (e.g., Cooper & Duncan, 1971). Other revisions of dissonance theory specified a different role for the self in dissonance arousal and reduction.

Moral Versus Hedonic Dissonance

Kelman and Baron (1974) proposed that the way in which behavioral discrepancies influence attitude change depends on the implications of the discrepancy for the actor. These authors distinguished between the concepts of moral and hedonic dissonance. Moral dissonance occurs when a person performs an action that violates a moral precept or value, whereas hedonic dissonance occurs when a person performs an action that has little intrinsic value, such as a boring, unpleasant, or effortful task. Kelman and Baron (1974) proposed that whereas dissonance researchers treat these two types of discrepancies as functionally equivalent, the discrepancies have different motivational implications for the actor and activate different reduction strategies.

Moral dissonance has direct implications for the actor's self-concept and should arouse feelings of guilt. The person would then be motivated to make reparations for the act, but if this were not possible, he or she could adjust the relevant attitude to justify the behavior. The response to moral dissonance also depends on the actor's self-concept. A person with a positive self-image might perceive the immoral act as a discrepancy, but rather than reducing dissonance by adjusting attitudes to fit the behavior, the actor may strengthen his or her resolve and manifest a boomerang effect. A person with a negative self-image, in contrast, might respond to the moral transgression not by changing the attitude toward the behavior, but by changing the attitude toward the self, leading to even more self-loathing.

Hedonic dissonance, in contrast, does not relate to self-concept concerns; it focuses the actor on issues of equity, profitability, reciprocity, and distributive justice. The discomfort that follows from hedonic dissonance is negative but undifferentiated and, according to Kelman and Baron (1974), is not typically reduced by attitude change. Hedonic dissonance will most likely be resolved by distorting perceptions of the experience, selective recall, or trivializing the effort involved, each of which will be transitory in nature.

For some reason, the richness of Kelman and Baron's framework was never influential in the progression of dissonance research (but see Holland, Meertens, & Van Vugt, 2002, for a recent exception). One explanation may be that some of the predictions made by the model did not hold up to theoretical or empirical scrutiny. For example, contrary to Festinger and Carlsmith (1959), Kelman and Baron proposed that when people engage in a moral transgression (e.g., lying), the higher the reward for doing so, the greater the dissonance that will be aroused. The model also expects that whereas choice and commitment may be central to dissonance that follows a moral discrepancy, "they are essentially irrelevant to hedonic dissonance" (Kelman & Baron, 1974, p. 562). There are some published studies, however, that appear to contradict these suppositions (e.g., Cohen, 1962; Harmon-Jones, Brehm, Greenberg, Simon, & Nelson, 1996).

Aversive Consequences Model

Cooper and Fazio presented an influential reformulation of dissonance theory in a 1984 review chapter. In their "new look" at the data generated by the induced compliance paradigm, Cooper and Fazio (1984) concluded that Festinger's original emphasis on psychological consistency was misguided; the existing evidence indicated that attitude change did not always occur when behavior and belief were inconsistent. They also proposed that data concerning the role of cognitions about the self was equivocal. Cooper and Fazio (1984) concluded that the evidence indicated that dissonance occurs when people take personal responsibility for having committed a behavior that produced an aversive outcome. People are then motivated to change their attitudes in order to reduce the perceived negative consequences of the unwanted act.

This aversive consequences revision adopted an attributional perspective on dissonance. Cooper and Fazio (1984) proposed that the dissonance process begins when people engage in a behavior and then evaluate the consequences of the act. When the consequences are perceived to fall outside individuals' latitudes of acceptance and to be irrevocable, people conclude that the behavioral outcome is aversive or unwanted. People then attempt to attribute responsibility for the negative consequence by evaluating two pieces of information: choice and foreseeability. If they perceive that they acted under their own volition and could have foreseen the outcome, they accept responsibility for the outcome of the behavior. The acceptance of responsibility for the aversive outcome causes dissonance arousal.

Evidence that the consequences of behavior matter came from studies in which attitude change did not occur in the absence of any negative outcome for the behavior. In one study, Cooper and Worchel (1970) replicated the Festinger and Carlsmith (1959) procedure in which a participant was asked to tell a confederate that a boring task was enjoyable for either $1 or

$20. Cooper and Worchel also manipulated whether the lie had an aversive consequence by having the confederate either accept or reject the lie. Results showed that participants rated the dull task as more interesting when their lie was accepted by the confederate than when the lie was disbelieved. In another study, Scher and Cooper (1989) showed that even when people perform a proattitudinal behavior, they will alter their attitudes about their behavior if the act leads to a negative, aversive outcome. Thus, according to the aversive consequences revision, unwanted behavioral consequences are a necessary condition for dissonance to be aroused.

The aversive consequences model was criticized by some researchers for presenting an overly narrow picture of cognitive dissonance phenomena (e.g., Aronson, 1992; Berkowitz & Devine, 1989). Thibodeau and Aronson (1992), for example, argued that the model ignores the evidence of self-concept moderation of dissonance processes, which suggests that cognitions about the self influence the interpretations of behavioral consequences. Moreover, research by Harmon-Jones et al. (1996) indicated that aversive consequences might not be a necessary component of the dissonance process. In one representative study, participants wrote an essay under conditions of high or low choice stating that a foul tasting beverage—Kool-Aid mixed with vinegar—was enjoyable and refreshing. They were then told to discard their essay in the trash, ostensibly eliminating any consequence of having written the essay. The results showed that despite the absence of an aversive consequence for the essay (i.e., there was no "product" of their behavior), participants in the high-choice condition reported significantly more favorable attitudes toward the foul-tasting beverage than did those who wrote the essay under conditions of low choice (see also Harmon-Jones, 2000). Harmon-Jones et al. (1996) argued that whereas aversive consequences are sufficient to arouse dissonance, they are not necessary; the only necessary condition for the arousal of cognitive dissonance is psychological inconsistency. Together, the evidence for self-concept moderation of dissonance processes and the finding that dissonance occurs in the absence of a negative behavioral outcome suggest that the aversive consequences model may not provide a comprehensive understanding of how behavior influences attitude change.

Self-Affirmation Theory

Another view of self-motives in dissonance processes was advanced in the theory of self-affirmation (Steele, 1988). Steele (1988) proposed that dissonance experiments typically induce participants to engage in actions that pose a threat to the integrity of their favorable self-beliefs system. One way to restore the integrity of the self-system is to eliminate the discrepancy by changing relevant attitudes or beliefs. But Steele (1988) proposed that dissonance reduction through attitude change is just one way people go about the business of maintaining the fidelity of their globally positive self. Steele suggested that, if the primary goal of dissonance reduction is to repair the positive status of the self, then any thought or action that restores the self-system is sufficient for dissonance reduction. Thus, if people can activate other positive aspects of their self-concept when threatened, dissonance will be reduced without having to change cognitions related to the discrepancy. Anything that brings to mind other cherished aspects of the self, such as virtues or past successes, can eliminate the need to change attitudes to reduce dissonance.

Steele and Lui (1983) induced dissonance through counterattitudinal behavior and then had half of the participants, who held strong sociopolitical values, complete a scale measuring their sociopolitical values prior to completing a measure of their attitudes toward the discrepant act. Dissonance-induced attitude change was eliminated when participants with strong sociopolitical values were allowed to re-affirm those values before their attitudes were assessed. Participants who were not value oriented, or who did not complete the sociopolitical value scale, reduced dissonance by changing their attitudes. Subsequent research supported the tenets of self-affirmation in the free-choice paradigm by demonstrating that the activation of positive self-resources, such as putting on a jacket or lab coat that represents an important value, can reduce the need to justify a difficult decision (Steele, 1988). Thus, drawing on valued aspects of the self or other affirmational resources has been shown to attenuate the attitude change that follows in many of the classic experimental dissonance paradigms.

A further tenet of self-affirmation theory concerns the dispositional availability of positive self-attributes. To affirm the self, people must think about positive self-attributes. People with high self-esteem presumably have a greater number of accessible, positive attributes than do people with low self-esteem, so affirmation of the self should be easier for people with high self-esteem. Steele, Spencer, and Lynch (1993) tested this prediction in an experiment in which participants with high or low self-esteem participated in the free-choice paradigm (Brehm, 1956). For some participants, self-attributes were primed when they completed a self-esteem scale before making their decision; the other participants made their decision without having their self-attributes primed. Results showed that when self-attributes were primed, participants with high self-esteem showed less change in their ratings of the alternatives than did participants with low self-esteem. In a no-prime control, both self-esteem groups showed similar levels of significant postdecision justification. Note that this pattern of self-esteem differences is exactly opposite to what is predicted by the self-consistency perspective (i.e., people with high self-esteem should show more dissonance reduction than people with low self-esteem).

Self-affirmation theory (Steele, 1988) introduced the possibility that a discrepant behavior may induce a more general motivation to restore self-worth. The research challenged the paradigmatic dogma of dissonance research by suggesting that people change their discrepant attitudes because this option for dissonance reduction is typically the only one provided by the experimenter. If alternate strategies for affirming self-worth are provided, people will use the strategy that most fully restores the integrity of the self, even when it is unrelated to the discrepant cognitions that caused discomfort.

Subsequent lines of research, however, raise questions about some of the assumptions of self-affirmation theory. One issue concerns whether people can affirm the self by focusing on positive self-attributes that are directly related to the behavioral discrepancy. In research by J. Aronson, Blanton, and Cooper (1995) and Blanton, Cooper, Skurnik, and Aronson (1997), participants wrote an uncompassionate essay under conditions of high choice. In one experiment (J. Aronson et al., 1995), when subsequently allowed the opportunity to read positive feedback on self-attributes that were either related to the essay (e.g., compassion) or unrelated (e.g., creative), participants chose to avoid positive feedback about attributes that were relevant to the discrepant behavior and focused instead on positive feedback that was unrelated to their discrepant act. Another study (Blanton et al., 1997) provided participants with either relevant or irrelevant positive feedback following an uncompassionate advocacy. When told they were highly compassionate individuals, participants showed *more* attitude change relative to participants in a no feedback–high-choice control condition. In contrast, when told they were highly creative individuals, participants showed *less* attitude change compared to high-choice control participants. These data suggest that for positive self-attributes to serve as resources for dissonance reduction, they must shift processing away from the relevant standards for behavior. Thinking about positive self-attributes that are directly related to the discrepancy can actually exacerbate the need to justify one's behavior through attitude change.

Also, other mechanisms have been shown to operate when self-affirmations occur following discrepant behavior. For example, in line with one of Festinger's (1957) original assertions, Simon, Greenberg, and Brehm (1995) proposed that contemplating positive self-attributes attenuates attitude change by reducing the importance of the behavioral cognition. Simon et al. (1995) found that after a counterattitudinal advocacy, participants were less likely to change their attitudes, and more likely to reduce the importance of what they had done, when self-affirmed before reporting their attitude toward the essay topic. Tesser (2000) proposed that the impact of self-affirmation might be mediated by positive affect. For example, Tesser and Cornell (1991) found that after writing a counterattitudinal essay under high choice, participants allowed to bask in the reflected glory of a close other or provided with a positive social comparison to a close other showed less attitude change than a high-choice control condition. Tesser (2000) observed that dissonance engenders negative affect, and various self-esteem maintenance mechanisms, such as affirmation, infuse the self with positive affect. Thus, affirmation of the self may reduce attitude change following a discrepant behavior because the "glow" people get from focusing on positive self-attributes reduces the discomfort.

Despite the fact that affirmation of the self appears to reduce defensive responses across a broad range of self-threats (e.g., Sherman & Cohen, 2002), the mechanism(s) by which affirmations attenuate attitude change following a discrepant behavior are not well understood (Galinsky, Stone, & Cooper, 2000). Affirmations may reduce the motivation to change attitudes through multiple mechanisms, including distraction, trivialization, and the induction of positive affect. The question of whether these mechanisms serve a higher order goal, such as self-enhancement or psychological consistency, awaits further research.

Strategic Impression Management Motives

It might be argued that attitude change observed in dissonance experiments is not real; the demands of the situation cause participants to report attitudes that are not veridical. Tedeschi, Schlenker, and Bonoma (1971) proposed that attitude change in the early dissonance studies reflected deliberate, deceptive attempts to maintain an image of consistency between reported attitudes and behavior. Participants who willingly wrote a counterattitudinal essay experienced evaluation apprehension (Rosenberg, 1965) and feared looking foolish if they then reported attitudes highly discrepant from the essay's position. A study by Gaes, Kalle, and Tedeschi (1978) showed that only participants who engaged in public counterattitudinal behavior reported attitudes that were more favorable toward their essay (but see Stults, Messé, & Kerr, 1984).

The impression management interpretation forced dissonance theorists to reexamine the veracity of their attitude findings. The field responded with several studies that challenged an impression management view. For instance, preference for consonant over dissonant information has been documented even when participants were unaware that their examination of information was being monitored (e.g., Olson & Zanna, 1979). Also, attitude change following a discrepant act has been found even when the attitude measure was taken by someone unconnected to (and unaware of) the discrepant behavior (e.g., Festinger & Carlsmith, 1959; Linder et al., 1967) and in very private settings that greatly reduced self-presentation motives (e.g., Harmon-Jones et al., 1996). In sum, the available data indicate that impression management theory does not provide a comprehensive explanation of the range of dissonance findings.

Schlenker (1980) extended the impression management analysis of dissonance effects by proposing that when people commit a discrepant act, they are motivated to explain it to both a public and private audience. According to the *identity-analytic model*, counterattitudinal behavior motivates people to construct accounts, or explanations, for what they have done. Some accounts, such as excuses, are designed to reduce responsibility for the outcome, whereas other accounts, such as justifications, are designed to reduce the negative consequences of the behavior. Thus, the identity-analytic model embraces both the role of the self-concept forwarded by Aronson (1968) and the impression management motive described by Tedeschi et al. (1971). It is important to note that the model acknowledged that attitude change following a counterattitudinal behavior can be a *real* attempt to justify the behavior to oneself.

A compelling illustration of how public and private audiences can differentially influence dissonance processes was reported by Scheier and Carver (1980). These investigators manipulated public and private audiences by adopting procedures from the self-awareness literature (Duval & Wicklund, 1972). In one experiment, participants wrote a counterattitudinal essay under high or low choice. To induce a state of private self-awareness, some high-choice participants wrote their essay sitting in front of a mirror that reflected their image back to them. To induce a state of public self-awareness, some participants wrote their essay with a video camera pointed at their face. All then reported their attitudes toward the essay topic and, in addition, rated the persuasive strength of their essay. The results showed that choice moderated the level of attitude change, but among self-aware participants, attitude change was greater for those in the public self-awareness condition than those in the private self-awareness condition. In contrast, those in the private self-awareness condition rated their essay as significantly weaker than those in the public self-awareness group, even though objective judges saw no difference in the essays. These findings imply that the privately focused group derogated their essay to reduce dissonance. A follow-up study replicated these results using dispositional measures of public and private self-consciousness.

Although it seems clear that impression management is not the only motive operating in the classic dissonance paradigms, Tedeschi et al.'s (1971) paper helped to launch a productive literature on self-presentation goals. This perspective has been applied to many domains of social behavior, including helping, bargaining, and self-esteem.

The Third Generation of Dissonance Research: Uncovering New Dissonance Phenomena

After a very active period during the 1960s and early 1970s, publications on dissonance theory, and consistency theories in general, declined in the major journals (Abelson, 1983; Aronson, 1992). In the last decade, however, dissonance theory has reemerged as a significant topic in social psychology. Numerous researchers have identified new dissonance phenomena and processes. These developments include investigations of the experience of psychological discomfort, hypocrisy as a source of dissonance, the role of groups and social identity in dissonance processes, and the possibility that dissonance operates outside of awareness.

Dissonance and the Experience of Psychological Discomfort

Festinger described cognitive dissonance as inducing a state of psychological discomfort that people are motivated to reduce. Elliot and Devine (1994) suggested that contemporary dissonance researchers have overlooked this central assumption. If dissonance is experienced as a state of discomfort, it should be possible to document elevated feelings of discomfort using self-report measures. Further, a *dissonance thermometer* should closely track dissonance reduction through attitude change. Elliot and Devine (1994) manipulated the level of dissonance using a counterattitudinal essay task, and then varied whether participants reported their level of psychological discomfort (e.g., *uncomfortable*, *uneasy*, *bothered*) before or after reporting their attitudes toward the essay topic. When discomfort was measured before attitudes, high-choice participants reported significantly more discomfort than did low-choice participants, but when attitudes were reported first, high-choice participants reported low levels of discomfort that were similar to those in the low-choice group. These data support the assertion that dissonance is a state of psychological discomfort that is reduced when people change their attitudes.

Subsequent studies have extended the use of the dissonance thermometer. Harmon-Jones (2000) found that participants who wrote a counterattitudinal statement reported more psychological discomfort under high choice than under low choice when negative affect was measured first, even when the essay would produce no aversive consequences. Galinsky et al. (2000)

replicated the difference in psychological discomfort between high- and low-choice groups reported by Elliot and Devine (1994) and also obtained evidence suggesting that self-affirmations attenuate attitude change by reducing psychological discomfort. However, Galinsky et al. also found no attitude change across the groups, suggesting that the measure of discomfort somehow eliminated the need to reduce dissonance through attitude change.

This latter result is consistent with other studies in which a measure of self-reported emotion taken before an attitude measure has eliminated the motivation to change attitudes (e.g., Elliott & Devine, 1994, Experiment 1; Pyszczynski, Greenberg, Solomon, Sideris, & Stubing, 1993). Pyszczynski et al. (1993) proposed that if the function of attitude change is to protect the individual from the negative emotional state of dissonance, then expressing feelings of discomfort may also diminish the negative affect associated with dissonance, which should then reduce the need to alter cognitions. Pyszczynski et al. reported that when high-choice participants were encouraged, prior to writing a counterattitudinal essay, to express any negative tension they were experiencing, they showed less attitude change than high-choice participants who wrote the essay without the opportunity to express their discomfort. Similarly, Stice (1992) found that participants encouraged to confess their feelings about a counterattitudinal behavior reported higher levels of guilt, but subsequently showed less attitude change, than did nonexpression control participants. Together, these studies suggest that acknowledging discomfort about a discrepant act may reduce the motivation for attitude change. Creating unobtrusive procedures for measuring psychological discomfort may be critical for documenting the mediating role of self-reported negative affect in attitude change (see also Tesser, 2000).

The Hypocrisy Paradigm

The development of the hypocrisy paradigm was inspired in part by the debate between the self-consistency and aversive consequences revisions. Hypocrisy was operationalized as a situation in which people make a proattitudinal statement about the value of a specific target behavior, such as the use of condoms to prevent AIDS (Aronson, Fried, & Stone, 1991), conserving water (Dickerson, Thibodeau, Aronson, & Miller, 1992), or recycling (Fried & Aronson, 1995). By itself, the proattitudinal statement was not predicted to arouse dissonance because it was neither inconsistent with beliefs nor capable of producing an aversive outcome. Dissonance can occur, however, when participants are made mindful of the fact that they, themselves, do not perform the behavior they have advocated to others. Moreover, rather than changing attitudes toward the issue in order to reduce discomfort, as in the classic dissonance paradigms, hypocrisy was predicted to motivate people to practice what they preach by bringing their behavior back into line with their advocacy.

In studies designed to motivate sexually active college students to use condoms to prevent AIDS (Aronson et al., 1991; Stone, Aronson, Crain, Winslow, & Fried, 1994), participants first made a videotaped speech arguing that college students should use condoms every time they have sexual intercourse. Participants then generated a list of their previous failures to use condoms during intercourse. This procedure caused participants to increase their intentions to use condoms (Aronson et al., 1991) and to purchase more condoms when given the opportunity (Stone et al., 1994), compared to those who just advocated the use of condoms, were just made mindful of past failures to use condoms, or merely read about the dangers of AIDS. Thus, the hypocrisy paradigm instigates changes to behavior (a route to dissonance reduction that Festinger believed was very common).

Research also indicates that the dissonance induced by hypocrisy procedures is moderated by factors known to be important in other paradigms. In a study on recycling, Fried and Aronson (1995) found that participants who were exposed to a misattribution cue before the induction of hypocrisy were less likely to volunteer to work at a recycling center than hypocrisy participants not exposed to the misattribution cue. Perceived choice can also moderate the hypocrisy effect: Barquissau and Stone (2000) had participants advocate the importance of regular exercise, after which they focused on perceptions of high- or low-choice over past failures to exercise. When asked to ride a stationary bike as far as possible in 10 minutes, hypocrisy participants who focused on volitional failures to exercise in the past rode farther than participants who focused on failures to exercise that were beyond their control. Finally, Son Hing, Li, and Zanna (2002) found that an act of hypocrisy about nonprejudiced behavior aroused guilt and discomfort in aversive racists, which was later reduced by allocating more resources to a minority group.

To test directly the claim that hypocrisy motivates people to alter their behavior, Stone, Wiegand, Cooper, and Aronson (1997) induced hypocrisy about AIDS and condom use and then simultaneously offered more than one behavioral option for dissonance reduction: One that would solve the hypocritical discrepancy directly (e.g., condom purchase) and one that would allow affirmation of the self without solving the discrepancy directly (e.g., donating to a homeless shelter). When offered only the affirmation option (donation), fully 83% of those in the hypocrisy condition used it. But when the direct option was offered alongside the affirmation option, 78% purchased condoms compared to only 13% who donated money. There may be conditions, however, under which people use attitude change rather than behavior change to resolve a hypocritical discrepancy. Fried (1998) reported in a study on recycling that if the experimenter read the hypocrisy participants' past failures to recycle aloud to them, they did not adopt recycling behavior when offered the opportunity; they changed their attitudes about the importance of recycling instead. In contrast, participants volunteered for a recycling center when their past failures to recycle were kept private from the experimenter. These data suggest that when people are publicly associated with past failures to practice what they preach, they may feel embarrassed or ashamed, which motivates them to justify their previous transgressions through attitude change. Or as Festinger might have said, if public scrutiny of one's past behavior makes future behavior resistant to change, then people will take the path of least resistance and change their attitudes about performing the behavior.

More research is needed to identify the conditions under which hypocrisy motivates behavior change (McGregor, Newby-Clark, & Zanna, 1999). Several studies indicate that making a public commitment to the proattitudinal behavior is necessary (Stone et al., 1994; Stone et al., 1997), but others suggest that simply focusing on important cognitions, such as previous attitudes or emotional responses, can motivate the behavior (e.g., Harmon-Jones, Peterson, & Vaughn, 2003). Also, there is little evidence that hypocrisy induces long-term behavior change. For example, Aronson et al. (1991) reported that hypocrisy participants were only marginally more likely to be using condoms regularly 3 months after their participation in the study, and Fried and Aronson (1995) reported that none of their hypocrisy participants called a phone number they were given for volunteering at a recycling center. Perhaps the discomfort associated with hypocrisy motivates an immediate need to alter behavior, but once the dissonance is reduced, people return to their previous (but less than perfect) routines.

Group Level Dissonance Processes

Some researchers have begun to explore interpersonal aspects of dissonance processes (e.g., Cooper & Stone, 2000; Zanna & Sande, 1987). One intriguing question is whether a discrepant behavior enacted by another individual can cause attitude change in an observer. Sakai (1999) reported a study in which two people (one a confederate) completed a boring task modeled after Festinger and Carlsmith (1959). The experimenter then asked the confederate to tell the next participant that the task was interesting. To introduce a feeling of common fate, the confederate proposed to the naive participant that they go tell the lie together; the confederate stated that he would do all the talking, but asked the participant if this would be okay. During the advocacy, the confederate and participant sat together facing the waiting individual (also a confederate), but the naive participant did not assist in telling the lie. In a control condition, the confederate agreed to tell the lie but did not address the participant as his partner, and during the advocacy, the participant stood off in a corner of the room while the confederate told the lie. Results showed that observers in the common-fate condition felt more familiar with their partner, took more responsibility for their partner's behavior, and, most important, rated the boring task as more interesting than did observers in the control condition. These data suggest that tacitly agreeing to participate in a counterattitudinal conspiracy, even if one is only tangentially involved, can cause dissonance.

Norton, Monin, Cooper, and Hogg (2003) investigated whether people can suffer *vicarious dissonance* when they share a social identity with someone whom they observe commit a counterattitudinal behavior. In one study, participants overheard an ingroup or outgroup member make a speech that was counterattitudinal for the observer. Observers who identified strongly with the ingroup showed the most attitude change in the direction of the actor's speech, and this occurred even before the speech was actually delivered. Another study showed that attitude change in the observers was moderated by the ingroup actor's choice to make the speech and also by whether the speech had foreseeable aversive consequences. These procedures did not induce *personal* psychological discomfort, however, such as that identified by Elliot and Devine (1994). Instead, vicarious dissonance induced a high level of vicarious discomfort— discomfort observers imagined feeling if they were in the actor's shoes. This extension of the role of discomfort represents an intriguing new direction in understanding how dissonance operates at an interpersonal level.

The Role of Simultaneous Accessibility and Explicit Memory in Dissonance Processes

Contemporary theory and research on social cognition has led to new perspectives on the processes underlying dissonance arousal and reduction. For example, McGregor et al. (1999) proposed that dissonance could be construed as a situation in which a person simultaneously holds two highly accessible but inconsistent cognitions. Like a state of ambivalence, McGregor et al. noted that dissonance might be increased by factors that focus attention on the inconsistent cognitions. They proposed that many previous findings in dissonance research, such as the role of attitude reminders in trivialization, the attenuating effect of alcohol on attitude change, and the effect of hypocrisy on behavior, can be interpreted as examples of how the simultaneous accessibility of two inconsistent cognitions influences attitude change following a discrepant act.

Recent work has also investigated whether dissonance requires conscious, effortful thinking. Lieberman, Ochsner, Gilbert, and Schacter (2001) noted that dissonance theorists typically assume that for a discrepant behavior to motivate attitude change, people must consciously attribute their discomfort to the action, which implies that people explicitly remember their behavior. They tested this assumption in two studies with patients suffering from anterograde amnesia, who are incapable of forming new memories that can be consciously retrieved. Using the free-choice paradigm, amnesiacs and control participants were offered a choice between two art prints. The attitude data showed that both amnesiacs and control participants spread the alternatives by ranking the chosen item more positively than the unchosen item. A second study replicated the attitude change observed in the first experiment, even when participants were put under cognitive load. These data suggest that dissonance-induced attitude change does not require conscious deliberation; attitude change may proceed automatically outside of awareness. It remains to be seen, however, whether attitude change occurs automatically following important, self-defining discrepancies, such as those that have been investigated using counterattitudinal advocacies. Developing new ways to investigate automatic processes in dissonance is an exciting direction for future research.

Third Generation Models of Dissonance Processes

The last decade has also seen the development of new models of dissonance processes, which have contributed novel empirical findings and conceptual integrations. Whereas the models may appear to offer new revisions to dissonance theory, most embrace the basic tenets of the original theory while extending the analysis in new directions.

The Self-Standards Model

In a model designed to integrate several of the earlier revisions of dissonance theory, Stone and Cooper (2001) used socio-cognitive principles from the study of action identification (Vallacher & Wegner, 1985), cognitive accessibility, and the structure of self-knowledge to develop a new process model of how cognitions about the self influence dissonance processes. Stone and Cooper proposed that each of the different theories of cognitive dissonance describes a process by which people interpret discrepant behavior, but each makes a different assumption about the type of information people use to interpret and evaluate that behavior. In their presentation of the self-standards model (SSM; Stone & Cooper, 2001), these researchers proposed that people can use important attitudes, beliefs, or self-knowledge to understand the meaning of their behavior, but which criterion people use depends on the type of information that is brought to mind or primed by cues in the situation.

The SSM maintains that once people have acted, they evaluate their behavior against a standard of judgment, and that standard of judgment may or may not relate to a cognitive representation of the self. For example, if *normative standards* of judgment are made salient in the context, then people interpret and evaluate their behavior using the rules and prescriptions followed by most people in the culture. If the behavior represents a discrepancy from the salient normative standard, then, as predicted by the aversive consequences model (Cooper & Fazio, 1984), dissonance will be aroused, but it will be *nomothetic* and will not be moderated by self-concept differences. Alternatively, as stipulated by self-consistency theory (Aronson, 1968), people can interpret and evaluate their behavior using information related to their own personal, idiosyncratic self-concept. The SSM predicts that if *personal standards* are made salient in the context, then the behavior is compared to one's own, idiosyncratic self-expectancies. As a result, people with high self-esteem, who hold more positive expectancies for their behavior, are more likely to perceive the behavior as a discrepancy and show more attitude change. In contrast, people with low self-esteem, who hold more negative expectancies for their behavior, will perceive less of a discrepancy and show less attitude change. Thus, the SSM predicts that when personal standards are used to assess a discrepant behavior, dissonance arousal will be *idiographic* and self-concept differences will moderate the arousal process.

The SSM also predicts that, once dissonance is aroused, the accessibility of certain cognitions about the self determines the motivation to change attitudes or affirm the self (Steele et al., 1993). Once dissonance is aroused, the SSM assumes that people will experience negative emotion and be motivated to reduce it. If no further self-relevant thought occurs, the discrepancy will remain salient, and people will change their attitudes to reduce their discomfort. If new positive cognitions about the self are made accessible in the context, however, the strategy for dissonance reduction turns on the *relevancy* of the self-attributes to the behavioral discrepancy and the level of a person's self-esteem. Specifically, if relevant positive attributes activate self-expectancies, people with high self-esteem should experience more discomfort than people with low self-esteem. Conversely, if cues in the situation make accessible positive attributes that are irrelevant to the discrepant act, the SSM predicts that people with high self-esteem will use them as a resource for dissonance reduction. Those with low self-esteem, however, who have fewer positive self-attributes in their self-knowledge structure, should instead rely on attitude change to reduce their discomfort (Steele et al., 1993).

Tests of the predictions made by the SSM have shown that across different classic paradigms, attitude change can be a function of the predicted interaction between self-esteem and the type of standard used to assess the behavior (Stone, 2001). For example, Stone (2003) had participants with high or low self-esteem write a counterattitudinal essay under conditions of high or low choice. In some high-choice conditions, personal or normative standards were primed using a trait-listing task. Results showed that in the absence of priming any standards, high and low self-esteem participants in the low-choice condition showed less attitude change than did high and low self-esteem participants in the high-choice condition. When normative standards were primed, high and low self-esteem participants showed the same high level of attitude change, which was not different from that exhibited by participants in the high-choice control (no priming) condition. When their personal standards were primed, however, high self-esteem participants showed significantly more justification than low self-esteem participants, whose attitude change scores did not differ from the low-choice control groups. In another study, Stone and Cooper (2003) reported that after participants wrote an uncompassionate essay, priming relevant positive self-attributes (e.g., compassion) caused more attitude change for participants with high self-esteem than for those with low self-esteem, whereas priming irrelevant positive self-attributes (e.g., creative) caused more attitude change for participants with low self-esteem than for those with high self-esteem. Thus, as predicted by the SSM, when and how self-esteem moderated attitude change was a function of the accessibility and relevancy of the positive self-attributes made salient after the discrepant act.

The SSM uses principles of social cognition to illuminate how people process different types of behavioral discrepancies (cf. Kelman & Baron, 1974). There are issues that the model needs to address, however. For example, several individual differences are known to moderate dissonance-induced attitude change, including repression-sensitization (Olson & Zanna, 1982), self-monitoring (Snyder & Tanke, 1976), Machiavellianism (Epstein, 1969), preference for consistency (Cialdini, Trost, & Newsom, 1995), and attributional complexity (Stalder & Baron, 1998). Must personal standards for behavior be the focus for these characteristics to moderate attitude change? There may also be individual differences in how people construe norms for behavior. Finally, future research will be necessary to evaluate how the predictions made by the model apply to other dissonance phenomena, such as the derogation of a forbidden behavior, selective exposure to consonant information, and the effect of hypocrisy on behavior.

The "Radical Model" of Dissonance

Beauvois and Joule (1996) recently presented a new theoretical model of dissonance phenomena that emphasizes the importance of the dissonance ratio, defined as the number of dissonant cognitions divided by the number of dissonant cognitions plus the number of consonant cognitions. According to Beauvois and Joule (1996), the dissonance ratio is the key element that sets the original theory of dissonance apart from any revisions.

To understand dissonance phenomena, the radical model introduces the *generative cognition*, which is the one cognitive element against which everything is determined to be consonant or dissonant. Beauvois and Joule defined the generative cognition as the representation of behavior and further proposed that the generative cognition lies outside of the dissonance ratio. That is, the dissonance ratio only includes the cognitions that are consonant (denominator) and dissonant (denominator and numerator) with the generative cognition (behavior). They proposed that all other theories of dissonance have assumed that an attitude or some other cognition, such as the self, was generative. Beauvois and Joule maintained that when behavior is assumed to be generative, novel predictions about dissonance can be made that fall outside of what other conceptions of dissonance predict. These derived novel predictions have led to the development of two new paradigms for testing dissonance processes.

One observation made by the authors was that in the original Festinger and Carlsmith (1959) experiment, participants not only completed a boring task (which, according to the radical model theory, aroused dissonance by itself), but also performed a second counterattitudinal act by lying about how much they enjoyed the task. Beauvois and Joule labeled this the *double-forced compliance* procedure and predicted that, because the second behavior is consistent with the first, it should produce less attitude change than if participants performed either act alone. Experiments (Beauvois & Joule, 1996) showed that participants liked the task more when they completed the boring task and then told a confederate that it was boring (i.e., the truth) than when participants either read a description of the task and told the truth or just completed the boring task by itself. The authors proposed that these data contradict the aversive consequences (Cooper & Fazio, 1984) and self-affirmation (Steele, 1988) revisions of dissonance. How can warning another person about the tediousness of an act constitute an aversive outcome, and how can it be a threat to the self to tell someone the truth about the task? These are interesting questions that deserve further empirical attention.

A second new paradigm is based on the hypothesis that people can rationalize a problematic behavior by engaging in a new act that is consistent with the first. The key observation is that people may use *act rationalization* (a second, equally or more costly dissonant behavior) if the opportunity for the second discrepant act presents itself immediately after the first discrepant act. Otherwise, if given time, people will reduce dissonance through cognitive rationalization (attitude change) and not be motivated to perform the second act. Beauvois and Joule (1996) reported studies showing that, after one discrepant behavior, participants chose to perform a second, even more costly act if they perceived volition for the first behavior or if they were asked to perform the second act before they had an opportunity to rationalize the first one.

The predictions and research inspired by the radical model are provocative and have led to the discovery of new dissonance phenomena. Awareness of these findings has been limited by the fact that many of the supporting studies are published in non-English language journals. The model will benefit from addressing how the *importance* of the cognitions in the dissonance ratio influence the radical model's predictions, and how factors that influence resistance to change account for the interesting patterns of data generated by the new paradigms.

The Action-Orientation Model

Harmon-Jones and Harmon-Jones (2002) recently proposed a new model that addresses a fundamental question about dissonance processes: Why do discrepancies between actions and attitudes motivate cognitive and behavioral changes? The action-orientation model posits that dissonance motivation evolved because it adaptively warns an organism that the ability to carry out effective action is at risk or threatened by inconsistent information in the behavioral context. Once an organism commits to a course of action, if other information becomes salient that is inconsistent with the cognitions facilitating effective action, the action will be conflicted, which will create an aversive arousal state (discomfort). The proximal motivation to reduce cognitive discrepancy resides in the need to reduce the negative affect associated with dissonance, whereas the distal motivation stems from the "requirement for effective action" (Harmon-Jones & Harmon-Jones, 2002, p. 2). Thus, negative affect triggers the overarching distal motivation for effective action, which provides the direction (action orientation) that causes cognitive and/or behavior change. The emphasis in the model on the regulation of effective action harkens back to early models of psychological consistency that stressed the need for prediction and control as the underlying motivation in consistency strivings (e.g., Heider, 1946; Lecky, 1945).

This model makes predictions for how action-orientation information will influence dissonance reduction. After a decision is made, people should focus on executing the decision. Any information that invokes action orientation should enhance dissonance reduction. In two studies (Harmon-Jones & Harmon-Jones, 2002), participants completed a free-choice procedure (Brehm, 1956) in which they made a difficult choice between two alternatives. In the key conditions, participants then wrote about implementing the decision (an action orientation) or wrote about orientation-neutral or irrelevant control topics. Results showed that priming action orientation increased the typical spreading of alternatives effect relative to control conditions in which dissonance was high but neutral information was primed. Although the results of these studies are consistent with the action-orientation model's predictions, future research is required to address alternative processes that may be invoked by priming action-orientation information, such as the importance and self-relevance of the cognitions activated by goal-directed thinking. Nevertheless, the action-orientation model offers novel predictions regarding how different mindsets influence the motivation to reduce dissonance through attitude change (see also Harmon-Jones et al., 2003).

Computational Models of Dissonance Theory

Computational modeling has found its way into the study of cognitive dissonance theory (Read & Miller, 1994; Shultz & Lepper, 1996). Shultz and Lepper (1999) suggested that attitude change observed in dissonance experiments can be understood as examples of constraint satisfaction. Constraint models view processes in psychology as problems that have various constraints, or *fixed parameters*, that influence how the problems can be solved. Using computer programs designed for artificial neural network research, constraint-satisfaction methods begin with a problem state where theoretically derived values for some of the known constraints are input, and the problem is then solved by allowing the computer to generate the other constraints from the inputted values. Shultz and Lepper (1996) proposed that cognitive dissonance experiments create problems (inconsistencies) with constraints that require the inconsistencies to be resolved through the simultaneous adjustment of attitudes and beliefs. Thus, creating values that represent the constraints inherent in classic dissonance paradigms, including values to represent the causal connections between cognitions and variables like the levels of reward, punishment, or choice, should allow computer models to reproduce many of the attitude change effects reported in published research.

Shultz and Lepper (1996) introduced the *consonance model* to test the role of constraint satisfaction in dissonance processes. The consonance network program is designed to increase consonance among cognitions under conditions of inconsistency. Dissonance experiments can be represented by a network containing a set of cognitions arranged with particular relations and initial activations. For example, to model the Linder et al. (1967) experiment that documented the role of choice in moderating attitude change following induced compliance, Shultz and Lepper (1996) began by inputting values for the most relevant cognitions in the situation: attitude, writing the essay, and payment for the statement. A different set of values was generated to reflect the causal relations between these cognitions under high- and low-choice conditions. For example, excitatory (causal) relations were input between the attitude toward the essay and the writing of the essay (the more one supports the position, the more this would be expressed in the essay) and between the essay and payment ("you get what you pay for"). The relation between the attitude and payment was set to negative, reflecting that the more one agrees with the topic, the less one needs to be paid to express it. In addition, the initial attitude was set to negative (against the essay topic), whereas the essay task was set to positive, reflecting one of the primary discrepancies assumed to drive dissonance reduction. The networks in the low-choice condition were set similarly, with two exceptions. First, the relation between attitude and essay was set to zero to reflect that attitudes are irrelevant to the essay when choice is low. Second, the relation between attitude and payment was set to positive, because in this condition, the more one is paid, the more positive the experience of writing the essay should be. The data produced by the computer network analysis reproduced the crossover interaction between choice and payment, such that attitudes were more favorable in high choice when payment was low, but more favorable in low choice when payment was high. The consonance model also successfully reproduced classic findings in the free-choice and forbidden toy paradigms.

Van Overwalle and Jordens (2002) noted that the consonance model presented by Shultz and Lepper (1996) does not allow learning: Researchers set the values for the connections between cognitions. A more realistic model of how dissonant information is processed would require the values to be developed and adjusted by the program itself. The *adaptive-connectionist* program developed by Van Overwalle and Jordens conceptualizes attitude change following a discrepant act as an adaptive, rational process of error reduction between expected and obtained outcomes. A discrepancy in the network between expected and actual outcomes reflects cognitive dissonance, whereas the adjustments in the connection weights determined by a feed-forward algorithm reflect dissonance reduction through attitude change. Modeling several of the classic paradigms, Van Overwalle and Jordens (2002) replicated many of the attitude change effects and showed that when the model adjusts for the presence of negative affect, it yields different parameter estimates than were reported by the consonance model.

The computational modeling approach to dissonance potentially permits a level of precision never obtained by dissonance researchers who use the classic paradigms to test their hypotheses. Whereas instructions delivered by an experimenter can effectively manipulate levels of high and low choice, the high-impact methodology originally developed by Festinger and his students would be hard pressed to create the specific levels of high and low choice that computer programming affords. Nevertheless, it remains to be seen whether computer programs can anticipate the human capacity to react to situational influences, and whether novel findings generated by computer programs will be replicated by humans under the same conditions.

Cultural Models of Dissonance Processes

Researchers in many areas of social psychology have recently begun to ask whether social processes are universal across cultures. Markus and Kitayama (1991) proposed that differences between individualistic and collectivistic cultures in the way the self is construed limit the generalizability of numerous processes, including cognitive dissonance. They proposed that because the self in collectivistic cultures is based more on social roles, positions, and relationships (an interdependent self), internal attributes such as individual attitudes are less central to how collectivists construe their behavior. In addition, whereas Westerners (from individualistic cultures) tend to take personal responsibility for discrepancies between attitudes and volitional behavior, the tendency for Asians to be more sensitive to social role requirements might lead them to attribute discrepancies to the situation, reducing their dissonance.

Research by Heine and Lehman (1997) showed that several assumptions made by dissonance researchers may not generalize across cultures. They reported that following a free-choice task, participants who were recent immigrants to Canada from Japan and China did not show evidence of attitude change, nor were they influenced by an affirmation manipulation, whereas Canadian participants replicated previous research. Heine and Lehman (1997) concluded, "Along with the myriad conditions necessary to observe dissonance reduction in forced-choice and free-choice paradigms ... we would add that the sample should not be from a culture representative of the interdependent view of self" (p. 397). This observation reflects the general sentiment in the work on cultural differences in dissonance that attitude–behavior inconsistencies do not cause discomfort in people who possess an interdependent view of self.

Although there are published studies that failed to replicate the classic dissonance effects among people from Japan and other interdependent cultures, cultural moderation of dissonance processes should not be surprising to students of Festinger's original theory. In his original book (1957), Festinger noted that one factor that determines whether two cognitions are inconsistent is the prevailing cultural mores and norms. Specifically, he wrote:

> Dissonance could arise because of cultural mores. If a person at a formal dinner uses his hands to pick up a recalcitrant chicken bone, the knowledge of what he is doing is dissonant with the knowledge of formal dinner etiquette. The dissonance exists simply because the culture defines what is consonant and what is not. In some other culture those two cognitions might not be dissonant at all. (p. 14)

Festinger provided many examples of how culture determines not only what cognitions are inconsistent, but also the choice of a dissonance reduction strategy. Thus, the idea that culture could moderate both dissonance arousal and reduction was an explicit element of the original theory of dissonance.

Also, studies conducted in Japan and other interdependent cultures have documented dissonance-induced attitude change. For instance, dissonance can occur in Japanese samples in the form of attitude change following a voluntary counterattitudinal act (Sakai, 1981; Sakai & Andow, 1980). Research has also shown that, as predicted by Festinger (1957), dissonance may occur in different conditions across cultures. Kitayama, Snibbe, Markus, and Suzuki (2004) showed that dissonance occurred among Japanese participants only when they viewed a counter-attitudinal act from the perspective of others. Hoshino-Browne, Zanna, Spencer, and Zanna (2002) found that Asian Canadians with strong Asian identities showed more post-decision justification when their decision would affect a close friend than when the decision would affect only the self, whereas European Canadians and Asian Canadians with weak Asian identities were more likely to justify a difficult decision they made for themselves than for a close friend.

In general, findings are consistent with the idea that culture will "define what is consonant and what is not" (Festinger, 1957, p. 14). Dissonance researchers, like many in the field of social psychology, were guilty of ignoring the role of culture until cross-cultural researchers questioned whether dissonance findings would generalize. By doing so, cultural scholars have called attention to factors that are important for understanding how cognitive dissonance influences the behavior–attitude relation.

Dissonance theory continues to provide a compelling theoretical framework for investigating when, how, and why behavior influences attitudes. Notwithstanding the diverse models we have described, one underlying assumption remains in virtually all of the approaches: The effect of behavior on attitudes is a motivated process, primarily driven by the need to reduce an unpleasant psychological state. As we will detail next, this assumption is not shared by another major approach to understanding how behavior influences attitudes.

SELF-PERCEPTION THEORY

In *self-perception theory*, Daryl Bem (1965, 1967, 1972) hypothesized a potent, causal influence of behavior on attitudes (and on other internal states). The key proposition in Bem's model was that self-perception and social perception are parallel processes: Individuals may often infer their own internal states, including attitudes, from the same external, visible cues they would use to infer another person's internal states.

> An individual's belief and attitude statements and the beliefs and attitudes that an outside ob-
> server would attribute to him are often functionally equivalent in that both sets of statements are
> "inferences" from the same evidence: the public events that the socializing community originally
> employed in training the individual to make such self-descriptive statements. (1965, p. 200)

What are the visible cues that observers use to judge another individual's attitudes and preferences? Typically, observers monitor the individual's actions, as well as external factors that might have facilitated or inhibited such actions. To the extent that external constraints are absent, internal states consistent with behavior will typically be inferred. Similarly, Bem proposed that people often infer their own attitudes from their previous behavior and the circumstances in which their behavior occurred. For instance, individuals may infer attitudes that are consistent with their previous volitional actions.

Self-Perception Theory as an Alternative Interpretation of Dissonance Theory

Bem (1965, 1967) initially proposed self-perception theory as an alternative interpretation of dissonance findings. Specifically, Bem proposed that participants in dissonance studies simply used information about their own behavior and external incentives to infer their attitudes. For example, participants in Festinger and Carlsmith's (1959) study knew that they had told another person that the tasks were enjoyable; participants in the $20 condition (but not the $1 condition) also knew that there had been a strong external incentive for doing so. Just as they would for another person, these participants doubted that an internal state motivated their behavior, whereas participants in the $1 condition inferred from the absence of strong incentives that an internal state compatible with the behavior probably existed. This rationale is consistent with the discounting principle later articulated by attribution theorist Harold Kelley (1973).

Interpersonal Replication Studies

If the assumption that self-perception mimics interpersonal perception is valid, then the inferences that observers draw about the internal states of participants in dissonance studies should be similar to those that were drawn by the participants themselves. To test this reasoning, Bem conducted several studies that he labelled *interpersonal replications* of dissonance experiments. In these studies, participants were given information about a participant in one condition of a dissonance experiment and were asked to infer that participant's attitude. For instance, participants in an interpersonal replication of the Festinger and Carlsmith experiment (Bem, 1967) listened to a tape recording that described in detail, but nonevaluatively, the tasks in the original study. These individuals also learned that the focal participant had accepted an offer of $1 (or $20) to tell a waiting subject that the tasks were fun and then listened to the participant describing the tasks positively to a young woman who made few responses (as in the original study). Individuals in this replication study estimated that the $1 participant actually enjoyed the tasks more than did the $20 participant—the same pattern of reported enjoyment as in the original experiment.

Bem provided interpersonal replication studies of other dissonance paradigms as well, including counter-attitudinal essay writing (Bem, 1965) and the free-choice paradigm (Bem, 1967). He suggested that it was more parsimonious to explain the findings without recourse to complex internal states and motives, such as dissonance arousal. (For a more recent example of using an interpersonal replication procedure to validate a self-perception interpretation of a finding, see Albarracín, Cohen, & Kumkale, 2003.)

Dissonance theorists responded by arguing that individuals in Bem's replication studies lacked one important piece of information that was available to participants in the actual dissonance experiments: the initial attitude before the counterattitudinal behavior (e.g., Jones, Linder, Kiesler, Zanna, & Brehm, 1968; Mills, 1967). These researchers showed that if people in an interpersonal replication study were given information about the dissonance participants' initial attitudes, the replication did not reproduce the pattern of the original dissonance study.

Bem and McConnell (1970) responded to this criticism by suggesting that participants in dissonance experiments were *not* aware of their initial attitude at the time of reporting their final attitude, so the interpersonal replication studies *did* reproduce the phenomenology of the original experiments. To test this point, Bem and McConnell had participants write a counterattitudinal essay, but after participants wrote the essay, they were asked to report their *pre-essay attitude* (measured in a previous session) instead of their current attitude. As predicted, participants' recall of their initial attitude was biased in the direction of the essay, suggesting that they were not aware of their initial attitude.

Even this finding did not end the controversy, however, because dissonance theorists argued that forgetting one's initial view after changing an attitude is an integral part of the dissonance reduction process. Over the next few years, several papers were published that manipulated the salience or extremity of the initial attitude in an attempt to test dissonance versus self-perception predictions. Some of these studies appeared to support dissonance theory (e.g., Green, 1974; Ross & Shulman, 1973) and some appeared to support self-perception theory (e.g., Snyder & Ebbesen, 1972). Other researchers concluded that both models were so flexible that it was impossible to design crucial tests of the theories (see Greenwald, 1975).

Role of Arousal

One difference between dissonance and self-perception theories has yielded data that seem conclusive: the role of arousal. Dissonance theory predicts that engaging in counterattitudinal behavior causes an unpleasant state of arousal or tension, which motivates attitude change or some other form of dissonance reduction. Self-perception theory, however, hypothesizes that attitude change following counterattitudinal behavior results from a cognitive, inferential process that is neither motivated by nor designed to reduce unpleasant arousal. As noted earlier in the section on dissonance theory, numerous studies have unequivocally supported the assumption of dissonance theory that unpleasant arousal occurs after counterattitudinal behavior (e.g., Pallak & Pittman, 1972; Zanna & Cooper, 1974).

Attitude-Incongruent Versus Attitude-Congruent Behavior

Fazio, Zanna, and Cooper (1977) proposed that dissonance theory explains the impact of attitude-incongruent behavior on attitudes better than self-perception theory, whereas self-perception theory explains the impact of attitude-congruent behavior on attitudes better than dissonance theory. They defined *attitude-congruent* behavior as behavior that falls within the actor's latitude of acceptance (i.e., actions that diverge only a little from the actor's most pre-ferred position). Attitude-incongruent behavior, in contrast, is behavior that falls outside of the actor's latitude of acceptance (i.e., behavior that is highly divergent from the actor's most pre-ferred position). Fazio and his colleagues observed that, based on dissonance principles, only attitude-incongruent behavior should lead to arousal, which could then be misattributed to an external source (Zanna & Cooper, 1974). Thus, attitude-incongruent behavior should not lead to attitude change in the presence of a misattribution cue, but attitude-congruent behavior should lead to attitude change even in the presence of a misattribution cue, because there is no arousal involved. To test this reasoning, the researchers asked participants to write an essay under either high- or low-choice conditions. Some participants wrote an essay that argued for a highly dis-crepant position (attitude-incongruent behavior), whereas other participants wrote an essay that argued for a position only slightly discrepant from their own initial view (attitude-congruent behavior). Finally, some participants were given information suggesting that the small, sound-proof booth in which they were completing the study might make them feel tense or uncomfortable, whereas nothing was said to other participants about any possible misattribution source.

Results supported the authors' predictions. Participants exhibited attitude change following attitude-incongruent behavior only when they had high choice and were *not* given an opportunity to misattribute their arousal; attitude change was eliminated when participants were led to believe that the small booth created their discomfort. In contrast, following attitude-congruent behavior, participants exhibited attitude change when they had high choice, and the misattribution manipulation did not affect this pattern. This latter finding is consistent with the self-perception assumption that no arousal will occur when an advocacy falls within an actor's latitude of acceptance.

Taken together, research on the arousal properties of dissonance and the applicability of self-perception to attitude-congruent behavior has indicated that self-perception theory is not a compelling interpretation of the attitudinal consequences of voluntary, attitude-incongruent behavior. Thus, Bem's original intent to replace dissonance theory was not achieved. Nevertheless, self-perception theory remains a viable explanation of the impact of behavior on attitudes in many other situations. In the following paragraphs, we elaborate on applications of self-perception theory to domains other than counter-attitudinal behavior.

Conditions Under Which Self-Perception Processes Occur

One of the important questions that researchers have attempted to answer concerns the conditions under which self-perception processes occur. In his initial papers, Bem (1965, 1967) did not specify these conditions, focusing instead on the relevance of self-perception to dissonance settings. In a 1972 paper, however, Bem proposed that self-perception occurs when "internal cues are weak, ambiguous, or uninterpretable" (p. 2). This hypothesis concedes that internal states, including attitudes, can be strong and unambiguous, in which case perceivers can presumably access the states directly and do not need to infer the states from external cues.

The clearest support for Bem's weak or ambiguous proposal was provided by Shelly Chaiken and Mark Baldwin (1981). These researchers measured participants' beliefs and feelings about environmental issues in a preliminary session. Some participants exhibited consistency between their cognitive and affective responses (e.g., they expressed favorable beliefs and positive feelings), whereas other participants exhibited inconsistency (e.g., they expressed favorable beliefs but ambivalent feelings). High cognitive–affective consistency was assumed to reflect a clear and well-formulated attitude, whereas low cognitive–affective consistency was assumed to reflect a weak and poorly formulated attitude. At a second session 2 weeks later, all participants completed a questionnaire that was designed to induce a biased review of their past environmental behaviors. Specifically, participants completed a questionnaire that either made their previous *pro*-environmental actions salient or made their previous *anti*-environmental actions salient. All participants then reported their attitudes toward environmental issues. The researchers assumed that if the manipulated salience of previous pro- or anti-environmental behaviors influenced participants' reported attitudes, then self-perception processes were implicated. As predicted, the responses of participants with well-formulated attitudes were not influenced by the manipulation of past behavior. In contrast, the responses of participants with poorly formulated attitudes differed depending on whether pro-environmental or anti-environmental behaviors were made salient; these individuals rated themselves as more pro-environmental when the questionnaire made previous pro-environmental behaviors salient than when the questionnaire made previous anti-environmental behaviors salient.

Researchers have identified at least two other conditions that increase the likelihood of self-perception effects. Taylor (1975) found that participants exhibited stronger self-perception effects when an attitude was relatively inconsequential than when it had important implications. Kiesler, Nisbett, and Zanna (1969) demonstrated that people were more likely to infer their attitudes from their actions when implicit or explicit cues in the environment suggested that actions reflected attitudes. In sum, these findings suggest that attitudes are more likely to be inferred from behavior when the preexisting attitude is weak, poorly formulated, or inconsequential, and when cues imply that behavior reflects attitudes (see also Fazio, 1987).

Attitude Domains Amenable to Self-Perception Effects

Self-perception processes have been investigated in a wide variety of attitude domains. For reasons of space, we review here only two, well-known applications of the theory. Other domains we will not review but to which self-perception theory has also been successfully applied include humorous enjoyment (e.g., Bem, 1965; Fazio, Sherman, & Herr, 1982; Olson, 1992), interpersonal attraction (e.g., Kellerman, Lewis, & Laird, 1989; Seligman, Fazio, & Zanna, 1980), heterosexual anxiety (e.g., Haemmerlie & Montgomery, 1982), religious attitudes (e.g., Zanna, Olson, & Fazio, 1981), attitudes toward university issues (e.g., Albarracín & Wyer, 2000; Allison & Messick, 1988), boredom (e.g., Damrad-Frye & Laird, 1989), and introversion-extraversion (e.g., Fazio, Effrein, & Falender, 1981). In each of these domains, participants have been shown to use their behavior and the circumstances in which their behavior occurred to infer an internal state.

Helpfulness: The Foot-in-the-Door Effect

Compliance with a small request increases the likelihood that an individual will also comply with a subsequent larger request, compared to someone who was not asked to perform the small request. Freedman and Fraser (1966) labelled this finding as the *foot-in-the-door effect*; they showed that people who had been asked 2 weeks earlier to sign a petition about keeping their state beautiful or to put a small "Be a safe driver" sticker in a window of their home were much more likely to agree subsequently to put a large, unattractive sign in their yard displaying the words "Drive Carefully" than were individuals who did not receive an initial small request. This finding has been replicated many times, using varied small and large requests (for reviews, see Burger, 1999; Dillard, 1991).

The most common explanation of the foot-in-the-door effect has been a self-perception account (e.g., DeJong, 1979; Snyder & Cunningham, 1975; but see Gorassini & Olson, 1995; Rittle, 1981). From this perspective, agreeing to perform a small favor stimulates a self-inference of helpfulness ("I am a helpful person" or "I am favorable toward being helpful"). This self-perception or self-labelling then increases the likelihood of further compliance, because the individual thinks, "I should help because I am favorable toward being helpful." Conditions that increase the likelihood of inferring an internal state congruent with the initial compliance, such as freedom of choice and incurring more than a trivial cost, have been shown to magnify the foot-in-the-door effect (e.g., Seligman, Bush, & Kirsch, 1976).

An intriguing twist on the relation between self-perception and compliance was made by Rind and Kipnis (1999), who showed that people who were instructed to use a particular influence strategy on another individual inferred relevant internal states if they were successful. For instance, participants who used rational arguments to successfully convince another individual described themselves as intelligent and friendly, whereas participants who successfully used authoritative influence described themselves as dominant and unfriendly.

Intrinsic Motivation: The Overjustification Effect

Another application of self-perception theory has been to judgments of *intrinsic motivation*— the pure enjoyment of an activity or task for its own sake. A basic tenet of self-perception theory is that when there are strong external justifications for behavior, individuals are less likely to infer that an internal state caused the action. An interesting dilemma can arise, then, when external incentives exist for performing an intrinsically enjoyable task. Self-perception theory predicts that perceivers might discount the role of internal states and infer that their behavior was caused by the incentives.

The detrimental effect of rewards on intrinsic motivation was labelled the *overjustification effect* by Lepper, Greene, and Nisbett (1973), because the external incentives overjustify the behavior (which would be sufficiently justified by its intrinsic enjoyableness). In an early study, preschool children drew pictures for an experimenter using attractive magic marker pens. Before agreeing to draw, some children were offered a reward for drawing (a Good Player Award); other children unexpectedly received this reward after drawing; and a third group of children never heard about any reward. After 1 or 2 weeks, the magic marker pens were reintroduced as a free play activity in the preschool, and children's spontaneous use of the pens was observed. Results showed that children who had been offered the reward for drawing pictures were less likely to play with the pens during the free play time than were children in the unexpected or no reward conditions. The researchers concluded that children who were offered a reward to draw pictures attributed their use of the pens to the reward rather than to the pens' intrinsic attractiveness, which decreased their subsequent interest in using the pens.

The overjustification effect has been replicated in many studies (see Condry, 1977; Lepper & Greene, 1978; Tang & Hall, 1995), but limiting conditions have been identified (see Deci & Flaste, 1995; Vallerand, 1997). Perhaps most important, if rewards communicate competence at a task, rather than seeming to be manipulative or controlling, they are less likely to impair intrinsic motivation. Also, if the reward is unusual for the activity (e.g., offering a monetary payment for reading), it is more likely to be seen as controlling and to have a detrimental effect on intrinsic motivation.

UNDERLYING DIMENSIONS AND FUTURE RESEARCH DIRECTIONS

In this final section of the chapter, we attempt to integrate existing research and theories on the influence of behavior on attitudes. We discuss several dimensions that can be used to classify existing theories, with the goals of locating the different models of the behavior–attitude relation within a broad, integrative framework and identifying common mechanisms that underlie the models. We close with some possible directions for future research on this topic.

Nature of the Attitude

One dimension that can be used to conceptualize the theories we have described is the nature of the attitudes on which the theories focus. All models deal with the effect of behavior on attitudes, but some are most useful for specific kinds of attitudes. Also, the models address somewhat different issues within the domain of attitudes. We elaborate on these points next.

Attitude Formation Versus Attitude Change

An issue that is addressed in almost every chapter of this book is the relevance of various theories to attitude formation versus attitude change. In the context of the present chapter, behavior can influence both attitude formation and attitude change. That is, behavior can contribute to the generation of an attitude that did not previously exist, and behavior can alter an existing attitude. The different models we described can be located along this dimension.

Attitude Formation.   Some theories describe the process by which behavior causes people to form or develop new attitudes toward objects or events in their social context. The theory that is focused most specifically on attitude formation is self-perception theory. Researchers have documented empirically that the self-perception of attitudes occurs mainly for weak, ambiguous, or poorly formulated attitudes (e.g., Chaiken & Baldwin, 1981). Also, researchers have suggested that being asked for one's attitude on an issue sometimes serves as the impetus for attitude formation via self-perception (e.g., Fazio, 1987). Further, it makes conceptual sense that going through the process of using past behavior to infer one's attitude would not occur if a strong and well-developed attitude could be easily accessed. Although self-perception theory applies best to attitude formation, it is unlikely that self-perception processes are *always* involved in the formation of every attitude; new evaluative predispositions can form in other ways, perhaps most obviously based on information about the target.

Can behavior lead to attitude formation in ways other than through self-perception? One possibility is via dissonance processes. Although dissonance theory deals primarily with attitude change, it is conceivable that in addition to changing previously held attitudes, people may also have to create new attitudes to help justify an especially painful discrepant act. Effort justification processes may also generate new attitudes when knowledge that one has invested effort or resources toward a previously neutral goal motivates a positive evaluation of the goal (e.g., Axsom & Cooper, 1985). For instance, an individual might agree to participate in a Neighborhood Watch program without having a clear attitude toward the program or without thinking about what the commitment will involve; after attending meetings, delivering flyers for the group, and patrolling the neighborhood, the individual might rationalize these efforts by deciding that the Neighborhood Watch program is important. Finally, a process of attitude formation is described in the aversive consequences version of dissonance theory. Cooper and Fazio (1984) observed that dissonance arousal might be a conditioned emotional response that is learned when the negative consequences of behavior generate negative sanctions from parents and/or peers. "Given a sufficient number of such experiences, an association is apt to develop between personally producing negative effects and arousal" (Cooper & Fazio, 1984, p. 244). It follows that attitudes toward objects and events may develop as children learn how to reduce their discomfort following punishments from their parents or peers. Similarly, if adults believe that their behavior has created aversive consequences for a previously neutral target, they might reduce dissonance by deciding that the target deserved the misfortune. For instance, people who voted for a politician who then introduced legislation that hurt small businesses might rationalize their role in the aversive consequences by deciding that people who own small businesses (previously a neutral group to this individual) are greedy.

Change of Preexisting Attitudes.   Behavior can also cause people to change their preexisting attitudes through a variety of mechanisms, the most investigated of which falls under the wide theoretical umbrella of dissonance theory. The original version of dissonance theory (Festinger, 1957) and the various revisions to dissonance theory, including self-consistency theory and self-affirmation theory, all view attitude change as a strategy for dissonance reduction. Whereas each viewpoint on dissonance posits that different processes contribute to attitude change (e.g., inconsistency between behavior and attitude versus threats to the self-concept), all perspectives share the assumption that behavior causes attitude change via motivational processes. That is, all assume that once people construe their actions as discrepant from some prevailing cognition, such as a specific attitude, belief, self-image, or standard, they experience aversive arousal that is reduced by changing a relevant attitude. Changing preexisting attitudes then serves to reduce the discomfort imposed by the errant behavior.

Biased scanning researchers have focused almost exclusively on attitude change (e.g., Janis & Gilmore, 1965). Participants in these studies have been asked to improvise arguments or to role play situations that are known to be inconsistent with current attitudes. The role playing is assumed to generate new, persuasive information that elicits attitude change.

Attitude–Behavior Consistency

Most of the theories we described address the influence of behavior on attitude formation and/or change. A few models, however, also have implications for understanding how to get people to act consistently with their previously held attitudes. These perspectives specify how behavior can motivate individuals to behave more consistently with their attitudes and values.

The clearest example of this application is dissonance research using the hypocrisy paradigm (e.g., Dickerson et al., 1992; Stone et al., 1994). The dynamics of hypocrisy induction, involving both public commitment to a position and private awareness of inconsistent behavior, motivate people to reduce dissonance by adopting an attitude-consistent course of action (e.g., purchasing condoms, taking shorter showers, or voting to provide more funding for a minority group organization), even when other options for dissonance reduction are present, like affirmation of an unrelated positive self-image (Stone et al., 1997). Thus, an act of hypocrisy appears to motivate people to practice what they preach by changing their behavior to bring it back into line with their attitudes about the topic.

Self-affirmation theory also can be seen as relevant to attitude–behavior consistency. Specifically, people can reduce dissonance by performing behaviors that affirm their values or self-worth—in other words, by performing behaviors that are consistent with their attitudes and values (e.g., Steele, 1988). For example, people can reduce dissonance by giving money to a charity (an attitude-consistent action) and thereby affirming their generosity. Research also indicates, however, that affirming values or self-images related to the attitude–behavior discrepancy may not always be a viable option (see Aronson et al., 1995; Stone & Cooper, 2003).

Attitude Accessibility

A final characteristic of attitudes addressed in the theories we have described is accessibility. Almost all of the theories would predict that attitude formation or attitude change is associated with increased accessibility of the attitude. A newly formed attitude will, by definition, be more accessible than a nonattitude, and an attitude that has recently changed (often in the direction of becoming more polarized) will be more accessible at least in the short term. Perhaps the only model that is silent on accessibility is self-perception theory, which rests on the assumption that people do not have direct access to internal states.

The mechanisms that set attitude formation and change into motion also depend on the accessibility of attitudes. The various versions of dissonance theory disagree, however, about which elements must be accessible for dissonance to be aroused. Many early models (e.g., Brehm & Cohen, 1962) and some recent approaches (Harmon-Jones et al., 1996) assume that the preexisting attitude must be accessible for dissonance arousal; other views, such as self-consistency (Aronson, 1968; 1992) and self-affirmation (Steele, 1988), assume that cognitions about the self must be accessible; and still others like the aversive consequences (Cooper & Fazio, 1984) and radical models (Beauvois & Joule, 1996) assume that cognitions about behavior must be accessible. Some recent models have integrated these assumptions by proposing that the nature of dissonance arousal is a function of the accessibility of different types of cognitions, including attitudes, beliefs, and cognitions about the self (McGregor et al., 1999; Stone & Cooper, 2001; Harmon-Jones & Harmon-Jones, 2002). Attitude accessibility may also play a role in dissonance reduction strategies. For example, Simon et al. (1995) showed that people will trivialize their behavior when their previous attitudes have been made salient or accessible in memory. It seems clear that factors associated with accessibility and memory will play a central role in future research on dissonance processes.

Nature of the Behavior

Another way of classifying the theories we have described is in terms of the type of behavior on which they focus. The various models make clear that different kinds of behavior can influence attitudes in different ways. In this section, we outline two dimensions underlying behavior that provide a useful framework for categorizing the theories: the extent to which the behavior is voluntary versus constrained, and the extent to which the behavior is attitude-incongruent versus attitude-congruent.

Voluntary Versus Constrained Behavior

One fundamental dimension of behavior concerns its degree of volition. Some actions are perceived to be purely voluntary, whereas others are perceived to reflect external constraints. (Of course, actions can also be partly voluntary and partly externally caused, but for our present purposes, the dichotomous classification is sufficient.) This dimension has important implications for the effect of behavior on attitudes.

Voluntary Behavior.   Most, but not all, of the theories we described in this chapter predict attitude change only when the behavior is voluntary. These theories propose that the effects of behavior on attitudes are mediated by psychological states that occur only when the actions are perceived to be volitional. For instance, in order for a state of dissonance (the mediator of attitude change according to dissonance theory) to be aroused, people must perceive that their actions were freely undertaken (e.g., Linder et al., 1967). Similarly, the various revisions of dissonance theory, including self-consistency theory, self-affirmation theory, the aversive consequences model, and the self-standards model, all begin with the assumption that actions were voluntary. Why is volition important? When someone's inconsistent, harmful, or irrational behavior was volitional, he or she will feel a strong need to justify that behavior (to the self or to others). Volitional behavior presumably reflects the actor's true self; if this (presumed) true self appears irrational or harmful, the actor will be motivated to rationalize his or her behavior.

Self-perception theory also focuses on voluntary behavior, this time because volitional behavior is presumed to reflect the actor's true intentions (Bem, 1972). Here, the presumption of veridicality does not arouse defensive motivation, but rather allows clear, rational inferences to be drawn about the self. When perceivers infer others' attitudes, they limit their attention to the others' volitional actions. Similarly, when perceivers engage in self-perceptions of attitudes, they limit their consideration to their own volitional actions. Thus, voluntary behavior generally has more "punch" than constrained behavior, for both motivational and cognitive reasons.

Constrained Behavior.   Biased scanning research has focused on constrained behavior; participants are instructed to play a role or to improvise a set of arguments without being given any opportunity to decline. Under these conditions, individuals should attribute their behavior to the assigned roles rather than personal beliefs. Nevertheless, people often change their attitudes in the direction of the advocated position. The hypothesized mediating process in this case is self-persuasion: People generate new arguments or thoughts that are consistent with the assigned role. The processes initiated by volitional behavior (dissonance, self-perception) do not occur.

Note that the effects identified by biased scanning research should also occur when people engage voluntarily in similar behaviors. If an individual voluntarily decides to play a role, the same processes should be initiated (of course, other processes may *also* occur, such as dissonance and self-perception). For instance, voluntary role playing should generate new arguments just as well as coerced role playing.

Attitude-Incongruent Behavior Versus Attitude-Congruent Behavior

A second fundamental dimension of behavior concerns its consistency with existing attitudes. Some actions are perceived to be inconsistent with the actor's existing attitudes, whereas others are perceived to be largely compatible with existing attitudes. This dimension has important implications for how behavior will affect attitudes.

Attitude-Incongruent Behavior.   Most of the theories we described emphasize the influence of counterattitudinal behavior on attitudes. For example, in biased scanning research, participants are required to argue for a position known to differ from their current attitudes. Dissonance theory also focuses on counterattitudinal behavior—in this case, the impact of realizing that one's voluntary actions have been inconsistent with one's relevant attitudes, knowledge, or values. It is precisely the inconsistency that causes the arousal of dissonance (Festinger, 1957). This focus is also true of the various revisions of dissonance theory; in each case, the motivational significance of behavior derives from its incompatibility with the self-concept or other salient and important cognitions (e.g., Aronson, 1968; Beauvois & Joule, 1996; Stone & Cooper, 2001).

In Fazio et al.'s (1977) proposed integration of dissonance and self-perception theories, the researchers used the notion of *latitudes* (borrowed from social judgment theory) to understand counterattitudinal versus proattitudinal behavior. These authors suggested that dissonance is aroused when behavior falls outside the acceptable range of actions—that is, outside whatever actions the actor would previously have identified as compatible with his or her attitude. This perspective underscores that, although we have talked about actions in terms of broad categories of counterattitudinal versus proattitudinal behavior, inconsistency is a continuum. Presumably, the intensity of the motivation aroused by counterattitudinal behavior will be positively related to its degree of discrepancy from the initial attitude.

Attitude-Congruent Behavior.   Self-perception theory is one model we have re-viewed that focuses primarily on the impact of attitude-congruent behavior on attitudes. The-orists have argued that because attitude-congruent behaviors typically do not activate the motivational processes outlined in such models as dissonance theory, congruent actions in-fluence attitudes mainly through cognitive, inferential processes (Fazio et al., 1977). Studies of the self-perception of helpfulness, intrinsic motivation, and other states have documented that perceivers make rational inferences based on personal behavior and the circumstances in which the behavior occurred.

The hypocrisy paradigm in dissonance theory also applies to proattitudinal behavior. Par-ticipants in these studies are induced to argue for positions with which they agree, which theoretically should not cause dissonance. However, when subsequently reminded of their per-sonal failures to adhere to this position, the discrepancy arouses dissonance, which is reduced by performing the proattitudinal behavior they advocated to others.

Other theories can be applied selectively to attitude-congruent behavior. For instance, the aversive consequences model of dissonance hypothesizes that even proattitudinal actions that result in aversive consequences will arouse dissonance (e.g., Scher & Cooper, 1989). It is the consequences of the behavior, rather than its consistency with one's attitudes, that is assumed to produce dissonance.

Nature of the Underlying Processes

A final dimension we will use to integrate the models described in this chapter is the nature of the processes assumed to underlie the impact of behavior on attitudes. Taken together, the various theories posit many mediating processes, reflecting the complexity of the behavior–attitude relation. Some models emphasize particular mechanisms, whereas others implicate multiple processes. We will examine this issue by distinguishing between automatic processes, deliberative processes, and motivational processes, though we should note at the outset that these categories are not mutually exclusive.

Automatic Versus Deliberative Processes

The theories covered in this chapter vary with respect to how much they assume that behavior influences attitudes through automatic or deliberative processes. Clearly, some effects of behavior on attitudes reflect relatively automatic processes. By automatic, we mean that the processes occur quickly, are spontaneous (i.e., unintentional or without conscious initiation), and require few cognitive resources (Bargh, 1994). These automatic processes often reflect a least-effort strategy of decision making; thus, they occur mainly under conditions of low importance or low personal relevance—conditions that elicit what has been labeled *heuristic processing* or the *peripheral route* in dual-process models of persuasion (Chaiken, 1987; Petty & Cacioppo, 1986). The effects of these judgments may be short-lived if people do not subsequently think about, consolidate, or act on the new attitude.

The processes described in self-perception theory can occur automatically, such as when one's past or current behavior is used as a simple heuristic for inferring one's attitude. This minimal-effort strategy of assuming behavior–attitude correspondence presumably occurs when the domain is not terribly important to the perceiver. Although effortful self-perception inferences do occur, minimal-effort, heuristic inferences are probably common manifestations of self-perception.

Other theories in this chapter assume that the influence of behavior on attitudes occurs via deliberative processes. By deliberative, we mean that the processes are consciously initiated, occur within the perceiver's awareness, and require significant cognitive resources. Because of the necessary cognitive resources, these processes occur mainly under conditions of high importance or high personal relevance—conditions that elicit what has been labeled *systematic processing* or the *central route* in dual-process models of persuasion (Chaiken, 1987; Petty & Cacioppo, 1986). The effects of deliberative processes are likely to be longer lasting than those of automatic processes, because the former involve conscious integration of the attitude into memory (see Albarracín, 2002; Zanna, Fazio, & Ross, 1994).

The biased scanning process hypothesized by researchers of role playing (e.g., Janis & Gilmore, 1965) provides an excellent example of a deliberative effect. When individuals are instructed to argue for a discrepant position, they consciously generate arguments in order to perform their assigned task effectively. These improvised arguments result in self-persuasion, such that participants decide that the advocated position has merit. Because the new attitude is based on cognitive support, it should be relatively permanent.

Self-perception theory also conceptualizes perceivers as engaging in reasoned thinking about their internal states, at least under certain conditions. For example, perceivers are assumed to exhibit discounting or augmentation effects based on information about external factors impinging on them (e.g., Damrad-Frye & Laird, 1989; Olson, 1992). Perceivers make causal judgments about their internal states based on salient information and attributional principles.

The wide varieties of processes falling under the rubric of dissonance theory are more difficult to characterize in terms of automatic versus deliberative processes. One reason is that much of the theory was developed before the social cognition revolution occurred in social psychology (Jones, 1998). Arguably, the perception and reduction of dissonance are conceptualized as involving deliberative processes in most early models of dissonance. Dissonance is assumed to occur when there is a conscious awareness of a discrepancy between two cognitions (one cognition usually concerns a behavior and the other an attitude). Moreover, dissonance reduction is often described as a conscious attempt to rationalize one's behavior: A dissonant cognition is altered, or consonant cognitions are added, in order to make sense of the behavior. The assumption that dissonance reduction is conscious is supported by evidence that distracting people from their counterattitudinal behavior can eliminate attitude change (e.g., Zanna & Aziza, 1976) and by evidence that when provided a choice, people show a preference for certain dissonance reduction strategies over others (Aronson et al., 1995; Stone et al., 1997). The various revisions of dissonance theory, including self-consistency theory, self-affirmation theory, and the aversive consequences model, also assume that deliberative processes mediate the effects of behavior on attitude. Each model postulates relatively complex reasoning about the status of the self or the consequences of one's behavior. Finally, the discomfort that mediates the effect of behavior on attitudes in these models is assumed to be consciously experienced (Elliot & Devine, 1994; Pyszczynski et al., 1993).

Some findings suggest that dissonance may not always be conscious or deliberative. For example, dissonance arousal itself may be automatic, so long as the necessary conditions occur. Also, research on misattribution indicates that people do not always know why they feel discomfort following a discrepant behavior. Recall that the misattribution approach was based on the two-factor theory of emotion (Schachter & Singer, 1962), with the assumption that for a discrepant behavior to motivate attitude change, it must cause arousal that is labeled negatively (see Cooper & Fazio, 1984). Research shows that if the arousal is attributed to a source other than one's behavior, or if it is labeled positively, people do not change their attitudes. The fact that people can misattribute their arousal to something like the lights in a laboratory or can interpret their arousal as positive indicates that they do not spontaneously attribute their arousal to their own actions, possibly because they are unaware of the role their behavior played in the arousal process. The research by Lieberman et al. (2001) on the role of explicit memory in dissonance-induced attitude change provides further evidence that conscious attention and deliberation over the meaning of a discrepant behavior may not be necessary for a difficult decision to motivate rationalization.

Finally, studies show that people often use the first strategy for dissonance reduction that is offered to them, regardless of whether the strategy directly reduces the discrepancy between attitudes and behavior (e.g., Simon et al., 1995; Steele & Lui, 1983; Tesser & Cornell, 1991). One reason people may be able to misattribute their arousal, fail to recall their behavior, and use indirect strategies for dissonance reduction is that they may sometimes be unaware of the discrepancy underlying their motivated state. The apparently pliable nature of dissonance indicates that behavior may influence attitudes through automatic processes that operate without much conscious control.

Certain consequences of dissonance arousal (or, perhaps more correctly, certain consequences of *avoiding* dissonance arousal) may also operate automatically. For example, the selective exposure hypothesis predicts that people are motivated to approach consonant information and avoid dissonant information; this motivation may sometimes influence spontaneous attentional processes that occur without individuals' awareness, perhaps especially for certain personality types (e.g., *repressors*, who perceptually defend themselves from threatening stimuli, see Olson & Zanna, 1979).

Some recent models of the dissonance process may be capable of accounting for both deliberative and automatic processes in dissonance arousal and reduction. For example, the self-standards model of dissonance (Stone & Cooper, 2001) was developed in part to address the role of implicit and explicit thought in dissonance-induced attitude change. The model hypothesizes that the accessibility of particular standards (e.g., personal vs. normative standards) determines the nature and consequences of dissonance arousal; and further, different standards for interpreting behavior can be activated without individuals' realization, such as by an implicit priming procedure (Stone, 2003; Stone & Cooper, 2003). Thus, the SSM encompasses automaticity in dissonance by emphasizing the impact of the relative accessibility of different cognitions. The processing assumptions of the model, however, do not preclude the possibility that the implicit accessibility of specific cognitions can activate deliberative thought about the implications of behavior, explicit attention to discomfort, and careful consideration about how to reduce dissonance. Similarly, the effect of simultaneously accessible cognitions in affective responses is consistent with the idea that an implicit process can influence the explicit experience of emotion when people act inconsistently with important attitudes or beliefs (Higgins, 1996; McGregor et al., 1999). Thus, contemporary models that integrate principles and methodologies from social cognition with classic dissonance assumptions and procedures hold promise for elucidating the role played by deliberate and automatic processing in dissonance phenomena.

Motivational Processes

The extent to which behavior guides attitudes through motivational processes is independent of the extent to which the process is relatively automatic or deliberative. That is, some motivational processes are automatic, whereas others are deliberative (and the same goes for nonmotivational processes). But a key feature of many of the perspectives we have described is that they have motivational significance for the individual.

Dissonance theory posits that motivational processes are initiated by the awareness of inconsistencies. In Festinger's (1957) original statement, cognitive dissonance was described as an aversive state that motivates changes to cognitions to reduce the state. Researchers who have manipulated factors that influence the magnitude of dissonance, such as through the *degree* of external justification for counterattitudinal behavior, have typically found parallel differences in the *amount* of attitude change, suggesting that dissonance is a motivational state that varies in strength depending on the degree of inconsistency and justification (e.g., Cohen, 1962). The fact that attitude change following counterattitudinal behavior is eliminated by alcohol consumption, which dulls emotional intensity, is also consistent with a motivational view (e.g., Steele et al., 1981). Indeed, all of the studies showing that dissonance is a state of arousal, or that dissonance reduction requires that the arousal be labeled as being due to counterattitudinal behavior, support the argument that dissonance is a motivational state (e.g., Zanna & Cooper, 1974).

Nevertheless, the precise nature of the motivation in terms of the goals achieved by dissonance reduction continues to be a matter of some debate (Harmon-Jones & Mills, 1999). The various revisions of dissonance theory, including self-consistency theory, self-affirmation theory, the aversive consequences model, and the new wave of models, retain the original theory's motivational perspective, but the source of the motivation is different (e.g., a need for self-consistency rather than a general need for psychological consistency). Models that predict moderating effects for individual difference variables like self-esteem assume that individuals experience different degrees of discomfort, which motivate different degrees of defensive response.

Two research areas we have discussed are explicitly nonmotivational: biased scanning research and self-perception theory. These models focus on cognitive processes that are initiated by behavior: biased scanning initiated by constrained counterattitudinal behavior in role playing research, or inferences about internal states based on voluntary neutral or attitude-congruent behavior in self-perception theory. These processes are neither defensive nor designed to protect the self, but instead reflect informational effects of arguments or knowledge on attitudes.

Future Research on the Influence of Behavior on Attitudes

We have reviewed and discussed a wide range of theories and research on the behavior–attitude relation. This literature has provided important insights about the influence of behavior on attitudes. Researchers have documented effects of both constrained and voluntary actions on both attitude formation and change. The mechanisms underlying these effects encompass both motivational and nonmotivational processes that occur both automatically and deliberatively.

Given the diversity of approaches to this topic, there are a multitude of directions that future research could take. Many avenues hold promise for important extensions to knowledge. In this final section, we outline a few possibilities that seem to us especially interesting.

Dissonance Processes

As the dominant approach in this literature, dissonance theory continues to receive a lot of attention and seems likely to do so for the foreseeable future. Earlier, we described numerous new topics and models in dissonance research, and these issues warrant further attention. For example, the experience of dissonance at the group level and cultural factors in dissonance arousal and reduction are important. Simply identifying differences between individual and group dissonance or between cultures in dissonance arousal/reduction would be worthwhile, but it would be even more significant to explore the mechanisms underlying these differences. For example, when people from one culture do not show attitude change following a free-choice task, is it because they did not perceive a discrepancy, or did they experience discomfort but use a strategy other than attitude change to reduce their dissonance? Exploring such questions will greatly clarify the meaning of group or cultural moderation of dissonance processes.

The new theoretical models of cognitive dissonance that have developed over the last decade are likely to lead to several new directions in dissonance research. The novel assumptions made by the self-standards model (Stone & Cooper, 2001), the radical model (Beauvois & Joule, 1996), the action-orientation model (Harmon-Jones & Harmon-Jones, 2002), and computational models of dissonance (Shultz & Lepper, 1996) not only account for classic dissonance effects, but also present new challenges for previous revisions of dissonance theory. Although each new model was developed in part to clarify the processes underlying classic dissonance effects, each also integrates contemporary theory in areas like social cognition and self-regulation with computer modeling and neuroimaging techniques. Thus, the new models offer new insights and make new predictions for how dissonance affects the behavior-to-attitude link. These models deserve careful testing and comparisons of their predictive validity. Whether integration of these models is possible will also be an interesting question over the next decade.

A long-standing issue in dissonance theory that continues to warrant attention is how people select a mode of dissonance reduction. Advances in our understanding of this question have been made (e.g., J. Aronson et al., 1995; Blanton et al., 1997; Galinsky et al., 2000; Simon et al., 1995; Stone & Cooper, 2003; Tesser, 2000), but a comprehensive model that accounts for all possibilities has yet to be developed. For example, what are the conditions that influence whether people will, following dissonance arousal, exhibit attitude change, trivialization, adding consonant cognitions, or behavior change? Are there factors like attitude strength that influence resistance to change, and are there other factors that influence the choices people make between various modes of dissonance reduction? Researchers need to identify both situational factors and stable individual differences that play a role in this process.

Mechanisms Underlying the Effects of Behavior on Attitudes

Researchers have rarely examined simultaneously the possible contributions of multiple processes to the impact of behavior on attitudes. For example, few researchers have included manipulations in their studies that would yield different predictions for dissonance versus biased scanning versus self-perception mechanisms. Instead, researchers have generally focused on a single theoretical perspective and looked for evidence of a specific psychological mechanism.

A laudable exception to the paucity of research on multiple mechanisms by which behavior might affect attitudes was reported by Albarracín and Wyer (2000). These researchers constructed a situation within which competing predictions could be derived for dissonance, biased scanning, self-perception, and heuristic models concerning how past behavior should affect measures of attitudes and future behavior. Results favored two of the mechanisms (biased scanning and self-perception) and raised doubts about the other two mechanisms in producing the findings. We need more research of this nature to identify the conditions under which various processes account for the effects of behavior on attitudes.

The respective roles of automatic and deliberative processes also need more investigation. Although both kinds of effects are involved, we need more detailed knowledge of when and why each occurs. With the exception of the importance or significance of the attitude topic (e.g., its personal relevance), researchers have paid little attention to variables that moderate whether automatic or deliberative processes are elicited in this domain.

Influence of Behavior on Multiple Attitudes

Researchers have typically examined the influence of behavior on a specific attitude, such as participants' attitudes toward an experimental task, the topic of an essay, or a choice alternative. It is very likely, however, that a single behavior can sometimes affect numerous attitudes. Research examining this broader influence would be welcome.

For example, an individual's decision to donate or not to donate to a charity in response to a door-to-door solicitation could potentially influence his or her attitudes toward the specific charitable organization, toward door-to-door solicitations in general, toward the gender, ethnic, or age group of the solicitor, and so on. This reasoning is similar to Ajzen and Fishbein's (1980) concept of *impact effects*, which are unanticipated effects of a persuasive message on beliefs that were not directly targeted in the message. Impact effects are probably the norm rather than the exception in persuasive campaigns, but researchers have rarely studied them. Similarly, behavior probably affects more than one attitude in many circumstances, but researchers have not examined this possibility.

In addition to investigating the influence of behavior on several related attitudes, it would be interesting to extend research to examine whether behavior can affect broader, higher order concepts like values and ideologies (Maio, Olson, Bernard, & Luke, 2003). Values can be defined as abstract ideals that function as important guiding principles in individuals' lives, such as equality, security, and freedom (Rokeach, 1973; Schwartz, 1992). Ideologies can be defined as systems of attitudes and values that are organized around an abstract theme, such as liberalism, conservatism, capitalism, or democracy (Converse, 1964; McGuire, 1985). Given that actions induced in previous behavior–attitude studies have often been related to important aspects of the self (e.g., rationality, compassion, truthfulness), it seems possible that values or ideologies could potentially be affected. To be sure, behavior would need to be very important and/or public for broad concepts like values to be affected, but these criteria may be met in some circumstances.

Dynamic, Reciprocal Relations Between Behavior and Attitudes

Perhaps the most important direction in which research and theorizing must go is toward developing models that represent the dynamic, bidirectional relations between behavior and attitudes. There is no doubt that behavior affects attitudes, and there is no doubt that attitudes affect behavior. The challenge is to design theories that capture this reciprocal interdependence. Theorists have long recognized the bidirectional nature of the relation between behavior and attitudes (e.g., see Eagly & Chaiken, 1993; Fazio & Zanna, 1981; Kelman, 1974), but such reciprocity has not often been incorporated into research.

An interesting exception to this scarcity of attention came from Holland, Verplanken, and van Knippenberg (2002), who measured the extremity and strength of participants' attitudes toward Greenpeace. Participants returned to the laboratory a week after reporting their attitudes and were given the opportunity to donate money to Greenpeace, after which their attitudes were measured again. Results showed that participants who held strong attitudes at the first session were more likely to behave consistently with their attitude when given the opportunity to donate money at the second session than were participants who held weak attitudes at the first session. Further, participants who held strong attitudes at the first session were not influenced by their donation behavior when reporting their attitudes at the second session, whereas participants who held weak attitudes at the first session reported attitudes at the second session that were affected by their donation behavior (reporting more favorable attitudes if they donated and more unfavorable attitudes if they did not donate). The authors concluded that strong attitudes guide behavior, whereas weak attitudes are influenced by behavior.

Holland et al.'s (2002) analysis provides a nice perspective on the reciprocal relations between behavior and attitudes, incorporating a feature of the attitude as an important moderating variable. We hope that future research will extend this perspective by incorporating additional factors into the dynamic interplay between behavior and attitudes. For instance, does the nature of the behavior (e.g., voluntary vs. constrained, or attitude-incongruent vs. attitude-congruent) differentially influence the strength of behavior-to-attitude and attitude-to-behavior effects? Some domains or conditions may produce symmetrical interdependence between behavior and attitudes, whereas other domains or conditions may produce asymmetrical interdependence. These issues will be fascinating to explore in future research.

CONCLUSION

We have discussed three theoretical perspectives on how behavior can influence attitudes: biased scanning, dissonance motivation, and self-perception inferences. This topic has yielded some of social psychology's most famous findings and theories. Although interest has waxed and waned to some extent over the years, the increasing sophistication of recent research gives us confidence that the effects of behavior on attitudes will continue to attract attention from scientists and to fascinate laypersons well into the foreseeable future.

REFERENCES

Abelson, R. P. (1983). Whatever became of consistency theory? *Personality and Social Psychology Bulletin, 9*, 37–54.

Abelson, R. P., Aronson, E., McGuire, W., Newcomb, T., Rosenberg, M., & Tannenbaum, P. (1968). *Theories of cognitive consistency: A sourcebook.* Chicago: Rand McNally.

Ajzen, I., & Fishbein, M. (1980). *Understanding attitudes and predicting social behavior.* Englewood Cliffs, NJ: Prentice-Hall.

Albarracín, D. (2002). Cognition in persuasion: An analysis of information processing in response to persuasive communications. In M. P. Zanna (Ed.), *Advances in experimental social psychology* (Vol. 34, pp. 61–130). New York: Academic Press.

Albarracín, D., Cohen, J. B., & Kumkale, G. T. (2003). When communications collide with recipients' actions: Effects of post-message behavior on intentions to follow the message recommendations. *Personality and Social Psychology Bulletin, 29*, 834–845.

Albarracín, D., & Wyer, R. S., Jr. (2000). The cognitive impact of past behavior: Influences on beliefs, attitudes, and future behavioral decisions. *Journal of Personality and Social Psychology, 79*, 5–22.

Allison, S. T., & Messick, D. M. (1988). The feature-positive effect, attitude strength, and degree of perceived consensus. *Personality and Social Psychology Bulletin, 14*, 231–241.

Andreoli, V. A., Worchel, S., & Folger, R. (1974). Implied threat to behavioral freedom. *Journal of Personality and Social Psychology, 30*, 765–771.

Aronson, E. (1968). Dissonance theory: Progress and problems. In R. Abelson, E. Aronson, W. McGuire, T. Newcomb, M. Rosenberg, & P. Tannenbaum (Eds.), *Theories of cognitive consistency: A sourcebook* (pp. 5–27). Chicago: Rand McNally.

Aronson, E. (1992). The return of the repressed: Dissonance theory makes a comeback. *Psychological Inquiry, 3*(4), 303–311.

Aronson, E., & Carlsmith, J. M. (1962). Performance expectancy as a determinant of actual performance. *Journal of Abnormal and Social Psychology, 65*, 178–182.

Aronson, E., & Carlsmith, J. M. (1963). Effect of the severity of threat on the devaluation of forbidden behavior. *Journal of Abnormal and Social Psychology, 66*, 584–588.

Aronson, E., Fried, C. B., & Stone, J. (1991). Overcoming denial and increasing the use of condoms through the induction of hypocrisy. *American Journal of Public Health, 81*, 1636–1638.

Aronson, E., & Mills, J. (1959). The effect of severity of initiation on liking for a group. *Journal of Abnormal and Social Psychology, 59*, 177–181.

Aronson, J., Blanton, H., & Cooper, J. (1995). From dissonance to disidentification: Selectivity in the self-affirmation process. *Journal of Personality and Social Psychology, 68*(6), 986–996.

Axsom, D., & Cooper, J. (1985). Cognitive dissonance and psychotherapy: The role of effort justification in inducing weight loss. *Journal of Experimental Social Psychology, 21*, 149–160.

Bargh, J. A. (1994). The four horsemen of automaticity: Awareness, intention, efficiency, and control in social cognition. In R. S. Wyer, Jr., & T. K. Srull (Eds.), *Handbook of social cognition* (Vol. 1, pp. 1–40). Hillsdale, NJ: Lawrence Erlbaum Associates.

Barquissau, M., & Stone, J. (2000). *When hypocrisy induced dissonance encourages exercise behavior.* Unpublished manuscript, University of Arizona, Tucson.

Beauvois, J. L., & Joule, R. V. (1996). *A radical dissonance theory.* Bristol, PA: Taylor & Francis.

Bem, D. J. (1965). An experimental analysis of self-persuasion. *Journal of Experimental Social Psychology, 1*, 199–218.

Bem, D. J. (1967). Self-perception: An alternative interpretation of cognitive dissonance phenomena. *Psychological Review, 74*, 183–200.

Bem, D. J. (1972). Self-perception theory. In L. Berkowitz (Ed.), *Advances in experimental social psychology* (Vol. 6, pp. 1–62). New York: Academic Press.

Bem, D. J., & McConnell, H. K. (1970). Testing the self-perception explanation of dissonance phenomena: On the salience of premanipulation attitudes. *Journal of Personality and Social Psychology, 14*, 23–31.

Berkowitz, L., & Devine, P. G. (1989). Research traditions, analysis, and synthesis in social psychological theories: The case of dissonance theory. *Personality and Social Psychology Bulletin, 15*, 493–507.

Blanton, H., Cooper, J., Skurnik, I., & Aronson, J. (1997). When bad things happen to good feedback: Exacerbating the need for self-justification with self-affirmations. *Personality and Social Psychology Bulletin, 23*, 684–692.

Brehm, J. W. (1956). Post-decision changes in desirability of alternatives. *Journal of Abnormal and Social Psychology, 52*, 384–389.

Brehm, J. W., & Cohen, A. R. (1962). *Explorations in cognitive dissonance.* San Diego, CA: Academic Press.

Brockner, J., Wiesenfeld, B. M., & Raskas, D. F. (1993). Self-esteem and expectancy-value discrepancy: The effects of believing that you cant (or can't) get what you want. In R. F. Baumeister (Ed.), *Self-esteem: The puzzle of low self-regard* (pp. 219–240). New York: Plenum.

Burger, J. M. (1999). The foot-in-the-door compliance procedure: A multiple-process analysis and review. *Personality and Social Psychology Review, 3*, 303–325.

Chaiken, S. (1987). The heuristic model of persuasion. In M. P. Zanna, J. M. Olson, & C. P. Herman (Eds.), *Social influence: The Ontario symposium* (Vol. 5, pp. 3–39). Hillsdale, NJ: Lawrence Erlbaum Associates.

Chaiken, S., & Baldwin, M. W. (1981). Affective-cognitive consistency and the effect of salient behavioral information on the self-perception of attitudes. *Journal of Personality and Social Psychology, 41*, 1–12.

Chapanis, N. P., & Chapanis, A. (1964). Cognitive dissonance: Five years later. *Psychological Bulletin, 61*, 1–22.

Cialdini, R. B., Trost, M. R., & Newsom, J. T. (1995). Preference for consistency: The development of a valid measure and the discovery of surprising behavioral implications. *Journal of Personality and Social Psychology, 69*, 318–328.

Cohen, A. R. (1962). An experiment on small rewards for discrepant compliance and attitude change. In J. W. Brehm & A. R. Cohen (Eds.), *Explorations in cognitive dissonance* (pp. 73–78). New York: Wiley.

Condry, J. (1977). Enemies of exploration: Self-initiated versus other-initiated learning. *Journal of Personality and Social Psychology, 35*, 459–477.

Converse, P. E. (1964). The nature of belief systems in mass publics. In D. E. Apter (Ed.), *Ideology and discontent* (pp. 206–261). New York: Free Press.

Cooper, J. (1980). Reducing fears and increasing assertiveness: The role of dissonance reduction. *Journal of Experimental Social Psychology, 16,* 199–213.

Cooper, J. (1998). Unlearning cognitive dissonance: Toward an underderstanding of the development of dissonance. *Journal of Experimental Social Psychology, 34,* 562–575.

Cooper, J., & Duncan, B. L. (1971). Cognitive dissonance as a function of self-esteem and logical inconsistency. *Journal of Personality, 39,* 289–302.

Cooper, J., & Fazio, R. H. (1984). A new look at dissonance theory. In L. Berkowitz (Ed.), *Advances in experimental social psychology* (Vol. 17, pp. 229–266). New York: Academic Press.

Cooper, J., & Stone, J. (2000). Cognitive dissonance and the social group. In D. J. Terry & M. A. Hogg (Eds.), *Attitudes, behavior, and social context: The role of norms and group membership* (pp. 227–244). Mahwah, NJ: Lawrence Erlbaum Associates.

Cooper, J., & Worchel, S. (1970). Role of undesired consequences in arousing dissonance. *Journal of Personality and Social Psychology, 16,* 199–206.

Cooper, J., Zanna, M. P., & Taves, P. A. (1978). Arousal as a necessary condition for attitude change following induced compliance. *Journal of Personality and Social Psychology, 36,* 1101–1106.

Damrad-Frye, R., & Laird, J. D. (1989). The experience of boredom: The role of self-perception of attention. *Journal of Personality and Social Psychology, 57,* 315–320.

Deci, E. L., & Flaste, R. (1995). *Why we do what we do: The dynamics of personal autonomy.* New York: Putnam.

DeJong, W. (1979). An examination of self-perception mediation of the foot-in-the-door effect. *Journal of Personality and Social Psychology, 37,* 2221–2239.

Dickerson, C., Thibodeau, R., Aronson, E., & Miller, D. (1992). Using cognitive dissonance to encourage water conservation. *Journal of Applied Social Psychology, 22,* 841–854.

Dillard, J. P. (1991). The current status of research on sequential-request compliance techniques. *Personality and Social Psychology Bulletin, 17,* 283–288.

Duval, S., & Wicklund, R. A. (1972). *A theory of objective self-awareness.* New York: Academic Press.

Eagly, A. H., & Chaiken, S. (1984). Cognitive theories of persuasion. In L. Berkowitz (Ed.), *Advances in experimental social psychology* (Vol. 17, pp. 267–359). San Diego, CA: Academic Press.

Eagly, A. H., & Chaiken, S. (1993). *The psychology of attitudes.* Fort Worth, TX: Harcourt Brace Jovanovich.

Elkin, R. A., & Leippe, M. R. (1986). Physiological arousal, dissonance, and attitude change: Evidence for a dissonance—arousal link and a "don't remind me" effect. *Journal of Personality and Social Psychology, 51,* 55–65.

Elliot, A. J., & Devine, P. G. (1994). On the motivational nature of cognitive dissonance: Dissonance as psychological discomfort. *Journal of Personality and Social Psychology, 67*(3), 382–394.

Elms, A. C. (1967). Role playing, incentive, and dissonance. *Psychological Bulletin, 68,* 132–148.

Elms, A. C., & Jains, I. L. (1965). Counter-norm attitudes induced by consonant versus dissonant conditions of role-playing. *Journal of Experimental Research in Personality, 1,* 50–60.

Epstein, G. F. (1969). Machiavelli and the devil's advocate. *Journal of Personality and Social Psychology, 11,* 38–41.

Fazio, R. H. (1987). Self-perception theory: A current perspective. In M. P. Zanna, J. M. Olson, & C. P. Herman (Eds.), *Social influence: The Ontario symposium* (Vol. 5, pp. 129–150). Hillsdale, NJ: Lawrence Erlbaum Associates.

Fazio, R. H., Effrein, E. A., & Falender, V. J. (1981). Self-perceptions following social interaction. *Journal of Personality and Social Psychology, 41,* 232–242.

Fazio, R. H., Sherman, S. J., & Herr, P. M. (1982). The feature-positive effect in the self-perception process: Does not doing matter as much as doing? *Journal of Personality and Social Psychology, 42,* 404–411.

Fazio, R. H., & Zanna, M. P. (1981). Direct experience and attitude–behavior consistency. In L. Berkowitz (Ed.), *Advances in experimental social psychology* (Vol. 14, pp. 161–202). San Diego, CA: Academic Press.

Fazio, R. H., Zanna, M. P., & Cooper, J. (1977). Dissonance and self-perception: An integrative view of each theory's proper domain of application. *Journal of Experimental Social Psychology, 13,* 464–479.

Festinger, L. (1957). *A theory of cognitive dissonance.* Evanston, IL: Row, Peterson.

Festinger, L. (1964). *Conflict, decision, and dissonance.* Stanford, CA.: Stanford University Press.

Festinger, L., & Carlsmith, J. M. (1959). Cognitive consequences of forced compliance. *Journal of Abnormal and Social Psychology, 58,* 203–210.

Festinger, L., Riecken, H., & Schachter, S. (1956). *When prophecy fails.* Minneapolis: University of Minnesota Press.

Freedman, J. L. (1965). Long-term behavioral effects of cognitive dissonance. *Journal of Personality and Social Psychology, 1,* 145–155.

Freedman, J. L., & Fraser, S. C. (1966). Compliance without pressure: The foot-in-the-door technique. *Journal of Personality and Social Psychology, 4,* 195–202.

Freedman, J. L., & Sears, D. O. (1965). Selective exposure. In L. Berkowitz (Ed.), *Advances in experimental social psychology* (Vol. 2, pp. 57–97). New York: Academic Press.

Frey, D. (1986). Recent research on selective exposure to information. In L. Berkowitz (Ed.), *Advances in experimental social psychology* (Vol. 19, pp. 41–80). New York: Academic Press.

Fried, C. B. (1998). Hypocrisy and identification with transgressions: A case of undetected dissonance. *Basic and Applied Social Psychology, 20*, 145–154.

Fried, C. B., & Aronson, E. (1995). Hypocrisy, misattribution, and dissonance reduction. *Personality and Social Psychology Bulletin, 21*(9), 925–933.

Gaes, G. G., Kalle, R. J., & Tedeschi, J. T. (1978). Impression management in the forced compliance situation. *Journal of Personality and Social Psychology, 14*, 493–510.

Galinsky, A. D., Stone, J., & Cooper, J. (2000). The reinstatement of dissonance and psychological discomfort following failed affirmations. *European Journal of Social Psychology, 30*, 123–147.

Gerard, H. B., & White, G. L. (1983). Post-decisional reevaluation of choice alternatives. *Personality and Social Psychology Bulletin, 9*, 365–369.

Glass, D. (1964). Changes in liking as a means of reducing cognitive discrepancies between self-esteem and aggression. *Journal of Personality, 32*, 531–549.

Gorassini, D. R., & Olson, J. M. (1995). Does self-perception change explain the foot-in-the-door effect? *Journal of Personality and Social Psychology, 69*, 91–105.

Green, D. (1974). Dissonance and self-perception analyses of "forced compliance": When two theories make competing predictions. *Journal of Personality and Social Psychology, 29*, 819–828.

Greenwald, A. G. (1969). The open-mindedness of the counterattitudinal role player. *Journal of Experimental Social Psychology, 5*, 375–388.

Greenwald, A. G. (1970). When does role playing produce attitude change? *Journal of Personality and Social Psychology, 16*, 214–219.

Greenwald, A. G. (1975). On the inconclusiveness of "crucial" cognitive tests of dissonance versus self-perception theories. *Journal of Experimental Social Psychology, 11*, 490–499.

Greenwald, A. G., & Albert, R. D. (1968). Acceptance and recall of improvised arguments. *Journal of Personality and Social Psychology, 8*, 31–34.

Haemmerlie, F. M., & Montgomery, R. L. (1982). Self-perception theory and unobtrusively biased interactions: A treatment for heterosexual anxiety. *Journal of Counseling Psychology, 29*, 362–270.

Harmon-Jones, E. (2000). Cognitive dissonance and experienced negative affect: Evidence that dissonance increases experienced negative affect even in the absence of aversive consequences. *Personality and Social Psychology Bulletin, 26*, 1490–1501.

Harmon-Jones, E., Brehm, J. W., Greenberg, J., Simon, L., & Nelson, D. E. (1996). Evidence that the production of aversive consequences is not necessary to create cognitive dissonance. *Journal of Personality and Social Psychology, 70*, 5–16.

Harmon-Jones, E., & Harmon-Jones, C. (2002). Testing the action-based model of cognitive dissonance: The effect of action orientation on postdecisional attitudes. *Personality and Social Psychology Bulletin, 28*, 711–723.

Harmon-Jones, E., & Mills, J. (Eds.). (1999). *Cognitive dissonance: Progress on a pivotal theory in social psychology.* Washington, DC: American Psychological Association.

Harmon-Jones, E., Peterson, H., & Vaughn, K. (2003). The dissonance-inducing effects of an inconsistency between experienced empathy and knowledge of past failures to help: Support for the action-based model of dissonance. *Basic and Applied Social Psychology, 25*, 69–78.

Heider, F. (1946). Attitudes and cognitive organization. *Journal of Psychology, 21*, 107–112.

Heine, S. J., & Lehman, D. R. (1997). Culture, dissonance, and self-affirmation. *Personality and Social Psychology Bulletin, 23*(4), 389–400.

Higgins, E. T. (1996). The "self-digest": Self-knowledge serving self-regulatory functions. *Journal of Personality and Social Psychology, 71*, 1062–1083.

Higgins, E. T., Rhodewalt, F., & Zanna, M. P. (1979). Dissonance motivation: Its nature, persistence, and reinstatement. *Journal of Experimental Social Psychology, 15*, 16–34.

Holland, R. W., Meertens, R. M., & Van Vugt, M. (2002). Dissonance on the road: Self-esteem as a moderator of internal and external self-justification strategies. *Personality & Social Psychology Bulletin, 28*, 1713–1724.

Holland, R. W., Verplanken, B., & van Knippenberg, A. (2002). On the nature of attitude–behavior relations: The strong guide, the weak follow. *European Journal of Social Psychology, 32*, 869–876.

Hoshino-Browne, E., Zanna, A. S., Spencer, S. J., & Zanna, M. P. (2002). Investigating attitudes cross culturally: A case of cognitive dissonance among East Asians and North Americans. In G. Haddock & G. R. Maio (Eds.), *Contemporary perspectives on the psychology of attitudes* (pp. 375–398). London, UK: Psychology Press.

Hovland, C. I., Janis, I. L., & Kelley, H. H. (1953). *Communication and persuasion: Psychological studies of opinion change.* New Haven, CT: Yale University Press.

Janis, I. L. (1968). Attitude change via role playing. In R. P. Abelson, E. Aronson, W. J. McGuire, T. M. Newcomb, M. J. Rosenberg, & P. H. Tannenbaum (Eds.), *Theories of cognitive consistency: A sourcebook* (pp. 810–818). Chicago: Rand McNally.

Janis, I. L., & Gilmore, J. B. (1965). The influence of incentive conditions on the success of role playing in modifying attitudes. *Journal of Personality and Social Psychology, 1*, 17–27.

Janis, I. L., & King, B. T. (1954). The influence of role playing on opinion change. *Journal of Abnormal and Social Psychology, 49*, 211–218.

Johnson, D. J., & Rusbult, C. E. (1989). Resisting temptation: Devaluation of alternative partners as a means of maintaining commitment in close relationships. *Journal of Personality and Social Psychology, 57*, 967–980.

Jones, E. E. (1998). Major developments in five decades of social psychology. In D. T. Gilbert, S. T. Fiske, & G. Lindzey (Eds.), *The handbook of social psychology* (4th ed., Vol. 1, pp. 3–57). Boston: McGraw-Hill.

Jones, S. C. (1973). Self- and interpersonal evaluations: Esteem theories versus consistency theories. *Psychological Bulletin, 79*(3), 185–199.

Jones, R. A., Linder, D. E., Kiesler, C. A., Zanna, M. P., & Brehm, J. W. (1968). Internal states or external stimuli: Observers' attitude judgments and the dissonance theory—self-persuasion controversy. *Journal of Experimental Social Psychology, 4*, 247–269.

Kellerman, J., Lewis, J., & Laird, J. D. (1989). Looking and loving: The effects of mutual gaze on feelings of romantic love. *Journal of Research in Personality, 23*, 145–161.

Kelley, H. H. (1973). The process of causal attribution. *American Psychologist, 28*, 107–128.

Kelman, H. C. (1953). Attitude change as a function of response restriction. *Human Relations, 6*, 185–214.

Kelman, H. C. (1962). The induction of action and attitude change. In S. Coopersmith (Ed.), *Personality research* (pp. 81–110). Copenhagen, Denmark: Munksgaard.

Kelman, H. C. (1974). Attitudes are alive and well and gainfully employed in the sphere of action. *American Psychologist, 29*, 310–324.

Kelman, H. C., & Baron, R. M. (1974). Moral and hedonic dissonance: A functional analysis of the relationship between discrepant action and attitude change. In S. Himmelfarb & A. H. Eagly (Eds.), *Readings in attitude change* (pp. 558–575). New York: Wiley.

Kiesler, C. A. (1971). *The psychology of commitment*. New York: Academic Press.

Kiesler, C. A., Nisbett, R. E., & Zanna, M. P. (1969). On inferring one's beliefs from one's behavior. *Journal of Personality and Social Psychology, 11*, 321–327.

Kitayama, S., Snibbe, A. C., Markus, H. R., & Suzuki, T. (2004). Is there any "free" choice? Self and dissonance in two cultures. *Psychological Science, 15*, 527–533.

Lecky, P. (1945). *Self-consistency: A theory of personality*. Garden City, NY: Anchor Books.

Lepper, M. R., & Greene, D. (Eds.). (1978). *The hidden cost of reward*. Hillsdale, NJ: Lawrence Erlbaum Associates.

Lepper, M. R., Greene, D., & Nisbett, R. E. (1973). Undermining children's interest with extrinsic rewards: A test of the "overjustification effect." *Journal of Personality and Social Psychology, 28*, 129–137.

Lieberman, M. D., Ochsner, K. N., Gilbert, D. T., & Schacter, D. L. (2001). Do amnesics exhibit cognitive dissonance reduction? The role of explicit memory and attention in attitude change. *Psychological Science, 121*, 135–140.

Linder, D. E., Cooper, J., & Jones, E. E. (1967). Decision freedom as a determinant of the role of incentive magnitude in attitude change. *Journal of Personality and Social Psychology, 6*, 245–254.

Losch, M. E., & Cacioppo, J. T. (1990). Cognitive dissonance may enhance sympathetic tonus, but attitudes are changed to reduce negative affect rather than arousal. *Journal of Experimental Social Psychology, 26*, 289–304.

Lowin, A. (1967). Approach and avoidance as alternative modes of selective exposure to information. *Journal of Personality and Social Psychology, 6*, 1–9.

Maio, G. R., Olson, J. M., Bernard, M. M., & Luke, M. A. (2003). Ideologies, values, attitudes, and behaviour. In J. Delamater (Ed.), *Handbook of social psychology* (pp. 283–308). New York: Kluwer Academic/Plenum.

Maracek, J., & Mettee, D. (1972). Avoidance of continued success as a function of self-steem, level of esteem certainty, and responsibility for success. *Journal of Personality and Social Psychology, 22*, 98–107.

Markus, H. R., & Kitayama, S. (1991). Culture and self: Implications for cognition, emotion, and motivation. *Psychological Review, 98*, 224–253.

McGregor, I., Newby-Clark, I. R., & Zanna, M. P. (1999). "Remembering" dissonance: Simultaneous accessibility of inconsistent cognitive elements moderates epistemic discomfort. In E. Harmon-Jones & J. Mills (Eds.), *Cognitive dissonance: Progress on a pivotal theory in social psychology* (pp. 325–355). Washington, DC: American Psychological Association.

McGuire, W. J. (1985). Attitudes and attitude change. In G. Lindzey & E. Aronson (Eds.), *Handbook of social psychology* (3rd ed., Vol. 2, pp. 233–346). New York: Random House.

Mettee, D. (1971). Rejection of unexpected success as a function of the negative consequences of accepting success. *Journal of Personality and Social Psychology, 17*, 332–341.

Mills, J. (1965a). Avoidance of dissonant information. *Journal of Personality and Social Psychology, 2*, 589–593.

Mills, J. (1965b). Effect of certainty about a decision upon postdecision exposure to consonant and dissonant information. *Journal of Personality and Social Psychology, 2*, 749–752.

Mills, J. (1967). Comment on Bem's "Self-perception: An alternative interpretation of cognitive dissonance phenomena." *Psychological Review, 74*, 535.

Newcomb, T. M. (1953). An approach to the study of communicative acts. *Psychological Review, 60*, 393–404.

Norton, M. I., Monin, B., Cooper, J., & Hogg, M. A. (2003). Vicarious dissonance: Attitude change from the inconsistency of others. *Journal of Personality and Social Psychology, 85*, 47–62.

Olson, J. M. (1992). Self-perception of humor: Evidence for discounting and augmentation effects. *Journal of Personality and Social Psychology, 62*, 369–377.

Olson, J. M., & Zanna, M. P. (1979). A new look at selective exposure. *Journal of Experimental Social Psychology, 15*, 1–15.

Olson, J. M., & Zanna, M. P. (1982). Repression-sensitization differences in responses to a decision. *Journal of Personality, 50*, 46–57.

Osgood, E. E., & Tannenbaum, P. H. (1955). The principle of congruity in the prediction of attitude change. *Psychological Review, 62*, 42–55.

Pallak, M. S., & Pittman, T. S. (1972). General motivational effects of dissonance arousal. *Journal of Personality and Social Psychology, 21*, 349–358.

Petty, R. E., & Cacioppo, J. T. (1986). The elaboration likelihood model of persuasion. In L. Berkowitz (Ed.), *Advances in experimental social psychology* (Vol. 19, pp. 123–205). San Diego, CA: Academic Press.

Pyszczynski, T., Greenberg, J., Solomon, S., Sideris, J., & Stubing, M. J. (1993). Emotional expression and the reduction of motivated cognitive bias: Evidence from cognitive dissonance and distancing from victims' paradigms. *Journal of Personality and Social Psychology, 64*, 177–186.

Read, S. J., & Miller, L. C. (1994). Dissonance and balance in belief systems: The promise of parallel constraint satisfaction processes and connectionist modeling approaches. In R. C. Schank & E. Langer (Eds.), *Beliefs, reasoning, and decision making: Psycho-logic in honor of Bob Abelson* (pp. 209–235). Hillsdale, NJ: Lawrence Erlbaum Associates.

Rhodewalt, F., & Agustsdottir, S. (1986). Effects of self-presentation on the phenomenal self. *Journal of Personality and Social Psychology, 50*(1), 47–55.

Rhodewalt, F., & Comer, R. (1979). Induced-compliance attitude change: Once more with feeling. *Journal of Experimental Social Psychology, 15*, 35–47.

Rind, B., & Kipnis, D. (1999). Changes in self-perception as a result of successfully persuading others. *Journal of Social Issues, 55*(1), 141–156.

Rittle, R. H. (1981). Changes in helping behavior: Self versus situational perceptions as mediators of the foot-in-the-door effect. *Personality and Social Psychology Bulletin, 7*, 431–437.

Rokeach, M. (1973). *The nature of human values.* New York: Free Press.

Rosenberg, M. J. (1965). When dissonance fails: On eliminating evaluation apprehension from attitude measurement. *Journal of Personality and Social Psychology, 1*, 28–42.

Ross, M., & Shulman, R. F. (1973). Increasing the salience of initial attitudes: Dissonance versus self-perception theory. *Journal of Personality and Social Psychology, 28*, 138–144.

Sakai, H. (1981). Induced compliance and opinion change. *Japanese Psychological Research, 22*, 32–41.

Sakai, H. (1999). A multiplicative power-function model of cognitive dissonance: Toward an integrated theory of cognition, emotion, and behavior after Leon Festinger. In E. Harmon-Jones & J. Mills (Eds.), *Cognitive dissonance: Progress on a pivotal theory in social psychology* (pp. 267–294). Washington, DC: American Psychological Association.

Sakai, H., & Andow, K. (1980). Attribution of personal responsibility and dissonance reduction. *Japanese Psychological Research, 22*, 32–41.

Schachter, S., & Singer, J. E. (1962). Cognitive, social and physiological determinants of emotional state. *Psychological Review, 69*, 379–399.

Scheier, M. F., & Carver, C. S. (1980). Private and public self-attention, resistance to change, and dissonance reduction. *Journal of Personality and Social Psychology, 39*, 390–405.

Scher, S. J., & Cooper, J. (1989). Motivational basis of dissonance: The singular role of behavioral consequences. *Journal of Personality and Social Psychology, 56*, 899–906.

Schlenker, B. R. (1980). *Impression management: The self-concept, social identity, and interpersonal relations.* Monterey, CA: Brooks/Cole.

Schlenker, B. R., & Trudeau, J. V. (1990). Impact of self-presentations on private self-beliefs: Effects of prior self-beliefs and misattribution. *Journal of Personality and Social Psychology, 58*, 22–32.

Schwartz, S. H. (1992). Universals in the content and structure of values: Theoretical advances and empirical tests in 20 countries. In M. P. Zanna (Ed.), *Advances in experimental social psychology* (Vol. 25, pp. 1–65). San Diego, CA: Academic Press.

Seligman, C., Bush, M., & Kirsch, K. (1976). Relationship between compliance in the foot-in-the-door paradigm and size of first request. *Journal of Personality and Social Psychology, 33*, 517–520.

Seligman, C., Fazio, R. H., & Zanna, M. P. (1980). Effects of salience of extrinsic rewards on liking and loving. *Journal of Personality and Social Psychology, 38*, 453–460.

Sherman, D. K., & Cohen, G. L. (2002). Accepting threatening information: Self-affirmation and the reduction of defensive biases. *Current Directions in Psychological Science, 11*, 119–123.

Shrauger, J. S. (1975). Responses to evaluation as a function of initial self-perceptions. *Psychological Bulletin, 82*(4), 581–596.

Shultz, T. R., & Lepper, M. R. (1996). Cognitive dissonance reduction as constraint satisfaction. *Psychological Review, 103*, 219–240.

Shultz, T. R., & Lepper, M. R. (1999). Computer simulation of cognitive dissonance reduction. In E. Harmon-Jones & J. Mills (Eds.), *Cognitive dissonance: Progress on a pivotal theory in social psychology* (pp. 235–265). Washington, DC: American Psychological Association.

Simon, L., Greenberg, J., & Brehm, J. (1995). Trivialization: The forgotten mode of dissonance reduction. *Journal of Personality and Social Psychology, 68*(2), 247–260.

Skinner, B. F. (1953). *Science and human behavior.* New York: Macmillan.

Snyder, M. L., & Wicklund, R. A. (1976). Prior exercise of freedom and reactance. *Journal of Experimental Social Psychology, 12*, 120–130.

Snyder, M., & Cunningham, M. R. (1975). To comply or not to comply: Testing the self-perception explanation of the "foot-in-the-door" phenomenon. *Journal of Personality and Social Psychology, 31*, 64–67.

Snyder, M., & Ebbesen, E. B. (1972). Dissonance awareness: A test of dissonance theory versus self-perception theory. *Journal of Experimental Social Psychology, 8*, 502–517.

Snyder, M., & Tanke, E. D. (1976). Behavior and attitude: Some people are more consistent than others. *Journal of Personality, 44*, 510–517.

Son Hing, L. S., Li, W., & Zanna, M. P. (2002). Inducing hypocrisy to reduce prejudicial responses among aversive racists. *Journal of Experimental Social Psychology, 38*(1), 71–78.

Stalder, D. R., & Baron, R. S. (1998). Attributional complexity as a moderator of dissonance-produced attitude change. *Journal of Personality and Social Psychology, 75*, 449–455.

Steele, C. M. (1988). The psychology of self-affirmation: Sustaining the integrity of the self. In L. Berkowitz (Ed.), *Advances in experimental social psychology* (Vol. 21, pp. 261–302). San Diego, CA: Academic Press.

Steele, C. M., & Lui, T. J. (1983). Dissonance processes as self-affirmation. *Journal of Personality and Social Psychology, 45*, 5–19.

Steele, C. M., Southwick, L. L., & Critchlow, B. (1981). Dissonance and alcohol: Drinking your troubles away. *Journal of Personality and Social Psychology, 41*, 831–846.

Steele, C. M., Spencer, S. J., & Lynch, M. (1993). Dissonance and affirmational resources: Resilence against self-image threats. *Journal of Personality and Social Psychology, 64*(6), 885–896.

Stice, E. (1992). The similarities between cognitive dissonance and guilt: Confession as a relief of dissonance. *Current Psychology: Research & Reviews, 11*, 69–77.

Stone, J. (1999). What exactly have I done? The role of self-attribute accessibility in dissonance. In E. Harmon-Jones & J. Mills (Eds.), *Cognitive dissonance: Progress on a pivotal theory in social psychology* (pp. 175–200). Washington, DC: American Psychological Association.

Stone, J. (2001). Behavioral discrepancies and construal processes in cognitive dissonance. In G. Moskowitz (Ed.), *Cognitive social psychology: The Princeton symposium on the legacy and future of social cognition* (pp. 41–58). Hillsdale, NJ.: Lawrence Erlbaum Associates.

Stone, J. (2003). Self-consistency for low self-esteem in dissonance processes: The role of self-standards. *Personality and Social Psychology Bulletin, 29*, 846–858.

Stone, J., Aronson, E., Crain, A. L., Winslow, M. P., & Fried, C. B. (1994). Inducing hypocrisy as a means of encouraging young adults to use condoms. *Personality and Social Psychology Bulletin, 20*(1), 116–128.

Stone, J., & Cooper, J. (2001). A self-standards model of cognitive dissonance. *Journal of Experimental Social Psychology, 37*, 228–243.

Stone, J., & Cooper, J. (2003). The effect of self-attribute relevance on how self-esteem moderates dissonance processes. *Journal of Experimental Social Psychology, 39*, 508–515.

Stone, J., Wiegand, A. W., Cooper, J., & Aronson, E. (1997). When exemplification fails: Hypocrisy and the motive for self-integrity. *Journal of Personality and Social Psychology, 72*(1), 54–65.

Stults, D. M., Messé, L. A., & Kerr, N. L. (1984). Belief discrepant behavior and the bogus pipeline: Impression management or arousal attribution. *Journal of Experimental Social Psychology, 20*, 47–54.

Tang, S., & Hall, V. C. (1995). The overjustification effect: A meta-analysis. *Applied Cognitive Psychology, 9*, 365–404.

Taylor, S. E. (1975). On inferring one's attitudes from one's behavior: Some delimiting conditions. *Journal of Personality and Social Psychology, 31*, 126–131.

Tedeschi, J. T., Schlenker, B. R., & Bonoma, T. V. (1971). Cognitive dissonance: Private ratiocination or public spectacle? *American Psychologist, 26*, 685–695.

Tesser, A. (2000). On the confluence of self-esteem maintenance mechanisms. *Personality and Social Psychology Review, 4*, 290–299.

Tesser, A., & Cornell, D. P. (1991). On the confluence of self processes. *Journal of Experimental Social Psychology, 27*, 501–526.

Thibodeau, R., & Aronson, E. (1992). Taking a closer look: Reasserting the role of the self-concept in dissonance theory. *Personality and Social Psychology Bulletin, 18*(5), 591–602.

Vallacher, R. R., & Wegner, D. M. (1985). *A theory of action identification.* Hillsdale, NJ: Lawrence Erlbaum Associates.

Vallerand, R. J. (1997). Toward a hierarchical model of intrinsic and extrinsic motivation. In M. P. Zanna (Ed.), *Advances in experimental social psychology* (Vol. 29, pp. 271–360). San Diego, CA: Academic Press.

Van Overwalle, F., & Jordens, K. (2002). An adaptive connectionist model of cognitive dissonance. *Personality and Social Psychology Review. 6*, 204–231.

Vrugt, A. (1992). Preferential treatment of women and psychological reactance theory: An experiment. *European Journal of Social Psychology, 22*, 303–307.

Walster, E. (1964). The temporal sequence of post-decision dissonance. In L. Festinger (Ed.), *Conflict, decision, and dissonance.* (pp. 112–128). Palo Alto, CA: Stanford University Press.

Ward, W. D., & Sandvold, K. D. (1963). Performance expectancy as a determinant of actual performance: A partial replication. *Journal of Abnormal and Social Psychology, 67*, 293–295.

Waterman, C. K. (1969). The facilitating and interfering effects of cognitive dissonance on simple and complex paired associates learning tasks. *Journal of Experimental Social Psychology, 5*, 31–42.

Watts, W. (1967). Relative persistence of opinion change induced by active compared to passive participation. *Journal of Personality and Social Psychology, 5*, 4–15.

Wicklund, R. A., & Brehm, J. W. (1976). *Perspectives on cognitive dissonance.* Hillsdale, NJ: Lawrence Erlbaum Associates.

Zanna, M. P., & Aziza, C. (1976). On the interaction of repression-sensitization and attention in resolving cognitive dissonance. *Journal of Personality, 44*, 577–593.

Zanna, M. P., & Cooper, J. (1974). Dissonance and the pill: An attribution approach to studying the arousal properties of dissonance. *Journal of Personality and Social Psychology, 29*, 703–709.

Zanna, M. P., Fazio, R. H., & Ross, M. (1994). The persistence of persuasion. In R. C. Schank & E. Langer (Eds.), *Beliefs, reasoning, and decision-making: Psycho-logic in honor of Bob Abelson* (pp. 347–362). Mahwah, NJ: Lawrence Erlbaum Associates.

Zanna, M. P., Higgins, E. T., & Taves, P. A. (1976). Is dissonance phenomenologically aversive? *Journal of Experimental Social Psychology, 12*, 530–538.

Zanna, M. P., Olson, J. M., & Fazio, R. H. (1981). Self-perception and attitude–behavior consistency. *Personality and Social Psychology Bulletin, 7*, 252–256.

Zanna, M. P., & Sande, G. N. (1987). The effect of collective actions on the attitudes of individual group members: A dissonance analysis. In M. P. Zanna, J. M. Olson, & C. P. Herman (Eds.), *Social influence: The Ontario symposium* (Vol. 5, pp. 151–163). Hillsdale, NJ: Lawrence Erlbaum Associates.

7

Belief Formation, Organization, and Change: Cognitive and Motivational Influences

Robert S. Wyer, Jr.
Hong Kong University of Science and Technology

Dolores Albarracín
University of Florida

This chapter is concerned with the representation of beliefs in memory and the factors that influence their formation and change. After discussing the nature of beliefs and their relation to other cognitions (e.g., attitudes, opinions, and other types of judgments), we review alternative conceptualizations of the way in which belief-relevant knowledge is organized in memory and the processes that underlie its retrieval and use. Then, we discuss factors that influence the computation of beliefs on the basis of criteria other than the knowledge to which they directly pertain. Finally, we consider motivational factors that affect responses to belief-relevant information and the change in beliefs that can result from these responses.

BASIC CONCEPTS

Beliefs are typically conceptualized as estimates of the likelihood that the knowledge one has acquired about a referent is correct or, alternatively, that an event or state of affairs has or will occur (Eagly & Chaiken, 1998; Fishbein & Ajzen, 1975). In much social psychological research (for a review, see Wood, 2000), the referent of a belief is a proposition (e.g., the assertion that the United States will become involved in a nuclear war within the next 10 years, or that one's secretary is having an affair with the department head). Beliefs can refer to subjective experiences as well. We are often uncertain about whether we actually saw or heard something, or whether the food we are eating at a local restaurant tastes as good as it did the last time. These uncertainties, like uncertainties about the validity of verbal information, also constitute beliefs.

Beliefs obviously vary in strength. We are completely confident that some things are true (e.g., that Abraham Lincoln was president of the United States) and confident that other things are not true (e.g., that Abraham Lincoln was tsar of Russia), but are relatively uncertain about still other things (e.g., that Abraham Lincoln had brown eyes). These beliefs can often be expressed in units of subjective probability ranging from 0 to 1. They can also be expressed in units of confidence or certainty. To this extent, beliefs could potentially pertain to virtually all

273

concepts and knowledge we have accumulated, including the definitions of semantic concepts, mathematical relations (e.g., $2 + 2 = 4$) and truisms (e.g., honesty is the best policy).

Beliefs can refer to a specific event or situation or a general one. Moreover, they can be about the present, the past, or the future. Beliefs about the future are often equated with *expectations* (Olson, Roese, & Zanna, 1996). The processes that underlie these different types of beliefs could differ. However, such differences are matters of theoretical and empirical inquiry and are not inherent in the conceptualization of beliefs per se.

Fishbein and Ajzen (1975) distinguished between *beliefs in* something and *beliefs about* it. Thus, I might believe in God, or in the principle of free speech. I might also believe that God is not all-powerful, and that free speech is guaranteed by the U.S. Constitution. However, a belief in God is equivalent to the belief in the proposition that God exists, and a belief in the principle of free speech is equivalent to the belief that free speech is desirable. In each case, therefore, the belief can be conceptualized as an estimate of subjective probability, or alternatively, of the certainty that a proposition is true.

Beliefs and Knowledge

As the preceding discussion indicates, beliefs pertain to knowledge. That is, they concern the likelihood that one's knowledge about a referent is correct or, alternatively, that this knowledge has implications for a past or future state of affairs. Beliefs can also concern the likelihood that new information one receives about a referent is true. But to say that beliefs *refer to* knowledge is not necessarily to say that beliefs are *part of* knowledge and are stored in memory as such. Rather, beliefs could simply be viewed as subjective probability estimates that are computed online at the time they become necessary to attain a goal to which they are relevant (e.g., to communicate information to others, or to make a behavioral decision). Once a belief is reported, this judgment might often be stored in memory and consequently might be recalled and used as a basis for judgments that are made at a later point in time. (For evidence of the effects of previously reported judgments on subsequent ones, see Carlston, 1980; Higgins & Lurie, 1983; Lingle & Ostrom, 1979; Sherman, Ahlm, Berman, & Lynn, 1978.) Of course, they may not be the *only* criterion that is brought to bear on these latter beliefs. Other concepts and knowledge one has accumulated could be retrieved and used in addition to, or instead of, these prior judgments. Schwarz and Bohner (2001; see also Wyer, 2004; Wyer & Srull, 1989) have argued that all judgments are computed online, and that the consistency of judgments over time simply reflects the fact that similar bodies of knowledge are involved in their computation. This possibility has obvious implications for the processes that underlie belief formation and change. For example, differences in the beliefs reported at different points in time may not indicate a conscious change in these beliefs, but rather, may only reflect the fact that different subsets of previously acquired knowledge have been used to compute them.

Be that as it may, a conceptualization of belief formation and change requires an understanding of how knowledge about the referents of beliefs is organized in memory, and of which aspects of this knowledge are actually considered in computing these beliefs. We begin by reviewing briefly the types of social knowledge that people acquire. We then discuss the distinction between the beliefs that are based on this knowledge and other knowledge-related constructs (e.g., attitudes, opinions, and judgments).

Referents of Knowledge

Knowledge can be about oneself, other persons, places, objects or events. It can also concern the relations among these entities. Thus, we know our name and where we live, that we like to go to movies, and that we ate dinner at Jaspa's Restaurant yesterday evening. Similarly, we know that Jimmy Carter won the Nobel Peace Prize, that Marilyn Monroe was blonde, that Chicago is west of New York, that the World Trade Center collapsed on September 11, 2001, and that drinking too much wine can make you sick. Knowledge can also describe procedures for performing a function or attaining a goal. Thus, for example, we know how to get a meal at a restaurant and how to drive a car.

Knowledge can often be statistical. For example, we might know that less than 50% of Americans voted for George W. Bush in the 2000 election, that there is a 90% chance of rain tomorrow, and that 51% of first marriages end in divorce. Beliefs, defined as subjective probabilities, can be directly influenced by this type of information. Nevertheless, beliefs do not always correspond to objective probabilities. For one thing, objective probabilities can be subjectively ambiguous and, therefore, the beliefs on which they are based can vary with the context in which they are evaluated. Windschitl, Martin, and Flugstad (2002) presented participants with information about two diseases. The diseases were described as equally prevalent among women but as differing in prevalence among men. Participants estimated the chances of a female target's having each disease to be lower than the objective probability they were given when the disease was highly prevalent among men, but to be higher than the objective probability when the disease was less common among men.

Sources of Knowledge

Knowledge is often acquired through direct experience with its referents. It can also be internally generated. That is, it can result from performing cognitive operations on information one has already acquired. Thus, for example, we might infer that a person is sadistic from evidence that he set fire to a cat's tail, and we might conclude that smoking is bad for the health from statistical evidence of its association with lung cancer and heart disease. Or, we could form a mental image from the description of a character in a novel, and we might experience a positive or negative affective reaction to a U.S. President's plan to permit logging in national forests. Cognitions about these subjective reactions could be stored as knowledge about their referents and could later be retrieved for use in making a judgment or decision.

The information that serves as a basis for beliefs is often conveyed verbally, in the form of propositions. It can also be transmitted in other sense modalities (auditory, visual, olfactory, etc.). However, there is clearly not an isomorphic relation between the modality of stimulus information and the modality of its representation in memory. Verbal information can often elicit visual images in the course of comprehending it (Black, Turner, & Bower, 1979; Garnham, 1981; Glenberg, Meyer, & Lindem, 1987; Reyes, Thompson, & Bower, 1980; Wyer & Radvansky, 1999). Moreover, nonverbal information is sometimes recoded verbally in the course of communicating about it to others. Note that when linguistically coded information is represented in memory as a mental image, features that were not specified in the information are likely to be added to the image in the course of constructing it. Correspondingly, many details of visually or acoustically coded information are likely to be lost when it is recoded verbally.

Specificity of Knowledge

Some of the knowledge we acquire refers to specific events that occurred at a particular time and place. This knowledge can often have the form of stories about a sequence of events that we learn about and later describe to others. Other knowledge can refer to more general types of persons and situations. Thus, for example, I may have a detailed memory of last night's dinner at Timpone's, when a waiter tripped over a chair and spilled wine on my new suit. At the same time, I also know the general sequence of events that occurs in restaurants (being shown to a table, ordering the meal, eating, paying, etc.). Many generalized sequences of events can constitute implicit theories about the causal relatedness of these events that can be used to comprehend and explain specific experiences and to predict their consequences. The construction and use of these theories and their role in belief formation are discussed in some detail in later sections of this chapter.

Distinguishing Beliefs From Other Constructs

The conceptualization of a belief as an estimate of subjective probability seems straightforward. However, its relation to other theoretical constructs is not as clear as one might like. Several ambiguities concerning these distinctions are worth noting.

Beliefs Versus Perceptions, Inferences, and Judgments

Three constructs—perceptions, inferences, and judgments—are often used interchangeably in social psychological research. It is useful to define them more precisely, however, as they are related to beliefs in different ways.

Although *perception* has a more technical meaning in research on psychophysics, we use the term in this chapter to refer to the interpretation of stimulus information in terms of concepts the information exemplifies. An *inference* refers to the construal of the implications of information or knowledge for an unspecified characteristic, based on cognitive rules of the sort we describe in later sections of this chapter. A *judgment* is the overt or implicit expression of an inference and can be either a verbal utterance ("ridiculous," "exciting," "nice") or a rating along a scale. Thus, for example, if we hear a man chew out his secretary for being late, we might perceive this behavior to be hostile. Based on this perception, we might infer that the man is generally mean and insensitive. This inference, in turn, could later provide the basis for describing the person to someone else or for rating his eligibility for a position as personnel director. Beliefs, as we have conceptualized them, are estimates that an inference is correct. As such, they may be influenced by perceptions and have consequences for judgments.

Beliefs Versus Attitudes and Opinions

Measurement Ambiguities.   Beliefs, attitudes, and opinions are obviously central constructs in social psychological theory and research. Nevertheless, there is a surprising lack of consensus about their meaning and the manner in which they are expressed. Agreement with a descriptive statement (e.g., "Cigarette smoking will be declared illegal"), for example, is often interpreted as a belief, whereas agreement with a prescriptive statement (e.g., "Cigarette smoking should be declared illegal") is assumed to reflect an opinion. To the extent that agreement with a statement is based on one's estimate of the likelihood that the statement is true, however, this distinction is illusory. The only difference might lie in the fact that the validity of a descriptive (belief) statement can often be verified empirically, whereas the validity of a prescriptive (opinion) statement cannot.

The fuzziness of the distinction between belief and opinion statements is further illustrated by comparing the belief statement, "Cigarette smoking is unhealthy," and the opinion statement, "Cigarette smoking is detestable." The statements are structurally similar, and both concern an association of a concept—cigarette smoking—with an undesirable attribute. Similarly, the assertion, "most Americans detest cigarette smoking," is often assumed to reflect a belief, whereas the assertion, "I detest cigarette smoking" is assumed to express an attitude. However, agreement with each of these propositions might be based on the subjective probability that the proposition is true. To this extent, responses to all of these statements would reflect beliefs. Whether individuals who make these various statements see differences in their implications or, alternatively, use the statements interchangeably, is of course an empirical question.

Theoretical Considerations.   Theoretical formulations of the relations among beliefs, attitudes, and opinions do not help much to clarify matters. For instance, tripartite conceptions of attitudes (Katz & Stotland, 1959; Krech & Crutchfield, 1948; for reviews, see Breckler, 1984a, 1984b) have assumed that attitudes have an affective component (feelings toward the attitude object), a cognitive component (beliefs and opinions), and a conative (behavioral) component. In this view, beliefs and opinions are both components of an attitude by definition.

A definition of attitude in terms of beliefs and opinions is also implied by Thurstone's (1959; see also Edwards, 1957) attitude scaling procedures. That is, people's attitudes toward a referent is based on their agreement with a set of statements that have been scaled on the basis of independent judges' beliefs about the favorableness of the statements' implications for the referent. A different conceptualization with similar implications was proposed by Wyer (1973). He found evidence that people's evaluation of an object along a category scale of liking (which is conceptually similar to scales along which attitudes are often measured) was the subjective expected value of a distribution of beliefs that the object belonged to each of the categories that compose the scale. Furthermore, people's subjective uncertainty about their evaluation of the object was predictable from the dispersion of their beliefs that it belonged to these categories. To the extent that an attitude is simply an expression of liking, this conceptualization also suggests that there is little conceptual difference between beliefs and attitudes. Moreover, it recognizes that people can be uncertain of their attitudes as well as the validity of statements that bear on them (beliefs).

Fishbein (1963; Fishbein & Ajzen, 1975) made a much clearer distinction between attitudes and beliefs. Borrowing largely from a subjective expected utility conceptualization (Peak, 1955; but see Fishbein, 1967, for a conceptualization in terms of social learning theory), he assumed that an attitude toward an object, A_O, can be predicted from the equation

$$A_O = \Sigma b_i e_i, \qquad\qquad [1]$$

where e_i is the evaluation of the ith attribute of the object and b_i is the belief that the object possesses the attribute. (Alternatively, if the attitude object is a behavior, e_i and b_i represent the evaluation of the ith consequence of the behavior and the belief that the consequence will occur, respectively.) According to this conception, beliefs about an object are theoretically determinants of an attitude toward the object but are not themselves an attitude.

Other conceptualizations also make distinctions. For example, Albarracín and Wyer (2001; see also Wyer, Clore, & Isbell, 1999) conceptualized attitudes toward an object as expressions of the affective reactions that people experience and attribute to their feelings about this object. According to them, attitudes can potentially be influenced by both (a) reactions that have actually become conditioned to the object through learning and are elicited by thoughts about it (e.g., b_i and e_i; see Equation 1), and (b) the affect that one happens to be experiencing for reasons that have nothing to do with the object being evaluated (e.g., moods) but is misattributed to one's feelings about the object (Schwarz & Clore, 1983, 1996). Along similar lines, Zanna and Rempel (1988) distinguished between evaluations that are based on feelings and evaluations that are based on other, nonaffective criteria (for empirical evidence of this difference, see Adaval, 2001; Pham, 1998; Yeung & Wyer, in press). To this extent, evaluations of an object along a scale of favorableness could sometimes be based on affect, sometimes on beliefs, and sometimes on both.

The controversy surrounding the relation between beliefs and attitudes cannot be fully resolved. To the extent that beliefs and attitudes are conceptually distinct, however, the relation between them is a matter of theoretical and empirical interest and does not exist by definition. In this chapter, we retain our conceptualization of beliefs as estimates of subjective probability which, in the case of propositions, are reflected in either (a) estimates of the likelihood that a proposition is true, (b) expressions of confidence or certainty that the proposition is valid, or, in some cases, (c) agreement with the proposition. In contrast, we reserve the term *attitude* for responses to an object along a continuum of favorableness. Many of the factors that underlie belief formation and change could govern attitude processes as well. In this chapter, however, we will generally restrict our review of the literature to research and theory in which beliefs, as we conceptualize them, have been the primary focus of attention.

THEORIES OF KNOWLEDGE BELIEF ORGANIZATION

As noted earlier, a question arises as to whether beliefs (i.e., estimates of certainty or subjective probability) are part of knowledge and are represented as such in memory, or alternatively, they are the result of cognitive operations that are performed on this knowledge at the time the beliefs are reported. Suppose a woman is asked her belief in the proposition that comprehensive examinations increase the quality of undergraduate education. On one hand, she could retrieve and use a previously formed estimate of the likelihood that the proposition is true. On the other hand, she might never have thought about the issue before. In this case, she might compute her estimate on the spot, based on previously acquired knowledge that appears to be relevant. Moreover, these possibilities are not mutually exclusive. Even when a previously formed belief (or the report of this belief) exists in memory, it might be only one of several pieces of knowledge that might be drawn on in computing one's belief at a later point in time.

These alternative possibilities have seldom been articulated. Some conceptualizations (e.g., McGuire, 1960, 1981; Wyer & Goldberg, 1970) implicitly assume that beliefs are themselves elements of a stable memory system that is organized according to certain a priori rules (see also Slovic & Lichtenstein, 1971). Theories of belief change, such as Fishbein and Ajzen's (1975), operate under similar assumptions. Other conceptions, however (see Bem, 1972; Hasher, Goldstein, & Toppin, 1977), suggest that beliefs are situation-specific expressions of certainty that people do not estimate until they are called on to do so, and that they compute on the basis of whatever criteria happen to come to mind at the time.

To the extent that beliefs are computed online on the basis of criteria that are accessible in memory at the time, a conceptualization of these computational processes requires an understanding of both (a) the manner in which belief-relevant knowledge is organized in memory (and consequently is likely to be activated and applied) and (b) the cognitive processes that underlie the use of this knowledge to make an estimate. The next sections of this chapter concern these matters. We first describe how knowledge might be organized in memory and then review how people compute beliefs on the basis of this knowledge.

General Theories of Knowledge Organization

Numerous theories of memory organization have been proposed, details of which are beyond the scope of this chapter (for a summary, see Carlston & Smith, 1996; Smith, 1994). Four general conceptualizations that provide the bases for more specific theories of belief organization are worth describing briefly. The theories differ in terms of the assumptions they make about the degree of interrelatedness of different units of knowledge and the processes that surround their retrieval.

Independent-Trace Theories

Hintzman (1986) assumed that information in memory is not organized at all. That is, each experience is stored in memory as a separate trace, independently of others. When information about a referent is required, a set of features, or *retrieval cues*, are compiled that specify the nature of the information being sought, and all existing representations that contain these features are activated. The features that are most frequently contained in the activated set of representations are weighted most heavily and, consequently, have the predominant influence on any judgment or decision that is made. Thus, for example, suppose someone is asked about war. The use of "war" as a retrieval cue might activate all of the knowledge that includes war as an element. The features common to this knowledge may be abstract and few in number, leading to a general description of war that is very nonspecific. "Vietnamese war" might activate only those representations that pertain to this more specific event, leading to a more detailed description whose implications could differ from those of war in general. As this example suggests, the more specific the retrieval cues, the fewer preexisting memory traces are likely to be identified and, therefore, the more detailed the memory.

Another implication of this conceptualization is that the more frequently a particular type of experience is encountered, the more representations containing the features of this experience are likely to be stored in memory and, therefore, the more likely it is that these features will have an influence on judgments and decisions. Moreover, each time information is retrieved, the features that are extracted from it form a new representation that is stored in memory along with the other representations on which it is based (Hintzman, 1986). Thus, abstract memory representations can come to function independently of the specific representations that were used to construct them.

Associative Network Theories

A second conceptualization has its roots in Collins and Loftus' (1975) spreading activation model of memory (see also Anderson & Bower, 1973; for a direct application to social memory, see Wyer & Carlston, 1979). This conceptualization assumes that concepts and knowledge units are represented in memory by *nodes* and that associations between them are denoted by *pathways*. Associations are presumably formed by thinking about one concept or knowledge unit in relation to another. The more often the two elements are thought about in combination, the stronger the association becomes.

The model assumes that when a particular unit of knowledge is thought about (i.e., activated), excitation spreads to other units along the pathways connecting them. When excitation that accumulates at a node reaches a minimum activation threshold, the knowledge stored at this node is activated, leading it to come to mind as well. Once a unit of knowledge is deactivated (no longer thought about), however, the excitation at the node does not dissipate immediately but decays gradually over time. Consequently, the unit is more likely to be reactivated by additional excitation that is transmitted from other sources. In effect, this assumption implies a recency effect of activating a concept or unit of knowledge on its later recall and use.

An associative network model contrasts with an independent-trace conceptualization in the emphasis it places on the associations that are formed between different units of knowledge as a result of the cognitive activities that surround their use. Moreover, it assumes that once two units of knowledge become associated as a result of thinking about them in relation to one another, the subsequent activation of one will stimulate the activation of the other as well. Many specific conceptualizations of belief organization and change are implicitly based on this assumption.

Schema Theories

Associative network theories of knowledge organization assume that different pieces of knowledge are discrete and are stored at different memory locations. A somewhat different conceptualization (Brewer & Nakamura, 1984; Rumelhart, 1984) assumes that many knowledge structures are organized in memory schematically, or configurally, as a set of interrelated features. In social psychology, the term *schema* has often been used to refer to any cluster of features that have become associated with a referent and stored in memory as a unit (Fiske & Taylor, 1991). However, it is useful to distinguish between *categorical* representations, which consist of a list of features without any inherent organization, and *schematic* representations whose features are interrelated according to a set of rules that can be specified a priori (see Bobrow & Norman, 1975; Brewer & Lichtenstein, 1981; Mandler, 1979; Wyer & Carlston, 1994). These relations can be spatial, temporal, or logical. A spatially organized schema is exemplified by a human face whose eyes, nose, and mouth are in specified positions in relation to one another. A temporally organized schema might be composed of the events that occur in a restaurant. The features of many event representations can be organized both spatially and temporally. For example, a mental representation of "The boy threw the ball to the girl" could consist of a mental image of the boy and the ball positioned in relation to one another, but might also depict the ball in the air, the girl waiting to catch it, and her actually doing so.

In contrast, a categorical representation might simply consist of a central concept denoting its referent along with a number of unrelated features that have no particular order. A lawyer, for example, might be represented as someone who prepares briefs, questions witnesses, and is both mercenary and articulate. However, the description would be equally meaningful if the attributes were conveyed in a different order (e.g., "is articulate, questions witnesses, is mercenary, and prepares briefs"). In contrast, order is critical is a schematic representation. For example, a description of a restaurant visit in which the person ate a meal, looked at the menu, paid the bill and was shown to a table would appear to make little sense.

The most important distinction between schematic and categorical representations arises when they are brought to bear on the comprehension of new information. That is, all of the features that are necessary to construct a schematic representation are not always specified. To this extent, they must be implicitly added in order to make the representation meaningful. Thus, the description of someone as having a big nose and a beard does not specify the nature of the eyes and hair color. Similarly, the statement "John went to a Chinese restaurant, ordered fried rice and paid $14" does not indicate that John actually ate the meal. These features may nevertheless be added spontaneously in the course of comprehending the information. These additions can often occur spontaneously (Graesser, Singer, & Trabasso, 1994). When this occurs, there may often be little distinction between the added features and those that were actually specified in the information presented.

This latter possibility is important. We noted earlier that when people have formed a representation on the basis of new information, they later use the representation as a basis for judgments and decisions without consulting the information on which it was based. To this extent, the added features, although not specified, may be recalled as actually having been mentioned. (For empirical evidence of these intrusions in a variety of domains, see Bransford, Barclay, & Franks, 1972; Graesser, Gordon, & Sawyer, 1979; Loken & Wyer, 1983; Spiro, 1977. Formal accounts of such intrusions are implied by connectionist and distributed processing models; see Smith, 1996). The implications of these intrusions for an understanding of belief formation and change are elaborated presently.

"Storage Bin" Models

A fourth conceptualization combines features of other approaches. This conceptualization assumes that information about a particular referent is stored in memory at a particular location, thereby constituting a *memory organization packet* (Schank, 1972) or, in terms of Wyer and Srull's (1986, 1989) conceptualization, a *referent bin*. The knowledge representations that are stored in a particular location can depend on the type of information being represented. Thus, they can include propositions, schemas, visual images, clusters of traits and behaviors, and sequences of temporally related events. Once each representation is formed, it is stored as a separate unit of knowledge and can later be retrieved independently of others for a purpose to which it is relevant.

Wyer and Srull (1989) assume that knowledge is stored in a bin in the order it is acquired, with the most recently formed representation on top. Moreover, when information about a referent is needed, a bin pertaining to the referent is identified and a probabilistic top-down search is performed for knowledge of the type required. If a knowledge representation is identified, a copy of it is formed and, once it has been used, is returned to the top of the bin. This means that knowledge representations that have been formed and used most recently (i.e., ones near the top of a bin) and frequently (that are represented in multiple copies) are most likely to be used again. In evaluating this possibility, note that the assumption that recently formed knowledge representations are most likely to be retrieved and used does not negate the influence of information acquired earlier. The first information one receives about a person or object may often influence the interpretation of later information and may provide a central concept around which later information is organized. In such instances, the first information obtained about a referent may have a disproportionate impact on judgments. (For a more detailed discussion of primacy vs. recency effects within the framework of this model, see Wyer & Srull, 1989.)

Summary

The four conceptualizations outlined are metaphorical and should be evaluated in terms of their utility in conceptualizing and predicting empirical findings rather than in their validity as a description of the physiology of the brain. The assumptions underlying the conceptualizations are implicit in many more specific formulations of belief formation and change to be discussed in this chapter. Moreover, the conceptualizations provide a basis for postulating four factors that are often assumed to underlie the retrieval and use of belief-relevant knowledge. The implications of these theories can be summarized in four postulates:

P1: (Recency). The likelihood of retrieving and using a piece of belief-relevant knowledge is a positive function of the recency with which the knowledge has been acquired or used in the past.

P2: (Frequency). The likelihood of retrieving and using a piece of belief-relevant knowledge is a positive function of the frequency with which it has been encountered and used in the past.

P3: (Strength of Association). The likelihood that exposure to one unit of knowledge stimulates the retrieval and use of a second unit increases with the extent to which the two units of knowledge have been thought about in relation to one another.

P4: (Schematic processing). If a configuration of information is comprehended in terms of a more general schema, features that are not mentioned in the information but instantiate features of the schema will be spontaneously added to the representation as it is formed and, therefore, will later be recalled as actually having been mentioned.

The implications of these postulates for belief formation and change become important in light of research and theory on knowledge accessibility (Bargh, 1994, 1997; Bargh, Chen, & Burrows, 1996; Bargh & Pietromonaco, 1982; Higgins, 1996; Wyer, 2003). As Taylor and Fiske (1978) pointed out, people typically do not bring all of the relevant knowledge they have available to bear on a judgment or decision. Rather, they rely on only a small amount of this information that comes to mind easily at the time. Chaiken (1987) provides a particularly clear theoretical analysis of this possibility. That is, when people are required to make a judgment or decision, they first apply the criterion that is quickest and easiest to use and assess their confidence that the implications of this criterion are valid. If their confidence is above a minimum threshold, they base their response on this criterion without further consideration. If, however, their confidence is below the threshold, they apply additional criteria, and continue in this manner until either their threshold is reached or, alternatively, they do not have the time to engage in further processing. Situational and individual difference factors that influence participants' confidence threshold will consequently determine the number of criteria they employ. In general, however, only a small amount of knowledge will be involved.

In the present context, these considerations suggest that the knowledge that people use as a basis for the beliefs they report is likely to be a function of the recency and frequency with which it has been encountered or thought about in the past (Postulates 1 and 2), or the strength of its association with other belief-relevant knowledge that happens to be accessible in memory (Postulate 3). For example, evidence that more extensively processed information is easier to recall (Craik & Lockhart, 1972; see also Wyer & Hartwick, 1980) could be partly a reflection of the effects of frequency and strength of association implied by Postulates 2 and 3. Knowledge accessibility may also depend on the information's relatedness to a more general schema that is brought to bear on the referent of the beliefs being reported. Theory and research that are based on these assumptions are described in the pages to follow.

Associative Theories of Belief Organization and Change

Some theoretical formulations of belief formation and change are based on assumptions similar to those of a general associative network conceptualization, whereas others exemplify schema-based conceptions of knowledge organization. Still other theories make minimal assumptions about the organization of knowledge in memory and, therefore, are more akin to independent-trace models. In this section of the chapter, we focus on network types of representations, giving primary emphasis to McGuire's (1960, 1981; McGuire & McGuire, 1991) formulations of knowledge organization.

The Content and Structure of Thought Systems

Perhaps the most extensive and far-reaching analysis of the organization of belief-relevant knowledge is embodied in William and Claire McGuire's (1991) conceptualization of the content, structure, and operation of thought systems. They proposed that in order to cope effectively with the situations and events they encounter in daily life, people attempt to explain events that have occurred in the past and to predict their occurrence in the future. This disposition stimulates them both to identify the antecedents of the events they encounter and to construe the consequences of these events. To confirm this assumption, the McGuires asked participants to free associate to propositions that described the possible occurrence of an event such as increasing admission prices to university sporting events. As they expected, over 65% of the responses to these propositions pertained to either reasons why the event might occur or to potential consequences of its occurrence.

McGuire and McGuire (1991) postulated four more specific strategies that people can use to cope with life experiences. These strategies take into account both people's desire to see the world in a favorable light and their desire to have an accurate perception of reality.

1. (Utility maximization) Events stimulate thoughts about consequences that are similar to the events in desirability. That is, desirable (undesirable) events stimulate thoughts about possible consequences that are also desirable (undesirable).

2. (Congruent origins) Events stimulate thoughts about antecedents that are similar to them in desirability. That is, desirable (undesirable) events stimulate thoughts about desirable (undesirable) causes.

3. (Wishful thinking) Desirable events stimulate thoughts about why the events are likely to occur, whereas undesirable events stimulate thoughts about why they will not occur.

4. (Rationalization) Events that appear likely to occur stimulate thoughts about desirable consequences, whereas events that are considered unlikely stimulate thoughts about undesirable consequences.

The first two of these hypotheses—utility maximization and congruent origins—received strong support in McGuire and McGuire's (1991) research. Although the other postulates were less convincingly supported on the basis of participants' spontaneous free responses in the McGuires' work, they have received confirmation in other paradigms. For example, participants who have formed a favorable attitude toward a behavior on the basis of the affect they are experiencing for objectively irrelevant reasons tend both (a) to increase their beliefs that the behavior will have consequences they consider to be desirable, and (b) to increase their liking for consequences of the behaviors that they believe are likely to occur (Albarracín & Wyer, 2001).

Empirical Evidence

According to an associative network conception of knowledge organization, thinking about two entities in relation to one another should increase their association in memory and, therefore, should increase the likelihood that calling attention to one of the events will stimulate thoughts about the other as well (Postulate 3). To this extent, the McGuires' research provides insight into the sort of associations that are formed spontaneously between causally related events in the absence of explicit requests to do so. As noted earlier, people who are called on to explain an event or construe its desirability may bring only a small amount of knowledge to bear on these judgments. Thus, people who are motivated to estimate the likelihood of the event described in a proposition may search for antecedents of it, whereas those who are motivated to construe the event's desirability may search for possible consequences of it. In each case, however, they are likely to identify and use the first relevant piece of previously acquired knowledge that comes to mind rather than searching for all of the information that might be relevant (Higgins, 1996). Therefore, the number of associations that are actually formed as a result of this activity may be limited.

Evidence that these associations are formed was obtained by Wyer and Hartwick (1984). Participants first read a list of randomly ordered propositions with instructions to indicate if they understood them. Some of the propositions were causally related; that is, the event that was described in one proposition, A (e.g., "Trucks carrying heavy cargo destroy highway paving") was the antecedent of the event that was described in a second, C (e.g., "the weight limit on truck cargo may be decreased"). After this familiarization task, some participants reported their belief in either the antecedent (A) or the consequence (C). Others reported the desirability of either A or C. Finally, in a second session several days later, participants recalled the propositions they had encountered in the earlier session.

The authors reasoned that if a judgment-relevant proposition had been made salient during the familiarization task, participants would identify and use it, thereby forming an association between this proposition and the one they were asked to judge. Thus, they should form an association between A and C if they are asked to report either their belief in C (which stimulates them to search for an antecedent) or the desirability of A (which leads them to search for a consequence). This association should be reflected in their recall of the propositions later.

Specifically, if A and C are associated in memory, thoughts about one proposition (e.g., C) should cue the recall of the second (A). Consequently, the likelihood of recalling A should be greater if C has been recalled than if it has not. This possibility was, in fact, the case when participants had reported either their beliefs in C or the desirability of A. When they had reported the desirability of C or their belief in A, however, no association between the two propositions was formed, and so the recall of A had no impact on the recall of C.

Implications for Belief Salience

Associations of the sort postulated by the McGuires (1991) and Wyer and Hartwick (1984) have implications for the sort of knowledge that is likely to be used as a basis for not only beliefs but attitudes as well. Fishbein and Ajzen (1975) assume that people's attitudes toward an object or behavior are determined by the subset of beliefs about the attributes of the referent that are *salient* (i.e., accessible) in memory. These attributes, and the beliefs pertaining to them, can vary over both individuals and situations. For example, a person might believe both that using condoms prevents AIDS and that using condoms decreases unwanted pregnancies. However, these beliefs may differ in the strength of their association with the notion that using contraceptives is desirable and, therefore, the likelihood that they come to mind when the possibility of using condoms is thought about.

As implied by Postulates 1 to 4, however, other situational factors can influence the retrieval of belief-relevant propositions from memory as well, including the frequency and recency with which the propositions have been thought about or the amount of thought that has been devoted to them in the past (Craik & Lockhart, 1972). To this extent, people are likely to report different attitudes, depending on which subset of belief-relevant cognitions happens to come to mind at the time (for a review of relevant evidence, see Albarracín, Wallace, & Glasman, 2004). These considerations suggest that attitudes, like other judgments, are not always stable, but rather, can depend on the time they are requested or become necessary for attaining a goal to which they are relevant (Schwarz & Bohner, 2001; but see Krosnick & Petty, 1995, for a different view).

Further Considerations

Although the associative processes postulated by McGuire and others have typically focused on small numbers of related propositions, these processes can potentially govern the relations among substantial bodies of knowledge. Several attempts have been made to assess individual differences in the differentiation and interrelatedness of persons' belief systems and to examine their implications (see Gruenfeld, 1995; Linville, 1982; Rokeach, 1954; Schroeder, Driver, & Streufert, 1967; Scott, 1969; Scott, Osgood, & Peterson, 1979). As Wyer (1964) showed, however, alternative measures of cognitive differentiation and integration are often uncorrelated and, therefore, may be tapping different underlying constructs. This makes general conclusions based on this research difficult to draw.

Probabilogical Models of Belief Organization and Change

The conceptualization of knowledge organization developed by the McGuires (1991) provides an indication of how different pieces of belief-relevant knowledge can become associated in memory. However, it does not describe the way in which beliefs themselves are related, or how beliefs in one piece of information can affect beliefs about others to which it is related. A conceptualization proposed by McGuire (1960, 1981) and extended by Wyer and Goldberg (1970; see also Wyer, 1974, 2003) addressed this matter. McGuire (1960) noted that the causal relatedness of two cognitions, A and C, can be described in a syllogism of the form "A;

if A, then C; C." To this extent, beliefs in C should be a function of the beliefs that these premises are true (that is, the beliefs that A is true *and* if A is true, C is true). Wyer (1970; Wyer & Goldberg, 1970) further noted that C might be true for reasons other than those embodied in these premises, and that beliefs in these reasons could be reflected in beliefs in the mutually exclusive set of premises, "not A; if not A, then C." If this is so, and if beliefs in the premises are in units of subjective probability (i.e., along a scale from 0 to 1), the belief that C is true, $P(C)$ should be a function of the beliefs in these two mutually exclusive sets of premises, or:

$$P(C) = P(A)P(C/A) + P(\sim A)P(C/\sim A),\qquad\qquad [2]$$

where $P(A)$ and $P(\sim A)$ $[= 1 - P(A)]$ are beliefs that A is and is not true, respectively, and $P(C/A)$ and $P(C/\sim A)$ are conditional beliefs that C is true if A is and is not true, respectively.

Several studies (Wyer, 1970, 1975) show that experimental manipulations of the beliefs composing the right side of Equation 2 confirm the multiplicative and additive effects of these beliefs on beliefs in the conclusion. Moreover, if people's estimates of the likelihood of each proposition are reported along a 0 to 10 scale and then divided by 10 to convert them to units of probability, the equation provides a quantitative description of the relations among the beliefs composing it that is typically accurate to within a half of a scale unit (.05) without requiring ad hoc curve-fitting parameters. This is true regardless of whether the beliefs involved pertain to abstract entities (e.g., genes and person attributes) that are described by the experimenter (Wyer, 1975), events described in stories about hypothetical events (Wyer, 1970), or events that might occur in the real world (Wyer & Goldberg, 1970).

Several studies (see Dillehay, Insko, & Smith, 1966; Holt, 1970; Watts & Holt, 1970) support the assumption that people attempt to maintain logical consistency among their beliefs and opinions. McGuire (1960) suggested one particularly interesting implication of this assumption. He noted that people's beliefs are not always consistent because they do not think about them in relation to one another. However, asking people to report syllogistically related beliefs in temporal proximity should call their attention to any inconsistency that exists and, therefore, should stimulate them to reduce or eliminate the inconsistency by changing one or more of the beliefs involved. If this is true, the beliefs that people report after engaging in this cognitive activity should be more consistent than they were at first. McGuire (1960) denoted this phenomenon to *Socratic effect*. Therefore, if Equation 2 provides a valid description of the relationship among syllogistically related beliefs, the accuracy of this equation in describing people's beliefs should increase over time once the beliefs to which the equation pertains have been made salient.

Rosen and Wyer (1972) confirmed this hypothesis. That is, participants reported their beliefs in propositions of the sort to which Equation 2 pertains in two sessions a week apart. These beliefs, converted to units of probability, were more consistent in the second session than the first. That is, participants appeared to revise their beliefs to eliminate inconsistencies among them once these inconsistencies were called to their attention.

Two contingencies in this conclusion are noteworthy. First, individual differences may exist in the disposition to eliminate logical inconsistencies of the sort that Equation 2 describes. For example, Norenzayan and Kim (2000) found evidence that the Socratic effect occurs only among representatives of Western cultures and is not evident among Asians. Easterners, who appear to have a less analytic thinking style than Westerners do (Choi, Nisbett, & Norenzayan, 1999), are apparently less motivated to engage in the syllogistic reasoning processes that underlie the Socratic effect.

Second, Henninger and Wyer (1976) found that the Socratic effect was only apparent when participants in the first administration of the questionnaire reported their beliefs in the conclusion, $P(C)$, before reporting their beliefs in the premises. When participants encountered the premises first, the consistency of their beliefs was high in the first session and did not increase further over time. People may find it easier to change their belief in a conclusion to make it consistent with their beliefs in premises than to change their beliefs in premises to make them consistent with their belief in the conclusion. Therefore, participants who encountered the conclusion at the time their beliefs in the premises were salient to them were able to modify their belief in it online to make it consistent with their beliefs in these premises. However, participants who encountered the premises after reporting their beliefs in the conclusion could not easily engage in this online inconsistency resolution. Alternatively, they might have eliminated the inconsistency by altering their beliefs in the conclusion, but this change (and, therefore, the reduction in inconsistency that resulted from it) was not evident until they reported this belief again in the second session.

To the extent that the Socratic effect generalizes beyond the situations in which it has been traditionally investigated, it has further implications. For one thing, it suggests that changes in people's beliefs can be induced simply by calling their attention to preexisting knowledge that bears on the beliefs rather than by providing new information. Moreover, to the extent that calling people's attention to an inconsistency among their beliefs stimulates cognitive work to eliminate it, the increased coherence of these beliefs might make them more resistant to change in the future. McGuire's (1964) research on resistance to persuasion is worth noting in this regard. He found that exposing people to a communication that attacked a previously formed belief increased their resistance to subsequent attacks. Furthermore, this increased resistance was true even when the arguments presented in the initial attack differed from those in the later one. McGuire suggests that the initial attack made participants aware of their vulnerability, leading them to bolster their defenses by counterarguing, and that the practice they had in performing this activity increased their ability to refute the attack they encountered subsequently. Another possibility, however, is that the initial attack made them aware of the inconsistency in their beliefs associated with the target proposition and stimulated inconsistency resolution processes similar to those that underlie the Socratic effect. This increased coherence of the beliefs increased resistance to influence by subsequent messages.

SCHEMATIC THEORIES OF KNOWLEDGE ORGANIZATION AND INFERENCE: IMPLICATIONAL MOLECULES

Wyer and Hartwick's (1984) research suggests that the associations that people form between propositions can sometimes be fortuitous, depending on the knowledge that happens to be accessible in memory at the time the events are contemplated. However, many causally related events or states of affairs may be encountered frequently in the course of daily life, leading to the formation of strong associations between the propositions and the events or states they describe (Postulate 3). As a result, the configuration of causally related propositions may come to function as a schema, being activated and applied as a unit in comprehending information and drawing inferences about states or events to which it is applicable. To this extent, the application of such a schema could have effects of the sort suggested by Postulate 4.

Implicational Molecules

Abelson and Reich (1969) formalized this possibility (see also Bear & Hodun, 1975; Kruglanski, 1989; Wyer, 2004; Wyer & Carlston, 1994). They postulated the existence of *implicational molecules*, or sets of psychologically related propositions that are bound together by psychological implication. These molecules, which can function as schemas (Wyer & Carlston, 1979,

1994), reflect generalizations about events that occur frequently in the real world. Thus, for example, the general conviction that smoking causes lung cancer might be embodied in the molecule:

$$[P \text{ smokes}; P \text{ has (will get) lung cancer}].$$

Alternatively, a person might have a *just deserts molecule* exemplifying the notion that people get what they deserve, composed of the propositions:

$$[P \text{ does something bad (good); bad (good) things befall } P].$$

Or, a *similarity-attraction molecule*, exemplifying the generalization that people who like the same thing like one another, might be:

$$[P_1 \text{ likes } X; P_2 \text{ likes X}; P_1 \text{ and } P_2 \text{ like one another}].$$

The schematic character of implicational molecules is exemplified by their use in comprehending new experiences. This comprehension is governed by a *completion principle* whose implications are similar to those implied by Postulate 4. That is, if a specific experience or set of experiences instantiates all but one proposition in a molecule, an instantiation of the other is inferred to be true as well. The principle applies regardless of which propositions are instantiated by the experiences and which are not. Thus, the just desserts molecule could be used to infer that a particular person who has done a bad deed will be punished or otherwise experience misfortune. However, it could also be used to infer that a person who has encountered misfortune has done something bad or is, for other reasons, a bad person (for evidence supporting this possibility, see Lerner & Miller, 1978; Lerner & Simmons, 1966; Walster, 1966).

The completion principle, which is consistent with processes that presumably occur in the construction of schemas, has extremely broad implications. Several more specific conceptualizations of belief formation and change can be viewed as special cases of the more general theory proposed by Abelson and Reich (1969). Two particularly well-known phenomena—cognitive balance and social attribution—are particularly worth discussing in this context. From different perspectives, each conceptualization calls attention to a more general question, concerning which of several alternative implicational molecules are activated and applied at any given time. The aforementioned principles of knowledge organization could potentially provide answers to this question.

Cognitive Balance Theory

According to Heider (1946, 1958), people's perceptions of interpersonal relationships are guided by the assumptions that people get along well with one another if they have similar interests, values, or attitudes; if they belong to the same group, organization, or social category; or if they have other characteristics in common. Correspondingly, they are not expected to get along well if their attitudes and values conflict, or if the individuals are dissimilar in terms of personality, group membership, or other characteristics. Note that these implications are very similar to those of the similarity-attraction molecule we described earlier.

One implication of balance theory is that balanced relations may be represented schematically in memory, whereas unbalanced relations may be stored as individual pieces of information. This possibility was confirmed on the basis of two criteria. First, if people comprehend new information they receive according to a balance principle, they are likely to spontaneously add unmentioned features to the representation they form that are consistent with these principles. Consistent with this prediction, Picek, Sherman, and Shiffrin (1975) gave participants sets of relations among four hypothetical persons. In some cases, some relations were unspecified but, if inferred, would produce balanced triads of relations (e.g., A likes B; B likes C; C dislikes D; D dislikes A). In other cases, the missing relations would not produce perfect balance (e.g., A likes B; B likes C; C likes D; D dislikes A). Later, participants recalled the relations they had learned. Participants who were exposed to the first sets of relations tended to recall the unspecified balance-producing relations as actually having been presented. When the unspecified relations could not produce balance, however, intrusion errors were not evident.

Second, if people organize sets of relations in memory according to balance principles, they should later respond to the information as a single unit of knowledge rather than in terms of its constituent elements. Sentis and Burnstein (1979) provided compelling evidence of this possibility. Participants were exposed to sets of three relations that were either balanced (e.g., "Al likes Bob; Al dislikes X; Bob dislikes X") or imbalanced (e.g., "George likes Peter; George dislikes X; Peter likes X"). Then, they were shown sets of either 1, 2, or 3 of the relations in each set and asked to verify that the relations were among the ones they had previously seen. When the original set of relations was imbalanced, the time that participants took to perform this task increased with the number of relations they were asked to verify. When the relations were balanced, however, the opposite was true; participants took less time to verify all three relations in combination than they took to verify any one of the relations when presented in isolation. In the latter case, participants had apparently stored the relations in memory as a unit, and so they could verify a configuration that matched this unit very quickly. However, more time was required to "unpack" the configuration in order to verify any given component.

Numerous applications of cognitive balance exist in the literature (for summaries, see Eagly & Chaiken, 1993). Moreover, the theory has been extended to larger configurations of cognitions (Abelson & Rosenberg, 1958; Cartwright & Harary, 1956; see also Gollob, 1974, for an interesting extension of the theory). In most successful tests of the conceptualization's utility in describing comprehension and inference, however, the persons and objects involved in the relations have been described abstractly, and the relations do not reflect the social context in which they occurred. When the information pertains to specific types of people and relations, the applicability of the principle is often unclear (see Wyer & Lyon, 1970).

Several of these contingencies are suggested by an implicational molecule conceptualization. In addition to a similarity-attraction molecule, for example, people are likely to have a *competitiveness molecule* that exemplifies the generalization that people who want the same thing dislike one another:

$$[P \text{ wants } X;\ O \text{ wants } X;\ P \text{ and } O \text{ dislike one another}]$$

In addition, they might have a *jealousy molecule* exemplifying the generalization that people dislike others who have what they want:

$$[P \text{ wants } X;\ O \text{ has } X;\ P \text{ dislikes } O]$$

The applicability of these molecules are likely to depend on the types of elements involved in the relations being described as well as the relations themselves. A similarity-attraction molecule is likely to be applied when P's and O's sentiment relations to the referent do not create interpersonal conflict. Thus, for example, two men, Bob and Alan, may both be believed to like one another if they have similar sentiments about George W. Bush. If Bob and Alan are both in love with the same woman, however, or if Bob covets Alan's wife, the competitiveness and jealousy molecules are more likely to be applied. To this extent, the beliefs may be governed by the completion principle in much the same way described earlier. However, the effects of applying the principle would not produce balance.

Beliefs About Causality

Several motives could potentially underlie a person's behavior. For example, people do things (a) because they like doing them, (b) because they are forced to do them, or (c) because their actions will attain some external objective that they consider desirable. These generalizations could be exemplified in three different molecules, which have a proposition in common:

1. [*P* enjoys *B*; *P* performs *B*]
2. [*O* controls *P*; *O* likes *B*; *P* performs *B*]
3. [*P* wants *X*; *B* facilitates *X*; *P* performs *B*]

Thus, suppose people hear a man express a favorable opinion of abortion, which exemplifies the proposition "*P* performs *B*." In the absence of any other information, only the first of the aforementioned molecules would stimulate an application of the completion principle. Thus, observers should infer that the man favors abortion (or, at least, likes to advocate it publicly). However, suppose observers learn that the person's employer favors abortion (an instantiation of "*O* likes *B*") or that the person is getting paid to advocate the position (an instantiation of "*B* facilitates *X*"). In these cases, the completion principle could be applied to the second and third molecules as well as the first. Assuming that all three molecules are equally accessible, therefore, people should be less likely to infer that the man personally favors abortion (or the behavior of advocating it) in this case than when only the first molecule applies.

This conclusion, of course, is consistent with correspondent inference theory (Jones & Davis, 1965). Moreover, note that the molecules are potentially applicable in comprehending and making inferences about one's own behavior as well as others'. To this extent, a similar analysis would suggest that a person would infer his/her own liking for abortion to be less when the second two molecules are potentially applicable than when they are not (see Bem, 1967, 1972).

Our analysis of attribution phenomena in terms of implicational molecule theory assumes that these phenomena occur spontaneously in the course of comprehending the information one receives. As such, it clearly does not capture all of the phenomena to which theory and research on social attribution is relevant. Many attributions are made deliberately to comply with social demands, or are stimulated by personal motives (e.g., the desire to maintain self-esteem). We consider these possibilities in a later section of this chapter.

Stereotypes as Implicational Molecules

People may form generalizations about the characteristics of individuals who belong to certain social groups or categories. These generalizations, which are typically viewed as *stereotypes*, can be conceptualized as implicational molecules of the form:

[*P* belongs to group *G*; Members of *G* have attribute *X*; *P* has attribute *X*].

Thus, if members of a group are believed to be aggressive, an individual member of the group may be inferred to have this attribute, and this inference may be made independently of other information available.

Research on stereotype-based beliefs and inferences is extensive (for reviews, see Fiske, 1998; Hamilton & J. Sherman, 1994), and a detailed review is beyond the scope of this chapter. To give but one example, Bodenhausen and Wyer (1985) found that individuals who read the transcript of a criminal case in which the defendant was accused of assault in a bar were more likely to believe that the defendant was guilty if his name was Carlos Ramirez than if his name was nondescript, and this effect occurred independently of the implications of the evidence contained in the transcript. The name of the defendant apparently activated a stereotype of Latinos as aggressive, and this stereotype influenced judgments independently of other considerations (but see Bodenhausen & Lichtenstein, 1987, for qualifications on this conclusion).

The conceptualization of stereotype-based representations of knowledge as implicational molecules has further implications. According to the completion principle, people should not only infer that a person has a stereotype-related attribute on the basis of information about his group membership, but should infer the individual's group membership on the basis of information that he has stereotype-consistent attributes. This prediction is essentially a recognition of the *representativeness* heuristic identified by Kahneman and Tversky (1972). That is, American college students who are told that a person is short, has black hair, and reads poetry infer that the individual is more likely to be a Chinese studies professor than to be an engineering professor despite the fact that few if any American university faculty members are Chinese studies professors and that the description is characteristic of many individuals who were not Chinese.

The Role of Implicit Theories in Belief Formation and Change

The implicational molecules we have described consist of only a few causally related propositions. Much more extensive scenarios can be constructed to describe entire sequences of events that occur over a period of time. These scenarios, which have the form of a narrative, theoretically exist in memory as a single unit of knowledge (Schank & Abelson, 1995; Wyer, 2004; Wyer, Adaval, & Colcombe, 2002). As such, they can function as *implicit theories* about the sequence of temporally and thematically related events that occur in situations of the sort to which they refer. Once these narrative-based theories are constructed, they can potentially be used to comprehend new experiences that exemplify them. To this extent, they can influence beliefs about unmentioned events and states of affairs through processes similar to those implied by Postulate 4.

The narrative representations that constitute implicit theories can be of several types (Wyer, 2004). Some representations may be mental simulations of situational- and temporally specific sequences of events (e.g., episode models; see Wyer & Radvansky, 1999). Others may have the character of stories about real or hypothetical experiences involving themselves and others that people communicate to one another for the purpose of informing, entertaining, or illustrating a point. More general representations (e.g., scripts; see Schank & Abelson, 1977; Todorov, 1973) can depict prototypic sequences of events that occur routinely in certain general types of situations (e.g., a restaurant). Still other generalized representations could resemble *story skeletons* (Schank & Abelson, 1995) that people use to comprehend the events that occur in a series of thematically related situations. A common example might be the romantic scenario of the sort that pervades movies and television shows—for example, a boy meets a girl, they fall in love, an unexpected event creates conflict, the boy and girl argue and break up, the misunderstanding is resolved, and the boy and girl make up and live happily ever after.

Comprehension and Memory Processes

The influence of implicit theories on beliefs could often be guided by a completion principle similar to that postulated to underlie the use of an implicational molecule. That is, once a preexisting representation is activated and used to comprehend new information, instantiations of unmentioned features that are required in order to comprehend the information may be added spontaneously to the representation that is formed of the information. Consequently, these features may be later recalled as actually having been presented. Thus, people who read that "John pounded a nail into the wall" might later recall that he used a hammer (Bransford, Barclay, & Franks, 1972). Similarly, people who are told that Bob went to an Italian restaurant, ordered chicken cacciatore, and paid $21.95 might later recall that he ate there (see Graesser et al., 1979), although he might actually have been picking up some food for a sick friend. These intrusions occur spontaneously at the time the information is comprehended (Wyer & Radvansky, 1999; but see Colcombe & Wyer, 2002, for a qualification on this conclusion).

Other intrusions can occur as a result of more deliberative processing. This processing may be stimulated by an attempt to explain an unexpected event, or could result from the need to comply with external demands. A study by Spiro (1977) exemplifies the former possibility. Participants in an initial experimental session read an ostensibly true story about an engaged couple. In some versions of the story, the man revealed that he did not want children, the woman objected, and a serious argument ensued. After reading the story, the participants were asked to perform an ostensibly unrelated task. While they were doing so, however, the experimenter incidentally remarked that the couple had gotten married and were still happily together.

Participants were then dismissed but returned for a second experimental session several weeks later, at which time they were asked to recall the story they had read earlier. They were explicitly cautioned to report only things that were mentioned in the story and not inferences they had made. Nevertheless, many participants recalled behaviors that had not been described but were consistent with the romantic relationship story skeleton described earlier. For example, one person recalled that the woman found she couldn't have children. Another recalled that the man changed his mind. Apparently, persons who heard the experimenter's incidental remark during the first session spontaneously speculated about how it might be true despite the serious conflict described in the story they had read, and made inferences about unstated events, based on the implications of the story skeleton. These inferences then became part of the representation that they stored in memory and later used as a basis of their recall (Postulate 4).

Similar effects can result from external demands. In a well-known demonstration by Loftus and Palmer (1974), participants who had been shown a picture of a traffic accident were asked either how fast the car was going when it "smashed into" the tree or, alternatively, how fast the car was going when it "hit" the tree. Participants estimated a faster speed in the first case than the second. In doing so, however, they reconstructed the picture they had seen, adding features to it that were consistent with implications of the question. Thus, they reported seeing broken glass at the scene of the accident, although it was not actually shown in the picture.

Loftus (1975) provides numerous other examples of this phenomena in her analysis of the questionable validity of eye-witness testimony. In other contexts (Loftus, 2000), she notes that similar phenomena can underlie adults' post-hoc memories of sexual abuse that occurred in early childhood. That is, individuals who have a very vague memory of an event that occurred in early life may be stimulated to apply an implicit theory of sexual abuse in reconstructing a story about it, adding features that they later remember as actually having taken place.

Reconstructing the Past

Loftus' (2000) examples of reconstructive memory for sexual abuse may exemplify a more general influence of implicit theories on people's beliefs about the past that occurs very frequently in daily life. That is, when people have only a vague recollection of specific events, they may use implicit theories as a basis for reconstructing these events instead of relying on their memory for what actually occurred. Research summarized by Michael Ross (1989) provides examples. In one study, female participants who had previously reported their typical emotional reactions during the period of their menstrual cycle were asked to keep a daily diary of their moods over the course of a month. At the end of the month, they were asked to recall the moods they had experienced during this period. Participants' recall was better predicted by their implicit theories about their emotional reactions during the time of their menstrual cycle than by the actual feelings they had reported experiencing at this time.

Students in a second study (Conway & Ross, 1984) participated in a program that they believed would increase their study skills. After participating, they were asked to recall their preprogram estimates of their ability. Their recall was governed primarily by their implicit theories that the program would be effective. Thus, participants whose skills after participating did not actually change over the course of the program recalled their preprogram ability as lower than it actually was, consistent with their theory that they had improved.

In a study by Goethals and Reckman (1973), students participated in a group discussion of bussing. The discussion was dominated by a confederate whose position contrasted with the opinion that participants had reported in an earlier session. The confederate's view had a substantial influence on not only participants' postdiscussion opinions but also their recall of the opinions they had reported earlier. Thus, participants apparently employed an implicit theory that their position on the issue was stable over time and, therefore, used their postdiscussion opinions to infer what their earlier position must have been before the discussion took place. This interpretation was confirmed by Ross (1989). Specifically, participants, after reporting their agreement with the position advocated in a persuasive message, were asked to list the thoughts they had had in the course of trying to recall the opinion they had reported 1 month earlier. Responses of over 50% of the participants suggested the use of an implicit *temporal consistency theory* (e.g., "I answered the question now and assumed that my opinion probably hadn't changed month in a month or so.").

Research conducted in the context of self-perception theory (Bem, 1967, 1972) provides further examples. Bem argued that when people are asked to report their stand on a social issue, they do not perform an exhaustive review of the large amount of self-knowledge they have stored in memory that bears on this position. Rather, they retrieve the judgment-relevant information that comes most easily to mind and base their response on the implications of this information alone. In many instances, this information is a behavior they have recently performed. Under these circumstances, people construe the implications of this behavior for the judgment they are asked to make and resort to additional information only if they consider its implications to be unclear or unreliable (see Chaiken, 1987).

In an interesting demonstration of this possibility, Bem and McConnell (1970) induced participants to advocate a position with which they had reported disagreement during an earlier experimental session. Some participants were given the opportunity to refuse to advocate the position, whereas others were not given a choice. Later, participants were asked to recall the belief they had reported in the earlier session. Participants who had voluntarily agreed to advocate the position recalled their beliefs as consistent with the position they had advocated, whereas those who were forced to advocate the position did not. Thus, the former participants appeared to invoke a theory that people believe in the positions they voluntarily agree to advocate publicly and used this theory to infer their prebehavior position on the issue they endorsed rather than recalling the position they had actually reported.

Spontaneous Versus Deliberative Processes of Belief Formation

The impact of implicational molecules and implicit theories on beliefs is due in part to their schematic character. That is, unmentioned features of information that instantiate elements of the molecule or theory that is used to comprehend it may be added spontaneously to the mental representation of the information's referent that is formed and stored in memory. As a consequence, these elements may later be recalled as actually having been mentioned (Postulate 4). As the research by Ross and his colleagues testifies, however, implicit theories are also used deliberately to make inferences about events to which they pertain. In these latter cases, the implicit theories might not be invoked unless participants are confronted with a task that requires them. In this regard, it is generally important to distinguish between beliefs that are formed spontaneously in the course of receiving information and beliefs that are only constructed on demand, or in the service of a goal to which they are relevant.

The Spontaneous Identification of True and False Statements

A theoretical discussion of the conditions that give rise to spontaneous and deliberative inferences in the course of comprehension is provided by Graesser, Singer, and Trabasso (1994). Two conceptualizations developed in social psychological research have implications for this question. Gilbert (1991; Gilbert, Krull, & Malone, 1990) postulated that people must entertain the possibility that an assertion is true in order to comprehend it. However, a second stage of processing is required to identify the statement as false. To demonstrate this two-stage process, participants in one study (Gilbert, 1991) received a series of stimulus statements along with indications that the statements were either true or false. Then, they were asked to verify the truth of these statements while performing either a simple or a distracting cognitive task. Participants who were distracted were presumably able to perform the first, comprehension stage of processing. Therefore, they were unlikely to misidentify true statements as false despite the distraction. In contrast, distraction significantly disrupted the second, falsification stage of processing, as evidenced by an increase in the tendency to misidentify false statements as true.

A somewhat different conceptualization proposed by Wyer and Radvansky (1999; see also Wyer, 2004). According to this theory, people who encounter a proposition comprehend it by forming a mental simulation of the situation it depicts (e.g., a situation model), based on a comparison of its features to those of a previously formed knowledge representation in memory. If the similarity of the statement to the representation they use to comprehend it exceeds a certain threshold, people not only comprehend the information but spontaneously recognize it as true. Correspondingly, if the similarity is below some minimal threshold, they spontaneously identify it as false. If the similarity falls in between these extremes, however, participants comprehend and store the proposition in memory without assessing its validity.

Wyer and Radvansky (1999) obtained support for this conceptualization. Participants were exposed to propositions about actual people and events about which they had prior knowledge. Some of the propositions were true (e.g., Jane Fonda acted in a movie), others were false (e.g., Jane Fonda played professional basketball) and others were of uncertain validity (e.g., Jane Fonda rode a motorcycle). Some participants were asked to indicate whether or not they understood each statement, whereas others were told to indicate whether the statements were likely to be true or false. The time required to verify true and false statements was very similar to the time required to comprehend them, suggesting that verification occurred spontaneously in the course of comprehension. In contrast, statements of unknown validity took much longer to validate than to comprehend.

Implications of Spontaneous Validation Processes

Wyer and Radvansky's (1999) theory has additional implications. Grice (1975) and others (e.g., Green, 1989; Higgins, 1981; Sperber & Wilson, 1986) note that social communication is often governed by certain normative principles (e.g., to be informative, to tell the truth, to be polite, etc.). Consequently, when a message that is conveyed in a social context appears to violate these principles, recipients may attempt to reinterpret its implications in a way that conforms to their expectations. For example, if people perceive that a statement's literal meaning is obviously true or obviously false, they may infer that the communicator intends the statement to be ironic and, therefore, to express the opposite point of view. Thus, the assertion "Central Illinois is a wonderful place to spend the summer—I simply love all that heat and high humidity" is likely to be interpreted by residents of the area as sarcastic (that is, as a disparagement of Illinois and not a true description of its virtues).

The effects of communication norms on responses to information have been discussed in detail elsewhere (Higgins, 1981; Schwarz, 1994, 1998b; Strack, 1994; Wyer, 2004; Wyer & Gruenfeld, 1995). Gruenfeld and Wyer (1992; see also Wegner, Wenzlaff, Kerker, & Beattie, 1981) provided an application of the effect of norm violations in a study of reactions to news. Participants read a series of statements that had ostensibly been taken from newspaper headlines. In one condition, some of the headlines affirmed the validity of propositions that participants in the study were unlikely to believe to be true (e.g., "Members of the U.S. Senate belong to the Ku Klux Klan"). In another condition, the headlines denied the propositions' validity ("Members of the U.S. Senate do *not* belong to the Ku Klux Klan") and therefore were consistent with participants' a priori beliefs. After reading the statements, participants estimated the likelihood that they were true.

Relative to control conditions, participants who read affirmations increased their beliefs in the propositions. However, participants who had read denials *also* increased their beliefs in the propositions' validity. In fact, this effect was similar in magnitude to the effect of affirmations. Statements that denied the validity of a proposition that participants already believed to be false appeared to violate the norm that communications are intended to convey new information. Consequently, participants questioned the reason why the statement was made and, in doing so, speculated that there might be some reason (albeit unknown to them) that the statement might in fact be true and, therefore, was actually intended to be informative. As a result of this speculation, however, they increased their belief in the proposition being denied. Aside from its specific implications, this research calls attention to the fact that the influence of information on beliefs is likely to depend on not only the nature of the information itself, but also the social context in which it is conveyed.

The attempt to reconcile information that violates normative principles of communication can have other effects as well. For example, favorable statements about oneself often violate norms to be modest, and unfavorable statements about others, at least in the others' presence, violate norms to be polite. Therefore, these statements can stimulate attempts to understand why the statements were made, and this additional processing can increase the accessibility of the statements in memory (Wyer, Budesheim, Lambert, & Swan, 1994). This heightened accessibility, in turn, could increase the likelihood of using the statements as bases for beliefs that are reported later.

FORMAL MODELS OF BELIEF FORMATION AND CHANGE

The effects of information on beliefs of the sort described in the previous section occur in the course of comprehension. However, belief formation and change can also depend on computational processes that surround the assessment and integration of the information's implications after it has been comprehended. In this section, we review formal models of the cognitive activities that occur in the course of construing the implications of information for one's beliefs. In the next section, we focus on the role of heuristic criteria that often do not involve a detailed analysis of the information or knowledge that is relevant to them.

Conditional Inference Processes

A model of belief formation proposed by Wyer and Hartwick (1980) is similar to the probabilogical conceptualization developed by McGuire (1960) and described earlier in this chapter. These authors assumed that when people are asked to estimate the likelihood that a target proposition (C) is true, they search their memory for a second, informational proposition (A) that has implications for its validity. Once this proposition is identified, they estimate both (a) the likelihood that the target proposition would be true if the informational proposition were true and (b) the likelihood that the target would be true if the informational proposition were false. Then, if their estimates of these two probabilities differ, people average them, weighting each by the likelihood that the informational proposition is true and false, respectively. This process can be described by Equation 2. That is, the equation essentially implies that the belief in C is a weighted average of the two conditional beliefs, with the beliefs that A is and is not true serving as estimates of the relative weights attached to these conditionals.

As indicated earlier, Equation 2 provides a surprisingly accurate description of the effect of information bearing on an informational proposition, A, on beliefs in a related proposition, C. This accuracy is maintained even when the latter proposition is not mentioned in the information bearing on A. Thus, the formulation potentially describes the impact of information bearing directly on one proposition on beliefs in other, unmentioned propositions to which the first is related. The formulation applies both when the propositions involved are descriptive such as "George Bush will not be reelected," and when they are evaluative such as "I dislike George Bush" (Wyer, 1972, 1973).

The conditional inference model can be applied in a number of content domains. For instance, Jaccard and King (1977) observed that perceptions of likelihood that an outcome will occur can function as the premise of a syllogism (e.g., "outcome X will occur; if X will occur, I will perform behavior B"). Thus, people may construe the probability that buying a new computer will allow them to run more programs simultaneously, and might then infer a high likelihood that they will buy the computer (Jaccard & King, 1977).

In applying the model, however, it is important to keep in mind that the accuracy of the equation does not in itself validate the cognitive processes that underlie it. That is, the equation's accuracy could be the product of syllogistic inference processes of the sort postulated by McGuire (1960) as well as the algebraic computations assumed by Wyer and Hartwick (1980). Moreover, if components of the equation were true probabilities, the equation would be a mathematical tautology. To this extent, the model's accuracy could reflect a more general tendency for subjective probabilities (beliefs) to combine in a manner consistent with the laws of mathematical probability (Wyer & Goldberg, 1970). Because other inference rules implied by this assumption are less effective in describing human inference processes (Wyer, 1976), this latter interpretation seems unlikely to be valid. Be that as it may, Equation 2 provides a clear illustration of an instance in which the quantitative accuracy of a model is not a sufficient basis for evaluating the assumptions that underlie its validity.

Linear Models of Belief Formation

A limitation of the conditional inference model described by Equation 2 is its focus on the implications of a single proposition that happens to come to mind at the time. Although the implications of other criteria are taken into account, these implications are lumped together in the value of $P(C/\sim A)$, or the belief that the conclusion is true for reasons other than A. Other formulations consider more directly the possibility that multiple factors are considered. Slovic and Lichtenstein (1971), for example, postulated that people who predict an unknown event from a set of cues are likely to combine these cues in an additive fashion. Therefore, regression procedures can be used to predict beliefs on the basis of the implications of several different pieces of information, with the regression weights assigned to each piece being used as an indication of its relative importance.

Multiple-regression approaches can be useful in identifying individual differences in the weights given to different types of cues (Wiggins, Hoffman, & Taber, 1969). Nevertheless, the assumptions that underlie these approaches are often incorrect (Anderson, 1974, 1981; Fishbein & Ajzen, 1975; Tversky, 1969; Wiggins & Hoffman, 1968). Birnbaum and Stegner (1979), for example, found that participants' estimates of a car's value was an *average* of its Blue Book value and the opinion of another person, with the weight of each piece of information depending on the credibility of its source.

In many instances, however, neither summative nor averaging models may be applicable. Kahneman and Tversky (1982a) provide strong evidence that people's estimates of the conjunction of two features (e.g., the likelihood that a woman is a feminist bank teller) are not predictable from their estimates of each feature (i.e., being a feminist or being a bank teller) considered in isolation. In these instances, people appear to configurally process the information rather than construing the implications of each piece of information separately. The conditions in which different combinatorial processes underlie the beliefs that people report (as well as other judgments they make) require more detailed analyses than can be provided in this chapter (see Wyer & Carlston, 1979, for a general discussion of these matters).

Information Processing Models of Belief Formation and Change

The preceding models pertain primarily to the computation of beliefs once the implications of the available information have been identified. Other models have been developed to account for the cognitive activities that occur in the course of assessing these implications. These formulations have been stimulated in large part by evidence that people's responses to belief-relevant information are unlikely to be predicted from the objective implications of the information that they can recall at the time their beliefs are reported. Rather, these responses reflect the number and implications of the thoughts that recipients had about the message at the time they encountered it (Greenwald, 1968; Osterhouse & Brock, 1970; Petty & Cacioppo, 1986). Two models, by McGuire (1968) and Fishbein and Ajzen (1975), provide examples.

McGuire (1968)

According to McGuire (1968), the likelihood of being influenced by a communication is a multiplicative function of (a) the likelihood of receiving and comprehending the implications of the message and (b) the cognitive elaboration of these implications that occurs subsequently. If the communication is counterattitudinal, this elaboration is likely to consist primarily of counterarguing. A simplified version of this conceptualization was proposed by Wyer (1974), namely,

$$P(I) = P(R)[1 - P(CA)],$$ [3]

where $P(I)$ is the probability that the information bearing specifically on a proposition has an impact on beliefs in its validity, $P(R)$ is the probability of receiving and comprehending this information, and $P(CA)$ is the probability of refuting its validity. Thus, situational and individual difference factors that independently influence the likelihood of comprehending and effectively counterarguing a communication should have a multiplicative impact on the communication's influence. An interesting implication of the conceptualization arises from the observation that influence is greater when reception and counterarguing are both moderate (e.g., $P[R] = P[CA] = .5$) than when they are either both low ($= 0$) or both high ($= 1$). Thus, variables that simultaneously influence both reception and counterarguing (e.g., intelligence, knowledge of the topic, or situational distraction) can have a nonmonotonic effect on communication impact.

Several studies support implications of this formulation. For example, Festinger and Maccoby (1964) and Osterhouse and Brock (1970) both showed that distracting recipients from thinking carefully about a message that contradicted their beliefs and opinions (and, therefore, decreased $P[CA]$) increased the impact of the communication. Contingencies of these effects on the quality of the communication (e.g., the ease of comprehending the message and the cogency of the arguments; see Regan & Cheng, 1973) can also be interpreted in terms of their effects on the model's components (Wyer, 1974). Finally, McGuire's (1964) research on resistance to persuasion can be conceptualized in terms of its effects on the extent to which exposure to an initial attack on one's position increases the ability to counterargue effectively and, therefore, decreases the influence of subsequent attacks.

Fishbein and Ajzen (1975)

A somewhat different formalization of belief processes was proposed by Fishbein and Ajzen (1975). These authors distinguished between the acceptance of a communication's implications as valid and the change in beliefs that results from this acceptance. Specifically, they postulated that the acceptance of a communication is a function of the quantity

$$p(A) = (1 - D)^{1/f}, \qquad [4]$$

where D is the discrepancy between the recipient's a priori belief in a proposition and the position advocated by a message $(0 < D < 1)$, and f denotes facilitating factors that increase acceptability of a communication, such as a persuasive source. The actual change in the belief induced by the message, C, is given by the equation:

$$C = D(A) = D(1 - D)^{1/f} \qquad [5]$$

Thus, change in the belief is greater when the discrepancy between the implications of the message and one's prior belief is moderate (e.g., $D = .5$) than when it is either large (e.g., $D = 1$) or small (e.g., $D = 0$). At the same time, the amount of change produced by a given discrepancy will be less when facilitation (f) is high (e.g., the source is highly credible). Evidence consistent with supporting this conceptualization was obtained by Hovland and Pritzker (1957). Although this conceptualization and McGuire's (1968) theory can both be brought to bear on the same phenomena, the different implications of the two conceptualizations have not been clearly articulated.

Belief–Attitude Relations

The aforementioned theories of belief formation and change could potentially be viewed as components of the more general theory of attitude formation and change proposed by Fishbein (1963; see also Fishbein & Ajzen, 1975). Fishbein postulated that people's attitude toward an object is an additive function of their evaluations of a set of attributes that happen to be salient at the time, each weighted by their belief that the object has the attribute (see Equation 1). To the extent that Equation 1 describes the process whereby people compute their attitudes on the basis of their beliefs and evaluations of individual features, situational and informational factors that influence people's beliefs about an object should have a predictable influence on their attitudes as well.

Implications of this possibility were confirmed by Albarracín and Wyer (2001; see also Albarracín, 2002). They concluded that people who receive a persuasive message first compute their beliefs in the arguments contained in it and then, if these beliefs are above a certain threshold of probability, assess the favorableness of their implications and increment their attitudes accordingly. This conclusion is consistent with evidence that beliefs are often formed spontaneously in the course of comprehending information, whereas evaluations may require more deliberative processing (Gilbert, 1991; Wyer & Radvansky, 1999).

HEURISTIC BASES OF BELIEF FORMATION AND CHANGE

As we discussed in the previous section, the beliefs that people form about the world in which they live are partly a function of the knowledge they have accessible in memory and use as a basis for computing them. To this extent, beliefs are often unstable, depending on situational factors that make different subsets of knowledge accessible in memory at the time the beliefs are reported.

However, beliefs are not based on the knowledge people acquire alone. They can also be influenced by factors that have little to do with the persons, objects, or events to which they pertain. That is, people may employ heuristic criteria in estimating the likelihood of an event, or the truth of an assertion, independently of the body of acquired knowledge that might potentially be brought to bear on it.

The use of judgmental heuristics to make inferences about real and hypothetical events is very well established. Research bearing on the influence of heuristics has been reviewed in some detail elsewhere (Ajzen, 1996; Kahneman, Slovic, & Tversky, 1982; S. Sherman & Corty, 1984) and is unnecessary to elaborate in the present context. Many heuristics can be viewed as a subset of the implicit theories or implicational molecules noted in an earlier section. However, they normally pertain to more general criteria for judgment rather than to specific domains of knowledge. In this section, we consider three such criteria: the ease of retrieving belief-relevant knowledge, subjective familiarity, and the ease of imaging the situations to which a belief pertains.

Ease of Retrieval

One of the best-known and well-established criteria for belief formation was identified by Tversky and Kahneman (1973) and was labeled, somewhat misleadingly, an *availability heuristic*. It is more appropriately referred to as an *ease-of-retrieval* heuristic and can be viewed as an application of the following implicational molecule:

[X occurs frequently (infrequently); Instances of X come to mind easily (with difficulty)]

This molecule can be used to infer that if things occur frequently, they are easy to remember. As already noted, this proposition is not always true. That is, novel or unexpected events are often thought about more extensively than common ones and, therefore, are relatively more likely to come to mind more easily (Wyer & Hartwick, 1980). Thus, it may be the frequency with which something is thought about, and not the frequency of its occurrence per se, that determines the ease of retrieving it from memory.

Be that as it may, the most interesting applications of the ease-of-retrieval molecule concern the converse, namely, that if instances of an object or event come to mind easily, they are likely to have occurred frequently. Thus, to use Tversky and Kahneman's (1973) classic example, people are likely to infer that more English words begin with the letter k than have k as the third letter. This inference is actually incorrect. However, words that begin with k come to mind more easily than words with k as the third letter, and people's beliefs are based on this criterion. Three quite different bodies of research that exemplify the role of ease of retrieval in belief formation are worth discussing in some detail.

The Effect of Ease of Retrieval on Inferences About Oneself and Others

One of the more imaginative applications of the ease-of-retrieval heuristic was made by Norbert Schwarz and his colleagues (for a review, see Schwarz, 1998a). In a typical study (Schwarz et al., 1991), some participants were asked to generate 6 instances of assertive behavior they had performed recently, whereas others were asked to generate 12. Then, they were asked to estimate the likelihood that they were assertive. Not surprisingly, participants typically reported more instances of assertiveness when they were asked to generate 12 than when they were asked to generate 6. Nevertheless, they judged themselves to be less assertive when asked to generate 12 rather than 6 instances of assertiveness. Participants who were told to generate 6 instances of the attribute apparently found it easy to do so and, therefore, inferred that they possessed the attribute. In contrast, participants found it difficult to generate 12 instances and, therefore, concluded that they did not have the attribute. In other words, participants did not base their beliefs on the actual number of instances of the behavior they were able to remember. Rather, they used the difficulty of generating these instances as the criterion.

People do not always ignore the implications of their past knowledge, of course. However, their computation of a belief on the basis of these implications is cognitively effortful. Consequently, they may only perform these operations when ease of retrieval is likely to be an unreliable criterion. In other conditions of Schwarz et al.'s (1991) research, for example, participants generated instances of assertiveness in the presence of distracting background music. In this case, participants apparently attributed their difficulty of generating instances to the distraction and to their lack of knowledge. In these conditions, therefore, they judged themselves as more assertive when they had generated 12 instances rather than 6.

The use of an ease-of-retrieval heuristic as a basis for judgment is quite pervasive, having been identified in research on consumer judgments as well as beliefs about oneself (see Menon & Raghubir, 1998). Further examples are described later in this chapter. The heuristic's implications can be quite ironic. For example, people may be less likely to believe that a proposition is true if they have attempted to generate a large number of reasons for its validity than if they have thought about only a few. Research by Wänke, Bless, and Biller (1996) supports this speculation. Some participants were asked to generate either three or seven arguments that either favored or opposed a specific issue, after which they were asked to report their own position on the issue. Other, yoked participants read the arguments that individuals in the first group had written. The yoked participants reported themselves to be more in favor of the position advocated when they had read seven-argument responses than when they had read three-argument responses, confirming the assumption that the substantive implications of the seven-argument sets were relatively more persuasive. Nevertheless, the participants who had actually generated the arguments judged themselves to be *less* in favor of the position when they had generated seven arguments than when they had generated only three. Thus, the effects of ease of retrieval overrode the effects of actual knowledge.

Perceptions of Social Reality

A more direct application of the ease-of-retrieval heuristic is exemplified by research on the impact of television on beliefs and opinions (O'Guinn & Shrum, 1997; Shrum, O'Guinn, Semenik, & Faber, 1991; Shrum, Wyer, & O'Guinn, 1998). Much of our knowledge about people and events comes from watching television; people watch an average of over $4\frac{1}{2}$ hours of television daily (Nielsen, 1995). However, the information acquired in this manner obviously does not provide an accurate picture of the world in general. For one thing, television newscasts usually focus on events that are newsworthy, and, therefore, give priority to things that occur infrequently. Fictitious events that are shown on television are biased in other ways. Soap operas, for example, are prone to portray individuals with affluent life styles. Other shows are prone to convey aggression and the individuals involved in it (police, shady characters, etc.). In short, the people and events that are seen on television are not representative of those that occur in real life.

Effects of Exposure Frequency.   People are likely to dissociate the information they receive from its source as time goes on (Cook, Gruder, Hennigan, & Flay, 1979; Hovland, Lumsdaine, & Sheffield, 1949: Moore & Hutchinson, 1995). This dissociation is partly a result of the fact that people think about the referents of information more extensively than they think about the context in which it was acquired. Consequently, people who are asked to infer the incidence of persons and events in the real world may draw on exemplars they have seen on television without considering where they encountered them. To this extent, they may tend to overestimate the incidence of events that are over-represented on television, particularly when they are frequent television viewers.

The *cultivation effect* of television is well documented (see Gerbner, Gross, Morgan, & Signorielli, 1994). Shrum and his colleagues provide strong support for an ease-of-retrieval interpretation of the effect. For example, frequent soap opera viewers are relatively more likely than infrequent viewers to overestimate the proportion of Americans who belong to a country club or who have a swimming pool in their back yard. Ironically, they are also more likely to overestimate the incidence of crime or the number of policemen (O'Guinn & Shrum, 1997). Moreover, they make these estimates more quickly than infrequent viewers do, confirming the assumption that frequent viewers have instances of the characteristics being judged relatively more accessible in memory. These effects are evident even when other factors that might intuitively account for the relation between television watching and perceptions (e.g., educational or socioeconomic level) are controlled.

It is worth noting, however, that the effects of viewing frequency on people's beliefs can be reduced or eliminated by calling their television watching habits to their attention (Shrum et al., 1998) or by increasing their motivation to make correct judgments (Shrum, 1999). These data suggest that people can distinguish between events they see on television and those they learn about through other sources if they motivated to do so. (Alternatively, they may apply other criteria than ease of retrieval.) Generally, however, this motivation does not exist.

Effects of Novelty.   Shrum et al.'s (1998) findings are consistent with more general evidence of the effects of exposure frequency on knowledge accessibility (Higgins, 1996; Srull & Wyer, 1979, 1980; see Postulate 1). As we have noted, however, the frequency of exposure to instances of a given type may often not be as critical as the frequency of thinking about them or the time devoted to doing so (Craik & Lockhart, 1972; Wyer & Hartwick, 1980). Thus, novel or unexpected events are likely to be thought about more extensively than common ones (Wyer & Hartwick, 1980). They should, therefore, become more accessible in memory and, as a result, should be more likely to influence judgments. Wyer and Hartwick (1980) found that implausible propositions, which may be thought about extensively at the time they are first encountered, were relatively more likely than plausible propositions to be retrieved and used as bases for beliefs in other propositions to which they were syllogistically related.

Although these results do not contradict the findings obtained by Shrum and his colleagues (1998), they raise an additional consideration. That is, novel events that are encountered on television or elsewhere in the media could stimulate more cognitive activity than familiar ones and, therefore, might become more accessible in memory for this reason. Therefore, according to the ease-of-retrieval principle, the likelihood of these novel events should be overestimated, and this should be true regardless of the amount of television one watches. Experimental evidence of this hypothesis was reported by Hamilton and Gifford (1976). In this research, participants were exposed to a set of behaviors that were ostensibly performed by different members of a social group. In some cases, 13 behaviors were presented, of which 4 were unfavorable. In other cases, 26 behaviors were presented, of which 8 were unfavorable. Therefore, the proportion of unfavorable behaviors was the same in each case, but the number of these behaviors was less in the first condition than in the second. After receiving the information, participants estimated the incidence of the unfavorable behaviors. They were more inclined to overestimate the incidence of the behaviors in the first condition than in the second. Moreover, they believed that members of the group were generally more likely to possess the trait implied by the behaviors. Analogous effects were observed when the favorableness of the minority and majority behaviors was reversed.

These findings have implications for an understanding of media effects on both beliefs and the behavior that is based on these beliefs. For example, airplane highjacking occurs very infrequently. Yet, instances of these events are often thought about extensively when they occur, and are, therefore, likely to be accessible in memory. Consequently, individuals are likely to overestimate the likelihood of the events' occurrence and, as a result, might be less willing to travel than they otherwise would.

The effects of exposure frequency identified by Shrum and his colleagues (1998) and the effects of novelty identified by Hamilton and Gifford (1976) could sometimes offset one another. However, the relative contributions of these factors can depend in part on the extent to which individuals are motivated to think about the information at the time they receive it. People are often passive recipients of the information transmitted in television sitcoms and are unlikely to think much about it. The effects of this information on perceptions of social reality may therefore increase with the frequency of exposure to it. In contrast, rare events of the sort that are seen in newscasts may stimulate substantial cognitive activity. In this case, the effects of this activity may influence frequency estimates despite the novelty of the event, thus overriding the cultivation effects observed by Shrum et al.

Contextual Influences on the Accessibility of Belief-Relevant Information

Perhaps a more general indication of the effect of ease of retrieval is found in the impact of knowledge accessibility on judgments. That is, people are likely to infer that the information that comes easily to mind is likely to be representative of the entire body of knowledge they have available. Consequently, they may often use this information as a basis for judgment without searching for other information that could also be relevant (Taylor & Fiske, 1978). This possibility is exemplified by research on the way that beliefs are influenced by the context in which they are solicited. Although this research has been summarized in detail elsewhere (e.g., Schwarz, 1994; Strack, 1994), two examples are particularly noteworthy.

The Effect of Prior Judgments on Subsequent Ones.   The criteria that are used to answer a question in a belief questionnaire can be influenced by concepts that have been activated and used to answer earlier questions. This influence is most apparent when the two beliefs are normally based on similar criteria. For example, consider the proposition that the American Nazi Party should be allowed to speak on campuses and the more general proposition that members of social and political organizations should be allowed to express their views in public. Many considerations that underlie beliefs in the first proposition are relevant to the second as well. To this extent, people who report their belief in the first proposition may activate concepts and knowledge that, having become accessible in memory, influence the belief they report in the second one.

However, this effect may be contingent on whether respondents think that the questioner expects them to use similar or different criteria. Strack, Martin, and Schwarz (1988) point out that when people encounter related items in a belief questionnaire, they often infer that the questioner considers the items to mean different things and, therefore, expects them to use different criteria for evaluating the items. (Otherwise, why is the questioner asking both questions?) Consequently, they may intentionally exclude the criteria they use in responding to the first item from consideration when computing their response to the second. To continue with our example, suppose people who have reported their belief that the American Nazi Party should be allowed to speak on campuses are likely to activate reasons why this should not be the case. Therefore, if they are subsequently asked their beliefs about groups in general, they might normally use these reasons as bases for reporting these beliefs as well, and, consequently, might report less strong beliefs in this proposition than they otherwise would. However, suppose participants assume that they are supposed to use different criteria in responding to the two questions. Then, they might intentionally exclude the criteria they used to answer the first question from consideration in responding to the second and, as a result, might report their belief in the second question to be stronger than they would otherwise.

A study by Ottati, Riggle, Wyer, Schwarz, and Kuklinski (1989) supports these possibilities. People reported their beliefs in a series of general propositions about free speech similar to that described in the preceding example. In some cases, however, a related proposition that referred to either a highly respected group (e.g., the American Civil Liberties Union) or a negatively regarded group (e.g., the American Nazi Party) was also included. When this group-specific item occurred six items before the general one, it had a positive effect on participants' responses to the second item; that is, participants reported stronger beliefs in the proposition if the earlier one had referred to the ACLU than if it had referred to the Nazi Party. When the group-specific item occurred immediately before the general one, however, it had a negative impact; that is, participants reported stronger beliefs in the general proposition if the preceding one had referred to the American Nazi Party.

The Effects of Comparative Judgments on Absolute Judgments.   A quite different effect of ease of retrieval on beliefs was identified in a series of studies by Mussweiler and Strack (1999a; 1999b; 2000a; 2000b; for a review, see Mussweiler, 2003). In a typical study, some participants might be asked to compare a target object to a high value (e.g., "Is the Nile longer or shorter than 3,000 miles?"). Others might be asked to compare it to a very low value ("Is the Nile longer or shorter than 50 miles?"). Then, after making this comparative judgment, participants are asked to estimate the actual value of the object in question (e.g., the actual length of the Nile). Participants typically make larger estimates in the first condition than in the second. Moreover, this is true regardless of plausibility of the high and low values specified in the comparative items and occurs even when participants perceive these values to have been selected at random.

In accounting for these effects, Mussweiler and Strack (1999a, 1999b, 2000a, 2000b) assumed that in responding to the first question, participants activate concepts associated with the value assigned to the standard, and that once these concepts become accessible in memory, they influence the criteria that participants use to generate the absolute estimates they report later. (Support for this assumption was confirmed by evidence that making comparative judgments increases the speed of identifying standard-related concepts in a later lexical decision task; see Mussweiler & Strack, 1999a).

Familiarity

The effect of ease of retrieval is particularly evident when people's beliefs are a function of the frequency with which instances of an event or state of affairs occurred. However, many beliefs are not of this type. Many beliefs, for example, pertain to the occurrence of a single object, event, or state of affairs (e.g., that George Washington had red hair, that the capital of Tanzania is Dar es Salaam, or that the Cleveland Indians won the 1920 World Series). Such beliefs are not based on estimates of frequency per se. Nevertheless, ease of retrieval may play a role in the computation of these beliefs as well.

Specifically, if the elements of a statement can be understood in terms of concepts or knowledge that come to mind quickly, the statement is likely to seem familiar and, therefore, to have been encountered at some time in the past. Therefore, it is assumed to be true. A well-known conceptualization of recognition memory by Gillund and Shiffrin (1984) supports this contention. They assumed that people's beliefs that an item was contained in a list they have encountered earlier are based on the item's subjective familiarity. They further predicted that although the item's familiarity is determined in part by its actual presence or absence in the original list, it could be influenced by a number of other factors as well, including the item's semantic or structural similarity to other, previously acquired concepts and knowledge and the similarity of the situational context in which the item being judged to situations the recipient has encountered in the past.

More generally, people's beliefs that they have encountered a piece of information in a particular situation may be a function of its similarity to other, previously formed concepts and knowledge that were acquired before this situation occurred. However, the reverse may also be true. That is, beliefs that an information item's familiarity is due to one's general knowledge about its referent could be influenced by exposure to the item in a particular, perhaps irrelevant situational context (e.g., an experiment). Two provocative demonstrations of this phenomenon were conducted by Hasher, Goldstein, and Toppin (1977) and Jacoby, Kelley, Brown, and Jasechko (1989). In Hasher et al.'s study, participants completed a belief questionnaire containing statements whose validity was likely to be unknown to college students (e.g., "The capital of Tanzania is Dar es Salaam"). Several days later, they completed a second questionnaire that contained some of the statements they had seen earlier. Participants reported stronger beliefs in these statements when they encountered them the second time than they had at first. Presumably, the statements seemed familiar to participants when they read them the second time, but they misattributed the statements' familiarity to their prior knowledge about the persons or events to which the statements referred rather than to the presence of the items in the questionnaire they had completed earlier. Consequently, they reported the statements as more likely to be true.

In a conceptually similar study, Jacoby et al. (1989) exposed participants to names of persons, some of whom were fictitious. Then, 24 hours later, participants were given a second list of names and asked to indicate which of them referred to well-known persons. The second list contained some of the same fictitious names that participants had encountered earlier. Participants were more likely to believe that these names referred to well-known persons than names they had not seen before. Thus, as Jacoby et al. (1989) suggested, the persons "became famous overnight."

Simulation: The Effects of Constructing Explanations for a Situation on Beliefs in its Occurrence

Ease of retrieval can influence beliefs in yet another way. In many cases, specific instances of a situation may not exist or, at least, may not easily come to mind. In this case, beliefs may be based on the plausibility of the antecedent conditions that might give rise to the situation at hand. The identification of these antecedents could often be based on an implicit theory of the causal relations among the events, as suggested earlier. However, when several alternative theory-based explanations of a situation might potentially be generated, the explanation that is easiest to construct is most likely to be applied. Moreover, the easier it is for someone to construct a particular explanation of a hypothetical event or state of affairs, the more likely the person is to believe that the situation has occurred in the past or might occur in the future.

This possibility is captured by the *simulation* heuristic proposed by Kahneman and Tversky (1982b). However, the general conception that easy-to-explain events are believed more likely to occur has general implications for a wide variety of specific phenomena that bear on the effects of constructing explanations for a situation on beliefs in its occurrence.

Informational and Situational Effects of Explanation Generation on Belief Formation

Evidence that the ease of constructing an explanation of an event can increase beliefs in its occurrence is provided by Pennington and Hastie (1986, 1988, 1992). In one study (Pennington & Hastie, 1988), participants read the transcript of a court case containing testimony for both the prosecution and the defense. Although the content of the transcript was the same in all conditions, the order of conveying the testimony for each side varied. In *witness-order* conditions, the testimony for a given side was organized according to the witness who provided it, as it was conveyed in the original trial. In *story-order* conditions, the testimony was conveyed in the order it became relevant in constructing a narrative of the events that led up to the crime, the crime itself, and its aftermath. After reading the transcript, participants recommended a verdict and estimated their confidence that their judgment was correct. Findings indicated that when the testimonies for each side were presented in a different order, over 70% of the participants favored the verdict implied by the testimony that was conveyed in story order. In contrast, when both sets of testimony were conveyed in the same order, an equal proportion of participants favored each side. Moreover, participants were more confident of their judgments when the testimonies were both conveyed in story order rather than witness order.

The Effect of Generating an Explanation on Predictions

Pennington and Hastie's findings provide convincing evidence that information about an event stimulates stronger beliefs when it is conveyed in a way that makes an explanation for the event easy to construct. A corollary of this conclusion is that if individuals are induced to explain an event whose occurrence is uncertain, this activity should increase the ease with which this explanation will come to mind in the future and, therefore, should increase beliefs that the event has occurred or will occur. Three studies bear on this possibility. In a study by Ross, Lepper, Strack, and Steinmetz (1977), participants read a clinical case study with instructions to explain why the protagonist might have engaged in a particular behavior (e.g., committing suicide or donating a substantial sum of money to the Peace Corps). They later predicted that the event they had explained was more likely to have occurred than the events they had not explained, despite being told that there was no evidence that the protagonist had engaged in either act. Analogously, Sherman, Skov, Hervitz, and Stock (1981) found that people who were arbitrarily asked to explain why they might succeed or fail on an anagrams task later predicted that they would attain the outcome they had explained. Moreover, their actual task performance confirmed this prophecy. Participants apparently retrieved a selective subset of self-knowledge for use in generating their explanation that they later brought to bear on their prediction. Their prediction, in turn, was used as a standard at the time they actually performed the task, motivating them to attain the performance level it implied.

The selective retrieval of self-knowledge to explain one's own behavior may occur sponta-neously. In a study by Ross, Lepper, and Hubbard (1975), participants received false feedback that they had done either well or poorly in distinguishing between actual and bogus suicide notes. Later, they were debriefed, being shown compelling evidence that the feedback they re-ceived bore no resemblance to their actual performance. Nevertheless, participants were more likely to predict they would do well on a similar task in the future if they had been led to believe that they had performed well on the first task than if they had been led to believe they had done poorly. It seems reasonable to suppose that participants who received feedback that deviated from their expectations spontaneously attempted to explain it and, in doing so, selectively retrieved a body of self-knowledge about their past experiences that provided a plausible narrative-based causal account of it. Later, they used this representation as a basis for their predictions without considering the validity of the feedback that stimulated its construction.

The Effects of Generating Explanations on Hindsight Bias

The preceding studies suggest that individuals use the first explanation of a situation that comes to mind (e.g., the explanation they can generate most quickly and easily) as a basis for their belief that the situation will occur, and that they seldom consider other possibilities that, although plausible, could come to mind less easily. This tendency could underlie the hindsight bias identified by Fischoff (1975, 1982; for a review, see Hawkins & Hastie, 1990). That is, people who know that an event has occurred often overestimate the likelihood that they would have predicted it. This could occur because people who are told that the event has occurred attempt to generate a plausible explanation for it and, if this can be done easily, conclude that its occurrence was foreordained.

If this interpretation is correct, however, the magnitude of the hindsight bias should be altered by either increasing or decreasing participants' perceptions of the ease of explaining the event they are asked to consider. This was demonstrated using procedures similar to that employed by Schwarz (1998a) and his colleagues to investigate the effects of ease of retrieval. For example, Sanna, Schwarz, and Stocker (2002) told participants that an event had occurred and to generate either 2 or 10 thoughts about why the event happened. Participants who generated few thoughts increased their belief that the event was inevitable, thereby strengthening the hindsight bias. However, participants who generated 10 thoughts, which was difficult to do, decreased their belief that the event was foreordained. Correspondingly generating a large number of reasons why the event might not have occurred increased beliefs in its inevitability (Sanna & Schwarz, 2003).

Affective Influences on Beliefs

As exemplified by the impact of ease of retrieval on beliefs, people often base their judgments on their subjective reactions to the stimuli being judged. The use of positive and negative affect as information about one's feelings toward an object and, therefore, evaluations of the object, is widely recognized (for reviews, see Schwarz & Clore, 1996; Wyer, Clore, & Isbell, 1999). Although affect is primarily relevant to evaluative judgments (e.g., attitudes), it can sometimes influence beliefs as well.

For example, people may base their estimates of the likelihood of a negative event on the anxiety they experience when they think about it, based on the assumption that their feelings are due to their concern that the event is likely to occur. In a study by Johnson and Tversky (1983), for example, people were induced to feel anxious by reading descriptions of an emotion-evoking tragic event (e.g., a fatal accident). These participants reported stronger beliefs than control subjects in the likelihood that other, unrelated events (cancer, an earthquake, etc.) would occur. Moreover, this effect did not depend on the similarity of the event they had read about to the events being predicted. Thus, participants misattributed the anxiety they were experiencing as a result of reading about the first event to their feelings about other events as well, and used these feelings as a basis for their judgments. To this extent, one might expect the impact of these feelings to decrease when people's attention is explicitly called to the actual source of their feelings. However, Gasper and Clore (1998) showed that this was the case only if the situation-induced anxiety that participants were experiencing was inconsistent with their chronic level of anxiety. Chronically anxious individuals were influenced by the anxiety they were experiencing in all cases.

The positive or negative affect that people experience can also have an indirect influence on their beliefs. Participants in a study by Albarracín and Wyer (2000) read a persuasive communication under conditions in which they were feeling happy or unhappy. When participants were able to concentrate on the message, they typically based their attitudes toward the position advocated on their beliefs in the arguments contained in the message, reporting more favorable attitudes when the arguments were strong than when they were weak. In some conditions, however, participants were distracted from thinking about the communication at the time it was presented (for a treatment of the role of distraction in this domain, see Albarracín & Kumkale, 2003). These individuals based their attitudes on the extraneous affect they were experiencing instead. Moreover, these attitudes, once formed, influenced their beliefs in the consequences of the policy being advocated independently of the quality of the arguments in the message they had read earlier.

MOTIVATIONAL BASES FOR BELIEFS

The research and theory we have described thus far has focused on the cognitive processes that underlie belief formation and change and the type of knowledge to which these processes are applied. In some cases, beliefs are formed spontaneously in the course of comprehension (Wyer & Radvansky, 1999). In other cases, however, beliefs can have motivational roots. That is, they are often formed for a purpose. Certain motives for belief formation and change have been implicit in our previous discussion. Others, however, are less apparent. An understanding of the role of motivation is complicated in part by the fact that people may often have more than one goal, and beliefs that satisfy one goal can conflict with the attainment of others. In this section, we review a number of these motives and describe representative research that bears on their influence.

Types of Motives

A comprehensive review of the motives that potentially influence the formation and change in beliefs, and the cognitive responses to information that bears on them, is provided by Kunda (1990). For example, people may be motivated to be accurate (Kruglanski, 1980), to be consistent (Festinger, 1957; Heider, 1946; McGuire, 1960), to maintain a positive self-image (Baumeister, 1997), to believe in a just world (Lerner, Miller, & Holmes, 1976), to gain closure (Kruglanski, 1980), to avoid uncertainty and ambiguity (Harvey, Hunt, & Schroder, 1961; Roney & Sorrentino, 1995), and to avoid engaging in excessive cognitive effort (Chaiken, 1987; Taylor & Fiske, 1978). A number of these motives, however, may be manifestations of a more general one: to construct a representation of oneself and the world that permits one to cope effectively with life situations and, therefore, to lead a happy and successful life. Effective coping presumably requires that perceptions of oneself and one's world are a sufficiently close approximation of reality to permit the consequences of social events to be predicted and interpreted. At the same time, it also requires personality characteristics and abilities that enable one to perform successfully in one's social and physical environment. Finally, it requires that one's efforts be rewarded, and that one does not encounter misfortune for circumstances beyond one's control. The beliefs that one constructs of oneself and the world may be partly motivated by a desire to believe that these conditions exist.

However, beliefs that satisfy one of these objectives may be incompatible with others. An accurate perception of oneself, for example, is not always favorable. Moreover, misfortunes do occur for fortuitous and uncontrollable reasons. Thus, the maintenance of favorable concepts about oneself and the world may often be at the expense of accuracy, and beliefs bearing on them can reflect a compromise between the implications of these motives (Kunda, 1990).

Responses to Belief Dilemmas

People often receive information that conflicts with the implications of the motive-based representation they have constructed of themselves and the world in general. For example, it might suggest that their previously formed beliefs are inaccurate. Alternatively, the information might imply that individuals do not have the personal qualities necessary to ensure a happy life, or that their pursuit of happiness might not be successful for reasons beyond their control. The acceptance of such information as valid might require a modification of not only the beliefs to which it is directly relevant, but also to others with which they are associated in the knowledge representation in which they are embedded. These modifications, however, not only could have negative implications for oneself and others but also might be cognitively effortful. For these reasons, people are often motivated to resist change in their beliefs or the adoption of new ones, if they can accommodate to information in other ways.

Several possible responses to belief-related information were postulated by Abelson (1959), and others have been identified elsewhere (e.g., Kunda, 1990). For example:

1. *Reinterpretation.* People might selectively activate concepts that permit them to interpret the information as either consistent rather than inconsistent with their prior beliefs and opinions or, alternatively, as irrelevant. For example, they might activate knowledge that calls into question the credibility of the information's source. Or, if the information pertains to their own behavior, people might attribute the behavior or its outcome to situational factors that minimize its implications for their previously formed beliefs.

2. *Counterarguing.* People might retrieve previously acquired knowledge that permits them to refute the validity of the information or its implications.

3. *Bolstering.* People might selectively retrieve and review information that implies that their existing beliefs are valid for other reasons, despite the implications of the new information presented.

4. *Compartmentalization.* People might attempt to divide the referent of the new information into components, with the information being relevant to one, relatively unimportant component.

5. *Transcendence.* People might attempt to view the implications of the information within a broader conceptual framework that renders its implications, although valid, to be relatively unimportant.

These various responses require different amounts of cognitive effort. Moreover, this effort might sometimes be greater than that required to accept the information's implications at face value. For example, information can often pertain to concepts or propositions that are remotely connected to other components of one's cognitive system. In this case, the acceptance of the information as valid is likely to require little modification of previously formed beliefs. However, if the beliefs that are implicated by the new information occupy a central position in one's cognitive network, acceptance of the information's implications might require a change in not only the beliefs to which it directly pertains but many others with which it is associated. To avoid this disruption, other responses to the information may be attempted.

More generally, responses to belief-discrepant information may be governed by a priority system in which the strategies that are easiest to apply are given priority, with more cognitively demanding strategies attempted only if the initial attempts prove to be unsuccessful (Chaiken, 1987). The number of strategies that are attempted may depend in part on situational and individual difference factors that influence the need for closure (Kruglanski, 1980).

In this regard, it is obviously difficult if not impossible to construct a completely accurate perception of oneself and the world, or to accommodate the implications of the competing motives that may underlie information processing (e.g., the motive to be accurate and, at the same time, to maintain a positive self-image). Therefore, it seems likely that people do not attempt to attain this ideal. Rather, they have a *tolerance threshold*, below which they are willing to accept the implications of the information without further attempts to reconcile its inconsistency with other beliefs or the goals to which it is relevant. In an analysis of decision making, Simon (1957) postulated that people engage in *satisficing*. That is, they often do not attempt to attain the best solution possible, but rather, settle for one that is above some minimal threshold of acceptability and, therefore, is good enough. A similar strategy might be employed in responding to belief-relevant information. Kunda (1990) also notes that people might often strike some compromise between accuracy and desirability in responding to belief-relevant experiences. The nature of this compromise might depend on the tolerance threshold that they invoke.

With these considerations in mind, we will review briefly some of the literature that bears on the role of motivational factors on belief formation and change and the cognitive responses that are stimulated by belief-relevant information. Our review is not intended to be exhaustive, but rather, to be representative of the concerns addressed in the areas to be covered.

Accuracy and Efficiency

People are presumably motivated to construct an accurate perception of themselves and their environment (see Kruglanski, 1980; Kruglanski & Stroebe, this volume). This motive may derive in part from pragmatic considerations. That is, people are undoubtedly better able to cope effectively with daily life experiences if they have an accurate perception of themselves, other persons, and more generally, the world in which they live. However, the acquisition of knowledge that would be necessary in order to attain perfect accuracy is difficult if not impossible. Moreover, as Kruglanski (1980) also notes, people may often be motivated by the desire to make a quick judgment or decision and, therefore, may be unwilling or unable to devote the time and energy required to be completely accurate even if it were possible to do so. That is, they may be satisfied with a construction of the world that is *sufficient* to permit them to cope effectively, even if it is not perfectly correct.

Chaiken's (1980, 1987) formulation of belief and attitude formation and change is based on similar assumptions. To reiterate, people who are called on to estimate the likelihood that a proposition is true may engage in belief-relevant cognitive activity until their confidence that their estimate exceeds a certain threshold, after which they make the judgment and terminate further processing. This threshold might depend on a number of situational and individual difference factors that influence the importance of the estimate to be made. Thus, participants who are extrinsically or intrinsically motivated to be accurate may adopt a high threshold and, therefore, may expend more effort in computing their belief than they would otherwise. For example, they may be more inclined to think extensively about the implications of the information they have acquired, and may retrieve and bring more previously acquired knowledge to bear on it. Moreover, they may be correspondingly less inclined to base their belief on the first relevant criterion that comes to mind.

The effects of numerous situational and individual difference factors on the impact of information can potentially be conceptualized in terms of their impact on the threshold that people adopt. For example, this threshold, and consequently the amount of cognitive activity they expend in the processing of this information, may increase with their need for cognition (Cacioppo & Petty, 1982; Petty & Cacioppo, 1986) or with their intolerance of ambiguity (Webster & Kruglanski, 1994). It could also vary with the importance of the belief to the information recipient. Transitory situational factors, such as the affect that people experience at the time they receive information, can also influence this threshold and, therefore, can affect the amount of effort they expend in using the information to form beliefs to which it is relevant (Bless, Bohner, Schwarz, & Strack, 1990; Bodenhausen, 1993; Clore & Schnall, this volume).

Desirability

People are frequently motivated to think well of themselves and the individuals they care about and to believe that neither they nor others will come to harm (see Weinstein, 1980; but see Chang, Asakawa, & Sanna, 2001; Heine & Lehmen, 1995; Shepperd, Ouellette, & Fernandez, 1996). This state of affairs, however, does not always exist in actuality; people are not always admirable, and the world is not always benevolent. Thus, beliefs that convey an accurate picture of reality can have unfavorable implications, and beliefs with favorable implications are not always correct. Under these conditions, the results of people's cognitive activity may reflect a compromise between accuracy and desirability.

McGuire (1960, 1981; McGuire & McGuire, 1991) postulated that individuals' beliefs are guided in part by wishful thinking. That is, people usually wish to maintain a positive view of themselves and the world in which they live. Therefore, they may be disposed to believe that desirable events or states of affairs are likely to occur and that undesirable events and states are unlikely. He further assumed that when beliefs that result from wishful thinking are inaccurate, they can become inconsistent with other beliefs (see Equation 2), and that when this occurs, calling attention to the inconsistency disposes people to eliminate it (McGuire, 1960; Rosen & Wyer, 1972). In fact, the evidence for wishful thinking within the paradigm used to test implications of McGuire's probabilogical model is very limited (McGuire & McGuire, 1991; Wyer, 1974). However, research in other paradigms provides much stronger confirmation of the tendency and the processes that underlie it.

For example, people appear to be motivated to maintain favorable conceptions of themselves and the attributes they possess. Consequently, they may selectively process new information and previously acquired knowledge that permits them to construct beliefs that are consistent with these conceptions (see Pyszcynski & Greenberg, 1987). This selective processing may be reflected in both their attention to new self-relevant information and their retrieval of previously acquired self-knowledge.

A compelling example of selective processing was reported by Arkin, Gleason, and Johnston (1976). Participants in this study received feedback that they had either succeeded or failed on a task under conditions that suggested that either they were personally responsible for this outcome or, alternatively, the outcome could have been due to external, situational factors. Participants who failed on the task accepted responsibility for this outcome only if no other plausible explanations existed. Conversely, participants who succeeded took responsibility regardless of whether extraneous factors could have accounted for the outcome or not.

Arkin et al.'s findings would be consistent with the priority system described earlier. That is, the implications of successful performance are quite consistent with the favorable self-concept that participants attempt to maintain of themselves and therefore could be easily assimilated into the beliefs that pertain to this concept. Therefore, participants did not bother to engage in more extensive processing. In contrast, the implications of failure, which were less consistent with their beliefs about themselves, stimulated them to seek information that would permit them to interpret this outcome as irrelevant, and they accepted the implications of this outcome only if this information was not available.

Results of a study by Wyer and Frey (1983) can be viewed similarly. In this study, participants who had ostensibly done either well or poorly on an intelligence test read a passage that conveyed both positive and negative arguments concerning the validity of intelligence tests in general. As one might expect, participants were more likely to disparage the validity of intelligence test when they had done badly than when they had not. At the same time, however, they recalled a greater proportion of arguments that supported the validity of intelligence test than other participants. The participants who did poorly apparently found it difficult to reconcile the implications of their poor performance with their previously formed beliefs about themselves, and so they attempted to refute the arguments that the intelligence tests were valid. However, their more extensive processing of this belief-discrepant information increased its accessibility in memory (Craik & Lockhart, 1972) and, therefore, increased their ability to recall it later.

Bolstering can come into play as well. This is particularly true when people receive information that a personal characteristic is important for success and well-being. In this event, people may selectively search for information that supports their belief that they have this characteristic. A study by Sanitioso, Kunda, and Fong (1990) suggests this possibility. Some participants were told that extroversion was conducive to success after leaving college, whereas others were told that introversion was conducive to success. Then, in an ostensibly unrelated study, they were asked to list behaviors they had performed in the past along a related trait dimension (shy vs. outgoing). Participants listed more behaviors that were congruent with the trait that was ostensibly conducive to success than behaviors that were incongruent with this trait. This and other studies suggested that people who have been told that a particular trait is associated with success selectively searched memory for personal experiences that confirmed their possession of the trait. Consequently, these experiences came to mind more quickly when they were called on to report instances of their behavior at a later point in time. Research in other paradigms has similar implications. For example, people are less likely to report engaging in a particular behavior (drinking coffee, brushing one's teeth) if they are told that the activity is bad for the health than if they are told it is healthy (Ross, McFarland, & Fletcher, 1981; B. Sherman & Kunda, 1989).

The information that people retrieve and use to bolster their belief that they will have a successful or happy life can also stimulate the construction of implicit theories about themselves and others that imply that they will be successful or will otherwise have desirable consequences. Kunda (1987), for example, found that college students are typically convinced that they will remain married to their first spouse for life despite knowledge that 50% of all marriages end in divorce. This belief is likely to result from their attempts to convince themselves that they personally have qualities that are uniquely conducive to marital happiness. To demonstrate this hypothesis, Kunda (1987) gave participants information about a target person who was either happily married or divorced, and whose demographic and personality characteristics either matched or did not match those of the participants themselves. Then, they asked the participants to indicate which of the target's attributes were most likely to contribute to his or her marital situation. Participants were more inclined to attribute the success of happily married targets to characteristics that matched their own than to characteristics that differed. Correspondingly, they were more likely to attribute the failure of divorced targets to traits that differed from their own than to traits that were similar. Studies in other domains yielded similar conclusions.

In combination, therefore, the series of studies described in this section suggest that despite the failure for wishful thinking to be identified in research performed by McGuire (1960, McGuire & McGuire, 1991), it seems clear that cognitive activities implied by this motive do, in fact, operate.

Beliefs in a Just World

The preceding studies suggest that people are motivated to believe that they personally have favorable attributes and, therefore, are able to cope effectively with the world in which they live. A byproduct of this motivation may be a desire to believe that the world is just and, therefore, that they (who presumably have desirable qualities) will not encounter adversity for reasons beyond their control. The just desserts molecule described in an earlier section may be partly a result of this desire. That is, people may be motivated to believe that people not only get what they deserve but also deserve what they get (Lerner & Miller, 1978; Lerner et al., 1976).

If this prediction is the case, experiences that threaten people's perceptions that the world as just may increase their motivation to adopt beliefs that bolster this perception. Wyer, Bodenhausen, and Gorman (1985) reported evidence of this tendency. Participants read a series of scenarios describing rape incidents and, in each case, reported both their belief that the defendant was convicted and their belief that the victim was partly responsible for the incident. Before doing so, however, participants (as part of a different experiment) were exposed to pictures showing acts of extreme nonsexual aggression (e.g., a lynching, a dead soldier with his skull torn apart by a bullet, a gory hit-and-run accident, etc.) that presumably called attention to injustice. These participants not only increased their belief that the defendant in the rape scenarios was convicted (that is, he got what he deserved) but also their belief that the victim was partly responsible for the incident (i.e., she deserved what she got). This pattern was true even when the defendant was a stranger and the victim vigorously resisted the attack.

Consistency

An additional motive that appears to guide belief formation and change is the desire to maintain an initial consistency among one's beliefs and opinions. This motive could be partly the result of a more general desire to construct an accurate representation of the world. The criterion for cognitive consistency, which has been studied extensively in social psychological research for decades (Heider, 1946, 1958; Festinger, 1957; for reviews, see Abelson et al., 1968), may vary. It may be conceptualized in terms of the compatibility of beliefs with the propositions that compose an implicational molecule or implicit theory. Alternatively, it might be defined in terms of Equation 2. Finally, it could be conceptualized in terms of a discrepancy between the implications of one's behavior and previously formed beliefs about the target of this behavior (Cooper & Fazio, 1984; Festinger, 1957; Wicklund & Brehm, 1976).

As noted earlier, some conceptualizations (e.g., McGuire, 1960) assume that the modification of beliefs to eliminate cognitive inconsistency occurs spontaneously once people become aware that the inconsistency exists. Other conceptualizations, however, assume that the awareness of inconsistency induces an unpleasant state of arousal or discomfort, and that changes in beliefs are motivated by a desire to eliminate this discomfort. The validity of this assumption has been convincingly established in research on cognitive dissonance theory (Festinger, 1957). This theory has typically been applied to inconsistencies between a person's behavior (e.g., publicly advocating a particular position on an issue, or a decision to perform a particular activity) and previously formed beliefs concerning the behavior's desirability (for a review, see Cooper & Fazio, 1984). In this context, Zanna and Cooper (1976), for example, showed that under conditions in which participants were led to believe that the arousal they were experiencing as a result of their belief-inconsistent behavior was attributable to other factors (e.g., to the effects of taking an arousal-inducing pill), the attempt to eliminate inconsistency through belief change is not evident.

Moreover, in a direct test of the assumption, Croyle and Cooper (1983) obtained physiological measures of participants' arousal while they voluntarily engaged in belief-discrepant behavior. Performing the behavior in these conditions induced arousal, as expected. Under conditions in which the measures of arousal were taken, however, participants' beliefs were not affected by their behavior. Apparently participants experienced arousal as a result of their dissonant behavior, but attributed it to their concern about the elaborate apparatus that was used to measure it rather than to their belief-discrepant behavior per se and, therefore, did not change these beliefs. The effects of belief-inconsistent behavior on beliefs is also eliminated by the presence of other situational factors that might account for this behavior, such as a lack of choice concerning whether or not to engage in the behavior, a high monetary incentive for performing it, or an unpleasant experimental room (for reviews, see Cooper & Fazio, 1984; Olson & Stone, this volume).

However, the arousal induced by belief-discrepant behavior and, therefore, the change in beliefs that results from it, could more fundamentally result from the implications of the behavior for one's self esteem (Cooper & Fazio, 1984). Thus, dissonance-induced belief change is most evident when one voluntarily engages in behavior that has negative consequences. Such behavior may be particularly threatening to one's concept of oneself as an intelligent person who engages in desirable activities, the outcome of which is under one's control. Thus, situational factors that permit one to preserve one's self-esteem without engaging in the cognitive activities required to change previously formed beliefs may decrease the likelihood of modifying these beliefs. (For more direct evidence that people do not engage in dissonance-induced belief change if they can bolster their self image in other ways, see Steele, 1988; Steele & Liu, 1983.)

In summary, the motivation underlying many belief-change phenomena can be conceptualized in terms of attempts to preserve a favorable self-concept and a view of the world as a place in which one's abilities and virtues are likely to be rewarded. As Kunda (1990) notes, however, the change in beliefs that results from this motivation may not always override the motive to be accurate. Thus, for example, people who voluntarily perform a behavior that is incompatible with their previously formed belief in a position may change this belief in a direction that is more consistent with the position they advocated, but they do not completely reverse it. That is, they do not totally ignore their prebehavior beliefs or the knowledge that bears on them. Rather, their beliefs appear to be a compromise between the implications of these conflicting criteria.

Other Motivational Determinants of Selective Information Processing

The motivation to cope effectively with life events can be manifested in selective information seeking of a different sort. Higgins (1998) has noted that people often have two different motivational orientations. One, *promotion* focus, disposes individuals to emphasize the desirable aspects of a present or future event to the exclusion of its negative aspects. The second, *prevention* focus, results from a desire to avoid negative features of a situation and stimulates attention to the undesirable features of an event without considering the desirable ones. These different orientations may bias the aspects of the information that one acquires in a situation and, consequently, beliefs that are based on it.

Chronic individual differences in prevention or promotion focus may exist as a result of social learning. Asians, for example, are more inclined to have a prevention focus than European-Americans are. This difference is manifested in both their attention to negative aspects of a situation in which they imagine themselves (Aaker & Lee, 2001) and their choices in multiple-attribute decision situations (Briley, Morris, & Simonson, 2000). Briley et al. (2000), for example, found that when participants were confronted with a choice between (a) a product with both extremely favorable and extremely unfavorable attributes and (b) a product with only moderately favorable and unfavorable features, European Americans typically preferred the former alternative, suggesting that they focused their attention on the potential benefits of having the products they considered without considering their potential costs. In contrast, Asians were more inclined to choose the second alternative, suggesting that they were concerned about avoiding negative attributes of the products without considering their advantages.

These different motivational orientations can be influenced by situational factors as well (see Higgins, 1998). Briley and Wyer (2002), for example, found that calling individuals' attention to their cultural identity, which made them conscious of their group membership, induced a prevention focus that influenced their choice behavior, and this was true of both Asians and Americans. These findings do not bear directly on belief formation and change. However, to the extent differences in prevention and promotion focus bias the attention that people pay to positive and negative aspects of a situation, it seems reasonable to suppose that this focus influences beliefs about this situation as well as what people choose to perform.

CONCLUDING REMARKS

This chapter has covered a lot of ground. After conceptualizing beliefs and distinguishing them from other types of cognitions, we discussed the content and organization of the knowledge in memory and the processes that lead a particular subset of knowledge to be brought to bear on the beliefs to which it is relevant. We then considered several more specific formulations of the way in which beliefs are formed both spontaneously in the course of comprehending new information and deliberately, in construing and evaluating the information's implications. In this discussion, the role of implicational molecules and implicit theories was emphasized. We then discussed heuristic bases for computing beliefs on the basis of criteria that do not involve a detailed analysis of belief-relevant knowledge. Finally, we considered the role of motivation in belief formation and change.

Despite the extensiveness of this discussion one ambiguity was not completely resolved. It remains unclear whether beliefs per se are organized and stored in memory, or whether they are computed online, based on the knowledge that happens to come to mind at the time. With few exceptions (e.g., the probabilogical model of belief organization proposed by McGuire, 1960; see also Wyer, 1974), the bulk of the research and theorizing we have discussed is compatible with the latter, constructivist point of view. It nevertheless seems reasonable to assume that beliefs, or judgments based on them, are often stored in memory as part of the knowledge people acquire and are, therefore, often available, along with other knowledge, for use as a basis for computing new beliefs. It, therefore, makes more sense to ask, not whether previously formed beliefs are formed and stored in memory, but rather, when these beliefs are stored and retrieved for use in making judgments to which they are relevant (see Albarracín, Wallace, & Glasman, in press). Future research and theorizing should address this matter.

ACKNOWLEDGMENTS

The writing of this chapter was supported in part by grants RGC HKUST 6022/00H and HKUST 6053/01H from the Research Grants Council of the Hong Kong Special Administrative Region, China, and grants K01-MH01861 and R01 NR08325 from the National Institutes of Health. We thank Ece Kumkale for assistance with the preparation of this manuscript.

REFERENCES

Aaker, J. L., & Lee, A. Y. (2001). I seek pleasures, we avoid pains: The role of self-regulatory goals in information processing and persuasion. *Journal of Consumer Research, 27,* 33–49.

Abelson, R. P. (1959). Modes of resolution of belief dilemmas. *Conflict Resolution, 3,* 343–352.

Abelson, R. P., Aronson, E., McGuire, W. J., Newcomb, T. M., Rosenberg, M. J., & Tannenbaum, P. H. (Eds.). (1968). *Theories of cognitive consistency: A sourcebook.* Chicago: Rand McNally.

Abelson, R. P., & Reich, C. M. (1969). Implicational molecules: A method for extracting meaning from input sentences. In D. E. Walker & L. M. Norton (Eds.), *Proceedings of the International Joint Conference on Artificial Intelligence.*

Abelson, R. P., & Rosenberg, M. J. (1958). Symbolic psycho-logic: A model of attitudinal cognition. *Behavioral Science, 3,* 1–13.

Adaval, R. (2001). Sometimes it just feels right: The differential weighting of affect-consistent and affect-inconsistent product information. *Journal of Consumer Research, 7,* 207–245.

Ajzen, I. (1996). The social psychology of decision making. In E. T. Higgins & A. W. Kruglanski (Eds.), *Social psychology: Handbook of basic principles* (pp. 297–325). New York: Guilford.

Albarracín, D. (2002). Cognition in persuasion: An analysis of information processing in response to persuasive communications. In M. P. Zanna (Ed.), *Advances in experimental social psychology* (Vol. 34, pp. 61–130). San Diego, CA: Academic Press.

Albarracín, D., & Kumkale, G. T. (2003). Affect as information in persuasion: A model of affect identification and discounting. *Journal of Personality and Social Psychology, 84,* 453–469.

Albarracín, D., Wallace, H. M., & Glasman, L. R. (2004). Survival and change of attitudes and other social judgments: A model of judgment activation and comparison. In M. P. Zanna (Ed.), *Advances in experimental social psychology* (Vol. 36). San Diego, CA: Academic Press.

Albarracín, D., & Wyer, R. S. (2000). The cognitive impact of past behavior: Influences on beliefs, attitudes and future behavioral decisions. *Journal of Personality and Social Psychology, 79,* 5–22.

Albarracín, D., & Wyer, R. S. (2001). Elaborative and nonelaborative processing of a behavior-related persuasive communication. *Personality and Social Psychology Bulletin, 27,* 691–705.

Anderson, J. R. (1983). *The architecture of cognition.* Cambridge, MA: Harvard University Press.

Anderson, J. R., & Bower, G. H. (1973). *Human associative memory.* Washington, DC: Winston.

Anderson, N. H. (1974). Cognitive algebra: Integration theory to applied social attribution. In L. Berkowitz (Ed.), *Advances in experimental social psychology* (Vol. 7, pp. 1–101). San Diego, CA: Academic Press.

Anderson, N. H. (1981). *Foundations of information integration theory.* New York: Academic Press.

Arkin, R. M., Gleason, J. M., & Johnston, S. (1976). Effect of perceived choice, expected outcome and observed outcome of an action on the causal attributions of actors. *Journal of Experimental Social Psychology, 12,* 151–158.

Bargh, J. A. (1994). The four horsemen of automaticity: Awareness, intention, efficiency, and control in social cognition. In R. S. Wyer & T. K. Srull (Eds.), *Handbook of social cognition* (2nd ed., Vol. 1, pp. 1–40). Hillsdale, NJ: Lawrence Erlbaum Associates.

Bargh, J. A. (1997). The automaticity of everyday life. In R. S. Wyer (Ed.), *Advances in social cognition* (Vol. 10, pp. 1–62). Mahwah, NJ: Lawrence Erlbaum Associates.

Bargh, J. A., Chen, M., & Burrows, L. (1996). Automaticity of social behavior: Direct effects of trait construct and stereotype activation on action. *Journal of Personality and Social Psychology, 71,* 230–244.

Bargh, J. A., & Pietromonaco, P. (1982). Automatic information processing and social perception: The influence of trait information presented outside of conscious awareness on impression formation. *Journal of Personality and Social Psychology, 43,* 437–449.

Baumeister, R. F. (1997). Identity, self-concept, and self-esteem: The self lost and found. In R. Hogan & J. A. Johnson (Eds.), *Handbook of personality psychology* (pp. 681–710). San Diego, CA: Academic Press.

Bear, G., & Hodun, A. (1975). Implicational principles and the cognition of confirmatory, contradictory, incomplete, and irrelevant information. *Journal of Personality and Social Psychology, 32,* 594–604.

Bem, D. J. (1967). Self-perception: An alternative interpretation of cognitive dissonance phenomena. *Psychological Review, 74,* 183–200.

Bem, D. J. (1972). Self-perception theory. In L. Berkowitz (Ed.), *Advances in experimental social psychology* (Vol. 6, pp. 1–62). New York: Academic Press.

Bem, D. J., & McConnell, H. K. (1970). Testing the self-perception explanation of dissonance phenomena: On the salience of premanipulation attitudes. *Journal of Personality and Social Psychology, 14,* 23–31.

Birnbaum, M. H., & Stegner, S. (1979). Source credibility in social judgment: Bias, expertise, and the judge's point of view. *Journal of Personality and Social Psychology, 37,* 48–74.

Black, J. B., Turner, T., & Bower, G. H. (1979). Point of view in narrative comprehension, memory, and production. *Journal of Verbal Learning and Verbal Behavior, 11,* 717–726.

Bless, H., Bohner, G., Schwarz, H., & Strack, F. (1990). Mood and persuasion: A cognitive response analysis. *Personality and Social Psychology Bulletin, 16,* 331–345.

Bobrow, D. G., & Norman, D. A. (1975). Some principles of memory schemata. In D. G. Bobrow & A. Collins (Eds.), *Representation and understanding: Studies in cognitive science* (pp. 131–149). New York: Academic Press.

Bodenhausen, G. V. (1993). Emotions, arousal, and stereotypic judgments: A heuristic model of affect and stereotyping. In D. M. Mackie & D. L. Hamilton (Eds.), *Affect, cognition, and stereotyping: Interactive processes in group perception* (pp. 13–37). San Diego: Academic Press.

Bodenhausen, G. V., & Lichtenstein, M. (1987). Social stereotypes and information processing strategies: The impact of task complexity. *Journal of Personality and Social Psychology, 52,* 871–880.

Bodenhausen, G. V., & Wyer, R. S. (1985). Effects of stereotypes on decision-making and information-processing strategies. *Journal of Personality and Social Psychology, 48,* 267–282.

Bower, G. H., Black, J. B., & Turner, T. J. (1979). Scripts in memory for texts. *Cognitive Psychology, 11,* 177–220.

Bransford, J. D., Barclay, J. R, & Franks, J. J. (1972). Sentence memory: A constructive versus interpretative approach. *Cognitive Psychology, 3,* 193–209.

Breckler, S. J. (1984a). Empirical validation of affect, behavior, and cognition as distinct components of attitude. *Journal of Personality and Social Psychology, 47,* 1191–1205.

Breckler, S. J. (1984b). Emotion and attitude change. In M. Lewis & J. M. Haviland (Eds.), *Handbook of emotion* (pp. 461–473). New York: Guilford.

Brewer, W. H., & Lichtenstein, E. H. (1981). Event schemas, story schemas, and story grammars. In J. Long & A. Baddeley (Eds.), *Attention and performance, IX* (pp. 363–379). Hillsdale, NJ: Lawrence Erlbaum Associates.

Brewer, W. H., & Nakamura, G. V. (1984). The nature and functions of schemas. In R. S. Wyer & T. K. Srull (Eds.), *Handbook of social cognition* (Vol. 1, pp. 119–160). Hillsdale, NJ: Lawrence Erlbaum Associates.

Briley, D. A., Morris, M., & Simonson, I. (2000). Reasons as carriers of culture: Dynamic versus dispositional models of cultural influence on decision making. *Journal of Consumer Research, 27,* 157–178.

Briley, D. A., & Wyer, R. S. (2002). The effect of group membership salience on the avoidance of negative outcomes: Implications for social and consumer decisions. *Journal of Consumer Research, 29,* 400–415.

Cacioppo, J. T., & Petty, R. E. (1982). The need for cognition. *Journal of Personality and Social Psychology, 42,* 116–131.

Carlston, D. E. (1980). Events, inferences and impression formation. In R. Hastie, T. Ostrom, E. Ebbesen, R. Wyer, D. Hamilton, & D. Carlston (Eds.), *Person memory: The cognitive basis of social perception* (pp. 89–119). Hillsdale, NJ: Lawrence Erlbaum Associates.

Carlston, D. E., & Smith, E. R. (1996). Principles of mental representation. In E. T. Higgins & A. W. Kruglanski (Eds.), *Social psychology: Handbook of basic principles* (pp. 184–210). New York: Guilford.

Cartwright, D., & Harary, F. (1956). Structural balance: A generalization of Heider's theory. *Psychological Review, 63,* 277–293.

Chaiken, S. (1980). Heuristic versus systematic information processing in the use of source versus message cues in persuasion. *Journal of Personality and Social Psychology, 39,* 752–766.

Chaiken, S. (1987). The heuristic model of persuasion. In M. P. Zanna, J. M. Olson, & C. P. Herman (Eds.), *Social influence: The Ontario Symposium* (Vol. 5, pp. 3–39). Hillsdale, NJ: Lawrence Erlbaum Associates.

Chang, E. C., Asakawa, K., & Sanna, L. J. (2001). Cultural variations in optimistic and pessimistic bias: Do Easterners really expect the worst and Westerners really expect the best when predicting future life events? *Journal of Personality & Social Psychology, 81,* 476–491.

Choi, I., Nisbett, R. E., & Norenzayan, A. (1999). Causal attribution across cultures: Variation and universality. *Psychological Bulletin, 125,* 47–63.

Colcombe, S. J., & Wyer, R. S. (2002). The role of prototypes in the mental representation of temporally-related events. *Cognitive Psychology, 44,* 67–103.

Collins, A. M., & Loftus, E. F. (1975). A spreading-activation theory of semantic processing. *Psychological Review, 82,* 407–428.

Conway, M., & Ross, M. (1984). Getting what you want by revising what you had. *Journal of Personality and Social Psychology, 47,* 738–748.

Cook, T. D., Gruder, C. L., Hennigan, K. M., & Flay, B. R. (1979). History of the sleeper effect: Some logical pitfalls in accepting the null hypothesis. *Psychological Bulletin, 86,* 662–679.

Cooper, J., & Fazio, R. H. (1984). A new look at dissonance theory. In L. Berkowitz (Ed.), *Advances in experimental social psychology* (Vol. 17, pp. 229–266). New York: Academic Press.

Craik, F. I. M., & Lockhart, R. S. (1972). Levels of processing: A framework for memory research. *Journal of Verbal Learning and Verbal Behavior, 11,* 671–684.

Croyle, R. T., & Cooper, J. (1983). Dissonance arousal: Physiological evidence. *Journal of Personality and Social Psychology, 45,* 782–791.

Dillehay, R. C., Insko, C. A., & Smith, M. M. (1966). Logical consistency and attitude change. *Journal of Personality and Social Psychology, 3*, 646–654.

Eagly, A. H., & Chaiken, S. (1993). *The psychology of attitudes*. Fort Worth, TX: Harcourt Brace.

Eagly, A. H., & Chaiken, S. (1998). Attitude structure and function. In D. T. Gilbert, S. T. Fiske, et al. (Eds.), *Handbook of social psychology*, 4th ed. (Vol. 1, pp. 269–322). Boston: McGraw-Hill.

Edwards. A. L. (1957). *Techniques of attitude scale construction*. New York: Appleton-Century-Crofts.

Festinger, L. (1957). *A theory of cognitive dissonance*. Stanford, CA: Stanford University Press.

Festinger, L., & Maccoby, E. (1964). On resistance to persuasive communications. *Journal of Abnormal and Social Psychology, 68*, 359–366.

Fischoff, B. (1975). Hindsight ≠ foresight: The effect of outcome knowledge on judgment under uncertainty. *Journal of Experimental Psychology: Human Perception and Performance, 1*, 288–299.

Fischoff, B. (1982). For those condemned to study the past: Heuristics and biases in hindsight. In D. Kahneman, P. Slovic, & A. Tversky (Eds.), *Judgment under uncertainty: Heuristics and biases* (pp. 332–351). New York: Cambridge University Press.

Fishbein, M. (1963). An investigation of the relationships between beliefs about an object and attitude toward that object. *Human Relations, 16*, 233–239.

Fishbein, M. (1967). A behavior theory approach to the relations between beliefs about an object and the attitude toward the object. In M. Fishbein (Ed.), *Readings in attitude theory and measurement* (pp. 389–400). New York: Wiley.

Fishbein, M., & Ajzen, I. (1975). Belief, attitude, intention, and behavior: An introduction to theory and research. Reading, MA: Addison-Wesley.

Fiske, S. T. (1998). Stereotyping, prejudice, and discrimination. In D. T. Gilbert, S. T. Fiske, & G. Lindzey (Eds.), *Handbook of social psychology*, 4th ed. (Vol. 2, pp. 357–414). New York: McGraw-Hill.

Fiske, S. T., & Taylor, S. E. (1991). *Social cognition*. New York: McGraw-Hill.

Garnham, A. (1981). Mental models as representations of text. *Memory & Cognition, 9*, 560–565.

Gasper, K., & Clore, G. L. (1998). The persistent use of negative affect by anxious individuals to estimate risk. *Journal of Personality and Social Psychology, 74*, 1350–1363.

Gerbner, G., Gross, L., Morgan, M., & Signorielli, N. (1994). Growing up with television: The cultivation perspective. In J. Bryant & D. Zillmann (Eds.), *Media effects: Advances in theory and research* (pp. 17–41). Hillsdale, NJ: Lawrence Erlbaum Associates.

Gilbert, D. T. (1991). How mental systems believe. *American Psychologist, 46*, 107–119.

Gilbert, D. T., Krull, D. S., & Malone, P. S. (1990). Unbelieving the unbelievable: Some problems in the rejection of false information. *Journal of Personality & Social Psychology, 59*, 601–613.

Gillund, G., & Shiffrin, R. M. (1984). A retrieval model for both recognition and recall. *Psychological Review, 91*, 1–67.

Glenberg, A. M., Meyer, M., & Lindem, K. (1987). Mental models contribute to foregrounding during text comprehension. *Journal of Memory and Language, 26*, 69–83.

Goethals, G. R., & Reckman, R. F. (1973). The perception of consistency in attitudes. *Journal of Experimental Social Psychology, 9*, 491–501.

Gollob, H. F. (1974). The Subject-Verb-Object approach to social cognition. *Psychological Review, 81*, 286–321.

Graesser, A. C., Gordon, S. E., & Sawyer, J. D. (1979). Memory for typical and atypical actions in scripted activities: Test of a script pointer + tag hypothesis. *Journal of Verbal Learning and Verbal Behavior, 18*, 319–322.

Graesser, A. C., Singer, M., & Trabasso, T. (1994). Constructing inferences during narrative text comprehension. *Psychological Review, 101*, 371–395.

Green, G. M. (1989). *Pragmatics and natural language understanding*. Hillsdale, NJ: Lawrence Erlbaum Associates.

Greenwald, A. G. (1968). Cognitive learning, cognitive responses to persuasion and attitude change. In A. G. Greenwald, T. C. Brock, & T. M. Ostrom (Eds.), *Psychological foundations of attitudes* (pp. 147–170) New York: Academic Press.

Grice, H. P. (1975). Logic and conversation. In P. Cole & J. L. Morgan (Eds.), *Syntax and semantics: Speech acts* (pp. 41–58). New York: Academic Press.

Gruenfeld, D. H. (1995). Status, ideology, and integrative complexity on the U.S. Supreme Court: Rethinking the politics of political decision making. *Journal of Personality & Social Psychology, 68*, 5–20.

Gruenfeld, D. H., & Wyer, R. S. (1992). Semantics and pragmatics of social influence: How affirmations and denials affect beliefs in referent propositions. *Journal of Personality and Social Psychology, 62*, 38–49.

Hamilton, D. L., & Gifford, R. K. (1976). Illusory correlation in interpersonal perception: A cognitive basis of stereotypic judgment. *Journal of Experimental Social Psychology, 13*, 392–407.

Hamilton, D. L., & Sherman, J. W. (1994). Stereotypes. In R. S. Wyer & T. K. Srull (Eds.), *Handbook of social cognition*, 2nd ed. (Vol. 2, pp. 1–68). Hillsdale, NJ: Lawrence Erlbaum Associates.

Harvey, O. J., Hunt, D., & Schroder, H. (1961). *Conceptual systems and personality organization*. New York: Wiley.

Hasher, L., Goldstein, D., & Toppin, T. (1977). Frequency and the conference of referential validity. *Journal of Verbal Learning and Verbal Behavior, 16*, 107–112.

Hawkins, S. A., & Hastie, R. (1990). Hindsight: Biased judgment of past events after the outcomes are known. *Psychological Bulletin, 107*, 311–327.

Heider, F. (1946). Attitudes and cognitive organization. *Journal of Psychology, 21*, 107–112.

Heider, F. (1958). *The psychology of interpersonal relations.* New York: Wiley.

Heine, S. J., & Lehman, D. R. (1995). Cultural variation in unrealistic optimism: Does the West feel more vulnerable than the East? *Journal of Personality & Social Psychology, 68*, 595–607.

Henninger, M., & Wyer, R. S. (1976). The recognition and elimination of inconsistencies among syllogistically-related beliefs: Some new light on the "Socratic effect." *Journal of Personality and Social Psychology, 34*, 680–693.

Higgins, E. T. (1981). The "communication game:" Implications for social cognition and persuasion. In E. T. Higgins, C. P. Herman, & M. P. Zanna (Eds.), *Social cognition: The Ontario Symposium* (Vol. 1, pp. 342–392). Hillsdale, NJ: Lawrence Erlbaum Associates.

Higgins, E. T. (1996). Knowledge activation: Accessibility, applicability, and salience. In E. T. Higgins & A. Kruglanski (Eds.), *Social psychology: Handbook of basic principles* (pp. 133–168). New York: Guilford.

Higgins, E. T. (1998). Promotion and prevention: Regulatory focus as a motivational principle. In M. P. Zanna (Ed.), *Advances in experimental social psychology* (Vol. 30, pp. 1–46). San Diego, CA: Academic Press.

Higgins, E. T., & Lurie, L. (1983). Context, categorization and recall: The "change-of-standard" effect. *Cognitive Psychology, 15*, 525–547.

Hintzman, D. L. (1986). "Schema abstraction" in a multiple-trace model. *Psychological Review, 93*, 411–428.

Holt, L. E. (1970). Resistance to persuasion on explicit beliefs as a function of commitment to and desirability of logically related beliefs. *Journal of Personality and Social Psychology, 16*, 583–591.

Hovland, C. I., Lumsdaine, A. A., & Sheffield, F. D. (1949). *Experiments on mass communication.* Princeton, NJ: Princeton University Press.

Hovland, C. I., & Pritzker, H. A. (1957). Extent of opinion change as a function of amount of change advocated. *Journal of Abnormal & Social Psychology, 54*, 257–261.

Jaccard, J. J., & King, G. W. (1977). The relation between behavioral intentions and beliefs: A probabilistic model. *Human Communication Research, 3*, 326–334.

Jacoby, L. L., Kelley, C. M., Brown, J., & Jasechko, J. (1989). Becoming famous overnight: Limits on the ability to avoid unconscious influences of the past. *Journal of Personality and Social Psychology, 56*, 326–338.

Johnson, E. J., & Tversky, A. (1983). Affect, generalization, and the perception of risk. *Journal of Personality and Social Psychology, 45*, 20–31.

Jones, E. E., & Davis, K. J. (1965). From acts to dispositions: The attributional process in person perception. In L. Berkowitz (Ed.), *Advances in experimental social psychology* (Vol. 2, pp. 220–266). New York: Academic Press.

Kahneman, D., & Miller, D. T. (1986). Norm theory: Comparing reality to its alternatives. *Psychological Review, 93*, 136–153.

Kahneman, D., Slovic, P., & Tversky, A. (Eds.). (1982). *Judgment under uncertainty: Heuristics and biases.* New York: Cambridge University Press.

Kahneman, D., & Tversky, A. (1972). Subjective probability: A judgment of representativeness. *Cognitive Psychology, 3*, 430–454.

Kahneman, D., & Tversky, A. (1982a). On the study of statistical intuitions. *Cognition, 11*, 143–157.

Kahneman, D., & Tversky, A. (1982b). The simulation heuristic. In D. Kahneman, P. Slovic, & A. Tversky (Eds.), *Judgment under uncertainty: Heuristics and biases* (pp. 201–208). New York: Cambridge University Press.

Katz, D., & Stotland, E. (1959). A preliminary statement to a theory of attitude structure and change. In S. Koch (Ed.), *Psychology: A study of science* (Vol. 3, pp. 423–475). New York: McGraw-Hill.

Krech, D., & Crutchfield, R. S. (1948). *Theory and problems of social psychology.* New York: McGraw-Hill.

Krosnick, J. A., & Petty, R. E. (1995). Attitude strength: An overview. In R. E. Petty & J. A. Krosnick (Eds.), *Attitude strength: Antecedents and consequences* (pp. 1–24). Hillsdale, NJ: Lawrence Erlbaurn Associates.

Kruglanski, A. W. (1980). Lay epistemologic process and contents: Another look at attribution theory. *Psychological Review, 87*, 70–87.

Kruglanski, A. W. (1989). *Lay epistemics and human knowledge: Cognitive and motivational bases.* New York: Plenum.

Kunda, Z. (1987). Motivated inference: Self-serving generation and evaluation of causal theories. *Journal of Personality and Social Psychology, 53*, 636–647.

Kunda, Z. (1990). The case for motivated reasoning. *Psychological Bulletin, 108*, 480–498.

Lerner, M. J., & Miller, D. T. (1978). Just world research and the attribution process: Looking back and ahead. *Psychological Bulletin, 85*, 1030–1051.

Lerner, M. J., Miller, D. T., & Holmes, J. G. (1976). Deserving and the emergence of forms of justice. In L. Berkowitz (Ed.), *Advances in experimental social psychology* (Vol. 19, pp. 133–162). New York: Academic Press.

Lerner, M. J., & Simmons, C. H. (1966). Observer's reaction to the "innocent victim: Compassion or rejection? *Journal of Personality and Social Psychology, 4*, 203–210.

Lingle, J. H., & Ostrom, T. M. (1979). Retrieval selectivity in memory-based impression judgments. *Journal of Personality and Social Psychology, 37*, 180–194.

Linville, P. W. (1982). The complexity-extremity effect and age-based stereotyping. *Journal of Personality and Social Psychology, 42*, 193–211.

Loftus, E. F. (1975). Leading questions and the eyewitness report. *Cognitive Psychology, 7*, 560–572.

Loftus, E. F. (2000). Remembering what never happened. In E. Tulving (Ed.), *Memory, consciousness and the brain: The Tallinn conference* (pp. 106–118). Philadelphia, PA: Taylor & Francis.

Loftus, E. F., & Palmer, J. (1974). Reconstruction of automobile destruction. *Journal of Verbal Learning and Verbal Behavior, 2*, 467–471.

Loken, B. A., & Wyer, R. S. (1983). Effects of reporting beliefs in syllogistically related propositions on the recognition of unmentioned propositions. *Journal of Personality and Social Psychology, 45*, 306–322.

Mandler, J. (1979). Categorical and schematic organization in memory. In C. R. Puff (Ed.), *Memory, organization and structure*. New York: Academic Press.

McGuire, W. J. (1960). A syllogistic analysis of cognitive relationships. In M. J. Rosenberg & C. I. Hovland (Eds.), *Attitude organization and change* (pp. 140–162). New Haven: Yale University Press.

McGuire, W. J. (1964). Inducing resistance to persuasion: Some contemporary approaches. In L. Berkowitz (Ed.), *Advances in experimental social psychology* (Vol. 1, pp. 191–229). New York: Academic Press.

McGuire, W. J. (1968). Personality and attitude change: An information-processing theory. In A. G. Greenwald, T. C. Brock, & T. M. Ostrom (Eds.), *Psychological foundations of attitudes* (pp. 171–196). New York: Academic Press.

McGuire, W. J. (1981). The probabilogical model of cognitive structure and attitude change. In R. E. Petty, T. M. Ostrom, & T. C. Brock (Eds.), *Cognitive responses in persuasion* (pp. 291–307). Hillsdale, NJ: Lawrence Erlbaum Associates.

McGuire, W. J., & McGuire, C. V. (1991). The content, structure and operation of thought systems. In R. S. Wyer & T. K. Srull (Eds.), *Advances in social cognition* (Vol. 4, pp. 1–78). Hillsdale, NJ: Lawrence Erlbaum Associates.

Menon, G., & Raghubir, P. (1998). *When automatic accessibility meets conscious content: Implications for judgment formation*. Unpublished manuscript, New York University.

Moore, D. L., & Hutchinson, J. W. (1995). The influence of affective reactions to advertising: Direct and indirect mechanisms of attitude change. In L. Alwitt & A. Mitchell (Eds.), *Psychological processes and advertising effects: Theory, research and application* (pp. 65–87). Hillsdale, NJ: Lawrence Erlbaum Associates.

Mussweiler, T. (2003). Comparison processes in social judgment: Mechanisms and consequences. *Psychological Review, 110*, 472–489.

Mussweiler, T., & Strack, F. (1999a). Hypothesis-consistent testing and semantic priming in the anchoring paradigm: A selective accessibility model. *Journal of Experimental Social Psychology, 35*, 136–164.

Mussweiler, T., & Strack, F. (1999b). Comparing is believing: A selective accessibility model of judgmental anchoring. In W. Stroebe & M. Hewstone (Eds.), *European review of social psychology* (Vol. 10, pp. 135–167). Chichester, UK: Wiley.

Mussweiler, T., & Strack, F. (2000a). The use of category and exemplar knowledge in the solution of anchoring tasks. *Journal of Personality and Social Psychology, 78*, 1038–1052.

Mussweiler, T., & Strack, F. (2000b). The "relative self": Informational and judgmental consequences of comparative self-evaluation. *Journal of Personality and Social Psychology, 79*, 23–38.

Nielsen, A. C. (1995). *Nielsen report on television*. Northbrook, IL: Nielsen.

Norenzayan, A., & Kim, B. (2000). Unpublished raw data.

O'Guinn, T. C., & Shrum, L. J. (1997). The role of television in the construction of social reality. *Journal of Consumer Research, 23*, 278–294.

Olson, J. M., Roese, N. J., & Zanna, M. P. (1996). Expectancies. In E. T. Higgins & A. Kruglanski (Eds.), *Social psychology: A handbook of basic principles* (pp. 211–238). New York: Guilford.

Osterhouse, R. A., & Brock, T. C. (1970). Distraction increases yielding to propaganda by inhibiting counterarguing. *Journal of Personality and Social Psychology, 15*, 344–358.

Ottati, V., Riggle, E., Wyer, R. S., Schwarz, N., & Kuklinski, J. (1989). The cognitive and affective bases of opinion survey responses. *Journal of Personality and Social Psychology, 57*, 404–415.

Peak, H. (1955). Attitude and motivation. In M. R. Jones (Ed.), *Nebraska symposium on motivation* (Vol. 3, pp. 149–188). Lincoln: University of Nebraska Press.

Pennington, N., & Hastie, R. (1986). Evidence evaluation in complex decision making. *Journal of Personality and Social Psychology, 51*, 242–258.

Pennington, N., & Hastie, R. (1988). Explanation-based decision making: Effects of memory structure on judgment. *Journal of Experimental Psychology: Learning, Memory and Cognition, 14*, 521–533.

Pennington, N., & Hastie, R. (1992). Explaining the evidence: Tests of the story model for juror decision making. *Journal of Personality and Social Psychology, 62*, 189–206.

Petty, R. E., & Cacioppo, J. T. (1986). *Communication and persuasion: Central and peripheral routes to attitude change.* New York: Springer-Verlag.

Pham, M. T. (1998). Representativeness, relevance and the use of feelings in decision making. *Journal of Consumer Research, 25*, 144–159.

Picek, J. S., Sherman, S. J., & Shiffrin, R. M. (1975). Cognitive organization and coding of social structures. *Journal of Personality and Social Psychology, 31*, 758–768.

Pyszczynski, T. A., & Greenberg, J. (1987). Toward an integration of cognitive and motivational perspectives on social inference: A biased hypothesis-testing model. In L. Berkowitz (Ed.), *Advances in experimental social psychology* (Vol. 20, pp. 297–340). San Diego, CA: Academic Press.

Regan, D., & Cheng, J. (1973). Distraction and attitude change: A resolution. *Journal of Experimental Social Psychology, 9*, 138–147.

Reyes, R. M., Thompson, W. C., & Bower, G. H. (1980). Judgmental biases resulting from differing availabilities of arguments. *Journal of Personality and Social Psychology, 39*, 2–12.

Rokeach, M. (1954). The nature and meaning of dogmatism. *Psychological Review, 61*, 194–204.

Roney, C. J. R., & Sorrentino, R. M. (1995). Reducing self-discrepancies or maintaining self-congruence? Uncertainty orientation, self-regulation, and performance. *Journal of Personality and Social Psychology, 68*, 485–497.

Rosen, N. A., & Wyer, R. S. (1972). Some further evidence for the "Socratic effect" using a subjective probability model of cognitive organization. *Journal of Personality and Social Psychology, 24*, 420–424.

Ross, M. (1989). Relation of implicit theories to the construction of personal histories. *Psychological Review, 96*, 341–357.

Ross, L., Lepper, M. R., & Hubbard, M. (1975). Perseverance in self-perception and social perception: Biased attributional processes in the debriefing paradigm. *Journal of Personality and Social Psychology, 32*, 880–892.

Ross, L., Lepper, M. R., Strack, F., & Steinmetz, J. (1977). Social explanation and social expectation: Effects of real and hypothetical explanations on subjective likelihood. *Journal of Personality and Social Psychology, 35*, 817–829.

Ross, M. (1989). Relation of implicit theories to the construction of personal histories. *Psychological Review, 96*, 341–357.

Ross, M., McFarland, C., & Fletcher, G. J. O. (1981). The effect of attitude on recall of past histories. *Journal of Personality and Social Psychology, 10*, 627–634.

Rumelhart, D. E. (1984). Schemata and the cognitive system. In R. S. Wyer & T. K. Srull (Eds.), *Handbook of social cognition* (Vol. 1, 161–188). Hillsdale, NJ: Lawrence Erlbaum Associates.

Sanitioso, R., Kunda, Z., & Fong, G. T. (1990). Motivated recruitment of autobiographical memories. *Journal of Personality and Social Psychology, 59*, 229–241.

Sanna, L. J., & Schwarz, N. (2003). Debiasing the hindsight bias: The role of accessibility experiences and (mis)attributions. *Journal of Experimental Social Psychology, 39*, 287–295.

Sanna, L. J., Schwarz, N., & Small, E. M. (2003). Accessibility experiences and the hindsight bias: I knew it all along versus it could never have happened. *Memory & Cognition, 30*, 1288–1296.

Sanna, L. J., Schwarz, N., & Stocker, S. L. (2002). When debiasing backfires: Accessible content and accessibility experiences in debiasing hindsight. *Journal of Experimental Psychology: Learning, Memory, and Cognition, 28*, 497–502.

Schank, R. C. (1972). *Dynamic memory: A theory of reminding in computers and people.* Cambridge, UK: Cambridge University Press.

Schank, R. C., & Abelson, R. P. (1977). *Scripts, plans, goals and understanding.* Hillsdale, NJ: Lawrence Erlbaum Associates.

Schank, R. C., & Abelson, R. P. (1995). Knowledge and memory: The real story. In R. S. Wyer (Ed.), *Advances in social cognition* (Vol. 8, pp. 1–85). Hillsdale, NJ: Lawrence Erlbaum Associates.

Schroeder. H. M., Driver, M. J., & Streufert, S. (1967). *Human information processing: Individuals and groups functioning in complex social situations.* New York: Holt, Rinehart & Winston.

Schwarz, N. (1994). Judgment in a social context: Biases, shortcomings, and the logic of conversation. In M. P. Zanna (Ed.), *Advances in experimental social psychology* (Vol. 24, pp. 123–162). San Diego, CA: Academic Press.

Schwarz, N. (1998a). Accessible content and accessibility experiences: The interplay of declarative and experiential information in judgment. *Personality and Social Psychology Review, 2*, 87–99.

Schwarz, N. (1998b). Communication in standardized research situations: A Gricean perspective. In S. Fussell & R. Kreuz (Eds.), *Social and cognitive approaches to interpersonal communication* (pp. 39–66). Mahwah, NJ: Lawrence Erlbaum Associates.

Schwarz, N., Bless, H., Strack, F., Klumpp, G., Rittenauer-Schatka, H., & Simons, A. (1991). Ease of retrieval as information: Another look at the availability heuristic. *Journal of Personality and Social Psychology, 61*, 195–202.

Schwarz, N., & Bohner, G. (2001). The construction of attitudes. In A. Tesser & N. Schwarz (Eds.), *Blackwell handbook of social psychology: Intraindividual processes* (Vol. 1, pp. 413–436). Oxford, UK: Blackwell.

Schwarz, N., & Clore, G. L. (1983). Mood, misattribution, and judgments of well-being: Informative and directive functions of affective states. *Journal of Personality and Social Psychology, 45*, 513–523.

Schwarz, N., & Clore, G. L. (1996). Feelings and phenomenal experiences. In E. T. Higgins & A. Kruglanski (Eds.), *Social psychology: A handbook of basic principles* (pp. 433–465). New York: Guilford.

Scott, W. A. (1969). Structure of natural cognitions. *Journal of Personality and Social Psychology, 12*, 261–278.

Scott, W. A., Osgood, D. W., & Peterson, C. (1979). *Cognitive structure: Theory and measurement of individual differences.* New York: Winston.

Sentis, K. P., & Burnstein, E. (1979). Remembering schema-consistent information: Effects of a balance schema on recognition memory. *Journal of Personality and Social Psychology, 37*, 2200–2212.

Shepperd, J. A., Ouellette, J. A., & Fernandez, J. K. (1996). Abandoning unrealistic optimism: Performance estimates and the temporal proximity of self-relevant feedback. *Journal of Personality and Social Psychology, 70*, 844–855.

Sherman, B. R., & Kunda, Z. (1989). *Motivated evaluation of scientific evidence.* Paper presented at the American Psychological Society convention, Arlington, VA.

Sherman, S. J., Ahlm, K., Berman, L., & Lynn, S. (1978). Contrast effects and the relationship to subsequent behavior. *Journal of Experimental Social Psychology, 14*, 340–350.

Sherman, S. J., & Corty, E. (1984). Cognitive heuristics. In R. S. Wyer & T. K. Srull (Eds.), *Handbook of social cognition* (Vol. 1, pp. 189–286). Hillsdale, NJ: Lawrence Erlbaum Associates.

Sherman, S. J., Skov, R. B., Hervitz, E. F., & Stock, C. B. (1981). The effects of explaining hypothetical future events: From possibility to probability to actuality and beyond. *Journal of Experimental Social Psychology, 17*, 142–158.

Shrum, L. J. (1999). The relationship of television viewing with attitude strength and extremity: Implications for the cultivation effect. *Media Psychology, 1*, 3–25.

Shrum, L. J., O'Guinn, T. C., Semenik, R. J., & Faber, R. J. (1991). Process and effects in the construction of normative consumer beliefs: The role of television. In R. H. Holman & M. R. Solomon (Eds.), *Advances in research* (Vol. 18, pp. 755–763). Provo, UT: Association for Consumer Research.

Shrum, L. J., Wyer, R. S., & O'Guinn, T. (1998). The effects of watching television on perceptions of social reality. *Journal of Consumer Research, 24*, 447–458.

Simon, H. (1957). *Models of man: Social and rational.* New York: Wiley.

Slovic, P., & Lichtenstein, S. (1971). Comparison of Bayesian and regression approaches to the study of information processing in judgment. *Organizational Behavior and Human Decision Processes, 6*, 649–744.

Smith, E. R. (1994). Procedural knowledge and processing strategies in social cognition. In R. S. Wyer & T. K. Srull (Eds.), *Handbook of social cognition* (Vol. 1, pp. 99–151). Hillsdale, NJ: Lawrence Erlbaum Associates.

Smith, E. R. (1996). What do connectionism and social psychology offer each other? *Journal of Personality and Social Psychology, 70*, 893–912.

Sperber, D., & Wilson, D. (1986). *Relevance: Communication and cognition.* Oxford, UK: Basil Blackwell.

Spiro, R. J. (1977). Remembering information from text: The "state of schema" approach. In R. C. Anderson, R. J. Spiro, & W. E. Montague (Eds.), *Schooling and the acquisition of knowledge.* Hillsdale, NJ: Lawrence Erlbaum Associates.

Srull, T. K., & Wyer, R. S. (1979). The role of category accessibility in the interpretation of information about persons: Some determinants and implications. *Journal of Personality and Social Psychology, 37*, 1660–1672.

Srull, T. K., & Wyer, R. S. (1980). Category accessibility and social perception: Some implications for the study of person memory and interpersonal judgments. *Journal of Personality and Social Psychology, 38*, 841–856.

Srull, T. K., & Wyer, R. S. (1989). Person memory and judgment. *Psychological Review, 96*, 58–63.

Steele, C. M. (1988). The psychology of self-affirmation: Sustaining the integrity of the self. In L. Berkowitz (Ed.), *Advances in experimental social psychology* (Vol. 21, pp. 261–302). New York: Academic Press.

Steele, C. M., & Liu, T. J. (1983). Dissonance processes as self-affirmation. *Journal of Personality and Social Psychology, 45*, 5–19.

Strack, F. (1994). Response processes in social judgment. In R. S. Wyer & T. K. Srull (Eds.), *Handbook of social cognition*, 2nd ed. (Vol. 1, pp. 287–322). Hillsdale, NJ: Lawrence Erlbaum Associates.

Strack, F., Martin, L. L., & Schwarz, N. (1988). Priming and communication: Social determinants of information use in judgments of life satisfaction. *European Journal of Social Psychology, 18*, 429–442.

Taylor, S. E., & Fiske, S. T. (1978). Salience, attention and attribution: Top of the head phenomena. In L. Berkowitz (Ed.), *Advances in experimental social psychology* (Vol. 11, pp. 249–288). New York: Academic Press.

Tetlock, P. E. (1989). Structure and function of political belief systems. In A. R. Pratkanis, S. J. Breckler, & A. G. Greenwald (Eds.), *Attitude structure and function* (pp. 129–151). Hillsdale, NJ: Lawrence Erlbaum Associates.

Thurstone, L. L. (1959). *The measurement of values.* Chicago: University of Chicago Press.

Todorov, T. (1973). The fantastic: A structural approach to a literary genre. (Richard Howard, Trans.). Cleveland, OH: Case Western Reserve University Press.

Tversky, A. (1969). Intransitivity of preferences. *Psychological Review, 76*, 31–48.

Tversky, A., & Kahneman, D. (1973). Availability: A heuristic for judging frequency and probability. *Cognitive Psychology, 5*, 207–232.

Walster, E. (1966). Assignment of responsibility for an accident. *Journal of Personality and Social Psychology, 3*, 73–79.

Wänke, M., Bless, H., & Biller, B. (1996). Subjective experience versus content of information in the construction of attitude judgments. *Personality and Social Psychology Bulletin, 22*, 1105–1113.

Watts, W. A., & Holt, L. E. (1970). Logical relationships among beliefs and timing as factors in persuasion. *Journal of Personality and Social Psychology, 116*, 571–582.

Webster, D. M., & Kruglanski, A. W. (1994). Individual differences in need for cognitive closure. *Journal of Personality and Social Psychology, 67*, 1049–1062.

Weinstein, N. D. (1980). Unrealistic optimism about future life events. *Journal of Personality & Social Psychology, 39*, 806–820.

Wegner, D. M., Wenzlaff, R., Kerker, R. M., & Beattie, A. E. (1981). Incrimination through innuendo: Can media questions become public answers? *Journal of Personality and Social Psychology, 40*, 822–832.

Wicklund, R. A., & Brehm, J. W. (1976). *Perspectives on cognitive dissonance*. Hillsdale, NJ: Lawrence Erlbaum Associates.

Wiggins, N., & Hoffman, P. J. (1968). Three models of clinical judgment. *Journal of Abnormal Psychology, 73*, 70–77.

Wiggins, N., Hoffman, P. J., & Taber, T. (1969). Types of judges and cue utilization in judgments of intelligence. *Journal of Personality & Social Psychology, 12*, 52–59.

Windschitl, P. D., Martin, R., & Flugstad, A. R. (2002). Context and the interpretation of likelihood information: The role of intergroup comparisons on perceived vulnerability. *Journal of Personality & Social Psychology, 82*, 742–755.

Wood, W. (2000). Attitude change: Persuasion and social influence. *Annual Review of Psychology, 51*, 539–570.

Wyer, R. S. (1964). Assessment and correlates of cognitive differentiation and integration. *Journal of Personality, 32*, 495–509.

Wyer, R. S. (1970). The quantitative prediction of belief and opinion change: A further test of a subjective probability model. *Journal of Personality and Social Psychology, 16*, 559–571.

Wyer, R. S. (1972). Test of a subjective probability model of social evaluation processes. *Journal of Personality and Social Psychology, 22*, 279–286.

Wyer, R. S. (1973). Category ratings as "subjective expected values": Implications for attitude formation and change. *Psychological Review, 80*, 446–467.

Wyer, R. S. (1974). *Cognitive organization and change: An information-processing approach*. Hillsdale, NJ: Lawrence Erlbaum Associates.

Wyer, R. S. (1975). Functional measurement analysis of a subjective probability model of cognitive functioning. *Journal of Personality and Social Psychology, 31*, 94–100.

Wyer, R. S. (1976). An investigation of the relations among probability estimates. *Organizational Behavior and Human Performance, 15*, 1–18.

Wyer, R. S. (2004). *Social comprehension and judgment: The role of situation models, narratives, and implicit theories*. Mahwah, NJ: Lawrence Erlbaum Associates.

Wyer, R. S., Adaval, R., & Colcombe, S. J. (2002). Narrative-based representations of social knowledge: Their construction and use in comprehension, memory and judgment. In M. P. Zanna (Ed.), *Advances in experimental social psychology* (Vol. 34, pp. 131–197). San Diego, CA: Academic Press.

Wyer, R. S., Bodenhausen, G. V., & Gorman, T. F. (1985). Cognitive mediators of reactions to rape. *Journal of Personality and Social Psychology, 48*, 324–338.

Wyer, R. S., Budesheim, T. L., Lambert, A. J., & Swan, S. (1994). Person memory and judgment: Pragmatic influences on impressions formed in a social context. *Journal of Personality and Social Psychology, 66*, 254–267.

Wyer, R. S., & Carlston, D. E. (1979). *Social cognition, inference and attribution*. Hillsdale, NJ: Lawrence Erlbaum Associates.

Wyer, R. S., & Carlston, D. E. (1994). The cognitive representation of persons and events. In R. S. Wyer, & T. S. Srull, (Eds.), *Handbook of social cognition* (pp. 41–98). Hillsdale, NJ: Lawrence Erlbaum Associates.

Wyer, R. S., Clore, G. L., & Isbell, L. M. (1999). Affect and information processing. In M. P. Zanna (Ed.), *Advances in experimental social psychology* (Vol. 31, pp. 1–77). San Diego, CA: Academic Press.

Wyer, R. S., & Frey, D. (1983). The effects of feedback about self and others on the recall and judgments of feedback-relevant information. *Journal of Experimental Social Psychology, 19*, 540–559.

Wyer, R. S., & Goldberg, L. (1970). A probabilistic analysis of the relationships among beliefs and attitudes. *Psychological Review, 77*, 100–120.

Wyer, R. S., & Gruenfeld, D. H. (1995). Information processing in social contexts: Implications for social memory and judgment. In M. P. Zanna (Ed.), *Advances in experimental social psychology* (Vol. 27, pp. 49–91). San Diego, CA: Academic Press.

Wyer, R. S., & Hartwick, J. (1980). The role of information retrieval and conditional inference processes in belief formation and change. In L. Berkowitz (Ed.), *Advances in experimental social psychology* (Vol. 13, pp. 241–284). New York: Academic Press.

Wyer, R. S., & Hartwick, J. (1984). The recall and use of belief statements as bases for judgments: Some determinants and implications. *Journal of Experimental Social Psychology, 20,* 65–85.

Wyer, R. S., & Lyon, J. D. (1970). A test of cognitive balance theory implications for social inference processes. *Journal of Personality and Social Psychology, 16,* 598–618.

Wyer, R. S., & Radvansky, G. A. (1999). The comprehension and validation of social information. *Psychological Review, 106,* 89–118.

Wyer, R. S., & Srull, T. K. (1986). Human cognition in its social context. *Psychological Review, 93,* 322–359.

Wyer, R. S., & Srull, T. K. (1989). *Memory and cognition in its social context.* Hillsdale, NJ: Lawrence Erlbaum Associates.

Yeung, C. W. M., & Wyer, R. S. (in press). Affect, pictures and consumer judgment: The impact of initial appraisals of a product on evaluations and expectancy–confirmatory information processing. *Journal of Consumer Research, 31,* 412–424

Zanna, M. P., & Cooper, J. (1976). Dissonance and the attribution process. In J. Harvey, W. Ickes, & R. Kidd (Eds.), *New directions in attribution research* (Vol. 1, pp. 199–217). Hillsdale, NJ: Lawrence Erlbaum Associates.

Zanna, M., & Rempel, J. K. (1988). Attitudes: A new look at an old concept. In D. Bar-Tal & A. Kruglanski (Eds.), *The social psychology of knowledge* (pp. 315–334). Cambridge, UK: Cambridge University Press.

8

The Influence of Beliefs and Goals on Attitudes: Issues of Structure, Function, and Dynamics

Arie W. Kruglanski
University of Maryland

Wolfgang Stroebe
University of Utrecht

Several decades have passed since Gordon Allport's (1935) famous statement that the concept of attitudes is the single most important social psychological notion, and his statement rings as true today as it did then. The volumes on attitudes and attitude change continue to mushroom (see Albarracín, Johnson, Zanna, & Kumkale this volume; Chaiken & Trope, 1999; Haddock & Maio, 2004; Olson & Maio, 1999; Petty & Krosnik, 1996) as does novel theoretical and empirical research on various aspects of attitude formation and change (e.g., Kruglanski & Thompson, 1999; Lord & Lepper, 1999; Schwarz & Bohner, 2001; Wilson, Lindsey, & Schooler, 2000).

The lively scene of attitude research is like "a circus tent over diverse side shows" (Kelley, 1989, p. XX) containing as it does a plethora of approaches and concept. That heterogeneity forestalls the formation of a coherent picture of what attitudes are, how they differ from kindred concepts, how they are formed and altered, and what their consequences may be. The present chapter attempts to identify the conceptual obstacles to a unified understanding of attitudes, and to present a point of view affording an integrative solution to some of the quandaries surrounding the attitude construct. Admittedly, ours is hardly a magical solution, and it requires a number of conceptual choices and commitments from the outset. We shall be explicit about those and about their implications for a unified perspective on attitudes.

As an advance organizer, we first discuss several problematic issues associated with the attitudes topic and develop a general framework, grounded in recent decades of research in social cognition, that affords a unified perspective on these issues. We then apply this framework to three major research domains related to the attitudes concept, dealing respectively with attitude structure, attitude function, and attitude dynamics (i.e., attitude change). We conclude by drawing the implications of our analysis for understanding attitudes and exploring them further.

ISSUES IN ATTITUDE RESEARCH

What Is an Attitude? A Matter of Definition

McGuire (1985, pp. 239–240) tellingly illustrates the considerable diversity in the conceptual definitions of the attitude concept and raises the issue of its distinctiveness from numerous related notions (including *schemata, templates, social representations*, and *frames of reference*, among others). Zanna and Rempel (1988) simplify the discussion by highlighting the distinction between single and three-component definitions of attitudes—the latter including *affective, cognitive*, and *behavioral* reactions to a stimulus object. Zanna and Rempel (1988) point to a basic problem with the tripartite definition: It presupposes a necessary relation between attitudinally relevant affect, cognition, and behavior, a matter best regarded as an empirical issue (Breckler, 1983, 1984). In light of these problems, Zanna and Rempel opt for a single component definition of an attitude as "the categorization of a stimulus object along an evaluative dimension" (1988, p. 319). In other words, an attitude is conceived of as an evaluative judgment of an object in terms of its degree of "goodness" (or "badness"). However, Zanna and Rempel (see also, Olson & Zanna, 1993) accept affective, cognitive, and behavioral reactions as correlates of attitudes. They argue that attitudes, as evaluative judgments, can be based on, or developed from, affective information (e.g., in the case of conditioning), cognitive information (e.g., in the case of knowledge-based evaluations), and behavioral information (e.g., in the case of self-perception inferences from previous actions). Moreover, those attitudes, as evaluative judgments, can generate affective, cognitive, and behavioral responses (see also, Eagly & Chaiken, 1993). If one remembers that earlier theorists used the term *affect* as a synonym for evaluation (Chaiken, Pomerantz, & Giner-Sorolla, 1995), Zanna and Rempel's (1988) suggestion that evaluation constitutes the predominant aspect of attitudes is consistent with the earlier definitions of Thurstone (1931) and Fishbein and Ajzen (1975). Furthermore, Zanna and Rempel's (1988) conception of attitudes corresponds closely to the way attitudes have been typically operationally defined and assessed in much attitudinal research (Dawes & Smith, 1985). Our first methodological commitment is, therefore, to accept Zanna and Rempel's (1988) definition and to treat attitudes, accordingly, as *evaluative judgments*.

Are Attitudes Dispositional or Episodic?

Accepting our conception of attitudes as (evaluative) judgments has implications for another definitional issue, namely, whether attitudes are *dispositional* or *episodic*, or whether they represent stable tendencies or ones that are induced by situational factors. Until recently, it has been so widely accepted that attitudes are stable dispositions that stability has often been included in definitions of the concept as one of the defining feature of attitudes. For example, Krech and Crutchfield (1948), in their influential textbook of social psychology, defined attitude as "an *enduring* organizational, motivational, emotional, perceptual, and cognitive process with respect to some aspect of an individual's world" (p. 152, emphasis ours). The notion that attitudes are *predispositions* (e.g., Campbell, 1963; Katz, 1960; Ostrom, 1984) also connotes stability referring as it does to a preexisting readiness, to "respond to an object or class of objects in a consistently favorable or unfavorable way" (Fishbein, 1967, p. 257). In line with these definitions, there is evidence that attitudes can persist for years or even a lifetime (e.g., Alwin, Cohen, & Newcomb, 1991; Marwell, Aiken, & Demerath, 1987).

The stability of attitudes has typically been attributed to the conception of attitudes as learned structures that reside in long-term memory and are activated when the issue or object of the attitude is encountered (e.g., Fazio & Williams, 1986). Underlying this conception is the assumption that, even though people consider the attributes of an attitude object as existing in the external world when they first evaluate it, they are likely to store their evaluations in memory following the initial evaluation. This storage enables individuals to subsequently retrieve the evaluation from memory on re-exposure to the attitude object, without a need for concomitant retrieval of information that gave rise to them in the first place. The fact that many attitudes appear to be stable over long periods of time would seem to support the notion that once stored in memory, attitudes will be recalled rather than reconstructed on the basis of momentarily accessible information. One explanation is that, as Eagly and Chaiken (1993) reasoned, "in daily life direct retrieval may be the rule rather than the exception" (p. 112). Recent evidence for a genetic basis of (some) attitudes would offer an additional explanation for attitude stability. Attitudes that are high in heritability are likely to be more resistant to change than attitudes that are low in heritability (Olson, Vernon, Harris, & Jang, 2001; Tesser, 1993). It is important to note that the assumption that attitudes are influenced by biological and genetic factors is complementary rather than incompatible with the view that attitudes are learned: Genetic factors exert their influence on an organism that is in a particular environment and, as a result, the final product is a combination of biological and experiential factors (Olson et al., 2001).

These views notwithstanding, there is also a growing body of research that suggests that attitudes may be much less enduring and stable than has been traditionally assumed (for reviews, see Erber, Hodges, & Wilson, 1995; Potter, 1998; Schwarz & Bohner, 2001; Schwarz & Strack, 1991; Tourangeau & Rasinski, 1988). According to this research, attitudes fluctuate over time, and appear to "depend on what people happen to be thinking about at any given moment" (Erber et al., 1995, p. 433). Or as Potter (1998) expressed it from the perspective of a "discursive social psychology," "the same individual can be found offering different evaluations on different occasions, or even during different parts of a single conversation" (p. 244). For example, Wilson and his colleagues have demonstrated that attitudes can change when people analyze their reasons for holding them, and this change occurs for a wide range of attitude objects, including political candidates (Wilson, Kraft, & Dunn, 1989) and dating partners, among others (Wilson & Kraft, 1993). Similarly, in a study of German students' attitudes toward an "educational contribution," attitudes were much more favorable when the target question was preceded by a question about the amount of financial support the Swedish government gives to every student than when it was preceded by a question about the tuition fees American students have to pay (Strack, Schwarz, & Wänke, 1991).

One would expect a certain extent of context dependence, even if evaluations were retrieved from memory, because all judgments are, after all, context dependent (Eiser & Stroebe, 1971). However, if attitude measures elicited the mere *retrieval* of evaluative judgments stored in memory, then these judgments should not depend on what people happen to think about at any given moment. In light of this expectation, the existing evidence of incidental or temporary influences on attitudes gave rise to various attitude-as-construction models (e.g., Bem, 1972; Erber et al., 1995; Schwarz & Bohner, 2001; Tourangeau & Rasinski, 1988; Wyer & Srull, 1989). These models assume that attitudes are constructed online at any given moment on the basis of a sampling of individual beliefs (or other reactions) about the attitude issue. Thus, according to these models, attitudes often reflect information about the attitude objects that is momentarily accessible to the individual (see also Bassili & Brown, this volume; Wyer & Srull, 1989).

Initially, evidence of the stability of some attitudes appeared to be inconsistent with the idea that attitudes are constructed online. However, as proponents of the attitudes-as-constructions view have argued, their perspective can account for attitude stability *as well as* malleability (Erber et al., 1995; Schwarz & Bohner, 2001). According to the attitude-as-construction model, attitudes should remain stable to the extent that respondents form similar mental representations of the attitude object at each time, or draw on similar sources of information. This assumption is consistent with findings that attitudes characterized by a high degree of evaluative–cognitive inconsistency or ambivalence are indeed less stable (e.g., Bargh, Chaiken, Govender, & Pratto, 1992; Jonas, Broemer, & Diehl, 2000a, 2000b).

The attitude representation theory of Lord and Lepper (1999) offers a position that is intermediate between theories of attitudes-as-constructions and as learned constructs. Lord and Lepper (1999) argued that the stability or instability of attitudes toward social categories depends on whether the same or different category exemplars come to mind at different times. Their *representation postulate* posits "that a person's response to any attitude-relevant stimulus will depend not only on the perceived properties of that stimulus and the situation surrounding it, but also on the subjective representation of that stimulus by the person" (p. 269). Their *matching postulate* suggests "that the closer the match between the subjective representations and perceived immediate stimuli to which a person is responding in one situation and the subjective representations and perceived immediate stimuli to which the person is responding in a different situation, the more consistency there will be in the person's responses" (p. 269). A similar matching assumption has been proposed by Ajzen (1996, p. 379) as an explanation for attitude–behavior (in)consistency.

Although difficult to disentangle empirically, there are important theoretical differences between the attitude-as-construction models (e.g., Erber et al., 1995; Schwarz & Bohner, 2001) and the attitude representation theory of Lord and Lepper (1999). The attitude representation theory is really a theory about attitude objects. As long as individuals retrieve the same exemplars of an object (e.g., a social category) when constructing their attitude, the attitude will remain stable. In contrast, attitudes are likely to vary when different beliefs about the attitude object become accessible at the different points of assessment (Schwarz & Bohner, 2001).

In a certain sense, Schwarz and Bohner's (2001) position is more general than that of Lord and Lepper (1999), because it does not preclude the retrieval of exemplars (e.g., specific concerts attended) treated as representative of the general category (e.g., classical music), while allowing also for the possibility that the category as such will be considered in light of the category's or the exemplar's attributes. It should be noted that even if one's attitude were based on different information at different points in time, the attitude would only differ to the extent that the evaluative content of this information was different. Thus, one could retrieve different exemplars (Sia, Lord, Blessum, Ratcliffe, & Lepper, 1997) or indeed different beliefs about the consequences of the attitude object, and the attitude would be still the same if the evaluative content of the beliefs about the exemplars (or about the general category) were the same.

In summary, our present commitment to the view of attitudes as evaluative judgments is compatible with the notion that they may vary in their stability. This does not necessarily mean that all attitudes must be constructed *de novo*. Some attitudinal judgments may be chronically accessible (hence, enduring and relatively stable over time), or they may be relatively inaccessible (Fazio, 1990), or even unavailable in an individual's memory (see Higgins, 1996). If no relevant attitude is available, it may need to be assembled from situationally given information. This information may include beliefs about exemplars deemed representative of given categories (Lord & Lepper, 1999) and the evaluative beliefs about the attributes or consequences of those exemplars, or of that category. As Eagly and Chaiken (1993) point out, a

> decline in attitudinal stability occurs because the relative accessibility of the favorable and unfavorable attributes ascribed to an attitude object would affect the attitude expressed at any one point in time. In (an) example of (a) good looking, charming, unreliable, and deceitful friend, some social contexts (e.g., a party) might increase the accessibility of good looks and charm, whereas other contexts (e.g., working with him on a demanding task) might increase the accessibility of unreliability and deceitfulness (p. 127).

As a consequence, one may have different attitudes about the same object on different occasions.

Is the Attitude–Object Relation a Unique One?

The uniqueness issue in attitude–object relations differs somewhat from the issue of stability. An instability of an attitude renders it nonunique, of course, but the opposite is not necessarily the case. This conclusion emerges from the notion of stability as attitudinal consistency over time, whereas the notion of nonuniqueness may include the contemporaneous existence of different attitudes toward the same object (with attitude object defined broadly as including behavior, proposals, or abstract ideas). This distinction, indeed, is a major implication of the work on *attitude ambivalence* (e.g., Kaplan, 1972), and is also suggested by Wilson and colleagues' (2000) dual attitude model (explicit and implicit). Both topics are considered at length in our subsequent section dealing with attitude structure. They show, however, that the relationship between an evaluative judgment and an object need not be unique and that the popular notion of love–hate relations is not incompatible with contemporary scientific research on attitudes.

Are Attitudes Distinctive From Related Constructs?

The literature on attitudes often discusses them in counter distinction from other concepts such as beliefs, affective states, behaviors, and goals. In the tripartite formulation of attitudes (for discussions see Breckler, 1984; McGuire, 1985), affect, cognition, and behavior are presumed to be the three components of attitudes. In the *means-goals* framework (McGuire, 1968; Rosenberg, 1960), attitude objects are viewed as means, instrumental to the attainment of various goals. Consequently, attitudes are determined by the belief that the attitude objects indeed bring about goal attainment, and that the goals in question are ones the individual cares about. In both cases, the relevant discussions highlight the *distinctiveness* between these constructs. In the tripartite framework, the relation between attitudes on the one hand and beliefs (or cognitions), affects, and behaviors on the other hand resembled that of a whole (the attitude) to its component parts. By contrast, in the means-goals framework. the relation between attitudes on the one hand, and beliefs and goals on the other is that of an effect (the attitude) and its causes. These treatments, however, obscure the fact that attitudes, as well as beliefs, goals, affect, and behavior all possess an important cognitive aspect: They are all mentally represented, and in that sense they should all behave in accordance with principles governing mental representations regardless of their content (Carlston & Smith, 1996).

In a sense, attitudes, affects, goals, and behavioral information are all beliefs, albeit of different sorts. An attitude is a belief that an object merits a certain (positive or negative) evaluation; a goal is a belief that a given state of affairs is desirable and attainable (see Gollwitzer & Bargh, 1996; Kruglanski, 1996; Wyer & Albarracín, this volume); behavioral information is often used to denote a belief that a given *action* has taken place; and affect involves (although it is not limited to) a mental representation of a given feeling or emotional experience (Averill, 1982; Schimmack & Crites, this volume; Schwarz & Clore, 1996). In this sense, the distinction among beliefs, goals, attitudes, behaviors, and affects is misleading.

Now, far be it for us to suggest that the cognitive, mental representation aspect is all there is to attitudes, goals, behaviors, or affects. The beliefs that represent these constructs have different contents, and these contents carry entirely different implications. Goals may have energizing properties, behaviors act on the environment, affects may have physiological underpinnings, etc. Nonetheless, the notion that they all constitute mental representations or beliefs is not trivial. Primarily, it suggests that (a) they can all vary in their degree of momentary activation or accessibility, (b) as beliefs, they can be proven or disproved on the basis of appropriate evidence, and (c) their formation and change does not occur in a motivational vacuum, but rather has a clear motivational basis in the individual's epistemic goals (Kruglanski, 1989).

The definition of attitudes as beliefs opens the door for considerable potential flexibility in one's expressed or experienced attitudes depending on their momentary accessibility and that of their determinants. Thus, if an attitude toward a given object was readily accessible, there would be no need to construct a new attitude, or to reconsider the old one, unless the motivational or informational conditions changed, and new arguments or other evidence led one to suspect that one's former attitude was no longer adequate. In fact, the entire domain of persuasion research (discussed later) is devoted to just such a case, wherein an attempt is made to alter preexisting attitudes by recruiting new relevant information or instilling the appropriate motivations to that end. Additionally, when the old attitude toward an object is inaccessible, a new attitude could be constructed on the basis of accessible informational pieces, possibly including behavioral, affective, or goal-related information. These points are discussed at length in subsequent portions of this chapter.

Summary: Attitudes as Evaluative Judgments

In summary, a commitment to the view of attitudes as evaluative judgments has a number of implications regarding attitudinal phenomena. First, it suggests that just like other judgments or knowledge structures, attitudes, too, may vary in their degree of stability, going from stable, seemingly *dispositional* to unstable or *episodic* attitudes. Second, the judgmental view of attitudes suggests that attitudes need not (though, they could) be uniquely associated with their objects. Individuals may have ambivalent feelings toward specific objects, and their implicit and explicit attitudes might differ. Third, the judgmental view of attitudes acknowledges their cognitive aspect as beliefs or mental representations carrying a specific (evaluative) content. As such, attitudes may vary in their degree of momentary activation or accessibility (see Fazio, 1995), and they may be constructed from relevant evidence that happens to be mentally accessible at a given point in time. Such evidence may come in the form of affective, behavioral, or goal-related information that can also vary in its degree of momentary activation. In this sense, the judgmental view of attitudes stresses their similarity to the constructs of goals, affective states, and behaviors when viewed from an informational perspective. In what follows we apply the present, judgmental view of attitudes to issues of attitude structure, functions, and dynamics.

ATTITUDE STRUCTURE

Expectancy–Value Models of Attitudes

Expectancy–value models have been (and still are) the most popular models used by attitude theorists to express the relationship between attitudes and beliefs. From this perspective, an individual's attitude toward a given attitude object (e.g., capital punishment, physical exercise, the French) depends on the subjective value attached to attributes of the object or its consequences (or outcomes), each weighted by the subjective probability that the object is associated with these attributes or consequences. Thus, one's attitude toward the French would be a function of how likely one thinks it is (i.e., expectancy, subjective probability) that the French possess certain attributes (e.g., are intellectual, charming, pleasure loving, etc.) and how positively or negatively one evaluates these attributes (i.e., their value, subjective utility). Similarly, one's attitude toward physical exercise would be a function of the perceived likelihood with which we associate physical exercise with certain consequences such as low blood pressure or physical fitness, and our evaluation of these consequences, which is the degree to which these consequences are seen to advance or impede the attainment of (more or less significant) objectives.

The general attitude toward an object is, thus, thought to reflect the sum total of the evaluations of the various attributes associated with the attitude object, each multiplied by the subjective probability ascribed to that association. In a general form, the expectancy–value model of attitudes can be represented as follows:

$$\text{Attitude} = \Sigma \text{Expectancy} \times \text{Value}$$

Stimulated by the work of Peak (1955), Rosenberg (1956, 1960) was probably the first to introduce an explicit expectancy–value model into the attitude area. He formulated his basic hypothesis as follows (using the term affect where we would speak of evaluation today):

> When a person has a relatively stable tendency to respond to a given object with either positive or negative affect, such a tendency is accompanied by a cognitive structure made up of beliefs about the potentialities of that object for attaining or blocking the realization of valued states; the sign (positive or negative) and the extremity of affect felt towards the object are correlated with the content of its associate cognitive structure. (Rosenberg, 1960, p. 18)

In those terms, one's attitude toward some object will be more positive, the more a given attitude object is perceived as *instrumental* to obtaining positively valued goals (or consequences) and to blocking negatively valued goals. This assumption can be expressed algebraically as follows:

$$A_o = \sum_{i=1}^{n} I_i V_i$$

where I_i is the instrumentality, which is the probability that the object o would promote or block the attainment of the goal or value i; V_i is the value importance or the degree of satisfaction or dissatisfaction individuals would experience if they obtained the value $_i$; and n reflects the number of goals or valued states mediated by the attitude object (Fishbein & Ajzen, 1975).

It was Fishbein, however, who developed the expectancy–value approach into a general theory of attitudes (1963; Fishbein & Ajzen, 1975). Whereas Rosenberg's formulation was restricted to goals (or values) as the attributes of interest and to instrumental relations as links between the attitude object and these goals, Fishbein's formulation does not limit the attributes of the attitude object or the relations between object and attribute in that way. In contrast to the notion of instrumentality as relevant to the attainment of goals extrinsic to the attitude object, the more general notion of *attribute* also encompasses features intrinsic to the object. For instance, one may have a positive attitude toward a Caravaggio painting because of its interplay of light and shade, which is an intrinsic property of the painting. Similarly, one might have a positive attitude toward Florida because of its warm climate, which also is an intrinsic feature. Fishbein's more general formulation is expressed algebraically as follows:

$$A_o = \sum_{i=1}^{n} b_i e_i,$$

where A_o is the attitude toward the object, action, or event o; b_i is the belief i about o (expressed as the subjective probability that o is associated with the attribute i); e_i is the evaluation of the attribute i; and n is the number of salient attributes. Fishbein and Ajzen (1975) not only demonstrated repeatedly that attitudes correlated highly with their summed expectancy–value products, but also that each attitude object was associated with a very limited number of beliefs *accessible* to individuals at a given time. In this sense, Fishbein and Ajzen's (1975) formulation anticipates the attitudes as construction view (Schwarz & Bohner, 2001) and the general notion that attitudes (Fazio, 1990), as well as their component parts, are subject to the vagaries of accessibility and knowledge activation.

Information Integration Versus Consistency

Although Fishbein's and Rosenberg's theories are both expectancy–value theories of attitudes, they differ in their assumptions about the *directionality* of the relationship between attitudes and beliefs. Fishbein's conception assumes that individuals form attitudes by learning about their attributes. Thus, attitudes are assumed to arise from a *bottom-up* integration of attribute information (Anderson, 1971, 1991).

By contrast, Rosenberg's (1956, 1960) theory is in essence a consistency theory (see Abelson, Aronson, et al., 1968), representing a *top-down* approach in which attitude formation and change occur in service of the *consistency motive*. On that basis, Rosenberg (1960) formulated the following hypothesis regarding the affective and cognitive components of an attitude:

> When the affective and cognitive components of an attitude are mutually consistent, the attitude is in a stable state; when the affective and cognitive components are mutually inconsistent ... the attitude is in an unstable state and will undergo spontaneous reorganizing activity until such activity eventuates either in (a) attainment of affective–cognitive consistency or (b) the placing of an "irreconcilable" inconsistency beyond the range of active awareness. (1960, p. 22)

There are two related predictions to be derived from Rosenberg's hypothesis; namely, that attitudes and beliefs are generally correlated, and that in cases where attitudes are inconsistent with beliefs (i.e., where there is a low evaluative–cognitive consistency), either the beliefs, or the attitudes, or both, are likely to change.

Much of Rosenberg's early research supported the viability of the first hypothesis, consistent with Fishbein's attitude model as well. This work demonstrated repeatedly that attitudes, operationalized as object evaluations, were generally consistent with beliefs, operationalized as instrumentality-value products (Chaiken, Pomerantz, & Giner-Sorolla, 1995). More interesting in the present context, however, are Rosenberg's experimental tests of the second hypothesis, which suggest that inconsistency *motivates* individuals to restore consistency by changing their attitudes, their beliefs, or both.

In a classic series of experiments on this topic, Rosenberg measured the cognitive structure of individuals' attitudes toward some high interest attitude issues (e.g., African Americans moving into White neighborhoods) twice, once before and once after a half hour interval. During the interval, these individuals were hypnotized and given an affect-modifying suggestion such as "when you wake up, the idea of Negroes moving into White neighborhoods will give you a happy, exhilarated feeling." Rosenberg was able to demonstrate that the hypnotic suggestion resulted in a significant change in the individuals' attitude toward the attitude object. In addition, he observed that this change resulted in a correspondent change in their cognitive structure, change that was not displayed by control individuals who had not been hypnotized.

Further predictions derived from Rosenberg's theory have been tested and empirically supported (see Chaiken et al., 1995, for a review). For example, if highly consistent attitudes are more stable than less consistent ones, they should also be more predictive of behavior. In support of this prediction, Norman (1975) demonstrated that the attitude toward volunteering for psychology experiments was more stable and predicted a relevant behavior more accurately when individuals displayed high-attitude consistency (signing up for a study; $r = .62$) than when they had low-attitiudinal consistency ($r = -.28$). This finding was present even though the two groups did not differ in the means or standard deviations of their attitude scores. In addition, there is evidence that high-consistency attitudes are more resistant to social influence than are low-consistency attitudes (Chaiken & Baldwin, 1981; Norman, 1975, Experiment 3).

Note that the information-integration and the consistency approaches are not actually competing or incompatible. Rather, they illuminate different aspects or ingredients of attitudinal structure. Information-integration refers to the *evidence* for a given attitude based on the attitude object's (positive or negative) consequences vis a vis the individuals' (active or accessible) goals. However, as evaluative judgments, attitudes are unlikely to be devoid of a motivational substrate. The consistency motive referred to by Rosenberg (1960) identifies one epistemic goal individuals may have in regard to attitude formation. Such a goal may represent the need for cognitive closure with respect to the attitudinal issue and an intolerance of ambiguity on this topic (see Kruglanski & Webster, 1996). This analysis suggests that the desire for consistency or coherence may vary across situations as well as across individuals. There is considerable evidence that both, in fact, are true (Cialdini, Trost, & Newsom, 1995). As we shall see, the distinction between evidential and goal aspects of attitudes is important in other domains of attitude research beyond that of attitude structure.

Ambivalence: The Dimensional Structure of Attitudes

As already noted, attitudes have been traditionally conceived of in bipolar terms, as points on a continuum of favorability and as related to an attitude object stably and uniquely, just like other properties of physical objects (e.g., the height of a table; Thurstone, 1931). As we have seen, however, subsequent theorizing and research have shown that some attitudes may be neither stable nor unique. An important version of such nonuniqueness relates to the concept of *attitudinal ambivalence*, which consists of simultaneously holding a positive and a negative attitude toward an object or an issue. Whereas evaluative-cognitive consistency refers to the degree of consistency between the overall evaluation of an attitude object and the evaluative meaning of beliefs about the object, research on attitudinal ambivalence has mainly focused on the evaluative inconsistencies that exist within a given component (e.g., Jonas, Broemer, & Diehl, 2000a; Maio, Bell, & Esses, 1996; Maio, Esses, & Bell, 2000; Thompson, Zanna, & Griffin, 1995).

Researchers have measured ambivalence either directly as an *experienced* state, or calculated it indirectly from a *formula* (Jonas et al., 2000a). When researchers use direct measures, individuals are asked to express their feeling of ambivalence (e.g., "I find myself torn between two sides of the issue of..."). The formula-based approach is related to the definition of ambivalence as the coexistence of positive and negative evaluations of the same object. Thus, it requires separate assessment of the two evaluations. With the *split semantic differential* method suggested by Kaplan (1972), respondents are first asked to evaluate the positive qualities of the attitude object while ignoring the negative aspects. After that, they are asked to evaluate the negative aspects, disregarding all positive qualities. These two ratings are then combined arithmetically into an index of ambivalence. Although no consensus has been reached about the properties of an ideal ambivalence formula (Jonas et al., 2000a), researchers do agree that such a formula should satisfy at least two conditions (Thompson et al., 1995). First, the two attitude components must be similar in magnitude. As the difference in magnitude between the two components increases, the attitude becomes more polarized in the direction of the stronger component. Second, for ambivalence to exist, the two attitude components have to be at least of a moderate intensity. With similarity held constant, ambivalence increases directly with intensity. There is evidence that experience-based and formula-based measures of ambivalence show a moderate degree of correlation (.35 to .45; Jonas et al., 2000a; also Fabrigar, MacDonald, & Wegener, this volume).

Superficially, there appears to be a great deal of conceptual overlap between the notions of ambivalence and evaluative-cognitive inconsistency. However, as Maio and colleagues (2000) have pointed out, this impression is deceptive. First, the assessment of evaluative-cognitive inconsistency focuses on the difference in evaluations *between* components; for example, evaluative-cognitive inconsistency reflects the extent to which the evaluative implications of an individual's beliefs about an attitude object are inconsistent with his or her overall evaluation of the object. In contrast, most research on ambivalence has focused on differences in evaluations *within* components (e.g., simultaneous positive and negative evaluation of an attitude object). Second, even when the between-components ambivalence and inconsistency are taken into account, a major difference remains: Ambivalence is a function of the *amount of conflict* within an attitude (i.e., *opposing* valences of *similar* magnitude), whereas inconsistency is a function of the *magnitude of the difference* between evaluations. As a hypothetical example, a positive dimension score of +4 and a negative dimension score of −4 would reflect greater ambivalence (more conflict) than a positive dimension score of +1 and a negative dimension score of −7. In contrast, inconsistency would be the same in both examples, because the degree of inconsistency is determined by the magnitude of the difference in evaluations. Consistent with this differentiation, Maio and colleagues (2000) found only weak or no association between various measures of inconsistency and ambivalence in attitudes toward Asian people.

With regard to the *consequences* of ambivalence and inconsistencies, both similarities and differences have been observed. Some of the similarities concern findings regarding attitude stability and impact on behavior. As with the evaluative-cognitive inconsistency, there is some evidence that attitudes show lower temporal stability at higher levels of ambivalence (e.g., Bargh et al., 1992; Jonas et al., 2000b, but for an inconsistent finding, see Bassili, 1996) and that they are also less predictive of behavior (Jonas et al., 2000b).

As for differences, evaluative-cognitive inconsistency appears to be related neither to accessibility nor to attitudinal extremity (for a review, see Chaiken et al., 1995). In contrast, several studies provide evidence that higher ambivalence is related to lower accessibility (i.e., higher response latencies) as well as to *less extreme* attitudes (see Jonas et al., 2000a, for a review). The attitude extremity finding is not surprising if one considers that ambivalence research was originally motivated by interest in individuals who hold neutral positions on evaluative dimensions. The lower accessibility of the overall evaluation is probably due to the fact that ambivalent attitudes correspond to attitude objects that have strong links in memory to both good and bad evaluations (Kaplan, 1972). In fact, high simultaneous accessibility of potentially conflicting evaluations has been shown to be positively related to experienced ambivalence (Newby-Clark, McGregor, & Zanna, 2002). Because both the good and the bad evaluations become active on exposure to the attitude object, the individual has to resolve the resulting response competition to arrive at an overall evaluation (Bargh et al., 1992).

There is some evidence that attitude ambivalence has motivating properties and drives cognitive activity in service of the goal of constructing a coherent attitude on a topic (Rosenberg's, 1960, notion of the consistency motive). In support of this assumption, Maio et al. (2000) found evidence that individuals with highly ambivalent attitudes toward Asian people processed a persuasive communication arguing for more immigration from Hong Kong more systematically than individuals with attitudes of low ambivalence.

It is noteworthy that we know more about the *consequences* of ambivalence than about its *antecedents*. However, there is some evidence about individual differences associated with the propensity for ambivalence. Need for cognition (Cacioppo & Petty, 1982) and fear of invalidity (Kruglanski, 1989) have been found to be associated with the amount of ambivalence that characterized individuals' attitudes on a range of issues (Thompson & Zanna, 1995). Individuals with high need for cognition, who engage and enjoy effortful cognitive endeavors and dislike ambiguity, tend to have lower levels of ambivalence than individuals low on need for cognition. In contrast, personal fear of invalidity, a heightened concern with making errors, is positively correlated with levels of ambivalence.

With regard to domain-specific antecedents, one would assume that ambivalence would result in domains characterized by goal conflicts (e.g., Kruglanski, Shah, et al., 2002; Stroebe, 2002). For example, Stroebe (2002) argued that chronic dieters (i.e., restrained eaters; Herman

& Polivy, 1984) experience a conflict between two incompatible goals: On the one hand, they enjoy food and love to eat (the eating enjoyment goal); on the other hand, in line with societal demands for slimness, they want to either lose weight (weight loss goal), or at least avoid gaining weight (weight control goal). As a consequence, they experience difficulties reducing their calorie intake, because eating enjoyment, as an affective reaction, is usually the first reaction to food stimuli. Because eating enjoyment and weight control are incompatible goals, the stimulation of eating enjoyment results in an inhibition of eating-control thoughts. In support of this hypothesis, Mensink, Stroebe, Schut, and Arts (2003) showed that increasing the accessibility of eating enjoyment through semantic priming of *eating-enjoyment* concepts reduced the accessibility of *eating-control* concepts.

Wensink, Stroebe, and Schut (reported in Stroebe, 2002) further demonstrated that the attitudes of restrained eaters toward eating are highly ambivalent. In line with Freud (1923), who described self-regulation as a continuous battle of the ego to reconcile the urges of the pleasure-driven id with the demands of the norm-imposing superego, we would argue that eating is only one of many domains where hedonism is difficult to reconcile with the demands of society.

Somewhat similarly, Katz and Hass (1988) have argued that ambivalence can be the result of conflicting values, citing as an example the domain of racial attitudes in the United States. There is evidence that, during the last few decades, the racial attitudes of European Americans toward African Americans have become more ambivalent, with feelings of friendliness and rejection toward this target group existing side by side. Thus, as has also been suggested by others (e.g., Gaertner & Dovidio, 1986; Kinder & Sears, 1981), modern, aversive, or symbolic racism differs in important ways from traditional forms of racism. Katz and Hass (1988) argued that for some individuals, African Americans are perceived as deserving of help, yet at the same time, as not doing enough to help themselves. Katz and Hass provided empirical evidence that these conflicting sentiments are rooted in two largely independent core value orientations in American culture: humanitarianism-egalitarianism on the one hand, and the Protestant work ethic on the other.

A different possibility of holding two incompatible attitudes at the same time is outlined by Wilson et al. (2000) in their model of dual attitudes. These authors argued against the widely held assumption that attitude change results in the replacement of the prior attitude by the new (changed) attitude and suggested that persuasive advocacies or new experiences may often result in the creation of a novel attitude without necessarily disposing of the old attitude. Dual attitudes are defined as different evaluations of the same attitude object, one on an automatic, implicit level, and one on a controlled, explicit level. For example, European Americans who are reared in racist families and learn to be prejudiced against African Americans may adopt egalitarian values as adults and learn to abhor prejudice of all kinds. Whereas the traditional view on attitude change would assume that the new egalitarian attitude has replaced the old racist attitudes from childhood, Wilson et al. (2000) argued that these individuals now hold dual attitudes toward African Americans: a habitual (or implicit) negative attitude and a more recently constructed (explicit) positive attitude. This model yields the intriguing prediction that the attitude individuals are likely to endorse at any given time will depend on whether they have the cognitive capacity to retrieve the explicit attitude, while suppressing the old attitude (Devine, 1989).

Wilson et al. (2000) argued that dual attitudes are distinct from the subjective state of ambivalence. Specifically, people may not feel conflicted about dual evaluations because, at any given moment, only one of the evaluations predominates and is treated as the sole evaluation. However, if one defines ambivalence as the *existence* of conflicting evaluations rather than the *experience* of conflict, then the model of Wilson and colleagues (2000) may indeed be considered to depict a kind of ambivalence. Furthermore, on a methodological note, the failure to find correlations between explicit and implicit measures of prejudice might not indicate an absence of awareness of the implicit attitude, but rather the operation of social desirability norms on explicit measures.

The Bases of Attitudes

In the important analysis of the attitude concept discussed earlier, Zanna and Rempel (1988, p. 319) treat attitudes as *beliefs*, potentially derivable from three classes of *evidence*: (a) utilitarian beliefs about the positive and/or negative consequences mediated by the attitude object (the cognitive basis or degree to which the object mediates the attainment of various goals), (b) feelings and emotions, and (c) behavioral information about instances in which one intended to or actually approached or avoided a stimulus.

It is noteworthy that the cognitive basis in this formulation corresponds directly to the expectancy-value and the means goals frameworks described earlier, wherein the motivationally relevant consequences that the object mediates, and/or the motivationally relevant features of the object as such, serve as evidence for one's attitude toward it. This inference is based on a rule, whereby the more an object promotes the satisfaction of positive goals and the avoidance of negative goals, the more it merits a positive evaluation.

The conception proposed by Zanna and Rempel (1988) goes beyond the means goals framework, however, in identifying additional evidential bases for attitudes. For instance, positive feelings in presence of an attitude object may signify to an individual that he or she likes or positively evaluates this object. This evaluation may be based on an inference rule whereby a positive feeling in presence of an object signifies a positive evaluation (see Schwarz & Clore, 1983). Finally, the belief (or perception) that one has exhibited an approach or an avoidance behavior toward an object may be considered evidence for a positive or a negative attitude in accordance with an inference rule that approach behaviors toward an object (e.g., choosing it, seeking it out, making a positive statement about it, etc.) signify liking or positive evaluation, whereas avoidance behaviors signify a dislike or a negative evaluation (e.g., Bem, 1965).

Is Zanna and Rempel's (1988) classification of attitudinal bases exhaustive? It seems possible to add at least two more general categories to the mix. There is increasing evidence for the role of genetic variables in attitude formation and change (Olson, Vernon, & Jang, 2001; Tesser, 1993). Although little is known about the mechanism by which genetic factors influence attitudes, it is extremely unlikely that there is a direct, one-to-one connection between genes and attitudes (Olson, Vernon, & Jang, 2001). However, genes may establish general predispositions that shape environmental experiences in ways that increase the likelihood of the individual developing specific attitudes.

A second, and rather different general basis for attitudes could be the *epistemic authority* of the source supporting a given attitudinal judgment (Ellis & Kruglanski, 1992; Kruglanski et al., in press; Raviv, Bar-Tal, Raviv, & Abin, 1993). Epistemic authority is maximal when a particular source is perceived as *infallibly knowledgeable* about a given domain (or even across domains, as a parent might be for a child). For instance, evaluations of a source considered expert in some field could lead one to adopt an attitude apparently held by the source based on an expertise inference rule or heuristic (Chaiken, Liberman, & Eagly, 1989). If one subscribed to the notions that whatever an expert says is valid, X is an expert, and X says that Y is good/bad, then one may directly infer that Y is indeed good/bad without having to consider utilitarian beliefs, affect, or behavioral evidence. In an identical fashion, a majority source could promote attitudinal acceptance based on a *consensus heuristic* to which some persons might subscribe. This heuristic assigns epistemic authority to a consensual opinion, such that a source with a negative epistemic authority, perhaps a minority source, can undermine the adoption of an attitude via an inference rule that an attitude endorsed by this particular source is likely to be unwarranted or invalid.

Even if the source's epistemic authority in the eyes of the recipient were impeccable, one might still suspect that the source's statements do not reflect his or her true opinions for other reasons. For instance, *information* that the source may receive a material benefit for persuading the recipient may detract from the source's perceived sincerity. This hypothesis is related to the notion of discounting (Kelley, 1972a), whereby the possible benefit to the source of persuading the recipient detracts from the perceived causal role of the source's true opinions in prompting the source's pronouncement (Eagly, Wood, & Chaiken, 1978). In counter distinction to discounting, the notion of augmentation (Kelley, 1972b) suggests that a loss the source may incur for expressing an opinion augments one's faith in the authenticity of the opinion. Though the processes of discounting and augmentation may seem complicated and laborious, they could be routinized and rendered relatively simple and independent of cognitive resources. Trope and Gaunt (2000), for example, observed that when the biasing information about a situational demand is particularly salient, discounting occurs independently of cognitive load.

Although in Zanna and Rempel's (1988) framework the attitudinal bases are implied to play a predominantly *informational* function, there may be more to the story. For example, mood states have been shown to influence the effort individuals spend on processing information: There is ample evidence that individuals are more highly motivated to scrutinize persuasive arguments (and therefore to be more influenced by the quality of these arguments) when in a bad rather than good or neutral mood (e.g., Mackie & Worth, 1989; Schwarz & Bless, 1991). It also seems plausible that intense feelings can produce a powerful motivational state that may appropriately bias the formation of attitudinal judgments (Dunning, 1999; Kunda, 1990; Kunda & Sinclair, 1999). Consider Zanna and Rempel's (1988, p. 319) example of a parent whose child has been killed by a drunk driver. This person's attitude (toward drunk driving) is likely to be affected not only by the extreme salience of the information about the terrible consequences of a given instance of drunk driving, but by a powerful *motivational bias* to judge this particular attitude object in highly negative terms. In other words, feelings typically stem from the satisfaction or frustration of various *goals*, and they often activate other goals (such as perpetuating positive feelings and removing or ameliorating negative ones) that may affect the formation of attitudinal judgments. In this sense, feelings may affect attitudes via a motivational route in addition to an informational route, namely, by giving rise to a directional *epistemic motivation* capable of affecting judgments. For instance, an intensely negative feeling associated with having lost a child in a drunk driving accident might evoke a powerful motivation to perceive alcohol consumption as evil. Such motivation may then bias the cognitive process by increasing the accessibility of arguments congruent with a desired conclusion and inhibiting the accessibility of arguments incongruent with it (Kunda, 1990). If this assumption is correct, feelings may constitute particularly powerful determinants of attitudes, and it appears that they do. Consistent with this notion, Abelson, Kinder, Peters and Fiske (1982) demonstrated that feeling states associated with various political candidates predicted research participants' attitudes toward these candidates over and above beliefs about those candidates (see also Lavine, Thompsen, Zanna, & Borgida, 1998).

Nor are feelings alone in their ability to engender motivational states. The knowledge that a given attitude was expressed or endorsed by a majority source, for example, may activate a goal to agree with this attitude in order to be accepted by the majority (e.g., Moscovici, 1980). In contrast, knowledge that an attitude characterizes a minority source might lead to its rejection, based on an evoked motivation to separate oneself from a powerless group. In other words, consistent with our prior notion that goals have a cognitive dimension and are mentally represented, they may be activated by information (e.g., about one's feelings, or about the source's status) that in and of itself may function as evidence for attitudinal judgments.

Do different attitudinal bases systematically differ in their consequences? Fazio & Zanna (1981) found that attitudes based on direct experience with the attitude object (i.e., based on past behaviors toward the attitude object) predict future behavior toward the object better than attitudes based on indirect experience (translatable as utilitarian beliefs). Would this be invariably so? One could argue that the value of any evidence for any judgment is subjective and is in the eye of the beholder.

Different persons may attach different degrees of credibility to various types of evidence in accordance with their source, including their own experience with the attitude object. Thus, personal experience could be assigned different evidential weight by individuals varying in their degree of self-ascribed epistemic authority (Ellis & Kruglanski, 1992; Kruglanski et al., in press; Raviv et al., 1993), defined as their subjective confidence in their knowledge in a domain or perceived competence to interpret the experience. Possibly, individuals with a high degree of self-ascribed epistemic authority would be more ready to use their personal experience as a basis from which to launch their behavior than individuals with a low degree of self-ascribed epistemic authority. Consistent with this reasoning, Ellis and Kruglanski (1992) found that, controlling for actual mathematical ability, people with a low self-ascribed epistemic authority in mathematics benefited less from experiential learning and actually learned better when the same mathematical principles were imparted by a teacher.

Similarly, individuals may ascribe differential epistemic authority to different sources of (utilitarian) beliefs about goals mediated by the attitude object. Presumably, attitudinal beliefs imparted by a source with a highly revered epistemic authority (e.g., a parent, a priest, or a respected professional in a relevant domain) would be held with greater confidence than beliefs imparted by a source with a less impeccable epistemic authority. In turn, it seems plausible to assume that the tendency to launch behavior in accordance with the attitude would vary positively with the confidence with which the attitude in question was held by the individual. Of course, the tendency to enact an attitudinally consistent behavior should depend on factors other than one's confidence in an attitude. Specifically, it should depend on the degree to which the attitude gave rise to a behavioral intention (Fishbein & Ajzen, 1975), which in turn should depend on the degree to which a given goal believed to be served by the attitude object was momentarily activated, and the conditions (time and place) were adjudged appropriate for enacting that behavior.

In summary, Zanna and Rempel's (1988) analysis suggests that the evidential (or informational) bases of attitudes may include a variety of evidence types beyond utilitarian beliefs about the attitude object, namely, behavioral information, as well as affect. In our analysis of this work, we added to it an evidential category having to do with source authority, and we pointed out that beyond the evidential bases, attitude formation is likely to be importantly affected by epistemic goals, possibly themselves evoked or activated by the information given.

Probabilogical Models

Whereas the Zanna and Rempel (1988) paper offers a useful taxonomy of evidential types, probabilogical models of cognitive functioning (McGuire, 1960, 1968, 1981; Wyer, 1974; Wyer & Carlston, 1979; Wyer & Goldberg, 1970) dwelled on the psycho-logic whereby *any* evidence may lead to evaluative (or other) conclusions. This view assumes that attitude systems accord with the "axioms of logic and probability theory" (McGuire, 1985, p. 244).

Consider the following propositions (adapted from McGuire, 1985, p. 244): (a) the number of 15- to 25-year-olds in the U.S. population will decline in the 1980s and the 1990s, (b) 15- to 25-year-olds commit a disproportionate number of all violent crimes, and (c) the per capita rate of violent crime in the United States should decline in the 1980s and the 1990s. The probabilogical model asserts that the relations between the foregoing three propositions will be expressed by the following equation:

$$P(c) = p[c/(a\&b)] \times p(a\&b) + p[c/-(a\&b)] \times p - (a\&b) \qquad [1]$$

In terms of the present discussion, the probabilities in this equation refer to the recipient's *beliefs* in various states of affairs including the major and the minor premises (a and b) that jointly determine a belief in the conclusion (c). Note also that the probabilogical models are *normative* in the sense of assuming that the individual considers not only situationally available evidence (represented by premises a and b) in relation to conclusion c, but also *all* alternative evidential bases (represented by the complement to a and b, that is, $-[a\&b]$) relevant to that conclusion. In that particular sense, the probabilogical model depicts an idealized state of affairs rather than the limited capacity and motivation conditions (central to Simon's, 1980, *bounded rationality* notion) of human information processing (see Pierro, Mannetti, Erb, Spiegel, & Kruglanski, in press; Kruglanski, Dechesne, & Chun, in press; Kruglanski, Pierro, Mannetti, & Spiegel, in press).

In addition to these probabilogical relations, the probabilogical model acknowledges a variety of *alogical* functioning principles affecting the formation and change of attitudes and opinions. One such principle that received a fair amount of research attention is the *Socratic effect* (McGuire, 1960) whereby attitude change can be effected not only by confronting the recipient with new information, but also by enhancing the salience of previously available information. Discussions of the probabilogical model (e.g., McGuire, 1985) also acknowledge the biasing effects on attitudinal conclusions of directional motivations of the *wishful thinking* variety, through which various epistemic goals may affect one's judgments. Research into such effects demonstrated high (in the order of .70) correlations between expected likelihoods and desirability of occurrence, attesting both to inferences of the object's likelihood from its desirability (Granberg & Brent, 1983) and of the object's desirability from its likelihood (Sjöberg, 1978). However, discussions of the probabilogical model do not typically integrate the assumed extralogical tendencies with the fundamentally logical reasoning structure being postulated. Thus, it is not clear which of the several terms in Equation (1) are influenced by increased informational salience, and/or the directional epistemic goals of the wishful thinking variety, and if so, how.

Summary

Over the years, research on attitude structure has addressed some fundamental issues concerning the essence of attitudes. Expectancy–value models have dealt with the notion that attitudes are constructed from beliefs about the positive or negative features of objects, in which the features' positivity/negativity is relative to goals and values to which individuals may subscribe. Subsequent theoretical analyses have broadened the evidential bases of attitudes to include behavioral and affective information (Zanna & Rempel, 1988) as well as the epistemic authority of the source (Kruglanski, 1989). Whereas the foregoing refer to *content* categories of evidence, the probabilogical models (McGuire, 1960; Wyer, 1974) addressed the logical structure of arguments whereby conclusions are drawn from evidence of any type.

Already early attitude research has recognized the fact that the saliency (or accessibility) of utilitarian beliefs (about positive and negative consequences of attitude objects, about behavior) may vary across situations as well as persons (Fishbein & Ajzen, 1975). Recent research on goals and values also suggests that their accessibility (or degree of momentary activation) may vary (Kruglanski et al., 2002; Stroebe, 2002), as may the accessibility of evidential beliefs about behaviors or affective states. To the extent that beliefs and goals/values enter into the construction of attitudes, then attitudes may be unstable across situations, with the consequence that an individual may experience and/or express different attitudes toward the same object on different occasions. Finally, because attitudes themselves constitute cognitive structures, just like other such structures they can be implicit and exert an automatic, out-of-awareness influence on relevant judgments and behaviors (Greenwald & Banaji, 1995; Wilson et al., 2000).

ATTITUDE FUNCTIONS

As stressed earlier, goals may relate to attitudes in two distinct ways: namely, as *evidence* that the attitude object merits a positive or a negative evaluation (because it promotes or impedes the attainment of various goals), and as *epistemic motivations* that influence attitude formation. The distinction between goals as evidence and goals as epistemic motivations is pertinent to a long-standing interest of social psychologists in *attitude functions*. Simply put, the two roles that goals may fulfill in their relation to attitudes have been occasionally confused in the functional research tradition. Whereas attitude functions primarily refer to the goals that an *attitude* may serve (i.e., answering the question of *why* should a given *attitude* be held), and in this sense may be thought of as *epistemic motivations* underlying attitude formation, often these have been confused with goals that an *attitude object* may serve, and that, therefore, serve as (utilitarian) *evidence* for the kind of evaluation (i.e., attitude) this object merits (i.e., answering the question of what kind of object evaluation is warranted).

Note, furthermore, that goals for attitude formation (i.e., attitude functions envisioned *before* the attitude was formed) need not be the same as goals or functions that the attitude fulfills (uses to which it can be put) *after* it has been formed. For instance, an attitude originally formed out of curiosity may be subsequently used to gain acceptance to a valued group, or an attitude whose formation was influenced by the need to belong to a group may function to boost one's self-esteem once the group norms have been internalized.

A Brief History

Brewster Smith (1947) was the first to explicitly theorize about attitude functions, and he distinguished several of those. For instance, attitudes may serve an *object appraisal function*, which may facilitate one's decisions of whether to approach or avoid a given object (or a class of objects). In this vein, Fazio (1990) demonstrated that the possession of accessible attitudes facilitates decision making with respect to those objects, as attested by quicker lexical decision times to the requisite judgments. Similarly, Katz (1960) proposed that attitudes may serve a *knowledge function*, which arguably is broader in conception than the utilitarian object appraisal function. The difference is that the acquisition of knowledge may be motivated by curiosity and be absent of any pragmatic or instrumental concerns, whereas the object appraisal function appears to be geared to the approach–avoidance issue with specific objects, and, hence, to be relatively instrumental or pragmatic in orientation.

Smith, Bruner, and White (1956) and Katz (1960) also agreed that attitudes may be held and expressed in order to cope with an intra-psychic conflict. Katz (1960) called this the *ego-defensive function* and Smith et al. (1956) referred to it as the *externalization function*. Both Smith et al. (1956) and Katz (1960) argued that attitudes may serve the purpose of *self-expression*, though the function of self-expression differed in the two frameworks. On the one hand, Smith et al. (1956) stressed the *social adjustment function* that the expression of attitudes serves in regulating one's relations with others. Katz (1960), on the other hand, highlighted the *self-expression function* in articulating one's internalized values and, thus, serving to strengthen a desirable sense of self.

Whereas the general taxonomies of Smith et al. (1956) and Katz (1960) have proven useful over the years, it is important to realize that an attitude can serve almost any goal at all (Olson & Maio, 1999). For example, an attitude may provide the function of cognitive closure, anxiety reduction, locomotion/assessment (Kruglanski et al., 2000), or promotion/prevention (Higgins, 1997). In some contexts, it may be more informative to identify the specific goals that an attitude object may serve, rather than viewing those as instances of the broader taxonomic categories of attitude functions.

The Primacy of the Knowledge Function

If, as we presently assume, an attitude may fruitfully represent an evaluative *judgment*, then *any* attitude, independent of the evidence on which it was based and of the epistemic motivations (or envisioned functions) affecting its formation, may be said to fulfill a knowledge function. As Fazio (2000, pp. 3–4) expressed it, "the object appraisal function can be considered the primary value of possessing an attitude. *Every* attitude, regardless of any other functional beliefs that it may also provide, serves this object appraisal function."

The knowledge function that attitudes serve yields numerous benefits for the individual. For instance, using measures of autonomic reactivity to assess effort expenditure during decision making, Blascovich, Ernst, Tomaka, Kelsey, Salomon, and Fazio (1993) as well as Fazio, Blascovich, and Driscoll (1992) found that individuals whose attitudes were relatively accessible as a result of their having rehearsed their evaluations displayed less autonomic reactivity when making decisions based on those attitudes than did individuals with less accessible attitudes. Additional research by Fazio and his colleagues (1992) suggests that accessible attitudes orient visual attention and categorization processes in a useful manner so that more resources are left for coping with other stressors an individual might be experiencing.

As with other accessible knowledge, accessible attitudes can exact costs as well. Specifically, they can inhibit the individual from noticing aspects of the object that are incongruent with the attitude (Fazio, Lednetter, & Towles-Schwen, 2000). Knowledge accessibility can result in a quick utilization of accessible knowledge at the expense of carefully monitoring possible changes in the object's functionality. Individuals with accessible attitudes tend to be slower in recognizing a change in the attitude object, and they may underestimate the degree of change that they do perceive. In short, because of their accessibility, strong attitudes may foster a closed mindedness that reduces individuals' sensitivity to possible shifts in an attitude object's utility or goals that the object may serve or hinder (Fazio, 1990).

Research on knowledge accessibility (e.g., Ford & Kruglanski, 1995; Thompson, Roman, Moscovitz, Chaiken, & Bargh, 1994) demonstrated that accessible constructs are particularly likely to influence judgments under a high need for cognitive closure and are unlikely to affect judgments under a high need to avoid closure, such as that induced by accuracy instructions. It is thus possible that the rigidity fostered by accessible attitudes can be at least partially mitigated under the appropriate motivational (i.e., goal-related) conditions.

Functions of Attitudes or of Attitude Objects?

Whereas the work by Fazio refers to the goals or functions served by *attitudes* as such, research described by Shavit and Nelson (1999) seems to refer more to goals or functions served by the attitude *objects*. Accordingly, Shavitt and Nelson (2000, p. 41) found that "for products that predominantly engage a utilitarian function, claims regarding product attributes and benefits are particularly persuasive (e.g., 'the special construction that makes Coolcraft air conditioners so efficient also makes them quiet')." In other words, one is likely to develop a positive attitude toward a Coolcraft air conditioner because efficiency and quietness constitute goals that an air conditioner could reasonably serve; hence, representing *evidence* for the goodness of this particular brand, warranting a positive attitude toward it. Obviously, this conception of functions is similar to the means-end structure of attitudes suggested by Rosenberg (1960).

Note that when goal satisfaction or function fulfillment serve as evidence for the value of the attitude object (or its goodness), the information that the object accomplishes these particular objectives has to be *credible*. One would not take seriously an assertion that an air conditioner is good because it improves the efficiency of one's immune system or the acuity of one's vision. In other words, it is not the attitude toward a product, but the product itself that serves the functions in question (e.g., of efficiency and quietness). Therefore, credibility that it indeed fulfills those functions influences the attitude toward the product accordingly.

Because evidence for an attitude comprises the goals served by the attitude object, evidence consisting of more desirable goals should elicit a more positive attitude than evidence consisting of less desirable goals. This is in accordance with the inference rule whereby *the more important the goals that the attitude object serves, the more positive would be the attitude that it merits*. Of course, the relative desirability of goals may differ across persons. Consistent with this notion, Snyder and DeBono (1985) found that product ads that were functionally phrased (social-adjustive or image-oriented ads for high self-monitors and value expressive or product-quality ads for low self-monitors) elicited a more positive attitudinal response and higher levels of purchasing intention than did functionally irrelevant ads.

In their chapter on attitudes function, Lavine and Snyder (1999) discussed functions in terms of goals served by the attitude object, rather than the attitude per se: "a person with a social-adjustive attitude should be especially interested in sizing up an attitude object's value-related qualities, whereas a person with a social-adjustive attitude should be more interested in sizing up the object's normative qualities" (p. 103). Indeed, research conducted by Lavine and Snyder (1996) contains impressive evidence that attitudes toward voting as well as actual voting behavior are affected by the degree to which the persuasive messages match the personality of the recipient. Thus, low self-monitors were persuaded more by messages extolling the value expressive function of voting, and high self-monitors were persuaded by messages extolling the social-adjustive value of voting. Similarly, low authoritarians perceived messages framed in terms of threats for not voting as of a higher quality than messages framed in terms of rewards for voting, and the opposite was the case for high authoritarians. Again, at issue in Lavine and Snyder's (1996) research was *voting* as an *attitude object* rather than the possession of a given attitude toward voting.

Prentice and Carlsmith's (1999) research focused, similarly, on functions served by attitude objects. One of their findings was that attitudes toward possessions whose primary value resided in their symbolic meaning (e.g., photographs, family heirlooms, a diary) differed from possessions whose primary value derived from the direct benefits they enabled (e.g., a stereo, a computer, a bicycle). This research, thus, also referred to functions served by the attitude objects and not functions served by possessing the attitudes as such.

In contrast to these findings, work by DeBono (1987) did address the functions of *attitudes*. This research found that low self-monitors adopted a more favorable attitude toward deinstitutionalization of the mentally ill, after learning that this *attitudinal position* was associated with their values (representing a value expressive goal) than after learning that it was supported by 70% of their peers (representing a social-adjustive goal). The opposite pattern of results was exhibited by high self-monitors.

Goal Magnitudes and Processing Extent

A claim that an attitude object serves (or undermines) an important goal is likely to affect attitudes through several pathways: It can serve as direct evidence for an attitude toward that object (i.e., heuristic cue, message argument), but it is also likely to enhance processing motivation, which is the extent to which the arguments contained in this claim will be scrutinized. Such an enhancement of processing motivation should increase the persuasive impact of strong and carefully reasoned (i.e., high quality) arguments and decrease the impact of low-quality arguments. Evidence consistent with this analysis was furnished by Petty and Wegener (1998a). These investigators found that when message content matched the functional basis of product attitudes—when the message content referred to functions deemed more important to participants (i.e., when image messages were presented to high self-monitors or quality messages were presented to low self-monitors)—the difference between high- and low-quality arguments was more pronounced than when the message content mismatched the functional base.

In other words, as we noted earlier, an activation of a goal served by an attitude object may not only provide evidence for the kind of evaluation the object merits but also evoke an epistemic motivation that may affect attitude formation. Whereas in Petty and Wegener's (1998a) work the goals or functions of the attitude object may have represented a nondirectional epistemic motivation (to arrive at an accurate attitudinal judgment), it is conceivable that goals may occasionally evoke a directional epistemic motivation as well. For instance, an individual who strongly wishes to improve his or her appearance may not only develop a positive attitude toward a cosmetic product that promised to do so, but would also be biased in the evaluation of arguments to that effect. Such individuals might overestimate the quality of arguments advocating the product, being more convinced by low-quality arguments than an individual with less strong an appearance goal. Such possibilities could be profitably examined in future research.

Summary

The functions that *possessing an attitude* may serve are not necessarily those served by the *attitude objects*. Functions served by the attitude object refer to goals that the attitude object may help to attain. In this sense, they constitute *evidence* for the degree of goodness assignable to the attitude objects or, in other words, *reasons* for holding the attitude in question. Goals served by possessing the attitude (attitude functions) may influence the formation or maintenance of attitudes without serving as evidence for the attitudes. In that sense, these goals are the *causes of*, rather than the *reasons for*, the attitude. The distinction between the functions of attitude objects and of attitudes as such has been glossed over in the literature on attitude functions. As a consequence, much of the recent research on attitude functions has centered on the functions on the attitude objects rather than on the attitudes per se.

Furthermore, goals that an attitude object may fulfill may also introduce a (directional or a nondirectional) epistemic motivation—that is, an epistemic goal affecting the formation of an attitude—by inducing a biased or an unbiased scrutiny of arguments. Finally, much of the work on attitude functions has demonstrated that such different functions exist and that different attitude objects are associated with different functions. It should be noted, however, that strictly speaking any goal can be served by an attitude or an attitude object under some circumstances. Therefore, although taxonomies of functions are useful and important, they are of necessity incomplete and inadequate to capture all the manifold nuances in possible goals or functions that attitudes and/or attitude objects can serve (Olson & Maio, 1999).

ATTITUDE DYNAMICS

A great deal of theoretical and empirical research on attitudes considered the dynamic issues of the formation and change of attitudes. This work explored the processes whereby attitudes are formed and altered as a consequence of new information. This work also considered the characteristics of attitude formation and change processes for attitude persistence, resistance to counterpersuasion, and the attitude–behavior relation.

Much of this work has treated attitudes as (evaluative) judgments or knowledge structures whose formation and change proceeds in accordance with the same general principles that govern the formation and change of all judgments and knowledge structures. Although, the concepts of *persuasion* and *attitude change* have been often used interchangeably in this literature, persuasion is only one form of social influence. Persuasion refers to attitude change in response to complex verbal messages that are intended to persuade an audience. However, as research on majority and minority influence has demonstrated, our attitudes and beliefs are also affected by the mere knowledge of the attitudes and beliefs of other group members (Asch, 1951, 1956; Moscovici, 1980). Our treatment of attitude dynamics will, therefore, review both types of social influence, namely, research on the influence of majorities and minorities as well as the traditional research on persuasion. However, before we review the impact of social influence processes on attitudes, we will discuss two learning theory approaches to the acquisition of attitudes, which could challenge the idea that attitudes constitute evaluative beliefs that are constructed from evidence.

The Learning of Attitudes: Mere Exposure and Evaluative Conditioning

There are essentially two pathways to the acquisition of evaluation that have received attention from within learning psychology, namely, mere exposure and evaluative conditioning.

Mere Exposure Effects

Mere exposure can be viewed as a nonassociative type of valence acquisition, because simple repeated exposure to stimuli is sufficient to increase their perceived favorability (Zajonc, 1968). This effect has been documented in many studies and quite different stimulus materials (e.g., nonsense words, ideographs, geometric forms, photographs) and with supraliminal as well as subliminal versions of the mere exposure paradigm (for a review, see Bornstein, 1989). Based on evidence that the mere exposure effect does not necessitate subjects' recognition of a stimulus as having been presented earlier, Zajonc (1980) argued that "preferences need no inferences," meaning that a stimulus may directly elicit affect without any cognitive mediation.

Although at present there is no single satisfactory account for the mere exposure effect (Bohner & Wänke, 2002), one of the more plausible explanations in terms of *perceptual fluency* suggests that the absence of awareness may not imply an absence of cognitions. According to this interpretation, individuals experience facilitated encoding when perceiving a stimulus at a repeated rate and this facilitated encoding is experienced as pleasant (Bornstein & D'Agostino, 1994). Individuals then attribute this pleasant experience of facilitated processing (i.e., perceptual fluency) to the favorability of the stimulus. Consistent with this assumption, the positive effects of high fluency on evaluative judgment are eliminated under conditions that invite misattribution of affect to an irrelevant source (Winkielman, Schwarz, Fazandeiro, & Reber, 2003). Thus, fluency effects on preference judgments are no longer obtained when the informational value of the affective reaction is undermined.

Evaluative Conditioning

The second pathway to the acquisition of evaluation that has received attention from within learning psychology is associative in nature. Evaluative conditioning is based on the contingent pairing of originally neutral stimuli with events that already have some positive or negative valence, prototypically a liked or a disliked face presented in a picture, with a neutral face. As a result of the pairing, the initially neutral face comes to acquire the valence of the face with which it was previously associated (e.g., Baeyens, Eelen, Crombez, & Van den Bergh, 1992; Olson & Fazio, 2001; Walther, 2002).

Earlier research conceived of evaluative conditioning as a form of classical conditioning. Thus, according to Staats and Staats (1958), the conditioning of attitudes is based on the pairing of an initially neutral attitude object (e.g., name of a nationality) serving as the conditioned stimulus (CS) with a (positively or negatively) valenced stimulus (e.g., words with positive or negative evaluative meaning) serving as the unconditioned stimulus (UCS), and followed by the attitude object's acquisition of the UCS's valence. In modern learning theories, classical conditioning processes are considered instances of signal learning wherein the organism learns that a conditional, if–then, relationship exists between the UCS (e.g., the food in a Pavlovian conditioning paradigm) and the CS (e.g., the bell). As Hermans and colleagues (2003) argued, the most important function of Pavlovian or classical conditioning is the detection of reliable predictors or signals (CSs) for the occurrence of biologically significant environmental stimuli (UCs). In humans, this type of learning depends on the individual's *awareness* of the relation between CS and UCS and is sensitive to extinction manipulations (Hermans, Bayens, & Eelen, 2003).

However, the contemporary view of classical conditioning as signal learning is not compatible with the pattern of findings observed with evaluative conditioning. Therefore, researchers have begun to recognize that evaluative conditioning differs from classical conditioning and cannot be explained in terms of signal learning (Hermans et al., 2003). In contrast to classical conditioning, evaluative conditioning is not dependent on participants' awareness of the contingencies involved. Furthermore, weakening of the contingency by single CS or UCS presentations does not automatically decrease conditioning. Finally, evaluative conditioning is apparently resistant to extinction, as shown by the findings that after successful evaluative learning, unreinforced (i.e., single) CS presentations do not alter its valence for the individuals. For instance, a positive evaluation of a soft drink established through its association with pleasant music is stable and relatively independent of its further co-occurrences with the music.

The mechanism underlying evaluative conditioning is not well understood at this time. Walther, Nagengast, and Trasselli (2003) plausibly hypothesize that evaluative conditioning may involve a simple Gestalt principle, namely, that things presented in close proximity acquire a similar meaning or valence. This principle evokes the notion of entitativity (Campbell, 1958; Hamilton & Sherman, 1996), implying that stimuli occurring in proximity are similar and/or share a common fate, are then perceived to compose the same entity. Thus, a negatively valued face lends its negative meaning to the group of which the neutral face is also a part. In turn, membership in a negatively valenced group may constitute evidence that that the initially neutral face also merits a negative evaluation.

Such interpretation allows that some sort of if–then rule is involved in the acquisition of attitudes through evaluative conditioning, though it might be a different rule than that involved in a prototypical classical conditioning paradigm. In classical conditioning, evidence for the valence of the CS has to do with its putative (positive or negative) *consequences*, whereas in evaluative conditioning the evidence has to do with the CS's *group membership*.

Such an analysis might also shed some light on the fact that classical, but not evaluative, conditioning is subject to extinction. When a classically conditioned CS is presented alone, apart from the UCS, the separation constitutes disconfirming evidence regarding its assumed positive or negative consequences (represented by the UCS). This separation may well undermine the individual's belief that the CS has such consequences, hence, removing the evidential basis for the (positive or negative) attitude toward the CS.

A different psychological situation might exist, however, when an evaluatively conditioned CS appears alone, for this isolation does not negate the CS's membership in the larger group of which the UCS too is a member. For instance, a lone encounter with an individual member of a negatively (e.g., a street gang) or a positively (e.g., an admired sports team) valued group does not deny her or his membership in those entities. Consequently, it does not undermine the reason (or, in present terms, the evidence) for the attitude one has previously developed toward this CS.

Goals.   In classical conditioning, a UCS such as food or a shock represents a goal-related affordance of a positive or negative nature. Similarly, in evaluative conditioning, the UCS (e.g., a liked or a disliked face) is goal-related, representing the kind of stimulus one is typically motivated to approach or to avoid. As we have noted earlier, such sense of goal-relatedness is tied to the UCS's function as *evidence* for an attitude formed toward the CS.

But goals (albeit different ones) could affect conditioning via the function of *epistemic motivation* as well, affecting the readiness to carry out learning or to form attitudes in the first place. In this vein, Schwarz and Bless (1991) suggested that whereas happy mood is more likely to elicit a top-down processing style, sad mood is more likely to elicit a detailed analysis of the information at hand, hence, contributing to learning. Consistent with this notion, Walther and Grigoriadis (2003) showed that participants in a sad mood tended to form attitudes (including positive attitudes) through an evaluative conditioning procedure to a greater extent than participants in a happy mood.

The formation of attitudes via evaluative conditioning procedures may seem very different from their formation of attitudes in response to persuasive communications. Whereas conditioning may occur outside of conscious awareness, thus exhibiting a feature of automaticity, change in response to persuasive communications appears to be conscious and deliberative. Nonetheless, it is possible that the same informational (i.e., evidence) and motivational (i.e., goals) variables play the same role in both types of processes. Inferences, after all, can be made extremely fast and outside of conscious awareness (Uleman, Newman, & Moscowitz, 1996), even when they are guided by strategic (i.e., goal-related) considerations (Bassili & Smith, 1986). Such potential commonality between automatic and deliberative processes of attitude formation suggests the potential for their synthesis within an overarching conceptual framework. This possibility may be fruitfully explored in future research.

Persuasion and Attitude Change

The Yale Program: Studying the Matrix of Persuasive Communications

Traditionally, most work on attitude change has focused on the impact of persuasion on attitudes (see also Johnson, Maio, & Smith-McLallen, this volume). Persuasion refers to attitude change in response to verbal messages, which often consist of an overall position that is advocated and one or more arguments designed to support this position. An influential early research program on communication and persuasion was initiated by Carl Hovland and his colleagues at Yale University (Hovland, Lumsdaine, & Sheffield, 1949; Hovland, Janis, & Kelley, 1953). This work was organized in accordance with Laswell's famous statement about "Who says what to whom and with what effect." It organized the variables pertinent to persuasion into the several categories contained in this slogan, namely, into those related to the communication's *source* (i.e., the persuader), its *target* (i.e., the audience), and aspects of its *effectiveness* (i.e., attitude or opinion change).

The two main source characteristics investigated by the Yale group were *expertise* and *trustworthiness*. Presumably, these two variables exert their persuasive effects interactively: An expert will be more persuasive than a nonexpert to the extent that the expert is perceived as trustworthy and absent of ulterior motives. Although source expertise is often defined in terms of objective or external source characteristics such as a high level of education, intelligence, social status, professional attainment, or familiarity with the issue (Hass, 1981), the recipients' subjective *beliefs* about what constitutes expertise in a given context seems critical. For instance, children are reportedly more influenced by children just a little older than themselves than by ones of the same age as themselves or by much older children (Stukat, 1958). This finding suggests that it is the perception of (or belief in) relevant expertise that matters, rather than the actual or objective expertise (which presumably varies monotonically with the children's age). Thus, depending on the individual and the persuasive context, different persons may be believed to be expert or bestowed with epistemic authority (Kruglanski et al., in press; Raviv, Bar-Tal, Raviv, & Abin, 1993) regarding a persuasion topic.

Beyond expertise and trustworthiness, the *sympathy* or perceived likability evoked by communicators seems to matter. For instance, the remoteness that ordinary receivers may sense from expert sources (Huston, 1973) may occasionally undermine the efficacy of persuasive communications. Similarly, an occasional indication of ineptness can augment the persuasiveness of an excessively distant source (Aronson, Willerman, & Floyd, 1966; Deaux, 1972) by humanizing and, hence, endearing that source to recipients. Whereas expertise and trustworthiness may affect persuasion because of *beliefs* about their relevance to the subject matter (i.e., an *expert* communicator who means what she says—or, is trustworthy—should probably be listened to), likeability of communicators may exert its persuasive effects by influencing the recipients' *goals* of being reciprocally liked by the communicators or receiving approval of their personal style and values from them.

Perceived lack of trustworthiness, defined as a perceived intent to persuade, may also affect recipients' reactions through the goals it may introduce. The work of McGuire (1961, 1969) suggests that a forewarning about a source's intent to persuade may arouse *resistance*, which in turn may prompt a rehearsal of arguments supporting the original beliefs, criticism of the persuasive arguments when these are delivered, dislike for the source, avoidance of the message, etc. However, in other circumstances, forewarning of the intent to persuade may introduce the goal to agree with the communicator, if he or she is liked or perceived as potentially instrumental to the recipient's objectives (Wood & Quinn, 2003).

Recipients' *goals* also figure prominently in discussions of *source power* variables (McGuire, 1985). A powerful source, capable of dispensing or withdrawing substantial rewards, is likely to be persuasive when it demands persuasion and has the ability to monitor whether compliance has taken place. In other words, accepting the source's position may serve as a *means* to goal-attainment through pleasing the powerful communicator. One might question whether persuasion in such instances is authentic or represents a merely public compliance unaccompanied by a private change. Work on motivated reasoning, however, (e.g., Dunning, 1999; Kunda, 1990; Kunda & Sinclair, 1999) suggests that an extrinsic directional goal to accept a given position (such as the goal of being liked by a powerful communicator) may induce authentic acceptance by biasing the reasoning process in a motivationally congruent direction. This presence of a directional goal does not mean that the recipient in such an instance lacks the goal of accuracy or is not motivated to adopt a valid position. After all, to believe in something means to hold it as true. The directional motivations (e.g., those stemming for the source's perceived power) may *bias* the processing of persuasively relevant information in a motivationally congruent direction, and outside of recipients' awareness. As a consequence, people may be convinced that the motivationally desirable positions they reach are, in fact, valid (e.g., see Higgins, 1981).

Message Variables Effects.   An intriguing factor related to the message of the persuasive communication (the "what" in Laswell's equation) has to do with the positivity/negativity of consequences conditional on the acceptance or the rejection of a persuasive advocacy. As noted earlier, such consequences may both constitute *evidence* for the advocated position and activate a *goal* to bring those consequences about. What may complicate matters, however, is that such a goal may instigate the search for the most adequate means to attain it, possibly leading to an identification of a means superior to that advocated in the message. For instance, research has suggested that acceptance of the advocated position is contingent on it being perceived as *instrumental* to fostering the desirable (or avoiding the undesirable) consequences depicted in the message (Leventhal Meyer & Nerenz, 1980; Rogers & Mewborn, 1976; Slovic, Fischoff, & Lichtenstein, 1988). If the advocated position is not perceived as instrumental, or if an alternative position is perceived as more instrumental to the recipients' goals, the persuasive communication may fall flat and ultimately fail to persuade.

In fact, the persuasive communication may induce several simultaneously operating goals, some deliberately induced, others unintended by the communicator. For instance, a high magnitude of threat may, in addition to the goal of removing the threat, foster the objective to do so instantaneously in order to eliminate the threat-induced and highly aversive fear experience. Defensive avoidance, or denial of the threat, may be subjectively perceived as a means that accomplishes both purposes: It removes the subjective experience of threat and it does so immediately, thus dispensing with the need to engage in laborious, long-term work often associated with acceptance of the communicators' recommendations (Janis, 1967). Alternatively, a threat that effectively induces feelings of vulnerability in the target audience can bias respondents to view the recommended protective action in a positive light and to accept the action recommendation even in the absence of strong supportive evidence (Das, DeWit, & Stroebe, 2003).

Implicit Versus Explicit Conclusions.   As already noted, attitudes are evaluative beliefs inferred from relevant evidence (as well as based on various epistemic motivations). This issue is pertinent to a classic problem in persuasion research, namely, whether the drawing of explicit or implicit conclusions has the greater persuasive impact. As McGuire (1985) has indicated, the putative efficacy of nondirective therapy suggests that refraining from explicit conclusions is often more effective. Similarly, early laboratory experiments on attitude-change (Fine, 1957; Marrow & French, 1945; Thistlewaite & Kamenetzky, 1955) suggest that receivers capable and motivated to draw the conclusion for themselves are more persuaded than participants for whom the conclusion was articulated in a clear-cut manner by the communicator. From the present perspective, if the rule linking the evidence with the attitude (e.g., that swimming is good for one's health) is highly accessible in the recipient's mind, the mere mention that a swimming opportunity exists at place X (e.g., that a given hotel has a swimming pool) might suffice for creating a positive attitude toward X. In contrast, if that rule is not particularly fresh or accessible, it might need to be explicitly refreshed or primed for the appropriate conclusion to be reached (e.g., one might need to be explicitly reminded of the health advantages of swimming). Priming the appropriate inference rule might be more essential if the recipient has limited cognitive capacity at the moment, and/or lacks a particularly strong goal to think about the issue, which may prevent her or him from activating the relevant rule in the absence of the prime (Chaiken et al., 1989). Of course, the very notion of *priming* assumes that there is something to be primed to begin with. Thus, the recipient must have the appropriate rule *available* in her or his memory (Chaiken, Axsom, Liberman, & Wilson, 1992; Higgins, 1996). Should the rule not be available in memory, it might need to be constructed *de noveau* for the recipient, making the conclusion-drawing process even more laborious and explicit.

The issue of implicit versus explicit conclusions relates not only to recipients' beliefs about the evidence presented in the persuasive communication but also to their metacognitive beliefs about their own versus the source's *epistemic authority* in a domain (Raviv et al., 1993). For instance, individuals with a high self-ascribed epistemic authority relative to that ascribed to the source might believe in a conclusion more if they drew it on their own. By contrast, individuals with a low self-ascribed authority (relative to that imputed to the source) might place greater faith in an externally derived conclusion, explicitly stated by the source.

Finally, the issue of implicit versus explicit conclusion drawing may not be devoid of motivational implications. For instance, individuals with a goal of verifying their self-concept as competent and independent thinkers might find the process of conclusion drawing pleasing and, hence, might be particularly motivated to believe the inferences they themselves have gleaned from the information given. By contrast, individuals with a strong affiliation goal might be more motivated to agree with a conclusion if it was delivered by an appealing communicator.

In summary, our analysis of classical message variables in persuasion affirms the multiple roles that beliefs and goals play in the persuasion process. Recipients' beliefs relate to (a) inference rules to which recipients may subscribe and which may determine the degree to which evidence made available in persuasive settings is found compelling, and (b) to recipients' metacognitive ascriptions of epistemic authority to various sources of information including themselves. As noted throughout, goals may enter as evidence for the attitude objects' goodness or badness and as epistemic motivations leading recipients to accept or resist various conclusions or to continue searching for the best available means for gratifying those particular goals.

Audience Effects.   Beliefs and goals are also involved in various audience effects (the "to whom" in Laswell's equation) of concern to attitude-change researchers. For instance, findings that women tend to be more persuadable than men on masculine topics, and men, more persuadable than women on feminine topics (e.g., Cacioppo & Petty, 1980; Karabecnick, 1983) may simply mean that people in general are less persuadable in areas where they have strongly formed *beliefs* to begin with. It is also possible that socialization differences between the genders in *goals* to be socially accepted and liked (Eagly, 1983; McGuire, 1985) may account for the greater overall tendency of women to be influenced by persuasive communications in laboratory studies. These possibilities that tie gender differences in persuasibility to socialization differences in beliefs or goals imply the potential transiency and instability of such differences corresponding to potential shifts in socialization patterns of men and women over time.

Gender is but one among the many individual difference variables on which members of recipient audiences may differ. Indeed, there appear to exist several individual differences that are related in various ways to persuasibility (McGuire, 1985, p. 286). Thus, complex and inconsistent findings exist about persuasibility and a host of other personality variables such as self-esteem, mental age, intelligence, and others (for reviews, see Briñol & Petty, this volume; McGuire, 1985, pp. 185–290). McGuire (1985) admonishes that the effect of any individual-difference variable on persuasibility needs to be evaluated in the context of its effects on the two main phases of the persuasion process: *comprehension* and *yielding* (McGuire, 1968). For instance, intelligence (encompassing as it does critical ability) may be negatively related to yielding and positively to comprehension. Insofar as either of these two variables may be more salient in some situations than in others, inconsistent effects over studies should be expected that overall tend to cancel each other out. McGuire (1985) hypothesizes that "such compensatory dynamics may be a cost-effective evolutionary adaptation for maintaining an optimal intermediate level of susceptibility, flexibly controlled by two opposing processes" (p. 286).

From the present conceptual perspective, the personality variables that have been historically studied in connection with persuasion may not have had a clear enough relation to actual factors affecting persuasion (and approximated in McGuire's, 1968, reception-yielding model). It is also of interest that the two basic components of McGuire's model correspond to the belief/goal distinction that we have discussed throughout. In those terms, the comprehension phase seems to emphasize the process of belief formation, whereas the yielding phase seems to emphasize goals evoked in the situation, such as the goals to resist or accept the persuasive conclusions. From the present theoretical perspective, the two phases involved in attitude change need not occur *sequentially*, however. Specifically, one's goals to accept or reject a persuasive communication may affect its very comprehension. One might be quicker to comprehend a desirable conclusion (e.g., by promptly retrieving or constructing the premises that lend it coherence) than an undesirable one. In general, if by comprehension means grasping the nature, significance and meaning of something (Webster's New Collegiate Dictionary, 9th ed.), which corresponds to the formation of subjective knowledge on a topic (e.g., what it was that the communicator was asserting), then informational processing goals (of directional and nondirectional varieties) may be strongly involved in both the comprehension and the yielding aspects of persuasion as well. To this extent, comprehension and yielding might not be readily separable (see Rhodes & Wood, 1992).

Be that as it may, McGuire's (1968) reception-yielding model signals an important departure from the variable-listing approach characteristic of the Yale communication and persuasion program, and constitutes an early step toward the construction of process models of attitude change. Major subsequent approaches with a similar process orientation are considered next.

Dual Process Models of Attitude Change

Over the last 2 decades, attitude research has been strongly influenced by two theoretical frameworks: Petty and Cacioppo's (e.g., 1986) elaboration likelihood model (ELM) and Chaiken and Eagly's heuristic systematic model (HSM; Chaiken, Liberman, & Eagly, 1989). Though they may significantly differ in some regards (for comparisons see Eagly & Chaiken, 1993; Petty, 1994), these two models share a substantial commonality: Both assume that persuasion may be accomplished by two *qualitatively different* modes. The ELM draws the distinction between the central and the peripheral routes to attitude change, whereas the HSM draws the distinction between the systematic and the heuristic modes. Both models also state that conditions that promote the extensive processing of message arguments produce attitude change via one of the modes (the central one in the ELM and the systematic one in the HSM), whereas conditions that reduce the thorough processing of message arguments foster attitude change via the remaining mode (the peripheral mode in the ELM and the heuristic mode in the HSM). In what follows, the unique features of each of these dual process models is considered in turn.

The Elaboration Likelihood Model.   The ELM proposes a continuum of elaboration likelihood bounded at one end by total absence of thought about issue-relevant information available in the persuasion situation and at the other end by a complete elaboration of all issue-relevant information (Petty, 1994, p. 1). Extensive elaboration of the message information corresponds to persuasion via the central route, whereas reliance on message irrelevant cues corresponds to persuasion via the peripheral route. According to the ELM "any variable that increases the likelihood of thinking increases the likelihood of engaging the central route" (Petty, 1994, p. 2). Prominent variables are (a) personal relevance of the message, (b) whether the source is expert, (c) whether it is attractive, (d) whether it consists of multiple communicators versus a single one, or (e) whether the message recipient is high (or low) in the need for cognition (Cacioppo & Petty, 1982).

Processing information via the central route can be objective or biased by prior knowledge or motivation. According to Petty (1994, pp. 1–2):

> The ELM assumes that the default mode in persuasion settings is to understand the world and develop accurate views. Bias can be produced, however, when other motives are made salient . . . For example, if people came to feel that their autonomy to hold a particular view was threatened, the reactance motive could lead to defensive processing of a persuasive message.

Similarly, when personal interests are very intense "as when an issue is intimately associated with central values . . . Processing will either terminate in the interest of self-protection or will become biased in service of one's own ego" (Petty & Cacioppo, 1986, p. 148).

Though the central and peripheral routes to persuasion are assumed to qualitatively differ and to be capable of operating in different circumstances, the ELM affirms that they may occasionally co-occur (Petty & Wegener, 1998b; Johnson, Maio, & Smith-McLallen, this volume). At most points along the elaboration continuum, there is likely to be some co-occurrence of processes and some joint impact. Thus, "as the elaboration likelihood is increased central route processes have a greater impact on attitudes and peripheral route processes—a reduced impact on attitudes" (Mackie, 1987, p. 4).

According to the ELM, the same variable can serve different functions in the persuasion process (e.g., Petty & Wegener, 1998b). Specifically, "a variable serving as a peripheral cue can have some persuasion *impact* or outcome under both high and low elaboration conditions but the underlying processes producing these outcomes are postulated to differ" (Petty, 1994, p. 6). When the elaboration likelihood is low, a variable (e.g., source attractiveness) could serve as a cue promoting attitude formation without much processing. When the elaboration likelihood is high, the same variable could serve as an issue argument (e.g., an advertisement by a physically attractive source of a beauty product may imply that use of the product may have contributed to her attractiveness). Finally, when the elaboration likelihood is intermediate, the very same variable could determine the elaboration likelihood (e.g., an attractive source may prompt a more extensive processing of her message). In a relevant study by Puckett, Petty, Cacioppo, and Fisher (1983), arguments were more carefully processed when they were associated with a socially attractive rather than a socially unattractive source.

Finally, according to the ELM, attitudes acquired via the central route differ in their consequences from attitudes acquired via the peripheral route. Attitudes acquired via the central route are expected to manifest greater temporal persistence, to be more predictive of behavior, and to exhibit greater resistance to counterpersuasion than attitudes acquired via the peripheral route. The greater resistance and persistence follow from the expectation that, under the central route, the issue-relevant attitude schema is accessed, rehearsed, and manipulated more often, thus strengthening the interconnections among the components and rendering the schema more internally consistent, accessible, enduring and resistant than under the peripheral route (for review see Petty & Cacioppo, 1986).

The Heuristic-Systematic Model. According to the HSM, systematic processing constitutes a "comprehensive, analytic orientation in which perceivers access all informational input for its relevance and importance to their judgmental task, and integrate all useful information in forming their judgments" (Chaiken, Liberman, & Eagly, 1989, p. 212). By contrast, "heuristic processing is viewed as a more limited processing mode requiring much less cognitive effort and capacity than systematic processing. When processing heuristically, people focus on a subset of available information enabling the use of simple inferential rules, schemata, or cognitive heuristics to formulate their judgments and decisions" (p. 213). Heuristic processing was furthermore characterized as "more exclusively theory driven than systematic processing," and the mode-of-processing distinction was assumed to be *not merely quantitative* (p. 213, italics added), but qualitative. In this view, heuristic processing is "more exclusively theory driven because recipients utilize minimal informational input in conjunction with simple (declarative or procedural) knowledge structures to determine message validity quickly and efficiently" (p. 216).

Like the ELM, the HSM too assumes that, in persuasion settings, persons' main motivation is the desire to formulate valid or accurate attitudes. Both heuristic and systematic processing are assumed capable of occurring in the service of that goal (Chaiken et al., 1989, p. 214). The HSM also holds that motivational variables have similar effects on systematic and heuristic processing. Thus, for instance, personal relevance is assumed to "influence not only the magnitude of systematic processing (but) also enhances the likelihood of heuristic processing, because (it increases) the cognitive accessibility of relevant persuasion heuristics and/or increases the vigilance with which people search (the setting or their memories) for relevant heuristic cues" (p. 226).

In its more recent versions (Chaiken et al., 1989; Eagly & Chaiken, 1993), the HSM is portrayed as a multiple-motive model, encompassing *defensive* and *impression* management motivations in addition to the accuracy motivation. The multiple motive HSM views processing mode and processing goals as orthogonal. According to this view, "... heuristic and systematic processing occur in the service of the individual's processing goal, whatever that goal may be" (Chaiken et al., 1989, p. 235).

Analogously to the ELM, the HSM, too, affirms that systematic and heuristic processing can co-occur. However, the HSM offers three specific ways in which such co-occurrence can take place: (a) the attenuation, (b) the bias, and (c) the additivity hypotheses. The *attenuation hypothesis* assumes that systematic processing may provide recipients with additional evidence regarding message validity, which may contradict the implications of the persuasion heuristics being utilized. Consequently, the impact of the heuristic cues may be attenuated. The *bias hypothesis* assumes that heuristic cues "... influence recipients' perceptions of the probable validity of persuasive messages, and they may also bias recipients' perceptions of message content. Thus, if a message is delivered by an expert, its arguments may be viewed more positively than if the message is delivered by a nonexpert" (p. 228). Finally, the *additivity hypothesis* assumes that both message factors and heuristics should exert significant effects on recipients' attitudes.

The Role of Goals and Beliefs in Dual Process Models of Attitude Change

Beliefs and goals play a variety of roles in the processes of persuasion assumed by the ELM and the HSM. Prior beliefs probably determine whether and to what degree a given message argument is convincing or unconvincing. For instance, an argument that comprehensive examinations are desirable because those who take them have a better shot at a successful professional career, probably rests on the belief that a successful career is a good thing (a belief that might be disputed by individuals who find the pace of careerism excessive and who prefer an alternative, less stressful life style). Similarly, the persuasive effects of *cues* or *heuristics* rest on beliefs in specific relations among cognitive categories. For instance, efficacy of the expertise cue probably rests on the belief that experts are right (Chaiken et al., 1992). Efficacy of the consensus cue, probably depends on recipients' belief that majorities are correct, etc. (Chaiken et al., 1989).

Prior beliefs and background knowledge may also play a role in determining a recipient's ability to generate responses to a persuasive communication. On the one hand, "Possessing an evaluatively biased store of knowledge may enhance recipients' abilities to rebut counterattitudinal arguments and to generate proattitudinal arguments (so that) more knowledgeable recipients may be less persuaded by counterattitudinal messages but more persuaded by proattitudinal messages" (Chaiken et al., 1989, p. 230). On the other hand, however, possessing extensive knowledge on a topic may enable one to appreciate a broader array of counterattitudinal arguments as well, increasing in this way the potential for attitude change. Whether prior knowledge would ultimately foster greater resistance to persuasive messages or greater acceptance could possibly depend on the individuals' *goals* in the situation. If the goal was to defend one's original attitudinal position, possession of prior knowledge might afford the basis for generating counterarguments. If the goal, however, was to agree with the communicator and allow oneself to be persuaded, possession of prior knowledge might enable one to engender supportive arguments and to use them to buttress the persuasive message.

Whether one's prior knowledge is used to generate resistance or to promote acceptance of the message, individuals with an extensive, well-differentiated network of prior beliefs about the topic probably self-ascribe considerable epistemic authority (Bar-Tal, Raviv, Raviv, & Brosh, 1991; Ellis & Kruglanski, 1992; Kruglanski, 1989; Kruglanski et al., in press; Raviv, Bar-Tal, Raviv, & Abin, 1993) on the issue and feel confident in their ability to comprehend the message arguments and to evaluate them on their own without resorting to information extrinsic to the message (e.g., information pertaining to source expertise or to the degree of consensus supporting the advocated conclusion). In other words, individuals with a high self-ascribed epistemic authority on the topic of the message (possibly deriving from their extensive background knowledge) may be in a position to compare the subjective relevance of information contained in the message per se with the subjective relevance of a particular source endorsing the advocacy or of the advocacy enjoying widespread consensus. By contrast, individuals with a low self-ascribed epistemic authority, or a low such authority in a given domain, may not feel competent to evaluate the merits of the arguments as such nor to compare them with other types of information exogenous to the message. Therefore, such individuals may tend to orient to the latter, exogenous information, regardless of what kind of messages are being presented to them. These interesting possibilities may be fruitfully pursued in further research.

The Unimodel

Recently, an alternative to the dual process models was offered and referred to as the *unimodel* (Chun, Spiegel, & Kruglanski, 2002; Erb, Kruglanski, Chun, Pierro, Mannetti, & Spiegel, 2003; Kruglanski & Thompson, 1999a, 1999b; Kruglanski, Thompson, & Spiegel, 1999; Pierro, Mannetti, Kruglanski, & Sleeth-Keppler, 2004). The unimodel depicts persuasion as a single process (see also Albarracín, 2002; Albarracín & Kumkale, 2003). Specifically, it suggests that the two qualitatively distinct informational inputs identified in the dual mode theories, namely, (peripheral or heuristic) cues on the one hand and message arguments on the other hand, are *functionally equivalent* in constituting two separate content categories of *evidence* for persuasive conclusions. The way such evidence is given to recipients may vary on a number of dimensions such as length, complexity, and ordinal position. These dimensions may, in turn, interact with recipients' motivation and capacity to determine persuasive impact.

More specifically, the unimodel views *subjectively relevant* evidence as the antecedent condition in an "if X than Y" assertion. It assumes that this reasoning structure applies equally to all sorts of evidence, that is to both message arguments and heuristic or peripheral cues. For instance, efficacy of the *expertise heuristic* involves the recipient's prior belief in the premise that "if someone is an expert, her or his pronouncements can be trusted." Likewise, efficacy of the *message argument* that comprehensive exams for college seniors increase the likelihood of landing an attractive job rests on a prior belief of the recipient in the premise "if an activity increases the likelihood of an attractive job, then it should be adopted."

According to the unimodel then, persuasion can be characterized by the (singular) process of drawing conclusions from available evidence. Moreover, if the information available to the recipient was experienced initially as lengthy, complex, or unclear, the appreciation of its evidential relevance may require considerable motivation and cognitive capacity. Should the recipient's motivation and capacity be low, only easy-to-process (e.g., brief and simple) information should exert persuasive impact. The order in which the information is presented may also determine processing difficulty: Early information may be easier to process than later information as it finds the recipient relatively fresh and mentally alert. Later information, by contrast, may encounter a mentally fatigued recipient, whose capacity is drained by the processing of preceding information.

Ordinal position of the information should also affect the *immediacy* with which conclusions are reached. Basing one's conclusions on early information affords a more immediate cognitive closure, for example, than basing them on later information. Indeed, prior research has established that the need for cognitive closure often leads to *primacy effects* in judgment formation (Kruglanski & Freund, 1983; Pierro et al., in press), reflecting the disproportionate impact that early versus later information may have on judgments under these conditions. Finally, the processing of early information could bias the interpretation of later information, especially if the latter was relatively less clear or more ambiguous than the earlier information (e.g., Chaiken & Maheswaran, 1994).

Note that the distinction between message arguments and cues is orthogonal to informational length/complexity or ordinal position. After all, some message arguments can be brief and simple, whereas others may be lengthy and complicated. Peripheral or heuristic cues, too, may be brief and succinct or, to the contrary, lengthy and complex (Petty & Cacioppo, 1986, p. 130). Finally, cues and message arguments need not systematically differ in their ordinal position because the specific location at which a given information is inserted is under the control of the presenter (see Kruglanski & Thompson, 1999a, 1999b). According to the unimodel, what matters to persuasion are such informational variables as length/complexity and ordinal position, which determine the parameter of task difficulty, rather than whether the information consists of message arguments or cues. Note that because the distinction between message arguments and cue is *qualitative* (as is *any distinction* between discrete informational types or contents), the notion that it is critical to persuasion sustains the concept of qualitatively distinct persuasion modes (Chaiken, Duckworth, & Darke, 1999; Petty, Wheeler, & Bizer, 1999). According to the unimodel, however, controlling for the pertinent quantitative parameters, cues, and message arguments should have identical effects on persuasion.

Reviews of evidence for the dual process notions revealed that in a large number of prior persuasion studies conducted from the dual mode perspective, length, complexity, order of presentation (Kruglanski & Thompson, 1999a, 1999b; Erb, Kruglanski, Pierro, Mannetti, & Spiegel, 2003), and subjective relevance (Pierro et al., in press) were confounded with the cue/message argument distinction. Specifically, the cues used in persuasion studies were typically briefer and less complex than the message arguments, were generally placed *before* the message arguments, and were typically perceived as *less relevant* to the communicator's conclusions than the message arguments. Furthermore, subsequent research guided by the unimodel demonstrated that when the message arguments are appropriately brief, are presented before the cues, and/or are less subjectively relevant than the cues, they replicate the previous cue effects: They, too, are persuasive primarily under low-processing motivation and low-cognitive capacity conditions. Similarly, when the cues are presented in a lengthier and a more complex format, are placed following the message arguments, and/or are perceived as more subjectively relevant to the communicator's conclusions than the message arguments, they replicate the previously found effects of the message arguments: They, too, are persuasive primarily under high-processing motivation and high-cognitive capacity conditions.

In other words, when the information (whether that typically referred to as message arguments or as cues) is relatively difficult to process, it requires a considerable amount of motivation and cognitive capacity to *appreciate* its (high or low) degree of relevance to the advocated conclusion. By contrast, when the information is relatively easy to process, it doesn't require much motivation and cognitive capacity to discern its relevance to the topic (or the lack thereof).

Beliefs and Goals From the Unimodel Perspective

Both *beliefs* and *goals* play a prominent role in the view of persuasion depicted by the unimodel. Beliefs, in particular, define the unimodel's critical quantitative parameter of subjective relevance conceived of as the *degree* to which an individual finds credible the connection between two informational categories (X and Y) in a conditional ("if X then Y") statement. In other words, the subjective relevance of a given item of information (x) depends on the extent of the individual's belief that the broader category (X) constitutes an antecedent term in a conditional statement relating it to (Y), and, hence, warranting the specific conclusion (Y).

Goals, however, refer to two motivational parameters assumed by the unimodel, namely, the *degree* of *processing* motivation and of *directional* motivation (Johnson & Eagly, 1989). Processing motivation may depend on the goals of accuracy or of cognitive activity per se (Cacioppo & Petty, 1982) and represents the amounts of energy and effort the individual is willing to invest in processing or elaborating the information given in a persuasive setting. As previously indicated, the processing-motivation parameter of the unimodel should interact with the difficulty-of-processing parameter to determine persuasive outcomes. The greater the processing difficulty, the more processing would be required to properly appreciate the relevance of the information given to the advocated conclusion. In turn, the amount of processing would be constrained by the recipient's cognitive and motivational resources.

The directional motivation parameter of the unimodel refers to the motivational desirability of specific conclusions and the biasing effect this may exert on the persuasion process. Specifically, a strong directional motivation might sharpen individuals' ability to realize (and occasionally exaggerate) the subjective relevance of information with motivationally desirable implications and to underestimate the subjective relevance of information with motivationally undesirable implications. It is possible that the directional motivation would be able to bias more the conclusions reached when the individuals' processing resources exceed those needed to cope with the demands imposed by the information processing task. The greater impact of directional motivations on the degree of bias that takes place in such a case may be due to the greater energy required to reach a directional conclusion than to simply decode the information given.

The Unimodel and Prior Attitude-Change Formulations

We view the unimodel as continuous with prior conceptions of attitude change in social psychology. Thus, its conception of evidence for attitudinal judgments is very much in line with the probabilogical models (McGuire, 1960, 1968, 1981; Wyer, 1974; Wyer & Carlston, 1979; Wyer & Goldberg, 1970). Unlike the probabilogical models, however, the unimodel is descriptive rather than normatively inspired. In other words, it does not imply that the individual considers the complement to a given set of premises (a and b) relevant to conclusion (c), represented by the term—(a and b), and representing, in effect, all the potential sets of premises relevant to c. In other words, the unimodel focuses on the derivation of a judgment from a single set of premises, allowing at the same time that under the appropriate motivational and cognitive resource conditions (underemphasized in the probabilogical formulations), multiple such sets of premises may be brought to bear on the judgment at hand.

In its emphasis on processing resources, the unimodel echoes the focus of the dual process models that, for their part, rather neglected the mechanisms of evidence and the way individuals reach conclusions on the basis of the available information (stressed in the probabilogical formulations). Finally, the unimodel draws particular attention to cognitive task demands, represented by the parameter of *processing difficulty* that may interact with motivation and cognitive capacity conditions to determine the (nondirectional and directional) impact that the information given may have on attitudinal (and other) judgments.

Summary

Like the dual process models of persuasion, the unimodel attempts to integrate belief and goal elements that enter into the formation of attitudes and opinions. Rather than drawing the distinction between qualitatively separate processing modes, however, intimately tied to the distinction between (peripheral or heuristic) cues and message arguments, the unimodel explicitly elaborates the function of beliefs in the persuasion process in terms of the *subjective relevance* parameter. It also identifies the parameter of processing difficulty and relates it to the role of processing goals (of nondirectional and directional variety) in affording the appreciation of informational relevance to the conclusions reached.

Majority and Minority Influence and Attitude Change

Although it is somewhat of a truism that the groups we belong to play an important role in shaping our (descriptive and evaluative) beliefs, for most of their short history, the social psychological study of persuasion and attitude change has developed rather independently from research on social or group influence. The two fields have used different stimulus materials, developed different theories, and, consequently, have been discussed in separate sections of social psychology textbooks (Franzoi, 2003; Hewstone & Stroebe, 2001; Hogg & Vaughan, 2002; Myers, 2002). Whereas research on persuasion has typically studied the impact of complex messages on individual attitudes, early studies of majority/minority influence focused mainly on the effect of knowledge of the judgments of other group members on individual members' judgments of simple physical stimuli (e.g., Asch, 1956; Moscovici, 1980; Moscovici & Facheux, 1972; Sherif, 1936). Only during the last few decades has there been a convergence between the two research traditions with students of group influence increasingly using complex messages and relating their analyses to various notions of persuasion (see also Ottati, Edwards, & Krumdick, this volume; Prislin & Wood, this volume).

Historically, research on majority and minority influence has gone through three distinct phases (Martin & Hewstone, 2001). The first phase was stimulated by the classic research of Sherif (1936) and Asch (1951, 1956). This research was conducted mostly in the United States (pre-1970), used predominantly simple perceptual stimulus material, and was concerned with the ability of the majority to induce conformity in individual group members. The second phase (late 1960s–1980), stimulated by the work of Moscovici, was conducted mainly in Europe, and focused on the ability of active minorities to influence the majorities in which they were embedded (Moscovici, 1980). Again, many of these studies used simple perceptual material as stimuli. Finally, in the third phase (1980–present), a fusion was achieved between the research traditions of social influence and persuasion research. In what follows, we briefly review these three historical phases highlighting the role that beliefs and goals have played in notions of social influence processes.

Conformity: The Study of Majority Influence

The Asch Paradigm.   In a series of classic studies, Asch (1951, 1956) demonstrated that exposure to a unanimous majority has a substantial impact on judgments (of the length of lines) by naïve participants. An important finding in this context concerned the effect of dissent or a breech of unanimity in the majority (Asch, 1956). If even one other individual in the group opposed the majority, the rate of conformity dropped precipitously from 35% to approximately 5%. This finding suggests that, although the social reality provided by a group is important to the maintenance of individuals' own judgments, such reality need not be provided by a majority and can, in fact, be obtained from a group containing only one other individual apart from oneself.

Theories of Conformity. It is noteworthy that Asch's conformity research was predominantly empirical in emphasis and did not contain much in the way of a theoretical analysis. Such theorizing was not late in appearing, however, embodied in the works of Festinger (1950, 1954), Deutsch and Gerard (1955), and Kelman (1961). Festinger (1950) argued that majorities exert pressures of uniformity on their members for two main reasons: *social reality* and *group locomotion*. The social reality idea relates to the notion that individuals have the need to evaluate the correctness of their attitudes and beliefs and that groups serve an important function in the satisfaction of this need. It will be noted that this analysis foreshadows the considerable emphasis of later persuasion researchers on the *accuracy motivation* (e.g., Chaiken, Liberman, & Eagly, 1989; Petty & Cacioppo, 1986) and on the *consensus heuristic*, which is the notion that people often subscribe to the belief that majorities are correct.

The locomotion idea states that groups often have goals they desire to move toward, and consensus or opinion uniformity is often necessary to enable such a movement. Festinger's (1950, 1954) theorizing does not address whether the social reality and locomotion needs are completely independent of each other. For instance, it could be that locomotion is based on group members' authentic understanding of their options, which are, in turn, grounded in their social reality. In this sense, social reality may be viewed as a precondition for, rather than as an alternative to, group locomotion.

A clearer conceptual distinction between two classes of needs underlying majority influence was drawn by Deutsch and Gerard (1955) in their differentiation between *informational* and *normative* social influence. Informational social influence by a group occurs when group members accept information from one another as evidence about reality. As can be seen, this notion parallels closely Festinger's (1950) concept of social reality. However, the notion of normative social influence is rather divergent from Festinger's notion of group locomotion. Specifically, normative influence is defined as the tendency to conform to the positive expectations of other group members. Thus, individuals may accept normative social influence because they do not want to stand out, be disliked, or be otherwise disadvantaged because of their deviant status. Normative social influence is assumed to result in a public compliance, but not in a private acceptance. Because normative social influence is dependent on the group's ability to monitor the individuals' responses, individuals will display a changed position publicly only as long as they are still in the group's sphere of influence. In contrast, informational social influence will result in a genuine belief change (reflecting a private acceptance or internalization). The changed positions will be maintained privately as well as publicly and remain intact even after the individual moves away from the group's sphere of influence.

It is noteworthy that the notion of normative influence assumes a necessary connection between the individual's goals (e.g., being accepted by the group or having a grasp of reality) and the authenticity of opinions and attitudes formed under its influence: The goal to understand one's reality is assumed to result in the formation of *authentic* beliefs, whereas the goal to belong and to be accepted results in the formation of *public expressions* but not genuine beliefs.

It is of interest that recent decades of research on motivated cognition (see, e.g., Dunning, 1999; Johnson & Eagly, 1989; Kruglanski, 1989, 1999, 2004; Kunda, 1999; Kunda & Sinclair, 1999) suggest that many goals having little to do with the formation of accurate beliefs or the formation of a firm social reality as such, can influence the formation of authentic judgments on all kinds of topics. This notion is also present in various revisions of dissonance theory (Festinger, 1957), whereby a (genuine) attitude change produced by the dissonant state may be in the service of various self-protective motives having little to do with accuracy or reality per se (Aronson, 1990; Cooper & Fazio, 1984; Steele, 1988). In this vein, Higgins (1981) in his communication game paradigm reports findings that the goal of being liked by the audience leads communicators to express attitudes congruent with the audience's preferences, that the communicators themselves end up believing (the "saying is believing" effect).

The notion of being liked by others arguably corresponds to Kelman's (1961) notion of the *identification* process in a trichotomy including also *compliance* (corresponding to Deutsch and Gerard's, 1955, *normative* influence) and *internalization* (corresponding to their notion of *informational* influence). It is noteworthy that the array of individuals' goals relevant to persuasion and the acceptance of social influence has swelled considerably since the publication of Deutsch and Gerard's (1955) and Kelman's (1961) seminal analyses. These goals now include the *accuracy, ego defense*, and *impression management* motives in Chaiken, Liberman, and Eagly's (1989) analysis, *accountability* in Tetlock's (1985) model, *the need for cognition* (Cacioppo & Petty, 1982), and *promotion and prevention* motives in Higgins' (1997) regulatory focus theory, amongs other. The realization that any goal can mediate authentic persuasion led Kruglanski (1989) to propose a more abstract classification of goals in terms of *nonspecific* and *specific* needs for closure. The nonspecific need for closure refers to a motivational continuum ranging from the goal of possessing clear and definite knowledge on a topic, to the goal of avoiding such knowledge. The points on this continuum are assumed to be affected by a variety of lower order goals such as the goals of accuracy (the fear of invalidity) or accountability, the need for cognition, and the need to act or locomote (Kruglanski, Thompson, Higgins, et al., 2000) to mention just a few.

The need for specific closure refers to a continuum of preferences for a given conclusion ranging from the avoidance of a specific conclusion to a strong desire to affirm it. The need for specific closure, closely related to notions of motivated reasoning (Kunda, 1990), is assumed to be affected by a broad variety of goals leading to preferences for a correspondingly broad variety of conclusions.

Minority Influence: The Early Studies

A Conflict Theory of Majority and Minority Influence.   Moscovici (Moscovici, 1980; Moscovici & Facheux, 1972) argued that in addition to influence that majorities exert on individual members, minorities can exert a potent reciprocal influence in some cases. In fact, it is precisely this type of influence that enables social change of various sorts. This theory is based on the assumption that "all influence attempts, no matter what their origin, create a conflict...." (Moscovici, 1980, p. 214). Confronted with such a conflict, the individual may have two primary objectives: (a) to seem consistent and acceptable, socially, to others and to himself or herself, and (b) to make sense out of the confusing physical and social environment in which she or he is plunged. Although both majority and minority sources might induce an informational conflict, it is finally the motive to be accepted and liked by the majority that determines conflict resolution in the direction of the majority, reflecting the extent of majority influence over the individual. Moscovici assumes that, when confronted with a disagreeing majority, the individual will engage in a *comparison process* and

> concentrate all his attention on what others say, so as to fit in with their opinions or judgments . . . even if privately, he has reservations . . . Once the interaction is over and the social pressure is removed, however, when the individual is alone in looking at and judging the property of the object, he sees and judges it as he did before, as it is. (Moscovici, 1980, p. 215)

It should be clear that Moscovici's (1980) depiction of majority influence bears a strong resemblance to Deutsch and Gerard's (1955) notion of *normative influence*, whereby acceptance of the majority position is motivated by the goal to be liked and accepted by the group.

Minority influence, by contrast, is assumed to be mediated by a qualitatively distinct *validation process*, which entails "an examination of the relations between its response and the object or reality" (Moscovici, 1980, p. 215). Specifically, consistent and vocal minorities are assumed to introduce a fear of invalidity in their audiences, based on a suspicion that the minority's self-assurance and behavioral persistence indicate that there is some validity to their viewpoint, after all. Thus, the minority viewpoint may be subjected to relentless criticism and thorough examination in which course some members of the majority may become converted. This "conversion produced by a minority implies a real change of judgments or opinions, not just an individual's assuming in private a response he has given in public" (p. 217). It is noteworthy that the foregoing conversion process bears a close resemblance to Deutsch and Gerard's (1955) notion of *informational influence*.

In an important way, the dual process of majority versus minority influence depicted by Moscovici (1980) hinges on which of two motives, that of belonging and being accepted versus that of having a veridical perception of reality, is dominant. Whereas Moscovici assumed that the evocation of these motives is correspondent to their (majority vs. minority) source, Kruglanski and Mackie (1990) pointed out that one may occasionally desire acceptance from an appealing (courageous, idealistic, rebellious) minority and use the majority opinion as a cue to its validity in accordance with the consensus heuristic whereby majorities are correct. According to this view, (a) the evocation of either motive need not be correlated with the source's minority/majority status, and (b) the motive to be accepted or liked may also lead to genuine conversion, leading to genuine persuasion or attitude change (Higgins, 1981).

One of the most comprehensive reviews of minority influence research is the meta-analysis by Wood, Lundgren, Ouelette, Busceme, and Blackstone (1994). Based on 97 independent research reports published between 1950 and 1991, Wood et al. (1994) examined the impact of minorities and majorities on measures of public as well as private change. This research revealed that majorities had more impact than minorities on public and direct private measures (those assessing the same attitude object as in the influence appeal). However, on indirect private measures (referring to objects similar to those in the influence appeal in content and dimension but not in concrete detail), the influence of minorities exceeded that of majorities. This suggests that the minority position may lead in some cases to a thorough rethinking of the issues involved, just as suggested by Moscovici (1980). Whereas on direct issues mentioned in the influence attempt, majorities might prevail, possibly for informational as well as motivational (social acceptance) reasons, a disidentification with deviant minorities may inhibit change on the directly related issues, yet the extensive rethinking processes instigated by minority influence may cause a shift on indirectly assessed issues.

The New Look: Dual Process Analyses of Minority and Majority Influence

With the rise of dual process theories of persuasion, the focus of social influence research has been broadened to incorporate the concepts and methods of persuasion research. A seminal study of this type was performed by Maass and Clark (1983), who tested the possibility that minorities induce active thinking (i.e., systematic or central route processing leading to permanent attitude change), whereas majorities trigger peripheral information processing, leading only to public compliance. Using the attitude issue of gay rights, the results of this research indicated that, as predicted, minority sources induced greater attitude change than majorities when the attitude measure was taken in private; whereas a greater majority effect was found when respondents believed that their attitudes would be disclosed in public. Support was also found for the notion that acceptance of the advocacy was mediated by the generation of arguments and counterarguments (assessed via the thought listing technique) in the private condition, but not in the public condition.

Mackie (1987), however, found that the majority had more impact than the minority on both public and private measures, and, furthermore, that majority positions stimulated more cognitive responding favorable to the position advocated. This finding suggests that (a) majorities may be capable of inducing informational influence (i.e., authentic attitude change), whether via the consensus heuristic, the goal to be accepted by the majority, or both, and (b) that a majority position need not result in shallow or heuristic processing. The consensus heuristic may be taken to suggest that the majority opinion is likely to be correct, and, hence, that its arguments need to be carefully scrutinized (see Maheswaran & Chaiken, 1991). That last proposal suggests that a majority position discrepant from one's own may have a motivational impact originally ascribed to minorities (see Moscovici, 1980), namely, through the implication that one's goal of holding valid opinions is not being met.

A doubt regarding the validity of one's own position may be induced by a departure from expectancy, which was the essential point made by Baker and Petty (1994) in their classic paper. According to these authors, people expect that their attitudes are shared with the majority of people (Ross, Greene, & House, 1977). Thus, a majority position that disagrees with that of the recipient, or, to the contrary, a minority position that agrees with it, both constitute a disconfirmation of expectancies and, hence, a sense that one's goal of accuracy and veridicality is frustrated. This frustration is likely to motivate careful processing of the information provided. Consistent with this analysis, Baker and Petty (1994) found that when the source/position pairing was imbalanced (majority discrepant, minority congruent), attitude change was driven mainly by argument quality. In contrast, when source/position pairing was balanced (majority congruent, minority discrepant), there was hardly any argument quality effect, and attitude change was mainly driven by the status of the source.

Summary

In recent years, the study of majority/minority effects began to adopt the paradigms of persuasion research. This adoption had considerable impact on the way in which minority influence effects have been studied. From the perspective of the persuasion paradigm, majorities and minorities are *sources* of messages, thus, often constituting peripheral cues. Accordingly, in much of this research, participants were merely informed that a large or small proportion of members of relevant reference groups indicated their agreement with the position advocated in the persuasive communication. The main finding of this work was that the impact of majority sources is much greater than that of minorities, at least for public as well as direct private measures. This majority advantage is consistent with the view that majority influence may often rest on an important belief component, namely, that consensus implies correctness, and possibly on two goal components, namely, the desire of being correct and of being accepted by the majority. If this analysis is correct, the majority advantage ought to be reduced for participants who do not subscribe to the belief equating consensus and correctness, do not care much about correctness with regard to the attitude issue, and/or whose goal is to be accepted by a given minority rather than a majority. Such possibilities could be profitably probed in subsequent research.

CONCLUSION

In this chapter, we examined social psychological research on attitudes highlighting, in particular, the relations between notions of attitudes, beliefs, and goals. We started by considering several general issues associated with the attitude concept and by making several conceptual commitments. Our foremost and primary commitment was to approach attitudes as evaluative judgments or knowledge structures with an evaluative content. This decision had implications for several subsequent issues of interest. One such issue was that of attitudes' stability. If attitudes are evaluative judgments (or knowledge structures), then they should behave like other such structures. They should be constructed from (subjectively) appropriate evidence, and they should vary in their accessibility over time. Both foregoing elements suggest that attitudes could vary in their temporal stability, some attitudes being more stable than other attitudes (for an analyses of the processes leading to stability, see Albarracín, Glasman, & Wallace, in press).

Another issue is that of uniqueness: Are attitudes uniquely associated with their objects or not? Again, attitudes' cognitive nature (as knowledge structures or evaluative judgments) implies an answer: All cognitions can be subject to mental control. They can be suppressed or inhibited (see Wegner & Wenzlaf, 1996). Accordingly, some attitudes, too, can be inhibited and other attitudes to the same objects can be then constructed. This construction allows that more than one attitude toward the same object may exist, ushering in the possibility of attitudinal ambivalence. In addition, some cognitions may exert their effects implicitly (i.e., outside of conscious awareness). The cognitive nature of attitudes allows that some of them, too, may be implicit or unconscious. In short, our cognitive treatment of attitudes as evaluative judgments suggests that attitudes may vary in the uniqueness of their association with their objects, and it allows the possibility of more than a single attitude to the same object.

Finally, we raised the issue of attitudes' distinctiveness from other kindred constructs, such as goals and beliefs. We noted that the construct of belief pertains to beliefs of all possible contents, including attitudinal contents of an evaluative nature. In so far as attitudes are evaluative judgments, they are a subcategory of beliefs. In that sense, a juxtaposition of beliefs and attitudes is, strictly speaking, incorrect and constitutes a category mistake (Ryle, 1949). Further goals, too, pertain to a belief that a given (desirable and attainable) state of affairs is one that the individual intends to pursue through action. Thus, in a sense, both attitudes and goals are beliefs, albeit of different contents. Because of their common cognitive nature, beliefs (regarding attitudes or goals) are subject to the vicissitudes of knowledge activation (Higgins, 1996), and they can vary in their accessibility. These properties cohere with the potentiality for attitudinal instability (and lack of uniqueness) previously mentioned.

We applied the foregoing notions to three major domains of research and theorizing about attitudes, namely, those concerned with *attitude structure, attitude functions,* and *attitude dynamics or change.* These areas of research have been typically treated as separate and as concerned with rather different issues. Yet the present, integrative perspective reveals that they share some fundamental commonalities. In all three domains, the relation between attitudes, beliefs, and goals (or values) was of importance though the different domains of study accorded differential relative emphasis to these concepts. Thus, in the expectancy/value formulations of attitude structure, an attitude is determined by beliefs about the attitude object mediating various goals. In subsequent formulations of attitude structure, the belief component of attitudes was assumed to refer, additionally, to information about behaviors, affective states (Zanna & Rempel, 1988), as well as epistemic authority of the source (Kruglanski, 1989; Kruglanski et al., in press). All these were assumed to constitute general categories of evidence from which attitudes may be constructed. The process of such construction (as distinct from contents) was highlighted in the probabilogical models of attitudes (McGuire, 1960; Wyer, 1974), and in the various theories of persuasion (Chaiken, Liberman, & Eagly, 1989; Kruglanski & Thompson, 1999a, 1999b; McGuire, 1968; Petty & Cacioppo, 1986; Staats & Staats, 1958).

Whereas the various *attitude structure* formulations did (implicitly) address the issue of evidence for attitudes and highlighted the role of goal fulfillment (or nonfulfillment) as one type of such evidence, they largely skirted the motivational function of goals as prompting a (biased or unbiased) process of attitude construction. Some mention of such function is inherent in McGuire's (1960) concept of wishful thinking and in Zanna and Rempel's (1988) discussion of the role of intense affect as a basis of attitudes. Generally, however, the various attitude structure models devoted considerably greater attention to the topic of evidence than to that of underlying motivations of attitude construction.

By contrast, discussions of *attitude functions* emphasize the various uses to which attitudes may be put and, hence, motivations on which attitude formation may be based. In parallel to the classification of evidence types from which attitudes can be constructed, theories of attitude functions (Katz, 1960; Smith, 1947; Smith et al., 1956) proposed a classification of motivations that may underlie the formation of attitudes (e.g., the acquisition of knowledge, self-expression, and ego defense). However, much recent research on attitude functions often failed to draw a sharp enough distinction between the role of goals as an evidence type for attitudes and as motivations underlying attitude formation.

Finally, models of attitude change contained numerous references to a variety of *evidence types* for an attitude, including the source's expertise, the amount of consensus supporting a given attitudinal advocacy, arguments contained in the message, mood, as well as epistemic motivations, including the propensity to yield or resist a persuasive communication, the desire to be accepted by the majority, the desire to avoid rejection, the motivations for accuracy, impression management, esteem enhancement, etc.

The present analytic framework, thus, provides a common terminology for discussing a wide variety of attitudinal formulations concerned with issues of attitudinal structure, functions, and dynamics. This framework affords both a comparative summary of what has been accomplished so far and points to possible novel directions in which future research on attitudes may be taken. To mention just a few, the notion that goals are cognitive constructs suggests, among other things, that attitude functions may vary across time, that message arguments may themselves activate various processing motivations, and, hence, that the phases of comprehension and yielding may be occurring concomitantly rather than serially. The notion of one's own and others' ascribed epistemic authority raises the issue of metacognition (Jost, Kruglanski, & Nelson, 1999) and its role in attitude formation and change. The separation between the evidential and motivational aspects of attitudes also suggests that minorities may not be necessarily tied to a validation motivation, nor majorities to the affiliation motivation. In short, considering attitudes as evaluative judgments permits their analysis in terms of recent developments in the field of motivated social cognition, promising fresh insights into this classical, and well-tilled, topic of social psychological inquiry.

REFERENCES

Abelson, R. P., Aronson, E., McGuire, W. J., Newcomb, T. M., Rosenberg, M. J., & Tannenbaum, P. H. (Eds.). (1968). *Theories of cognitive consistency: A source book.* Chicago: Rand McNally.

Abelson, R. P., Kinder, D. R., Peters, M. D., & Fiske, S. T. (1982). Affective and semantic components in political person perception. *Journal of Personality and Social Psychology, 42*, 619–630.

Ajzen, I. (1984). Attitudes. In R. J. Corsini (Ed.), *Wiley encyclopedia of psychology* (Vol. I, pp. 99–100). New York: Wiley.

Ajzen, I. (1996). The directive influence of attitudes on behavior. In P. M. Gollwitzer & J. A. Bargh (Eds.), *The psychology of action* (pp. 385–403). New York: Guilford Press.

Albarracín, D. (2002). Cognition in persuasion: An analysis of information processing in response to persuasive communications. In M. P. Zanna (Ed.), *Advances in experimental social psychology* (Vol. 34, pp. 61–130). San Diego, CA: Academic Press.

Albarracín, D., Glasman, L. R., & Wallace, H. M. (in press). Survival and change in attitudes: A model of judgment activation and comparison. In M. P. Zanna (Ed.), *Advances in experimental social psychology*. San Diego: Academic Press.

Albarracín, D., & Kumkale, G. T. (2003). Affect as information in persuasion: A model of affect identification and discounting. *Journal of Personality and Social Psychology, 84*, 453–469.

Allport, G. W. (1935). Attitudes. In C. Murchison (Ed.), *Handbook of Social Psychology* (pp. 798–884). Worchester, MA: Clark University Press.

Alwin, D. F., Cohen, R. L., & Newcomb, T. (1991). *Political attitudes over the life span: The Bennington women after fifty years.* Madison: University of Wisconsin Press.

Anderson, N. H. (1971). Information integration theory and attitude change. *Psychological Review, 78*, 171–206.

Anderson, N. H. (Ed.). (1991). *Contributions to information integration theory* (Vols. 1, 2, & 3). Hillsdale, NJ: Lawrence Erlbaum Associates.

Aronson, E. (1990, December). *The return of the repressed: Dissonance theory makes a comeback.* Presidential address presented at the meeting of the Western Psychological Association, Los Angeles.

Aronson, E., Willerman, B., & Floyd, J. (1966). The effect of pratfall on increasing interpersonal attraction. *Psychonomic Science, 4*, 227–228.

Asch, S. E. (1951). Effects of group pressure on the modification and distortion of judgments. In H. Guetzkow (Ed.), *Group, leadership and men* (pp. 177–190). Pittsburgh, PA: Carnegie University Press.

Asch, S. E. (1956). Studies of independence and conformity: A minority of one against a unanimous majority. *Psychological Monographs, 70* (9, Whole No. 416).

Averill, J. R. (1982). *Anger and aggression: An essay on emotion.* New York: Springer.

Baeyens, F., Eelen, P., Crombez, G., & Van den Bergh, O. (1992). Human evaluative conditioning: Acquisition trials, presentation schedule, evaluative style and contingency awareness. *Behavior Research and Therapy, 30*, 133–142.

Baker, S. M., & Petty, R. E. (1994). Majority and minority influence: Source-position imbalance as a determinant of message scrutiny. *Journal of Personality and Social Psychology, 67*, 5–19.

Bargh, J. A., Chaiken, S., Govender, R., & Pratto, F. (1992). The generality of the automatic attitude activation effect. *Journal of Personality and Social Psychology, 62*, 893–912.

Bar-Tal, D., Raviv, A., Raviv, A., & Brosh, M. (1991). Perception of epistemic authority and attribution for its choice as a function of knowledge area and age. *European Journal of Social Psychology, 21*, 477–492.

Bassili, J. N. (1996). Meta-judgmental versus operative indexes of psychological attributes: The case of measures of attitude strength. *Journal of Personality and Social Psychology, 71*, 637–653.

Bassili, J. N., & Brown, R. (in press). The influence of attitudes on affect: A potentiated recruitment framework. In D. Albarracín, B. T. Johnson, & M. P. Zanna (Eds.), *Handbook of attitudes and attitude change: Basic principles.* Mahwah, NJ: Lawrence Erlbaum Associates.

Bassili, J. N., & Smith, M. C. (1986). On the spontaneity of trait attribution: Converging evidence for the role of cognitive strategy. *Journal of Personality and Social Psychology, 50*, 239–245.

Bem, D. J. (1965). An experimental analysis of self-persuasion. *Journal of Experimental Social Psychology, 1*, 199–218.

Bem, D. J. (1972). Self-perception theory. In L. Berkowitz (Ed.), *Advances in experimental social psychology* (Vol. 6, pp. 1–62). New York: Academic Press.

Blascovich, J., Ernst, J. M., & Tomaka, J. (1993). Attitude accessibility as a moderator of autonomic reactivity during decision making. *Journal of Personality and Social Psychology, 64*, 165–176.

Blascovich, J., Ernst, J. M., Tomaka, J., Kelsey, R. M., Salomon, K. L., & Fazio, R. H. (1993). Attitude accessibility as a moderator of autonomic reactivity during decision making. *Journal of Personality and Social Psychology, 64*, 165–176.

Bohner, G., & Wänke, M. (2002). *Attitude and attitude change.* Hove, UK: Psychology Press.

Bornstein, R. F. (1989). Exposure and affect: Overview and meta-analysis of research, 1968–1987. *Psychological Bulletin, 106*, 265–289.

Bornstein, R. F., & D'Agostino, P. R. (1994). The attribution and discounting of perceptual fluency: Preliminary tests of a perceptual fluency/attribution model of the mere exposure effect. *Social Cognition, 12*, 113–148.

Breckler, S. J. (1983). *Validation of affect, behavior, and cognition as distinct components of attitude.* Unpublished doctoral dissertation, Ohio State University, Columbus.

Breckler, S. J. (1984). Empirical validation of affect, behavior, and cognition as distinct components of attitude. *Journal of Personality and Social Psychology, 47*, 1191–1205.

Cacioppo, J. T., & Petty, R. E. (1980). Sex differences in influenceabililty: Toward specifying the underlying process. *Personality and Social Psychology Bulletin, 6*, 651–656.

Cacioppo, J. T., & Petty, R. E. (1982). The need for cognition. *Journal of Personality and Social Psychology, 42*, 116–131.

Campbell, D. T. (1958). Common fate, similarity, and other indices of the status of aggregates of persons as social entities. *Behavioral Science, 3*, 14–25.

Campbell, D. T. (1963). Social attitudes and other acquired behavioral dispositions. In S. Koch (Ed.), *Psychology: A study of a science* (Vol. 6, pp. 94–172). New York: McGraw-Hill.

Carlston, D. E., & Smith, E. R. (1996). Principles of mental representation. In E. T. Higgins & A. W. Kruglanski (Eds.), *Social psychology: Handbook of basic principles* (pp. 184–210). New York: Guilford.

Chaiken, S., Axsom, D., Liberman, A., & Wilson, D. (1992). *Heuristic processing of persuasive messages: Chronic and temporary sources of rule accessibility.* Unpublished manuscript, New York University.

Chaiken, S., & Baldwin, M. W. (1981). Affective–cognitive consistency and the effect of salient behavioral information on the self-perception of attitudes. *Journal of Personality and Social Psychology, 41*, 1–12.

Chaiken, S., Duckworth, K. L., & Darke, P. (1999). When parsimony fails . . . *Psychological Inquiry, 10*, 118–123.

Chaiken, S., Liberman, A., & Eagly, A. (1989). Heuristic and systematic information processing within and beyond the persuasion context. In J. S. Uleman & J. A. Bargh (Eds.), *Unintended thought* (pp. 212–252). New York: Guilford.

Chaiken, S., & Maheswaran, D. (1994). Heuristic processing can bias systematic processing: Effects of source credibility, argument ambiguity, and task importantance on attitude judgment *Journal of Personality and Social Psychology, 66*, 460–473.

Chaiken, S., Pomerantz, E. M., & Giner-Sorolla, R. (1995). Structural consistency and attitude strength. In R. E. Petty & J. A. Krosnick (Eds.), *Attitude strength: Antecedents and consequences* (pp. 387–412). Mahwah, NJ: Lawrence Erlbaum Associates.

Chaiken, S., & Tzope, Y. (1999). (Eds.). *Dual process theories in social psychology*. New York: Guilford.

Chun, W. Y., Spiegel, S., & Kruglanski, A. W. (2002). Assimilative behavior identification can also be resource dependent: A unimodel-based analysis of dispositional attribution phases. *Journal of Personality and Social Psychology, 83*, 542–555.

Cialdini, R. B., Trost, M. R., & Newsom, J. T. (1995). Preference for consistency: The development of a valid measure and the discovery of surprising behavioral implications. *Journal of Personality and Social Psychology, 69*, 318–328.

Cooper, J., & Fazio, R. H. (1984). A new look at dissonance theory. In L. Berkowitz (Ed.), *Advances in experimental social psychology* (Vol. 17, pp. 229–266). San Diego, CA: Academic Press.

Das, E. H. H. J., DeWit, J. B. F., & Stroebe, W. (2003). Fear appeals motivate acceptance of action recommendation. Evidence for a positive bias in the processing of persuasive messages. *Personality and Social Psychology Bulletin, 29*, 650–664.

Dawes, R. M., & Smith, T. L. (1985). Attitude and opinion measurement. In G. Lindzey & E. Aronson (Eds.), *The handbook of social psychology* (3rd ed., pp. 509–566).

Deaux, K. (1972). Anticipatory attitude change: A direct test of the self-esteem hypothesis. *Journal of Experimental Social Psychology, 8*, 143–155.

DeBono, K. G. (1987). Investigating the social-adjustive and value-expressive functions of attitudes: Implications for persuasion processes. *Journal of Personality and Social Psychology, 52*, 279–287.

Devine, P. G. (1989). Stereotypes and prejudice: Their automatic and controlled components. *Journal of Personality and Social Psychology, 56*, 5–18.

Deutsch, M., & Gerard, H. B. (1955). A study of normative and informational social influence upon individual judgment. *Journal of Abnormal and Social Psychology, 51*, 629–636.

Dunning, D. (1999). A newer look: Motivated social cognition and the schematic representation of social concepts. *Psychological Inquiry, 10*, 1–11.

Eagly, A. H. (1983). Gender and social influence: A social psychological analysis. *American Psychologist, 38*, 971–981.

Eagly, A. H., & Chaiken, S. (1993). *The psychology of attitudes*. New York: Harcourt Brace Jovanovich.

Eagly, A. H., Wood, W., & Chaiken, S. (1978). Causal inferences about communicators and their effects on opinion change. *Journal of Personality and Social Psychology, 36*, 424–435.

Eiser, J. R., & Stroebe, W. (1971). *Categorization and social judgement*. London: Academic Press.

Ellis, S., & Kruglanski, A. W. (1992). Self as epistemic authority: Effects on experiential and instructional learning. *Social Cognition, 10*, 357–375.

Erb, H. P., Kruglanski, A. W., Chun, Y. W., Pierro, A., Mannetti, L., & Spiegel, S. (2003). Searching for commonalities in human judgment: The Parametric unimodel and its dual-model alternatives. In W. Stroebe & M. Hewstone (Eds.), *European Review of Social Psychology, 14*, 1–47.

Erber, M. W., Hodges, S. D., & Wilson, T. D. (1995). Attitude strength, attitude stability, and the effects of analyzing reasons. In R. E. Petty & J. A. Krosnick (Eds.), *Attitude strength: Antecedents and consequences* (pp. 433–454). Mahwah, NJ: Lawrence Erlbaum Associates.

Fazio, R. H. (1990). Multiple processes by which attitudes guide behavior: The MODE model as an integrative framework. In M. P. Zanna (Ed.), *Advances in experimental social psychology* (Vol. 23, pp. 75–109). San Diego, CA: Academic Press.

Fazio, R. H. (1995). Attitudes as object-evaluation associations: Determinants consequences and correlates of attitude accessibility. In R. E. Petty & J. A. Krosmick (Eds.), *Attitude strength antecedents and consequences* (pp. 247–282). Mahwah, NJ: Erlbaum.

Fazio, R. H., Blascovich, J., & Driscoll, D. M. (1992). On the functional value of attitudes: The influence of accessible attitudes on the ease and quality of decision making. *Personality and Social Psychology Bulletin, 18*, 388–401.

Fazio, R. H., Lednetter, J. E., & Towles-Schwen, T. (2000). On the costs of accessible attitudes: Detecting that the attitude object has changed. *Journal of Personality and Social Psychology, 78*, 197–210.

Fazio, R. H., & Williams, C. J. (1986). Attitude accessibility as moderator of the attitude–behavior relation: An investigation of the 1984 presidential election. *Journal of Personality and Social Psychology, 51*, 505–514.

Fazio, R. H., & Zanna, M. P. (1981). Direct experiance and attitude-behavior consistency. In L. Berkowitz (Ed.), *Advances in experimental social psychology* (Vol. 14, pp. 161–202). San Diego, CA: Academic Press.

Festinger, L. (1950). Informal social communication. *Psychological Review, 57*, 271–282.

Festinger, L. (1954). A theory of social comparison processes. *Human Relations, 7*, 117–282.

Festinger, L. (1957). *A theory of cognitive dissonance*. Stanford, CA: Stanford University Press.

Fine, B. J. (1957). Conclusion drawing, communicator credibility, and anxiety as factors in opinion change. *Journal of Abnormal and Social Psychology, 54*, 369–374.

Fishbein, M. (1963). An investigation of the relationship between beliefs about an object and the attitude towards the object. *Human Relations, 16*, 233–240.

Fishbein, M. (1967). A consideration of beliefs and their role in attitude measurement. In M. Fishbein (Ed.), *Readings in attitude theory and measurement.* (pp. 257–266). New York: Wiley.

Fishbein, M., & Ajzen, I. (1975). *Belief, attitude, intention, and behavior*. Reading, MA: Addison-Wesley.

Ford, T. E., & Kruglanski, A. W. (1995). Effects of epistemic motivations on the use of accessible contructs in social judgments.*Personality and Social Psychology Bulletin, 21*, 950–962.

Forgas, J. P. (2002). Feeling and doing: Affective influences on social behavior. *Psychological Inquiry, 13*, 1–28.

Franzoi, S. L. (2003). *Social Psychology* (3rd. ed.). Boston: McGraw-Hill.

Freud, S. (1923). *Das Ich und das Es*. [The ego and the id]. Leipzig, Germany: Internationaler Psychoanalytischer Verlag.

Gaertner, S. L., & Dovidio, J. F. (1986). The aversive form of racism. In J. F. Dovidio & S. L. Gaertner (Eds.), Prejudice, discrimination, and racism (pp. 61–86). Orlando, FL: Academic Press.

Gollwitzer, P., & Bargh, J. A. (1996). (Eds.) *The psychology of action: Linking cognition and motivation to behavior.* New York: Guilford.

Granberg, D., & Brent, E. E. (1983). When prophecy leads: The preference expectation link in U.S. presidential elections, 1952–1980. *Journal of Personality and Social Psychology, 45*, 477–491.

Greenwald, A. G., & Banaji, M. R. (1995). Implicit social cognition: Attitudes, self-esteem, and stereotypes. *Psychological Review, 102*, 4–27.

Hass, G. (1981). Effects of source characteristics on cognitive responses and persuasion. In R. E. Petty, T. M. Ostrom, & T. C. Brock (Eds.), *Cognitive responses in persuasion* (pp. 142–172). Hillsdale, NJ: Lawrence Erlbaum Associates.

Haddock, G., & Maio, G. R. (Eds.). (2003). *Theoretical perspectives on attitudes for the 21st century: The Gregynog Symposium.* New York: Psychology Press.

Hamilton, D. L., & Sherman, S. J. (1996). Perceiving persons and groups. *Psychological Review, 103*, 336–355.

Heaton, A. W., & Kruglanski, A.W. (1991). Person perception by introverts and extroverts under time pressure: Need for closure effects. *Personality and Social Psychology Bulletin, 17*, 161–165.

Herman, C. P., & Polivy, J. (1984). A boundary model for the regulation of eating. In A. J. Stunkard & E. Stellar (Eds.), *Eating and its disorders* (pp. 141–156). New York: Raven.

Hermans, D., Bayens, F., & Eelen, P. (2003). On the acquisition and activation of evaluative information in memory: The study of evaluative learning and affective priming combined. In J. Much & K. C. Klauer (Eds.), *The psychology of evaluation* (pp. 139–168). Mahwah, NJ: Lawrence Erlbaum Associates.

Hewstone, M., & Stroebe, W. (Eds.). (2001). *Introduction to social psychology* (3rd ed.). Oxford, UK: Blackwell.

Higgins, E. T. (1981). The "communication game": Implications for social cognition and persuasion. In E. T. Higgins, C. P. Herman & M. P. Zanna (Eds.), *Social cognition: The Ontario symposium* (Vol. 1, pp. 343–392). Hillsdale, NJ: Lawrence Erlbaum Associates.

Higgins, E. T. (1996). Knowledge activation. In E. T. Higgins & A. W. Kruglanski (Eds.), *Social psychology: A handbook of basic principles.* (pp. 133–168). New York: Guilford.

Higgins, E. T. (1997). Beyond pleasure and pain. *American Psycologist, 52*, 1280–1300.

Hogg, M. A., & Vaughan, G. A. (2002). *Social Psychology* (3rd ed.). Harlow, UK: Prentice-Hall.

Hovland, C. I. (Ed.). (1957). *The order of presentation in persuasion.* New Haven, CT: Yale University Press.

Hovland, C. I., Janis, I., & Kelley, H. H. (1953). *Communication and persuasion.* New Haven, CT: Yale University Press.

Hovland, C. I., Lumsdaine, A. A., & Sheffield, F. D. (1949). *Experiments on mass communication.* Princeton, NJ: Princeton University Press.

Huston, T. L. (1973). Ambiguity of acceptance, social desirability, and dating choice. *Journal of Experimental Social Psychology, 9*, 32–42.

Janis, I. L. (1967). Effects of fear arousal on attitude change: Recent developments in theory and experimental research. In L. Berkowitz (Ed.), *Advances in experimental social psychology* (Vol. 3, pp. 122–224). New York: Academic Press.

Johnson, B. T., & Eagly, A. H. (1989). The effects of involvement on persuasion: A meta-analysis. *Psychological Bulletin, 17*, 290–314.

Johnson, B. T., Maio, G. R., & Smith McLallen, A. (in press). Communication and attitude change: Causes, processes and effects. In D. Albarracín, B. T. Johnson, & M. P. Zanna (Eds.), *Handbook of attitudes and attitude change: Basic principles.* Mahwah, NJ: Lawrence Erlbaum Associates.

Jonas, K., Broemer, P., & Diehl, M. (2000a). Attitudinal ambivalence. In W. Stroebe & M. Hewstone (Eds.), *European review of social psychology* (Vol. 11, pp. 35–74). Chichester, UK: Wiley.

Jonas, K., Broemer, P., & Diehl, M. (2000b). Experienced ambivalence as a moderator of consistency between attitudes and behavior. *Zeitschrift für Sozialpsychologie, 31,* 153–165.

Jost, J. T., Kruglanski, A. W., & Nelson, T. O. (1999). Social meta-cognition: An expansionist review. *Personality and Social Psychology Review, 1,* 23–46.

Kaplan, K. J. (1972). On the ambivalence-indifference problem in attitude theory and measurement: A suggested modification of the semantic differential technique. *Psychological Bulletin, 77,* 361–372.

Karabecnick, S. A. (1983). Sex-relevance of content and influenceability: Sistrunk and McDavid revisited. *Personality and Social Psychology Bulletin, 9,* 243–252.

Katz, D. (1960). The functional approach to the study of attitudes. *Public Opinion Quarterly, 24,* 163–204.

Katz, I. (1981). *Stigma: A social psychological analysis.* Hillsdale, NJ: Lawrence Erlbaum Associates.

Katz, I., & Hass, R. G. (1988). Racial ambivalence and American value conflict: Correlational and priming studies of dual cognitive structures. *Journal of Personality and Social Psychology, 55,* 893–905.

Kelley, H. H. (1972a). Attribution in social interaction. In E. E. Jones, D. E. Kanause, H. H. Kelley, R. E. Nisbett, S. Valins, & B. Weiner (Eds.), *Attribution: Perceiving the causes of behavior* (pp. 1–26) . Morristown, NJ: General Learning Press.

Kelley, H. H. (1972b). Causal schemata and the attributuion process. In E. E. Jones, D. E. Kanause, H. H. Kelley, R. E. Nisbett, S. Valins, & B. Weiner (Eds.), *Attribution: Perceiving the causes of behavior* (pp. 151–174) . Morristown, NJ: General Learning Press.

Kelley, H. H. (1989). Foreword. In A. W. Kruglanski. *Lay epistemics and human knowledge: Cognitive and motivational bases.* (pp. vii–ix). New York: Plenum.

Kelman, H. C. (1961). Three processes of social influence. *Public Opinion Quarterly, 25,* 57–78.

Kinder, D. R., & Sears, D. O. (1981). Prejudice and politics: Symbolic racism versus racial threats to the good life. *Journal of Personality and Social Psychology, 40,* 414–431.

Krech, D., & Crutchfield, R. S. (1948). *Theories and problems in social psychology.* New York: McGraw-Hill.

Kruglanski, A. W. (1989). *Lay epistemics and human knowledge: Cognitive and motivational bases.* New York: Plenum.

Kruglanski, A. W. (1996). Goals as knowledge structures. In P. M. Gollwitzer and J. A. Bargh (Eds.), *The psychology of action: Linking cognition and motivation to behavior* (pp. 599–618). New York: Guilford.

Kruglanski, A. W. (1999). Motivation, cognition, and reality: Three memos for the next generation of research. *Psychological Inquiry, 10,* 54–58.

Kruglanski, A. (in press). *The psychology of closed mindedness.* New York: Psychology Press.

Kruglanski, A. W., Raviv, A., Bar-Tal, D., Raviv, A., Ellis, S., Bar, R., Pierro, A., & Mannetti, L. (in press). Says Who?: Epistemic Authority Effects in Social Judgment. In M. P. Zanna (Ed.) *Advances in Experimental Social Psychology*, Vol. 36.

Kruglanski, A., & Freund, T. (1983). The freezing and un-freezing of lay-inferences: Effects on impressional primacy, ethnic stereotyping and numerical anchoring. *Journal of Experimental Social Psychology, 19,* 448–468.

Kruglanski, A., & Mackie, D. (1990). Majority and minority influence: A judgmental process analysis. In W. Stroebe & M. Hewstone (Eds.), *European review of social psychology* (Vol. 1, pp. 230–261). Chichester, UK: Wiley.

Kruglanski, A., Shah, J. Y., Fishbach, A., Friedman, R., Chun, W. Y., & Sleeth-Keppler, D. (2002). A theory of goal systems. In M. P. Zanna (Ed.), *Advances in experimental social psychology* (Vol. 34, pp. 331–378). San Diego: Academic Press.

Kruglanski, A. W., & Thompson, E. P. (1999a). Persuasion by a single route: A view from the unimodel. *Psychological Inquiry, 10,* 83–110.

Kruglanski, A. W., & Thompson, E. P. (1999b). The illusory second mode, or the cue *is* the message. *Psychological Inquiry, 10,* 182–193.

Kruglanski, A. W., Thompson, E. P., Higgins, E. T., Atash, M. N., Pierro, A., Shah, J. Y., Spiegel, S. (2000). To do the *right* thing! or to just *do* it!: Locomotion and assessment as distinct self-regulatory imperatives. *Journal of Personality and Social Psychology.*

Kruglanski, A. W., Thompson, E. P., & Spiegel, S. (1999). Separate or equal?: Bimodal notions of persuasion and a single-process "unimodel." In S. Chaiken and Y. Trope (Eds.), *Dual process models in social cognition: A source book.* New York: Guilford.

Kruglanski, A. W., & Webster, D. M. (1996). Motivated closing of the mind: "Seizing" and "freezing." *Psychological Review, 103,* 263–283.

Kunda, Z. (1990). The case for motivated reasoning. *Psychological Bulletin, 108,* 480–498.

Kunda, Z. (1999). *Social cognition: Making sense of people*. Cambridge, MA: MIT Press.

Kunda, Z., & Sinclair, L. (1999). Motivated reasoning with stereotypes: Activation, application, and inhibition. *Psychological Inquiry, 10*, 12–22.

Lavine, H., & Snyder, M. (1996). Cognitive processing and the functional matching effect in persuasion: The mediating role of subjective perceptions of message quality. *Journal of Experimental Social Psychology, 32*, 580–604.

Lavine, H., & Snyder, M. (1999). Cognitive processes and the functional matching effect in persuasion: Studies in personality and political behavior. In J. M. Olson & G. R. Maio (Eds.), *Why we evaluate? : Functions of attitudes*. (pp. 97–132). Mahwah, NJ: Lawrence Erlbaum Associates.

Lavine, H., Thomsen, C. J., Zanna, M. P., & Borgida, E. (1998). On the primacy of affect in the determination of attitudes and behavior: The moderating role of affective–cognitive ambivalence. *Journal of Experimental Social Psychology, 34*, 398–421.

Leventhal, H., Meyer, D., & Nerentz, D. (1980). The common sense representation of illness danger. In S. Rachman (Ed.), *Medical psychology* (Vol. 2. pp. 7–30). New York: Pergamon.

Lord, C. G., & Lepper, M. R. (1999). Attitude representation theory. In M. P. Zanna (Ed.), *Advances in experimental social psychology* (Vol. 31, 265–344). San Diego, CA: Academic Press.

Maass, A., & Clark, R. D. III (1983). Internalization versus compliance: Differential processes underlying minority influence and conformity. *European Journal of Social Psychology, 13*, 197–215.

Maheswaran, D., & Chaiken, S. (1991). Promoting systematic processing in low motivation settings: The effect of incongruent information on processing and judgment. *Journal of Personality and Social Psychology, 61*, 13–25.

Mackie, D. M. (1987). Systematic and nonsystematic processing of majority and minority persuasive communications. *Journal of Personality and Social Psychology, 53*, 41–52.

Mackie, D. M., & Worth, L. T. (1989). Processing deficits and the mediation of positive affect in persuasion. *Journal of Personality and Social Psychology, 57*, 27–40.

Maio, G. R., Bell, D. W., & Esses, V. M. (1996). The formation of attitudes towards new immigrant groups. *Journal of Experimental Social Psychology, 24*, 1762–1776.

Maio, G. R., Esses, V. M., & Bell, D. W. (2000). Examining conflict between components of attitudes: Ambivalence and inconsistency are distinct constructs. *Canadian Journal of Behavioural Science, 32*, 58–70

Marrow, A. J., & French, J. R. P. (1945). Changing a stereotype in industry. *Journal of Social Psychology 1*, (3), 33–37.

Martin, R., & Hewstone, M. (2001). Determinants and consequences of cognitive processes in majority and minority influence. In J. P. Forgas & K. D. Williams (Eds.), *Social influence: Direct and indirect processes* (pp. 315–330). Philadelphia: Psychology Press.

Marwell, G., Aiken, M., & Demerath, N. J. (1987). The persistence of political attitudes among 1960s civil rights activists. *Public Opinion Quarterly, 51*, 359–375.

McGuire, W. J. (1960). A syllogistic analysis of cognitive relationships. In M. J. Rosenberg & C. I. Hovland (Eds.), *Attitude organization and change* (pp. 65–111). New Haven, CT: Yale University Press.

McGuire, W. J. (1961). Resistance to persuasion conferred by active and passive prior refutation of the same and alternative counterarguments. *Journal of Abnormal and Social Psychology, 63*, 326–332.

McGuire, W. J. (1968). The nature of attitudes and attitude change. In G. Lindzey & E. Aronson (Eds.), *The handbook of social psychology* (Vol. 3, pp. 136–315). Reading, MA: Addison-Wesley.

McGuire, W. J. (1969). The nature of attitudes and attitude change. In G. Lindzey & E. Aronson (Eds.), *Handbook of social psychology*, 2nd ed. (Vol. 3, pp. 136–314). Reading, MA: Addison-Wesley.

McGuire, W. J. (1981). The probabilogical model of cognitive structure and attitude change. In R. E. Petty, T. M. Ostrom, & T. C. Brock (Eds.), *Cognitive responses in persuasion* (pp. 291–307). Hillsdale, NJ: Lawrence Erlbaum Associates.

McGuire, W. J. (1985). Attitudes and attitude change. In G. Lindzey & E. Aronson (Eds.), *Handbook of social psychology 3rd ed.* (Vol. 2, pp. 233–346). New York: Random House.

Mensink, W., Stroebe, W., Schut, H., & Aarts, H. (2003). Waarom lijnen niet lukt: Het conflict tussen lekker eten en lijnen [Why dieting fails: The conflict between eating enjoyment and weight control]. In E. van Dijk, E. Kluwer, & D. Wigoboldus (Eds.), *Jaarboek Social Psychologie 2002* (pp. 219–226). Delft, Netherlands: Eburon.

Moscovici, S. (1980). Toward a theory of conversion behavior. In L. Berkowitz (Ed.), *Advances in experimental social psychology* (Vol. 13, pp. 209–239). San Diego, CA: Academic Press.

Moscovici, S., & Facheux, C. (1972). Social influence, conformity bias, and the study of active minorities. In L. Berkowitz (Ed.), *Advances in experimental social psychology* (Vol. 6, pp. 150–202). New York: Academic Press.

Myers, D. G. (2002). *Social psychology* (7th ed.). Boston: McGraw-Hill.

Newby-Clark, I. R., McGregor, I., & Zanna, M. P. (2002). Thinking and caring about cognitive inconsistency: When and for whom does attitudinal ambivalence feel uncomfortable? *Journal of Personality and Social Psychology, 82*, 157–166.

Norman, R. (1975). Affective–cognitive consistency, attitudes, conformity, and behavior. *Journal of Personality and Social Psychology, 32*, 83–91.

Olson, M. A., & Fazio, R. (2001). Implicit attitude formation through classical conditioning. *Psychological Science, 5*, 413–417.

Olson, J. M., & Maio, G. R. (1999). *Why we evaluate? : Functions of attitudes.* Mahwah, NJ: Lawrence Erlbaum Associates.

Olson, J. M., Vernon, P. A., Harris, J. A., & Jang, K. L. (2001). The heritability of attitudes: A study of twins. *Journal of Personality and Social Psychology, 80*, 845–860.

Olson, J. M., Vernon, P. A., & Jang, K. L. (2001). The heritability of attitudes: A study of twins. *Journal of Personality and Social Psychology, 80*, 845–860.

Olson, J. M., & Zanna, M. P. (1993). Attitude and attitude change. *Annual Review of Psychology, 44*, 117–154.

Osgood, C. E., Suci, G. E., & Tannenbaum, P. H. (1957). *The measurement of meaning.* Urbana: University of Illinois Press.

Ostrom, T. M. (1984). The sovereignty of social cognition. In R. S. Wyer, Jr., & T. K. Srull (Eds.), *Handbook of social cognition* (Vol. 1, pp. 1–38). Hillsdale, NJ: Lawrence Erlbaum Associates.

Peak, H. (1955). Attitude and motivation. In M. R. Jones (Ed.), *Nebraska symposium on motivation* (pp. 149–188). Lincoln: University of Nebraska Press.

Petty, R. E. (1994). Two routes to persuasion: State of the art. In G. d'Ydewalle, P. Eelen, & P. Berteleson (Eds.), *International perspectives on psychological science* (Vol. 2, pp. 229–247). Hillsdale, NJ: Lawrence Erlbaum Associates.

Petty, R. E., & Cacioppo, J. T. (1986). The elaboration likelihood model of persuasion. In L. Berkowitz (Ed.), *Advances in experimental social psychology* (Vol. 19, pp. 123–205). San Diego, CA: Academic Press.

Petty, R. E., & Krosnik, J. A. (1996). *Attitude strength: Antecedents and consequences.* Hillsdale, NJ: Lawrence Erlbaum Associates.

Petty, R. E., & Wegener, D. T. (1998a). Matching versus mismatching attitude functions: Implications for scrutiny of persuasive messages. *Personality and Social Psychology Bulletin, 24*, 227–240.

Petty, R. E., & Wegener, D. T. (1998b). Attitude change: Multiple roles for persuasion variables. In D. Gilbert, S. T. Fiske, & G. Lindzey (Eds.), *Handbook of social psychology, 4th ed.* (Vol. 1, pp. 323–390). New York: McGraw-Hill.

Petty, R. E., Wheeler, S. C., & Bizer, G. Y. (1999). Is there one persuasion process or more? Lumping versus splitting in attitude change theories. *Psychological Inquiry, 10*, 156–163.

Pierro, A., Mannetti, L., Kruglanski, A. W., & Sleeth-Keppler, D. (2004). Relevance Override: On the reduced impact of "cues" under high motivation conditions of persuasion studies. *Journal of Personality and Social Psychology, 86*, 251–264.

Potter, J. (1998). Discursive social psychology: From attitudes to evaluative practices. In W. Stroebe & M. Hewstone (Eds.), *European review of social psychology* (Vol. 9, pp. 233–266). Chichester, UK: Wiley.

Prentice, D. A., & Carlsmith, K. M. (1999). Opinions and personality: On the psychological functions of attitudes and other valued possessions. In J. M. Olson & G. R. Maio (Eds.), *Why we evaluate? : Functions of attitudes* (pp. 223–248). Mahwah, NJ: Lawrence Erlbaum Associates.

Puckett, J. M., Petty, R. E., Cacioppo, J. T., & Fisher, D. L. (1983). The relative impact of age and attractiveness stereotypes on persuasion. *Journal of Gerentology, 38*, 340–343.

Raviv, A., Bar-Tal, D., Raviv, A., & Abin, R. (1993). Measuring epistemic authority. *European Journal of Personality, 7*, 119–138.

Rhodes, N., & Wood, W. (1992). Self-esteem and intelligence affect influencability: The mediating role of message perception. *Psychological Bulletin, 111*, 156–171.

Rogers, R. W., & Mewborn, C. R. (1976). Fear appeals and attitude change: Effects of anxiousness probability of occurrence and the efficacy of coping responses. *Journal of Personality and Social Psychology, 34*, 54–61.

Rosenberg, M. J. (1956). Cognitive structure and attitudinal affect. *Journal of Abnormal and Social Psychology, 53*, 367–372.

Rosenberg, M. J. (1960). An analysis of affective-cognitive consistency. In C. I. Hovland & M. J. Rosenberg (Eds.), *Attitude organization and change* (pp. 15–64). New Haven, CT: Yale University Press.

Ross, L., Greene, D., & House, P. (1977). The "false consensus effect": An egocentric bias in social perception and attribution processes. *Journal of Experimental Social Psychology, 13*, 279–301.

Ryle, G. (1949). *The concept of mind.* Chicago: The University of Chicago Press.

Schwarz, N., & Bless, H. (1991). Happy and mindless, but sad and smart? The impact of affective states on analytic reasoning. In J. P. Forgas (Ed.), Emotion and social judgments (pp. 55–72). Oxford, UK: Pergamon.

Schwarz, N., & Bohner, G. (2001). The construction of attitudes. In A. Tesser & N. Schwarz (Eds.), *Blackwell handbook of social psychology: Intraindividual processes* (pp. 436–457). Oxford, UK: Blackwell.

Schwarz, N., & Clore, G. L. (1983). Mood, misattribution and judgment of well being: Informative and directive functions & affective states. *Journal of Personality and Social Psychology, 45*, 513–523.

Schwarz, N., & Clore, G. L. (1996). Feelings and phenomenal experiences. In E. T. Higgins & A.W. Kruglanski (Eds.), *Social psychology: Handbook of basic principles* (pp. 433–465). New York: Guilford.

Schwarz, N., & Strack, F. (1991). Context effects in attitude surveys: Applying cognitive theory to social research. In W. Stroebe & M. Hewstone (Eds.), *European review of social psychology* (Vol. 2, pp. 31–50). Chichester, UK: Wiley.

Shavit, S., & Nelson, M. R. (1999). The social identity function in person perception: Communicated meaning of product preferences. In J. M. Olson & G. R. Maio (Eds.), *Why we evaluate? : Functions of attitudes* (pp. 37–58). Mahwah, NJ: Lawrence Erlbaum Associates.

Sherif, M. (1936). *The psychology of social norms.* New York: Harper.

Sherif, M., & Cantril, H. (1947). *The psychology of ego-involvement: Social attitudes and identifications.* New York: Wiley.

Sia, T. L., Lord, C. G., Blessum, K. A., Ratcliff, D. D., & Lepper, M. R. (1997). Is a rose always a rose? The role of social category exemplar change in attitude stability and attitude–behavior consistency. *Journal of Personality and Social Psychology, 72,* 501–514.

Simon, H. A. (1980). Problem solving in education. In D. T. Tuma & F. Reif (Eds.), *Problem solving and education: Issues in teaching and research* (pp. 81–96). Hillsdale, NJ: Lawrence Erlbaum Associates.

Sjöberg, L. (1978, Oct.). *Beliefs and values as attitude components.* Paper presented at the International symposium on social psychophysics. Mannheim, Germany.

Slovic, P., Lichtenstein, S., & Fischoff, B. (1988). Decision making. In R. C. Atkinson, R. J. Hernstein, G. Lindzey & R. Duncan Luce (Eds.). Sterens' handbook of experimental psychology 2nd ed., (Vol. 2, pp. 673–738). New York: Wiley.

Smith, M. B. (1947). The personal setting of public opinions: A study of attitudes toward Russia. *Public Opinion Quarterly, 11,* 507–523.

Smith, M. B., Bruner, J. S., & White, R. W. (1956). *Opinions and personality.* New York: Wiley.

Snyder, M., & DeBono, K. G. (1985). Appeals to images and claims about quality: Understanding the psychology of advertising. *Journal of Personality and Social Psychology, 49,* 586–597.

Staats, A. W., & Staats, C. K. (1958). Attitudes established by classical conditioning. *Journal of Abnormal and Social Psychology, 57,* 37–40.

Steele, C. M. (1988). The psychology of self-affirmation: Sustaining the integrity of the self. In L. Berkowitz (Ed.), *Advances in experimental social psychology* (Vol. 21, pp. 261–302). San Diego, CA: Academic Press.

Strack, F., Schwarz, N., & Wänke, M. (1991). Semantic and pragmatic aspects of context effects in social and psychological research. *Social Cognition, 9*(111), 876–889.

Stroebe, W. (2002). Übergewicht als Schicksal? Die cognitive Steuerung des Essverhaltens [Obesity as fate? The cognitive regulation of eating behavior]. *Psychologische Rundschau, 53,* 14–22.

Stukat, K. G. (1958). Suggestibility: A factorial and experimental analysis. Oxford: Alinquist & Wiksell.

Tesser, A. (1993). The importance of heritability in psychological research: The case of attitudes. *Psychological Review, 100,* 129–142.

Tetlock, P. E. (1985). Accountability: The neglected social context of judgment and choice. In B. Staw & L. Cummings (Eds.). Research in organizational behavior (Vol. 7, pp. 297–332). Greenwhich, CT: JAI Press.

Thistlewaite, D. L., & Kamenetzky, J. (1955). Attitude change through refutation and elaboration of audience counterarguments. *Journal of Abnormal and Social Psychology, 51,* 3–12.

Thompson, E. P., Roman, R. J., Moscovitz, G. B., Chaiken, S., & Bargh, J. A. (1994). Accuracy motivation attenuates covert priming: The systematic reprocessing of social information. *Journal of Personality and Social Psychology, 66,* 474–489.

Thompson, M. M., & Zanna, M. P. (1995). The conflicted individual: Personality-based and domain-specific antecedents of ambivalent social attitudes. *Journal of Personality, 63,* 259–288.

Thompson, M. M., Zanna, M. P., & Griffin, D. W. (1995). Let's not be indifferent about (attitudinal) ambivalence. In R. E. Petty & J. A. Krosnick (Eds.), *Attitude strength: Antecedents and consequences* (pp. 361–412). Mahwah, NJ: Lawrence Erlbaum Associates.

Thurstone, L. L. (1931). The measurement of attitudes. *Journal of Abnormal and Social Psychology, 26,* 249–269.

Tourangeau, R., & Rasinski, K. A. (1988). Cognitive processes underlying context effects in attitude measurement. *Psychological Bulletin, 103,* 299–314.

Trope, Y., & Gaunt, R. (1999). A dual-process model of overconfident attributional inferences. In S. Chaiken & Y. Trope (Eds.), *Dual process theories in social psychology* (pp. 161–179). New York: Guilford.

Trope, Y., & Gaunt, R. (2000). Processing alternative explanations of behaviour: Correction or integration. *Journal of Personality and Social Psychology, 79,* 837–852.

Tybout, A. M., & Scott, C. A. (1983). Availability of well-defined internal knowledge and the attitude formation process: Information aggregation versus self-perception. *Journal of Personality and Social Psychology, 44,* 474–491.

Uleman, J. S., Newman, L. S., & Moscowitz, G. B. (1996). Unintended social inference: The case of spontaneous trait inference. In M. P. Zanna (Ed.), *Advances in experimental social psychology* (Vol. 28, pp. 211–279). San Diego, CA: Academic Press.

Walther, E. (2002). Guilt by mere association: Evaluative conditioning and the spreading attitude effect. *Journal of Personality and Social Psychology, 82*, 919–934.

Walther, E., & Grigoriadis, S. (2003). *Why sad people like shoes better: The influence of mood on the evaluative conditioning of consumer attitudes*. Unpublished manuscript. Heidelberg University, Germany.

Walther, E., Nagengast, B., & Trasselli, C. (2003). *Evaluative conditioning in social psychology: Facts and speculations*. Unpublished manuscript. Heidelberg University, Germany.

Webster, D. M., Richter, L., & Kruglanski, A. W. (1996). On leaping to conclusions when feeling tired: Mental fatigue effects on impressional primacy. *Journal of Experimental Social Psychology, 32*, 181–195.

Wegner, D. M., & Wenzlaf, R. M. (1996). Mental control. In E. T. Higgins & A.W. Kruglanski (Eds.), Social psychology: Handbook of basic principles (pp. 466–492). New York: Guilford.

Winkielman, P., Schwarz, N., Fazandeiro, T., & Reber, R. (2003). The hedonic marking of processing fluency: Implications for evaluative judgment. In J. Musch & K. C. Klauer (Eds.), *The psychology of evaluation* (pp. 189–218). Mahwah, NJ: Lowrence Erlbaum Associates.

Wilson, T. D., & Kraft, D. (1993). Why do I love thee? Effects of repeated introspections about a dating relationship on attitudes toward the relationship. *Personality and Social Psychology Bulletin, 19*(4), 409–418.

Wilson, T. D., Kraft, D., & Dunn, D. S. (1989). The disruptive effects of explaining attitudes: The moderating effects of knowledge about the attitude object. *Journal of Experimental Social Psychology, 25*, 379–400.

Wilson, T. D., Lindsey, S., & Schooler, T. Y. (2000). A model of dual attitudes. *Psychological Review, 107*, 101–126.

Wood, W. (1982). Retrieval of attitude-relevant information from memory: Effects on susceptibility to persuasion and on intrinsic motivation. *Journal of Personality and Social Psychology, 42*, 798–810.

Wood, W., Lundgren, S., Oullette, J. A., Busceme, S., & Blackstone, T. (1994). Minority influence: A meta-analytic review of social influence processes. *Psychological Bulletin, 115*, 323–345.

Wood, W., & Quinn, J. M. (2003). Forewarned and forearmed? Two meta-analysis syntheses of forewarnings of influence appeals. *Psychological Bulletin, 129*, 119–138.

Wyer, R. S., Jr. (1974). *Cognitive organization and change: An information processing approach.* New York: Wiley.

Wyer, R. S., Jr., & Carlston, D. E. (1979). *Social cognition, inference and attribution*. Hillsdale, NJ: Lawrence Erlbaum Associates.

Wyer, R. S., Jr., & Goldberg, L. (1970). A probabilistic analysis of the relationships between beliefs and attitudes. *Psychological Review, 77*, 100–120.

Wyer, R. S., Jr., & Srull, T. K. (1989). Memory and cognition in its social context. Hillsdale, NJ: Lawrence Erlbaum Associates.

Zajonc, R. B. (1968). Attitudinal effects of mere exposure. *Journal of Personality and Social Psychology: Monograph Supplement, 9*, 1–27.

Zajonc, R. B. (1980). Feeling and thinking: Preferences need no inferences. *American Psychologist, 39*, 117–123.

Zanna, M. P., & Rempel, J. K. (1988). Attitudes: A new look at an old concept. In D. Bar-Tal & A. W. Kruglanski (Eds.), *The social psychology of knowledge* (pp. 315–334). Cambridge, UK: Cambridge University Press.

9

The Influence of Attitudes on Beliefs: Formation and Change

Kerry L. Marsh
University of Connecticut

Harry M. Wallace
Trinity University

Through direct or indirect contact with an object or event, we experience what attributes that object may have, what feelings it evokes in us, and what actions we can take with regard to it. Our response to those experiences generally does not stop with a cataloguing of these believed features, affective reactions, and perceived action-possibilities, however. Often, the resulting beliefs people form regarding whether the object has desirable or undesirable attributes leads individuals to form a general evaluative tendency, that is, an attitude toward that object. In this chapter we review research on one way in which forming such attitudes is useful: in aiding the subsequent retrieval, formation, or change in beliefs about the object. Because of the nature of conceptual structures such as attitudes, and because of the motivation to resist information that contradicts our current preferences, attitudes often have attitude-congruent effects on beliefs. Attitude–belief congruence means that individuals accept or revise their beliefs about attributes of the object in a way that makes these beliefs congenial with their attitudes. Although the more traditional way of conceptualizing the link between beliefs and attitudes is to view beliefs as causally prior to attitudes (see Kruglanski & Stroebe, this volume, for a review of these perspectives), there is evidence that attitudes also distort our beliefs, through information processing that is biased for motivational or cognitive reasons. Attitudes can influence beliefs by influencing the perception of an attitude object, by affecting the mere retrieval of beliefs on which the attitude was originally formed, or by constructing new beliefs on-the-fly. Moreover, circumstances that lead one to reflect on or change an attitude can strengthen attitude–belief associations and yet, paradoxically, cause distorted beliefs *about the beliefs* that formed those attitudes (an attitude–belief disconnect). This chapter reviews theoretical perspectives on attitude–belief effects and reviews the evidence for a causal impact of attitudes on beliefs, discussing the conditions under which attitude–belief congruence effects are strengthened or eliminated.

ATTITUDES INFLUENCE BELIEFS THROUGH
BIASED PERCEPTIONS

Social Judgment Theory

According to the social judgment theory perspective (Sherif, Sherif, & Nebergall, 1965), prior attitudes serve as an anchor against which to judge other stimuli. At minimum, our attitudes influence our beliefs about others' attitudes—for example, how extreme or moderate their attitudes seem to us. Depending on where others' attitudes fall within one's latitude of acceptance, rejection, and noncommitment, one may assimilate or contrast others' positions with one's own position (e.g., Sherif et al., 1965). A belief about the validity of another person's position is contrasted in an unflattering light (toward disbelief) if it is in one's latitude of rejection, and assimilated and seen as more valid if another's position falls within one's latitude of acceptance. One implication of social judgment theory is that prior attitudes could influence retrieval of beliefs in the process of judging persuasive messages. Consistent with the tenets of social judgment theory, a number of studies provide correlational evidence that prior attitudes play an important role in belief retrieval (e.g., Johnson, Lin, Symons, & Campbell, 1995; Wood, 1982; Wood & Kallgren, 1988). Another implication of social judgment theory supported by research is that through assimilation and contrast processes, prior attitudes can lead to biased perceptions of information in a persuasive message, resulting in beliefs about the validity of the information in the message (Johnson, Smith-McLallen, Killeya, & Levin, 2004). Thus, a message that falls within one's latitude of acceptance will lead to beliefs that the arguments are valid and good, whereas arguments in a message that advocates a position far from one's current attitudinal position will be seen as weak.

ATTITUDES' EFFECTS ON BELIEF RETRIEVAL

Social judgment theory indicates that the initial judgmental process of responding to a persuasive message may affect beliefs about the message content. The outcomes of this judgmental process may subsequently be stored in memory, to presumably have additional impact when attitudes are retrieved from memory. A number of theoretical perspectives suggest that attitudes have an effect on the accessibility of beliefs stored in memory. One fundamental issue, however, is whether retrieval will be biased in an attitude-congruent direction. A recent meta-analysis of memory for attitude-relevant information suggests that this issue cannot be concluded by simply assuming that attitude-congruent information that an individual receives will be stored and then retrieved when beliefs are assessed. Rather, an individual's memory for information that was received in a persuasive message is not necessarily biased in a congenial direction (Eagly, Chen, Chaiken, & Shaw-Barnes, 1999; Eagly, Kulesa, Chen, & Chaiken, 2001). Therefore, in the following section, we discuss what explanations better account for the retrieval of beliefs from memory.

Cognitive Consistency Theories

A number of cognitive consistency and structural accounts suggest that retrieved beliefs should be consistent with attitudes. Consistency theories (Abelson et al., 1968; Rosenberg, Hovland, McGuire, Abelson, & Brehm, 1960) postulate consistency between the organization of relevant attitudinal/belief components. These include theories involving consistency in cognitive organization (Abelson & Rosenberg, 1958; Osgood & Tannenbaum, 1955; Rosenberg, 1956, 1960b), perceptual consistency–balance theory (Heider, 1958), and motivated inconsistency reduction–dissonance theory (Festinger, 1957). From each of these perspectives, attitudes and beliefs will normally be psychologically consistent. According to Rosenberg (1960b), for in-stance, the magnitude and direction of one's attitude toward some object (termed *affect* in his writings) varies as a function of the summed beliefs regarding whether the object would be useful for achieving values, weighted by the importance of those values (Rosenberg, 1956). Thus, retrieval of the summary attitude should also lead to retrieval of relevant beliefs about the object, including values and beliefs about the instrumental potency of that object for attaining a value (Rosenberg, 1960a).

Other Structural Perspectives

Other structural perspectives that have implications for attitude–belief relations make specific predictions regarding the way cognitive structures are organized. McGuire's early probabilog-ical research (McGuire, 1960a, 1960c) and his later research on the organization, content, and operation of thought systems (McGuire, 1960a, 1960c; McGuire & McGuire, 1991) suggests that people develop "connected and coherent thought systems around core events that might befall him or her" (McGuire & McGuire, 1991, p. 4) that help the individual cope realistically and autistically with these events. In McGuire's studies using syllogisms to test probabilogical models (McGuire, 1960a, 1960b, 1960c; see Wyer & Albarracín, this volume), participants rated the desirability of sets of three propositions, and rated the subjective probability that each proposition was true. The propositions were syllogistically related such that if premises A and B were true, conclusion C should be true.

One way in which individuals are believed to cope with an event is by thinking of the pleasantness of the event's antecedents or consequences and the degree to which the antecedents promote the event. For example, the desirability of a potential event such as whether admission prices to major sporting events will increase will be judged on the basis of logical reasoning about the positivity of the consequences and antecedents. Thus, raised prices to the events will be viewed more negatively if they will lead one to not be able to attend as many sporting events and if it follows from negative antecedents such as rising operating costs. McGuire's model (McGuire & McGuire, 1991) also makes predictions about individuals' beliefs regarding the core event's likelihood of happening. *Sufficient reason* for the event's occurrence implies that individuals make realistic judgments based on how many antecedents promote or prevent it. Thus, an individual might view rising sports ticket costs as likely to the degree to which he or she believes that there are a number of antecedents such as decreasing sports profits, and as less likely if there are antecedents such as strict price control laws.

The implication of these principles is that attitude–belief systems are formed in an orga-nized and coherent manner. The realistic and coping principles of McGuire's model, therefore, suggest that accessing one's attitude should also result in retrieval of beliefs that are consis-tent with the attitude. Other models that make more explicit assumptions regarding memory representations also suggest that there should be cognitive links between attitudes and attitude-relevant beliefs. Whether models assume a tripartite structure (Breckler, 1984), or view some attitudes as bipolar and others as unipolar, the structural assumptions imply that one's eval-uative summary will be linked to supportive beliefs. For instance, attitudes can be viewed as involving object label, evaluative summary (attitude), and a knowledge structure that supports that evaluation (Pratkanis, 1989; Pratkanis & Greenwald, 1989). Such associative network models imply that through spreading activation, retrieving one's attitude will lead to activation of linked nodes such as beliefs (Sherman, 1987).

Cognitive Processing Principles

Cognitive consistency and structural accounts, as well as social judgment theory, suggest that the congruence between attitude and beliefs is in large part a consequence of the assessment of the truth-value of some event (the likelihood that the object has some attribute). This attitude–belief congruence is based either on the standard set by one's own attitude, the logical link between antecedents and consequences, or the ways attitudes and beliefs are stored as a consequence of forming attitudes through weighted beliefs. Modern social-cognitive models of persuasion have implications for the underlying cognitive processes by which attitudes influence beliefs. Current models of persuasion include the elaboration likelihood model (e.g., Petty & Cacioppo, 1986; Petty & Wegener, 1999), heuristic-systematic model (Chaiken, Liberman, & Eagly, 1989; Chen & Chaiken, 1999), the MODE model of attitude–behavior consistency (Fazio, 1990b; Fazio & Towles-Schwen, 1999), and single-process models of persuasion (Albarracín, 2002; Kruglanski, Thompson, & Spiegel, 1999). Although models differ in the specific message reception (Albarracín, 2002) and yielding processes (e.g., Chaiken et al., 1989; Petty & Cacioppo, 1986) they describe, there are commonalities in the underlying information processing principles they assume. For instance, all models speak in some way to the consequences of cognitive limitations (i.e., lack of capability—limits that are due to cognitive content, or lack of cognitive capacity; Kruglanski et al., 1999), and variations in motivational engagement in the attitudinal issue. These cognitive process models have general implications for the processes of retrieving beliefs in response to retrieval of an attitude.

For attitudes to lead to belief retrieval, attitudes must first be formed online, that is, at the time of exposure to information (Mackie & Asuncion, 1990) rather than merely formed at the time of attitude expression. If attitudes are not formed online, then correlations between attitudes and beliefs cannot be caused by attitudes preceding belief formation. Moreover, even if attitudes are formed at the time when people are exposed to information about attributes of the attitude object, attitudes might not be used to cue retrieval of beliefs. Rather, if time is sufficient and accuracy motivation is high, beliefs might be retrieved directly (Sanbonmatsu & Fazio, 1990). For instance, assume one formed a more positive attitude about one department store over another, while also learning details such as the preferred store's particular strengths in some departments and weaknesses in others. If one has to make an expensive purchase and has time to choose a store to patronize, one would go to the store one believed was better for that purchase rather than relying on one's attitude toward the store (Sanbonmatsu & Fazio, 1990). With online formation of attitudes, the belief-related information that affected its formation could have been relatively unelaborated, as in the case where the individual was not motivated to deliberate and a message cue allowed for simple acceptance of the information (e.g., the message was presented by an expert). Alternatively, individuals who were exposed to a message on an issue of importance to them, for which they had sufficient knowledge and cognitive resources to ponder, might form beliefs (and attitudes) that diverge considerably from the message content. Because attitudes formed online can be stored separately from the beliefs that served as the basis for attitude formation (Hastie & Park, 1986), attitudes would only lead to retrieval of (attitude-consistent) beliefs to the extent that an individual makes sufficient effort to retrieve them. In this case, attitudes will likely lead to a bias to retrieve those beliefs that were most strongly elaborated and, thus, most congruent with the attitudes.

For example, research testing the cognition in persuasion model indicates that relatively more effortful processing (that is, moderate motivation and high ability) is required for beliefs to be used in the formation of attitudes (Albarracín, 2002). When cognitive resources are more limited, individuals will use other information to form their attitudes (e.g., affective state). The implication of this premise for subsequent retrieval is that attitudes that are formed from more elaborative processes (central route or systematic processing rather than peripheral cues) are most likely to lead to biased retrieval—albeit the beliefs retrieved may not be the equivalent in content to information that the individual received. That is, beliefs that are retrieved in such a situation will be biased in an attitude-consistent direction—and it may be the case that original information that was attitude-*uncongenial* might well have been most strongly counterargued (Eagly, Kulesa, Brannon, Shaw, & Hutson-Comeaux, 2000) and, thus, least believed. In contrast, for attitudes that are formed through more shallow processing, for example, using an affective cue about one's emotional state at the time of attitude formation, retrieval of one's attitude necessarily cannot yield retrieval of beliefs that formed those attitudes. However, these attitudes can affect the subsequent formation of beliefs (Albarracín & Wyer, 2001).

Implications of Attitude–Belief Retrieval for Belief Formation

Approaches that emphasize that retrieving one's attitude will increase the accessibility of beliefs in memory also have implications for constructing beliefs on-the-fly from the retrieved attitude. For instance, from McGuire's perspective, there are logical cognitive ramifications of attitudes for the belief system. Attitudes have an impact on logically related propositions as well as relatively remote logical ramifications (McGuire, 1981). For example, if one has a positive attitude toward teacher competency testing, and then encounters new information that a teacher failed or passed such a test, one's positive attitude toward such testing is likely to form beliefs that follow logically: One's inferences about the teacher's competence will be affected by this information (Mackie, Ahn, Asuncion, & Allison, 2001). Individuals with negative attitudes toward such testing will not be affected by such information, because such inferences do not follow logically from a position opposing the validity of such tests.

However, the implication of more complex analyses of attitudinal processes yielded by information processing principles lead to the conclusion that motivated inference processes will more commonly occur than will logical reasoning processes. In the next section we detail evidence that attitudes lead to the formation of beliefs that are distorted in an attitudinally congenial manner.

ATTITUDES INFLUENCE MOTIVATED INFERENCES

When individuals form an attitude online (Mackie & Asuncion, 1990), and such attitudes are sufficiently accessible from memory (Fazio, 1990b), these attitudes can often have a direct effect on an individual's beliefs that an object or event has certain qualities. The most common effects reflect motivated inferences that yield attitude–belief congruency. Such effects of attitudes on beliefs are not merely limited to beliefs about the attitude object (Lord, Ross, & Lepper, 1979; Rosenberg, 1960b) but can extend to beliefs about related events or objects (Hastorf & Cantril, 1954), beliefs about future outcomes (Babad & Katz, 1991; Markman & Hirt, 2002; McGuire, 1960a), and beliefs about other people's attitudes (Krosnick, 1990a).

Wishful Thinking

Despite the assumptions of cognitive consistency and structural models, the effects of attitudes on inferences do not always adhere to logical consistency. Individuals may display logical inconsistencies between available information and their preferred attitude-consistent conclusions, distorting judgments in an attitude-consistent direction. One autistic coping principle of McGuire's thought system analysis is a *rationalization* principle that suggests that one adjusts the desirability of the core event based on its likelihood. Thus, one might come to feel that rising sports ticket prices would not have such devastating consequences after all, if it seemed inevitable that this was to occur. McGuire's research indicated that when inconsistencies in subjective probability ratings in syllogism triads occurred, they tended to be a function of the desirability of the consequences (McGuire & McGuire, 1991). The total evidence of wishful thinking from McGuire's studies, however, offers only weak support that the attitudinal valence of statements has an effect on whether we believe them to be true (see Wyer & Albarracín, this volume). Dillehay and colleagues (Dillehay, Insko, & Smith, 1966) also found mixed support for wishful thinking, finding effects of belief distortions in some, but not all, circumstances. Both McGuire (1960a) and Dillehay et al., however, found support for validity-seeking processes. Namely, presenting participants with messages that argued for the truth of a proposition led to changes in unmentioned, though logically related, beliefs.

Results of more recent research examining moderators of attitude strength in persuasion (Johnson et al., 2004) suggests that attitudes' impact on beliefs may be more consistent overall with wishful thinking than with logical, validity-seeking processes. Johnson et al. (2004) examined the relationship between desirability of a proposition and beliefs about the likely truth of the proposition, and these variables' effects on judgments of argument strength. Johnson et al.'s valence hypothesis suggests that the label of *argument strength* is usually a proxy for the degree to which an argument is positive in valence, or implies desirable consequences, and that perceived validity of an argument is not the basis for argument strength. For example, their research indicated that commonly used arguments viewed as strongly supportive of having senior comprehensive exams were positively valenced statements such as maintaining academic excellence at the university, or attracting more corporations for job recruitment (e.g., Petty, Harkins, & Williams, 1980). In contrast, weak arguments about difficult exams preparing one for life implied undesirable consequences such as the possibility of failure and unpleasant difficulties in the future. Moreover, propositions that implied more desirable consequences were perceived as more likely, but it was the valence of the position—that is, the degree of congruence with desired consequences—that affected attitudes, not the likelihood of the consequences (Johnson et al., 2004).

Although McGuire (1960c) suggested that the events for which subjective probability and desirability were being assessed could involve any object of judgment, including physical entities or combination of entities (McGuire, 1960c, 1981), most of his research involved propositions about future states of affairs or occurrences (e.g., McGuire & McGuire, 1991). Thus, results of these studies have the most implications for *wishful thinking* in which beliefs about the likelihood of a future event are biased by an individual's attitudes toward that event. Evidence for wishful thinking is particularly abundant in the area of political attitudes. Analyses of nonsystematic surveys of college students and community members conducted prior to World War II (Cantril, 1938; McGregor, 1938) suggested that participants' attitudes toward the occurrence of political events affected their attitudes toward events for which predictive data were ambiguous (Roosevelt being elected) but not for events with strong external evidence (another world war, Hitler being in power). More systematic survey research during the last 55 years also offers evidence for wishful thinking bounded by reality, though the correlational nature of these investigations leaves the causal direction of the attitude–beliefs relationship open to interpretation. In elections, preferences for a political candidate strongly influence predictions of who will win an election in the United States (Granberg & Brent, 1983; Lewis-Beck & Skalaban, 1989) as well as in other countries such as Israel and New Zealand (e.g., Babad & Yacobos, 1993). For instance, for both state and national elections, candidate preferences predicted citizen forecasts (Dolan & Holbrook, 2001). For other political predictions (Granberg & Holmberg, 1986) and predictions in other arenas, evidence for wishful thinking or an *allegiance bias* (Markman & Hirt, 2002) is equally strong. For instance, Babad and colleagues (Babad, 1987; Babad & Katz, 1991) found that soccer fans in soccer stadiums and betting stations in Israel displayed wishful thinking regarding the outcome of the games. Such results have been replicated in the United States for fans of college sports teams (e.g., Markman & Hirt, 2002).

Breadth and Mechanisms of Effects

A wide range of studies, covering domains as diverse as sporting events and the political arena find that wishful thinking is pervasive. In contrast, the effects for a reverse association between desirability of outcome and beliefs about it coming true are more limited. Research examining people's predictions of who would win U.S. presidential elections from 1952 to 1980 indicated a *bandwagon effect* (i.e., implying more rationalization processes) only in 1960, when a significant number of individuals who initially preferred Nixon but expected Kennedy to win voted for Kennedy (Granberg & Brent, 1983). Apart from this single example, most data from these elections are consistent with wishful thinking rather than rationalization, but these effects are also bounded by reality constraints. If a citizen wants a particular candidate to become mayor of her town, she is more likely to predict that her candidate will win (Dolan & Holbrook, 2001), and she is likely to view arguments that imply that outcome as stronger than arguments implying a loss (Johnson et al., 2004). One reason for such autistic thinking is that it serves a coping function (McGuire & McGuire, 1991), psychologically defending oneself against undesired outcomes. But even as it might serve an irrational function of making something appear to be more likely to come true, it might also serve an adaptive and rational function—an overgeneralization of the promotive effects of positive expectations on reality.

Wishful thinking might be a form of superstitious behavior designed to influence reality. For instance, one might refuse to harbor negative expectations about a desired reality in the case of wanting a particular horse to win a race. Violating such superstitions by betting against one's preferred horse might be seen as bad karma that could in some way cause that horse to lose. Second, and more realistically, for outcomes over which one does have some control over the outcome, a bias to believe in one's preferred reality is adaptive for creating such a reality because of the positive effects on motivation and action that result from holding that bias (Nasco & Marsh, 1999). Thus, having some confidence about one's political candidate's chances to win might lead one to more effectively work for that outcome (donate money, campaign, be an effective persuader of others), whereas extreme doubt of the personal controllability of that outcome would decrease effective action (Bandura, 1997; Wortman & Brehm, 1975). Wishful thinking in this context, however, is also bounded by reality. In cases where a negative outcome is likely and consequential, likelihood judgments may show the opposite of optimism, where individuals "brace for the worst" by anticipating a feared future (Shepperd, Findley-Klein, Kwavnick, Walker, & Perez, 2000).

Current Attitudes Yield Biased Predictions Regarding Others' Attitudes and One's Own Past Attitudes

Attitudes also affect our beliefs about others, an effect frequently examined in the political arena. People whose policy attitudes are important to them are likely to believe that candidates have substantial differences in their attitudes on policy issues (Krosnick, 1990a). On rare occasions, partisans hold negative beliefs about others such as in the negative media bias, in which medias are viewed as hostile toward one's side (Vallone, Ross, & Lepper, 1985). However, most distortions of beliefs about others are in an attitude-supportive direction. For instance, according to the attitude projection hypothesis, individuals' attitude toward a policy may lead them to distort their perceptions of a favored (or disfavored) candidate's position on a policy relevant to their attitude (e.g., research by Granberg & Brent, 1980; Shaffer, 1981). To conduct a strong test of this projection hypothesis, studies must look at how attitude position and prior perceptions of candidate positions before an election predict *subsequent* perceptions of candidate's perceptions. One such study (Krosnick, 1990a) found little evidence that *change* in perceptions of a candidate's position was predicted by prior attitudes, suggesting that the evidence for attitude projection is weaker than political psychologists have thought. However, other research suggests that forming a positive attitude toward someone (e.g., having a friendly instructor) can lead us to believe they have other positive attributes (e.g., are intelligent), an effect termed the *halo effect* (Kozlowski & Kirsch, 1987; Lance, LaPointe, & Stewart, 1994; Nisbett & Wilson, 1977a). This tendency to make attitude-congruent inferences about others may even extend to situations where we evaluate the validity of information about individuals. For instance, students who were asked to identify facts about liked and disliked personalities were more likely to identify attitude-congruent facts as true (Pratkanis, 1988).

Moreover, similar processes occur when people use their current attitudes as a guide for forming beliefs about themselves. Considerable research by Ross and colleagues indicates that individuals' beliefs about what their attitudes were in the past are distorted by their current attitudes. Individuals whose attitudes have been changed showed selective retrieval of their past beliefs, and faulty reconstruction of autobiographical memories (e.g., Ross & Conway, 1986). Thus, a woman who supports a conservative candidate, currently owns her own business, and makes considerably more money than when she was much younger may falsely recollect her previous beliefs about her political positions. She may be likely to forget that as a student she had more liberal beliefs and supported political positions that were less conservative than her current political attitudes.

Summary

Effects such as projection, the halo effect, and biased assessments about facts regarding others or oneself in the past occur for reasons similar to that of wishful thinking. These effects occur both because of motivational reasons as well as for cognitive appraisal reasons—that attitudes are handy tools for assessing reality (Pratkanis, 1988). In addition, such effects as inferring one's own past beliefs also reflect faulty retrieval and reasoning processes, including implicit theories regarding attitude–belief congruence and beliefs about personal stability (Ross, 1989; Ross & Conway, 1986). Although the outcomes of resulting judgmental processes can often be biased, it is important to recognize that using one's attitude to make inferences can be useful, for instance, in a situation in which one would otherwise have no information. Thus, one's own attitude has some informational value that can improve predictive accuracy (e.g., Hoch, 1987; Murphy, Jako, & Anhalt, 1993; Solomonson & Lance, 1997). An individual from a different culture, dropped into a completely alien society would dramatically improve his ability to guess about other people's beliefs if he were given any member of that society's attitudes as a starting point for his judgments. On the other hand, the individual would do well to document his current attitudes so that once the attitudes he reported changed, he would not have to rely on highly faulty reconstructive processes to recall what they had been.

Biased Processing of New Information

Considerable evidence suggests that acceptance of new beliefs, or updating of old beliefs, are biased in an attitude-consistent direction. First, individuals are less likely to expose themselves to information that contradicts their attitudes. For example, people are less likely to be around people whose views differ from their own, or to choose to listen to a talk show host whose views strongly contradict their own. Both de facto exposure and selective exposure that is dissonance driven (Frey, 1986; Sweeney & Gruber, 1984) contribute to individuals' continued exposure to attitude-confirming information.

Second, individuals' prior attitudes may often serve to bias the new beliefs they form (or old beliefs they update) because of ability limitations. Individuals who have an attitude supportive of one political candidate have knowledge bases that are consistent with their attitude; thus, their understanding, interpretation, and storage of new information is likely to be attitude-consistent. In examining the hostile media phenomenon (that the media is perceived is being unduly biased against one's own side), researchers suggested that part of the reason pro-Israeli and pro-Arab students believed that media coverage of highly charged events in West Beirut in 1982 was biased (Vallone et al., 1985) was because their informational bases (e.g., the content and analyses *not* covered by the media) differed. To the extent that biases are informationally based rather than motivationally driven, individuals who are aware of the potential biasing effects of their attitude could potentially correct their beliefs to adjust for these biases if they were motivated and able (Wegener & Petty, 1997).

Third, individual's prior attitudes distort the processing of new information for motivational reasons. As detailed in the following, considerable evidence suggests that individuals process new information in an attitude-congruent manner so as to defend themselves against a wide range of unwanted conclusions, from believing that one's attitudes are incorrect, to believing that one's health is in danger. These processes reflect, in part, the natural conservatism of the cognitive system: Individuals show a status quo effect in their decisions, resisting making a different choice unless the new choice is substantially better, so they tend to avoid accepting that their attitudes are contradicted by new information about the attitude object. Motivated reasoning processes (Kunda, 1990) regarding the probable attributes of an entity may serve to bolster and maintain attitudes and maintain an inherent sense of the continuity and consistency of self (Abelson, 1986). Moreover, the beliefs we form after exposure to information may serve motivational purposes much the way other cognitive biases do, such as attributions about the causes of events that are biased in a self-flattering manner (Bradley, 1978; Greenwald, 1980). From the perspective of the heuristic-systematic model, attitudes will be particularly likely to bias forming or updating beliefs when an individual experiences defense motivation, the "desire to hold attitudes and beliefs that are congruent with one's perceived material interests or existing self-definitional attitudes and belief" (Chen & Chaiken, 1999, p. 77). In addition to evidence that attitudes distort beliefs in an attitude-congruent direction (Bothwell & Brigham, 1983; Ditto & Lopez, 1992; Hastorf & Cantril, 1954; Houston & Fazio, 1989; Lord et al., 1979; Pomerantz, Chaiken, & Tordesillas, 1995; Proshansky, 1943), there is considerable evidence that general self-interest or hedonic relevance of an attitude increases belief distortion (Ditto & Lopez, 1992; Giner-Sorolla & Chaiken, 1997; Liberman & Chaiken, 1992). In the studies that provide this evidence, participants are typically presented with novel belief-relevant information that contradicts their preferred beliefs, implying for instance that the individual may be sick or at risk for disease, or arguing for a position that goes against the individual's vested interest. In many cases, such research is not dealing with the effects of existing attitudes, but attitudes that are constructed on-the-fly in the experimental context. For instance, even if one did not know about a given disease prior to an experiment, one's intrinsic attitude toward personal physical well-being will lead to automatic generation of a negative evaluative response to the idea of being infected with this previously unknown disease. Thus, a positive evaluative tendency toward being healthy and alive, performing well, or being viewed positively by others can lead to defensive distortion in beliefs (e.g., unwillingness to believe a negative outcome).

Empirical Evidence for Motivational Distortions

The strongest evidence that attitudes' effects on beliefs are motivationally driven comes from situations in which individuals are exposed to ambiguous information such as at sporting events, in research reports, or in information about an individual. Attitudes frequently lead to the formation of attitude-congenial beliefs through biased processing of ambiguous information. Two classic examples stand out. Hastorf and Cantril (1954) found that Princeton and Dartmouth students who viewed the same Princeton versus Dartmouth football game had different beliefs regarding the infractions each team had committed. Two decades later, Lord, Ross, and Lepper (1979) had participants who held extreme attitudes for or against capital punishment read articles that presented mixed evidence regarding capital punishment as a deterrent for crime. Attitudes affected their beliefs. For example, participants viewed the proattitudinal report in the experiment as more convincing than the counterattitudinal report, and they devoted more critical scrutiny regarding the methodological flaws in studies yielding counterattitudinal findings. Other studies have replicated Lord et al.'s results using their capital punishment materials (Houston & Fazio, 1989; Pomerantz et al., 1995). Comparable biasing effects have been demonstrated using other materials (Bothwell & Brigham, 1983; Proshansky, 1943) and in different domains such as impression formation (e.g., Lott, Lott, Reed, & Crow, 1970). For instance, college students who watched the 1980 Reagan–Carter U.S. presidential debate believed that the candidate they preferred prior to the debate had won the debate (Bothwell & Brigham, 1983).

Mechanisms of Motivational Distortion

Researchers have specified a number of mechanisms by which defense motivation results in attitudes having a biasing effect on beliefs. Many of the principles are not specified in any particular model of persuasion (e.g., modern dual process models), but are derived from social cognition and information processing principles relevant to persuasion (e.g., Albarracín, 2002; McGuire, 1968; Sherman, 1987; Wegener & Carlston, this volume).

Biased Information Seeking.   Defense motivation engages what lay epistemic theory would label a need for specific closure—that is, a desire to reach a particular conclusion. One way to achieve this particular closure is to prematurely freeze the search for information if the search yields information that supports the desired conclusion (Kruglanski, 1989, 1990). Ditto and Lopez (1992, Experiment 1) induced a positive or negative attitude toward a potential interaction partner. Participants were then allowed to see their partner's responses to analogy items, on which the person was shown to perform well or poorly. Participants ended their examination of the other person's performance on the items more quickly when the performance allowed them to develop beliefs about the person that were consistent with their attitude. In addition, defense motivation is associated with delayed freezing in an epistemic search (Kruglanski, 1989, 1990) when incoming information is disconfirming of one's preferred conclusions. Ditto and Lopez (1992, Experiment 2) found, for instance, that when participants testing themselves for a fictitious medical condition believed that a test indicator needed to change color in order to indicate absence of the condition, participants not only waited much longer to conclude the test, but sought to test themselves again.

Biased Analysis and Evaluation of Information.   For belief-relevant information that is not congenial with one's attitude or personal interests, one may show more extensive analysis and critical evaluation of the information. Considerable evidence suggests that individuals engage in biased hypothesis testing (Snyder & Swann, 1978), a process that often is motivated toward confirmation of an existing bias. One way in which individuals might confirm a desired hypothesis, for instance, is by setting higher standards for validity of a less preferred belief. For instance, Ditto and Lopez (1992) found that participants were more likely to take multiple tests if an initial test diagnosing some presumed illness yielded an undesirable outcome. Moreover, the individual might selectively focus on weaknesses of the opposing position but ignore the weaknesses of evidence that supports one's position (e.g., Hastorf & Cantril, 1954; Lord et al., 1979), or combine information in a biased manner (Petty & Wegener, 1999). For instance, Liberman and Chaiken (1992) had coffee drinkers (versus nondrinkers) read an essay discussing different reports arguing for and against the hypothesis that coffee drinking was associated with development of disease. Each report had methodological limitations, allowing for biased interpretations to have an effect. Thus, the coffee drinkers processed the threatening aspects of the reports the most, finding methodological flaws in the reports that supported a link between coffee drinking and disease.

Biased Cognitive Responses. In addition to more critically evaluating and analyzing the content of messages that contradict one's attitude or desired conclusion, individuals' self-generated arguments will be biased in a direction toward their preferred conclusion. The role of cognitive responses in mediating persuasion has been verified by experimental procedures that direct an individual's thoughts in a message-agreeing or message-disagreeing manner (Killeya & Johnson, 1998). Instructing an individual to engage in favorable thoughts about a message or to engage in unfavorable thoughts can overcome the effects of weak and strong arguments, respectively (Killeya & Johnson, 1998). Therefore, individuals who are motivated to direct their thoughts toward discounting a message's undesired conclusion may often be successful. For example, Ditto and Lopez (1992, Experiment 3) found that participants were able to come up with more potential excuses for why a test might be wrong when the test result implied an undesirable outcome.

Biased Use of Heuristics. Both the heuristic-systematic model and the elaboration likelihood model suggest that biased processing that occurs for motivational reasons can lead to biased assessment of persuasion cues as well as biased elaboration of message arguments if elaboration likelihood is high (Petty & Wegener, 1999). In general, attitude-biased or self-interest-biased processing leads individuals to use heuristics if heuristics are congenial with one's attitude or interests, but they are ignored or actively discounted if they are contrary to one's attitude or interest. For instance, participants who had a vested interest in validating the importance of essay exams (i.e., they believed they performed better on these) or invalidating essay exams responded differently to a consensus cue depending on whether a message was supportive of their vested interest (Giner-Sorolla & Chaiken, 1997). Thus, people who received only the consensus cue saw it as less reliable if it contradicted their vested interest. For people who also received a message and the consensus cue was hostile to their vested interest, the effects of vested interests on attitude change were partially mediated by participants' cognitive elaborations.

Whether one or another of these processes will occur should depend on the reality constraints of the situation—these processes will be used strategically and flexibly given the constraints of the particular situation. Each of these effects implies that relevant attitudes (e.g., regarding being healthy) are automatically accessed in that situation and then they bias perception of the attitude object (Fazio, 1990a). If the relevance of the information to one's attitudes or beliefs was not apparent to an individual, or the relevant attitude or hedonic relevance were not highly accessible, these biases would not occur. Moreover, an individual's ability to engage in more thought-intensive strategies will also be important. Individuals who cannot engage in more elaborative processes because of cognitive distractions or time pressure for instance, may simply reject or accept the belief-relevant information, or strategically assess the validity of salient peripheral cues (Petty & Wegener, 1999). In addition, other situational factors may reduce individuals' needs to distort their beliefs in an attitude-consistent direction. For example, individuals who have recently affirmed their values respond more objectively to information in a message rather than showing a proattitudinal distortion (Correll, Spencer, & Zanna, in press).

MODERATORS OF ATTITUDE–BELIEF CONGRUENCE IN RETRIEVAL AND FORMATION OF BELIEFS

A number of moderators of the tendency for attitudes to increase the accessibility of beliefs stored in memory and for attitudes to yield distorted beliefs have received empirical support. In general, these moderators fall into two categories—those that reflect circumstances about which beliefs are being retrieved or formed and serve as reality constraints, and those that reflect qualities of the attitudes themselves (e.g., attitude strength; for a review, see Fabrigar, MacDonald, & Wegener, this volume).

Situational Constraints

Ambiguity increases the congruence between attitude and belief for numerous phenomena, including wishful thinking (Cantril, 1938). People's tendency to distort information in an attitude-congruent direction is bounded by reality. To paraphrase Singer (1980), a distinguishing feature of belief systems is that they all are apparently true—people do not intentionally choose to believe something they know is false. The strongest evidence for attitude–belief congeniality comes from situations where evidence for and against one's attitudinal position in a new situation is mixed, ambiguous, or incomplete, and not in situations where the objective outcome of some attitude-relevant situation is highly salient (Allison, Beggan, Midgley, & Wallace, 1995). In predicting future political outcomes, for instance, evidence of wishful thinking is reduced when there is overwhelming evidence for the likely outcome (Cantril, 1938; McGregor, 1938). Analysis of U.S. presidential elections over 30 years also indicated that wishful thinking was weaker in years when the outcome of the election was relatively unambiguous (Granberg & Brent, 1983). Strong evidence of attitudes' distorting influence on beliefs comes from experimental contexts in which mixed information is presented, such as evidence for and against capital punishment (Lord et al., 1979), or mixed research evidence for a caffeine–disease link (Liberman & Chaiken, 1992).

The source of attitude–belief congruence effects is clarified by examining the variables that are *not* sufficient for reducing attitude–belief congruence. In general, imposition of external motivators to reduce biased distortions has little effect. Instructing people to be objective in their judgments can have small effects for limited groups, reducing wishful thinking (Babad, 1987), but it often does not (Babad, Hills, & O'Driscoll, 1992; Babad & Katz, 1991). Similar manipulations, such as making individuals more accountable for their judgments or other attempts to explicitly direct individuals' processing in an objective direction, have also typically not had much effect (Babad, 1997).

Additional evidence for the limited effectiveness of external inducements is that monetary inducements do not eliminate wishful thinking in sports fans (Babad & Katz, 1991) or in voters (Babad, 1997). The limitations of external instructions and external incentives in moderating wishful thinking suggests that when attitudes distort beliefs, they do so either because of limitations in cognitive capabilities or because of an automatic (and difficult to override) orientation toward attitude-maintenance. Cognitive content is less likely to play a role in moderating attitude effects on beliefs for many of the contexts that have been studied. For instance, during a game, biased access to knowledge about each team's strengths and weaknesses should be substantially less important during the immediacy of a game. In contrast, knowledge during exposure to a political persuasion attempt would be substantially more important. Overall, for thinking about the future, the evidence is more supportive of a motivated distortion.

Attitudinal Features

Other moderators of attitude–belief congruence pertain to aspects of the attitude itself. When considered along a nonattitude (Converse, 1964) to attitude dimension, true attitudes are likely to lead to more generation or retrieval of beliefs than nonattitudes, especially beliefs that are congruent with the valence of the prior or changed attitude. In particular, attitudes that are highly accessible, meaning that they are automatically evoked by presentation of an attitude object, will be associated with a strong tendency to retrieve beliefs and interpret attitude-relevant information (the foundation of beliefs) in an attitude consistent manner (Houston & Fazio, 1989). Fazio and Williams (1986) found that individuals' beliefs about the performance of Reagan in a TV debate were biased in the direction of their attitudes, an effect that was stronger in individuals with more accessible attitudes regarding Reagan. Moreover, attitudes that have been formed by means that increase attitude accessibility (e.g., direct experience; Fazio, Chen, McDonel, & Sherman, 1982) or attitudes that have been made temporarily more accessible (e.g., through repeated expression; Houston & Fazio, 1989; Schuette & Fazio, 1995) have more effects on subsequently expressed beliefs. For instance, participants with more accessible attitudes toward the death penalty had stronger correlations between their attitudes and their beliefs about the capital punishment studies used in Lord et al. (1979; Houston & Fazio, 1989). Such effects were not present, however, when participants had high concern about making valid judgments (Schuette & Fazio, 1995). These effects were, therefore, consistent with the MODE model's predictions that attitude effects on perceptions will diminish with increased motivation to process information in a deliberative fashion.

Another important moderator of attitude–belief congruence effects is whether the attitude is one about which an individual has knowledge or not. For instance, instructions to reflect on one's attitude would not be expected to lead to polarization if participants do not have access to the reasons they formed their attitude (e.g., Wilson, Dunn, Bybee, Hyman, & Rotondo, 1984). For wishful thinking phenomena, although political knowledge attenuates wishful thinking (Babad, 1997; Babad et al., 1992; Dolan & Holbrook, 2001), there is some evidence (Babad, 1997) that it does so only weakly. In general, individuals who are able to successfully defend their attitudes against new belief-inconsistent information must have sufficient, accessible knowledge. For instance, Chaiken and Yates (1985) found that high consistency subjects generated refutational thoughts in response to discrepant information. Knowledge works as a moderator for cognitive as well as motivational reasons—one has adequate knowledge to adequately defend one's prior attitude, but even under high accuracy motivation, having access to a complex base of knowledge that is homogeneous, that is, involves highly correlated dimensions (Millar & Tessar, 1986b), can yield attitude-congruent beliefs.

Perhaps the most important attitudinal dimension that moderates attitude–belief congeniality effects is attitude strength. By definition, attitudes that are strong rather than weak should have more influence on beliefs, generally in a congruent direction. Strong attitudes are those that are durable (persistent and resistant) and impactful (influence information processing and judgments; Petty & Krosnick, 1995). Stronger attitudes can reflect a number of different dimensions. For instance, individuals vary in the degree to which their attitudes are consistent with their beliefs. Individuals with high evaluative-cognitive consistency should have stronger congruence and more highly organized beliefs (Chaiken & Baldwin, 1981). Moreover, attitudes that individuals subjectively experience as important are believed to involve more knowledge that is primarily accurate (which implies more attitude–belief consistency); such attitudes should have more influence in guiding interpretations (Boninger, Krosnick, & Berent, 1995). For example, people whose policy attitudes are important to them are more likely to believe that candidates have substantial differences in their attitudes on policy issues (Krosnick, 1990a). Attitude importance is associated with having more accessible attitudes, being more knowledgeable about issues, having the attitude linked to more core values, and having more internal consistency (Krosnick, 1990b)—all factors that may increase the likelihood that attitudes will lead to consistent beliefs. The emphasis of attitude importance research, however, is that beliefs are congenial with attitudes for relatively objective reasons (attitude-consistent knowledge and beliefs that result from cognitive elaborations of one's attitude position). The most plausible explanation for the link between attitude importance and attitude–belief consistency is that importance involves highly accessible attitudes (Lavine, Borgida, & Sullivan, 2000; Lavine, Sullivan,

Borgida, & Thomsen, 1996) toward objects that one has extensive knowledge about and that one is motivated to think about. Important attitudes are likely high in *embeddedness*, that is, linkage to the self, values, or knowledge, but moderate in degree of commitment or certainty (Pomerantz et al., 1995). Although in some cases high motivation to deliberate about incoming information could reduce the direct impact of attitudes on perceptions (Fazio, 1990b; Schuette & Fazio, 1995), this effect is compensated for by the tendency for attitude importance to increase approach tendencies toward proattitudinal information (Visser, Krosnick, & Simmons, 2003).

The attitude strength concepts of *personal relevance* or *vested interest* are more commonly used to refer to attitude objects that have an impact on pragmatic or hedonically relevant outcomes and are less inherently linked to personal values. In particular, many manipulations of personal relevance were intentionally chosen to involve attitude objects for which individuals have limited knowledge and counterarguments (Petty, Cacioppo, & Haugtvedt, 1992). Issues that are more personally relevant because they have implications for one's own practical outcomes are likely to induce more thoughtful analysis. Merely engaging in thought about issues that are logically related to one's attitudes can lead to more consistency between cognitive elements such as attitudes and beliefs (the *Socratic effect*; McGuire, 1960a). Moreover, self-threat also engages motivated defense against attitude-inconsistent belief formation. Personal relevance and vested interest manipulations vary considerably in the degree to which they evoke threats to the self. The degree to which the outcomes threaten pragmatic outcomes (e.g., tuition hikes, senior thesis exams), self-identity, or self-existence (e.g., ego-involving issues that evoke personal values; Johnson & Eagly, 1989; and threats to one's health or life) likely determines whether attitude–belief congruency is a function of cognitive biases versus more radically distorted motivated reasoning. In support of the former process is evidence that personally involving attitude issues lead to increased thought and polarization and, thus, heightened attitude accessibility (Thomsen, Borgida, & Lavine, 1995). Moreover, structural accounts similarly argue for this process. McGuire's model (McGuire & McGuire, 1991) predicts stronger links among thought elements for highly desirable and personally involving events.

There is some evidence, however, that vested interest can lead to defensively distorted beliefs. For example, in one study, students at a university who believed they would be most affected by a tuition surcharge had stronger beliefs that all other students (even those unaffected by the surcharge) would have attitudes similar to their own (Crano, 1983). In addition, evidence that vested interest's effect occurs in part for self-protective reasons is reflected by the fact that the false consensus bias is stronger after a failure manipulation (Sherman, Presson, & Chassin, 1984). Moreover, studies in which the potential outcomes threaten one's health find that participants distort their beliefs about the accuracy of the implied information (Ditto & Lopez, 1992; Liberman & Chaiken, 1992).

Caveats to Attitude Strength as a Moderator

Having more elaboratively structured, that is, stronger, attitudes means more thoughtfulness in response to counterattitudinal information. For example, one should have well-elaborated thoughts regarding why counterattitudinal information that has been encountered is believed to be incorrect. As a result, although one's attitudes should be congenial with one's stored beliefs, there may be no congeniality effect reflected in the correlation between remembered information one was exposed to (because one's active refutation of them might have yielded quite contrary beliefs) and one's attitude (Eagly et al., 1999; Eagly et al., 2000).

Moreover, many attitude–belief effects are quite robust and occur even when attitude strength dimensions are apparently low. For instance, Granberg and Brent (1983) found that the effects of preferences for a U.S. presidential candidate on individuals' expectations that they would win were not much weaker for nonvoters and those who said that the candidate choice was not that important to them. Thus, although some conditions (such as stronger attitudes) lead to stronger attitude–belief congeniality effects, few conditions lead to the complete elimination or reversal of congeniality effects.

One final caveat comes from Tetlock's value pluralism model of ideological reasoning (Tetlock, 1983b, 1986; Tetlock, Armor, & Peterson, 1994; Tetlock & Boettger, 1989; Tetlock, Peterson, & Lerner, 1996). This model suggests that certain ideologies may lend themselves to more integrative complexity, which involves holding equally strong, conflicting values. In such cases one might infer that the beliefs yielded from such political attitudes and attitude systems will not show simple congruency.

Conclusions

In sum, the mechanisms by which attitudes bring about the formation or retrieval of congruent beliefs are structural as well as motivational. That is, the mechanisms reflect either the outcomes of judgmental processes (Sherif et al., 1965) or the way attitudes and beliefs are perceptually (Heider, 1958) or cognitively organized (Osgood & Tannenbaum, 1955; Rosenberg, 1960a), but they also reflect the tendency for preferences to bias beliefs, as in wishful thinking phenomena (McGuire, 1960a). For some moderators such as attitude strength and knowledge, attitude–belief congruence probably reflects cognitive effects rather than substantial motivational distortion. For other situations (predicting an unknown outcome, receiving new information about a previously unknown danger), motivational explanations dominate. The total evidence for attitudes' effects on beliefs, however, offers particularly strong support that even when the effects reflect predominantly motivational processes (e.g., wishful thinking effects), the process is marked not by passive selection or storage of attitude-congruent information and overlooking of incongruent information (Eagly et al., 1999). Instead, when attitude–belief congruencies occur, they are the result of highly active cognitive processing involving actively refuting attitude-discrepant information in the process of reconstructing past beliefs (Ross & Conway, 1986) or forming beliefs about new information (Ditto & Lopez, 1992).

CHANGING BELIEFS BY CHANGING THE CONTENT OR EXTREMITY OF ATTITUDES

Cognitive Consistency, Information Processing, and Belief Change

Meta-analytic and experimental studies (Eagly et al., 1999; Eagly et al., 2000; Eagly et al., 2001; Hastie & Park, 1986) provide compelling evidence that the valence of information remembered from a persuasive message is often uncorrelated with the attitude that was formed. Given this demonstrated independence, one might infer that a change in attitude should not necessarily have an impact on relevant beliefs. Theoretical perspectives that address cognitive consistency processes and cognitive structural issues, however, make predictions that contradict this inference. Moreover, empirical evidence also contradicts this inference and indicates that there are reciprocal links between changes in attitudes, retrieval of beliefs, and strengthening of changed attitudes. After attitude change, for instance, individuals who are induced to recall past behaviors indicate beliefs about their past behavior that are biased by their new attitudes (Ross, McFarland, Conway, & Zanna, 1983). Furthermore, engaging in such recollections strengthens the persistence of the changed attitudes (Lydon, Zanna, & Ross, 1988).

Cognitive consistency theories assume that the reason a change in one's attitude leads to cognitive reorganization of related thoughts is to maintain psychological consistency. Direct, early evidence that change in one's attitudes can precede change in beliefs about the attitude object's attributes comes from approaches testing expectancy–value models of cognitive consistency (Rosenberg, 1960b) and models regarding the organization of thought systems. Two weeks after assessing participants' attitudes and cognitive structures (values and beliefs) for different social issues, Rosenberg (1960b) hypnotized participants and gave them a posthypnotic suggestion to change their evaluative responses (i.e., attitudes) on two of the social issues, one of low and one of high personal interest. Afterward, attitudes, values, and beliefs about whether an attitude object would achieve those values (instrumentality) were assessed. Attitudes were changed as expected, especially on the low interest item. Moreover, Rosenberg found that related beliefs changed—both the intensity of participants' values and their beliefs about instrumentality. For example, a woman under posthypnotic suggestion who was induced to feel much more positively about a city-manager plan changed her beliefs regarding whether it would lead to a more democratic system and promote equal rights (Rosenberg & Gardner, 1958). In contrast, control participants asked to role play different attitude responses on their high- and low-interest topics showed more exaggerated responses than hypnotized participants. For the manipulated topics, the control participants indicated more extreme changes on their attitudes and cognitions, but primarily changes in the values, not on instrumentality. More important, they also reported attitude change on nonmanipulated attitude objects. In contrast, changes in attitudes and beliefs occurred only on manipulated items for hypnotized participants (Rosenberg, 1960b). Thus, presumably the hypnotized participants' belief changes were due to the hypnosis-induced attitude change rather than being due to experimental demand. Although the experimental use of hypnosis is somewhat unusual and is invalid for studying memory (Lynn, Lock, Myers, & Payne, 1997), it has acceptable validity for creating cognitive and emotional states (e.g., Forgas, Bower, & Krantz, 1984; Kirsch & Lynn, 1999). Nevertheless, a methodological confound in the study raises other questions about the validity of the results. Namely, the experimental group was not equivalent to the control group; the former group was selected on the basis of being highly hypnotizable.

Most other expectancy–value models, most notably the theories of reasoned action and planned behavior (Ajzen, 1991; Ajzen & Fishbein, 1980), have exclusively conceptualized weighted beliefs as being causally prior to attitudes and, thus, have not included tests analogous to Rosenberg's. Nor do cognitive dissonance researchers test the causal direction of attitudes preceding belief change. Rather researchers typically use behavioral manipulations such as induced compliance combined with manipulations of beliefs (e.g., about negative consequences of their actions, Cooper & Fazio, 1984) and measure attitude change as a consequence (see Olson and Stone, this volume).

An early study by McGuire using triads of syllogism, however, did offer support for Rosenberg's finding (McGuire, 1960a). Some participants received a message that argued that one of the propositions was true. As a consequence, other related beliefs were changed, but less extensively than expected. Therefore, changes in beliefs as a function of changes in attitudes may occur somewhat imperfectly (McGuire & McGuire, 1991). The components of the thought system are apparently only loosely linked unless the issues are personally involving, in which case the thought system may be tightly articulated. According to this perspective, although changing attitudes should influence beliefs, there will be some cognitive inertia such that change in belief may be slow and delayed, and the extent of the change is not as extensive as logic implies (McGuire, 1960a).

Thus, approaches that focus on the structural analysis of attitudes and beliefs suggest that attitude change will lead to belief change. However, of particular concern, given that modern cognitive perspectives on attitudes and memory reveal a lack of congeniality effects in memory for attitude-relevant information (Eagly et al., 2001; Hastie & Park, 1986), is whether current cognitive models of persuasion would similarly expect changes in beliefs as a function of attitude change. Albarracín (2002) has argued that most current information-processing models focus extensively on yielding processes (e.g., whether it results from cognitive responses or responses to simple message cues), and do not specify detailed predictions regarding the reception processes. As such, current dual process models do not provide a sufficient framework for organizing the myriad of findings relevant to these reception and retrieval processes (e.g., Chaiken et al., 1989; Petty & Cacioppo, 1986). In contrast, the cognition in persuasion model describes the sequential steps involved in the retrieval, selection, and use of information in cognitive processing of messages (Albarracín, 2002). Recent research testing these processes verifies that changes in attitudes can precede changes in beliefs under some circumstances (Albarracín & Wyer, 2001). The researchers presented strong or weak arguments about a moderately relevant topic after students received a positive or negative mood induction. Some participants read the persuasive message while receiving a moderate distraction. The distraction was weak enough that participants were responsive to argument strength—their beliefs about the likely consequences of such a policy were affected accordingly. The distraction was strong enough, however, that it disrupted participants' abilities to combine belief-based information in forming their attitudes. For these participants, a causal model in which attitudes preceded message-relevant beliefs was a better fit to the correlations than a model in which beliefs predicted attitudes (Albarracín & Wyer, 2001). Participants' beliefs were influenced by the strength of the message arguments as well as by the attitudes participants formed based on the affective cue from the mood manipulation. For participants who had sufficient ability to engage in more complete processing of the message (e.g., they did not receive a distraction, or they had extra processing time if they had a distraction), the correlations better supported a model in which beliefs predicted attitudes.

In summary, limited research testing cognitive consistency and structural perspectives on thought systems demonstrates that belief change can follow changes in attitudes. Moreover, more recent research focusing on the role of cognition in persuasion processes suggests that under some circumstances, belief change can follow rather than precede attitude change. All of these studies, however, involve an explicit attempt to directly change an individual's attitudes by presenting them with persuasive information. Another way in which attitudes have been shifted is through procedures that merely have individuals focus on their attitudes in some way—either introspecting on the attitude itself (e.g., Sadler & Tesser, 1973)—or with a metacognitive focus, introspecting on the reasons for holding their attitude (e.g., Wilson et al., 1984). These two areas of research, attitude polarization and thought introspection research, respectively, have very different consequences for beliefs, as we discuss in the following.

Attitude Polarization

One implication of both structural accounts (Rosenberg et al., 1960) as well as motivational explanations (Lord et al., 1979) of attitudes' effects on beliefs is that greater activation of attitudes should lead to increased coherence in expressed beliefs congenial to one's attitudes. This notion is supported by research on thought-induced attitude polarization. In one study involving pairs of participants (Sadler & Tesser, 1973), participants were induced to form negative or positive attitudes of their fellow participant. Some participants were instructed to think about their partner; other participants were distracted from thinking. Afterward they wrote down their beliefs about their partner. Participants in the thought inducement condition had more extreme attitudes than control participants, they wrote more negative thoughts about dislikable partners than control participants, and they also wrote more positive thoughts about likable partners than control participants. Numerous other studies have supported the basic processes that in some circumstances, having people think about their attitudes can lead to attitude extremity (Cialdini, 1976; Cialdini & Petty, 1981; Fitzpatrick & Eagly, 1981; Liberman & Chaiken, 1991; Tesser & Conlee, 1975; Tesser & Cowan, 1975; Tetlock, 1983a), with beliefs mediating this effect (Clary, Tesser, & Downing, 1978; Tesser, 1978; Tesser & Conlee, 1975; Tesser & Cowan, 1975).

Thought Introspection

Recent research directly contradicts the general finding that increasing thought about one's attitudes leads to congruence in the existing attitude and one's generated beliefs during the introspection. Instead, research suggests that one consequence of thinking about the reasons one holds an attitude is that it can lead to beliefs that are disconnected from the original attitudes. This research mostly stems from studies in which individuals focus on the reasons for holding attitudes, specifically ones for which they have limited access to the correct foundation of their original preferences (e.g., Nisbett & Wilson, 1977b). For example, over the course of five sessions, Wilson and Kraft (1993) had dating couples repeatedly introspect on the reasons their relationships were going the way they were. Individuals' attitudes toward their relationship were changed by this manipulation, but there wasn't any common pattern of shift across the group. In contrast to Tesser's typical findings (Tesser, 1978), polarization of attitudes did not occur. This research reveals that attitudes can often be disconnected from related beliefs (e.g., Wilson et al., 1984). Wilson and his colleagues suggested that the reason for this disconnect is that people bring to mind reasons that are accessible and easy to verbalize (i.e., highly shareable; Freyd, 1983) but not necessarily in line with an individual's initial attitude. As a result of such thought, the attitudes that participants report will be different than if they had not engaged in such thought. Wilson's work (e.g., Wilson & Dunn, 1986; Wilson, Dunn, Kraft, & Lisle, 1989; Wilson & Kraft, 1993; Wilson, Kraft, & Dunn, 1989) suggests that reflecting on the reasons for holding one's attitude leads to (often transient) change in those attitudes, and as a result, a disconnect between attitude and behavior, as a result of inability to access the correct beliefs (or feelings) that are related to the formation of that attitude.

One question regarding the thought introspection studies is whether the manipulation leads individuals to form a different attitude than they would have otherwise (e.g., in cases where attitudes are being newly formed), whether an existing attitude is being changed by the manipulation, or whether a new attitude is created, without updating the old attitude. Although in the earliest studies, premanipulation attitudes were not measured (e.g., Wilson et al., 1984); later studies did so, verifying that participants' reported attitudes were shifting (Wilson & Kraft, 1993). Thus, early research suggested that actual attitude change was occurring. For example, an individual who enjoys a particular puzzle but introspects on the reasons would be viewed as changing her attitude as a result of the process. However, the reduced correlations that resulted from these attitudes and the actual behavior suggested that somehow the real reasons for taking pleasure in the behavior continued to direct behavior by some means (Wilson et al., 1984). This lowered attitude–behavior correlation directly contradicted the findings of attitude polarization research, in which similar experimental manipulations led to an increase in attitude–behavior consistency (Millar & Tesser, 1986a, 1989).

A resolution of the odd paradox that a changed attitude was not also reflected in behavior change is offered by the recent introduction of a dual attitudes system for explaining these results (Wilson, Lindsey, & Schooler, 2000). When one engages in metacognitive processing, introspecting about why one holds an attitude might not allow one to access the source of information that formed that attitude (e.g., verbalizable beliefs and unarticulatable experiential qualities). Alternatively, one might be unable to use this information. In either case, a new attitude may be created (Wilson et al., 2000) rather than the old one further polarized (Tesser,

1978). This dual attitudes system suggests, however, that older attitudes may be automatically evoked in some situations (and hence would guide behavior) unless an individual has the capability and motivation to reflect on their newer, explicit attitudes.

More important than what this research says about attitudes and beliefs is perhaps what it says about the link between attitudes and *metabeliefs*—beliefs about the original sources of one's attitude formation or lay theories about attitudinal processes. A more general demonstration of this phenomena occurs in affective forecasting (Gilbert & Ebert, 2002; Gilbert & Wilson, 2000). In affective forecasting, individuals estimate the extent or durability of the feelings that they will experience should they receive certain positive or negative outcomes in the future. In making such forecasts, people's use of their attitudes and current preferences lead them to make biased predictions. Thus, an individual will likely overestimate how long their joy will last if they win a lottery or how awful they will feel if they fail a test. Their beliefs reflect an exaggerated reliance on their current preferences for outcomes and indicate poor lay theories about the strength and stability of people's emotional responses to outcomes. People are not aware of the psychological processes by which desired outcomes, once received, might be less satisfactory than anticipated, or how less preferred outcomes may be less distressing than anticipated (e.g., Crawford, McConnell, Lewis, & Sherman, 2002).

In sum, a variety of studies that involve reflecting on current attitudes suggest that those attitudes can be an incorrect basis for formation of beliefs, whether they are beliefs about the foundation of one's current attitudes, or beliefs about one's affective responses to future, attitude-relevant outcomes. An individual may know what they currently feel, but using those attitudes to form beliefs may be faulty. For instance, one could be wrong about *why* one cares for a romantic partner (e.g., Wilson et al, 1984), and wrong about how *lasting* the angst will be should that relationship end (e.g., Gilbert & Ebert, 2002).

Moderators for Changing Beliefs Through Attitude Change

At first reflection, lack of attitude congeniality effects in memory for persuasive messages and rather poor access to beliefs about why we hold certain attitudes seem at odds with research finding change in beliefs in response to message-induced attitude change or research on attitude polarization. Resolving these effects requires understanding the moderators of attitude–belief effects and moderators of the attitude–belief disconnection.

According to cognitive consistency approaches, consistency pressures will only be apparent when an individual's needs or expectations cause them to focus on their attitudes (Abelson & Rosenberg, 1958). McGuire's thought system research similarly suggests that not all changes in attitudes will result in belief changes (McGuire & McGuire, 1991). Rather, events that are highly desirable and personally involving are expected to have stronger links between cognitive elements. Both analyses suggest that changes in attitudes that are not of particular importance to an individuals' needs or desires may result in relatively little change in beliefs. However, if individuals are exposed to persuasive arguments of importance to them, other research suggests that change in their beliefs is more likely to *precede* attitude change unless their cognitive resources are low (Albarracín & Wyer, 2001). Regardless of the situations, cognitive approaches to persuasion clarify why congeniality effects in memory are not common (Eagly et al., 2001)—because information is actively transformed in the process of forming attitude. Thus, it is the *belief* about information that is presented that will commonly be congenial with related attitudes, not the untransformed information presented in a message.

Several moderators of attitude polarization effects have also been identified. Attitude polarization is more likely to occur in ambiguous situations (Tesser & Cowan, 1975). Moreover, polarization occurs more commonly for issues about which one has extensive knowledge (Tesser & Leone, 1977), and issues for which one has high evaluative-cognitive consistency

(Chaiken & Yates, 1985). In addition, attitude depolarization would be more likely to occur in situations that induce an individual to generate attitude-inconsistent cognitive responses (e.g., Killeya & Johnson, 1998). Such a situation might occur when one is exposed to an accountability manipulation in which one anticipates discussing an issue with someone with different views (Tetlock, 1983a). These findings suggest that the situations in which increased accessibility to attitudes (via thought) will lead to attitude-consistent beliefs are those in which the content of one's attitudes makes congruence more readily possible and when the thought focus is open-ended rather than directed into specific directions.

More generally, resolving the issue of when introspection will lead to more insight into the beliefs that are relevant to one's attitudes (Tesser, 1978) versus reduced insight (Wilson et al., 1984) is a particular challenge. Several moderators of the attitude–belief disconnect, however, offer clues. Analyzing reasons will modify attitudes (i.e., lead to a disconnect) mostly when one is less knowledgeable about a topic (Wilson, Kraft et al., 1989). Moreover, when task demands require focus on one's attitudes, one may need time to show a change in attitudes as a result of reflecting on beliefs about that attitude (Wilson et al., 2000). When individuals experience time pressure during this process, they may revert to their old attitude. In addition, Hodges and Wilson (1993) found that people with less accessible attitudes changed their attitudes more than people who had highly accessible attitudes (as assessed by response time).

Attitude–belief disconnect is most likely to occur when real reasons are poorly defined and difficult to articulate (Wilson & Schooler, 1991). Millar and Tesser (1986a; 1989), for instance, demonstrated that focusing on an ill-fitting dimension of one's attitudes (*reasons* or cognitive aspects of a puzzle task) led to a poor attitude–behavior correlation (e.g., when one's playing with puzzles was an expression of affective dimensions: enjoyment). For the most part, the laboratory creates unique constraints in task and dimensions of focus that may be less common in the real world. Within the laboratory context, one can make individuals think analytically about tasks for which they might otherwise trust intuition (their romantic partner) or they would not bother analyzing (puzzles). Thus, it seems likely that inadvertently focusing on the wrong dimensions of one's attitude will occur much less often for attitudes in naturally occurring settings that are important enough for one to bother reflecting about. For example, Kmett and colleages (Kmett, Arkes, & Jones, 1999) used an issue of considerably more importance—choosing a college—than typical topics studied by Wilson (e.g., selecting jams, posters, or reregistering for a course for the next term). High school seniors analyzed reasons in advance of attending college; thus, they had existing attitudes that they then analyzed. In all groups, analysis led to greater satisfaction with college—regardless of whether recall was accurate or not at follow-up. Therefore, introspecting about real reasons is helpful during attitude formation (Kmett et al., 1999), but introspecting about pseudo-reasons for existing attitudes is unhelpful.

The implication of this account for persistence and change is that attitudes and beliefs may overtly seem quite transient, affected by the current context and hindered by our inability to access or use veridical sources of our attitude formation. However, in most recent accounts (Wilson et al., 2000), researchers suggest that those original attitudes and beliefs might persist. Moreover, an unresolved question is just how pervasive the tendency to engage in meta-cognitive processes regarding the affective bases of one's attitudes is. Accessing one's attitude should frequently result in access to beliefs. This process will commonly occur automatically through spreading activation for highly accessible attitudes, or more effortfully, when an individual actively retrieves his or her attitude. Thus, accessing attitudes is likely to be relatively spontaneous. In contrast, however, the tendency to engage in thoughts *about* one's attitudes is not likely to be very spontaneous. One might not spontaneously think about the reasons for holding one's current attitudes, and one might not spontaneously think about how one's current attitudes will influence one's feelings about future outcomes. For example, individuals do not necessarily spontaneously anticipate how much regret they would feel regarding lost opportunities or incorrect choices in the future (Crawford et al., 2002).

A broader perspective (i.e., taking into account decision-making theory and research) suggests boundary conditions to the findings of Wilson and colleagues (e.g., Wilson, Dunn, et al., 1989). For instance, cognitive neuroscience research seems to suggest that individuals' reasoned choices involve veridical assessment of their evaluative responses to phenomena for individuals with intact cognitive systems (Damasio, 1994). Although contrived situations that force individuals to verbally articulate intuitive and implicit reactions to stimuli may create disconnection between attitude, belief, and behavior, research on decision making (Wagar & Thagard, 2004), attempts to self-regulate impulses (Mischel, Cantor, & Feldman, 1996), and risk assessment (Loewenstein, Weber, Hsee, & Welch, 2001) suggest that individuals have access to their evaluative responses (albeit distorted) and attempt to regulate their actions accordingly. That is, approaches that focus on getting individuals to control their behavior in the fact of attractive but potentially harmful stimuli (e.g., in a risky sexual situation), convincingly postulate that people have direct access to their reactions to stimuli that are present (e.g., sexual interest). Not all such reactions, however, are well verbalized. For instance, individuals' intuitive assessments of the future, based somatically on their experiences in the present (how well or how poorly they are feeling about something) may be intuitive and not well articulated. Thus, making good choices about the future, such as which deck of cards to choose from, in an experiment that has some decks with bad but nonobvious payoffs, may be based on awareness of emotional reactions that is not yet articulated in verbal beliefs (Bechara, Damasio, Tranel, & Damasio, 1997). Individuals may naively and correctly assess their evaluative reactions to events and, thus, correctly form beliefs about them, and yet not be well able to articulate that *somatically marked* (Damasio, 1994) information in typical experimental procedures.

CONCLUSIONS

This chapter addressed aspects of attitude-related processes that have traditionally received less systematic examination. Most attitudinal models focus on a causal direction of beliefs preceding attitudes rather than the opposite. One consequence of most attitude research traditions is that they may have unduly restricted thought regarding the causal direction of these links. Relevant research on these less-studied causal directions, however, reveals rich consequences of attitudes for beliefs and suggests some promising areas of future study that have been relatively neglected. Evidence that attitudes influence beliefs has grown dramatically since Hastorf and Cantril (1954) first examined how Princeton and Darmouth fans "saw a game." Current evidence extends from reconstructions of the past and projections onto the present as well as wishful interpretations of the future, extending across topics that involve personal self-interest to those that have political impact. With the continued development of cognitive processing principles comes an articulation of *why* we "see the game" differently: Attitudes bias the retrieval and formation of beliefs both because of cognitive processes (more accessible attitude-congruent knowledge) as well as motivated distortions (e.g., to protect the self). In addition, considerable understanding of some of the moderators of these effects has been gained, most notably attitude accessibility and attitude importance. The most intriguing and recent wrinkle in these findings is the development of research that splits with previous findings (Sadler & Tesser, 1973; Tesser, 1976) of how thinking about one's attitude leads to attitude polarization, and more important, attitude–belief coherence. This newest research harkens back to the classic finding nearly 30 years ago that we do not always know why we form certain preferences (Nisbett & Wilson, 1977b). Out of this understanding that there can often be a disconnect between ill-formed or affectively formed attitudes and our beliefs about why we hold those attitudes

(Wilson, Kraft et al., 1989; Wilson, Lisle, Schooler, & Hodges, 1993), is the implication that our metacognitions regarding the origins of our attitudes (and indeed, our guesses about our future attitudinal reactions; Crawford et al., 2002; Gilbert & Ebert, 2002) are often flawed. Resolving these disparate understandings of the attitude–belief congruence versus attitude–belief disconnect is tentatively offered here, but is clearly something that encourages further study.

REFERENCES

Abelson, R. P. (1986). Beliefs are like possessions. *Journal for the Theory of Social Behaviour, 16*, 223–250.

Abelson, R. P., Aronson, E., McGuire, W. J., Newcomb, T. M., Rosenberg, M. J., & Tannenbaum, P. H. (Eds.). (1968). *Theories of cognitive consistency: A sourcebook*. Chicago: Rand McNally.

Abelson, R. P., & Rosenberg, M. J. (1958). Symbolic psycho-logic: A model of attitudinal cognition. *Behavioral Science, 3*, 1–13.

Ajzen, I. (1991). The theory of planned behavior. *Organizational Behavior and Human Decision Processes, 50*, 179–211.

Ajzen, I., & Fishbein, M. (1980). *Understanding attitudes and predicting social behavior*. Englewood Cliffs, NJ: Prentice-Hall.

Albarracín, D. (2002). Cognition in persuasion: An analysis of information processing in response to persuasive communications. In M. P. Zanna (Ed.), *Advances in experimental social psychology* (Vol. 34, pp. 61–130). San Diego, CA: Academic Press.

Albarracín, D., & Wyer, R. S., Jr. (2001). Elaborative and nonelaborative processing of a behavior-related communication. *Personality and Social Psychology Bulletin, 27*, 691–705.

Allison, S. T., Beggan, J. K., Midgley, E. H., & Wallace, K. A. (1995). Dispositional and behavioral inferences about inherently democratic and unanimous groups. *Social Cognition, 13*, 105–126.

Babad, E. (1987). Wishful thinking and objectivity among sports fans. *Social Behaviour, 2*, 231–240.

Babad, E. (1997). Wishful thinking among voters: Motivational and cognitive influences. *International Journal of Public Opinion Research, 9*, 105–125.

Babad, E., Hills, M., & O'Driscoll, M. (1992). Factors influencing wishful thinking and predictions of election outcomes. *Basic and Applied Social Psychology, 13*, 461–476.

Babad, E., & Katz, Y. (1991). Wishful thinking—against all odds. *Journal of Applied Social Psychology, 21*, 1921–1938.

Babad, E., & Yacobos, E. (1993). Wish and reality in voters' predictions of election outcomes. *Political Psychology, 14*, 37–54.

Bandura, A. (1997). *Self-efficacy: The exercise of control*. New York: Freeman.

Bechara, A., Damasio, H., Tranel, D., & Damasio, A. R. (1997). Deciding advantageously before knowing the advantageous strategy. *Science, 275*, 1293–1294.

Boninger, D. S., Krosnick, J. A., & Berent, M. K. (1995). Origins of attitude importance: Self-interest, social identification, and value relevance. *Journal of Personality and Social Psychology, 68*, 61–80.

Bothwell, R. K., & Brigham, J. C. (1983). Selective evaluation and recall during the 1980 Reagan–Carter debate. *Journal of Applied Social Psychology, 13*, 427–442.

Bradley, G. W. (1978). Self-serving biases in the attribution process: A reexamination of the fact or fiction question. *Journal of Personality and Social Psychology, 36*, 56–71.

Breckler, S. J. (1984). Empirical validation of affect, behavior, and cognition as distinct components of attitude. *Journal of Personality and Social Psychology, 47*, 1191–1205.

Cantril, H. (1938). The prediction of social events. *Journal of Abnormal and Social Psychology, 33*, 364–389.

Chaiken, S., & Baldwin, M. W. (1981). Affective-cognitive consistency and the effect of salient behavioral information on the self-perception of attitudes. *Journal of Personality and Social Psychology, 41*, 1–12.

Chaiken, S., Liberman, A., & Eagly, A. H. (1989). Heuristic and systematic information processing within and beyond the persuasion context. In J. S. Uleman & J. A. Bargh (Eds.), *Unintended thought* (pp. 212–252). New York: Guilford.

Chaiken, S., & Yates, S. (1985). Affective-cognitive consistency and thought-induced attitude polarization. *Journal of Personality and Social Psychology, 49*, 1470–1481.

Chen, S., & Chaiken, S. (1999). The heuristic-systematic model in its broader context. In S. Chaiken & Y. Trope (Eds.), *Dual-process theories in social psychology* (pp. 73–96). New York: Guilford.

Cialdini, R. B. (1976). Elastic shifts of opinion: Determinants of direction and durability. *Journal of Personality and Social Psychology, 34*, 663–672.

Cialdini, R. B., & Petty, R. E. (1981). Anticipatory opinion shifts. In R. E. Petty, T. M. Ostrom, & T. C. Brock (Eds.), *Cognitive responses in persuasion* (pp. 217–235). Hillsdale, NJ: Lawrence Erlbaum Associates.

Clary, E. G., Tesser, A., & Downing, L. L. (1978). Influence of a salient schema on thought-induced cognitive change. *Personality and Social Psychology Bulletin, 4*, 39–43.

Converse, P. E. (1964). The nature of belief systems in mass publics. In D. E. Apter (Ed.), *Ideology and discontent* (pp. 206–261). New York: Free Press.

Cooper, J., & Fazio, R. H. (1984). A new look at dissonance theory. In L. Berkowitz (Ed.), *Advances in experimental social psychology* (Vol. 17, pp. 229–266). San Diego, CA: Academic Press.

Correll, J., Spencer, S. J., & Zanna, M. P. (2004). An affirmed self and an open mind: Self-affirmation and sensitivity to argument strength. *Journal of Experimental Social Psychology, 40*, 350–356.

Crano, W. D. (1983). Assumed consensus of attitudes: The effects of vested interest. *Personality and Social Psychology Bulletin, 9*, 597–608.

Crawford, M. T., McConnell, A. R., Lewis, A. C., & Sherman, S. J. (2002). Reactance, compliance, and anticipated regret. *Journal of Experimental Social Psychology, 38*, 56–63.

Damasio, A. R. (1994). *Descartes' error: Emotion, reason, and the human brain.* New York: Putnam.

Dillehay, R. C., Insko, C. A., & Smith, M. B. (1966). Logical consistency and attitude change. *Journal of Personality and Social Psychology, 3*, 646–654.

Ditto, P. H., & Lopez, D. F. (1992). Motivated skepticism: Use of differential decision criteria for preferred and nonpreferred conclusions. *Journal of Personality and Social Psychology, 63*, 568–584.

Dolan, K. A., & Holbrook, T. M. (2001). Knowing versus caring: The role of affect and cognition in political perceptions. *Political Psychology, 22*, 27–44.

Eagly, A. H., Chen, S., Chaiken, S., & Shaw-Barnes, K. (1999). The impact of attitudes on memory: An affair to remember. *Psychological Bulletin, 125*, 64–89.

Eagly, A. H., Kulesa, P., Brannon, L. A., Shaw, K., & Hutson-Comeaux, S. (2000). Why counterattitudinal messages are as memorable as proattitudinal messages: The importance of active defense against attack. *Personality and Social Psychology Bulletin, 26*, 1392–1408.

Eagly, A. H., Kulesa, P., Chen, S., & Chaiken, S. (2001). Do attitudes affect memory? Tests of the congeniality hypothesis. *Current Directions in Psychological Science, 10*, 5–9.

Fazio, R. H. (1990a). How do attitudes guide behavior? In R. M. Sorrentino & E. T. Higgins (Eds.), *Handbook of motivation and cognition: Foundations of social behavior* (pp. 204–243). New York: Guilford.

Fazio, R. H. (1990b). Multiple processes by which attitudes guide behavior: The MODE model as an integrative framework. In M. P. Zanna (Ed.), *Advances in experimental social psychology* (Vol. 23, pp. 75–109). San Diego, CA: Academic Press.

Fazio, R. H., Chen, J., McDonel, E. C., & Sherman, S. J. (1982). Attitude accessibility, attitude–behavior consistency, and the strength of the object-evaluation association. *Journal of Experimental Social Psychology, 18*, 339–357.

Fazio, R. H., & Towles-Schwen, T. (1999). The MODE model of attitude–behavior processes. In S. Chaiken & Y. Trope (Eds.), *Dual process theories in social psychology* (pp. 97–116). New York: Guilford.

Fazio, R. H., & Williams, C. J. (1986). Attitude accessibility as a moderator of the attitude–perception and attitude–behavior relations: An investigation of the 1984 presidential election. *Journal of Personality and Social Psychology, 51*, 505–514.

Festinger, L. (1957). *A theory of cognitive dissonance.* Stanford, CA: Stanford University Press.

Fitzpatrick, A. R., & Eagly, A. H. (1981). Anticipatory belief polarization as a function of the expertise of a discussion partner. *Personality and Social Psychology Bulletin, 7*, 636–642.

Forgas, J. P., Bower, G. H., & Krantz, S. E. (1984). The influence of mood on perceptions of social interactions. *Journal of Experimental Social Psychology, 20*, 497–513.

Frey, D. (1986). Recent research on selective exposure to information. In L. Berkowitz (Ed.), *Advances in experimental social psychology* (Vol. 19, pp. 41–80). San Diego, CA: Academic Press.

Freyd, J. J. (1983). Shareability: The social psychology of epistemology. *Cognitive Science, 7*, 191–210.

Gilbert, D. T., & Ebert, J. E. J. (2002). Decisions and revisions: The affective forecasting of changeable outcomes. *Journal of Personality and Social Psychology, 82*, 503–514.

Gilbert, D. T., & Wilson, T. D. (2000). Miswanting: Some problems in the forecasting of future affective states. In J. P. Forgas (Ed.), *Feeling and thinking: The role of affect in social cognition* (pp. 178–197). New York: Cambridge University Press.

Giner-Sorolla, R., & Chaiken, S. (1997). Selective use of heuristic and systematic processing under defense motivation. *Personality and Social Psychology Bulletin, 23*, 84–97.

Granberg, D., & Brent, E. E. (1980). Perceptions of issue positions of presidential candidates. *American Scientist, 68*, 617–646.

Granberg, D., & Brent, E. E. (1983). When prophecy bends: The preference-expectation link in U.S. presidential elections, 1952–1980. *Journal of Personality and Social Psychology, 45*, 477–491.

Granberg, D., & Holmberg, S. (1986). Prior behavior, recalled behavior, and the prediction of subsequent voting behavior in Sweden and the U.S. *Human Relations, 39*, 135–148.

Greenwald, A. G. (1980). The totalitarian ego: Fabrication and revision of personal history. *American Psychologist, 35*, 603–618.

Hastie, R., & Park, B. (1986). The relationship between memory and judgment depends on whether the judgment task is memory-based or on-line. *Psychological Review, 93*, 258–268.

Hastorf, A. H., & Cantril, H. (1954). They saw a game; a case study. *Journal of Abnormal and Social Psychology, 49*, 129–134.

Heider, F. (1958). *The psychology of interpersonal relations*. Hillsdale, NJ: Lawrence Erlbaum Associates.

Hoch, S. J. (1987). Perceived consensus and predictive accuracy: The pros and cons of projection. *Journal of Personality and Social Psychology, 53*, 221–234.

Hodges, S. D., & Wilson, T. D. (1993). Effects of analyzing reasons on attitude change: The moderating role of attitude accessibility. *Social Cognition, 11*, 353–366.

Houston, D. A., & Fazio, R. H. (1989). Biased processing as a function of attitude accessibility: Making objective judgments subjectively. *Social Cognition, 7*, 51–66.

Johnson, B. T., & Eagly, A. H. (1989). Effects of involvement on persuasion: A meta-analysis. *Psychological Bulletin, 106*, 290–314.

Johnson, B. T., Lin, H. Y., Symons, C. S., & Campbell, L. A. (1995). Initial beliefs and attitudinal latitudes as factors in persuasion. *Personality and Social Psychology Bulletin, 21*, 502–511.

Johnson, B. T., Smith-McLallen, A., Killeya, L. A., & Levin, K. D. (2004). Truth or consequences: Overcoming resistance to persuasion with positive thinking. In E. S. Knowles & J. Linn (Eds.), *Resistance and persuasion*. (pp. 215–233). Mahwah, NJ: Lawrence Erlbaum Associates.

Killeya, L. A., & Johnson, B. T. (1998). Experimental induction of biased systematic processing: The directed-thought technique. *Personality and Social Psychology Bulletin, 24*, 17–33.

Kirsch, I., & Lynn, S. J. (1999). Automaticity in clinical psychology. *American Psychologist, 54*, 504–515.

Kmett, C. M., Arkes, H. R., & Jones, S. K. (1999). The influence of decision aids on high school students' satisfaction with their college choice decision. *Personality and Social Psychology Bulletin, 25*, 1293–1301.

Kozlowski, S. W., & Kirsch, M. P. (1987). The systematic distortion hypothesis, halo, and accuracy: An individual-level analysis. *Journal of Applied Psychology, 72*, 252–261.

Krosnick, J. A. (1990a). Americans' perceptions of presidential candidates: A test of the projection hypothesis. *Journal of Social Issues, 46*, 159–182.

Krosnick, J. A. (1990b). Government policy and citizen passion: A study of issue publics in contemporary America. *Political Behavior, 12*, 59–92.

Kruglanski, A. W. (1989). *Lay epistemics and human knowledge: Cognitive and motivational bases*. New York: Plenum.

Kruglanski, A. W. (1990). Lay epistemic theory in social-cognitive psychology. *Psychological Inquiry, 1*, 181–197.

Kruglanski, A. W., Thompson, E. P., & Spiegel, S. (1999). Separate or equal? Bimodal notions of persuasion and a single-process "unimodel." In S. Chaiken & Y. Trope (Eds.), *Dual process theories in social psychology* (pp. 293–313). New York: Guilford.

Kunda, Z. (1990). The case for motivated reasoning. *Psychological Bulletin, 108*, 480–498.

Lance, C. E., LaPointe, J. A., & Stewart, A. M. (1994). A test of the context dependency of three causal models of halo rater error. *Journal of Applied Psychology, 79*, 332–340.

Lavine, H., Borgida, E., & Sullivan, J. L. (2000). On the relationship between attitude involvement and attitude accessibility: Toward a cognitive-motivational model of political information processing. *Political Psychology, 21*, 81–106.

Lavine, H., Sullivan, J. L., Borgida, E., & Thomsen, C. J. (1996). The relationship of national and personal issue salience to attitude accessibility of foreign and domestic policy issues. *Political Psychology, 17*, 293–316.

Lewis-Beck, M. S., & Skalaban, A. (1989). Citizen forecasting: Can voters see into the future? *British Journal of Political Science, 19*, 146–153.

Liberman, A., & Chaiken, S. (1991). Value conflict and thought-induced attitude change. *Journal of Experimental Social Psychology, 27*, 203–216.

Liberman, A., & Chaiken, S. (1992). Defensive processing of personally relevant health messages. *Personality and Social Psychology Bulletin, 18*, 669–679.

Loewenstein, G. F., Weber, E. U., Hsee, C. K., & Welch, N. (2001). Risk as feelings. *Psychological Bulletin, 127*, 267–286.

Lord, C. G., Ross, L., & Lepper, M. R. (1979). Biased assimilation and attitude polarization: The effects of prior theories on subsequently considered evidence. *Journal of Personality and Social Psychology, 37*, 2098–2109.

Lott, A. J., Lott, B. E., Reed, T., & Crow, T. (1970). Personality-trait descriptions of differentially liked persons. *Journal of Personality and Social Psychology, 16*, 284–290.

Lydon, J., Zanna, M. P., & Ross, M. (1988). Bolstering attitudes by autobiographical recall: Attitude persistence and selective recall. *Personality and Social Psychology Bulletin, 14,* 78–86.

Lynn, S. J., Lock, T. G., Myers, B., & Payne, D. G. (1997). Recalling the unrecallable: Should hypnosis be used to recover memories in psychotherapy? *Current Directions in Psychological Science, 6,* 79–83.

Mackie, D. M., Ahn, M. N., Asuncion, A. G., & Allison, S. T. (2001). The impact of perceiver attitudes on outcome-biased dispositional inferences. *Social Cognition, 19,* 71–93.

Mackie, D. M., & Asuncion, A. G. (1990). On-line and memory-based modification of attitudes: Determinants of message recall–attitude change correspondence. *Journal of Personality and Social Psychology, 59,* 5–16.

Markman, K. D., & Hirt, E. R. (2002). Social prediction and the "allegiance bias." *Social Cognition, 20,* 58–86.

McGregor, D. (1938). The major determinants of the prediction of social events. *Journal of Abnormal and Social Psychology, 33,* 179–204.

McGuire, W. J. (1960a). Cognitive consistency and attitude change. *Journal of Abnormal and Social Psychology, 60,* 345–353.

McGuire, W. J. (1960b). Direct and indirect persuasive effects of dissonance-producing messages. *Journal of Abnormal and Social Psychology, 60,* 354–358.

McGuire, W. J. (1960c). A syllogistic analysis of cognitive relationships. In M. J. Rosenberg, C. I. Hovland, W. J. McGuire, R. P. Abelson, & J. W. Brehm (Eds.), *Attitude organization and change: An analysis of consistency among attitude components* (pp. 65–111). New Haven, CT: Yale University Press.

McGuire, W. J. (1968). Personality and attitude change: An information-processing theory. In A. G. Greenwald, T. C. Brock, & T. M. Ostrom (Eds.), *Psychological foundations of attitudes* (pp. 171–196). San Diego, CA: Academic Press.

McGuire, W. J. (1981). The probabilogical model of cognitive structure and attitude change. In R. E. Petty, T. M. Ostrom, & T. C. Brock (Eds.), *Cognitive responses in persuasion* (pp. 291–307). Hillsdale, NJ: Lawrence Erlbaum Associates.

McGuire, W. J., & McGuire, C. V. (1991). The content, structure, and operation of thought systems. In R. S. Wyer, Jr. & T. K. Srull (Eds.), *Advances in social cognition* (Vol. 4, pp. 1–78). Hillsdale, NJ: Lawrence Erlbaum Associates.

Millar, M. G., & Tesser, A. (1986a). Effects of affective and cognitive focus on the attitude–behavior relation. *Journal of Personality and Social Psychology, 51,* 270–276.

Millar, M. G., & Tesser, A. (1986b). Thought-induced attitude change: The effects of schema structure and commitment. *Journal of Personality and Social Psychology, 51,* 259–269.

Millar, M. G., & Tesser, A. (1989). The effects of affective-cognitive consistency and thought on the attitude–behavior relation. *Journal of Experimental Social Psychology, 25,* 189–202.

Mischel, W., Cantor, N., & Feldman, S. (1996). Principles of self-regulation: The nature of willpower and self-control. In E. T. Higgins (Ed.), *Social psychology: Handbook of basic principles* (pp. 329–360). New York: Guilford.

Murphy, K. R., Jako, R. A., & Anhalt, R. L. (1993). Nature and consequences of halo error: A critical analysis. *Journal of Applied Psychology, 78,* 218–225.

Nasco, S. A., & Marsh, K. L. (1999). Gaining control through counterfactual thinking. *Personality and Social Psychology Bulletin, 25,* 556–568.

Nisbett, R. E., & Wilson, T. D. (1977a). The halo effect: Evidence for unconscious alteration of judgments. *Journal of Personality and Social Psychology, 35,* 250–256.

Nisbett, R. E., & Wilson, T. D. (1977b). Telling more than we can know: Verbal reports on mental processes. *Psychological Review, 84,* 231–259.

Osgood, C. E., & Tannenbaum, P. H. (1955). The principle of congruity in the prediction of attitude change. *Psychological Review, 62,* 42–55.

Petty, R. E., & Cacioppo, J. T. (1986). The elaboration likelihood model of persuasion. In L. Berkowitz (Ed.), *Advances in experimental social psychology* (Vol. 19, pp. 123–205). New York: Academic Press.

Petty, R. E., Cacioppo, J. T., & Haugtvedt, C. P. (1992). Ego-involvement and persuasion: An appreciative look at the Sherifs' contribution to the study of self-relevance and attitude change. In D. Granberg & G. Sarup (Eds.), *Social judgment and intergroup relations: Essays in honor of Muzafer Sherif* (pp. 147–174). New York: Springer-Verlag.

Petty, R. E., Harkins, S. G., & Williams, K. D. (1980). The effects of group diffusion of cognitive effort on attitudes: An information-processing view. *Journal of Personality and Social Psychology, 38,* 81–92.

Petty, R. E., & Krosnick, J. A. (1995). Attitude strength: An overview. In R. E. Petty & J. A. Krosnick (Eds.), *Attitude strength: Antecedents and consequences* (pp. 1–24). Hillsdale, NJ: Lawrence Erlbaum Associates.

Petty, R. E., & Wegener, D. T. (1999). The elaboration likelihood model: Current status and controversies. In S. Chaiken & Y. Trope (Eds.), *Dual-process theories in social psychology* (pp. 37–72). New York: Guilford.

Pomerantz, E. M., Chaiken, S., & Tordesillas, R. S. (1995). Attitude strength and resistance processes. *Journal of Personality and Social Psychology, 69,* 408–419.

Pratkanis, A. R. (1988). The attitude heuristic and selective fact identification. *British Journal of Social Psychology, 27,* 257–263.

Pratkanis, A. R. (1989). The cognitive representation of attitudes. In A. R. Pratkanis (Ed.), *Attitude structure and function* (pp. 71–98). Hillsdale, NJ: Lawrence Erlbaum Associates.

Pratkanis, A. R., & Greenwald, A. G. (1989). A sociocognitive model of attitude structure and function. In L. Berkowitz (Ed.), *Advances in experimental social psychology* (Vol. 22, pp. 245–285). San Diego, CA: Academic Press.

Proshansky, H. M. (1943). A projective method for the study of attitudes. *Journal of Abnormal and Social Psychology, 38*, 393–395.

Rosenberg, M. J. (1956). Cognitive structure and attitudinal affect. *Journal of Abnormal and Social Psychology, 53*, 367–372.

Rosenberg, M. J. (1960a). An analysis of affective-cognitive consistency. In M. J. Rosenberg, C. I. Hovland, W. J. McGuire, R. P. Abelson, & J. W. Brehm (Eds.), *Attitude organization and change: An analysis of consistency among attitude components* (pp. 15–64). New Haven, CT: Yale University Press.

Rosenberg, M. J. (1960b). Cognitive reorganization in response to the hypnotic reversal of attitudinal affect. *Journal of Personality, 28*, 39–63.

Rosenberg, M. J., & Gardner, C. W. (1958). Some dynamic aspects of posthypnotic compliance. *Journal of Abnormal and Social Psychology, 57*, 351–366.

Rosenberg, M. J., Hovland, C. I., McGuire, W. J., Abelson, R. P., & Brehm, J. W. (Eds.). (1960). *Attitude organization and change: An analysis of consistency among attitude components*. New Haven, CT: Yale University Press.

Ross, M. (1989). Relation of implicit theories to the construction of personal histories. *Psychological Review, 96*, 341–357.

Ross, M., & Conway, M. (1986). Remembering one's own past: The reconstruction of personal histories. In R. M. Sorrentino & E. T. Higgins (Eds.), *Handbook of motivation and cognition: Foundations of social behavior* (pp. 122–144). New York: Guilford.

Ross, M., McFarland, C., Conway, M., & Zanna, M. P. (1983). Reciprocal relation between attitudes and behavior recall: Committing people to newly formed attitudes. *Journal of Personality and Social Psychology, 45*, 257–267.

Sadler, O., & Tesser, A. (1973). Some effects of salience and time upon interpersonal hostility and attraction during social isolation. *Sociometry, 36*, 99–112.

Sanbonmatsu, D. M., & Fazio, R. H. (1990). The role of attitudes in memory-based decision making. *Journal of Personality and Social Psychology, 59*, 614–622.

Schuette, R. A., & Fazio, R. H. (1995). Attitude accessibility and motivation as determinants of biased processing: A test of the MODE model. *Personality and Social Psychology Bulletin, 21*, 704–710.

Shaffer, S. D. (1981). Balance theory and political cognitions. *American Politics Quarterly, 9*, 291–320.

Shepperd, J. A., Findley-Klein, C., Kwavnick, K. D., Walker, D., & Perez, S. (2000). Bracing for loss. *Journal of Personality and Social Psychology, 78*, 620–634.

Sherif, C. W., Sherif, M., & Nebergall, R. E. (1965). *Attitude and attitude change: The social judgment-involvement approach*. Philadelphia: Saunders.

Sherman, S. J. (1987). Cognitive processes in the formation, change, and expression of attitudes. In M. P. Zanna (Ed.), *Social influence: The Ontario Symposium Vol. 5* (pp. 75–106). Hillsdale, NJ: Lawrence Erlbaum Associates.

Sherman, S. J., Presson, C. C., & Chassin, L. (1984). Mechanisms underlying the false consensus effect: The special role of threats to the self. *Personality and Social Psychology Bulletin, 10*, 127–138.

Singer, J. E. (1980). Social comparison: The process of self-evaluation. In L. Festinger (Ed.), *Retrospections on social psychology* (pp. 158–179). New York: Oxford University Press.

Snyder, M., & Swann, W. B., Jr. (1978). Hypothesis-testing processes in social interaction. *Journal of Personality and Social Psychology, 35*, 1202–1212.

Solomonson, A. L., & Lance, C. E. (1997). Examination of the relationship between true halo and halo error in performance ratings. *Journal of Applied Psychology, 82*, 665–674.

Sweeney, P. D., & Gruber, K. L. (1984). Selective exposure: Voter information preferences and the Watergate affair. *Journal of Personality and Social Psychology, 46*, 1208–1221.

Tesser, A. (1976). Attitude polarization as a function of thought and reality constraints. *Journal of Research in Personality, 10*, 183–194.

Tesser, A. (1978). Self-generated attitude change. In L. Berkowitz (Ed.), *Advances in experimental social psychology* (Vol. 11, pp. 289–338). New York: Academic Press.

Tesser, A., & Conlee, M. C. (1975). Some effects of time and thought on attitude polarization. *Journal of Personality and Social Psychology, 31*, 262–270.

Tesser, A., & Cowan, C. L. (1975). Thought and number of cognitions as determinants of attitude change. *Social Behavior and Personality, 3*, 165–173.

Tesser, A., & Leone, C. (1977). Cognitive schemas and thought as determinants of attitude change. *Journal of Experimental Social Psychology, 13*, 340–356.

Tetlock, P. E. (1983a). Accountability and complexity of thought. *Journal of Personality and Social Psychology, 45*, 74–83.

Tetlock, P. E. (1983b). Cognitive style and political ideology. *Journal of Personality and Social Psychology, 45*, 118–126.

Tetlock, P. E. (1986). A value pluralism model of ideological reasoning. *Journal of Personality and Social Psychology, 50*, 819–827.

Tetlock, P. E., Armor, D., & Peterson, R. S. (1994). The slavery debate in antebellum America: Cognitive style, value conflict, and the limits of compromise. *Journal of Personality and Social Psychology, 66*, 115–126.

Tetlock, P. E., & Boettger, R. (1989). Accountability: A social magnifier of the dilution effect. *Journal of Personality and Social Psychology, 57*, 388–398.

Tetlock, P. E., Peterson, R. S., & Lerner, J. S. (1996). Revising the value pluralism model: Incorporating social content and context postulates. In C. Seligman, J. M. Olson, & M. P. Zanna (Eds.), *The psychology of values: The Ontario Symposium Vol. 8* (pp. 25–51). Hillsdale, NJ: Lawrence Erlbaum Associates.

Thomsen, C. J., Borgida, E., & Lavine, H. (1995). The causes and consequences of personal involvement. In R. E. Petty & J. A. Krosnick (Eds.), *Attitude strength: Antecedents and consequences* (pp. 191–214). Hillsdale, NJ: Lawrence Erlbaum Associates.

Vallone, R. P., Ross, L., & Lepper, M. R. (1985). The hostile media phenomenon: Biased perception and perceptions of media bias in coverage of the Beirut massacre. *Journal of Personality and Social Psychology, 49*, 577–585.

Visser, P. S., Krosnick, J. A., & Simmons, J. P. (2003). Distinguishing the cognitive and behavioral consequences of attitude and certainty: A new approach to testing the common-factor hypothesis. *Journal of Experimental Social Psychology, 39*, 118–141.

Wagar, B. M., & Thagard, P. (2004). Spiking Phineas Gage: A neurocomputational theory of cognitive-affective integration in decision-making. *Psychological Review, 111*, 67–79.

Wegener, D. T., & Petty, R. E. (1997). The flexible correction model: The role of naive theories of bias in bias correction. In M. P. Zanna (Ed.), *Advances in experimental social psychology* (Vol. 29, pp. 141–208). San Diego, CA: Academic Press.

Wilson, T. D., & Dunn, D. S. (1986). Effects of introspection on attitude–behavior consistency: Analyzing reasons versus focusing on feelings. *Journal of Experimental Social Psychology, 22*, 249–263.

Wilson, T. D., Dunn, D. S., Bybee, J. A., Hyman, D. B., & Rotondo, J. A. (1984). Effects of analyzing reasons on attitude–behavior consistency. *Journal of Personality and Social Psychology, 47*, 5–16.

Wilson, T. D., Dunn, D. S., Kraft, D., & Lisle, D. J. (1989). Introspection, attitude change, and attitude–behavior consistency: The disruptive effects of explaining why we feel the way we do. In L. Berkowitz (Ed.), *Advances in experimental social psychology* (Vol. 22, pp. 287–343). San Diego, CA: Academic Press.

Wilson, T. D., & Kraft, D. (1993). Why do I love thee?: Effects of repeated introspections about a dating relationship on attitudes toward the relationship. *Personality and Social Psychology Bulletin, 19*, 409–418.

Wilson, T. D., Kraft, D., & Dunn, D. S. (1989). The disruptive effects of explaining attitudes: The moderating effect of knowledge about the attitude object. *Journal of Experimental Social Psychology, 25*, 379–400.

Wilson, T. D., Lindsey, S., & Schooler, T. Y. (2000). A model of dual attitudes. *Psychological Review, 107*, 101–126.

Wilson, T. D., Lisle, D. J., Schooler, J. W., & Hodges, S. D. (1993). Introspecting about reasons can reduce post-choice satisfaction. *Personality and Social Psychology Bulletin, 19*, 331–339.

Wilson, T. D., & Schooler, J. W. (1991). Thinking too much: Introspection can reduce the quality of preferences and decisions. *Journal of Personality and Social Psychology, 60*, 181–192.

Wood, W. (1982). Retrieval of attitude-relevant information from memory: Effects on susceptibility to persuasion and on intrinsic motivation. *Journal of Personality and Social Psychology, 42*, 798–810.

Wood, W., & Kallgren, C. A. (1988). Communicator attributes and persuasion: Recipients' access to attitude-relevant information in memory. *Personality and Social Psychology Bulletin, 14*, 172–182.

Wortman, C. B., & Brehm, J. W. (1975). Responses to uncontrollable outcomes: An integration of reactance theory and the learned helplessness model. In L. Berkowitz (Ed.), *Advances in experimental social psychology* (Vol. 8, pp. 277–336). New York: Academic Press.

10

The Structure of Affect

Ulrich Schimmack
University of Toronto at Mississauga

Stephen L. Crites, Jr.
University of Texas, El Paso

THE ORIGINS AND STRUCTURE OF AFFECT

Affect is a prevalent concept in contemporary psychology. However, it is also a relatively new concept in psychology. Before 1960 "affect" appeared in only 175 publication titles. The number increased first gradually (923 references between 1960 and 1980) and then exponentially (4,170 citations between 1980 and 2000 in PsychINFO). In the 1960s, affect became an established concept in attitude research. For example, Rosenberg (1956) introduced the concept *attitudinal affect*, and it became popular to distinguish an affective component of attitudes from its cognitive and behavioral counterparts. At the same time, the term affect was increasingly used in the slowly developing area of emotion research. For example, Tomkins (1962, 1963) published two influential volumes on *affect*, and Zuckerman and colleagues published a widely used mood measure called the "Multiple Affect Adjective Checklist" (MAACL) (e.g., Zuckerman & Lubin, 1965).

In both literatures, affect has been defined as an evaluation/appraisal of an object, person, or event as good or bad, favorable or unfavorable, desirable or undesirable (see Thurstone, 1931; Ortony, Clore, & Collins, 1988). As attitudes are themselves defined as evaluations, attitude researchers initially equated affect with the valence of an attitude (Giner-Sorolla, 1999). However, this broad definition of affect leads to several conceptual problems. For example, if affect is the evaluation of an object, it is impossible to study the influence of affect on attitudes (Clore & Schnall, this volume) or the influence of attitudes on affect, because something cannot be the cause or the effect of itself. As a result, modern attitude theories often use a narrower definition of affect that is more consistent with the definition of affect in the emotion literature as a momentary pleasant or unpleasant state. The present chapter focuses exclusively on affective states such as emotions, moods, and sensory affects.

Conscious and Unconscious Affect

An important distinction can be made between conscious affect and unconscious affect. Emotion researchers have struggled for a long time with the notion of unconscious affects. Emotional states are typically seen as types of feelings (Clore, Ortony, & Foss, 1987), and feelings imply a conscious experience. Hence, many emotion theories define affect as conscious experiences (e.g., Clore, 1994). As a result, the notion of unconscious affect would be contradictory because it is impossible to have an unconscious experience (Berridge & Winkielman, 2003). However, the notion of unconscious affect and unconscious influences on attitudes is widespread and deserves to be examined more carefully.

The most common notion of unconscious affect stems from the famous mere exposure paradigm (Zajonc, 1980). In this paradigm, repeated exposures to an object lead to more favorable evaluations of the object when it is presented later with full awareness. Most important, the mere exposure effect occurs even when people do not recall previous incidences of exposure and after subliminal exposure to the stimulus. In this paradigm, affect is unconscious because participants are unaware of the *reason* for their evaluation. That is, they like a stimulus, but they do not know why they like it. It is important to note that participants in mere exposure studies are clearly aware of the immediate source of their affect, namely the stimulus that is presented during the evaluation task. For example, in a forced choice task participants can identify which object they like better, but they do not know that their choice is influenced by the frequency of prior exposure. As a result, mere exposure effects do not constitute a paradox "unconscious experience" because neither the affective reaction nor the object of the affective reaction is unconscious. Rather, mere exposure effects show dissociation between a conscious experience and a reason for this experience ("I feel good, but I don't know why"). In this regard, mere exposure effects are similar to other unexplained affective experiences such as being in a good or bad mood for no particular reason. Affective experiences without an identifiable reason play an important role in attitude research, such as the arousal-transfer effects on attraction (Foster, Witcher, Campbell, & Green, 1998) and mood effects on life-satisfaction judgments (Schwarz & Clore, 1983; Schimmack, Oishi, & Diener, 2002; Siemer & Reisenzein, 1998). Importantly, theories like the mood-as-information model (see Clore & Schnall, this volume) explicitly assume that the effects of affect on attitudes are based on conscious experiences of affect rather than unconscious affective processes.

Berridge and Winkielman (2003) proposed an alternative definition of unconscious affect as "an affective reaction of which one was simply not aware, even upon introspection" (p. 184). One of the greatest challenges for this definition of unconscious affect is to find measures of affect that do not rely on self-reports. Another challenge is to distinguish between unconscious affective and cognitive processes. There exist only a few empirical demonstrations of unconscious affect. Winkielman, Zajonc, and Schwarz (1997) subliminally presented a smiling or frowning face immediately before the presentation of a Chinese ideograph. Ideographs that followed a smiling face were evaluated more favorably than ideographs followed by frowning faces. Moreover, subliminal presentations of smiling and happy faces failed to elicit affective experiences (Berridge & Winkielman, 2003). Hence, the effect of the emotional stimuli on evaluations of the Chinese ideographs was not mediated by a conscious affective experience. In another study by Winkielman and colleagues, participants' consumption of a soft drink increased after subliminal priming with a smiling face and decreased after subliminal priming with a frowning face. Once more, this effect did not appear to be mediated by conscious affective experiences. Strahan, Spencer, and Zanna (2002) found that emotional stimuli outside awareness influence evaluations without changing affective experiences. Participants were subliminally exposed to a sad facial expression. Afterwards they rated how they were feeling, and they rated the emotion expressed in a piece of music. Exposure to the sad facial expression had no influence on people's affective experiences, but they rated the music as sadder after subliminal exposure to sad faces. In sum, these studies suggest that affective stimuli can influence attitudes without eliciting affective experiences.

Another question in the literature on unconscious affective experiences concerns the relation between conscious awareness of an affective stimulus and affective experiences. Can affective stimuli outside awareness still elicit an affective experience? The answer to this question may depend on the nature of the affective stimulus. Dijksterhuis and Aarts (2003) presented positive and negative words subliminally (11 ms with forward and backward mask). In one study, participants had to guess whether the word was positive or negative. Participants performed above chance for negative words, but not for positive words. The authors suggest that subliminal affective stimuli elicit an unconscious affective response. When this response is above a certain threshold, the affect becomes consciously accessible. The higher detection rate of negative stimuli arises from a lower threshold of unconscious negative affect to become consciously accessible.

However, a series of studies with affective pictures (sharks, feces, babies, puppies) found that neither subliminal presentations of pleasant nor unpleasant pictures elicited affective experiences (Schimmack, 2004). In two studies participants saw backward masked, brief presentations of varying durations (10 ms, 30 ms, 50 ms). Afterwards participants saw a pair of pictures, which included the picture that was presented briefly (target) and a new picture (foil). Importantly, the valence of the foil was manipulated. On some trials, the target and the foil had the same valence. On other trials, the foil had the opposite valence as the target. If subliminal presentations of emotional stimuli elicit an emotional experience, then participants should be able to pick the target on the basis of its valence when the valence of the target and the foil was different, but not when target and foil had the same valence. Contrary to this prediction, valence of the foil had no impact on recognition of the target. Participants' performance was entirely based on the length of the stimulus presentation and the nature of the mask, indicating that participants' judgments were based on perceptual cues rather than emotional experiences. Another study examined whether subliminal presentations of pictures altered participants' mood state. Participants were randomly assigned to four groups. Participants were either exposed to 20 positive or 20 negative pictures. Half the participants could clearly see the pictures, whereas others were exposed to subliminal presentations of the pictures. Participants who saw the pictures showed significant differences in their affective experiences after positive or negative picture presentations. However, subliminal exposure of the same pictures had no effect on affective experiences after the experiment.

One salient difference between the picture studies and the word studies by Dijksterhuis and Aarts (2003) is the stimulus material. Subliminal presentations of affective words have been shown to elicit a skin-conductance response (Lazarus & McCleary, 1951; Van den Hout, De Jong, & Kindt, 2000). Hence, words seem to be able to activate affective responses that sometimes become consciously accessible. One important distinction between words and emotional pictures is that words contain evaluative meaning, whereas novel pictures need to be appraised before their valence can be determined. The former process may occur automatically and unconsciously, whereas the latter process may be more complex and require at least some awareness of stimulus features (see Smith & Kirby, 2001). An alternative explanation could be that Dijksterhuis and Aarts (2003) failed to control for guessing and participants may simply have guessed that negative stimuli were presented more frequently than positive stimuli (see Schimmack, 2004, for details). One interesting avenue for future research is to examine whether subliminal presentations of facial expressions can elicit conscious affective experiences. Subliminal presentations of facial expressions elicit activation in emotional brain areas and in the facial muscles of participants (Dimberg, Thunberg, & Elmehed, 2000; Whalen et al., 1998; Sheline et al., 2001). Whether these responses are sufficient to produce conscious affective experiences remains to be determined.

The dissociation of conscious and unconscious components of affective responses has some interesting implications for attitude researchers. An influential study by Devine (1989) demonstrated that participants who were exposed to subliminal primes of an African American stereotype had a more negative impression of a fictitious character that was introduced after the priming task (see also Wittenbrink, Judd, & Park, 1997; Lepore & Brown, 1997). This finding has typically been attributed to cognitive processes of construct accessibility. However, it is also possible that the subliminal presentation of stereotype-related stimuli activates some un-conscious affective processes, which may in part mediate the influence of these stimuli on conscious evaluations (see Wheeler & Petty, 2001). One challenge for attitude researchers will be the measurement of unconscious affect. For example, primes of negative stereotypes may produce changes in facial electromyogram (EMG), which may predict evaluative judgments independently of changes in affective experiences. A first step would be to include measures of affective experiences in these studies to examine whether the subliminal stimuli produced a change in affective experiences.

In sum, a growing literature suggests that affective stimuli can influence neurological and physiological components of affect, evaluative judgments, and approach-avoidance behavior without eliciting conscious affective experiences. The influence of these unconscious processes on attitudes provides an intriguing avenue for future research. At the same time, Berridge and Winkielman's (2003) definition of unconscious affect also implies that most of the attitude literature has examined the role of consciously accessible affect, with or without an identifiable source, in the formation of attitudes. Therefore our subsequent review of the affect literature focuses on conscious affective experiences.

Facets of Affective Experiences

Schimmack, Oishi, Diener, and Suh (2000) proposed a taxonomy of affective experiences for personality research. The same taxonomy can also serve as a framework for studies of affec-tive experiences in attitude research. The taxonomy distinguishes between *facets* of affective experiences. Each facet is defined by a *type*, a *quality*, and an *aspect* of an affective experience. The original taxonomy distinguished two types of affective experiences (emotions vs. moods), two qualities (pleasant vs. unpleasant), and three aspects (intensity, duration, and frequency). In this chapter, we also review *sensory affects* as a third type of affective experience. In total, the facet framework distinguishes 18 facets (3 types × 2 qualities × 3 aspects). To illustrate, the frequency (aspect) of pleasant (quality) moods (type) would be one facet, whereas the intensity (aspect) of unpleasant (quality) emotions (type) would be another. Subsequently, we review types, qualities, and aspects of affective experiences and point out the importance of these distinctions for attitude research.

Types of Affective Experiences: Distinct Origins of Affect

The distinctions among types of affective experiences are closely related to their origins. The notion of affect seems to imply that all types of affective experiences share a common set of affective qualities (i.e., pleasant vs. unpleasant). Accordingly, it does not matter how an affective experience is elicited. For example, thinking about a wonderful vacation or eating delicious ice cream elicits the same pleasant experience, whereas the death of a loved pet and hitting a thumb with a hammer elicits the same unpleasant experience. The facet framework takes a different view. Accordingly, different types of affect have distinct causes and consequences. Many emotion researchers distinguish at least two types of affects: emotions and moods (e.g., Frijda, 1993; Ortony et al., 1988). Schimmack and Siemer (1998) examined lay people's distinction between these two types of affect. They found that participants in the United States and Germany considered some affects more typical examples of emotions than moods and others more typical examples of moods than emotions (Table 10.1). U.S. participants also rated affect words on a number of dimensions that have been proposed to distinguish emotions and moods, such as the intensity, duration, object directedness (feeling about something; e.g., I am disappointed about my performance), and knowing the cause of the affective experience.

TABLE 10.1
Typical Examples of Emotions and Moods Based on English
and German Typicality Ratings

High Emotion *Low Mood Typicality*	*High Mood* *Low Emotion Typicality*
hate	crabby
ashamed	confident
jealous	nostalgic
envious	indifferent
love	restless
pity	tense
hurt	optimistic
loathing	balanced
terrified	at peace
outraged	good-humored
disgust	grouchy
angry	pensive
guilty	bored
dismayed	relaxed
disappointed	tired

Note: Based on Schimmack and Siemer (1998).

Typical emotion words referred to more intense affects that were directed at objects and had a known cause than typical mood words. Duration ratings were not related to the mood versus emotion distinction. This finding is consistent with the distinction between emotions and moods most commonly made in the emotion literature. Accordingly, emotions are object-directed, intentional states, whereas moods do not have an object (Frijda, 1993).

In the present chapter, we include sensory affects as a third type of affective experiences. Sensory affects are affective experiences that are elicited by sensations such as touch, taste, smell, sound, and vision. Examples of sensory affects are the pleasant touch of velvet, the unpleasant sound of a crying baby, the pleasant taste of mango, and the pleasant smell of lavender. Sensory affects differ from emotions in that they are triggered by immediate sensory inputs, whereas emotions are elicited by the appraisal of events for one's well-being. This distinction is similar to Hoffman's (1986) distinction between affects that are caused directly by physical and sensory aspects of stimuli (sensory affects) and those that are caused by the meaning of a stimulus (emotions). Sensory affects differ from moods in that sensory affects have an easily identifiable cause because the affective experience is closely connected to the sensation.

Emotions.   Of the different types of affects, emotions have received most of the attention by psychologists. The first influential theory of emotions was the James-Lange theory (James, 1894). The main aim of the theory was to account for the immediate causes of emotional experiences and their qualitative distinctions. Why does anger feel different from fear? The James-Lange theory saw the answer to this question in the bodily reactions to an emotional stimulus. Accordingly, emotional stimuli triggered bodily responses, and feedback of these bodily responses produced the emotional experience. Qualitative distinctions, for example, between anger and fear, were due to different patterns of physiological activity. Due to the strong influence of the James-Lange theory on emotion research, numerous studies have tried to uncover correlations between qualitatively distinct emotions (e.g., anger and fear) and measures of peripheral physiological activity (skin conductance, blood pressure, EMG). In general, the search for peripheral correlates of emotions has been disappointing (Frijda, 1986; Gray, 1994; Panksepp, 1994). The reason appears to be that the function of peripheral physiological processes is mostly related to energy requirements (Gray, 1994), which are only loosely related to emotions. Sometimes intense emotions require immediate availability of energy. However, at other times intense emotions can occur with minimal energy (in a movie theater) and at other times high energy levels can occur with minimal emotions (e.g., running up some stairs).

One major problem of the James-Lange theory is the lack of physiological correlates of the valence of affective experiences in the body. That is, one of the most salient qualitative distinctions among emotions is whether the emotional experience is pleasant (e.g., happy, proud, grateful) or unpleasant (e.g., sad, angry, fearful). If peripheral physiological arousal would be the basis of qualitative distinctions among emotional experiences, then one should be able to find peripheral physiological indicators that correlated with the valence of emotional experiences. However, 100 years of research have produced little evidence for bodily correlates of valence (see Eagly & Chaiken, 1993). Lang, Greenwald, Bradley, and Hamm (1993) found a significant but small relation between valence ratings and heart rate changes in response to emotional pictures. Bradley, Codispoti, Cuthbert, and Lang (2001) provided a more detailed analysis of this finding. Accordingly, both positive and negative pictures produce a larger heart rate deceleration than neutral pictures after the onset of a picture. Hence, initial heart rate deceleration is not an indicator of valence, but reflects the emotionality or arousal level of an emotional stimulus. Afterwards, heart rate accelerates faster after positive pictures than after negative pictures. Even under laboratory conditions, the effect size of this difference is small (Cohen's d = .47) compared to the effect size of emotional experiences in response to positive and negative pictures (Cohen's d = 4.25). The relation between heart rate and valence of emotional experiences also does not generalize to other emotion-induction methods. For example, Rottenberg, Kasch, Gross, and Gotlib (2002) found no differences in heart rate when participants were viewing amusing or sad movies, and Levenson and Ekman (2002) report *higher* heart rates for three negative emotions (anger, fear, sadness) than for happiness when participants posed facial expressions of emotions. Hence, it is impossible to use heart rate as an indicator of the valence of emotional experiences. In sum, the James-Lange theory had a strong influence on emotion research, but failed to provide a coherent theory of the origin of emotional experiences.

Emotion researchers proposed two solutions to the problems of the James-Lange theory. The first solution was to look for a response system that was more differentiated than the autonomic nervous system. Empirical studies showed that facial muscles allow the expression of at least six distinct emotions (happiness, surprise, anger, fear, sadness, disgust; see Ekman, 1973; Izard, 1977). Based on this finding, several researchers proposed that emotional experiences are based on the sensory feedback of the facial muscles. Facial feedback theory generated a considerable number of studies that manipulated the activity of facial muscles and examined the influence on emotional experiences. A meta-analysis of these studies suggests that facial feedback has only a small to moderate effect on emotional experiences, and the effect is too weak for facial feedback to be the immediate determinant of emotional experiences (Matsumoto, 1987). The influence of facial feedback may also vary across emotions. Kleinke, Peterson, and Rutledge (1998) found that imitating a smile increased experiences of pleasure, but facial expressions of negative emotions did not induce unpleasant emotions. Similarly, Soussignan (2002) found that smiling increased pleasure, but did not diminish displeasure elicited by positive and negative film clips. Most recently, Keillor, Barrett, Crucian, Kortenkamp, and Heilman (2002) tested the facial-feedback theory with a patient, whose face had been bilaterally paralyzed. According to the facial-feedback theory, this condition should severely diminish the intensity of emotional experiences. Contrary to this prediction, the patient reported normal emotional experiences in everyday life, and an experimental study showed normal reactions to emotional pictures. In sum, facial feedback is neither necessary nor sufficient to generate emotional experiences.

The second solution to the problems of the James-Lange theory was Schachter and Singer's (1962) two-factor theory of emotions. Accordingly, peripheral physiological arousal is responsible for the intensity of an emotion, while cognitions are responsible for the qualitative distinctions between different emotions like anger and fear. The two-factor theory solves the problem of the James-Lange theory that bodily responses failed to account for qualitative distinctions between emotions. However, the theory still maintained the key assumption of the James-Lange theory that peripheral physiological activation is a necessary component of emotions. Without peripheral activation, people may evaluate situations and appraise them as good or bad, but the cognitions will not feel like an emotion. In other words, peripheral physiological arousal distinguished emotions (cognitions plus arousal) from mere cognitions. Although the Schachter and Singer (1962) theory made an important contribution by highlighting the importance of cognitions for emotions, empirical evidence failed to support the hypothesis that peripheral arousal is an important aspect of emotional experiences (see Reisenzein, 1983, for an extensive review). One test of the theory is based on the study of emotional experiences in patients with spinal-cord injury, which reduces the feedback of peripheral arousal. According to the two-factor theory, this should reduce the intensity of emotional experiences. However, empirical evidence does not support this prediction (e.g., Chwalisz, Diener, & Gallagher, 1988; Cobos, Sanchez, Garcia, Vera, & Vila, 2002). For example, a recent study examined the influence of erotic films on experiences of sexual arousal in spinal-cord injured women compared to normal women (Sipski, Alexander, & Rosen, 2001). When just seeing an erotic film, normal and spinal-cord injured participants experienced the same intensity of sexual arousal. However, when the film was combined with manual stimulation of the vagina, healthy women reported more intense sexual arousal than spinal-cord injured women. This finding shows that peripheral arousal can add to the intensity of emotional experiences, but it is not necessary for the experience of emotions.

Other studies used Schachter and Singer's (1962) original paradigm of inducing arousal by injections of adrenalin. Mezzacappa, Katkin, and Palmer (1999) injected adrenalin or a placebo into the blood of healthy volunteers before they watched emotional film clips. A manipulation check showed a strong increase in heart rate in response to adrenaline but not in the placebo condition. However, adrenalin injections had only a small significant effect on the intensity of fear and non-significant effects on other emotions. In sum, empirical evidence does not support Schachter and Singer's (1962) hypothesis that the intensity of emotional experiences is based on the amount of peripheral physiological activation.

Despite the shortcomings of the two-factor theory, it was in part responsible for the reemergence of cognitive emotion theories that had been overshadowed by the James-Lange theory (Frijda, 1986; Lazarus, 1991; Reisenzein & Schönpflug, 1992; Roseman, 1984; Roseman & Smith, 2001; Scherer, 1984; Smith & Ellsworth, 1985; Weiner, 1986). Cognitive emotion theories assume that cognitions play two important roles for emotions (Frijda & Zeelenberg, 2001). First, cognitions are important for the generation of an emotional response. Second, cognitions play a major role in differentiating specific emotions from each other. Lazarus and colleagues provided first empirical evidence for the powerful influence of cognitions on emotional experiences (e.g., Lazarus & Alfert, 1964). In one experiment, participants watched a film, in which older males of a tribal culture cut deeply into the penis and scrotum of adolescents with a stone knife as part of an initiation ritual. Some participants were shown this clip with the (mis)information that this procedure was neither painful nor dangerous and that the adolescents welcomed the procedure to become men. The information altered the appraisal of the ritual, reduced the intensity of emotional experiences, and lowered skin conductance and heart rate during the film clip.

Early efforts of appraisal theorists were devoted to structural issues. Structural theories related dimensions of cognitive appraisals to specific emotions (Frijda, Kuipers, & ter Shure, 1989; Lazarus, 1991; Reisenzein & Spielhofer, 1994; Roseman, 1984; Scherer, 1984; Smith & Ellsworth, 1985). Typical appraisal dimensions are the evaluation of an event as desirable or undesirable (evaluation), the attribution of causality as internal or external, the attribution of responsibility, and the temporal perspective (i.e., whether the event is in the past or future). For example, pride and guilt are caused by internal attributions whereas anger and gratitude are caused by external attributions. Disappointment and happiness are caused by events that actually happened, whereas anxiety and hope are caused by anticipation of future events.

Cognitive theories of emotions have often been criticized on the grounds that they neglect non-cognitive determinants of affect. However, most of the criticism is due to vague definitions of cognition and emotion. Cognitive theories of emotions appear ridiculous if one defines cognitions as a long, deliberate process similar to cognitions in a chess game. Clearly, emotional experiences are too fast to be elicited by extended deliberation. However, many cognitive processes occur more quickly. For example, recognition judgments are often made within a few hundred milliseconds and recognition is typically considered a cognitive process. On the other hand, the term emotion is often used so broadly as to include moods or primitive motor responses. If one limits the concept of emotion to experiences of paradigmatic examples of emotions (see Table 10.1), empirical evidence for non-cognitive causes of emotional experiences is scarce.

Another problem of cognitive emotion theories is the difficulty of separating affective and cognitive components of an emotional experience. Many appraisal theories failed to specify the nature of those aspects of an emotional experience that are caused by appraisals and provide emotions with their characteristic quality that distinguishes them from mere cognitions. This problem was highlighted in an article by Frijda and Zeelenberg (2001) titled "Appraisal: What is the dependent?" The authors propose action tendencies as one major group of outcomes of an appraisal process. Accordingly, the appraisals of anger lead to action tendencies to attack. Other researchers have proposed that feelings of pleasure and displeasure, or positive and negative affect, constituted the affective component of emotional experiences (Frijda & Zeelenberg, 2001; Ortony, Clore, & Collins, 1988; Reisenzein, 2001; Wierzbicka, 1999). Sometimes, additional affective components such as arousal are added to pleasure and displeasure (Reisenzein, 1994; Russell & Barrett, 1999). One alternative hypothesis is that a small set of basic emotions provides the non-cognitive, hot component of emotional experiences that differentiates them from pure cognitions (Oatley & Johnson-Laird, 1987). This issue will be examined in more detail in the following section on qualities of affective experiences.

In sum, emotion research has moved from purely bodily theories of emotions to more cognitive theories of emotions. Cognitive theories can better account for the differences between distinct emotions and provide an explanation for the influence of cognitions on emotional experiences. However, despite various process models of emotions, the understanding of the cognitive and affective processes underlying emotional experiences is still limited (see Scherer, Schorr, & Johnstone, 2001), and it has been difficult to separate cognitive and affective components of emotions.

Moods.   Typical moods are experiences of alertness, drowsiness, tension and relaxation, grouchiness and feeling down or blue (see Table 10.1). These experiences are typically not covered by emotion theories; for a good reason. Neither feedback theories nor cognitive theories of emotions provide a sensible account of moods. Moods are not characterized by distinct facial expressions (see Ekman & Davidson, 1994), and moods are not linked to appraisal dimensions. The difference between emotions and moods also produced different literatures. While emotions have been studied since the beginning of the 20th century, mood research did not start until the middle of the last century. Nowlis and colleagues created the first mood questionnaire to examine the influences of drugs on affective experience (Nowlis, 1965, 1961). It is no accident that Nowlis created a mood questionnaire for this purpose, rather than relying on a list of emotions. It was intuitively evident that drugs could influence moods (e.g., restless, tired, relaxed), but that drugs do not induce emotions (e.g., hate, shame, guilt) because drug induced affects lack an object. Of course, somebody may feel ashamed about taking a drug, but in this case one needs to distinguish the emotion that is elicited by the cognitive appraisal of the act and its implications from the direct physiological effects of a drug on affective experiences.

One major function of moods appears to be the monitoring and evaluation of internal bodily states. Feelings of wakefulness and tiredness track mental and physical energy levels. Based on an influential theory by Thayer (1989), the dimension ranging from extreme alertness to extreme tiredness is often called energetic arousal (Matthews, Jones, & Chamberlain, 1990; Schimmack & Grob, 2000; Schimmack & Reisenzein, 2002). Energetic arousal shows a circadian rhythm; that is, it rises from the early morning to midday and decreases from afternoon to the late evening. Energetic arousal is also related to the availability of energy; that is, glucose levels in blood. Experimentally induced low blood-glucose levels lead to experiences of less energetic arousal (Gold, MacLeod, Deary, & Frier, 1995; McCrimmon, Frier, & Deary, 1999). Moods also appear to provide feedback about invasion of the body by infections and diseases (Maier & Watkins, 1998). The immune system seems to play the role of a sense organ that provides the central nervous system with information about bodily states. This information is not consciously accessible, but the brain may transform the input from the immune system into consciously accessible states. These states may then change organisms' behavior in an adaptive manner. For example, information from the immune system may lead to experiences of low energetic arousal. As a result, an individual will refrain from strenuous activities, which provides more energy for the immune system to fight off a disease. Empirical support for a link between health and mood stems from experience-sampling studies that show a significant correlation between illness-symptoms and mood (Clark & Watson, 1988; Watson, 1988; Williams, Colder, Lane, McCaskill, Feinglos, & Surwit, 2002).

Mood states do not only track states of peripheral systems. Rather, they are also related to neurological states. Extensive research on mood disorders (anxiety, depression) has revealed that experiences of anxiety and depression are directly related to neurochemical processes in the brain. In particular, levels of neurotransmitters such as serotonin and dopamine influence mood experiences (Frei et al., 2001; Liechti, Baumann, Gamma, & Vollenweider, 2000). Drugs like Prozac and other Selective Serotonin Reuptake Inhibitors (SSRIs) reduce depression and anxiety by influencing the neurotransmitter serotonin. The illegal drug Ecstasy also influences mood experiences by releasing large amounts of serotonin. Other legal (nicotine) and illegal (cocaine) drugs seem to influence mood experiences by altering dopamine levels. Drugs that lower dopamine levels, which are used for the treatment of schizophrenia, tend to induce unpleasant mood experiences (Kumari, Hemsley, Cotter, Checkley, & Gray, 1998).

The reviewed findings demonstrate that moods are at least in part influenced by endogenous biological factors. However, moods are also influenced by exogenous factors. One of the most common and salient factors is music (e.g., Husain, Thompson, & Schellenberg, 2002; Scherer & Zentner, 2001). Stratton and Zalanowski (2003) asked students to keep a music and mood diary. Participants recorded when they listened to music, the type of music, and their mood states before and after listening to music. Most students listened to music while they were carrying out other activities, with the most frequent type of music being rock music, which frequently produced a more positive mood state. People are aware of music's ability to change moods, and they use music to alter their moods (Knobloch & Zillmann, 2002). The influences of music on mood can persist after the end of musical stimulation (Siemer & Reisenzein, 1998). Music also influences behavior (and maybe experiences) of animals, and researchers started to investigate the neurological processes that mediate these effects (e.g., Panksepp & Bernatzky, 2002). Besides music, many other exogenous factors influence moods. For example, Schwarz and Clore (1983) took advantage of the fact that people are in a better mood on sunny days than on rainy days to study mood effects on attitude judgments.

Arguably, the most widely used method to induce moods in laboratory studies relies on residual affective experiences after an experience of an emotion or sensory affect (see Clore & Schnall, this chapter). For example, some studies have used pleasant and unpleasant odors or tastes to induce affective experiences (e.g., Albarracín & Kumkale, 2003; Ehrlichman & Halpern, 1988). Other studies have asked participants to vividly recall a past emotional event (e.g., Gasper & Clore, 1998). The affect-induction period is followed by a period in which participants perform a cognitive task. For example, they listen to a persuasive message. It is assumed that participants' affect at this time is still influenced by the affect-inducing task. These residual affective experiences can be considered moods because they are no longer directed at something or attached to a sensory experience. For example, after recalling an experience of anger, participants may still feel irritated or annoyed, but they are no longer angry about the event they recalled. Although the assumption that emotions and sensory affects persist after the eliciting condition is reasonable, little empirical work has been devoted to the scientific investigation of these effects (see Ekman & Davidson, 1994; Hemenover, 2003). Everyday examples suggest that affective experiences may end quickly or even reverse in hedonic tone after the eliciting factors are removed. For example, inhaling the exhaust of a passing truck may cause momentary displeasure. This experience, however, ends quickly or is even followed by pleasant relief when the odor is no longer experienced. For example, Ehrlichman and Halpern (1988) argued that pleasant and unpleasant odors influenced memory retrieval while the odors were present, but did not influence affect ratings of the memories five minutes after the odor was removed. Indeed, one problem of experimental mood-inductions is the short duration of the induced moods. For example, Isbell and Wyer (1999) failed to find reliable effects when the manipulation check was conducted more than 30 minutes after the mood induction. Studies of affective experiences in natural environments suggest that these events can sometimes have longer lasting effects that extend over a couple of hours (Peeters et al., 2003), but even strong emotional events often do not have effects on the mood the next day (David, Green, Martin, & Suls, 1997). In sum, moods are influenced by endogenous and exogenous factors. They are not based on a cognitive analysis of the situation and the cause is often not salient. Residual affective experiences after an emotional event are often used to induce moods in the laboratory, but these experiences do not last long.

Sensory Affects.   Sensory affects are, as the name suggests, affects that are elicited in response to sensory stimulation (see Reisenzein, 2001; Reisenzein & Schonpflug, 1992). Scientific studies of sensory affects have a long tradition (e.g., Beebe-Center, 1932). All sense organs provide information about the type and intensity of stimulation (e.g., quality and intensity of taste), which is often accompanied by an affective experience. Sensory stimuli may elicit affective experiences in several ways. Some sensory stimuli are likely to have an innate association with affect, whereas most affective experiences in response to sensory stimuli are learned or at least influenced by learning (Rolls, 1999). The influence of learning on sensory affects has been demonstrated in twin studies (Greene, Desor, & Maller, 1975; Rissanen, Hakala, Lissner, Mattlar, Koskenvuo, & Roennemaa, 2002; Rozin & Millman, 1987), by developmental changes in affective reactions (Rozin & Fallon, 1987), and by cross-cultural differences in affective reactions to sensory stimuli (e.g., Ayabe-Kanamura et al., 1998). Affective responses to sensory stimuli may already be learned in the uterus (Schaal, Marlier, & Soussignan, 2000). The most common learning mechanisms for sensory affects are based on simple associative learning (Rolls, 1999) and mere exposure (Zajonc, 1980). Furthermore, affective responses may be generalized from an affective stimulus to other stimuli that are similar or otherwise associated (Rhodes, Halberstadt, & Brajkovich, 2001; Rozin & Fallon, 1987; Walther, 2002; Zanna, Kiesler, & Pilkonis, 1970).

Innate sensory affects. Some sensory stimuli provide important information for survival. Charles Darwin already speculated that some affective reactions to stimuli with survival value are inherited. "Fears of children, which are quite independent of experience, are the inherited effects of real dangers ... during savage times" (Poulton & Menzies, 2002). Empirical evidence for this hypothesis stems from taste preferences in newborns. Gustatory sensations provide important information about the survival value of foods. Sweetness is a sign of nutritious food, whereas bitterness is a sign of potentially dangerous substances. Not surprisingly, sweetness is associated with pleasure, whereas bitterness is associated with displeasure. This association is already present in newborns and shared with other primates (Rosenstein & Oster, 1988; Steiner, Glaser, Hawilo, & Berridge, 2001). Newborns also seem to discriminate between pleasant and unpleasant odors, although the evidence is more ambiguous (Soussignan, Schaal, Marlier, & Jiang, 1997). Innate individual differences in the sensitivity to sensory stimulation can also influence a wide variety of affective experiences. For example, inherited differences in sensitivity to bitterness influence affective reactions and attitudes to a variety of bitter foods (Bartoshuk & Beauchamp, 1994). Individual differences in the liking of spicy foods also appear to have an inherited, biological component (Rozin & Millman, 1987).

Many sensory affects are present very early in life but require some minimal learning experiences (Poulton & Menzies, 2002). For example, fear of heights does not occur until infants start moving and their perceptual system can process three-dimensional information (Adolph, 2000; Campos, Langer, & Krowitz, 1970). Similarly, infants' preference for attractive faces seems to depend on the abstraction of a prototype from encounters with different faces. Like adults, infants show a preference for the average, prototypical face (Rubenstein, Kalakanis, & Langlois, 1999).

Classical conditioning. One form of learning is based on classical conditioning, which was first demonstrated by Pavlov in animal research (Pavlov, 1927). After several trials in which a stimulus (e.g., the sound of a bell) that does not elicit a behavior is paired with a stimulus (e.g., smell of food) that elicits a behavior (e.g., salivation), the presentation of the (initially) neutral stimulus alone elicits the behavior. While behaviorism explained this phenomenon purely in terms of associations between stimuli and responses, subsequent research has demonstrated the involvement of affect in classical conditioning. In a recent study, Hermans, Spruyt, and Eelen (2003) demonstrated the affective consequences of classical conditioning on an explicit and implicit measure of affect. A neutral human face was arbitrarily paired with electric shock, while another face signaled the non-occurrence of shock. After eight presentations of the faces, participants rated the face paired with shock as unpleasant, while the other face was rated as pleasant. The implicit measure was based on the affective priming task. In this task, one stimulus is presented briefly (300 ms) before the onset of a second stimulus. Participants have to judge the valence of a second stimulus as fast as possible. Although participants are supposed to ignore the first stimulus, evidence shows that the first stimulus influences responses. When the two stimuli have the same valence, responses are faster than when the two stimuli have a different valence. In Hermans et al.'s (2003) study, responses to positive words were faster when they followed the face that was not paired with shock, whereas responses to negative words were faster when they followed the face paired with shock. In sum, classical conditioning is an important mechanism for the learning of affective responses to many stimuli that do not possess intrinsic affective qualities.

Extinction. Extinction can be considered reverse conditioning. Extinction consists of re-peated presentations of a stimulus that signals positive or negative consequences without the typically associated consequences. For example, a stimulus that signaled the occurrence of electroshock is presented several times without electroshock. Extinction reduces the affective reaction to a stimulus. Typically, extinction has been studied with stimuli that acquired affective value through conditioning. However, extinction can also influence innate responses to stimuli. For example, monkeys show an innate avoidance of snakes, which influences their response to the initial encounter of a toy snake. However, after repeated encounters without negative consequences, monkeys quickly learn to ignore the harmless toy snakes (Nelson, Shelton, & Kalin, 2003). Snake phobia and related anxieties in humans may be based on a lack of extinction learning. That is, everybody is born with a set of innate fears (e.g., heights, dark), but repeated encounters of the feared objects without negative consequence reduces these fears in most people to normal levels. Conditioning and extinction provide alternative explanations for individual differences in fears and phobias. Fears that are not innate (dental fear) are mostly due to conditioning experiences, whereas fears with an innate component (fear of heights) are mostly due to a lack of extinction experiences (Poulton & Menzies, 2002). Due to the higher number of extinction experiences, non-anxious individuals even tend to have more negative experiences with a fear-eliciting stimulus than high anxious individuals. For example, people with fear of heights have fewer experiences of falling than people without fear of heights.

Evaluative conditioning. Evaluative conditioning is similar to classical conditioning in that the acquisition of affective reactions is based on the learning of associations. However, evaluative conditioning also seems to differ in several ways from classical conditioning (De Houwer, Thomas, & Baeyens, 2001; Rozin, Wrzesniewski, & Byrnes, 1998). First, classical conditioning relies on the signal function of a stimulus. Hence, classical conditioning tends to be most effective when the conditioned stimulus precedes the unconditioned stimulus. However, in evaluative conditioning a neutral stimulus acquires the affective properties of an affective stimulus even when the two stimuli are presented concurrently (e.g., van Reekum, van den Berg, & Frijda, 1999). Based on this distinction between classical and evaluative conditioning, many earlier studies of classical conditioning are actually examples of evaluative conditioning. For example, Staats and Staats (1957) demonstrated that pairing nonsense syllabus with positive or negative words changed the affective response to the nonsense syllabus. In these studies, nonsense syllabus did not signal the occurrence of a positive or negative word. Rather, the affect of the valence stimulus seems to have been transferred automatically to the initially neutral stimulus.

A second distinction between classical and evaluative conditioning concerns awareness of the contingency between the two stimuli. Classical conditioning is based on awareness of a contingency between the conditioned and the unconditioned stimulus. For example, if people are not aware that a red light signals the occurrence of electric shock, then the red light does not produce an affective response. In contrast, evaluative conditioning is assumed to take place without awareness of stimulus contingencies (de Houwer, 2001; Olson & Fazio, 2001).

Third, affective responses that are acquired through classical conditioning are quickly unlearned when the conditioning stimulus is no longer paired with the unconditioned stimulus (extinction). Presumably, extinction has this effect because people learn that the conditioned stimulus no longer signals the occurrence of the unconditioned stimulus. In contrast, affective reactions that are acquired through evaluative conditioning tend to be more resistant to extinction (Hermans et al., 2003; but see Stevenson, Boakes, & Wilson, 2000).

Most of the evidence on evaluative conditioning relies on acquisition and testing within a single experimental session. Hence, one concern may be that these effects are rather short-lived. However, a few studies have demonstrated that the effects of a brief evaluative conditioning procedure last several weeks (Grossman & Till, 1998). On the other hand, it is noteworthy that several studies failed to demonstrate evaluative conditioning effects (see de Houwer et al., 2001; Rozin et al., 1998, for reviews). De Houwer et al. (2001) speculate that the relation between stimuli may moderate the effectiveness of evaluative conditioning. For example, evaluative conditioning seems to be more effective for two related stimuli such as odors and tastes, than for two unrelated stimuli such as colors and tastes.

Another limitation of the existing evidence is the reliance on the traditional conditioning paradigm to establish associations. It is possible that humans also learn associations in different ways. Baeyens, Eelen, Crombez, and De Houwer (2001) demonstrated that affective reactions can be acquired by observational learning. Rozin and Royzman (2001) found that merely informing participants that a sweater had been worn by a liked or disliked person influenced affective reactions to the sweater. Many irrational likes and dislikes such as prejudices may be based on such learning mechanisms rather than on actual covariation learning. In sum, the evidence suggests that any association between two stimuli can transfer affective information from one stimulus to another. Not surprisingly, conditioning is often used in advertising to infuse rather mundane products with affective value (e.g., Shimp, Stuart, & Engle, 1991). However, it remains to be determined whether advertising effects are based on evaluative or classical conditioning. For example, Shimp et al. (1991) observed effects only when participants were aware of the association between a product and the unconditioned stimulus. This finding suggests that the effects were not due to evaluative conditioning, which should have produced effects even without awareness of the association.

Mere exposure. Whereas the previous learning mechanisms were all based on some form of associative learning, mere exposure is typically assumed to be a different process. The basic finding is that repeated presentations of a neutral stimulus produce a mild pleasant response to the stimulus (Zajonc, 1968; see Bornstein, 1989, for a review). Most studies have examined mere exposure effects under tightly controlled laboratory conditions. However, the effect is also evident in more naturalistic settings and lasts at least for one week. For example, Law, Schimmack, and Braun (2003) showed participants brief video sketches. The sketches incidentally included everyday products of one of two brands (pasta, coffee). One week later participants rated their liking and made forced choice judgments of the two brands. Participants liked the brands that were included in the sketches significantly more and this preference was independent of explicit recall or recognition and occurred even after warning about the possible effect of exposure.

Although the mere exposure effect is robust, it has been more difficult to provide a theoretical explanation for it (see Bornstein, 1989). One explanation assumes that unfamiliar stimuli are potentially dangerous, whereas familiar stimuli are not. Mere exposure is considered a form of extinction; that is, repeated presentations without negative consequences reduce the initial unpleasant response. This theory encounters two problems. First, the mere exposure effect has been most consistently demonstrated with stimuli that are initially neutral rather than negative or threatening. For example, participants report neither displeasure nor anxiety when they are presented with a Chinese character that they have never seen before. Furthermore, repeated exposure of stimuli that are negative increases displeasure rather than rendering these stimuli more pleasurable (Ortony et al., 1988; Schimmack, 2004).

Other explanations assume that repetition facilitates the processing of a stimulus (e.g., Bornstein & D'Agostino, 1994; Mandler, Nakamura, & Van Zandt, 1987). Fluency of processing has been used to explain mere exposure effects in several ways. Some models assume that fluency of processing generates a conscious experience, which can be misattributed as arising from the affective properties of the stimulus (e.g., Mandler et al., 1987). Initially, it was assumed that experiences of fluency could be misattributed to any characteristic of a stimulus. If pleasantness judgments are required, fluency increases pleasantness ratings. If unpleasantness judgments are requested, fluency increases unpleasantness judgments. However, experimental evidence shows that mere exposure increases pleasantness ratings but not unpleasantness ratings (see Reber, Winkielman, & Schwarz, 1998; Seamon, McKenna, & Binder, 1998). An alternative model proposed that experiences of fluency are intrinsically pleasant (Winkielman

& Cacioppo, 2001). Accordingly, mere exposure induces pleasure due to enhanced fluency of processing, and people fail to distinguish between fluency-based pleasure and pleasure elicited by the attributes of an object. This version of the fluency hypothesis can explain why mere exposure to neutral and positive stimuli increase pleasantness ratings. However, some mere exposure findings are inconsistent with the model. First, according to the misattribution model, mere exposure effects should be weaker when participants recognize a stimulus. The reason is that they should be less inclined to attribute fluency to positive attributes of the stimulus. Contrary to this prediction, Szpunar, Schellenberg, and Pliner (2004) found that liking of musical pieces sometimes increased with increased recognition of the musical piece. Second, the model cannot explain why mere exposure to already negative stimuli increases displeasure (Ortony et al., 1988; Schimmack, 2003a).

A slight modification of the fluency hypothesis may be able to do so. Accordingly, repeated exposure makes it easier to process a stimulus, which enhances the affective reaction to it. This hypothesis can account for increased liking of so-called neutral stimuli due to a positivity offset in the affect system (Cacioppo & Berntson, 1994; Ito, Cacioppo, & Lang, 1998). Neutral stimuli are often not really neutral but elicit mild pleasant experiences. Repeated exposure may intensify this affective response. Consistent with this model, mere exposure also intensifies affective reactions to relatively strong positive stimuli and it produces more intense negative responses to unpleasant stimuli (Schimmack, 2004).

Zajonc (2001) recently proposed a conditioning explanation of mere exposure. Accordingly, organisms learn to associate the stimulus with the non-occurrence of unpleasant stimuli, which renders them pleasant. In other words, the neutral stimuli become safety signals that nothing bad is going to happen. This interpretation would be consistent with the finding in conditioning studies, in which one stimulus is paired with shock, while another stimulus is not paired with shock. While the former stimulus elicits displeasure, the latter stimulus elicits pleasure (e.g., Hermans et al., 2003). The conditioning hypothesis could also explain why repeated presentation of an unpleasant stimulus intensifies displeasure. Repeated presentations of a stimulus only serve as a safety signal if they are not accompanied by unpleasant experiences. However, a negative stimulus induces displeasure, which precludes the association of the stimulus with the absence of displeasure. However, the conditioning hypothesis also encounters some problems. First, it contradicts the common finding that classical conditioning requires awareness of the contingency between the conditioned and unconditioned stimulus. As mere exposure effects occur without awareness, this precondition is not met. Second, the conditioning hypothesis assumes that exposure during negative contexts leads to unpleasant affect. However, Saegert, Swap, and Zajonc (1973) found that exposure increased liking even when exposure was paired with a negative stimulus (an unpleasant taste).

In sum, mere exposure is a robust and important determinant of affective reactions. However, mere exposure is only one of many mechanisms that influence sensory affects and its underlying mechanisms are less well understood than those underlying associative learning. The mere exposure effect does not predict that affective reactions to sensory stimuli are closely related to the frequency of exposure. Many children may like ice cream more than broccoli, even if their parents feed them more broccoli than ice cream. In fact, economic theories of supply and demand predict an inverse relation between frequency and affect. Most people have seen more fieldstones than diamonds and more Fords than Jaguars, although many people are likely to prefer diamonds and Jaguars to fieldstones and Fords.

Implications of Types for Attitude Research.   We propose that the different types of affective experiences play different roles in the formation and change of attitudes (Eagly & Chaiken, 1993). Emotions and sensory affects are tightly connected to cognitions or sensations. Therefore, the cause of these affective experiences is typically very salient. As a result, these affective experiences provide relevant information for attitudes if the cognitions or sensations are related to an attitude object. For example, the pleasant taste of pistachio gelato provides valid information about attitudes towards gelato and pistachio. It does not provide relevant information about other features of the tasting situation such as the salesperson, the table at which the gelato is eaten, or other irrelevant characteristics associated with the eating of gelato.

A study by Bushman and Baumeister (1998) on displaced aggression provides a scientific example of the specific effects of emotions. To induce anger, participants first wrote an essay, which received a very negative evaluation by a second participant (who did not really exist). Afterwards, participants played a competitive game with a second participant, in which they could administer a loud noise to the competitor after they won. The intensity and duration of the noise was used as a measure of aggression. Some participants were told that they were playing with the participant who had evaluated their essay. Others were told that they were playing with a different participant. Participants showed aggressive behavior when they believed they were playing with the participant who had evaluated their essay, but not when they believed they were playing with a new participant. Hence, the frustration and anger that was elicited by a negative essay influenced behavior toward the competitor who had evaluated the essay, but it did not influence behavior toward an unrelated individual. On some occasions anger may influence behavior toward people who are neither the cause nor the object of anger (Marcus-Newhall, Pedersen, Carlson, & Miller, 2000; Miller, Pedersen, Earleywine, & Pollock, 2003; Twenge & Campbell, 2003). However, these cases do not contradict the general idea that emotions typically influence attitudes toward related objects. First, when other factors are equal, people are more likely to aggress against the individual who elicited anger than at somebody else. Second, it has not been demonstrated that displaced aggression has effects on attitudes that last beyond the anger episode.

Moods are influenced by many factors that have nothing to do with an attitude object. Nevertheless, moods may influence the momentary appraisal of an attitude object. The reason is that undirected affect can be misattributed; that is, people may confuse a mood with an emotional reaction to the object (Clore & Schnall, this volume; Schwarz & Clore, 1983). Mood effects on the evaluation of an attitude object in a specific situation may sometimes have lasting effects on an attitude, especially when people have very little other accessible information about the attitude object. For example, Dutton and Aron (1974) examined the influence of arousal on attraction. Male participants walked over a high suspension bridge that elicited arousal or a lower stable bridge that did not elicit arousal. At the end of the bridge, an attractive woman asked participants to answer a few survey questions and participants could later call her for the results. Men who had walked over the suspension bridge rated the experimenter as more attractive and, more importantly, were more likely to call her several days later. Hence, a mood, the residual affect after walking over the suspension bridge, influenced the emotional reaction to an attitude "object," which had lasting effects on the attitude and behavior toward the attitude object.

In other situations, however, mood effects may not last beyond the situation in which the mood is experienced. For example, seeing a product in a store when experiencing a good mood may increase liking of the product, but returning to the store later and seeing the same product in a bad mood is likely to have the reverse effect. Moreover, the bias of the first encounter is unlikely to influence the evaluation of the product during the second encounter. Schimmack, Diener, and Oishi (2002) found evidence for short-lived effects of moods on life satisfaction judgments. Mood influenced life satisfaction judgments at the same time a judgment was made, but this effect did not lead to a lasting attitude change when life satisfaction was assessed later.

When will mood effects have lasting effects and when are the biases limited to the momentary situation, in which the mood is experienced? There exists no research on this question. A plausible hypothesis is that mood will only have lasting effects to the extent that it changes the processing of other information about the attitude object. In contrast, a simple affective bias will have no effect or even lead to a contrast effect when the same attitude object is encountered again in a different mood state.

In sum, attitude research may benefit from the distinction between types of affective experiences. Emotions and sensory affects are likely to provide more relevant information about attitude objects and to have a longer-lasting influence on attitudes. In contrast, moods may bias momentary evaluations and behaviors towards attitude objects, but they are less likely to have lasting effects on attitudes.

Qualities of Affective Experiences

Affective experiences have different qualities. Anger feels different from fear, and the pleasant taste of raspberry is different from the displeasure of a bloated stomach. Most studies of affective qualities have examined qualities of affective experiences separately for emotions, moods, and sensory affects, although emotions and moods are not always clearly differentiated. Hence, we review the work on qualitative distinctions among affective experiences in separate sections for each type of affect.

Emotions. Most of the work on qualities of affective experiences is concerned with qualitative differences among emotions. Wundt (1896) proposed one of the first structural theories of emotions. Accordingly, each emotion could be reduced to a specific mixture of three basic affect dimensions: pleasure-displeasure, tension-relaxation, and arousal-calmness (Reisenzein, 1992). Today, three major classes of taxonomies can be differentiated. One class of theories follows Wundt's tradition and argues that emotions, or at least their affective core, can be reduced to a few basic dimensions that do not correspond to any particular emotion (Morgan & Heise, 1988; Reisenzein, 1994; Russell & Barrett, 1999). A second class of theories postulates sets of basic emotions that cannot be reduced to more primitive components. Each emotion has a unique evolutionary function and is based on separable neurological substrates in the brain (Ekman, 1992; Izard, 1993; Oatley & Johnson-Laird, 1987). A third class of theories postulates that most of the distinctions among emotions are based on cognitions and that only the salient difference between pleasant and unpleasant emotions is based on different affective qualities (Ortony et al., 1988; Wierzbicka, 1999). According to these theories, all emotions either share pleasant affect or unpleasant affect, and finer qualitative distinctions between emotions are based on additional cognitions. For example, fear is an unpleasant affect about the prospect of an undesirable event, whereas anger is an unpleasant affect about a blameworthy act (Ortony et al., 1988).

Emotion researchers have taken three approaches to developing taxonomies of emotions: (a) linguistic analysis of emotion words (Oatley & Johnson-Laird, 1987; Wierzbicka, 1999), (b) scaling of similarity judgments of emotion words (e.g., Shaver, Schwartz, Kirson, & O'Connor, 1987), and (c) examining the covariations of emotions in emotional events or scenarios (Izard, 1977; Reisenzein, 1995). Shaver et al. (1987; see also Shaver, Wu, & Schwartz, 1992) conducted one of the largest and most comprehensive investigations. They first asked students to rate the typicality of several hundreds of words as emotion words. Based on this first study, they selected over 100 typical exemplars of emotions. Another group of students made similarity sortings of the emotion words. The more frequently two emotions are sorted into the same pile, the more similar they are to each other. The sorting data were analyzed with Multidimensional Scaling (MDS) as well as Hierarchical Cluster Analysis. The authors concluded that the Hierarchical Cluster Analysis provided a more meaningful description of the data than a two- or three-dimensional MDS solution. Figure 10.1 illustrates the main elements of the hierarchical solution (see Table 7.1 in Shaver et al., 1992). The hierarchical tree first distinguishes pleasant

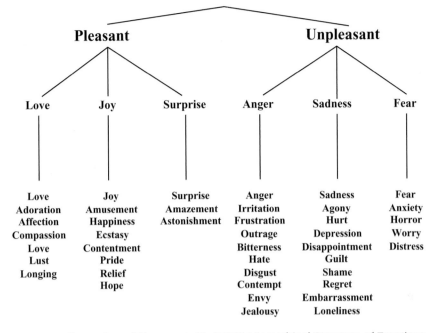

FIG. 10.1. Illustration of Shaver et al.'s (1987) Hierarchical Structure of Emotions.

emotions (e.g., love, happiness, gratitude, pride) and unpleasant emotions (e.g., shame, anger, fear, sadness, regret). Shaver et al. (1987) also identified a group of six clusters, which represent the basic level of emotion concepts, according to Rosch's prototype theory of categories (Rosch, Mervis, Gray, Johnson, & Boyes-Braem, 1976). Shaver et al. (1987) labeled these clusters love, joy, surprise, anger, sadness, and fear. Each cluster includes several subordinate emotion concepts. For example, the anger cluster includes anger, frustration, hate, envy, and jealousy.

Although a hierarchical model captures some salient features of perceived similarities between emotions, Fig. 10.1 also illustrates some problems of a strict hierarchical structure. First, the hierarchical arrangement of some emotions is questionable. Whereas jealousy may be a subtype of anger and homesickness a subtype of sadness, it is questionable that guilt is a subtype of sadness, or that surprise is always a pleasant experience. Second, it is questionable that all subordinate emotions are only related to one basic emotion. For example, hurt is as much associated with anger as with sadness, and longing is associated with sadness as well as love. Finally, hierarchical cluster analysis does not provide labels for the basic level emotions. The labels at this level were chosen by Shaver et al. (1987) and they may not correspond to the shared affective quality of the subordinate emotions.

The use of similarity judgments to develop a taxonomy of qualitative distinctions among emotions is also questionable. The (implicit) assumption was that similarity judgments of emotions are made in a similar manner as similarity judgments of colors. Red is judged as similar to orange because these colors look similar. In analogy, people may judge envy and anger to be similar because they feel similar. However, empirical studies of the cognitive processes underlying similarity judgments have suggested that these judgments are based, at least in part, on implicit knowledge about the covariation of emotions (Barrett & Fossum, 2001; Conway & Bekerian, 1987; Reisenzein & Schimmack, 1999; Schimmack & Reisenzein, 1997). For example, jealousy and anger are judged to be similar because these two emotions often co-occur. As a result, similarity judgments of emotions do not provide direct information about the qualities of emotions. Rather, they may only provide indirect information about the quality of emotion that has to be inferred from the pattern of co-occurrence. For this purpose, it seems better to rely on actual covariation data than on people's implicit beliefs of covariations – although these measures are highly related (Reisenzein & Schimmack, 1999).

Data of the actual covariations of emotions also provide a much more stringent test of hierarchical relations between emotions than scaling solutions of similarity judgments. The reason is that hierarchical relations make powerful predictions about the conditional probabilities of experiencing one emotion given the experience of another emotion (Reisenzein, 1995). For example, if anger is the basic emotion underlying jealousy, then experiences of jealousy should always be accompanied by experiences of anger. The reason is that jealousy is nothing but a special type of anger (e.g., anger at a sexual rival). Reisenzein (1995) found support for weak hierarchical relations between emotions, but not for strict hierarchical relations. That is, jealousy was more likely to occur with anger than anger with jealousy, but jealousy did not always co-occur with anger. In sum, the existing evidence does not suggest that most emotions can be reduced to a few basic emotions that lend each emotion a distinct affective quality.

The taxonomy in Fig. 10.1 is also consistent with theories that postulate pleasure or displeasure as the affective core of emotional experiences (Ortony et al., 1988). Accordingly, people should always experience pleasure when they experience pride, love, lust, and relief, and they should always experience displeasure when they experience sadness, shame, guilt, frustration, jealousy, or fear. Surprisingly, rigorous tests of this proposition with co-occurrence data are lacking. The reason may be that nobody has attempted to test a hypothesis that seems so self-evident. People find it very easy to rate emotions as either pleasant or unpleasant (Morgan & Heise, 1988; Schimmack & Siemer, 1998). However, the relation between experiences of pleasure and displeasure and specific emotions may be more complex. For example, people voluntarily engage in activities that elicit unpleasant emotions such as fear (roller coaster rides). In some of these cases, the specific emotion (fear) may be dissociated from its typical valence (unpleasant). In sum, the research on qualitative distinction between emotions has shown that people make broad and fine distinctions between emotions. Pleasure and displeasure are more viable candidates for the affective core of emotions than basic emotions such as anger, fear, or sadness (see also Ortony & Turner, 1990).

Mood.   Research on the qualitative distinctions of moods has been dominated by factor analyses of mood questionnaires (see Watson & Tellegen, 1985; Schimmack, 1997, for reviews). Initially, researchers extracted 6 to 12 monopolar factors, which represented qualities such as relaxation, boredom, tiredness, depression, cheerfulness, tension, irritation, excitement, and energy. These qualities also emerge in similarity sortings of moods (Reisenzein & Schimmack, 1999; Schimmack, 1997). However, these factors were often highly correlated with each other. As a result, Tellegen and colleagues proposed that the structure of mood can be represented more parsimoniously by two orthogonal factors, which they called *Positive Affect (PA)* and *Negative Affect (NA)* (Watson & Tellegen, 1985; Zevon & Tellegen, 1982). Watson, Clark, and Tellegen (1988) published the Positive Affect and Negative Affect Schedule (PANAS) for a relatively brief assessment of these two factors. With 2000 citations, the PANAS is arguably the most widely used contemporary mood measure.

The two-factor model of moods and the PANAS have produced a controversy in the affect literature. Several researchers have argued that the names Positive Affect and Negative Affect misrepresent the nature of the two factors (e.g., Feldman, Barrett, & Russell, 1998; Larsen & Diener, 1992). The PANAS-PA scale is comprised of items such as alert, inspired, excited, and proud. It does not include items such as happiness, cheerfulness, or relaxation. The PANAS-NA scale is comprised of items such as tension, irritation, guilt, and shame, but it does not include items such as sadness, unhappiness, displeasure, or boredom. Hence, the PANAS scales do not assess directly whether somebody is feeling pleasant (positive) or unpleasant (negative) because people can be in a pleasant mood without experiencing excitement, and they can be in an unpleasant mood without feeling tension (see Schimmack & Grob, 2000; Schimmack & Reisenzein, 2002). In response to this criticism, Watson, Wiese, Vaidya, and Tellegen (1999) suggested calling PA Positive Activation and NA Negative Activation. These labels provide a more adequate description of the nature of the PANAS scales. Egloff, Schmukle, Burns, Kohlmann, and Hock (2003) demonstrated that the PANAS-PA scale is comprised of three more specific affects, labeled Joy, Interest, and Activation. The inclusion of interest and activation in the PANAS-PA scale explains why PANAS-PA and other measures of pleasant moods often show divergent findings.

Patrick and Lavoro (1997) examined affective reactions to pictures from the International Affective Picture System (IAPS). The IAPS contains a wide range of pictures that range from extremely positive to extremely negative ones. The authors hypothesized that positive pictures influence PANAS-PA, but have no effect on PANAS-NA and negative pictures influence PANAS-NA but have no effect on PANAS-PA. Contrary to this prediction, negative pictures produced an increase in PANAS-PA. Patrick and Lavoro (1997) found that the increase in PANAS-PA in response to negative pictures was due to the activation items of the PANAS-PA scale such as alert, attentive, and interested in the PANAS-PA. These items reflect engagement with a stimulus, but do not reveal the evaluation of a stimulus. With regard to pictures, ample evidence shows that both positive and negative pictures are engaging (Lang et al., 1993). Thus, the inclusion of activation items in the PANAS-PA scales explains why PANAS-PA shows an increase in response to negative pictures. In contrast, other measures of pleasant affect that do not include activation items show no increase in pleasant affect in response to negative pictures (Ito et al., 1998).

A typical finding in the mood literature is that people have more pleasant experiences on weekends than on weekdays (Stone, Hedges, Neale, & Satin, 1985). In contrast, Clark and Watson (1988) found no differences in PANAS-PA between weekdays and weekends. Egloff, Tausch, Kohlmann, and Krohne (1995) directly compared PANAS-PA and a more traditional measure of pleasant affect and found significant effects of weekend versus weekday for the measure of pleasant affect, but not for the PANAS-PA. Once more, this finding can be attributed to the activation component of the PANAS, which is likely to be higher during weekdays than weekends. The authors also found different effects of time of day on PANAS-PA and other measures of pleasant affect (Egloff et al., 1995; Kennedy-Moore, Greenberg, Newman, & Stone, 1992). In sum, numerous studies have demonstrated divergent findings between the PANAS-PA scale and other measures of pleasant affect. The discrepancies are most likely due to the inclusion of activation items in the PANAS scale.

The activation component of the PANAS-PA scale may create a problem for its use in attitude research, which may benefit more from pure measures of the valence of affective experience. Researchers interested in the separate assessment of valence and activation could use one of several measures that include separate measures of valence and different types of activation (Steyer, Schwenkmezger, Notz, & Eid, 1994; Matthews et al., 1990; Schimmack & Grob, 2000). For example, Schimmack and Grob (2000) demonstrated that scales with three items for pleasant affect (pleasant, positive, good) and three items for unpleasant affect (unpleasant, negative, bad) have good psychometric properties (see also Schimmack & Reisenzein, 2002). Schimmack, Diener, and Oishi (2002) demonstrated that these three-item scales were reliable measures of the valence of past emotional experiences as well as current mood. Both measures predicted life-satisfaction, which can be considered an attitude toward one's life.

Sensory Affects.   There have been comparatively few studies on qualities of sensory affects. The reason may be the assumption that sensory affects lack any qualitative distinctions other than the obvious difference between pleasant and unpleasant sensory affects. Several studies have examined similarity judgments of odors (e.g., Berglund, Berglund, Engen, & Ekman, 1973). Most of these studies find support for a distinction between pleasant and unpleasant odors, although hedonic tone may be a more salient feature for novices than for experts (Yoshida, 1964), and hedonic tone is less salient when judgments are based on memories of odors than on actual sensory stimulation (Carrasco & Ridout, 1993). Clearly, valence is not the only dimension that distinguishes odors. Additional distinctions are based on the sensory qualities of odors. For example, fruity odors (e.g., strawberry) are different from spicy odors (e.g., mint), and earthy ones (e.g., mushrooms) (e.g., Carrasco & Ridout, 1993; Sulmont, Issanchou, & Köster, 2002). However, more research needs to examine the structure of sensory affects. Wundt's (1896) theory was heavily based on sensory affects, and he suggested that arousal-calmness and tension-relaxation discriminate between affects. It is conceivable that some odors increase activation (e.g., mint), whereas others induce calmness (e.g., lavender). The same may be true for other sensory affects.

Pleasure and Displeasure: Opposite or Distinct Qualities.   Although the nature of qualitative distinctions between affects remains elusive, evidence for all three types of affects shows a marked distinction between pleasant affects and unpleasant affects. One unresolved question in the affect literature has been the nature of this distinction (Beebe-Center, 1932; Diener & Iran-Nejad, 1986; Reisenzein, 1992; Russell & Carroll, 1999; Schimmack, 2001). Is displeasure merely the opposite of pleasure, or are pleasure and displeasure two distinct affective qualities?

Aside from some early empirical studies (see Beebe-Center, 1932), the issue was first examined by means of correlations and factor analysis of mood scales. The initial studies often found independent factors of pleasant moods and unpleasant moods (e.g., Nowlis, 1965). Some researchers proposed that this result was an artifact of ambiguous response formats and found a bipolar pleasure-displeasure factor with other response formats (Meddis, 1972; Green, Goldman, & Salovey, 1993). However, Schimmack, Böckenholt, and Reisenzein (2002) demonstrated that a bipolar factor only emerges when participants interpret the response format in a bipolar manner. Unipolar scales of pleasant affect and unpleasant affect are only moderately negatively correlated. In recent years it has become clear that psychometric approaches are unlikely to resolve the controversy, and that experimental data are needed (Cacioppo & Berntson, 1994; Diener, 1999; Schimmack, 2001).

Experimental studies have rediscovered the importance of mixed feelings for structural models of affect (see Beebe-Center, 1932). Mixed feelings are defined as concurrent experiences of pleasant affect and unpleasant affect (Beebe-Center, 1932; Kahneman, 1992; Ortony et al., 1988; Schimmack, 2001; Williams & Aaker, 2002). If pleasant affect and unpleasant affect were opposite ends of a single continuum, then it should be impossible to experience pleasure and displeasure at the same time. An analogy is the dimension of height. Short and tall are opposite ends of a single dimension and somebody cannot be short and tall. However, if pleasant affect and unpleasant affect are not opposite ends of a single dimension, then it should be possible to experimentally induce experiences of pleasant affect and unpleasant affect.

A few early studies examined mixed feelings in the realm of sensory affects (see Beebe-Center, 1932). For example, Henning (1915, in Beebe-Center, 1932) observed in some self-studies that pleasant and unpleasant odors elicit mixed feelings when the two odors were presented separately to each nostril, but not if both nostrils were exposed to both odors. Other studies exposed participants to different sensations such as a pleasant smell and unpleasant tactile stimulation (e.g., smell of vanilla and rubbing sandpaper on forehead; Wohlgemuth, 1925) or two rapidly alternating pictures (Kellogg, 1915). Unfortunately, measurement problems and the lack of significance tests rendered the findings of these studies inconclusive. These problems have been addressed in a small number of recent studies (Hemenover & Schimmack, in press; Larsen, McGraw, & Cacioppo, 2001; Larsen, McGraw, Mellers, & Cacioppo, 2004; Schimmack, 2001, 2003b; Schimmack & Colcombe, in press; Hunter, Schellenberg & Schimmack, 2004). Schimmack (2001) demonstrated mixed feelings by inducing mild unpleasant affect in participants who were initially in a good mood. Although the mild unpleasant affect reduced the intensity of pleasant affect, it was not strong enough to fully eliminate pleasant affect. As a result, participants experienced more intense mixed feelings after, rather than before, the mood induction. Hemenover and Schimmack (in press) demonstrated that disgusting humor elicits disgust and amusement. Larsen et al. (2001) demonstrated that happy-sad situations (e.g., the movie "Life is Beautiful") elicit mixed feelings of happiness and sadness. Hunter, Schellenberg & Schimmack (2004) manipulated tempo, mode, and instrumentation of musical pieces to induce mixed feelings of happiness and sadness. Fast temp, major key, and wood instrumentation all increased happiness, whereas slow tempo, minor key, and string instruments increased sadness. Pieces that combined happy and sad elements elicited significantly stronger mixed feelings than pieces that were unambiguously happy or sad.

One concern about these findings has been the question of strict co-occurrence versus alternation. Do people really feel pleasant and unpleasant at the same time, or do these two feelings alternate? To address this question, Larsen et al. (2004) created a conflicting situation in a gambling paradigm. Participants could win or lose money. Before each gamble they were informed how much money they could win or lose. Some games were designed to elicit mixed feelings by having participants win the smaller of two wins (a disappointing win). Indeed, participants reported the strongest experiences of mixed feelings when they won $5 but could have won $12. In a second study, participants could press two separate buttons, one to report feelings of pleasure and one to report feelings of displeasure. In response to disappointing wins, participants pressed both buttons for an extended period of time rather than alternating the two buttons. This finding suggests that the two experiences were indeed concurrent rather than alternating. Additional support stems from a follow-up study of Schimmack's (in press) demonstration of mixed feelings. In the new study, the computer presented the 14 affect items in a random order. As a result, some participants rated pleasant affect and unpleasant affect in close temporal proximity, whereas other participants made these judgments with several other items in between. In a large sample of 900 participants, the number of items between ratings of pleasure and displeasure had no effect on the reported level of pleasant affect and unpleasant affect. This finding also suggests that feelings of pleasure and displeasure existed concurrently for a longer period of time. In another test of the coexistence of pleasure and displeasure, Schimmack, Colcombe, and Crites (2001) forced participants to respond on a 3-point bipolar scale (pleasant, neutral, unpleasant) to unambiguous and conflicting picture pairs. Participants needed more time to respond to conflicting pairs, indicating that they indeed experienced a state of conflict rather than feeling pleasant at one time and unpleasant at another time. In sum, all recent tests of co-occurrence versus alternation are supportive of co-occurrence. However, more research is needed.

A two-dimensional conceptualization of pleasure and displeasure raises the interesting question of the empirical relation between pleasant affect and unpleasant affect (Cacioppo & Berntson, 1994; Diener & Iran-Nejad, 1986). Cacioppo and Berntson (1994) proposed three modes of activation. Reciprocal activation implies that activation of one quality leads to a decrease in the other quality. Uncoupled activation implies that activation in one affective quality can occur without changes in the other affective quality. Coactivation implies that an increase in one quality is accompanied by an increase in the other affect. Reciprocal activation is most typical. For example, Diener and Iran-Nejad (1986) obtained reports of thousands of everyday emotional experiences. They found that participants reported mixed feelings of mild to moderate intensity, but intense mixed feelings were virtually absent. Hence, intense experiences of pleasure seem to inhibit concurrent experiences of intense displeasure and vice versa. Schimmack (2001) also found that an induction of mild displeasure was accompanied by a decrease in pleasure. As a result, participants did experience mild mixed feelings, but strong mixed feelings were again absent. Schimmack and Colcombe (in press) used Kellogg's (1915) paired-picture paradigm to induce mixed emotional reactions. Participants saw pairs of pleasant, unpleasant, and neutral pictures either side-by-side or in rapid alternation (400 ms each). After each picture pair, participants rated how pleasant and how unpleasant they felt during the 4 s presentation. Conflicting picture-pairs elicited more mixed feelings than unambiguous pairs. However, positive pictures reduced the intensity of displeasure and negative pictures reduced the intensity of pleasure. The strength of this inhibition effect depended on the nature of the pictures. Positive arousing pictures (erotic pictures) produced a stronger inhibition effect and were more resistant to inhibition from negative pictures than positive calm pictures (e.g., cute animals, landscapes). The same was true for highly arousing negative pictures (mutilated bodies) versus less arousing negative pictures (graveyards, dirty objects).

In sum, mixed feelings are receiving renewed attention in emotion research. Although more research is urgently needed, the first findings show that people can experience feelings of opposite valence in the same situation. This finding supports a conceptualization of pleasure and displeasure are two distinct affective qualities, which are best represented along two unipolar dimensions (Cacioppo & Berntson, 1994; Diener & Iran-Nejad, 1986; Larsen et al., 2001; Schimmack, 2001). At the same time, the intensity of pleasure and displeasure tend to be reciprocally related. With increasing intensity of one quality, the intensity of the other quality tends to decrease.

Aspects of Affective Experiences

Schimmack et al. (2000) distinguished three aspects of affective experiences: intensity, duration, and frequency. Intensity refers to the magnitude of an affective experience at one moment in time. For example, one minute after winning a prize, people experience more intense happiness in response to winning $1,000,000 than in response to winning $1,000. Duration refers to the time from onset to offset of an affective experience. For example, the happiness about winning $1,000 may last 3 hours, whereas the happiness about winning $1,000,000 may last 6 hours. Finally, the frequency of affect refers to the number of onsets of an affective experience over a certain time interval (e.g., the number of experiences of pride in one week). The distinction between aspects of affective experiences plays an important role in research on affective determinants of attitudes. In particular, frequency, intensity, and duration may have different influences on memories of past affective experiences, which have a strong influence on attitudes.

Frequency of Affective Experiences.   The influence of affective experiences on attitudes is often mediated by the memory representation of past affective experiences. Eagly, Mladinic, and Otto (1994) found that attitudes toward Democrats or Republicans were related to emotions that respondents typically felt in response to members of each group. Lavine, Thomsen, Zanna, and Borgida (1998) found that attitudes toward candidates of the U.S. Presidency were influenced by memories of past emotional experiences in response to the U.S. Presidents. To fully understand the influence of affective experiences on attitudes in these studies, it is important to know how accurately people remember past affective experiences and how memories of affective experiences may be biased.

Empirical evidence shows accuracy and biases in frequency judgments of affective experiences (Klumb & Baltes, 1999; Parkinson, Briner, Reynolds, & Totterdell, 1995; Schimmack, 2002; Schimmack & Hartmann, 1997; Schimmack & Reisenzein, 1997; Thomas & Diener, 1990). Schimmack (2002) demonstrated high accuracy for the relative frequency of different emotions using daily diary data as a standard of comparison. Memory based judgments and diary data showed highly similar rank orders of the frequency of distinct emotions. For example, happiness is more frequent than anger, which is more frequent than jealousy. However, memory for the absolute frequency of emotions is relatively poor. People tend to underestimate the frequency of emotions, and this bias becomes more severe for frequent emotions. The strength of this bias varies across individuals. As a result, comparisons of individual differences show only moderate accuracy.

Some studies have started to examine the nature of these biases. Most pertinent to attitude research, Eagly, Chen, Chaiken, and Shaw-Barnes (1999) reviewed the literature on attitude-consistent memory. That is, attitude-consistent memories may be more accessible than attitude-inconsistent information. However, evidence for such biases is weak. In the affect literature, Schimmack and Hartmann (1997) examined the influence of a repressive coping style; that is a personality characteristic linked to the suppression or denial of unpleasant affect. The authors found that repression was linked to the experience and encoding of emotional events but had no influence on memory biases. That is, memory-based judgments accurately reflected the lower frequency of repressors' unpleasant emotions that they recorded during encoding. Oishi and Schimmack (2003) found evidence that prototypical emotional events are more memorable. U.S. Americans provided more accurate frequency judgments of emotional events that were typical of U.S. experiences, whereas Japanese participants provided more accurate frequency judgments of typical Japanese events.

Another important issue is the influence of valence on memory. If attitudes are based on memories of past emotional experiences and unpleasant experiences are more memorable, then attitudes would tend to be negatively biased. Different results have been obtained in laboratory studies (Bradley, Greenwald, Petry, & Lang, 1992; Buchanan, Denburg, Tranel, & Adolphs, 2001; Cahill & McGaugh, 1995; Hamann, Ely, Grafton, & Kilts, 1999; Ochsner, 2000; Reisberg, Heuer, McLean, & O'Shaughnessy, 1988) and studies of autobiographical memories (Menzies, 1933; Seidlitz & Diener, 1993; Thomas & Diener, 1990). Laboratory studies tend to find that negative events are more memorable, whereas studies of autobiographical memories tend to find a positive bias. One problem of laboratory studies is the possibility of confounds. Few laboratory studies have controlled for purely cognitive factors (e.g., frequency or uniqueness) that may be confounded with the valence of emotional pictures. For example, pictures of beaches are more common than pictures of burn victims. One common finding is that emotional or arousing events are more memorable than neutral events.

One important, yet neglected issue is the context-sensitivity of memories of past emotional experiences. For example, past experiences of anger can only influence attitudes toward political candidates if people are able to distinguish anger in response to one candidate from anger in response to another candidate. Confusion is unlikely when people rely on the conscious retrieval of individual episodes. However, often impressions about the frequency of affective experiences are based on fast and implicit processes that do not involve retrieval of specific episodes (Schimmack, 2002; Schimmack & Reisenzein, 1997; Robinson & Clore, 2002). Schimmack and Reisenzein (1997) found evidence for context-sensitivity in conditional probability judgments. People reported different frequencies of emotions in the context of other emotions. For example, anger was judged to be more frequent in the context of jealousy than in the context of guilt. Schimmack (1997) found that people accurately distinguished the frequency of the same emotion in two consecutive weeks, using daily diary data as a standard of comparison. In contrast, Robbinson and Clore (2002) suggested that people often rely on generalized semantic information to judge the frequency of emotions. To the extent that people rely on semantic information, their impressions are bound to be insensitive to the frequency of emotions in specific contexts. Another important question for future research may be the weight of individual affective experiences in determining the affective component of attitudes.

It is possible that respondents discount some affective experiences. For example, liking for peaches may not be based on the frequency of all pleasant and unpleasant experiences with peaches. Rather, people may discount atypical experiences (e.g., a rotten peach). Thus, the frequency of pleasant and unpleasant experiences with an attitude object may be an imperfect indicator of the affective component of an attitude. In sum, the existing evidence suggests a fair amount of accuracy in memories of the frequency of past affective experiences. At the same time, it is likely that the accessibility of affective memories is also influenced by systematic biases, although many plausible biases do not seem to have a strong effect.

Intensity. Although many attitudes are based on numerous affective experiences, some attitudes toward rare attitude-objects may be based on a single affective experience. For example, attitudes towards vacation destinations may be based on a single visit. Attitudes based on a single affective experience also influence the frequency of future experiences. For example, people tend to return to restaurants after a positive experience and may never return to restaurants where they had a negative experience. Hence, it is also important to know how people remember a single affective experience. No study has reported hedonic reversals in memory, probably because instances of recalling a pleasant experience as unpleasant and vice versa are rare. It is more likely that people forget an affective experience. For example, sometimes people rent a movie or buy a book, only to discover after a short while that they already saw the movie or read the book. This may typically occur when the affective experience was low in intensity and arousal (see previous section). Whether people can forget very intense emotional experiences (e.g., traumatic events) or may falsely remember intense affective experiences that never happened is a controversial issue (see Loftus, 1994) but not very important for attitude research. In general, "people remember their emotions fairly accurately" (p. 2, Levine & Safer, 2002). Nevertheless, memories of affective experiences are also subject to several biases (Levine, 1997; Levine, Prohaska, Burgess, Rice, & Laulhere, 2001; Levine & Safer, 2002; Safer, Levine, & Drapalski, 2002). One bias is related to changes in the cognitive appraisal of the same event. Memory based judgments of past emotions are biased by the appraisals of the same event from the present situation. For example, Safer, Bonanno, and Field (2001) found that memories of grief 6 months after the death of a loved one were more strongly predicted by current grief 5 years later than by the ratings of grief that were made 6 months after the death of a loved one. Levine et al. (2001) found that memories of emotional responses to the O. J. Simpson verdict were influenced by present appraisals of his guilt. Typically, biases increase with the time between the occurrence of an event and memory retrieval. Furthermore, biases tend to be stronger if relevant cognitions changed (Levine & Safer, 2002). Hence, memories of recent affective experiences that influence current attitudes are likely to be relatively accurate, whereas memories of past affective experiences and past attitudes are more likely to be biased.

Duration. Rationally we would assume that prolonged experiences of pleasure or displeasure have a stronger influence on attitudes than brief experiences of the same intensity. However, in a series of studies, Fredrickson and Kahneman (1993) demonstrated *duration neglect* in attitude judgments. Fredrickson and Kahneman (1993) obtained online ratings of affective experiences while participants watched brief film clips, which varied in length. Afterwards participants evaluated all film clips from memory. The retrospective ratings were mostly influenced by the intensity at the peak moment and at the end, while participants neglected duration. An everyday example may be movies. Although an excellent 3-hour movie provides a larger amount of pleasure than an equally excellent 2-hour movie, it is unlikely that playing time influences attitudes toward movies. Subsequent studies have demonstrated some limitations of the peak-end rule (Ariely & Loewenstein; 2000; Ariely, Kahneman, & Lowenstein, 2000; Schreiber & Kahneman, 2000). Schreiber and Kahneman (2000) examined evaluations of noise sequences. An important difference to previous studies was the presence of a notable change in intensity within a sequence. For example, one sequence played intense noise for 4 s and mild noise for 8 s, while another sequence played intense noise for 8 s and mild noise for 4 s. The peak-end rule predicts that the two sequences are evaluated equally because they have the same peak and end. Contrary to this prediction, participants rated the sequences with the longer intense noise as more annoying than the sequence with the shorter intense noise. However, this effect was relatively small. Duration also appears to be a significant predictor of evaluations in within-subject studies, which render the duration of an episode salient (Schreiber & Kahneman, 2000; Ariely & Lowenstein, 2000). However, even in these studies duration effects are quite small. In sum, retrospective evaluations of affective episodes are largely influenced by peak and end intensity, whereas duration plays a minor role.

Implications of Aspects for Attitude Research. The distinction between aspects of affective experiences raises the interesting question of the relation between aspects of affective experiences and attitudes. Research on the peak-end rule and duration neglect starts to address this question, but the research is limited to evaluations of brief episodes. Thus, frequency is irrelevant for these evaluations. It is possible that other results are obtained for attitude objects with repeated experiences that may even differ in valence. Research on the affective determinants of life satisfaction judgments suggests that this is indeed the case. Ample evidence shows that past experiences of pleasant affect and unpleasant affect are a strong determinant of life satisfaction (Diener, Sandvik, & Pavot, 1991; Schimmack, Diener, & Oishi, 2002). Schimmack and Diener (1997) pointed out that the amount of affect can be decomposed into a frequency and an intensity component. Diener et al. (1991) found that the frequency of pleasant and unpleasant affect was a stronger predictor of life-satisfaction judgments than the intensity. That is, an individual with a few extremely positive experiences has a less positive attitude toward his or her life than an individual with many mild positive experiences. Schimmack (2003) examined the influence of frequency, intensity, and duration on life-satisfaction judgments. Once more, frequency played an important role in life-satisfaction judgments. However, intensity did interact with frequency. That is, when two individuals had the same frequency of negative emotions, the individual with more intense emotions was less satisfied.

At first sight, the relative neglect of intensity in life satisfaction judgments seems to contradict the peak-end rule, which implies that intensity at two moments can predict the final attitude very well. However, the peak-end rule only applies to evaluations of a single episode, whereas life-satisfaction judgments are based on a heterogeneous set of affective experiences. Schimmack (2005) examined attitudes (i.e., like vs. dislike judgments) toward complex affective events. The affective events were several series of five affective pictures. The pictures varied in intensity, duration, and frequency of pleasant and unpleasant pictures. Consistent with Fredrickson and Kahneman (1993), duration of a single picture had no effect on subsequent liking judgments. Consistent with Diener et al. (1991), frequency of pleasant or unpleasant pictures had a strong effect on liking of affect series.

In sum, affective experiences vary in intensity, duration, and frequency. These aspects of affective experiences can play different roles in the formation of an attitude. For some attitude objects people may neglect duration, for others they may neglect the intensity or frequency. More research should examine how aspects of affective experiences influence attitudes toward traditional attitude objects such as political opinions, consumer products, and prejudice.

Affective Neuroscience

We conclude our chapter with a brief review of the rapidly growing literature on affective processes in the brain. Ultimately, we hope that an understanding of the biological processes underlying affect can contribute to our understanding of affective experiences and their influences on attitudes. At the simplest level, the brain must (a) analyze and make sense of sensory information, and (b) prepare and execute appropriate motor responses to this sensory information (Berntson, Boysen, & Cacioppo, 1993). Furthermore, both processes can involve memory, as sensory information can be compared to previous sensory representations and plans or possible motor responses can be compared against previous motor representations. The difficulty in studying the association between affect and the neural systems that are associated with it is that affect is closely associated with both sensory and motor functions. For example, the link between sensory functions and affect is illustrated by research investigating the neural systems that are responsible for evaluating biologically relevant stimuli such as food (Berridge, 1996) and research exploring the neural systems that are need for affective learning (Armony, Servan-Schreiber, Cohen, & LeDoux, 1995). Alternatively, the link between motor functions and affect is illustrated by research exploring the neural systems that are involved in action tendencies to approach or withdrawal from stimuli (Davidson & Irwin, 1999) and research investigating autonomic (e.g., cardiac and vascular) somatic (e.g., skeletomotor) responses that are associated with affective experiences (e.g., see Cacioppo, Berntson, & Klein, 1992).

The neural systems associated with affect not only serve as a bridge between sensory and motor functions; they also span diverse neural systems within both these functional divisions. We are endowed with a diverse set of sensory systems that are each specialized for detecting different types of stimuli (e.g., molecules, light, pressure, etc.) and nearly any type of stimulus and the neural activity it evokes has the potential to either (a) evoke an affective reaction and/or (b) moderate an affective reaction caused by a stimulus in a completely different sensory system. An essential function of the chemical senses of taste and smell, for instance, is to identify stimuli that are either beneficial (e.g., food) or harmful (e.g., toxin).

Research on anencephalic infants who are born without a cortex suggest that neural systems in the brainstem are sufficient for (a) identifying and evaluating these beneficial and harmful classes of stimuli, (b) evoking facial motor responses associated with either pleasure or disgust, and (c) initiating the appropriate behavioral action (i.e., intake or rejection). Thus, these biologically beneficial and harmful classes of chemical stimuli appear to evoke reflexive affective responses that are initiated by neural systems in the brainstem. In spite of this very close link between a stimulus and affective/evaluative response, the nature of these affective reactions can vary dramatically depending on the activity of interoceptive sensory systems that monitor the internal environment. That is, the pleasure people derive from stimuli such as sugar depends on hunger/satiation – sugars are evaluated more positively when people are transiently or chronically food deprived than when they are satiated (Cabanac, 1971; Cabanac, Duclaux, & Spector, 1971).

After neural systems finish analyzing and evaluating an external stimulus (or even an internal stimulus such as an affective memory or thought), they must transmit this information to other neural systems that can prepare and implement the appropriate motor functions. An early step in this process is likely to be comparing possible behaviors to memory representations and sensory analyses. For example, the 98-pound kicker who spent a night in the hospital after punching a 300-pound defensive tackle who angered him might elect for a different course of action the next time he becomes angry with someone 3 times his size. Just as contextual factors can dramatically alter affective sensory processing (i.e., hunger's impact on the evaluation of sugar), motor output of affective processes can vary dramatically depending on contextual information. For example, if a person's cardiac functioning, electrodermal activity (sweating), or zygomaticus major activity (muscle responsible for pulling the corners of the mouth up and back for smiling) is already significantly elevated before an affective experience, the activity in these systems may not increase as much as they might normally do. Alternatively, the ability of neural motor systems to inhibit or control various output systems can vary so it is possible to see changes in one output system that is preparing for a certain action that is not matched by output in a second system because the second system is being inhibited. The autonomic nervous system of our 98-pound kicker, for instance, may be preparing for a fight when he becomes angry at the 300-pound defensive tackle, while the somatic nervous system, which controls voluntary skeletomotor activity, is being effectively inhibited.

A complicating factor in understanding the diverse research investigating the association between affect and neural processes is that different research approaches have tended to focus on different species. Much of the research exploring the link between affect and sensory functions has used nonhumans, primarily rodents, whereas much of the research exploring the link between affect and executive/motor functions has used humans. Given the enormous similarities between the phylogenetically older areas of human and nonhuman brains and the biological importance of affective processes, one might expect considerable overlap across different species. However, despite the similarities among different mammalian species, there are some important differences in very rudimentary processes. Thus, it is important to validate research findings in nonhumans with human participants. For example, gustatory neurons in the brain stem change their responsiveness to food based on interoceptive signals of hunger/satiety in rats but not monkeys (Yaxley, Rolls, Sienkiewicz, & Scott, 1985). Thus, in rats the brainstem appears to be adjusting the affective significance of a gustatory stimulus based on interoceptive sensations of hunger. In monkeys, however, this process of evaluative adjustment based on interoceptive feedback appears to occur in the cortex (Scott & Plata-Salamán, 1999). The same evaluative process, therefore, appears to be occurring at two different levels of the brain hierarchy in rodents and primates. There may even be significant differences between humans and other primates in neural structures such as the amygdala, which is an important neural structure associated with affect (Zald, 2003). Recent advances in neural imaging, especially functional magnetic resonance imaging (fMRI), allow for the first time to study the neurological processes underlying human affective experience that heretofore have been very difficult to examine.

The easy part of associating affective processes with neural processes is identifying regions of the brain that are important for the affective process. Certain brain regions have long been known to be important for affective processes because damage to those brain regions disrupts discrete affective processes. For example, certain regions of the brain (e.g., amygdala, prefrontal cortex) and/or discrete neural systems that use particular neurotransmitters (e.g., dopamine, endorphins) are universally accepted as being important for affective processes. However, the specific functions of these areas are still under dispute. The remainder of this section provides a brief overview of research programs linking specific affective processes to specific neurological systems.

There has been a substantial body of research, primarily in rodents and other nonhuman animals, that has investigated the neural substrates that are important for affective or hedonic processing of motivationally relevant stimuli such as food. This research illustrates that these affective neural systems are hierarchically organized and there are parallel interacting systems that perform slightly different affective functions. In a hierarchical evaluative system, successive neural processing units elaborate upon previous evaluative outputs by incorporating heretofore unavailable information (Berridge, 1996). For example, decerebrate rats (brain stem separated from forebrain) display positive evaluative reactions and behaviors toward sucrose when it is placed in their mouths, suggesting that evaluative mechanisms located in the brainstem are sufficient for evaluative coding. The affective reactions and behavior of decerebrate rats, however, are not altered if sucrose is paired with illness caused by LiCl injections (Grill & Norgren, 1978b). Thus, decerebrate rats do not learn to associate the food with illness as do rats that have intact brains suggesting that neural units located in the forebrain (cortex) are necessary for associating taste with illness and altering evaluative reactions to stimuli accordingly.

Evidence for the parallel evaluative systems is demonstrated by research using multiple measures of affective output. Rats display a characteristic set of expressive behaviors when pleasant (e.g., sweet) substances are placed in their mouths and a different set of expressive behaviors when unpleasant (e.g., bitter) substances are placed in their mouths (Grill & Norgren, 1978a, 1978b). Researchers have measured these taste reactivity responses and compared them to ingestive responses (e.g., food seeking and intake) to elucidate the affective mechanisms that are associated with food intake and also drug abuse. Although research examining these two types of behaviors has revealed that many factors influence both taste reactivity and ingestive responses to food (e.g., hunger, satiety, conditioned taste aversion), it is possible to alter either taste reactivity or ingestive responses without changing the other (e.g., see Berridge, 1996; Berridge & Robinson, 1998 for reviews). Based on these findings, Berridge and his colleagues have proposed that there are two neural systems that give rise to affective behaviors—one that affectively or hedonically evaluates stimuli ("liking") and another that instigates goal-directed behavior toward that stimulus ("wanting") (see Berridge, 1996; Berridge & Robinson, 1998 for reviews).

There has been substantial research investigating the role of the amygdala in affective neural processing since Klüver and Bucy (1937) reported that temporal lobe lesions in monkeys dramatically altered their normal affective reactions to stimuli and Weiskrantz (1956) demonstrated that the amygdala accounted for this effect. In some ways the amygdala is ideal for affective sensory processing because it has extensive and reciprocal connections with exteroceptive and interoceptive senses (see Zald, 2003). For example, the amygdala receives direct input from the thalamus, a primary sensory processing structure in the brain. This connection may explain the speed and automaticity of some affective processes (Zajonc, 1980). Most visual information travels from the retina to the lateral geniculate nuclei of the thalamus and then to the primary visual cortex; if this route is damaged, animals are functionally blind. Recent research suggests that the amygdala receives information from a secondary visual pathway that travels from the retina to the superior colliculi in the brainstem and through the pulvinar in the thalamus before going to the amygdala and that this path might account for emotional reactions to unseen stimuli (Morris, Scott, & Dolan, 1999; see also Zald, 2003). Finally, because the amygdala projects back to primary sensory areas, it may be able to influence or enhance sensory processing (i.e., focus attention) of affective stimuli.

Although the amygdala responds to a wide variety of affective stimuli, there is considerable evidence that the amygdala is particularly important for affective learning. LeDoux and his colleagues (see Armony, Servan-Schreiber, Cohen, & LeDoux, 1995; LeDoux, 1996) have conducted extensive research demonstrating the critical role the amygdala plays in fear conditioning – that is, learning to associate an initially neutral stimulus with a fear-evoking stimulus. Also consistent with the idea that the amygdala is important for affective learning and memory is research suggesting that the amygdala (a) responds to novel stimuli and (b) habituates fairly rapidly to affective stimuli (Cahill & McGaugh, 1998; LeDoux, 1996; Zald, 2003). Thus, the amygdala may be important for learning associations between new stimuli and stimuli that evoke affective responses and also for learning to ignore affectively laden stimuli that are not associated with significant pleasant or unpleasant consequences.

In spite of considerable evidence that the amygdala is important for affective sensory processes and learning, it is clear that it is not the only neural structure that is involved in these functions. For instance, the amygdala is important in learning the relation between water and electric shock, but not between water and bitter taste (Cahill & McGaugh, 1990). In addition, the amygdala seems to be more important for highly arousing affective stimuli and less important for low or moderately arousing affective stimuli (Adolphs, Tranel, & Damasio, 1998; Cahill & McGaugh, 1990) and appears more important for affective sensory processing than affective production (Anderson & Phelps, 2000).

Studies with humans also suggest that the amygdala plays a different role in humans than in other species. Cheng, Knight, Smith, Stein, and Helmstetter (2003) found that amygdala activity was correlated with the peripheral physiological skin conductance response to a conditioning stimulus, but not with the learning of the significance of the conditioning stimulus. This finding has two implications. First, amygdala activity may be more strongly related to the response side of an emotion than with the appraisal component. Second, its correlation with the skin conductance response suggests that amygdala activity is related to arousal, but not the valence of emotional experiences. This conclusion is also supported by evidence that the amygdala is activated by both positive and negative emotional stimuli (Hamann & Mao, 2002; Hamann, Ely, Hoffman, & Kilts, 2002; Karama et al., 2002; Sander & Scheich, 2001). Hence, amygdala activity does not provide the salient distinction between pleasant and unpleasant experiences. Furthermore, the amygdala does not seem to be necessary for the experience of emotions. Anderson and Phelps (2002) examined emotional experiences of 20 patients with unilateral amygdala damage and 1 patient with bilateral amygdala damage. The results showed no differences between affective experiences of patients with amygdala damage and normal controls. In sum, it seems unlikely that the amygdala is a causal factor in the generation of emotional experiences, in particular the hedonic tone of emotional experiences.

Another structure that receives a lot of attention is the nucleus accumbens in the ventral striatum (Rolls, 1999). Animal studies suggest that this structure plays an important role in the regulation of approach motivation. Animal models show that self-stimulation in this area is reinforcing and leads to the neglect of all other needs and activities. Not surprisingly, the structure has been implicated in addiction research. Rewards and approach behavior can be linked to positive emotional experiences. However, the link does not imply that the nucleus accumbens is a cause of pleasant emotions. Indeed, approach motivation can co-occur with strong displeasure; for example, when somebody is frantically looking for a lost key. At the same time, many experiences of pleasant emotions can occur without approach motivation (e.g., gratitude, relief, pride). For example, pride is typically experienced after achieving a goal that was pursued with much effort. Hence, the pleasant experience starts exactly at the time when approach motivation ends. In support of the distinction between approach motivation and pleasant experiences, Knutson, Fong, Adams, Varner, and Hommer (2001) found fMRI activity in the nucleus accumbens during the anticipation of a rewarded-response, but not during the receiving of a reward. No measures of subjective experiences were obtained, but it is plausible to assume that the anticipation of an uncertain reward was less pleasant and probably more unpleasant than the receiving of an actual reward. Further evidence stems from a comparison of two studies that measured fMRI activity in response to attractive faces. In one study, attractive female faces were shown as a reward for performance on a reaction time task (Aharon et al., 2001). In the other study, attractive male and female faces were shown while participants had to judge the sex of the person in the picture (O'Doherty et al., 2003). Only the former study found fMRI activity in the nucleus accumbens, suggesting that it was the approach motivation underlying the reaction time (RT) task that produced the activity, not the presentation of attractive faces themselves.

Another area that has been implicated in the processing of affective information is the orbitofrontal cortex (Rolls, 1999). Rolls (1999) reviews animal research with primates and human fMRI work indicating that neurons in the orbitofrontal cortex respond to the reward value of numerous stimuli, including responses to positive and negative events. O'Doherty, Kringelbach, Rolls, Hornak, and Andrews (2001) assessed brain activity during a gambling task, in which participants choose between two options. Gains and losses varied in magnitude and probability and across stimuli. The study revealed activation in the orbitofrontal cortex that correlated with the magnitude of rewards and punishment, with different areas being more sensitive to rewards or punishments. O'Doherty et al. (2003) also found increased activation in the orbitofrontal cortex in response to pictures of attractive faces. Additional evidence stems from brain imaging studies of sexual arousal. Several studies have reported increased activity in the orbitofrontal cortices of men and women while watching erotica (Karama et al., 2002; Redoute et al., 2000). A PET scan study found activation in the orbitofrontal cortex in response to olfactory (e.g., mint, butyric acid), visual (a beach, a surgical operation), and auditory (a flowing river, a woman crying) emotional stimuli (Royet et al., 2000). Anderson et al. (2003) found that activity in the orbitofrontal cortex correlated with the valence of olfactory stimuli, whereas amygdala activity was related to the intensity, but not the valence of stimuli. In sum, these studies suggest that the orbitofrontal cortex plays an important role in the evaluation of stimuli and the elicitation of pleasant and unpleasant experiences, in particular sensory affective experiences. Anderson et al. (2003) even found significant correlations between subjective reports of the pleasantness and unpleasantness of odors and the strength of activation in areas of the orbitofrontal cortex. This finding suggests that activation in the orbitofrontal cortex is the most promising candidate for an objective, neurological measure of the valence of affective experiences.

CONCLUSION

We reviewed the literature on affect, with a special emphasis on affective experience. We proposed a taxonomy of affective experience that distinguishes types, qualities, and aspects of affective experience. Different types of affective experience have different origins and have different consequences for the formation and change of attitudes. Emotions and sensory affects are more likely to have lasting effects on attitudes than moods. A salient distinction between qualities of affective experience is valence (pleasant vs. unpleasant). Recent evidence of mixed feelings suggests that pleasure and displeasure are distinct affective qualities. One important avenue for future research is relating mixed affective experience to ambivalent attitudes (Priester & Petty, 1996). We also believe that attitude research can benefit from the distinction among aspects of affective experience. Some attitudes may be based on a few intense experiences, whereas others may be based on frequent mild affective experiences. Finally, the rapid progress in affective neuroscience provides new opportunities to study the neurological underpinning of the affective component of attitudes.

REFERENCES

Adolph, K. E. (2000). Specificity of learning: Why infants fall over a veritable cliff. *Psychological Science, 11*, 290–295.

Adolphs, R., Tranel, D., & Damasio, A. R. (1998). The human amygdala in social judgment. *Nature, 393*(6684), 470–474.

Aharon, I., Etcoff, N., Ariely, D., Chabris, C. F., O'Connor, E., & Breiter, H. C. (2001). Beautiful faces have variable reward value. fMRI behavioral evidence. *Neuron, 32*, 537–551.

Albarracin, D., & Kumkale, G. T. (2003). Affect as information in persuasion: A model of affect identification and discounting. *Journal of Personality and Social Psychology, 84*, 453–469.

Anderson A. K., Christoff, K., Stappen, I., Panitz, D., Ghahremani, D. G., Glover, G., Gabrieli, J. D. E., & Sobel, N. (2003). Dissociated neural representations of intensity and valence in human olfaction. *Nature Neuroscience, 6*, 196–202.

Anderson, A. K., & Phelps, E. A. (2000). Expression without recognition: Contributions of the human amygdala to emotional communication. *Psychological Science, 11*, 106–111.

Anderson, A. K., & Phelps, E. A. (2002). Is the human amygdala critical for the subjective experience of emotion?: Evidence of intact dispositional affect in patients with amygdala lesions. *Journal of Cognitive Neuroscience, 14*, 709–720.

Ariely, D., Kahneman, D., & Loewenstein, G. (2000). [Joint comment] on "When does duration matter in judgment and decision making?" (Ariely & Loewenstein, 2000). *Journal of Experimental Psychology: General, 129*, 524–529.

Ariely, D., & Loewenstein, G. (2000). When does duration matter in judgment and decision making? *Journal of Experimental Psychology: General, 129*, 508–523.

Armony, J. L., Servan-Schreiber, D., Cohen, J. D., & LeDoux, J. E. (1995). An anatomically constrained neural network model of fear conditioning. *Behavioral Neuroscience, 109*, 246–257.

Ayabe-Kanamura, S., Schicker, I., Laska, M., Hudson, R., Distel, H., Kobayakawa, T., & Saito, S. (1998). Differences in perception of everyday odors: A Japanese-German cross-cultural study. *Chemical Senses, 23*, 31–38.

Baeyens, F., Eelen, P., Crombez, G., & De Houwer, J. (2001). On the role of beliefs in observational flavor conditioning. *Current Psychology: Developmental, Learning, Personality, Social, 20*, 183–203.

Barrett, L. F., & Fossum, T. (2001). Mental representations of affect knowledge. *Cognition & Emotion, 15*, 333–363.

Bartoshuk, L. M., & Beauchamp, G. K. (1994). Chemical senses. *Annual Review of Psychology, 45*, 419–449.

Beebe-Center, J. G. (1932). *The psychology of pleasantness and unpleasantness*. Oxford, England: Van Nostrand.

Berglund, B., Berglund, U., Engen, T., & Ekman, G. (1973). Multidimensional analysis of twenty-one odors. *Scandinavian Journal of Psychology, 14*, 131–137.

Berntson, G. G., Boysen, S. T., & Cacioppo, J. T. (1993). Neurobehavioral organization and the cardinal principle of evaluative bivalence. In F. M. Crinella & J. Yu (Eds.), *Brain mechanisms: Papers in memory of Robert Thompson* (pp. 75–102). New York: New York Academy of Sciences.

Berridge, K. C. (1996). Food reward: Brain substrates of wanting and liking. *Neuroscience & Biobehavioral Reviews. Special Issue: Society for the Study of Ingestive Behavior, Second Independent Meeting, 20*, 1–25.

Berridge, K. C., & Robinson, T. E. (1998). What is the role of dopamine in reward: Hedonic impact, reward learning, or incentive salience? *Brain Research Reviews, 28*, 309–369.

Berridge, K. C., & Winkielman, P. (2003). What is an unconscious emotion? The case for unconscious "liking." *Cognition & Emotion, 17*, 181–211.

Bornstein, R. F. (1989). Exposure and affect: Overview and meta-analysis of research, 1968–1987. *Psychological Bulletin, 106*, 265–289.

Bornstein, R. F., & D'Agostino, P. R. (1994). The attribution and discounting of perceptual fluency: Preliminary tests of a perceptual fluency/attributional model of the mere exposure effect. *Social Cognition, 12*, 103–128.

Bradley, M. M., Codispoti, M., Cuthbert, B. N., & Lang, P. J. (2001). Emotion and motivation I: Defensive and appetitive reactions in picture processing. *Emotion, 1*, 276–298.

Bradley, M. M., Greenwald, M. K., Petry, M. C., & Lang, P. J. (1992). Remembering pictures: Pleasure and arousal in memory. *Journal of Experimental Psychology: Learning, Memory, & Cognition, 18*, 379–390.

Breckler, S. J., & Wiggins, E. C. (1993). Emotional responses and the affective component of attitude. *Journal of Social Behavior and Personality, 8*, 281–296.

Buchanan, T. W., Denburg, N. L., Tranel, D., & Adolphs, R. (2001). Verbal and nonverbal emotional memory following unilateral amygdala damage. *Learning & Memory, 8*, 326–335.

Bushman, B. J., & Baumeister, R. F. (1998). Threatened egotism, narcissism, self-esteem, and direct and displaced aggression: Does self-love or self-hate lead to violence? *Journal of Personality and Social Psychology, 75*, 219–229.

Cabanac, M. (1971). Physiological role of pleasure. *Science, 173*, 1103–1107.

Cabanac, M., Duclaux, R., & Spector, N. H. (1971). Sensory feedback in regulation of body weight: Is there a ponderostat. *Nature, 229*, 125–127.

Cacioppo, J. T., & Berntson, G. G. (1994). Relationship between attitudes and evaluative space: A critical review, with emphasis on the separability of positive and negative substrates. *Psychological Bulletin, 115*, 401–423.

Cacioppo, J. T., Berntson, G. G., & Klein, D. J. (1992). What is an emotion? The role of somatovisceral afference, with special emphasis on somatovisceral "illusions." In M. S. Clark (Ed.), *Review of personality and social psychology: Emotion and social behavior*. (Vol. 14, pp. 63–98). Thousand Oaks, CA, US: Sage.

Cahill, L., & McGaugh, J. L. (1990). Amygdaloid complex lesions differentially affect retention of tasks using appetitive and aversive reinforcement. *Behavioral Neuroscience, 104*, 532–543.

Cahill, L., & McGaugh, J. L. (1995). A novel demonstration of enhanced memory associated with emotional arousal. *Consciousness & Cognition, 4*, 410–421.

Cahill, L., & McGaugh, J. L. (1998). Mechanisms of emotional arousal and lasting declarative memory. *Trends in Neurosciences, 21*, 294–299.

Campos, J. J., Langer, A., & Krowitz, A. (1970). Cardiac responses on the visual cliff in prelocomotor human infants. *Science, 170*(3954), 196–197.

Carrasco, M., & Ridout, J. B. (1993). Olfactory perception and olfactory imagery: A multidimensional analysis. *Journal of Experimental Psychology: Human Perception & Performance, 19*, 287–301.

Chaiken, S., & Eagly, A. H. (1983). Communication modality as a determinant of persuasion: The role of communicator salience. *Journal of Personality and Social Psychology, 45*, 241–256.

Cheng, D. T., Knight, D. C., Smith, C. N., Stein, E. A., & Helmstetter, F. J. (2003). Functional MRI of human amygdala activity during Pavlovian fear conditioning: Stimulus processing versus response expression. *Behavioral Neuroscience, 117*, 3–10.

Chwalisz, K., Diener, E., & Gallagher, D. (1988). Autonomic arousal feedback and emotional experience: Evidence from the spinal cord injured. *Journal of Personality and Social Psychology, 54*, 820–828.

Clark, L. A., & Watson, D. (1988). Mood and the mundane: Relations between daily life events and self-reported mood. *Journal of Personality and Social Psychology, 54*, 296–308.

Clore, G. L. (1994). Why emotions are never unconscious. In P. Ekman and R. J. Davidson (Eds.), *The nature of emotion* (pp. 285–290). Oxford, UK: Oxford University Press.

Clore, G. L., Ortony, A., & Foss, M. A. (1987). The psychological foundations of the affective lexicon. *Journal of Personality and Social Psychology, 53*, 751–766.

Cobos, P., Sanchez, M., Garcia, C., Vera, M. N., & Vila, J. (2002). Revisiting the James versus Cannon debate on emotion: Startle and autonomic modulation in patients with spinal cord injuries. *Biological Psychology, 61*, 251–269.

Conway, M. A., & Bekerian, D. A. (1987). Situational knowledge and emotions. *Cognition & Emotion, 1*, 145–191.

Davidson, R. J., & Irwin, W. (1999). The functional neuroanatomy of emotion and affective style. *Trends in Cognitive Sciences, 3*, 11–21.

David, J. P., Green, P. J., Martin, R., & Suls, J. (1997). Differential roles of neuroticism, extraversion, and event desirability for mood in daily life: An integrative model of top-down and bottom-up influences. *Journal of Personality and Social Psychology, 73*, 149–159.

De Houwer, J. (2001). Contingency awareness and evaluative conditioning: When will it be enough? *Consciousness & Cognition: An International Journal, 10*, 550–558.

De Houwer, J., Thomas, S., & Baeyens, F. (2001). Association learning of likes and dislikes: A review of 25 years of research on human evaluative conditioning. *Psychological Bulletin, 127*, 853–869.

Devine, P. G. (1989). Stereotypes and prejudice: Their automatic and controlled components. *Journal of Personality and Social Psychology, 56*, 5–18.

Diener, E. (1999). Introduction to the special section on the structure of emotion. *Journal of Personality and Social Psychology, 76*, 803–804.

Diener, E., & Emmons, R. A. (1984). The independence of positive and negative affect. *Journal of Personality and Social Psychology, 47*, 1105–1117.

Diener, E., & Iran-Nejad, A. (1986). The relationship in experience between various types of affect. *Journal of Personality and Social Psychology, 50*, 1031–1038.

Diener, E., Sandvik, E., & Pavot, W. (1991). Happiness is the frequency, not the intensity, of positive versus negative affect. In F. Strack, M. Argyle, & N. Schwarz (Eds.), *Subjective well-being: An interdisciplinary perspective* (pp. 119–139). Elmsford, NY: Pergamon.

Dijksterhuis, A., & Aarts, H. (2003). On wildebeests and humans: The preferential detection of negative stimuli. *Psychological Science, 14*, 14–18.

Dimberg, U., Thunberg, M., & Elmehed, K. (2000). Unconscious facial reactions to emotional facial expressions. *Psychological Science, 11*, 86–89.

Dutton, D. G., & Aron, A. P. (1974). Some evidence for heightened sexual attraction under conditions of high anxiety. *Journal of Personality and Social Psychology, 30*, 510–517.

Eagly, A. H., & Chaiken, S. (1993). *The psychology of attitudes.* Orlando, FL: Harcourt Brace Jovanovich College Publishers.

Eagly, A. H., Chen, S., Chaiken, S., & Shaw-Barnes, K. (1999). The impact of attitudes on memory: An affair to remember. *Psychological Bulletin, 125*, 64–89.

Eagly, A. H., Mladinic, A., & Otto, S. (1994). Cognitive and affective bases of attitudes toward social groups and social policies. *Journal of Experimental Social Psychology, 30*, 113–137.

Egloff, B., Schmukle, S. C., Burns, L. R., Kohlmann, C., & Hock, M. (2003). Facets of dynamic Positive Affect: Differentiating joy, interest, and activation in the Positive and Negative Affect Schedule (PANAS). *Journal of Personality and Social Psychology, 85*, 528–540.

Egloff, B., Tausch, A., Kohlmann, C., & Krohne, H. W. (1995). Relationships between time of day, day of the week, and positive mood: Exploring the role of the mood measure. *Motivation & Emotion, 19*, 99–110.

Ehrlichman, H., & Halpern, J. N. (1988). Affect and memory: Effects of pleasant and unpleasant odors on retrieval of happy and unhappy memories. *Journal of Personality and Social Psychology, 55*, 769–779.

Ekman, P. (1973). Universal facial expressions in emotion. *Studia Psychologica, 15*, 140–147.

Ekman, P. (1992). Are there basic emotions? *Psychological Review, 99*, 550–553.

Ekman, P., & Davidson, R. J. (Eds.). (1994). *The nature of emotion.* New York: Oxford University Press.

Feldman Barrett, L., & Russell, J. A. (1998). Independence and bipolarity in the structure of current affect. *Journal of Personality and Social Psychology, 74*, 967–984.

Foster, C. A., Witcher, B. S., Campbell, W. K., & Green, J. D. (1998). Arousal and attraction: Evidence for automatic and controlled processes. *Journal of Personality and Social Psychology, 74*, 86–101.

Fredrickson, B. L., & Kahneman, D. (1993). Duration neglect in retrospective evaluations of affective episodes. *Journal of Personality and Social Psychology, 65*, 45–55.

Frei, E., Gamma, A., Pascual-Marqui, R., Lehmann, D., Hell, D., & Vollenweider, F. X. (2001). Localization of MDMA-induced brain activity in healthy volunteers using low resolution brain electromagnetic tomography (LORETA). *Human Brain Mapping, 14*, 152–165.

Frijda, N. H. (1986). *The emotions*. Cambridge, UK: Cambridge University Press.

Frijda, N. H. (1993). Moods, emotion episodes, and emotions. In M. Lewis & J. M. Haviland (Eds.), *Handbook of emotions; Handbook of emotions* (pp. 381–403). New York: Guilford.

Frijda, N. H., Kuipers, P., & ter Schure, E. (1989). Relations among emotion, appraisal, and emotional action readiness. *Journal of Personality and Social Psychology, 57*, 212–228.

Frijda, N. H., & Zeelenberg, M. (2001). Appraisal: What is the dependent? In K. R. Scherer & A. Schorr (Eds.), *Appraisal processes in emotion: Theory, methods, research* (pp. 141–155). London: Oxford University Press.

Gasper, K., & Clore, G. L. (1998). The persistent use of negative affect by anxious individuals to estimate risk. *Journal of Personality and Social Psychology, 74*, 1350–1363.

Giner-Sorolla, R. (1999). Affect in attitude: Immediate and deliberative perspectives. In S. Chaiken & Y. Trope (Eds.), *Dual-process theories in social psychology; Dual-process theories in social psychology* (pp. 441–461). New York: Guilford.

Gold, A. E., MacLeod, K. M., Deary, I. J., & Frier, B. M. (1995). Hypoglycemia-induced cognitive dysfunction in diabetes mellitus: Effect of hypoglycemia unawareness. *Physiology & Behavior, 58*, 501–511.

Gray, J. A. (1994). Three fundamental emotion systems. In P. Ekman and R. J. Davidson (Eds.), *The nature of emotion* (pp. 243–248). Oxford, UK: Oxford University Press.

Green, D. P., Goldman, S. L., & Salovey, P. (1993). Measurement error masks bipolarity in affect ratings. *Journal of Personality and Social Psychology, 64*, 1029–1041.

Greene, L. S., Desor, J. A., & Maller, O. (1975). Heredity and experience: Their relative importance in the development of taste preference in man. *Journal of Comparative & Physiological Psychology, 89*, 279–284.

Grill, H. J., & Norgren, R. (1978a). The taste reactivity test: I. Mimetic responses to gustatory stimuli in neurologically normal rats. *Brain Research, 143*, 263–279.

Grill, H. J., & Norgren, R. (1978b). The taste reactivity test: II. Mimetic responses to gustatory stimuli in chronic thalamic and chronic decerebrate rats. *Brain Research, 143*, 281–297.

Grossman, R. P., & Till, B. D. (1998). The persistence of classically conditioned brand attitudes. *Journal of Advertising, 27*, 23–31.

Hamann, S. B., Ely, T. D., Grafton, S. T., & Kilts, C. D. (1999). Amygdala activity related to enhanced memory for pleasant and aversive stimuli. *Nature Neuroscience, 2*, 289–293.

Hamann, S. B., Ely, T. D., Hoffman, J. M., & Kilts, C. D. (2002). Ecstasy and agony: Activation of human amygdala in positive and negative emotion. *Psychological Science, 13*, 135–141.

Hamann, S., & Mao, H. (2002). Positive and negative emotional verbal stimuli elicit activity in the left amygdala. *NeuroReport: For Rapid Communication of Neuroscience Research, 13*, 15–19.

Hemenover, S. H. (2003). Individual differences in rate of affect change: Studies in affective chronometry. *Journal of Personality and Social Psychology, 85*, 121–131.

Hemenover, S. H., & Schimmack, U. (in press). That's disgusting! . . . , But very amusing: Mixed feelings of amusement and disgust. *Cognition and Emotion*.

Hermans, D., Spruyt, A., & Eelen, P. (2003). Automatic affective priming of recently acquired stimulus valence: Priming at SOA 300 but not at SOA 1000. *Cognition & Emotion, 17*, 83–99.

Hoffman, M. L. (1986). Affect, cognition, and motivation. In R. M. Sorrentino & E. T. Higgins (Eds.), *Handbook of motivation and cognition: Foundations of social behavior* (pp. 244–280). New York: Guilford.

Hunter, P. G., Schellenberg, E. G., & Schimmack, U. (2004, November). Music evokes mixed emotions. Paper presented at the 3rd annual Auditory Perception, Cognition, and Action meeting. Minneapolis, MN.

Husain, G., Thompson, W. F., & Schellenberg, E. G. (2002). Effects of musical tempo and mode on arousal, mood, and spatial abilities. *Music Perception, 20*, 151–171.

Isbell, L., & Wyer, R. S. Jr. (1999). Correcting for mood-induced bias in the evaluation of political candidates: The roles of intrinsic and extrinsic motivation. *Personality and Social Psychology Bulletin, 25*, 237–249.

Ito, T. A., Cacioppo, J. T., & Lang, P. J. (1998). Eliciting affect using the International Affective Picture System: Trajectories through evaluative space. *Personality and Social Psychology Bulletin, 24*, 855–879.

Izard, C. E. (1977). *Human emotions*. New York: Plenum.

Izard, C. E. (1993). Four systems for emotion activation: Cognitive and noncognitive processes. *Psychological Review, 100*, 68–90.

James, W. (1894). The physical basis of emotion. *Psychological Review*, I, 516–529.

Kahneman, D. (1992). Reference points, anchors, norms, and mixed feelings. *Organizational Behavior and Human Decision Processes, 51*, 296–312.

Karama, S., Lecours, A. R., Leroux, J-M., Bourgouin, P., Beaudoin, G., Joubert, S., & Beauregard, M. (2002). Areas of brain activation in males and females during viewing of erotic film excerpts. *Human Brain Mapping, 16*, 1–13.

Keillor, J. M., Barrett, A. M., Crucian, G. P., Kortenkamp, S., & Heilman, K. M. (2002). Emotional experience and perception in the absence of facial feedback. *Journal of the International Neuropsychological Society, 8*, 130–135.

Kellogg, C. E. (1914–1915). Alteration and interference of feelings. *Psychological Monographs, 18*, 1–94.

Kennedy-Moore, E., Greenberg, M. A., Newman, M. G., & Stone, A. A. (1992). The relationship between daily events and mood: The mood measure may matter. *Motivation & Emotion, 16*, 143–155.

Kleinke, C. L., Peterson, T. R., & Rutledge, T. R. (1998). Effects of self-generated facial expressions on mood. *Journal of Personality and Social Psychology, 74*, 272–279.

Klüver, H., & Bucy, P. C. (1937). "Psychic blindness" and other symptoms following bilateral temporal lobectomy in Rhesus monkeys. *American Journal of Physiology, 119*, 352–353.

Klumb, P. L., & Baltes, M. M. (1999). Time use of old and very old Berliners: Productive and consumptive activities as functions of resources. *Journals of Gerontology: Series B: Psychological Sciences & Social Sciences, 54*, S271–S278.

Knobloch, S., & Zillmann, D. (2002). Mood management via the digital jukebox. *Journal of Communication, 52*, 351–366.

Knutson, B., Fong, G. W., Adams, C. M., Varner, J. L., & Hommer, D. (2001). Dissociation of reward anticipation and outcome with event-related fMRI. *NeuroReport: For Rapid Communication of Neuroscience Research, 12*(17), 3683–3687.

Kumari, V., Hemsley, D. R., Cotter, P. A., Checkley, S. A., & Gray, J. A. (1998). Haloperidol-induced mood and retrieval of happy and unhappy memories. *Cognition & Emotion, 12*, 497–508.

Lang, P. J., Greenwald, M. K., Bradley, M. M., & Hamm, A. O. (1993). Looking at pictures: Affective, facial, visceral, and behavioral reactions. *Psychophysiology, 30*, 261–273.

Larsen, J. T., McGraw, A. P., & Cacioppo, J. T. (2001). Can people feel happy and sad at the same time? *Journal of Personality and Social Psychology, 81*, 684–696.

Larsen, J. T., McGraw, A. P., Mellers, B. A., & Cacioppo, J. T. (2004). The Agony of victory and Thrill of Defeat: Mixed emotional reactions to disappointing wins and relieving losses. *Psychological Science, 15*(5), 325–330.

Larsen, R. J., & Diener, E. (1992). *Promises and problems with the circumplex model of emotion.* In M. S. Clark (Ed.), *Emotion. Review of personality and social psychology* (Vol. 13, pp. 25–59). Thousand Oaks, CA: Sage.

Lavine, H., Thomsen, C. J., Zanna, M. P., & Borgida, E. (1998). On the primacy of affect in the determination of attitudes and behavior: The moderating role of affective-cognitive ambivalence. *Journal of Experimental Social Psychology, 34*, 398–421.

Law, S., Schimmack, U., & Braun, K. A. (2003). Cameo appearances of branded products in TV shows: How effective are they? Manuscript in preparation.

Lazarus, R. (1991). *Emotion and adaptation.* New York: Oxford University Press.

Lazarus, R. S., & Alfert, E. (1964). Short-circuiting of threat by experimentally altering cognitive appraisal. *Journal of Abnormal & Social Psychology, 69*, 195–205.

Lazarus, R. S., & McCleary, R. A. (1951). Autonomic discrimination without awareness: A study of subception. *Psychological Review, 58*, 113–122.

LeDoux, J. E. (1996). *The emotional brain: The mysterious underpinnings of emotional life.* New York: Simon & Schuster.

Lepore, L., & Brown, R. (1997). Category and stereotype activation: Is prejudice inevitable? *Journal of Personality and Social Psychology, 72*, 275–287.

Levenson, R. W., & Ekman, P. (2002). Difficulty does not account for emotion-specific heart rate changes in the directed facial action task. *Psychophysiology, 39*, 397–405.

Levine, L. J. (1997). Reconstructing memory for emotions. *Journal of Experimental Psychology: General, 126*, 165–177.

Levine, L. J., Prohaska, V., Burgess, S. L., Rice, J. A., & Laulhere, T. M. (2001). Remembering past emotions: The role of current appraisals. *Cognition & Emotion, 15*, 393–417.

Levine, L. J., & Safer, M. A. (2002). Sources of bias in memory for emotions. *Current Directions in Psychological Science, 11*, 169–173.

Liechti, M. E., Baumann, C., Gamma, A., & Vollenweider, F. X. (2000). Acute psychological effects of 3,4-methylenedioxymethamphetamine (MDMA, "Ecstasy") are attenuated by the serotonin uptake inhibitor citalopram. *Neuropsychopharmacology, 22*, 513–521.

Loftus, E. F. (1994). The repressed memory controversy. *American Psychologist, 49*, 443–445.

Maier, S. F., & Watkins, L. R. (1998). Cytokines for psychologists: Implications of bidirectional immune-to-brain communication for understanding behavior, mood, and cognition. *Psychological Review, 105*, 83–107.

Mandler, G., Nakamura, Y., & Van Zandt, B. J. (1987). Nonspecific effects of exposure on stimuli that cannot be recognized. *Journal of Experimental Psychology: Learning, Memory, & Cognition, 13*, 646–648.

Marcus-Newhall, A., Pedersen, W. C., Carlson, M., & Miller, N. (2000). Displaced aggression is alive and well: A meta-analytic review. *Journal of Personality and Social Psychology, 78*, 670–689.

Matsumoto, D. (1987). The role of facial response in the experience of emotion: More methodological problems and a meta-analysis. *Journal of Personality and Social Psychology, 52*, 769–774.

Matthews, G., Jones, D. M., & Chamberlain, A. G. (1990). Refining the measurement of mood: The UWIST Mood Adjective Checklist. *British Journal of Psychology, 81*, 17–42.

McCrimmon, R. J., Frier, B. M., & Deary, I. J. (1999). Appraisal of mood and personality during hypoglycemia in human subjects. *Physiology & Behavior, 67*, 27–33.

Meddis, R. (1972). Bipolar factors in mood adjective checklists. *British Journal of Social & Clinical Psychology, 11*, 178–184.

Menzies, R. N. (1933). Memory for pleasant, unpleasant, and indifferent events of the recent past. *Psychological Bulletin, 30*, 574.

Mezzacappa, E. S., Katkin, E. S., & Palmer, S. N. (1999). Epinephrine, arousal, and emotion: A new look at two-factor theory. *Cognition & Emotion, 13*, 181–199.

Miller, N., Pedersen, W. C., Earleywine, M., & Pollock, V. E. (2003). A theoretical model of triggered displaced aggression. *Personality and Social Psychology Review, 7*, 75–97.

Morgan, R. L., & Heise, D. (1988). Structure of emotions. *Social Psychology Quarterly, 51*, 19–31.

Morris, J. S., Scott, S. K., & Dolan, R. J. (1999). Saying it with feeling: Neural responses to emotional vocalizations. *Neuropsychologia, 37*, 1155–1163.

Nelson, E. E., Shelton, S. E., & Kalin, N. H. (2003). Individual differences in the responses of naive rhesus monkeys to snakes. *Emotion, 3*, 3–11.

Nowlis, V. (1961). Methods for studying mood changes produced by drugs. *Revue de Psychologie Appliquee, 11*, 373–386.

Nowlis, V. (1965). Research with the Mood Adjective Check List. In S. S. Tomkins & C. E. Izard (Eds.), *Affect, cognition, and personality* (pp. 352–389). New York: Springer.

Oatley, K., & Johnson-Laird, P. N. (1987). Towards a cognitive theory of emotions. *Cognition & Emotion, 1*, 29–50.

Ochsner, K. N. (2000). Are affective events richly recollected or simply familiar? The experience and process of recognizing feelings past. *Journal of Experimental Psychology: General, 129*, 242–261.

O'Doherty, J., Kringelbach, M. L., Rolls, E. T., Hornak, J., & Andrews, C. (2001). Abstract reward and punishment representations in the human orbitofrontal cortex. *Nature Neuroscience, 4*, 95–102.

O'Doherty, J., Winston, J., Critchley, H., Perrett, D., Burt, D. M., & Dolan, R. J. (2003). Beauty in a smile: The role of medial orbitofrontal cortex in facial attractiveness. *Neuropsychologia. Special Issue: The cognitive neuroscience of social behavior, 41*, 147–155.

Oishi, S., & Schimmack, U. (2003). *Frequency judgments of emotion: A congruence effect of culture and emotion-eliciting situations.* Manuscript under review.

Olson, M. A., & Fazio, R. H. (2001). Implicit attitude formation through classical conditioning. *Psychological Science, 12*, 413–417.

Ortony, A., Clore, G. L., & Collins, A. (1988). *The cognitive structure of emotions.* New York: Cambridge University Press.

Ortony, A., & Turner, T. J. (1990). What's basic about basic emotions? *Psychological Review, 97*, 315–331.

Panksepp, J. (1994). The clearest physiological distinctions between emotions will be fond among the circuits of the brain. In P. Ekman and R. J. Davidson (Eds.), *The nature of emotion* (pp. 258–260). Oxford, UK: Oxford University Press.

Panksepp, J., & Bernatzky, G. (2002). Emotional sounds and the brain: The neuro-affective foundations of musical appreciation. *Behavioural Processes, 60*, 133–155.

Parkinson, B., Briner, R. B., Reynolds, S., & Totterdell, P. (1995). Time frames for mood: Relations between monetary and generalized ratings of affect. *Personality and Social Psychology Bulletin, 21*, 331–339.

Patrick, C. J., & Lavoro, S. A. (1997). Ratings of emotional response to pictorial stimuli: Positive and negative affect dimensions. *Motivation & Emotion, 21*, 297–322.

Pavlov, I. P. (1927). *Conditioned reflexes: an investigation of the physiological activity of the cerebral cortex.* Oxford, UK: Oxford University Press.

Peeters, F., Nicolson, N. A., Berkhof, J., Delespaul, P., & deVries, M. (2003). Effects of daily events on mood states in major depressive disorder. *Journal of Abnormal Psychology, 112*, 203–211.

Poulton, R., & Menzies, R. G. (2002). Fears born and bred: Toward a more inclusive theory of fear acquisition. *Behaviour Research and Therapy, 40*, 197–208.

Priester, J. R., & Petty, R. E. (1996). The gradual threshold model of ambivalence: Relating the positive and negative bases of attitudes to subjective ambivalence. *Journal of Personality and Social Psychology, 71*, 431–449.

Reber, R., Winkielman, P., & Schwarz, N. (1998). Effects of perceptual fluency on affective judgments. *Psychological Science, 9*, 45–48.

Redoute, J., Stoleru, S., Gregoire, M., Costes, N., Cinotti, L., Lavenne, F., Le Bars, D., Maguelone, G. F., & Pujol, J.-F. (2000). Brain processing of visual sexual stimuli in human males. *Human Brain Mapping, 11*, 162–177.

Redoute, J., Stoleru, S., Gregoire, M.-C., Costes, N., Cinotti, L., Lavenne, F., Le Bars, D., Forest, M. G., & Pujol, J.-F. (2000). Brain processing of visual sexual stimuli in human males. *Human Brain Mapping, 11*(3), 162–177.

Reisberg, D., Heuer, F., McLean, J., & O'Shaughnessy, M. (1988). The quantity, not the quality, of affect predicts memory vividness. *Bulletin of the Psychonomic Society, 26*, 100–103.

Reisenzein, R. (1983). The Schachter theory of emotion: Two decades later. *Psychological Bulletin, 94*, 239–264.

Reisenzein, R. (1992). A structuralist reconstruction of Wundt's three-dimensional theory of emotion. In H. Westmeyer (Ed.), *The structuralist program in psychology: Foundations and applications* (pp. 141–189). Ashland, OH: Hogrefe & Huber Publishers.

Reisenzein, R. (1994). Pleasure-arousal theory and the intensity of emotions. *Journal of Personality and Social Psychology, 67*, 525–539.

Reisenzein, R. (1995). On Oatley and Johnson-Laird's theory of emotion and hierarchical structures in the affective lexicon. *Cognition & Emotion, 9*, 383–416.

Reisenzein, R. (2001). Appraisal processes conceptualized from a schema-theoretic perspective: Contributions to a process analysis of emotions. In K. R. Scherer & A. Schorr (Eds.), *Appraisal processes in emotion: Theory, methods, research* (pp. 187–201). London: Oxford University Press.

Reisenzein, R., & Schimmack, U. (1999). Similarity judgments and covariations of affects: Findings and implications do affect structure research. *Personality and Social Psychology Bulletin, 25*, 539–555.

Reisenzein, R., & Schönpflug, W. (1992). Stumpf's cognitive-evaluative theory of emotion. *American Psychologist, 47*, 34–45.

Reisenzein, R., & Spielhofer, C. (1994). Subjectively salient dimensions of emotional appraisal. *Motivation & Emotion, 18*, 31–77.

Rhodes, G., Halberstadt, J., & Brajkovich, G. (2001). Generalization of mere exposure effects to averaged composite faces. *Social Cognition, 19*, 57–70.

Rissanen, A., Hakala, P., Lissner, L., Mattlar, C., Koskenvuo, M., & Roennemaa, T. (2002). Acquired preference especially for dietary fat and obesity: A study of weight-discordant monozygotic twin pairs. *International Journal of Obesity & Related Metabolic Disorders, 26*, 973–977.

Robinson, M. D., & Clore, G. L. (2002). Belief and feeling: Evidence for an accessibility model of emotional self-report. *Psychological Bulletin, 128*, 934–960.

Rolls, E. T. (1999). *The Brain and Emotion*. Oxford, UK: Oxford University Press.

Rosch, E., Mervis, C. B., Gray, W. D., Johnson, D. M., & Boyes-Braem, P. (1976). Basic objects in natural categories. *Cognitive Psychology, 8*, 382–439.

Roseman, I. J. (1984). Cognitive determinants of emotions: A structural theory. In P. Shaver (Ed.). Review of personality and social psychology: Vol. 5, Emotions, relationships, and health (pp. 11–36). Beverly Hills, CA: sage.

Roseman, I. J., & Smith, C. A. (2001). Appraisal theory: Overview, assumptions, varieties, controversies. In K. R. Scherer & A. Schorr (Eds.), *Appraisal processes in emotion: Theory, methods, research* (pp. 3–19). London: Oxford University Press.

Rosenberg, M. J. (1956). Cognitive structure and attitudinal affect. *Journal of Abnormal & Social Psychology, 53*, 367–372.

Rosenstein, D., & Oster, H. (1988). Differential facial responses to four basic tastes in newborns. *Child Development, 59*, 1555–1568.

Rottenberg, J., Kasch, K. L., Gross, J. J., & Gotlib, I. H. (2002). Sadness and amusement reactivity differentially predict concurrent and prospective functioning in major depressive disorder. *Emotion, 2*, 135–146.

Royet, J., Zald, D., Costes, N., Lavenne, F., Koenig, O., & Gervais, R. (2000). Emotional responses to pleasant and unpleasant olfactory, visual, and auditory stimuli: A positron emission tomography study. *Journal of Neuroscience, 20*(20), 7752–7759.

Rozin, P., & Fallon, A. E. (1987). A perspective on disgust. *Psychological Review, 94*, 23–41.

Rozin, P., & Millman, L. (1987). Family environment, not heredity, accounts for family resemblances in food preferences and attitudes: A twin study. *Appetite, 8*, 125–134.

Rozin, P., & Royzman, E. B. (2001). Negativity bias, negativity dominance, and contagion. *Personality & Social Psychology Review, 5*, 296–320.

Rozin, P., Wrzesniewski, A., & Byrnes, D. (1998). The elusiveness of evaluative conditioning. *Learning & Motivation, 29*, 397–415.

Rubenstein, A. J., Kalakanis, L., & Langlois, J. H. (1999). Infant preferences for attractive faces: A cognitive explanation. *Developmental Psychology, 35*, 848–855.

Russell, J. A., & Barrett, L. F. (1999). Core affect, prototypical emotional episodes, and other things called emotion: Dissecting the elephant. *Journal of Personality and Social Psychology, 76*, 805–819.

Russell, J. A., & Carroll, J. M. (1999). On the bipolarity of positive and negative affect. *Psychological Bulletin, 125,* 3–30.

Saegert, S., Swap, W., & Zajonc, R. B. (1973). Exposure, context, and interpersonal attraction. *Journal of Personality and Social Psychology, 25,* 234–242.

Safer, M. A., Bonanno, G. A., & Field, N. P. (2001). "It was never that bad": Biased recall of grief and long-term adjustment to the death of a spouse. *Memory, 9,* 195–204.

Safer, M. A., Levine, L. J., & Drapalski, A. L. (2002). Distortion in memory for emotions: The contributions of personality and post-event knowledge. *Personality & Social Psychology Bulletin, 28,* 1495–1507.

Sander, K., & Scheich, H. (2001). Auditory perception of laughing and crying activates human amygdala regardless of attentional state. *Cognitive Brain Research, 12,* 181–198.

Schaal, B., Marlier, L., & Soussignan, R. (2000). Human fetuses learn odours from their pregnant mother's diet. *Chemical Senses, 25,* 729–737.

Schachter, S., & Singer, J. (1962). Cognitive, social, and physiological determinants of emotional state. *Psychological Review, 69,* 379–399.

Scherer, K. R. (1984). Emotion as a multicomponent process: A model and some cross-cultural data. In P. Shaver (Ed.). Vol 5. Review of Personality and Social Psychology: Vol 5. Emotions, relationships, and health (pp. 37–63). Beverly Hills, CA: Sage

Scherer, K. R., Banse, R., & Wallbott, H. G. (2001). Emotion inferences from vocal expression correlate across languages and cultures. *Journal of Cross-Cultural Psychology, 32,* 76–92.

Scherer, K. R., Schorr, A., Johnstone, T. (Eds.) (2001). Appraisal process in emotion. Oxford: Oxford University Press.

Scherer, K. R., & Zentner, M. R. (2001). Emotional effects of music: Production rules. In P. N. Juslin & J. A. Sloboda (Eds.), *Music and emotion: Theory and research* (pp. 361–392). London: Oxford University Press.

Schimmack, U., & Hartmann, K. (1997). Interindividual differences in the memory representation of emotions: Exploring the cognitive processes in repression. *Journal of Personality and social Psychology, 73,* 1064–1079.

Schimmack, U. (1997). The Berlin Everyday Language Mood Inventory (BELMI): Toward the content valid assessment of moods [Das Berliner-Alltagssprachliche-Stimmungs-Inventar (BASTI): Ein Vorschlag zur kontentvaliden Erfassung von Stimmungen.]. *Diagnostica, 43,* 150–173.

Schimmack, U. (2001). Pleasure, displeasure, and mixed feelings: Are semantic opposites mutually exclusive? *Cognition & Emotion,* 15(1), 81–97.

Schimmack, U. (2002). Frequency judgments of emotions: The cognitive basis of personality assessment. In P. Sedelmeier & T. Betsch (Eds.), *Frequency processing and cognition* (pp. 189–204). Oxford, UK: Oxford University Press.

Schimmack, U. (2003). Affect measurement in experience Sampling research. *Journal of Happiness Studies, 4,* 79–106.

Schimmack U. (2004). *Emotional experiences require awareness of the eliciting stimulus.* Manuscript under review.

Schimmack, U. (in press). *Response latencies of pleasure and displeasure ratings: Further evidence for mixed feelings. Cognition and Emotion.*

Schimmack, U. (2005). *Attitudes towards multi-peaked affective episodes: The impact of frequency, intensity, duration, and position.* Manuscript in preparation.

Schimmack, U., Böeckenholt, U., & Reisenzein, R. (2002). Response styles in affect ratings: Making a mountain out of a molehill. *Journal of Personality Assessment, 78,* 461–483.

Schimmack, U., & Colcombe, S. (in press). Eliciting mixed feelings with the paired-picture paradigm: A tribute to Kellogg (1915). *Cognition and Emotion.*

Schimmack, U., Colcombe, S., & Crites, S. (2001). *Pleasure and displeasure in reaction to conflicting picture pairs: Examining appealingness and appallingness appraisals.* Unpublished manuscript (http://www.erin.utoronto.ca/%7Ew3psyuli/ulipubs.htm).

Schimmack, U., & Diener, E. (1997). Affect intensity: Separating intensity and frequency in repeatedly measured affect. *Journal of Personality and Social Psychology, 73,* 1313–1329.

Schimmack, U., Diener, E., & Oishi, S. (2002). Life-satisfaction is a momentary judgment and a stable personality characteristic: The use of chronically accessible and stable sources. *Journal of Personality, 70,* 345–384.

Schimmack, U., & Grob, A. (2000). Dimensional models of core affect: A quantitative comparison by means of structural equation modeling. *European Journal of Personality, 14,* 325–345.

Schimmack, U., Oishi, S., & Diener, E. (2002). Cultural influences on the relation between pleasant emotions and unpleasant emotions: Asian dialectic philosophies or individualism-collectivism? *Cognition & Emotion, 16,* 705–719.

Schimmack, U., Oishi, S., Diener, E., & Suh, E. (2000). Facets of affective experiences: A framework for investigations of trait affect. *Personality & Social Psychology Bulletin, 26,* 655–668.

Schimmack, U., & Reisenzein, R. (1997). Cognitive processes involved in similarity judgments of emotions. *Journal of Personality and Social Psychology, 73,* 645–661.

Schimmack, U., & Reisenzein, R. (2002). Experiencing activation: Energetic arousal and tense arousal are not mixtures of valence and activation. *Emotion, 2,* 412–417.

Schimmack, U. & Siemer, M. (1998). *Mood and emotions: Folk psychology's contribution to scientific taxonomies of affective experiences.* Unpublished manuscript.

Schreiber, C. A., & Kahneman, D. (2000). Determinants of the remembered utility of aversive sounds. *Journal of Experimental Psychology: General, 129,* 27–42.

Schwarz, N., & Clore, G. L. (1983). Mood, misattribution, and judgments of well-being: Informative and directive functions of affective states. *Journal of Personality and Social Psychology, 45,* 513–523.

Scott, T. R., & Plata-Salaman, C. R. (1999). Taste in the monkey cortex. *Physiology & Behavior, 67,* 489–511.

Seamon, J. G., McKenna, P. A., & Binder, N. (1998). The mere exposure effect is differentially sensitive to different judgment tasks. *Consciousness & Cognition: An International Journal, 7,* 85–102.

Seidlitz, L., & Diener, E. (1993). Memory for positive versus negative life events: Theories for the differences between happy and unhappy persons. *Journal of Personality and Social Psychology, 64,* 654–663.

Shaver, P., Schwartz, J., Kirson, D., & O'Connor, C. (1987). Emotion knowledge: Further exploration of a prototype approach. *Journal of Personality and Social Psychology, 52,* 1061–1086.

Shaver, P. R., Wu, S., & Schwartz, J. C. (1992). Cross-cultural similarities and differences in emotion and its representation. In M. S. Clark (Ed.), *Emotion. Review of personality and social psychology* (Vol. 13, pp. 175–212). Thousand Oaks, CA: Sage.

Sheline, Y. I., Barch, D. M., Donnelly, J. M., Ollinger, J. M., Snyder, A. Z., & Mintun, M. A. (2001). Increased amygdala response to masked emotional faces in depressed subjects resolves with antidepressant treatment: An fMRI study. *Biological Psychiatry, 50,* 651–658.

Shimp, T. A., Stuart, E. W., & Engle, R. W. (1991). A program of classical conditioning experiments testing variations in the conditioned stimulus and context. *Journal of Consumer Research, 18,* 1–12.

Siemer, M., & Reisenzein, R. (1998). Effects of mood on evaluative judgements: Influence of reduced processing capacity and mood salience. *Cognition & Emotion, 12,* 783–805.

Sipski, M. L., Alexander, C. J., & Rosen, R. (2001). Sexual arousal and orgasm in women: Effects of spinal cord injury. *Annals of Neurology, 49,* 35–44.

Smith, C. A., & Ellsworth, P. C. (1985). Patterns of cognitive appraisal in emotion. *Journal of Personality and Social Psychology, 48,* 813–838.

Smith, C. A., & Kirby, L. D. (2001). Toward delivering on the promise of appraisal theory. In K. R. Scherer & A. Schorr (Eds.), *Appraisal processes in emotion: Theory, methods, research* (pp. 121–138). London: Oxford University Press.

Soussignan, R. (2002). Duchenne smile, emotional experience, and autonomic reactivity: A test of the facial feedback hypothesis. *Emotion, 2,* 52–74.

Soussignan, R., Schaal, B., Marlier, L., & Jiang, T. (1997). Facial and autonomic responses to biological and artificial olfactory stimuli in human neonates: Re-examining early hedonic discrimination of odors. *Physiology & Behavior, 62,* 745–758.

Staats, C. K., & Staats, A. W. (1957). Meaning established by classical conditioning. *Journal of Experimental Psychology, 54,* 74–80.

Steiner, J. E., Glaser, D., Hawilo, M. E., & Berridge, K. C. (2001). Comparative expression of hedonic impact: Affective reactions to taste by human infants and other primates. *Neuroscience & Biobehavioral Reviews, 25,* 53–74.

Stevenson, R. J., Boakes, R. A., & Wilson, J. P. (2000). Resistance to extinction of conditioned odor perceptions: Evaluative conditioning is not unique. *Journal of Experimental Psychology: Learning, Memory, & Cognition, 26,* 423–440.

Steyer, R., Schwenkmezger, P., Notz, P., & Eid, M. (1994). Theoretical analysis of a multidimensional mood questionnaire (MDBF) [Testtheoretische Analysen des Mehrdimensionalen Befindlichkeitsfragebogen (MDBF)]. *Diagnostica, 40,* 320–328.

Stone, A. A., Hedges, S. M., Neale, J. M., & Satin, M. S. (1985). Prospective and cross-sectional mood reports offer no evidence of a "blue Monday" phenomenon. *Journal of Personality and Social Psychology, 49,* 129–134.

Storm, C., & Storm, T. (1987). A taxonomic study of the vocabulary of emotions. *Journal of Personality and Social Psychology, 53,* 805–816.

Strahan, E. J., Spencer, S. J., & Zanna, M. P. (2002). Subliminal priming and persuasion: Striking while the iron is hot. *Journal of Experimental Social Psychology, 38,* 556–568.

Stratton, V. N., & Zalanowski, A. H. (2003). Daily music listening habits in college students: Related moods and activities. *Psychology & Education, 40,* 1–11.

Sulmont, C., Issanchou, S., & Köster, E. P. (2002). Selection of odorants for memory tests on the basis of familiarity, perceived complexity, pleasantness, similarity and identification. *Chemical Senses, 27,* 307–317.

Szpunar, K. K., Schellenberg, E. G., & Pliner, P. (2004). Liking and memory for musical stimuli as a function of exposure. *Journal of Experimental Psychology: Learning, Memory, and Cognition, 30*(2), 370–381.

Thayer, R. E. (1989). *The biopsychology of mood and arousal.* London: Oxford University Press.

Thomas, D. L., & Diener, E. (1990). Memory accuracy in the recall of emotions. *Journal of Personality and Social Psychology, 59,* 291–297.

Thurstone, L. L. (1931). The measurement of social attitudes. *Journal of Abnormal & Social Psychology, 26,* 249–269.

Tomaka, J., Blascovich, J., Kibler, J., & Ernst, J. M. (1997). Cognitive and physiological antecedents of threat and challenge appraisal. *Journal of Personality and Social Psychology, 73*, 63–72.

Tomkins, S. S. (1962). *The positive affects. Affect, imagery, consciousness* (Vol. 1). New York: Springer.

Tomkins, S. S. (1963). *The negative affects. Affect, imagery, consciousness* (Vol. 2). New York: Springer.

Twenge, J. M., & Campbell, W. K. (2003). "Isn't it fun to get the respect that we're going to deserve?" Narcissism, social rejection, and aggression. *Personality and Social Psychology Bulletin, 29*, 261–272.

Van den Hout, M. A., De Jong, P., & Kindt, M. (2000). Masked fear words produce increased SCRs: An anomaly for Ohman's theory of pre-attentive processing in anxiety. *Psychophysiology, 37*, 283–288.

van Reekum, C. M., van den Berg, H., & Frijda, N. H. (1999). Cross-modal preference acquisition: Evaluative conditioning of pictures by affective olfactory and auditory cues. *Cognition & Emotion, 13*, 831–836.

Walther, E. (2002). Guilty by mere association: Evaluative conditioning and the spreading attitude effect. *Journal of Personality and Social Psychology, 82*, 919–934.

Watson, D. (1988). Intraindividual and interindividual analyses of positive and negative affect: Their relation to health complaints, perceived stress, and daily activities. *Journal of Personality and Social Psychology, 54*, 1020–1030.

Watson, D., Clark, L. A., & Tellegen, A. (1988). Development and validation of brief measures of positive and negative affect: The PANAS scales. *Journal of Personality and Social Psychology, 54*, 1063–1070.

Watson, D., & Tellegen, A. (1985). Toward a consensual structure of mood. *Psychological Bulletin, 98*, 219–235.

Watson, D., Wiese, D., Vaidya, J., & Tellegen, A. (1999). The two general activation systems of affect: Structural findings, evolutionary considerations, and psychobiological evidence. *Journal of Personality and Social Psychology, 76*, 820–838.

Weiner, B. (1986). Attribution, emotion, and action. In R. M. Sorrentino & E. T. Higgins (Eds.), *Handbook of motivation and cognition: Foundations of social behavior* (pp. 281–312). New York: Guilford.

Weiskrantz, L. (1956). Behavioral changes associated with ablation of the amygdaloid complex in monkeys. *Journal of Comparative & Physiological Psychology, 49*, 381–391.

Whalen, P. J., Rauch, S. L., Etcoff, N. L., McInerney, S. C., Lee, M. B., & Jenike, M. A. (1998). Masked presentations of emotional facial expressions modulate amygdala activity without explicit knowledge. *Journal of Neuroscience, 18*, 411–418.

Wheeler, S. C., & Petty, R. E. (2001). The effects of stereotype activation on behavior: A review of possible mechanisms. *Psychological Bulletin, 127*, 797–826.

Wierzbicka, A. (1999). *Emotions across languages and cultures: Diversity and universals.* New York: Cambridge University Press.

Williams, P., & Aaker, J. L. (2002). Can mixed emotions peacefully coexist? *Journal of Consumer Research, 28*, 636–649.

Williams, P. G., Colder, C. R., Lane, J. D., McCaskill, C. C., Feinglos, M. N., & Surwit, R. S. (2002). Examination of the neuroticism-symptom reporting relationship in individuals with type-2 diabetes. *Personality and Social Psychology Bulletin, 28*, 1015–1025.

Winkielman, P., & Cacioppo, J. T. (2001). Mind at ease puts a smile on the face: Psychophysiological evidence that processing facilitation elicits positive affect. *Journal of Personality and Social Psychology, 81*, 989–1000.

Winkielman, P., Zajonc, R. B., & Schwarz, N. (1997). Subliminal affective priming resists attributional interventions. *Cognition & Emotion, 11*, 433–465.

Wittenbrink, B., Judd, C. M., & Park, B. (1997). Evidence for racial prejudice at the implicit level and its relationship with questionnaire measures. *Journal of Personality and Social Psychology, 72*, 262–274.

Wohlgemuth, A. (1925). The coexistence and localization of feeling. *British Journal of Psychology, 16*, 116–122.

Wundt, W. (1896). *Grundrisse der Psychologie* [Outlines of psychology]. Leipzig, Germany: Engelmann.

Yaxley, S., Rolls, E. T., Sienkiewicz, Z. J., & Scott, T. R. (1985). Satiety does not affect gustatory activity in the nucleus of the solitary tract of the alert monkey. *Brain Research, 347*, 85–93.

Yoshida, M. (1964). Studies in the psychometric classification of odors. *Japanese Journal of Psychology, 35*, 1–17.

Zajonc, R. B. (1968). Attitudinal effects of mere exposure. *Journal of Personality and Social Psychology, 9*, 1–27.

Zajonc, R. B. (1980). Feeling and thinking: Preferences need no inferences. *American Psychologist, 35*, 151–175.

Zajonc, R. B. (2001). Mere exposure: A gateway to the subliminal. *Current Directions in Psychological Science, 10*, 224–228.

Zald, D. H. (2003). The human amygdala and the emotional evaluation of sensory stimuli. *Brain Research Reviews, 41*, 88–123.

Zanna, M. P., Kiesler, C. A., & Pilkonis, P. A. (1970). Positive and negative attitudinal affect established by classical conditioning. *Journal of Personality and Social Psychology, 14*, 321–328.

Zevon, M. A., & Tellegen, A. (1982). The structure of mood change: An idiographic/nomothetic analysis. *Journal of Personality and Social Psychology, 43*, 111–122.

Zuckerman, M., & Lubin, B. (1965). Normative data for the multiple affect adjective check list. *Psychological Reports, 16*, 438.

11

The Influence of Affect on Attitude

Gerald L. Clore
Simone Schnall
University of Virginia

AFFECTIVE INFLUENCE ON ATTITUDE

Priests of the medieval Catholic Church understood something about the relationship between affect and attitude. To instill the proper attitude in parishioners, priests dramatized the power of liturgy to save them from Hell in a service in which the experience of darkness and fear gave way to light and familiar liturgy. These ceremonies "were written and performed so as to first arouse and then allay anxieties and fears" (Scott, 2003, p. 227):

> The service usually began in the dark of night with the gothic cathedral's nave filled with worshippers cast into total darkness. Terrifying noises, wailing, shrieks, screams, and clanging of metal mimicked the chaos of hell, giving frightened witnesses a taste of what they could expect if they were tempted to stray. After a prolonged period of this imitation of hell, the cathedral's interior gradually became filled with the blaze of a thousand lights. As the gloom diminished, cacophony was supplanted by the measured tones of Gregorian chants and polyphony. Light and divine order replaced darkness and chaos (R. Scott, personal correspondence, March 15, 2004).

This ceremony was designed to buttress beliefs by experience and to transfigure abstractions into attitudes. In place of merely hearing about "the chaos and perdition of hell that regular performances of liturgy were designed to hold in check" (Scott, 2003), parishioners should actually feel reactions of fear and confusion when contemplating Hell, and of hope and relief at the familiar sounds of liturgy.

By what processes do such momentary affective reactions become attitudes? This chapter explores some of the answers that social psychologists give to that question. Before proceeding, however, we discuss three sets of distinctions that underlie our treatment of affect and attitude. The first concerns the similarities and differences among attitudes and affective conditions. The second concerns the evaluative and importance information conveyed by the valence and arousal dimensions of affect. The third concerns direct versus indirect influences of affect on attitude.

437

Three Orienting Distinctions

Attitudes and Other Evaluative Conditions

"Affect" refers to evaluative reactions that are embodied. Two common forms of affect are moods and emotions, both of which are affective states. "States" exist when multiple systems of the organism simultaneously reflect the same condition. Thus, emotional states exist when the same affective reaction to the same object is manifest in multiple systems at the same time (Clore & Ortony, 2000). For example, a person who is in a state of fear may simultaneously look, feel, think, and act afraid, as well as have fearful patterns of physiology and brain activation. If emotions are particular kinds of evaluative reactions to objects, and attitudes are also evaluative tendencies toward objects, how do attitudes differ from emotions?

That question is addressed elsewhere (Schimmack & Crites, this volume; Fabrigar, Mac-Donald, & Wegener, this volume), but a useful additional comparison is that the evaluative meanings basic to both emotions and attitudes act differently because they are differently constrained (Clore & Colcombe, 2003). Table 11.1 depicts two of these constraints–temporal and object constraints. For example, moods and emotions are ephemeral and cannot be stored. Whatever evaluative information they carry is temporally constrained, existing only as long as the supporting cognitions, perceptions, or other elicitors are active, and vanishing as soon as one is no longer in that state. The same is not true of attitudes, because attitudes are not evaluative states, but evaluative tendencies, that do not necessarily vanish when one stops thinking about the attitude object. Thus, the evaluative meanings of attitudes are not constrained by time and may be either temporary or enduring (Eagly & Chaiken, 1993).

Another kind of constraint concerns whether or not the evaluative meaning is focused on a specific object. In that regard, attitudes and emotions are similar. Both are evaluations of something specific. By contrast, moods and temperaments are examples of conditions that are not dedicated to specific objects. Both are evaluative orientations without built-in direction; without being constrained by an object. Thus, cheerful moods and cheerful temperaments may make things in general seem positive. But, as shown in Table 11.1, moods differ from temperaments in part because the evaluative inclinations of moods are momentary or constrained by time. In contrast, evaluative inclinations based in temperament are neither object-specific nor temporally-specific. Thus, one can be said to have a cheerful temperament, even if one is momentarily cheerless.

According to Table 11.1, both emotions and attitudes have objects. If so, then understanding how emotion influences attitude might involve asking how the evaluative aspects of emotions, which are necessarily ephemeral, become an attitudinal evaluation, which has no such temporal constraint.

Table 11.1 indicates that the evaluative inclinations of moods also differ from those of attitudes in their object constraints. Hence, understanding how moods influence attitudes involves asking how an evaluative state, which was not about anything in particular, becomes constrained to be about a specific attitude object. For example, how might simply being in a foul

TABLE 11.1
Some Constraints on Evaluative Meaning That Differentiate Attitudes From
Other Evaluative Conditions

	Temporally Constrained State	Temporally Unconstrained Tendency
Object-focused	Emotion	Attitude
No Object Constraint	Mood	Temperament

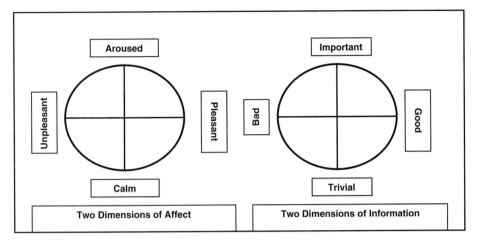

FIG. 11.1. Valence and Arousal as Two Dimensions of Embodied Affective Experience. The subjective experience of affect is generally found to vary along two dimensions (valence and arousal), which serve as embodied information (evaluation and importance) about the object of the affect.

mood influence one's attitude toward something? One approach to answering that question lies in the information about value and importance that is conveyed in affect.

Affective Value and Importance

Affective experience appears to have both valence and arousal components. These are depicted here as independent, bipolar dimensions (Russell, 2003). Valence can also be separated into two dimensions, each of which varies in arousal or intensity (Watson & Tellegen, 1985). With respect to attitude formation, the valence component can be thought of as embodied evaluation, and the arousal component can be thought of as an embodied perception of importance (Frijda, Ortony, Sonnemans, & Clore, 1992). This characterization of the experience and the information inherent in valence and arousal cues is depicted in Fig. 11.1.

As discussed by Schimmack and Crites (this volume), emotions arise when situations are perceived as positive or negative in some way and also as personally relevant, urgent, or important. These appraisals of value and importance are represented in embodied form as feelings that are pleasant or unpleasant and that are characterized by high or low arousal. The experience of such feelings in turn conveys information that something in a situation is good or bad and important or trivial. According to the affect-as-information hypothesis (Clore et al., 2001; Schwarz & Clore, 1983) affect influences attitude. Positively or negatively valenced feelings then signal positive or negative evaluations and attitudes, whereas feelings of arousal commandeer attention (Simon, 1967) and make attitude-relevant information memorable (Cahill & McGaugh, 1998).

The fact that embodied evaluations signal both Value and Importance is reflected in the organization of this chapter. In addition, at a higher level of organization, one can also distinguish between affective influences on both the "What" and the "How" of attitude formation and change, as we see next.

Affect and the "What" and "How" of Attitude Formation and Change

The impact of affect depends not only on the affect itself, but on what the affect appears to be about. Affect tends to transfer its goodness or badness to whatever is in mind at the time. Thus, if one is focused on some object, that object may be experienced as correspondingly good or bad. But if one is focused not on an object, but on a task, then the same affective cues can influence how information is processed. Thus, one's focus can determine either "What" object is good or bad (direct influences) or "How" one should process attitude relevant information (indirect influences).

In the following sections, we review several forms of direct influence, including affective conditioning, mere exposure, social influence, and causal attribution. Through *direct* association, conditioning, and attribution, positive and negative affect can become positive and negative attitudes. By contrast, when one focuses on tasks and coping, rather than on objects and judgment, affect can have *indirect* effects on attitude. For example, affect can influence whether people use categorical information (e.g., stereotypes, brand names, political party affiliation) as opposed to individuating information (e.g., actions of a person, attributes of a product, or votes of a candidate).

We are suggesting that the specific influence of affect depends on the object of one's attention at the time. At the broadest level, organisms can attend either to objects or to actions. With respect to attitudes, an *object focus* allows organisms to learn what is good and what is bad in their physical and social worlds, whereas an *action focus* allows them to evaluate how well they are coping in that world.

These two kinds of focus can also be seen in two forms of reward learning: *classical conditioning* and *instrumental learning*. Like the two forms of affective influence on attitudes, the two forms of affective influence on learning involve a transfer of value from affect to object. The two forms (whether of affective influence or of learning) differ from each other mainly in the kinds of objects to which affective value becomes associated. Pavlov's dogs attended to the stimulus of a bell, and the associated affect from the delivery of food presumably generated a positive attitude toward that conditioned stimulus. But in the instrumental learning of Skinner's pigeons and Thorndike's rats, the affect from reward conferred its value on actions or responses that were instrumental in obtaining reward.

These two kinds of learning correspond to the distinction in cognitive psychology between *semantic knowledge* and *procedural knowledge*. Semantic knowledge, too, involves information about objects in the world, whereas procedural memory involves information about action. We raise these distinctions here because they map onto the two kinds of affective influence on which we focus. Affect provides evaluative information that can either modify evaluative representations of objects in the world (semantic knowledge) or modify evaluations of possible responses to such objects (procedural knowledge). Thus, affect can either influence attitude by serving directly as information about the value of the attitude object, or indirectly by serving as information about the value of one's thoughts or inclinations regarding the object. Finally, we distinguish between two kinds of direct effects. One concerns the role of the *valence component* of affect in determining the valence component of attitude, and the other concerns the role of the *arousal component* of affect in making lasting or memorable attitudes.

Summary

Three kinds of distinctions are helpful in reviewing research on affect and attitude. One distinction is between the evaluative aspects of attitudes and the evaluative aspects of affect. The secret to affective influences on attitude is ultimately that both affect and attitudes, despite their differences, are evaluative. Thus, the evaluation embodied in affect can be conditioned, associated, inferred, attributed or otherwise transformed into the evaluative tendencies of attitude. Conversely, when attitudes are strong, attitude objects can also elicit affect. Table 11.1 suggested that two kinds of constraints on the generality of these kinds of evaluations distinguish attitude from emotion, mood, and temperament. For example, the evaluative meanings in attitude and emotion are both about specific objects. However, since emotions are ephemeral, their evaluative meanings are constrained by time, whereas attitudes and their evaluative tendencies need not be ephemeral and hence have no such temporal constraints.

The second distinction is between evaluation and importance. We suggest that the valence and arousal components of affective experiences may have different influences on attitude. Whereas affective valence signals the goodness-badness of an event, the arousal component signals its urgency or importance.

The third distinction is between affective influences on the "What" and the "How" of attitude formation and change. We suggest that the influence of affect depends not only on the affect itself, but on what the affect appears to be about. We distinguish whether affect becomes associated with a stimulus or with a response. Within a stimulus focus, affect can have a direct influence on attitude. Within a response focus, it can have an indirect effect by influencing how one processes attitude relevant information such as stereotypes and persuasive messages. We suggest that the value transfer from affect to attitude in these two kinds of influence correspond to a similar transfer of value from rewards to stimuli in classical conditioning and to responses in instrumental learning. We turn next to the first of these—direct influences of affect on attitude.

Direct Influence of Affect on Attitude

Classical Conditioning and Affective Association

Thinking of attitudes as conditioned affective responses is an old and familiar idea (e.g., Razran, 1954; Staats & Staats, 1958). Hence, one would think that attitudinal conditioning would be well understood, and issues about how it works long settled. On the contrary, basic questions remain. Moreover, interest in affect and conditioning has never been higher, and recent research includes some surprising conclusions (for reviews, see De Houwer, Thomas, & Baeyens, 2001; Hermans, Baeyens, & Eelen, 2003; Kruglanski & Stroebe, this volume). For example, despite the fact that classical conditioning would seem to be the mother of all primitive, noncognitive explanations for behavior, some reviewers conclude that there is no convincing evidence of classical conditioning in humans without conscious awareness of the contingency between conditioned and unconditioned stimuli (Lovibond & Shanks, 2002). In addition, despite appearances, the associational process whereby rewards and punishments influence attitudes is apparently not really an example of classical or Pavlovian conditioning (De Houwer et al., 2001). A review of simple evaluative associations versus Pavlovian conditioned responses shows a number of instructive differences, which we describe. Before touching on those issues, however, a bit of history is in order.

Associationism. There has long been a desire among philosophers and psychologists to use physical principles to understand psychological phenomena. The conditioned reflex is one example. Descartes suggested that just as mirrors automatically reflect light, we also have "reflexes" that automatically reflect aspects of the environment, as when people withdraw their hands from fire. Using that idea, associationist philosophers from Locke to Hume tried to explain how moral, cognitive, and affective life might be generated from associations involving such reflexes. At the time, this issue was controversial because there was a tension between the idea of randomness implied by such associationism and the dominant rationalist theories, which were especially concerned with questions of moral order.

John Sutton (1998), a current day neurophilosopher, suggests that Descartes' associationism, which today may seem too mechanistic, was in his day seen as too random. The concern was that without executive control over the construction of meaning, people would not be able to maintain a stable moral sense or even a stable self. In contrast, today we seem less concerned with people's moral sense (for better or worse), and research suggests a diminished role for central processing (Cooney & Gazzaniga, 2003). Indeed, some conclude that our sense of executive control (Clark, 1997) and conscious will (Wegner, 2002) are illusory. These trends in cognitive science seem quite compatible with the associationism we see in conditioning approaches to attitudes.

Classical Conditioning of Attitude.   Most reviews of conditioning and attitude start with Razran's early experiments in which such stimuli as musical selections, paintings, photographs, and slogans were presented during free luncheons. In one such experiment, he obtained measures of ethnic prejudice from New Yorkers by having them rate photographs of college women presented once unlabeled and again two weeks later with Jewish, Italian, or Irish names. He then applied the luncheon technique to 12 of the participants. For this part, he presented the items that had shown the most bias as they ate a free lunch. Their subsequent rerating of the items appeared to show that the free lunch had conditioned away the ethnic bias. It is hard to know whether conditioning was actually shown, because items chosen on the basis of extremity of response tend to regress to the mean by chance when rerated. Such changes in rating might look like attitude change, but not be. However, Razran did other luncheon studies that were not subject to such shortcomings. For example, in one, Razran (1954) presented music and pictures that had been associated with eating and found that they increased "frequencies of food-related free verbalizations, frequencies of food-related rhyme finding, and speed of unscrambling food-related letter-scrambled words" (Razran, 1954, p. 274). A second point, however, as noted by Razran, is that despite the visceral nature of the stimuli involved, these conditioned responses were actually cognitive ones. For example, although the pictures and music did remind people of food-related material, there was no evidence for conditioned hunger or desire for food, as might have been expected.

Another early study that is particularly relevant to affect and attitude is Watson and Raynor's (1920) famous demonstration of conditioned aversion in Little Albert, a 9-month-old child. The study is one of the most cited pieces of research in psychology. However, it consists simply of Watson's description of how Little Albert reacted when Watson struck a metal rod with a hammer behind the child's head when a white rat (and later a rabbit) was placed before him. Textbooks generally overstate the evidence for generalization (as did Watson himself subsequently). Little Albert did not, as some suggest (Wolpe, 1958), develop a phobia for rats and other furry objects. Also, the study did not illustrate "preparedness" to learn to fear furry things (Seligman, 1970). There was clear evidence of some aversion, but the evidence for generalization and resistance to extinction was not as impressive as often claimed in textbooks (Harris, 1979). Indeed, a week later, reactions were sufficiently weak that Watson instituted new conditioning trials to strengthen the aversion.

Another touchstone in discussions of conditioning and attitude are early experiments by Staats and Staats (1958). They showed changes in the evaluation of words referring to nationalities (e.g., Dutch, Swedish) or of male names (e.g., Tom, Bill) after repeatedly being associated with positive or negative words. For example, the words Swedish and Dutch were paired with positive or negative words, whereas the words German, Italian, French, and Greek were paired with random words. So, Dutch might be paired with such words as gift, sacred, and happy, whereas Swedish might be paired with such words as bitter, ugly, and failure. Afterwards, participants were given a booklet with six pages. On each was one of the national names and a pleasant to unpleasant rating scale. They were told to indicate how they felt about each word in order to see if their feelings influenced their recall. After eliminating nearly 20% of the participants who indicated awareness of the pairings, they found that the stimuli associated with positive or negative words were rated more and less positively, respectively.

In the intervening years, there were several other pivotally important demonstrations of attitude conditioning, including studies by Zanna, Kiesler, and Pilkonis (1970) and research by Krosnik, Betz, Jussim, and Lynn (1992), which used subliminal affective pictures as a UCS in order to control for awareness of the conditioned stimulus-unconditioned stimulus (CS-UCS) contingency. More recently, Olson and Fazio (2001) have examined the classical conditioning of evaluative reactions by looking at implicit measures of attitude. They paired pictures of two Pokemon characters with positive and negative words and images. Each was paired 20 times with valence words, and these trials were embedded in 430 other trials. Subjects were told that the slides were random, and that their task was simply to hit a response key as fast as possible when an image appeared. The task was said to concern video surveillance. They later assessed participants' recognition of the pairings and conducted a funnel interview, neither of which suggested much awareness.

The results showed conditioning both on explicit evaluations and on the Implicit Association Test (IAT). It is not clear how adequate the funnel interview was, but they eliminated the six of 56 participants who mentioned one of the contingencies in response to a direct question. An evaluation might have emerged only after participants were asked for their opinion (Experiment 1) or were asked to make evaluative responses as part of the IAT assessment procedure (Experiment 2). In support of this possibility, Olson and Fazio (2002) note that a previous study (Fazio, Lenn, & Effrein, 1984) had shown consolidation of evaluative information into an attitude only after direct questions about attitude.

To test this possibility, they repeated the study, but assessed attitude formation by presenting the previously conditioned Pokemon characters subliminally. The procedure involved both forward and backward masking. Attitude conditioning was still evident even though participants were not asked to consciously evaluate the figures. That is, positive and negative words were evaluated more quickly when preceded by subliminal exposure to the Pokemon figure of the same (conditioned) valence.

The authors argue that the associations were formed without awareness. The basis of this claim is that the results were unaffected by eliminating the 10% of participants who explicitly mentioned the associations in response to the question, "Did you notice anything unusual about the items that were presented with the Pokemon Shielder and Metapod?" In the original Olson and Fazio (2001) studies, awareness was measured by explicit memory for specific CS-UCS pairs. Participants were classified as aware only if they could accurately recognize which specific items had appeared together, and recognition of such specific item pairings was at chance.

The results suggested that the prior results were not due to procedure-induced, conscious evaluation of the attitude objects. On the other hand, the evidence for attitude was the reaction time to evaluate the associated words, a procedure which may have kept any prior evaluations active. Also, the attitude assessment took place immediately after the association procedure and in the same basic situation.

Awareness. Is awareness of the contingency between the CS and the UCS necessary for conditioning? In a 1974 paper, the cognitive psychologist William Brewer reviewed the literature and made the surprising conclusion that there was no convincing evidence of classical conditioning in humans without awareness. To prepare this chapter, we wrote to him to see if the evidence over the intervening 30 years had changed his mind. His response was fascinating. He said that despite the lack of evidence, he never doubted the possibility of unconscious conditioning in humans. He noted the following quote from his original review: ". . . given that Homo sapiens evolved from much simpler organisms and that the lower brain centers still function, it would seem strange if human beings showed no unconscious, automatic learning at all" (p. 28).

He said that this would have been his reply to our request a week earlier, but that he had just learned of a new review (Lovibond & Shanks, 2002) that reaffirmed his original claim and of still another, earlier review (Boakes, 1989, p. 389), which stated that "[Brewer's] conclusion still stands that there is no convincing evidence for conditioning in human subjects without awareness of the contingencies." The gist of the argument made by Lovibond and Shanks (2002) is that most of the attempts to assess awareness have simply been inadequate, with the result that any evidence that might support the idea of unconscious conditioning is ambiguous.

Interestingly, just as social psychologists are investing their faith more and more in unconscious determinants of behavior, investigators of conditioning are concluding that classical Pavlovian conditioning, the great hope for a peripheralist explanation of behavior, may require consciousness (Walther, 2002). However, several researchers have recently argued that the kinds of evaluative associations studied by social psychologists are actually not examples of classical conditioning of the Pavlovian variety, an issue to which we turn next.

Evaluative Association vs. Classical Conditioning

An interesting development in this literature lies in the distinction made by Baeyens, Eelen, Crombez, and Van den Bergh (1992) between what they call Pavlovian conditioning and evaluative conditioning (or simple association). The distinction is easily made, because classical or Pavlovian conditioning is an association of two events, and it concerns developing expectations that the UCS will follow the CS, which simply acts as a signal that the UCS is about to occur. Thus, when Pavlov sounded a bell, dogs in his lab came to expect food powder in their mouths. Expecting food triggered various responses, including salivation, which Pavlov measured, and perhaps dopamine and positive affect, which he did not measure.

The evaluative conditioning done by social psychologists, on the other hand, simply involves ensuring that participants process the meaning of two stimuli together, so that one then tends to think of them together. Without any electric shock or food powder being involved, no activity is required, and there is no necessity to marshal bodily resources to cope with such events. All that is required is for the organism to passively process lexical, pictorial, or other valenced items. It is rather like a concept learning task (Davey, 1994) or an impression formation task. Thus, when neutral Chinese ideographs (CS) are processed at the same time as smiling or angry faces (UCS), later thoughts about the ideographs are likely to include the pleasantness or unpleasantness of the faces with which they had consistently been paired (Winkielman, Zajonc, & Schwarz, 1997).

Pavlovian conditioning is a form of expectancy learning that allows the organism to prepare for responses to an expected event. By contrast, evaluative association simply induces a change in valence by making one also think about an associated positive or negative stimulus. The difference is in whether the CS makes one prepare for the UCS, or simply think (consciously or unconsciously) of the UCS, without expecting it to occur.

This characterization makes it easy to understand various other differences that have come to light between these phenomena. For example, Pavlovian conditioning extinguishes when the CS is presented without being followed by the UCS, but evaluative associations show no such extinction. Of course, if evaluative associations are more like impression formation or concept learning than like conditioning, extinction would not be expected. Our attitude toward a person who has been rude to us may not change even if he does not continue to be rude on subsequent occasions.

De Houwer et al. (2001) note that the preparation to cope with a UCS elicited by Pavlovian conditioning may be expensive in terms of resources and energy, which may explain why it is sensitive to extinction, and why it generally involves awareness of the CS-UCS relation. By contrast, evaluative "conditioning" or evaluative association is a simpler process of determining the valence of a stimulus by averaging across the valence of the stimuli with which it co-occurred in the past (Baeyens, Eelen, & Crombez, 1995).

Although De Houwer et al. (2001) still use the term "conditioning," some question whether the conditioning metaphor is really helpful in thinking about results from the evaluative association paradigm. For instance, Davey (1994) suggests conceptual categorization might be a more accurate characterization of the process. If a CS is processed in the context of a positive UCS, for example, then aspects of the CS that can be considered positive become salient. One essentially recategorizes the CS on the basis of these newly salient features within the context provided by the UCS. More generally, perhaps what contexts do is to get one to respond to contextually appropriate aspects or subvarieties of a stimulus.

This idea also explains context effects in studies using the IAT (Greenwald, McGhee, & Schwartz, 1998). The results of IAT studies often make people look both sexist and racially prejudiced. However, if one changes the usual context, the prejudiced pattern of response times can be made to disappear. For example, Lowery, Hardin, and Sinclair (2001) found that responses by White participants that would reflect negative stereotypes of African Americans did not appear in an IAT study with a black experimenter. Presumably, in that context, the category "Black" suggested people like the experimenter, rather than nameless, faceless, stereotypic black persons.

Regardless of how one thinks about studies of attitude conditioning, it seems clear that attitude responses can be created or altered by pairing neutral stimuli with stimuli that already have evaluative meaning. DeHouwer et al. (2001) suggest that the method provides a means to shape the way people behave toward new or previously neutral stimuli such as products, people, or ideas. Conditioning has long enjoyed the status of a basic process in terms of which other more complex processes might be explained. But it may be illuminating to consider still more basic processes.

The Gestalt Basis of Conditioning, Priming, and Mood Effects

In their review of affective conditioning, Hermans et al. (2003) suggested that priming and conditioning are curiously similar techniques. Both involve one stimulus followed by a second. In priming, the first influences reactions to the second, whereas in conditioning, the second influences responses to the first. At some level, the processes involved are presumably similar or identical. Indeed, at a still more basic level, they are also similar to the processes involved in the affective influence of mood on judgment.

These three processes are similar in the sense that in each an evaluation of one thing is influenced by its association with something else. In priming studies, the evaluative meaning of an initial prime influences responses to a later target. Both conditioning and priming employ evaluative words or pictures, but they involve different temporal relations. In conditioning, the target to be influenced comes before the source of evaluation, whereas in priming, the order is reversed. In both, reactions to the target are influenced by reactions to other stimuli presented at about the same time. In mood studies, both the nature of the evaluative stimulus and the timing of stimuli are different. The source of evaluation is the affect from background mood (rather than of affect from an evaluative word or picture), and the target is presented during the mood (rather than before, as in priming, or after, as in conditioning). When asked for a judgment, one may attend to how one feels, and an association is thus formed between affect and the target stimulus or object of judgment. But the processes seem very similar regardless of whether the effective stimulus is the positive meaning of a word or pleasant affect, and whether the affective information comes before, after, or during the processing of the target.

Underlying the particulars of these paradigms of attitude research, one can find a unity of process. Not only attitude formation, but also everyday sense-making depends on an automatic tendency to knit the separate experiences of each moment into a seamless narrative fabric. In filmmaking, this process is known by the French term *montage* (editing). Exploited today in all films, it was originally developed by the early Russian filmmaker Serge Eisenstein, who appreciated that successive scenes in a film are automatically linked together, which makes a compelling way to tell a story. Thus, if frames of a crouching tiger are followed by frames of a woman screaming, we seem to have witnessed the heroine's fear of a charging tiger, but if the initial scene had depicted a small child crawling along a window ledge, we would have experienced her fear of the child falling. The alternative technique for filming, *mise en scene* shows all of the relevant elements in a single scene. The French term meaning "placing on stage," is now used in film studies to designate how a particular scene is framed. As in film, so in reality, the emotional meaning of a moment depends on what experiences succeed each other or are associated in time. We are suggesting simply that just as successive sequences of scenes on film become a narrative whole, so the experience of affect also joins with whatever else is in mind at the time to form a narrative. This tendency for current mental content to be taken as the object of affect has been referred to as the "affective immediacy principle" (Clore et al., 2001).

One way to view all these phenomena is in terms of the Gestalt principle by which stimuli experienced closely in time and space are automatically seen as connected (Heider, 1958). At each unfolding moment, we rely on the content of short-term memory to provide coherence. Brain-damaged individuals with short-term memory deficits frequently find themselves confused, because without some short-term carryover from the last moment, the current moment makes no sense (Sacks, 1985). Normal individuals sometimes have related experiences when they make comments such as, "I know I came in here to get something, but I can't remember what it was."

In this segment, we have suggested that conditioning, priming, and mood effects may rest on a more basic mechanism that might be called "experiential montage." Before leaving the conditioning topic, we examine in the next segment some limitations of conditioning as an explanation of the role of affect in attitude. In that discussion, we make two points. The second of those is that cognitive, cultural, and interpersonal processes, rather than conditioning, often mediate the influence of affect on attitude. The first point, to which we now turn, concerns the assumption that almost anything can become conditioned to almost anything else. We noted earlier that this randomness assumption was seen as objectionable during the era of the Enlightenment because it threatened belief in a moral order. In the next section we suggest that the assumption is objectionable today because it appears to be false.

Limitations of Conditioning Explanations

The enthusiasm with which we pursue conditioning as a primary explanation of everyday attitudes should perhaps also be tempered by other evidence, such as the findings of a study of attitudes toward dogs (Doogan & Thomas, 1992; see also Rimm, Janda, Lancaster, Nahl, & Dittmar, 1977). A survey of 100 college students and 30 children showed that only about half had early experiences that could have directly conditioned a fear of dogs, and many of these were simply additional recollections of being afraid rather than instances of harm. The other individuals seemed to have learned primarily by observation, parental warnings, and TV news stories about dog attacks.

Biological Preparedness.   Not all stimuli have an equal potential of becoming conditioned stimuli. For example, simply by virtue of being primates, we are likely to develop a more or less negative attitude to snakes and spiders. Neither we nor our chimpanzee cousins are apparently born with this attitude, but rather we come "prepared" (Seligman, 1970) to learn the attitude. The evolutionary argument is simply that primates who readily learned to avoid snakes, spiders, and angry faces had a greater chance to become one of our grandparents than those who did not. It is assumed that such preparedness for fear learning can operate automatically and be independent of conscious processing. The best known evidence comes from Mineka, Davidson, Cook and Keir (1984) showing that young monkeys readily learn to fear snakes simply by seeing another monkey show fear.

A systematic examination using pictures of snakes as conditioning stimuli has been done by the Swedish investigator Arne Öhman (Öhman & Soares, 1998). He and his collaborators find that when briefly presented pictures of snakes are visually masked and followed by electric shock, skin conductance responses readily become conditioned. The remarkable part of these experiments is that the unconscious exposure to snakes or spiders or angry faces readily led to conditioning, but pairing unconscious presentations of pictures of flowers, mushrooms, or happy faces did not result in conditioned skin conductance responses.

Even when associated images of mushrooms were equally reliable signals of shock onset, there was little attitude conditioning. Such results suggest that we are more prepared to dislike snakes than we are to dislike mushrooms. However, if ingestion of mushrooms were followed by nausea and vomiting, they too could become intensely disliked, an example of the well known Garcia effect (Garcia & Koelling, 1966). In the original demonstration, Garcia discovered that rats will readily associate taste, but not visual or auditory cues, with nausea. Amazingly, an association is formed even when a taste is separated from nausea by hours. Further, if the food is novel, a single association can establish an aversion that lasts for years.

Öhman and Soares (1998) concluded that such "prepared" stimuli are detected by an automatic preattentive system that acts independently of controlled attentional processes. Similarly, Garcia showed taste aversion conditioning even with unconscious animals. On the other hand, might the preparedness studied by Öhman simply be some weak dislike? Then, when subliminal exposure triggers reactions that are weak, but compatible with the reactions elicited by shock, conditioning might occur more easily than to stimuli without such a headstart. The different reaction to mushrooms when associated with shock and with nausea might mean that a match between the mode of exposure (e.g., ingestion) and the locus of negative outcome (e.g., nausea in the stomach) is critical. In any case, the notion that conditioning involves random association of stimulus and response may not be tenable on biological grounds.

Cognitive Preparedness.   Analogous limitations concern our cognitive preparedness to make certain associations between affect and attitude objects. Affective reactions to stimuli are usually embedded in mental and causal models that support their association. Thus, adults who burn their finger on the stove may be surprised at their clumsiness, but they are not surprised that pain could follow such an act. They need not have the experience again and again to establish an association. Even the least sophisticated of us have a crude mental model of heat transfer that supports associations between the stimulus of heat and the pain of being burned. Associations are involved, of course, but the experience of being burned enlivens an already existing, nonrandom association based in a latent mental model that supports and maintains the association. Similarly, an experience of being bullied by adolescent males with tattoos would likely be enmeshed in at least a half-baked model that makes that association more likely than one that might support an expectation that one would be bullied by the class president or the valedictorian. Once one has the idea that certain kinds of individuals may present certain kinds of threats under certain conditions, one has an attitude. But the critical association is likely to be one based on cognitive structures of knowledge and belief.

Cultural Preparedness.   The appeal of affect and of conditioning as explanations for attitude lies partly in their apparent simplicity and seemingly non-cognitive nature. However, the affective influence on some attitudes comes not from conditioning, but from cultural

ideology. For example, cross-cultural research on negative attitudes toward obese people suggests that the ability of obesity to elicit negative affect depends on implicit inferences about
blame, which in turn implicate ideological and cultural assumptions. Crandall et al. (2001)
found evidence that prejudice against obese people is based on assumptions of individual responsibility, which are predominant in individualistic, but not collectivist cultures. Crandall
et al. refer to their approach as an "ideological theory of prejudice." They define ideology as
a network of interrelated beliefs and values that "not only enshrine ideas and explanations but
entail evaluation and affect" (Brown, 1973, p. 13).

In the foregoing, we suggest that psychologists have placed too much faith in the infinite
malleability of associations and hence of attitudes. In the following section, we suggest that
we may also have placed too much faith in the correlated assumption that affective meaning
comes from simple, primitive processes.

In the experiments by Staats and Staats (1958) the names of countries were presented with
positive or negative words. These studies suggest that people learn attitudes by associating
positive or negative concepts to persons or groups. Presumably affective comments from others
do influence our attitudes, but some (Sinclair, Huntsinger, Skorinko, & Hardin, 2003) suggest
that such influences arise as part of a process of maintaining our own identities, rather than by
classical conditioning. In addition, linguists realized early on that mere association probably
would not take us very far in understanding semantic learning (Chomsky, 1968).

Bottom-up explanations dominated psychology until the cognitive revolution highlighted
the top-down role played by cognitive structure. Analogously, it should not be a surprise that
social attitudes often also reflect social structure and interpersonal relations. In that regard, an
alternative understanding of how we learn word meanings (including evaluative meanings), is
known as "Theory of Mind." That approach, to which we now turn, serves as our final limitation
of bottom-up, classical conditioning approaches to attitude learning.

Theory of Mind.   "Theory of mind" refers to the understanding that people have mental
states such as thoughts, beliefs, and desires that can be inferred from behavior. Although
Premack and Woodruff (1978), who coined the term, investigated mind-reading abilities in
chimpanzees, "theory of mind" entered into the study of human development and has generated
a great amount of empirical research on how children acquire this fundamental aspect of social
cognition (e.g., Astington, 2000; Leslie, 1987; Lewis & Mitchell, 1994; Wellman, 1990; Zelazo,
Astington, & Olson, 1999).

In his book on the learning of word meaning, Paul Bloom (2000) proposes that theory of
mind is crucial for understanding how children learn what things mean. In a comparison that
is potentially informative for attitude theorists, he contrasts two forms of learning. One was
suggested by John Locke and the other by St. Augustine. Locke proposed that we learn word
meanings by association. With repeated association between hearing a name and seeing an
object, a child will respond to the presentation of the stimulus object with the response of the
name. Augustine, on the other hand, suggested that word meanings are actually learned from
one's elders in context as the child infers the intent of others who use particular words. Bloom
proposes that Augustine had the right idea, and that research bears him out. His elaboration
of the Augustinian account of how he learned the meanings of words as a child is framed in
terms of theory of mind.

Theory of mind research is based on the idea that much of a child's cognitive development
hinges on the child coming to understand what other people have in mind when they do or
say something. The focus is not limited to figuring out specific and localized references, but
assumes also that we operate out of a more general theory of other people's perspectives.
It is important to note that investigators of theory of mind do not assume that children are
engaged in deep philosophical thought. On the contrary, the power of the approach lies in the

idea that under the broad umbrella of "theory of mind" are a host of inferential moves, which children (and the rest of us) employ more or less automatically. For instance, at some point in development, children come automatically to use the gaze of others to disambiguate what they mean when they refer to something in the room. Indeed, even in the second year of life, children develop an intense interest in the behavior of others and can already make accurate inferences about false beliefs on the part of others (Onishi & Baillargeon, 2002).

The importance of such automatic social information processing can be seen dramatically by considering the difficulty of interacting with autistic children (Baron-Cohen, Tager-Flusberg, & Cohen, 1993). An important way of understanding many of the cognitive aspects of autism is precisely that they are deficient in theory of mind. They tend to be focused on the non-living, mechanical aspects of their environment, and often have special difficulty with language and communication. For example, autistic children experience another person's words to refer to what they themselves are looking at, rather than using the speaker's gaze. Normally, automatic social inference processes are quite fundamental for social interaction and for cognitive development generally.

If understanding how word meanings are learned requires a theory of mind perspective, then understanding how affective meanings are learned may too. The potential explanatory power of the approach recommends it to social psychologists, but theory of mind is also appealing because it provides an appropriately social perspective on attitude learning.

Category-Triggered Affect

Another socially-derived, top-down approach to affect and attitude draws on schema theory. Fiske (1982) pointed out that we can have strong affective reactions to individuals we have never encountered simply by thinking of them as members of a category to which we already have affective reactions. In her treatment of schema-triggered affect, she proposed that as we apply a schema or category to others, they tend to inherit whatever affective reaction we have to the category. Thus, in political discourse, or what passes for political discourse during elections, candidates attempt to get voters to place their opponents in undesirable categories and to place themselves in desirable categories. They do so in the knowledge that individuals are painted with the same brush as the categories of which they are seen to be members.

When individuals are stereotyped, they are assumed to have all of the attributes that are stereotypically seen as characteristic of the group to which they belong. However, in addition, Fiske and Pavelchek (1986) provided a model of both piecemeal and category-based evaluation, suggesting that categorization occurs first, and is followed by piecemeal processing if categorization is not successful. According to the model, encountering an attitude object elicits existing attitudes toward the object. Other attribute information may be ignored if it is inconsistent with the category activated by the stimulus.

The model has also been applied in marketing contexts. At great expense, producers of consumer goods attempt to create positive stereotypes about their brand name. They bank on the idea that products introduced within a positive brand name will inherit the brand-based affect. Conversely, companies involved in direct mail marketing have the reverse problem. They often attempt to disguise the mail they send out to avoid it being categorized as "junk mail," because it is a negative category and mail thus categorized is more likely to be thrown away than read (Zhao, 1993). Thus, they may include category-inconsistent features, such as the use of handwriting, rather than printing, or the use of the recipient's name, rather than a generic address such as "Resident."

We discuss the affective dynamics of categorization and stereotyping further in a later section. For now, however, we turn our attention from such molar processes to a very molecular process of affective influence–mere exposure.

Mere Exposure

Mere exposure describes the observation that the repeated, unreinforced presentation of a stimulus is sufficient to increase positive affect toward that stimulus, relative to a stimulus that has not been presented repeatedly. In a classic study, Zajonc (1968) presented Chinese-looking characters, nonsense words, or yearbook photographs for either 0, 2, 5, 10, or 25 times to participants. Participants subsequently rated how "good" or "bad" the meanings of the Chinese characters or of the nonsense words were, and how much they liked the person shown in the photographs. For all three kinds of stimuli, participants' ratings increased with increasing numbers of presentations. Many studies have since replicated and extended this basic effect, suggesting that the mere exposure effect is a robust phenomenon (Bornstein, 1989). The effect has been documented for a great number of different stimuli, including ecologically relevant stimuli, such as foods (Crandall, 1984; Rogers & Hill, 1989), drinks (Pliner, 1982), music (Peretz, Gaudreau, & Bonnel, 1998), brand names (Baker, 1999; Janiszwewski, 1993), and urban environments (Herzog, Kaplan, & Kaplan, 1976).

Bornstein and colleagues (Bornstein, Leone, & Galley, 1987) also investigated the applicability of the mere exposure effect to social situations of everyday life. Participants were subliminally primed with the photograph of a person they later interacted with (a confederate in the experiment), or a blank slide. Subsequently, the participant and two confederates were asked to evaluate poems to determine if their author was a man or a woman. Participants were more likely to agree with the confederate with whose face they had been primed. These and other findings (e.g., Moreland & Beach, 1992) suggest that the mere exposure effect is relevant to phenomena occurring outside of the psychological laboratory.

Increased liking of a stimulus also occurs when participants are not consciously aware of having been repeatedly exposed to that stimulus. The first demonstration of a mere exposure effect with subliminal stimulus presentation was documented by Kunst-Wilson and Zajonc (1980). Polygons were shown for 1 ms, five times each. Participants consistently preferred previously seen polygons over new ones, although they indicated recognizing those previously exposed only at chance level. Thus, conscious awareness of the stimuli does not appear to be necessary for mere exposure effects to occur (Monahan, Murphy, & Zajonc, 2000; see Bornstein, 1992).

Bornstein and D'Agostino (1992) specifically compared the magnitude of mere exposure effects of consciously perceived versus subliminally presented stimuli. Either polygons or yearbook photographs were presented for either 5 ms or 500 ms, and were subsequently masked. They were presented for 0, 1, 5, 10, or 20 exposures. After repeated exposure, participants rated each on scales measuring affect (like–dislike) and recognition (old–new). Consistent with previous findings, frequently exposed figures and faces received more positive ratings than infrequently exposed figures. In addition, the effects were significantly larger for stimuli presented for 5 ms, compared with stimuli presented for 500 ms. Because effect sizes tended to be greater when stimuli were not recognized, Bornstein (1989) concluded that awareness tends to inhibit the mere exposure effect.

Although mere exposure has been documented in hundreds of studies, explanations regarding its mechanism remain controversial. Whereas some have argued for an affective basis (Zajonc, 1980, 2001), others have argued for a cognitive basis (Bornstein & D'Agostino, 1992; Klinger & Greenwald, 1994).

Early attempts to explain mere exposure effects did not fare well in empirical tests, because they were unable to explain the later emerging findings involving stimuli presented outside of conscious awareness (see Harrison, 1977; Stang, 1974, Bornstein, 1989 for reviews). More recent explanations have identified a central role of perceptual fluency or ease of processing as a result of repeated stimulus exposure.

Theories that account for the mere exposure effect in terms of fluency fall into two categories. Some investigators propose that fluency has no affective valence (Bornstein & D'Agostino, 1994; Jacoby, Kelley, & Dywan, 1989; Mandler, Nakamura, & Van Zandt, 1987). Others propose that fluency has a positive valence (e.g., Harmon-Jones & Allen, 2001; Reber, Winkielman, & Schwarz, 1998; Winkielman, Schwarz, Fazendeiro, & Reber, 2003).

As an example of the first approach, Mandler et al. (1987) proposed a nonspecific activation model in which repeated exposure leads to increased accessibility of the stimulus representation. As a consequence, participants should rate any stimulus property, including affective judgments of liking, as more extreme. Evidence for this hypothesis is that participants rate nonaffective properties (e.g., brightness or darkness of stimuli) more highly for frequently exposed stimuli (Mandler et al., 1987). Hence, an important aspect of this model is that fluency leads to more extreme judgments of *any* kind, whether positive or negative, affective or nonaffective. Related to this view is the perceptual fluency/attributional model (Bornstein, 1992; Bornstein & D'Agostino, 1994; Jacoby et al., 1989). It suggests that perceptual fluency is simply misattributed as liking. Support for this position comes from the finding that the effect size depends on the delay between stimulus presentation and ratings (Bornstein, 1989). The higher the delay, the more positive the ratings, suggesting that time passing after stimulus exposure reduces the likelihood that participants correctly attribute affective responses to previous exposure. In other words, when participants are aware of having seen the stimulus previously, the experience of fluency is simply attributed to frequency of exposure and not to liking. Similarly, lower ratings are found when participants are explicitly given alternate explanations for the experience of fluency (Bornstein & D'Agostino, 1994). Conversely, subliminal presentation makes the correct attribution of fluency impossible, leading to larger effects than supraliminally presented stimuli (Bornstein, 1989). When presentation times allow awareness, effects are strongest for very brief exposure times (< 1 s) and get increasingly weaker with larger exposure times (Bornstein, 1989).

If fluency is indeed the driving force behind the mere exposure effect, then manipulations that increase fluency should lead to more positive evaluations. In other words, perceived fluency by itself should create the mere exposure effect in the absence of repeated stimulus presentations. Precisely this effect was found in several studies (Reber et al., 1998). For example, in one study pictures of objects were shown to participants. In order to manipulate fluency, some pictures were preceded by a subliminal presentation of their contours, whereas other pictures were preceded by contours of other objects. As expected, those pictures whose own contours had appeared first were liked better than the other pictures. Thus, a "mere exposure" effect was created even when all pictures were presented only once. Additional studies manipulating fluency demonstrated that similar effects to those of perceptual fluency have been obtained with conceptual fluency (see Winkielman et al., 2003).

However, Winkielman and colleagues (Reber et al., 1998; Winkielman & Cacioppo, 2001; Winkielman et al., 2003) argue that high fluency, that is, fast and effortless processing of information, may signal positive states of the environment, and of one's own cognitive processes. As a result, fluency leads to positive affect as well as to positive evaluations of target stimuli. Repeated stimulus exposure results in higher ratings of positive affect than single exposures (Monahan et al., 2000). The same picture arises from EMG measures in that high fluency is associated with activation of the zygomaticus muscle used for smiling, but not with the corrugator muscle used for frowning. Thus high fluency appears to involve positive affect, but not negative affect (Harmon-Jones & Allen, 2001; Winkielman & Cacioppo, 2001).

The nonspecific activation model proposed by Mandler and colleagues (1987) and the related perceptual fluency/attributional model (Bornstein, 1992; Bornstein & D'Agostino, 1994) suggest that repeated exposure leads to higher ratings of any stimulus-relevant dimension. However, Winkielman et al. (2003) note that the data on this issue are equivocal. Although

Mandler et al. (1987) found increases in ratings for brightness and darkness, they did not find increased "disliking" of frequently exposed stimuli. A similar finding was reported by other researchers (Seamon, McKenna, & Binder, 1998), who in fact were not able to replicate Mandler et al.'s (1987) findings on stimulus brightness and darkness.

Further, studies of affective evaluations demonstrate an asymmetric effect, such that only positive evaluations, but not negative evaluations, are influenced by fluency manipulations, regardless of how questions concerning the ratings are worded. For instance, Reber et al. (1998) found that high fluency led to increased judgments of liking and decreased judgments of disliking. Similarly, Winkielman and Cacioppo (2001) instructed half of their participants to report their positive affect, and half to report their negative affect after a fluency manipulation. Only positive affect increased when exposed to high fluency. Those reporting negative affect did not show similar increases. In addition, as noted above, measures of facial muscle activity only revealed activation for muscles involved in positive affect, but not for those involved in negative affect (Harmon-Jones & Allen, 2001; Winkielman & Cacioppo, 2001).

To summarize, recent research on the mere exposure effect has focused on whether experiences of perceptual fluency have an affective valence or not. Data by Winkielman using multiple methods suggest that fluency does have a positive affective quality. Given that we all have implicit goals to comprehend our surroundings (Kelly, 1955), cognitive fluency should indeed be positive (see Mackie & Smith, 2002). Thus, an affective component appears to be part of the processes that result in the mere exposure effect. Zajonc (2001) recently proposed another affective mechanism involved in the mere exposure effect. He argued that it can be viewed as an example of classical conditioning in which the absence of negative consequences serves as a rewarding unconditional stimulus. However, direct data supporting this conjecture are currently lacking, and would perhaps be difficult to obtain. Yet, evidence has been accumulating that the mere exposure effect is mediated by affect, albeit not in the manner that Zajonc (1980) initially envisioned.

Zajonc (1980) saw the mere exposure effect as an example of affect that was not mediated by cognition. The critical finding was that the effect is larger when people are unaware of having previously been exposed to the relevant stimulus. If one assumes that most cognitive operations are unconscious, however, then that finding takes on a different significance. From an affect-as-information perspective, the finding mirrors the dynamics also seen in mood research (see Clore & Colcombe, 2003). Affect (regardless of whether it is from mood, frequent prior exposure, or some other source) is likely to influence liking of unrelated objects only if the true source of the affect is ambiguous or unknown. In the mere exposure paradigm, the positive affect is from fluency of processing rather than anything inherent in the stimulus. When the fluency is experienced as familiarity from prior exposure rather than as spontaneous liking, then the mere exposure effect is less likely to be observed. To explore further the role of unexplained affect in attitude, we turn next to the mood and judgment paradigm.

Mood and Evaluative Judgment

Affective feelings elicited by objects routinely influence evaluative judgments of them. In addition, irrelevant feelings arising from associated happy or sad moods can also affect such evaluative judgments (e.g., Esses & Zanna, 1995; Forgas, Bower, & Krantz, 1984; Forgas & Moylan, 1991; Gasper & Clore, 1998; Keltner, Locke, & Audrain, 1993; Ottati & Isbell, 1996). However, as in the case of mere exposure, affect from mood tends to influence liking only when the cause of the affect is not obvious. But before reviewing relevant research, some background is in order.

Background. In the 1960s and 1970s social psychologists were not receptive to the idea that phenomenal experience played a role in attitude and evaluative judgment. The emphasis was on how people combine information in attitudes and impressions. Research focused on whether people add (Fishbein, 1963), average (Anderson, 1965), or respond to proportions (Byrne & Clore, 1966) of positive and negative information (see Wyer & Albarracín, this volume). Less often asked were questions about what information enters into attitudes. Fishbein and Ajzen (1975) maintained that attitudes are based on beliefs and evaluations concerning properties of attitude objects, whereas Clore and Byrne (1974) emphasized the role of affective feelings. Progress in resolving such disputes was slow because feelings and beliefs about particular objects tend to be highly correlated. Although problematic for research, such a confounding of beliefs and feelings is advantageous in everyday life. If people's feelings and beliefs routinely conflicted (see Fabrigar, MacDonald, & Wegener, this volume), making ordinary decisions could be laborious and unreliable.

Method.   Charles Gouaux (1971) solved the research problem by showing mood-inducing films to his subjects. In this way, he varied feelings independently of beliefs. At about the same time, Griffitt and Veitch (1971) did something similar by conducting an experiment in either a normal room or a hot and crowded room. These investigators found that feelings could influence attitude and attraction independently of beliefs, but more importantly, they devised a new research tool. Since then, mood induction procedures have become a staple in social psychology. The technique is valuable as a way of independently varying thoughts and feelings, despite the fact that they are ordinarily thoroughly entwined.

Memory-Based Models.   Despite demonstrations that affect does influence judgment, investigators were reluctant to assign a primary role to feelings. The mood method caught on, but initial explanations reverted to the traditional idea that judgments must be based on beliefs about objects of judgment. At about the same time, both Isen (Isen, Shalker, Clark, & Karp, 1978) and Bower (Bower, Monteiro, & Gilligan, 1978) proposed memory-based models of affective influence. Using the idea of spreading activation from Anderson and Bower's (1973) human associative memory (HAM) model, they treated mood as a node in a memory network. When moods are induced, they suggested, activation spreads from the mood node to mood-congruent concepts in semantic memory and to mood-congruent events in episodic memory. In this way, mood could influence judgment by making accessible a biased sample of information from memory. For example, in happy moods, one is more likely to recall positive information about a target object, and hence bias judgment in a positive way. A virtue of these models was that they were consistent with traditional approaches (Arkes & Hammond, 1986), which emphasized that judgments are based on beliefs. The role of emotion, therefore, was assumed to be indirect, determining which beliefs were retrieved from memory to serve as the basis for judgment.

Affect-as-Information Model.   The affect-as-information view is a general approach to which many investigators have made contributions, elaborations, and variations. Wyer and Carlston (1979) suggested that the knowledge or information that one was in a mood might itself influence attitude and attraction. They focused on affective knowledge or *information about* one's feelings. Schwarz and Clore (1983) applied the idea but have emphasized the embodied information of feelings, rather than conceptual information about feelings. They examined the role of mood in judgments of life satisfaction in two experiments.

In one experiment, they asked participants ostensibly to help in the construction of a Life Event Inventory (LEI). Participants were to supply a detailed description of a happy or sad experience in their recent past which in fact served as a mood induction technique. In a second experiment, the researchers relied on warm and sunny versus cold and rainy spring weather to induce happy and sad moods. In that study, they asked questions about life satisfaction during a telephone interview conducted on either warm and sunny or cold and rainy days. Each experiment showed that happy moods led to higher ratings of life satisfaction compared to those by individuals in sad moods.

The experiments also included attribution manipulations, which consisted of making salient a plausible alternative cause of participants' feelings. The first experiment was conducted in an odd, sound-proofed room covered in insulation and electrical shielding. The oddness of the room was exploited in a cover story suggesting that spending time in the room might make them feel tense (or pleasantly relaxed). Participants were given an opportunity to rate how much the room contributed to their current feelings before making their life satisfaction ratings.

In the second experiment, the telephone interviewer had said that he was calling from Chicago, so that for half of the respondents, he could ask at the beginning, "By the way, how is the weather down there?" The purpose of that pleasantry was to make salient an external possible cause for their feelings, which was in this case the true cause.

Schwarz and Clore (1983) found that in both experiments, the effects of mood on judgments of life satisfaction disappeared in the condition in which an external plausible cause for their feelings was salient (the sound-proofed room or the sunny or rainy weather). At the end of the interview, respondents were also asked about their current mood, and it is important to note that the external attribution manipulation had no effect on self-reported mood. Rather than changing how they felt, the external attributions changed the apparent relevance of the experienced information of happy and sad feelings for determining life satisfaction. Once attributed to being in an odd room or experiencing foul weather, feelings of sadness, for example, were not experienced as informative about their level of life satisfaction.

The results suggested that affect can influence judgment directly, provided that it is experienced as a reaction to the object of judgment. Moreover, the effect did not appear to be an obligatory consequence of affect, but instead was contingent on how it was experienced; that is, on the apparent information value of the affect. This account contrasts with the idea that mood automatically activates mood-congruent material in memory and then serves as the basis for judgment. It is common, of course, to make judgments on the basis of what comes to mind about the object of judgment. But independently of such belief-based judgments, it appears that people also (implicitly) ask themselves, "How do I feel about it?" (Schwarz & Clore, 1988).

The misattribution paradigm is useful for analytic purposes to disentangle affect from beliefs. The results do not imply that the affect of attitude is easily misattributed. Indeed, specific attitudes, like specific emotions, should be resistant to misattribution, because their affect is already dedicated to an object (see Table 11.1).

Research showing that mood effects on evaluative judgments are actually due to mood can be seen from a study by Strack, Schwarz, and Gschneidinger (1985). They asked participants to describe happy or sad life events either in a vivid or in a pallid way. They found that only vivid accounts produced moods and mood-congruent judgments. In contrast, pallid accounts tended to produce the opposite. Specifically, they judged their life satisfaction to be greater after recalling unpleasant experiences than after recalling pleasant ones. Their judgments contrasted their current lives to the positivity or negativity of the events they had recalled. Thus, event recall by itself does not have the same effect on judgment as mood.

The difference between an affect-as-information explanation and a memory-based explanation can be seen by imagining being asked how much one likes one's meal at a restaurant. Traditional judgment theory (Anderson, 1981) would suggest that we answer such questions by retrieving stored evaluations from memory. Essentially one would be saying, "I know that I am enjoying my meal because it is lasagna, and I know that I like lasagna." Alternatively, people may simply taste the food and answer on the basis of the on-line experience of pleasure or displeasure. In other words, they may use their affect directly as information, rather than indirectly as a cue to retrieve stored knowledge about one's likes.

When Is Affect Used as Information?   Isbell and colleagues (Isbell & Wyer, 1999; Ottati & Isbell, 1996) found mood effects on liking for stimulus persons described as political candidates. However, these effects occurred mainly when judges were not well informed about politics. For those high in political expertise, happy moods led to lower, rather than higher, evaluations of candidates, suggesting that they corrected their judgments for the influence of feelings and relied instead on their expertise. It would be a mistake, however, to conclude that affect plays a role only in the attitudes of novices. Lodge and Taber (2004) note that affect actually plays a larger role in the judgments of politically sophisticated individuals because politically relevant stimuli are more likely to elicit affect in them. Thus, when affect is from an irrelevant source, such as induced moods (e.g., Ottati & Isbell, 1996), we should expect less influence of affect, whereas when the affect stems from the attitude object itself, we might expect more affect and hence more effect with greater sophistication (Lodge & Taber, 2004).

Forgas (1995) concurs that affect should have no influence on judgment when prior judgments can be retrieved. His affect infusion model differentiates situations into those that are "open" versus "closed" and that involve high versus low effort. It says that mood should have an influence in "open," but not "closed" situations. A "closed" situation is one in which a specific answer already exists in memory or is dictated by motivation. An "open" situation involves some amount of processing, which can be either heuristic (low effort) or substantive (high effort). Forgas categorizes the affect-as-information approach (Clore, Schwarz, & Conway, 1994; Schwarz & Clore, 1983) as low effort or heuristic, and the memory-based approach (Forgas & Bower, 1987) as high effort or substantive.

An Affect Heuristic.   The idea of a "How do I feel about it?" heuristic was proposed in Schwarz and Clore (1988), who suggested that use of the heuristic is likely when little other information is available and when time constraints put a premium on attentional resources. Since then, Slovic and colleagues (Slovic, Finucane, Peters, & MacGregor, 2002) have also proposed an "affect heuristic."

The idea that affect is used as a heuristic suggests that mood effects should be found mainly when judgments are made quickly. However, Forgas (1995) reports greater mood effects on tasks that take longer, providing evidence for two kinds of mood effects, one that is a heuristic shortcut, and another that involves more effortful, substantive processing. But for many judgments, asking oneself how one feels about an object is not a shortcut, but is the most relevant data to be considered. Indeed, even in choices that are backed up by considerable research, one may still ask how the tentative decision feels. If it does not feel right, good decision makers may go back to the drawing board.

Affective Bias?   Investigators of judgment and decision making tend to see affective influences on judgment as biases. Such language assumes that pure, unbiased judgments would not involve affect. But we assume that affect did not evolve to conflict with common sense. Indeed, work on emotional intelligence (Mayer & Salovey, 1997) suggests that it is important for judgments to be informed by emotion. Damasio (1994) arrives at similar conclusions from studies of patients with damage to the prefrontal cortex. He argues that the poor judgment among these individuals does not result from deficits in intelligence, but from deficits in their ability to use affective reactions as feedback.

Alternative Affective Representations

Investigations of affective influences often focus on mood or other affective feelings. However, other forms of affective information appear to have similar influences. For example, evidence

(Clore & Colcombe, 2003) suggests that without necessarily changing people's moods, unconsciously primed affective thoughts can have the same cognitive consequences as affective feelings of mood. The same also appears to be true of facial expressions (Schnall & Clore, 2002; Strack, Martin, & Stepper, 1988), and even colors (Soldat, & Sinclair, 2001). Although unconscious priming, posed expressions, and related stimuli can affect mood under certain circumstances, it is also useful to entertain a broader view, recognizing that multiple representations of affective meaning can each have similar effects.

According to Clore and Colcombe (2003), parallel effects can be expected for mood, unconsciously primed evaluative concepts, feedback from facial expressions, and perhaps other affectively meaningful cues to the extent that they all convey information about goodness or badness. Indeed, even in studies of felt mood, according to the affect-as-information approach, it is not the feelings per se that are important but their information value. What is critical for affective information to influence judgment is that it is experienced as compelling by virtue of seeming to arise spontaneously from within. The spontaneity and compellingness of the evaluative information is more important than whether the medium of the information is facial muscles, motor action, visceral feelings, or thoughts. We have argued that the influence of affective feedback on judgment and processing is not limited to feelings, but that affective information can be represented in multiple media.

Affect in Attitudes Toward Actions

Complementing research on affect and judgment is theorizing about affect and decision making. From an attitude framework, we might think of affective influences on decision making as influences of affect on attitudes toward actions (Fishbein & Ajzen, 1975).

Risk-as-Feeling.   Loewenstein, Weber, Hsee, and Welch (2001) have proposed a risk-as-feeling model. They suggest that feelings often constitute a major component in decision making processes, and lead to decisions that are primarily made on the basis of feelings rather than cognitive processes. In particular, risky decisions are often governed by fear and anxiety that work independently of cognitive considerations of risks. Decision-relevant feelings might come from vividly imagined consequences of a decision, and from personal experiences or familiarity of the consequences of making a decision. For example, Loewenstein et al. (2001) consider the case of deciding whether or not to get insurance against floods or earthquakes. Most people are likely to overestimate the occurrence of such adverse events when confronted with anecdotal reports, rather than actual probabilities of floods and earthquakes. Thus, personally knowing somebody who witnessed an earthquake, and the resulting fear of the same event happening to oneself, can override other pieces of information, and lead to decisions that neglect cognitive factors. Loewenstein et al. refer to their model as dealing with "anticipatory" emotion: feelings experienced while the decision is being pondered. In contrast, "anticipated" affect comes into the picture when considering the emotional implications of having made a certain decision.

Affect Decision Theory.   A model that deals with such anticipated emotion is the affect decision theory proposed by Mellers, Schwartz, Ho and Ritov (1997). These authors argue that a person's expectation about an outcome has important consequences on the emotional response to that outcome. In their research, participants were given certain expectations about the amount of money they would win or lose in a gamble, and these expectations were either confirmed or violated. The results indicated that affective responses were not a linear function of the absolute amount of money. A greater win was not necessarily perceived as more pleasant than a smaller win. Instead, the amount of the win interacted with the participant's expectation of the win: Unexpected wins were experienced as more pleasant than expected wins. Participants engaged in counterfactual reasoning so that they considered not only what actually happened, but what *could* have happened. As noted by Mellers et al., this reasoning led to the counterintuitive finding that an unexpected win of $5.40 produced more positive affect than an expected win of $9.70. Thus, expectations about predicted outcomes form the basis for counterfactual comparisons so that certain wins lead to disappointment, whereas certain losses lead to relief.

Specific Emotions and Attitude

Thus far, we have focused on the role of positive and negative affect in positive and negative attitudes. But some investigators have begun to examine specific emotions (Lerner, Small, & Loewenstein, 2004). For example, DeSteno, Dasgupta, Bartlett, and Cajdric (2004) focused on anger. They proposed that anger should influence automatic evaluations of outgroups because of its functional relevance to intergroup conflict and competition, whereas other negative emotions that are less relevant to intergroup relations (e.g., sadness) should not. In two experiments, they created minimal ingroups and outgroups. The minimal groups situation involved asking New Yorkers to estimate "How many people ride the New York subway everyday?" Participants were then told (on a random basis) whether they were an under- or an over-estimator. Experimenters gave red wristbands to the underestimators and blue wristbands to the overestimators. They then induced anger, sadness, or a neutral state. Automatic attitudes toward the in- and outgroups were assessed using pictures in an evaluative priming measure (Experiment 1) and the Implicit Association Test (Experiment 2). The results showed that anger created automatic prejudice toward the outgroup, whereas sadness and neutrality resulted in no automatic intergroup bias.

Mackie, Devos, and Smith (2000) also examined the role of specific emotions in attitudes toward outgroups. They proposed that emotions such as fear are characterized by different action tendencies than emotions such as anger. They proposed that groups that are feared should be avoided, whereas groups responded to with anger may elicit an aggressive stance. In three experiments, they found evidence that people had different inclinations toward outgroups to which they felt fear as opposed to anger. When the ingroup was strong (enjoyed collective support of group members), people were more willing to entertain such actions as arguing with, confronting, opposing, and attacking the outgroup. Moreover, they found that the relation between appraisal of group strength and offensive action tendencies was mediated by self-reported anger.

In addition to specificity of behavioral inclinations, some attitudes may also involve specificity in the kind of evaluation involved. For example, Haidt (2001) has proposed an emotion-based account of what might be thought of as moral attitudes. He argues that many of our moral evaluations are based on disgust or other emotional reactions. In his view, moral reasoning of the sort studied by Kohlberg (1969) may often be after-the-fact justifications for moral judgments, rather than causes of them. For example, in what he calls demonstrations of "moral dumbfounding," Haidt asked students to consider such scenarios as one involving consensual sex between a brother and sister. The students tend to find such actions morally objectionable. However, when asked why, their reasons are often insubstantial and faltering, leading some to say essentially, "I don't know why, it is just disgusting." He suggests that what may appear to be a lack of insight may actually be an accurate account of the emotional basis of moral attitudes.

In the foregoing sections, we have discussed in some depth the many ways in which affective valence may influence attitudinal valence. Before leaving this discussion of the direct influences of affect on attitude, we consider the role played by the other major facet of affect–arousal.

Arousal as Importance

Affective feelings are evanescent. One does not store feelings in memory; they last only as long as they are being experienced, and no longer. Of course, a person might remember the fact that he or she was happy on some occasion, but one cannot look into memory and find the happy feelings. One can even mentally replay an emotional event, and elicit feelings, but those are new feelings, not memories of the original ones. Long ago, Bartlett (1932) showed that we do not store experiences as experiences, but rather that we reconstruct them later. The same is true of visceral feelings (Loewenstein, 1996), including emotions (Wyer et al., 1999). If so, how can momentary affect become attitudes, which are not necessarily momentary?

One answer may lie in the arousal aspect of affect. The arousal aspect of affect conveys information about urgency and importance (Fig. 11.1), and that embodiment of importance makes events memorable. Indeed, recent research on the neuroscience of memory shows how the adrenaline elicited during affective experience acts to consolidate memory for those events over time (Cahill & McGaugh, 1998). Presumably, a psychologically important event is one that may be affectively arousing, and that arousal makes it more memorable. If so, similar subsequent events may remind one of that event and elicit related affective reactions experienced as an affective attitude.

William James (1890) said that, "If we remembered everything, we should on most occasions be as ill off as if we remembered nothing." The key, he suggested, lies in selecting what to remember. One hundred years later, it is becoming clearer that emotion helps us in selecting what is important to remember.

Memory is generally thought of as divided into short-term and long-term memory, and "memory consolidation" refers to the process by which memories get transferred from the short-term to the long-term store. This is where emotion comes in. The brain has to decide what is worth retaining from all of the experiences that pass through short-term memory. We can try to make something more memorable by consciously attending to it or by practicing it. But when an event triggers the release of adrenaline, we will remember it even without trying to. As things get emotional, the stress hormone adrenaline stimulates the amygdala, which tags the experience as important for storage in other areas of the brain.

Arousal appears to be a way to give information preferential weighting for storage. Thus, the most important experiences result in the strongest memories. Moreover, since it is the arousal rather than the valence of an experience that matters, it can make both good news and bad news more memorable.

The primary work on arousal and memory has been done by McGaugh and colleagues (Cahill & McGaugh, 1998). For example, one study showed that a series of emotionally evocative film clips were better recalled than a series of neutral clips taken from the same films (Cahill et al., 1996). The emotional clips depicted themes of animal mutilation or violent crime, whereas the neutral clips were similar in style, but less emotionally arousing, including scenes of court proceedings, travel, and so on.

Students watched the films while glucose utilization in the brain was measured by positron emission tomography (PET). Three weeks later they were contacted by telephone and asked to recall the film clips. The results showed that mean activity in the amygdala showed a clear relationship to later mean recall of the emotional clips, but not of the nonemotional clips. Thus, amygdala activity during emotional experiences is related to long-term, conscious recall of those experiences, but such amygdala activity is not relevant to recall of nonemotional situations.

These findings support the view that although neutral experiences can be remembered without involvement of stress hormones or amygdala activation, when one is emotionally aroused, stress hormones stimulate the amygdala to influence storage of that material in memory.

Irrelevant Arousal Is Also Effective.   As it happens, arousal-induced memory en-hancement can occur even when the source of the arousal is irrelevant, and even if it comes after learning has already taken place. For example, Nielson (2003) found such effects when she showed an arousing film after people memorized a list of words such as fire, queen, and butterfly (see also Pearson, 2002). Half of the participants watched a film of a dentist pulling a tooth, complete with blood and screeching drill. Twenty-four hours later, these traumatized participants' memory for the list was about 10% better than the memory of participants who watched a dull film about tooth brushing. Apparently even if the material is not personally meaningful, emotion can aid memory.

We have long known that emotionally charged events are easier to remember. Psychologists have usually assumed that this occurs because people focus more on emotional events or because they essentially engage in more practice of emotional events as they ruminate about them. Now, it appears that adrenaline does the work, by activating the amygdala, which signals the hippocampus, which helps decide what to remember. These results are consistent with animal data showing that memory can be enhanced by administering adrenalin shortly after aversive training at the time that it would normally have been released by aversive stimulation. It thus appears that, "Long-term memories are not made instantaneously: they consolidate over time after learning (Cahill & McGaugh, 1998, p. 294)."

Arousal Can Hinder as Well as Help.   It should be noted, however, that arousal can interfere with memory, as well as enhance it. The dose-response curve for adrenaline is an inverted U, so that either too much or too little adrenaline does not improve memory. We may fail to remember either mundane events or events accompanied by truly extreme emotion, but in general, strong emotion yields strong memories.

Implications.   What are the implications of these discoveries about emotion and memory for the establishment of attitude? LeDoux (1996) has suggested that "emotion is memory." In other words, he thinks of an emotion that is triggered in some situation as an embodied memory of the significance of such situations. If so, then it may be equally sensible to say that "attitude is memory" (at least for attitudes originating in personal affective experience). The research to date, however, has not focused on whether emotion during an experience makes the emotional significance, as opposed to making the situational details, memorable.

From research in which volunteers watched a grim film of a rabbit-processing factory, Cahill found that the more viewers ruminated over the next two days on what they had seen, they more they could remember. He suggests that replaying a memory reelicits adrenaline and reactivates the amygdala (Pearson, 2002). Indeed, some (Pittman, 1989) suggest that the problem in cases of posttraumatic stress disorder (PTSD) is that in addition to the memorability of the original trauma, each time it is remembered, new arousal further increases its memorability until the memory becomes disabling.

To the extent that the remembered details support the ability of a situation to reelicit emotion, then the processes we have discussed may be important in transforming momentary emotional experiences into attitudes. On the other hand, mood research suggests that the generality of affective influences may depend specifically on forgetting about the details of the situation in which the affect originated (Keltner et al., 1993). Jacobs and Nadel (1985) too say that old phobias recur when the activity of the hippocampus, which is responsible for situating memories, is dampened. Under such conditions the emotional significance of experience with the phobic object becomes unconstrained by the time and place of its original occurrence. Thus, stereotyped and persistent reactions may be elicited that are not constrained by an appropriate context in memory. And similar spreading of fearful reactions can occur over time as animals forget the aspects of the environment that served as safety signals (Hendersen,

1978). Thus, to develop a generic attitude may require that the affect become attached to some attribute of the stimulus object divorced from a particular time and place. It is possible, therefore, that remembering well the situational details of emotional moments would limit or constrain emotional memories to be relevant only to that situation, thus inhibiting production of a generalized attitude. On the other hand, well remembered situations should have a greater capacity to elicit an emotional and attitudinal response.

Summary of Direct Effects

This large segment covers the direct influences of affect on attitude, including, most notably, classical conditioning. The idea of reducing complex phenomena to simple reflexes dates at least to Descartes, who envisioned explanations based on behavioral reflexes that were as automatic as the physical reflections of light from mirrors.

Classical Conditioning.   We reviewed classic studies of attitude conditioning (Razran, 1954; Watson & Raynor, 1920; Staats & Staats, 1958), as well as recent ones (Olson & Fazio, 2001). However, some investigators (Baeyens et al., 1992; DeHouwer et al., 2001) suggest that the simple affective associations involved in attitude development do not fit the Pavlovian conditioning mold. Pavlovian conditioning, on the one hand, involves expectations about the occurrence of an event (UCS), awareness of event contingency, and extinction of expectancies when the conditioned stimulus is no longer followed by such events. The simple associations involved in affect and attitude, on the other hand, do not depend on expectations of events, do not appear to require awareness, and do not show extinction effects. In these respects, such associations may be more like impression formation than like conditioned responding.

Narrative Coherence.   We suggested that a single gestalt principle may underlie various phenomena, including affective conditioning or association, affective priming, and mood effects on judgment. In all of these, succeeding moments of experience tend to form perceptual groupings. This automatic process of linking successive experiences together is presumably also responsible for the narrative coherence that makes everyday experiences meaningful.

Limitations to Conditioning Models.   An additional limitation of classical conditioning as a paradigm for attitude development is the implication that the relevant associations are random and haphazard. This criticism was anticipated even during the Enlightenment by critics of associationism (Sutton, 1998). Modern research suggests that we are evolutionarily prepared (Seligman, 1970) to learn particular kinds of responses to particular classes of stimuli, as is evident in phenomena such as the Garcia effect (Garcia & Koelling, 1966). In addition, certain things become associated with affect not haphazardly or by conditioning, but because we are cognitively or culturally prepared to associate them (as components of structured knowledge and cultural assumptions). As a further counterpoint to associationistic explanations, we discussed how theory of mind provides a social and cognitive account of how children learn affective meaning (Bloom, 2000). Finally, we emphasized that objects may also simply inherit the affective reactions to the groups or categories to which they are seen to belong (Fiske, 1982).

Mere Exposure.   We next turned to studies of mere exposure (Zajonc, 1968; 2001), the observation that increased exposure to novel stimuli increases liking. The effect is greatest when people are unaware of the prior exposures (Kunst-Wilson & Zajonc, 1980), interpreted initially as evidence that affect can be processed prior to and independently of cognition. Critics emphasized that since most cognitive processing takes place outside of awareness, lack of awareness does not imply lack of cognition. Others offered cognitive interpretations in terms of familiarity and fluency of processing (e.g., Bornstein & D'Agostino, 1992). Recent evidence (Winkielman et al., 2003) suggests, however, that cognitive fluency (in the context of goals to understand) elicits positive affect, which in turn elicits liking. Thus, mere exposure is an affective phenomenon, but not one that bypasses ordinary cognitive processing.

Mood and Judgment.   Research on mood and judgment was a final example of direct influences of affect. As with mere exposure, induced affect from mood influences judgment mainly when its source is not obvious. Clear demonstrations of affect in attitude involved inducing mood independently of beliefs in research on interpersonal attraction (Gouaux, 1971; Griffitt & Veitch, 1971). Early explanations reconciled these observations with traditional notions that judgments depend on beliefs. Theorists (Bower et al., 1978; Isen et al., 1978) proposed that affect served to activate cognitive material in memory–the real bases for judgment. Others (Schwarz & Clore, 1983) proposed that affect itself can act as information about the value of attitude objects. According to the affect-as-information approach, judgments are sometimes made by (implicitly) asking, "How do I feel about it?" (Schwarz & Clore, 1988). Although sometimes called a judgment "heuristic" (Slovic et al., 2002), others note that affective influences need not be viewed as shortcuts (Forgas, 1995; Wyer et al., 1999), nor as sources of "bias" to be overcome (Ketelaar & Clore, 1997; Damasio, 1994; Salovey & Mayer, 1990).

We noted that sources of affective information other than mood show mood-like effects on judgment and information processing. To the extent that expressions, colors, and subliminal primes also provide compelling information about value, they should function the same as mood regardless of whether or not they induce mood.

Attitude Toward Action.   Affect can also influence attitudes toward actions, as seen in hypotheses aimed at explaining affect in decision making. These include both risk-as-feeling (Loewenstein et al., 2001) and affect decision theory (Mellers et al., 1997). In addition, research is increasingly focused on the role of specific emotions such as disgust (Lerner et al., 2004) and anger (DeSteno et al., 2004). Mackie et al. (2000), for example, suggest that outgroups eliciting anger may incline people toward aggression, whereas those eliciting fear may simply be avoided.

Arousal and Memory.   Finally, research on long term memory for arousing events (Cahill & McGaugh, 1998) suggests that the arousal component of affect may also be important for attitude formation. We ended this section by asking whether remembering well the details of emotional moments would establish or limit the establishment of general attitudes.

Although affect has many *direct* influences on attitude, as described in this section, there are also *indirect* influences that are important. We turn to these indirect influences now.

Indirect Influence of Affect on Attitudes

When people focus directly on attitude objects with the goal of evaluating them, then positive and negative affective cues are likely to be experienced as manifestations of liking and disliking. This represents a direct effect on attitude. But in task situations when people focus on their own expectations and inclinations to respond and have a performance goal, then the same affective cues may be experienced as information about their own efficacy, rather than as liking. In such situations, individuals who feel efficacious (by virtue of being in a happy mood) tend to rely on cognitively accessible information, such as stereotypes, whereas those who do not (by virtue of being in a sad mood) tend to focus on individuating information. In this way, affect may have an indirect effect on attitude, for example, by governing whether people rely on categorical or individuating information (Fiedler, 1988; Schwarz, 1990).

Affect and Stereotyping

Few areas of social psychology have received as much attention in the past decade as stereotyping. A thorough review is beyond the scope of this chapter. Nevertheless, two salient points in this literature are relevant to a treatment of affect and attitude. The first is the development during the 1990s of a dual process view of stereotyping (Devine, 1989). The second is research on affective triggers for stereotyping (Bodenhausen, 1993).

The idea that stereotyping follows naturally as a response to ethnic labeling was explicit in Allport's (1954) initial writing on the topic, as was the idea that people sometimes put the brakes on their prejudices. Thus, in a sense Allport also anticipated the current dual-process view of stereotyping. In the meantime, some social psychologists also have treated stereotype activation as an automatic consequence of intergroup contact. But these same investigators have often emphasized that people can and do control such automatic stereotyping (Brewer, 1988; Fiske & Neuberg, 1990; for a review see Devine & Montieth, 1999).

Interestingly, these treatments of stereotyping have tended to take emotion out of stereotyping. Rather than assuming that the impulse to stereotype ethnic minorities results from deep seated anger, which motivates displacement and scapegoating (Dollard & Miller, 1950), this view sees stereotyping as just another instance of cognitive categorization. Recent work using the IAT has also contributed to the idea that ethnic stereotypes are part of most people's world knowledge and stereotypic names and labels tend to activate such knowledge even among minority group members.

Despite the fact that the existence of stereotypes may not implicate emotion, some research does suggest that affect plays a role in the use of stereotypes in judgments and decisions. Specifically, studies of mood and processing show that stereotypes are more likely to be used when individuals are in happy than in sad moods.

Bodenhausen, Sheppard, and Kramer (1994) asked participants induced to be happy and sad to act as jurors. Before reading about the crime, participants read the target's name and home town, which identified him in half of the cases as Hispanic. This identification was intended to activate a stereotype, and the research examined when this information would and would not be used in judgments of guilt. They found that the stereotype had more impact on the judgments of jurors in happy, rather than in sad, moods.

The research shows clearly that affective cues can play a role in the use of stereotypes. However, the role played by affect is not unique to stereotyping. Indeed, happy mood appears to have the same influence on the use of any categorical information. For example, Bless and colleagues (Bless et al., 1996) examined the role of mood in people's use of scripts (schemas about action sequences) to process information from stories. In a recognition task, they found that individuals in happy moods made more script-consistent errors. That is, they falsely recognized information that they had not actually heard, but which was consistent with the restaurant script they had used to encode the story.

Additional findings in the study by Bless et al. (1996) help explain why happy mood increases reliance on stereotypes, scripts, and other general knowledge structures. Older explanations had assumed that individuals in happy moods might be sufficiently preoccupied that they had limited attentional resources for systematic processing (Worth & Mackie, 1987). Or perhaps positive feelings implied that systematic processing was unnecessary (Schwarz, 1990). To test these explanations, Bless et al. (1996) included a secondary task as participants listened to the story. They found that participants in happy moods did not lack the ability or motivation for systematic processing. In fact, they performed better than those in sad moods on the secondary task. Instead, it appeared that their reliance on the restaurant script to process the story left them with extra attentional resources for doing the secondary task.

The greater use of the accessible cognitions on the part of happy mood participants suggests that in task situations positive affect serves as efficacy feedback (Clore et al., 2001). That is, positive affective cues provide a green light for relying on expectations, inclinations, and accessible cognitions. They confer value on the processor's own constructive efforts (Fiedler, 2001) and cue a relational orientation, in which people process incoming information in relation to accessible cognitions and general knowledge structures (Bless & Fiedler, 1995). Negative affect serves as a stop sign that tends to reduce reliance on accessible cognitions and increases reliance on external information in the environment.

Subsequent research by Isbell (1999, 2004) has provided further evidence for an affect-as-information interpretation of mood and stereotyping results. In a series of studies, her participants read one of a series of narratives in which a character engages in behaviors, some of which imply one stereotype and some of which imply another. Beforehand, they were given an expectation intended to cue one of the two stereotypes. For example, the character in the story was described either as an introverted librarian or an extraverted salesperson. When she asked later for ratings of the character, she consistently found that individuals in happy, but not those in sad moods, used their initial expectations and activated stereotypes. Her results were thus consistent with those of Bodenhausen et al. (1994).

Attribution.   As a test of the affect-as-information interpretation, Isbell (2004) also introduced an attribution manipulation. Participants rated how the writing task, which had been used as a method of mood induction, had made them feel. This process made salient the true cause of their positive or negative affective feelings. Once their true cause became salient, these irrelevant feelings were no longer experienced as feedback about the value of their accessible cognitions. As predicted, the results were reversed for individuals in the attribution groups, so that sad but not happy individuals now relied on the activated stereotype. Why do attribution manipulations not simply eliminate mood effects? Presumably, reversals occur because ordinary processing already involves both top-down and bottom-up processing. Inhibiting the kind of processing style encouraged by their now discounted feelings leaves only the opposing tendency, resulting in reversed results in which sad mood individuals now use stereotypes and happy mood individuals do not.

In addition to her attribution results, in other versions of the same paradigm, Isbell also asked her participants to recall the story they had heard. She found, as expected, that individuals in happy moods recalled significantly more stereotype-inconsistent behaviors from the story. Consistent with the prior person memory literature (Wyer & Srull, 1989), increased schema-inconsistent recall is a clear indication that individuals in happy moods were actively using the accessible stereotype to process the story. That is, behaviors that do not fit the stereotype tended to stick out and received more practice, leading to greater recall.

Anger.   One further surprising but important fact about mood and stereotyping concerns the effects of anger. Bodenhausen at al. (1994) manipulated anger in addition to happy and sad mood. He found that responses of participants in angry moods showed that they also relied on stereotypes. Thus, happy and angry mood led to the same results, even though happy is considered a positive emotion and anger a negative emotion. But the affect-as-information hypothesis concerning mood effects on processing maintains that the nature of affective influences should depend on the information conveyed by the affect in that situation. If feelings of anger (like positive affective feelings) are experienced as information that one's own position is correct, then it is not surprising that in angry, as well as in happy moods, people rely on accessible cognitions, including stereotypes. Tiedens and Linton (2001) also provide evidence that emotions associated with certainty (e.g., disgust) promote heuristic processing, whereas emotions associated with uncertainty (e.g., fear) promote systematic processing.

Egalitarian Goals.   Most research on mood and stereotyping concerns the tendency for individuals in happy or angry moods, but not in sad moods, to use stereotypes. According to the affect-as-information approach, however, this result occurs because stereotypes are fairly accessible for most people (at least in the usual experimental situations studied). But what if the people studied were chronic egalitarians? Would positive mood make chronic egalitarians stereotype less? Dunn and Clore (2004) tested this hypothesis with participants who possessed a chronic goal to treat women in an egalitarian fashion. Following the approach used by Moskowitz, Gollwitzer, Wasel, and Schaal (1999), they first asked men to rate women as a group on various gender-stereotypical attributes. Next, participants completed a survey that forced them to endorse stereotypical statements about women. Finally, they were again asked to rate women on stereotypical attributes. The idea is that people with egalitarian goals who have been forced to endorse stereotypical statements should compensate by describing women in counter-stereotypical ways at the next opportunity. Thus, participants who rated women as substantially less stereotypic on the final survey than the initial survey were classified as "chronic egalitarians."

A week later, they first listened to happy or sad music to induce mood and then completed a lexical decision task involving a series of pictures and letter strings. On each trial, a picture of a male or female appeared followed by a stereotypically female word, a gender-neutral word, or a nonword. Stereotype activation was measured by the degree to which pictures of women facilitated detection of stereotypically female words.

Consistent with previous research, they found that non-chronic egalitarians exhibited greater stereotyping on the lexical decision task in happy, rather than in sad, moods. In contrast, chronic egalitarians exhibited the opposite pattern, showing greater stereotyping in sad, rather than in happy, moods. This finding indicates that rather than exerting a direct influence on stereotyping, positive affect simply influences reliance on accessible strategies of social perception. For people who typically avoid stereotyping, happy moods apparently minimize rather than promote stereotypical thinking.

Category-Triggered Affect.   In the first section of the chapter, we discussed Fiske's work on schema-triggered affect. We noted that Fiske and Pavelchek (1986) proposed a theory concerning when one would focus on categorical information and when one would focus on individuating information. That work predated the research on mood and stereotyping, which implies that affect is one of the important conditions determining whether people focus on categorical or individuating information. As in the case of stereotyping, whether or not the affective reactions to individuals are dictated by affective reactions to their group depends on whether perceivers focus on their group identity or individual identity. That, in turn, appears to depend partly on mood.

This tendency for certain emotions to foster the use of stereotypes when accessible does not imply that happy or angry individuals would be more likely to form stereotypes in the first place. For example, happy and sad mood participants show no greater tendency to include stereotypic attributes in lists of characteristics of various ethnic groups (Esses & Zanna, 1995). Also, within the illusory correlation paradigm, both happy and sad mood inductions have been found to disrupt both the formation of illusory stereotypes (Hamilton, Stroessner, & Mackie, 1993) and accurate judgments of the variability of individuals within groups (Stroessner & Mackie, 1992).

Brand Names.   We noted earlier that reliance on brand names in the consumer domain may operate somewhat like stereotyping. In line with such an interpretation, Adaval (2001) examined influences of mood on intentions to buy various products, including sneakers and jeans. She provided information about both brand names (e.g., Levi's vs. Rustler) and product quality (e.g., high vs. low quality workmanship). She found that variation in the favorability of the brands had significantly more impact on the decisions of individuals in happy moods than on decisions of those in sad moods. Thus, regardless of the kind of attitude object, positive affect appears to promote a tendency to focus on global, categorical information, whereas in negative states, individuals focus more on individuating details.

Party Identification.   In a related vein, some observations suggest that voters in positive moods are also more likely to rely on the party identification of candidates. Consistent with the insights from mood research, Marcus and MacKuen (1993) show that anxiety inhibits reliance on predispositions such as partisan identification and ideological conviction, making voters learn more about issues and candidates. Instead of voting on the basis of category-level information, anxious voters rely on more individuated information (Marcus, Neuman, & MacKuen, 2000). This process lays the groundwork for change from habitual voting patterns. For example, in the 1988 presidential election, Republican attacks made Democrats more anxious about their candidate, opening up the possibility of defection of Democratic voters. Such defections often hold the key factor in elections (e.g., Clinton Republicans in 1996 and Reagan Democrats in 1984). Marcus suggests (personal communication, March 2, 2004) that who gets anxious is also a key factor. For example, when things go bad in Iraq or in the economy during a Republican administration, Republican voters would be more likely to get anxious than Democrats.

Summary.   When associated with attitude objects, positive affect may be experienced as liking. But during task performance, it may be experienced as efficacy (Clore et al., 2001) or fluency (Mackie & Smith, 2002). In turn, such positive feedback should lead to the confident use of accessible cognitions, including stereotypes. Indeed, Bodenhausen et al. (1994) showed greater stereotype use in happy than in sad moods. We emphasized an affect-as-information interpretation of mood effects on stereotyping. Consistent with that view, Isbell (2003) showed that the effect could be reversed by changing attributions. Also consistent are findings of increased stereotype use for other emotions that implicate either confidence in one's own view, including anger (Bodenhausen et al., 1994) and disgust (Tiedens & Linton, 2001). Finally, that stereotype accessibility is the key can be seen from research showing that individuals for whom egalitarianism is accessible show less rather than more stereotype use in happy moods (Dunn & Clore, 2004).

Stereotype use was seen as part of a general tendency to adopt a category-level focus (Fiske & Pavelchek, 1986; Gasper & Clore, 2002) when positive affect empowers current thoughts. Applications of this idea can be seen in related affective influences on attention to brand names as opposed to product attributes by consumers (Adaval, 2001) and political party identification as opposed to specific candidate attributes among voters (Marcus & MacKuen, 1993). A second kind of indirect influence, to which we turn next, concerns the role of affect in determining whether individuals scrutinize persuasive arguments or tend to accept them as presented.

Affect and Persuasion

As discussed extensively by Johnson, Maio, and Smith-McLallen (this volume), two basic ways of processing persuasive messages have been identified (Chaiken, Liberman, & Eagly, 1989; Petty & Cacioppo, 1986). One way is to focus on the actual content of a persuasive message, and to scrutinize the message content with regard to the quality of its arguments. This strategy of dealing with persuasive messages has been termed "central" (Petty & Cacioppo, 1986) or "systematic" (Chaiken et al., 1989) processing. In contrast, "peripheral" or "heuristic" processing involves disregarding the content of the message, focusing instead on additional cues irrelevant to the actual content, such as the source of the information or the status or the expertise of the person conveying it. As a consequence of the different routes of processing, when participants use the central/systematic route of responding to message content, they tend to be persuaded more by strong arguments, and less by weak arguments. However, the strength of the argument matters less when the peripheral route is chosen. In that case, other "peripheral" factors, such as the credibility of the source of the message or the intention of the communicator become important in the persuasive process.

The model assumes also that the same information can be processed in either or both a central or a peripheral manner (Petty & Cacioppo, 1986). For example, the attractiveness of a woman advertising beauty products could either be a relevant cue, indicating that the beauty products work, or an irrelevant cue, consisting of positive affective reactions to her beauty that become associated with the product. The model thus emphasizes that multiple roles can be played by particular factors. The influence of mood or extraneous affect is an example of a factor that can either be relevant or irrelevant. For example, the positive feelings of a person processing the proposals of a political candidate may act as a valid argument, whereas the positive feelings from hearing the "Star-Spangled Banner" in the background may act as an irrelevant cue, rather than a valid argument. Indeed, a whole literature has been generated investigating the effects of mood on persuasion (for reviews, see Mackie, Ascuncion, & Rosselli, 1992; Schwarz, Bless, & Bohner, 1991; Eagly & Chaiken, 1993).

Persuasion and Affective States.   One robust finding is that in happy moods, people are persuaded equally by strong and weak arguments, whereas in sad moods, people are persuaded more by strong, and less by weak arguments (Bless, Bohner, Schwarz, & Strack, 1990; Bless, Mackie, & Schwarz, 1992; Mackie & Worth, 1989; Sinclair, Mark, & Clore, 1994; Worth & Mackie, 1987). For example, Bless et al. (1990) induced moods by having students contemplate a pleasant or an unpleasant event from their own lives. Participants then considered strong or weak arguments supporting an increase in student services fees at their university. A positive mood resulted in a propensity to use the peripheral route, by paying little attention to the message content, such as the quality of arguments. In contrast, participants in the negative mood condition were persuaded only by strong arguments; presumably, they paid more attention to argument content and elaborated on it more.

However, these effects were malleable: When they were distracted by a secondary task, people in negative moods elaborated less, and in fact, performed much like participants in happy moods (Bless et al., 1990). In contrast, participants in happy moods showed no effects of the distracter task, suggesting that they did not engage in elaborative processing in the first place. Further, when given explicit instructions to evaluate argument quality, happy mood participants were persuaded only by strong arguments, an indication that they were able to engage in elaborative processing when explicitly asked to do so (Bless et al., 1990).

Several explanations have been offered for the effects of moods on persuasion (for an extensive discussion of this issue, see Bless & Schwarz, 1999). The findings described above were initially interpreted by Bless and colleagues (1990) as indicating that when in a happy mood, people are simply not *motivated* to pursue effortful processing, and instead, rely on less demanding styles of processing. Since this deficit can be overcome by specific instructions, it does not reflect a deficit in cognitive capacity, as suggested by others (Mackie & Worth, 1989). The cognitive capacity hypothesis postulates that because positive mood states activate large amounts of connected positive content in memory (Isen, 1987), cognitive resources are not available for systematic elaboration of the message content for individuals experiencing a positive mood (Mackie & Worth, 1989; Worth & Mackie, 1987). Support for this position comes from the finding that when participants in happy moods were given additional time to elaborate message content, the effects of positive mood on persuasion were eliminated (Mackie & Worth, 1989).

However, several empirical findings are inconsistent with a cognitive capacity account. It has also been suggested that negative mood states (rather than positive ones) limit cognitive processing capacity (Ellis & Ashbrook, 1988). Further, if participants experiencing positive moods are indeed unable to engage in elaborative processing, instructions should not make a difference, but they did in the studies reported by Bless et al. (1990). In addition, investigators (Isen, 1987) have repeatedly found that happy moods in fact lead to better performance, relative to neutral or sad moods, for example, on creative problem solving tasks. A series of experiments that is particularly instructive in this context was reported by Bless and colleagues (Bless et al., 1996). They found that, compared to sad or neutral moods, happy moods increased reliance on script-based information, which led to better rather than worse performance on a secondary task. Thus, positive mood did not compromise performance, as would be expected according to limited capacity accounts.

Although in earlier work they argued for a motivational explanation of mood on persuasion (Bless et al., 1990), in later accounts, Bless and Schwarz (1999) rephrased their position as reflecting reliance on "general knowledge structures" that can function independently of motivational or cognitive capacity constraints. For example, as noted by Bless and colleagues (1996), in some situations, happy individuals actually outperform individuals in sad or neutral moods, because they can use general knowledge structures such as schemas, expectations, and stereotypes. Thus, limitations on cognitive capacity do not seem to be responsible for the effects of mood on persuasion. It seems more plausible that participants in positive moods process persuasive arguments less systematically because their affective cues signal that they have already done sufficient processing (Martin, Ward, Achee, & Wyer, 1993).

This notion is consistent with the view that affective states confer informational value when it comes to cognitive processing (Clore, 1992; Clore et al., 1994; Schwarz & Clore, 1983, 1988, 1996). According to this account, negative moods indicate a problematic environment, whereas positive moods signal a safe and benign environment. As a cognitive consequence, people in bad moods are more likely to engage in systematic processing, whereas people in good moods are less likely to engage in effortful processing, and instead, do more heuristic processing. Consistent with the assumption that mood states signal processing requirements, Sinclair et al. (1994) found that the impact of mood states on persuasion can be eliminated when their informational value is called into question. Following the procedure described earlier (Schwarz & Clore, 1983), students were approached on either a sunny or a rainy day. While they were exposed to persuasive messages, their attention was, or was not, drawn to the weather as an external, irrelevant source of their mood. Only when participants did not focus on the weather as the cause of their feelings did the usual influence of mood on persuasion occur, with happy participants being equally persuaded by strong and weak arguments and sad participants being persuaded by strong arguments only. When attention was drawn to the weather, participants discounted the affective information, eliminating its influence on persuasion. Thus, affect serves as an implicit signal for the kind of cognitive processing strategy to pursue, but it loses this function when the feelings are experienced as task irrelevant.

A somewhat different perspective has been put forward by Petty and colleagues (Petty, DeSteno, & Rucker, 2001; Petty, Schumann, Richman, & Strathman, 1993). In line with their elaboration likelihood model (Petty & Cacioppo, 1986), they argue that affective cues serve different functions depending on the likelihood of cognitive elaboration. According to this model, classical conditioning is an example of a *direct* affective influence under conditions of low elaboration: An attitude object that has become associated with positive affect is evaluated positively, whereas an attitude object that has become associated with negative affect is evaluated negatively (Razran, 1940). In other words, mood functions as a direct, peripheral cue when elaboration likelihood is low. In contrast, when elaboration likelihood is high, such as when the attitude object is highly personally relevant, the relevance of the mood itself is judged, and mood has an influence on attitudes that is mediated by the affectively toned thoughts generated by the mood. Finally, moderate elaboration conditions are hypothesized to influence persuasion in the manner that resulted in the differential interaction effects of mood state and argument quality observed by Mackie and Worth (1989), and Bless and colleagues (1990, 1992).

The affect as information and elaboration-likelihood positions are not entirely dissimilar. Petty and colleagues suggest that negative affect should lead to more central processing and positive affect to more peripheral processing. Similarly, a cognitive tuning explanation suggests that negative affect implies a problematic situation, leading participants to engage in systematic processing, and positive affect signals a benign situation, leading participants to engage in heuristic processing. There are variations on how best to phrase an informational view. An alternative, for example, would be to predict that positive moods lead to the use of accessible information and negative moods to decreased use of such information. If one assumes that the most accessible information in the persuasion studies is the persuasive argument presented, then happy recipients may be prone to accept them, and sad recipients prone not to rely on such accessible information, but to scrutinize the details of the arguments. Such systematic processing leads them to accept or reject the arguments on their merits: to reject weak and accept strong arguments.

Loose ends in these explanations have been pointed out by Wyer et al. (1999) who noted that even in the original data by Bless et al. (1990), happy recipients were found to counterargue more than sad recipients, which is inconsistent with the idea that positive affect leads to less systematic processing.

Although some evidence favors the elaboration-likelihood model (see Wegener & Petty, 2001), other data are harder to reconcile with it. For example, findings from the Bless et al. (1990) studies appear inconsistent. These researchers included a condition that led to high elaboration (specific instructions to evaluate argument quality), but they did not find the main effect of mood that would be predicted by the elaboration likelihood model. Further, working while being distracted could be considered a low elaboration condition, but it also did not result in a direct effect of mood. Finally, Sinclair et al. (1994) also used a manipulation that could be characterized as a high elaboration condition. The participants consisted of students for whom comprehensive final exams were very relevant, because the introduction of the exams in the near future was presented as a distinct possibility. One concern about the multiple role model of affect has been that it does not unambiguously determine what factors count as low, moderate or high levels of elaboration (Eagly & Chaiken, 1993).

In addition to specifying when people use affect in persuasive messages, a model of when they correct for its influence has also been outlined (Petty & Wegener, 1993; Wegener & Petty, 1997). A related, two-step model that specifies one process for both the usage and the discounting of affective information has recently been proposed by Albarracín and Kumkale (2003). These authors propose that affect confers information in persuasion situations if, and only if, two conditions are met: First, message recipients must notice their affective reaction, and second, they must judge it as relevant. If people either fail to attend to their feelings or do attend to them, but attribute them to an irrelevant cause, then affect may play no role in persuasion. To actually have an influence, affect must be noticed, but not be judged irrelevant. One implication of their model is that at low levels of thought, increases in attention to one's feelings may increase the role of irrelevant affective influences, whereas further increases in attention may decrease affective influences (see also Gasper & Clore, 2000; Gohm & Clore, 2000). They suggest, therefore, that the motivation and ability to process arguments systematically should be associated with persuasion in a curvilinear manner, so that irrelevant affect should influence persuasion primarily for moderate levels of motivation and ability.

Although such irrelevant affective influences implicate low motivation or ability to correctly attribute feelings, the influence of relevant affect generated by considering the arguments themselves do not. Indeed, argument-induced affect might play the biggest role among individuals most motivated and able to make correct attributions. Specifically, Albarracín and Kumkale (2003) predicted that reduced ability and motivation should have a curvilinear effect on the impact of irrelevant (mood-based) affect, but should linearly reduce the impact of message-induced (relevant) affect.

Indeed, they found that when either motivation or ability was low, participants' attitudes were strongly influenced by the experimental mood induction. Presumably, low ability in combination with high motivation, or low motivation in combination with high ability allowed participants to go through the first step of the model, affect identification, but prevented them from proceeding to the next stage, discounting the affective reaction as irrelevant. In contrast, when both ability and motivation were high, participants were able to discount the effects of the mood induction, and thus eliminated its influence on their attitude. Finally, when both ability and motivation were low, participants were unlikely to even complete the first stage of the process, affect identification, and thus, also showed no effects of affect on their attitudes. Overall, this research integrates the motivational and attentional capacity aspects of earlier models into the affect-as-information framework, and provides compelling evidence for it.

Persuasion and Affect Regulation.   In the studies reviewed thus far, affect can be seen as providing information about the persuasion situation or the quality of the arguments. Such informational functions come into play under conditions of performance motivation. Sometimes, however, people may be more motivated to feel good than to perform well. Thus, when driving to work, one might switch from a news station to a music station on the radio if one's momentary motivation to maintain one's mood were greater than one's motivation to be well informed. Wegener, Petty, and Smith (1995) induced such hedonic motivation by emphasizing the enjoyable versus depressing nature of their persuasive material. When individuals expected the persuasive arguments to be uplifting, those in happy moods were more, rather than less, likely than those in sad moods to differentiate strong and weak arguments. The authors proposed the hedonic contingency model (HCM) which suggests that the usual mood effects on the processing of strong and weak arguments can also reflect the unpleasantness of thinking deeply about counterattitudinal material. That is, if individuals were momentarily focused more on enjoyment than performance, those in happy moods might want to avoid such unpleasant thoughts, producing the reverse of the usual mood and processing effect. Similar reversals of mood effects were reported by Martin et al. (1993) on liking, as opposed to persuasion, when they similarly manipulated emphasized hedonic over performance concerns.

Persuasion and Affective Messages.   All of the research reviewed above deals with the effects of emotional states on processing persuasive communications. Additional work has been conducted where the affective component is not in the mood state of the recipient, but in the persuasive message itself. This research falls into two categories, namely, the work on fear appeals (for a detailed review, see Eagly & Chaiken, 1993), and the work that compares cognitive and emotional message content (Edwards, 1990; Edwards & von Hippel, 1995; Fabrigar & Petty, 1999; Rosselli, Skelly, & Mackie, 1995).

In a classic study, Janis and Feshbach (1953) investigated the influence of various levels of fearful content on compliance with a persuasive appeal. Participants received information about the benefits of brushing one's teeth. For the high fear appeal, participants were presented with very graphic images of tooth decay, whereas for the low fear appeal, participants were presented with X rays of cavities and pictures of healthy teeth. A medium fear appeal condition consisted of pictures with a moderate level of depicted tooth decay. Two findings were noteworthy: First, compared to the other two fear conditions, participants in the high fear condition showed the lowest amount of reported compliance with the message of the communication, tooth brushing. Second, these participants were also more susceptible to counterarguments that they were exposed to one week after the original study. Thus, these authors and others (Hovland, Janis, & Kelley, 1953) suggested that high fear appeals tend to result in a defensive reaction, where message recipients actively try to minimize the threat's reality and relevance in their own life.

However, research in the years to follow did not necessarily find the same kind of evidence (Eagly & Chaiken, 1993), and others concluded that high fear appeals in fact do lead to increased persuasion (Boster & Mongeau, 1984). Extensions of the work on fear appeals (Rogers, 1983) went on to include mediating cognitive aspects, such as one's own perceived vulnerability to the threat, and one's sense of efficacy in dealing with it. Recent work has also addressed the match of the persuasive message with the mood state of the perceiver. For instance, Sengupta and Johar (2001) found that under some conditions, anxiety leads to improved elaboration of the persuasive message. When participants experiencing high levels of anxiety were given a message that was very relevant to their anxiety, they elaborated it extensively. In contrast, interference of high anxiety was found when they were given a message that was unrelated to the source of their anxiety. These authors argue that higher motivation to process the message can compensate for cognitive deficits associated with high anxiety (cf. Eysenck, 1982). Along similar lines, Petty and colleagues (Petty et al., 2001) concluded in their review of the literature on persuasion using fear appeals that when people feel competent and motivated to bring about an action in the face of likely threat, then fear appeals can be very effective. If, on the other hand, people feel that they do not possess the necessary skills or resources to deal with the threatening message, then messages with fear appeal can have the unintended effect of resulting in denial of the persuasive message, and as a consequence, less elaboration of its content.

Rather than being specific to fear, persuasive messages can differ in whether the content focuses on affective or on cognitive information (Edwards, 1990; Edwards & von Hippel, 1995; Fabrigar & Petty, 1999). For example, Edwards (1990) found that persuasive appeals were more successful when the appeal matched the content of the initial attitude formation, such that attitudes that had been formed on an affective basis were more easily changed by affectively toned appeals, whereas attitudes that had been formed on a cognitive basis were more easily changed by a cognitive appeal. However, mismatching effects for affective and cognitive appeals have also been reported (Millar & Millar, 1990). In Edwards' (1990) work, participants had either tasted a beverage (affective appeal) or read about its benefits (cognitive appeal), so it could be objected that the affective appeal involved a direct experience of the attitude objects, whereas the cognitive appeal did not. In subsequent work, Fabrigar and Petty (1999, experiment 2) conducted a study where both kinds of appeals consisted of an indirect experience. Participants learned about an unfamiliar animal, a "lemphur," and were exposed to either affective or cognitive information about it. They were able to confirm the presence of matching effects when controlling for direct versus indirect experience.

Zanna and Rempel (1988) suggested that there may be individual differences in whether people's attitudes are more consistent with the favorability of their feelings or more consistent with the favorability of their beliefs. Huskinson and Haddock (2004) recently pursued this idea and found considerable individual differences. In addition, they found that attempts to change attitudes that were affective or cognitive were more successful when they were consistent with the individual's general tendency to base their attitudes on affect or beliefs.

Summary. In happy moods, people tend to be persuaded equally by strong and weak arguments, whereas in sad moods, people are persuaded only by strong arguments and reject weak arguments. Whereas some investigators (Worth & Mackie, 1987) assume that happy moods reduce processing resources, others (Bless & Schwarz, 1999) propose that individuals in happy moods engage in heuristic processing because of the positive information conveyed by their feelings. In addition, Bless et al. (1996) showed that rather than engaging in heuristic processing because of reduced resources, individuals in happy moods actually have spare resources because they are engaging in heuristic processing. Still others (Sinclair et al., 1993) have shown that such mood effects can be eliminated if the feelings of mood are attributed to the weather.

From a somewhat different perspective, Petty and colleagues (1993; 2001) show that mood can have multiple effects depending on the likelihood of cognitively elaborating persuasive messages. Extending this logic, Albarracín and Kumkale (2003) proposed a two stage model of mood effects. They suggest that whether mood has an effect or not depends first on whether or not the message recipients notice their affect, and second, whether or not they judge it as relevant.

Finally, research has also been done on affect elicited by persuasive messages themselves. For example, Janis and Feshbach's (1953) classic work on the effectiveness of fear appeals has been revisited (Petty et al., 2001) with the suggestion that whether fear appeals are effective or not depends on the ability of message recipients to cope. It was finally noted that whether factual or emotional appeals work best may depend on how the attitudes in question were originally established (Edwards, 1990).

Affect and Cognitive Dissonance

In addition to changing attitudes via persuasive arguments, another method of attitude change beloved by social psychologists is through cognitive dissonance. In everyday life, too, an effective method of change can be to point out to people their inconsistencies. Young children are often alarmingly observant in spotting inconsistencies in parental rules and pronouncements. The traditional explanation for dissonance emphasized the role of uncomfortable tension elicited by an awareness of the inconsistency between beliefs and freely chosen actions (Festinger, 1957). In contrast to the original theory and later attributional interpretations (Cooper & Fazio, 1984), recent treatments of dissonance have emphasized affect rather than arousal, by assuming that dissonance is an emotional state of discomfort (Elliott & Devine, 1994; Harmon-Jones, 2001; Higgins, Rhodewalt, & Zanna, 1979; Losch & Cacioppo, 1990; Van Overwalle & Jordens, 2002). Olson and Stone (this volume) provide a fuller discussion of these studies. Moore (2003) has proposed an affect-as-information interpretation of dissonance-based attitude change. He had participants write counterattitudinal essays supporting tuition increases at their university. Counterattitudinal behavior under choice conditions is expected to produce cognitive dissonance, which Moore characterized as a negative state. After their essays, participants wrote about happy or sad life events to induce mood. As predicted, positive affect provided an "all clear" that eliminated dissonance-based attitude change.

Rather than increasing attitude change, as might be expected, sad moods can also reduce change for a different reason. Sad participants took the opportunity to attribute all their negative affect, including the negative affect of dissonance, to the immediately preceding, and relatively salient, mood induction procedure. Prior research (Schwarz & Clore, 1983) had shown that people are more likely to explain negative than positive affect, since negative affect signals a problem that needs attention. Accordingly, the negative mood group attributed their affect to the mood induction procedure and tended not to engage in dissonance-based attitude change. The salience of the negative mood manipulation appears to have served as a lightning rod to draw off dissonance-based affect by changing its meaning. Thus, taking an affect-as-information approach, Moore (2003) has provided a contemporary reinterpretation of cognitive dissonance as negative affect. His data suggested that dissonance effects could be eliminated either by providing positive affect as an antidote to dissonance or by changing the apparent source, (and hence the information value), of the negative affect of dissonance. The attribution of affect finding is similar to the attribution of arousal finding obtained much earlier (Zanna & Cooper, 1976).

Persuasion and the Affective Immediacy Principle.   Although positive affect reduced attitude change in Moore's (2003) experiments, Rhodewalt and Comer (1979) have reported the opposite result. Comparing the two studies, one suspects that the influence of affective cues on attitude change and persuasion depends on when affect enters the picture. Moore (2003) found less attitude change when he introduced happy mood *after* essay writing, because positive mood nullified the dissonance-induced discomfort that usually elicits attitude change. But Rhodewalt and Comer (1979) found more attitude change when participants smiled *during* their writing of the counterattitudinal essays. This occurred presumably because smiling informed participants that they were happy about the persuasive message (which would have been their focus) rather than being happy about their own attitude. These findings are consistent with our assumption that the impact of affect ultimately depends on what is in focus at the time (Clore et al., 2001).

Further support comes from results reported by Briñol and Petty (2003), who found that affective cues from head nodding and shaking could either increase or decrease persuasion, depending on whether participants were having positive or negative thoughts about persuasive messages at the time. More generally, these results are all consistent with the idea expressed in the "affective immediacy principle" (Clore et al., 2001), which says that, "affective feelings tend to be experienced as reactions to current mental content."

Affect as Evidence

Another indirect influence of affect on attitude formation stems from the fact that people tend to believe what they feel. This observation has been expressed as a feelings-as-evidence hypothesis (Clore & Gasper, 2000):

> *The Feelings-as-Evidence hypothesis is that belief-consistent feelings may be experienced as confirmation of those beliefs.* Evidence from the sensations of feeling may be treated like sensory evidence from the external environment, so that something both believed propositionally and also felt emotionally may seem especially valid. In this sense ... feeling is believing. (p. 25)

The hypothesis suggests that, for example, feeling negative affect at the same time as one entertains negative thoughts may validate them and give them gravity. Indeed, the subjective experience of affect can serve almost like a sixth sense, dedicated not to vision, audition, or touch, but to evaluation. Versions of this idea have recently been expressed in other related hypotheses, which we describe briefly.

Affect Confirmation.   The affect confirmation hypothesis is that people weight affect-consistent information more than affect-inconsistent information in evaluative judgments. Adaval (2001) tested her idea in a consumer study, mentioned earlier. She manipulated mood using videos, and then collected judgments about several consumer products. Product information included brand names and positive or negative product attributes (e.g., for sneakers, a soft, flexible sole vs. a hard, inflexible sole). Analyses showed that as raters evaluated the products, they gave more weight to positive attributes when they were themselves in positive moods, and more weight to negative information when they were in negative moods. The experienced affect seemed to serve as evidence of the importance of similarly-valenced attributes.

Affective Certainty.   Tamir, Robinson, and Clore (2002) propose a related model to explain enhanced performance on self-relevant reaction time tasks when actual feelings (of mood) matched beliefs about usual feelings (trait affect). The idea again was that affective experience could provide confirming data for self theories, and that (relative to states of affective disconfirmation) such affective certainty would make people more efficient at accessing their attitudes or deciding between wanted things (e.g., love) and unwanted things (e.g., disease). Four experiments found just such performance benefits on attitude-relevant tasks, and not on tasks with no personal relevance (e.g., recognizing animal words).

Self-Validation.   A different, but related idea has been proposed independently by Briñol and Petty (2003). This hypothesis does not focus on experienced affect, but suggests that cues such as head nods and arm flexion may be experienced as validation of thoughts that come to mind. They note that one's ideas would seem to be validated if others nodded their heads and invalidated if others shook their heads. In several experiments they examined whether one's own head movements would serve a similar validating or invalidating function (see also Epley & Gilovich, 2001, 2004).

In a persuasion paradigm, they presented either strong or weak persuasive arguments. They reasoned that people would have positive thoughts about strong arguments and negative thoughts about weak arguments. Moreover, head nods should validate and head shaking should invalidate whatever thoughts were current. As expected, they found that in response to strong arguments, people were more persuaded when they nodded and less persuaded when they shook their heads. Especially interesting was confirmation of the expectation that in response to weak arguments, the reverse should occur. Indeed, shaking one's head "no" after weak arguments produced more persuasion than after strong ones. Essentially, the double negative of head shaking in response to negative thoughts increased the persuasiveness of weak arguments. They also measured thought confidence and showed that it played a mediational role. More generally, they showed that self-produced affective information (in the form of head nodding and shaking) acted like an experiential validation of participants' thoughts.

Summary.   In this final segment of the indirect effects section of the chapter, we noted that renewed interest in cognitive dissonance effects has begun to emphasize the negativity rather than the arousal components of dissonance. For example, some investigators have found that positive affect seems to nullify the motivation for dissonance reduction. Indeed, examination of an affect-as-information model of dissonance phenomena (Moore, 2003) found elimination of dissonance effects, either from positive affect or from misattributions of the negative affect of dissonance.

Another kind of indirect influence occurs when affect acts as evidence for some affectively similar belief. We proposed that affect functions rather like a sixth sense. Positive and negative feelings provide affective experiences of value, just as rough and smooth feelings provide tactile experiences of texture, or sensations of lightness and darkness provide visual experiences of illumination. Adaval (2001) found *affect confirmation* effects in which feelings of mood seemed to confirm the positive or negative value of product attributes. Similarly, Tamir et al. (2002) found *affective certainty* effects when people's general affective beliefs about themselves were confirmed by their current feelings. Such congruence made them fast in making decisions about things they wanted or did not want. And Briñol and Petty (2003) found that persuasion effects could be altered by nodding or shaking one's head when these movement were experienced as *self-validation* or invalidation of thoughts about persuasive messages. This sample of research rounds out our consideration of the indirect influences of affect and affect-relevant action on attitude.

We turn next to a consideration of some larger issues about affect and cognition in attitude.

Issues About Affect and Cognition

Western thought has tended to cast emotion and cognition into conflicting roles. But social psychologists (Salovey & Mayer, 1990) and neuroscientists (Damasio, 1994) now suggest that emotion fosters rather than hinders adaptive rationality. For these and other reasons, research on emotion has skyrocketed in recent years, becoming one of the most sought-after intellectual exports from psychology (McLemee, 2003). Indeed, the pace of development and export has been so rapid that natural corrective forces have not kept pace. In this section, we review work that suggests that second thoughts are in order about some widely held ideas about affect, including the "automatic evaluation effect" and the "low road to emotion."

Automatic Evaluation Effect?

Attitudes help us anticipate the consequences of situations so that we can act accordingly. Hence, it can be important for attitude objects to be able to elicit affect readily (Fazio & Powell, 1997). One of the most important demonstrations of such automatic evaluative reactions was a study of affective priming by Fazio, Sanbonmatsu, Powell, and Kardes (1986). They found faster evaluations of target words when primes of similar valence preceded the words by about 300 ms. Thus, seeing a positive word (e.g., "friend") facilitated categorizing another word (e.g., "birthday") as positive relative to categorizing a negative word (e.g., "anger") as negative (see Klauer, 1998, for a review).

The effectiveness of such evaluative congruence in speeding performance suggests that people may automatically evaluate stimuli. The fact that a similar effect occurs even when the task is not explicitly about evaluative categorization led Bargh (1997) to conclude that objects are processed evaluatively before they are processed descriptively. However, others (Rolls, 1999) assume that objects are first classified descriptively (at some level) before affective analysis.

Storbeck and Robinson (2004) explicitly examined whether evaluative or descriptive priming is more basic. They noted that most studies of evaluative priming include words (as primes and targets) that vary systematically in evaluative meaning but not also in descriptive meaning. As a result, research participants are left with no choice but to implicitly categorize primes and targets evaluatively, because no descriptive categories are consistently available. If so, then such studies may provide evidence that people engage in automatic stimulus classifications of some kind, but may be relevant to whether evaluative classifications have a favored status.

To test this hypothesis, Storbeck and Robinson (2004) repeated standard priming studies, varying evaluative and descriptive similarity independently. Thus, their words included positive and negative animal words (e.g., puppy, spider) and positive and negative texture words (e.g., silky, rough), or in some cases, religious words (e.g., angel, Hell). In three experiments, they consistently found descriptive priming, but not evaluative priming. Three different methods–an evaluative task, a descriptive task, and a lexical decision task–all led to the same conclusion. Evaluative priming was found only when they eliminated the possibility of using descriptive similarity between primes and targets, as other investigators had inadvertently done before them.

These results suggest that declarative memory is organized descriptively, rather than evaluatively. Indeed, the utility of a system in which the activation of one negative concept would activate all other negative concepts, even a little bit, is unclear. Storbeck and Robinson (2004) review a variety of behavioral, neurological, and electrophysiological studies relevant to the question and conclude: "These results are rather dramatic in suggesting that affective analysis is typically dependent, or parasitic, on some prior semantic analysis." Similar conclusions about the priority of semantic analysis have also been reached by De Houwer and Randell (2004) using a pronunciation task.

Of course, people probably do evaluate just about everything they encounter, and they presumably do so automatically. Evaluation, moreover, is the most powerful dimension of connotative meaning, and according to Osgood, this is true of all words in all languages (Osgood, Suci, & Tannenbaum, 1957). Also, people can decode evaluative meaning independently of semantic meaning in the real world via tone of voice, prosody of speech, and manner of expression. Indeed, automatic inferences about evaluative word meanings can occur even on such extrasemantic bases as whether words are printed in light or dark fonts (Meier, Robinson, & Clore, 2004) and whether words appear up or down on a computer screen (Meier & Robinson, 2004). But apart from such presentational considerations, the evaluative meanings of the words themselves probably cannot be processed independently of their descriptive meanings. Thus, evidence for the "automatic evaluation effect" adduced from studies of affective priming may need a second look, as recent data suggest an "automatic *categorization* effect" rather than an "automatic *evaluation* effect."

The "Low Road" to Emotion?

A related issue in psychology concerns whether or not emotion arises out of cognitive appraisals (interpretations of stimuli) or whether emotion plays by its own rules. One position in this debate is captured in Zajonc's (1980) proposal that, "Preferences need no inferences." Zajonc (2001) and others taking a related view (Berkowitz & Harmon-Jones, 2004) often cite as supporting evidence LeDoux's discovery of a possible "low road" to emotion (e.g., LeDoux, Romanski, & Xagoraris, 1989). This work established aversive conditioning in rats by pairing electric shock with a change in the illumination of a light. The procedure was successful despite the fact that lesions had eliminated the visual cortex from the circuit. Conditioning was accomplished via a subcortical pathway going directly from the sensory thalamus (where sensory signals are processed) to the amygdala (which is important in emotional reactions) without first going to the cerebral cortex. The results were important because they showed activation of emotion-relevant reactions (avoidance) without involvement of the cortex. These results show that an emotion-relevant response can occur before the object of the emotion could be identified (even implicitly) at the cortical level and before one could feel an emotion. By this low route, information about possible threat could apparently reach the amygdala by a direct route 7 ms before it could arrive indirectly via the cortex. It has been argued that these few milliseconds would have conferred a survival advantage.

These findings and their subsequent dissemination (LeDoux, 1996) have fired the imagination of social science writers (Goleman, 1995) as potential ways of explaining phenomena in social psychology (Zajonc, 1998), political science (McDermott, 2003), advertising, and related disciplines. Does this low road to affect really offer a new view of attitude formation? The amygdala may be important for attitude, since this small, almond-shaped organ plays a critical role in fear and possibly other emotions. But can attitudes be created via the "low road" to the amygdala without cortical involvement?

Storbeck (2004) has recently reviewed the literature relevant to LeDoux's discovery for its relevance to social psychologists. He concluded that the low route discussed by LeDoux probably has little relevance to phenomena in social psychology. The evidence suggests that only very simple stimuli can be detected using this low road, such as changes in illumination, which is what LeDoux used as a CS. Without the involvement of the visual cortex, the pictures, faces, or words generally used as stimuli in social psychological experiments cannot be discriminated. Hence, the "low road" to emotion that LeDoux found for rats probably does not hold much promise for explaining human attitudes.

Some findings also suggest that direct connections between the thalamus and the amygdala diminish as one moves up the phylogenetic scale, and that they may not exist at all in primates and humans (Dolan, 2000; Kudo, Glendenning, Frost, & Masterson, 1986). Of course, there are other subcortical routes to the amygdala in humans. However, the larger conclusion is that evaluative reactions appear to be generally dependent on cortical analyses. Even the subcortical routes that play a role in visual detection are thoroughly intertwined with cortical areas. A similar interplay between cortical and subcortical processes is apparent in affect (see Davidson & Irwin, 1999; Davidson, Jackson, & Kalin, 2000, for reviews). It is probably not the case, therefore, that attitudes, judgments, and behaviors in humans are adequately explained by the "low road" idea.

It should be clear, however, that success in tracing pathways to the amygdala has been a major breakthrough, which has spurred examination of subcortical affective processes generally. We assume that further research will show additional subcortical contributions to affect, and hence to attitude in humans. However, the surprisingly popular idea that affect is fundamentally subcortical is not consistent with the data (Davidson, 2003). Hence, contrary to the wealth of recent citations by social scientists, low road accounts are implausible explanations of affective influences on attitudes, consumer choices, or political preferences.

Summary

Because affective forces seem powerful and resist control, many psychologists believe that affective and evaluative processes occur earlier and are more fundamental than cognitive and descriptive processes. However, research increasingly suggests that this conclusion may be misguided. Many aspects of affective processing are automatic and unconscious, of course, but that is also true of ordinary cognitive processing. Also, organisms do place a high priority on evaluative information, but in head to head comparisons, descriptive priming appears to trump evaluative priming unless evaluative categorization is made salient.

Recent research also casts doubt on the relevance for social psychology of what has been called the "low road to emotion." LeDoux's (1996) demonstration of aversive conditioning in rats via a rapid subcortical route from the sensory thalamus directly to the amygdala was a landmark achievement. However, the assumption that such findings might illuminate human emotions may be unwarranted. Although subcortical processing doubtlessly plays an important role in emotion, such processes are thoroughly intertwined with higher, cortical processing.

In the final section, we turn from existing ideas about affect that we think have been misapplied to a discussion of three new ideas that may be useful in understanding affect and attitudes.

Affective Attitudes as Emergent and Embodied
Evaluative Constancy

Multiple Kinds of Affect

Our review of affective influences on attitude has examined a variety of processes as though they act in isolation. In fact, however, we expect that powerful attitudes often emerge from multiple affective sources. Strack and colleagues (see Neumann & Strack, 2000; Neumann, Förster, & Strack, 2003) have discussed multiple affective *manifestations* such as positive and negative feelings and approach and avoidance behavior, but our point concerns multiple *kinds* of affect.

If affect and attitude are both representations of value, what is the source of that value? How do we know that something is good or bad? As indicated at the beginning, Ortony et al. (1988) propose three sources of value (goals, standards, and tastes), which underlie three kinds of affect (being pleased at outcomes, approving of actions, and liking objects). These in turn are bases for three kinds of evaluation (e.g., utilitarian, moral, and aesthetic). These different kinds of good are not really comparable. Thus, one cannot fix a price on morality. Indeed, attempts to do so are the stuff of tragedy, as dramatized in Goethe's *Faust*.

In addition, the case can be made that sensations become compelling perceptions of reality to the extent that they transcend simple sensory accounting. For example, we see objects in hologram-like reality when both eyes provide parallel, but slightly different images of the same thing. Presumably, such emergence reflects the fact that it is computationally simpler to perceive one object as "out there" rather than seeing two highly redundant sensory images. In analogous fashion, we suggest that emotional realities may emerge from parallel perceptions of multiple kinds of good or bad in a single object. Consider a leader whose policies are seen as good in a utilitarian sense, whose actions seem moral, and who is also personally attractive or eloquent. A combination of these different affective reactions (being pleased, approving, liking) might command a degree of loyalty to the leader none of them by themselves could elicit. Similarly, people fall in love, not only because their beloved may be good for them in some way (being pleased), but perhaps also because the person's actions may seem excellent or admirable (approving), and because the person him or herself may be beautiful or handsome (liking). From such diverse sources, the person's goodness may be beyond mental accounting, creating what may be experienced as a transcendent reality that may not be shared in the perceptions of others. In a different, but related formulation, Thagard and Nerb (2002) conceptualize affective processes as "emotional gestalts," reflecting the dynamical nature of an "emotional state as a gestalt that emerges from a complex of interacting environmental, bodily, and cognitive variables" (Thagard & Nerb, 2002, p. 275).

We are suggesting that to the extent that, like emotions, attitudes have multiple constituents, they can take on a life of their own, because of the incommensurability of the multiple affective reactions from which they stem. Research on mood (Schwarz & Clore, 1983) suggests that the influence of affect on judgment depends on the implicit mental accounting for the affect. Thus, attitudes from multiple, incomparable sources may be powerful, as love and hate are powerful, in part because they resist attributional accounting and transcend the constraints on evaluation that such accounting seem to bring (Wilson, Gilbert, & Centerbar, 2003). In addition to this process, however, affectively-based attitudes may also be powerful because they are embodied.

Embodied Evaluation

Traditionally psychologists have focused on the *belief* components of attitude. Fishbein and Ajzen (1975), however, have pointed out that it is the *evaluative* component of belief that contributes the main portion of an attitude. The point of an affective approach to attitude is to broaden the concept to include evaluative aspects that go beyond evaluative beliefs. Research increasingly makes it clear that evaluative feelings, in addition to evaluative beliefs, influence attitudes. Attitude objects about which one has strong beliefs also have the capacity to elicit evaluative feelings (Fazio & Powell, 1997). The power of attitude, like the power of emotion, lies in the fact that attitudes can be *experienced* as well as known. Thus, it is possible that the study of attitudes, certainly the study of affect and attitudes, may be informed by the idea of *embodiment*. Affective processes are fundamentally embodied: Bodily processes such as expressive behaviors, physiological changes, and actions are central components of the subjective experience of affect.

In recent years, a related concept of "embodied cognition" has become prominent in cognitive science. Investigators of embodied cognition assume that cognitive processes are influenced and constrained by the way we function in the world with our bodies (Barsalou, 1999; Clark, 1997; Glenberg, 1997; Lakoff & Johnson, 1999; Varela, Thompson, & Rosch, 1991). The same assumptions that underlie the idea of embodied cognition are applicable to embodied affect (Schnall, 2004). For example, central to the embodied cognition position is the assumption that cognition ultimately serves action, and a similar assumption can be made about affect and emotion. Thus, affect provides information about the liking or disliking of objects and situations, and about the value of pursuing or avoiding particular actions. Similarly, we assume that attitudes serve not merely as mental structures of preference, but also as a compass for action.

A second assumption is that both cognitive and affective processes are constrained not only contextually, but also by the nature of the human body. Affectively relevant bodily cues can consist of facial expressions, postures, or general behaviors of approach and avoidance, and all of these provide powerful influences on attitudes, as discussed by Olson and Stone (this volume). Finally, a third shared assumption concerns emergent properties. Both affective and cognitive processes involve emergent properties that arise in nonlinear ways and that result in action-relevant consequences. Overall, this position derives from the realization that investigators need to treat the evolution of human cognitive and affective processes as components of the evolution of human bodies (Schnall, 2003). In line with this functional orientation toward affect and attitudes, we conclude this chapter with the thought that one function served by attitude is to provide affective constancy, which would appear to be important in everyday social relations.

Attitudes Afford Evaluative Constancy

How do one's momentary affective experiences become attitudes? It can be instructive to think about attitudes as analogous to perceptions. An overarching aim of the perceptual system appears to be to construct perceptual constancy from sensory variation. Thus, a tabletop exists as a rectangle of constant size in our perception, even though our actual retinal image of the table top may change dramatically in size and shape as we pass by. With this perceptual constancy as a model, one can view attitudes as the outcome of processes directed toward affective constancy. We do not react to visual or auditory stimuli as such, but rather to a model of the thing seen or heard (Bregman, 1990). Thus, for example, when a car passes between us and a person across the street, we do not assume that she ceased to exist, despite the fact that she disappears from our retina momentarily. Perception is aimed at establishing the constancies that lie behind our changing sensory representations.

Person perception also deals with constructed models of others, rather than with specific behaviors. We do not cease to perceive others as "friendly" or "trustworthy" during their absence. Momentary disagreements with friends and family do not usually end the relationship or make us adopt new attitudes toward them. This is true, we assume, because the others with whom we interact are really *virtual* others or models of others. We do not simply react to the words and behaviors we hear and see in an online, bottom-up fashion. They are framed and given meaning as the words and behaviors of an idealized mental entity (Blascovich, 2002; Heise, 1979).

Such affective models help maintain love, loyalty, and commitment to partners, teams, organizations, causes, political parties, candidates, products, and ideas. We may retain our identities as fans even when our team loses, and we remain loyal Americans, Israelis, or Japanese even when our candidate or party is not in power. One's mental models of objects allows us to maintain object constancy despite visual occlusion or gaps in attention. So too one's attitude toward others affords the evaluative constancy so indispensable to social life.

Conclusions and Summary

In this section we summarize what we have covered and list (in italics) 20 tentative conclusions. The first half of this chapter is titled, "Direct Influence of Affect on Attitude," which is divided into valence-based and arousal-based influences. We suggested that: *(1) Two dimensions of affect, valence and arousal, each play a different role in attitude formation. The valence component can be thought of as embodied evaluation and the arousal component as embodied importance or urgency.* The valence-based phenomena include affective conditioning, affective priming, category-triggered affect, mere exposure, and mood-congruent judgment.

Reflecting recent trends in the literature, we distinguished classical, Pavlovian conditioning (which involves preparation for coping with an expected rewarding or punishing event) from affective association (which involves simply processing a target stimulus and a valenced stimulus together). The two processes turn out to be distinguishable empirically. We reviewed the classical studies of attitude conditioning, and suggested that, *(2) Despite appearances, the associational process whereby rewards and punishments influence attitudes may not be an example of classical or Pavlovian conditioning.* Attitude formation is better captured by a process of simple affective association than by Pavlovian classical conditioning. We also discussed limitations of conditioning as a model of attitude formation. For example, *(3) Not only biological preparedness, but also cognitive and cultural preparedness constrain the affective associations people make.* Moreover, we suggested that, *(4) All associational phenomena from conditioning to affect-as-information may depend on the same underlying Gestalt processes, whereby temporally contiguous experiences become a unit, providing a narrative flow from one moment to the next.* We also discussed social psychological implications of Bloom's (2000) theory of mind approach to how children learn the meanings of words. His work implies that, *(5) Children learn (affective) meanings not by bottom-up associations (John Locke), but by top-down inferences about what others mean (Augustine).*

Returning to more molecular processes, we reviewed research on the mere exposure phenomenon, concluding that rather than as originally envisioned, *(6) Mere exposure effects are due to the positive affective consequences of the experience of cognitive fluency.*

The status of the mood and judgment literature was the next topic. Taking an affect-as-information approach, we suggested that, *(7) Implicit attributions underlie both mere exposure effects and mood effects on attitude.* Although investigators of judgment and decision making refer to affective influences as "biases," and several investigators consider the use of affect as a judgment heuristic, we emphasized that, *(8) Rather than being solely a source of judgment bias, affect plays an essential role in effective judgment and decision making.*

Next we noted that the influence of affective feedback on judgment and processing is not limited to feelings, but that similar effects can be seen with other affective cues, including facial expressions, subtly or unconsciously primed concepts, and even colors. We concluded that, *(9) The spontaneity and compellingness of the evaluative information is more important than whether the information is in the form of visceral feelings, facial muscle contraction, motor action, or primed thoughts.*

Under the heading of "Attitudes toward Actions," we briefly discussed other models of affect and decision making, including the idea of *Risk as Fear* and *Affect Decision Theory.* Finally, we departed from simple notions of valence to consider how specific emotions might mediate attitudes toward outgroups. We reviewed Mackie and Smith's (2002) proposal that,

(10) Groups that are feared tend to be avoided, whereas groups responded to with anger may elicit an aggressive stance.

We proposed that in addition to valence, the arousal component of affect also has direct effects as a marker of the importance of events. Recent work on hormones and memory show that, *(11) The arousal elicited by important events facilitates consolidation of experiences into lasting attitude-relevant memories.*

In the second half of the chapter, we turned from direct to indirect influence of affect on attitudes. This represented a shift from an "object focus," in which affect influences evaluations of physical and social objects in the world, to an "action focus," in which affect influences the processing of attitude relevant information. We suggested that differences in whether or not value is transferred from affective reaction to object versus action parallels differences in the transfer of value from reward in classical versus instrumental conditioning or in semantic versus procedural learning. For example, by empowering one's own point of view, *(12) Individuals in happy (and perhaps also angry) moods use their own categorical cognitions, including stereotypes, brand names, and party identification, whereas those in sad moods focus on individuating information about persons, products, and candidates.*

Affect also influences reactions to persuasive messages. A consistent finding is that, *(13) Individuals in positive moods tend to be moderately persuaded by both strong and weak persuasive arguments, whereas individuals in sad moods tend to be persuaded only by strong arguments and not by weak ones.* We also considered affective interpretations of cognitive dissonance (as opposed to traditional arousal interpretations). Research suggests that the influence of affect on dissonance-induced attitude change may depend on the timing of affect inductions. Such findings are consistent with the immediacy principle, which says that, *(14) The object of affective reactions, and hence of affect-based attitudes, depends on what is in mind when affect is experienced.* As in classical conditioning, the associations that occur in the real world tend to reflect the constraints imposed by cognitive and situational structure.

A final indirect effect implicates an "affect-as-evidence" hypothesis, which predicts that, *(15) Feelings may serve as experiential evidence for compatible thoughts and beliefs occurring at the time.* In addition, head nods or other positive after-relevant cues may similarly serve to validate (and head shakes may invalidate) concurrent thoughts.

Subsequently, two phenomena with implications for the relationship between affect and cognition were considered. Recent research suggests that, *(16) Contrary to the "automatic evaluation" hypothesis, descriptive priming takes precedence over evaluative priming when the two are directly compared.* In addition, recent contributions from cognitive neuroscience leads to the conclusions that, *(17) Popular assumptions about a rapid "low road" to emotion, which elicits affect before cortical interpretation is possible, appear to be inapplicable to human attitude research.*

We suggested that attitudes of love and loyalty may occur when different, incommensurate kinds of affective information converge in the same object. We speculated that, *(18) Diverse sources of good (or bad) may confound mental accounting to be experienced as transcendent goodness (or badness).* We suggested, too, that, *(19) The power of affect arises in part from the embodied nature of affect.* Finally, taking a functional view, we suggested that, *(20) Despite constantly changing affective experience, attitudes can afford an evaluative constancy that is indispensable to social life.*

ACKNOWLEDGMENTS

Support is acknowledged from NIMH grants RO1MH 50074 to Gerald Clore and RO3MH67580 to Simone Schnall.

REFERENCES

Adaval, R. (2001). Sometimes it just feels right: The differential weighting of affect-consistent and affect-inconsistent product information. *Journal of Consumer Behavior, 28,* 1–17.

Albarracín, D., & Kumkale, G. T. (2003). Affect as information in persuasion: A model of affect identification and discounting. *Journal of Personality and Social Psychology, 84,* 453–469.

Allport, G. W. (1954). *The nature of prejudice.* Reading, MA: Addison-Wesley.

Anderson, J. R., & Bower, G. H. (1973). *Human associative memory.* Washington, D.C: Winston.

Anderson, N. H. (1965). Averaging versus adding as a stimulus-combination rule in impression formation. *Journal of Experimental Psychology, 70,* 394–400.

Anderson, N. H. (1981). *Foundations of information integration.* New York: Academic Press.

Arkes, H. R., & Hammond, K. R. (Eds.). (1986). *Judgment and decision making: An interdisciplinary reader.* New York: Cambridge University Press.

Astington, J. W. (Ed.). (2000). *Minds in the making: Essays in honor of David R. Olson.* Malden, MA: Blackwell.

Baeyens, F., Eelen, P., & Crombez, G. (1995). Pavlovian associations are forever: On classical conditioning and extinction. *Journal of Psychophysiology, 9,* 127–141.

Baeyens, F., Eelen, P., Crombez, G., & Van den Bergh, O. (1992). Human evaluative conditioning: Acquisition trials, presentation schedule, evaluative style and contingency awareness. *Behaviour Research and Therapy, 30,* 133–142.

Baker, W. E. (1999). When can affective conditioning and mere exposure directly influence brand choice? *Journal of Advertising, 28,* 31–46.

Bargh, J. A. (1997). The automaticity of everyday life. In R. S. Wyer (Eds.), *Advances in social cognition* (Vol. 10, pp. 1–61). Mahwah, NJ: Lawrence Erlbaum Associates.

Baron-Cohen, S., Tager-Flusberg, H., & Cohen, D. J. (Eds.). (1993). *Understanding other minds: Perspectives from autism.* Oxford, UK: Oxford University Press.

Barsalou, L. W. (1999). Perceptual symbol systems. *Behavioral and Brain Sciences, 22,* 577–660.

Bartlett, F. C. (1932). *Remembering: A study in experimental and social psychology.* Cambridge: Cambridge University Press.

Berkowitz, L., & Harmon-Jones, E. (2004). Toward an understanding of the determinants of anger. *Emotion, 4,* 107–130.

Blascovich, J. (2002). Social influence within immersive virtual environments. In R. Schroeder (Ed.), *The social life of avatars* (pp. 127–145). London: Springer-Verlag.

Bless, H., Bohner, G., Schwarz, N., & Strack, F. (1990). Mood and persuasion: A cognitive response analysis. *Personality and Social Psychology Bulletin, 16,* 331–345.

Bless, H., Clore, G. L., Schwarz, N., Golisano, V., Rabe, C., & Wölk, M. (1996). Mood and the use of scripts: Does happy mood really lead to mindlessness? *Journal of Personality and Social Psychology, 71,* 665–679.

Bless, H., & Fiedler, K. (1995). Affective states and the influence of activated general knowledge. *Personality and Social Psychology Bulletin, 21,* 766–778.

Bless, H., Mackie, D. M., & Schwarz, N. (1992). Mood effects on attitude judgments: Independent effects of mood before and after message elaboration. *Journal of Personality and Social Psychology, 63,* 585–595.

Bless, H., & Schwarz, N. (1999). Sufficient and necessary conditions on dual processing models: The case of mood and information processing. In S. Chaiken & Y. Trope (Eds.), *Dual process theories in social psychology* (pp. 423–440). New York: Guilford.

Bloom, P. (2000). *How children learn the meaning of words.* Cambridge, MA: MIT Press.

Boakes, R. A. (1989). How one might find evidence for conditioning in adult humans. In T. Archer & L. G. Nilsson (Eds.), *Aversion, avoidance and anxiety: Perspectives on aversively motivated behavior* (pp. 381–402). Hillsdale, NJ: Lawrence Erlbaum Associates.

Bodenhausen, G. V. (1993). Emotions, arousal, and stereotypic judgments: A heuristic model of affect and stereotyping. In D. M. Mackie & D. L. Hamilton (Eds.), *Affect, cognition and stereotyping: Interactive processes in group perception* (pp. 13–37). San Diego, CA: Academic Press.

Bodenhausen, G. V., Sheppard, L. A., & Kramer, G. P. (1994). Negative affect and social judgment: The differential impact of anger and sadness. *European Journal of Social Psychology, 24,* 45–62.

Bornstein, R. F. (1989). Exposure and affect: Overview and meta-analysis of research, 1968–1987. *Psychological Bulletin, 106,* 265–289.

Bornstein, R. F. (1992). Subliminal mere exposure effects. In R. F. Bornstein & T. S. Pittman (Eds.), *Perception without awareness: Cognitive, clinical, and social perspectives* (pp. 191–210). New York: Guilford.

Bornstein, R. F., & D'Agostino, P. R. (1992). Stimulus recognition and the mere exposure effect. *Journal of Personality and Social Psychology, 63,* 545–552.

Bornstein, R. F., & D'Agostino, P. R. (1994). The attribution and discounting of perceptual fluency: Preliminary tests of a perceptual fluency/attributional model of the mere exposure effect. *Social Cognition, 12,* 103–128.

Bornstein, R. F., Leone, D. R., & Galley, D. J. (1987). The generalizability of subliminal mere exposure effects: Influence of stimuli perceived without awareness on social behavior. *Journal of Personality and Social Psychology, 53*, 1070–1079.

Boster, F. J., & Mongeau, P. (1984). Fear-arousing persuasive messages. In R. N. Bostrom (Ed.), *Communication yearbook* (Vol. 8, pp. 330–375). Beverly Hills, CA: Sage.

Bower, G. H., Monteiro, K. P., & Gilligan, S. G. (1978). Emotional mood as a context of learning and recall. *Journal of Verbal Learning and Verbal Behavior, 17*, 573–585.

Bregman, A. S. (1990). *Auditory scene analysis: The perceptual organization of sound.* Cambridge, MA: Bradford Books, MIT Press.

Brewer, M. B. (1988). A dual process model of impression formation. In T. Srull & R. Wyer (Eds.), *Advances in social cognition* (Vol. 1). Hillsdale, NJ: Lawrence Erlbaum Associates.

Brewer, W. F. (1974). There is no convincing evidence for operant or classical conditioning in adult humans. In W. B. Weimer & D. S. Palermo (Eds.), *Cognition and the symbolic processes* (pp. 1–42). Hillsdale, NJ: Lawrence Erlbaum Associates.

Briñol, P., & Petty, R. E. (2003). Overt head movements and persuasion: A self-validation analysis. *Journal of Personality and Social Psychology, 84*, 1123–1139.

Brown, L. B. (1973). *Ideology.* Harmondsworth, UK: Penguin.

Byrne, D., & Clore, G. L. (1966). Predicting interpersonal attraction toward strangers presented in three different stimulus modes. *Psychonomic Science, 4*, 239–240.

Cahill, L., Haier, R. J., Fallon, J., Alkire, M. T., Tang, C., Keator, D., Wu, J., &. McGaugh, J. L. (1996). Amygdala activity at encoding correlated with long-term, free recall of emotional information. *Proceedings of the National Academy of Sciences, 93*, 8016–8021.

Cahill, L., & McGaugh, J. L. (1998). Mechanisms of emotional arousal and lasting declarative memory. *Trends in Neuroscience, 21*, 294–299.

Chaiken, S., Liberman, A., & Eagly, A. H. (1989). Heuristic and systematic processing within and beyond the persuasion context. In J. S. Uleman & J. A. Bargh (Eds.), *Affect and social behavior* (pp. 152–206). New York: Cambridge University Press.

Chomsky, N. (1968). *Language and mind.* New York: Harcourt, Brace, Jovanovich.

Clark, A. (1997). *Being there: Putting the brain, body, and world together again.* Cambridge, MA: MIT Press.

Clore, G. L. (1992). Cognitive phenomenology: Feelings and the construction of judgment. In L. L. Martin & A. Tesser (Eds.), *The construction of social judgments* (pp. 133–163). Hillsdale, NJ: Lawrence Erlbaum Associates.

Clore, G. L., & Byrne, D. (1974). A reinforcement-affect model of attraction. In T. L. Huston (Ed.), *Foundations of interpersonal attraction* (pp. 143–170). New York: Academic Press.

Clore, G. L., & Colcombe, S. (2003). The parallel worlds of affective concepts and feelings. In J. Musch & K. C. Klauer (Eds.), *The psychology of evaluation: Affective processes in cognition and emotion* (pp. 335–369). Mahwah, NJ: Lawrence Erlbaum Associates.

Clore, G. L., & Gasper, K. (2000). Feeling is believing: Some affective influences on belief. In N. H. Frijda, A. S. R. Manstead, & S. Bem (Eds.), *Emotions and beliefs: How do emotions influence beliefs?* (pp. 10–44). Cambridge: Cambridge University Press.

Clore, G. L., & Ortony, A. (2000). Cognition in emotion: Never, sometimes, or always? In R. D. Lane & L. Nadel (Eds.), *The cognitive neuroscience of emotion* (pp. 24–61). New York: Oxford University Press.

Clore, G. L., Schwarz, N., & Conway, M. (1994). Affective causes and consequences of social information processing. In R. S. Wyer & T. K. Srull (Eds.), *Handbook of Social Cognition* (pp. 323–417). Hillsdale, NJ: Lawrence Erlbaum Associates.

Clore, G. L., Wyer, R. S., Dienes, B., Gasper, K., Gohm, C. L., & Isbell, L. (2001). Affective feelings as feedback: Some cognitive consequences. In L. L. Martin & G. L. Clore (Eds.), *Theories of mood and cognition: A user's handbook* (pp. 27–62). Mahwah, NJ: Lawrence Erlbaum Associates.

Cooney, J. W., & Gazzaniga, M. S. (2003). Neurological disorders and the structure of human consciousness. *Trends in Cognitive Sciences, 7*, 161.

Cooper, J., & Fazio, R. (1984). A new look at dissonance theory. In L. Berkowitz (Ed.), *Advances in experimental social psychology* (Vol. 17, pp. 229–266). New York: Academic Press.

Crandall, C. S. (1984). The liking of food as a result of exposure: Eating doughnuts in Alaska. *Journal of Social Psychology, 125*, 187–194.

Crandall, C. S., D'Anello, S., Sakall, N., Lazarus, E., Wieczorkowska, G., Feather, N. T. (2001). An attribution-value model of prejudice: Anti-fat attitudes among six nations. *Personality and Social Psychology Bulletin, 27*, 30–37.

Damasio, A. R. (1994). *Descartes' error: Emotion, reason and the human brain.* New York: Putnam.

Davey, G. C. L. (1994). Defining the important questions to ask about evaluative conditioning: A reply to Martin and Levey (1994). *Behaviour Research and Therapy, 32*, 307–310.

Davidson, R. J. (2003). Seven sins in the study of emotion: Correctives from affective neuroscience. *Brain and Cognition, 52,* 129–132.

Davidson, R. J., & Irwin, W. (1999). The functional neuroanatomy of emotion and affective style. *Trends in Cognitive Science, 3,* 11–21.

Davidson, R. J., Jackson, D. C., & Kalin, N. H. (2000). Emotion, plasticity, context, and regulation: Perspectives from affective neuroscience. *Psychological Bulletin, 126,* 890–906.

De Houwer, J., & Randell, R. (2004). Robust affective priming in a conditional pronunciation task: Evidence for the semantic representation of evaluative information. *Cognition and Emotion, 18,* 251–264.

De Houwer, J., Thomas, S., & Baeyens, F. (2001). Associative learning of likes and dislikes: A review of 25 years of research on human evaluative conditioning. *Psychological Bulletin, 127,* 853–869.

DeSteno, D., Dasgupta, N., Bartlett, M.Y., & Cajdric, A. (2004). The effect of emotion on automatic intergroup attitudes. *Psychological Science, 15,* 319–324.

Devine, P. G. (1989). Stereotypes: Their automatic and controlled components. *Journal of Personality and Social Psychology, 56,* 5–18.

Devine, P. G., & Montieth, M. J. (1999). Automaticity and control in stereotyping. In S. Chaiken & Y. Trope (Eds.), *Dual process theories in social psychology* (pp. 339–360). New York: Guilford.

Dolan, R. (2000). Functional neuroimaging of the amygdala during emotional processing and learning. In J. P. Aggleton (Ed.), *The amygdala: A functional analysis* (pp. 631–654). New York: Oxford University Press.

Dollard, J., & Miller, N. E. (1950). *Personality and psychotherapy.* New York: McGraw-Hill.

Doogan, S., & Thomas, G. V. (1992). Origins of fear in adults and children: The role of conditioning processes and prior familiarity with dogs. *Behaviour Research and Therapy, 30,* 387–394.

Dunn, L. W., & Clore, G. L. (2004, August). *Mood and stereotyping: The moderating role of egalitarian goals.* Poster presented to the American Psychological Association, Honolulu.

Eagly, A. H., & Chaiken, S. (1993). *The psychology of attitudes.* Orlando, FL: Harcourt Brace.

Edwards, K. (1990). The interplay of affect and cognition in attitude formation and change. *Journal of Personality and Social Psychology, 59,* 202–216.

Edwards, K., & von Hippel, W. (1995). Hearts and minds: The priority of affective versus cognitive factors in person perception. *Personality and Social Psychology Bulletin, 21,* 996–1011.

Elliott, A. J., & Devine, P. G. (1994). On the motivational nature of dissonance: Dissonance as psychological discomfort. *Journal of Personality and Social Psychology, 67,* 382–394.

Ellis, H. C., & Ashbrook, P. W. (1988). Resource allocation model of the effect of depressed mood states on memory. In K. Fiedler & J. P. Forgas (Eds.), *Affect, cognition and social behavior.* Toronto: Hogrefe International.

Epley, N., & Gilovich, T. (2001). Putting adjustment back in the anchoring and adjustment heuristic: Divergent processing of self-generated and experimenter-provided anchors. *Psychological Science, 12,* 391–396.

Epley, N., & Gilovich, T. (2004). Are adjustments insufficient? *Personality and Social Psychology Bulletin, 30,* 447–460.

Esses, V. M., & Zanna, M. P. (1995). Mood and the expression of ethnic stereotypes. *Journal of Personality and Social Psychology, 69,* 1052–1068.

Eysenck, M. (1982). *Attention and arousal, cognition and performance.* Berlin, Germany: Springer.

Fabrigar, L. R., & Petty, R. E. (1999). The role of the affective and cognitive bases of attitudes in susceptibility to affectively and cognitively based persuasions. *Personality and Social Psychology Bulletin, 25,* 363–381.

Fazio, R. H., Lenn, T. M., & Effrein, E. A. (1984). Spontaneous attitude formation. *Social Cognition, 2,* 217–234.

Fazio, R. H., & Powell, M. C. (1997). On the value of knowing one's likes and dislikes: Attitude accessibility, stress, and health in college. *Psychological Science, 8,* 430–436.

Fazio, R. H., Sanbonmatsu, D. M., Powell, M. C., & Kardes, F. R. (1986). On the automatic activation of attitudes. *Journal of Personality and Social Psychology, 50,* 229–238.

Festinger, L. (1957). *A theory of cognitive dissonance.* Evanston, IL: Row, Peterson.

Fiedler, K. (1988). Emotional mood, cognitive style, and behavior regulation. In K. Fiedler & J. Forgas (Eds.), *Affect, cognition, and social behavior* (pp. 100–119). Toronto: Hogrefe International.

Fiedler, K. (2001). Affective states trigger processes of assimilation and accommodation. In L. L. Martin & G. L. Clore (Eds.), *Theories of mood and cognition: A user's handbook* (pp. 85–98). Mahwah, NJ: Lawrence Erlbaum Associates.

Fishbein, M. (1963). An investigation of the relationship between beliefs about an object and the attitude toward that object. *Human Relations, 16,* 233–240.

Fishbein, M., & Ajzen, I. (1975). *Belief, attitude, intention and behavior.* Reading, MA: Addison-Wesley.

Fiske, S. T. (1982). Schema-triggered affect: Applications to social perception, in M. S. Clark & S. T. Fiske (Eds.), *Affect and cognition: The seventeenth annual Carnegie symposium on cognition* (pp. 55–78). Hillsdale, New Jersey: Lawrence Erlbaum Associates.

Fiske, S. T., & Neuberg, S. L. (1990). A continuum of impression formation, from category-based to individuating processes: Influence of information and motivation on attention and interpretation. In M. P. Zanna (Ed.), *Advances in experimental social psychology* (Vol. 23, pp. 1–74). New York: Academic Press.

Fiske, S. T., & Pavelchek, M. A. (1986). Category-based versus piecemeal-based affective responses: Developments in schema-triggered affect. In R. M. Sorrentino & E. T. Higgins (Eds.), *Handbook of motivation and cognition: Foundations of social behavior* (pp. 167–203). Chichester, UK: Wiley.

Forgas, J. P. (1995). Mood and judgment: The affect infusion model (AIM). *Psychological Bulletin, 117*, 39–66.

Forgas, J. P., & Bower, G. H. (1987). Mood effects on person perception judgments. *Journal of Personality and Social Psychology, 53*, 53–60.

Forgas, J. P., Bower, G. H., & Krantz, S. E. (1984). The influence of mood on perception of social interactions. *Journal of Experimental Social Psychology, 20*, 497–513.

Forgas, J.P. & Moylan, S. (1991). Affective influences on stereotype judgments. *Cognition and Emotion, 5,* 379–395.

Frijda, N., Ortony, A., Sonnemons, J., & Clore, G. (1992). The complexity of intensity: Issues concerning the structure of emotion intensity. In M. Clark (Ed.), *Emotion. Review of personality and social psychology* (Vol. 13, pp. 60–89). Newbury Park, CA: Sage.

Garcia, J., & Koelling, R. A. (1966). Relation of cue to consequence in avoidance learning. *Psychonomic Science, 4*, 123.

Gasper, K. & Clore, G. L. (1998). The persistent use of negative affect by anxious individuals to estimate risk. *Journal of Personality and Social Psychology, 74*, 1350–1363.

Gasper, K., & Clore, G. L. (2000). Do you have to pay attention to your feelings to be influenced by them? *Personality and Social Psychology Bulletin, 26*, 698–711.

Gasper, K. & Clore, G. L. (2002). Attending to the big picture: Mood and global vs. local processing of visual information. *Psychological Science, 13,* 34–40.

Glenberg, A. M. (1997). What memory is for. *Behavioral and Brain Sciences, 20*, 1–55.

Gohm, C. L., & Clore, G. L. (2000). Individual differences in emotional experience: Mapping scales to processes. *Personality and Social Psychology Bulletin, 26*, 679–697.

Goleman D. (1995). *Emotional Intelligence.* New York: Bantam.

Gouaux, C. (1971). Induced affective states and interpersonal attraction. *Journal of Personality and Social Psychology, 20*, 37–43.

Greenwald, A. G., McGhee, D., & Schwartz, J. L. K. (1998). Measuring individual differences in cognition: The Implicit Association Task. *Journal of Personality and Social Psychology, 74*, 1469–1480.

Griffitt, W., & Veitch, R. (1971). Hot and crowded: Influences of population density and temperature on interpersonal behavior. *Journal of Personality and Social Psychology, 17*, 92–98.

Haidt, J. (2001). The emotional dog and its rational tail: A social intuitionist approach to moral judgment. *Psychological Review. 108*, 814–834.

Hamilton, D. L., Stroessner, S. J., & Mackie, D. M. (1993). The influence of affect on stereotyping: The case of illusory correlations. In D. M. Mackie & D. L. Hamilton (Eds.), *Affect, cognition, and stereotyping: Interactive processes in group perception* (pp. 39–61). New York: Academic Press.

Harmon-Jones, E. (2001). The role of affect in cognitive dissonance processes. In J. P. Forgas (Ed.), *Handbook of affect and social cognition* (pp. 237–255). Mahwah, NJ: Lawrence Erlbaum Associates.

Harmon-Jones, E., & Allen, J. J. B. (2001). The role of affect in the mere exposure effect: Evidence from psychophysiological and individual differences approaches. *Personality and Social Psychology Bulletin, 27,* 889–898.

Harris, B. (1979). Whatever happened to Little Albert? *American Psychologist, 34*, 151–160.

Harrison, A. A. (1977). Mere exposure. In L. Berkowitz (Ed.), *Advances in experimental social psychology* (Vol. 10, pp. 39–82). New York: Academic Press.

Heider, F. (1958). *The psychology of interpersonal relations.* New York: Wiley.

Heise, D. R. (1979). *Understanding events: Affect and the construction of social action.* New York: Cambridge University Press.

Hendersen, R. (1978). Forgetting of conditioned fear inhibition. *Learning and Motivation, 8,* 16–30.

Hermans, D., Baeyens, F., & Eelen, P. (2003). On the acquisition and activation of evaluative information in memory: The study of evaluative learning and affective priming combined. In J. Musch & K. C. Klauer (Eds.), *The Psychology of Evaluation: Affective Processes in Cognition and Emotion* (pp. 139–168). Mahwah, NJ: Lawrence Erlbaum Associates.

Herzog, T. R., Kaplan, S., & Kaplan, R. (1976). The prediction of preference for familiar urban places. *Environment and Behavior, 8*, 627–645.

Higgins, E. T., Rhodewalt, F., & Zanna, M. P. (1979). Dissonance motivation: Its nature, persistence, and reinstatement. *Journal of Experimental Social Psychology, 15*, 16–34.

Hovland, C. I., Janis, I. L., & Kelley, H. H. (1953). *Communication and persuasion: Psychological studies of opinion change.* New Haven, CT: Yale University Press.

Huskinson, T. L. H., & Haddock, G. (2004). Individual differences in attitude structure: Variance in the chronic reliance on affective and cognitive information. *Journal of Experimental Social Psychology 40,* 82–90.

Isbell, L. (1999). Beyond heuristic information processing: Systematic processing in happy and sad moods. Unpublished Doctoral Dissertation, University of Illinois at Urbana-Champaign.

Isbell, L. M. (2004). Not all happy people are lazy or stupid: Evidence of systematic processing in happy moods. *Journal of Experimental Social Psychology, 40,* 341–349.

Isbell, L. M., & Wyer, R. S. (1999). Correcting for mood-induced bias in the evaluation of political candidates: The roles of intrinsic and extrinsic motivation. *Personality and Social Psychology Bulletin, 25,* 237–249.

Isen, A. (1987). Positive affect, cognitive processes and social behavior. In L. Berkowitz (Ed.), *Advances in experimental social psychology* (Vol. 20, pp. 203–253). New York: Academic Press.

Isen, A. M., Shalker, T. E., Clark, M., & Karp, L. (1978). Affect, accessibility of material in memory, and behavior: A cognitive loop? *Journal of Personality and Social Psychology, 36,* 1–11.

Jacobs, W. J., & Nadel, L. (1985). Stress-induced recovery of fears and phobias. *Psychological Review, 92,* 512–531.

Jacoby, L. L., Kelley, C. M., & Dywan, J. (1989). Memory attributions. In H. L. Roediger & F. I. M. Craik (Eds.), *Varieties of memory and consciousness: Essays in honor of Endel Tulving* (pp. 391–422). Hillsdale, NJ: Erlbaum.

James, W. (1890). *The principles of psychology* New York: Dover Publication.

Janis, I. L., & Feshbach, S. (1953). Effects of fear-arousing communications. *Journal of Abnormal and Social Psychology, 48,* 78–92.

Janiszewski, C. (1993). Preattentive mere exposure effects. *Journal of Consumer Research, 20,* 376–392.

Kelly, G. A. (1955). *The psychology of personal constructs.* New York: Narton.

Keltner, D., Locke, K. D., & Audrain, P. C. (1993). The influence of attribution on the relevance of negative feelings to personal satisfaction. *Personality and Social Psychology Bulletin, 19,* 21–29.

Ketelaar, T., & Clore, G. L. (1997). Emotions and reason: Proximate effects and ultimate functions. In G. Matthews (Ed.), *Personality, Emotion, and Cognitive Science* (pp. 355–396), Amsterdam: Elsevier Science Publishers (North-Holland).

Klauer, K. (1998). Affective priming. In W. Stroebe and M. Hewstone (Eds.), *European Review of Social Psychology* (Vol. 8, pp. 67–103). New York: Wiley.

Klinger, M. R., & Greenwald, A. G. (1994). Preferences need no inferences: The cognitive basis of unconscious mere exposure effects. In P. M. Niedenthal & S. Kitayama (Eds.), *The heart's eye: Emotional influences in perception and attention* (pp. 67–85). San Diego, CA: Academic Press.

Kohlberg, L. (1969). Stage and sequence: The cognitive-developmental approach to socialization. In D. A. Goslin (Ed.), *Handbook of socialization theory and research* (pp. 347–480). Chicago: Rand McNally.

Krosnik, J. A., Betz, A. L., Jussim, L. J., & Lynn, A. R. (1992). Subliminal conditioning of attitudes. *Journal of Personality and Social Psychology, 18,* 152–162.

Kudo, M., Glendenning, K., Frost, S., & Masterson, R. (1986). Origin of mammalian thalamocortical projections. I. Telencephalic projection of the medial geniculate body in the opossum (Didelphis virginiana). *Journal of Comparative Neurology, 245,* 176–197.

Kunst-Wilson, W., & Zajonc, R. (1980). Affective discrimination of stimuli that can not be recognized. *Science, 207,* 557–558.

Lakoff, G., & Johnson, M. (1999). *Philosophy in the flesh: The embodied mind and its challenge to Western thought.* New York: Basic Books.

LeDoux, J. (1996). *The emotional brain: The mysterious underpinnings of emotional life.* New York: Simon & Schuster.

LeDoux, J., Romanski, L., & Xagoraris, A. (1989). Indelibility of subcortical emotional memories. *Journal of Cognitive Neuroscience, 1,* 238–243.

Lerner, J. S., Small, D. A., & Loewenstein, G. (2004). Heart strings and purse strings: Carry-over effects of emotions on economic decisions. *Psychological Science, 15,* 337–341.

Leslie, A. M. (1987). Pretense and representation: The origins of "Theory of Mind". *Psychological Review, 94,* 412–426.

Lewis, C., & Mitchell, P. (Eds.). (1994). *Children's early understanding of mind: Origins and development.* Hillsdale, NJ: Lawrence Erlbaum Associates.

Lodge, M., & Taber, C. S. (2004). *The primacy of affect for political candidates, parties, and issues: An experimental test of the hot cognition hypothesis.* Unpublished manuscript, State University of New York at Stony Brook.

Loewenstein, G. (1996). Out of control: Visceral influences on behavior. *Organizational Behavior and Human Decision Processes, 65,* 272–292.

Loewenstein, G. F., Weber, E. U., Hsee, C. K., & Welch, N. (2001). Risk as feelings. *Psychological Bulletin, 127,* 267–286.

Losch, M. E., & Cacioppo, J. T. (1990). Cognitive dissonance may enhance sympathetic tonus, but attitudes are changes to reduce negative affect rather than arousal. *Journal of Experimental Social Psychology, 26,* 289–304.

Lovibond, P. F., & Shanks, D. P. (2002). The role of awareness in Pavlovian conditioning: Empirical evidence and theoretical implications. *Journal of Experimental Psychology: Animal Behavior Processes, 28,* 3–26.

Lowery, B., Hardin, C., & Sinclair, S. (2001). Social influence effects on automatic racial prejudice. *Journal of Personality and Social Psychology, 81*, 842–855.

Mackie, D. M., Ascuncion, A. G., & Rosselli, F. (1992). The impact of positive affect on persuasion processes. In M. S. Clark (Ed.), Emotion and social behavior. *Review of Personality and Social Psychology* (Vol. 14, pp. 247–270). Newbury Park, CA: Sage.

Mackie, D. M., Devos, T., & Smith, E. R. (2000). Intergroup Emotions: Explaining offensive action tendencies in an intergroup context. *Journal of Personality and Social Psychology, 79*, 602–616.

Mackie, D. M., & Smith, E. R. (Eds.). (2002). *Beyond prejudice: From outgroup hostility to intergroup emotions.* Philadelphia: Psychology Press.

Mackie, D. M., & Worth, L. T. (1989). Processing deficits and the mediation of positive affect in persuasion. *Journal of Personality and Social Psychology, 57*, 27–40.

Mandler, G., Nakamura, Y., & Van Zandt, B. J. (1987). Nonspecific effects of exposure on stimuli that cannot be recognized. *Journal of Experimental Psychology: Learning, Memory and Cognition, 13*, 646–648.

Marcus, G. E., & Mackuen, M. B. (1993). Anxiety, enthusiasm, and the vote: The emotional underpinnings of learning and involvement during presidential campaigns. *American Political Science Review, 87*, 672–685.

Marcus, G. E., Neuman, W. R., & Mackuen, M. B. (2000). *Affective intelligence and political judgment.* Chicago: University of Chicago Press.

Martin, L. L., Ward, D. W., Ahee, J. W., & Wyer, R. S. (1993). Mood as input: People have to interpret the motivational implication of their moods. *Journal of Personality and Social Psychology, 64*, 317–326.

Mayer, J. D., & Salovey, P. (1997). What is emotional intelligence? In P. Salovey & D. Sluyter (Eds.), *Emotional development and emotional intelligence: Educational implications.* New York: Basic Books.

McDermott, R. (2003). *The feeling of rationality: The meaning of neuroscientific advances for political science.* Working paper. Department of Political Science, University of California, Santa Barbara. (Paper delivered at Harvard University, March 20, 2003).

McLemee, S. (2003). Getting emotional. *The Chronicle of Higher Education, 49*, (24) (Feb 21), A14.

Meier, B. P., Robinson, M. D., & Clore, G. L. (2004). Why good guys wear white: Automatic inferences about stimulus valence based on color. *Psychological Science, 15*, 82–87.

Meier, B. P., & Robinson, M. D. (2004). Why the sunny side is up: Associations between affect and vertical position. *Psychological Science, 15*, 243–247.

Mellers, B. A., Schwartz, A., Ho, K., & Ritov, I. (1997). Decision affect theory: Emotional reactions to the outcomes of risky options. *Psychological Science, 8*, 423–429.

Millar, M. G., & Millar, K. U. (1990). Attitude change as a function of attitude type and argument type. *Journal of Personality and Social Psychology, 59*, 217–228.

Mineka, S., Davidson, M., Cook, M., & Keir, R. (1984). Observational conditioning of snake fear in rhesus monkeys. *Journal of Abnormal Psychology, 93*, 355–372.

Monahan, J. L., Murphy, S. T., & Zajonc, R. B. (2000). Subliminal mere exposure: Specific, general, and diffuse effects. *Psychological Science, 11*, 462–466.

Moore, S. E. (2003). *Inconsistency-as-Information: An examination of the effects of incidental positive and negative affect on the cognitive dissonance reduction process.* Unpublished doctoral dissertation, University of Alberta.

Moreland, R. L., & Beach, S. R. (1992). Exposure effects in the classroom: The development of affinity among students. *Journal of Experimental Social Psychology, 28*, 255–276.

Moskowitz, G. B., Gollwitzer, P. M., Wasel, W., & Schaal, B. (1999). Preconscious control of stereotype activation through chronic egalitarian goals. *Journal of Personality and Social Psychology, 77*, 167–184.

Neumann, R., Förster, J., & Strack, F. (2003). Motor compatibility: The bidirectional link between behavior and evaluation. In J. Musch & K. C. Klauer (Eds.), *The psychology of evaluation: Affective processes in cognition and emotion* (pp. 371–391). Mahwah, NJ: Lawrence Erlbaum Associates.

Neumann, R., & Strack, F. (2000). Experiential and nonexperiential routes of motor influence on affect and evaluation. In H. Bless & J. P. Forgas (Eds.), *The message within: The role of subjective experience in social cognition and behavior* (pp. 52–68). Philadelphia: Psychology Press.

Nielson, K. (Nov. 17, 2003). *Society for Neuroscience.* Orlando, FL.

Öhman, A., & Soares, J. J. F. (1998). Emotional conditioning to masked stimuli: Expectancies for aversive outcomes following nonrecognized fear-relevant stimuli. *Journal of Experimental Psychology: General, 127*, 68–82.

Olson, M. A., & Fazio, R. H. (2001). Implicit attitude formation through classical conditioning. *Psychological Science, 12*, 413–417.

Olson, M. A., & Fazio, R. H. (2002). Implicit acquisition and manifestation of classically conditioned attitudes. *Social Cognition, 20*, 89–103.

Onishi, K., & Baillargeon, R. (2002, April). 15-month-old infants' understanding of false belief. Paper presented at the Biennial International Conference on Infant Studies, Toronto.

Ortony, A., Clore, G. L., & Collins, A. (1988). *The cognitive structure of emotions*. New York: Cambridge University Press.

Osgood, C. E., Suci, G. J., & Tannenbaum, P. H. (1957). *The measurement of meaning*. University of Illinois Press, Chicago.

Ottati, V., & Isbell, L. (1996). Effects of mood during exposure to target information on subsequently reported judgments: An on-line model of misattribution and correction. *Journal of Personality and Social Psychology, 71*, 39–53.

Pearson, H. (2002). Bloody teeth boost memory. *Nature: Science Update*. [Nature News Service]. www.nature.com

Peretz, I., Gaudreau, D., & Bonnel, A.-M. (1998). Exposure effects on music preference and recognition. *Memory and Cognition, 26*, 884–902.

Petty, R. E., & Cacioppo, J. T. (1986). *Communication and persuasion: Central and peripheral cues to attitude change*. New York: Springer.

Petty, R. E., DeSteno, D., & Rucker, D. D. (2001). The role of affect in attitude change. In J. P. Forgas (Ed.), *Handbook of affect and social cognition* (pp. 212–233). Mahwah, NJ: Lawrence Erlbaum Associates.

Petty, R. E., Schumann, D. W., Richman, S. A., & Strathman, A. J. (1993). Positive mood and persuasion: Different roles for affect under high- and low-elaboration conditions. *Journal of Personality and Social Psychology, 64*, 5–20.

Petty, R. E., & Wegener, D. T. (1993). Flexible correction processes in social judgment: Correcting for context-induced contrast. *Journal of Experimental Social Psychology, 29*, 137–165.

Pittman, R. K. (1989) Post-traumatic stress disorder, hormones, and memory. *Biological Psychiatry, 26*, 221–223.

Pliner, P. L. (1982). The effects of mere exposure on liking for edible substances. *Appetite, 3*, 283–290.

Premack, D., & Woodruff, G. (1978). Does the chimpanzee have a theory of mind? *Behavioral and Brain Sciences, 1*, 515–526.

Razran, G. H. S. (1940). Conditional response changes in rating and appraising sociopolitical slogans. *Psychological Bulletin, 37*, 481.

Razran, G. H. S. (1954). The conditioned evocation of attitudes (cognitive conditioning?) *Journal of Experimental Psychology, 48*, 278–282.

Reber, R., Winkielman, P., & Schwarz, N. (1998). Effects of perceptual fluency on affective judgments. *Psychological Science, 9*, 45–48.

Rhodewalt, F., & Comer, R. (1979). Induced-compliance attitude change: Once more with feeling. *Journal of Experimental Social Psychology, 15*, 35–48.

Rimm, D. C., Janda, L. H., Lancaster, D. W., Nahl, M., & Dittmar, K. (1977). An exploratory investigation of the origin and maintenance of phobias. *Behavior Research and Therapy*, 15, 231–238.

Rogers, P. J., & Hill, A. J. (1989). Breakdown of dietary restraint following mere exposure to food stimuli: Interrelationships between hunger, salivation and food intake. *Addictive Behaviors, 14*, 387–397.

Rogers, R. W. (1983). Cognitive and physiological processes in fear appeals and attitude change: A revised theory of protection motivation. In J. T. Cacioppo & R. E. Petty (Eds.), *Social psychophysiology: A sourcebook* (pp. 153–176). New York: Guilford.

Rolls, E.T. (1999). *The Brain and Emotion*. Oxford, UK: Oxford University Press.

Rosselli, F., Skelly, J. J., & Mackie, D. M. (1995). Processing rational and emotional messages: The cognitive and affective mediation of persuasion. *Journal of Experimental Social Psychology, 31*, 163–190.

Russell, J. A. (2003). Core affect and the psychological construction of emotion. *Psychological Review, 110*, 145–172.

Sacks, O. (1985). *The man who mistook his wife for a hat*. New York: Summit Books.

Salovey, P., & Mayer, J. D. (1990). Emotional intelligence. *Imagination, Cognition and Personality*, 9, 185–211.

Schnall, S. (2004). Embodiment in affect and cognition. Unpublished Manuscript.

Schnall, S., & Clore, G. L. (2002, June). *Enacted affect as information: How facial expressions influence recall of emotional events*. Paper presented at the meeting of the American Psychological Society, New Orleans.

Schwarz, N. (1990). Feelings as information: Informational and motivational functions of affective states. In E.T. Higgins & R. Sorrentino (Eds.), *Handbook of motivation and cognition: Foundations of social behavior* (Vol. 2, pp. 527–561). New York: Guilford.

Schwarz, N., Bless, H., & Bohner, G. (1991). Mood and persuasion: Affective states influence the processing of persuasive communication. In M. P. Zanna (Ed.), *Advances in experimental social psychology* (Vol. 24, pp. 161–199). San Diego, CA: Academic Press.

Schwarz, N., & Clore, G. L. (1983). Mood, misattribution, and judgments of well-being: Informative and directive functions of affective states. *Journal of Personality and Social Psychology, 45*, 513–523.

Schwarz, N., & Clore, G. L. (1988). How do I feel about it? Informative functions of affective states. In K. Fiedler & J. Forgas (Eds.), *Affect, cognition and social behavior* (pp. 44–62). Toronto: Hogrefe International.

Schwarz, N., & Clore, G. L. (1996). Feelings and phenomenal experience. In E. T. Higgins & A. W. Kruglanski (Eds.), *Social psychology: A handbook of basic principles* (pp. 433–465). New York: Guilford.

Scott, R. (2003). *The Gothic Enterprise*. Berkeley, CA: University of California Press.

Seamon, J. G., McKenna, P. A., & Binder, N. (1998). The mere exposure effect is differentially sensitive to different judgment tasks. *Consciousness and Cognition, 7*, 85–102.

Seligman, M. E. P. (1970). On the generality of the laws of learning. *Psychological Review, 77*, 406–418.

Sengupta, J., & Johar, G.V. (2001). Contingent effects of anxiety on message elaboration and persuasion. *Personality and Social Psychology Bulletin, 27*, 139–150.

Simon, H. A. (1967). Motivational and emotional controls of cognition. *Psychological Review, 74*, 29–39.

Sinclair, R. C., Mark, M. M., & Clore, G. L. (1993). Mood-related persuasion depends on (mis)attributions. *Social Cognition, 12*, 309–326.

Sinclair, S. Huntsinger, J., Skorinko, J., & Hardin, C. (2003). *Social tuning of the self: Consequences for the self-evaluations of stereotype targets.* Unpublished manuscript, University of Virginia.

Sinclair, R. C., Mark, M. M., & Clore, G. L. (1994). Mood-related persuasion depends on (mis)attributions. *Social Cognition. 12*, 309–326.

Slovic, P., Finucane, M., Peters, E., & MacGregor, D. G. (2002). The affect heuristic. In T. Gilovich, D. Griffin, & D. Kahneman (Eds.), *The psychology of intuitive judgment heuristics and biases* (pp. 397–420). Cambridge: Cambridge University Press.

Soldat, A. S., & Sinclair, R. C. (2001). Colors, smiles, and frowns: External affective cues can directly affect responses to persuasive communications in a mood-like manner without affecting mood. *Social Cognition, 19*, 469–490.

Stang, D. J. (1974). Methodological factors in mere exposure research. *Psychological Bulletin, 81*, 1014–1025.

Staats, A. W., & Staats, C.K. (1958). Attitude established by classical conditioning. *Journal of Abnormal and Social Psychology, 11*, 187–192.

Strack, F., Martin, L. L., & Stepper, S. (1988). Inhibiting and facilitating conditions of the human smile: A nonobtrusive test of the facial feedback hypothesis. *Journal of Personality and Social Psychology, 54*, 768–777.

Strack, F., Schwarz, N., & Gschneidinger, E. (1985). Happiness and reminiscing: The role of time perspective, mood, and mode of thinking. *Journal of Personality and Social Psychology, 49*, 1460–1469.

Storbeck, J. (2004). *Cleaning-up the "quick and dirty" low route to affective analysis: Implications for social psychologists.* Unpublished Manuscript, University of Virginia.

Storbeck, J., & Robinson, M. (2004). Preferences and inferences in encoding visual objects: A systematic comparison of semantic and affective priming. *Personality and Social Psychology Bulletin, 30*, 81–93.

Stroessner, S. J., & Mackie, D. M. (1992). The impact of induced affect on the perception of variability in social groups. *Personality and Social Psychology Bulletin, 18*, 546–554.

Sutton, J. (1998). *Philosophy and memory traces: Descartes to connectionism.* Cambridge, UK: Cambridge University Press.

Tamir, M., Robinson, M. D., & Clore, G. L. (2002). The epistemic benefits of trait-consistent mood states: An analysis of extraversion and mood. *Journal of Personality and Social Psychology, 83*, 663–677.

Thagard, P., & Nerb, J. (2002). Emotional gestalts: Appraisal, change, and the dynamics of affect. *Personality and Social Psychology Review, 6*, 274–282.

Tiedens, L. Z., & Linton, S. (2001). Judgment under emotional certainty and uncertainty: The effects of specific emotions on information processing. *Journal of Personality and Social Psychology, 81*, 973–988.

Van Overwalle, F., & Jordens, K. (2002). An adaptive connectionist model of cognitive dissonance. *Personality and Social Psychology Review, 6*, 204–231.

Varela, F. J., Thompson, E., & Rosch, E. (1991). *The embodied mind: Cognitive science and human experience.* Cambridge, MA: MIT Press.

Walther, E. (2002). Guilty by mere association: Evaluative conditioning and the spreading attitude effect. *Journal of Personality and Social Psychology, 82*, 919–934.

Watson, D., & Tellegen, A. (1985). Toward a consensual structure of mood. *Psychological Bulletin, 98*, 219–235.

Watson, J. B., & Raynor, R. (1920). Conditioned emotional reactions. *Journal of Experimental Psychology, 3*, 1–14.

Wegener, D. T., & Petty, R. E. (1997). The flexible correction model: The role of naive theories of bias in bias correction. In M. P. Zanna (Ed.), *Advances in experimental social psychology* (Vol. 29, pp. 141–208). New York: Academic Press.

Wegener, D. T., & Petty, R. E. (2001). Understanding the effects of mood through the elaboration likelihood and flexible correction models. In L. L. Martin & G. L. Clore (Eds.), *Theories of mood and cognition: A user's handbook* (pp. 177–210). Mahwah, NJ: Lawrence Erlbaum Associates.

Wegener, D. T. , Petty, R. E., & Smith, S.M. (1995). Positive moods can increase or decrease message scrutiny: The hedonic contingency view of mood and message processing. *Journal of Personality and Social Psychology, 69*, 5–15.

Wegner, D. M. (2002). *The illusion of conscious will.* Cambridge, MA: MIT Press.

Wellman, H. M. (1990). *The child's theory of mind.* Cambridge, MA: MIT Press.

Wilson, T. D., Gilbert, D. T., & Centerbar, D. B. (2003). Making sense: The causes of emotional evanescence. In I. Brocas & J. Carrillo (Eds.), *The psychology of economic decisions. Vol. 1: Rationality and well being* (pp.209–233). New York: Oxford University Press.

Winkielman, P., & Cacioppo, J. T. (2001). Mind at ease puts a smile on the face: Psychophysiological evidence that processing facilitation increases positive affect. *Journal of Personality and Social Psychology, 81*, 989–1000.

Winkielman, P., Schwarz, N., Fazendeiro, T. A., & Reber, R. (2003). The hedonic marking of processing fluency: Implications for evaluative judgment. In J. Musch & K. C. Klauer (Eds.), *The psychology of evaluation: Affective processes in cognition and emotion.* Mahwah, NJ: Lawrence Erlbaum Associates.

Winkielman, P., Zajonc, R.B., & Schwarz, N. (1997). Subliminal affective priming resists attributional interventions. *Cognition and Emotion, 11*, 433–465.

Wolpe, J. (1958). *Psychotherapy by reciprocal inhibition.* Stanford, CA: Stanford University Press.

Worth, L. T., & Mackie, D. M. (1987). Cognitive mediation of positive mood in persuasion. *Social Cognition, 5*, 76–94.

Wyer, R. S., & Carlston, D. E. (1979). *Social cognition inference and attribution.* Hillsdale, NJ: Lawrence Erlbaum Associates.

Wyer, R. S., Clore, G. L., & Isbell, L. (1999). Affect and information processing. In M. Zanna (Ed.), *Advances in Experimental Social Psychology* (pp. 1–77). New York: Academic Press.

Wyer, R. S., & Srull, T. K. (1989). *Memory and cognition in its social context.* Hillsdale, NJ: Lawrence Erlbaum Associates.

Zajonc, R. B. (1968). Attitudinal effects of mere exposure. *Journal of Personality and Social Psychology: Monograph Supplement, 9*, 1–27.

Zajonc, R. B. (1980). Feeling and thinking: Preferences need no inferences. *American Psychologist, 35*, 117–123.

Zajonc, R.B. (1998). Emotions. In D. T. Gilbert, S. T. Fiske, & G. Lindzey (Eds.), *The handbook of social psychology* (pp. 591–632). Boston, MA: McGraw-Hill.

Zajonc, R. B. (2001). Mere exposure: A gateway to the subliminal. *Current Directions in Psychological Science, 10*, 224–228.

Zanna, M. P., & Cooper, J. (1976). Dissonance and the attribution process. In J. H. Harvey, W. J. Ickes, & R. F. Kidd (Eds.), *New directions in attribution research* (Vol. 1, pp. 199–217). Hillsdale, NJ: Lawrence Erlbaum Associates.

Zanna, M., P., Kiesler, C. A., & Pilkonis, P. A. (1970). Positive and negative attitudinal affect established by classical conditioning. *Journal of Personality and Social Psychology, 14*, 321–328.

Zanna, M. P., & Rempel, J. K. (1988). Attitudes: A new look at an old concept. In D. Bar-Tal & A. Kruglanski (Eds.), *The social psychology of knowledge* (pp. 315–334). New York: Cambridge University Press.

Zelazo, P. D., Astington, J. W., & Olson, D. R. (Eds.). (1999). *Developing theories of intention: Social understanding and self control.* Mahwah, NJ: Lawrence Erlbaum Associates.

Zhao, K. (1993). *How categorization and deliberative processing explain consumer response to direct mail advertising.* Unpublished honor's thesis in marketing. Baruch College, City University of New York.

III

Integrative Views on Attitudes

12

Cognitive Processes in Attitude Formation and Change

Duane T. Wegener
Donal E. Carlston
Purdue University

One could argue that cognitive process has been at the heart of research on attitudes virtually since that research began (e.g., Thurstone, 1928; Peterson & Thurstone, 1933). With the advent of the social cognition movement, the concept of what qualifies as "cognition" has undergone considerable development, but the centrality of cognition to studies of attitude formation and change remains. This centrality is evident even though recent studies of attitude change have more thoroughly incorporated concepts such as motivation and affect than was true when social cognition researchers focused almost exclusively on "cold" cognition. We lay the groundwork for our chapter by clarifying definitions associated with the terms "attitude," "cognition," and "process." Then, we review and organize the specific types of cognitive processes that have been studied in attitude formation and change. Our goal in doing so is not only to cover both classic and recent approaches to attitudinal processes, but also to address central issues about the definition and nature of such processes.

DEFINITIONAL ISSUES: ATTITUDES, COGNITION, AND PROCESS

Attitudes

Like most attitude researchers, we treat the terms "evaluation" and "attitude" as synonyms (see Albarracín, Johnson, Zanna, & Kumkale, chap. 1, this volume). That is, attitudes are overall evaluations of objects, which can be physical objects, people, policies, behaviors, etc.[1] Because overall evaluations inform people whether to approach or avoid an object, it makes sense for an adaptive cognitive system to represent those evaluations in memory (Fazio & Olson, 2003a). What form this representation might take, however, has been a matter of some debate.

One useful metaphor for attitude representation is the associative network, with attitudes being primarily composed of an evaluative node linked to a node representing the attitude object (Fazio, 1995). Attitude-relevant knowledge is represented with additional nodes that are often linked to both the attitude object and the evaluation (though some knowledge associated with the attitude object might be associated with the opposite overall evaluation, thereby creating ambivalence; see Fabrigar, MacDonald, & Wegener, chap. 3, this volume). An alternative metaphor is that of a connectionist network (see Bassili & Brown, chap. 3, this volume). In this metaphor, attitudes are generally represented by a pattern of activation within a module (Smith & DeCoster, 1998) or set (Kashima & Kerekes, 1994) of units.[2] In a connectionist framework, the cognitive representation of the attitude is "stored" in the connection weights among units. These weights determine the amount of activation that flows from any one unit to another after an initial set of units is activated by an encounter with, or thought about, the attitude object. Although there are a variety of ways in which distributed representations and connectionist models differ from symbolic representations (such as associative networks), most attitude effects can be conceptualized within either metaphor without much conceptual cost.

A cognitive system built to facilitate action seems likely to include cognitive elements that help guide those actions. A common perspective assumes that evaluations are stored in memory, as are observations, inferences, judgments and a variety of other products of cognition (Carlston, 1994; Eagly & Chaiken, 1993; Lingle & Ostrom, 1981; Hovland, Janis, & Kelley, 1953). Although some attitudes are surely "constructed" at some point (see later discussion), we assume that many attitudes are stored in memory (though some are "stronger" than others, i.e., more accessible, based on greater knowledge, etc., see Petty & Krosnick, 1995).[3]

Cognitive Processes

In the attitudes and social cognition areas, one could almost drop the "cognitive" from the term "cognitive process" with little change in meaning. When one speaks of process in much of social psychology, those processes involve interpretation of stimuli, use of existing knowledge, and storage of resulting perceptions or judgments in memory. The term "cognitive" is used so broadly today that it is virtually a synonym for "psychological" or "mental." If the human brain is involved, a process is cognitive, and because the human brain is almost always involved, few human activities fall outside the cognitive umbrella. Even automatic, implicit, thoughtless, and habitual responses are embraced by contemporary cognitive theory, and traditional alternatives to cognition such as motivation and emotion are treated as having cognitive antecedents, as operating on knowledge structures stored in memory, and as having cognitive consequences. As Markus and Zajonc (1985) put it, "the change since [the fifties and sixties] has been of revolutionary proportions, impelling nearly all investigators to view social psychological phenomena from the cognitive perspective. Social psychology and cognitive social psychology are today nearly synonymous." (p. 137). These words are as true today as when Markus and Zajonc first wrote them (see also Mischel, 1998).

During this transformation, definitions of what people consider to be a "cognitive approach" have shifted. As intimated earlier, attitudes research has included many sorts of cognitive processes and constructs, such as comprehension, retention, balance, cognitive dissonance, and cognitive response. Yet, many of the original treatments of these processes would not have been identified as "social cognition" in the early days of that approach because the original attitude theories said little about how the relevant cognitive elements were encoded, structured, or retrieved or about the specific cognitive operations that would bring about the hypothesized outcomes (e.g., "consistency").

Especially in the 1970s and early 1980s, the emphasis in social cognition was on "cold" cognition—a cognition essentially void of extracognitive motives or emotion. This emphasis was perhaps ushered into prominence by developments in the 1960s and early 1970s in areas such as causal attribution (Jones & Davis, 1965; Kelley, 1967), aided by the computer analogy and mathematical/computational models of cognitive systems and processes (Fishbein, 1963; McGuire, 1960; Wyer, 1974). However, social cognition of the 1990s and 2000s is considerably more diverse (some might say "diffuse"). The topics of motivation and emotion have been rediscovered, though thoroughly couched in terms of cognitive antecedents, processes, and consequences. Psychological mechanisms that occur outside of consciousness and without intention are also incorporated into cognitive models (Wegner & Bargh, 1998).

In the current chapter, we retain the general definition of cognition that permeates current work in social cognition. As best we can tell, any process that stores knowledge structures in memory or that operates on stored knowledge structures is considered "cognitive." This definition is admittedly broad, as is the common inclusion of phenomena as diverse as inconsistency resolution, heuristics and biases, piecemeal processing, and behavior priming under the umbrella of "social cognition." Taking this broad definition into account, the various mental processes studied throughout the history of attitudes research (e.g., balance, comprehension, retention, elaboration) would, without a doubt, qualify as "cognitive" (even if they might not have qualified as such in the early days of social cognition).

Defining Process

Surprisingly, the term "process" is undefined by most psychological dictionaries, including the *Blackwell Dictionary of Cognitive Psychology* (Eysenck, Ellis, Hunt, & Johnson-Laird, 1994). Consequently, we suggest the following definition, which seems to capture standard understandings of process in cognitive contexts: A *cognitive process* involves one or more recurrent mental events that, in concert, add to, alter, or act upon representations in memory with detectable consequences. As this definition implies, cognitive processes are not directly observable (like other hypothetical constructs, see later discussion), but must be inferred from their "detectable consequences." This permits considerable latitude in defining and describing processes, so that their nature and existence are closely tied to theories of mental phenomena. In other words, processes are essentially latent constructs that are understood principally from the broader theories in which they are embedded.

As components of broader theories, processes may be described (and defined) at varying levels of generality and scope. At the broadest level, *universal* process descriptions reflect general rules, operations, or metaphors that could characterize almost any form of thought and that encompass a wide variety of disparate phenomena. *Bounded* process descriptions depict processes as having narrower domains of application, the assumption being that different processes, described at roughly the same level of scope, predominate in different circumstances or for different people. Finally, *component* processes (which at the lowest level may even be tied closely to neurological events) have very limited responsibilities, such that several (if not more) must be linked together to account for even relatively simple phenomena.

Individual theories include process descriptions that differ in level of generality and scope, and theories may describe one, two, or several cognitive processes, depending on the functional goals of the theorist. As a rule, however, theorists who assume universal processes tend to view these processes as alternatives to the more bounded processes posited by most attitude theorists. And theorists who describe bounded processes vary considerably in the extent to which their theories explicitly touch base with the kinds of component processes common in early social cognition. Whether reflected in a single theory or not, many cognitive processes are undoubtedly interconnected, sometimes serially, so that the output of one serves as input for others; sometimes hierarchically, so that higher level processes subsume lower level ones; and sometimes interactively, so that they affect the execution of one another.

Although theorists have considerable latitude in characterizing cognitive processes, there are ground rules (and some of these ground rules are becoming more restrictive, as discussed later.) One important rule is to distinguish process from content. If one were to adopt a plumbing metaphor, one might describe the pipes as the structure, the transported liquid as the content, and the pressure and gravitationally-induced movement of liquid through the pipes as the process. Of course, the mind is not a kitchen sink, and in the mind, content, process and structure may be less clearly distinguishable than this metaphor suggests. Structure and process are especially intimately intertwined, and even in our plumbing metaphor, the structure of the piping determines the nature of the process.

Yet, processes are generally more ephemeral than structures in that processes are expected to come and go. They are not always active, but rather they occur recurrently, becoming active each time some mental operation must be performed on some set of representational contents or stimulus inputs. We would not likely characterize any one-time operation as a cognitive process, nor would we be likely to so characterize mental activity that never ceases as one. Processes should be turned on, and then after they have done their work, they should turn off. This ephemeral nature can make processes more difficult to observe than cognitive representations–often the outputs of process—because representations are expected to persist for some time after the process has ended.

Evaluation as Structure Versus Process

The term "evaluation" can sometimes create misunderstandings because it can mean either the attitudinal content represented in memory or the process of arriving at an attitude. Although most attitudes research includes an assumption that at least some attitudes are stored in memory, some theorists have claimed that they are not. Rather, attitudes are described as the outcome of evaluative processes operating on information available in memory and in the environment (Schwarz & Bohner, 2001; Wilson, & Hodges, 1992).

As pointed out by Fazio and Olson (2003a), the strongest "constructionist" assumptions face certain logical difficulties (see also Wyer & Albarracín, chap. 7, this volume). If evaluations are always constructed, on what basis are such constructions formed? For example, in studies that show "inclusion" or "exclusion" of a salient exemplar to influence overall evaluations of a category (Coats & Smith, 1999; Stapel & Schwarz, 1998), these effects seem to be driven at least in part by evaluations of the exemplar. Even if the evaluation of the exemplar was constructed, how is the positivity or negativity of exemplars determined? If the "goodness" or "badness" of some core information (or criteria for judging information) is stored, then clearly some attitudes are stored in memory.

It seems likely that a middle ground is more defensible (see also Bassili & Brown, chap. 13, this volume, and Kruglanski & Stroebe, chap. 8, this volume). Because attitude reports include question interpretation, scale interpretation, and generation of standards of comparison (Tourangeau & Rasinski, 1988; Schwarz & Bohner, 2001), reports of attitudes will often include some level of "construction" (see Lord & Lepper, 1999, for discussion of how representations and context combine in producing attitudinal responses). Yet, the extent of construction probably depends on both situational and attitudinal factors. If respondents view the judgment or object as particularly important or relevant, they may be likely to actively consider as much information as possible, especially if they do not already have an established evaluation on which to rely. If respondents already have a strong evaluation of the object, and, especially, if there is little reason to go beyond this initial perception, then constructive activities seem less likely. Also, if construction occurs with strong evaluations, the evaluations themselves seem likely to guide that construction.

In fact, research suggests that accessible attitudes are less likely than inaccessible attitudes to be influenced by constructive activities (Hodges & Wilson, 1993). A strong version of the construction or "construal" model (Schwarz & Bohner, 2001) could account for such effects by saying that oft-used knowledge decreases the likelihood of context effects. Yet, a model in which people must always construct their attitudes would have more difficulty accounting for results obtained in recent studies by Priester, Nayakankuppum, Fleming, and Godek (2004). If attitudes are constructed (the result of a quick "review" of object attributes), then (a) reporting an attitude should result in fast and easy subsequent recognition of attributes and (b) judgments of attributes should make subsequent attitude judgments faster. This mutual facilitation should not occur, however, if attitudes are stored and accessed independent of the attribute information. In a series of studies, Priester et al. found that the "construction" pattern was more likely when attitudes were "weak" (inaccessible or ambivalent) but the "independent access" pattern was more likely when attitudes were strong (accessible or univalent).

Content Versus Process

As our definition of process suggests, cognitive content is also implicated in every cognitive process, suggesting some degree of inseparability there, as well. But there is a useful distinction between content and process, even if it has a stronger conceptual than biological reality. Processes are more general and more ephemeral than representations. Processes are generally thought to operate on different cognitive representations at different times: they are not in the exclusive employ of one content alone (though some may be thought to operate primarily on certain classes of content or combinations of content and target–one could also define content at different levels of generality). For example, one may have specific mental representations of the President or his tax policies, but few would characterize mental activities associated with one and only one of these representations as a cognitive process. Instead, a process ought to act on many different representations. To return to our metaphor, the processes that move liquids through pipes (e.g., pressure) presumably operate on many different liquids, though they might operate differentially, depending on attributes of the liquids (e.g., viscosity).

Caveats

There are other rules for identifying cognitive processes as well, which we discuss in the following section. Several caveats will be useful, however. First, as already noted, processes can be described at varying levels of generality. The appropriate level of generality is determined by one's goals: that is, by what one wishes to explain or predict. When the goal is integration, process can be described with broad, sweeping strokes that make commonalities obvious and suggest extensions to new domains. When the goal is specific prediction, process can be described with more limited scope, including the necessary contingencies for turning a given process on and off in order to articulate well with accumulated data. Special caution is required when comparing or contrasting processes that may be defined at altogether different levels of generality, in satisfaction of different objectives.

Second, processes are fuzzy categories (McCloskey & Glucksberg,1979); they lack defining features, despite periodic attempts to frame them in such terms. Instead, they can only be identified and distinguished from other processes through collections of features. For the psychologist, this fuzziness generally means that processes can best be understood through multiple pieces of evidence and different kinds of measures. Despite regular advances in process measures, any one method is generally most useful in examining a limited range of processes. Even then, that utility increases when the method is supplemented with alternative approaches.

These issues become especially relevant when controversies erupt over which of two processes better accounts for a phenomenon, or whether it takes one, two, or more processes to do so. There is general agreement that quantitative differences in amount of a process can influence outcomes, as can qualitative differences in type of process. Yet, especially in recent critiques of dual process models (Fishbein & Middlestadt, 1995; Kruglanski & Thompson, 1999a), claims have been made that there are no qualitative differences (or that none have been shown), and that one ought not confuse different levels of a single process with qualitatively different processes. Some methods for distinguishing process focus on this consideration.

It is not always clear, however, whether differences in processes are qualitative versus quantitative. Even when different processes can be arrayed along a single quantitative continuum, it may be useful to characterize these using qualitatively different process labels. Note, for example, that running, walking, strolling, and loitering all lie on a single speed dimension, yet they are distinguished in language because they spring from different antecedents and motives, and they can have different consequences. To illustrate, consider the different implications of being arrested while running, walking, or loitering in a shopping mall.

Because some distinctions might be characterized in either quantitative or qualitative ways, efforts to delineate separable processes are often complex. Such efforts have proliferated nonetheless, an inevitable consequence of the decision to cast aside behaviorist restraint and to speculate openly about the operations of the black box of the mind. Because we cannot absolutely know what transpires between stimulus and response, we can never be certain whether that transpiration implicates one process or more. Even if we could know exactly what occurs between stimulus and response, there might be considerable debate about how to "chunk" the mental events into processes. Therefore, attempts to identify and disambiguate processes will inevitably involve some degree of speculation, combined with judicious, but subjective, interpretation of evidence from a range of theoretical and empirical sources.

Although a wide variety of specific techniques have been developed, most rely in one way or another on theories (process descriptions) predicting certain outcomes (on judgments, response times, electrical activity, or some other dimension). When the predicted outcomes occur, and especially when the predicted outcomes differ significantly from outcomes predicted by an alternative process description, this is taken as evidence in support of the theory in question. In a later section of the chapter, we illustrate general process testing in social psychology. Before doing so, however, we address some possible counterarguments to our general characterization of process description and testing. In particular, some might argue that developments such as the information processing approach remove many of the "fuzzy" elements of process definition, making process description quite straightforward. Also, researchers might hold up specific methods as a "best approach" to identifying processes (such as methods adapted from discriminant construct validity, the process dissociation method, and new brain imaging technologies in neuropsychology). Although each of these methods provides some leverage in process identification, we believe that none of these methods represents the "holy grail" of process identification. Rather than concluding that defining process is futile, we would take any ambiguities in specific methods to mean that no single method will suffice in isolation.

Information Processing

Development of the information-processing model provided a framework for breaking down and organizing processes. Information input, storage, retrieval, and computation suggested stimulus perception, storage, recall, and judgment, and the impossibly complex human information processor was reduced to manageable subprocesses that could be examined separately (Broadbent, 1958). In the early days of social cognition, the cold logic of the computer metaphor predominated, and social cognition was identified with the information-processing approach (e.g., Hastie & Carlston, 1980), perhaps too strongly (Forgas, 1983; Zajonc, 1980). During this period, interest in "hotter" psychological mechanisms languished (Fiske & Taylor, 1991). Eventually this imbalance was noted and redressed (e.g., Dunning, 1999; Kruglanski, 1996), though the information-processing model remains the implicit arbiter of what kinds of mechanisms some psychologists admit as "processes." From this perspective, recall is clearly a process, elaboration is probably one, and ego-defense is less clearly so. Such norms are useful–they do, at least, provide common language for describing cognition in terms of tasks the mind must typically accomplish. But information processing mechanisms represent only one (fairly low) level of scope (what we have termed *component* processes), and the goals of social psychologists often pertain to higher levels (involving *bounded* or even *universal* processes).

The reification of information processing also does little to necessarily differentiate one process from another. Characterizing impression formation as the perception, encoding, storage, retrieval, combination, and summarization of observed behaviors applies conventional labels to what could be a singular process or an aggregation of 30 different processes. From a connectionist point of view, for example, all of these varieties of information processing could be accomplished through a single process: the spreading of activation across nodes in accordance with weights derived from previous experience (Rumelhart, 1997; Smith & DeCoster, 1998).

Alternatively, each stage of information processing might be viewed as comprising dozens of separate processes, ranging from memory activation to incongruity resolution to self comparison. How we choose to characterize cognitive processes depends on our working theory of the mind, and though the information processing model informs that theory, it doesn't necessarily offer uniquely accurate insights into what is going on in the black box.

Discriminant Construct Validity

Campbell and Fiske (1959) proposed that measures of the same construct should be correlated (convergent validity) and that measures of different constructs ought to be relatively uncorrelated (discriminant validity). In application to personality measures, for example, use of a multitrait, multimethod design allows one to assess and compare correlations between all trait-measure combinations to assess the validity of underlying constructs (see Visser, Fabrigar, Wegener, & Browne, 2004, for a review). Processes might be treated as latent constructs, discriminable through the same general methods.

As Miller and Pederson (1999) noted, however, "The issue of discriminative process validity is more subtle and complex than is discriminative construct validity" (p. 150). One complexity is that other latent constructs are generally hypothesized to be stable entities, whereas processes exist only when instigated, so they cannot be measured without procedures to activate them. A second complexity is that direct or pure measures of cognitive processes are difficult (perhaps impossible) to devise (Jacoby, 1991), and devising the multiple measures suggested by Campbell and Fiske (1959) is likely to be especially difficult. When they can be devised, and when methods exist to prompt the processes of interest (especially selectively) then the general logic of construct validation might be applicable. That is, different measures of the same process should be correlated, whereas measures of different processes might not be (unless the different processes are part of the same causal chain or are both instigated by the same factor or factors).

Cognitive Approaches

Cognitive psychologists have developed procedures for distinguishing one process from another in order to address thorny issues such as whether different kinds of memory (e.g., semantic vs. episodic, implicit vs. explicit) truly reflect different systems and processes or are simply different manifestations of the same system and process. A common approach is to manipulate or measure different processes while holding other aspects of a procedure constant. For example, different groups of participants might be instructed to process the same stimulus information differently in order to assess the differential impact of the engaged processes on a single dependent measure. Imagine that participants are given a poem, with half told to engage in rote repetition and the other half told to focus on the poem's meaning. If the two groups then differ on some dependent measure (perhaps, recognition of lines from the poem), this could indicate that the participants engaged in fundamentally different mnemonic processes. Alternatively, this result could simply suggest that the two groups engaged in essentially the same mnemonic process, but to different degrees. To achieve greater clarity, the method might be expanded to incorporate two separate dependent measures (perhaps memory for language and memory for gist) in the hope that one might better reflect rote learning and the other gist learning.

However, Jacoby (1991) has noted how difficult it is to find pure, independent measures of cognitive processes. An alternative strategy is to hold the dependent variable constant and to vary the stimulus in a manner that should affect the hypothesized processes. For example, one group of participants might receive meaningful poetry, and another, a list of nonsense syllables. Then if gist memory instructions prove more effective for the former group, and rote memory instructions prove more effective for the latter, this finding would provide stronger evidence that separate processes are implicated. Conceptually equivalent is the effort to find a set of factors that affects one hypothesized process, but not the second, and vice versa. When two processes can be manipulated independently, it makes sense that they are, in fact, two separate processes.

But this kind of reasoning is not bulletproof. For purposes of illustration, consider whether or not small and large trees (or the processes affecting them) differ in qualitative ways. Consistent with the previous rationale, one could easily find different factors that affect small and large trees differently. Small trees are more vulnerable to hungry deer denuding their branches, whereas large trees are more vulnerable to thunderstorms, as lightning strikes tall trees and their full limbs catch the wind, leading to blow downs. Yet, small trees clearly grow into large trees, so one could argue that they are, in essence, qualitatively the same (differing only along a quantitative dimension). To be sure, small and large trees both employ the same basic processes of drawing water and nutrients from the soil and photosynthesizing glucose from carbon dioxide in the leaves; moreover, these processes are disrupted by the denuding of branches or breakage of limbs in the wind. However, a purely quantitative theory focusing on these general processes might not produce predictions useful to a person who wants to prevent tree mortality. In some circumstances at least, a theory conceptualizing branch denuding, limbs breaking, and trees falling over as distinct processes might prove more useful for understanding how to protect trees from destruction. We reiterate our earlier point that (for social psychologists, especially) theoretical utility is a primary consideration in describing processes.

Cognitive psychologists have developed related methods to identify processes, including signal detection (Green & Swets, 1974), the Stroop technique (Cohen, Dunbar, & McClelland, 1990), process-dissociation and inclusion-exclusion (Jacoby, 1991). The latter three methods rely on situations where processes that normally function in parallel instead operate at cross purposes. For example, the process-dissociation and inclusion-exclusion methods involve the priming of incorrect responses, so that implicit familiarity (which normally facilitates accuracy) results in inaccuracy. On some trials, subjects are told to try to correct for familiarity, allowing the researcher to tease out the separate impact of implicit and explicit influences on memory (for refinements see McElree, Dolan, & Jacoby, 1999; Stern, McNaught-Davis, & Barker, 2003).

Such methods promise an advance over identification of factors that independently affect each hypothesized process. However, process-dissociation methods are not readily extendable to processes that differ along dimensions other than awareness. Moreover, critics have cautioned that the assumptions of the process dissociation method do not always hold (Dodson & Johnson,

1996; Komatsu, Graf, & Uttl, 1995; Wilson & Horton, 2002), though, of course, such claims are controversial (Toth, Reingold, & Jacoby, 1995).

Social Neuroscience

Some researchers regard the most promising candidates for process identification as lying in contemporary neuroscience. Recent developments have greatly enhanced psychologists' ability to determine which areas of the cerebral cortex are most involved in the cognitive processes of normal individuals. For example, functional magnetic resonance imaging (fMRI) can measure increases in concentrations of oxygenated hemoglobin, averaging across repeated measurements to produce the now-familiar two-dimensional, colorized brain slices that show one or another area "lighting up" in apparent response to some cognitive task. Such techniques seem to hold promise for distinguishing among discrete processes by showing that they implicate different "localized" areas of cortex.

Specifically, the dissociative method in neuroscience involves demonstrating that a process implicates one area in the brain and not another. When possible, this dissociative approach seeks to demonstrate a "double dissociation" in which one area of the brain "lights up" in response to a cognitive task, whereas other areas do not light up, and instead respond to a different task. The strongest inferences can be made if this second task does NOT implicate the area affected by the first task, creating the "double dissociation." Critics have noted that the dissociative method assumes modularity in the brain (Shallice, 1988), that double dissociation can occur even with inseparable processes (Plaut, 1995) and that the double dissociation method relies on a number of unproven premises (Dunn & Kirsner, 2003). Consequently, Dunn and Kirsner suggested that the method is not the ultimate answer that some seem to believe (cf., Baddeley, 2003).[4]

Summary

It seems that there is no magic formula for determining equivalence or nonequivalence of processes. Despite encouraging developments in information processing, construct validation, cognitive psychology, and social neuroscience, the identification and discrimination of mental processes remains complex. These developments provide a set of guidelines for accumulating evidence for the existence of one or more cognitive processes, and they help define what psychologists in different areas mean by cognitive process. But none of these areas have devised a single foolproof technique for identifying or distinguishing processes, and the techniques that have been devised tend to reflect differing emphases and objectives within different approaches to psychological phenomena. Consequently the techniques must be used judiciously and often as part of a "triangulation" strategy, though even this approach may not address questions of how to best characterize a given process in relation to other processes.

Process Identification in Social Psychology

Most efforts at process identification in social psychology are not "pure" applications of the previously discussed methods. Scattered efforts have been made to use process dissociation procedures in social cognition research (Lambert, Payne, Jacoby, Shaffer, Chasteen, & Khan, 2003; Zarate, Sanders, & Garza, 2000). For the most part, however, social psychologists have attempted to discriminate hypothesized processes using the basic approach of mapping theoretical predictions (especially different predictions across competing theories) onto observed outcomes. A classic example of efforts to disambiguate competing processes pitted dissonance theory (Festinger, 1957, 1964) against self-perception theory (Bem, 1967, 1972). These theories provided alternative explanations for a variety of phenomena, including the attitude change that occurs after people advocate attitudinal positions other than their own.

According to Festinger, counterattitudinal advocacy creates a state of discomfort or arousal (called dissonance) that individuals are motivated to reduce, and they often accomplish this by changing their attitudes to fit their advocacy. In contrast, Bem suggested that dissonance need not be involved, as people can simply infer their own attitudes from the things they do or hear themselves say. Although essentially a conflict between two different characterizations of self-persuasion processes, the effort to distinguish dissonance from self-perception assumed greater importance as a test of motivational versus cognitive explanations for social phenomena. After initial efforts to devise tasks that would uniquely show the effects of one process rather than the other, some theorists (e.g., Greenwald, 1975) concluded that the hypothesized processes differed more in wording than in substance, and thus could never truly be distinguished. Nonetheless, self-perception and dissonance processes did differ in one important regard, namely the negative state of arousal that dissonance theory posited. This difference ultimately allowed the two processes to be dissociated, at least to the satisfaction of most social psychologists.

A role for unpleasant arousal was first demonstrated using misattribution procedures. Zanna and Cooper (1974) showed that providing research participants with a pill that allegedly created unpleasant arousal significantly reduced attitude change from writing a counterattitudinal essay. Because self-perception theory posited no role for psychological discomfort (the point was that this was unnecessary), misattribution results served as critical tests between the theories. Critical tests between theories have been common in social psychology–especially tests of moderators that apply to one theory and not another, or for which different theories predict different effects (Sigall & Mills, 1998). Such tests rely heavily on theories being specific enough to make clear predictions regarding the factor or moderator, but when this is the case, critical tests can constitute compelling evidence supporting different process explanations.

Later dissonance research directly measured psychological discomfort using physiological measures (Elkin & Leippe, 1986) or self-reports (Elliot & Devine, 1994). Measurement of proposed mediating processes has become more and more common in social psychology, to the point that studies without some form of mediation evidence are difficult to publish in top journals. In many cases, alternative theories differ not in terms of the ultimate judgment outcome or behavior measured in a particular study, but in the mediating process responsible for the outcome. If one theory proposes a certain mediating process whereas the other theory does not, evidence of mediation can be taken as evidence in support of the first theory. Also, sometimes different theories suggest different mediators, which can be competitively examined.

It is unclear whether dissonance and self-perception could have been disentangled were it not for the hypothesized role of arousal in the former process. However, the ultimate resolution of the conflict might have been anticipated on theoretical grounds. It seems unlikely that people would misinterpret highly discrepant positions as their own or that people would feel much discomfort in advocating positions close to their own. Consequently, the former situation was more likely to implicate dissonance and the latter, more likely to implicate self-perception, as research eventually demonstrated (Fazio, Zanna, & Cooper, 1977). But theoretical grounds alone are rarely accepted as a basis for distinguishing cognitive processes. The theories have to make empirical predictions that differ in some demonstrable way, and then data must be collected to demonstrate one outcome or the other (or domains in which each outcome occurs).

Self-perception and dissonance retained their independent stature because they included different constructs *and* because the different constructs were shown to play a role in some circumstances but not in others. If psychological discomfort had always played a role in counterattitudinal advocacy, then self-perception would probably receive little or no attention. In contrast, if psychological discomfort never played a role in counterattitudinal advocacy, dissonance might have fallen by the wayside. But because discomfort sometimes plays a role, both dissonance and self-perception have remained.

PROCESSES IN ATTITUDE FORMATION AND CHANGE

In the remainder of this chapter, we discuss processes relevant to the area of attitude formation and change. Some of these processes have received greater attention in other areas, such as impression formation or attitude-behavior relations, but most have traditionally received attention in discussions of persuasion processes. As mentioned previously, different researchers have focused on process descriptions at varying levels of generality. Some theories and processes are pitched at very high levels of generality, to the point of saying that all of attitude change is, in essence, the same, universal process. Other theories and processes are bounded, in that they have a limited domain of applicability and must be supplemented by other processes to completely capture phenomena of interest to attitude theorists and practitioners. Finally, some processes, especially those associated with the so-called information processing approach, can reasonably be thought of as implicating low level, *component* processes. In the rest of the chapter, we begin by discussing universal process descriptions in attitude change, followed by bounded process descriptions and concluding with component process descriptions. Because the processes themselves are fuzzy categories, as are the distinctions we make among levels, we acknowledge that many processes could be placed at more than one level of generality.

Universal Process Descriptions

Perhaps the greatest draw to universal process descriptions is that they seem parsimonious. Scientists generally prefer to use the fewest distinctions necessary to explain phenomena of interest. Therefore, it should not be surprising that some people prefer explanations that employ a single process, rather than two or more, to explain a given set of phenomena. It is probably not necessary to remind readers that models positing relatively effortless (automatic, peripheral, heuristic) and relatively effortful (controlled, central, systematic) processes are common in social psychology today (Chaiken & Trope, 1999). Interestingly, some theorists have argued that all of this research can be captured by a single process (Kruglanski & Thompson, 1999a). More generally, over the years, a number of processes have been described as virtually universal (for additional discussion, see Johnson, Maio, & Smith-McLallen, chap. 15, this volume).

The Expectancy-Value Approach

Martin Fishbein and his colleagues have argued that all attitude change is "cognitive." By this, he does not mean that definitions of cognition have become so inclusive that all evaluation (as well as affect, motivation, or other alternative concepts) has its basis in "cognition," although this might be true to some extent. Rather, Fishbein uses the label "cognition" for belief structures (measured using the techniques he and his colleagues have studied since the 1960s—e.g., Fishbein, 1963). In these techniques, attributes of attitude objects are often solicited from one set of participants in efforts to identify salient beliefs associated with the object. Then, with another set of participants, the perceived likelihood of the object possessing the attribute (expectancy) and evaluation of the attribute (value) are measured, and likelihood X evaluation products are created for each attribute and summed across attributes (Fishbein & Ajzen, 1975).

In a wide variety of settings, overall evaluations of objects are strongly predicted by such belief structures. For example, Ottati, Fishbein, and Middlestadt (1988) found that an expectancy-value index of beliefs about Ronald Reagan significantly predicted attitudes toward Ronald Reagan. Similarly, Middlestadt, Fishbein, and Chan (1993) found that an expectancy-value index of modal beliefs about drinking a brand of apple juice significantly predicted attitudes toward drinking that brand of apple juice. Notably, an expectancy-value index of beliefs significantly predicted attitudes when the index included all modal beliefs identified in a previous belief-elicitation study, but not when the index included only beliefs associated with verbal content in a previous advertisement.[5] Within the expectancy-value approach, a persuasive message can have an impact because it influences perceptions of likelihood or desirability associated with beliefs directly addressed by the message, because it influences perceptions of likelihood or desirability associated with beliefs not addressed by the message, or because it influences which beliefs are salient to the individual (Fishbein & Ajzen, 1981). Because most studies of "noncognitive" processes have not measured beliefs in the ways outlined by Fishbein and colleagues, Fishbein and Middlestadt (1995, 1997) concluded that there has been little or no evidence provided for "noncognitive" attitude change.[6]

Though not stated directly, Fishbein and Middlestadt (1995) seem to regard Fishbein's expectancy-value approach as superior to dual-process theories, at least to the extent that dual-process models postulate "noncognitive" effects that, according to Fishbein and Middlestadt, have not been found. On some level, it seems to us that the so-called dual-process models and the expectancy-value approach focus on different goals. Although the expectancy-value approach allows for various distal factors to influence attitudes, it focuses on the mediating process of belief change as the universal mechanism for these effects. In contrast, dual-process models focus on predicting which distal factors influence attitudes in which situations, potentially predict which beliefs should be responsible for attitude changes and which should not, and also allow for mechanisms other than belief change in explaining effects of some distal factors. Given the ubiquity of approaches and processes that do not postulate belief-based mechanisms, future research is likely to address whether and when attitude change occurs separate from changes in beliefs.

Information Integration

In a manner similar to expectancy-value models' multiplicative treatment of likelihood and desirability, information integration theory (Anderson, 1971) posits that salient pieces of information are weighted (multiplied) by their importance in arriving at an overall evaluation of an object. However, in contrast to the additive rule used to combine information in Fishbein and Ajzen's (1975) expectancy-value approach, information integration theory posits an averaging process. That is, a person's initial evaluation is given a weight, as is each piece of additional information or each thought prompted by the message (cf. Anderson, 1981), and a weighted average of the entire set constitutes the overall evaluation of the object. In this formulation, factors such as source credibility can be viewed as influencing the weights of information provided by a source (Birnbaum, Wong, & Wong, 1976). Unfortunately, the utility of the model is limited by its relative silence regarding a priori determinants of these weights (see Eagly & Chaiken, 1984; Petty & Cacioppo, 1981).

Probabilogical/Syllogistic/If-Then Reasoning

Attitudes and beliefs have long been analyzed as relating to formal rules of logic and probability. For example, an attitude that exercise is valuable can be conceptualized as following from the premises that exercise leads to longer life and that longer life is valuable (see Eagly & Chaiken, 1998; McGuire, 1960; Wyer, 1974). Of course, people could differ in the extent to which they believe that exercise leads to long life and even to which long life is viewed as valuable. Also, other premises, such as "exercise is hard work" and "hard work is unpleasant" could influence the same attitudinal conclusion. When many premises are relevant to the same conclusion, the belief system is said to have extensive horizontal structure (McGuire, 1981).

The previous example parallels aspects of the expectancy-value approach in that the first premise addresses an attribute (consequence) of exercise and the second premise addresses the desirability of that attribute. This need not be the case for the logical properties to apply. Also, in the probabilogical approach, the probability of a conclusion is a function of the probability that the two premises are true, the probability of the conclusion given that the two premises are true, the probability that the two premises are not true, and the probability of the conclusion given that the premises are not true (see Eagly & Chaiken, 1993; McGuire, 1981; Wyer, 1970; for equations and comparisons of the McGuire and Wyer approaches).

Simple inferences, such as "experts can be trusted" and "the source is an expert," "therefore, I agree with the message" (Chaiken, 1987) can be thought of in syllogistic terms. The probabilogical approach can also be easily applied to message-based persuasion (see Eagly & Chaiken, 1993; McGuire, 1981). Each argument in a persuasive message can be viewed as posing a syllogism that supports the advocated position. For example, in a message designed to persuade a person to buy a car, each argument might describe a positive feature of the car (e.g., reliability, gas mileage, comfort). The message could result in a series of syllogisms of the form "the car is comfortable," "comfort is desirable," therefore, "the car is desirable." Wyer (1970) provided research participants with persuasive messages aimed at changing beliefs in a premise and found that observed changes strongly predicted changes in conclusions. Moreover, because any premise or conclusion can become a premise for other syllogisms, changes in one element of the system could result in changes in other, unmentioned attitudes (see Dillehay, Insko, & Smith, 1966; Mugny & Perez, 1991; for a review, see Wyer & Albarracín, chap. 7, this volume).

Building upon the probabilogical approach, Kruglanski and his colleagues (Kruglanski & Thompson, 1999a; Kruglanski, Thompson, & Spiegel, 1999) characterize all of attitude change as manifestations of "if-then" reasoning. One could also think of expectancy-value structures in such terms (i.e., "if an object possesses positive attributes and does not possess negative attributes, then the object is good;" see Kruglanski & Thompson, 1999a). The "unimodel" view connects more closely to the dual-process theories, which treat persuasion processes as bounded, in that the unimodel includes the dual-process inspired idea that attitude change is sometimes relatively thoughtful and sometimes relatively nonthoughtful. Yet, the unimodel characterizes this difference in terms of the extent of the same underlying hypothesis-testing process, rather than allowing for different (bounded) processes to dominate across different circumstances. For example, a researcher using "bounded" theories such as the heuristic-systematic model (HSM; Chaiken, Liberman, & Eagly, 1989) or the elaboration likelihood model (ELM; Petty & Cacioppo, 1986) might conceptualize impact of an attractive message source as including processes such as use of heuristics, balance, or classical conditioning (see later discussions). In contrast, the unimodel would conceive the attractive source as simply one type of evidence used to test the hypothesis that the advocacy is good. Other types of evidence, such as message arguments, might be more complex and difficult to process, thereby determining their differential impact at different levels of processing within the same fundamental hypothesis-testing process.

Benefits of describing processes at this high level of generality might include highlighting commonalities across many types of phenomena. As an example, basically the same unimodel has also been applied to attribution (Chun, Spiegel, & Kruglanski, 2002) and to a wide variety of judgment phenomena (Kruglanski, Chun, Erb, Pierro, Mannetti, & Spiegel, 2003). The unimodel is touted as being more parsimonious than dual- or multi-process models, because two or more processes are replaced by different amounts of a single process in accounting for phenomena. Yet, as we discuss later in the chapter, moderators such as evidence complexity are still distinctions, which can reduce the apparent parsimony. Also, there are potential costs anytime a theory "lumps" into one process category mental operations that other theories treat as separable processes.

Bounded Process Descriptions

Most process descriptions in the attitude change area implicate a more restricted domain of application. Recall that by "bounded" we mean that the described processes are posited to capture a portion of the attitudes domain and that other processes are assumed to capture other portions of that domain. Like dissonance and self-perception, different bounded processes generally have different antecedents, and are theorized to have at least some nonoverlapping consequences (in terms of judgment, thought, or behavior). Moreover, from our perspective, bounded processes may be composed of component processes that represent the basic building blocks of social cognition. There may be no clear demarcation between bounded and component processes, but, in organizing this chapter, we have attempted to focus our component process section on basic information processing processes that may be involved in more than one bounded process. Consequently, our component process section is aligned with the encoding and memory processes that more closely connect social cognition to cognitive psychology.

USING THE ELABORATION CONTINUUM TO ORGANIZE BOUNDED PROCESSES

Motivation and Ability as Determinants of Elaboration

Following past treatments, especially those using the ELM (Petty & Cacioppo, 1981, 1986), we organize our discussion of the bounded processes using the dimension of "amount of elaboration" (see Petty & Cacioppo, 1981; Petty & Wegener, 1998). Although people want to hold reasonable, defensible attitudes, people are not always willing and able to put in the cognitive effort necessary to ensure optimal evaluations. Therefore, motivation and ability to think carefully about attitude-relevant information determine the processes along the elaboration continuum in which people are most likely to engage. In fact, when investigating moderators of which processes are operating, many of the moderators are interpreted in terms of how they influence motivation and/or ability to process object-relevant information (see Eagly & Chaiken, 1993; Petty & Wegener, 1998, Johnson et al., chap. 15, this volume).

Quantitative and Qualitative Distinctions Among Bounded Processes

Theories describing bounded processes have proposed both quantitative and qualitative distinctions among those processes. The elaboration continuum directly captures the quantitative dimension ("amount of processing"). One could evaluate an object with minimal elaboration by only considering one piece of information about the object. Often that piece will be the first received, leading to low-thought primacy effects (see Petty, Tormala, Hawkins, & Wegener, 2001), though motivation or ability can be so low that no information is evaluated until the message is completed and an attitude question is encountered (see Mackie & Asuncion, 1990). Evaluating one piece of information might be more or less effortful than using a stored heuristic or a simple attribution, but is certainly less effortful than similarly evaluating more pieces of information. Other quantitative differences could involve equal attention to all available information, but less to each piece in one condition than another or less effortful integration of information in one condition than another.

Within any level of thinking, theories using bounded processes often allow for "qualitative" distinctions. In essence, these qualitative distinctions are between different mental operations. For example, in mathematics, many long division and algebra problems might be similar in requisite effort, but they involve somewhat different cognitive manipulations and operations.

Among persuasion processes, classical conditioning, balance, and self-perception may all fall toward the low end of the elaboration continuum, but qualitative distinctions can also be made among these. On some level, if a given distinction allows one to predict people's future thoughts, judgments, or behaviors, it may not matter in any practical respect whether the distinction was, in fact, quantitative or qualitative (Ajzen, 1999). In fact, debates over whether a given attitude-change distinction is quantitative or qualitative in nature have arisen only recently, principally in contrasting universal versus bounded descriptions of persuasion processes. Regardless of whether one accepts conceptions of persuasion processes as qualitatively distinct, there is general agreement that attitude-change processes can be usefully arrayed along the (quantitative) elaboration continuum.

Low to Moderate Elaboration Processes

A variety of processes are alleged to influence attitudes without the necessity of deep or effortful thinking. These processes are generally found to operate when motivation or ability to think is lacking. Perhaps the lowest level of elaborative thinking corresponds to processes that represent "mere associations" between the attitude object and some other positive or negative cognitive element. Other relatively low-thought processes involve simple inferences about the attitude object, but often on the basis of information "peripheral" to the qualities of the object.

Mere Association

Classical/Evaluative Conditioning.   In attitudinal studies of classical (Pavlovian) conditioning, the attitude object is temporally paired with another positively- or negatively-valenced object or experience. For example, Staats and Staats (1958) showed that unfamiliar nationalities or disembodied names (i.e., conditioned stimuli, CS) were evaluated more positively if their presentation was consistently followed by words with positive rather than negative meanings (i.e., unconditioned stimuli, US). Similar effects have been shown with a wide range of attitude objects (CSs; Gresham & Shimp, 1985; Griffitt, 1970; Razran, 1940) and USs (see De Houwer, Thomas, & Baeyens, 2001). Classical conditioning has also been shown to influence evaluations of attitude objects previously associated with the target (Walther, 2002). Moreover, trait-implying statements (the US) influence impressions of a person whose photograph accompanies them (the CS) even when the statements are clearly about someone else and are said to be randomly paired with the photograph (i.e., trait transference; Skowronski, Carlston, Mae, & Crawford, 1998). The associations formed with the photographed person are not only evaluative in nature, but also convey trait-specific information. Therefore, the evaluative influences are but one facet (albeit a central one) of associative mechanisms.

In traditional studies of classical conditioning, the CS comes before the US (i.e., "forward conditioning"). However, as in the studies of trait transference, pairing of a US and CS also influences attitudes when the CS and US are presented simultaneously (Cacioppo, Priester, & Berntson, 1993; Strack, Martin, & Stepper, 1988). In fact, although effects are typically smaller than with the "forward conditioning" procedures, evaluative influences also consistently occur with "backward conditioning," when the US precedes the CS (De Houwer et al., 2001).[7] As discussed by Walther (2002), some researchers have suggested that a better term for this general type of learning is "evaluative conditioning" and that this learning is distinguishable from the "signal learning" aspect of classical conditioning, which depends more heavily on the timing of CS and US (see De Houwer et al., 2001).

Some researchers have expressed concerns that classical conditioning requires participants to recognize the CS-US contingency (i.e., that certain targets were consistently followed by stimuli of a particular valence; e.g., Lovibond & Shanks, 2002; see also Kruglanski & Stroebe, chap. 8, this volume, and Clore & Schnall, chap. 11, this volume) and perhaps to be aware of how the experimenter expects participants to respond (Page, 1974). Because the signal learning aspect of classical conditioning depends heavily on the CS preceding and predicting occurrence of the US, it could be that signal learning depends on some level of contingency awareness. Yet, a number of findings suggest that neither type of awareness is necessary for evaluative conditioning (which presumably occurs in forward, backward, and simultaneous conditioning paradigms). Conditioning effects have been found when the experimenter is no longer present and responses are made in an unrelated context (Berkowitz & Knurek, 1969; Zanna, Kiesler, & Pilkonis, 1970). Conditioning also influences responses difficult to control, such as Implicit Association Test (IAT) assessments of evaluative associations (Olson & Fazio, 2001) or speed of responding when the attitude object later serves as a "prime" (even after the explicit evaluation of the object has been changed, e.g., Petty, Briñol, Tormala, & Jarvis, 2003). Finally, and most importantly, conditioning can influence evaluations when the US (De Houwer, Baeyens, & Eelen, 1994) or both the CS and US (Dijksterhuis, 2004) are presented subliminally. These results suggest that neither explicit awareness of pairings of stimuli nor "demand" effects of recognizing such pairings is necessary for evaluative conditioning to occur.

Consistent with the notion that classical/evaluative conditioning requires little effortful thinking, classical/evaluative conditioning studies have generally used impoverished stimuli that would not provide much content to elaborate (and generally not much opportunity to elaborate, with many stimuli presented one after the other). Also, such conditioning has greater impact on targets initially associated with weak or nonexistent evaluations (e.g., nonsense syllables) rather than existing neutral evaluations (e.g., neutral words; see Priester, Cacioppo, & Petty, 1996; see also Cacioppo, Marshall-Goodell, Tassinary, & Petty, 1992; Shimp, Stuart, & Engle, 1991).

Operant Conditioning.   When people express some initial favor or disfavor toward an attitude object, this favor or disfavor can be enhanced by rewarding that expression. For example, in studies that randomly assign telephone interviewers to provide positive responses (e.g., "good") to either favorable or unfavorable statements made toward the attitude object by respondents, the number of responses consistent with the rewarded valence is increased (Hildum & Brown, 1956). Also, these rewards result in more favorable or unfavorable responses (whichever is rewarded) after some delay and in an unrelated context (Insko, 1965). Straightforward application of this persuasion technique requires that there be some favorable or unfavorable responses to be rewarded. If there are no favorable responses toward the attitude object, for instance, then there can be no rewarding of favorable responses.

If there are no naturally occurring responses to be rewarded, punishment of the opposing responses could help create some of the desired responses. One might also use operant conditioning to "shape" behaviors (e.g., rewarding less negative responses initially, but requiring gradually more positive responses for additional rewards until, eventually, quite positive responses occur when they once did not; Skinner, 1953). In any case, one has to administer effective rewards. In the phone interviewing paradigm, it is necessary for the interviewer to be likeable for him or her to use positive reactions (e.g., "good") to effectively reward the recipient of the conditioning (e.g., Insko & Butzine, 1967; Insko & Cialdini, 1969).[8]

For some years, there have been debates about whether operant and classical conditioning are, in essence, the same (for a recent claim of sameness, see Donahoe & Vegas, 2004). For current purposes, each represents relatively simple associations between the attitude object and some valenced object or event. Yet, operationally, studies of classical conditioning generally start with an object toward which few or no valenced associations exist, whereas studies of operant conditioning typically begin with an object toward which there are some existing associations, so that evaluative responses occur that can be rewarded and enhanced.

Mere Exposure.   When novel objects are encountered repeatedly, they are often evaluated more favorably (Zajonc, 1968, 1998), even when people cannot report whether or not
they have previously seen the attitude object (Kunst-Wilson & Zajonc, 1980). Bornstein (1989;
Bornstein & D'Agostino, 1994) has attributed exposure effects to increases in perceptual fluency (Jacoby, Kelley, Brown, & Jasechko, 1989) that can be attributed to liking for the object,
but might also be attributed to other stimulus dimensions (Mandler, Nakamura, & Shebo
Van Zandt, 1987) perhaps including disliking if the stimulus is already negatively valenced
(Klinger & Greenwald, 1994). When familiarity can be attributed to previous presentations
rather than liking, perceptions are "corrected," and mere exposure effects are diminished. For
example, mere exposure effects are reduced when stimuli are exposed for longer periods of time
(Bornstein & D'Agostino, 1992) or when people are told that the stimuli have been presented
previously (Bornstein & D'Agostino, 1994). The fact that thinking about the origin of fluency
can diminish or remove effects of previous exposure does not mean that the original effects
of fluency depended on thinking, however (cf., Kruglanski & Stroebe, chap. 8, this volume).
A person could directly perceive an object as good based on associative or exposure-based
processes that relied on little or no thought about the object, but more thoughtful attributions
and corrections could change the effects of those originally nonthoughtful influences.

In fact, some theorists argue that perceptual fluency is directly perceived as pleasant. That
is, rather than a neutral fluency experience being attributed to liking or other dimensions,
some have argued that fluency itself is experienced directly as positive affect. For example,
Winkielman and Cacioppo (2001) proposed a hedonic fluency model (HFM) in which easy
processing of a stimulus results in a brief positive affective experience. Support for this approach includes ease of processing being associated with physiological markers associated
with positive affect (such as increased electrical activity in the zygomaticus region) as well
as self-reports of positive reactions (Winkielman & Cacioppo, 2001; see also Harmon-Jones
& Allen, 2001). Apparently, these affective reactions can sometimes become diffuse enough
to be attributed to different items. For example, Monahan, Murphy, and Zajonc (2000) found
that increased 5ms repetitions of Chinese ideographs increased participant reports of positive
mood, and polygons visually dissimilar to the ideographs were also liked to a greater extent
when ideographs had been repeatedly encountered (see Clore & Schnall, chap. 11, this volume,
for additional discussion).

Whether mere exposure belongs with "associative" processes could certainly be debated,
but mere exposure is similar to these types of processes in that there is little reason to expect
the sense of familiarity to require more than minimal thought about the attitude object. Mere
exposure effects occur when the object is presented very briefly (Bornstein, 1989) or even
subliminally (Bornstein & D'Agostino, 1992). Mere exposure is also strongest when motivation
to process available information is minimal (as when evaluation apprehension is low rather
than high; Kruglanski, Freund, & Bar-Tal, 1996).

Inferential Approaches

On some level, virtually all cognitive processes could be deemed "associative" in that stored
knowledge or evaluations must become associated with an attitude object for attitudes to form
or change. In the previous section, we described processes that do little more than directly
associate some type of evaluation or feeling with the attitude object. In other situations, people
briefly consider some piece of information, but use this information as a relatively simple way
to determine whether a positive or negative evaluation is appropriate, without taking the time
or effort that would be involved in more extensive processing of other available information.
Because these processes go beyond direct association of the object with an evaluation, they
are often referred to as inferences.

Use of Heuristics.   Simple inferences may involve decision rules or "heuristics" (Chaiken, 1987). For example, when a person receives a message from an expert source but is unmotivated or unable to think carefully about what the source has to say, that person might simply acknowledge that "experts can be trusted." Coupled with the knowledge that "this expert likes the proposal," the heuristic would result in the inference that the proposal is good. This process differs from "mere association" processes because people receive the same pairing between the proposal and "good" regardless of whether the source of the message is expert or not. But previously stored knowledge about expert versus nonexpert sources influences the extent to which the "goodness" of the proposal stated in the message is imparted to the object in memory.

As with mere association processes, heuristic use has the greatest impact when motivation and ability to think are relatively low. For example, sources or other features of communications that might be associated with heuristics (e.g., sources that are attractive/likeable, expert, similar, or numerous and messages that appear long or with many arguments, regardless of quality) influence post-message attitudes most when messages are relatively low in personal relevance (Chaiken, 1980; Petty, Cacioppo, & Goldman, 1981) and when message recipients have relatively little knowledge about the attitude object (Wood & Kallgren, 1988; Wood, Kallgren, & Preisler, 1985) or are distracted during message presentation (Kiesler & Mathog, 1968; see Petty & Wegener, 1998, for additional discussion). Also, these heuristics are most likely to operate when they are accessible or salient (Eagly & Chaiken, 1993; Pallak, 1983; Roskos-Ewoldsen & Fazio, 1992).[9] Of course, the kinds of inferences underlying heuristic use are quite minimal. However, the inferences made when multiple pieces of information about the attitude object must be considered or combined undoubtedly require considerably more cognitive effort. These more elaborative inferences are discussed later in the chapter.

Balance.   When people simply know that an admired other supports a position, likes a product, etc., use of a source-related heuristic (e.g., experts are usually correct) can lead to outcomes similar to those predicted by balance theory (Heider, 1958) or congruity theory (Osgood & Tannenbaum, 1955). These theories are cognitive consistency theories, which rest on the general idea that inconsistency is uncomfortable. For these theories, the inconsistency comes from agreeing with a disliked other or disagreeing with a liked other. Because "balance" or "congruity" feels better, people should gravitate toward agreeing with liked others or disagreeing with disliked others. Evidence does suggest that agreeing with disliked others and especially, disagreeing with liked others is perceived as uncomfortable (Jordan, 1953; Priester & Petty, 2001). Yet, the role of this discomfort in balance or congruity effects has not been explored as fully as in dissonance effects (see Olson & Stone, chap. 6, this volume).

Balance or congruity processes might often involve a relatively low level of elaboration, because neither balance nor congruity requires consideration of the qualities of the attitude object per se (Petty & Wegener, 1998). Yet, balance and congruity involve three pieces of knowledge (i.e., attitude toward another person, the other person's attitude toward the object, and one's own attitude toward the object). Consideration of all three might require greater cognitive effort than thinking only about one's liking for the other person ("attraction") or agreement with the other person ("agreement," Zajonc, 1968; Miller & Norman, 1976), which require consideration of only one or two pieces of information, respectively (Cacioppo & Petty, 1981).

Attribution.   Attribution (i.e., inferences about the causes of behavior, see Gilbert, 1998) can also vary in the amount of cognitive effort required. At least some attributional processes that explain approach or avoidance (e.g., inferring a positive attitude from approach behavior) probably require much less effort than inferences that incorporate various pieces of information about the attitude object and compare those pieces of information to object-relevant knowledge in memory (see later discussions of the concept of elaboration).

The most common example of simple attributions of approach or avoidance is captured in self-perception theory (Bem, 1967, 1972). Bem suggested that when they do not already have strong attitudes, people must infer their attitudes rather than retrieving them from memory. For some time, self-perception theory was thought to be an alternative explanation for dissonance effects (Bem, 1972; Greenwald, 1975). Yet, self-perception alone could not account for all dissonance effects (Beauvois, Bungert, & Mariette, 1995; Zanna & Cooper, 1974). For the current discussion, it is important to note that self-perception effects appear most likely when people are less likely to think carefully about object-relevant information. The tendency to infer one's attitudes from past behavior is more likely when people possess little, rather than much, knowledge about the attitude object (Wood, 1982) and when the attitude object is unimportant rather than important to perceivers (Taylor, 1975; see also Chaiken & Baldwin, 1981). Finally, self-perception effects are more likely when behavior is proattitudinal (within one's latitude of acceptance) rather than counterattitudinal (in one's latitude of rejection; Fazio et al., 1977), with proattitudinal information often being processed less thoroughly than counterattitudinal information (Cacioppo & Petty, 1979b; Ditto & Lopez, 1992; Edwards & Smith, 1996).

Although self-perception was hypothesized to operate when existing attitudes are weak, differences in attributions might also influence attitudes that are relatively long lived. For example, children who already enjoy coloring with markers do so less if they receive expected rewards for this activity, so that they attribute the behavior to the reward rather than to their own enjoyment (Deci, 1975; Lepper, Greene, & Nisbett, 1973). Ironically, this suggests that an effective way to decrease agreement with an idea is to repeatedly reward a person for expressing the view and then later remove the reward (Scott & Yalch, 1978).

Some attributions might also influence how much people process attitude-relevant information. For example, when a source speaks against his or her own self interest, message recipients might infer that the person is being honest and the message is true (Eagly, Chaiken, & Wood, 1981). This attribution could decrease the need for scrutiny of the message itself (Wood & Eagly, 1981), especially if the message recipient is sensitive to possible reasons to forgo active processing of information (Priester & Petty, 1995). If, however, the message recipient questions the truthfulness of a source (e.g., because the source speaks *for* his or her own self interest), potential untrustworthiness could signal that scrutiny of the message is necessary, even for people who would prefer to find reasons not to think (Priester & Petty, 1995).[10]

Moderate to High Elaboration Processes

The term "elaboration" reflects the idea that scrutiny of an attitude object goes beyond memorization of presented information. Though "scrutiny," "effortful processing," "careful thinking," and similar terms are used as synonyms, the "elaboration" term perhaps best captures the range of activities involved. Elaboration includes comparison of such information with background knowledge and standards, including one's previous evaluations of the object (Petty & Cacioppo, 1986; see also Albarracín, Wallace, & Glasman, in press). As Petty and Cacioppo (1986) put it, elaboration includes attention to any presented information, attempts to access relevant information from both external (message) and internal (knowledge) sources, attempts to scrutinize and make inferences about attitude-relevant arguments in light of other available information, drawing conclusions about merits of the attitude object or recommendation, and derivation of an overall evaluation that combines the outputs of these efforts.[11]

Persuasion researchers have identified a number of ways to assess the extent of elaboration in processing of persuasive communications. Perhaps the most popular procedure has been to vary the quality of the arguments contained in a message and to gauge the extent of elaboration by the relative size of the argument quality effect on attitudes (Petty, Wells, & Brock, 1976). Greater argument quality effects suggest greater argument scrutiny. Other procedures include measuring the number and profile of generated thoughts relevant to the attitude object or issue (Petty, Ostrom, & Brock, 1981). High elaboration is associated with more thoughts (Burnkrant & Howard, 1984) and thoughts that better reflect the quality of the arguments presented (Harkins & Petty, 1981). In addition, correlations between thought favorability and post-message attitudes tend to be greater when argument scrutiny is high (Chaiken, 1980; Petty & Cacioppo, 1979), and higher levels of elaboration can produce longer reading or exposure times to messages (Mackie & Worth, 1989).

As we discuss in the following sections, processes relatively high in elaboration might focus on particular types of thinking. For example, some proposed processes focus on inferences, others focus on use of background knowledge, and still others focus on the ways in which multiple pieces of information might be combined into overall evaluations.

Combinatorial/Integrative Processes

As discussed earlier, one might construe simple inferences using a syllogistic framework: two pieces of information form premises that suggest a conclusion. Of course, consistent with quantitative distinctions embodied in the elaboration continuum, such syllogistic reasoning could also be more complex. For example, when people possess greater knowledge or are more motivated to process information related to the attitude object, they are more likely go beyond the presented information to make inferences about omitted information (see Kardes, 1994). In terms of syllogistic reasoning, this would expand the number of syllogisms that determine the conclusion (i.e., the evaluation of the attitude object).

When multiple pieces of information support (or when some support and some oppose) a given conclusion, mental operations are undoubtedly initiated that combine the pieces of information in some way (see Chaiken, Duckworth, & Darke, 1999). The expectancy-value, information integration, and probabilogical approaches discussed earlier provide somewhat different views of how people combine multiple pieces of information to arrive at an attitude. However, each view deals in some way with perceptions of the desirability of object attributes and the likelihood that the object possesses that attribute. In each view, one could change attitudes by influencing the perceived desirability or likelihood of attributes (see Eagly & Chaiken, 1993; Petty & Wegener, 1991).

When creating "strong" versus "weak" messages (Petty & Cacioppo, 1986), researchers have generally created messages that differ in the desirability of described attributes rather than in the likelihood that the attitude object possesses the attributes (Johnson, Smith-McLallen, Killeya, & Levin, 2004; Areni & Lutz, 1988). Even so, evidence suggests that attitudes can be changed by influencing either attribute desirability or likelihood (Lutz, 1975; MacKenzie, 1986). Although some theorists have suggested that perceptions of likelihood are more easily changed than perceptions of desirability (McGuire & McGuire, 1991), data are mixed regarding the impact of likelihood versus desirability on attitudes (see Johnson et al., 2004).

If combining perceptions of arguments into an overall evaluation takes effort, then variations in likelihood or desirability perceptions should have greatest impact on attitudes when motivation and ability to process information are high. In fact, people high in need for cognition (Cacioppo & Petty, 1982) do show mood effects on attitudes that are mediated by the perceived likelihood of events, whereas people low in need for cognition do not (DeSteno, Petty, Rucker, Wegener, & Braverman, 2004; Wegener, Petty, & Klein, 1994). Similarly, likelihood-by-desirability products predict overall attitudes better when people are high rather than low in topic relevant knowledge (see Albarracín & Wyer, 2001; Lutz, 1977).

Although it seems reasonable that, at some point, people must integrate pieces of information into an overall attitude, an unresolved issue regards when (before, during, or after a message) people form and consolidate their attitudes. One might argue that people consolidate their attitudes to a greater extent when elaboration is high rather than low (see Petty, Haugtvedt, & Smith, 1995). However, it could be that opportunities to consolidate also matter. For example, when two opposing messages are sequentially presented, high levels of personal relevance result in primacy effects (i.e., greater impact of the first message, Haugtvedt & Wegener, 1994). This suggests that high-relevance message recipients consolidate their attitudes before receiving the second message, which is then counterargued. However, if the same information is collapsed into a single message, with no gap between presentation of the two sides, then high levels of thinking result in recency (i.e., greater impact of the last information, Petty et al., 2001). Recency with an "unchunked" message implies that attitude consolidation did not fully occur until the end of the message. Opportunities to consolidate may also have consequences beyond the immediate attitudinal judgment. For instance, Haugtvedt and Strathman (1990) found that providing a consolidation period after a message increases the persistence of the attitude over time.

Cognitive Responses

In Response to Messages. Initially, the term "cognitive response" was applied broadly to include source derogations and other thoughts not germane to the attitude object (Brock, 1967; Greenwald, 1968). With development of the elaboration likelihood model (ELM), however, distinctions were made between thoughts about "central merits" of attitude objects versus thoughts about more "peripheral" aspects of a persuasive attempt. In many cases, thoughts about sources or other potential cues should predict attitudes best when elaboration is low. Thoughts about the issue or object per se should predict attitudes better when elaboration is high (see Chaiken, 1980; Petty & Cacioppo, 1979, 1984). In contemporary research, the term "cognitive response" is often limited to object- or issue-relevant thoughts, and these thoughts are then used to index the extent of elaboration (see Wegener, Downing, Krosnick, & Petty, 1995; see also Albarracín, 2002).

A variety of studies have produced data consistent with the idea that people generate cognitive responses and that these responses predict post-message attitudes (see Eagly & Chaiken, 1993; Petty et al., 1995). Past studies have produced (a) patterns of thought favorability that mirror the valence of attitudes as they change in response to manipulations of messages or situations (Cacioppo & Petty, 1979b; Johnson et al., 2004; Osterhouse & Brock, 1970), (b) indices of thought valence (e.g., positive thoughts minus negative thoughts, divided by total thoughts) that correlate with attitudes more highly when motivation or ability to process is hypothesized to be high (Chaiken, 1980; Petty & Cacioppo, 1979), and (c) data consistent with thoughts serving as mediators between independent variables and attitudes (Chaiken & Maheswaran, 1994; Petty, Schumann, Richman, & Strathman, 1993; see also Petty, Wegener, Fabrigar, Priester, & Cacioppo, 1993). Physiological activity has also been consistent with the theorized valence of cognitive activity during a message (Cacioppo & Petty, 1979a). Of course, for as long as cognitive responses have been measured, researchers have expressed concerns that thoughts might sometimes serve as justifications for attitudes, rather than causes of them (see Miller & Colman, 1981). Yet, substantial evidence suggests that cognitive responses can also influence, rather than justify, attitudes (see Petty et al., 1993, for a review; see also Albarracín & Wyer, 2001).

When There Is No Message. The influence of self-generated thoughts and information has been of interest since the early days of attitudes research. For example, Janis and King (1954) had three participants each generate one message and listen to the others' messages.

When attitudes were compared at the end of the session, participants were generally more per-suaded by the message they generated than by the messages generated by the other participants (see also Culbertson, 1957; Elms, 1966). This pattern might occur because the person gener-ating the message focuses thoughts on support for his or her advocated position (Greenwald, 1969) or because the person finds his or her own thoughts to be more compelling than the thoughts of others (Greenwald & Albert, 1968). If the generated arguments include events, such as events that would lead to discovery of a cure for the common cold (Janis & King, 1954), it is important to note that imagination of an event can make the event seem more likely if the event is relatively easy to imagine (Anderson, Lepper, & Ross, 1980; Sherman, Cialdini, Schwartzman, & Reynolds, 1985). If the arguments generated are generally "strong," it is also possible that differential persuasion is due to people thinking more about the topic when they are self-generating than when they are receiving messages from others. In the Janis and King (1954) procedure, at least, the person generates the message while alone, but listens to the messages with another person. Individual identifiability and responsibility are known to lead to greater processing than when messages are received as part of a group (Petty, Harkins, & Williams, 1980). Increased persistence of attitudes based on self-generated arguments (Mann & Janis, 1968; Watts, 1967) is also consistent with this possibility.

Although participants in self-generation studies are generally given a position to take and a rough outline of potential points to make, other research has simply asked participants to think about an issue, with no guidance about what to think. Tesser and his colleagues have generally found that opportunities to think about an attitude object make the attitudes more extreme (Sadler & Tesser, 1973; Tesser, 1978). But extremity primarily results when people have a clear, unambivalent attitude toward the target (Liberman & Chaiken, 1991; Tesser & Leone, 1977) and are committed to their attitude (Millar & Tesser, 1986). When prethought attitudes are not clear and consistent, mere thought leads to more moderate, rather than more extreme, attitudes (Judd & Lusk, 1984; see Tesser, Martin, & Mendolia, 1995).

In research on reasons analysis (i.e., introspection; see Wilson, Dunn, Kraft, & Lisle, 1989), respondents are asked to explain or think about why they hold the attitudes that they do. This procedure is similar to mere thought, because people are given little guidance other than their own attitude itself, and similar to self-generation, in that people generate their own reasons. Because people are often poor at determining what influences them (Nisbett & Wilson, 1977), Wilson and colleagues believed that asking people to explain why they feel the way they do should "cognitivize" the attitude, highlighting features or factors that were not the "true" basis for the preintrospection attitude. Emphasizing cognitive, easily-verbalized features could lead to moderation or greater extremity for different people (Wilson, Dunn, et al., 1989). Even so, the clarity or strength of one's attitude should matter. If one possesses a strong attitude, then the attitude should guide reasons generation, minimizing effects on (temporary) attitude change (Hodges & Wilson, 1993; Wilson, Kraft, & Dunn, 1989).

Objectivity and Bias in Thinking.   Many motivational or ability factors can be viewed as "objectively" increasing or decreasing the sheer amount of processing, without favoring certain types of thoughts. For example, Petty et al. (1976) showed that distraction disrupts whatever the dominant thoughts are, regardless of whether these generally favor or oppose the message advocacy. From an ELM perspective, motivation is relatively objective when no judgment outcome is preferred over another, and when the person's goal is to seek "correct" attitudes, whatever they might be (Petty & Cacioppo, 1986). In contrast, motivated biases push people toward a particular preferred outcome, as when people want to view them-selves positively (Brown, 1986), to take "forbidden" positions (Brehm, 1966), or to identify with admired others (Snyder, 1974). When people elaborate, motivation could influence the thoughts that come to mind or the attention given to particular features of the attitude object.[12]

Yet, one has to be careful in assuming motivation as the source of a bias, because ability biases could be responsible for similar results, even in the absence of biasing motivations. For example, consider the fact that people often judge potential interaction partners more positively than people they will not meet (Berscheid, Graziano, Monson, & Dermer, 1976). This could be due to motivated biases to view one's interaction partner positively. However, if most of the available information about the partner is positive (either in the experimental setting or in the mind of the perceiver), then simple increases in amount of thought could enhance the positivity of judgments. Such results might reflect differences in people's ability to generate thoughts in one direction versus another. For example, even in the absence of biasing motivations, knowledge that is slanted in one direction could lead to judgments that move in that direction to varying degrees, depending on the amount of "objective" motivation present.

Many factors could foster selective thoughts. For example, happiness makes positive events seem more likely and negative events seem less likely, compared with neutral moods (see Wegener & Petty, 1996). Even more specifically, anger makes angering (but not saddening) events seem likely to occur, but sadness makes saddening (not angering) events seem likely (DeSteno, Petty, Wegener & Rucker, 2000). Therefore, when elaboration likelihood is high, angry people are more influenced by messages that focus on angering consequences of inaction, but sad people are more influenced by those that focus on saddening consequences of inaction (DeSteno et al., 2004). As discussed later in the section on bias correction, people might become aware of these or other biases, and might consequently seek to avoid "biased" outcomes. But in circumstances where the issue of bias is not salient, or if perceptions of bias are erroneous, high levels of elaboration can produce strong biases, despite motivations to seek "correct" attitudes (see Petty & Cacioppo, 1986; Petty & Wegener, 1999). Biases in processing are especially likely when available information is somewhat mixed or ambiguous and open to alternative interpretations (Chaiken & Maheswaran, 1994; Lord, Ross, & Lepper, 1979).

Cognitive Dissonance

Building on earlier notions of cognitive consistency (Heider, 1946; Osgood & Tannenbaum, 1955), Festinger (1957, 1964) developed a general and widely applicable theory concerning responses to inconsistent (dissonant) cognitions. Like the previous consistency theories, inconsistency was regarded as creating an unpleasant affective state, which would create pressure to change one or more cognitions to restore or bring about consistency (consonance). Because one typical path to reduce dissonance is to engage in cognitive activity aimed at changing one of the dissonant cognitions, cognitive dissonance is often viewed as producing relatively high levels of processing. The processing is biased in that dissonance creates motivation to prefer interpretations or thoughts most consistent with other salient cognitions (Schultz & Lepper, 1996).

Because dissonance is often produced by behaviors that conflict with beliefs or evaluations, and because the behaviors are often difficult to "undo" (see Steele, 1988), attitude or belief change–making the attitude or belief more similar to the behavior–is often the result. These beliefs and attitudes are then maintained by a variety of processes, including selective exposure and attention to attitude-consistent, rather than inconsistent, information, especially in dissonance producing situations (Festinger, 1964). As summarized by Frey (1986), selective exposure effects are stronger when people are told they must expose themselves to chosen material (Brock, 1965), when they freely choose to perform an attitude-relevant behavior (Frey & Wicklund, 1978), when they are committed to their preselection attitudes (Brock & Balloun, 1967; Sweeney & Gruber, 1984), and when available information strongly supports each position (Kleinhesselink & Edwards, 1975; see also Marsh & Wallace, chap. 9, this volume).

Dissonance can also be reduced through means other than belief or attitude change (see Abelson, 1959). For example, dissonance reduces with the generation of consonant cognitions (i.e., thoughts that make the dissonant cognitions consistent). The effects of sufficient versus insufficient justification can be thought of in these terms. For example, in the famous Festinger and Carlsmith (1959) study, $20 was sufficient compensation for telling a white lie so that the belief-inconsistent behavior did not result in belief change. The high level of compensation for the behavior provided a cognition consonant with the behavior. Similarly, in the "forbidden toys" studies, a "severe threat" justified avoidance of a desired toy, providing a consonant cognition and shielding children from dissonance-induced devaluation of the toy (e.g., Aronson & Carlsmith, 1963). Dissonance can also be reduced or avoided through trivialization (i.e., viewing the attitude or belief as less important). Interestingly, trivialization has been used to explain why being reminded of domains in which one excels (i.e., self-affirmation, Steele, 1988) can decrease dissonance (Simon, Greenberg, & Brehm, 1995).

An amazing number of revisions and reinterpretations of dissonance have been developed over the years, for example, self-perception (Bem, 1967); self-consistency (Aronson, 1969); impression management (Tedeschi, Schlenker, & Bonoma, 1971); aversive consequences (Cooper & Fazio, 1984); self-affirmation (Steele, 1988); radical model (Beauvois & Joule, 1996); self-standards (Stone & Cooper, 2001); and the action-based model (Harmon-Jones & Harmon-Jones, 2002); see Olson & Stone, chap. 6, this volume, for a review). Even so, several core aspects of Festinger's original theory have continued to ring true. For example, conditions designed to produce dissonance do bring about states of unpleasant arousal, as measured by self-report (Elliot & Devine, 1994; Harmon-Jones, 2000) or physiological measures (Elkin & Leippe, 1986; Losch & Cacioppo, 1990) and as indicated by misattribution paradigms (Zanna & Cooper, 1974). As noted earlier, conditions proposed to produce dissonance increase the likelihood of selective exposure effects. Also, some evidence suggests that inconsistency per se can create dissonance (Harmon-Jones, Brehm, Greenberg, Simon, & Nelson, 1996; Harmon-Jones, 2000), though clearly, the attitude change that accompanies dissonance is most likely to be found when people freely choose counterattitudinal action (Sherman, 1970) and harmful consequences of the action are likely to occur (Calder, Ross, & Insko, 1973). Finally, dissonance-induced changes in attitudes or beliefs can be reduced through removal of unpleasant feelings by drinking alcohol (Steele, Southwick, & Critchlow, 1981), experiencing pleasant events (Cooper, Fazio, & Rhodewalt, 1978), or reminding oneself of other successes or abilities (Steele, 1988; Tesser & Cornell, 1991).

Metacognition

The notion of metacognition (i.e., cognition about cognition) is only beginning to be explored in attitude change. One could discuss virtually any work on attribution, and much on mere exposure and other persuasion topics as involving metacognition (see Jost, Kruglanski, & Nelson, 1998). Yet, this direct link has not generally been made. Metacognition clearly has the potential to influence peoples' beliefs and actions. For example, perceptions of one's own psychological functioning can influence whether a word is judged as "new" or "old" (Strack & Förster, 1998), perceptions that one "knows" an unretrievable word can lead people to spend time searching memory for the word (Costermans, Lories, & Ansay, 1992), and perceptions of one's own self-efficacy in cognitive tasks can influence intellectual performance (Bandura, 1991, 1995). Although relatively simple forms of metacognition might exist (e.g., perceptions of what created familiarity in mere exposure studies), some metacognitive effects may depend on high levels of thought. That is, to the extent that metacognition involves thinking about the appropriateness or potential causes of one's thoughts, metacognition seems more likely to occur when people are already motivated and able to think in the first place (see Briñol & Petty, in press; Petty, Briñol, Tormala, & Wegener, in press).

Self-Validation.   A recent example of "thoughtful" metacognition concerns research on the self-validation hypothesis (e.g., Petty, Briñol, & Tormala, 2002). According to this view, people's thoughts only guide their attitudes to the extent that people possess confidence in the correctness of those thoughts. This premise suggests that one might usefully add the dimension of *confidence* in thinking to the dimensions of *amount* of thinking and *direction* of thinking, which have received most attention in persuasion research (see Briñol & Petty, in press).

Thought confidence has been measured as well as manipulated in a variety of ways. People are more confident when asked to recall previous experiences in which they possessed much versus little confidence (Petty et al., 2002), when nodding their head up-and-down rather than side-to-side (Briñol & Petty, 2003), when writing with their dominant rather than nondominant hand (Briñol & Petty, 2003), when learning after a message that the message came from an expert rather than a nonexpert source (Briñol, Tormala, & Petty, 2004), and when generation of thoughts is easy rather than difficult (Tormala, Petty, & Briñol, 2002). Therefore, one can confidently conclude that thought confidence plays a causal role in determining whether attitudes are based on the thoughts people produce about an attitude object. Consistent with the argument that metacognition often requires relatively high levels of motivation and ability, thought confidence has been shown to matter most for people who report high levels of thinking about the attitude object (Petty et al., 2002). Also, the majority of metacognition research in persuasion has created relatively high levels of motivation and ability for all participants. Although the current evidence suggests that metacognition is more likely to spontaneously occur under conditions of high elaboration, future research will undoubtedly compare metacognitive processes across high and low elaboration settings.

Bias Correction.   One type of metacognition that has received a fair amount of attention in social cognition and attitude change involves correction of perceived biases (Petty & Wegener, 1993; Strack, 1992; Wilson & Brekke, 1994). In general, corrections can be said to take place when a person attempts to remove or avoid the inappropriate or otherwise unwanted influence of some factor. The "biasing" factor could be part of the target, the judgment setting, or the perceiver. For example, a person could try not to be influenced by the biological sex of a leader–an aspect of the target–because the person's sex should not be a central dimension in determining whether a person is a good leader or not (Sczesny & Kühnen, 2003). Or, a person could try not to be influenced by assimilation or contrast with stimuli presented prior to the target, an aspect of the judgment setting (Martin, Seta, & Crelia, 1990; Petty & Wegener, 1993). Finally, perceivers could try to avoid influences of their own mood when evaluating the qualities of a political candidate (Ottati & Isbell, 1996; see also Berkowitz, Jaffee, Jo, & Troccoli, 2000; Wegener & Petty, 2001). Just as elaboration is higher when people have both the motivation and the ability to think, corrections for bias should be most likely when people have both the motivation and the ability to avoid bias.

Motivation and ability to correct should be somewhat distinct from motivation and ability to elaborate. As noted earlier, people might be motivated and able to elaborate but unaware of any potential for bias. In such circumstances, elaboration can be biased by factors such as previous attitudes (Houston & Fazio, 1989; Lord, Ross, & Lepper, 1979), primed or salient concepts (Lingle & Ostrom, 1981; Sherman, Mackie, & Driscoll, 1990), or recipient mood (Petty, Schumann, et al., 1993). Yet, when the potential for bias becomes salient and motives and abilities to correct are increased, people are more likely to try to reduce or avoid effects of these and other factors (see Wegener & Petty, 1995, 1997).

When social perceivers are left to identify potential biases on their own, some data suggest that a high level of thinking encourages correction (DeSteno et al., 2000; Martin et al., 1990). Yet, when people are alerted to a particular bias, and the metacognitive work of identifying biases and deciding which might be operating is reduced, then the same corrections have been observed in both high and low elaboration settings. For example, Petty, Wegener, & White (1998) alerted people to potential source biases after a persuasive message and showed that the same corrections can occur regardless of whether initial processing of the message is high (when impact of sources is unlikely, if messages are unambiguous) or low (when impact of sources is likely). Alerting people to potential "bias" of a likeable or dislikeable source removed effects of the source when initial processing had been low, but produced the opposite bias (dislikeable source being more persuasive than the likeable source) when initial processing had been high.

Making corrections may often require greater mental effort than not making corrections, although the overall mental effort in corrections could potentially differ across people, targets, and settings (see Wegener & Petty, 1997; Wegener, Dunn, & Tokusato, 2001). For example, practice in making corrections could routinize the process, see Smith, Stewart, & Buttram, 1992; Wegener & Petty, 1997; see also Moskowitz, Gollwitzer, Wasel, & Schoal, 1999). If effort differs across corrections, in some situations, corrective efforts may be less effortful than initial processing of a message. If so, corrections may be relatively ineffective or fleeting in impact. This might be one reason for sleeper effects in persuasion (i.e., delayed impact of a message; Hovland, Lumsdaine, & Sheffield, 1949; Pratkanis, Greenwald, Leippe, & Baumgartner, 1988). The sleeper effect is most likely when message recipients have thought carefully about the message prior to receipt of a reason to "discount" (correct for) the implications of the message (Petty & Cacioppo, 1986; Petty, Wegener, et al., 1993; see Kumkale & Albarracín, 2004, for a recent review). Such effects may reflect instances where processing of the merits of the attitudinal position was more extensive (more elaborated) than the corrective attempt to discount the message.

Consequences of Elaboration

The concept of elaboration has played a central role in theorizing about bounded processes, in part, because it has been tied to demonstrable and practical consequences of attitude change. Such consequences have been summarized under the rubric of the overall "strength" of attitudes, with strength defined in terms of the forces the attitude can withstand and create (see Fabrigar et al., chap. 3, this volume). Krosnick and Petty (1995) defined strength in terms of the persistence of the attitude over time (withstanding the force of time), the resistance of the attitude to attack (withstanding the force of opposing persuasive appeals), and the ability of the attitude to guide related thoughts and behavior (creating a force that guides cognition and action; see also Eagly & Chaiken, 1993, 1998; Petty & Wegener, 1998). Attitudes based on high, rather than low, levels of elaboration have been found to persist longer over time (Petty, Haugtvedt, & Smith, 1995), to resist opposing persuasive messages better (Haugtvedt & Petty, 1992; Shestowsky, Wegener, & Fabrigar, 1998), and to better predict future behavior (Cacioppo, Petty, Kao, & Rodriguez, 1986).

Component Process Descriptions

As noted earlier, many processes associated with the information processing approach could be regarded as components of the bounded processes. For example, the concept of elaboration could be viewed as implicating the activation of an attitude and/or attitude-relevant information in memory, attention to attitude-relevant information, encoding/comprehension of that information (perhaps using the attitude as a schema with which to interpret the information), retrieval of information and evaluations already stored in memory, comparison of these cognitive elements with new information or evaluations, evaluation of the merits of available information, integration of new and previous evaluations, storage of new information or evaluations in memory, and so on (see Petty et al., 1995; Petty & Cacioppo, 1986). We discuss such component processes in the following sections.

Activation of Attitudes/Knowledge

The concepts of construct activation and accessibility have long been central to social cognition (Bruner, 1957; Higgins, 1996; Higgins & King, 1981; Taylor & Fiske, 1978). Moreover, Nobel prize winner Daniel Kahneman has suggested that many, if not all, of the judgment biases that he documented with Amos Tversky may simply be manifestations of the accessibility principle: That people tend to rely or over-rely on whatever information is most accessible at the moment (Kahneman, 2003). However, research on the role of attitude activation in attitude change has been somewhat limited. A good deal of research shows that accessible attitudes are more likely than inaccessible attitudes to predict future behavior (Fazio, 1995; Fazio & Olson, 2003a). This implies that accessible attitudes remain more stable over time (Fabrigar et al., chap. 3, this volume), a possibility that has received direct empirical support (Zanna, Fazio, & Ross, 1994). One reason for this persistence may be that accessible attitudes are more likely to resist change in the face of social influence (Bassili, 1996; Bassili & Fletcher, 1991).

Attitude activation could serve as a component or contributor to many of the bounded processes described earlier. For example, accessible attitudes might be more likely to be used as "cues" or in "heuristics" to judge a message as acceptable or unacceptable (Fabrigar et al., chap. 3, this volume). Accessible attitudes more powerfully bias processing of attitude relevant information (Houston & Fazio, 1989; Schuette & Fazio, 1995). Accessible attitudes could receive greater weight in information integration or could more powerfully direct selective attention. Research has also shown that attitude accessibility can influence the amount of thinking in which one engages (Fabrigar, Priester, Petty, & Wegener, 1998).

As discussed in more detail by Fabrigar et al. (chap. 3, this volume), popular measures of working knowledge also undoubtedly reflect the amount of object-relevant knowledge that is accessible and activated rather than the total amount available in memory. In many ways, it seems that activated knowledge could serve a role similar to that played by accessible attitudes. Activated knowledge would be more likely to influence interpretations of new information, or to combine with it in some fashion. Activated knowledge might also influence perceptions of the extent of one's knowledge, which could undermine confidence in a current attitude when little knowledge is readily accessible or enhance confidence when a great deal of knowledge is readily accessible.

It is important to distinguish the effects of accessible/activated knowledge and the effects of knowledge accessibility (see Schwarz & Vaughn, 2002; Wyer & Albarracín, chap. 7, this volume). The former stems from the implications of information that is retrieved or generated (Taylor & Fiske, 1978), whereas the latter stems from the perceived ease with which that information is retrieved or generated (Tversky & Kahneman, 1973). The ease with which knowledge can be generated can influence the valence and extremity of attitudes. For example, if asked to generate reasons to use public transportation, people are more likely to hold positive attitudes toward public transportation if asked to generate only a few reasons (making generation easy) rather than many reasons (making generation more difficult; Wänke, Bless, & Biller, 1996). Some researchers have characterized such effects as an ease-of-generation heuristic (see Haddock, 2000; Rothman & Schwarz, 1998). In contrast, Tormala et al. (2002) conceptualized ease of generation as a type of metacognition, mediated by confidence in thoughts. Tormala et al. found that ease of generation had greater effects on attitudes when the attitude object was high rather than low in personal relevance (cf., Rothman & Schwarz, 1998).

Categorization and Perceptual Distortions

Categorization is a fundamental cognitive process that is inextricably intertwined with issues of activation (Lingle, Altom & Medin, 1984; Macrae & Bodenhausen, 2000). Social objects can usually be categorized in multiple ways, with individuals focusing on those alternatives that have most recently or frequently been used (Higgins, Bargh, & Lombardi, 1985), and those that are linked to the most accessible attitudes (Smith, Fazio, & Cejka, 1996). Once an object has been categorized in terms of one alternative (e.g., race), other alternatives (e.g., gender) are actually inhibited, making individuals less aware of the attributes (and presumably, the attitudes) associated with the unchosen alternatives (Macrae, Bodenhausen & Milne, 1995). Moreover, once an object has been categorized, it becomes associated with attitudes linked to that category, even if category attributes are no longer salient (Castelli, Zogmaister, Smith, & Arcuri, 2004). In sum, such results suggest (for example) that if a black comedian is categorized as a comedian (either because this category is more salient or linked to more accessible attitudes), the fact that he is black will be inhibited, and he will evoke comedian-consistent attitudes even when no longer looking or acting like someone in that role.

When attitudes are activated and function as schemas to guide interpretations of new, especially ambiguous, information, the information is generally encoded as consistent with the attitude (e.g., Houston & Fazio, 1989). Yet, this is not always the case. According to social judgment theory (Sherif & Hovland, 1961), perceivers spontaneously categorize stimuli along meaningful dimensions, including favorability, without necessarily being aware of the process. Yet, this categorization process (in reference to one's own attitude) can distort views of a communicator's position. Especially when people hold strong views, they perceive advocacies relatively close to their own as even closer (assimilation) and perceive relatively discrepant advocacies as even farther away (contrast) than they objectively are (Sherif & Sherif, 1967). These perceptual distortions (or perceptions of the message that result from the distortions) were hypothesized to mediate changes in attitudes. Although the proposed curvilinear effects of message discrepancy have been found in a number of studies (Bochner & Insko, 1966; Eagly & Telaak, 1972), evidence of the social judgment theory mediators has been more illusive.

Both categorization and perceptual distortion could influence a variety of thoughtful and nonthoughtful processes. For example, when thinking about an object, categorization of the object would surely determine which new information is viewed as most informative about the object. To the extent that different categorizations call up different stored evaluations, the different evaluations could be used as "cues" to accept or reject new advocacies (Wegener, Petty, Smoak, & Fabrigar, 2004). Distortions in perceptions of the message position would also influence the likelihood of such nonthoughtful acceptance or rejection. But, of course, perceptual distortions would also influence interpretations of the information as cognitive responses are generated and multiple pieces of information and knowledge are integrated into an overall evaluation.

Attention and Memory

From early in the development of persuasion theory, it was assumed that learning and retention of message content was important for the long-term impact of persuasive messages (Hovland et al., 1953). That is, the working assumptions of the Yale group headed by Carl Hovland in the 1950s were that people had to attend to the message, comprehend its meaning, yield to the message (accept it as true), and retain the message content over time. One could think of attention as relating to concepts such as motivation and ability to think about attitude-relevant information. In many of the Hovland-group studies, incentives were said to increase the likelihood of paying attention to a message (a motivational effect). Also, when ability to process is manipulated through distraction (such as distraction created by a secondary task, e.g., Petty et al., 1976), this is essentially an attentional manipulation. Attention would also be implicated in motivational biases in processing, where the motivation essentially focuses attention on certain types of informational content (see Sherman, 1987, for extensive discussions of attention in relating cognitive processes to message-based attitude change).

Greater attention to attitude-relevant information could come in a number of forms. Sometimes, increased attention would be reflected in longer times spent reading or thinking about information that is somehow relevant to the message recipient. In studies of impression formation and attitudes, time spent reading information has been assessed as an indication of amount of attention paid to (and effort spent processing) information (Neuberg & Fiske, 1987; Mackie & Worth, 1989).

As discussed within the dissonance framework, people can also selectively expose themselves to information consistent rather than inconsistent with their attitudes. Of course, this selective exposure could lead to greater memory for attitude-consistent information. In studies of the attitude congeniality effect in memory, however, presentation of attitude-relevant information is often externally paced, so the recipient of the information can pay differential attention, but cannot control the length of time a given piece of information is available. This external pacing may be one reason that attitude congeniality effects in memory have been relatively small and inconsistent (Eagly, Chen, Chaiken, & Shaw-Barnes, 1999). When recipients have limited time to seek information and must choose which information to consider, significant attitude congeniality effects can occur (Smith et al., 2004). The effect especially occurs when attitude-expression is made salient to research participants, even when presentation of information is controlled (Smith et al., 2004). One important aspect of attention not generally noted within the message learning approach is that attention need not be "positive" attention. For example, sometimes attitude-inconsistent information can be memorable because people pay attention in the process of arguing against it (Eagly, Kulesa, Brannon, Shaw, & Hutson-Comeaux, 2000).

Reception Processes

McGuire (1968, 1989) grouped attention, comprehension, and, to some extent, retention, into the concept of "reception" of a message and contended that some variables might primarily influence persuasion through their effects on reception, whereas others might influence persuasion because they affect yielding to the message. Also, McGuire proposed that certain variables might serve to increase reception at the same time as they decrease yielding (and vice versa). For example, as intelligence increases, people might be more able to understand (receive) messages, but might also be less willing to yield to the message (e.g., because they are confident of their premessage opinions). With these types of variables, persuasion should be greatest when the variable is at a moderate level (the compensation principle, McGuire, 1968). A meta-analysis of studies involving self-esteem and intelligence showed the hypothesized curvilinear pattern for self-esteem, but only a negative relation between intelligence and persuasion (Rhodes & Wood, 1992). From the reception/yielding perspective, this pattern could occur because past studies did not include participants at low enough levels of intelligence (so that reception was always relatively high) or because the messages used were simple enough for yielding to become the primary determinant of persuasion (see also Briñol & Petty, chap. 14, this volume).

Incongruity Resolution

In attitude congeniality effects (as in mere thought effects), attitudes seem to be operating as schemas, directing attention to attitude-consistent information (though not equally strongly across settings). In contrast, incongruity resolution research in social cognition focuses on how people consider and remember information that is incongruent with their expectancies or conclusions (Hastie & Kumar, 1979; Srull, 1981). People tend to recall incongruent pieces of information better than congruent ones, a finding of special interest because it seemingly violates implications of schema theories that predominated early in the social cognition era (Fiske & Taylor, 1984). This inconsistency was somewhat resolved through recognition that expectancy-congruent information does possess a recall advantage compared with expectancy-irrelevant information, but that incongruent information is even more memorable. In an early form of incongruency theory, that additional memory was attributed to additional attention given to incongruent information because it was unexpected (Hastie & Kumar, 1979). Later, the more elaborate Hastie/Srull model (Wyer & Srull, 1989) attributed the advantage to a reconciliation process that involved comparison of incongruent and congruent items, building up associative links that ultimately favored retrieval of the highly-interconnected incongruent material.[13]

The effects of incongruity-resolution were generally on memory for behavioral evidence rather than on impressions drawn from the behaviors. By extension, it might appear that incongruent attitudinal evidence could have little impact on attitudes, even if such incongruity did introduce anomalies into recall for the evidence. To our knowledge, however, studies involving mixed information have not demonstrated recall advantages for incongruent information (though some studies have found increased memory for counterattitudinal rather than proattitudinal messages when the message is entirely counter or pro, Cacioppo & Petty, 1979b).[14]

Still untested are some interesting implications of the incongruity work, for example, relating to patterns of interconnections formed among different pieces of attitude-related evidence. It seems probable that high effort, elaborative processing entails a certain amount of comparison and reconciliation of disparate pieces of evidence, though this processing likely focuses on the overall attitude, rather than on congruence among opposing pieces of information (cf., Wyer & Srull, 1989). Regardless of what material high effort perceivers attempt to reconcile, however, such elaborative processing should result in a more complex, fully-articulated network of inter-item attitudinal associations than produced by low effort processing (see Fabrigar et al., chap. 3, this volume; Petty et al., 1995).

Memory for Messages

Although the working assumptions of the Hovland group featured a primary role for memory of message arguments, results were less than encouraging. In the late 1950s and early 1960s, a number of studies failed to produce significant correlations between memory for the message and resultant attitudes, or found that changes in attitudes over time failed to mirror changes in memory (Insko, 1964; Miller & Campbell, 1959; Watts & McGuire, 1964). There might have been many reasons for this, but the most recognized is that a pure learning or reception model does not take into account individuals' unique evaluations of the information. Two people could both remember a piece of information, but one might find that argument very persuasive, whereas the other finds the same argument entirely specious (see Petty, Ostrom, et al., 1981). Consistent with speculations by McGuire (1968), correlations between memory and attitudes are markedly increased when the recalled information is weighted by the person's evaluation of that information (Chattopadhyay & Alba, 1988).

The Hovland group assumed that memory would follow high levels of attention, good comprehension of information, and trust that the information was correct. Yet, research has shown, somewhat paradoxically, that message memory predicts attitudes better when initial attention to (and processing of) the message is low rather than high (Haugtvedt & Petty, 1992; Haugtvedt & Wegener, 1994; Mackie & Asuncion, 1990). This could happen if people make memory-based judgments (Hastie & Park, 1986) when processing is disrupted or low for other reasons (perhaps especially if no other salient cues are available at the time of judgment, Petty & Wegener, 1998). In essence, if people did not form evaluations of the advocated position when the message was first encountered, when they are ultimately asked for their opinions, they have little choice but to rely on whatever they can remember.

One might be tempted to associate the level of elaboration (high versus low) with the Hastie and Park (1986) distinctions between on-line and memory-based judgments. Motivations that would lead to high levels of elaboration might lead to on-line processing, whereas low levels of motivation seemingly leave people with little other choice than to make memory-based judgments (using presented information if there were no prior attitudes toward the object). Yet, the relation between the on-line and memory-based judgment modes and amount of elaboration is likely to be somewhat more complex. For example, even when people make memory-based judgments, they might engage in "thoughtful" evaluation of recalled information, or they might use the volume of information recalled as a "cue" to the amount of information supporting the advocated position (Petty & Cacioppo, 1984). Some of the low-elaboration processes described earlier could occur in a relatively on-line fashion as the object or advocacy is encountered (e.g., conditioning), whereas others may be more post hoc, based on recalled information (e.g., self-perception). In general, however, many low-elaboration processes may proceed in both on-line and memory-based ways.

CONTENT, PROCESSES, AND MEASURES: IMPLICIT OR EXPLICIT?

Much ado is made about implicit processes, and many of the processes discussed in the preceding sections would be candidates for inclusion (perhaps especially those involving activation and categorization). Unfortunately, a great deal of confusion surrounds the term "implicit" in this context, as it has also in the cognitive literature on implicit memory (Roediger, 2003). A defining feature of implicit measures and processes is often that they operate outside of awareness (Greenwald & Banaji, 1995). It is not always evident, however, exactly of what people are unaware. Wegener and Petty (1998) distinguished awareness of represented content (in the context of judgmental theories), awareness of process, and awareness of outcomes. Individuals may or may not realize that they associate Republicans with wealth, may or may not realize how this belief might influence their impressions of Republicans (or rich people), and may or may not be aware of the favorable or unfavorable attitudes that they hold because of these beliefs and processes. In another context (spontaneous trait inference), Uleman (1989) distinguished seven different kinds of awareness, including awareness that one is thinking.

Clearly, people may have varying degrees of awareness of stimuli, beliefs, processes, and attitudes. Yet, it is extremely important to be precise about whether one is applying the "implicit/explicit" distinction to measures, to processes, or to the attitude construct itself (in part, because any one of these need not, in any way, imply the others; see also Dulany, 1997). Researchers can measure attitudes directly and transparently, with what is sometimes termed an explicit measure, or they can be more circumspect, measuring attitudes indirectly, with what is sometimes termed an implicit measure. These implicit measures typically take advantage of attitudinal processes, such as activation of knowledge that is directionally consistent with the attitude (Hammond, 1948) or spreading activation of the evaluation, such that respondents are better prepared to identify like-valenced stimuli rather than stimuli that mismatch the valence of the attitude (Fazio, Jackson, Dunton, & Williams, 1995). The critical difference between "explicit" and "implicit" measures would seem to be that the latter measures typically assess the activation of an attitude under conditions where respondents are relatively unaware that their attitude is being assessed or, perhaps, where respondents might be aware of the measurement attempt, but have some difficulty controlling the impact of the attitudinal processes on responses, as in the IAT (Greenwald, McGhee, & Schwartz, 1998).

Thus, the term "implicit measure" can, at the least, be reasonably applied when respondents do not realize that their attitudes are being measured. Whether a given implicit measure primarily taps one's attitude per se is another matter, however. Though perhaps less technologically advanced than current measures, indirect attitude measures have been around for some time (see Himmelfarb, Chapter 2 in Eagly & Chaiken, 1993; Petty & Cacioppo, 1981), and early criticisms that they sometimes measure something other than attitude (Kidder & Campbell, 1970) resurface with each new generation of indirect measures (see Fazio & Olson, 2003b). With careful attention to measure construction, however, it should be possible to use reliable and valid indirect or implicit measures (see Wegener & Fabrigar, 2004).

Unfortunately, whether a measure is implicit or explicit does not determine whether the attitude or process being measured is similarly implicit or explicit. Clearly, for example, one can use implicit measures to measure attitudes of which people are fully aware. In fact, one might use such situations as opportunities to test whether an implicit and explicit measure are tapping the same or different constructs. One might also inquire explicitly about attitudes people have never considered "explicitly," or that are derived from a process of which people are completely unaware. Clearly, implicit measures can be influenced by explicit processes, and explicit measures can be influenced by implicit processes (and, conceivably, by evaluations of which people are not aware). Because of the possible non-correspondence between measures and processes, a number of cognitive theorists now prefer the terms "direct" and "indirect" measures in preference to "explicit" and "implicit measures" (Roediger, 2003). This is an interesting development, given the long history of the "direct" versus "indirect" terminology in measurement of attitudes (Hammond, 1948; Kidder & Campbell, 1970).

Some researchers have used unawareness of the source of one's attitudes as definitive of an "implicit attitude," even if people might be aware of the evaluation itself (Wilson, Lindsey, & Schooler, 2000). This seems problematic, because if the term "implicit" is to mark constructs that are outside awareness, then using the term "implicit" with attitude should mean that the attitude itself is outside awareness. Such usage would parallel traditional use of the terms in cognitive psychology, where an "implicit memory" has referred to effects of memory that occur in the absence of explicit recall. For example, measures such as savings in relearning can show that a concept or association is in memory, despite inability of respondents to recall or recognize the original stimuli (Carlston & Skowronski, 1994; Vakil, Langleben-Cohen, Frenkel, Groswasser, & Aberbuch, 1996). To us, at least, it would seem most appropriate to apply the term "implicit" to attitudes in much the same way. That is, we would reserve the term "implicit attitude" for detectable evaluations that differ from those of which people are aware. For example, there might be situations in which people report positive attitudes toward a group, but the group label serves as a neutral or negative prime in a priming task (Fazio et al., 1995). In such cases, it would seem justifiable to refer to measures of the primed evaluations as measures of "implicit attitude." Yet, when evaluations measured by an implicit measure are (or would be) the same as those reported on a self-report scale, it seems unnecessary and potentially misleading to refer to those attitudes as "implicit." The measure may be implicit, but there is little evidence that the attitude is, in such cases.

Identifying an attitude as implicit using such criteria would not mean that the processes underlying that attitude must be implicit, nor would this use of terms imply that the processes underlying explicit attitudes must be explicit. In fact, people are probably often aware of (explicit) attitudes whose origins are in processes that occur outside of awareness. For example, most of the research on mere exposure used explicit measures to demonstrate that repeated exposure results in increasingly favorable attitudes. Yet, in many studies, respondents could not even report whether they had previously seen the stimuli, let alone report the processes at work. Even with more "thoughtful" processes, people are probably often unaware of the operation of the specific activities in which their minds have engaged. In such cases, the process may be implicit, but the attitude is not.

Essentially by definition, implicit processes occur outside of awareness. Among such processes may be attitude activation leading to speeded attitude-consistent evaluative (Fazio, 1995; Fazio et al., 1995) or nonevaluative responses (Bargh, Chaiken, Raymond, & Hymes, 1996). The greatest difficulty in defining implicit processes in terms of awareness is that most attitudinal processes discussed in this chapter probably occur outside of awareness, at least some of the time. For example, people may often fail to realize that they are relying on a particular heuristic or that they are weighting particular information more heavily than other information. Similarly, they seem unlikely to know that they are evaluating an object more favorably because they have seen it often or because they felt happy when they received the persuasive message. This lack of awareness of specific cognitive processes is essentially the "lack of knowing" noted by Nisbett and Wilson (1977). Even cognitive processes that were at one time deliberate and apparent (including, perhaps, some forms of elaborative analysis) may ultimately achieve a degree of automaticity, reducing awareness of their functioning (Smith et al., 1992). Therefore, with regard to process, it is not at all clear how, and with what utility, particular processes should be labeled as implicit. It may well be that much of the fascination with things implicit comes from the development of *implicit measures* that might bypass respondent attempts to answer disingenuously or from the existence of *implicit attitudes* of which people are unaware. But it is far too easy to find *implicit processes* that operate under the radar of consciousness.

WHITHER THE LEVEL OF PROCESS DESCRIPTION

In this chapter, we have organized our discussion of process, in part, by referring to the level of generality at which processes are described. The higher the level of generality, the greater process commonality one is likely to see across phenomena and across research domains. Yet, in order to account for accumulated data, "universal" process descriptions must be supplemented with moderators articulating how outcomes of the one process are changed across settings. As noted earlier, the fact that few or even one process can be viewed as explaining an entire domain has been touted as a reason to prefer theories positing a universal process. After all, one process is more parsimonious than two or more, is it not?

Benefits of Parsimony: Apparent or Real?

In our reading, there would seem to be a number of potential costs associated with universal process descriptions. At some level of generality, virtually any two processes can be described in similar terms. For example, the birth, growth, reproduction, and ultimate death of virtually all living things can be described similarly. Yet, for practical and understandable reasons, few psychologists would view the reproduction (or birth, growth, or death) of human beings and mushrooms as involving essentially the same processes. More generally, at least for the purposes of training and practice, physicians and botanists are best prepared using markedly different curricula, markedly different tools, etc.. Despite the potential benefits of emphasizing similarities across different phenomena (i.e., lumping processes into one superordinate category), "lumping" can also obscure important differences. As Petty, Wheeler, and Bizer (1999) put it:

> When constructing persuasion theories, researchers need to decide what distinctions are impor-
> tant... For example, is "tying one's shoe" quantitatively or qualitatively different from "engaging
> in an ax murder"? These behaviors might be lumped if you see them as falling along a dimension
> going from effortless to effortful physical action. However, most state legislators have decided to
> see them as qualitatively different from the point of view of the law (different antecedent mind
> states bring these actions about, their consequences are different, etc.). Our point is that you can
> lump (or see as quantitatively rather than qualitatively different) almost any psychological or phys-
> ical process depending on how you define the underlying continuum. What categorizations make
> sense depend on your purpose, the conceptual understanding the distinctions bring, their ability
> to allow unique predictions, and so forth. (p. 162)

We would also note that lumping different processes within the same process description does not necessarily lead to a more parsimonious theory. If the theory attempts to explain and predict results that diverge across contexts, a single process explanation will generally need to be expanded. It may retain its simple characterization of a single process, but only by adding moderators that explain how this process produces one pattern rather than another under a particular set of circumstances. For example, the unimodel uses concepts such as length or complexity of information (Kruglanski & Thompson, 1999a) and relevance of information to a conclusion (Pierro, Mannetti, Kruglanski, & Sleeth-Keppler, 2004) to determine when a given source or set of arguments will most influence attitudes. Yet, as might be expected, these moderators are generally the same moderators as those identified (and previously studied) using theories that refer to bounded processes to capture various phenomena across the entire domain of attitude change (Chaiken et al., 1999; Wegener & Claypool, 1999; cf. Darke et al., 1998, with Pierro et al., 2004).

In our view, if the same concepts are used to explain phenomena (even if the two theories use different terminology for those concepts), then the two theories are, for all intents and purposes, the same theory. Therefore, the level of parsimony achieved by defining process at a higher level of generality may be more apparent than real. The theory using one universal process might be parsimonious in terms of describing process ("process description parsimony"). Yet, if the same number of total concepts (moderators) are retained, the theory has not produced any parsimony in the overall explanation of the phenomena ("explanatory parsimony"). Differences between theories then become primarily semantic (see Wegener & Claypool, 1999).[15]

Bounded Versus Component Process Descriptions

The astute reader will note that "lumping" also occurs as one moves from component process descriptions to bounded process descriptions. Unlike comparisons between universal process descriptions and the other levels, however, we are unaware of any "bounded process" theorists touting parsimony as a reason to prefer the bounded process compared with component processes. In addition, "bounded process" theorists seem quite willing to investigate component processes when necessary. For example, researchers have noted that elaboration could produce cognitive biases by changing the perceived likelihood of events described in a persuasive message or by changing perceptions of the desirability of those events; and further, that these two processes might be influenced by different factors and processes, and might also influence each other (see McGuire, 1960; 1981; McGuire & McGuire, 1991). This does not mean that an elaboration researcher taking this approach would always separate perceptions of likelihood and desirability, but doing so poses little or no challenge to theorizing at the "lumped" level of elaboration.[16] In contrast, when a single process is hypothesized to be universal, the-
orizing at a lower level of process generality is discarded and taken as unnecessary or even

counterproductive. This is not to say that one approach is entirely good or bad, but it is to say that the "bounded" and "component" levels of process description seem to share more in their approaches than the "universal" level shares with either of the other levels.

Summary and Conclusions

Readers may have noted the integration or juxtaposition of material from the social cognition and attitudes areas in this chapter. Combining work from both areas seems appropriate at many levels, as the two areas are closely allied, even sharing a subsection of the *Journal of Personality and Social Psychology*. Moreover, the social cognition approach has served to emphasize the importance of cognitive processes, which represent the central focus of this chapter. The social cognition approach also suggests that process theories, issues, and measures can often be derived from cognitive psychology in particular, as well as from other approaches to psychology that can contribute to our understanding of the unobservable processes of the mind. The attitude concept's history and broad relevance within social psychology make it an ideal area in which to raise process issues and discussions that have implications for the entire field. Consequently, we have tried to delve into a number of debates relating to the definition and measurement of cognitive processes in general, as well as to their identification in the attitude area in particular. Although it is unrealistic to try to resolve all such issues in limited space, we hope we have at least outlined some of the relevant considerations for future process theorists.

We also endeavored to review the massive literature on attitude change processes on several different levels. Our emphasis was on "bounded" processes, where, in fact, the bulk of attitude change theory and research has been developed. In our review, we used the elaboration continuum as an organizational device for discussing a wide variety of attitudinal processes. This is arguably appropriate given the extent to which this area has become oriented around the issue of how "thoughtful" (elaborative) people are in dealing with attitude-relevant information, a focus that seems justified given the amount of leverage it provides in predicting which circumstances lead to attitudes with lasting impact. Future research will undoubtedly continue to isolate the specific reasons elaboration has such effects, and, by doing so, may also discover new dimensions that also meaningfully organize persuasion processes.

We also delved into both more general (in fact, "universal") process descriptions and into lower level "component" process descriptions. The most general process descriptions address single mechanisms that relate to virtually the entire domain of attitude change, and that are often proposed as alternatives to more pervasive bounded theories. At the least general (component) level, the information processing model (and related attitudinal approaches) describe a host of basic processes that are implicated in many of the bounded processes on which we primarily focused. One finds these basic component processes primarily in areas that have developed outside the prominent dual- or multi-process theories of attitude change (i.e., the ELM and HSM). Perhaps this reflects, in part, the different level of process descriptions in these prominent bounded-process theories compared with the information-processing (social cognition) focus on component processes. A number of researchers have explicitly discussed relations between the two levels of analysis (Albarracín, 2002; Lingle & Ostrom, 1981; Sherman, 1987), and we outlined some of these relations as well. Clearly there is considerable room for fuller integration of the social cognition and attitude change areas.

Our ultimate goal in this overview was to bring together a number of ideas about how to define, identify, and organize attitudinal processes along with a great deal of research about what those processes are and when and how they operate. It is our hope that this discussion will help to advance understanding of attitudinal processes, not only with regard to their nature and identification, but also in regard to the many different domains in which they may operate.

ACKNOWLEDGMENTS

Preparation of this chapter was aided by grant BCS 0094510 from the National Science Foundation, by grant MOP - 64197 from the Canadian Institutes of Health Research, and by a Fellowship in the Center for Behavioral and Social Sciences at Purdue University.

ENDNOTES

[1] Although the processes involved in attitude formation and change might often be similar across different types of attitude objects, it is clear that the specificity of an attitude object influences the utility of a measured attitude in predicting future behaviors toward the object (see Ajzen and Fishbein, chap. 5, this volume, for a review).

[2] Some connectionist models have represented attitude using a single unit receiving input from a network (Eiser, Fazio, Stafford, & Prescott, 2003, Study 2), but most connectionist models distribute representations of attitudes across a set of units.

[3] Some models of attitude structure discuss maintenance of multiple evaluations of the same object at the same time. Little research has addressed which process(es) promote creation of dual- or multiple-attitude representations (see Fabrigar, MacDonald, and Wegener, chap. 3, this volume).

[4] More generally, Cacioppo, Berntsen, Lorig, Norris, Rickett and Nussbaum (2003) noted a number of limitations in using localization procedures to identify social psychological processes. Among these are that "almost all cerebrocortical tissue serves more than one function" (p. 654) and that "activation may not reflect the locus in which a particular information processing component originates, but rather may reflect a region that is part of a more distributed network of processing mechanisms that work together to perform the task or a region that is an earlier (or later) stage in an information processing sequence" (p. 654). Cacioppo and colleagues noted further that "vigilance is especially important when one is examining integrative mechanisms responsible for orchestrating complex social behaviors – that is, the kind of information processes in which social psychologists tend to be interested. Localization is more apparent at the lowest levels of organization (i.e., lower sensory and motor processes)." (p. 655; see also Willingham & Dunn, 2003). As Cacioppo et al. (2003) put it, "just because you're imaging the brain doesn't mean you can stop using your head" (p. 656).

[5] Fishbein and Middlestadt (1995, 1997) detail how "noncognitive" factors might appear to predict attitudes when belief measures do not include all salient beliefs and when attitude and belief measures are not "correspondent" (Fishbein & Ajzen, 1974).

[6] Albarracín and Wyer (2001) provided a possible example of direct effects of affect on attitudes (see also Petty, Schumann, Richman, & Strathman, 1993; Schwarz, 1997) and of influences of attitudes on assessments of attribute likelihood and desirability (see Fabrigar et al., chap. 3, this volume; Herr, 1995), both occurring under conditions of high distraction. Evidence of "justifying" attitudes on belief measures was suggestive, but not conclusive, because evidence of the impact of attitudes on likelihood and desirability assessments depended on comparisons of model fit when paths between beliefs and attitudes were in opposite directions. Unfortunately, the models are not nested, so no direct test of these differences was presented. Comparisons could be made using confidence intervals for certain measures of model fit (see Wegener & Fabrigar, 2000), but such comparisons await future research.

[7] Backward conditioning affects attitudes with both supraliminal (e.g., Stuart et al., 1987) and subliminal presentations of the US (e.g., Krosnick, Betz, Jussim, & Lynn, 1992). Such effects are sometimes stronger when the same US is subliminal rather than supraliminal (Murphy & Zajonc, 1993; Murphy, Monahan, & Zajonc, 1995), perhaps when a supraliminal US leads to attempts to avoid its influence (see Martin, Seta, & Crelia, 1990; Wegener & Petty, 1997).

[8] One could theoretically consider many types of rewards, but these interpersonal rewards make the operant conditioning studies very similar to balance effects (in which one prefers to agree with liked others and to disagree with disliked others, Heider, 1958).

[9] Salience of a heuristic could, in some circumstances, undermine its use. For example, although people might use a "how do I feel about it?" heuristic (Schwarz & Clore, 1983) more if the mood itself is salient, factors that make the mood salient could also alert people that the source of the mood makes its use inappropriate. Alerting people to the possible impact of a heuristic might generally get people to correct for its impact if the influence of the heuristic does not satisfy the perceiver's goals (e.g., see Petty et al., 1998; Wegener, Dunn, & Tokusato, 2001).

[10] When message sources present unexpected information that does not relate to their own self interests, this can result in surprise-induced increases in information processing (Petty, Fleming, Priester, & Feinstein, 2001).

[11] In social cognition, "elaboration" might be viewed as "relational processing" (see Hunt & Einstein, 1981; Carlston & Smith, 1996). In contrast to item-specific processing, relational processing emphasizes comparison and integration of different pieces of information resulting in a relatively complex knowledge structure. Relational processing might also involve comparison and integration of information with prior knowledge, which is traditionally characterized as

"depth of processing" (Craik & Lockhart, 1972; see Petty & Cacioppo, 1986, for links between elaboration and depth of processing).

[12] Although motivated biases have often been discussed in relation to thoughtful processes, motivated bias can also occur when elaboration is low. The same motivation that biases thoughts when elaboration is high could be used as a cue to accept (or reject) a message that matches (or mismatches) the goal, or could guide use of other cues in the persuasive setting (see also Chaiken et al., 1989; Giner-Sorolla & Chaiken, 1997; Wegener, Petty, Smoak, & Fabrigar, 2004).

[13] In attitudes research, a number of papers have documented greater processing of surprising or unexpected information (e.g., Baker & Petty, 1994; Ziegler, Diehl, & Ruther, 2002). Under the rubric of elaboration, this processing would be conceptualized as "relational" (like the Hastie/Srull model) rather than being directed only at the specific unexpected information in the message. Yet, elaboration would generally be conceptualized as including integration of the information with an overall evaluation. In the Hastie/Srull approach, incongruity resolution creates behavior-behavior links, not integration of behaviors with summary traits.

[14] Observed null effects could be because the incongruity paradigm differs from most attitude change research in important respects. Participants in the incongruity paradigm are explicitly told to form a coherent impression of a novel person who engages in disparate behaviors, and, in most studies, the experimenter provides participants with this person's "true" trait (as an expectancy) prior to presentation of the conflicting behavioral information (see Srull, 1981, for an exception). Because the target is novel and the expectancy provided, attending to the information (and perhaps, reconciling it with the expectancy) may seem "called for" by the task. In contrast, most attitudes studies provide a cover story that gives message recipients some reason for exposure to the message other than evaluating it, and it is not implicitly or explicitly suggested that their task is to form a "coherent" attitude.

[15] Another common criterion for evaluating new theories concerns the generative potential for the theory compared with existing theories. To be sure, the dual- and multi-process theories of attitude change generated many (at the time) novel predictions about traditional persuasion variables such as involvement (see Petty & Cacioppo, 1979) and distraction (see Petty, Wells, & Brock, 1976). To date, it is less clear whether recent theories positing a universal process do more than repackage the predictions that followed from previous dual-process perspectives.

[16] This need not always be the case. If a "bounded" process description assumes that a number of component processes all work in the same evaluative direction, but research on the separate components shows that some of the components routinely work in unrelated or opposite directions, this could threaten the "lumped" conception and be used to argue for a focus on the individual components.

REFERENCES

Abelson, R. P. (1959). Modes of resolution of belief dilemmas. *Journal of Conflict Resolution, 3*, 343–352.

Ajzen, I. (1999). Dual-mode processing in the pursuit of insight is no vice. *Psychological Inquiry, 10*, 110–112.

Albarracín, D. (2002). Cognition in persuasion: An analysis of information processing in response to persuasive communications. In M. P. Zanna (Ed.). *Advances in experimental social psychology* (Vol. 34, pp. 61–130). San Diego, CA: Academic Press.

Albarracín, D., & Wyer, R. S. (2001). Elaborative and nonelaborative processing of a behavior-related communication. *Personality and Social Psychology Bulletin, 27,* 691–705.

Anderson, C. A., Lepper, M. R., & Ross, L. (1980). Perseverance of social theories: the role of explanation in the persistence of discredited information. *Journal of Personality and Social Psychology, 39*, 1037–1049.

Anderson, N. H. (1971). Integration theory and attitude change. *Psychological Review, 78*, 171–206.

Anderson, N. (1981). Integration theory applied to cognitive responses and attitudes. In R. E. Petty, T. M. Ostrom, & T. D. Brock (Eds.), *Cognitive responses in persuasion* (pp. 361–397). Hillsdale, NJ: Lawrence Erlbaum Associates.

Areni, C. S., & Lutz, R. J. (1988). The role of argument quality in the Elaboration Likelihood Model. *Advances in Consumer Research, 15*, 197–203.

Aronson, E. (1969). The theory of cognitive dissonance: A current perspective. In L. Berkowitz (Ed.), *Advances in experimental social psychology* (Vol. 4, pp. 1–34). San Diego, CA: Academic Press.

Aronson, E., & Carlsmith, J. M. (1963). Effect of the severity of threat on the devaluation of forbidden behavior. *Journal of Abnormal and Social Psychology, 66,* 584–588.

Baddeley, A. (2003). Double dissociations: Not magic but still useful. *Cortex, 39*, 129–131.

Baker, S. M., & Petty, R. E. (1994). Majority and minority influence: Source-position imbalance as a determinant of message scrutiny. *Journal of Personality and Social Psychology, 67*, 5–19.

Bandura, A. (1991). Self-regulation of motivation through anticipatory and self-reactive mechanisms. In R. A. Dienstbier (Ed.), *Perspectives on motivation: Nebraska Symposium 1990* (Vol. 38, pp. 69–164). Hillsdale, NJ: Lawrence Erlbaum Associates.

Bandura, A. (1995). *Self efficacy in changing societies*. New York: Cambridge University Press.

Bargh, J. A., Chaiken, S., Raymond, P., & Hymes, C. (1996). The automatic evaluation effect: Unconditional automatic attitude activation with a pronunciation task. *Journal of Experimental Social Psychology, 31*, 104–128.

Bassili, J. N. (1996). Meta-judgmental versus operative indexes of psychological attributes: The case of measures of attitude strength. *Journal of Personality & Social Psychology, 71*, 637–653.

Bassili, J. N., & Fletcher, J. F. (1991). Response-time measurement in survey research: A method for CATI and a new look at nonattitudes. *Public Opinion Quarterly, 55*, 331–346.

Beauvois, J. L., Bungert, M., & Mariette, P. (1995). Forced compliance: Commitment to compliance and commitment to activity. *European Journal of Social Psychology, 25*, 17–26.

Beauvois, J. L., & Joule, R. V. (1996). *A radical dissonance theory*. Philadelphia: Taylor & Francis, Inc.

Bem, D. J. (1967). Self-perception: An alternative interpretation of cognitive dissonance phenomena. *Psychological Review, 74*, 183–200.

Bem, D. J. (1972). Self-perception theory. In L. Berkowitz (Ed.), *Advances in experimental social psychology* (Vol. 6, pp. 1–62). New York: Academic Press.

Berkowitz, L., Jaffee, S., Jo, E., & Troccoli, B. (2000). On the correction of feeling-induced judgmental biases. In J. P. Forgas (Ed.), *Feeling and thinking: The role of affect in social cognition: Studies in emotion and social interaction* (Second Series, pp. 131–152). New York: Cambridge University Press.

Berkowitz, L., & Knurek, K. A. (1969). Label-mediated hostility generalization. *Journal of Personality and Social Psychology, 13*, 200–206.

Berscheid, E., Graziano, W. G., Monson, T., & Dermer, M. (1976). Outcome dependency, attention, attribution, and attraction. *Journal of Personality and Social Psychology, 34*, 987–989.

Birnbaum, M. H., Wong, R., & Wong, L. K. (1976). Combining information from sources that vary in credibility. *Memory and Cognition, 4*, 330–336.

Bochner, S., & Insko, C. A. (1966). Communicator discrepancy, source credibility, and opinion change. *Journal of Personality and Social Psychology, 4*, 614–621.

Bornstein, R. F. (1989). Exposure and affect: Overview and meta-analysis of research, 1968–1987. *Psychological Bulletin, 106*, 265–289.

Bornstein, R. F., & D'Agostino, P. R. (1992). Stimulus recognition and the mere exposure effect. *Journal of Personality and Social Psychology, 63*, 545–552.

Bornstein, R. F., & D'Agostino, P. R. (1994). The attribution and discounting of perceptual fluency: Preliminary tests of a perceptual fluency/attributional model of the mere exposure effect. *Social Cognition, 12*, 103–128.

Brehm, J. W. (1966). *A theory of psychological reactance*. San Diego, CA: Academic Press.

Briñol, P., & Petty, R. E. (2003). Overt head movements and persuasion: A self-validation analysis. *Journal of Personality and Social Psychology, 84*, 1123–1139.

Briñol, P., & Petty, R. E. (in press). Self-validation processes: The role of thought confidence in persuasion. To appear in G. Haddock & G. Maio (Eds.). *Theoretical perspectives on attitudes for the 21st century*. Philadelphia: Psychology Press.

Briñol, P., Tormala, Z. L., & Petty, R. E. (2004). Self-validation of cognitive responses to advertisements. *Journal of Consumer Research, 30*, 559–573.

Broadbent, D. E. (1958). *Perception and Communication*. London: Pergamon.

Brock, T. C. (1965). Commitment to exposure as a determinant of information receptivity. *Journal of Personality and Social Psychology, 2*, 10–19.

Brock, T. C. (1967). Communication discrepancy and intent to persuade as determinants of counterargument production. *Journal of Experimental Social Psychology, 3*, 296–309.

Brock, T. C., & Balloun, J. L. (1967). Behavioral receptivity to dissonant information. *Journal of Personality and Social Psychology, 6*, 413–428.

Brown, J. D. (1986). Evaluations of self and others: Self-enhancement biases in social judgments. *Social Cognition, 4*, 353–376.

Bruner, J. S. (1957). On perceptual readiness. *Psychological Review, 64*, 123–152.

Burnkrant, R. E., & Howard, D. J. (1984). Effects of the use of introductory rhetorical questions versus statements on information processing. *Journal of Personality and Social Psychology, 47*, 1218–1230.

Cacioppo, J. T., Berntson, G. G.; Lorig, T. S., Norris, C. J., Rickett, E., & Nusbaum, H. (2003). Just because you're imaging the brain doesn't mean you can stop using your head: A primer and set of first principles. *Journal of Personality and Social Psychology, 85*, 650–661.

Cacioppo, J. T., Marshall-Goodell, B. S., Tassinary, L. G., & Petty, R. E. (1992). Rudimentary determinants of attitudes: Classical conditioning is more effective when prior knowledge about the attitude stimulus is low than high. *Journal of Experimental Social Psychology, 28*, 207–233.

Cacioppo, J. T., & Petty, R. E. (1979a). Attitudes and cognitive response: An electro-physiological approach. *Journal of Personality and Social Psychology, 37*, 2181–2199.

Cacioppo, J. T., & Petty, R. E. (1979b). Effects of message repetition and position on cognitive responses, recall, and persuasion. *Journal of Personality and Social Psychology, 37*, 97–109.

Cacioppo, J. T., & Petty, R. E. (1981). Effects of extent of thought on the pleasantness ratings of P-O-X triads: Evidence for three judgmental tendencies in evaluating social situations. *Journal of Personality and Social Psychology, 40*, 1000–1009.

Cacioppo, J. T., & Petty, R. E. (1982). The need for cognition. *Journal of Personality and Social Psychology, 42*, 116–131.

Cacioppo, J. T., Petty, R. E., Kao, C. F., & Rodriguez, R. (1986). Central and peripheral routes to persuasion: An individual difference perspective. *Journal of Personality & Social Psychology, 51*, 1032–1043.

Cacioppo, J. T., Priester, J. R., & Berntson, G. G. (1993). Rudimentary determinants of attitudes II: Arm flexion and extension have differential effects on attitudes. *Journal of Personality and Social Psychology, 65*, 5–17.

Calder, B. J., Ross, M., & Insko, C. A. (1973). Attitude change and attitude attribution: Effects of incentive, choice, and consequences. *Journal of Personality and Social Psychology, 25*, 84–99.

Campbell, D. T., & Fiske, D. W. (1959) Convergent and discriminant validation in the multitrait-multimethod matrix. *Psychological Bulletin, 56*, 81–105.

Carlston, D. E. (1994). Associated Systems Theory: A systematic approach to the cognitive representation of persons and events. In R. S. Wyer (Ed.), *Advances in Social Cognition: Vol. 7. Associated Systems Theory* (pp. 1–78). Hillsdale, NJ: Lawrence Erlbaum Associates.

Carlston, D. E., & Skowronski, J. J. (1994). Savings in the relearning of trait information as evidence for spontaneous inference generation. *Journal of Personality and Social Psychology, 66*, 840–856.

Carlston, D. E., & Smith, E. R. (1996). Principles of mental representation. In E. T. Higgins & A. W. Kruglanski (Eds.). *Social Psychology: Handbook of Basic Principles* (pp. 194–210). New York: Guilford Press.

Castelli, L., Zogmaister, C., Smith, E. R., Arcuri, L. (2004). On the automatic evaluation of social exemplars. *Journal of Personality & Social Psychology, 86*, 373–387.

Chaiken, S. (1980). Heuristic versus systematic information processing in the use of source versus message cues in persuasion. *Journal of Personality and Social Psychology, 39*, 752–766.

Chaiken, S. (1987). The heuristic model of persuasion. In M. P. Zanna, J. M. Olson, & C. P. Herman (Eds.), *Social influence: The Ontario symposium* (Vol. 5, pp. 3–39). Hillsdale, NJ: Lawrence Erlbaum Associates.

Chaiken, S., & Baldwin, M. W. (1981). Affective-cognitive consistency and the effect of salient behavioral information on the self-perception of attitudes. *Journal of Personality and Social Psychology, 41*, 1–12.

Chaiken, S., Duckworth, K. L., & Darke, P. (1999). When parsimony fails . . . *Psychological Inquiry, 10*, 118–123.

Chaiken, S., Liberman, A., & Eagly, A. H. (1989). Heuristic and systematic processing within and beyond the persuasion context. In J. S. Uleman & J. A. Bargh (Ed.), *Unintended thought* (pp. 212–252). New York: Guilford.

Chaiken, S., & Maheswaran, D. (1994). Heuristic processing can bias systematic processing: Effects of source credibility, argument ambiguity, and task importance on attitude judgment. *Journal of Personality and Social Psychology, 66*, 460–473.

Chaiken, S., & Trope, Y. (Eds.). (1999). *Dual-process theories in social psychology.* New York: Guilford.

Chattopadhyay, A., & Alba, J. W. (1988). The situational importance of recall and inference in consumer decision making. *Journal of Consumer Research, 15*, 1–12.

Chun, W. Y., Spiegel, S., & Kruglanski, A. W. (2002). Assimilative behavior identification can also be resource dependent: A unimodel perspective on personal-attribution phases. *Journal of Personality and Social Psychology, 83*, 542–555.

Coats, S., & Smith, E. R. (1999). Perceptions of gender subtypes: Sensitivity to recent exemplar activation and in-group/out-group differences. *Personality and Social Psychology Bulletin, 25*, 515–526.

Cohen, J. D., Dunbar, K., & McClelland, J. L. (1990). On the control of automatic processes: A parallel distributed processing account of the Stroop effect. *Psychological Review, 97*, 332–361.

Cooper, J., & Fazio, R. H. (1984). A new look at dissonance theory. In L. Berkowitz (Ed.), *Advances in experimental social psychology* (Vol. 17, pp. 229–266). New York: Academic Press.

Cooper, J., Fazio, R. H., & Rhodewalt, F. (1978). Dissonance and humor: Evidence for the undifferentiated nature of dissonance arousal. *Journal of Personality and Social Psychology, 36*, 280–285.

Costermans, J., Lories, G., & Ansay, C. (1992). Confidence level and feeling of knowing in question answering: The weight of inferential processes. *Journal of Experimental Psychology: Learning, Memory, & Cognition, 18*, 142–150.

Craik, F. I. M., & Lockhart, R. S. (1972). Levels of processing: A framework for memory research. *Journal of Verbal Learning and Verbal Behavior, 11*, 671–684.

Culbertson, F. M. (1957). Modification of an emotionally held attitude through role playing. *Journal of Abnormal and Social Psychology, 54*, 230–233.

Darke, P. R., Chaiken, S., Bohner, G., Einwiller, S., Erb, H. P., & Hazelwood, J. D. (1998). Accuracy motivation, consensus information, and the law of large numbers: Effects on attitude judgment in the absence of argumentation. *Personality and Social Psychology Bulletin, 24*, 1205–1215.

Deci, E. L. (1975). *Intrinsic motivation*. New York: Plenum.

De Houwer, J., Baeyens, F., & Eelen, P. (1994). Verbal evaluative conditioning with undetected US presentations. *Behavior Research and Therapy, 32*, 629–633.

De Houwer, J., Thomas, S., & Baeyens, F. (2001). Associative learning of likes and dislikes: A review of 25 years of research on human evaluative conditioning. *Psychological Bulletin, 127*, 853–869.

DeSteno, D., Petty, R. E., Rucker, D. D., Wegener, D. T., & Braverman, J. (2004). Discrete emotions and persuasion: The role of emotion-induced expectancies. *Journal of Personality and Social Psychology, 86*, 43–56.

DeSteno, D., Petty, R. E., Wegener, D. T., & Rucker, D. D. (2000). Beyond valence in the perception of likelihood: The role of emotion specificity. *Journal of Personality and Social Psychology, 78*, 397–416.

Dijksterhuis, A. (2004). I like myself but I don't know why: Enhancing implicit self-esteem by subliminal evaluative conditioning. *Journal of Personality and Social Psychology, 86*, 345–355.

Dillehay, R. C., Insko, C. A., & Smith, M. B. (1966). Logical consistency and attitude change. *Journal of Personality and Social Psychology, 3*, 646–654.

Ditto, P. H., & Lopez, D. F. (1992). Motivated skepticism: Use of differential decision criteria for preferred and nonpreferred conclusions. *Journal of Personality and Social Psychology, 63*, 568–584.

Dodson, C. S., Johnson, M. K. (1996). Some problems with the process-dissociation approach to memory. *Journal of Experimental Psychology: General, 125*, 181–194.

Donahoe, J. W., & Vegas, R. (2004). Pavlovian Conditioning: The CS-UR Relation. *Journal of Experimental Psychology: Animal Behavior Processes, 30*, 17–33.

Dulany, D. E. (1997). Consciousness in the explicit (deliberative) and implicit (evocative). In J. D. Cohen & J. W. Schooler (Eds.), *Scientific approaches to consciousness: Carnegie Mellon Symposia on cognition* (pp. 179–212). Mahwah, NJ: Lawrence Erlbaum Associates.

Dunn, J. C., & Kirsner, K. (2003). What can we infer from double dissociations? *Cortex, 39*, 1–7.

Dunning, D. (1999). A newer look: Motivated social cognition and the schematic representation of social concepts. *Psychological Inquiry, 10*, 1–11.

Eagly, A. H., & Chaiken, S. (1984). Cognitive theories of persuasion. In L. Berkowitz (Ed.), *Advances in experimental social psychology* (Vol. 17, pp. 268–361. New York: Academic Press.

Eagly, A. H., & Chaiken, S. (1993). *The psychology of attitudes*. Forth Worth, TX: Harcourt, Brace, Jovanovich.

Eagly, A. H., & Chaiken, S. (1998). Attitude structure and function. In D. Gilbert, S. Fiske, & G. Lindzey (Eds.), *The handbook of social psychology* (4th edition, pp. 269–322). New York: McGraw-Hill.

Eagly, A. H., Chaiken, S., & Wood, W. (1981). An attribution analysis of persuasion. In J. H. Harvey, W. J. Ickes, & R. F. Kidd (Eds.), *New direction in attribution research* (Vol. 3, pp. 37–62). Hillsdale, NJ: Lawrence Erlbaum Associates.

Eagly, A. H., Chen, S., Chaiken, S., & Shaw-Barnes, K. (1999). The impact of attitudes on memory: An affair to remember. *Psychological Bulletin, 125*, 64–89.

Eagly, A. H., Kulesa, P., Brannon, L. A., Shaw, K., & Hutson-Comeaux, S. (2000). Why counterattitudinal messages are as memorable as proattitudinal messages: The importance of active defense against attack. *Personality and Social Psychology Bulletin, 26*, 1392–1408.

Eagly, A. H., & Telaak, K. (1972). Width of the latitude of acceptance as a determinant of attitude change. *Journal of Personality and Social Psychology, 23*, 388–397.

Edwards, K., & Smith, E. E. (1996). A disconfirmation bias in the evaluation of arguments. *Journal of Personality and Social Psychology, 71*, 5–24.

Eiser, J. R., Fazio, R. H., Stafford, T., & Prescott, T. J. (2003). Connectionist simulation of attitude learning: Asymmetries in the acquisition of positive and negative evaluations. *Personality and Social Psychology Bulletin, 29*, 1221–1235.

Elkin, R. A., & Leippe, M. R. (1986). Physiological arousal, dissonance, and attitude change: Evidence for a dissonance-arousal link and a "Don't remind me" effect. *Journal of Personality and Social Psychology, 51*, 55–65.

Elliot, A. J., & Devine, P. G. (1994). On the motivational nature of cognitive dissonance: Dissonance as psychological discomfort. *Journal of Personality and Social Psychology, 67*, 382–394.

Elms, A. C. (1966). Influence of fantasy ability on attitude change through role-playing. *Journal of Personality and Social Psychology, 4*, 36–43.

Eysenck, M. W., Ellis, A. W., Hunt, E. B., & Johnson-Laird, P. N. (Eds). (1994). *The Blackwell Dictionary of Cognitive Psychology*. Oxford, UK: Blackwell.

Fabrigar, L. R., Priester, J. R., Petty, R. E., & Wegener, D. T. (1998). The impact of attitude accessibility on elaboration of persuasive messages. *Personality and Social Psychology Bulletin, 24,* 339–352.

Fazio, R. H. (1995). Attitudes as object-evaluation associations: Determinants, consequences, and correlates of attitude accessibility. In R. E. Petty & J. A. Krosnick (Eds.), *Attitude strength: Antecedents and consequences* (pp. 247–282). Mahwah, NJ: Lawrence Erlbaum Associates.

Fazio, R. H., Jackson, J. R., Dunton, B. C., & Williams, C. J. (1995). Variability in automatic activation as an unobtrusive measure of racial attitudes: A bona fide pipeline? *Journal of Personality and Social Psychology, 69*, 1013–1027.

Fazio, R. H., & Olson, M. A. (2003a). Attitudes: Foundations, functions, and consequences. In M. A. Hogg & J. Cooper (Eds.), *The SAGE handbook of social psychology* (pp. 139–160). Thousand Oaks, CA: Sage.

Fazio, R. H., & Olson, M. A. (2003b). Implicit measures in social cognition research: Their meaning and use. *Annual Review of Psychology, 54*, 297–327.

Fazio, R. H., Zanna, M. P., & Cooper, J. (1977). Dissonance and self-perception: An integrative view of each theory's proper domain of application. *Journal of Experimental Social Psychology, 13*, 464–479.

Festinger, L. (1957). *A theory of cognitive dissonance.* Evanston, IL: Row, Peterson.

Festinger, L. (1964). *Conflict, decision, and dissonance.* Stanford, CA: Stanford University Press.

Festinger, L., & Carlsmith, J. M. (1959). Cognitive consequences of forced compliance. *Journal of Abnormal and Social Psychology, 58*, 203–210.

Fishbein, M. (1963). An investigation of the relationship between beliefs about an object and the attitude toward that object. *Human Relations, 16*, 233–240.

Fishbein, M., & Ajzen, I. (1974). Attitudes toward objects as predictors of single and multiple behavioral criteria. *Psychological Review, 81*, 59–74.

Fishbein, M., & Ajzen, I. (1975). *Belief, attitude, intention, and behavior: An introduction to theory and research.* Reading, MA: Addison-Wesley.

Fishbein, M., & Ajzen, I. (1981). Acceptance, yielding and impact: Cognitive processes in persuasion. In R. E. Petty, T. M. Ostrom, & T. D. Brock (Eds.), *Cognitive responses in persuasion* (pp. 339–359). Hillsdale, NJ: Lawrence Erlbaum Associates.

Fishbein, M., & Middlestadt, S. E. (1995). Noncognitive effects on attitude formation and change: Fact or artifact? *Journal of Consumer Psychology, 4*, 181–202.

Fishbein, M., & Middlestadt, S. E. (1997). A striking lack of evidence for nonbelief-based attitude formation and change: A response to five commentaries. *Journal of Consumer Psychology, 6*, 107–115.

Fiske, S. T., & Taylor, S. E. (1984). *Social cognition.* Reading, MA: Addison-Wesley.

Fiske, S. T., & Taylor, S. E. (1991). *Social cognition* (2nd ed.). New York: McGraw-Hill.

Forgas, J. P. (1983). What is social about social cognition? *British Journal of Social Psychology, 22*, 129–144.

Frey, D. (1986). Recent research on selective exposure to information. In L. Berkowitz (Ed.), *Advances in experimental social psychology* (Vol. 19, pp. 41–80). San Diego, CA: Academic Press.

Frey, D., & Wicklund, R. (1978). A clarification of selective exposure: The impact of choice. *Journal of Experimental Social Psychology, 14*, 132–139.

Gilbert, D. T. (1998). Ordinary Personalogy. In D. Gilbert, S. Fiske, & G. Lindzey (Eds.) *Handbook of social psychology* (pp. 89–150).

Gilbert, D. (1999). What the mind's not. In S. Chaiken & Y. Trope (Eds.). *Dual Process Theories in Social Psychology* (pp. 3–11). New York: Guilford.

Giner-Sorolla, R., & Chaiken, S. (1997). Selective use of heuristic and systematic processing under defense motivation. *Personality and Social Psychology Bulletin, 23*, 84–97.

Green, D. M., & Swets, J. A. (1974). *Signal detection theory and psychophysics.* Oxford, UK: Rober E. Kríe.

Greenwald, A. G. (1968). Cognitive learning, cognitive response to persuasion, and attitude change. In A. G. Greenwald, T. C. Brock, & T. M. Ostrom (Ed.), *Psychological foundations of attitudes* (pp. 147–170). New York: Academic Press.

Greenwald, A. G. (1969). The open-mindedness of the counterattitudinal role player. *Journal of Experimental Social Psychology, 5*, 375–388.

Greenwald, A. G. (1975). On the inconclusiveness of "crucial" cognitive tests of dissonance versus self-perception theories. *Journal of Experimental Social Psychology, 11*, 490–499.

Greenwald, A. G., & Albert, R. D. (1968). Acceptance and recall of improvised arguments. *Journal of Personality and Social Psychology, 8*, 31–34.

Greenwald, A. G., & Banaji, M. R. (1995). Implicit social cognition: Attitudes, self-esteem, and stereotypes. *Psychological Review, 102*, 4–27.

Greenwald, A. G., McGhee, D. E., & Schwartz, J. L. K. (1998). Measuring individual differences in implicit cognition: The implicit association test. *Journal of Personality and Social Psychology, 74*, 1464–1480.

Gresham, L. G., & Shimp, T. A. (1985). Attitude toward the advertisement and brand attitude: A classical conditioning perspective. *Journal of Advertising, 14*, 10–17.

Griffitt, W. B. (1970). Environmental effects on interpersonal affective behavior: Ambient effective temperature and attraction. *Journal of Personality and Social Psychology, 15*, 240–244.

Haddock, G. (2000). Subjective ease of retrieval and attitude-relevant judgments. In H. Bless & J. P. Forgas (Eds.), *The message within: The role of subjective experience in social cognition and behavior* (pp. 125–142). Philadelphia: Taylor & Francis.

Hammond, K. R. (1948). Measuring attitudes by error choice: An indirect method. *Journal of Abnormal and Social Psychology, 43*, 38–48.

Harkins, S. G., & Petty, R. E. (1981). The effects of source magnification of cognitive effort on attitudes: An information processing view. *Journal of Personality and Social Psychology, 40*, 401–413.

Harmon-Jones, E. (2000). Cognitive dissonance and experienced negative affect: Evidence that dissonance increases experienced negative affect even in the absence of aversive consequences. *Personality and Social Psychology Bulletin, 26*, 1490–1501.

Harmon-Jones, E., & Allen, J. J. B. (2001). The role of affect in the mere exposure effect: Evidence from psychophysiological and individual differences approaches. *Personality and Social Psychology Bulletin, 27*, 889–898.

Harmon-Jones, E., Brehm, J. W., Greenberg, J., Simon, L., & Nelson, D. E. (1996). Evidence that the production of aversive consequences is not necessary to create cognitive dissonance. *Journal of Personality and Social Psychology, 70*, 5–16.

Harmon-Jones, E., & Harmon-Jones, C. (2002). Testing the action-based model of cognitive dissonance: The effect of action orientation on postdecisional attitudes. *Personality and Social Psychology Bulletin, 28*, 711–723.

Hastie, R., & Carlston, D. E. (1980). Theoretical issues in person memory. In R. Hastie, T. M. Ostrom, E. B. Ebbeson, R. S. Wyer, Jr., D. L. Hamilton, & D. E. Carlston (Eds.), *Person memory: the cognitive basis of social perception*. Hillsdale, NJ: Lawrence Erlbaum Associates.

Hastie, R., & Kumar, A. P. (1979). Person memory: Personality traits as organizing principles in memory for behaviors. *Journal of Personality and Social Psychology, 37*, 25–34.

Hastie, R., & Park, B. (1986). The relationship between memory and judgment depends on whether the judgment task is memory-based or on-line. *Psychological Review, 93*, 258–268.

Haugtvedt, C. P., & Petty, R. E. (1992). Personality and persuasion: Need for cognition moderates the persistence and resistance of attitude changes. *Journal of Personality and Social Psychology, 63*, 308–319.

Haugtvedt, C. P., & Strathman, A. (1990). Situational personal relevance and attitude persistence. *Advances in Consumer Research, 17*, 766–769.

Haugtvedt, C. P., & Wegener, D. T. (1994). Message order effects in persuasion: An attitude strength perspective. *Journal of Consumer Research, 21*, 205–218.

Heider, F. (1946). Attitudes and cognitive organization. *Journal of Psychology, 21*, 107–112.

Heider, F. (1958). *The psychology of interpersonal relations*. New York: Wiley.

Herr, P. M. (1995). Whither fact, artifact, and attitude: Reflections on the theory of reasoned action. *Journal of Consumer Psychology, 4*, 371–380.

Higgins, E. T. (1996). Knowledge activation: Accessibility, applicability, and salience. In E. T. Higgins & A. W. Kruglanski (Eds.), *Social Psychology: Handbook of Basic Principles* (pp. 133–168). New York: Guilford.

Higgins, E. T., Bargh, J. A., & Lombardi, W. J. (1985). Nature of priming effects on categorization. *Journal of Experimental Psychology: Learning, Memory, & Cognition, 11*, 59–69.

Higgins, E. T., & King, G. A. (1981). Accessibility of social constructs: Information processing consequences of individual and contextual variability. In N. Cantor & J. Kihlstrom (Eds.), *Personality, Cognition, and Social Interaction* (pp. 69–121). Hillsdale, NJ: Lawrence Erlbaum Associates.

Hildum, D. C., & Brown, R. W. (1956). Verbal reinforcement and interviewer bias. *Journal of Abnormal and Social Psychology, 53*, 108–111.

Hodges, S. D., & Wilson, T. D. (1993). Effects of analyzing reasons on attitude change: The moderating role of attitude accessibility. *Social Cognition, 11*, 353–366.

Houston, D. A., & Fazio, R. H. (1989). Biased processing as a function of attitude accessibility: Making objective judgments subjectively. *Social Cognition, 7*, 51–66.

Hovland, C. I., Janis, I. L., & Kelley, H. H. (1953). *Communication and persuasion: Psychological studies of opinion change*. New Haven, CT: Yale University Press.

Hovland, C. I., Lumsdaine, A. A., & Sheffield, F. D. (1949). *Experiments on mass communication*. Princeton, NJ: Princeton University Press.

Hunt, R. R., & Einstein, G. O. (1981). Relational and item-specific information in memory. *Journal of Verbal Learning and Verbal Behavior, 20*, 497–514.

Insko, C. A. (1964). Primacy versus recency in persuasion as a function of the timing of arguments and measures. *Journal of Abnormal and Social Psychology, 69*, 381–391.

Insko, C. A. (1965). Verbal reinforcement of attitude. *Journal of Personality and Social Psychology, 2*, 621–623.

Insko, C. A., & Butzine, K. W. (1967). Rapport, awareness, and verbal reinforcement of attitude. *Journal of Personality and Social Psychology, 6*, 225–228.

Insko, C. A., & Cialdini, R. B. (1969). A test of three interpretations of attitudinal verbal reinforcement. *Journal of Personality and Social Psychology, 12*, 333–341.

Jacoby, L. L. (1991). A process dissociation framework: Separating automatic from intentional uses of memory. *Journal of Memory and Language, 30*, 513–541.

Jacoby, L. L., Kelley, C. M., Brown, J., & Jasechko, J. (1989). Becoming famous overnight: Limits on the ability to avoid unconscious influences of the past. *Journal of Personality and Social Psychology, 56*, 326–338.

Janis, I. L., & King, B. T. (1954). The influence of role playing on opinion change. *Journal of Abnormal and Social Psychology, 49*, 211–218.

Johnson, B. T., Smith-McLallen, A., Killeya, L. A., & Levin K. D. (2004). Truth or consequences: Overcoming resistance to persuasion with positive thinking. In E. S. Knowles & J. A. Linn (Eds.), *Resistance and persuasion* (pp. 215–233). Mahwah, NJ: Lawrence Erlbaum Associates.

Jones, E. E., & Davis, K. E. (1965). From acts to dispositions: The attribution process in person perception. In L. Berkowitz (Ed.), *Advances in experimental social psychology* (Vol. 2, pp. 219–266). New York: Academic Press.

Jordan, N. (1953). Behavioral forces that are a function of attitudes and of cognitive organization. *Human Relations, 6*, 273–287.

Jost, J. T., Kruglanski, A. W., & Nelson, T. O. (1998). Social metacognition: An expansionist review. *Personality and Social Psychology Review, 2*, 137–154.

Judd, C. M., & Lusk, C. M. (1984). Knowledge structures and evaluative judgments: Effects of structural variables on judgment extremity. *Journal of Personality and Social Psychology, 46*, 1193–1207.

Kahneman, D. (2003). A perspective on judgment and choice: Mapping bounded rationality. *American Psychologist, 58*, 697–720.

Kardes, F. R. (1994). Consumer judgment and decision processes. In R. S. Wyer and T. K. Srull (Eds.), *Handbook of social cognition* (2nd ed., Vol. 2; pp. 399–466). Hillsdale, NJ: Lawrence Erlbaum Associates.

Kashima, Y., & Kerekes, A. R. Z. (1994). A distributed memory model of averaging phenomena in person impression formation. *Journal of Experimental Social Psychology, 30*, 407–455.

Kelley, H. H. (1967). Attribution theory in social psychology. In D. Levine (Ed.), *Nebraska symposium on motivation* (Vol. 15, pp. 192–238). Lincoln, NE: University of Nebraska Press.

Kidder, L. H., & Campbell, D. T. (1970). The indirect testing of social attitudes. In G. F. Summers (Ed.), *Attitude measurement* (pp. 333–385). Chicago: Rand McNally.

Kiesler, S. B., & Mathog, R. (1968). The distraction hypothesis in attitude change. *Psychological Reports, 23*, 1123–1133.

Kleinhesselink, R. R., & Edwards, R. E. (1975). Seeking and avoiding belief-discrepant information as a function of its perceived refutability. *Journal of Personality and Social Psychology, 31*, 787–790.

Klinger, M. R., & Greenwald, A. G. (1994). Preferences need no inferences?: The cognitive basis of unconscious mere exposure effects. In P. M. Niedenthal & S. Kitayama (Eds.), *The hear's eye: Emotional influences in perception and attention* (pp. 67–85). San Diego, CA: Academic Press.

Komatsu, S., Graf, P., & Uttl, B. (1995). Process dissociation procedure: Core assumptions fail, sometimes. *European Journal of Cognitive Psychology, 7*, 19–40.

Krosnick, J. A., Betz, A. L., Jussim, L. J., & Lynn, A. R. (1992). Subliminal conditioning of attitudes. *Personality and Social Psychology Bulletin, 18*, 152–162.

Krosnick, J. A., & Petty, R. E. (1995). Attitude strength: An overview. In R. E. Petty & J. A. Krosnick (Eds.), *Attitude strength: Antecedants and consequences* (pp. 1–24). Mahwah, NJ: Lawrence Erlbaum Associates.

Kruglanski, A. W. (1996). Motivated social cognition: Principles of the interface. In E. T. Higgins and A. W. Kruglanski (Eds.), *Social Psychology: Handbook of Basic Principles* (pp. 493–520). New York: Guilford.

Kruglanski, A. W., Chun, W. Y., Erb, H. P., Pierro, A., Mannetti, L., & Spiegel, S. (2003). A parametric unimodel of human judgment: Integrating dual-process frameworks in social cognition from a single-mode perspective. In J. P. Forgas, K. D. Williams, & W. von Hippel (Eds.), *Social judgments: Implicit and explicit processes* (pp. 137–161). New York: Cambridge University Press.

Kruglanski, A. W., Freund, T., & Bar-Tal, D. (1996). Motivational effects in the mere-exposure paradigm. *European Journal of Social Psychology, 26*, 479–499.

Kruglanski, A. W., & Thompson, E. P. (1999a). Persuasion by a single route: A view from the unimodel. *Psychological Inquiry, 10*, 83–109.

Kruglanski, A. W., Thompson, E. P., & Spiegel, S. (1999). Separate or equal?: Bimodal notions of persuasion and a single-process "Unimodel." In S. Chaiken & Y. Trope (Eds.), *Dual process theories in social psychology* (pp. 293–313). New York: Guilford.

Kumkale, G. T., & Albarracin, D. (2004). The Sleeper Effect in Persuasion: A Meta-Analytic Review. *Psychological Bulletin, 130*, 143–172.

Kunst-Wilson, W. R., & Zajonc, R. B. (1980). Affective discrimination of stimuli that cannot be recognized. *Science, 207*, 557–558.

Lambert, A. J., Payne, B. K., Jacoby, L. L., Shaffer, L. M., Chasteen, A. L., & Khan, S. R. (2003). Stereotypes as dominant responses: On the "social facilitation of prejudice in anticipated public contexts. *Journal of Personality and Social Psychology, 84*, 277–295.

Lepper, M. R., Greene, D., & Nisbett, R. E. (1973). Undermining children's intrinsic interest with extrinsic reward: A test of the "overjustification" hypothesis. *Journal of Personality and Social Psychology, 28*, 129–137.

Liberman, A., & Chaiken, S. (1991). Value conflict and thought-induced attitude change. *Journal of Experimental Social Psychology, 27*, 203–216.

Lingle, J. H., Altom, M. W. & Medin, D. L. (1984). Of cabbages and kings: Assessing the extendibility of natural object concept models to social things. In R. S. Wyer & T. K. Srull (Eds.). *Handbook of Social Cognition, Volume 1* (pp. 71–117). Hillsdale, NJ: Lawrence Erlbaum Associates.

Lingle, J. H., & Ostrom, T. M. (1981). Principles of memory and cognition in attitude formation. In R. E. Petty, T. M. Ostrom, & T. D. Brock (Eds.), *Cognitive responses in persuasion* (pp. 399–420). Hillsdale, NJ: Lawrence Erlbaum Associates.

Lord, C. G., & Lepper, M. R. (1999). Attitude representation theory. In M. P. Zanna (Ed.), *Advances in experimental social psychology* (Vol. 31, pp. 265–343). Mahwah, NJ: Lawrence Erlbaum Associates.

Lord, C. G., Ross, L., & Lepper, M. R. (1979). Biased assimilation and attitude polarization: The effects of prior theories on subsequently considered evidence. *Journal of Personality and Social Psychology, 37*, 2098–2109.

Losch, M. E., & Cacioppo, J. T. (1990). Cognitive dissonance may enhance sympathetic tonus, but attitudes are changed to reduce negative affect rather than arousal. *Journal of Experimental Social Psychology, 26*, 289–304.

Lovibond, P. F., & Shanks, D. R. (2002). The role of awareness in Pavlovian conditioning: Empirical evidence and theoretical implications. *Journal of Experimental Psychology: Animal Behavior Processes, 28*, 3–26.

Lutz, R. J. (1975). Changing brand attitudes through modification of cognitive structure. *Journal of Consumer Research, 1*, 49–59.

Lutz, R. J. (1977). An experimental investigation of causal relations among cognitions, affect, and behavioral intention. *Journal of Consumer Research, 3*, 197–208.

MacKenzie, S. B. (1986). The role of attention in mediating the effect of advertising on attribute importance. *Journal of Consumer Research, 13*, 174–195.

Mackie, D. M., & Asuncion, A. G. (1990). On-line and memory-based modification of attitudes: Determinants of message recall-attitude change correspondence. *Journal of Personality and Social Psychology, 59*, 5–16.

Mackie, D. M., & Worth, L. T. (1989). Processing deficits and the mediation of positive affect in persuasion. *Journal of Personality and Social Psychology, 57*, 27–40.

Macrae, C. N., & Bodenhausen, G. V. (2000). Social cognition: Thinking categorically about others. *Annual Review of Psychology, 51*, 93–120.

Macrae, C. N., Bodenhausen, G. V., & Milne, A. B. (1995). The dissection of selection in person perception: Inhibitory processes in social stereotyping. *Journal of Personality & Social Psychology, 69*, 397–407.

Mandler, G., Nakamura, Y., & Shebo Van Zandt, B. J. (1987). Nonspecific effects of exposure on stimuli that cannot be recognized. *Journal of Experimental Psychology: Learning, Memory, and Cognition, 13*, 646–648.

Mann, L., & Janis, I. L. (1968). A follow-up study on the long-term effects of emotional role playing. *Journal of Personality and Social Psychology, 8*, 339–342.

Markus, H., & Zajonc, R. B. (1985). The cognitive perspective in social psychology. In G. Lindzey & E. Aronson (Eds.), *The handbook of social psychology* (3rd ed., Vol. 1, pp. 137–230). New York: Random House.

Martin, L. L., Seta, J. J., & Crelia, R. A. (1990). Assimilation and contrast as a function of people's willingness and ability to expend effort in forming an impression. *Journal of Personality and Social Psychology, 59*, 27–37.

McCloskey, M., & Glucksberg, S. (1979). Decision processes in verifying category membership statements: Implications for models of semantic memory. *Cognitive Psychology, 11*, 1–37.

McElree, B., Dolan, P. O., & Jacoby, L. L. (1999). Isolating the contributions of familiarity and source information to item recognition: A time course analysis. *Journal of Experimental Psychology: Learning, Memory, & Cognition, 25*, 563–582.

McGuire, W. J. (1960). A syllogistic analysis of cognitive relationships. In C. I. Hovland & M. J. Rosenberg (Eds.), *Attitude organization and change: An analysis of consistency among attitude components* (pp. 65–111). New Haven, CT: Yale University Press.

McGuire, W. J. (1968). Personality and attitude change: An information-processing theory. In A. G. Greenwald, T. C. Brock, & T. M. Ostrom (Eds.), *Psychological foundations of attitudes* (pp. 171–196). New York: Academic.

McGuire, W. J. (1981). The probabilogical model of cognitive structure and change. In R. E. Petty, T. M. Ostrom, & T. D. Brock (Eds.), *Cognitive responses in persuasion* (pp. 291–307). Hillsdale, NJ: Lawrence Erlbaum Associates.

McGuire, W. J. (1989). Theoretical foundations of campaigns. In R. E. Rice & C. K. Atkin (Eds.), *Public communication campaigns* (pp. 43–66). Newbury Park: Sage.

McGuire, W. J., & McGuire, C. V. (1991). The content, structure, and operation of thought systems. In R. S. Wyer Jr., & T. Srull (Ed.), *Advances in social cognition* (Vol. 4, pp. 1–78). Hillsdale, NJ: Lawrence Erlbaum Associates.

Middlestadt, S. E., Fishbein, M., & Chan, D. K.-S. (1993). The effect of music on brand attitude: Affect or belief based change? In E. M. Clark, T. Brock, & D. Stewart (Eds.), *Attention, attitude, and affect in response to advertising* (pp. 149–167). Hillsdale, NJ: Lawrence Erlbaum Associates.

Millar, M. G., & Tesser, A. (1986). Thought-induced attitude change: The effects of schema structure and commitment. *Journal of Personality and Social Psychology, 51*, 259–269.

Miller, C. E., & Norman, R. M. G. (1976). Balance, agreement, and attraction in hypothetical social situations. *Journal of Experimental Social Psychology, 12*, 109–119.

Miller, N., & Campbell, D. T. (1959). Recency and primacy in persuasion as a function of the timing of speeches and measurements. *Journal of Abnormal and Social Psychology, 59*, 1–9.

Miller, N., & Colman, D. E. (1981). Methodological issues in analyzing the cognitive mediation of persuasion. In R. E. Petty, T. M. Ostrom, & T. D. Brock (Eds.), *Cognitive responses in persuasion* (pp. 105–125). Hillsdale, NJ: Lawrence Erlbaum Associates.

Miller, N., & Pederson, W. C. (1999). Assessing process distinctiveness. *Psychological Inquiry, 10*, 150–155.

Mischel, W. (1998). Metacognition at the hyphen of social-cognitive psychology. *Personality and Social Psychology Review, 2*, 84–86.

Monahan, J. L., Murphy, S. T., & Zajonc, R. B. (2000). Subliminal mere exposure: Specific, general, and diffuse effects. *Psychological Science, 11*, 462–466.

Moskowitz, G. B., Gollwitzer, P. M., Wasel, W., & Schaal, B. (1999). Preconscious control of stereotype activation through chronic egalitarian goals. *Journal of Personality and Social Psychology, 77*, 167–184.

Mugny, G., & Perez, J. A. (1991). *The social psychology of minority influence.* Translated by V. W. Lamongie. New York: Cambridge University Press.

Murphy, S. T., Monahan, J. L., & Zajonc, R. B. (1995). Additivity of nonconscious affect: Combined effects of priming and exposure. *Journal of Personality and Social Psychology, 69*, 589–602.

Murphy, S. T., & Zajonc, R. B. (1993). Affect, cognition, and awareness: Affective priming with optimal and suboptimal exposures. *Journal of Personality and Social Psychology, 64*, 723–739.

Neuberg, S. L., & Fiske, S. T. (1987). Motivational influences on impression formation: Outcome dependency, accuracy-driven attention, and individuating processes. *Journal of Personality and Social Psychology, 53*, 431–444.

Niedenthal, P. M. (1990). Implicit perception of affective information. *Journal of Experimental Social Psychology, 26*, 505–527.

Nisbett, R. E., & Wilson, T. D. (1977). Telling more than we can know: Verbal reports on mental processes. *Psychological Review, 84*, 231–259.

Olson, M. A., & Fazio, R. H. (2001). Implicit attitude formation through classical conditioning. *Psychological Science, 12*, 413–417.

Osgood, C. E., & Tannenbaum, P. H. (1955). The principle of congruity in the prediction of attitude change. *Psychological Review, 62*, 42–55.

Osterhouse, R. A., & Brock, T. C. (1970). Distraction increases yielding to propaganda by inhibiting counterarguing. *Journal of Personality and Social Psychology, 15*, 344–358.

Ottati, V., Fishbein, M., & Middlestadt, S. E. (1988). Determinants of voters' beliefs about the candidates' stands on the issues: The role of evaluative bias heuristics and the candidates' expressed message. *Journal of Personality and Social Psychology, 55*, 517–529.

Ottati, V. C., & Isbell, L. M. (1996). Effects of mood during exposure to target information on subsequently reported judgments: An on-line model of misattribution and correction. *Journal of Personality and Social Psychology, 71*, 39–53.

Page, M. M. (1974). Demand characteristics and the classical conditioning of attitudes experiment. *Journal of Personality and Social Psychology, 30*, 468–476.

Pallak, S. R. (1983). Salience of a communicator's physical attractiveness and persuasion: A heuristic versus systematic processing interpretation. *Social Cognition, 2*, 158–170.

Peterson, R. C., & Thurstone, L. L. (1933). *The effect of motion pictures on the social attitudes of high school children.* Chicago: University of Chicago Press.

Petty, R. E. (1997). The evolution of theory and research in social psychology: From single to multiple effect and process models of persuasion. In C. McGarty & S. A. Haslam (Eds.), *The message of social psychology: Perspectives on mind in society.* Oxford, UK: Basil Blackwell.

Petty, R. E., Briñol, P, & Tormala, Z. L. (2002). Thought confidence as a determinant of persuasion: The self-validation hypothesis. *Journal of Personality and Social Psychology, 82*, 722–741.

Petty, R. E., Briñol, P., Tormala, Z. L., & Jarvis, W. B. G. (2003). *Implications of implicit ambivalence: An exploration of the PAST model.* Unpublished manuscript, Ohio State University.

Petty, R. E., & Cacioppo, J. T. (1979). Issue-involvement can increase or decrease persuasion by enhancing message-relevant cognitive responses. *Journal of Personality and Social Psychology, 37*, 1915–1926.

Petty, R. E., & Cacioppo, J. T. (1981). *Attitudes and persuasion: Classic and contemporary approaches.* Dubuque, IA: Brown.

Petty, R. E., & Cacioppo, J. T. (1984). The effects of involvement on responses to argument quantity and quality: Central and peripheral routes to persuasion. *Journal of Personality and Social Psychology, 46*, 69–81.

Petty, R. E., & Cacioppo, J. T. (1986). *Communication and persuasion: Central and peripheral routes to persuasion.* New York: Springer-Verlag.

Petty, R. E., Cacioppo, J. T., & Goldman, R. (1981). Personal involvement as a determinant of argument-based persuasion. *Journal of Personality and Social Psychology, 41*, 847–855.

Petty, R. E., Fleming, M. A., Priester, J. R., & Feinstein, A. H. (2001). Individual versus group interest violation: Surprise as a determinant of argument scrutiny and persuasion. *Social Cognition, 19*, 418–442.

Petty, R. E., Harkins, S. G., & Williams, K. D. (1980). The effects of group diffusion of cognitive effort on attitudes: An information processing view. *Journal of Personality and Social Psychology, 38*, 81–92.

Petty, R. E., Haugtvedt, C. P., & Smith, S. M. (1995). Elaboration as a determinant of attitude strength. In R. E. Petty & J. A. Krosnick (Eds.), *Attitude strength: Antecedents and consequences* (pp. 93–130). Mahwah, NJ: Lawrence Erlbaum Associates.

Petty, R. E., & Krosnick, J. A. (Eds.). (1995). *Attitude strength: Antecedents and consequences*. Mahwah, NJ: Lawrence Erlbaum Associates.

Petty, R. E., Ostrom, T. M., & Brock, T. D. (Eds.). (1981). *Cognitive responses in persuasion*. Hillsdale, NJ: Lawrence Erlbaum Associates.

Petty, R. E., Schumann, D. W., Richman, S. A., & Strathman, A. J. (1993). Positive mood and persuasion: Different roles for affect under high- and low-elaboration conditions. *Journal of Personality and Social Psychology, 64*, 5–20.

Petty, R. E., Briñol, P., Tormala, Z. L., & Wegener, D. T. (in press). Metacognitive processes in social judgment. In A. Kruglanski & E. T. Higgins (Eds.), *Social psychology: A handbook of basic principles* (2nd ed.). New York: Guilford.

Petty, R. E., Tormala, Z. L., Hawkins, C., & Wegener, D. T. (2001). Motivation to think and order effects in persuasion: The moderating role of chunking. *Personality and Social Psychology Bulletin, 27*, 332–344.

Petty, R. E., & Wegener, D. T. (1991). Thought systems, argument quality, and persuasion. In R. S. Wyer Jr., & T. K. Srull (Eds.), *Advances in social cognition* (Vol. 4, pp. 147–161). Hillsdale, NJ: Lawrence Erlbaum Associates.

Petty, R. E., & Wegener, D. T. (1993). Flexible correction processes in social judgment: Correcting for context-induced contrast. *Journal of Experimental Social Psychology, 29*, 137–165.

Petty, R. E., & Wegener, D. T. (1998). Attitude change: Multiple roles for persuasion variables. In D. Gilbert, S. Fiske, & G. Lindzey (Eds.), *The handbook of social psychology* (4th ed., pp. 323–390). New York: McGraw-Hill.

Petty, R. E., & Wegener, D. T. (1999). The Elaboration Likelihood Model: Current status and controversies. In S. Chaiken & Y. Trope (Eds.), *Dual process theories in social psychology* (pp. 41–72). New York: Guilford.

Petty, R. E., Wegener, D. T., Fabrigar, L. R., Priester, J. R., & Cacioppo, J. T. (1993). Conceptual and methodological issues in the elaboration likelihood model of persuasion: A reply to the Michigan State critics. *Communication Theory, 3*, 336–363.

Petty, R. E., Wegener, D. T., & White, P. (1998). Flexible correction processes in social judgment: Implications for persuasion. *Social Cognition, 16*, 93–113.

Petty, R. E., Wells, G. L., & Brock, T. C. (1976). Distraction can enhance or reduce yielding to propaganda: Thought disruption versus effort justification. *Journal of Personality and Social Psychology, 34*, 874–884.

Petty, R. E., Wheeler, S. C. & Bizer, G. Y. (1999). Is there one persuasion process or more? Lumping versus splitting in attitude change theories. *Psychological Inquiry, 10*, 156–162.

Pierro, A., Mannetti, L., Kruglanski, A. W., & Sleeth-Keppler, D. (2004). Relevance override: On the reduced impact of "cues" under high-motivation conditions of persuasion studies. *Journal of Personality and Social Psychology, 86*, 251–264.

Plaut, D. C. (1995). Double dissociation without modularity: Evidence from connectionist neuropsychology. *Journal of Clinical & Experimental Neuropsychology, 17*, 291–321.

Pratkanis, A. R., Greenwald, A. G., Leippe, M. R., & Baumgardner, M. H. (1988). In search of reliable persuasion effects: III. The sleeper effect is dead. Long live the sleeper effect. *Journal of Personality and Social Psychology, 54*, 203–218.

Priester, J. R., Cacioppo, J. T., & Petty, R. E. (1996). The influence of motor processes on attitudes toward novel versus familiar semantic stimuli. *Personality and Social Psychology Bulletin, 22*, 442–447.

Priester, J. R., Nayakankuppum, D., Fleming, M. A., & Godek, J. (2004). The A^2SC^2 model: *The Journal of Consumer Research, 30*, 574–587.

Priester, J. R., & Petty, R. E. (1995). Source attributions and persuasion: Perceived honesty as a determinant of message scrutiny. *Personality and Social Psychology Bulletin, 21*, 637–654.

Priester, J. R., & Petty, R. E. (2001). Extending the bases of subjective attitudinal ambivalence: Interpersonal and intrapersonal antecedents of evaluative tension. *Journal of Personality and Social Psychology, 80*, 19–34.

Razran, G. H. S. (1940). Conditioned response changes in rating and appraising sociopolitical slogans. *Psychological Bulletin, 37*, 481.

Rhodes, N., & Wood, W. (1992). Self-esteem and intelligence affect influenceability: The mediating role of message reception. *Psychological Bulletin, 111*, 156–171.

Roediger, H. L. (2003). Reconsidering implicit memory. In J. S. Bowers & C. J. Marsolek (Eds.), *Rethinking implicit memory* (pp. 3–18). New York: Oxford University Press.

Roskos-Ewoldsen, D. R., & Fazio, R. H. (1992). The accessibility of source likability as a determinant of persuasion. *Personality and Social Psychology Bulletin, 18*, 19–25.

Rothman, A. J., & Schwarz, N. (1998). Constructing perceptions of vulnerability: Personal relevance and the use of experiential information in health judgments. *Personality and Social Psychology Bulletin, 24*, 1053–1064.

Rumelhart, D. E. (1997). The architecture of mind: A connectionist approach. In J. Haugeland (Ed)., *Mind design 2: Philosophy, psychology, artificial intelligence* (pp. 205–232). Cambridge, MA: MIT Press.

Sadler, O., & Tesser, A. (1973). Some effects of salience and time upon interpersonal hostility and attraction. *Sociometry, 36*, 99–112.

Schuette, R. A., & Fazio, R. H. (1995). Attitude accessibility and motivation as determinants of biased processing: A test of the MODE model. *Personality and Social Psychology Bulletin, 21*, 704–710.

Schwarz, N. (1997). Mood and attitude judgments: A comment on Fishbein and Middlestadt. *Journal of Consumer Psychology, 6*, 93–98.

Schwarz, N., & Bohner, G. (2001). The construction of attitudes. In A. Tesser & N. Schwarz (Eds.), *Blackwell handbook of social psychology: Intraindividual processes* (pp. 436–457). Malden, MA: Blackwell.

Schwarz, N., & Clore, G. L. (1983). Mood, misattribution, and Judgments of well-being: Informative and directive functions of affective states. *Journal of Personality and Social Psychology, 45,* 513–523.

Schwarz, N., & Vaughn, L. A. (2002). The availability heuristic revisited: Ease of recall and content of recall as distinct sources of information. In T. Gilovich & D. Griffin (Eds.), *Heuristics and biases: The psychology of intuitive judgment* (pp. 103–119). New York: Cambridge University Press.

Scott, C. A., & Yalch, R. J. (1978). A test of the self-perception explanation of the effects of rewards on intrinsic interest. *Journal of Experimental Social Psychology, 14*, 180–192.

Sczesny, S., & Kühnen, U. (2003). Meta-cognition about biological sex and gender-stereotypic physical appearance: Consequences for the assessment of leadership competence. *Personality and Social Psychology Bulletin, 30*, 13–21.

Shallice, T. (1988). *From neuropsychology to mental structure*. New York: Cambridge University Press.

Sherif, M., & Hovland, C. I. (1961). *Social judgment: Assimilation and contrast effects in communication and attitude change*. New Haven, CT: Yale University Press.

Sherif, M., & Sherif, C. W. (1967). Attitude as the individual's own categories: The social judgment-involvement approach to attitude and attitude change. In C. W. Sherif & M. Sherif (Eds.), *Attitude, ego-involvement, and change* (pp. 105–139). New York: Wiley.

Sherman, S. J. (1970). Effects of choice and incentive on attitude change in a discrepant behavior situation. *Journal of Personality and Social Psychology, 15*, 245–252.

Sherman, S. J. (1987). Cognitive processes in the formation, change, and expression of attitudes. In M. P. Zanna, J. M. Olson, & C. P. Herman (Eds), *Social influence: The Ontario symposium*, (Vol. 5, pp. 75–106). Hillsdale, NJ: Lawrence Erlbaum Associates.

Sherman, S. J., Cialdini, R. B., Schwartzman, D. F., & Reynolds, K. D. (1985). Imagining can heighten or lower the perceived likelihood of contracting a disease: The mediating effect of ease of imagery. *Personality and Social Psychology Bulletin, 11*, 118–127.

Sherman, S. J., Mackie, D. M., & Driscoll, D. M. (1990). Priming and the differential use of dimensions in evaluation. *Personality and Social Psychology Bulletin, 16*, 405–418.

Shestowsky, D., Wegener, D. T., & Fabrigar, L. R. (1998). Need for cognition and interpersonal influence: Individual differences in impact on dyadic decisions. *Journal of Personality and Social Psychology, 74*, 1317–1328.

Shimp, T. A., Stuart, E. W., & Engle, R. W. (1991). A program of classical conditioning experiments testing variations in the conditioned stimulus and context. *Journal of Consumer Research, 18*, 1–12.

Shultz, T. R., Lepper, M. R. (1996). Cognitive dissonance reduction as constraint satisfaction. *Psychological Review, 103*, 219–240.

Sigall, H., & Mills, J. (1998). Measures of independent variables and mediators are useful in social psychology experiments: But are they necessary? *Personality and Social Psychology Review, 2*, 218–226.

Simon, L., Greenberg, J., & Brehm, J. (1995). Trivialization: The forgotten mode of dissonance reduction. *Journal of Personality and Social Psychology, 68*, 247–260.

Skinner, B. F. (1953). *Science and human behavior*. New York: Macmillan.

Skowronski, J. J., Carlston, D. E., Mae, L., & Crawford, M. T. (1998). Spontaneous trait transference: communicators take on the qualities they describe in others. *Journal of Personality and Social Psychology, 74*, 837–848.

Smith, E. R. (1996). What do connectionism and social psychology offer each other? *Journal of Personality and Social Psychology, 70*, 893–912.

Smith, E. R., & DeCoster, J. (1998). Knowledge acquisition, accessibility, and use in person perception and stereotyping: Simulation with a recurrent connectionist network. *Journal of Personality and Social Psychology, 74*, 21–35.

Smith, E. R., & DeCoster, J. (2000). Dual-process models in social and cognitive psychology: Conceptual integration and links to underlying memory systems. *Personality & Social Psychology Review, 4*, 108–131.

Smith, E. R., Fazio, R. H., & Cejka, M. A. (1996). Accessible attitudes influence categorization of multiply categorizable objects. *Journal of Personality and Social Psychology, 71*, 888–898.

Smith, E. R., Stewart, T. L., & Buttram, R. T. (1992). Inferring a trait from a behavior has longterm, highly specific effects. *Journal of Personality and Social Psychology, 62*, 753–759.

Smith, S. M., Fabrigar, L. R., Powell, D. M., Estrada, M., Houde, S. J. R. J., & Prosser, M. A. (2004). *The role of processing motivation and ability in the relationship between attitudes and recall.* Unpublished manuscript, St. Mary's University, Halifax, Nova Scotia.

Snyder, M. (1974). The self-monitoring of expressive behavior. *Journal of Personality and Social Psychology, 30*, 526–537.

Srull, T. K. (1981). Person memory: Some tests of associative storage and retrieval models. *Journal of Experimental Psychology: Human Learning and Memory, 7*, 440–463.

Staats, A. W., & Staats, C. K. (1958). Attitudes established by classical conditioning. *Journal of Abnormal and Social Psychology, 57*, 37–40.

Stapel, D. A., & Schwarz, N. (1998). The Republican who did not want to become president: An inclusion/exclusion analysis of Colin Powell's impact on evaluations of the Republican party and Bob Dole. *Personality and Social Psychology Bulletin, 24*, 690–698.

Steele, C. M. (1988). The psychology of self-affirmation: Sustaining the integrity of the self. In L. Berkowitz (Ed.), *Advances in experimental social psychology* (Vol. 21, pp. 261–302). New York: Academic Press.

Steele, C. M., Southwick, L., & Critchlow, B. (1981). Dissonance and alcohol: Drinking your troubles away. *Journal of Personality and Social Psychology, 41*, 831–846.

Stern, L. D., McNaught-Davis, A. K., & Barker, T. R. (2003). Process dissociation using a guided procedure. *Memory and Cognition, 31*, 641–655.

Stone, J., & Cooper, J. (2001). A self-standards model of cognitive dissonance. *Journal of Experimental Social Psychology, 37*, 228–243.

Strack, F. (1992). The different routes to social judgments: Experiential versus informational based strategies. In L. L. Martin and A. Tesser (Eds.), *The Construction of social judgments.* Hillsdale, NJ: Lawrence Erlbaum Associates.

Strack, F., & Förster, J. (1998). Self-reflection and recognition: The role of metacognitive knowledge in the attribution of recollective experience. *Personality and Social Psychology Review, 2*, 111–123.

Strack, F., Martin, L., & Stepper, S. (1988). Inhibiting and facilitating conditions of the human smile: A nonobtrusive test of the facial feedback hypothesis. *Journal of Personality and Social Psychology, 54*, 768–777.

Stuart, E. W., Shimp, T. A., & Engle, R. W. (1987). Classical conditioning of consumer attitudes: Four experiments in an advertising context. *Journal of Consumer Research, 14*, 334–349.

Sweeney, P. D., & Gruber, K. L. (1984). Selective exposure: Voter information preferences and the Watergate affair. *Journal of Personality and Social Psychology, 46*, 1208–1221.

Taylor, S. E. (1975). On inferring one's attitude from one's behavior: Some delimiting conditions. *Journal of Personality and Social Psychology, 31*, 126–131.

Taylor, S. E., & Fiske, S. T. (1978). Salience, attention, and attribution: Top of the head phenomena. In L. Berkowitz (Ed.), *Advances in Experimental Social Psychology* (Vol. 11, pp. 249–288). New York: Academic Press.

Tedeschi, J. T., Schlenker, B. R., & Bonoma, T. V. (1971). Cognitive dissonance: Private ratiocination or public spectacle? *American Psychologist, 26*, 685–695.

Tesser, A. (1978). Self-generated attitude change. In L. Berkowitz (Ed.), *Advances in experimental social psychology* (Vol. 11, pp. 289–338). New York: Academic Press.

Tesser, A., & Cornell, D. P. (1991). On the confluence of self processes. *Journal of Experimental Social Psychology, 27*, 501–526.

Tesser, A., & Leone, C. (1977). Cognitive schemas and thought as determinants of attitude change. *Journal of Experimental Social Psychology, 13*, 340–356.

Tesser, A., Martin, L., & Mendolia, M. (1995). The impact of thought on attitude extremity and attitude-behavior consistency. In R. E. Petty & J. A. Krosnick (Eds.), *Attitude strength: Antecedents and consequences* (pp. 73–92). Mahwah, NJ: Lawrence Erlbaum Associates.

Thurstone, L. L. (1928). Attitudes can be measured. *American Journal of Sociology, 33*, 529–544.

Tormala, Z., Petty, R. E., & Briñol, P. (2002). Ease of retrieval effects in persuasion: The roles of elaboration and thought confidence. *Personality and Social Psychology Bulletin, 28*, 1700–1712.

Toth, J. P., Reingold, E. M., & Jacoby, L. L. (1995). A response to Graf and Komatsu's critique of the process dissociation procedure: When is caution necessary? *European Journal of Cognitive Psychology, 7*, 113–130.

Tourangeau, R., & Rasinski, K. A. (1988). Cognitive processes underlying context effects in attitude measurement. *Psychological Bulletin, 103*, 299–314.

Tversky, A. & Kahneman, D. (1973). Availability: A heuristic for judging frequency and probability. *Cognitive Psychology, 5*, 207–232.

Uleman, J. S. (1989). A framework for thinking intentionally about unintended thought. In J. S. Uleman & J. A. Bargh (Eds.) *Unintended thought* (pp. 425–449). New York: Guilford Press.

Vakil, E., Langleben-Cohen, D., Frenkel, Y., Groswasser, Z., & Aberbuch, S. (1996). Saving during relearning as an implicit measure of memory in closed-head-injured patients. *Neuropsychiatry, Neuropsychology, and Behavioral Neurology, 9*, 171–175.

van Overwalle, F., & Jordens, K. (2002). An adaptive connectionist model of cognitive dissonance. *Personality and Social Psychology Review, 6*, 204–231.

Visser, P. S., Fabrigar, L. R., Wegener, D. T., & Browne, M. (2004). *Analyzing multi-trait multi-method data in personality and social psychology*. Unpublished manuscript.

Walther, E. (2002). Guilty by mere association: Evaluative conditioning and the spreading attitude effect. *Journal of Personality and Social Psychology, 82*, 919–934.

Wänke, M., Bless, H., & Biller, B. (1996). Subjective experience versus content of information in the construction of attitude judgments. *Personality and Social Psychology Bulletin, 22*, 1105–1113.

Watts, W. A. (1967). Relative persistence of opinion change induced by active compared to passive participation. *Journal of Personality and Social Psychology, 5*, 4–15.

Watts, W. A., & McGuire, W. J. (1964). Persistence of induced opinion change and retention of the inducing message contents. *Journal of Abnormal and Social Psychology, 68*, 233–241.

Wegener, D. T., & Claypool, H. M. (1999). The elaboration continuum by an other name does not smell as sweet. *Psychological Inquiry, 10*, 176–181.

Wegener, D. T., Downing, J., Krosnick, J. A., & Petty, R. E. (1995). Measures and manipulations of strength-related properties of attitudes: Current practice and future directions. In R. E. Petty and J. A. Krosnick (Eds.), *Attitude strength: Antecedents and consequences* (pp. 455–487). Hillsdale, NJ: Lawrence Erlbaum Associates.

Wegener, D. T., Dunn, M., & Tokusato, D. (2001). The Flexible Correction Model: Phenomenology and the use of naive theories in avoiding or removing bias. In G. B. Moskowitz (Ed.), *Cognitive social psychology: The Princeton symposium on the legacy and future of social cognition* (pp. 277–290). Mahwah, NJ: Lawrence Erlbaum Associates.

Wegener, D. T., & Fabrigar, L. R. (2000). Analysis and design for nonexperimental data: Addressing causal and noncausal hypotheses. In H. T. Reis & C. M. Judd (Eds.), *Handbook of research methods in social and personality psychology* (pp. 412–450). New York: Cambridge University Press.

Wegener, D. T., & Fabrigar, L. R. (2004). Constructing and evaluating quantitative measures for social psychological research: Conceptual challenges and methodological solutions. In C. Sansone, C. C. C. Morf, & A. T. Panter (Eds.), *The SAGE handbook of methods in social psychology* (pp. 145–172). New York: Sage.

Wegener, D. T., & Petty, R. E. (1995). Flexible correction processes in social judgment: The role of naive theories in corrections for perceived bias. *Journal of Personality and Social Psychology, 68*, 36–51.

Wegener, D. T., & Petty, R. E. (1996). Effects of mood on persuasion processes: Enhancing, reducing, and biasing scrutiny of attitude-relevant information. In L. L. Martin and A. Tesser (Eds.), *Striving and feeling: Interactions among goals, affect, and self-regulation* (pp. 329–362). Mahwah, NJ: Lawrence Erlbaum Associates.

Wegener, D. T., & Petty, R. E. (1997). The flexible correction model: The role of naive theories of bias in bias correction. In M. P. Zanna (Ed.), *Advances in experimental social psychology* (Vol. 29, pp. 141–208). Mahwah, NJ: Lawrence Erlbaum Associates.

Wegener, D. T., & Petty, R. E. (1998). The naive scientist revisited: Naive theories and social judgment. *Social Cognition, 16*, 1–7.

Wegener, D. T., & Petty, R. E. (2001). Understanding effects of mood through the Elaboration Likelihood and Flexible Correction Models. In L. L. Martin & G. L. Clore (Eds.), *Theories of mood and cognition: A user's guidebook* (pp. 177–210). Mahwah, NJ: Lawrence Erlbaum Associates.

Wegener, D. T., Petty, R. E., & Klein, D. J. (1994). Effects of mood on high elaboration attitude change: The mediating role of likelihood judgments. *European Journal of Social Psychology, 24*, 25–43.

Wegener, D. T., Petty, R. E., Smoak, N. D., & Fabrigar, L. R. (2004). Multiple routes to resisting attitude change. In E. Knowles & J. Linn (Eds.), *Resistance and persuasion* (pp. 13–38). Mahwah, NJ: Lawrence Erlbaum Associates.

Wegner, D. M., & Bargh, J. A. (1998). Control and automaticity in social life. In D. Gilbert, S. Fiske, & G. Lindzey (Eds.), *The handbook of social psychology* (4th ed., pp. 446–496). New York: McGraw-Hill.

Willingham, D. T., & Dunn, E. W. (2003). What neuroimaging and brain localization can do, cannot do and should not do for social psychology. *Journal of Personality and Social Psychology, 85*, 662–671.

Wilson, D. E., & Horton, K. D. (2002). Comparing techniques for estimating automatic retrieval: Effects of retention interval. *Psychonomic Bulletin and Review, 9*, 566–574.

Wilson, T. D., & Brekke, N. (1994). Mental contamination and mental correction: Unwanted influences on judgments and evaluations. *Psychological Bulletin, 116*, 117–142.

Wilson, T. D., Dunn, D. S., Kraft, D., & Lisle, D. J. (1989). Introspection, attitude change, and attitude-behavior consistency: The disrupting effects of explaining why we feel the way we do. In L. Berkowitz (Ed.), *Advances in experimental social psychology* (Vol. 22, pp. 287–343). San Diego: Academic Press.

Wilson, T. D., & Hodges, S. D. (1992). Attitudes as temporary constructions. In L. L. Martin & A. Tesser (Eds.), *The construction of social judgments* (pp. 37–65). Hillsdale, NJ: Lawrence Erlbaum Associates.

Wilson, T. D., Kraft, D., & Dunn, D. S. (1989). The disruptive effects of explaining attitudes: The moderating effect of knowledge about the attitude object. *Journal of Experimental Social Psychology, 25*, 379–400.

Wilson, T. D., Lindsey, S., & Schooler, T. Y. (2000). A model of dual attitudes. *Psychological Review, 107*, 101–126.

Winkielman, P., & Cacioppo, J. T. (2001). Mind at ease puts a smile on the face: Psychophysiological evidence that processing facilitation elicits positive affect. *Journal of Personality and Social Psychology, 81*, 989–1000.

Wood, W. (1982). Retrieval of attitude-relevant information from memory: Effects on susceptibility to persuasion and on intrinsic motivation. *Journal of Personality and Social Psychology, 42*, 798–910.

Wood, W., & Eagly, A. H. (1981). Stages in the analysis of persuasive messages: The role of causal attributions and message comprehension. *Journal of Personality and Social Psychology, 40*, 246–259.

Wood, W., & Kallgren, C. A. (1988). Communicator attributes and persuasion: Recipients access to attitude-relevant information in memory. *Personality and Social Psychology Bulletin, 14*, 172–182.

Wood, W., Kallgren, C. A., & Preisler, R. M. (1985). Access to attitude-relevant information in memory as a determinant of persuasion: The role of message attributes. *Journal of Experimental Social Psychology, 21*, 73–85.

Wyer, R. S., Jr. (1970). Quantitative prediction of belief and opinion change: A further test of a subjective probability model. *Journal of Personality and Social Psychology, 16*, 559–570.

Wyer, R. S., Jr. (1974). *Cognitive organization and change: An information-processing approach.* Hillsdale, NJ: Lawrence Erlbaum Associates.

Wyer, R. S., Jr., & Srull, T. K. (1989). *Memory and cognition in its social context.*

Zajonc, R. B. (1968). Attitudinal effects of mere exposure. *Journal of Personality and Social Psychology Monograph Supplements, 9*, 1–27.

Zajonc, R. B. (1980). Feeling and thinking: Preferences need no inferences. *American Psychologist, 35*, 151–175.

Zajonc, R. B. (1998). Emotions. In D. Gilbert, S. Fiske, & G. Lindzey (Eds.), *Handbook of social psychology* (4th ed., pp. 591–632). New York: McGraw-Hill.

Zanna, M. P., & Cooper, J. (1974). Dissonance and the pill: An attribution approach to studying the arousal properties of dissonance. *Journal of Personality and Social Psychology, 29*, 703–709.

Zanna, M. P., Fazio, R. H., & Ross, M. (1994). The persistence of persuasion. In R. C. Schank & E. Langer (Eds.), *Beliefs, reasoning, and decision making: Psycho-logic in honor of Bob Abelson* (pp. 347–362). Hillsdale, NJ: Lawrence Erlbaum Associates.

Zanna, M. P., Kiesler, C. A., & Pilkonis, P. A. (1970). Positive and negative attitudinal affect established by classical conditioning. *Journal of Personality and Social Psychology, 14*, 321–328.

Zarate, M. A., Sanders, J. D., & Garza, A. A. (2000). Neurological disassociations of social perception processes. *Social Cognition, 18*, 223–251.

Ziegler, R., Diehl, M., & Ruther, A. (2002). Multiple source characteristics and persuasion: Source inconsistency as a determinant of message scrutiny. *Personality and Social Psychology Bulletin, 28*, 496–508.

13

Implicit and Explicit Attitudes: Research, Challenges, and Theory

John N. Bassili
University of Toronto at Scarborough

Rick D. Brown
University of Florida

THEORETICAL BACKGROUND AND CHALLENGES

Assumptions about the mental representation of attitudes are critical to our understanding of attitudes. Research findings from the past two decades have added to the challenges that must be met by any representational system of attitudes. Two challenges stand out in particular. The first challenge arises from the increasingly apparent dual nature of attitudinal processes: deliberate or explicit on the one hand, and automatic or implicit on the other (Devine, 1989; Fazio, 1990; Wilson, Lindsey, & Schooler, 2000), whereas the second challenge arises from the pervasiveness of context effects in attitude experience and expression (see Blair, 2002; Schwarz & Bohner, 2001). In addition to being able to accommodate deliberative as well as relatively automatic attitude expression, the attitudinal constructs that are posited by a representational system of attitudes have to be able to account for attitudinal malleability. We begin with a discussion of the challenges created by the apparent duality of attitude expression and experience and by context effects. Given the relative novelty of research on implicit attitudes, we review this area in particular detail.

Two Significant Challenges to Contemporary Theories of Attitudes

Implicit Versus Explicit Attitudes: The Challenge to the Unity of the Attitude Construct

Our growing understanding of implicit psychological processes as powerful contributors to thought and behavior has formed what is undoubtedly one of the most important contributions of psychological research at the end of the 20th century. By their very nature, implicit processes exert a subtle influence on the way we think and behave, and this very subtlety has kept them for long in the shadow of experimental research. Though a multitude of historical observations

543

of unconscious psychological processes have been reported, it is only recently that they have been brought together under the umbrella of implicit psychological phenomena (see Schacter, 1987, for a review). Most of these observations were made in the domain of human memory, but it was not long before the notion of implicit processes became central to the discourse about attitudes.

The first clear application of implicit procedures to the study of attitudes was reported by Fazio and his colleagues (Fazio, Sanbonmatsu, Powell, & Kardes, 1986) who used a priming procedure to investigate the automatic activation of attitudes. This methodology was seminal because of its ability to reveal the automatic activation of evaluations toward an object, presented as a prime, by detecting the extent to which it facilitates or interferes with the subsequent judgment of a target word's valence. Two features of the priming paradigm are particularly noteworthy. First, because facilitation or interference of the target judgment is computed against a baseline condition in which no prime is presented, many extraneous features of the task are controlled (see Bassili, 2000). Second, by keeping the temporal parameters of the task very brief with a stimulus onset asynchrony of 350 ms, any effects of the prime on the target judgments cannot be influenced by controlled processes and can be assumed to be automatic.

At present, the most prominent implicit measure of attitudes is the implicit association test (IAT) introduced by Greenwald, McGhee, and Schwartz (1998) (see Krosnick, Judd, & Wittenbrink, chap. 2, this volume). The IAT procedure is based on categorization tasks involving two sets of stimuli. For example, one set may consist of White faces and of African American faces, and the other set of words with a positive connotation and others with a negative connotation. The participant's task across a series of blocked trials is to discriminate between the stimuli. On the first block the discrimination may be between White faces and African American faces and on the second between pleasant words and unpleasant words. The IAT procedure hinges on trials in which the same response has to be made for either of two stimuli–African American faces or pleasant words, for example. Response latency on such trials serves as an index of the participant's implicit preference of the two target categories. For example, some participants are much slower at the discrimination task when the same key has to be pressed for African American faces and pleasant words, than for White faces and pleasant words, revealing an implicit preference for Whites over African American.

Nosek and Banaji (2001) introduced the Go/No-go Association Task (GNAT), which is a variant of the IAT that involves a single target category. On one block of trials, participants respond to stimuli representing the target category and pleasant words and do nothing in response to other stimuli. On another block of trials participants respond to stimuli representing the target category and unpleasant words. As in the case of the IAT, the comparison of response latencies or error rates to such trials serves as an index of a participant's evaluation of the target category.

There are a variety of other types of implicit measures of attitudes that include word fragment completion tasks (Dovidio, Kawakami, Johnson, Johnson, & Howard, 1997), name letter preference tasks (Koole, Dijksterhuis, & van Knippenberg, 2001), a modified evaluative priming procedure that uses a word pronunciation task in place of the word-valence task (Bargh, Chaiken, Raymond, & Hymes, 1996), and an evaluative variant of the spatial Simon task (De Houwer & Eelen, 1998; see Krosnick et al., chap. 2, this volume).

Importantly, implicit measures of attitudes have been shown to uniquely predict certain types of behavior–particularly spontaneous behavior. For example, implicit measures of prejudice have been shown to predict several spontaneous negative behaviors of Whites when interacting with African Americans (Dovidio et al., 1997; Dovidio, Kawakami, & Gaertner, 2002; McConnell & Liebold, 2001; Wilson et al., 2000). In a similar vein, Bessenoff and Sherman (2000) reported correspondence between a priming measure that used overweight and thin exemplars, and the distance at which participants later placed their own chair from an overweight woman. Futhermore, the link between implicit attitudes and spontaneous behaviors has been demonstrated in domains other than prejudice and stereotypes. For example, Marsh, Johnson, and Scott-Sheldon (2001) showed a link between implicit attitudes toward condom use and behavior. This link, shown for casual partners but not main partners, could not be explained by explicit attitudes.

In short, what has been learned about implicit attitudes over the past two decades has presented attitude theorists with the challenge of reconciling two dramatically different modes of attitude expression. This challenge has not been trivial, as the relation between implicit and explicit attitudes has varied from strong to weak depending on many factors. A comprehensive account of both types of attitudes and of the relationship between them is, accordingly, of utmost importance at this juncture in attitude theorizing.

A note of caution is in order as we proceed with our discussion of what we will call implicit and explicit attitudes in this chapter. The use of the labels "explicit attitude" and "implicit attitude" is not meant to convey that two distinct types of attitudes are necessarily represented in memory. The framework we adopt here is distinctly more integrative than these labels suggest. The labels are used for efficiency to refer to two modes of attitudinal experience and expression, an explicit one that involves reflection on, and awareness of, the judgmental process, and an implicit one that does not.

Context Effects: The Challenge to Attitudes as Enduring Representations

The tension between the properties of attitude stability and malleability has long played an important role in theorizing about attitudes (see Kruglanski & Stroebe, chap. 8, this volume). Traditional conceptions of attitudes assume that they are enduring psychological constructs that exercise a guiding function on thought and behavior. This perspective is evident in Allport's (1935) classic definition of attitudes and prominent in theories of how attitudes should relate to behavior (Ajzen & Fishbein, chap. 5, this volume). Despite reasonable and intuitive expectations of stability in the attitude domain, this quality has proven elusive, especially in the mass public. In his classic research, Philip Converse (1964, 1974) tracked political opinions expressed by the respondents who were interviewed on a number of occasions at two-year intervals. The lack of stability of expressed opinions was dramatic, prompting Converse to develop a "black and white model" in which a small proportion of respondents give answers in a stable manner and the rest give answers at random. The black and white model fit the data unnervingly well! This pattern, along with other indications of vacuity in mass public attitudes prompted Converse to suggest that what is often measured in attitude surveys are "nonattitudes" that reflect little by means of stable sympathies.

Converse's non-attitude thesis has been criticized on a number of grounds (for reviews see Kinder & Sears, 1985; Krosnick et al., chap. 2, this volume). Yet these skirmishes were but minor precursors to the battle about the stability of attitudes that would ensue. Schuman and Presser (1981) presented the results of an elaborate program of research on response effects, showing variations in answers caused not by substantive variations in the question but by apparently immaterial variations in things like the wording or order of questions. When asked whether the United States should forbid public speeches against democracy, for example, a larger percentage of respondents appear to be in favor of free speech than when asked if the United States should allow such speeches (Krosnick & Schuman, 1988; Rugg, 1941; for a review see Krosnick et al., chap. 2, this volume).

The apparent vacuity and lability of attitudes suggested by these findings was recently further emphasized by Norbert Schwarz and his colleagues (Schwarz & Strack, 1991; Schwarz & Bohner, 2001; for reviews, see Fabrigar et al., chap. 3, this volume; Kruglanski & Stroebe, chap. 8, this volume; Wyer & Albarracín, chap. 7, this volume). Whereas past demonstrations of context effects were usually interpreted as revealing error that one must guard against in attitude measurement, Schwarz and colleagues' claim has been that there is little evidence that attitude expression ever rests on anything other than on-the-spot construction (Schwarz & Strack, 1991; Schwarz & Bohner, 2001).

Schwarz's case is premised on the observation that context effects impact information processing at every phase of the question answering. Question comprehension is impacted by inferences based on the nature of previous questions and other contextual considerations (Sudman, Bradburn, & Schwarz, 1996). Recall and judgment processes are also impacted by contextual influences such as information that is included versus excluded from a consideration set, a process that can variously result in assimilation or contrast effects (Stapel & Schwarz, 1998; Schwarz & Bless, 1992). Context effects are also evident at output, with respondents being sensitive to the necessity to format their answers in a way that is compatible with the response scale (Strack, 1994), as well as to social desirability expectations and self-presentational motives (DeMaio, 1984).

The growing realization that attitude expression and experience can manifest themselves implicitly as well as explicitly has raised the possibility that implicit attitudes represent a more accurate reflection of people's inner feelings than explicit attitudes, thus providing a window that is free of the effects of self-censorship. The prospect that these "true attitudes" may prove to be more enduring and less susceptible to context effects than explicit attitudes has, in fact, been the source of early optimism in meeting the challenge of attitude malleability raised by survey data. As we will see later in this chapter, the optimism went unsatisfied, implicit attitudes also proving susceptible to context effects, including effects of training and of various motives (see the section on the malleability of implicit attitudes below).

In short, the challenge presented by context effects for the conceptualization of attitudes is not insubstantial. Survey researchers have found this challenge particularly tenacious, encountering it repeatedly through the years and worrying about its impact on the validity of the attitudes they measure (Hyman & Sheatsley, 1950; Rugg, 1941; Schuman & Presser, 1981). The challenge has now come to its social psychological home to roost, and it must be met by any comprehensive theory of attitudes.

Understanding Implicit/Explicit Attitudes and Context Effects

The building blocks of theories limit the scope of the phenomena the theories can explain. In this section we discuss the attitudinal primitives posited by popular theories of attitudes. By primitives, we mean theoretical elements that are helpful in explaining observed phenomena, and that do not themselves beg for explanation at approximately the same level as the phenomena they aim to explain. As we will see, the attitudinal primitives of most extant theories of attitudes have difficulty meeting the challenges posed by the variable relationship between implicit and explicit attitudes, and by context effects.

Object-Evaluation Associations as Primitives

Fazio (1986, 1995, 2001) offered what has arguably been the most influential view of the representation of attitudes for the past two decades. According to this view, attitudes consist of summary evaluations that are associated with the attitude object. These object-evaluation associations are presumed to be part of much broader associative networks, but the emphasis is on the object-evaluation association because its strength is assumed to be highly consequential for the way attitudes guide thought and behavior. The central tenet of the theory is that attitudes fall on a continuum defined at one end by representations of attitude objects that are not associated with a summary evaluation, and at the other end by representations of attitude objects that are strongly associated with a summary evaluation. When the object-evaluation is strong, the attitude is accessible, so that exposure to the attitude object will activate the evaluation. The process is thought to be automatic and important to the attitude-behavior relationship because activated evaluations serve to guide thought and behavior in the presence of the attitude object (Fazio, Powell, & Herr, 1983; for a review, see Ajzen & Fishbein, chap. 5, this volume). This phenomenon has been demonstrated in experiments in which the repeated expression of an attitude makes it more accessible and more likely to guide behavior. Related research has shown that accessible attitudes are less pliable and more stable than inaccessible attitudes (Bassili, 1996; Fazio & Williams, 1986), that they guide attention and categorization (Smith, Fazio, & Cejka, 1996; Roskos-Ewoldsen & Fazio, 1992), and that they prime evaluations automatically upon exposure to the attitude object (Fazio et al., 1986; Fazio, Jackson, Dunton, & Williams, 1995).

From the perspective of associative network theories, Fazio's approach is minimalistic, keeping a singular focus on the link between the attitude object node and a corresponding evaluative node. Yet, this theory underlies a most significant development in research in the social cognition of attitudes, namely the demonstration that evaluations can be triggered automatically. Automatic evaluation activation is at the heart of implicit attitudes, and most of the present interest in implicit attitudes can be traced to Fazio's theory and research. Fazio's contribution is all that more important because it provides a framework for understanding implicit attitudes that is lacking from other accounts based on constructs such as beliefs or exemplars, that we discuss below.

Useful as object-evaluation associations have proven to be in the attitudinal domain, they are not good theoretical candidates for attitudinal primitives. Ironically, the problem is not that object-evaluation associations are too specific, because the summarizing of an entire history of experience with an attitude object in a single evaluation represents a major step in abstraction and generalization. Instead, object-evaluation associations fail as attitudinal primitives because they are too static. If attitudes consisted entirely of a summary evaluation, we should expect measures of attitudes to yield the same results across time and situations. Yet, as we have already suggested, an overwhelming amount of research over the past several decades demonstrates that attitudes are highly susceptible to context effects (see Schwarz & Bohner, 2001).

Because the object-evaluation association approach posits that attitudes fall on a continuum of strength, they should not, according to this framework, all be assumed to be stable and resistant to context effects. In fact, intuition is consistent with the object-evaluation association approach in suggesting that strong attitudes should be less susceptible to context effects than weak attitudes (Payne, 1951). One may think, for example, that feelings that are accessible, that are held with certainty, that are considered important to the self, and that are felt with intensity, ought to resist the influence of suggestions contained in an attitudinal query. Under most circumstances, however, this is not the case (Bassili & Krosnick, 2000; Krosnick & Schuman, 1988; for a review see Krosnick et al., chap. 2, this volume).

All in all, therefore, it appears that attitude malleability in the face of context shifts is the norm rather than the exception, and that this malleability is characteristic of strong and weak attitudes alike, as well as of deliberative or explicit attitudes, and of automatically activated or implicit attitudes. Any theory of attitudes, therefore, has to have the flexibility to accommodate malleability just as readily as it accommodates stability.

Beliefs as Primitives

Combinatorial models of attitudes stipulate that attitudes are formed from the combination of beliefs (for reviews, see Kruglanski & Stroebe, chap. 8, this volume; Wyer & Albarracín, chap. 7, this volume). The probabilogical model introduced by McGuire (1960) and extended by Wyer (1970), for example, posits that people hold beliefs that are related logically to a conclusion. If one thinks of the belief in the conclusion as the attitude, then beliefs in various premises relevant to that conclusion can be thought of as the elements from which the attitude is formed.

The most popular approach to the relationship between beliefs and attitudes consists of expectancy-value models that posit that attitudes are the sum of expected values of attributes associated with the object. At the heart of Fishbein and Ajzen's (Ajzen & Fishbein, 1980; Fishbein & Ajzen, 1975; for reviews, see Ajzen & Fishbein, chap. 5, this volume; Wyer & Albarracín, chap. 7, this volume) influential theorizing about the relationship between attitudes and behavior is the notion that attitudes are determined by salient beliefs. The approach is thought to be "reasonable" because people form beliefs about an object by taking note of features, characteristics, outcomes and consequences associated with the object. These attributes are valued more or less positively by the person, and it is the values associated with the beliefs that ultimately yield evaluations of attitude objects.

Although people can hold a large number of beliefs about an attitude object, cognitive capacity limits the number that are salient at any given time (Doll & Ajzen, 1992; Miller, 1956). In this approach, therefore, attitudes are based on a sampling of salient beliefs about the attitude object and an integration of the values associated with these beliefs. In this fashion, we evaluate favorably objects that we believe at the moment to have largely desirable attributes or consequences, and we evaluate unfavorably objects that we believe to have largely undesirable attributes or consequences.

Beliefs are obvious candidates for attitudinal primitives, and in this capacity they offer an important advantage, but they also suffer from an important limitation. The advantage is that attitudes are composed of a sampling of evaluative elements that are salient at any moment in time. Context effects, therefore, are easily accounted for by variations in salience caused by temporary influences on the attributes of the attitude object that are brought to mind in a particular context. The limitation of belief sampling as a means of accounting for context effects is that beliefs themselves are susceptible to these effects. To illustrate, consider the belief assessed by the statement "having a baby within the next two years would make my marriage stronger" (Davidson & Jaccard, 1979). Given what we know about context effects on attitudes, it is very likely that this belief is abundantly susceptible to context effects. Is there any doubt, for example, that there would be a tendency for the answer to this question to be different if the question was preceded by a question about the stresses of child care than if it was preceded by a question about the joys of family outings? And if belief sampling is used to account for the influence of context on attitudes, how are we to account for the effect of context on beliefs?

The notion of sampling makes eminent sense for accounting for context effects. The problem is that the elements that are integrated into an attitude are defined at too high a level and share too many conceptual properties of attitudes to serve as primitives.

Exemplars as Primitives

Exemplar theories stipulate that knowledge representation comprises specific instances of previously encountered exemplars. In its strict form, this approach does not postulate any abstraction from the exemplars, a judgment about a stimulus being made from the match between that stimulus and exemplars that it brings to mind. As applied to attitudes, the exemplar approach stipulates that as attitude objects are encountered, known attributes of similar exemplars that are brought to mind from memory influence judgments about the attitude object (Smith & Zárate, 1992).

Exemplar approaches have enjoyed substantial success in explaining a variety of judgment effects related to attitudes. For example, Lord and Lepper (1999) have proposed an exemplar approach to attitude representation that posits that people sample from exemplars when they answer attitude questions. When the same exemplars are sampled at two separate times or situations, the attitude judgment tends to be stable. This point is illustrated in a study by Sia and colleagues (Sia, Lord, Blessum, Ratcliff, & Lepper, 1997) in which participants were asked to think of social categories and to name the first exemplar that came to mind to represent the category. Participants engaged in the same task about a month later. The results showed that the attitudes of students who named the same exemplar on the two occasions were much more stable than the attitudes of participants who named different exemplars.

The effect of exemplars can generalize to attitude objects with which they are associated. The inclusion/exclusion model proposed by Schwarz and his colleagues provides a particularly interesting example of this phenomenon (Schwarz & Bless, 1992; Stapel & Schwarz, 1998). The model stipulates that information that is included in the mental representation of the attitude object at the time of judgment results in assimilation effects, whereas information that is excluded from the mental representation of the attitude object results in contrast effects. In one study, for example, participants were asked what party Colin Powell recently joined (Stapel & Schwarz, 1998). The question led participants to think of Colin Powell (a highly popular military leader at the time) as being part of the Republican Party, resulting in more positive evaluations of the party than when no question about Colin Powell was asked.

The exemplar approach to attitude research has produced dramatic demonstrations of how the exemplars that are brought to mind by the attitude object influence judgments about the object. The very fact that attitude judgments involve a sampling process among exemplars imparts substantial flexibility to this approach in accommodating context effects. As a theory of attitudes, however, the exemplar approach suffers from an important shortcoming. To explain an attitude in terms of the exemplar that it brings to mind begs the question: How is the attitude toward the exemplar to be explained? Whether or not the processes responsible for evaluation can influence our judgments through exemplar activation, these processes must also operate at earlier stages to impart value and affective qualities to stored exemplars.

Schemas as Primitives

Greenwald and colleagues (Greenwald et al., 2002) recently provided a unified account of implicit social cognition focused on the relationships between the self and other social elements. According to this framework, information about the self is represented in schematic social knowledge structures where it is linked with constructs such as self-esteem, stereotypes, and attitudes. For example, the self concept includes a "ME" node that is linked to roles (e.g., graduate student) and traits (e.g., hard working). Self esteem is the collection of links between self concept nodes and corresponding positive and negative valence, represented as bipolar opposites. Stereotypes are collections of links with group concepts such as young person, graduate student, athlete, male and female, the last two also represented as bipolar opposites.

One interesting feature of this framework is that relations between constructs appear to conform to the principles of Heiderian balance (Heider, 1958) when measured using the IAT, but not when measured explicitly through self-report. Greenwald et al. (2002) attribute this difference to the fact that implicit measures such as the IAT are more sensitive to associations that the respondent is not aware of, and are also less susceptible to demand characteristics (Orne, 1962), evaluation apprehension (Rosenberg, 1969), and role playing (Weber & Cook, 1972), than are self-reports.

Issues of measurement aside, Greenwald et al.'s (2002) unified theory is particularly valuable because it provides a theoretical integration of some of social psychology's most important cognitive (self-concept, stereotypes) and affective (attitude, self-esteem) constructs. In general, however, schemas do not constitute good theoretical primitives because their focus is more on structural relationships among represented constructs than on the building blocks from which the constructs are assembled. In the case of Greenwald et al.'s (2002) unified theory, for example, self-concept, stereotypes, attitudes, self-esteem, and so forth, are high level constructs that bear analysis at a lower level of primitives. In the case of attitudes, such analysis is precisely the focus of the present discussion. Thus, while schematic theories can be very valuable in providing an integrated view of knowledge representation, such theories are poor candidates for primitives.

Multiple Attitudes as Primitives

One perspective on the relation between implicit and explicit attitudes is that old attitudes do not fade away, but linger in an implicit form (Wilson et al., 2000). According to the dual attitudes model, attitude change can result in a new evaluation that is explicit and consciously accessible, while the old evaluation lingers below awareness as an implicit attitude. When dual attitudes exist, the implicit attitude is more accessible and activated automatically, whereas the retrieval of an explicit attitude requires motivation and deliberate processing. Following this logic, the relative influence of implicit and explicit attitudes depends, therefore, upon the processing conditions under which a response is made. Explicit attitudes will influence deliberative responses that may occur if an individual has the opportunity to consider the consequences of his or her actions. Implicit attitudes will influence spontaneous or uncontrollable responses and responses that an individual does not view as an expression of inner feelings, and therefore does not attempt to control.

The dual attitudes model advanced by Wilson et al. (2000) provides a new perspective on attitude malleability by positing that context effects on attitude expression result from the elicitation of distinct attitudes in different circumstances. Pushed farther, the dual attitude model allows for the possibility that multiple implicit and explicit attitudes can coexist, and that a wide variety of attitudes can manifest themselves across contexts. Though theoretically possible, we believe that this perspective provides an unwieldy solution to the challenge posed by the susceptibility of attitudes to context effects. This lack of economy stems from the quasi-infinite potential diversity of contexts in which attitude objects can be encountered and far exceeds the capacity for memory to store autonomous representations of attitudes corresponding to each. There is simply too much diversity in attitude eliciting contexts for attitudinal primitives to be restricted to a set of autonomously represented attitudes, especially since these contexts are often instantiated linguistically and can thus be immensely varied.

Another problem we find with the dual attitude perspective is that it sets up an inherent opposition between implicit and explicit attitudes. Given that attitudes are relegated to the implicit realm by the formation of new explicit attitudes, one has to assume that implicit and explicit attitudes are usually different. In fact, Wilson et al. (2000) often invoke a process of "overriding" to account for the emergence of explicit attitudes in place of implicit ones. Yet, research on the relationship between implicit and explicit attitudes reveals that although the correlation between attitudes measured implicitly and explicitly is sometimes low, there are circumstances under which it is substantial (see section on response modes later in this chapter). It is unlikely, therefore, that the attitudinal primitives that underlie implicit attitudes are distinctly different from the attitudinal primitives that underlie explicit ones.

Connectionist Networks as Attitudinal Primitives

In contrast to models that rely on symbolic constructs such as object-evaluation associations, beliefs, or exemplars to represent the elements responsible for aspects of psychological functioning, connectionist models convey meaning at the level of patterns of activation distributed across units within a network (McClelland & Rumelhart, 1986). To this end, all stored knowledge is encoded in sets of connection weights that regulate the flow of activation among the individual units of a network. Retrieval of this knowledge involves reinstatement of a previously experienced pattern of activation, which can be evoked by a particular set of cues presented to the network as inputs. Within this framework, attitudinal primitives can be conceptualized as sets of units and connection weights that contribute to the emergence of distributed patterns of activation that may be associated with judgments, affect, and previous experiences with an attitude object.

Connectionist models provide explanations for many attitude relevant phenomena such as temporary and chronic accessibility, evaluative priming, and implicit processing of social information (see Smith, 1996 for a review; Masson, 1991; Smith, 1997; Wiles & Humphreys, 1993). Furthermore, by assuming differential involvement of areas of the brain that support feelings and cognition, connectionist systems can be designed to involve several types of elements that serve distinct functional roles. In this manner, affective elements that give rise to different experiential properties but that follow the same operational rules as purely evaluative ones can evoke patterns of activation associated with affective states and can interact with each other to produce the rich mix of human attitudinal and affective experience.

The flexibility and context sensitivity of connectionist networks is particularly relevant to the challenge posed by context effects in the attitude domain. Connectionist networks can be designed to satisfy parallel constraints that enable a network to settle into an overall activation pattern that best accommodates the current input in light of encoded representations of past experiences (Smolensky, 1989). As a consequence, it is unlikely that a given stored item will be evoked in precisely the same form as it was initially encoded. As a norm, encoded representations will be evoked or re-created in an imprecise form, as activation patterns are subject to influence from a person's accumulation of encoded knowledge (Smith, 1996). Furthermore, connectionist models are inherently context sensitive. Any other current sources of activation such as self-presentation concerns, expectancies, or affect, will also influence or constrain the resulting representation (Blair, Ma, & Lenton, 2001; Smith, 1996).

Connectionism can account for automatic processing in a variety of ways. For example, exposure to an attitude object that results in the automatic activation of evaluations and affect associated with the object can be modeled using pattern-completion properties of connectionist networks. Simply put, a partial pattern such as an input pattern representing the attitude object could evoke a much more elaborate pattern that incorporates several components of one's attitude toward the object (Moll, Miikkulainen, & Abbey, 1994). Automatic processing can also be modeled using a multimodule approach in which specific modules receive input patterns from sensory and perceptual modules and operate independent of, or prior to, conscious processing (Smith, 1997). In such a system, an input representing a perceived individual could result in the automatic categorization of this individual as a member of a particular stigmatized group and the automatic activation of attitudes toward this group independent of, or prior to, conscious processing of the individual.

Finally, several proponents of connectionism point out that these models are attractive because they provide a neural-like architecture for cognitive modeling (Bechtal & Abrahamsen, 1991). Generally speaking, connectionist networks are designed with a concern for neural plausibility. Although these models still involve simplifications and idealizations rather than actual matches of properties of biological neurons, their architecture is much more similar to the architecture of the brain than is the case for other extant symbolic models (Smith, 1996, 1997).[1]

The general properties of distributed connectionist networks make them good candidates for explaining implicit and explicit attitudes, which led us to organize our review around such a framework. For the purpose of our discussion, the inspiration afforded by connectionist networks is more important than specific instantiations aimed at modeling attitudes and affect. Accordingly, we will be unrestricted in the presentation of our framework by the type of detail that would normally be part of a workable connectionist model. Our aim is to present a perspective on what have become challenging theoretical issues in the domain of attitudes, and to do so in a comprehensive manner. For this purpose, abstractions from connectionism are likely to be more useful to our understanding of implicit and explicit attitudes than a fully specified but more narrow connectionist model. For example, the molecularity of the elements that make up connectionist networks affords substantial flexibility in the production of implicit and explicit attitudes. Further, context effects can be understood as a recruitment of elements that are constrained by both their internal dynamics (interconnections) and by the potentiation of contextualized eliciting conditions.

POTENTIATED RECRUITMENT: A FRAMEWORK FOR IMPLICIT AND EXPLICIT ATTITUDES

Overview of the Framework

We propose a framework in which attitudes are emergent properties of the activity of microconceptual networks that are potentiated by contextually situated objects, goals, and task demands. We chose the term "potentiation" over the more common term "activation" because "potentiation" places more emphasis on the source in the excitation process, an emphasis that is important in our framework. The evaluative phenomenology of attitudes in this framework derives from the potentiated recruitment of microconcepts that are imbued with evaluative information. Activity in microconceptual networks is highly fluid, its dynamic interplay being captured nicely by observations made by McIntosh (1999) on the basis of findings derived from functional neural imaging:

> Most parts of the brain possess the rudimentary properties necessary for cognition... When several brain regions interact at a larger scale, these rudimentary features will combine to produce a particular cognitive function (Bressler, 1995). Whether or not a region is part of a neurocognitive system depends on the specifics of the processing demands (what is the person doing?) and the interactions with other regions (what is the rest of the brain doing?). Just as an instrument in an orchestra may switch from a lead to a support role in different pieces of music, some regions may play a more prominent role in certain cognitive functions and then play a supporting role in others. (p. 540)

Likewise, we suggest that evaluation is an emergent property of activity in microconceptual networks that are recruited to a greater or lesser extent in different situations, and that imbue experience with distinct tonal quality.

Figure 13.1 depicts a framework consisting of a number of components, some representational, others stemming from conditions that impinge on the individual and others yet reflecting psychological processes. At the heart of the framework is the representational system that we term the *attitudinal cognitorium*. We borrow this label from Milton Rosenberg (1968), who coined it in the context of a discussion of cognitive consistency theories. The attitudinal cognitorium consists of microconcepts that are associated with each other in varying degrees and that have, at any given moment, a certain level of activation. Microconcepts are molecular elements of knowledge that yield meaning when assembled into networks with other microconcepts.

Several other elements of the framework identify sources of potentiation that influence the level of activation of microconcepts in the attitudinal cognitorium. There are four primary sources of such potentiation (Fig. 13.1: eliciting conditions). One source is recent information processing experiences that prime particular microconcepts in memory. Another source is current information about the attitude object. Eliciting conditions, which comprise such things as encounters with the attitude object and queries about it, are particularly powerful sources of potentiation. Because such eliciting conditions are steeped in a context, properties of the context also exert powerful potentiating influences on the attitudinal cognitorium. The third source of potentiation consists of spreading activation between linked concepts. The cueing of one stored concept by another is well known in memory research (Anderson, 1983; Srull, 1983) and we suggest that it is responsible for the influence of general knowledge and of culture on attitudes and affect. Finally, cognitive activity in working memory (see Fig. 13.1) is an important source of potentiation, as well.

The combined effect of potentiation from preexisting activation, eliciting conditions, and prior experiences gives rise to patterns of microconcept activation from which attitudes and affect emerge. The interpretation (Fig. 13.1: Appraisal and construal) of objects and events in the social environment determines our evaluative and emotional reactions to them (Ellsworth, 1991; Scherer, Schorr, & Johnstone, 2001). We posit that microconcepts differ in their capacity to engender evaluations and feelings. The developmental history of microconcepts (whether they stem from learned evaluations or conditioned affect, for example) will produce projections onto parts of the brain that specialize in cognition (e.g., the neocortex) or emotion (e.g., the amygdala). Activation of microconcepts will engender corresponding experiences. We propose that meaning and feelings emerge from these patterns of activation in a configural manner. That is, a best fit is achieved among the informational properties of the microconcepts so as to produce coherent evaluations and feelings. Patterns of activation are highly fluid, microconcepts that are recruited into one pattern in one set of potentiating circumstances having the potential of being recruited, in combination with other microconcepts, in a different pattern in another set of circumstances. This potential for recombination is, in our opinion, essential to explain the malleability of attitudes and affect.

The response side of the potentiated recruitment framework is critical for understanding the relationship between explicit and implicit attitudes. By definition, explicit attitudes involve means of expression in which the respondent is aware of the assessment of the attitude. This type of attitude assessment is familiar and historically ubiquitous. From survey questions about matters of government policy, to friends' queries about how one liked a movie, to private commiserations about one's feelings or moods, the expression of explicit attitudes requires the involvement of controlled processes in working memory. Implicit means of attitude assessment focus the respondent's attention on features of the task that are irrelevant to those that are of interest to the researcher. The indirect nature of such assessment, therefore, minimizes the involvement of controlled processes relevant to the focal task (Krosnick et al., chap. 2, this volume). Speeded means of assessment also minimize the involvement of controlled processes in the attitudinal task. This relative uncontrollability is achieved either by using extremely quick intervals in priming procedures, or by getting the participant to make judgments in a hurry. The potentiated recruitment framework, therefore, posits that the main difference between explicit and implicit attitudes is the involvement of controlled processes at output (curved lines in Fig. 13.1).

An Example

Evaluations are correlates of activity in networks of microconcepts. These microconcepts contain information, and this information carries evaluative and affective implications. Take the example of a woman who played competitive tennis as an adolescent. What evaluations and feelings will the sport engender in her? We propose that tennis will be represented in this woman's mind as a collection of microconcepts having to do with competition, discipline, pressure, fairness, the joys of winning, the disappointments of losing, traveling to tournaments, hanging out with other competitors, interacting with her parents, character building, etc. The list goes on, and is that much more elaborate because every one of these microconcepts is linked

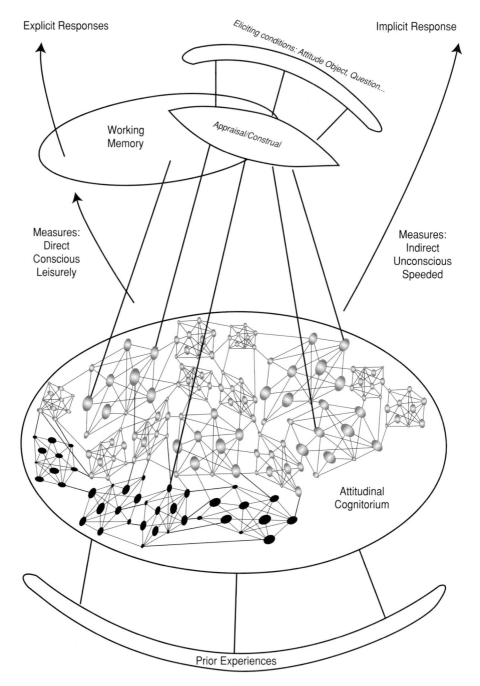

Explicit Responses

Implicit Response

Eliciting conditions: Attitude Object, Question...

Working
Memory

Appraisal/Construal

Measures:
Direct
Conscious
Leisurely

Measures:
Indirect
Unconscious
Speeded

Attitudinal
Cognitorium

Prior Experiences

FIG 13.1.   The Potentiated Recruitment Framework
Note: Potentiating factors are depicted as straight lines to, or within, the attitudinal cognitorium, whereas curved lines indicate output paths. Microconcepts in the cognitorium are depicted in two shades to indicate that some are pertinent to evaluation, whereas others are pertinent to feelings.

to information about specific instances where the concept was manifested. Competition may be linked to specific matches and tournaments, discipline to various training schedules over the years, fairness to disputes over line calls, the joys of winning to the outcome of matches, or interactions with parents, discussions and/or quarrels.

Where does this woman's attitude toward tennis come from? We propose that microconcepts are infused with evaluative and affective information and that attitudes are correlates of activation of microconcepts. Competing, winning, character building as well as many of the specific manifestations of these concepts may, for this woman, be positive and have the potential to engender positive feelings. Pressure, traveling to tournaments and quarreling with parents, along with their specific manifestations, are negative and have the potential to engender negative feelings. Evaluation at any given moment is the upshot of activity in the microconcepts that have been potentiated by eliciting, as well as prior processing conditions, and by cueing across interconnections among linked concepts (see Fig. 13.1).[3]

Implicit and Explicit Attitudes

In the following sections, we review the literature on implicit and explicit attitudes. For the reasons outlined above, a potentiated recruitment framework appears ideal to explain these phenomena. Our review is, accordingly, organized around this framework.

Features of the Context Potentiate Implicit and Explicit Attitudes

Perceptual information about the attitude object constitutes one of the most powerful potentiating forces acting on the attitudinal cognitorium. As Higgins (1996) discussed, knowledge activation depends on the relation between stored knowledge units and stimulus information. "Applicability" plays a central role in the synergy between attended features of the stimulus object and those of stored information: The greater the overlap between them, the greater the potentiating force that the stimulus will exert on stored knowledge (Higgins, 1989, 1996). Likewise, the power of the attitude object to potentiate attitudes plays a crucial role in the potentiated recruitment framework. Because there are preexisting interconnections among microconcepts in the cognitorium, complex patterns of activation usually result from exposure to a subset of features of the attitude object, such patterns allowing for the influence of general knowledge.

Recent research has investigated the influence of specific features of attitude objects on the expression of implicit evaluations. For example, Livingston and Brewer (2002) demonstrated that specific physical features of faces used as primes significantly influenced automatic evaluations as measured by a race evaluative priming procedure. Mitchell, Nosek, and Banaji (2003) have also investigated the role that specific exemplars play in the expression of implicit attitudes. In a study of particular relevance, participants completed two race IATs. One IAT included racial stimuli consisting of admired African American individuals and disliked White individuals. Conversely, the other IAT included racial stimuli consisting of disliked African American individuals and admired White individuals. If IAT effects are dependent exclusively on evaluations associated with category labels (see De Houwer, 2001), the exemplars comprising each stimulus set should not affect the results. However, consistent with the findings of Livingston and Brewer (2002), implicit evaluations were dependent on the exemplars. As expected, a significant preference for Whites was demonstrated when the stimuli consisted of admired White individuals and disliked African American individuals. However, the preference for Whites was reduced when the stimuli consisted of disliked White individuals and admired African American individuals.

Another important aspect of potentiation by the attitude object is that the object is always encountered in a context, and features of the context are just as involved in the potentiation as features of the attitude object. Context effects caused by the position of a question in the midst of others in a questionnaire are well known in survey research. A person's attitude toward free choice in abortion, for example, will appear less permissive if the issue is raised after questions in which abortion is contemplated to reduce a health risk for the fetus or the mother (Schuman & Presser, 1981). For the potentiated recruitment framework, such context effects are the norm rather than the exception, because context is part of the eliciting conditions for attitudes and affect.

Wittenbrink, Judd, and Park (2001, Study 2) provided compelling evidence that the context in which an attitude object is encountered can affect the potentiation of attitude-relevant microconcepts. In an otherwise typical race evaluative priming procedure, the images used as primes not only varied in the race of the depicted individual (White/African American), but also in social context. Independent of race, half the primes consisted of images of individuals in a positive context stereotypic of African Amercans (a church) and half consisted of images of individuals in a negative context stereotypic of African Americans (a dilapidated street corner). The results indicated that facilitation scores were generally related to the context in which the target individuals were presented. Most notably, African American target individuals presented in the positive context resulted in stronger facilitation of positive words compared to negative words. This finding supports a basic tenet of the potentiated recruitment network, namely that variations in the context in which the attitude object appears influences the configuration of information that is activated in the cognitorium.

Implicit Affect and Mere Exposure

Zajonc (1980, 2000) has argued that evaluative tendencies often emerge prior to, and independently of, cognition. This assumption of independence between cognition and affect has its roots in the distinction between "reason" and "passion" (Aristotle, trans. 1991; Le Bon, 1995) and usually posits that people differ a lot more in the former propensity than the latter. As advanced by Zajonc, the notion of affective primacy is supported by phenomena in which evaluation of a stimulus is driven by processes, often subconscious, that do not appear to involve explicit cognitive processes.

The mere exposure effect (Zajonc, 1968) is one source of evidence that Zajonc (2000) has interpreted as being consistent with the notion of affective primacy. In this well-known phenomenon, repeated exposure to a stimulus increases liking for it, a finding that has proven ubiquitous and robust (Bornstein, 1989; Harrison, 1977; Smith & Bond, 1993; for a review, see Clore & Schnall, chap. 11, this volume). In some mere exposure experiments, the stimuli are presented below the threshold of awareness (Kunst-Wilson & Zajonc, 1980) and participants are unable to subsequently recognize the stimuli to which they were exposed. Yet, preferences based on mere exposure still emerge. Such findings have prompted Zajonc to argue not only that affect may stem from a separate system than cognition, but also that this system is faster acting and often takes primacy over cognition (see Damasio, 1994).

Another experimental paradigm that has yielded results consistent with Zajonc's interpretation involves subliminal primes (Murphy & Zajonc, 1993). In the relevant conditions of these experiments targets consisting of Chinese ideographs were preceded by an "affective prime" consisting of a smiling or frowning face. The participants' task on each trial was to indicate how much they liked the ideograph. When the prime was presented subliminally (for 4 ms) judgments shifted in the affective direction of the prime, participants expressing a preference for the ideograph when it was preceded by a smiling face than when it was preceded by a frowning face. When the prime was presented supraliminally (for 1 s), the effect was reversed. This pattern of results led Zajonc and his colleagues to conclude that emotional reactions can occur with minimal stimulation and can influence subsequent cognitions. An important aspect of this logic is that the origin of affect that is elicited outside of conscious awareness is un-specified and can spill over onto the target, whereas the origin of affect that is elicited within the participant's awareness is specified and cannot easily be transferred to other stimuli.

The importance of subliminal stimulus presentation in mere exposure and priming studies for Zajonc's theory is that it presumably engages the affective system without simultaneously engaging the cognitive one. The potentiated recruitment framework does not share in this logic. A basic assumption of the potentiated recruitment framework is that most of cognition and affect is subconscious and that the potentiation of microconcepts relevant to both cognition and affect is also mostly subconscious. The finding that affective priming did not spill over onto the target in the supraliminal priming conditions of the Murphy and Zajonc (1993) studies is easily accommodated by the potentiated recruitment framework: Presumably, the engagement of working memory in these conditions (see Fig. 13.1) opened the door to untold numbers of processes with the potential to interact with the microconcepts potentiated by the subliminal prime (Martin, 1986; Strack, Schwartz, Bless, & Kuebler, 1993; Wegener & Petty, 1997). The overlaying of reflective working memory processes on top of subliminal microconcept potentiation can yield results that are very difficult to attribute to particular causes. For this reason, we do not feel that the dissociation in the effects of subliminal and supraliminal primes reported by Murphy and Zajonc (1993) provides strong evidence for either the primacy or the separateness of an affect system.

Another important element of Zajonc's distinction between cognition and affect is that cognition is always about something whereas unconscious affect is diffuse and can "become attached to any stimulus, even totally unrelated to its origin" (Zajonc, 2000, p. 54). Here again, we find the assumption regarding the delimitation of properties of affect to be overly restrictive. Cognition, like affect, is susceptible to diffuse associative effects. To illustrate, consider a study on spontaneous trait inference (Brown & Bassili, 2002). Under the guise of a study on the effects of distraction on information processing, participants were presented with trait implying information side by side with either faces or inanimate objects. The savings in relearning procedure used in this study revealed that traits were spontaneously associated with purported actors as well as with inanimate objects. The trait of superstition, for example, came to be associated with a banana! The fact that incongruous associations can develop between human characteristics such as superstition and inanimate objects such as bananas underscores the power of associative processes in the cognitorium, and raises doubts about the distinct status of affect or cognition in this regard.

The challenge of explaining the mere exposure and subliminal affective priming effects is easily met by the potentiated recruitment framework. The most common contemporary explanation of mere exposure is that repeated processing of a stimulus increases the fluency with which it is processed, an outcome that is hedonically positive and that is associated with the stimulus (Bornstein, 1989; Winkielman, Schwartz, Fazendeiro, & Reber, 2003). Fluency is a property that is very similar to accessibility, and is explained in terms of increased efficiency in the activation of assemblies of microconcepts in the potentiated recruitment framework. Subliminal affective priming can similarly be explained in terms of the recruitment by the subliminal prime of affectively laden microconcepts. In these two criterial phenomena closely related to implicit attitudes, therefore, processes that are native to potentiated recruitment replace the need for stipulation of distinct processes or systems.

Implicit Attitudes and Classical Conditioning

Classical conditioning phenomena are also relevant to understanding implicit and explicit at-titudes. The relevance of this quintessential learning mechanism for attitude formation has long been recognized (Razran, 1938; Staats & Staats, 1958). There has been an important controversy, however, about whether evaluations and feelings are formed on the basis of temporal associations between the attitude object and affect-producing, unconditioned stimuli. Keisler, Collins, and Miller (1969), for example, have argued that participants' awareness of CS-UCS contingencies and of the purpose of attitude conditioning experiments may underlie all apparent attitude conditioning (see also Page, 1974; Fishbein & Middlestadt, 1995).

Concerns about the artifactual nature of the classical conditioning of attitudes, however, has recently been allayed by experiments that effectively eliminate this bias. One approach has relied on cover stories to reduce the likelihood that participants will notice the contingency between the US and CS. Tracking the extent to which participants are aware of the contingency is important in this approach. Baeyens and his colleagues (Baeyens, Eelen, & Van den Bergh, 1990) measured participant awareness of the CS-UCS contingency in a conditioning procedure that involved the association of neutral pictures with strongly liked or disliked ones. Their results revealed some level of contingency awareness, but this awareness was not related to attitude conditioning.

Other studies have addressed the possible impact of contingency awareness in attitude conditioning by relying on subliminal presentation of the US (De Houwer, Baeyens, & Eelen, 1994; De Houwer, Hendrickx, & Baeyens, 1997; Krosnick, Betz, Jussim, Lynn, & Stephens, 1992; Niedenthal, 1990). Krosnick et al. (1992) presented participants with a series of photographs of a person engaged in mundane activities such as getting into a car. For some participants, each photograph was preceded by the subliminal presentation of either positive-affect-arousing photos (a large Mickey Mouse doll) or by a negative-affect-arousing photo (e.g., a skull). The subliminal affect-arousing photos influenced attitudes toward the target person as well as beliefs about the target person's personality traits. Subliminal effects of this sort have proven somewhat inconsistent and open to alternative interpretations (Eagly & Chaiken, 1993; Olson & Fazio, 2001). A meta-analysis of five relevant experiments did, however, reveal a small reliable effect of subliminal conditioning on attitudes (De Houwer et al., 1997).

Recently, Olson and Fazio (2001) have developed a paradigm for implicit learning that uses supraliminal exposures of the US. The paradigm is based on the observation that rules can be learned in the absence of the ability to articulate them or conscious knowledge of information relevant to them (for a review see Seger, 1994). Participants are presented a series of several hundred images that can appear anywhere on the computer screen, either alone or in pairs. Their task is to hit a response key as quickly as possible when a specified target image appears. Many of the images are of Pokemon cartoon characters, two of which are of particular importance for the procedure because they serve as CS. On a number of trials, one of the Pokemon characters is paired with a positive US consisting of a word (e.g., awesome) or an image (e.g., puppies) and the other character is paired with a negative word (e.g., awful) or image (e.g., cockroach). Despite the use of supraliminal exposures, participants in these experiments do not become aware of covariation between CS-US pairs. Yet, conditioning does occur as indicated by more positive ratings in a surprise evaluation task of the Pokemon associated with the positive items than for the Pokemon associated with negative ones. This attitude conditioning effect is also manifested on an implicit measure (the IAT in Experiment 2).

Classical conditioning is undoubtedly a very important mechanism for the formation of associations in the attitudinal cognitorium. Research on fear conditioning (see LeDoux, 2000) provides a particularly compelling illustration of the power and tractability of attitude-relevant affective conditioning. In a typical animal study of fear conditioning, a rat receives a tone (the CS) followed by an electric shock (the US). Following a few tone-shock pairings (sometimes a single pairing is sufficient), defense responses such as freezing, changes in autonomic and hormonal activity, as well as changes in pain sensitivity and reflex expressions occur following the CS. This form of conditioning is widespread across species, having been observed as low in the phyla as in flies and worms, and as high as in monkeys and humans. Although fear may be distinct among emotions in its urgent mobilization of means of protection for the organism, the lessons learned from this research, along with social psychological research on the conditioning of attitudes, have contributed important insights into processes of attitude formation.

Priming and Implicit Attitudes

Higgins (1996) defined accessibility as the activation potential of available information. Activation potential has a stable component that stems from chronic accessibility of microconcepts (Higgins, King, & Mavin, 1982), and a variable component that stems from temporary influences on the activation of microconcepts (e.g., Higgins, Rholes, & Jones, 1977). It is the latter property of temporary influences on activation potential that explains the ubiquitous effect of priming on the likelihood that microconcepts will be used at a subsequent time.

The impact of priming on accessibility effects and knowledge potentiation has been the subject of substantial attention in the study of social cognition (for reviews see Higgins, 1996; Macrae & Bodenhausen, 2000). Early studies of person perception processes (Higgins et al., 1977; Srull & Wyer, 1979) usually focused on the effect of prior exposure to category information on the subsequent interpretation of ambiguous or vague behavioral information. The finding that prior use of category information renders the subsequent use of the category more likely had such an impact on social cognition research that it was once dubbed "the law of cognitive structure activation" (Sedikides & Skowronski, 1991, p. 169).

The effect of priming is usually assimilative because judgments about the target are swayed in the direction of the prime. Assimilation effects are usually attributed to heightened accessibility of primed knowledge, which raises the likelihood of its being recruited in the interpretation of the stimulus input. This ubiquitous phenomenon is fundamental to the potentiated recruitment framework. Contrast effects, in which the judgment of the stimulus is pushed away from the prime, however, have also been observed. These have been attributed to the activation of information that serves as a standard of comparison for the target (Higgins, 1989) and to motivated inhibitory processes engendered by participants' awareness of their susceptibility to being biased by the prime (Martin, 1986).

The tension between activation and inhibition in knowledge representations continues to be the subject of intense interest and conjecture (Macrae & Bodenhausen, 2000). From the perspective of the potentiated recruitment framework, what is important is that accessibility of information in the attitudinal cognitorium is in a state of flux. Passing experiences have a temporary impact on the potentiation of microconcepts, and therefore, on their recruitability in evaluative processes. The possibility that inhibitory processes can occur in the cognitorium is theoretically significant because it can help account for the malleability of attitude expression.

Awareness in Implicit and Explicit Attitudes

A controversial issue relevant to the conceptualization of implicit attitudes concerns one's level of awareness of these evaluations. In their seminal review of implicit social cognition, Greenwald and Banaji (1995, p. 8) defined implicit attitudes as "introspectively unidentified (or inaccurately identified) traces of past experience that mediate favorable or unfavorable feeling, thought, or action toward social objects." One implication of this definition is that people lack awareness of implicit evaluations. The definition, therefore, has ramifications for the conceptualization of attitudes and their measurement. Researchers who endorse dual-attitude models (Wilson et al., 2000) and those who do not (Fazio & Olson, 2003) agree that people may often have awareness, even if fleetingly, of automatically activated evaluations. Furthermore, Fazio and Olson (2003) have argued that current implicit measurement procedures do little to ensure that participants are unaware of these attitudes. For these reasons, Fazio and Olson concluded that it is more appropriate to view the measure rather than the constructs as "implicit" or "explicit." From this perspective, participants may be unaware that their attitudes are being measured while being aware that they possess these attitudes.

The focus on awareness in our framework is on whether activity in working memory adds new elements to the potentiation of microconcepts, and whether goal directed thought processes promote or block the recruitment of microconcepts underlying attitude expression (see Fig. 13.1). To the extent that conscious symbolic thought becomes involved in processing attitudinal information, there is a potential for attitude experience and expression to be influenced and modified by conscious thought. The issue, in our view, is not one of switching from one system or one process to another, but of the addition of sources of potentiation and control to the recruitment and expression of microconcepts.

Implicit and Explicit Attitudes as Response Modes

There are many important factors that can influence explicit expression of attitudes. The most notable factors are related to motivational concerns such as self-presentation, consistency, and accuracy, and are primarily associated with deliberative processes. It is because implicit attitude expression is thought to preclude the involvement of deliberate processes that some theorists have been tempted to think of attitudes expressed through implicit means as "true" attitudes. According to the potentiated recruitment framework, however, this dichotomy is much too demarcated (see also Fazio & Olson, 2003). Our framework suggests that explicit and implicit attitudes share a vast base from which microconcepts conjoin into attitudes and feelings (see Fig. 13.1). Furthermore, we suggest that any factor that influences the potentiation of micro-concepts, and therefore their recruitability in evaluative processes, can influence explicit and implicit expression of attitudes. By contrast, the notion of "true attitude" implies a singularity and stability that is not consistent with the pervasive context effects that influence implicit attitudes as they do explicit ones.

Malleability of Implicit Attitudes

As we saw earlier, the question of whether implicit attitudes show the same kind of malleability in the face of shifting contexts as explicit attitudes is central to the conceptualization of the implicit/explicit attitude construct. The potentiated recruitment framework predicts variability in implicit attitude expression because several factors can have an impact on the potentiation of microconcepts. In addition to potentiation factors associated with chronic accessibility, implicit attitude expression can reflect the temporary influence of factors associated with recent thoughts or feelings and the construal of an attitude object in a particular goal state or social context. A review of the evidence of malleability in implicit attitude expression highlights the success researchers have had manipulating these types of potentiation factors.

Training and Explicit Instructions to Suppress Stereotypes and Prejudice.
Kawakami and colleagues (Kawakami, Dovidio, Moll, Hermsen, & Russin, 2000) demon-strated that training in stereotype negation can significantly reduce the automatic activation of stereotypes upon category activation. The stereotype negation training exercise involved 6 blocks of 80 trials. In each trial, the image of a target individual was presented followed by the presentation of a trait word. Participants were instructed to press "NO" if the trait presented was associated with the social group to which the target individual belonged and "YES" if the trait was not associated with the social group. Stereotype negation training reduced automatic activation of stereotypic traits associated with skinheads and African Americans. The large number of repetitive trials in this research suggest that racial judgments may be proceduralized

skill-like reactions that run their course upon exposure to relevant stimulus conditions (Anderson, 1983; Smith, 1989).

In a similar vein, Karpinski and Hilton (2001) demonstrated that learning new associations with a target social group can interfere with implicit attitude expression. In particular, participants completed a bogus memory exercise attempting to learn 200 word pairings. In the experimental condition, the targets consisted of an equal number of pairings of the word "youth" with a negative word, and of the word "elderly" with a positive word. Examination of pre- and post-memory-task IAT scores revealed that participants in the experimental condition demonstrated a significant reduction in their preference for the "youth" category. In contrast, the IAT scores of participants who attempted to memorize targets consisting of an equal number of pairings of the word "youth" with a positive word and the word "elderly" with a negative word were unaffected.

In a related line of research, Rudman, Ashmore, and Gary (2001) demonstrated that the implicit expression of racial attitudes can be significantly reduced through extensive diversity training. In two studies, race (African American/White) IATs were conducted prior to and upon completion of a 14-week prejudice and conflict seminar taught by an African American instructor. In both studies, participants who had completed the diversity training exhibited significant improvement in their attitudes toward African Americans. This improvement was not observed for participants who were enrolled in an unrelated course (control group).

The preceding results come from studies in which participants are not explicitly instructed to suppress their stereotypes or prejudice. The malleability of attitudes and stereotypes in response to explicit suppression instructions has also been explored, albeit with less consistent findings. In a study by Lowery, Hardin, and Sinclair (2001, Study 3), participants who were instructed "to be as non-prejudiced as possible" demonstrated significantly less preference for Whites when compared with African Americans as indexed by error rates on a race IAT. By contrast, Blair, Ma, and Lenton (2001, Study 4) found no effect of explicit instructions to suppress the activation of stereotypes toward gender. Prior to completing a GNAT, participants in a suppression condition were told that the subsequent word detection task was a measure of gender stereotyping and they should attempt to suppress stereotypical associations between females and weakness. Yet, the results provided no evidence that these explicit instructions moderated stereotype expression.

Other studies have shown that explicit suppression instructions ultimately lead to hyper-accessibility of the target constructs. For example, Macrae, Bodenhausen, Milne, and Jetten (1994, Study 3) presented participants with the photograph of a skinhead and instructed them to describe a typical day in the life of this individual. Afterwards, participants completed an ostensibly unrelated lexical decision task that included several words associated with the skinhead stereotype. Although participants who had been instructed to suppress stereotypical thoughts during the original writing task created passages containing less stereotype content than controls, they responded more quickly to stereotype-related target words in the subsequent lexical decision task.

In a similar study, Galinsky and Moskowitz (2000, Study 1) presented participants an image of an elderly man sitting near a newspaper stand. Participants were initially instructed to write a narrative essay about a typical day in the life of this individual. Before constructing their essay, participants in a stereotype suppression condition were further instructed to try to avoid the influence of stereotypic preconceptions when thinking about the individual. Participants in a perspective-taking condition were further instructed to adopt the perspective of the individual by trying to see the world through his eyes. Stereotype accessibility was subsequently measured using a lexical decision task. Both stereotype suppressors and perspective-takers wrote less stereotypical essays of the elderly than did participants in a control condition that received no further instructions. However, participants in the stereotype suppression condition demonstrated significantly shorter response times to stereotypic words compared to stereotype irrelevant words. This effect was not observed for participants in the perspective-taking or control conditions. In addition to supporting the notion of suppression rebound effects, therefore, this study also suggests that the expression of implicit attitudes toward stigmatized groups may be moderated by conscious perspective-taking strategies.

From the point of view of contemporary theories of thought suppression it is not surprising that strategies involving explicit instruction have met with limited success in moderating the automatic activation of evaluations and stereotypes. Theories of thought suppression suggest that conscious monitoring of unwanted thoughts can paradoxically result in repetitive priming and thus greater accessibility of the unwanted thoughts. It is only through vigilant conscious inhibitory mechanisms that expression of these thoughts is prevented (Macrae et al., 1994; Wegner & Erber, 1992; Wegner, 1994).

Promotion of Counter Stereotypes.   Researchers have attempted to moderate the automatic activation of negative attitudes toward stigmatized groups by increasing the accessibility of counter stereotypes. Although most people have a mental representation of an admired "exception" or counter exemplar for a given stigmatized social group, this representation is usually not highly accessible. Manipulations that increase the focus of attention on positive exemplars of stigmatized groups have had significant effects on implicit measures of attitudes. For example, Blair, Ma, and Lenton (2001) demonstrated that mental imagery can be a successful strategy for moderating the automatic activation of attitudes. In a series of studies, participants who completed a counter stereotype mental imagery task demonstrated reduced expression of gender-related attitudes compared with participants who completed neutral, stereotypic, or no mental imagery tasks. Specifically, participants in the critical counter stereotype condition were instructed to imagine several aspects of a "strong woman" and then to describe their mental image in a short paragraph. This exercise had significant effects on the automatic activation of information associated with gender as measured by the IAT, the GNAT, and a false memory paradigm.

In a similar vein, Dasgupta and Greenwald (2001, Study 1) demonstrated that implicit expression of attitudes toward stigmatized groups such as African Americans and the elderly can be moderated by repeated exposure to admired group members. Prior to completing a race IAT, participants in the experimental condition were exposed to several admired African American individuals and disliked White individuals under the guise of a general knowledge test. These participants demonstrated significantly less preference for Whites than participants who had been exposed to disliked African Americans and admired Whites or to nonracial exemplars. This effect was observed immediately after the manipulation and 24 hours later. A similar pattern of reduced ageism appeared in a subsequent study using admired elderly individuals and disliked young individuals.

Wittenbrink et al. (2001, Study 1) demonstrated that the relative accessibility of counter stereotype representations can also be manipulated in more subtle ways. In one study, participants watched a short video clip and wrote an essay about the events it depicted. In the counterstereotype condition, the video showed several African American individuals enjoying a harmonious family barbecue. Participants in this condition demonstrated significantly less preference for Whites compared to participants who had viewed a video depicting several African American individuals engaged in negative stereotypic behavior.

Ego-Defensive Motives.   Other lines of research have investigated the influence of ego-defensive motives on the construal of attitude objects. Spencer, Fein, Wolfe, Fong, and Dunn (1998) demonstrated that the motivation to restore one's self image can affect the automatic activation of attitude-relevant associations. Participants were given positive or negative feedback ostensibly based on their performance on a bogus IQ test. Afterwards, the accessibility of stereotypic Asian (Study 1) or African American (Study 3) traits was measured using a word fragment completion task in the presence or absence of a stereotype-relevant cue. Participants whose self-esteem had been threatened by negative feedback demonstrated significant stereotype activation upon exposure to a stereotype-relevant cue. This finding is noteworthy because all participants were kept cognitively busy during the word fragment task and previous research suggested that the automatic activation of stereotypes does not occur when a person's cognitive resources are tasked (see Gilbert & Hixon, 1991).

Sinclair and Kunda (1999, 2000) suggest that the motivation to form a particular impression of an individual can influence the accessibility of the mental representations associated with the social categories to which a target individual belongs. For example, in one study (Sinclair & Kunda, 1999, Study 3) participants received positive or negative feedback, ostensibly from an African American or White medical doctor, about their performance on an interpersonal skills questionnaire. A subsequent lexical decision task was used to measure the accessibility of words associated with doctors and African Americans. The accessibility of words associated with the African American stereotype was greatest for participants who received negative feedback from the African American doctor and lowest for participants who received positive feedback from the African American doctor. In contrast, the accessibility of words associated with doctors was greatest for participants who received positive feedback from the African American doctor and lowest for participants who received negative feedback from the White doctor. In other words, participants who were motivated to decrease the credibility of an African American doctor who had criticized them, inhibited words associated with doctor and activated traits stereotypic of African Americans. In contrast, participants who were motivated to increase the credibility of African American doctor who had praised them activated words associated with doctor and inhibited traits stereotypic of African Americans.

In a related line of research, Richeson and Ambady (2001) demonstrated that the social role that a male anticipates playing with a female coworker affected his implicit expression of gender-related attitudes. Specifically, male participants who anticipated working in a subordinate position to a female on a future task demonstrated a preference for males over females as indexed by a gender IAT. Male participants who anticipated playing the role of partner or a superior, however, demonstrated a preference for females over males. Interestingly, female participants' implicit expression of gender-related attitudes was not affected by their anticipated role relative to a male coworker in a future task.

Social-Regulatory Motives.   Research has also focused on the link between global social motives and implicit measures of attitudes. For example, Lowery, Hardin, and Sinclair (2001, Study 1) demonstrated that basic social-regulatory motives can moderate the expression of implicit attitudes toward stigmatized groups. Starting with the notion of "social tuning," Lowery et al. hypothesized that individuals would be highly motivated to reduce the expression of bias toward African Americans in the presence of an African American individual. Consistent with this prediction, White participants who interacted with an African American experimenter prior to completing a race (African American/White) IAT, revealed less preference for Whites compared to those participants who had interacted with a White experimenter. The moderating effect of social tuning was also found using a subliminal priming procedure (Lowery et al., 2001, Study 4).

Social Desirability and the Relation Between Implicit and Explicit Attitudes

According to the potentiated recruitment framework, microconcepts involved in the explicit and implicit expression of attitudes are recruited from a common base we have called the "attitudinal cognitorium" (see Fig. 13.1). In contrast to models of dual attitudes (Devine, 1989;

Karpinski & Hilton, 2001; Wilson et al., 2000), this framework does not assume unique mental representations for explicit and implicit attitudes. Instead, implicit and explicit attitudes differ in their output paths. In particular, working memory acts as a way station in the expression of explicit attitudes, whereas the expression of implicit attitudes goes through a relatively direct path. Simply put, deliberate processes active in working memory may contribute additional sources of potentiation and control to the recruitment and expression of microconcepts. This theoretical perspective is similar to that presented by Fazio as part of his motivation and opportunity as determinants of behavior model (MODE) (Fazio, 1990; Fazio & Towles-Schwen, 1999; Fazio & Olson, 2003) and by others who have distinguished between automatic and controlled aspects of attitudes (Devine, 1989).

Given the differential involvement of working memory in explicit and implicit attitude processes, the correspondence between measures of explicit and implicit attitudes should decrease as motivational influences are activated by the attitude object and social context. Researchers have long suggested that people are often more prejudiced than they would care to admit (Crosby, Bromley, & Saxe, 1980; Gaertner & Dovidio, 1986; Sigall & Page, 1971). Research examining the link between explicit and implicit measures of prejudice and stereotypes generally supports this view, as the correspondence between explicit and implicit measures of prejudice has usually been found to be low (for reviews see Blair, 2001; Brauer, Wasel, & Niedenthal, 2000; Dovidio, Kawakami, & Beach, 2001; Fazio & Olson, 2003).

The potentiated recruitment framework suggests that involvement of motivational factors operating in working memory may moderate the relationship between implicit and explicit measures of attitudes. If so, the correspondence between these measures should be weaker when the attitude object is of a nature that invokes motivational influences than when it is not. Fazio, Williams, and Sanbonmatsu (1990) offer evidence that is supportive of this view. Their research compared participants' explicit and implicit attitudes toward a variety of attitude objects ranging from the mundane (e.g., snakes, dentists) to more sensitive issues (e.g., pornography, African Americans). When the attitude object was not controversial, the correlation between implicit and explicit attitudes was high (r = .63). When the attitude object was controversial, the correlation was weak (r = −.11). Likewise, Nosek, Banaji, and Greenwald (2002) recently reported the results of thousands of IATs completed on an IAT internet site. As part of the online procedure, respondents completed both explicit and implicit measures of attitudes. High correlations were reported for attitude objects that are not particularly susceptible to social desirability pressures (preference for math vs. arts and for candidates in the 2000 federal election, r = .47 and .52, respectively). By contrast, much smaller correlations were found for more sensitive attitudes such as those relating to race, age, gender, and self-esteem, with correlations ranging from .08 to .24.[4]

Evidence that motivation plays a role in the overt expression of prejudice provides further support to the view that processes that operate in working memory may moderate the relationship between implicit and explicit attitudes. In one of their studies, Fazio et al. (1995, Study 4) included a measure of the motivation to control racial prejudice (see Dunton & Fazio, 1997 for details of an updated scale). The results showed that participants low in motivation to control prejudice exhibited explicit racial bias that was more consistent with their implicit attitudes than respondents high in motivation to control prejudice.

In a similar vein, Plant and Devine (1998) introduced the internal and external motivation to respond without prejudice scales (the IMS and EMS respectively). The IMS measures the extent to which one endorses, and has internalized, nonprejudiced beliefs. Higher scores on the IMS are associated with lower scores on typical explicit measures of prejudice. The EMS measures the extent to which individuals are motivated to conceal prejudiced beliefs in order to avoid negative evaluations resulting from their expression. High EMS scores were found to be associated with higher scores on traditional prejudice measures. Devine, Plant, Amodio,

Harmon-Jones, and Vance (2002) revealed that participants' levels of IMS and EMS moderated dissociation among implicit and explicit measures of prejudice. Most notably, participants with low IMS and high EMS scores exhibited highly prejudiced responses on both implicit and explicit measures. Participants with low EMS scores demonstrated consistency across the implicit and explicit measures, regardless of their IMS score.

Measurement Issues.   As is always the case when examining relationships between different measures, one needs to be mindful of methodological factors that mitigate strong correlations. It has long been known, for example, that when different methods are used to measure a common construct, the observed correlations tend to be smaller than when a common methodology is used (Campbell & Fiske, 1959; Krosnick et al., chap. 2, this volume). Explicit and implicit measures tend to differ in specificity. Explicit measures typically target the attitude object directly (e.g., one's feelings toward an outgroup), whereas implicit measures are typically indirect and relative (e.g., response latencies from trials involving exemplars from an ingroup compared to response latencies from trials involving exemplars from an outgroup). Moreover, as we just saw, explicit measures are susceptible to systematic error resulting from motivational factors. Similarly, whereas implicit measures may not be particularly susceptible to motivational biases, they often rely on response latency and can suffer from measurement error associated with it (Cunningham, Preacher, & Banaji, 2001). For these reasons, the overall correspondence between explicit and implicit measures of attitudes may be reduced because they rely on different methodologies and response formats (see Blair, 2000; Brauer et al., 2000; Dovidio et al., 2001).

In response to such concerns, recent research by Cunningham and his colleagues (Cunningham et al., 2001) has elucidated several measurement issues associated with the use of implicit measures of attitudes. Participants completed three implicit measures and one explicit measure of racial prejudice. Each measure was taken four times at 2-week intervals. Latent variables in structural equation modeling were used to correct for measurement error. These analyses revealed that implicit measures of attitudes demonstrated a high degree of measurement error. As a consequence, Cunningham and colleagues advise caution when attempting to use implicit measures of attitudes as indices of individual differences in the absence of analytic techniques that can separate measurement error from individual differences. However, after correction for measurement error, the implicit measures of attitudes demonstrated consistency across time and measures. Of particular interest, the implicit measures formed a single latent construct that was robustly correlated with a latent construct formed by the explicit measure. These results, therefore, provide strong support for single construct models of attitudes such as the potentiated recruitment framework. Nonetheless, given the two-factor solution, the two types of attitude measures also capture unique sources of variance. This finding is consistent with aspects of the framework, such as working memory, that are posited to be involved differentially in explicit and implicit measures (see Fig. 13.1).

General Discussion

The past decade has seen an explosion of interest in what is variously referred to as implicit or automatic attitudes. Implicit attitudes are important because of their potentially immediate impact on social functioning, and because cognitive methodologies can be used to identify evaluative reactions over which participants have little control. The first important step in this direction was taken by Fazio et al. (1986) who developed a priming methodology to reveal automatic evaluation activation upon exposure to the attitude object. As we have seen, other methodologies like the IAT have also proven successful in revealing preferences in contexts that elicit social desirability pressures (Dovidio et al., 1997; Dovidio et al., 2002;

Wilson et al., 2000). By contrast, explicit measures of attitudes often fail to correlate with behavioral or physiologicals indexes of preference (see Ajzen & Fishbein, chap. 5, this volume). A comprehensive theory of attitudes, therefore, must be able to accommodate characteristics of implicit and explicit attitude expression.

Given the important distinction between implicitly and explicitly measured attitudes, an understanding of the relationship between these constructs is essential. Research has revealed a high level of variability in the concordance between implicit and explicit attitudes (Fazio et al., 1990; Nosek et al., 2002) raising doubts about the independence of these constructs. The potentiated recruitment framework (see Fig. 13.1) accommodates these findings by positing that, with the exception of working memory involvement, the same processes are responsible for the emergence of implicit and explicit attitudes. Several motives can operate in working memory to influence or inhibit explicit attitudinal expression. Social desirability concerns are particularly important in some domains of attitudes, which is consistent with the potentiated recruitment framework's assumption that the relationship between explicit and implicit measures of attitudes drops as these concerns rise.

In addition to the focus on implicit attitudes as important psychological constructs, it has become increasingly apparent over the past several decades that attitudes are not necessarily enduring mental representations that are retrieved from memory at the time of judgment. As we saw earlier, Schwarz and his colleagues (Schwarz & Strack, 1991; Schwarz & Bohner, 2001) have presented a construal model of attitudes that rejects the notion that attitudes stem from stored memory representations. The strong form of this model not only suggests that attitudes are on-the-spot constructions, but by its very emphasis implies that these constructions are based on elements present in the external eliciting context rather than on elements that are represented in memory. According to this strong view, an attitudinal cognitorium plays only a minor role in judgment processes, working memory providing the forum for most attitudinal activity.

To the extent that the construal model does away with representational aspect of attitudes, we believe that it is wrong. The preponderance of evidence used to support the construal model comes from experiments that are more attuned to detecting change than to detecting stability. This is because the evidence is based on procedures in which a property of the context is manipulated to assess its effect on the reported attitude. The statistical focus is on whether the impact of the manipulation is significant, little attention being paid to the magnitude of the component of the response that remains stable across conditions. To conclude that an attitude that changes with shifting contexts is not based on a stable representation is akin to concluding that a flag that changes direction with shifting winds is not attached to a flagpole.

Schwarz's case against memory storage is focused entirely on the idea that attitudes are stored in a unitary fashion in memory, and that they can be retrieved intact regardless of the conditions that elicit them or the conditions that precede the elicitation. While it is true that some theorists like Fazio (1995) posit that attitudes consist of summary evaluations that are associated with the attitude object, there are other ways to conceive of the representation of attitudes that assume substantive representations without assuming that these representations are unitary or fixed. According to the potentiated recruitment framework, attitudes are represented as molecular elements that have the potential of being recruited in various mixes depending on the eliciting context and other potentiating factors. It is the fluidity of this process, rather than the lack of attitudinal representations, that accounts for malleability.

The emphasis in the potentiated recruitment framework is primarily on processes that are common to the emergence of all attitudes. However, the distinction between an attitudinal cognitorium in which the information is represented subsymbolically, and working memory in which symbolic processes predominate, conforms to a dual process view of attitudinal functioning. Dual process approaches are not new to research on attitudes (see Chaiken &

Trope, 1999 for a collection of such models, and Johnson, Maio, & Smith-McLallen, chap. 15, this volume, for a review). This notion is congenial to the potentiated recruitment framework, and has very wide application in psychology. In a recent article, for example, Kahneman (2003) attributed the effect of judgment heuristics to an intuitive system characterized by effortless and automatic associative processes that operate in parallel. The output of this system consists of accessible impressions that dominate judgment unless corrective steps are taken by rule governed reasoning processes that are slow, effortful, and serial in nature.

The interplay between the attitudinal cognitorium and working memory in the potentiated recruitment framework shares many of the elements of Fazio's (1990) MODE model. In both cases, automatic processes are responsible for the emergence of evaluations in consciousness, and effortful deliberative processes only occur when the motivation and cognitive capacity required by working memory are available. There is, however, a fundamental difference between the MODE model and the potentiated recruitment framework. Automatic processes in the MODE model involve the activation of attitude objects in which features are preassembled into coherent symbolic representations to which summary evaluations are attached. For reasons we presented early in this chapter, the potentiated recruitment framework dispenses with this view in favor of a representational system that is subsymbolic. That is, features of attitude objects (what we have called microconcepts) are assembled as they are recruited by potentiating influences that operate in a particular context. We contend that only such a subsymbolic system, where evaluations are attached to microconceptual features, can account for the fluidity of attitudes in changing contexts.

The MODE model accounts for attitude malleability by distinguishing between accessible attitudes that are activated automatically, and less accessible attitudes that are put together deliberately. The implication of this two-process approach is that deliberative processes are more susceptible to context effects than automatic ones. The finding that implicit attitudes are very susceptible to context effects poses a challenge to this explanation of attitude malleability. By contrast, the potentiated recruitment framework accommodates widespread malleability by positing that the sources of potentiation for an attitude are highly variable across contexts. Because implicit attitudes are as much the product of potentiating factors as explicit ones, there is no surprise in the fact that they are also as susceptible to context effects.

We began by noting that advancement in attitude research currently faces two particular challenges. The first challenge is in understanding the relationship between explicit and implicit attitudes. The correlation between explicitly and implicitly measured attitudes having varied across studies, it becomes important to reconcile these constructs in a coherent theoretical framework. The second challenge comes from the pervasive susceptibility of attitude experience and expression to context effects. Although it has been tempting to think of these context effects as applying only to weakly held attitudes (see Fabrigar, MacDonald, & Wegener, chap. 3, this volume), and to be driven by conscious influences on response processes, it has become apparent that context effects run deep and that they affect implicit as well as explicit attitude experience and expression. Given this malleability, it appears that attitudes emerge from a constructive process rather than from the retrieval of precomputed stored evaluations. Research on implicit and explicit attitudes has gone a long way in illuminating this process.

ACKNOWLEDGMENTS

The writing of this chapter was supported by Social Sciences and Humanities Research Council of Canada grant 410-2001-0554.

ENDNOTES

[1]Connectionism is not new to social psychology. In the title of his influential paper on the approach, Smith (1996) raises the question "What do connectionism and social psychology offer each other?" The outlook in the answer he provides is optimistic, with phenomena like accessibility, social interaction, and affect and motivation, standing to gain from the synergy between the two approaches. In a similar paper that explores the import of connectionism for social psychology, Read, Vanman, and Miller (1997) argued that connectionist modeling "has great importance for understanding issues of both historical and current concern for social psychologists" (p. 26). They went on to point out similarities between connectionist models and fundamental Gestalt principles as manifested in impression formation, cognitive consistency and goal-directed behavior. It is not without fanfare, therefore, that the connectionist revolution that has unfolded in cognitive psychology has been greeted in some social psychological circles.

Despite the attention given to the promise of connectionism in social psychology, a relatively small number of models that focus specifically on social psychological phenomena have been produced. A few examples of these models will help situate elements of the approach that hold substantial promise for theorizing about attitudes. First, we need to highlight an important distinction between types of connectionist models. The distinction is between "localist" or "symbolic" models, and "distributed" or "subsymbolic" models. In localist models, each processing unit, or node, represents an entire concept, whereas in distributed models nodes represent features, or subsymbolic microconcepts, with higher order concepts emerging from activity in networks of nodes. Although this distinction may appear minor and inconsequential in the connectionist bag of tools, it is crucial to the challenge paused by context effects to attitude theories, subsymbolic models offering a lot more flexibility for dealing with context effects than localist models.

Several localist connectionist approaches have been formulated to model social psychological phenomena. In one such model, Read and Marcus-Newhall (1993) focus on the evaluation of explanations by postulating connection weights between explanations such as "Cheryl is pregnant" and the fact that "she has an upset stomach," "has been gaining weight" and "is feeling tired." The constraints imposed by these connection weights in the spreading of activation among the nodes eventually lead the network to settle in a state where the broadest, most parsimonious, unique, and best developed explanation has a higher state of activation than competing explanations. In a similar parallel constraint satisfaction model, Kunda and Thagard (1996) account for the joint effect of stereotype and individuating information in impression formation by postulating that upon observing, for example, that an African American (or White) person pushed someone, activation spreads between conceptual representations of these observations and other concepts such as "aggressive," "violent push," and "jovial shove." Connection weights between these concepts cause it to settle with activation levels that conform to empirical findings regarding how stereotypes, behaviors, and traits affect each other's meanings, and how multiple stereotypes have an impact on impressions.

The preceding examples illustrate localist models where nodes contain entire concepts. Localist models that are more directly relevant to attitudes are also possible. For example, Read and Miller (1994) present a parallel constraint satisfaction model of the Festinger and Carlsmith (1959) cognitive dissonance experiment where the nodes contain concepts such as "I do not lie without a good reason," "I was paid $20," "the task was boring," "the task was interesting," etc. Beliefs, of course, are excellent candidates for concepts in localist connectionist networks. We have already seen, however, that beliefs are themselves susceptible to context effects. The assessment that a task is boring, for example, depends on what task preceded it, alternative available tasks, the thoughts one had while engaging in the task, etc. This is why we do not feel that localist networks built on entire symbolic concepts are ideally suited to meeting the challenge posed by the highly fluid nature of attitudinal experience.

By contrast to localist networks in which each unit represents an entire concept, subsymbolic networks posit that semantically meaningful representations consist of patterns of activation across a number of processing units (McClelland & Rumelhart, 1986). In a recent model of stereotyping processes, for example, each stimulus consisted of 40 activation values that were applied to 40 units in the network (Queller & Smith, 2002). Learning rules controlled changes in weights over a large number of training inputs. The stereotypicality of the output of the network was tested by comparing the activation values on the units with missing inputs with those on stereotypic activation values. In another recent subsymbolic model, Eiser, Fazio, Stafford, and Prescott (2003) trained a network consisting of three layers of processing units to discriminate "good" from "bad" inputs. Outputs from this network were characterized by "landscapes" of activation patterns, successful learning being revealed when the topology of these landscapes mimicked that of "good" and "bad" inputs.

Subsymbolic distributed networks are, by necessity, abstract. That is, mental representations and processes in these networks do not map in a simple linear manner onto people's responses or onto the symbolic constructs that theorists often find useful in accounting for thought, feelings, and behavior. This lack of correspondence may have been responsible for the slow adoption of such models in social psychology, and to Carlston and Smith's (1996) observation that "In coming years, social psychologists' theoretical thinking will no doubt mature beyond the simple tendency to assume a one-to-one correspondence between function (e.g., semantic priming) and structure (an associative link between two concepts)" (p. 198).

Matters of theoretical maturity aside, we believe that conceiving of attitudes as emergent properties of activity in networks of subsymbolic elements holds substantial promise in meeting the two challenges that we outlined at the outset, namely the challenge of context effects in attitude responses and experience, and the challenge of understanding the relationship between implicit and explicit attitudes.

[2] As we saw in our earlier discussion of attitudinal primitives, distributed knowledge representations offer a number of advantages over localized ones. One property that is of particular importance in the domain of attitudes is flexibility in accounting for context effects.

[3] The microconcepts used in the present example are, by necessity, described at a fairly abstract level. We suggest, however, that in the same way that a global attitude toward tennis is made up of microconcepts like the ones described here, so too are these microconcepts made up of finer elements. Quarreling, for example, may be made up of microconcepts such as disagreement, hostility, dominance, frustrations, etc. For communicative purposes, it is more fruitful to focus on microconcepts at a level of analysis that matches the evaluations under consideration than to aim for the finest level of analysis possible.

[4] Some studies, however, have failed to find correspondence between explicit and implicit attitudes toward mundane objects (Karpinski & Hilton, 2001).

REFERENCES

Ajzen, I., & Fishbein, M. (1980). *Understanding attitudes and predicting social behavior.* Englewood Cliffs, NJ: Prentice-Hall.

Allport, G. W. (1935). Attitudes. In C. Murchinson (Ed.), *A handbook of social psychology* (pp. 798–844). Worcester, MA: Clark University Press.

Anderson, J. R. (1983). A spreading activation theory of memory. *Journal of Verbal Learning & Verbal Behavior, 22,* 261–295.

Aristotle. (1991). *The art of rhetoric.* H. C. Lawson-Tancred, Trans. London: Penguin.

Baeyens, F., Eelen, P., & Van den Bergh, O. (1990). Contingency awareness in evaluative conditioning: A case for unaware affective-evaluative learning. *Cognition & Emotion. Special Issue: Evaluative Conditioning, 4,* 3–18.

Bargh, J., Chaiken, S., Raymond, P., & Hymes, C. (1996). The automatic evaluation effect: Unconditional automatic attitude activation with a pronunciation task. *Journal of Experimental Social Psychology, 32,* 104–128.

Bassili, J. N. (1996). Meta-judgmental versus operative indexes of psychological attributes: The case of measures of attitude strength. *Journal of Personality & Social Psychology, 71,* 637–653.

Bassili, J. N. (2000). Cognitive Indices of Social Information Processing. In A. Tesser & Norbert Schwarz (Eds.), *Blackwell handbook of social psychology: Intraindividual processes* (pp. 68–88). Malden, MA: Blackwell.

Bassili, J. N., & Krosnick, J. A. (2000). Do strength-related attitude properties determine susceptibility to response effects? New evidence from response latency, attitude extremity, and aggregate indices. *Political Psychology. Special Issue: Response latency measurement in telephone surveys, 21,* 107–132.

Bechtal, W., & Abrahamsen, A. (1991). *Connectionism and the mind: An introduction to parallel processing in networks.* Cambridge, MA: Basil Blackwell.

Bessenoff, G. R., & Sherman, J. W. (2000). Automatic and controlled components of prejudice toward fat people: Evaluation versus stereotype activation. *Social Cognition, 18,* 329–353.

Blair, I. (2001). Implicit stereotypes and prejudice. In G. B. Moskowitz (Ed.), *Cognitive social psychology: The Princeton symposium on the legacy and future of social cognition* (pp. 359–374). Mahwah, NJ: Lawrence Erlbaum Associates.

Blair, I. (2002). The malleability of automatic stereotypes and prejudice. *Personality and Social Psychology Review, 6,* 242–261.

Blair, I., Ma, J., & Lenton, A. (2001). Imagining stereotypes away: the moderation of automatic stereotypes through mental imagery. *Journal of Personality and Social Psychology, 81,* 828–841.

Bornstein, R. F. (1989). Exposure and affect: Overview and meta-analysis of research, 1968–1987. *Psychological Bulletin, 106,* 265–289.

Brauer, M., Wasel, W., & Niedenthal, P. (2000). Implicit and explicit components of prejudice. *Review of General Psychology, 4,* 79–101.

Bressler, S. L. (1995). Large-scale cortical networks and cognition. *Brain Research Reviews, 20,* 288–304.

Brown, R. D., & Bassili, J. N. (2002). Spontaneous trait associations and the case of the superstitious banana. *Journal of Experimental Social Psychology, 38,* 87–92.

Campbell, D., & Fiske, D. (1959). Convergent and discriminant validation by the multitrait-multimethod matrix. *Psychological Bulletin, 56,* 81–105.

Carlston, D. E., & Smith, E. R. (1996). Principles of mental representation. In E. T. Higgins & A. W. Kruglanski (Eds.), *Social psychology: Handbook of basic principles* (pp. 184–210). New York: Guilford.

Chaiken, S., & Trope, Y. (1999). *Dual-Process Theories in Social Psychology.* New York: Guilford.

Converse, P. E. (1964). The nature of beliefs systems in mass publics. In D. Apter (Ed.), *Ideology and discontent* (pp. 206–261). New York: The Free Press.

Converse, P. E. (1974). Comment: The status of nonattitudes. *American Political Science Review, 68*, 650–660.

Crosby, F., Bromley, S., & Saxe, L. (1980). Recent unobtrusive studies of Black and White discrimination and prejudice: A literature review. *Psychological Bulletin, 87*, 546–563.

Cunningham, W. A., Preacher, K. J., & Banaji, M. R. (2001). Implicit attitude measures: consistency, stability, and convergent validity. *Psychological Science, 12*, 163–170.

Damasio, A. R. (1994). *Descartes' error: Emotion, reason, and the human brain.* New York: Putnam.

Dasgupta, N., & Greenwald, A. G. (2001). On the malleability of automatic attitudes: Combating automatic prejudice with images of admired and disliked individuals. *Journal of Personality and Social Psychology, 81*, 800–814.

Davidson, A. R., & Jaccard, J. J. (1979). Variables that moderate the attitude-behavior relation: Results of a longitudinal survey. *Journal of Personality and Social Psychology, 37*, 1364–1376.

De Houwer, J. (2001). A structural and process analysis of the Implicit Association Test. *Journal of Experimental Social Psychology, 37*, 443–451.

De Houwer, J., Baeyens, F., & Eelen, P. (1994). Verbal evaluative conditioning with undetected US presentations. *Behaviour Research and Therapy, 32*, 629–633.

De Houwer, J., & Eelen, P. (1998). An affective variant of the Simon paradigm. *Cognition and Emotion, 12*, 45–61.

De Houwer, J., Hendrickx, H., & Baeyens, F. (1997). Evaluative learning with "subliminally" presented stimuli. *Consciousness and Cognition, 6*, 87–107.

DeMaio, T. J. (1984). Social desirability and survey measurement: A review. In C. F. Turner & E. Martin (Eds.), *Surveying Subjective Phenomena* (Vol. 2, pp. 257–281). New York: Russell Sage Foundation.

Devine, P. (1989). Stereotypes and prejudice: Their automatic and controlled components. *Journal of Personality and Social Psychology, 56*, 5–18.

Devine, P. G., Plant, E. A., Amodio, D. M., Harmon-Jones, E., & Vance, S. L. (2002). The regulation of explicit and implicit race bias: The role of motivations to respond without prejudice. *Journal of Personality and Social Psychology, 82*, 835–848.

Doll, J., & Ajzen, I. (1992). Accessibility and stability of predictors in the theory of planned behavior. *Journal of Personality and Social Psychology, 63*, 754–765.

Dovidio, J. F., Kawakami, K., & Beach, K. R. (2001). Implicit and explicit attitudes: Examination of the relationship between measures of intergroup bias. In R. Brown & S. L. Gaertner (Eds.), *Blackwell handbook of social psychology: Intergroup processes.* Malden, MA: Blackwell.

Dovidio. J. F., Kawakami, K., & Gaertner, S. L. (2002). Implicit and explicit prejudice and interracial interactions. *Journal of Personality and Social Psychology, 82*, 62–68.

Dovidio, J. F., Kawakami, K., Johnson, C., Johnson, B., & Howard, A. (1997). On the nature of prejudice: automatic and controlled processes. *Journal of Experimental Social Psychology, 33*, 510–540.

Dunton, B. C., & Fazio, R. H. (1997). An individual difference measure of motivation to control prejudiced reactions. *Personality and Social Psychology Bulletin, 23*, 316–326.

Eagly, A. H., & Chaiken, S. (1993). *The Psychology of Attitudes.* New York: Harcourt Brace Jovanovich.

Eiser, J. R., Fazio, R. H., Stafford, T., & Prescott, T. J. (2003). Connectionist simulation of attitude learning: Asymmetries in the acquisition of positive and negative evaluations. *Personality and Social Psychology Bulletin, 10*, 1221–1235.

Ellsworth, P. C. (1991). Some implications of cognitive appraisal theories of emotion. In K. Strongman (Ed.), *International review of studies on emotion* (pp. 143–161). New York: Wiley.

Fazio, R. H. (1986). How do attitudes guide behavior? In R. M. Sorrentino & T. E. Higgins (Eds.), *Handbook of motivation and cognition: Foundations of social behavior* (pp. 204–243). New York: Guilford.

Fazio, R. H. (1990). Multiple processes by which attitudes guide behavior: The MODE model as an integrated framework. In M. P. Zanna (Ed.), *Advances in experimental social psychology* (Vol. 23, pp. 75–109). New York: Academic Press.

Fazio, R. H. (1995). Attitudes as object-evaluation associations: Determinants, consequences, and correlates of attitude accessibility. In R. E. Petty & J. A. Krosnick (Eds.), *Attitude strength: Antecedents and consequences. Ohio State University series on attitudes and persuasion* (Vol. 4, pp. 247–282). Hillsdale, NJ: Lawrence Erlbaum Associates.

Fazio, R. H. (2001). On the automatic activation of associated evaluations: An overview. *Cognition & Emotion. Special Issue: Automatic Affective Processing, 15*, 115–141.

Fazio, R. H., Jackson, J. R., Dunton, B. C., & Williams, C. J. (1995). Variability in automatic activation as an unobtrusive measure of racial attitudes: A bona fide pipeline? *Journal of Personality and Social Psychology, 69*, 1013–1027.

Fazio, R. H., & Olson, M. A. (2003). Implicit measures in social cognition research: Their meaning and uses. *Annual Review of Psychology, 54*, 297–327.

Fazio, R. H., Powell, M. C., & Herr, P. M. (1983). Toward a process model of the attitude-behavior relation: Accessing one's attitude upon mere observation of the attitude object. *Journal of Personality and Social Psychology, 44,* 723–735.

Fazio, R. H., Sanbonmatsu, D. M., Powell, M. C., & Kardes, F. R. (1986). On the automatic activation of attitudes. *Journal of Personality and Social Psychology, 50,* 229–238.

Fazio, R. H., & Towles-Schwen, T. (1999). The MODE model of attitude-behavior processes. In S. Chaiken & Y. Trope (Eds.), *Dual-process theories in social psychology* (pp. 97–116). New York: Guilford.

Fazio, R. H., & Williams, C. J. (1986). Attitude accessibility as a moderator of the attitude-perception and attitude-behavior relations: An investigation of the 1984 presidential election. *Journal of Personality and Social Psychology, 51,* 505–514.

Fazio, R. H., Williams, C. J., & Sanbonmatsu, D. M. (1990). *Toward an unobtrusive measure of attitude.* Unpublished manuscript, Indiana University, Bloomington, IN.

Festinger, L., & Carlsmith, J. M. (1959). Cognitive consequences of forced compliance. *Journal of Abnormal and Social Psychology, 58,* 203–210.

Fishbein, M., & Ajzen, I. (1975). *Beliefs, attitude, intention, and behavior: An introduction to theory and research.* Reading, MA: Addison-Wesley.

Fishbein, M., & Middlestadt, S. (1995). Noncognitive effects on attitude formation and change: Fact or artifact? *Journal of Consumer Psychology, 4,* 1469–1480.

Gaertner, S. L., & Dovidio, J. F. (1986). The aversive form of racism. In J. F. Dovidio & S. L. Gaertner (Eds.), *Prejudice, discrimination, and racism* (pp. 61–89). San Diego, CA: Academic Press.

Galinsky, A. D., & Moskowitz, G. D. (2000). Perspective-taking: Decreasing stereotype accessibility and in-group favortism. *Journal of Personality and Social Psychology, 78,* 708–724.

Gilbert, D., & Hixon, G. (1991). The trouble of thinking: Activation and application of stereotypic beliefs. *Journal of Personality and Social Psychology, 60,* 509–517.

Greenwald, A. G., & Banaji, M. R. (1995). Implicit social cognition: Attitudes, self-esteem, and stereotypes. *Psychological Review, 102,* 4–27.

Greenwald, A. G., Banaji, R. M., Rudman, L. A., Farnham, S. D., Nosek, B. A., & Mellot, D. S. (2002). A unified theory of implicit attitudes, stereotypes, self-esteem and self-concept. *Psychological Review, 109,* 3–25.

Greenwald, A. G., McGhee, D. E., & Schwartz, L. K. (1998). Measuring individual differences in implicit cognition: The implicit association test. *Journal of Personality and Social Psychology, 74,* 1464–1480.

Harrison, A. A. (1977). Mere exposure. In L. Berkowitz (Ed.), *Advances in experimental social psychology* (Vol. 10, pp. 39–83). San Diego, CA: Academic Press.

Heider, F. (1958). *The psychology of interpersonal relations.* Oxford, UK: Wiley.

Higgins, E. T. (1989). Knowledge accessibility and activation: Subjectivity and suffering from unconscious sources. In J. S. Uleman & J. A. Bargh (Eds.), *Unintended thought: The limits of awareness, intention and control* (pp. 75–123). New York: Guilford.

Higgins, E. T. (1996). Knowledge activation: Accessibility, applicability, and salience. In E. T. Higgins & A. W. Kruglanski (Eds.), *Social psychology: Handbook of basic principles* (pp. 133–168). New York: Guilford.

Higgins, E. T., King, G. A., & Mavin, G. H. (1982). Individual construct accessibility and subjective impressions and recall. *Journal of Personality and Social Psychology, 43,* 35–47.

Higgins, E. T., Rholes, W. S., & Jones, C. R. (1977). Category accessibility and impression formation. *Journal of Experimental Social Psychology, 13,* 141–154.

Hyman, H. H., & Sheatsley, P. B. (1950). The current status of American public opinion. In J. C. Payne (Ed.), *The teaching of contemporary affairs* (pp. 11–34). New York: National Education Association.

Kahneman, D. (2003). A perspective on judgment and choice. *American Psychologist, 58,* 697–720.

Karpinski, A., & Hilton, J. L. (2001). Attitudes and the implicit association test. *Journal of Personality and Social Psychology, 81,* 774–788.

Kawakami, K., Dovidio, J. F., Moll, J., Hermsen, S., & Russin, A. (2000). Just say no (to stereotyping): Effects of training in the negation of stereotypic associations on stereotype activation. *Journal of Personality and Social Psychology, 78,* 871–888.

Keisler, C., Collins, B. E., & Miller, N. (1969). *Attitude change.* New York: Wiley.

Kinder, D. R., & Sears, D. O. (1985). Public opinion and political action. In G. Lindzey & E. Aronson (Eds.), *The handbook of social psychology* (3rd ed., Vol. 2, pp. 659–741). New York: Random House.

Koole, S. L., Dijksterhuis, A., & van Knippenberg, A. (2001). What's in a name: Implicit self-esteem and the automatic self. *Journal of Personality and Social Psychology, 80,* 669–685.

Krosnick, J. A., Betz, A. L., Jussim, L. J., Lynn, A. R., & Stephens, L. (1992). Subliminal conditioning of attitudes. *Personality and Social Psychology Bulletin, 18,* 152–162.

Krosnick, J. A., & Schuman, H. (1988). Attitude intensity, importance, and certainty and susceptibility to response effects. *Journal of Personality and Social Psychology, 54,* 940–952.

Kunda, Z., & Thagard, P. (1996). Forming impressions from stereotypes, traits, and behaviors: A parallel-constraint-satisfaction theory. *Psychological Review, 103*, 284–308.

Kunst-Wilson, W. R., & Zajonc, R. B. (1980). Affective discrimination of stimuli that cannot be recognized. *Science, 207*, 557–558.

Le Bon, G. (1995). *The crowd.* Somerset, NJ: Transaction Publishers.

LeDoux, J. E. (2000). Emotion circuits in the brain. *Annual Review of Neuroscience, 23*, 155–184.

Livingston, R. W., & Brewer, M. B. (2002). What are we really priming? Cue-based versus category-based processing of facial stimuli. *Journal of Personality and Social Psychology, 82*, 5–18.

Lord, C. G., & Lepper, M. R. (1999). Attitude Representation Theory. In M. P. Zanna (Ed.), *Advances in experimental social psychology* (Vol. 31, pp. 265–343). San Diego, CA: Academic Press.

Lowery, B. S., Hardin, C. D., & Sinclair, S. (2001). Social influence effects on automatic racial prejudice. *Journal of Personality and Social Psychology, 81*, 842–855.

Lowery, B. S., & Sinclair, S. (2001). Social influence effects on automatic racial prejudice. *Journal of Personality and Social Psychology, 81*, 842–855.

Macrae, C. N., & Bodenhausen, G. V. (2000). Social cognition: Thinking categorically about others. *Annual Review of Psychology, 51*, 93–120.

Macrae, C. N., Bodenhausen, G. V., Milne, A. B., & Jetten, J. (1994). Out of mind but back in sight: Stereotypes on the rebound. *Journal of Personality and Social Psychology, 67*, 808–817.

Marsh, K. L., Johnson, B. T., & Scott-Sheldon, L. A. J. (2001). Heart versus reason in condom use: Implicit versus explicit attitudinal predictors of sexual behavior. *Zeitschrift fur Experimentelle Psychologie, 48*, 161–175.

Martin, L. L. (1986). Set/reset: Use and disuse of concepts in impression formation. *Journal of Personality and Social Psychology, 51*, 493–504.

Masson, M. E. J. (1991). A distributed memory model of context effects in word identification. In D. Besner & G. W. Humphreys (Eds.), *Basic processes in reading: Visual word recognition* (pp. 233–263). Hillsdale, NJ: Lawrence Erlbaum Associates.

McClelland, J. L., & Rumelhart, D. E. (1986). A distributed model of human learning and memory. In J. L. McClelland & D. E. Rumelhart (Eds.), *Parallel distributed processing: explorations in the microstructure of cognition* (Vol. 2, pp. 170–215). Cambridge, MA: MIT Press.

McConnell, A. R., & Liebold, J. M. (2001). Relations between the implicit association test, explicit racial attitudes, and discriminatory behavior. *Journal of Experimental Social Psychology, 37*, 435–42.

McGuire, W. J. (1960). A syllogistic analysis of cognitive relationships. In C. I. Hovland & M. J. Rosenberg (Eds.), *Attitude organization and change: An analysis of consistency among attitude components* (pp. 65–111). New Haven, CT: Yale University Press.

McIntosh, A. R. (1999). Mapping cognition to the brain through neural interactions. *Memory, 7*, 523–548.

Miller, G. A. (1956). The magical number seven, plus or minus two: some limits on our capacity for processing information. *Psychological Review, 63*, 81–97.

Mitchell, J. P., Nosek, B. A., & Banaji, M. R. (2003). Contextual variations in implicit evaluation. *Journal of Experimental Psychology: General, 132*, 455–469.

Moll, M., Miikkulainen, R., & Abbey, J. (1994). The capacity of convergence-zone episodic memory. In *Proceedings of the twelfth national conference on artificial intelligence* (Vol. 1, pp. 68–73). Menlo Park, CA: American Association for Artificial Intelligence.

Murphy, S. T., & Zajonc, R. B. (1993). Affect, cognition, and awareness: Affective priming with optimal and suboptimal stimulus exposures. *Journal of Personality and Social Psychology, 64*, 723–739.

Niedenthal, P. M. (1990). Implicit perception of affective information. *Journal of Experimental Social Psychology, 26*, 505–527.

Nosek, B. A., & Banaji, M. R. (2001). The go/no-go association task. *Social Cognition, 19*, 625–666.

Nosek, B. A., Banaji, M. R., & Greenwald, A. G. (2002). Harvesting implicit group attitudes and beliefs from a demonstration website. *Group Dynamics, 6*, 101–115.

Olson, M. A., & Fazio, R. H. (2001). Implicit attitude formation through classical conditioning. *Psychological Science, 12*, 413–417.

Orne, M. T. (1962). On the social psychology of the psychological experiment: With particular reference to demand characteristics and their implications. *American Psychologist, 17*, 776–783.

Page, M. M. (1974). Demand characteristics and the classical conditioning of attitudes experiment. *Journal of Personality and Social Psychology, 30*, 468–476.

Payne, S. L. (1951). *The art of asking questions.* Princeton, NJ: Princeton University Press.

Plant, E. A., & Devine, P. G. (1998). Internal and external motivation to respond without prejudice. *Journal of Personality and Social Psychology, 75*, 811–832.

Queller, S., & Smith, E. R. (2002). Subtyping versus bookkeeping in stereotype learning and change: Connectionist simulations and empirical findings. *Journal of Personality and Social Psychology, 82*, 300–313.

Razran, G. H. S. (1938). Conditioning away social bias by the luncheon technique. *Psychological Bulletin, 37*, 481.

Read, S. J., & Marcus-Newhall, A. (1993). Explanatory coherence in social explanations: A parallel distributed processing account. *Journal of Personality and Social Psychology, 65*, 429–447.

Read, S. J., & Miller, L. C. (1994). Dissonance and balance in belief systems: The promise of parallel constraint satisfaction processes and connectionist modeling approaches. In R. C. Schank & E. Langer (Eds.), *Beliefs, reasoning, and decision making: Psycho-logic in honor of Bob Abelson* (pp. 209–235). Hillsdale, NJ: Lawrence Erlbaum Associates.

Read, S. J., Vanman, E. J., & Miller, L. C. (1997). Connectionism, parallel constraint satisfaction processes, and Gestalt principles: (Re)introducing cognitive dynamics to social psychology. *Pesonality and Social Psychology Review, 1*, 26–53.

Richeson, J. A., & Ambady, N. (2001). Who's in charge? Effects of situational roles on automatic gender bias. *Sex Roles, 44*, 493–512.

Roskos-Ewoldsen, D. R., & Fazio, R. H. (1992). On the orienting value of attitudes: Attitude accessibility as a determinant of an object's attraction of visual attention. *Journal of Personality and Social Psychology, 63*, 198–211.

Rosenberg, M. J. (1968). Hedonism, inauthenticity, and other goads toward expansion of a consistency theory. In R. P. Abelson, E. Aronson, W. J. McGuire, T. M. Newcomb, M. J. Rosenberg, & P. H. Tannenbaum (Eds.), *Theories of cognitive consistency: A sourcebook* (pp. 73–111). Chicago: Rand McNally.

Rosenberg, M. J. (1969). The conditions and consequences of evaluation apprehension. In R. Rosenthal & R. L. Rosnow (Eds.), *Artifacts in behavioral research* (pp. 279–349). New York: Academic Press.

Rudman, L. A., Ashmore, R. D., & Gary, M. L. (2001). "Unlearning" automatic biases: The malleability of implicit prejudice and stereotypes. *Journal of Personality and Social Psychology, 81*, 856–868.

Rugg, D. (1941). Experiments in wording questions: II. *Public Opinion Quarterly, 5*, 91–92.

Schacter, D. L. (1987). Implicit memory: History and current status. *Journal of Experimental Psychology: Learning, Memory and Cognition, 13*, 501–518.

Scherer, K. R., Schorr, A., & Johnstone, T. (2001). Appraisal processes in emotion: Theory, methods, research. *Series in affective science*. London: Oxford University Press.

Schuman, H., & Presser, S. (1981). *Questions and answers in attitude surveys: Experiments on question form, wording, and context*. New York: Academic Press.

Schwarz, N. (1996). Survey research: Collecting data by asking questions. In G. Semin, R. Guen, & R. K. Fiedler (Eds.), *Applied social psychology* (pp. 65–90). London: Sage.

Schwarz, N., & Bless, H. (1992). Scandals and the public's trust in politicians: Assimilation and contrast effects. *Personality and Social Psychology Bulletin, 18*, 574–579.

Schwarz, N., & Bohner, G. (2001). The construction of attitudes. In A. Tesser & Norbert Schwarz, (Eds.), *Blackwell handbook of social psychology: Intraindividual processes* (pp. 436–457). Malden, MA: Blackwell.

Schwarz, N., & Strack, F. (1991). Context effects in attitude surveys: Applying cognitive theory to social research. In W. Stroebe & M. Hewstone (Eds.), *European Review of Social Psychology* (Vol. 2, pp. 31–50). Chichester, UK: Wiley.

Sedikides, C., & Skowronski, J. J. (1991). The law of cognitive structure activation. *Psychological Inquiry, 2*, 169–184.

Seger, C. A. (1994). Implicit learning. *Psychological Bulletin, 115*, 163–196.

Sia, T. L., Lord, C. G., Blessum, K. A., Ratcliff, C. D., & Lepper, M. R. (1997). Is a rose always a rose? The role of social category exemplar change in attitude stability and attitude-behavior consistency. *Journal of Personality and Social Psychology, 72*, 501–514.

Sigall, H., & Page, R. (1971). Current stereotypes: A little fading, a little faking. *Journal of Personality and Social Psychology, 18*, 247–255.

Sinclair, L., & Kunda, Z. (1999). Reactions to a Black professional: Motivated inhibition and activation of conflicting stereotypes. *Journal of Personality and Social Psychology, 77*, 885–904.

Sinclair, L., & Kunda, Z. (2000). Motivated stereotyping of women: She's fine if she praised me but incompetent if she criticized me. *Personality and Social Psychology Bulletin, 26*, 1329–1342.

Smith, E. R. (1984). Model of social inference processes. *Psychological Review, 91*, 392–413.

Smith, E. R. (1989). Procedural efficiency and on-line social judgments. In J. N. Bassili (Ed.), *On-line cognition in person perception* (pp. 19–37). Hillsdale, NJ: Lawrence Erlbaum Associates.

Smith, E. R. (1991). Illusory correlation in a simulated exemplar-based memory. *Journal of Experimental Social Psychology, 27*, 107–123.

Smith, E. R. (1996). What Do Connectionism and Social Psychology Offer Each Other? *Journal of Personality and Social Psychology, 70*, 893–912.

Smith, E. R. (1997). Preconscious Automaticity in a Modular Connectionist System. In R. R. Wyer, Jr. (Ed.), *Advances in social cognition* (Vol. 10, pp. 187–202). Mahwah, NJ: Lawrence Erlbaum Associates.

Smith, E. R., Fazio, R. H., & Cejka, M. A. (1996). Accessible attitudes influence categorization of multiply categorizable objects. *Journal of Personality and Social Psychology, 71*, 888–898.

Smith, E. R., & Zárate, M. A. (1992). Exemplar-based model of social judgment. *Psychological Review, 99*, 3–21.

Smith, P. B., & Bond, M. H. (1993). *Social psychology across cultures: Analysis and perspectives.* New York: Harvester Wheatsheaf.

Smolensky, P. (1989). Connectionist modeling: Neural computation/mental connections. In L. Nadel, L. A. Cooper, P. Culicover, & R. M. Harnish (Eds.), *Neural connections, mental computation* (pp. 49–67). Cambridge, MA: MIT Press.

Spencer, S. J., Fein, S., Wolfe, C. T., Fong, C., & Dunn, M. A. (1998). Automatic activation of stereotypes: The role of self-image threat. *Personality and Social Psychology Bulletin, 24*, 1139–1152.

Srull, T. K. (1983). Organizational and retrieval processes in person memory: An examination of processing objectives, presentation format, and the possible role of self-generated retrieval cues. *Journal of Personality and Social Psychology, 44*, 1157–1170.

Srull, T. K., & Wyer, R. S. (1979). The role of category accessibility in the interpretation of information about persons: Some determinants and implications. *Journal of Personality and Social Psychology, 37*, 1660–1672.

Staats, A. W., & Staats, C. K. (1958). Attitudes established by classical conditioning. *Journal of Abnormal and Social Psychology, 11*, 182–192.

Stapel, D. A., & Schwarz, N. (1998). The Republican who did not want to become president: Colin Powell's impact on evaluations of the Republican party and Bob Dole. *Personality and Social Psychology Bulletin, 24*, 690–698.

Strack, F. (1994). Response processes in social judgment. In R. S. Wyer, Jr. & T. K. Srull (Eds.), *Handbook of social cognition, Vol. 1: Basic processes; Vol. 2: Applications* (pp. 287–322). Hillsdale, NJ: Lawrence Erlbaum Associates.

Strack, F., Schwartz, N., Bless, H., & Kuebler, A. (1993). *European Journal of Social Psychology, 23*, 53–62.

Sudman, S., Bradburn, N. M., & Schwarz, N. (1996). *Thinking about answers: The application of cognitive processes to survey methodology.* San Francisco: Jossey-Bass/Pfeiffer.

Weber, S. J., & Cook, T. D. (1972). Subject effects in laboratory research: An examination of subject roles, demand characteristics, and valid inference. *Psychological Bulletin, 77*, 273–295.

Wegener, D. T., & Petty, R. E. (1997). The flexible correction model: The role of naive theories of bias in bias correction. In M. P. Zanna (Ed.), *Advances in experimental social psychology* (Vol. 29, pp. 141–208). San Diego, CA: Academic Press.

Wegner, D. M. (1994). Ironic processes of mental control. *Psychological Review, 101*, 34–52.

Wegner, D. M., & Erber, R. (1992). The hyperaccessibility of suppressed thoughts. *Journal of Personality and Social Psychology, 69*, 903–912.

Wiles, J., & Humphreys, M. S. (1993). Using artificial neural nets to model implicit and explicit memory test performance. In P. Graf & M. E. J. Masson (Eds.), *Implicit memory: New directions in cognition, development, and neuropsychology* (pp. 141–165). Hillsdale, NJ: Lawrence Erlbaum Associates.

Wilson, T. D., Lindsey, S., & Schooler, T. Y. (2000). A model of dual attitudes. *Psychological Review, 107*, 101–126.

Winkielman, P., Schwartz, N., Fazendeiro, T. A., & Reber, R. (2003). The hedonic making of processing fluency: Implications for evaluative judgment. In J. Musch & K. C. Klauer (Eds.), *Affective processes in cognition and emotion* (pp. 189–217). Mahwah, NJ: Lawrence Erlbaum Associates.

Wittenbrink, B., Judd, C. M., & Park, B. (2001). Spontaneous prejudice in context: Variability in automatically activated attitudes. *Journal of Personality and Social Psychology, 81*, 815–827.

Wyer, R. S. (1970). Quantitative predictions of belief and opinion change: A further test of a subjective probability model. *Journal of Personality and Social Psychology, 16*, 559–570.

Zajonc, R. B. (1968). Attitudinal effects of mere exposure. *Journal of Personality and Social Psychology, 9*, 1–27.

Zajonc, R. B. (1980). Feeling and thinking: Preferences need no inferences. *American Psychologist, 35*, 151–175.

Zajonc, R. B. (2000). Feeling and thinking: Closing the debate over the independence of affect. In J. P. Forgas (Ed.), *Feeling and thinking: The role of affect in social cognition. Studies in emotion and social interaction, second series* (pp. 31–58). New York: Cambridge University Press.

14

Individual Differences in Attitude Change

Pablo Briñol
Universidad Autónoma de Madrid

Richard E. Petty
Ohio State University

The term *individual differences* refers to how people differ with respect to a wide variety of factors such as personality, motives, and abilities. Conceptualizations of individual differences in human temperament can be traced from the ancient typologies of Hippocrates and Galen to the somatotypes of Kretschmer and Sheldon, the work of Galton on mental testing and Binet on intelligence, to the most contemporary multitrait personality inventories, such as the Big Five (Costa & McCrae, 1985; Digman, 1990). Individual differences can emerge from a large variety of heritable and non-heritable sources, and some of the innumerable ways in which individuals differ may be more adaptive than others (see Buss & Greiling, 1999, for a review).

Individual differences contribute to explaining phenomena ranging from historical revolutions to scientific innovation and progress (Sulloway, 1996). For example, why, when faced with the same biological evidence that caused Darwin to accept evolution, did his closest colleagues refuse to abandon their creationist convictions? In part, this refusal may be because some people are predisposed to resist any radical innovation, whereas others tend to challenge any conviction and come up with revolutionary ideas. In this chapter, we examine how individual differences can influence attitudes and attitude change.

We organize our review of social psychology's leading individual difference constructs around four major motives that govern human thought and action. We focus on motives because of their pivotal role in determining social behavior, and because motivational ideas have profoundly influenced the study of attitudes and persuasion. Nevertheless, we will also cover some prominent nonmotivational individual differences, as well.

The general motives used to organize our review are: (a) knowledge, (b) consistency, (c) self-worth, and (d) social approval. Briefly described, the need to know refers to the desire to possess knowledge about and understanding of the social world. Knowledge gives people predictability and control over their social environments, allows individuals to adapt their behavior toward ways that provide pleasure and avoid pain, and provides a sense of individual freedom and competence (Brehm, 1966; Maslow, 1962; Murray, 1955). Second, the internal coherence or consistency of the explanatory system is a key aspect of understanding the world. Part of making sense of things is that perceptions and beliefs hang together without contradiction. The need for consistency leads people to avoid dissonance within or between the affective, cognitive, and behavioral components of the psychological system. Third, developing and maintaining positive self-perceptions is another fundamental human activity (Allport, 1955; James, 1890; Maslow, 1943; Tesser, 1988). Positive self-regard is a sign of social acceptance and liking (Leary, Tambor, Terdal, & Downs, 1995), is essential for achieving happiness and mental health (e.g., Taylor & Brown, 1988), and for coping with the stresses of life (Steele, 1988). The fourth human motive highlighted in this chapter is the need for social inclusion and approval. Affiliation with others can provide a sense of self-worth, and inclusion in a group can provide a desired social status or power (Deci, 1995; Guisinger & Blatt, 1994).

These four motives are widely used in the literatures on the self, identity, personality, human motivation, and social cognition (Baumeister, 1998; Dunning, 1999; Epstein, 2003; Kruglanski, 1996; see also Prislin & Wood, chap. 16, this volume). The precise distinctions among the motives are, of course, somewhat arbitrary and overlapping, but they capture much of the current motivational thinking in social psychology (see also Fiske, 2004). They have the advantage of being broad, basic, and more fundamental to the nature of human desire than particular specific motives that are the result of relatively specific situations. For that reason, the four major motives can be linked to a number of more specific individual differences that have been shown to be relevant to attitudes and attitude change.

Of course, the extent to which these motives are chronically or temporarily activated can vary not only from individual to individual, but can also vary within the same individual from situation to situation. However, this chapter examines individual rather than situational differences in motives. It is worth noting that in addition to these four motives, other motives are surely relevant for understanding attitudes that have not been captured as individual differences. For example, terror management theory–dealing with the fear of death–has important implications for understanding people's desires to protect and defend their cultural world views (i.e., value laden attitudes), but death anxiety has not been assessed as an individual difference (Pyszczynski et al., 1997).

Although some authors have studied the relationship of the four key motives to each other in order to establish a hierarchy among them (Sedikides, 1993), in attitude change situations, we suspect that any of the motives can be supreme depending on a number of individual and situational factors. In addition, any one motive can sometimes be subsumed by another. For example, the consistency motive could be seen as stemming from the knowledge motive because people may want to keep their explanatory system without contradictions in order to better understand and predict the world. Alternatively, the consistency motive could be incorporated into the self-worth motive because people may want to be coherent in order to feel good about themselves. Or, they may want to be consistent in order to be accepted by others. As these examples illustrate, the motive of consistency could possibly be subsumed into any of the other three human needs. But, the motives can also operate independently. For example, one could argue that a true need to know requires accepting the fact of ambivalence rather than consistency. Furthermore, the motives sometimes act in opposite ways allowing them to balance each other (Epstein, 2003). For example, although the need for self-worth could motivate people to seek self-enhancing information from others, the need for inclusion exerts pressure against such norm-violating behavior.

In this chapter, the four motives are used mostly as a practical way to organize the ever growing number and variety of specific individual differences relevant to attitudes and attitude change. Thus, the many possible interdependences among the motives are not problematic. The main function of our organizing structure is to facilitate access to the diversity of individual differences that have been examined. By using this motivational framework to organize the chapter, we do not imply that a particular individual difference was originally designed to assess a specific motive. In fact, due to the overlap among the motives, some of the individual differences described under one motive could plausibly be discussed under a different motive. For example, the Need for Closure (Webster & Kruglanski, 1994) is discussed under the knowledge motive, but it could plausibly fit under the need for consistency.

The focus of our analysis is on examining the impact of individual differences on attitude change (i.e., when an evaluation moves from one position to another, such as going from slightly favorable to very favorable) and attitude strength (i.e., how impactful and durable the attitudes are). We do not focus on how individual differences may determine the particular attitudinal positions that individuals hold. For example, Jost, Glaser, Kruglanski, and Sulloway (2003) have argued that people adopt conservative ideologies in an effort to satisfy their motives. In particular, they postulated that conservatism is partially determined by a variety of individual differences related to the motives of knowledge and consistency. Similar approaches can be found in the literature on sensation seeking predicting particular attitudes toward drugs and protective behaviors (Hoyle, Stephenson, Palmgreen, Lorch, & Donohew, 2002). In this chapter, rather than focusing on the study of specific attitudinal positions (or sets of related attitudes or ideologies), we examine the role of individual differences in affecting the psychological processes relevant to attitude change and strength.

The chapter is divided into four sections. We describe: (a) the core motives and the key psychological processes underlying attitude strength and change, (b) the relationship between motives and attitude change processes and their implications for attitude strength, (c) individual differences regarding preferences between motives, and (d) some remaining issues regarding individual differences and attitudes.

MOTIVES AND FUNDAMENTAL PROCESSES LEADING TO ATTITUDE CHANGE

We have already briefly described the four general human motives that serve as the organizing framework for the individual differences relevant to attitudes and persuasion. Table 14.1 summarizes the particular individual difference variables that we have grouped under the more general motives. Before turning to the specific research on individual differences, however, it is useful to consider the particular psychological processes through which individual differences in human motives are likely to influence attitude change. In Table 14.2, we have summarized the key processes along with the key motives. As implied by the matrix, our conceptual position is that each of the core motives can influence attitudes by one or more of the core processes underlying attitude change.

In specifying the underlying processes of attitude change, we rely on the mechanisms outlined in the elaboration likelihood model of persuasion (ELM) (Petty & Cacioppo, 1986; Petty, Priester, & Briñol, 2002; Petty & Wegener, 1999). The ELM outlines several distinct ways in which variables can have an impact on attitudes at different points along an elaboration continuum ranging from little or no thought about the information presented to complete and extensive thought about the information. Each of the four major motives described above can influence attitudes by affecting one or more of the underlying processes by which variables induce persuasion: (a) affecting the *amount* of issue-relevant thinking that occurs, (b) producing a *bias* to the thoughts that come to mind, (c) affecting structural properties of the thoughts, (d) serving as persuasive evidence or arguments, and (e) serving as simple cues to change in the absence of much thinking. Obviously, there are many persuasion theories that might have been used as an organizing framework (e.g., cognitive dissonance theory, Festinger, 1957; the heuristic-systematic model (HSM), Chaiken, Liberman, & Eagly, 1989), but we rely on the ELM mainly because it has guided numerous studies of individual differences and is

TABLE 14.1

Individual Differences Related to Four General Human Motives and Preferences Among Them

(1) Knowledge	Need for cognition (Cacioppo & Petty, 1982); Need to evaluate (Jarvis & Petty, 1996); Need for closure (Webster & Kruglanski, 1984); Causal uncertainty (Weary & Edwards, 1994) Self-awareness (Carver & Scheier, 1981)
(2) Consistency	Authoritarianism (Altemeyer, 1981); Dogmatism (Rokeach, 1954); Preference for consistency (Cialdini et al., 1995); Resistance to persuasion (Briñol et al., 2004); Bolster and counterargue (Briñol et al., 2004); Defensive Confidence (Albarracín & Mitchell, 2002); Argumentativeness (Infante & Rancer, 1982); Implicit theories of change (Dweck, Chiu, & Hong, 1995)
(3) Self-worth	Self-esteem (Rosenberg, 1979); Optimism (Scheier, Carver, & Bridges, 1994); Self-doubt (Oleson, Poehlmann, Yost, Lynch, & Arkin, 2000)
(4) Social Approval	Need for uniqueness (Snyder & Fromkin, 1977); Individualism-collectivism (Triandis, McCusker, & Hui, 1990); Field dependence (Witkin et al., 1954); Machiavellianism (Christie & Geis, 1970); Individual differences in disposition toward minority groups and identity (e.g., social dominance orientation, Pratto et al., 1994); Individual differences in the motivation to control for prejudice (e.g., internal and external motivation to respond without prejudice, Plant & Devine, 1998)
Preferences Between Motives	Self-Monitoring (Snyder, 1974); Uncertainty Orientation (Sorrentino & Short, 1986)

comprehensive in outlining the multiple processes by which variables–including individual differences–might impact persuasion. We outline these processes next.

Amount of Thinking

First, a certain motive can influence attitudes by influencing the amount of thinking in which people engage when making a social judgment. This effect on extent of information processing is likely to occur when the likelihood of thinking is not constrained to be high or low by other variables (e.g., neither high nor low amounts of external distraction) and thus thinking is free to vary (i.e., become greater or lesser). Importantly, an attitude formed based on effortful issue-relevant information processing will be well articulated and bolstered by supporting information, and as a consequence it should be strong (Petty, Haugtvedt, & Smith, 1995).

TABLE 14.2

Matrix of Motives and Psychological Processes Relevant to Attitude Change

	Knowledge	Consistency	Self-Worth	Social Approval
Amount of thinking				
Direction of thinking				
Features of thoughts (meta-cognition)				
Assessment of evidence (arguments)				
Use of peripheral cues				

Direction of Thinking

Second, motives can have an impact on persuasion by influencing not the amount, but the direction of the thinking that takes place. Perhaps the most extensively explored direction that thinking can take is whether it is aimed at supporting or derogating the position advocated, though other dimensions of thinking have been explored as well (e.g., whether the thoughts are directed at the source or the message; see Cacioppo, Harkins, & Petty, 1981). Attitude change is postulated to be a function of the number and valence of thoughts that come to mind, at least when elaboration is high (see reviews by Eagly & Chaiken, 1993; Petty & Cacioppo, 1986).

The distinction between amount and direction of thinking suggests that some motives may be more likely to be associated with affecting relatively objective (undirected) thinking whereas others may be more likely to affect biased (directed) thinking. For example, the need to know is likely to be associated with extensive and largely objective elaboration because the motive to understand is relatively independent of the content. In contrast, the need for self-worth could focus information processing activity in a particular direction if one side or the other reflected more favorably on the self. Other motives such as consistency and social approval might also guide information processing in a particular direction.

Structural Features of Thoughts

According to the ELM, variables can affect various structural features of thoughts such as how confident people are in them or how accessible they are. For example, when thoughts are held with high confidence, people will use them in forming their judgments (self-validation processes; Petty, Briñol, & Tormala, 2002; Briñol & Petty, 2004). On the other hand, if people doubt the validity of their thoughts, they will discard them. Furthermore, if people believe that their thoughts are biased in some way, they can adjust their judgments in a direction opposite to the implication of the thoughts (correction processes; Petty & Wegener, 1993; Wegener & Petty, 1997; Wilson & Brekke, 1994). Both validation and correction processes are generally more likely to occur when the extent of thinking is high, though with considerable practice, they can be automatized (e.g., Maddux, Barden, Brewer, & Petty, 2005). Thus, individual differences in the extent of thinking or in practice can moderate these metacognitive effects.

In addition, individual differences can determine what information is used to validate thoughts or attitudes. For example, under a high need to know, people might assess validity by using information related to the credibility of the source or other indicators of accuracy. However, if other motives such as the need for inclusion were salient, people might instead look to consensual validation of their thoughts and attitudes.

Use of Arguments

When thinking is high, people assess the relevance of all of the information in the context for assessing the merits of the attitude object under consideration. That is, the information in the context–whether originating in the source, message, recipient, or surroundings–is examined as a possible argument or reason for favoring or disfavoring the attitude object (Petty, 1994; Pierro, Mannetti, Kruglanski, & Sleeth-Keppler, 2004). Individual differences can influence what type of information serves as persuasive evidence for the attitude object. For example, positive information related to image would provide more persuasive evidence for high than low self-monitors (Snyder & DeBono, 1985).

Use of Cues

Finally, when conditions do not foster thinking, attitudes are influenced by a variety of low effort processes such as mere association (Cacioppo, Marshall-Goodell, Tassinary, & Petty,

1992) or reliance on heuristics (Chaiken, 1987). Motivational factors can influence attitude change in these circumstances by affecting the selection of cues or by having an impact on what cues would be more effective. For example, if the need to know is high but people are unable to carefully process information for whatever reason (e.g., distraction, noise), they are likely to look for cues related to knowing and accuracy, such as source credibility. In contrast, social cues would likely have a greater impact when the need for social inclusion is high.

Summary

In sum, individual differences in each of the four motives outlined earlier can be related to the fundamental processes of attitude change. In the present chapter, the literature on attitude change and strength is reviewed using this motivational framework. Before specific individual differences are examined, however, it is important to briefly mention a few additional assumptions of our framework. First, we assume that any one motive can be associated with different outcomes in different situations and for different individuals. Second, in different situations or for different individuals, the same attitude can be the result of the operation of different motives. A final theoretical assumption is that attitudes are not necessarily more accurate or stronger when they are formed or changed through one motive or the other. For example, an attitude shifted as a result of the need to know should not necessarily be more "accurate" than an attitude that results from the need to be coherent or the search for self-worth. That is, the need to know does not assure objectivity and other motives do not always produce biased attitudes. Obviously, as noted earlier, the strength of those attitudes depends on the extent to which the are based on extensive thinking regardless of whether they are actually grounded in reality or not.

It is noteworthy that these conceptual assumptions differentiate the present approach from other frameworks, such as the HSM (Chen & Chaiken, 1999). For example, the HSM distinguishes an "accuracy" motive which leads to objective processing from "defensive" and "impression" motives which lead to biased processing. As noted above, we do not tie the four key motives to any particular outcome or mechanism. For example, people who "defend" their current attitude might do so because they believe their attitude is accurate and therefore want to protect it, or because holding their ground makes them feel knowledgeable or competent, or because they think that defending their attitude will make them attractive to others, or because they value consistency per se.

THE RELATIONSHIP BETWEEN MOTIVES AND ATTITUDE CHANGE PROCESSES AND THEIR IMPLICATIONS FOR ATTITUDE STRENGTH

In this part of the chapter, we explain how particular individual differences falling under the four motives can influence attitude change through the various psychological processes just outlined. We first consider the impact of each motive as a whole. Then, we examine research on each of the particular individual differences related to this motivation.

Individual Differences Relevant to the Need for Knowledge and Their Impact on Attitude Change and Strength

The need for knowledge can influence attitude change processes in a variety of ways. Most notably, the need to know may require that people carefully process whatever information might be relevant in order to form an adaptive attitude, and thus gain predictability and control over the social environment. Thus, the need to know can influence attitude change and strength by affecting the amount of information processing that occurs (Chaiken & Maheswaran, 1994: Tormala, Briñol, & Petty, 2003). On the one hand, when the need to know is high, people may assess the validity of their own thoughts by using information related to the credibility of the source or other indicators of accuracy (Briñol, Petty, & Tormala, 2004). On the other hand, if the need to know is high but people are unable to process for whatever reason (e.g., distraction, noise), they are likely to look for simple cues related to knowing and accuracy, such as source credibility (Petty & Cacioppo, 1981). Next, we describe the specific individual difference measures related to the need to know and their influence on attitude change and strength through these psychological processes.

Need for Cognition.   Need for cognition (NC) (Cacioppo & Petty, 1982) refers to stable individual differences in the tendency to engage in and enjoy effortful thought. NC is commonly measured with a self-report scale containing statements such as, "I prefer complex to simple problems" (Cacioppo, Petty, & Kao, 1984). People high in NC tend to devote attention to an ongoing task, searching all the information available, especially information based on empirical and rational considerations.

Individuals high in NC consistently have been found to engage in greater elaboration of persuasive messages than those low in NC and to put forth more mental effort on a variety of cognitive tasks (see Cacioppo, Petty, Feinstein, & Jarvis, 1996 for a review). For example, people high in NC tend to form attitudes on the basis of an effortful analysis of the quality of the relevant information in a persuasive message, whereas people low in NC tend to be more reliant on simple peripheral cues in the persuasion context (Cacioppo, Petty, and Morris, 1983). However, even low NC individuals can be motivated to scrutinize the message arguments and eschew reliance on cues if situational circumstances are motivating–such as when the message is of high personal relevance (Axsom, Yates, & Chaiken, 1987), the source is potentially untrustworthy (Priester & Petty, 1995; Tormala et al., 2003), or the message content is surprising (Smith & Petty, 1996). Importantly, NC also has consequences for attitude strength, and people high in NC tend to have stronger attitudes than those low in NC (Petty et al., 1995). Additionally, because individuals high (vs. low) in NC tend to engage in deeper thinking, they also tend to form stronger automatic associations between attitude objects (Briñol, Petty, et al., 2004).

There are two important aspects to note regarding the effortful cognitive activity characteristic of individuals high in NC. First, the extent of the thinking is not the only process that can be affected by NC because the more extensive thinking of individuals high in NC is not necessarily objective. In fact, other variables such as mood can introduce a significant bias to the thought content of people high in NC (Petty, Schumann, Richman, & Strathman, 1993). Second, individuals high in NC not only tend to think more about any given attitude object, but they also devote more attention to their own thinking. As a result, high NC has been related to metacognitive processes such that individuals high in NC are more likely to evaluate their own thoughts for validity (Briñol & Petty, 2003; Briñol et al., 2004; Petty et al., 2002; Tormala et al., 2002, 2003), to engage in controlled (Wegener & Petty, 1997) and automatic (Petty, Briñol, Horcajo, & Jarvis, 2003) bias correction processes, and to draw different metacognitive inferences based on the intensity or efficiency with which they respond to persuasive messages (Tormala & Petty, 2002, 2004).

The need for cognition has been found to relate to a number of other well-established attitudinal phenomena. For example, NC has implications for the mere thought polarization effect, in which thinking about one's attitude leads to more extreme attitudes (Tesser, 1978). Given the greater propensity to engage in spontaneous thought, Smith, Haugtvedt, and Petty (1994) found that high NC individuals showed greater attitude polarization following a period of reflection on their attitudes. However, when explicit instructions to think are provided, low

NC individuals can show greater polarization than high NC individuals (Lassiter, Apple, & Slaw, 1996; Leone & Ensley, 1986). This finding suggests that when thinking is instructed rather than spontaneous, high NC individuals may consider all sides of the issue and thus show moderation rather than polarization.

Need for cognition has also been studied in the context of primacy and recency effects. High NC individuals tend to show greater primacy in judgment when the information is "chunked"— presented as consisting of two distinct sides of an issue (Kassin, Reddy, & Tulloch, 1990). In these situations, when a particular point of view is presented first, highly thoughtful individuals think about this information. As a consequence, the conclusions they draw from it bias pro-cessing of subsequent information (Haugtvedt & Petty, 1992; Haugtvedt & Wegener, 1994). In contrast, when the information presented is not clearly divided into two sides but rather comes in a continuous stream, low NC individuals have shown greater primacy in judgments than individuals high in NC (Ahlering & Parker, 1989). This result is consistent with the view that low amounts of thinking can cause individuals to freeze on the early information and ignore subsequent information (Kruglanski & Webster, 1996) (for additional discussion on this topic, see Petty & Jarvis, 1996; and for empirical evidence on the role of "chunking" and NC in moderating primacy/recency effects, see Petty, Tormala, Hawkins, & Wegener, 2001).

The need for cognition can also have important consequences for attitude change in the context of interpersonal influence. For example, Shestowsky, Wegener, and Fabrigar (1998) found that in the context of dyadic decision making, high NC individuals are perceived as more effective persuaders and are more capable of generating valid arguments to support their views than are low NC individuals. Consistent with the notion that high NC individuals tend to hold stronger attitudes than low NC individuals, high NC people were not only better at persuading their partners, but were also found to be more resistant to others' counterattitudinal persuasive attempts.

Finally, research has examined the notion that matching a persuasive message to the char-acteristic traits of individuals high versus low in NC can affect attitudes in multiple ways along the elaboration continuum (Petty & Cacioppo, 1986). For example, when the elaboration like-lihood is free to vary, matching can serve to enhance information processing activity (Wheeler, Petty, & Bizer, in press). Thus, a message that appears to be aimed at people who are not thoughtful could enhance the information processing activity of people low in NC (because it matches their self-schema), but reduce the information processing activity of individuals high in NC (because it mismatches their self-schema; see also Petty, Wheeler, & Bizer, 2000).

Recent research has also found that under low elaboration conditions NC-matching can also serve as a peripheral cue. In one study (Wheeler, Briñol, & Petty, 2002), individuals high and low in NC were exposed to products of different brands that were described as "intelligent, technical, and corporate" or as "glamorous, upper-class, and good looking." As expected, individuals high in NC assessed the brand as more favorable in the former than in the latter frame condition, whereas participants low in NC did the opposite. Importantly, these results were replicated when NC was assessed with an implicit measure (the implicit association test (IAT) (Greenwald, McGhee, & Schwartz, 1998). Future work might profitably address differences between implicit and explicit personality measures.

Need to Evaluate.   The need to evaluate (NE) (Jarvis & Petty, 1996; Petty & Jarvis, 1996) refers to individual differences in people's tendencies to engage in evaluative thought. People who are high in the need to evaluate tend to chronically assess whether things are good or bad (see also the "need to assess," Kruglanski, Thompson, Higgins, Atash, Pierro, Shah, & Spiegel, 2000). Knowing whether things in the world are good or bad helps people to understand the environment. Probably because of this and other functions (Maio & Olson, 2000), people tend to form attitudes about nearly everything (Bargh, Chaiken, Govender, &

Pratto, 1992; Roskos-Ewoldsen & Fazio, 1992). Nevertheless, some people are more chronic and spontaneous than others in their tendency to evaluate, and the NE scale assesses this. The NE scale contains items such as "I form opinions about everything." Worth noting, NE can be distiguished from other constructs, such as the Need for Affect (Maio & Esses, 2001), which assesses individual differences in the preference to approach or avoid situations that induce emotions. Recently, Huskinson and Haddock (2004) have shown that whereas individuals high in Need for Affect tend to base their evaluations mostly on affective information, individuals high in NE tend to use both affective and cognitive information.

Jarvis and Petty (1996) demonstrated that, compared to people low in NE, those high in the NE are more likely to form attitudes toward a variety of social and political issues. In other studies, Jarvis and Petty also found people high in NE to be more likely to generate evaluative thoughts when responding to both relatively novel stimuli (e.g., positive, negative, and neutral paintings from various styles and periods) and personally relevant stimuli (e.g., participants' autobiographical narratives describing a day in their lives). In addition, Petty and Jarvis (1996) reported that people high in NE were quicker to respond to a measure of their attitudes suggesting that their attitudes were more accessible (see also Albarracín, Wallace, & Glasman, in press). Also consistent with this idea are findings with measures of automatic attitude evaluation. Using an evaluative priming procedure (Fazio, Sanbonmatsu, Powell, & Kardes, 1986) in which positive or negative words precede target words, Hermans, DeHouwer, and Eelen (2001) found that high NE individuals responded more quickly to evaluatively congruent than to evaluatively incongruent target words. For those low in NE, however, there was no difference, as if their evaluations were not spontaneously accessible.

Because the attitudes of high NE individuals are spontaneously accessible, their attitudes would tend to be more stable across contexts, whereas individuals low in NE are more likely to base their attitudes on whatever information is salient in the immediate environment rather than their prior evaluations. Interestingly, Albarracín and colleagues (2004) suggested that if individuals high in NE are engaged in an explicit comparison of their old attitudes with new information that is consistent with these attitudes, they are more likely to polarize their positions because the new information validates the initial attitude. Low NE individuals are less likely to polarize because their initial attitudes are not as salient.

One reason attitudes come to mind more quickly for high than low NE individuals is that those high in NE tend to engage in online versus memory-based evaluative processing (Hastie & Park, 1986). In fact, Tormala and Petty (2001) found that high NE individuals formed attitudes toward an unfamiliar person in a spontaneous, online fashion, whereas low NE individuals formed them in a less spontaneous, more memory-based fashion. Thus, attitudes were more highly correlated with information retrieved from memory for low than for high NE persons.

Finally, recent research has shown that NE is useful in predicting a variety of important attitude-relevant cognitive, behavioral, and affective political processes (Bizer et al., 2004). Using data from national election surveys, Bizer and his colleagues found that NE predicted how many evaluative beliefs about political candidates a person held, the likelihood that a person would use evaluations of issue stances to determine candidate preferences, the extent to which a person engaged in political activism, the likelihood that a person voted or intended to vote, the extent to which a person used the news media for gathering information, and the intensity of emotional reactions a person felt toward political candidates.

The Need for Closure.   Need for closure (Webster & Kruglanski, 1994) refers to the desire for a definitive answer on some topic, as opposed to confusion and ambiguity. Need for closure represents a dimension of stable individual differences as well as a situationally evocable state. As a chronic dimension, the desire for definitive knowledge has been measured with the *Need for Closure Scale*, which includes items such as "I would rather know bad news than stay in a state of uncertainty" (for properties of the scale, see Webster & Kruglanski, 1994; see also Neuberg, West, Judice, & Thompson, 1997). In general, the need for closure appears to function similar to other treatments of open-mindedness and closed-mindedness. Being high in need for closure has been shown to reduce the extent of information processing, to magnify primacy effects, to increase reliance on theory-driven versus data-driven processing, and also to enhance reliance on initial anchors and primes (see Kruglanski and Webster, 1996, for a review).

With respect to interpersonal influence, those high in need for closure have sometimes been easier to persuade and sometimes more difficult to persuade. In general, when people do not possess any prior information on a topic, individuals high in need for closure have been found to be more open to attitude change and show a preference for persuasive partners, as this helps them to achieve closure. In contrast, when people have a prior opinion, high need for closure individuals are less open to change and show a preference for persuadable partners (Kruglanski, Webster, & Klem, 1993). In addition, those high in need for closure tend to be rejecting of opinion deviates, but accepting of conformists (Kruglanski & Webster, 1991). In sum, the most direct effects of need for closure are accepting an alternative opinion that can bring quick closure, but maintaining one's old attitude when it provides easy closure.

Need for closure can also influence attitude change by affecting the extent of thinking about information. For example, Klein and Webster (2000) exposed participants to a persuasive message about a new XT-100 answering machine composed of three or nine arguments that were either strong or weak. The results indicated that attitudes toward the product were more affected by the number of arguments (i.e., a peripheral cue; Petty & Cacioppo, 1984) than by the argument quality manipulation for individuals high in need for closure. In contrast, individuals low in need for closure scrutinized the message content more as revealed by the greater argument quality effect on their attitudes. In a second study, Klein and Webster (2000) found that individuals high in need for closure processed a message extensively if a peripheral cue was unavailable to provide an easy means for closure.

Causal Uncertainty.   Causal Uncertainty (Weary & Edwards, 1994) is defined as uncertainty about one's ability to identify and understand the causal conditions for social events. Individual differences in causal uncertainty can be assessed with the causal uncertainty scale (CUS) (Weary & Edwards, 1994). The CUS is a self-report inventory that measures chronic individual differences in the strength of causal uncertainty beliefs, including items such as "When I receive poor grades, I usually do not understand why I did so poorly." Individuals high in CU are motivated to resolve feelings of uncertainty by gaining a more accurate understanding of causal relations in the social world. For that reason, high scores on CU have been found to enhance social information search and processing (Weary & Jacobson, 1997; Weary, Jacobson, Edwards, & Tobin, 2001).

In the domain of attitude change, individuals high in CU are more persuaded by arguments providing causal explanations for events than arguments that do not contain causal information (Tobin, 2003). Additionally, CU has been examined together with individual differences in preference for type of information processing. Specifically, CU has been studied in relation to the Myers-Briggs Type Indicator (MBTI) (Myers & McCaulley, 1985), which measures the extent to which people prefer to make judgments based on conscious, rational processes, or on the output of more automatic processes (see Edwards, Lanning, & Hooker, 2002, for a review; see Epstein, Pacini, Denes-Raj, & Heier, 1996, for a similar conceptualization). Edwards (2003) has recently argued that the effect of causal uncertainty on effortful information processing depends on the extent to which a person typically prefers to process with conscious effort. In one study in which participants received a persuasive message, thoughts and attitudes of those high (vs. low) in causal uncertainty and "judgment" (i.e., preference for conscious effort) were more affected by the quality of the arguments contained in the message than individuals who were low in either causal uncertainty or judgment. This study suggests that causal uncertainty and a preference for rational conscious thought lead people to engage in controlled processing.

It is also noteworthy that causal uncertainty has been related to the propensity to engage in bias correction processes (see Vaughn &Weary, 2003). Just as those high in causal uncertainty sometimes engage in greater information processing, they also appear more likely to engage in attempts to debias their judgments when a bias is salient. As suggested by Vaughn and Weary (2003), future research should explore whether casual uncertainty can affect attitudes by influencing the extent to which individuals assess the validity of their own thoughts in response to persuasive messages.

Self-Awareness (Carver & Scheier, 1981).   One way in which people can try to understand their worlds is by knowing who they are and learning about themselves. Some individuals are more self-aware than others. That is, people differ in the extent to which they attend to their own attitudes, feelings, needs, and concerns. Fenigstein, Scheier, and Buss (1975) referred to these individual differences as private self-consciousness. Private self-consciousness is a trait that can be assessed with a self-reported questionnaire including items, such as "I'm always trying to figure myself out." Self-awareness is also a temporary state that can be manipulated.

Individuals high (vs. low) in private self-consciousness are more aware of their cognitive processes and are more cognizant of what factors influence their decisions. Private self-consciousness has been found to be associated with more attitude-behavior correspondence, presumably because it promotes introspection (Pryor, Gibbons, Wicklund, Fazio, & Hood, 1977). Also, because private self-consciousness makes people more aware of their existing attitudes it can be associated with more resistance to persuasion. Consistent with this view, individuals high in private self-awareness have been found to maintain their beliefs in the face of opposition more than individuals low in self-awareness (Froming, Walker, & Lopyan, 1982; Gibbons & Wright, 1983; Hutton & Baumeister, 1992). Scheier and Carver (1980) also found that high private self-consciousness increased resistance to attitude change in a cognitive dissonance paradigm.

The psychological processes by which private self-consciousness leads to resistance to attitude change are likely to vary as a function of the likelihood of thinking. For example, increasing private self-consciousness might bias one's thoughts in favor of previous attitudes under high elaboration conditions, and increase the impact of one's attitude as a simple cue when elaboration is relatively low. When elaboration is moderate, self-consciousness can influence persuasion by affecting the amount of thinking. In fact, Hutton and Baumeister (1992) found that increasing self-consciousness (temporarily induced with a mirror rather than measured with a self-report) increased the impact of argument quality on participants' attitudes. In contrast, participants who were not made self-aware showed equal degrees of persuasion regardless of the strength of the arguments.

Finally, self-consciousness might influence attitude change by other mechanisms under other circumstances. For example, self-consciousness might lead people to pay more attention to their own thoughts in response to a message, thus affecting persuasion by influencing thought-confidence. As described for other individual differences, this metacognitive role would be more likely to occur under relatively high elaboration conditions.

Individual Differences Relevant to the Need for Consistency and Their Impact on Attitudes and Persuasion

A wide variety of attitudinal frameworks are relevant to understanding the need for consistency. This variety includes work on cognitive dissonance (Festinger, 1957), self-perception

(Bem, 1972), attitudinal ambivalence (Kaplan, 1972; Priester & Petty, 1996; Thompson, Zanna, & Griffin, 1995), tolerance for ambiguity (Bem & Allen, 1974), impression management (Baumeister, 1982), commitment (Cialdini, 1993), self-persuasion (Janis & King, 1954), and attitude strength (Petty & Krosnick, 1995).

Once people make commitments or engage in behavior, they tend to act in consistent ways over time (Greenwald, Carnot, Beach, & Young, 1987). There are many strategies related to persuasion that may be used to generate an initial commitment, such as the foot-in-the-door technique (Freedman & Fraser, 1966), the lowball technique (Cialdini, Cacioppo, Bassett, & Miller, 1978), and making previous commitments salient (see also Pratkanis, 2000). Of course, people do not always behave in a manner consistent with prior commitments or actions, but when discrepancies occur, they are often experienced as unpleasant. In such situations, individuals are motivated to change their attitudes so as to undermine or eliminate the inconsistency, or at least the discomfort that results from the discrepancy (Abelson, Aronson, McGuire, Newcomb, Rosenberg, & Tannenbaum, 1968; Aronson, 1969; Festinger, 1957; Heider, 1958; Higgins, 1987).

The need to be consistent with prior commitments can help to explain why people are sometimes highly resistant to attitude change. When people are committed to an attitude, they are more certain the attitude is correct, they are more confident they will not change it, their position on the issue is more extreme, and their attitude is more stable, enduring, accessible and capable of predicting future behavior (Gross, Holtz, & Miller, 1995; Pomerantz, Chaiken, & Tordesillas, 1995). Although resistance to persuasion can be understood in multiple ways (for a review, see Petty, Tormala, & Rucker, 2004)—as an *outcome* (e.g., showing little or no change to a persuasive message), as a psychological *process* (e.g., one can resist by counterarguing), or as a *motivation* (i.e., having the goal of not being persuaded)—in this section we deal primarily with resistance as a *quality* of a person (i.e., being resistant to persuasion). We begin by providing a brief review of past classic work on individual differences in resistance to undermining internal consistency, and then we describe a number of more recent perspectives.

Authoritarianism and Dogmatism.   Research attempting to identify individual differences in persuasion and resistance originated in the early 1950s, when several scholars were focused on the study of different forms of cognitive rigidity—the stability of individuals' beliefs. One of the most ambitious attempts is represented by work on the "Authoritarian personality" (Altemeyer, 1981). The authoritarian personality arose out of the idea that some people were predisposed to agree with statements related to the fascist ideology (Stanger, 1936). Altemeyer's scale included items such as "What our country really needs, instead of more civil rights, is a good stiff dose of law and order." The initial measures of authoritarianism had a great deal of historic interest and inspired similar measures, such as the anti-semitism scale (Levinson & Sanford, 1944), the ethnocentrism scale (Adorno, Frenkel-Brunswik, Levinson, & Sanford, 1950), and the california F scale (Adorno et al., 1950)—forerunners of more contemporary prejudice measures. As an alternative to the authoritarian personality, Rokeach (1954) developed the dogmatism scale designed to measure individual differences in open versus closed belief systems. Items of the dogmatism scale include assertions such as "A man who does not believe in some great cause has not really lived." Attitudes about resistance to social and political change can also be assessed with Wilson and Patterson's (1968) conservatism scale (see Jost et al., 2003, for a review).

Because people high in authoritarianism support established authority and traditional values, they have sometimes been associated with prejudice, discrimination, and hostility against members of outgroups (Altemeyer, 1998; Duncan, Peterson, & Winter, 1997). According to Altemeyer (1981, 1998), authoritarianism is rooted in the acceptance of the attitudes and values advocated by authority figures. Importantly, attitudes formed or changed by those high (vs. low) in authoritarianism and dogmatism are more likely to be held with greater degrees of subjective confidence (Davies, 1998), and as a consequence are more difficult to change. However, because the sources of such confidence are not always necessarily accurate and accessible, those attitudes could be modified by other authority figures (Briñol & Petty, 2004).

There are some indications that authoritarianism measures, including dogmatism, can predict change in response to external pressures. For example, Crutchfield (1955) reported a correlation of .39 between authoritarianism and yielding to group pressure in a variation of the Asch (1956) conformity paradigm. Altemeyer (1981) also reported a correlation of .44 between authoritarianism and obedience in a replication of Milgram's (1974) obedience to authority paradigm. In both examples, individuals low in authoritarianism were more likely to resist group conformity and obedience pressures. These findings suggest that measures of authoritarianism can be at least partially useful in predicting susceptibility or resistance to overt social influence. Although there is little work examining the link between authoritarianism and verbal persuasion, individuals high (vs. low) in authoritarianism might be expected to be especially susceptible to authority cues when the likelihood of thinking is low, and to be influenced in their extent of thinking by authority figures when elaboration is free to vary. When elaboration is likely to be high, individuals high (vs. low) in authoritarianism might bias their thoughts in the direction of the authority when source information precedes message exposure, and gain confidence in their thoughts when authorities agree with them after message exposure.

Preference for Consistency.   The preference for consistency (PFC) (Cialdini, Trost, & Newsom, 1995) is measured with a scale that includes items such as "I typically prefer to do things the same way." The scale has been found to be useful in predicting individuals who would and would not be susceptible to cognitive consistency effects such as the foot-in-the-door technique (Freedman & Fraser, 1966) and cognitive dissonance (Festinger, 1957). For example, in one study, Cialdini et al. (1995) found that an initial public commitment (accomplished with acceptance of a small request) only led participants to agree to a second larger favor when they had high scores on the PFC scale. Subsequent research has shown that this effect can be shown even after long delays between that initial and the subsequent request (Guadagno, Asher, Demaine, & Cialdini, 2001). In contrast, after the delay, individuals low in PFC showed a reverse foot-in-the-door effect when their prior helpfulness was made salient. In another experiment, Cialdini et al. (1995) showed that free choice in writing a counterattitudinal essay (advocating increased tuition) resulted in more positive attitudes toward the proposal only among participants with a relatively strong preference for consistency. In a different paradigm, Nail et al. (2001) asked participants to vividly imagine being stood-up for dinner by a friend for no good reason. Being stood-up without a good justification should cause dissonance, and participants derogated the friend more when they were high (vs. low) in PFC.

The PFC has been found to moderate other important phenomena related to attitudes, such as attitude ambivalence. For example, Newby-Clark, McGregor, and Zanna (2002) found that when conflicting evaluations of attitude objects come to mind equally quickly (i.e., simultaneous accessibility), individuals high (but not low) in PFC felt more unpleasant feelings of uncertainty. That is, the relation between objective ambivalence and subjective ambivalence was strongest for individuals high in both PFC and in simultaneous accessibility of the conflicting beliefs.

Resistance to Persuasion.   The resistance to persuasion scale (RPS) (Briñol, Rucker, et al., 2004) was developed to assess peoples' metabeliefs and perceptions of their own vulnerability to persuasion, willingness to change, and motivation and ability to resist persuasion. The scale contains statements such as "It is hard for me to change my ideas." As described previously for other constructs, individual differences in beliefs about resistance to persuasion may have different effects on persuasion depending on the amount of elaboration. When elaboration is low, participants can use their beliefs about their own persuadability as a cue, adjusting their attitudes in the direction of their metabeliefs. That is, if people believe they are generally resistant to change, they can rely on this belief and change little in response to a persuasive message. When elaboration is high, individuals' beliefs might influence attitudes by inducing a bias in information processing (e.g., causing people to engage in intense counterarguing of a message if they believe that they are resistant to change). However, under high elaboration conditions, if situational cues suggest that being overly easy or difficult to persuade is inappropriate (e.g., when on a jury or in scientific research), they may attempt to correct for their self-conception (e.g., "I am too difficult to persuade, so I should be more open to new information").

In accord with this multiple roles perspective, in two studies Briñol and colleagues (2004) predicted and found that individuals exhibited attitude change consistent with their metabeliefs about their persuadability when the likelihood of thinking was low, but they appeared to correct for their beliefs under high elaboration conditions. Specifically, among participants low in NC, individuals who believed that they were generally resistant to persuasion showed less attitude change when exposed to various messages than did individuals who believed that they were generally susceptible to persuasion. However, participants high in NC showed a tendency for a reverse effect, demonstrating more persuasion when they thought they were difficult to persuade. This line of research suggests that some individual difference variables such as NC can moderate the effect of other individual differences (e.g., resistance to persuasion) on attitude change.

Bolstering Versus Counterarguing.   The bolster-counterargue scale (BCS) (Briñol et al., 2004) assesses individuals' beliefs about *how* they resist influence. For example, even if two individuals see themselves as fairly resistant to change, they may believe that they resist influence through very different means. An example item geared toward those who prefer to counterargue is: "I take pleasure in arguing with those who have opinions that differ from my own." An item geared toward those who prefer to bolster is: "When someone gives me a point of view that conflicts with my attitudes, I like to think about why my views are right for me."

In a study designed to examine the impact of people's perceptions of the effortful strategies they use to resist persuasion, Briñol, Rucker, et al. (2004) found that higher scores on the bolstering and counterarguing scales were each significantly associated with less attitude change in response to various messages. Notably, in a second experiment, this finding was replicated and the bolstering subscale was positively correlated with the number of bolstering thoughts, whereas the counterarguing subscale was positively correlated with the number of counterarguments generated (but not vice versa). Thus, the spontaneous generation of each type of cognitive response when trying to resist a message may vary from one individual to another, and the BCS may prove useful in assessing these individual differences.

There might be a number of important consequences resulting from differences in how people tend to resist persuasion. For example, classic research on inoculation showed that counterarguing an initially weak message led attitudes to be more resistant to a subsequent stronger message, but simply bolstering one's attitude prior to receiving an attacking message did not result in the same degree of resistance when participants were forced to confront new message arguments (McGuire, 1964).

In general, the bolstering and counterarguing strategies might be differentially effective as a function of message strength. If a message contains only weak or mildly persuasive arguments, counterarguing may be more effective than bolstering because counterarguing is likely to be successful and lead to inoculation type effects. Trying to bolster in the face of weak arguments, however, may not lead to the same success or knowledge that an individual was capable of resisting the message, rendering the attitude more susceptible to future persuasive attempts (McGuire, 1964). In the case of very strong arguments, attempting to counterargue may prove relatively ineffective leading to attitude change and high certainty in one's new attitude (Rucker & Petty, 2004). However, bolstering may prove relatively more effective in preventing attitude change if individuals simply focus on why their initial attitude is correct and do not try to confront the strong message arguments. In sum, understanding individuals' predispositions to various resistance strategies may enhance our understanding of when they are most likely to be able to resist persuasion and the consequences thereof.

Defensive Confidence. The defensive confidence scale (DCS) (Albarracín & Mitchell, 2004) assesses individuals' beliefs that they can defend their positions and contains items such as "I have many resources to defend my point of view when I feel my ideas are under attack." According to research by Albarracín and Mitchell, the beliefs people have about their ability to defend their attitudes moderate their approach to attitude-consistent information. Specifically, individuals who feel confident in their ability to defend their beliefs ignore information that threatens their beliefs less than individuals who do not feel confident about their abilities. This recent line of research suggests that the beliefs people have about their own abilities to defend their attitudes can influence information exposure.

Argumentativeness. Infante and Rancer (1982, p. 72) defined argumentativeness as "a generally stable trait that predisposes individuals in communication situations to advocate positions on controversial issues and to attack verbally the positions which other people hold on these issues." Infante and Rancer (1996) developed a scale to tap argumentativeness that includes items such as "I enjoy defending my point of view on an issue" (for a similar measure of argumentative competence, see Trapp, Yingling, & Wanner, 1987). There is some empirical evidence suggesting that individuals high in argumentativeness are more inclined to use a greater range of influence strategies and to be less apt to use their power to goad others into accepting their positions than those low in this trait (Infante & Rancer, 1996). As a consequence, people high in this construct also tend to be seen as more credible and capable communicators.

Although all of the research on argumentativeness conducted thus far has focused on individual differences in the persuader's skill of developing cogent arguments, individual differences in argumentativeness might be also relevant for the recipient of a persuasion attempt. In particular, individuals high in argumentativeness would likely be more resistant to persuasion, similar to the effect observed for individuals high in resistance to persuasion (Briñol, Rucker, et al., 2004).

Individual Differences in Implicit Theories of Change. Just as people can have beliefs about their *own* resistance to change, Dweck, Chiu, and Hong (1995) have shown that there are individual differences in the extent to which people see *others'* traits as fixed and stable (entity theorists) or as malleable and changeable (incremental theorists). These implicit theories about change can be measured by the implicit theory questionnaire, which assesses people's agreement with statements such as "All people can change even their most basic qualities." Research has shown that the implicit theory questionnaire possesses good psychometric qualities, and unique predictive power above other personality measures (Dweck, Chiu, & Hong, 1995; Hong, Chiu, Dweck, & Sacks, 1997; Levy, Stroessner, & Dweck, 1998). For example, individuals who score as entity theorists (compared to incremental theorists) have been found to draw stronger inferences from behavior, blame themselves more following failure, and form and endorse more extreme group stereotypes (see Dweck, 2000, for a review). In the context of evaluation, Hong et al. (1997) found that entity theorists, relative to incremental theorists, engage in more evaluative processing of information about target individuals when forming an impression. More recently, McConnell (2001) extended that research by showing that entity theorists tend to form online judgments, whereas incremental theorists tend to form memory-based judgments of target individuals. This effect is notable because research has demonstrated that online judgments tend to lead to more accessible evaluations, and thus are more likely to relate to behavior than are memory-based judgments (see Tormala & Petty, 2001).

Individual Differences Relevant to the Need for Self-Worth and Their Impact on Attitudes and Persuasion

People have a need to view themselves positively. Nevertheless, there are individual and cultural differences in the extent to which people possess positive self-views (Baumeister, Tice, & Hutton, 1989), actively seek information that maintains a positive self-view (Steele, 1988; Tesser, 1988), and wish to enhance the positivity of their self-views (Taylor & Brown, 1988; for a detailed review on cultural differences see Heine, Lehman, Markus, & Kitayama, 1999). For example, in a review of Western self-esteem studies, Baumeister et al. (1989) observed that the mean or median self-esteem scores were clearly and consistently higher than the conceptual midpoints of the scales, regardless of the measures used. Research on self-enhancement reveals that individuals' self-evaluations are distorted by self-protective tactics that foster these positive illusions (Taylor & Brown, 1988). For example, people seem to remember their past performance as better than it actually was (Crary, 1966), judge positive personality attributes to be more appropriate in describing themselves than in describing others (Alicke, 1985), tend to take credit for success, yet attribute failure to the situation (see Zuckerman, 1979, for a review), and tend to think that their good traits are unusual, but that their faults and flaws are common (Campbell, 1986). Research on favorable self-evaluation maintenance also documents the variety of compensatory self-protective responses that are elicited when people encounter threats to their self-esteem (Tesser, 1988).

Many self-esteem tactics have been identified in the literature that might have implications for attitude change. For example, people minimize the amount of time they spend processing critical feedback (Baumeister & Cairns, 1992), and when such unflattering feedback is processed, people often discover flaws and derogate whoever the source might be (Kunda, 1990). As described earlier under the motive for consistency, this research is consonant with the idea that people tend to be resistant to attitude change, especially when it comes to changing favorable attitudes toward themselves.

Perhaps one of the most interesting illustrations of how the motive of self-worth is related to attitude change comes from recent research on self-affirmation processes (Steele, 1988). Cohen, Aronson and Steele (2000) argued that because affirming oneself may reduce the perception of threat, it would decrease the need to defend one's attitudes thereby making one more vulnerable to persuasion. Consistent with this view, several experiments have found that resistance to persuasion is undermined when people are affirmed (e.g., by expressing personal values) before receiving a persuasive message (Cohen et al., 2000; Sherman, Nelson, & Steele, 2000). Correll, Spencer, and Zanna (2004) found that the openness to persuasion among affirmed individuals stemmed from more objective processing of the arguments presented, at least when the issue is personally important. Furthermore, in line with the ELM's notion of multiple roles, Briñol, Petty, Gallardo, and Horcajo (2004) found that when an affirmation followed rather than preceded a message, affirmed individuals were more confident in their thoughts to the arguments presented, which in turn determined the extent of influence.

There are a number of constructs and scales relevant to the need for self-worth such as the self-doubt scale (Oleson, Poehlmann, Yost, Lynch, & Arkin, 2000), the judgmental self-doubt scale (Mirels, Greblo, & Dean, 2002), the consumer self-confidence scale (Bearden, Hardesty, & Rose, 2001), and the subjective knowledge scale (Flynn & Goldsmith, 1999), but we focus on two that have achieved the most research attention with respect to attitude change: self-esteem and optimism.

Self-Esteem. The primary measure of self-esteem (SE), defined as the regard people have for themselves, used in social psychological research, is Rosenberg's (1965) *self-esteem scale*. The literature on attitudes and SE usually has been interpreted in terms of McGuire's (1968) reception/yielding model. McGuire (1968) proposed that the relationship between SE and persuasion should be positive when reception processes dominate (Berkowitz & Lundy, 1957), but negative when yielding processes dominate (Janis, 1954). That is, recipients low in SE might have difficulty receiving the message, whereas those high in SE would tend not to yield. If both processes operate simultaneously, then one would expect a curvilinear relationship between SE and persuasion. A meta-analysis of the literature revealed evidence for this curvilinear relationship, with people of moderate SE tending to be more influenceable than those low or high in SE (Rhodes & Wood, 1992). Although the curvilinear finding is consistent with the predictions derived from the reception-yielding model, it is also possible that differences in type or direction of thinking could help to explain the effect.

As described earlier, the ELM holds that any *one* variable can have an impact on persuasion by serving in different roles in different situations depending on the elaboration likelihood. When motivation and/or ability to process the information is low, people can be guided by their SE when deciding whether to accept or reject the persuasive message. In such situations, high SE individuals might be more resistant to persuasion than low SE individuals because they may be more likely to reason that their own opinion was as good or better than that of the source. The sense that one's opinion is better than another's opinion is a specific instance of the ownness bias or endowment effect (i.e, what is associated with me is good; Perloff & Brock, 1980; Kahneman, Knetsch, & Thaler, 1991).

When elaboration is high, SE can play a different role, such as biasing one's thoughts. Thus, high SE individuals would be likely to engage in thinking that supported their initial attitudes but that derogated alternative positions. Alternatively, under high elaboration conditions, SE can influence persuasion by affecting the confidence people have in the validity of the thoughts they have in response to the message. For example, in one study (Briñol & Petty, 2002), thought-direction was manipulated by exposing participants to strong or weak persuasive messages. As expected, the message composed of compelling arguments produced mostly favorable thoughts toward the proposal, whereas the weak arguments produced mostly negative thoughts. After the message was processed and thoughts generated, but prior to assessing attitudes toward the proposal, participants reported their SE. An interaction between SE and argument quality was obtained, such that for the strong message, high SE individuals showed more persuasion than low SE, whereas for the weak message the reversed pattern was observed. Consistent with the self-validation notion (Petty et al., 2002), SE influenced the extent to which participants relied on their own cognitive responses to the message.

Under high elaboration conditions, the role that SE plays depends on a number of factors. SE can either bias the direction of the thoughts or can affect a person's confidence in the thoughts that are generated. The biasing role is more likely when SE is made salient or measured before the message where it can influence thought generation, but if SE is made salient after the message, the latter role is more likely (Briñol & Petty, 2002). In addition, if people were made aware of the potentially biasing impact of SE (either on information processing or on judgment), they might attempt to correct for this influence (Petty, Wegener, & White, 1998). Finally, we speculate that SE might even serve as a message argument if it contains information central to the merits of the object, as might be the case in some personal selling scenarios, such as a job interview (e.g., I should get the job because I'm the best!).

When elaboration is moderate, SE can influence attitudes by affecting the extent of information processing, with low SE being associated with less elaboration than high SE. For example, low SE individuals might have little need to scrutinize the merits of a communication because they would believe that most people are more competent than they are and thus, the message can be accepted on faith. A high SE person, however, would have the confidence to scrutinize the message. This view is consistent with the results of Skolnick and Heslin (1971) who found that argument quality was more important in determining the attitudes of high than low SE individuals. To the extent that people who are high in self-esteem are reminded of this prior to a message and feel a sense of confidence that is misattributed to their attitudes, this confidence could reduce the extent of message processing in cases where elaboration is not constrained to be high or low.

Optimism.   The optimism-pessimism questionnaire (Dember, Martin, Hummer, Howe, & Melton, 1989) and the revised life orientation test (Scheier, Carver, & Bridges, 1994) assess the extent to which people take an optimistic or pessimistic view of life with items such as "I'm always optimistic about my future." Geers, Handley, and McLarney (2003) argued that because of their ability to cope better with unwanted and stressful information, optimists (vs. pessimists) are especially likely to elaborate on valenced information that is of high personal relevance. Consistent with this view, Geers et al., (2003) found that optimists (as measured with the two questionnaires mentioned above) were more persuaded than pessimists by personally relevant messages framed positively (i.e., a new tuition plan was described as a beneficial opportunity to reduce costs) and less persuaded by personally relevant messages framed negatively (i.e., the tuition plan would require all students to work part time for the university). Importantly, when the message was not personally relevant, optimism did not influence attitude change. The finding that optimists were more influenced by positively framed messages and pessimists by negatively framed messages under high thinking conditions (high relevance) may have been due to the fact that "matching" biased processing of the arguments. If the elaboration likelihood was low however, such matching might have served as a simple cue, or if elaboration was moderate, matching might have enhanced information processing activity.

Individual Differences Relevant to the Need for Social Inclusion and Their Impact on Attitudes and Persuasion

The need for social inclusion refers to the need for human approval, connection, relatedness, belonging, caring, and attachment. Although the degree to which a person is interdependent and bound up with others, as compared with the degree to which the individual is independent and separate, can vary as a function of culture (Kitayama, Markus, Matsumoto, & Norasakkunkit, 1997; Markus & Kitayama, 1991), all individuals value to some extent being included by and approved of by others (Baumeister & Leary, 1995).

Groups exert influence on individual attitudes because other people provide an informational standard of comparison for evaluating people's own attitudes (social comparison function) and because they provide social norms through which people can gain or maintain group acceptance (normative function). Applied to our analysis in this chapter, this distinction suggests that what particular pieces of information (e.g., source credibility versus consensus opinions) serve as peripheral cues or in other roles may depend on whether people are governed by informational or normative factors.

The distinction between informational and normative motives has been useful to provide an organizing framework to explain social influence phenomena ranging from an individual's agreement with groups, as in minority group influence (Moscovici, Mucchi-Faina, & Maass, 1994), to group-level shifts in attitude, as in group polarization (Isenberg, 1986). For a detailed review of the motive for social inclusion and approval with respect to attitude change see Prislin and Wood (chap. 16, this volume), Wood (1999), and Cialdini and Trost (1998). In this section of the chapter, we focus more specifically on the impact of individual differences in this motive on attitudes and persuasion. First, we cover individual differences in general motives toward collective versus individual orientation, and then we describe some individual differences toward specific minority groups.

Need for Uniqueness.   The need for uniqueness (Snyder & Fromkin, 1977) refers to the need to feel autonomous, independent, and different from other people. Thus, people who score low on the scale are those who do not want to be different from others. The scale includes items such as "As a rule, I strongly defend my own opinions." Individual differences in the need for uniqueness have been found to predict attitude change in conformity paradigms. For example, when induced to comply with the majority, those who score high (vs. low) in need for uniqueness tend to change their attitudes in the opposite direction as a way to reestablish their sense of uniqueness (Snyder & Fromkin, 1980). Subsequent research has identified at least 15 additional measures that can be used to assess individual differences in the sense of uniqueness and autonomy (see Hmel & Pincus, 2002, for a review). For example, Lynn and Harris (1997) developed a scale to assess the desire for unique consumer products.

As is the case for most individual differences, the need for uniqueness can be easily used to match the frame of persuasive messages with personal characteristics. For example, Tian, Bearden, and Hunter (2001) found that individuals who scored high (vs. low) in their version of the consumer need for uniqueness scale showed a greater preference for ads with unique product designs as compared with common designs. Similar person-message matching findings have been found for individual differences in the separateness-connectedness scale (Wang & Mowen, 1997). As described earlier in this chapter, the specific processes by which matching individual differences and messages results in more persuasion can vary as a function of the elaboration likelihood.

Individualism-Collectivism.   One of the most important ways in which individuals differ from each other has to do with their culture (Triandis, McCusker, & Hui, 1990). Cultural differences have been found to play a major role in a wide variety of phenomena relevant to social cognition and behavior (Markus & Kitayama, 1991; Oyserman, Coon, & Kemmelmeier, 2002). Individualism-collectivism is perhaps the most basic dimension of cultural variability identified in cross-cultural research (Triandis, 1995). Individualism refers to the idea that individuals are independent of one another, whereas collectivism refers to the assumption that groups bind and mutually obligate individuals. Although the distinction between individualism and collectivism has been used to distinguish between Western and East Asian societies, there are also individual differences within each of those two broad cultural axes. Such individual differences can be assessed with a variety of methods, including self-report questionnaires (Triandis & Gelfand, 1998; Triandis et al., 1990).

In the domain of attitude change, individualism and collectivism differences have been found to produce persuasive matching effects similar to those described for other variables. For example, Han and Shavitt (1994) found that, compared to Koreans, Americans were more persuaded by advertisements emphasizing individualistic benefits. In contrast, ads emphasizing family or ingroup benefits were more persuasive for Koreans than for Americans.

Another cultural finding is that Americans report finding individuating information more useful when they are in uncertain situations than relational information, with the reverse being true for Chinese (Gelfand, Spurlock, Sniezek, & Shao, 2000). This pattern of results has been replicated when instead of comparing individuals from different cultures, differences based on individualism/collectivism scales were used. For example, Cialdini, Wosinska, Barrett, Butner, and Gornik-Durose (1999) found that individuals (both American and Polish) high in individualism were more persuaded by an individualistic appeal based on their own prior behavior, whereas those who scored high in collectivism were more persuaded by a collectivistic appeal based on their peer group's prior behavior. Again, whether this matching effect reflects a simple cue, an argument, enhanced thinking, biased thinking, or validation of one's thoughts is an open research question.

Field Dependence.   The term field dependence (Witkin et al., 1954) refers to the extent to which individuals use self-produced as opposed to situational cues, such as the social group, in defining their attributes. This variable is often defined operationally as the extent to which people can use postural and inner ear (self-produced) cues to adjust a luminous rod to the vertical and ignore distracting cues from the perceptual "field," as opposed to the field dependent tendency to locate the vertical in terms of the field rather than one's body orientation. In brief, according to Witkin and his colleagues, field-dependent individuals' perceptions are influenced by the surrounding field or given context.

Field dependence/independence is also measured using the Embedded Figures Test (Witkin, Oltman, Raskin, & Karp, 1971), the Test of Field Dependence (Ekstrom, French, Harman, & Derman 1976), and the linear logistical Rasch model (Fischer & Molenaar, 1995). In these tests, people are provided with a number of items and are asked to select which one of various simple figures is embedded within a complex figure. Because field-dependent individuals are more aware of and responsive to aspects of their social situation than field independent persons, they were found to be more vulnerable to conformity situations (Witkin, 1964). In recent research, Hergovich (2003) found that field dependence was related to suggestibility and belief in paranormal phenomena. Conversely, in the forced-compliance situations in which change arises from an individuals' own behavior rather than external pressures, Laird and Berglas (1975) found that field-independent individuals changed their attitudes more after engaging in counter-attitudinal behavior.

Heesacker, Petty, and Cacioppo (1983) demonstrated that the field dependence can influence attitude change by affecting the extent of thinking. In a study in which both argument quality and source credibility were manipulated, Heesacker et al. (1983) found that the attitudes of field-independent individuals were significantly affected by the quality of the arguments regardless of whether the credibility of the source was high or low. This presumably stemmed from their general propensity to differentiate stimuli. However, field-dependent individuals only showed argument quality effects when source credibility was high (i.e., when it was worthwhile to think). Conceptually similar to the findings described for need for cognition, these results are consistent with the idea that situational variables such as source credibility can enhance information processing for people who typically are not motivated to scrutinize message content.

It is also possible that field dependence can influence attitude change by other psychological processes under different circumstances. For example, field dependence may affect the nature of the cues that people use to form an attitude under low elaboration conditions, to bias their thoughts, or to validate their thoughts in high elaboration settings. As suggested by the study by Heesacker et al. (1983), field dependents can be more affected by source credibility, whereas field independents might be more sensitive to their own behavioral reactions (Laird & Berglas, 1975).

Machiavellianism.   The manipulation of others for personal gain is referred to as Machiavellianism (Mach). Individual differences in Mach can be assessed with a Mach test that measures people's agreement with statements such as "Never tell anyone the real reason you did something unless it is useful to do so." In general terms, high-Machs are extremely pragmatic, have limited commitment to anything other than themselves, tend to adopt leadership roles, and are unconcerned with morality. A complete review of the literature on the issue by Wilson, Near, and Miller (1996) revealed that high-Mach individuals frequently outperform low-Machs in short-term social interactions, especially to the extent that three conditions are met: The experiments (a) involve face-to-face interactions, (b) allow room for innovation, and (c) involve situations that are emotionally charged (high in "irrelevant affect"), which tend to distract low-Machs more than high-Machs.

In the domain of persuasion, these characteristics imply that high-Machs may be more persuasive than low-Machs. For example, even though high-Machs are not more intelligent than low-Machs, they are perceived by their peers as more intelligent and attractive (Cherulnik, Way, Ames, & Hutto, 1981), easily beat low-Machs in bargaining and alliance-forming situations (Gunnthorsdottir, McCabe, & Smith, 2002), and have a superior talent for improvisation and advocating a position contrary to their own beliefs (Burgoon, Miller, & Tubbs, 1972). In research conducted out of the laboratory, Shultz (1993) studied the sales performance of stockbrokers and found that high-Machs had more clients and earned twice as much in commissions as low-Machs. Although this effect occurred only in loosely structured organizations, Shultz's study demonstrated that the Mach scale has implications for both short and long term forms of influence.

Evidence that high-Machs are better at persuading and influencing others is quite extensive (Christie & Geis, 1970; Wilson et al., 1996), but less is known regarding the role of this trait with respect to receiving persuasion. Based on their experiments, Christie and Geis (1970) argued that low-Machs appear to be more susceptible to emotional involvement in interactions on an interpersonal level and tend to be somewhat easily manipulated. To test this notion, Briñol and Petty (2002) gave participants either a set of strong or weak arguments in favor of consuming more vegetables in their diet. Consistent with the above notion, low Machs were more influenced by both messages than high Machs. Also consistent with this view, Bogart, Geis, Levy, and Zimbardo (1970) found that low-Machs changed their attitudes in a dissonance paradigm, whereas high-Machs resisted such an induction.

Individual Differences in Identity and Evaluation of Minority Groups.   Social psychologists have developed numerous measures to assess individual differences in attitudes toward many groups considered to be stigmatized in some way. For example, the modern racism scale (McConahay, Hardee, & Batts, 1981), the pro-Black and anti-Black scale (Katz & Hass, 1988), and the attitude toward blacks scale (Brigham, 1993) measure attitudes toward African Americans. The heterosexual attitudes toward homosexuality scale (Larsen, Reed, & Hoffman, 1980) assesses dispositions toward homosexuals, and the ambivalent sexism inventory (Glick & Fiske, 1996) measures negative attitudes toward women. Finally, individual differences in general dispositions toward minorities and other groups can be assessed with the social dominance orientation scale (Pratto et al., 1994), which assesses the extent to which an individual wants his or her group to dominate and be superior to outgroups.

As we have argued for other variables, individual differences in attitudes toward minority groups can influence attitude change through multiple processes depending on the elaboration likelihood. For example, under low thinking conditions, high (vs. low) prejudiced individuals are more likely to reject persuasive messages originating from stigmatized sources (Mackie, Worth, & Asuncion, 1990), especially for individuals high in identification with the ingroup (Fleming & Petty, 2000). This assumption is due to the fact that the group toward which one is prejudiced can serve as a simple negative cue.

Individual differences in prejudice and group identity can also affect attitudes in similar ways under high elaboration conditions, but through a different process–biasing thinking (Fleming & Petty, 2000). Finally, in situations where elaboration is moderate, individual differences in prejudice can affect attitude change by influencing how much thinking a minority source elicits. For example, Petty, Fleming, and White (1999) found that source stigmatization increased message scrutiny only among those who were low in prejudice toward the stigmatized group. In two studies, thoughts and attitudes of low-prejudiced individuals were more influenced by the quality of the arguments presented by a stigmatized (Black, Experiment 1; homosexual, Experiment 2) than a non-stigmatized (White, Experiment 1; heterosexual, Experiment 2) source. In subsequent research, this same effect was obtained when a persuasive message was about, rather than from, a stigmatized individual (Fleming, Petty, & White, 2004).

Individual Differences in the Motivation to Control for Prejudice. There are not only individual differences in evaluations of minority groups, but also chronic motivations to control for prejudice toward these groups. Among these measures are the motivation to control prejudiced reactions scale (Dunton & Fazio, 1997), the internal and external motivation to respond without prejudice scale (Plant & Devine, 1998), and the humanitarianism-egalitarianism and Protestant ethic scales (Katz & Hass, 1988). These instruments are effective in predicting differences in public and private endorsement of stereotypes as well as motivation to correct one's social judgments.

As described above, individuals low in prejudice scrutinize messages from stigmatized sources to guard against possibly unfair reactions by themselves or others (Petty et al., 1999). This enhanced elaboration activity is also likely to occur for individuals with high scores in motivation to control prejudice, as measured with the scales listed above (Sherman, Stroessner, & Azam, 1997).

Receiving and carefully elaborating relevant information is not the only mechanism through which people can try to correct for potential biases, however. For example, when the elaboration likelihood is relatively low, instead of gathering additional information, individuals motivated to correct for prejudice might rely on heuristics and peripheral cues. Under such circumstances, these individuals might correct simply by activating their heuristic belief, "I am an egalitarian person" (Blair & Banaji, 1996; Moskowitz, Gollwitzer, Wasel, & Schaal, 1999).

At the other extreme of the continuum, when elaboration likelihood is high, motivation to correct for prejudice might influence attitudes by biasing the direction of the thoughts. Consistent with this idea, when low-prejudice individuals were highly motivated to correct for the generation of prejudice-related responses, their thoughts and attitudes have been found to be nonstereotypic (Monteith, 1993). Also, when the likelihood of thinking is high, individual differences in the motive to control for prejudice might influence attitudes by inducing explicit correction processes. There is ample evidence in the domain of prejudice of correction for the unwanted effects of activated stereotypes on attitudes under high elaboration likelihood conditions (Devine, 1989; Dovidio, Kawakami, Johnson, Johnson, & Howard, 1997; Plant & Devine, 1998; Monteith, 1993). When such corrections become highly practiced, as they might be for individuals high in their chronic motive to control prejudice, these corrections may be executed automatically (Maddux et al., 2004).

INDIVIDUAL DIFFERENCES IN PREFERENCES BETWEEN MOTIVES

In this section, we describe two measures that can be used to distinguish between individuals who are more or less dominated by some of the preceding four motives. In particular, we review work on (a) Self-Monitoring (Snyder, 1974), and (b) Uncertainty Orientation (Sorrentino & Short, 1986).

Self-Monitoring

Snyder's (1974) self-monitoring scale differentiates between high self-monitors who are oriented toward social approval and inclusion and low self-monitors who are more motivated to be consistent with their internal beliefs and values. Self-monitoring can be assessed with a reliable and valid individual difference measure (Snyder, 1974) that includes items such as "I have considered being an entertainer."

In the domain of attitudes, high and low self-monitors differ in a number of ways. For example, because internal beliefs are more important to low self-monitors, these individuals are more susceptible to dissonance effects (Snyder & Tanke, 1976) and less susceptible to false feedback about their attitudes (Kendzierski, 1987; Valins, 1966; but see Fiske & Von Hendy, 1992). Also, because high self-monitors pay less attention to internal states and focus more on what the situation requires, they show lower attitude-behavior consistency than low self-monitors (Zanna, Olson, & Fazio, 1980).

Most research on self-monitoring has examined the notion that attitudes serve different functions for people who are high versus low in self-monitoring (Lavine & Snyder, 1996). According to the multiple-roles framework of the ELM, matching of a message to the function served by one's attitude can influence attitudes in multiple ways at different points along the elaboration continuum. Functional matching refers to presenting a message that is in some way relevant to the underlying function served by the attitudes of high and low self-monitors (e.g., presenting a message with value-oriented arguments to a low self-monitor and image-oriented arguments to a high self-monitor).

The most common initial finding in this literature was that high and low self-monitors were more persuaded by messages that were matched (versus mismatched) to the function served by their attitudes. For example, Snyder and DeBono (1985) exposed high and low self-monitors to advertisements for a variety of products that contained arguments appealing either to the social adjustment function (i.e., describing the social image that consumers could gain from the use of the product) or to the value-expressive function (i.e., presenting content regarding the intrinsic quality or merit of the product). They found that high self-monitors were more influenced by ads with image content than ads with quality content. In contrast, the attitudes of low self-monitors were more vulnerable to messages that made appeals to values or quality (see also DeBono, 1987; Lavine & Snyder, 1996; Snyder & DeBono, 1989).

Later research showed that the persuasive effect observed for matching can be determined by different psychological processes depending on the situation. When the likelihood of elaboration is high, matching the content of the message to the functional basis of the attitude is more likely to influence attitudes by biasing the direction of processing. For example, a high self-monitor would be more motivated to generate favorable thoughts to a message that made an appeal to image rather than an appeal to values (Lavine & Snyder, 1996). On the other hand, when the circumstances constrain the likelihood of elaboration to be very low, a functional match is more likely to influence attitudes by serving as a simple cue (DeBono, 1987). For example, even when the content of the message is not processed, if a source simply asserted that the arguments are consistent with a person's values, a low self-monitor may more inclined to directly agree than a high self-monitor by reasoning, "if it links to my values, it must be good."

Functional argument matching not only can influence attitude change by making matched arguments more persuasive than non-matched arguments, but also by influencing the amount of information processing. For example, functional argument matching can result in increased message scrutiny when the elaboration likelihood is free to vary. Some evidence for this was provided by DeBono and Harnish (1988). Their research showed that high self-monitors engaged in greater scrutiny of the arguments when they were presented by an attractive source (who might be expected to make an image appeal) than an expert source (who presumably would make a quality appeal), whereas low self-monitors demonstrated the reverse pattern. In other research, Petty and Wegener (1998) had high and low self-monitors read image (e.g., how good a product makes you look) or quality (e.g., how efficient a product is) appeals that contained strong (e.g., beauty or efficacy that last) or weak arguments (e.g., momentary beauty or efficacy). As expected, the cogency of the arguments had a larger effect on attitudes when the message contained arguments that matched rather than mismatched the functional basis of the attitude. In summary, the accumulated research suggests that matching of a message to the function served by one's attitude can influence attitudes by serving as a peripheral cue (when elaboration is low), by biasing thoughts (when elaboration is high), or by enhancing the amount of information processing (when elaboration is moderate).

Matching also has implications for the generation or production of persuasive messages. For example, Shavitt and her colleagues (Nelson, Shavitt, Schennum, & Barkmeier, 1997; Shavitt, 1990; Shavitt, Lowrey, & Han, 1992) studied the role of self-monitoring by asking participants to write their own advertisements for different types of products. Consistent with the matching notion, it was found that when writing for products that can serve multiple functions (e.g., watch, sunglasses), high self-monitors tended to use more image-based arguments and headlines, whereas low self-monitors tended to use more quality-based arguments and headlines. Thus, when there is opportunity to focus on multiple dimensions of an attitude object, differences in the types of functions that individuals focus on may emerge depending on differences in self-monitoring. Importantly, the above studies also revealed that when only utilitarian or social identity products (i.e., single-function attitude objects) were used, no differences between high and low self-monitors emerged, unless they were provided with several balanced claims (i.e., messages that included both utilitarian and social identity claims). These findings emphasized the importance of testing other unexplored ways in which matching message contents and/or frames with personality types might play a role in persuasion.

Uncertainty Orientation

Sorrentino and Short (1986) have differentiated between uncertainty-oriented individuals who are motivated toward knowledge seeking and understanding, and certainty-oriented individuals who are more interested in avoiding inconsistency. That is, uncertainty-orientation reflects interest in resolving uncertainty and gaining new knowledge, whereas certainty-orientation reflects a primary concern with avoiding ambiguity or confusion. Similar to other variables described under the need to know, to the extent that a situation can be seen as an opportunity to learn something about oneself or the world, uncertainty-oriented individuals will be motivated to think effortfully. In contrast, certainty-oriented individuals will only think carefully to the extent that a situation provides familiarity and certainty about their abilities and opinions. Similar to other individual differences related to the need for consistency, and as a result of the lack of interest in exploring or understanding, certainty-oriented individuals are seen as relatively closed to new beliefs and ideas, and they are likely to be intolerant of others who are different (Sorrentino & Roney, 2000). The measure of uncertainty orientation includes the assessment of two independent dimensions, Uncertainty and Authoritarianism, that assess one's desire to resolve uncertainty (with a projective test) and one's desire to maintain clarity (with a self-report scale), respectively.

Recall that research on self-monitoring has demonstrated that matching a message with a motive can influence attitude change by enhancing the extent of thinking, at least when elaboration is moderate (Petty & Wegener, 1998). A similar argument can be made for the case in which messages match uncertainty orientation. For example, Sorrentino and his colleagues (Sorrentino & Roney, 2000) postulate that situations that activate concerns relevant to one's uncertainty orientation lead to increases in effortful processing relative to situations irrelevant to one's uncertainty orientation. To test this prediction, Sorrentino, Bobocel, Gitta, Olson, & Hewitt (1988) conducted a study in which students were induced to think about a proposal that was high or low in personal relevance. The message contained either strong or weak arguments that came from a source that was high or low in expertise. Sorrentino et al. (1988) found that uncertainty-oriented persons were more influenced by the quality of the arguments contained in the message and less influenced by source expertise as personal relevance increased, replicating past research (Petty, Cacioppo, & Goldman, 1981). However, certainty-oriented participants showed the opposite pattern–being more influenced by source expertise and less influenced by argument quality as personal relevance increased. Whereas uncertainty-oriented individuals obtained certainty by processing the message arguments carefully when relevance was high, certainty-oriented individuals relied on experts to obtain certainty when the issue was of high relevance. Thus, this work suggests that uncertainty orientation can affect attitudes by affecting the extent of information processing, and the conditions that foster thinking are different for high and low certainty individuals.

REMAINING ISSUES IN INDIVIDUAL DIFFERENCES AND ATTITUDES

The bulk of the chapter has dealt with explicit motives–motives of which people are aware and that are assessed with explicit self-reports. In fact, all the individual differences relevant to attitudes and persuasion described so far in this chapter are measured by directly asking people about their self-views. However, just as people can hold conscious, easily reportable motives, personality theorists have suggested that there can be less consciously held motives as well (McClelland, Koestner, & Weinberger, 1989). Early on, these types of motives were assessed with projective tests (Thematic Apperception Test, Proshansky, 1943) and other indirect measures. More recently, investigators have begun to assess these motives with more contemporary implicit measures, such as the Implicit Association Test (IAT) (Greenwald et al., 1998). Implicit motives are important because they can influence information processing and behavior in certain contexts. For example, McClelland (1985) showed that measures of implicit motives are very effective in predicting behavior in relatively unconstrained and spontaneous situations. Furthermore, implicit motives have sometimes predicted action trends over time better than explicit measures of the same motives (McClelland, 1965). Similar arguments have been made for implicit versus explicit attitudes (Greenwald & Banaji, 1995; Wilson et al., 2000).

The importance of the distinction between explicit and implicit motives and its implications for the study of individual differences and attitude change has been noted by Epstein in his cognitive-experiential self-theory (CEST) (see Epstein, 2003, for a review). Epstein identified the same four basic motives used in this chapter as the major human needs, and noted that each of those explicit motives is associated with implicit beliefs able to influence thoughts and behavior. The CEST argues that there are two independent information-processing systems that operate in parallel (see also Smith & DeCostner, 2000). The experiential system is driven by emotion, is associative, rapid, and primarily nonverbal. In contrast, the rational system is analytic, logical, and slower in information processing. Importantly, Epstein and his colleagues have developed an instrument to assess individual differences in rational and experiential thinking styles, the rational-experiential inventory (REI) (Epstein et al., 1996; for a refined version, see Pacini & Epstein, 1999). The rational subscale of the REI is based largely on the need for cognition scale (Cacioppo & Petty, 1982), and has been able to predict intellectual performance and adjustment, including measures of ego strength and self-esteem, and is correlated with measures of openness, conscientiousness, and physical well-being. The experiential subscale is positively associated with measures of extroversion, agreeableness, empathy, creativity, emotionality, and sense of humor. Given different ways of processing information, Rosenthal and Epstein (2000; see Epstein, 2003) found matching effects for REI and persuasion. That is, in a study in which a rational message (emphasizing objective information) and an experiential message (including vivid individual cases) in favor of breast self-examination were presented, Rosenthal and Epstein (2000) found more persuasion when the message matched participants' thinking style.

This example demonstrates the relevance of considering implicit aspects of the self for the purpose of potential matching effects (see also Wheeler et al., 2002). However, individual differences in implicit constructs might influence attitudes and attitude change through a multitude of processes. For example, because independence between the implicit and explicit motives is a well-established finding (McClelland et al., 1989), there might be individuals with discrepancies between their explicit and implicit motives (Kehr, 2004). Briñol, Petty, and Wheeler (2004) have suggested that such discrepancies can have important consequences for information processing and attitude change. For example, because internal inconsistencies that are explicit are often associated with aversive feelings (Abelson et al., 1968) and enhanced information processing (Maio, Bell, & Esses, 1996), individuals with discrepancies between their implicit and explicit self-conceptions might similarly be (implicitly) motivated to reduce this ambivalence by seeking and processing discrepancy-relevant information. In order to test this assumption, Briñol, Petty, et al. (2004) conducted a study in which both explicit and implicit self-dimensions (e.g., self-esteem) were measured. Results showed that as implicit-explicit self-discrepancies increased, participants engaged in more thinking about a persuasive message framed as relevant to the discrepancy. In this research, message processing was assessed by the impact of strong versus weak arguments on attitudes and valenced thoughts. These findings suggest that discrepancies between explicit and implicit self-conceptions are important to understand because such discrepancies can influence attitudes by affecting the extent of information processing.

In the last part of the chapter, we examine a number of other individual differences that are related to persuasion, but for which the link with explicit or implicit motives is not as clear as the ones already described. For example, individual differences can be examined among relatively enduring demographic aspects of a person (e.g., gender and age), individual skills and abilities (e.g., intelligence), and general traits of personality (e.g., the Big Five). In this section, we cover the impact on attitude strength and change of the most studied measures of individual differences regarding ability, demographic, and other personality characteristics, noting the links to the four motivational constructs when relevant.

Gender

Women are sometimes viewed as more easily persuaded than men. Although this difference may reflect a cultural stereotype, research has tended to show that women are more susceptible to influence than men (Cooper, 1979; Janis & Field, 1959). The basis for this difference may be early socialization experiences because women are expected to conform and maintain harmony (Hovland & Janis, 1959; Eagly, 1978; Eagly & Wood, 1991). These expectations might suggest that gender could be particularly related to the motive of social approval. Another possibility is the greater message reception skills of women (McGuire, 1969), which would relate gender to the need to know. McGuire (1968) also speculated that the effect might be due to the gender of the influence agent, the experimenter, or the person who made the experimental materials. Additionally, Eagly and Carli (1981; see also Petty & Wegener, 1998) noted that some of the gender effect may be attributed to the nature of the influence topic and to the content of the message arguments often used in persuasion studies.

Each of these factors can probably account for part of the variance in gender effects. For example, the gender difference can be undermined or eliminated when the gender of the influence agent (Weitzenhoffer & Weitzenhoffer, 1958) or the gender of the investigator (Cooper, 1979) is controlled. The gender difference can also be reduced when the appeal is based on reciprocity rather than sympathy (Fink et al., 1975). Gender effects can even be reversed, with men being more influenceable than women, for those topics for which women have stronger attitudes or more knowledge (Cacioppo & Petty, 1980; Sistrunk & McDavid, 1971; see Eagly & Carli, 1981 for a review).

Much of this research suggests that there may not be much of a gender difference in persuadability once other factors are controlled (e.g., gender of source, knowledge differences in the audience). If there were an effect of gender itself on persuadability, little if any research has examined the mechanisms that might underlie its impact. Thus, it is not clear if gender affects persuasion because one's gender is used as a simple cue (e.g., "as a man, I must resist"), affects the extent of information processing, biases its direction, counts as an argument itself, or affects thought confidence. As described for other variables, each of these roles is more likely to occur under some circumstances and with different consequences for attitude strength.

Age

Popular wisdom suggests that young people are more susceptible to persuasion than are older adults. Laboratory research has generally confirmed this assumption. Different studies have shown that young children (vs. older individuals) are more open to different forms of suggestion and hypnosis (Ceci & Bruck, 1993) and that their attitudes are less stable (Alwin, Cohen, & Newcomb, 1991). Some authors have argued that this effect is due to a gradual decrease in susceptibility with age (Glenn, 1980). Others have proposed that this effect is the result of an abrupt change in resistance to persuasion after young adulthood (Mannheim, 1952), and still others have suggested a curvilinear relationship with younger and older individuals being most susceptible to change (Sears, 1981). Recent evidence has provided empirical support for the curvilinear hypothesis, with susceptibility to attitude change shown to be greater during early and late adulthood than during middle adulthood (Visser & Krosnick, 1998). However, it seems unlikely that age per se relates to influenceability. Perhaps age is related to the motive for consistency. Age is often confounded with other variables that would foster this effect, such as attitude strength, likelihood of challenging experiences, and people's naïve theories about aging (Petty & Wegener, 1998). Consonant with this view, Visser and Krosnick (1998) found that attitude importance, certainty, and perceived quantity of attitude-relevant knowledge are in fact greater in middle adulthood than during early or late adulthood.

Intelligence

Individual differences in intelligence are often measured with standardized, multitest reliable instruments (for a review, see Sternberg & Grigorenko, 2003). Traditional analyses of intelligence have focused on how intelligence affects a recipient's ability to receive and yield to messages (McGuire, 1969; for a review, see Wyer & Albarracín, chap. 7, this volume). Because intelligent individuals have greater ability to understand and to scrutinize the merits of a message than relatively less intelligent people, intelligence can presumably increase persuasion when reception factors are important (Cooper & Dinerman, 1951). In contrast, because intelligent individuals likely have a greater ability to defend their attitudes, intelligence can also lead to resistance to persuasion (Crutchfield, 1955). A meta-analytic examination of the accumulated literature on intelligence and attitude change revealed that increased intelligence was generally associated with decreased persuasion (Rhodes & Wood, 1992). There are a number of reasons why this might be the case.

Perhaps highly intelligent people have a greater ability to counterargue messages. However, if the message were especially strong (and not easily counterargued), highly intelligent people might show more persuasion. If we assume that intelligence increases the ability to discern the merits of strong arguments and the flaws in weak ones, then the ability to process associated with intelligence works similarly to the need to know. As described earlier in this chapter, the need to know often influences attitude change by enhancing the extent of information processing. Like other variables, intelligence might also be capable of serving in multiple roles. For example, although it has not been studied explicitly, the perceived intelligence of an individual could function as a peripheral cue (e.g., "I am likely smarter than the source, so why should I change my view?"), especially when the elaboration likelihood is low. Intelligence might not only influence attitudes by serving as a simple cue or by affecting the extent of elaboration, but also by biasing the information processing or by influencing thought confidence. For example, if one's intelligence is made salient after carefully processing the message, it might affect persuasion by influencing the confidence with which people hold their cognitive responses to the message (e.g., "Because I am usually right, I should trust and follow what I am thinking about the proposal").

Of course, we do not imply that only intelligence as measured with traditional questionnaires can play a role in persuasion. As noted previously, an individual's perceived intelligence could also have an impact on attitudes through different roles. Not only how intelligent a person thinks he or she is, but also other related metabeliefs can have an impact on attitudes, such as people's theories about the malleability of their own intelligence (Dweck et al., 1995). Future research might also benefit from exploring the role of individual differences in emotional intelligence or the ability to perceive, interpret and regulate peoples' own (and others) emotional states in influencing attitudes. The study of individual differences in birth order might provide another alternative for future research. For example, Sulloway (1996) linked higher intelligence to first-born children and to less rebellion against the status quo, which might lead in turn to more resistance to change and to accept new ideas.

The Big Five

Using cluster and factor analytic techniques, personality theorists have reduced the universe of possible personality traits to a limited set of dimensions. The most well-established example is the Big Five of personality (Costa & McCrae, 1985; Digman, 1990). The five orthogonal factors it proposes are usually referred to as (a) Extraversion or Dominance and Submissiveness, (b) Agreeableness, (c) Conscientiousness (Dependability), (d) Emotional Stability (Neuroticism), and (e) Openness to Experience. Most of the research studying the influence of these five factors on attitudes change has shown matching effects.

For example, dominant and submissive individuals have been found to be more responsive to individual persuaders (Blankenship, Hnat, Hess, & Brown, 1984) and to messages (Moon, 2002) that match their personality styles. In one study, Moon (2002) found that dominant individuals changed their attitudes more in the direction of a dominant message (defined as one that expressed greater confidence in its claims and was more commanding of others, relative to submissive messages; Dillard, Kinney, & Cruz, 1996), whereas submissive individuals were more influenced by messages with a submissive style. In conceptually similar research, Chang (2002) found that extravert individuals (as measured by the Eysenck, Eysenck, & Barrett, 1985 introvert/extravert scale) were more vulnerable to messages containing arguments presenting extravert characteristics of an object (e.g., for people who enjoy meeting others), whereas those scoring high in introversion showed more attitude change in response to a message containing introvert characteristics (e.g., for those who are mostly quiet with others). Wheeler et al. (in press) showed that matching the message frame to one's introversion/extraversion can enhance thinking about the arguments presented leading to persuasion only when the arguments are strong. Of course, the psychological processes through which matching messages and traits result in more persuasive effects can vary depending on the elaboration likelihood. Finally, recent research (Schaefer, Williams, Goodie, & Campbell, 2004) has shown that Extraversion tends to be associated with overconfidence (defined as the difference between confidence and accuracy) in a task in which participants had to rate how confident they were in their responses to general knowledge questions. Due to the important role of confidence in the domain of attitudes, this finding suggest that Extraversion and other basic personality dimensions may be capable of influencing attitude change by affecting the confidence with which people hold their cognitive responses.

Other Specific Traits

We noted earlier that individuals can differ in a variety of ways other than the five major factors, though many of the more specific traits may share some variance with the Big five (e.g., need for cognition is related to openness; Cacioppo et al., 1996). In concluding this section we note some other specific individual differences that have been related to persuasion. For example, consider individual differences in anxiety proneness as measured by the trait anxiety component of the State–Trait Anxiety Inventory (Spielberger, Gorsuch, & Lushene, 1970). Consistent with the notion that individuals classified by this scale as high (vs. low) in trait anxiety tend to exhibit more difficulties in processing and encoding information, DeBono and McDermott (1994) found that anxious people used the attractiveness of the source to decide their position in response to a persuasive message, whereas less anxious individuals relied on the cogency of the arguments contained in the message. Other research has demonstrated that the individual difference variable of repression-sensitization also identifies some people, sensitizers, who may be more attentive to argument quality and others, repressors, who may be more prone to using heuristics (DeBono & Snyder, 1992).

Obviously, individuals can differ in countless other ways. For many of these more specific individual differences, similar matching effects between the type of persuasive message and individual characteristics have been found. For example, different lines of research have found persuasive matching effects for ideal versus ought self-guides (Evans & Petty, 2003; Herbst, Gaertner, & Insko, 2003; Tykocinski, Higgins, &Chaiken, 1994), for individuals with a dominant independent vs. interdependent self-construals (Lee, Aaker, & Gardner, 2000; see also individualism-collectivism individual differences), for individuals who are high versus low in their consideration of future consequences (Strathman, Gleicher, Boninger, & Edwards, 1994), and for other more narrow variables, such as the centrality of visual product aesthetics (Bloch, Brunel, & Arnold, 2003). Sometimes these matching effects seem to be produced by the match serving as a simple cue, biasing processing, or affecting the extent of processing. As should be obvious by now, we suspect that each type of specific matching would be operative in different situations along the elaboration continuum.

Finally, in order to facilitate the understanding of possible personality differences among people, some scholars have taken single indicators of personality and aggregated them in multiple traits or cognitive styles. An example of this strategy can be found in the distinction between adaptors and innovators (e.g., Goldsmith, 1984). Adaptors like security and prudence, and are characterized by traits such as dogmatism, conservatism, intolerance of ambiguity, practicality, and group dependence. Innovators like challenge and are described by traits such as extroversion, flexibility, adventurousness, impulsiveness, impatience, risk taking, and independence. It seems plausible to expect that these two cognitive styles differ in the motives outlined in this chapter as well as in the type of information people consider when forming or changing their attitudes. For example, Bathe (1999) found that adaptators (vs. innovators) tended to be more vulnerable to different ads and also more sensitive to the source of messages.

CONCLUSIONS

In the present chapter, social psychology's major research findings regarding the role of individual differences on attitude change have been described. A large number of individual differences have been examined in persuasion research. We organized most of them into several meaningful categories of motivational factors: (a) knowledge seeking, (b) consistency, (c) self-worth, and (d) social approval. The main psychological processes by which variables within those four motives can influence attitude change are by: (a) affecting the amount of information processing; (b) biasing the thoughts that are generated, or (c) influencing one's confidence in those thoughts and thus whether they are used; (d) making certain information more likely to serve as arguments, or (e) affecting the selection and use of simple cues and heuristics. By grouping the many specific individual differences and persuasion processes into meaningful categories, we aimed to provide a useful guide to organize and facilitate access to key findings in this literature.

Individual differences in nonmotivational variables, such as demographic, ability, and cultural factors were also considered. Perhaps the most common finding in the literature on individual differences has been that matching persuasive messages to people's characteristics increases persuasion. The present review has provided a detailed examination of the different psychological mechanisms through which such persuasive matching effects and exceptions might occur. Consistent with the multiple roles notion of the ELM, matching messages with personality has been found to influence persuasion by different processes depending on the likelihood of thinking. Additionally, recent research has shown that matching can produce processing fluency or a feeling of fit (Lee & Aaker, 2004). Future research should explore whether such a sense of processing fluency or "feeling right" can also influence attitudes through the multiple processes described in the present chapter.

An additional feature of the current review is the proposition that individual differences can affect persuasion both when an individual is a target and an agent of persuasion. Although most of the research conducted in the domain of social psychology has focused on individuals as targets of influence, individual differences are also relevant for the study of the persuasive agent, as shown for variables such as need for cognition, Machiavellianism, and argumentativeness.

This review also makes it clear that the same basic human motives might be assessed with multiple individual difference measures. Although each of the particular measures focuses on different aspects of the motive, each presumably has in common the reliance on what people consciously report about their self-concept. However, we have noted that there might be other less consciously accessible individual differences relevant to attitude change. As described in this chapter, matching persuasive messages to implicit aspects of the self-concept, and studying the combinatory effects associated with both explicit and implicit individual differences constitutes an important avenue for future research.

REFERENCES

Abelson, R. P., Aronson, E., McGuire, W. J., Newcomb, T. M., Rosenberg, M. J., & Tannenbaum, P. H. (1968). *Theories of cognitive consistency: A sourcebook.* Chicago: Rand McNally.

Adorno, T. W., Frenkel-Brunswik, E., Levinson, D. J., & Sanford, R. N. (1950). *The authoritarian personality.* New York: Harper & Row.

Ahlering, R. F., & Parker, L. D. (1989). Need for cognition as a moderator of the primacy effect. *Journal of Research in Personality, 23,* 313–317.

Albarracín, D., & Mitchell, A. L. (2004). The role of defensive confidence in preference for proattitudinal information: How believing that one is strong can sometimes be a defensive weakness. *Personality and Social Psychology Bulletin, 30,* 1565–1584.

Albarracín, D., Wallace, H. M., & Glasman, L. R. (2004). Survival and change of attitudes and other social judgments: A model of activation and comparison. In M. P. Zanna (Ed.), *Advances in Experimental Social Psychology* (Vol. 36, pp. 252–315). San Diego, CA: Academic Press.

Alicke, M. D. (1985). Global self-evaluation as determined by desirability and controllability of trait adjectives. *Journal of Personality and Social Psychology, 49*, 1621–1630.

Allport, G. W. (1955). *Becoming; basic considerations for a psychology of personality.* New Haven, CT: Yale University Press.

Altemeyer, B. (1981). *Right-wing authoritarianism.* Winnipeg: University of Manitoba Press.

Altemeyer, B. (1998).The other "authoritarian personality." In M. P. Zanna (Ed.), *Advances in experimental social psychology* (Vol. 30, pp. 47–92). San Diego, CA: Academic Press.

Alwin, D. F., Cohen, R. L., & Newcomb, T. M. (1991). *The women of Benington: A study of political orientations over the life span.* Madison, WI: University of Wisconsin Press.

Aronson, E. (1969). Cognitive dissonance: A current perspective. In L. Berkowitz (Ed.), *Advances in experimental social psychology* (Vol. 4, pp. 1–34). New York: Academic Press.

Asch, S. E. (1956). Studies of independence and conformity: a minority of one against a unanimous majority. *Psychological Monographs, 70* (9, no. 416).

Avtgis, T. A. (1998). Locus of control and persuasion, social influence, and conformity: A meta-analytic review. *Psychological Reports, 83*, 899–903.

Axsom, D., Yates, S. M., & Chaiken, S. (1987). Audience response as a heuristic cue in persuasion. *Journal of Personality and Social Psychology, 53*, 30–40.

Bargh, J. A., Chaiken, S., Govender, R., & Pratto, F. (1992). The generality of the automatic attitude activation effect. *Journal of Personality and Social Psychology, 62*, 893–912.

Bathe, S. (1999). Cognitive style differences and their impact on responses to message sources. *Marketing, Intelligence, and Planning, 17*, 280–287.

Baumeister, R. F. (1982). A self-presentational view of social phenomena. *Psychological Bulletin, 91*, 3–26.

Baumeister, R. F. (1998). The self. In D. Gilbert, S. Fiske, & G. Lindzey (Eds.), *The handbook of social psychology* (4th ed., Vol. 2, pp. 680–740). New York: McGraw-Hill.

Baumeister, R. F., & Cairns, K. J. (1992). Repression and self-presentation: When audiences interfere with self-deceptive strategies. *Journal of Personality and Social Psychology, 62*, 851–862.

Baumeister, R. F., & Leary, M. R. (1995). The need to belong: Desire for interpersonal attachments as a fundamental human motivation. *Psychological Bulletin, 117*, 497–529.

Baumeister, R. F., Tice, D. M., & Hutton, D. G. (1989). Self- presentational motivations and personality differences in self-esteem. *Journal of Personality, 57*, 547–579.

Bearden, R. G., Netemeyer, M. F., & Teel, J. E. (1989). Measurement of consumer susceptibility to interpersonal influence. *Journal of Consumer Research, 15*, 473–481.

Bearden, W. O., Hardesty, D., & Rose, R. L. (2001). Consumer self-confidence: Refinements in conceptualization and measurement. *Journal of Consumer Research, 28*, 121–134.

Bem, D. J. (1972). Self-perception theory. In L. Berkowitz (Ed.), *Advances in experimental social psychology* (Vol. 6, pp. 1–62). New York: Academic Press.

Bem, D. J., & Allen, A. (1974). On predicting some of the people some of the time: The search for cross-situational consistencies in behavior. *Psychological Review, 81*, 506–520.

Berkowitz, L., & Lundy, R. M. (1957). Personality characteristics related to susceptibility to influence by peers or authority figures. *Journal of Personality, 25*, 306–316.

Bizer, G. Y., Krosnick, J. A., Holbrook, A. L., Wheeler, C. S., Rucker, D. D., & Petty, R. E. (2004). The impact of personality on cognitive, behavioral, and affective political processes: The effects of need to evaluate. *Journal of Personality, 72*, 995–1027.

Blair, I. V., & Banaji, M. R. (1996). Automatic and controlling processes in stereotype priming. *Journal of Personality and Social Psychology, 70*, 1142–1163.

Blankenship, V., Hnat, S. M., Hess, T. G., & Brown, D. R. (1984). Reciprocal interaction and similarity of personality attributes. *Journal of Social and Personal Relationships, 1*, 415–432.

Bloch, P. H., Brunel, F. F., Arnold, T. J. (2003). Individual differences in the centrality of visual product aesthetics: Concept and measurement. *Journal of Consumer Research, 29*, 551–565.

Bogart, K., Geis, F., Levy, M., & Zimbardo, P. (1970). No dissonance for Machiavellians. In R. Christie & F. L. Geis (Eds.), *Studies in Machiavellianism* (pp. 251–263). New York: Academic Press.

Brehm, J. W. (1966). *A theory of psychological reactance.* San Diego, CA: Academic Press.

Brewer, M. B. (1991). The social self: On being the same and different at the same time. *Personality and Social Psychology Bulletin, 17*, 475–482.

Brigham, J. C. (1993). College students' racial attitudes. *Journal of Applied Social Psychology, 23*, 1933–1967.

Briñol, P., & Petty, R. E. (2002). *Individual differences in confidence: A self-validation analysis.* Unpublished manuscript, Ohio State University, Columbus, OH.

Briñol, P., & Petty, R. E. (2003). Overt head movements and persuasion: A self-validation analysis. *Journal of Personality and Social Psychology, 84*, 1123–1139.

Briñol, P., & Petty, R. E. (2004). Self-validation processes: The role of thought confidence in persuasion. In G. Haddock & G. Maio (Eds.), *Contemporary perspectives on the psychology of attitudes* (pp. 205–226). London: Psychology Press.

Briñol, P., Petty, R. E., Barden, J., & Horcajo, J. (2004, February). *Changing automatic attitudes with persuasive messages*. Paper presented at the annual meeting of the Society for Personality and Social Psychology. Austin, TX.

Briñol, P., Petty, R. E., Gallardo, I., & Horcajo, J. (2004, February). *Multiple roles of self-affirmation in persuasion*. Paper presented at the annual meeting of the Society for Personality and Social Psychology. Austin, TX.

Briñol, P., Petty, R. E., & Tormala, Z. L. (2004). The self-validation of cognitive responses to advertisements. *Journal of Consumer Research, 31*, 559–573.

Briñol, P., Petty, R. E., & Wheeler, C. S. (2004). *Discrepancies between explicit and implicit self-concepts: Consequences for information processing and persuasion*. Manuscript under review.

Briñol, P., Rucker, D., Tormala, Z. L., & Petty, R. E. (2004). Individual differences in resistance to persuasion: The role of beliefs and meta-beliefs. In E. S. Knowles & J. A. Linn (Eds.), *Resistance and persuasion* (pp. 83–104). Mahwah, NJ: Lawrence Erlbaum Associates.

Burgoon, M., Miller, G. R., & Tubbs, S. L. (1972). Machiavellianism, justification, and attitude change following counterattitudinal advocacy. *Journal of Personality and Social Psychology, 22*, 366–371.

Buss, D. M., & Greiling, H. (1999). Adaptive individual differences. *Journal of Personality, 67*, 209–243.

Cacioppo, J. T., Harkins, S. G., & Petty, R. E. (1981). The nature of attitudes and cognitive responses and their relationships to behavior. In R. E. Petty, T. M. Ostrom, & T. C. Brock (Eds.), *Cognitive responses in persuasion* (pp. 31–54). Hillsdale, NJ: Lawrence Erlbaum Associates.

Cacioppo, J. T., Marshall-Goodell, B. S., Tassinary, L. G., & Petty, R. E. (1992). Rudimentary determinants of attitudes: Classical conditioning is more effective when prior knowledge about the attitude stimulus is low than high. *Journal of Experimental Social Psychology, 28*, 207–233.

Cacioppo, J. T., & Petty, R. E. (1980). Sex differences in influenceability: Toward specifying the underlying processes. *Personality and Social Psychology Bulletin, 6*, 651–656.

Cacioppo, J. T., & Petty, R. E. (1982). The need for cognition. *Journal of Personality and Social Psychology, 42*, 116–131.

Cacioppo, J. T., Petty, R. E., Feinstein, J. A., & Jarvis, W. B. G. (1996). Dispositional differences in cognitive motivation: The life and times of individuals varying in need for cognition. *Psychological Bulletin, 119*, 197–253.

Cacioppo, J. T., Petty, R. E., & Kao, C. F. (1984). The efficient assessment of need for cognition. *Journal of Personality Assessment, 48*, 306–307.

Cacioppo, J. T., Petty, R. E., & Morris, K. J. (1983). Effects of need for cognition on message evaluation, recall, and persuasion. *Journal of Personality and Social Psychology, 45*, 805–818.

Campbell, J. D. (1986). Similarity and uniqueness: The effects of attribute type, relevance, and individual differences in self-esteem and depression. *Journal of Personality and Social Psychology, 50*, 281–294.

Carver, C. S., & Scheier, M. F. (1981). *Attention and self-regulation: A control-theory approach to human behavior*. New York: Springer-Verlag.

Ceci, S. J., & Bruck, M. (1993). Suggestibility of the child witness: A historical review and synthesis. *Psychological Bulletin, 113*, 403–439.

Chaiken, S. (1987). The heuristic model of persuasion. In M. P. Zanna, J. M. Olson, & C. P. Herman (Eds.), *Social influence: The Ontario symposium* (Vol. 5, pp. 3–39). Hillsdale, NJ: Lawrence Erlbaum Associates.

Chaiken, S., Liberman, A., & Eagly, A. H. (1989). Heuristic and systematic processing within and beyond the persuasion context. In J. S. Uleman & J. A. Bargh (Eds.), *Unintended thought* (pp. 212–252). New York: Guilford.

Chaiken, S., & Maheswaran, D. (1994). Heuristic processing can bias systematic processing: Effects of source credibility, argument ambiguity, and task importance on attitude judgment. *Journal of Personality and Social Psychology, 66*, 460–473.

Chang, C. (2002). Self-congruency as a cue in different advertising-processing contexts. *Communication Research, 29*, 503–536.

Chen, S., & Chaiken, S. (1999). The Heuristic-systematic model in its broader context. In S. Chaiken and Y. Trope (Eds.), *Dual-process theories in social psychology* (pp. 73–96). New York: Guilford Press.

Cherulnik, P. D., Way, J. H., Ames, S., & Hutto, D. B. (1981). Impressions of high and low machiavellian men. *Journal of Personality, 49*, 388–400.

Christie, R., & Geis, F. L. (1970). *Studies in machiavellianism*. New York: Academic Press.

Cialdini, R. B. (1993). *Influence: science and practice* (3rd ed.). New York: HarperCollins.

Cialdini, R. B., & Trost, M. R. (1998). Social influence: Social norms, conformity and compliance. In D. T. Gilbert & S. T. Fiske (Eds.), *The handbook of social psychology*, (4th ed., Vol. 2, pp. 151–192). New York: McGraw-Hill.

Cialdini, R. B., Trost, M. R., & Newsom, J. T. (1995). Preference for consistency: The development of a valid measure and the discovery of surprising behavioral implications. *Journal of Personality and Social Psychology, 69*, 318–328.

Cialdini, R. B., Cacioppo, J. T., Bassett, R., & Miller, J. A. (1978). Low-ball procedure for producing compliance: Commitment then cost. *Journal of Personality and Social Psychology, 36*, 463–476.

Cialdini, R. B., Wosinska, W., Barrett, D. W., Butner, J., & Gornik-Durose, M. (1999). Compliance with a request in two cultures: The differential influence of social proof and commitment/consistency on collectivists and individualists. *Personality and Social Psychology Bulletin, 25*, 1242–1253.

Cohen, G., Aronson, J., & Steele, C. (2000). When beliefs yield to evidence: Reducing biased evaluation by affirming the self. *Personality and Social Psychology Bulletin, 26*, 1151–1164.

Cooper, E., & Dinerman, H. (1951). Analysis of the film "Don't Be a Sucker": A study of communication. *Public Opinion Quarterly, 15*, 243–264.

Cooper, H. M. (1979). Statistically combining independent studies: meta-analysis of sex differences in conformity research. *Journal of Personality and Social Psychology, 37*, 131–146.

Correll, J., Spencer, S. J., & Zanna, M. P. (2004). An affirmed self and an open mind: self-affirmation and sensitivity to argument strength. *Journal of Experimental Social Psychology, 40*, 350–356.

Costa, P. T., Jr., & McCrae, R. R. (1985). The NEO Personality Inventory manual. Odessa, FL: Psychological Assessment Resources, Inc.

Crary, R. W. (1966). Reactions to incongruent self-experiences. *Journal of Consulting Psychology, 30*, 246–252.

Crutchfield, R. S. (1955). Conformity and character. *American Psychologist, 10*, 191–198.

Davies, M. F. (1998). Dogmatism and belief formation: Output interference in the generation of consistent and inconsistent cognitions. *Journal of Personality and Social Psychology, 75*, 456–466.

DeBono, K. G. (1987). Investigating the social-adjustive and value-expressive functions of attitudes: Implications for persuasion processes. *Journal of Personality and Social Psychology, 52*, 279–287.

DeBono, K. G., & Harnish, R. J. (1988). Source expertise, source attractiveness, and processing or persuasive information: A functional approach. *Journal of Personality and Social Psychology, 55*, 541–546.

DeBono, K. G., & McDermott, J. B. (1994). Trait anxiety and persuasion: Individual difference in information processing strategies. *Journal of Research in Personality, 28*, 395–411.

DeBono, K. G., & Snyder, A. (1992). Repressors, sensitizers, source expertise, and persuasion. *Social Behavior and Personality, 20*, 263–272.

Deci, E. L. (1995). *Why we do what we do.* New York: Putnam.

Dember, W., Martin, S., Hummer, M., Howe, S., & Melton, R. (1989). The measurement of optimism and pessimism. *Current Psychology: Research & Reviews, 8*, 102–119.

Devine, P. G. (1989). Stereotypes and prejudice: Their automatic and controlled components. *Journal of Personality and Social Psychology, 44*, 20–33.

Digman, J. M. (1990). Personality structure: Emergence of the five factor model. *Annual Review of Psychology, 41*, 417–440.

Dillard, J. P., Kinney, T. A., & Cruz, M. G. (1996). Influence, appraisals, and emotions in close relationships. *Communication Monographs, 63*, 105–130.

Dovidio, J. F., Kawakami, K., Johnson, C., Johnson, B., & Howard, A. (1997). On the nature of prejudice: Automatic and controlled processes. *Journal of Experimental Social Psychology, 33*, 510–540.

Duncan, L. E., Peterson, B. E., & Winter, D. G. (1997). Authoritarianism and gender roles: Toward a psychological analysis of hegemonic relationships. *Personality and Social Psychology Bulletin, 23*, 41–49.

Dunning, D. (1999). A newer look: Motivated social cognition and the schematic representation of social concepts. *Psychological Inquiry, 10*, 1–11.

Dunton, B. C., & Fazio, R. H. (1997). An individual difference measure of motivation to control prejudiced reactions. *Personality and Social Psychology Bulletin, 23*, 316–326.

Dweck, C. S. (2000). *Self theories: Their role in motivation, personality and development.* Philadelphia: Taylor & Francis.

Dweck, C. S., Chiu, C., & Hong, Y. (1995). Implicit theories and their role in judgments and reactions: A world from two perspectives. *Psychological Inquiry, 6*, 267–285.

Eagly, A. H. (1978). Sex differences in influenceability. *Psychological Bulletin, 85*, 86–116.

Eagly, A. H., & Carli, L. L. (1981). Sex of researchers and sex-typed communications as determinants of sex differences in influenceability: A meta-analysis of social influence studies. *Psychological Bulletin, 90*, 1–20.

Eagly A. H., & Chaiken, S. (1993). *The psychology of attitudes.* Fort Worth, TX: Harcourt, Brace, Jovanovich.

Eagly, A. H., & Wood, W. (1991). Explaining sex differences in social behavior: A meta-analytic perspective. *Personality and Social Psychology Bulletin, 17*, 306–315.

Edwards, J. A. (2003). The interactive effects of processing preference and motivation on information processing: Causal uncertainty and the MBTI in a persuasion context. *Journal of Research in Personality, 37*, 89–99.

Edwards, J. A., Lanning, L., & Hooker, K. A. (2002). Jungian personality theory and social information processing. *Journal of Personality Assessment, 78*, 432–450.

Ekstrom, R. B., French, J. W., Harman, H. H., & Derman, D. (1976). Manual for kit of factor-referenced cognitive tests. Princeton, NJ: Educational Testing Service.

Epstein, S. (2002). Cognitive-Experiential Self-Theory of personality. In T. Millon & M. J. Lerner (Eds.), *Handbook of psychology* (Vol. 5, pp. 159–184). Hoboken, NJ: John Wiley & Sons.

Epstein, S., Pacini, R., Denes-Raj, V., & Heier, H. (1996). Individual difference in intuitive experiential and analytical rational thinking styles. *Journal of Personality and Social Psychology, 71*, 390–405.

Evans, L. M., & Petty, R. E. (2003). Self-guide framing and persuasion: Responsibly increasing message processing to ideal levels. *Personality and Social Psychology Bulletin, 29*, 313–324.

Eysenck, S. B. G., Eysenck, H. J., & Barrett, P. (1985). A revised version of the psychoticism scale. *Journal of Personality and Individual Differences, 6*, 21–29.

Fazio, R. H., Sanbonmatsu, D. M., Powell, M. C., & Kardes, F. R. (1986). On the automatic activation of attitudes. *Journal of Personality and Social Psychology, 50*, 229–238.

Fenigstein, A., Scheier, M. F., & Buss, A. H. (1975). Private self-consciousness: Assessment and theory. *Journal of Consulting and Clinical Psychology, 43*, 522–527.

Festinger, L. (1957). *A theory of cognitive dissonance.* Stanford, CA: Stanford University Press.

Fink, E. L., Rey, L. D., Johnson, K. W., Spenner, K., Morton, D. R., & Flores, E. T. (1975). The effects of family occupational type, sex, and appeal style on helping behavior. *Journal of Experimental Social Psychology, 54*, 369–374.

Fischer, G. H., & Molenaar, I. W. (1995). *Rasch models. Foundations, recent developments and applications.* New York: Springer-Verlag.

Fiske, S. T. (2004). *Social beings: A core motives approach to social psychology.* New York: Wiley.

Fiske, S. T., & Von Hendy, H. M. (1992). Personality feedback and situational norms can control stereotyping processes. *Journal of Personality and Social Psychology, 62*, 577–596.

Fleming, M. A., & Petty, R. E. (2000). Identity and persuasion: An elaboration likelihood approach. In M. A. Hogg & D. J. Terry (Eds.), *Attitudes, behavior, and social context: The role of norms and group membership* (pp. 171–199). Mahwah, NJ: Lawrence Erlbaum Associates.

Fleming, M. A., Petty, R. E., & White, P. H. (2004). Stigmatized targets and evaluation: Prejudice as a determinant of attribute scrutiny and polarization. *Personality and Social Psychology Bulletin.*

Flynn, L. R., & Goldsmith, R. E. (1999). A short, reliable measure of subjective knowledge. *Journal of the Academy of Marketing Science, 46*, 5766.

Freedman, J. L., & Fraser, S. C. (1966). Compliance without pressure: The foot-in-the-door technique. *Journal of Personality and Social Psychology, 4*, 195–203.

Froming, W. J., Walker, G. R., & Lopyan, K. J. (1982). Public and private self-awareness: When personal attitudes conflict with societal expectations. *Journal of Experimental Social Psychology, 18*, 476–487.

Geers, A. L., Handley, I. M., & McLarney, A. R. (2003). Discerning the role of optimism in persuasion: The valence-enhancement hypothesis. *Journal of Personality and Social Psychology, 85*, 554–565.

Gelfand, M. J., Spurlock, D., Sniezek, J., & Shao, L. (2000). Culture and social prediction: The role of information in enhancing confidence in social predictions in the U.S. and China. *Journal of Cross-Cultural Psychology, 31*, 498–517.

Gibbons, F. X., & Wright, R. A. (1983). Self-focused attention and reactions to conflicting standards. *Journal of Research in Personality, 17*, 263–273.

Glenn, N. O. (1980). Values, attitudes, and beliefs. In O. G. O'Brim & J. Kagan (Eds.), *Constancy and change in human development.* Cambridge, MA: Harvard Press.

Glick, P., & Fiske, S. T. (1996). The Ambivalent Sexism Inventory: Differentiating hostile and benevolent sexism. *Journal of Personality and Social Psychology, 70*, 491–512.

Goldsmith, R. E. (1984). Personality characteristics associated with adaptation-innovation. *Journal of Psychology, 117*, 159–165.

Greenwald, A. G., & Banaji, M. (1995). Implicit social cognition: Attitudes, self-esteem, and stereotypes. *Psychological Review, 102*, 4–27.

Greenwald, A. G., Carnot, C. G., Beach, R., & Young, B. (1987). Increasing voting behavior by asking people if they expect to vote. *Journal of Applied Psychology, 72*, 315–318.

Greenwald, A. G., McGhee, D. E., & Schwartz, J. L. K. (1998). Measuring individual differences in implicit cognition: The Implicit Association Task. *Journal of Personality and Social Psychology, 74*, 1464–1480.

Gross, S. R., Holtz, R., & Miller, N. (1995). Attitude certainty. In R. E. Petty & J. A. Krosnick (Eds.), *Attitude strength: Antecedents and consequences* (pp. 215–246). Hillsdale, NJ: Lawrence Erlbaum Associates.

Guadagno, R. E., Asher, T., Demaine, L. J., & Cialdini, R. B. (2001). When saying yes leads to saying no: Preference for consistency and the reverse foot-in-the door effect. *Personality and Social Psychology Bulletin, 27*, 859–867.

Guisinger, S., & Blatt, S. J. (1994). Individuality and relatedness: Evolution of a fundamental dialectic. *American Psychologist, 49*, 104–111.

Gunnthorsdottir, A., McCabe, K., & Smith, V. (2002). Using the machiavellianism instrument to predict trustworthiness in a bargaining game. *Journal of Economic Psychology, 23*, 49–66.

Han, S., & Shavitt, S. (1994). Persuasion and culture: advertising appeals in individualistic and collectivist societies. *Journal of Experimental Social Psychology, 30*, 326–350.

Hastie, R., & Park, B. (1986). The relationship between memory and judgment depends on whether the judgment task is memory-based or on-line. *Psychological Review, 93*, 258–268.

Haugtvedt, C. P., & Petty, R. E. (1992). Personality and persuasion: Need for cognition moderates the persistence and resistance of attitude changes. *Journal of Personality and Social Psychology, 63*, 308–319.

Haugtvedt, C. P., & Wegener, D. T. (1994). Message order effects in persuasion: An attitude strength perspective. *Journal of Consumer Research, 21*, 205–218.

Heesacker, M., Petty, R. E., & Cacioppo, J. T. (1983). Field dependence and attitude change: Source credibility can alter persuasion by affecting message-relevant thinking. *Journal of Personality, 51*, 653–666.

Heider, F. (1958). *The psychology of interpersonal relations.* New York: Wiley.

Heine, S. H., Lehman, D. R., Markus, H. R., & Kitayama, S. (1999). Is there a universal need for positive self-regard? *Psychological Review, 106*, 766–794.

Herbst, K. C., Gaertner, L., & Insko, C. A. (2003). My head says "yes," but my heart says "no:" Cognitive and affective attraction as a function of similarity to the ideal self. *Journal of Personality and Social Psychology, 84*, 1206–1219.

Hergovich, A. (2003). Field dependence, suggestibility and belief in paranormal phenomena. *Personality and Individual Differences, 34*, 195–209.

Hermans, D., De Houwer J., & Eelen, P. (2001). A time course analysis of the affective priming effect. *Cognition and Emotion, 15*, 143–165.

Higgins, E. T. (1987). Self-discrepancy: A theory relating self and affect. *Psychological Review, 94*, 319–340.

Hmel, B. A., & Pincus, A. L. (2002). The meaning of autonomy: On and beyond the interpersonal circumplex. *Journal of Personality, 70*, 277–310.

Hong, Y., Chiu, C., Dweck, C. S., & Sacks, R. (1997). Implicit theories and evaluative processes in person cognition. *Journal of Experimental Social Psychology, 33*, 296–323.

Hovland, C. I., & Janis, I. L. (1959). *Personality and persuadability.* New Haven, CT: Yale University Press.

Hoyle, R. H., Stephenson, M. T., Palmgreen, P., Lorch, E. P., & Donohew, L. (2002). Reliability and validity of scores on a brief measure of sensation seeking. *Personality and Individual Differences, 32*, 401–414.

Huskinson, T. L. H., & Haddock, G. (2004). Individual differences in attitude structure: Variance in the chronic reliance on affective and cognitive information. *Journal of Experimental Social Psychology, 40*, 82–90.

Hutton, D. G., & Baumeister, R. F. (1992). Self-awareness and attitude change: Seeing oneself on the central route to persuasion. *Personality and Social Psychology Bulletin, 18*, 68–75.

Infante, D. A., & Rancer, A. S. (1982). A conceptualization and measure of argumentativeness. *Journal of Personality Assessment, 46*, 72–80.

Infante, D. A., & Rancer, A. S. (1996). Argumentativeness and verbal aggression: A review of recent theory and research. In B. R. Burleson (Ed.), *Communication yearbook* (Vol. 19, pp. 319–351). Thousand Oaks, CA: Sage.

Isenberg, D. J. (1986). Group polarization: A critical review and meta-analysis. *Journal of Personality and Social Psychology, 50*, 1141–1151.

James, W. (1890). *The principles of psychology* (Vol. 1). Cambridge, MA: Harvard University Press.

Janis, I. L. (1954). Personality correlates of susceptibility to persuasion. *Journal of Personality, 22*, 504–518.

Janis, I. L., & Field, P. B. (1959). Sex differences and personality factors related to persuadability. In C. I. Hovland & I. L. Janis (Eds.), *Personality and persuadability* (pp. 55–68). New Haven, CT: Yale University Press.

Janis, I. L., & King, B. T. (1954). The influence of role-playing on opinion change. *Journal of Abnormal and Social Psychology, 49*, 211–218.

Jarvis, W. B. G., & Petty, R. E. (1996). The need to evaluate. *Journal of Personality and Social Psychology, 70*, 172–194.

Javalgi, R. G., Cutler, B. D., & Malhotra, N. K. (1995). Print advertising at the component level: A cross-cultural comparison of the United States and Japan. *Journal of Business Research, 34*, 117–124.

Jost, J. T., Glaser, J., Kruglanski, A. W., & Sulloway, F. J. (2003). Political conservatism as motivated social cognition. *Psychological Bulletin, 129*, 339–375.

Kahneman, D., Knetsch, J., & Thaler, R. (1991). The endowment effect, loss aversion, and status quo bias. *Journal of Economic Perspectives, 5*, 193–206.

Kaplan, K. J. (1972). On the ambivalence-indifference problem in attitude theory and measurement: A suggested modification of the semantic differential technique. *Psychological Bulletin, 77*, 361–372.

Kassin, S. M., Reddy, M. E., & Tulloch, W. F. (1990). Juror interpretations of ambiguous evidence: The need for cognition, presentation order, and persuasion. *Law and Human Behavior, 14*, 43–55.

Katz, I., & Hass, R. G. (1988). Racial ambivalence and American value conflict: Correlational and priming studies of dual cognitive structures. *Journal of Personality and Social Psychology, 55*, 893–905.

Kehr, H. M. (2004). Implicit/Explicit motive discrepancies and volitional depletion among managers. *Personality and Social Psychology Bulletin, 30*, 315–327.

Kemmelmeier, M., Burnstein, E., & Peng, K. (1999). Individualism and authoritarianism shape attitudes toward physician-assisted suicide. *Journal of Applied Social Psychology, 29*, 2613–2631.

Kendzierski, D. (1987). Effects of positive and negative behavioral feedback on subsequent attitude-related action. *Journal of Personality, 55*, 55–74.

Kitayama, S., Markus, H. R., Matsumoto, H., & Norasakkunkit, V. (1997). Individual and collective processes in the construction of the self: Self-enhancement in the United States and self-criticism in Japan. *Journal of Personality and Social Psychology, 72*, 1245–1267.

Klein, C., & Webster, D. M. (2000). Individual differences in susceptibility to persuasion as motivated by the need for cognitive closure. *Basic and Applied Social Psychology, 22*, 119–129.

Kruglanski, A. W. (1996). Motivated social cognition: Principles of the interface. In E. T. Higgins and A. W. Kruglanski (Eds.), *Social Psychology: A Handbook of Basic Principles*. New York: Guilford.

Kruglanski, A. W., Atash, M. N., De Grada, E., Mannetti, L., & Pierro, A. (1997). Psychological theory testing versus psychometric nay saying: Need for closure scale and the Neuberg et al. critique. *Journal of Personality and Social Psychology, 73*, 1005–1016.

Kruglanski, A. W., Peri, N., & Zakai, D. (1991). Interactive effects of need for closure and initial confidence on social information seeking. *Social Cognition, 9*, 127–148.

Kruglanski, A. W., Thompson, E. P., Higgins, E. T., Atash, M. N., Pierro, A., Shah, J. Y., & Spiegel, S. (2000). To "do the right thing" or to "just do it": Locomotion and assessment as distinct self-regulatory imperatives. *Journal of Personality and Social Psychology, 79*, 793–815.

Kruglanski, A. W., & Webster, D. M. (1991). Group member's reaction to opinion deviates and conformist at varying degrees of proximity to decision deadline and of environmental noise. *Journal of Personality and Social Psychology, 61*, 212–225.

Kruglanski, A. W., & Webster, D. M. (1996). Motivated closing of the mind: Seizing and Freezing. *Psychological Review, 103*, 263–283.

Kruglanski, A. W., Webster, D. M., & Klem, A. (1993). Motivated resistance and openness in the presence or absence of prior information. *Journal of Personality and Social Psychology, 65*, 23–35.

Kunda, Z. (1990). The case for motivated reasoning. *Psychological Bulletin, 108*, 480–498.

Laird, J. D., & Berglas, S. (1975). Individual differences in the effects of engaging in counter-attitudinal behavior. *Journal of Personality, 43*, 286–305.

Larsen, K. S., Reed, M., & Hoffman, S. (1980). Attitudes of heterosexuals toward homosexuality: A Likert- type scale and construct validity. *Journal of Sex Research, 16*, 245–257.

Lassiter, G. D., Apple, K. J., & Slaw, R. D. (1996). Need for cognition and thought induced attitude polarization: Another look. *Journal of Social Behavior and Personality, 11*, 647–665.

Lavine, H., & Snyder, M. (1996). Cognitive processing and the functional matching effect in persuasion. The mediating role of subjective perceptions of message quality. *Journal of Experimental Social Psychology, 32*, 580–604.

Leary, M. R., Tambor, E. S., Terdal, S. K., & Downs, D. L. (1995). Self-esteem as an interpersonal monitor: The sociometer hypothesis. *Journal of Personality and Social Psychology, 68*, 518–530.

Lee, A. Y., & Aaker, J. L. (2004). Bringing the frame into focus: The influence of regulatory fit on processing fluency and persuasion. *Journal of Personality and Social Psychology, 86*, 205–218.

Lee, A. Y., Aaker, J. L., & Gardner, W. L. (2000). The Pleasures and Pains of Distinct Self-Construals: The Role of Interdependence in Regulatory Focus. *Journal of Personality and Social Psychology, 78*, 1122–1134.

Leone, C., & Ensley, E. (1986). Self-generated attitude change: A person by situation analysis of attitude polarization and attenuation. *Journal of Research in Personality, 20*, 434–446.

Levinson, D. J., & Sanford, R. N. (1944). A scale for the measurement of anti-Semitism. *Journal of Psychology, 17*, 339–370.

Levy, S., Stroessner, S., & Dweck, C. S. (1998). Stereotype formation and endorsement: The role of implicit theories. *Journal of Personality and Social Psychology,74*, 1421–1436.

Lynn, M., & Harris, J. (1997). Uniqueness desire for unique consumer products. In W. O. Bearden, R. G. Netemeyer, & M. F. Mobley. (Eds.), *Handbook of marketing scales: Multi item measures for marketing and consumer behavior research* (100–101). Newbury Park, CA: Sage.

Mackie, D. M., Worth, L. T., & Asuncion, A. G. (1990). Processing of persuasive in-group messages. *Journal of Personality and Social Psychology, 58*, 812–822.

Maddux, W. W., Barden, J., Brewer, M. B., & Petty, R. E. (2005). Saying no to negativity: The effects of context and motivation to control prejudice on automatic evaluative responses. *Journal of Experimental Social Psychology, 41*, 19–35.

Maio, G. R., Bell, D. E., & Esses, V. M. (1996). Ambivalence and persuasion: The processing of messages about immigrant groups. *Journal of Experimental Social Psychology, 32*, 513–536.

Maio, G. R., & Esses, V. M. (2001). The need for affect: Individual differences in the motivation to approach or avoid emotions. *Journal of Personality, 69*, 583–615.

Maio, G. R., & Olson, J. (2000). *Why we evaluate: Functions of attitudes.* Mahwah, NJ: Lawrence Erlbaum Associates.

Mannheim, K. (1952). The problem of generations. In P. Keeskemeti (Ed.), *Essays on the sociology of knowledge* (pp. 276–322). London: Routledge & Kegan Paul.

Markus, H. R., & Kitayama, S. (1991). Culture and the self: implications for cognition, emotion, and motivation. *Psychological Review, 98*, 224–253.

Maslow, A. H. (1943). A Theory of Human Motivation. *Psychological Review, 50*, 370–396.

Maslow, A. H. (1962). *Toward a Psychology of Being.* Oxford, England: Van Nostrand.

McAdams, D. P. (1985). Motivation and friendship. In S. Duck & D. Perlman (Eds.), *Understanding personal relationships: An interdisciplinary approach* (pp. 85–105). Beverly Hills, CA: Sage.

McClelland, D. C. (1965). Achievement and entrepreneurship: A longitudinal study. *Journal of Personality and Social Psychology, 1*, 389–392.

McClelland, D. C. (1985). How motives, skills, and values determine what people do. *American Psychologist, 40*, 812–825.

McClelland, D. C., Koestner, R., & Weinberger, J. (1989). How do self-attributed and implicit motives differ? *Psychological Review, 96*, 690–702.

McConahay, J. B., Hardee, B. B., & Batts, V. (1981). Has racism declined in America? It depends on who is asking and what is asked. *Journal of Conflict Resolution, 25*, 563–579.

McConnell, A. R. (2001). Implicit theories: Consequences for social judgments of individuals. *Journal of Experimental Social Psychology, 37*, 215–227.

McCrae, R. R., & Costa, P. T., Jr. (1987). Validation of the five-factor model of personality across instruments and observers. *Journal of Personality and Social Psychology, 52*, 81–90.

McGuire, W. J. (1964). Inducing resistance to persuasion: Some contemporary approaches. In L. Berkowitz (Ed.), *Advances in experimental social psychology* (Vol. 1, pp. 191–229). New York: Academic Press.

McGuire, W. J. (1968). Personality and attitude change: An information-processing theory. In A. G. Greenwald, T. C. Brock, & T. M. Ostrom (Eds.), *Psychological foundations of attitudes* (pp. 171–196). New York: Academic Press.

McGuire, W. J. (1969). The nature of attitudes and attitude change. In G. Lindzey & E. Aronson (Eds.), *Handbook of social psychology* (2nd ed., Vol. 3, pp. 136–314). Reading, MA: Addison-Wesley.

Milgram, S. (1974). *Obedience to authority: An experimental view.* New York: Harper & Row.

Mirels, H. L., Greblo, P., & Dean, J. B. (2002). Judgmental self-doubt: beliefs about one's judgmental prowess. *Personality and Individual Differences, 33*, 741–758.

Monteith, M. J. (1993). Self-regulation of prejudiced responses: Implications for progress in prejudice reduction efforts. *Journal of Personality and Social Psychology, 65*, 469–485.

Moon, Y. (2002). Personalization and personality: Some effects of customizing message style based on consumer personality. *Journal of Consumer Psychology, 12*, 313–326.

Moscovici, S., Mucchi-Faina, A., & Maass, A. (1994). *Minority influence.* Chicago: Nelson-Hall Publishers.

Moskowitz, G. B., Gollwitzer, P. M., Wasel, W., & Schaal, B. (1999). Preconscious control of stereotype activation through chronic egalitarian goals. *Journal of Personality and Social Psychology, 77*, 167–184.

Murray, H. A. (1955). Types of human needs. In D. C. McClelland (Ed.), *Studies in motivation* (pp. 63–70). New York: Appleton-Century-Crofts.

Myers, I. B., & McCaulley, M. H. (1985). *Manual: A guide to the development and use of the Myers-Briggs Type Indicator.* Palo Alto, CA: Consulting Psychologists Press.

Nail, P. R., Correll, J. S., Drake, C. E., Glenn, S. B., Scott, G. M., & Stuckey, C. (2001). A validation study of the Preference for Consistency Scale. *Personality and Individual Differences, 31*, 1193–1202.

Nelson, M. R., Shavitt, S., Schennum, A., & Barkmeier, J. (1997). Prediction of long-term advertising effectiveness: New cognitive response approaches. In W. Wells (Ed.), *Measuring advertising effectiveness* (pp. 133–155). Hillsdale, NJ: Lawrence Erlbaum Associates.

Neuberg, S. L., West, S. G., Judice, T. N., & Thompson, M. M. (1997). On dimensionality, discriminant validity, and the role of psychometric analyses in personality theory and measurement: Reply to Kruglanski et al.'s (1997) defense of the Need for Closure Scale. *Journal of Personality and Social Psychology, 73*, 1017–1029.

Newby-Clark, I. R., McGregor, I., & Zanna, M. P. (2002). Thinking and caring about cognitive inconsistency: When and for whom does attitudinal ambivalence feel uncomfortable? *Journal of Personality and Social Psychology, 82*, 157–166.

Newcomb, T. M. (1943). *Personality and Social Change.* Ft. Worth, TX: Dryden Press.

Norem, J. K., & Cantor, N. (1986). Defensive pessimism: Harnessing anxiety as motivation. *Journal of Personality and Social Psychology, 51*, 1208–1217.

Oleson, K. C., Poehlmann, K. M., Yost, J. H., Lynch, M. E., & Arkin, R. M. (2000). Subjective overachievement: Individual differences in self-doubt and concern with performance. *Journal of Personality, 68*, 491–524.

Oyserman, D., Coon, H., & Kemmelmeier, M. (2002). Rethinking individualism and collectivism: evaluation of theoretical assumptions and meta-analyses. *Psychological Bulletin, 128*, 3–73.

Pacini, R. & Epstein, S. (1999). The relation of rational and experiential information processing styles to personality, basic beliefs, and the ration-bias phenomenon. *Journal of Personality and Social Psychology, 76*, 972–987.

Perloff, R. M., & Brock, T. C. (1980). And thinking makes it so: Cognitive responses to persuasion. In M. E. Roloff & G. R. Miller (Eds.), *Persuasion: New directions in theory and research* (pp. 67–99). Beverly Hills, CA: Sage.

Peterson, B. E., Doty, R. M., & Winter, D. G. (1993). Authoritarianism and attitudes toward contemporary social issues. *Personality and Social Psychology Bulletin, 19*, 174–184.

Petty, R. E. (1994). Two routes to persuasion: State of the art. In G. d'Ydewalle, P. Eelen, & P. Bertelson (Eds.), *International perspectives on psychological science* (Vol. 2, pp. 229–247). Hillsdale, NJ: Erlbaum.

Petty, R. E., & Briñol, P. (2002). Attitude Change: The Elaboration Likelihood Model of Persuasion. In G. Bartels & W. Nielissen (Eds.), *Marketing for Sustainability: Towards Transactional Policy Making* (pp. 176–190). Amsterdam, The Netherlands:IOS Press.

Petty, R. E., Briñol, P., Horcajo, J., & Jarvis, W. B. G. (2004). *Chronic accessibility and need for cognition.* Working paper. Ohio State University, Columbus, OH.

Petty, R. E., Briñol, P, & Tormala, Z. L. (2002). Thought confidence as a determinant of persuasion: The self-validation hypothesis. *Journal of Personality and Social Psychology, 82*, 722–741.

Petty, R. E., & Cacioppo, J. T. (1981). *Attitudes and persuasion: Classics and contemporary approaches.* Dubuque, IA: Brown.

Petty, R. E., & Cacioppo, J. T. (1984). The effects of involvement on responses to argument quantity and quality: Central and peripheral routes to persuasion. *Journal of Personality and Social Psychology, 46*, 69–81.

Petty, R. E., & Cacioppo, J. T. (1986). *Communication and persuasion: Central and peripheral routes to attitude change.* New York: Springer-Verlag.

Petty, R. E., & Cacioppo, J. T. (1996). Addressing disturbing and disturbed consumer behavior: Is it necessary to change the way we conduct behavioral science? *Journal of Marketing Research, 33*, 1–8.

Petty, R. E., Cacioppo, J. T. & Goldman, R. (1981). Personal involvement as a determinant of argument- based persuasion. *Journal of Personality and Social Psychology, 41*, 847–855.

Petty, R. E., Fleming, M. A., & White, P. (1999). Stigmatized sources and persuasion: Prejudice as a determinant of argument scrutiny. *Journal of Personality and Social Psychology, 76*, 19–34.

Petty, R. E., Haugtvedt, C., & Smith, S. M. (1995). Elaboration as a determinant of attitude strength: Creating attitudes that are persistent, resistant, and predictive of behavior. In R. E. Petty & J. A. Krosnick (Eds.), *Attitude strength: Antecedents and consequences* (pp. 93–130). Hillsdale, NJ: Lawrence Erlbaum Associates.

Petty, R. E., & Jarvis, B. G. (1996). An individual differences perspective on assessing cognitive processes. In N. Schwarz & S. Sudman (Eds.), *Answering questions: Methodology for determining cognitive and communicative processes in survey research* (pp. 221–257). San Francisco: Jossey-Bass.

Petty, R. E., & Krosnick, J. A. (1995). *Attitude strength: Antecedents and consequences.* Hillsdale, NJ: Lawrence Erlbaum Associates.

Petty, R. E., Priester, J. R., & Briñol, P. (2002). Mass media attitude change: implications of the Elaboration likelihood model of persuasion. In J. Bryant and D. Zillmann, (Eds.), *Media Effects: Advances in theory and research* (2nd ed., pp. 155–199). Mahwah, NJ: Lawrence Erlbaum Associates.

Petty, R. E., Schumann, D. W., Richman, S. A., & Strathman, A. J. (1993). Positive mood and persuasion: different roles for affect under high and low elaboration conditions. *Journal of Personality and Social Psychology, 64*, 5–20.

Petty, R. E., Tormala, Z., Hawkins, C., & Wegener, D. T. (2001). Motivation to think and order effects in persuasion: The moderating role of chunking. *Personality and Social Psychology Bulletin, 27*, 332–344.

Petty, R.E., Tormala, Z., & Rucker, D. D. (2004). Resistance to persuasion: An attitude strength perspective. In J. T. Jost, M. R. Banaji, & D. Prentice (Eds.), *Perspectivism in social psychology: The yin and yang of scientific progress* (pp. 37–51). Washington, D.C.: American Psychological Association.

Petty, R.E., & Wegener, D. T. (1993). Flexible correction processes in social judgment: Correcting for context induced contrast. *Journal of Experimental Social Psychology, 29*, 137–165.

Petty, R.E., & Wegener, D. T. (1998). Attitude change: Multiple roles for persuasion variables. In D. Gilbert, S. Fiske, & G. Lindzey (Eds.), *The handbook of social psychology* (4th ed., Vol. 1, pp. 323–390). New York: McGraw-Hill.

Petty, R. E., & Wegener, D. T. (1998). Matching versus mismatching attitude functions: Implications for scrutiny of persuasive messages. *Personality and Social Psychology Bulletin, 24*, 227–240.

Petty, R. E., & Wegener, D. T. (1999). The Elaboration Likelihood Model: Current status and controversies. In S. Chaiken & Y. Trope (Eds.), *Dual process theories in social psychology* (pp. 41–72). New York: Guilford Press.

Petty, R. E., Wegener, D. T., & White, P. (1998). Flexible correction processes in social judgment: Implications for persuasion. *Social Cognition, 16*, 93–113.

Petty, R. E., Wheeler, S. C., & Bizer, G. (2000). Matching effects in persuasion: An elaboration likelihood analysis. In G. Maio & J. Olson (Eds.), *Why we evaluate: Functions of attitudes* (pp. 133–162). Mahwah, NJ: Lawrence Erlbaum Associates.

Pierro, A., Mannetti, L., Kruglanski, A. W., & Sleeth-Keppler, D. (2004). Relevance override: On the reduced impact of "cues" under high motivation conditions of persuasion studies. *Journal of Personality and Social Psychology*, 86, 251–264.

Plant, E. A., & Devine, P. G. (1998). Internal and external motivation to respond without prejudice. *Journal of Personality and Social Psychology*, 75, 811–832.

Pomerantz, E. M., Chaiken, S., & Tordesillas, R. S. (1995). Attitude strength and resistance processes. *Journal of Personality and Social Psychology*, 69, 408–419.

Pratkanis, A. R. (2000). Altercasting as an influence tactic. In D. J. Terry & M. A. Hogg (Eds.), *Attitudes, behavior, and social context: The role of norms and group membership* (pp. 201–226). Mahwah, NJ: Lawrence Erlbaum Associates.

Pratto, F., Sidanius, J., Stallworth, L.M., & Malle, B.F. (1994). Social dominance orientation: A personality variable predicting social and political attitudes. *Journal of Personality and Social Psychology*, 67, 741–763.

Priester, J. M., & Petty, R. E. (1995). Source attributions and persuasion: Perceived honesty as a determinant of message scrutiny. *Personality and Social Psychology Bulletin*, 21, 637–654.

Priester, J. M., & Petty, R. E. (1996). The gradual threshold model of ambivalence: Relating the positive and negative bases of attitudes to subjective ambivalence. *Journal of Personality and Social Psychology*, 71, 431–449.

Pryor, J. B., Gibbons, F. X., Wicklund, R. A., Fazio, R. H., & Hood, R. (1977). Self-focused attention and self-report validity. *Journal of Personality*, 45, 514–527.

Proshansky, H. M. (1943). A projective method for the study of attitudes. *Journal of Abnormal and Social Psychology*, 38, 393–395.

Pyszczynski, T., Greenberg, J., Solomon, S. (1997). Why do we need what we need? A terror management perspective on the roots of human social motivation. *Psychological Inquiry*, 8, 1–20.

Rhodes, N., & Wood, W. (1992). Self-esteem and intelligence affect influenceability: The mediating role of message reception. *Psychological Bulletin*, 111, 156–171.

Rokeach, M. (1954). The nature and meaning of dogmatism. *Psychological Review*, 61, 194–204.

Rosenberg, M. (1979). *Conceiving the self*. New York: Basic Books.

Rosenthal, L., & Epstein, S. (2000). *Rational and experiential thinking styles as related to receptivity to messages syntonic and dystonic with thinking style*. Unpublished manuscript, University of Massachusetts at Amherst.

Roskos-Ewoldsen, D. R., & Fazio, R. H. (1992). On the orienting value of attitudes: Attitude accessibility as a determinant of an object's attraction of visual attention. *Journal of Personality and Social Psychology*, 63, 198–211.

Rucker, D. D., & Petty, R. E. (2004). When resistance is futile: Consequences of failed counterarguing for attitude certainty. *Journal of Personality and Social Psychology*, 86, 219–235.

Schaefer, P. S., Williams, C. C., Goodie, A. S., & Campbell, W. K. (2004). Overconfidence and the Big Five. *Journal of Research in Personality*, 38, 473–480.

Scheier, M. F., & Carver, C. S. (1980). Private and public self-attention, resistance to change, and dissonance reduction. *Journal of Personality and Social Psychology*, 39, 390–405.

Scheier, M. F., Carver, C. S., & Bridges, M. W. (1994). Distinguishing optimism from neuroticism (and trait anxiety, self-mastery, and self-esteem): A reevaluation of the Life Orientation Test. *Journal of Personality and Social Psychology*, 67, 1063–1078.

Sears, D. O. (1981). Life stage effects on attitude change, especially among the elderly. In S. B. Kiesler, J. N. Morgan, & V. K. Oppenheimer (Eds.), *Aging: Social change* (pp. 183–204). San Diego, CA: Academic Press.

Sedikides, C. (1993). Assessment, enhancement, and verification determinants of the self-evaluation process. *Journal of Personality and Social Psychology*, 65, 317–338.

Shavitt, S. (1990). The role of attitude objects in attitude functions. *Journal of Experimental Social Psychology*, 26, 124–148.

Shavitt, S., Lowrey, T. M., & Han, S. (1992). Attitude functions in advertising: The interactive role of products and self-monitoring. *Journal of Consumer Psychology*, 1, 337–364.

Sherif, M. (1936). *The psychology of social norms*. New York: Harper.

Sherman, D., Nelson, L., & Steele, C. (2000). Do messages about health risks threaten the self? Increasing the acceptance of threatening health messages via self affirmation. *Personality and Social Psychology Bulletin*, 26, 1046–1058.

Sherman, J. W., Stroessner, S. J., & Azam, O. (1997). *The role of personal attitudes in motivated individuation*. Unpublished manuscript, Northwestern University.

Shestowsky, D., Wegener, D. T., & Fabrigar, L. R. (1998). Need for cognition and interpersonal influence: Individual differences in impact on dyadic decisions. *Journal of Personality and Social Psychology*, 74, 1317–1328.

Shultz, J. S. (1993). Situational and dispositional predictions of performance: A test of the hypothesized Machiavellianism X structure interaction among sales persons. *Journal of Applied Social Psychology*, 23, 478–498.

Sistrunk, F., & McDavid, J. W. (1971). Sex variable in conforming behavior. *Journal of Personality and Social Psychology*, 17, 200–207.

Skolnick, P., & Heslin, R. (1971). Quality versus difficulty: Alternative interpretations of the relationship between self-esteem and persuadability. *Journal of Personality, 39*, 242–251.

Smith, E. R., & DeCostner, J. (2000). Dual-process models in social and cognitive psychology: Conceptual integration and links to underlying memory systems. *Personality and Social Psychology Review, 4*, 108–131.

Smith, S. M., & Petty, R. E. (1996). Message framing and persuasion: A message processing analysis. *Personality and Social Psychology Bulletin, 22*, 234–237.

Smith, S. M., Haugtvedt, C. P., & Petty, R. E. (1994). Need for cognition and the effects of repeated expression on attitude accessibility and extremity. *Advances in Consumer Research, 21*, 234–237.

Snyder, C. R., & Fromkin, H. L. (1977). Abnormality as a positive characteristic: The development and validation of a scale measuring need for uniqueness. *Journal of Abnormal Psychology, 86*, 518–527.

Snyder C. R., & Fromkin H. L. (1980). *Uniqueness: The human pursuit of difference*. New York: Plenum.

Snyder, M. (1974). Self-monitoring of expressive behavior. *Journal of Personality and Social Psychology, 30*, 526–537.

Snyder, M., & DeBono, K. G. (1985). Appeals to image and claims about quality: Understanding the psychology of advertising. *Journal of Personality and Social Psychology, 49*, 586–597.

Snyder, M., & DeBono, K. G. (1989). Understanding the functions of attitudes: Lessons from personality and social behavior. In A. Pratkanis, S. Breckler, & A. Greenwald (Eds.), *Attitude structure and function* (pp. 339–359). Hillsdale, NJ: Lawrence Erlbaum Associates.

Snyder, M., & Tanke, E. D., (1976). Behavior and attitude: Some people are more consistent than others. *Journal of Personality, 44*, 510–517.

Sorrentino, R. M., Bobocel, D. R., Gitta, M. Z., Olson, J. M., & Hewitt, E. C. (1988). Uncertainty orientation and persuasion: Individual differences in the effects of personal relevance on social judgments. *Journal of Personality and Social Psychology, 55*, 357–371.

Sorrentino, R. M., & Roney, C. J. R. (2000). *The uncertain mind: Individual differences in facing the unknown*. Philadelphia: Psychology Press.

Sorrentino, R. M., & Short, J. C. (1986). Uncertainty orientation, motivation, and cognition. In R. M. Sorrentino & E. T. Higgins (Eds.), *Handbook of motivation and cognition: Foundations of social behavior* (pp. 379–403). New York: Guilford.

Spielberger, C. D., Gorsuch, R. L., & Lushene, R. E. (1970). *The State-Trait Anxiety Inventory (STAI): Test manual*. Palo Alto, CA: Consulting Psychologists Press.

Stanger, R. (1936). Fascist attitudes: An exploratory study. *Journal of Social Psychology, 6*, 309–319.

Steele, C.M. (1988). The psychology of self-affirmation: Sustaining the integrity of the self. In L. Berkowitz (Ed.), *Advances in experimental social psychology* (Vol. 21, pp. 261–302). New York: Academic Press.

Sternberg, R. J., & Grigorenko, E. L. (2003). *The psychology of abilities, competencies, and expertise*. New York: Cambridge University Press.

Strathman, D., Gleicher, F., Boninger, D. S., & Edwards, C. S. (1994). The consideration of future consequences: Weighing outcomes of behavior. *Journal of Personality and Social Psychology, 66*, 742–752.

Sulloway, F. J. (1996). *Born to rebel*. New York: Pantheon.

Taylor, S. E., & Brown, J. D. (1988). Illusion and well-being: A social psychological perspective on mental health. *Psychological Bulletin, 103*, 193–210.

Tesser, A. (1978). Self-generated attitude change. In I. Berkowitz (Ed.), *Advances in experimental social psychology* (Vol. 11, pp. 289–338). New York: Academic Press.

Tesser, A. (1988). Toward a self-evaluation maintenance model of social behavior. In L. Berkowitz (Ed.), *Advances in experimental social psychology* (Vol. 21, pp. 181–227). New York: Academic Press.

Thompson, M. M., Zanna, M. P., & Griffin, D. W. (1995). Let's not be indifferent about (attitudinal) ambivalence. In R. E. Petty & J. A. Krosnick (Eds.), *Attitude strength: Antecedents and consequences* (pp. 361–386). Hillsdale, NJ: Lawrence Erlbaum Associates.

Tian, K.T., Bearden, W. O., & Hunter, G. L. (2001) Consumers need for uniqueness: Scale development and validation. *Journal of Consumer Research, 28*, 50–66.

Tobin, S. J. (2003). *Causal uncertainty and persuasion*. Unpublished doctoral dissertation, Ohio State University, Columbus, OH.

Tormala, Z. L., Briñol, P., & Petty, R. E. (2003). *Source credibility and self-validation processes in persuasion: An extension of the multiple roles hypothesis*. Manuscript under review.

Tormala, Z. L., & Petty, R.E. (2001). On-line versus memory-based processing: The role of 'need to evaluate' in person perception. *Personality and Social Psychology Bulletin, 27*, 1599–1612.

Tormala, Z. L., & Petty, R. E. (2002). What doesn't kill me makes me stronger: The effects of resisting persuasion on attitude certainty. *Journal of Personality and Social Psychology, 83*, 1298–1313.

Tormala, Z. L., & Petty, R. E. (2004). Resisting persuasion and attitude certainty: A meta-cognitive analysis. In E. S. Knowles & J. A. Linn (Eds.), *Resistance and persuasion* (pp. 65–82). Mahwah, NJ: Lawrence Erlbaum Associates.

Tormala, Z. L., Petty, R. E., & Briñol, P. (2002). Ease of retrieval effects in persuasion: the roles of elaboration and thought-confidence. *Personality and Social Psychology Bulletin, 28*, 1700–1712.

Trapp, R., Yingling, J., & Wanner, J. (1987). Measuring argumentative competence. In F. H. van Eemeren, R. Grooten-dorst, J. A. Blairr, & C. A. Willard (Eds.), *Argumentation: Across the lines of discipline* (pp. 253–261). Dordrecht, The Netherlands: Foris.

Triandis, H. C. (1995). *Individualism and Collectivism.* Boulder, CO: Westview Press.

Triandis H. C., & Gelfand M. (1998). Converging measurements of horizontal and vertical individualism and collectivism. *Journal of Personality and Social Psychology, 74*, 118–128.

Triandis, H. C., McCusker, C., & Hui, C. H. (1990). Multimethod probes of individualism and collectivism. *Journal of Personality and Social Psychology, 59*, 1006–1020.

Tykocinski, O., Higgins, T., & Chaiken, S. (1994). How message framing and self discrepancies influence persuasion: The motivational significance of psychological situations. *Personality and Social Psychology Bulletin, 20*, 107–115.

Valins, S. (1966). Cognitive effects of false heart-rate feedback. *Journal of Personality and Social Psychology, 4*, 400–408.

Vaughn, L. A., & Weary, G. (2003). Causal uncertainty and correction of judgments. *Journal of Experimental Social Psychology, 39*, 516–524.

Visser, P. S., & Krosnick, J. A. (1998). The development of attitude strength over the life cycle: Surge and decline. *Journal of Personality and Social Psychology, 75*, 1388–1409.

Wang, C. L., & Mowen J. C. (1997). Separateness connectedness self schema: Scale development and application to message construction. *Journal of Psychology and Marketing, 14*, 185–207.

Weary, G., & Edwards, J. A. (1994). Individual differences in causal uncertainty. *Journal of Personality and Social Psychology, 67*, 308–318.

Weary, G., & Jacobson, J. A. (1997). Causal uncertainty beliefs and diagnostic-information seeking. *Journal of Personality and Social Psychology, 73*, 839–848.

Weary, G., Jacobson, J. A., Edwards, J. A., & Tobin, S. J. (2001). Chronic and temporarily activated causal uncertainty beliefs and stereotype usage. *Journal of Personality and Social Psychology, 81*, 206–219.

Webster, D. M., & Kruglanski, A. W. (1994). Individual differences in need for cognitive closure. *Journal of Personality and Social Psychology, 67*, 1049–1062.

Wegener, D. T., & Petty, R. E. (1995). Flexible correction processes in social judgment: The role of naive theories in corrections for perceived bias. *Journal of Personality and Social Psychology, 68*, 36–51.

Wegener, D. T., & Petty, R. E. (1997). The flexible correction model: The role of naïve theories in bias correction. In M. P. Zanna (Ed.), *Advances in experimental social psychology* (Vol. 29, pp. 141–208). San Diego, CA: Academic Press.

Weitzenhoffer, A. M., & Weitzenhoffer, G. B. (1958). Sex, transference, and susceptibility to hypnosis. *American Journal of Clinical Hypnosis, 1*, 15–24.

Wheeler, S. C., Briñol, P., & Petty, R. E. (2002). Consumer persuasion as a function of explicit and implicit self-beliefs. *Asia Pacific Advances in Consumer Research, 5*, 209–211.

Wheeler, S. C., Petty, R. E., & Bizer, G. Y. (in press). Self-schema matching and attitude change: Situational and dispositional determinants of message elaboration. *Journal of Consumer Research.*

Wilson, D. S., Near, D., & Miller, R. R. (1996). Machiavellianism: A synthesis of the evolutionary and psychological literatures. *Psychological Bulletin, 119*, 285–299.

Wilson, G. D., & Patterson, J. R. (1968). A new measure of conservatism. *British Journal of Social and Clinical Psychology, 7*, 264–269.

Wilson, T. D., & Brekke, N. (1994). Mental contamination and mental correction: Unwanted influences on judgments and evaluations. *Psychological Bulletin, 116*, 117–142.

Wilson, T. D., Lindsey, S., & Schooler, T. Y. (2000). A model of dual attitudes. *Psychological Review, 107*, 101–126.

Witkin, H. A. (1964). Origins of cognitive style. In C. Scheerer (Ed.), *Cognition theory, research, promise.* New York: Harper & Row.

Witkin, H. A., Lewis, H. G., Hertzman, M., Machover, K., Meissner, P. B., & Wapner, S. (1954). *Personality Through Perception.* New York: Harper & Row.

Witkin, H., Oltman, P., Raskin, E., & Karp, S. (1971). *A manual for the embedded figures test.* Palo Alto, CA: Consulting Psychologists Press.

Wood, W. (1982). Retrieval of attitude-relevant information from memory: Effects on susceptibility to persuasion and on intrinsic motivation. *Journal of Personality and Social Psychology, 42*, 798–910.

Wood, W. (1999). Motives and modes of processing in the social influence of groups. In S. Chaiken & Y. Trope (Eds.), *Dual-process theories in social psychology* (pp. 547–570). New York: Guilford.

Zanna, M. P., Olson, J. M., & Fazio, R. H. (1980). Attitude-behavior consistency: An individual difference perspective. *Journal of Personality and Social Psychology, 38*, 432–440.

Zuckerman, M. (1979). Attribution of success and failure revisited: The motivational bias is alive and well in attribution theory. *Journal of Personality, 47*, 245–287.

15

Communication and Attitude Change: Causes, Processes, and Effects

Blair T. Johnson
University of Connecticut

Gregory R. Maio
Cardiff University

Aaron Smith-McLallen
University of Connecticut

INTRODUCTION

Human life is replete with communications that have persuasive intent and seemingly always has been. Biblical Eve fell prey to the serpent's arguments to eat from the tree of the knowledge of good and evil and then convinced Adam to follow suit. Modern politicians persuade voters to support them. Advertisers target mass-market segments who will buy their products. Spammers send the masses unrelenting barrages of unwanted promotions. In science, scholars craft their manuscripts' arguments to induce acceptance of their reported evidence on the topic. These examples merely touch the surface of communication and attitude change. Lest they lead to the misconceptions that communication and attitude change are solely human affairs, it is important to note that the phenomenon appears in varying levels of sophistication across species, but especially in those that are social in nature. The great apes persuade through gestures and vocalizations. Even bees communicate and induce behavior change in other bees, though it may be doubtful whether attitudes mediate this relation. In humans, messages may meet with responses ranging from enthusiastic embrace to vehement resistance. Even when people are unaware of changing their attitudes, others' communications may induce subtle shifts in related cognitions.

Because communication and persuasion play such a prominent role in human life and culture, it is a scholarly topic of immense complexity and breadth. Scholars have often been interested in understanding persuasion in hopes of improving human welfare and of reducing wars and conflicts. Yet, while it is tempting to think of communication and persuasion as serving higher aims, like any technology, such tools can serve many ill aims. One of the most infamous uses of persuasion knowledge was Hitler's propaganda ministry in Nazi Germany, which successfully solicited the tacit or explicit support of a majority behind the government's goals to seek a "permanent solution" to the presence of "undesirables" or "inferiors" in their country

(Sternberg, 2003). The Holocaust bears witness to the power of persuasion: Orchestrated with other public events, deliberate mass communication campaigns sought and succeeded in this goal until Germany surrendered to the Allies. Ironically, the perception that people can so easily be swayed by such propaganda added fuel to the fire of communication researchers, who responded by further studying the processes by which such effects occur. Significant advances in knowledge of communication and persuasion came on the heels of one of history's great atrocities.

Although attitudes have been both a phenomenon and a scholarly interest since Antiquity, systematic scientific knowledge did not accrue until the 20th century (McGuire, 1985). Following some early rich sociological case studies of culture that highlighted attitudes (Thomas & Znaniecki, 1918), initial empirical work on measures of attitudes began in the 1920s (Bogardus, 1925; F. H. Allport & Hartman, 1925). Perhaps because the first empirical studies appeared in sociological or political science outlets, psychologists found it something of a revelation that "attitudes can be measured" (Thurstone, 1928; see Krosnick, Judd, & Wittenbrink, chap. 2, this volume). Subsequent work proceeded to related topics, such as whether attitudes predict behavior or the means by which they might change. As Ostrom's (1989) review makes clear, researchers' definitions of attitude have varied quite widely across this time, from the schema-like multidimensional view of G. W. Allport (1935) to the current consensus that an *attitude* is a mental tendency to evaluate some entity with some degree of favor or disfavor (Eagly & Chaiken, 1993, chap. 18, this volume; Zanna & Rempel, 1988). Even though definitions have varied, researchers who have examined communication and persuasion uniformly have examined variables such as favorability toward the message position or evaluative ratings of the message entity, which map neatly on to the attitude concept.

As we have implied, the domain of communication and persuasion can be quite broad, as shown by its frequent appearance across the entries in this Handbook. There are potential elements of communication and persuasion possible whenever two people interact, whether they are in the presence of each other or merely virtual or imagined. The mere presence of another person—connoting potential or actual communication—may impact attitudes toward that person, often without either people realizing it is happening. To take an extreme example, a classic social psychological finding is that multiple exposures to another person often create more positive attitudes toward that person (e.g., Saegert, Swap, & Zajonc, 1973). Similarly, people may use tactics of authority or coercion to change others' behavior (see Prislin & Wood, chap. 16, this volume, for a review). Although a persuader may use such tactics to convince another person to like them or to adopt their advocacies, communication and persuasion research typically focuses around the more-or-less deliberate attempts of one source to convince an audience of the value in a message position or positions. Although this chapter will generally focus on the more deliberate persuasion contexts, we also provide some coverage of nonverbal and nonconscious sources of persuasion.

In studies of communication and persuasion, results may take two basic empirical forms. The first form is a simple comparison of attitude levels before and after message presentation, which gauges the direction and amount of any change that occurs. Yet, because this comparison may reflect the influence of other factors such as maturation or testing (Cook & Campbell, 1979), researchers usually elaborate their experiments to include controls, such as a no-message group. Hence, actual persuasion can be gauged comparing post-message attitudes either to attitudes measured at baseline or against a no-message control group. Although such designs were relatively frequent in early persuasion studies, they have become less frequent in contemporary designs. The second and most common form of persuasion experiment in the last 25 years involves after-only designs in which participants typically do not provide baseline attitudes for comparison. In such studies, persuasion is assessed by comparing attitude levels in one group relative to another group or groups in the design. Such designs eliminate problems such as maturation and testing and permit a determination of whether a manipulated factor affected attitudes, but—unless baseline attitudes have been assessed—it is ambiguous as to which group has actually changed (Cook & Campbell, 1979; Johnson, Smith-McLallen, Killeya, & Levin, 2004).

We structure the remainder of our review in three general clusters. First, we discuss major theoretical perspectives on the processes by which communication-induced attitude change occurs and affects other variables. These theories illuminate when messages should be successful and when they should fail. Second, in keeping with the emphasis of this Handbook on the interrelations of key attitudinally-relevant variables, we examine causes of communication-induced attitude change, including factors that relate to change at message exposure and following it. Finally, we review the effects of communication-induced attitude change on such other potential outcomes as behavior, affects, beliefs, and awareness of change. We conclude with some thoughts about the future of research on communication and attitude change.

THEORETICAL PERSPECTIVES ON HOW COMMUNICATIONS CAN CHANGE ATTITUDES

The earliest fragments of recorded history bear witness not only to the phenomenon of one person persuading another but also to organized efforts to develop knowledge about this process. Early Greek philosophers dedicated considerable efforts toward understanding the nature of persuasion. Aristotle, in particular, focused on the subject in his *Rhetoric*, a work revered to this day for its careful dissection of argumentation. Aristotle described rhetoric in three main types of communication settings, including judicial, public speeches, and epideictic interpersonal dialogues. Persuasive success hinged on such principles as the character of the speaker, the emotional state of the audience, and especially the argument itself. To succeed, an orator ought to use appeals that the target already holds, building toward the orator's desired conclusion. Embellishing this tradition is Machiavelli's *The Prince*, which gained fame for its tacit recommendation that rulers might remain in power by sacrificing lofty ideals such as honesty in favor of clever self-serving deceit. In short, a powerful persuader might lie when it suits his or her interests even while maintaining an apparently trustworthy façade. The audience falls prey to the false arguments of a persuader who they wish to believe extols such Aristotellian virtues as mercy, honesty, humaneness, uprightness, and even religiousness; we discuss research on such dissimulations in the following pages (see *Signs of dissimulation*). Although philosophical treatises such as these may have held particular sway over the centuries, it is probably best to view them as having produced only hypotheses, many of which have not been tested (McGuire, 2000). The earliest research on communication and persuasion documented that change could occur in such settings as intergroup prejudice reduction (Remmers & Morgan, 1936; Thurstone, 1931) and alcohol prohibition (Knower, 1936). These early efforts notwithstanding, persuasion research remained relatively exploratory and unorganized until the seminal work of the Yale School of Communication and Persuasion (McGuire, 1996), which had its roots in the Allied Forces' efforts to win World War II (WWII) (see Johnson & Nichols, 1998). In the remainder of this section, we review the Yale group's theoretical perspective and other major models of persuasion that have proven especially generative over the years.

The Yale Communication and Attitude Change Program

The U.S. Army supported the initial work of the Yale group, which investigated how best to induce preparedness for members of the armed forces by using mass media techniques such as documentary films extolling the Allied cause and condemning the Axis counterpart (Hovland, Lumsdaine, & Sheffield, 1949). The Yale group's founder, Carl I. Hovland, seized upon Harold D. Lasswell's (1948, p. 37) classic statement that the communication process could be captured by the phrase, "who says what in which channel to whom with what effect." Beginning with research on U.S. armed forces members during WWII, and following the war in various locales, the group systematically broke down the persuasion process into the steps of this statement, attempting to hold other elements of the process constant while varying another part and examining its persuasive impact as an independent variable. To give only a brief sample of the many studies this group conducted, studies manipulating communicator credibility addressed "who says"; studies on fear appeals, order effects, and sidedness of communications addressed "what"; studies on a series of individual difference features addressed "whom"; and different dependent variables were investigated within and across studies to address the "what effect" portion of the statement. Only the "which channel" portion was left unsystematically explored (but see Hovland's 1954 review of others' work on this subject). Across the tradition, the Yale group strove to apply elements of reinforcement theory to the persuasion process. Although the Yale group was theoretically eclectic (McGuire, 1996), most of their work was steeped in the predominant framework of the day, behaviorism (Hull, 1943). Thus, the Yale group's work typically assumed that message recipients passively received and integrated information. Persuasive effects hinged on principles of reinforcement and drive: Persuasive messages elicit attitude change when they present reinforcements for attitude change (Hovland, Janis, & Kelley, 1953). The reinforcements could vary from the release of emotions to the experience of positive mood upon presentation of the attitude object. For example, a source may be attractive and elicit positive feelings in an audience, who may agree with the source in order to become more similar to him or her. Or, the source might wield great power and elicit fear in the audience members, thereby motivating them to agree in order to avoid suffering at the hands of the source. Further, the communicator may seem to be an expert and trustworthy individual, who can elicit message acceptance because the audience assumes that the communicator is correct and sincere. Thus, in essence, the Yale model specified that reinforcements are a function of attributes of the source of the messages, the message content, the message setting, and the message recipients.

The Yale group proved highly prolific, publishing many articles and books on different aspects of persuasion (e.g., Hovland et al., 1949, 1953; Hovland, 1959; Hovland & Janis, 1959; M. Sherif & Hovland, 1961). Yet, while it was extolled for its highly programmatic research and its series of scholarly volumes, their findings were often characterized as conflicting, difficult to replicate, and difficult to integrate (Eagly & Chaiken, 1993; Fishbein & Ajzen, 1975; Petty & Cacioppo, 1981), possibly because scholars had only narrative rather than quantitative literature review tools (Johnson & Nichols, 1998). Similarly, as we discuss in the following pages (see *Cognitive Response Model*), evidence that the framework's central process, reinforcement-based learning mechanisms, underpin persuasion was scant. For example, some studies found that communicator credibility induced persuasion whereas others found no relation or even reversals (see Petty & Cacioppo's, 1981, review). Although conflicting research findings often are more apparent than real, subsequent research syntheses addressing communication and persuasion typically do reveal significant variability among study results that require more complex modeling to explain (Johnson, 1991; Johnson & Nichols, 1998). Although formally speaking the Yale group's communication and attitude program ceased to function following Hovland's sudden death in 1961, others at or allied with the Yale group developed enhanced models in subsequent decades.

Social Judgment Model

Muzafer and Carolyn Wood Sherif and their colleagues' social judgment model (SJM) posited that perceptual displacements mediate persuasion such that a person's existing attitudes provide an interpretive context for an incoming message (C. W. Sherif, 1980; C. W. Sherif & Sherif, 1967; C. W. Sherif, Sherif, & Nebergall, 1965; M. Sherif & Cantril, 1947; M. Sherif & Hovland, 1961). Attitudes further rest on latitudes of acceptance, rejection, and noncommitment, which are ranges of positions on the issue that a person accepts, rejects, or toward which he or she is noncommittal, respectively. According to the theory, individuals with relatively wide latitudes of rejection or narrow latitudes of acceptance on an issue have high *ego involvement* with it. Such attitudes are components of the ego or self-concept, that is, as aspects of the "self-picture—intimately felt and cherished" (C. W. Sherif et al., 1965, p. vi). In perhaps the most famous example of this research, Hovland, Harvey, and Sherif (1957) examined attitudes toward prohibition, a controversial issue at the time in Oklahoma. These researchers compared "dry" ego-involved participants, who typically were sampled from such groups as the Salvation Army, with "wet" ego-involved participants sampled from college students. Because of the model's emphasis on the relation of an attitude to the individual's values, in their synthesis of involvement studies, Johnson and Eagly (1989) labeled this construct *value-relevant involvement* to differentiate it from other forms of involvement.

In the SJM, persuasion is a combination of the message position in relation to the message recipient's attitudes and involvement in the issue. When the message position falls in, or very near to, a person's latitude of acceptance, the result is an attitudinal shift toward the position; that is, the person *assimilates* the message position. If the position falls in the latitude of rejection, the message seems more distant from the attitude than it truly is and no attitude change occurs; that is, the person *contrasts* the message position. For those for whom involvement is very high, very discrepant messages might result in negative attitude change, or *boomerang*. Message recipients with high value-relevant involvement have in fact exhibited greater resistance to message-based attitude change than those with low involvement (Johnson & Eagly, 1989, 1990; Johnson, Lin, Symons, Campbell, & Ekstein, 1995; Lampron, Krosnick, Shaeffer, Petty, & See, 2003; Maio & Olson, 1995a). This resistance may result because latitudes of acceptance and value-relevant involvement reflect subjective certainty about one's own attitude position (Eagly & Telaak, 1972; Hovland et al., 1957) and/or because this form of involvement rests on attitudes that are more central or more linked to cognitive structure (Krosnick, Boninger, Chuang, Berent, & Carnot, 1993; Lampron et al., 2003).

Given that Muzafer and Carolyn Wood Sherif and their colleagues developed the SJM contemporarily and in partial collaboration with Carl Hovland, it is an anachronism that it gave such a large role to active processes originating within rather than outside the message recipient. The SJM inspired a good bit of research in the 1960s and 1970s, and its involvement construct has recently enjoyed something of a revival (cf. Johnson & Eagly, 1989; Lampron et al., 2003). The SJM is unique among persuasion theories in emphasizing assimilation and contrast, yet, as Eagly and Chaiken (1993) discuss, its central prediction that assimilation and contrast underlie persuasion has fared poorly in empirical tests (e.g., Eagly & Telaak, 1972). Nonetheless, significant assimilation and contrast effects have appeared in attitude contexts as widely varying as evaluations of political candidates (Judd, Kenny, & Krosnick, 1983), consumer judgments (Stapel, Koomen, & Velthuijsen, 1998), mood (Abele & Gendolla, 1999; Geers & Lassiter, 1999), and stereotypes (Dijksterhuis et al., 1998). Given the apparent ease with which researchers have documented these effects, the case against the SJM's primary processing mechanism would seem somewhat weaker and deserving of greater scrutiny in research using more modern techniques, such as these recent studies have employed. Finally, a shortcoming of the SJM is that it gives little attention to message content dimensions such as the number and quality of arguments, emphasizing instead the message's position.

McGuire's Information Processing Theory

William J. McGuire developed an information processing theory that, while maintaining the Yale group's emphasis on steps involved in persuasion (Hovland, 1959), shared the SJM's emphasis on an active role by the participant. The steps in McGuire's reception-yielding model expanded and contracted in different versions across three decades (cf. McGuire, 1968, 1989), but each iteration included three main steps: attention, comprehension, and yielding. In other words, one first had to attend to a message for any influence to occur, then one had to comprehend it, and finally one could agree or disagree. Consistent with the Yale group's conceptions of persuasion processes, McGuire acknowledged the moderating roles of ability and motivation to "receive" information, ideas that became foundational for modern models of persuasion. The model predicts that some variables can have contrasting effects on different processes. High self-esteem, for example, might increase reception (because it enhances comprehension) but decrease yielding (because it enhances skepticism), a pattern that Rhodes and Wood (1992) meta-analytically confirmed. Other research has shown that the actual sequence of processes sometimes may be not as linear as McGuire theorized. As in the example with mere exposure to another person, message recipients might skip the comprehension phase altogether and yield based on simple attention to the target (McGuire, 1968). Similarly, intriguing evidence suggests that comprehension of a phrase instantaneously elicits its acceptance, which only later is modified if more deliberate thinking concludes that a correction is necessary (see Gilbert, 1991), similar to Tversky and Kahneman's (1974) anchor-and-adjust heuristic. Similarly, Edwards and Smith (1996) showed that arguments disconfirming one's beliefs receive greater scrutiny, which suggests that message recipients sometimes restart the sequence. Although these complications cloud the use of the information processing theory in persuasion, modern theories of persuasion have recognized that reception-related processes are at work.

Combinatorial Models of Persuasion

Combinatorial models posit that beliefs combine in some way to predict or cause attitude; these perspectives share a core assumption that one influence is through estimates of the *probabilities* associated with individual beliefs (McGuire, 1960; Wyer, 1974). Put another way, the logicality of the premises supporting or opposing an entity is a main determinant of attitudes toward the entity. Other combinatorial models combine judgments of probability with judgments of the desirability of the dimension in question (Anderson, 1971; Fishbein, 1963; McGuire & McGuire, 1991; for discussions in this volume, see Wyer & Albarracín, chap. 7, and Kruglanski & Stroebe, chap. 8). In this way, the positive or negative valence of a dimension affects attitude only if it is likely to be characteristic of the judged entity. Similarly, the likelihood of a dimension affects attitude only to the extent that it has a positive or negative valence to the person. Although combinatory models of attitude have been quite generative in research on attitude structure and on the attitude-behavior link (e.g., Albarracín, Johnson, Fishbein, & Muellerleile, 2001), they have borne much less fruit regarding message-based persuasion, even though there are versions of these models that do make predictions for persuasion contexts (see Eagly & Chaiken's, 1993, review). In particular, Fishbein and Ajzen's (1981) treatment of this subject recommends that, to change attitudes, one must first determine the primary beliefs underlying the targeted attitude and then tailor arguments to change these beliefs. Thus, the perspective places a high importance on the careful selection and use of arguments to create belief-mediated attitude change. With the unimodel (Kruglanski & Thompson, 1999) as the only exception (see *Unimodel*, in the following pages), Fishbein and Ajzen's theory remains unique among currently popular theories of persuasion in emphasizing how messages might affect beliefs that are related to attitudes. Nonetheless, as Eagly and Chaiken (1993) argued in their review of this persuasion theory, the model is not informative regarding how elements such as credibility, message order, or participant mood might influence persuasion nor about the particular processes involved in attitude change. The model remains relatively unexplored on an empirical basis (but see Albarracín & Wyer, 2001; Johnson et al., 2004), although it has inspired related social influence models (e.g., Fisher & Fisher, 1992).

Cognitive Response Model of Persuasion

Despite the Yale group's overall emphasis on passive learning, the eclectic interests of its members produced some intriguing results that apparently clashed with its simple behavioral learning philosophy. On the one hand was the finding that active role playing extolling a position produced greater attitude change than being the target of such a communication (Janis & King, 1954), an effect that proved quite robust and helped to kindle the cognitive dissonance revolution (see Olson and Stone's review, chap. 6, this volume). On the other hand were the repeated demonstrations of null or weak relations between learning of message content and attitude change (e.g., Insko, 1964). If message learning was the active process mediating change, then these results were discouraging, to say the least. Greenwald (1968), in an attempt to "salvage an associative learning interpretation of persuasion" (p. 281), took a cue from the role-playing literature and formally suggested that message recipient's thoughts about the message mediated attitude change. This formulation offered the hope that maintaining an associative learning model of persuasion implies that the idiosyncratic cognitive responses spurred by the message and retained by the message recipient could be tracked and potentially more closely linked to persuasion. Empirical tests soon showed moderate to large correlations between the valence of cognitive responses and attitude (Brock, 1967; Osterhouse & Brock, 1970; Petty & Cacioppo, 1979b; Petty, Wells, & Brock, 1976).

Following Greenwald's (1968) lead, other scholars also refined methodologies related to cognitive responding, resulting in an edited volume of such contributions (Petty, Ostrom, & Brock, 1981). Typically, following exposure to a message, researchers ask participants to write their thoughts they had while they heard or read the message, and then either they or independent judges code whether each thought is positive, neutral, or negative with respect to the position taken by the message; consequently, measures of cognitive responses bear strong resemblance to cognitive measures of attitude, particularly in Fishbein and Ajzen's (e.g., 1975) formulation. In other instances, participants list thoughts as they receive a message (e.g., Hovland et al., 1949; Killeya & Johnson, 1998); in rarer instances still, listings are taken both during and after message exposure (Killeya & Johnson, 1998). As Eagly and Chaiken (1993) reviewed, tests of the cognitive response model remained in essence only correlational rather than experimental. Because studies only correlated cognitive responses with attitudes or only showed parallel effects of experimental manipulations on cognitive responses and attitudes, it remained possible that cognitive responses were simply a measure of attitudes and not of the processes leading to attitudes (for suggestive data, see Albarracín & Wyer, 2000). Killeya and Johnson experimentally manipulated the valence of cognitive responses by directing participants to list only positive or only negative thoughts about the message; control participants were simply asked to list any thoughts they wished. In two experiments, positive instructions induced positive thoughts and positive attitudes (even with weak arguments), whereas (in one experiment) negative instructions induced negative thoughts and relatively negative attitudes (even with strong arguments). Such results are consistent with the conclusion that cognitive responding is a bona fide causal process underlying persuasion. Reflecting its explanatory power, the cognitive response model has influenced every subsequent major theory of persuasion, which we review in the next section, and these models have incorporated cognitive responding as a process moderated by other variables.

Contemporary Process Models of Persuasion

With the possible exception of the SJM, models of persuasion developed from the 1940s to 1970s assumed explicitly or implicitly that attitude change is simply a matter of drawing a logical conclusion for message recipients. This emphasis seems to assume that mental and behavioral life is relatively reasoned and volitional (cf. Fishbein & Ajzen, 1975; Eagly & Chaiken, 1984). In contrast, the possibility that mental life may often be neither very reasoned nor all that volitional has recently taken center stage in persuasion research, as it has in a range of theories across several disciplines (see Chaiken & Trope, 1999). Indeed, an emerging consensus considers mental and behavioral life almost completely driven by automatic and relatively non-conscious processes (Bargh & Ferguson, 2000; Baumeister, Muraven, & Tice, 2000). Largely consistent with that consensus, contemporary models of persuasion concur that recipients often process messages in ways that economize on time and energy, but reserve the possibility that recipients may expend considerable energy processing message-relevant information. Specifically, four contemporary process models, the elaboration likelihood model (ELM) (Petty & Cacioppo, 1981, 1986; Petty & Wegener, 1999), heuristic-systematic model (HSM) (Chaiken, 1980; Chaiken, Liberman, & Eagly, 1989; Chen & Chaiken, 1999), unimodel of persuasion (Thompson, Kruglanski, & Spiegel, 2000), and cognition in persuasion model (CPM) (Albarracín, 2002) explicitly contrast relatively effortful modes of cognition with those that are much less effortful. Table 15.1 provides a comparison of these four models along a wide range of dimensions. As the table shows, of these four, only the ELM and HSM explicitly posit qualitatively different dual processes; the other two models posit one process or a process sequence that accounts for both low- and high-effort contexts, which the theories examine in terms of ability and motivation to think about the communication.

Elaboration Likelihood Model.   Central to the ELM is its *elaboration continuum*, a motivational factor that determines the extent to which processing of message content is likely to occur. Essentially, the ELM argues that cognitive responses determine attitudes under high elaboration circumstances, when message recipients have sufficient ability and motivation to process the message. In such cases, recipients carefully scrutinize the information value of the message for clues about its validity; messages with strong arguments persuade and those with weak arguments should not. In the terms of the model, message participants follow the *central route* to persuasion, basing their attitudes on the information in the message. If the information is strong—that is, if it elicits primarily positive cognitive responses—then attitudes should change toward the appeal. In contrast, if the information is weak—that is, if it elicits primarily negative cognitive responses—then attitudes should move away from the appeal. Researchers have customarily used manipulations of strong versus weak messages, often pretested to produce the desired cognitive response profiles, in order to detect and to gauge the impact of high elaboration on persuasion.

Under low elaboration circumstances, when ability and motivation are low, a host of other non-message-content dimensions determine reactions. In terms of the model, low elaboration message participants follow the *peripheral route* to persuasion. The long list of factors known to act as *peripheral cues* includes such dimensions as the credibility of the communicator, his or her attractiveness, the length of the message presented, the recipient's mood, and so on (see Petty & Wegener, 1998a, for a review). A great deal of research has supported the central ELM predictions that (a) argument quality should matter more under high elaboration circumstances and that peripheral cues should not, and (b) argument quality should not matter under low elaboration circumstances but that peripheral cues should (for reviews, see Eagly & Chaiken, 1993; Perloff, 2003; Petty & Wegener, 1998a). Another prediction of the model is that attitude change through the central route should be longer lasting and more predictive of behavior than attitude change through the peripheral route, a pattern found in several studies (see Petty, Haugtvedt & Smith, 1995, for a review).

The ELM also specifies that the effects of elaboration, message content, and peripheral cues may depend on certain other factors. Although in general the ELM assumes relatively objective message processing on the part of the target, it also considers the roles that variables

TABLE 15.1

Comparison of Four Contemporary Process Models of Persuasion Along Key Conceptual Dimensions

	Models of Persuasion			
Dimension	Elaboration Likelihood Model (ELM)	Heuristic Systematic Model (HSM)	Unimodel	Cognition in Persuasion Model (CPM)
Psychological tradition(s)	Cognitive (cognitive response model; attributional; learning)	Cognitive	Attributional	Social-cognitive
Number of qualitatively distinct general processing modes	Two, central and peripheral routes; the latter has several processes	Two, heuristic and systematic processing	One, epistemic thought	One with stages (identification, interpretation, selection)
Processing modes can co-occur	No, but see Petty (1994)	Yes	Has only one general process	Assumes one process with various stages, but predicts influences of all identified pieces of information
Motives affecting persuasion	Primarily accuracy; other motives affect but bias processing	Primarily accuracy, but defense, and impressions possible	Accuracy, defense, and impressions	Primarily accuracy, but defense and impression possible
Assumes motivation and ability affect processing	Yes	Yes	Yes	Yes
Effects of high motivation and ability to process information	Processed via central route	Systematic processing	Increased epistemic thinking	Message content more important
Effects of moderate motivation and ability to process information	Generally not discussed (predicted effects implied as monotonic)	Not discussed	Not discussed because predicted effects are monotonic	Extra-message factors are identified but not discounted and thus have an influence
Effects of low motivation and ability to process information	Use of peripheral route processes	Heuristic processing	Decreased epistemic thinking	Decreased identification of message-content and of subjectively less relevant factors
Degree of explicitness regarding processing of message content	Moderate (empirically driven)	Moderate (empirically driven)	High (belief inference, similar to McGuire's, 1960, and Wyer's, 1974, combinatorial models)	High (stages of cognitive processing in persuasion)

(Continued)

TABLE 15.1
(Continued)

Models of Persuasion

Dimension	Elaboration Likelihood Model (ELM)	Heuristic Systematic Model (HSM)	Unimodel	Cognition in Persuasion Model (CPM)
Effect of argument quality on attitude change	Processed via central route, increases monotonically with ability and motivation to process messages	Processed systematically, increases monotonically with ability and motivation to process messages but may interact with heuristics	Increases monotonically with ability and motivation to process messages	Increases monotonically for strong but not weak arguments as motivation and ability increase; for weak arguments and ability increase, curvilinear under moderate levels
Effect of recipient mood	Positive moods increase reliance on peripheral cues under moderate ability and motivation but can be used as information or bias processing under high and low ability	Positive moods generally associated with increased reliance on heuristics but mood itself can be used as a source of information	Mood can be used as relevant information in some instances, increasing monotonically when mood-inducing stimuli require ability and motivation	Mood should affect attitude under moderate ability and motivation but have less influence otherwise
Behavior elicited in favor of message	More likely following strong arguments and unbiased use of the central route	More likely following strong arguments processed systematically under an accuracy motive	More likely following extensive epistemic thought of information implying truth value	More likely following strong arguments when temporally near the behavior point
Theoretical focus on reception vs. yielding processes	Primarily focused on variables that moderate yielding	Primarily focused on variables that moderate yielding	Prior knowledge and selective attention impact reception; depth of information processing affects yielding	Specifies cognitive processes involved in both reception and yielding
Key citations	Petty & Cacioppo (1981, 1986); Petty & Wegener (1999)	Chaiken (1980); Chaiken, Liberman, & Eagly (1989); Chen & Chaiken (1999)	Kruglanski, Thompson, & Spiegel (1999); Kruglanski & Thompson (1999)	Albarracín (2002); Albarracín & Kumkale (2003); Albarracín & Wyer (2000, 2001)

might play in creating relatively biased processing, which predisposes either disconfirming or confirming the message position. Knowledge, prior attitudes, need for cognition, and other individual differences can predispose a message recipient to relatively biased processing (see Briñol & Petty, chap. 14, this volume). Moreover, variables can potentially play multiple roles within the ELM, influencing elaboration, acting as arguments, or acting as peripheral cues. For instance, expertise information is typically considered a peripheral cue, but it may be processed as an argument that increases persuasion (Petty, Wheeler, & Bizer, 1999).

Appearing at a time when cognitive psychologists demonstrated depth-of-processing effects of shallow versus deeper processing of stimuli (cf. Craik & Lockhart, 1972; for similar points, see Moskowitz, Skurnik, & Galinsky, 1999; Symons & Johnson, 1997), the ELM had a certain appeal because its elaboration continuum maps loosely onto this dimension. The model has seen wide application within and outside social psychology and has proven to be a highly generative model capable of explaining a wide array of persuasive effects (Eagly & Chaiken, 1993; Perloff, 2003). Some critics have argued that the model is so explanatory and flexible that no study can falsify it (Stiff & Boster, 1987), pointing to the fact that the ELM permits individual variables to play more than one role in the persuasion process. Reviewers have also noted the model's reliance on empirical rather than a priori means of establishing argument quality (Eagly & Chaiken, 1993), which is a central construct in research on this model. Indeed, even Petty and Cacioppo (1986) have recognized that the ELM ultimately does not explain why variables such as argument quality have the effects that they have. Some (Chaiken, Duckworth, & Darke, 1999) have argued that the ELM's reliance on a single motive, accuracy or validity seeking, is a handicap, given a long history of scholarship and research supportive of multiple motives (cf. Smith, Bruner, & White, 1956; Katz, 1960; Kunda, 1990; Maio & Olson, 2000). Instead, the ELM explains the operation of such variables through its mechanism of biased processing. That is, people may believe they are engaged in validity seeking when processing information, yet motives such as ego-defense may bias information processing. Finally, labeling the ELM a dual-process model is something of a misnomer in that it explicitly specifies far more than two processes. While the central route might be characterized as involving one process (cognitive responding), Petty and colleagues include in their peripheral route what Eagly and Chaiken (1993, p. 323) characterized as "a heterogeneous lot" of processes, including classical conditioning, operant conditioning, attributions, heuristic processing, and so on. Nevertheless, any process can be broken down into more molecular processes. The description of the ELM as a dual-process model is appropriate insofar as the two routes are understood as classes of processes.

Heuristic-Systematic Model.   Simultaneous to the development of the ELM, Shelley Chaiken and her colleagues borrowed cognitive psychology concepts to develop the HSM, which contrasts how message recipients may deploy systematic or heuristic processing, or both, in the service of a processing goal that may be accuracy, defense of a prior attitude, or an impression conveyed to others. The HSM's *systematic processing* construct is analogous to processing in the ELM's central route, with the emphasis on analytical thinking with regard to message-relevant information. According to both the ELM and HSM, when ability and motivation are high, message recipients ought to engage in considerable systematic processing and, similar to the cognitive response model, the valence of their thoughts ought to be highly predictive of attitudes. Thus, the HSM makes the same predictions about systematic processing as the ELM does regarding the central route. For example, when motivation to elaborate, or to attend to message content is high, the persuasive impact of message quality is such that strong arguments produce more persuasion than do weak ones (Martin & Hewstone, 2001).

Heuristic processing, in contrast, is the application of simple if-then rules to decision making; for example, people usually follow the rule that experts are believeable. When ability or motivation are low, and a source who is obviously an expert presents the message, then this heuristic will likely be used to determine attitudes toward the message's recommendation. For example, Ito's (2002) low (but not high-) involvement message recipients' attitudes were influenced by source credibility and not by argument quality (see also Bohner, Ruder, & Erb, 2002; Kiesler & Mathog, 1968).

The HSM has received a great deal of attention as a model of persuasion (Eagly & Chaiken, 1993; Perloff, 2003) and has even been developed into a more general judgmental model (Chen & Chaiken, 1999). Despite the interest and sophistication of the HSM, scholars have often misconstrued the model as essentially equivalent to the ELM, basically using different labels for the same phenomena. Although the ELM and HSM do indeed make the same predictions about persuasion in many popularly examined contexts, this parallelism should not be taken to mean that the models are identical. For example, although the HSM agrees with the ELM that validity-seeking or accuracy is the primary processing motive that drives processes, the HSM also posits that message recipients may sometimes have defense or impression motives that drive and bias processing. Although dual-process theories often contrast deliberate versus spontaneous processes (see Bargh & Ferguson, 2000), this distinction applies less well to the HSM, which explicitly predicts that in situations conducive to both modes of processing, both will occur (Eagly & Chaiken, 1993). Supporting this *additivity hypothesis*, Ito (2002) found that argument quality and source credibility each affected attitudes under conditions of moderate motivation. Thus, in contrast to the ELM, the HSM requires no necessary trade-off in using these two processes, and studies support the conclusion that heuristic and systematic processing may appear in parallel (Bohner et al., 2002; Chaiken & Maheswaran, 1994; Ito, 2002; Sengupta & Johar, 2001). Also unlike the ELM, the HSM truly is a dual-process model, specifying heuristic and systematic processing as two qualitatively different processes involved in persuasion, whereas, as we noted above, the ELM contrasts two general classes of processes. Moreover, the HSM specifies that deficits in actual, relative to desired, confidence drive systematic and heuristic processing. That is, people engage in systematic processing when they desire a higher confidence level than they can attain through relatively effortful, heuristic modes of processing. Thus, either or both increases or decreases in desired confidence promote systematic processing. Recent work has shown that confidence can affect persuasion (Rucker & Petty, 2004; Tormala & Petty, 2002), but the HSM's confidence hypothesis apparently has received little direct attention (see Wyer & Albarracín, chap. 7, this volume).

Unimodel.   Though dual-process models are the most widely used theoretical perspectives in persuasion research, Kruglanski and his colleagues (Kruglanski & Thompson, 1999; Kruglanski, Thompson, & Spiegel, 1999) recently argued for a more parsimonious single-process model, the *unimodel*. This model takes as its starting point lay epistemic theory (Kruglanski, 1989), which addresses the processes governing the formation of subjective knowledge (e.g., judgments, opinions, attitudes, and impressions). Specifically, persuasion is a process of hypothesis testing and inference that is influenced by (a) the structure of the evidence presented, (b) cognitive-ability factors that affect inferential activity, and (c) motivational factors impacting the extent and direction of information processing and persuasion. The unimodel stipulates a number of influences on the persuasion process, but unlike the HSM and ELM dual-process approaches, the unimodel argues for a single-route to persuasion that treats central/systematic and peripheral/heuristic routes as incorporating functionally equivalent types of evidence. Evidence is any information relevant to the conclusion and may be understood as an if-then linkage between relevant information and possible conclusions. Relevance means that the information is pertinent to the conclusion that a person makes. Evidence can be processed explicitly or implicitly in relation to the idiosyncratic knowledge goal.

According to the unimodel, elements of the message itself (e.g., quality, complexity, and humor), source information (e.g., credibility, attractiveness, and speech), and context variables or environmental cues (e.g., ambient noise, lighting, and message modality) can all be considered relevant to the conclusion that a person makes about an issue. There are no a priori differences in degree of relevance in the two types of information specified by the ELM and HSM because the overall importance of each may differ across contexts or issues. Based on the assumption that there is only one broad process at work, the unimodel holds that availability and accessibility of relevant information are important to the persuasion process but that whether they occur centrally or peripherally is immaterial. Like the ELM and HSM, the unimodel also acknowledges the importance of motivation to process information. Unlike dual-process models, the unimodel considers motivation as important only to the extent that some motives affect the extent of message processing (e.g., need for cognition or motivation for accuracy) and others impact the direction of processing (e.g., ego-defensive or ego-enhancing motives), but they do not interact with the evidential category (e.g., heuristic cues or message arguments). The primacy of relevance judgments in the unimodel makes it essentially a functional theory of attitude change similar to those of Katz (1960), Kelman (1958, 1992), and Smith et al. (1956). These theoretical approaches to attitudes and attitude change emphasize how message recipients' goals relate to what information is considered relevant (Kruglanski, 1989) or legitimate (Kelman, 1992) and how that information is interpreted.

Despite the appeal of the apparent parsimony of the unimodel over the ELM and HSM, comparatively few published studies have documented the validity of its claims. Although the unimodel and the handful of studies providing support for it allude to some problems with the dual-process tradition, the lack of published evidence limits conclusions about the import of the model. Moreover, as Wegener and Carlston (chap. 12, this volume) review, the ELM appears able to explain key predictions of the unimodel. Of particular note is the fact that, in the ELM, variables can play several roles: Whereas the unimodel would emphasize the epistemic implications of received information to the recipient whether the information is source-specific or message content, the ELM would argue that even source information can serve as an argument under certain circumstances (Petty et al., 1999). A series of experiments by Piero, Mannetti, Kruglanski, and Sleeth-Keppler (2004) recently documented just this phenomenon. In their research, cues that typically have appeared in abbreviated forms in past persuasion research were made more salient by providing more information about them. For example, providing more elaborate information regarding the degree of consensus (cue) often affected the attitudes of high-relevance recipients, even in the face of traditional argumentation. The pattern especially occurred when the cue information followed the argumentation, which Piero and colleagues labeled a *relevance override*.

Cognition in Persuasion Model.   Taking inspiration from social cognitive theories (e.g., Srull & Wyer, 1989), Albarracín's (2002) recent cognition in persuasion model (CPM) details a series of processing stages that underlie persuasive effects that usually appear in a particular temporal ordering. Briefly, in stage one, a message recipient initially interprets the presented information in semantic terms using permanent memory. In stage two, the recipient identifies the information in the message or other information available at the time in order either to validate or to refute the information. In stage three, the recipient generates potential bases for judgment and then selects the most relevant information for use. In the fourth stage, the recipient uses the selected information in his or her judgment, which may modify attitudes or intentions to engage in relevant action. In the fifth and final stage, the recipient may act on their attitudes and intentions.

Like the unimodel, the CPM eschews the classic dual-process distinctions of the ELM and the HSM (see Table 15.1), instead specifying that the cognition-in-persuasion processing stages underlie persuasive effects regardless of ability and motivation levels. For example, Albarracín and Wyer (2001) showed that when distracted, participants relied on the affect induced by the message content as a basis for their attitudes rather than the content of the message itself. Moreover, the cognitive processes involved in forming judgments were quite similar at both high and low levels of elaboration, but the order of the stages and the information used in each case were distinct. Although distracted participants were able to make judgments of likelihood and desirability of outcomes suggested in the message, they were unable to combine them to form the basis for their attitudes; instead, they used the affect attributed to the message to rationalize their mood-based attitudes. Non-distracted participants also made judgments of likelihood and desirability of suggested outcomes but were able to combine them such that the implications suggested by the message became the primary basis for their attitudes.

Similar to McGuire's (1969) reception-yielding model, other variables can affect the likelihood of any particular stage promoting persuasion, meaning that some persuasion variables may have non-linear effects on persuasion. For example, on the basis of the CPM, Albarracín and Kumkale (2003) predicted and found that participants were more likely to use their moods as judgment cues under conditions of moderate thought than under either higher or lower levels of thought. The rationale is that two stages are involved in the selection of affective information. For example, for mood to have an influence, people must identify it but must not conclude that it is irrelevant as a source of evaluations of the message proposal. Consequently, mood has greater impact when ability and motivation are as high as is necessary to induce identification, but not so high as to induce discounting of the affect. Thus, in contrast to the ELM or HSM, the CPM predicts that extramessage cues are more likely to affect persuasion under conditions that promote moderate rather than either small or large amounts of message-relevant thinking.

In contrast to the ELM and HSM's treatment of prior knowledge as a potential moderator of the amount of deliberative processing in which a message recipient engages upon presentation of a persuasive message, the CPM is more similar to the SJM in that it views prior knowledge as a biasing filter through which information passes. Accordingly, Albarracín's (2002) review of studies suggested that people access only those memories and concepts that are relevant for understanding the content of the persuasive message at hand. For example, Albarracín and Wyer (2001) compared judgment-relevant dimensions that were either present in the message arguments or not present and therefore only memory based; path analyses revealed that message-present dimensions linked more closely to attitudes than memory-only dimensions. Although this conclusion conflicts with Greenwald's (1968) predictions that recipient-generated thoughts should have greater impact, Albarracín's (2002) reanalysis of Greenwald's own data as well as more recent findings using different methodologies to measure beliefs appear to support the CPM.

Relative to the other process models, the strengths of the CPM are at least two: (a) it offers very specific processes that underlie persuasive effects; and (b) it attempts to integrate reception and yielding, whereas the other models would seem to be primarily theories of yielding. Granted, the ELM, HSM, and unimodel each specify some role for reception variables, but these roles are relatively passive. As Table 15.1 shows, the CPM maintains the predictions that the models make about persuasion in high versus low motivation and ability settings, but makes novel predictions about moderate motivation and ability settings. Some of these predictions have been supported by research, as we have noted, but the model is deserving of further such work.

Summary and Integration

Models of persuasion, coupled with thousands of empirical studies, have provided a rich picture of communication and attitude change. The highly programmatic research of the Yale group of the 1950s set the stage for the decades of persuasion research that followed. Although their results did not paint a very coherent picture of the landscape of persuasion variables and their effects, they laid the foundation for research exploring source variables (e.g., expertise, attractiveness, and status), message variables (e.g., high- and low-fear appeals), and recipient variables (e.g., initial attitudinal position). McGuire's (1960, 1968a) work on information processing expanded the importance of the interaction between recipient and message variables by stressing the role of a message recipient's active participation in the persuasion process. In particular, he recognized that persuasion could be moderated by individual differences such as intelligence or self-esteem, variables that logically influence ability or motivation to "receive" information or to yield. Social judgment theorists also contended that responses to persuasive messages were largely dependent upon the recipient's existing attitudes and perspectives: Latitudes of acceptance and rejection differ across recipients; thus, responses to any given messages are likely to differ as a result. Later, Greenwald (1968) began to specify a cognitive process that could account for different responses to the same message. In particular, he suggested that the thoughts generated in response to a persuasive communication mediated attitude change. To the extent that a message's arguments evoked different thoughts in different people, different results can be expected. Contemporary process models of attitude change incorporate all of these ideas and make their own unique contributions. For example, the ELM, HSM, the unimodel, and the CPM each explicitly address the impact of ability and motivation to process information, the notion of thought-mediated persuasion, and the potential moderating effects of personality variables (see Table 15.1). These process models have been able to account for the impact of a significant portion of the effects that early persuasion researchers obtained. For example, the ELM and HSM in particular have guided numerous studies outlining specific effects of message-relevant thinking, source expertise and attractiveness, targeting issues of high personal relevance, and implications for behavior. In addition to cognitive responses to persuasive messages, process models are able to account for more affectively based processes such as mood and attraction to the source, and recognize that stimuli outside conscious awareness can impact our attitudes and behaviors. Yet the ultimate impact of the unimodel and the CPM is at this point unknown, owing to the relatively few empirical tests of these models. A challenge for researchers will be to develop comparative tests with the potential to support one model over another (see Albarracín & Kumkale, 2003).

CAUSES OF COMMUNICATION-INDUCED ATTITUDE CHANGE

As highlighted by the Yale model, one can divide causes of communication-induced attitude change into communicator, message, and recipient variables, and these three sets of variables are conceptually interrelated. For example, visual messages may convey the communicator's physical attractiveness better than an audio message. In addition, as described below, communicator and message variables may influence heuristics (e.g., overheard messages are trustworthy) and message-relevant thoughts (e.g., decisions that the arguments are novel) *within* the recipient. Such interrelations make it important to examine the ways in which the message, communicator, and recipient variables may interact, in addition to examining the effects of each set of variables separately. This section reviews these separate and combined effects.

Nature of the Message Communicator

Sources of a message directly and indirectly bring their own expectations, beliefs, feelings, motives, traits, physical characteristics, and social networks into the communication context. For instance, message communicators may wish to deceive the audience or to give an open and frank account; they may be physically attractive or unattractive; and a majority or minority of their peers may support them. These variables are important because they are frequently present in everyday contexts. As modern-day Machiavellians, used car salespeople might not be completely honest about the vehicles they sell; brand spokespeople are often above average in physical attractiveness; and advertiser claims are often made about a "majority" or a "minority" of people. Consequently, past research has examined cues that we use to detect dissimulation, the effects of dissimulation on the message recipients' and sources' attitudes, and the effects of source reinforcers (e.g., attractiveness) and source numeracy on attitudes. We summarize much of the abundant evidence on each of these variables below.

Signs of Dissimulation.   Perhaps the most important thing about the process of detecting dissimulation is that people tend to believe that particular facial cues (e.g., deviated gaze) signal deception, but people are actually better at detecting dissimulation when they do not see the communicator (DePaulo, 1994). When facial cues are absent, people rely on more valid cues to deceit, including voice pitch, speech errors, and speech hesitations (DePaulo, Stone, & Lassiter, 1985; Zuckerman, DePaulo, & Rosenthal, 1981; Zuckerman & Driver, 1985). In contrast, when facial cues are present, accuracy at detecting lies is barely greater than chance (Ekman & O'Sullivan, 1991).

An important caveat to these results is that the accuracy of dissimulation detection from facial cues improves when the deceiver is highly motivated to lie (DePaulo & Friedman, 1999) and when the message recipients are expert at lie detection (Ekman, O'Sullivan, & Frank, 1999). Researchers should therefore develop a model of how message recipients' attitudes are shaped by the cues to deception in nonvisual and visual modalities. Many interesting questions can be asked about the effects of these cues. Reynolds and Gifford (2001) recently took this approach with regard to judgments of intelligence, using a Brunswikian lens model to examine whether physical and nonverbal features associated with intelligence were used as cues to judge intelligence. Similar tactics could be employed in persuasion research. For example, are the effects of cues to dissimulation similar to the effects of forewarning of persuasive intent? As described below, forewarning of persuasive intent reduces persuasion by causing recipients to counterargue the content of the persuasive communication. This counterargumentation may also be elicited by nonvisual and visual cues to dissimulation, which may prime the message recipients to be skeptical or wary (see also Sagarin, Cialdini, Rice, & Serna, 2002). Thus, the effects of forewarning and cues to dissimulation on resistance to persuasion may be similar.

Effects on the Deceivers' Attitudes.   As Olson and Stone (chap. 6, this volume) describe, Festinger and Carlsmith's (1959) classic demonstration of the effects of behavior on attitudes had a tremendous impact on the study of attitudes. Their experiment is also relevant to understanding the effects of attitude dissimulation on the deceiver's attitudes, because the target behavior in their experiment was the act of communicating a false opinion about several experimental tasks to a new participant in the experiment. When the incentive offered for this counterattitudinal advocacy was low (i.e., $1 rather than $20), the dissimulation caused participants to change their attitude to more closely resemble their dissimulation. Since Festinger and Carlsmith's (1959) experiment, abundant research has replicated and extended this effect of attitude dissimulation on the deceiver's own attitude (see Harmon-Jones & Mills, 1999). This newer research has added the observation that attitude change occurs more strongly when people freely express false attitudes in a manner that produces aversive consequences (Cooper & Fazio, 1984; Cooper & Scher, 1994; R. W. Johnson, Kelly, & LeBlanc, 1995), although aversive consequences are not necessary for attitude change to occur (Harmon-Jones, 2000; Harmon-Jones, Brehm, Greenberg, Simon, & Nelson, 1996; Prislin & Pool, 1996).

Two major social psychological theories have been used to explain these effects of dissimulation: cognitive dissonance theory (Festinger, 1957) and self-perception theory (Bem, 1972). Dissonance theory proposes that attitude change occurs because the discrepancy between the dissimulation and the true attitude elicits an uncomfortable tension or "dissonance" in the deceiver, especially when there appears to be no external justification for the dissimulation and there are aversive consequences for having performed the dissimulation. In this situation, deceivers should attempt to reduce their dissonance by changing their attitude to match their false attitude expression (Elliot & Devine, 1994). In contrast, self-perception theory proposes that individuals performing the deception simply infer their true attitude from their behavior; no aversive arousal is involved (Bem, 1972). That is, in situations that present no incentive for the dissimulation, people guess that they must at least partly believe what they said, because they can see no other plausible reason for having expressed the false attitude.

Extant evidence, however, indicates that aversive arousal can be elicited by attitude dissimulation and that this arousal can mediate the effect of dissimulation on attitude change (Fazio, Zanna, & Cooper, 1977; Zanna & Cooper, 1974; Zanna, Higgins, & Taves, 1976). Nonetheless, arousal is less likely to play a role when the dissimulation is close to the true attitude than when it is very discrepant from the true attitude (Fazio et al., 1977). In other words, some dissimulation-induced attitude change may occur through a dissonance reduction mechanism, whereas other dissimulation-induced attitude change may occur through a self-perception mechanism (Fazio et al., 1977). An additional complication is that dissimulation-induced attitude change may be more likely to occur when the dissimulation threatens the people's self-concept than when the dissimulation does not threaten the self-concept (Heine & Lehman, 1997; Steele, Spencer, & Lynch, 1993). Thus, it could be argued that the dissonance and self-perception accounts of dissimulation-induced attitude change should be broadened to incorporate the role of the self-concept (see Steele, 1988). However, the precise role of the self-concept also may vary across cultures (Hoshino-Browne, Zanna, Spencer, & Zanna, in press).

Although attitude dissimulation that occurs with high external justification and without aversive consequences does not typically produce dissonance-motivated or self-perception–motivated attitude change, it can nonetheless affect the accessibility (i.e., ease of retrieval) of the dissimulator's attitude. Specifically, when people are asked to indicate the opposite of their true attitude without the elicitation of any aversive consequences, attitudes become more accessible (i.e., more quickly recalled), even though the dissimulation in these circumstances elicits no attitude change. This effect arises both when the initial attitudes are strong (Maio & Olson, 1995b) and weak (Johar & Sengupta, 2002). More important, subsequent attitude-relevant judgments become more compatible with the true attitude after such attitude dissimulation (Maio & Olson, 1998).

Source Reinforcers. Abundant evidence supports the hypothesis that source reinforcers such as attractiveness, status, likeability, expertise, and trustworthiness increase persuasion (see Cialdini, 1993), although each effect appears to hinge somewhat on whether message recipients have the motivation and ability to process message content and may rest on individual differences (Livingston, 2001). A frequent explanation for the effects of source variables is that they act as heuristic guides or cues for attitude formation (Chaiken, 1987). For example, source attractiveness may operate through simple heuristics such as the audience's belief that "people I like usually have correct opinions on issues" (Chaiken, 1987, p. 4), and source expertise may operate through the audience's belief that "statements by experts can be trusted" (Chaiken, 1987, p. 4). As a result of having these simple decision rules, people need not carry out an exhaustive examination of presented arguments–they can simply agree with messages that are delivered by the desirable sources. As we have discussed, contemporary process models of persuasion (see Table 15.1) agree that source characteristics can exert their effects in this easy, nonelaborate manner, although the processes involved may be complex. At the time of message processing, the heuristics must be accessible (Chaiken, 1987; Chaiken & Eagly, 1983; Darke et al., 1998) and the source characteristics (e.g., "Oprah Winfrey is likeable," "Einstein is an expert") must be easy to retrieve from memory if they are to have an effect on message acceptance. For example, source likeability increases persuasion more strongly when the positive attitude toward the source is highly accessible from memory than when it is less accessible (Roskos-Ewoldsen, Bichsel, & Hoffman, 2002; Roskos-Ewoldsen & Fazio, 1992).

Other evidence supports the ELM's position that source characteristics can occasionally act as message arguments or influence the nature of message processing, in addition to acting as simple cues. For instance, the high attractiveness of a spokeswoman for a beauty product might be an argument for the effectiveness of the product, a cue to evaluate the product favorably, or lead people to process the other information about the product more closely. Consistent with the notion that source characteristics can bias message processing, they affect message processing when other factors (e.g., recipients' personality) do not constrain people to process the messages in an elaborate or nonelaborate manner (Heesacker, Petty, Cacioppo, 1983; Puckett, Petty, Cacioppo, & Fisher, 1983), and when the source characteristics conflict (e.g., an expert and dislikeable source; Ziegler, Diehl, & Ruther, 2002). Finally, researchers testing the unimodel of persuasion (Thompson, Kruglanski, & Spiegel, 2000) have predicted and found that source characteristics are more likely to function as arguments when they are described in very complex ways (e.g., the communication of expertise through a curriculum vitae). The complex format makes it necessary to utilize systematic processing in order to discover the source characteristics in the first place.

It is worth noting that such research does not distinguish between different types of influence from sources. In contrast, French and Raven (1959; Raven, 1992) described six bases of social power that sources may employ in the service of persuasive messages: reward, coercion, expertise, information, referent power, and legitimate authority. As Prislin and Wood's (chap. 16, this volume) review of research suggests, this model encompasses the aforementioned effects of source likeability (referent power) and source expertise (expertise and, to a lesser extent, information power), in addition to the effects of sources that possess legitimate authority, the ability to distribute rewards (reward power), or the ability to punish (coercive power). An important issue for future research is whether the effects of sources vary across the types of power they employ. According to Kelman (1958, 1974), sources with control over message recipients' outcomes (i.e., sources that possess reward and coercive power) elicit superficial, public agreement with their messages, but no true attitude change. In contrast, sources who are attractive to message recipients (i.e., sources that possess referent power) elicit public and private agreement with the message, but primarily in the contexts that are relevant to the relationship between the source and the message recipient. Agreement with the message is independent of both the public-private dimension and the relationship between the source and message recipient only when the source appears to convey useful and valid information (i.e., expertise and information power). Kelman (1958) labeled these three processes as compliance, identification, and integration, respectively, and there is some evidence for the validity of this distinction (Kelman & Eagly, 1965; Oriña, Wood, & Simpson, 2002; cf. Nail, 1986; Nail, MacDonald, & Levy, 2000).

Despite these intriguing theories, the power of a message source over a message recipient is an underinvestigated source variable. Some early studies found, perhaps not surprisingly, that powerful sources persuade more than weak ones (French & Raven, 1959). However, if a recipient perceives that the message source has power over outcomes important to the recipient, apparent changes in attitude and behavior may be indicative of acquiescence or coercion (Kelman, 1958) rather than true attitude change, the hallmark of persuasion. Nonetheless, even mere changes in overt behavior can lead to attitude change (see Olson & Stone, chap. 6, this volume). Therefore, it is possible that most attitude "change" in response to powerful sources is volitional, and not merely acquiescence.

Sources of low power can also be persuasive. Petty, Fleming, and White (1999) showed that for low prejudice people, stigmatized sources stimulated message relevant thinking, and aversive racism may motivate this increased elaboration (White & Harkins, 1994). Consistent with this view, Fiske, Morling, and Stevens (1996) found that messages from sources who had power over task outcomes increased message scrutiny; if the source had power over evaluations of the recipient, the message processing was positively biased. Targets may also infer source status from speech variables. For example, faster speech or use of passive voice has been associated with high source credibility (Hurwitz, Miron, & Johnson, 1992; Miller, Maruyama, Beaber, & Valone, 1976; Smith & Shaffer, 1995). Powerless speech, characterized by verbal hedging and disfluencies, may convey low social status (O'Barr, 1982). Finally, lower status communicators adopt their higher status partners' subtle communication styles (Gregory & Webster, 1996).

Sometimes messages from sources with low credibility can elicit persuasion even when recipients initially discount the message because of the low source credibility. The sleeper effect occurs when (a) the quality of argumentation contained in a persuasive communication is strong enough to elicit persuasion (b) a discounting cue (e.g., low source credibility) is strong enough to negate the initial persuasive effects of the message, and (c) the association between the discounting cue and the message conclusion is forgotten more quickly than the arguments contained in the message. Over time, if recipients are able to recall the content of the message and forget the discounting cue (often a source cue) delayed persuasion has been shown to occur (Gruder et al., 1978; Pratkanis, Greenwald, Leippe, & Baumgardner, 1988). Recent research has demonstrated that the sleeper effect is mediated by message-relevant thinking at the time of message presentation (Priester, Wegener, Petty, & Fabrigar, 1999). Kumkale and Albarracín's (2004) recent meta-analytic review confirmed each of these points.

Source Numeracy. Research on situations wherein the source of a message is a minority or majority of people within a group, and the audience is composed of the other group members, echoes French and Raven's (1959) and Kelman's (1958, 1974) distinctions. Research in this context has focused on the difference between (a) agreement as a function of the validity of information from a source and (b) agreement as a function of the attractiveness of the source. Convention labels these types of influence in groups as informational and normative influence, respectively (see Prislin & Wood, chap. 16, this volume).

This importance of informational and normative influence in the group context was first made evident in classic experiments by Sherif (1935) and Asch (1956). Sherif found that individual participants converged with the majority's answer to a question about an ambiguous, difficult problem, which involved identifying the amount of movement of a light in a darkened room. Asch extended the demonstration of conformity by showing that participants frequently agreed with a majority's patently incorrect solution to an easy problem, which involved deciding whether pairs of lines of unambiguously different lengths were equal or different in length. Sherif's results seemed consistent with the notion that people use the majority's response as a practical and valid cue for identifying the correct solution, whereas Asch's results seemed consistent with the notion that people agree with the group in order to maintain positive regard from other group members (see Deutsch & Gerard, 1955).

Subsequent research has indicated that both informational and normative influence contribute to the effect of majority sources. With regard to informational influence, Hochbaum (1954) found that majority influence is greater when the participants are made to feel less competent beforehand. In addition, Coleman, Blake, and Mouton (1958) found that participants conformed to a majority's incorrect responses to difficult questions more than to the majority's incorrect responses to easy questions (see also Asch, 1952; Deutsch & Gerard, 1955).

Presumably, the reduced sense of competence in Hochbaum's experiment and the difficulty of items in Coleman et al.'s experiment made people place more value on information obtained from others. With regard to normative influence, evidence indicates that conformity increases when attitudes are expressed in public rather than in private (Asch, 1956), the group provides important rewards (Crutchfield, 1955), recipients of the group pressure strongly desire group approval (Crowne & Marlowe, 1964), and the group itself is made to seem more attractive to the recipients of group pressure (Festinger, Gerard, Hymovitch, Kelley, & Raven, 1952). Thus, the extant support for an informational route to majority influence is matched by strong evidence for a normative route to majority influence (see also Argyle, 1957; Deutsch & Gerard, 1955; Insko, Smith, Alicke, Wade, & Taylor, 1985; Mouton, Blake, & Olmstead, 1956). Thus, it is likely that most majority influence involves a blend of both types.

Note that informational and normative influence resemble the affective and cognitive antecedents of attitudes that are core themes in this volume. Recent research demonstrates a role for the behavioral component as well. Specifically, the biased interpretation of the stimulus can occur after the decision to agree with the majority, in addition to occurring beforehand (Buehler & Griffin, 1994; Griffin & Buehler, 1993). Moreover, the post-conformity change in interpretation increases over time (Buehler & Griffin, 1994). This evidence is consistent with the previously discussed research on dissonance theory (Festinger, 1957) and self-perception theory (Bem, 1972). Both of these theories argue that people can alter their thinking and judgments to become more consistent with behaviors (e.g., conformity) that they have recently performed. Together with the evidence for informational and normative influence, these theories are consistent with the conclusion that majority influence can reflect a blend of affective, cognitive, and behavioral information.

Minorities in groups can influence majority opinion when they express their opinions consistently, thereby appearing more confident, competent, and honest (Bassili & Provencal, 1988; Maass & Clark, 1984). In fact, the perception of trustworthiness can also increase when the people with the minority opinion are otherwise similar to people in the majority, because the similar minorities are seen as having less of a personal investment in the decision. For example, heterosexual advocates of gay rights influence heterosexual opinion on gay rights more than do gay male, lesbian, and bisexual advocates of gay rights (Maass, Clark, & Haberkorn, 1982).

Although both majorities and minorities elicit attitude change, there has been ample speculation that they do so through different processes. One set of perspectives argues that majorities stimulate simple conformity to group views without much concomitant thought, whereas minorities stimulate attitude change through systematic thought about the issue (Moscovici, 1980; Peterson & Nemeth, 1996). In contrast, other perspectives argue that majority sources elicit more message scrutiny than minority sources (Mackie, 1987), because people usually assume that consensus views are correct (see Cialdini, 1993) and, therefore, deserving of attention (see also Harkins & Petty, 1981, 1987). Yet another set of perspectives describes majority and minority influence as a mathematical function of the strength (abilities, power, status), immediacy (proximity in space or time), and number of majority group members present in the persuasion context versus the strength, immediacy, and number of the minority group members present (Latané, 1981; Latané & Wolf, 1981; Tanford & Penrod, 1984). In this model, the faction with the greatest strength, immediacy, and numeracy exerts the largest influence, and the strength of both factions is also held to depend on their capacity to exert informational and normative power, as has been emphasized in studies of majority influence (Wolf, 1987).

Additional models retain a dual-process point of view, but do not link majorities and minorities exclusively to either process. These models suggest that either majorities or minorities may elicit heuristic or systematic processing, depending on other factors. For instance, messages from both sources may receive systematic processing when the personal relevance of the issue is high (Kerr, 2002). Presumably, personal relevance motivates systematic processing to such an extent that the majority versus minority status of the source becomes less relevant (Baker & Petty, 1994). In contrast, Erb, Bohner, Schmälzle, and Rank (1998) found that exposure to majority and minority views reduced message scrutiny when the participants held no strong prior attitude and the issues and groups were of low personal relevance. Even in conditions of low relevance, however, the effects of majority and minority sources can be more complex. Compared to majorities, minorities elicit more attention to argument quality when the minorities are aware of the unpopularity of their position, expect interaction with the majority group, and are at least somewhat dependent on the majority group—the absence of these factors may cause neither majorities nor minorities to elicit systematic processing (Kerr, 2002).

When the personal relevance of the issue is moderate or uncertain, however, both sources can elicit systematic processing. In particular, Baker and Petty (1994) predicted and found that people often feel surprised when they encounter a majority view that differs from their own. As a result of this feeling of surprise, participants processed a majority message that was incongruent with their initial attitude more carefully than a majority message that was congruent with their attitude. Similarly, participants processed a minority message that was congruent with their initial attitude more carefully than a minority message that was incongruent with their attitude. Thus, the effect of majorities and minorities was moderated by the surprisingness of the communicators' positions (see Erb et al., 2002).

Summary

Attributes of the source of a message complicate the effects of the messages. For example, in many persuasion contexts, the source provides facial and nonfacial cues to deception. Ironically, message recipients are better at detecting deception when nonfacial cues are present than when deception is accompanied by facial cues, and an interesting issue is how the presence or absence of the cues affects message processing. Another interesting issue is the effect of the dissimulations on the sources' own attitudes (i.e., an effect of behavior on attitude). Abundant evidence indicates that message sources may become convinced by their own deceptions, either as a means of reducing discomfort from their dissimulation or through a simple inference process. When the dissimulation does not elicit attitude change, however, it may indirectly reinforce the strength of the deceiver's preexisting attitude.

Attributes of the source of a message can also elicit particular incentives for attitude change. Consistent with seminal models of attitude change and attitude function, messages from sources who are attractive, high in status, likeable, expert, trustworthy, and powerful are more effective than messages from sources who do not possess these attributes. Contemporary models of persuasion indicate that these source characteristics might elicit persuasion through the activation of relevant heuristics (e.g., "experts can be trusted"), provided that the heuristics are accessible from memory at the time of message processing. In addition, these models indicate that the source characteristics might sometimes act as persuasive arguments in their own right or bias the nature of message scrutiny. Also, the extent to which different source attributes elicit public versus private agreement may depend on the type of social power that they reflect.

Research has also focused on the effects of variations in the number of message sources. Majority pressures may affect judgments through a normative route, an informational route, or both. Both routes are also relevant to understanding minority influence, although analyses of minority influence have focused on several aspects of behavioral style that predict minorities' effectiveness (e.g., consistency, similarity to majority). The research has led to provocative proposals that majorities and minorities elicit different levels of message scrutiny. Although much evidence is consistent with this hypothesis, other evidence indicates that majorities and minorities elicit similar levels of processing when other factors are controlled (e.g., personal relevance, position expectations).

EFFECTS OF THE NATURE AND STRUCTURE
OF MESSAGES

Anticipated Communication

Before receiving a persuasive message, people can receive information indicating (a) the content of the message and (b) the persuasive intent within the message (Papageorgis, 1968). Sometimes, the warning of content accompanies a warning of persuasive intent. For instance, people typically know that someone will try to sell them a time-share when they are invited to "visit" a resort. On other occasions, the warning is informative not about the message's point of view, but merely its topic. For example, promotions of a book about cancer might indicate that it describes the author's struggles with the disease, without noting that the author uses his or her experience to press specific points, such as the hazards of smoking and a lack of adequate care for cancer patients. On yet other occasions, we may know that the message is intended to persuade us, but the content of the arguments may be unclear. For instance, a reader of the book about cancer may warn a new reader that the text is "preachy," and presses specific points, but the new reader may not be told which points will be argued.

Research has examined the effects of these types of forewarning separately (Hass & Grady, 1975; Petty & Cacioppo, 1979a) or in combination (Allyn & Festinger, 1961; Brock, 1967). In general, forewarning causes more resistance to persuasion, at least among message recipients who possess stronger initial attitudes (Allyn & Festinger, 1961; Jacks & Devine, 2000), higher involvement with the topic (Wood & Quinn, 2003), and are not distracted at the time of message processing (Chen, Reardon, Rea, & Moore, 1992; Watts & Holt, 1979). This pattern of effects is consistent with the hypothesis that forewarning can increase counterarguing of the message, either in advance of message presentation (i.e., after a content forewarning) or during message presentation (Wood & Quinn, 2003).

Nevertheless, the aforementioned research focused on a context wherein the forewarnings were followed by a simple message from a source, but there is no potential interaction with the source. Although forewarning often increases resistance in this noninteractional context, it may actually decrease resistance when the message recipients anticipate potential dialogue with the source of the message. Indeed, people show anticipatory attitude change when they are asked to be the source of a message to an audience. For example, Tetlock (1983) manipulated whether participants were aware or unaware of the attitudes of a person to whom they had to express an opinion. Aware participants subsequently altered their attitude to be consistent with the attitude of the message recipient, whereas unaware participants adopted more neutral attitudes, which were supported by evaluatively inconsistent and complex thoughts. Chen, Shechter, and Chaiken (1996) predicted and found that this pattern of attitude change was highest among participants with high impression management concerns, which were identified using an individual difference measure (self-monitoring; Snyder, 1987) or manipulated using a priming technique (see Bargh, 1990). In their meta-analytic review of such evidence, Wood and Quinn (2003) concluded that message recipients modify their attitudes to fit the position of a message source with whom they expect to interact, but primarily when the issue is less personally involving. When the interaction partner's attitudes are unclear, message recipients again seem to stick to relatively neutral territory and are unaffected by argument quality (Johnson & Eagly, 1989).

Argument Quality and Quantity.   Although it appeared only relatively recently, argument quality appears to be the most-manipulated communication dimension (Petty et al., 1976). Its popularity stems primarily from its use as a gauge of the extent to which targets process message content—as scrutiny increases, the logic goes, the impact of argument quality should increase (Petty & Cacioppo, 1986). Another reason for this variable's popularity may be that it is also one of the more robust manipulations at researchers' disposal: Basically, strong arguments are more persuasive than weak arguments, as numerous research syntheses have shown directly (Johnson et al., 2004; Stiff, 1986) or indirectly (Johnson & Eagly, 1989; Wood & Quinn, 2003). The robustness of this effect should be no surprise given that scholars frequently pretest their messages to produce profiles of strongly favorable versus unfavorable cognitive response profiles, following Petty and Cacioppo's (1986) example. More interesting is that the effects of argument quality vary quite widely across the literature, hinging on message recipients' levels of involvement, message length, and the position taken by the messages. Argument quality appears to have a larger effect when involvement is outcome- rather than value- or impression-relevant (Johnson & Eagly, 1989; Maio & Olson, 1995a), when messages or message arguments are longer rather than shorter (Johnson & Eagly, 1989; Friedrich, Fetherstonhaugh, Casey, & Gallagher, 1996; Wood, Kallgren, & Preisler, 1985), and when the message position is counter- rather than pro-attitudinal (Johnson et al., 2004). When the message position is pro-attitudinal, recipients will find their own reasons to agree more following the messages, whether the arguments are strong or weak; when arguments are counterattitudinal, strong arguments appear to induce actual attitude change, whereas weak arguments appear to induce maintenance of initial attitudes (Johnson et al., 2004). Boomerang effects, wherein recipients' attitudes move significantly away from the message position are rare, but may occur when outcome-relevant involvement is high (Johnson et al., 2004). Finally, although longer messages tend to be more persuasive, their effects hinge on their argument quality and on message recipients' involvement. When message recipients have high outcome-relevant involvement, the typical argument quality effect is observed, with strong arguments more persuasive than weak arguments; in contrast, under low involvement circumstances, message length may act as a persuasion cue yielding equivalent persuasion for both strong and weak arguments sets (Petty & Cacioppo, 1984).

Given that argument quality has been defined on a more-or-less empirical basis, one might question what it means, ultimately, to show that strong arguments are more persuasive than weak arguments. Scholars such as Petty and Cacioppo (1986, pp. 31–32) have recognized that their own use of the argument quality construct is not informative about what makes any particular argument persuasive. More generally, attitudes scholars have recognized that failure to understand how message information relates to attitude change "is probably the most serious problem in communication and persuasion research" (Fishbein & Ajzen, 1975, p. 359). Although a merit of the argument quality variable is its experimental nature, it is of course possible that variables other than logical plausibility or cogency drive its effects. Indeed, research suggests that argument quality is more closely related to valence (good vs. bad; positive vs. negative) than to cogency (likely vs. unlikely; low vs. high probability of being true) or to the interaction of valence and cogency (Areni & Lutz, 1988; Johnson et al., 2004). Thus, strong arguments tend to make good consequences salient whereas weak arguments tend to make bad consequences salient. This research suggests that the past argument quality effects should be recast as argument valence effects (Eagly & Chaiken, 1993).

Valence and cogency are not the only possible argument dimensions that may underlie persuasion, and rhetoric scholars have provided many detailed possible analyses (Areni, 2003; McGuire, 2000). Beyond these qualitative analyses, experimentation has shown that causal arguments appear to be quite convincing relative to simple descriptions of what consequences will occur (Slusher & Anderson, 1996). Moreover, arguments viewed as novel and valid have been judged as more persuasive than arguments that are viewed as less valid and non-novel (Garcia-Marques & Mackie, 2001; Vinokur & Burnstein, 1978). Argument complexity or comprehensiveness may also be related to persuasion. Supporting McGuire's reception-yielding perspective, studies have tended to show that comprehensible arguments are more persuasive than less comprehensible arguments (Eagly, 1974).

Message Framing.   Another area of burgeoning research is that of message framing. Such research typically holds the arguments constant and varies how the message position is stated so that it has either a loss focus or a gain focus (for reviews, see Devos-Comby & Salovey, 2002; Rothman & Salovey, 1997). Loss frames typically emphasize the costs that will accrue if an action is not taken (e.g., "if you don't stop action X, you will die!") whereas gain frames emphasize the benefits that will result if an action is taken ("if you stop action X, you will live longer"). Typically, loss frames are more persuasive than gain-frame messages (Meyerowitz & Chaiken, 1987), although this effect may depend on having sufficient motivation and ability to process the message (Maheswaran & Meyers-Levy, 1990). Similarly, the personality trait of optimism appears to heighten such effects (Geers, Handley, & McLarney, 2003). Finally, a series of experiments by Lee and Aaker (2004) consistently found that loss frames were more persuasive than gain frames only when participants were motivated to pursue positive outcomes. In contrast, when participants were motivated to prevent negative events, gain frames were more persuasive than loss frames.

Other Message Dimensions.   Persuasion researchers have examined a huge array of other message-related dimensions. Posing arguments in the form of rhetorical questions tends to increase motivation to process the arguments, resulting in larger argument quality effects even when involvement is low (Petty, Cacioppo, & Heesacker, 1981). Although scholars have long regarded two-sided messages as more persuasive than one-sided messages for targets holding more opposed vs. favorable attitudes (Hovland et al., 1949), a meta-analysis of this literature produced little support for this prediction (Allen, 1991). Fear appeals generally enhance persuasion, as shown by meta-analyses of this literature (Boster & Mongeau, 1985; Sutton, 1982; Witte & Allen, 2000), possibly because they contain recommended actions that, if adopted, would help to negate the basis of the fear (Das, de Wit, & Stroebe, 2003; for more on this topic, see *Arousal and Message Effects*, in the following pages). Finally, early theories such as the SJM predicted that as message positions take more extreme stands in relation to the recipients' own views, agreement may be less likely, but attitude change more likely. For example, Bochner and Insko (1966) found that highly discrepant messages elicited more (message congruent) changes in post-communication attitudes, but also greater amounts of communication disparagement. Because such findings have proven difficult to replicate (see Eagly, 1974; Ostrom, Steele, & Smilansky, 1974), renewed attention to communication discrepancy would be worthwhile.

NATURE OF THE MESSAGE RECIPIENT

As noted above, many effects of communicator and message variables occur because they activate relevant heuristics and message-relevant thoughts for the message recipients. However, a variety of individual differences moderate the persuasive impact of message and communicator variables, as Briñol and Petty (chap. 14, this volume) review. The nature of an individual difference is that some variability in recipients' attitudes, abilities, and motivations exists prior to message exposure. For example, before receiving a persuasive message, recipients' attitudes toward the message topic may vary in structural attributes, the conviction with which they are held, and the psychological needs that they fulfill. Recipients may also vary in their ability and motivation to process the messages. The impact of each communication factor described in this chapter may depend on one or more individual differences. In this section, we discuss variability in dimensions of attitude structure, attitude function, and ability and motivation.

Variability in Attitude Structure

According to the popular tripartite view of attitudes (Zanna & Rempel, 1988), affective, cognitive, and behavioral information can influence attitudes, and the contribution of each type of information can vary. For example, some attitudes might express relevant feelings more than any specific beliefs and behaviors (e.g., attitudes toward abstract art), whereas other attitudes might express all three types of information simultaneously (e.g., attitudes toward war). This variability in the potential bases of attitude is important because it should influence the strength and structural integrity in attitudes. For example, extreme attitudes presumably reflect an abundance of consistent cognitive, affective, and behavioral information that supports either a favorable or unfavorable evaluation of the attitude object. As a result, it may be difficult for message arguments to overwhelm this consistent database with new evidence supporting a different attitude. Indeed, extreme attitudes are not only more stable across time (Prislin, 1996) but also more resistant to change (Bassili, 1996; Pomerantz, Chaiken, & Tordesillas, 1995).

Although the cohesiveness of attitude structure may explain effects of attitude extremity on attitude stability and resistance, scholars may examine attitude structure more directly, as Fabrigar, MacDonald, and Wegener (chap. 3, this volume) describe. One method involves counting the number of beliefs, feelings, and/or behaviors that people report when asked to describe their attitudes. This procedure helps to assess attitudinal embeddedness, which can be defined as the extent to which the attitude is associated with many beliefs, feelings, and behaviors in memory (Esses & Maio, 2002; Prislin & Ouellette, 1996). These associations are important because attitudes should be stronger when they are embedded in many cognitive, affective, and behavioral associates than when they are embedded in few cognitive, affective, and behavioral associates (Eagly & Chaiken, 1995). Indeed, Wood, Rhodes, and Biek (1995) found that persuasive messages are less effective among those who report more cognitive and behavioral associates of their attitudes than among those who report few of these associates.

It is also possible to examine the consistency between attitudinal elements and the net attitude. In theory, someone could report a positive attitude toward something (e.g., smoking), while having numerous beliefs, feelings, and behaviors that are evaluatively inconsistent with it (e.g., smoking causes cancer, smoking makes my food taste bad). For this reason, it is important to also assess the magnitude (i.e., absolute value) of the difference between the favorability implied by one's overall attitude and the favorability implied by one's beliefs, feelings, and behaviors regarding the attitude object (Esses & Maio, 2002). The importance of this assessment is demonstrated by evidence indicating that high evaluative-cognitive inconsistency is associated with lower attitude stability (Chaiken, Pomerantz, & Giner-Sorolla, 1995). It is therefore tempting to regard indices of inconsistency as useful predictors of resistance to change. Nevertheless, attitudes that possess high inconsistency with one component (e.g., high evaluative-cognitive inconsistency) may often exhibit low inconsistency with other components (e.g., low evaluative-affective inconsistency; Chaiken et al., 1995). Thus, it is essential that effects of inconsistencies between attitudes and all other attitude elements be examined simultaneously. As of yet, few studies have used this approach (Chaiken et al., 1995; Haddock & Huskinson, in press; Huskinson & Haddock, in press), and the implications of inconsistency for resistance to change are unclear.

In addition, it is important to examine conflict between elements of attitudes within components (e.g., positive versus negative beliefs) as well as conflict between elements of attitudes across components (e.g., positive beliefs versus negative emotions). These two types of conflict are often labeled as intra- and inter-component ambivalence, respectively (Esses & Maio, 2002;

MacDonald & Zanna, 1998; Thompson, Zanna, & Griffin, 1995). Research has assessed this intra- and intercomponent ambivalence by asking participants either (a) to rate their feelings of ambivalence or (b) to rate the favorability of their attitude elements so that these favorability ratings could be entered into formulae for calculating ambivalence (Bassili, 1996; Priester & Petty, 1996). Regardless of which method is used, people who report ambivalence toward an issue tend to scrutinize messages more carefully, causing them to resist weak arguments more than strong arguments (Jonas, Diehl, & Brömer, 1997; Maio, Bell, & Esses, 1996; Maio, Esses, & Bell, 2000).

Ambivalence is also one of several features of attitude structure that is associated with greater difficulty retrieving attitudes from memory (Bargh, Chaiken, Govender, & Pratto, 1992; Fazio, 1995). This relation is important because attitudes that are difficult to retrieve from memory are presumed to be less strongly associated in memory with the attitude object (Fazio, 1995). Ambivalence and other structural inconsistencies may interfere with this close association, which, in turn, makes it less likely that the attitude will be activated spontaneously when people encounter the attitude object (Fazio, Sanbonmatsu, Powell, & Kardes, 1986; Fazio, 1993; cf. Bargh et al., 1992; Chen & Bargh, 1999). As a result, attitudes with low accessibility are less likely to bias the processing of incoming information in a manner that is congruent with the attitude (see Fazio, 1995, 2000). Thus, attitude accessibility is another property of message recipients' attitude structure that predicts resistance to persuasive communications, and the effect of this property may potentially help to explain the effects of other structural properties (e.g., ambivalence).

Subjective Conviction.   As we reviewed above, the proponents of the SJM predicted and found that ego-involved individuals are more resistant to persuasion than those without this form of involvement. One reason may be that these individuals' narrow latitudes of acceptance reflect subjective certainty about their own attitude position (Eagly & Telaak, 1972). Certainty about the beliefs associated with those attitudes also moderates persuasion. Petty, Briñol, and Tormala (2002) found that increasing confidence in one's thoughts in response to a message by manipulating thought confidence or self-reported thought confidence moderated persuasion. In particular, increasing confidence in positive thoughts augmented persuasion, while increasing confidence in negative thoughts attenuated persuasion. Self-reports can assess many other ways in which attitudes are held with high subjective conviction. Attitude importance, attitude certainty, and attitude intensity are examples of some of the conviction-relevant variables that can be assessed by self-report. All of these variables are important because they can exert independent effects on stability and resistance processes (Pomerantz, Chaiken, & Tordesillas, 1995; Visser, Krosnick, & Simmons, 2003), despite strong relations among them (Krosnick et al., 1993).

Attitude Function

Like many other psychological constructs (e.g., stereotypes, traits), attitudes exist because they fulfill important psychological needs. These needs are varied and can affect the manner in which people form and maintain attitudes during exposure to persuasive communications. Smith et al. (1956) and Katz (1960) suggested a number of important attitude functions. One, Smith et al.'s (1956) object-appraisal function, exists when attitudes serve to simplify interactions with the attitude object. This function is served by any accessible attitude, regardless of whether the attitude is negative or positive. For example, people who have highly accessible attitudes toward different abstract paintings have less difficulty choosing which paintings they prefer most than do people who have less accessible attitudes toward the paintings (Blascovich et al., 1993; Fazio, Blascovich, & Driscoll, 1992). The usefulness of these accessible attitudes for decisions may make people reluctant to relinquish or change them, and the aforementioned evidence that accessible attitudes are more resistant to change supports this hypothesis (Fazio, 1995, 2000). Thus, the ability of highly accessible attitudes to serve the object-appraisal function may explain people's tendencies to protect these attitudes.

Other psychological functions may elicit resistance to attitude change by causing people to adopt specific attitude positions. For example, Katz's (1960) utilitarian function exists when people like things that are beneficial for them and dislike things that are harmful. Similarly, Katz (1960) proposed that a value-expressive function occurs when people like things that affirm or express important values and dislike things that threaten the values. Also, Smith et al.'s (1956) social-adjustive function is served when people like objects that are popular among people whom they like, but dislike objects that are unpopular among people whom they like.

An interesting feature of the utilitarian, value-expressive, and social-adjustive functions is that they may inspire different message processing objectives. According to the heuristic-systematic model of persuasion (Chaiken et al., 1989; Chen & Chaiken, 1999), people's processing of persuasive messages can be directed toward the attainment of attitudes that fulfill one or some combination of three goals (see also Johnson & Eagly, 1989): accuracy, self-defense, and social-impression management. The accuracy motivation directs people to process persuasive messages carefully and respond to both the strengths and weaknesses in the arguments (see also Petty & Wegener, 1999). This consideration of strengths and weaknesses increases persuasion when the arguments are strong and decreases persuasion when the arguments are weak.

It is more difficult to elicit persuasion when self-defense or impression-management motives exist. The self-defense motivation causes people to protect their perceived interests and their self-defining attitudes and beliefs (Chen & Chaiken, 1999). Self-defense can be achieved by selectively invoking heuristics that oppose the message (e.g., the speaker is unattractive) or by counterarguing the message arguments (Giner-Sorolla & Chaiken, 1997). Either way, the message must overcome significant resistance in order to elicit attitude change. Similarly, impression-management motives lead people to adopt whichever attitude satisfies current social goals, using both heuristics and message scrutiny (Chaiken, Giner-Sorolla, & Chen, 1996). For example, people might process message information in a way that affirms the attitude that is held by an important person with whom they expect to interact (Chen et al., 1996). Thus, defense and impression-management motives may elicit more closed-minded processing than the accuracy motives.

Ability and Motivation Dimensions

As Table 15.1 makes clear, prominent contemporary models of persuasion rest heavily on the ability and motivation of the message recipient to scrutinize the persuasive message itself. As ability or motivation are reduced, message recipients rely on other factors, such as number of arguments presented (e.g., Petty & Cacioppo, 1984; Wood et al., 1985) and source credibility (Petty, Cacioppo, & Goldman, 1981) to evaluate the message. As such, any individual difference that may impact motivation or ability to process message content accurately and efficiently is a potential moderator of the persuasive effects of the message and the source (see Briñol & Petty, chap. 14, this volume; Petty & Wegener, 1998a).

A variety of variables have been shown to impact a recipient's ability to process the message arguments systematically. Scrutiny of the arguments decreases in the presence of several constraints in the persuasive context, including distractions (Petty et al., 1976), physical discomfort or arousal (Petty, Wells, Heesacker, Brock, & Cacioppo, 1983; Sanbonmatsu & Kardes, 1988), time limitations (Smith & Shaffer, 1995), inability to read messages at the recipient's own pace (Chaiken & Eagly, 1976), message repetition (Cacioppo & Petty, 1979b; Gorn &

Goldberg, 1980), low recipient knowledge about the communication topic (Johnson et al., 1995; Wood et al., 1995), and inability to comprehend complex message content (Hafer, Reynolds, & Obertynski, 1996). Clinically diagnosed attention deficit disorders may also determine ability to elaborate. As the core symptoms of attention deficit disorders are impulsivity, inattention, and hyperactivity, individuals with such symptoms may process messages in unique and largely unexplored ways.

A variety of other individual differences may underlie motivation to elaborate on message content. The most widely studied variable is Need for Cognition (NC) (Cacioppo, Petty, Feinstein, & Jarvis, 1996), which has been shown to moderate the persuasive impact of argument quality such that the impact of argument quality is greater for those high in NC than for those low in NC. This moderating effect is understood to occur because of differential levels of motivation to process information systematically between those high and low in NC. Similarly, message scrutiny motivation is increased when feelings of accountability are heightened (Tetlock, 1983), and when people believe that they are solely responsible for message evaluation (Petty, Harkins, & Williams, 1980). Similarly, needs for non-specific and specific cognitive closure are motivational variables that impact the depth and direction of processing (Kruglanski, 1989; Kruglanski & Webster, 1996). Other specific motivations may also influence message processing. For example, those high in need for affiliation who find themselves in a minority may cave in to majority influences more quickly, and may be more susceptible to the effects of heuristic cues such as source credibility and attractiveness than those low in need for affiliation.

Message recipients' intelligence and self-esteem are two other variables that might influence ability and motivation. According to McGuire (1968), high levels of both variables should help make people able and motivated to understand and comprehend persuasive messages, because high intelligence involves greater thinking ability and high self-esteem reduces anxiety and heightens social engagement. On the other hand, high intelligence should also make people more able to counterargue messages, and high self-esteem should make people more certain about their views. The result of these competing influences should be more persuasion at moderate levels of the variables and lower at the low and high extremes—a pattern that Rhodes and Wood (1992) found in their meta-analysis of the self-esteem literature. The pattern they obtained in the intelligence literature was not curvilinear, but simply showed that with higher intelligence individuals exhibited less persuasion.

Differences on the optimism-pessimism dimension may moderate the impact of certain message frames. Some research suggests that the most persuasive aspect of a message's arguments is the valence of the consequences it suggests for the message recipient, rather than the likelihood that the argument is true (Johnson et al., 2004). From this perspective, optimists may respond more favorably to positively valenced arguments, regardless of truth value, whereas pessimists might be more persuaded if the argument is likely to be true. In other words, strong arguments might be true arguments for pessimists, but positively valenced ones for optimists. This prediction is in line with results found by Wegener, Petty, and Smith (1995).

Despite separate descriptions of ability and motivation factors, it is important to consider that many persuasion variables affect both ability and motivation to process messages. For example, Neimeyer, Metzler, and Dongarra (1990) found that depression increased reliance on peripheral cues, and Sayers, Baucom, and Tierney (1993) found that depressed individuals were less successful at persuading another participant than non-depressed individuals. It is unclear, however, whether depression inhibits ability or motivation to elaborate on message content. Mood is a prime example of a variable that biases message processing through its effects on both ability and motivation to process messages. Raghunathan and Trope (2002) revealed three ways in which these effects occur. First, positive mood may act as a resource that helps people to elaborate on presented information that is negative but self-relevant. For example, a positive mood might help a heavy caffeine user to elaborate on the details of a message citing the negative effects of caffeine on health, because the positive mood buffers against any negative implications of the message for self-evaluations. Second, a negative mood may cause people to process diagnostic and relevant information in a manner that helps them attain a positive mood (Wegener & Petty, 1994). The third effect is that, compared to a negative mood, a positive mood acts as a cue that goals are being met and everything is well. As a result, a positive mood can lead people to process a message without elaboration (Bless, Bohner, Schwarz, & Strack, 1990), at least when the information is not diagnostic or personally relevant. These findings indicate that mood can act as a resource (ability), a goal state (motive), or as information about the environment, thereby affecting the ability and motivation to process persuasive messages and the post-message attitude.

Clore and Schnall (chap. 11, this volume) provide an in-depth discussion of the relations between affect and attitudes. Although many of the relationships discussed in this section are moderately well established, others have scarcely been addressed. Relatively little is known about the effects of persuasive messages within clinically diagnosed populations, and many of the motivational dimensions that personality researchers have investigated remain untested in the persuasion literature. Broadening our approach to the investigation of moderators of persuasion will lead to a more robust understanding of persuasion and attitude change in general.

COMMUNICATOR-MESSAGE-RECIPIENT INTERACTIONS

Most of the above research focused on simple effects of communicator, message, and recipient variables on message processing strategies (use of heuristics). Additional evidence has examined how these variables interact to predict message processing. For example, Misra and Beatty (1990) suggested that source characteristics should fit the content and tenor of the message: People are more favorable toward advertised brands when the products are paired with celebrity sources who have compatible traits (e.g., a humorous product with a comedian) than when the products are paired with celebrity sources who have incompatible traits (e.g., a medical device with a liked comedian). Jarring combinations of sources and message may prevent the simple transfer of positive affect from the source to the message.

Notwithstanding the importance of such interactions involving source characteristics and message content, most studies have focused on how attributes of participants' initial attitudes toward the message interact with message and source characteristics to predict persuasion. This research focuses primarily on the role of the valence, function, and structure of message recipients' initial attitudes. Other research focuses on the role of arousal in the persuasion context, as a function of the message recipient and aspects of the message. All of these interactive processes are considered below.

Attitude Valence and Message Effects

Knowledge of the message recipients' pre-message attitude toward the topic of the message is vital for predicting their postmessage attitudes. In addition to the obvious prediction that people should agree more strongly with communications that support their attitude than with communications that refute their attitude, it is possible that people are influenced by different considerations in their processing of pro-and counter-attitudinal messages. This hypothesis is made plausible, in part, by evidence that pro- and counter-attitudinal messages elicit different physiological responses. Specifically, the facial muscles in control of frowning are more strongly activated during exposure to counterattitudinal messages than in response to proattitudinal messages, whereas the facial muscles in control of smiling are less strongly activated in response to counterattitudinal messages than in response to proattitudinal messages (Cacioppo & Petty, 1979a).

In addition, it is interesting that messages containing a coercive element (e.g., by saying "You *must* agree") reduce attitude change when the messages are counterattitudinal (Brehm, 1966), but they actually reverse attitude change (i.e., oppose the position in the message) when the message is proattitudinal (Worchel & Brehm, 1970). A potential explanation for this difference is that coercive elements in a message threaten people's sense of personal freedom, which they are motivated to restore (Brehm, 1966). When a message is counterattitudinal, mere maintenance of the pre-message attitude can restore freedom. In contrast, when the message is proattitudinal, freedom can be restored only by changing the attitude in the direction opposite to that argued in the message, as predicted by reactance theory (Brehm & Brehm, 1981).

Together the physiological results and the effects of threats to freedom provide a provocative indication that individuals process proattitudinal and counterattitudinal messages differently. Nonetheless, we know of no research directly testing this hypothesis, and it remains an interesting issue for future research.

Attitude Function and Message Effects

Despite the potential interaction between attitude valence and message valence, the importance of communicator-message-recipient interactions was first illustrated in publications on attitude function (Katz, 1960; Smith et al., 1956). Appearing just prior to these treatises, Hovland et al.'s (1953) *Communication and Persuasion* indicated that persuasive communications are more effective when they highlight an incentive for attitude change. For example, an advertisement promoting exercise might describe the utilitarian benefits of vigorous activity (e.g., better energy levels), or the ad might describe the social-adjustment benefits of vigorous activity (e.g., a more attractive physique). This theory suggested that message recipients change their attitude in response to a communication only when it highlights incentives that are important to message recipients. In practice, one of the major determinants of the importance of the incentives should be the function that is served by the initial attitude (Katz, 1960; Smith et al., 1956). If a person is experiencing a strong need to look attractive to others, then a social-adjustment argument for exercise should hold more incentive value for the individual than a utilitarian argument.

In the past two decades, many experiments have supported the conclusion that messages are more persuasive when their content addresses the dominant functions of the message recipients' attitudes than when the content is irrelevant to these functions. For instance, across many experiments, DeBono (2000) has used the personality measure of self-monitoring to tap the extent to which participants' attitudes served utilitarian versus social-adjustment functions. He then presented advertisements that focused on the benefits of a product for either utilitarian or social-adjustment goals. Results have indicated that high self-monitors, who tend to possess social-adjustment attitudes, are more persuaded by messages that address social adjustment concerns than by messages that address utilitarian concerns. In contrast, low self-monitors, who tend to possess utilitarian attitudes, are more persuaded by messages that address utilitarian concerns than by messages that address social adjustment concerns. Murray, Haddock, and Zanna (1996) confirmed this pattern of results using experimental variables. Similarly, Prentice (1987) found that participants who attached high importance to symbolic values (e.g., love, self-respect) and symbolic possessions (e.g., family heirlooms) were less persuaded by messages that contained instrumental (utilitarian) arguments than by messages that contained symbolic (value-expressive) arguments. Shavitt (1990) extended this pattern using different types of attitude objects as a means of identifying the recipients' likely attitude function. Specifically, she found that instrumental ads for instrumental products (e.g., an air conditioner) were more persuasive than symbolic ads for instrumental products.

Of interest is that function-match effects depend primarily on a persuasion context that elicits high or low message elaboration (Petty, Wheeler, & Bizer, 2000). When the persuasion context compels neither high amounts of message processing nor low amounts, the effects of the message's content depend on the cogency of the arguments: Matching effects may occur when the arguments are strong, but mismatching effects occur when the arguments are weak (Petty & Wegener, 1998b). This pattern supports the hypothesis that function matching sometimes causes people to scrutinize message arguments more carefully (Petty & Wegener, 1998b). Because of this scrutiny, people are able to detect flaws and strengths in messages that target their attitude function and react accordingly.

Attitude Structure and Message Effects

An interesting issue is whether similar matching effects occur when messages address the affective, cognitive, and behavioral information that underlies message recipients' attitudes. Edwards (1990) found some evidence to support this hypothesis. When her participants' initial attitudes were based on affective experience, a persuasive intervention that focused on inducing new (counterattitudinal) feelings toward an object was more effective than an intervention that presented (counterattitudinal) cognitive argumentation. In contrast, Millar and Millar (1990) proposed that matching messages should be less persuasive, because these messages directly challenge the way in which the recipients have been thinking about the attitude object, thereby eliciting feelings of threat and defensiveness. Their hypothesis about the negative effect of structural matches received support in three experiments that used different methodologies.

Given the conflicting evidence, Fabrigar and Petty (1999) attempted to provide a more definitive test of the effects of structure match by controlling for several factors that varied across the Edwards (1990) and Millar and Millar (1990) experiments. Fabrigar and Petty's first experiment examined the effects of matching messages with the affective and cognitive bases of recipients' attitudes, while controlling for matches in different affective and cognitive attributes. For example, message recipients were exposed to a novel beverage by sampling its pleasant taste, and then later were exposed to either a bad taste for the beverage or a bad odor from the beverage. Other message recipients were exposed to information about the beverage's positive taste, followed by information describing a negative taste or a bad odor. Regardless of whether the attribute dimensions matched (e.g., good taste vs. bad taste) or mismatched (e.g., good taste vs. bad smell), affective interventions were more effective at changing affective than cognitive attitudes. Similar match effects were obtained in their second experiment, which used written materials to manipulate the original bases of attitude and the subsequent persuasive information.

As was the case in the examination of attitude-function matching effects, an interesting issue is whether the effects of attitude structure matching depend on the levels of message processing that are elicited by the persuasion context, which Petty et al. (2000) proposed should occur. An important basis for this prediction is their observation that messages elicit more detailed processing when they are relevant to an important aspect of the recipients' self-concept than when they are not relevant to this aspect (Cacioppo, Petty, & Sidera, 1982; Evans & Petty, 2003). Because this effect is similar to the effect of attitude function matches on message processing (Petty & Wegener, 1998b), Petty et al. proposed that, in general, matches to attitude function or structure might operate by making a message seem more self-relevant. This relevance may act as a persuasive cue in conditions that elicit little message elaboration (e.g., high distraction), bias systematic processing in conditions that elicit high message elaboration, and encourage more systematic processing when the persuasion context does not specify either level of elaboration. Research has not yet fully tested this provocative hypothesis.

Arousal and Message Effects

The effects of messages can also depend on arousal states in message recipients. Anxiety is one such predictor of the ability and motivation to process messages. On the one hand, anxiety tends to decrease the ability to process messages by distracting people from the task at hand (e.g., Nottleman & Hill, 1977; see Eysenck, 1982). On the other hand, anxiety may enhance performance when the source of the anxiety is relevant to the task at hand (Eysenck, 1979). In the persuasion context, for example, a message might occasionally be relevant to a person's current anxieties and fears or irrelevant to them. Sengupta and Johar (2001) predicted and found that anxiety-relevant messages do in fact receive more elaborative processing (and more use of heuristic cues) in anxious than in nonanxious message recipients. When the message was not relevant to the source of anxiety, elaborate processing was lower in anxious than in nonanxious participants.

The effects of threatening and fear-inducing messages are also relevant, because these messages elicit a short-term anxiety that may affect the ability and motivation to process the messages. Hovland et al.'s (1953) seminal volume proposed that fear-inducing messages should elicit more yielding when contemplation of their recommendations helps to reduce the fear than when contemplation of their recommendations does not help to reduce the fear. Subsequent models extended this hypothesis by proposing that there should be curvilinear effects of the level of fear in messages, such that fear-inducing messages are more effective at moderate levels of fear than at low or high levels of fear (see also Janis, 1967; McGuire, 1968). Nonetheless, the obtained evidence has most often revealed more message acceptance in conditions of high fear than in conditions of low fear, rather than the predicted curvilinear pattern (see Ruiter, Abraham, & Kok, 2001).

More recent theoretical models suggested that effects of fear are best understood by distinguishing the affective and cognitive effects of fear arousal (Leventhal, 1970) and that the cognitive effects may involve both the appraisal of a threat and the appraisal of how to cope with the threat (Rogers, 1983). Ironically, examinations of the effects of threat appraisal and coping appraisals provide more precise tests of Hovland et al.'s (1953) prediction that message recommendations must help to reduce fear than did the earlier research that focused on curvilinear relations between fear and persuasion. That is, according to Rogers, severe threats that are salient in a message (i.e., high threat appraisal) should evoke more message yielding when the recommended protective actions are seen as being effective and easy to enact than when they are seen as being too ineffective or difficult to enact (i.e., low coping appraisal). However, even this more specific test has received only modest empirical support (Rogers & Prentice-Dunn, 1997).

A more fruitful approach may be to examine the process through which fear-inducing messages affect attitudes. One possibility is that fear-inducing messages cause people to process the message's recommendations more systematically, enabling greater attitude change when the recommendations are easy to achieve and compelling (Baron, Logan, Lilly, Inman, & Brennan, 1994). Gleicher and Petty (1992), in contrast, found that moderate fear elicited message scrutiny only when participants expected (but were not certain) that the message would provide a reassuring recommendation for action. Additional evidence indicates that high fear may elicit biased, critical scrutiny of messages when the message topic is of high personal relevance (Liberman & Chaiken, 1992). Thus, the general pattern of fear effects is consistent with the notion that fear elicits message scrutiny (see Hale, Lemieux, & Mongeau, 1995), although the extent and nature of the scrutiny may depend on other factors (e.g., reassurance, personal relevance).

Summary

Clearly, communication structure factors can have dramatic effects on the amount of attitude change the communication produces. Yet, studies have only rarely examined more than one message effect in the same design, with the consequence that it is difficult to know the boundaries on many of these effects. A message order effect may succumb to a dramatically large argument quality effect. A large fear appeal effect may reduce the impact of argument quality. Yet each of the observed message effects is also highly variable in its impact, suggesting the need for further research to determine boundary conditions for the effects.

EFFECTS OF COMMUNICATION-INDUCED ATTITUDE CHANGE

As the review above testifies, a substantial body of research has outlined and explored a multitude of variables that moderate persuasion. Yet far less research has explored the persistence and subsequent effects of communication-induced attitude change. This section summarizes the extant literature dealing with the behavioral and psychological consequences of communication-induced attitude change. In particular, we examine maintenance of attitude change, direct behavioral effects of attitude change, the relationship between attitude change and attitude functions, and awareness of attitude change.

Persistence of Attitude Change

Whether attitude changes persist following exposure to communications is an issue that greatly interested early scholars. Clearly, for behavior to change following changes in an attitude, the attitude changes must persist long enough to affect behavior. Consequently, early persuasion research routinely included both attitude and behavioral measures and frequently had multiple assessments of attitude. The paucity of such measures in contemporary work may in part be due to Cook and Flay's (1978) extensive narrative review of persistence, which concluded that attitude changes in experimental settings showed little staying power. Most contemporary studies are poorly suited to show persisting effects of attitude change, owing in part to the use of artificial issues such as instituting comprehensive exams as a requirement for graduation. Typically, experimenters debrief participants after completing the immediate dependent measures and researchers neither desire nor expect that effects will persist.

Despite the pessimism stemming from frequent failures of laboratory-induced attitude changes to persist, persuasion *can* last over the lifespan. Religious conversion, for example, often endures for a lifetime and is frequently accompanied by changes in attitudes toward others, the self, and religious practices. Similarly, Newcomb's (1943) Bennington College studies documented a liberal shift in the attitudes and values of a freshman class resulting from the influence of their upper-class leaders. The changes were still evident 50 years later (Alwin, Cohen, & Newcomb, 1991). In the health psychology literature, classroom-delivered HIV prevention (message-based) interventions produced increases in condom use that persisted as long as one year later (Fisher, Fisher, Bryan, & Misovich, 2002); yet it would be difficult to attribute all of this change to mere communication and persuasion.

Nevertheless, compelling examples of persistent attitude change have been documented in the laboratory. For example, Ross, McFarland, Conway and Zanna (1983) used messages to induce shifts in attitudes; then, they gave half of the participants the chance to recall attitude-relevant behaviors. These participants' attitudes were more resistant to change and persisted longer than those not recalling behaviors. Another example of persistence is the sleeper effect, which as we reviewed above, occurs when a message recipient initially discounts a persuasive set of arguments because of a perceived deficiency in the source, but later forgets the source and remembers the message. Upon recalling the message, the recipient's attitude shifts in the direction of the advocated position. Attitude change occurring via the sleeper effect is generally persistent. Sleeper effects have persisted as long as six weeks (Florack, Piontkowski, Knocks, Rottmann, & Thiemann, 2002; Pratkanis et al., 1988, Experiment 16; see Kumkale & Albarracín's, 2004, meta-analytic review). Similarly, McGuire's (e.g., 1964) inoculation research may be viewed as an attitude persistence paradigm. Specifically, exposure to the weakened dose of opposing arguments coupled with a refutation permits participants to retain their initial attitudes. Subsequently, participants show greater resistance to the full dose of opposing arguments compared to participants who were not so inoculated. Inoculation theory asserts that people can resist attitude change if they are trained to consciously generate responses to anticipated persuasive messages targeting a particular attitude or value (e.g., Bernard, Maio, & Olson, 2003; Sagarin, Cialdini, Rice, & Serna, 2002). Thus, when inoculations against future attacks follow successful persuasive communications, attitude change should be robust and persistent. In some senses, two-sided arguments incorporate a mild form of inoculation (see McGuire, 1964; Wyer & Albarracín, chap. 7, this volume).

There are at least two contemporary and successful theories of persistence, which identify conditions under which a new or modified attitude is likely to persist. First, according to the ELM, communication-induced attitude change will endure when message recipients carefully process the message; that is, when people process the message via central rather than peripheral routes. To the extent that communicators are able to increase elaboration, they increase the likelihood that any impact of the communication will be a lasting one (Mackie, 1987; van Schie, Martijn, and van der Pligt, 1994). As the review above attests, research has identified a number of variables associated with increased elaboration. For example, attitude changes in people high in need for cognition are generally more persistent than for those who are low in need for cognition (Haugtvedt & Petty, 1992). Similarly, relatively high persistence results when (a) people generate their own arguments (Elms, 1966), (b) are exposed to highly involving (Petty & Cacioppo, 1979b, Experiment 2) or (c) interesting (Ronis, Baumgardner, Leippe, Cacioppo, & Greenwald, 1977) issues, (d) are encouraged to produce self-generated thoughts (Killeya & Johnson, 1998), (e) are distracted less (Watts & Holt, 1979), (f) anticipate justifying their attitudes to others (Boninger, Brock, Cook, Gruder, & Romer, 1990), (g) experience multiple message exposures (H. H. Johnson & Watkins, 1971), and (h) produce message-consistent thoughts and memories (Albarracín & McNatt, 2003). Although this listing would suggest that all elaboration increases persuasion and persistence of attitude change, reflecting on beliefs and behavioral outcomes can also inhibit temporal attitude stability (Albarracín & McNatt, 2003; Wilson & Schooler, 1991).

The other theory of persistence is Albarracín, Wallace's, and Glasman (2004) model of judgment survival, which posits that three processes are involved in attitude change and maintenance of change: (a) activating the prior attitude (retrieving it from memory), (b) activating information related to the prior attitude (which can come from memory or an external source), and (c) comparing the prior attitude with the related information. Though sequential, the model does not assume that any of the processes are inevitable. For example, although activating the prior attitude is necessary to compare it to new information, it does not guarantee that comparison will occur. Situational or individual factors may inhibit the process of comparison; the individual may not be motivated or able to move from attitude activation to comparative validation. Each process can have different implications for attitude change and maintenance. For example, activating an existing attitude or attitude-relevant information alone may be sufficient for attitude maintenance. In contrast, attitude change will generally occur when reconstructing an existing attitude online in response to attitude-inconsistent information and when comparing a prior attitude that has been activated with either attitude-consistent or inconsistent information. Nonetheless, the activation and comparison processes are not necessarily independent; Albarracín and colleagues argued that considering them together results in a better understanding of attitude change and the maintenance of change. For example, if attitude activation and comparison are a sequential process, then activating a prior attitude ought to facilitate comparison. Yet, activation of both the prior attitude and attitude-related information may not be sufficient to induce comparison; attitude activation may not stimulate comparison if situational or individual factors discourage it. This intriguing theory is certainly deserving of further empirical tests.

Behavioral Effects of Communication-Induced Attitude Change

One fundamental task of social psychology is the prediction of social behavior. It is no wonder that one of the most frequently investigated consequences of attitude change is change in behavior and behavioral intentions, though the number of studies examining behavior in addition to behavior intentions seems to be in decline. As early as the 1930s, scholars have contested the causal relationship between attitudes and behaviors (LaPiere, 1934). Some proposed that attitudes follow from behavior (Festinger, 1957), whereas others argued that attitudes are not sufficient to predict behavior, but that "behavior is the result of many intrapsychic and interpersonal forces which may be quite independent of the attitude in question" (Sarnoff & Katz, 1954; pp. 119–120).

Contemporary attitude theories such as the theory of reasoned action (TRA) (Fishbein & Ajzen, 1975) and the theory of planned behavior (TPB) (Ajzen, 1985) recognize that attitudes are only one of the psychological determinants of volitional social behavior. In particular, the TRA and TPB stipulate that behavior follows from intentions to behave, and that these intentions, in turn, rest on subjective norms and attitudes. The TPB adds perceived behavioral control as a third predictor of intentions and a sometimes direct predictor of behavior. Still other models of behavior include the actor's past behavior (Bentler & Spekart, 1979) or habit (Triandis, 1977, 1980) as predictors of future behavior. Although these models specify a multitude of behavioral predictors, research suggests that the attitude component is usually the most important, and research using TPB and TRA often finds that attitudes are significant predictors of behavioral intentions and future behavior even when controlling for other sources of variance (see Ajzen & Fishbein, chap. 5, this volume).

Although many studies do not examine specific effects of communication-induced attitude change on behaviors, health interventions are often based on communications intended to produce positive evaluations of the object (e.g., condoms) and performance of the behavior (e.g., Albarracín et al., 2003). Communications that produce attitude change should result in subsequent behavior change to the extent that attitudes are directly and causally linked to behavior. Glasman and Albarracín's (2003) research synthesis revealed greater correspondence between attitudes and behaviors when participants received manipulations that (a) increased motivated to think about the object, (b) provided direct experience with the object, or (c) gave one- rather than two-sided information.

The direct impact of attitude change on behavior can also be seen in the domains of marketing and advertising, which are predicated on the notion that many types of communications create positive cognitive or affective associations with a product or brand, thereby impacting purchase behavior. In a meta-analysis of 77 studies, Grewal, Kavanoor, Fern, Costley, and Barnes (1997) found that, although advertisements comparing two or more brands generated more negative attitudes toward the advertisements themselves, they produced more favorable attitudes toward the sponsored brand, and significant increases in purchase intentions and purchase behavior.

In general, theories suggest communication-induced attitude change is likely to produce greater changes in behaviors and behavioral intentions when messages target attitudes toward the behavior, rather than attitudes toward the object (Albarracín, 2002; Fishbein & Ajzen, 1981). The effects of attitude change on behavior relative to other factors such as subjective norms may be moderated by cultural and interpersonal differences. For instance, the contribution of subjective norms to the prediction of behavior may be more important for those who identify highly with the reference group (Terry & Hogg, 1996), possess more interdependent self-construals, or are high in collectivism (Park & Levine, 1999). In addition, attitudes may be more important predictors of behavioral intentions for people with higher capacities for action-oriented mental strategies, but subjective norms may be more important for those with more state-oriented mental strategies (Bagozzi, Baumgartner, & Yi, 1992). Attitudes are most likely to influence behavior when they are closely linked to performing the behavior and when other factors such as subjective norms and perceived behavioral control, or indirect attitudes are not main causal agents. Nevertheless, including factors such as subjective norms and past behavior in addition to attitudes generally leads to significant increases in accurate behavioral prediction. For example, Albarracín et al.'s (2003) meta-analysis of HIV prevention interventions revealed that the communications improved attitudes toward condoms, but condom use remained unchanged unless the intervention also included a skills training element.

Implicit Attitudes and Attitude Change

To this point, we have not considered how effects of messages on attitudes may depend on the way in which the attitudes are later measured. As Krosnick and colleagues (chap. 2, this volume) describe, most procedures use explicit techniques, which ask participants to rate their own attitudes using provided scales. Krosnick and colleagues also describe how recent research has added a plethora of implicit techniques, which elicit attitude scores without reliance on self-reports (e.g., by examining response times to tasks that present the attitude object with positive or negatively valenced adjectives). In some contexts, people's scores on explicit and implicit measures differ considerably. For example, with regard to many socially sensitive issues such as racial attitudes, research has found only small correlations between explicit and implicit measures of attitude (see Fazio & Olson, 2003). If the attitude responsible for an action is tapped only via an implicit measure, then communications that are effective in changing attitudes on an explicit measure of the attitude may nonetheless have little impact on the relevant (implicit-attitude–based) behavior. This phenomenon appears with regard to prejudice and discrimination. For example, Dovidio and colleagues (1997) observed that, whereas explicitly measured racial attitudes predicted overall evaluations of the African American and White interviewers in an experiment, implicit measures of racial attitudes predicted amount of visual contact and eye blinking. In another study examining the relationship between discriminatory behavior and implicit and explicit measures of racial attitudes, McConnell and Leibold (2001) found that more favorable evaluations of Whites in comparison to African Americans on the Implicit Association Test (IAT) were predictive of more positive interactions with the White than the African American experimenter in general. Greater speaking time, more extemporaneous social comments, fewer speech errors, and fewer speech hesitations in interactions with the White (vs. African American) experimenter were also predicted by preferences for Whites as measured by the IAT. None of these outcomes was associated with explicit measures of racial attitudes (see Word, Zanna, & Cooper, 1974).

These studies again indicate that attitudes can predict behavior. Yet, attitudes measured in different ways predict different sets of behavior. Communications targeting racial attitudes may be effective in changing self-reported racial attitudes, but have little if any impact on behavior in interracial interactions (see Maio, Watt, & Hewstone, 2003). Nonverbal behavior is an important predictor of social interactions, and to the extent that implicit measures of attitude predict this behavior, explicit measures of attitude may have little impact. Currently, researchers are beginning to investigate ways to modify implicitly measured attitudes. The next step for such research is to demonstrate when and how modifications of implicitly measured attitudes can change behavior.

Awareness of Attitude Change

One of the principle goals of a persuasive communication is to induce attitude change. If and when a communication produces attitude change, are individuals aware that their attitude has been modified? If they are aware that their attitude has been modified, how accurate are they in assessments of the amount of attitude change that took place? Awareness of attitude change assumes that one is to some extent aware of the targeted attitude in the sense that they acknowledge it. As Petty, Wheeler, and Tormala (2003) described, an explicit attitude is one that a person can consciously acknowledge, though they may be unaware of its basis (Bornstein & D'Agostino, 1992) or its impact on other judgments and behaviors. In terms of communication-induced attitude change, numerous mere exposure studies have found that increased exposure to advertising messages can create positive attitudes toward a brand or product (see Vuokko, 1997 for a review). The effects of repeated exposure on attitudes are often unnoticed by those exposed to the stimuli. Thus, to the extent that a message can surreptitiously alter the basis of an attitude, attitude change may occur outside conscious awareness. Moreover, as Ross and McFarland (1988) indicated, people may believe the new attitude to be the one they held all along, or they may believe they have changed their attitudes when they have not. Several studies have demonstrated such failures of awareness. For example, Lowenthal and Lowenstein (2001) found that although people conceded that their attitude toward a presidential candidate might change over time, they underestimated the degree to which their own attitudes toward political candidates would change or had changed during the course of a presidential election campaign. Using an induced compliance paradigm, Bem and McConnell (1970) found that people who had a choice but were encouraged to write a counterattitudinal essay were significantly less accurate when asked to recall their initial attitude than were those in the no choice or control conditions, and recalled attitudes were not well correlated with initial attitudes for those in the choice condition ($r = .26$). However, even when those in the no-choice condition showed significant attitude change in comparison to the control group, there was a considerably higher degree of correspondence between their initial attitudes and their recalled attitudes ($r = .71$).

In contrast, the social judgment tradition would seem to assume that people are aware of their attitudes and changes in them. For instance, one of core propositions of the SJM is that people use their current attitudes as a judgmental anchor when evaluating other attitudinally relevant information (Sherif & Hovland, 1961). From this perspective, people evaluate new information in the light of the current attitude, a proposition that suggests attitude awareness. Similarly, whether or not a person has the ability to evaluate the functional fit of their new attitude may predict whether people are aware that attitude change has occurred.

As fundamental as these questions appear, relatively few studies have directly assessed awareness and accuracy of perceived attitude change. The paucity of research in this area is reflected in several notable reviews of the attitudes and attitude change literature that are silent on the issue of awareness of attitude change (e.g., Petty, Wegener, & Fabrigar, 1997; Wood, 2000). This omission stands in contrast to the developing body of metacognitive research in other domains. Our knowledge about awareness of attitude change is also limited because predominant paradigms in persuasion research incorporate factorial designs with no measures of pretest attitudes to determine the impact of any of a number of independent variables. These designs do not allow for within-subject comparisons of attitude change. In any case, a complete understanding of the effects of communication-induced attitude change calls for scientific inquiry into the how and when of people's awareness of attitude change.

Summary

Research on the effects of message-based communications has focused mainly on their direct impact on behavior (see Ajzen & Fishbein, chap. 5, this volume), but considerably less is known about other psychological implications of communication-induced attitude change. Attitude-behavior relation research generally supports the conclusion that messages targeting attitudes toward performing a behavior are more effective in producing behavior change than are those targeting an attitude object. Although messages that target consciously accessible attitudes (explicit attitudes) may be effective, such messages may have little impact on relevant behavior when the behavior (e.g., nonverbal behavior) is automatically activated and difficult to control. Lasting change occurs when people are exposed to an abundance of strong arguments, are motivated and able to elaborate on the message content, and cognitive responding is consonant with the message position.

Awareness of attitude change requires attitude awareness and introspection with regard to the attitude. In general, awareness of attitude change has received little direct attention to date. Awareness may be moderated by initial attitude, such that people may be more aware of attitude change when acquiescing to counterattitudinal messages than when becoming more extreme in response to a proattitudinal message. Similarly, persuasion occurring via the sleeper effect or mere exposure processes may decrease awareness of attitude change, whereas contexts that encourage cognitive elaboration in response to the message may enhance awareness of attitude change. Attitude function approaches imply that attitude change occurs in order to meet a functional need. Evaluating the function fit of modified attitudes may involve some degree of attitude awareness, although studies have yet to test this assumption directly. Though awareness of attitude change has not been the focus of prior research, it may be fertile ground for future research.

CONCLUSION

As this chapter testifies, modern research on communication and persuasion has yielded much fruit, accumulating extensive knowledge about when and how communications affect persuasion and other outcomes, such as behavior. This research has been inspired by philosophical thought and nurtured within diverse disciplines, not the least of which are advertising, political science, sociology, human communications, and psychology. That said, as in any scientific field, there are some interesting problems that remain largely unaddressed. Throughout this chapter, we have described many areas of potential future research. Whereas our review highlighted parochial interests for a particular domain of attitude research, some of these actually have broader implications. For example, which factors make arguments strong? We noted earlier that there is little research on these factors, which makes it difficult for researchers to know, a priori, when an argument will be strong, or for practitioners to design message arguments. For example, if you were a politician trying to win votes, what precisely should you say to receive this support? Similarly, if you are trying to design advertisements for an anti-racism campaign, what message content should you employ? The solution to such questions has been to pretest potential messages and select those with greatest impact. Although practical, the solution lacks theoretical insight.

This issue of defining argument quality is relevant to the process of persuasion in many ways. Specifically, it is conceivable that the strength of arguments depends intimately on many of the source, message, and recipient factors that we have described, while also influencing the nature of attitude change (e.g., stability and subsequent strength). For instance, politicians may frequently endorse popular values as a means of earning voter support, but how do they know which values to support? A cursory examination of party leadership campaigns would reveal that conservative and liberal leaders cite different values to match their respective audiences. In other words, they intuitively use arguments that address the functions of their recipients' attitudes. An interesting question is what would happen if a politician tried to convince people that he or she could effectively support the party values *and* other important values that are shared, but not emphasized by the party. Would this approach make the appeal more or less effective? Also, should the arguments be phrased rhetorically or directly, concretely or abstractly, metaphorically or plainly? Do the effects of these variables depend on other message and recipient factors as well as on the desired effects of the message?

Similar attention could profit an understanding of communication discrepancy's effects on persuasion. The sometimes-powerful impact of message framing suggests that communication discrepancy could be similarly powerful. Yet, while early persuasion researchers considered this factor extremely important, contemporary researchers have given the subject short shrift. The availability of enhanced methods, coupled with the interesting theoretical insights of contemporary theories, ought to infuse the subject of communication discrepancy renewed vigor (see Zanna, 1994, for some plausible directions). Given that the effects of message framing and argument quality appear to rest on the same evaluative processes, it would make sense that the effects of both of these variables rest on more general principles such as framing research has pursued (Rothman & Salovey, 1997). Unfortunately, the two variables rarely if ever appear in the same study and an intellectual integration has not yet appeared.

With regard to the desired effects of the message, an important issue is the extent to which the source, message, and recipient factors exert different effects on explicit and implicit measures of attitude. Prior research informs us that some of these factors (e.g., source attractiveness) receive less conscious scrutiny under conditions of high personal relevance. Consistent with the past research, this lack of scrutiny should cause the factors to be less likely to emerge in people's conscious deliberations of their attitude during the completion of explicit measures. In contrast, they may influence implicit measures of attitude, which may tap information that has been seen but not necessarily recognized at a conscious level. Other persuasion variables (e.g., detailed message content) receive more scrutiny in conditions of high personal relevance, enabling them to influence both the explicit and implicit measures (see also Wilson, Lindsey, & Schooler, 2000). Such potential effects are deserving of comprehensive consideration.

In closing this chapter, we note that the world continues to face such major challenges as poverty, terrorism, and the spread of diseases such as AIDS and SARS. These and other serious issues in our society involve attitudes toward social groups (e.g., people with AIDS). Advances in theory, methods, and analysis have given researchers an abundance of tools with which to examine communication and persuasion processes, yet comparatively little research has examined changing group-based attitudes. Although some attitude researchers have broached the subjects of prejudice and discrimination or used persuasion to gauge prejudice (Saucier & Miller, 2003), there have been few advances with respect to changing group-based attitudes. For example, how do we change attitudes toward the poor, such that new attitudes would lead to actions aimed at remediating poverty and the inequities created by poverty (Harman & Johnson, 2003)? Similarly, how can persuasion researchers use the tools available to them to change negative and hostile attitudes toward members of religious outgroups? Although attitude change research targeting real-world issues such as those mentioned above is difficult, this chapter bears testimony to the fact that across history, industrious and creative researchers have overcome many theoretical, methodological, and practical obstacles in pursuit of a greater understanding of communication and attitude change. If turned to real-world issues rather than relatively trivial laboratory issues, communication and persuasion theory and research may hold the keys to better life.

ACKNOWLEDGMENTS

The writing of this chapter was facilitated by National Institutes of Health grant R01-MH58563 to Blair T. Johnson.

REFERENCES

Abele, A. E., & Gendolla, G. H. E. (1999). Satisfaction judgments in positive and negative moods: Effects of concurrent assimilation and contrast producing processes. *Personality and Social Psychology Bulletin, 25*, 883–895.

Ajzen, I. (1985). From intentions to actions: A theory of planned behavior. In J. Kuhl & J. Beckmann (Eds.), *Action control: From cognition to behavior* (pp. 11–39). New York: Springer-Verlag.

Albarracín, D. (2002). Cognition in persuasion: An analysis of information processing in response to persuasive communications. In M. P. Zanna (Ed.), *Advances in experimental social psychology* (Vol. 34, pp. 61–130). San Diego, CA: Academic Press.

Albarracín, D., Johnson, B. T., Fishbein, M., & Muellerleile, P. A. (2001). Theories of reasoned action and planned behavior as models of condom use: A meta-analysis. *Psychological Bulletin, 127*, 142–161.

Albarracín, D., & Kumkale, G. T. (2003). Affect as information in persuasion: A model of affect identification and discounting. *Journal of Personality and Social Psychology, 84*, 453–469.

Albarracín, D., & McNatt, P. S. (in press). Change maintenance and decay of the influences of past behavior: Anchoring attitudes on beliefs following inconsistent actions. *Personality and Social Psychology Bulletin.*

Albarracín, D., McNatt, P. S., Klein, C. T. F., Ho, R. M., Mitchell, A. L., & Kumkale, G. T. (2003). Persuasive communications to change actions: An analysis of behavioral and cognitive impact in HIV prevention. *Health Psychology, 22*, 166–177.

Albarracín, D., Wallace, H. M., & Glasman, L. R. (2004). Survival and change of attitudes and other social judgments: A model of activation and comparison. In M. P. Zanna (Ed.), *Advances in experimental social psychology* (Vol. 36, pp. 252–315). San Diego, CA: Academic Press.

Albarracín, D., & Wyer, R. S. (2000). The cognitive impact of past behavior: Influences on beliefs, attitudes, and future behavioral decisions. *Journal of Personality and Social Psychology, 79*, 5–22.

Albarracín, D., & Wyer, R. S. (2001). Elaborative and non-elaborative processing of a behavior-related communication. *Personality and Social Psychology Bulletin, 27*, 691–705.

Allen, M. (1991). Meta-analysis comparing the persuasiveness of one-sided and two-sided messages. *Western Journal of Speech Communication, 55*, 390–404.

Allport, F. H., & Hartman, D. A. (1925). The measurement and motivation of atypical opinion in a certain group. *American Political Science Review, 19*, 735–760.

Allport, G. W. (1935). Attitudes. In C. Murchison (Ed.), *Handbook of social psychology* (pp. 798–844). Worcester, MA: Clark University Press.

Allyn, J., & Festinger, L. (1961). The effectiveness of unanticipated persuasive communications. *Journal of Abnormal and Social Psychology, 62*, 35–40.

Alwin, D. F., Cohen, R. E., & Newcomb, T. M. (1991). *Political attitudes over the life span: The Bennington women after fifty years.* Madison, WI: University of Wisconsin Press.

Anderson, N. H. (1971). Integration theory and attitude change. *Psychological Review, 78*, 171–206.

Areni, C. S. (2003). The effects of structural and grammatical variables on persuasion: An elaboration likelihood model perspective. *Psychology & Marketing, 20*, 349–375.

Areni, C. S., & Lutz, R. J. (1988). The role of argument quality in the elaboration likelihood model. *Advances in Consumer Research, 15*, 197–203.

Argyle, M. (1957). Social pressures in public and private situations. *Journal of Abnormal and Social Psychology, 54*, 172–175.

Asch, S. E. (1952). *Social psychology.* Englewood Cliffs, NJ: Prentice-Hall.

Asch, S. E. (1956). Studies of independence and conformity: A minority of one against a unanimous majority. *Psychological Monographs, 70* (9, Whole No. 416).

Bagozzi, R. P., Baumgartner, H., & Yi, Y. (1992). State versus action orientation and the theory of reasoned action: An application to coupon usage. *Journal of Consumer Research, 18*, 505–518.

Baker, S. M., & Petty, R. E. (1994). Majority and minority influence: Source-position imbalance as a determinant of message scrutiny. *Journal of Personality and Social Psychology, 67*, 5–19.

Bargh, J. A. (1990). Auto-motives: Preconscious determinants of social interaction. In E. T. Higgins & R. M. Sorrentino (Eds.), *Handbook of motivation and cognition* (Vol. 2, pp. 93–130). New York: Guilford.

Bargh, J. A., Chaiken, S., Govender, R., & Pratto, F. (1992). The generality of the automatic attitude activation effect. *Journal of Personality and Social Psychology, 62*, 893–912.

Bargh, J. A., & Ferguson, M. J. (2000). Beyond behaviorism: On the automaticity of higher mental processes. *Psychological Bulletin, 126*, 925–945.

Baron, R., Logan, H., Lilly, J., Inman, M., & Brennan, M. (1994). Negative emotion and message processing. *Journal of Experimental Social Psychology, 30*, 181–201.

Bassili, J. N. (1996). Meta-judgmental versus operative indexes of psychological attributes: The case of measures of attitude strength. *Journal of Personality and Social Psychology, 71*, 637–653.

Bassili, J. N., & Provencal, A. (1988). Perceiving minorities: A factor-analytic approach. *Personality and Social Psychology Bulletin, 14*, 5–15.

Baumeister, R. F., Muraven, M., & Tice, D. M. (2000). Ego depletion: A resource model of volition, self-regulation, and controlled processing. *Social Cognition, 18*, 130–150.

Bem, D. J. (1972). Self-perception theory. In L. Berkowitz (Ed.), *Advances in experimental social psychology* (Vol. 6, pp.1–62). San Diego, CA: Academic Press.

Bem, D. J., & McConnell, H. K. (1970). Testing the self-perception explanation of dissonance phenomena: On the salience of premanipulation attitudes. *Journal of Personality and Social Psychology, 24*, 23–31.

Bentler, P. M., & Speckart, G. (1979). Models of attitude-behavior relations. *Psychological Review, 86*, 452–464.

Bernard, M., Maio, G. R., & Olson, J. M. (2003). The vulnerability of values to attack: Inoculation of values and value-relevant attitudes. *Personality and Social Psychology Bulletin, 29*, 63–75.

Blascovich, J., Ernst, J. M., Tomaka, J., Kelsey, R. M., Salomon, K. L., & Fazio, R. H. (1993). Attitude accessibility as a moderator of autonomic reactivity during decision making. *Journal of Personality and Social Psychology, 64*, 165–176.

Bless, H., Bohner, G., Schwarz, N., & Strack, F. (1990). Mood and persuasion: A cognitive response analysis. *Personality and Social Psychology Bulletin, 16*, 331–345.

Bochner, S., & Insko, C. A. (1966). Communicator discrepancy, source credibility, and opinion change. *Journal of Personality and Social Psychology, 4*, 614–621.

Bogardus, E. S. (1925). Measuring social distances. *Journal of Applied Sociology, 9*, 299–308.

Bohner, G., Ruder, M., & Erb, H. P. (2002). When expertise backfires: Contrast and assimilation effects in persuasion. *British Journal of Social Psychology, 41*, 495–519.

Boninger, D. S., Brock, T. C., Cook, T. D., Gruder, C. L., & Romer, D. (1990). Discovery of reliable attitude change persistence resulting from a transmitter tuning set. *Psychological Science, 1*, 268–271.

Bornstein, R. F., & D'Agostino, P. R. (1992). Stimulus recognition and the mere exposure effect. *Journal of Personality and Social Psychology, 63*, 545–552.

Boster, F. J., & Mongeau, P. (1985). Fear-arousing persuasive messages. In R. N. Bostrom (Ed.), *Communication Yearbook* (Vol. 8, pp. 330–375). Beverly Hills, CA: Sage.

Brehm, J. W. (1966). *A theory of psychological reactance*. San Diego, CA: Academic Press.

Brehm, S. S., & Brehm, J. W. (1981). *Psychological reactance: A theory of freedom and control*. San Diego, CA: Academic Press.

Brock, T. C. (1967). Communication discrepancy and intent to persuade as determinants of counterargument production. *Journal of Experimental Social Psychology, 3*, 269–309.

Buehler, R., & Griffin, D. (1994). Change-of-meaning effects in conformity and dissent: Observing construal processes over time. *Journal of Personality and Social Psychology, 67*, 984–996.

Cacioppo, J. T., & Petty, R. E. (1979a). Attitudes and cognitive response: An electrophysiological approach. *Journal of Personality and Social Psychology, 37*, 2181–2199.

Cacioppo, J. T., & Petty, R. E. (1979b). Effects of message repetition and position on cognitive response, recall, and persuasion. *Journal of Personality and Social Psychology, 37*, 97–109.

Cacioppo, J. T., Petty, R. E., Feinstein, J. A., & Jarvis, W. B. G. (1996). Dispositional differences in cognitive motivation: The life and times of individuals varying in need for cognition. *Psychological Bulletin, 119*, 197–253.

Cacioppo, J. T., Petty, R. E., & Sidera, J. (1982). The effects of salient self-schema on the evaluation of pro-attitudinal editorials: Top-down versus bottom-up message processing. *Journal of Experimental Social Psychology, 18*, 324–338.

Chaiken, S. (1980). Heuristic versus systematic information processing and the use of source versus message cues in persuasion. *Journal of Personality and Social Psychology, 39*, 752–766.

Chaiken, S. (1987). The heuristic model of persuasion. In M. P. Zanna, J. M. Olson, & C. P. Herman (Eds.), *Social influence: The Ontario Symposium* (Vol. 5, pp. 3–39). Hillsdale, NJ: Lawrence Erlbaum Associates.

Chaiken, S., Duckworth, K. L., & Darke, P. (1999). When parsimony fails ... *Psychological Inquiry, 10*, 118–123.

Chaiken, S., & Eagly, A. H. (1976). Communication modality as a determinant of message persuasiveness and message comprehensibility. *Journal of Personality and Social Psychology, 34*, 605–614.

Chaiken, S., & Eagly, A. H. (1983). Communication modality as a determinant of persuasion: The role of communicator salience. *Journal of Personality and Social Psychology, 45*, 241–256.

Chaiken, S., Giner-Sorolla, R., & Chen, S. (1996). Beyond accuracy: Defense and impression motives in heuristic and systematic information processing. In P. M. Gollwitzer & J. A. Bargh (Eds.), *The psychology of action: Linking cognition and motivation to behavior* (pp. 553–578). New York: Guilford.

Chaiken, S., Liberman, A., & Eagly, A. H. (1989). Heuristic and systematic processing within and beyond the persuasion context. In J. S. Uleman & J. A. Bargh (Eds.), *Unintended thought* (pp. 212–252). New York: Guilford.

Chaiken, S., & Maheswaran, D. (1994). Heuristic processing can bias systematic processing: Effects of source credibility, argument ambiguity, and task importance on attitude judgment. *Journal of Personality and Social Psychology, 66*, 460–473.

Chaiken, S., Pomerantz, E. M., & Giner-Sorolla, R. (1995). Structural consistency and attitude strength. In R. E. Petty & J. A. Krosnick (Eds.), *Attitude strength: Antecedents and consequences* (pp. 387–412). Hillsdale, NJ: Lawrence Erlbaum Associates.

Chaiken, S., & Trope, Y. (Eds.) (1999). *Dual-process theories in social psychology*. New York: Guilford.

Chen, H. C., Reardon, R., Rea, C., & Moore, D. J. (1992). Forewarning of content and involvement: Consequences for persuasion and resistance to persuasion. *Journal of Experimental Social Psychology, 28*, 523–541.

Chen, M., & Bargh, J. A. (1999). Consequences of automatic evaluation: Immediate behavioral predispositions to approach or avoid the stimulus. *Personality and Social Psychology Bulletin, 25*, 215–224.

Chen, S., & Chaiken, S. (1999). The heuristic-systematic model in its broader context. In S. Chaiken & Y. Trope (Eds.), *Dual-process theories in social psychology* (pp. 73–96). London: Guilford.

Chen, S., Shechter, D., & Chaiken, S. (1996). Getting at the truth or getting along: Accuracy versus impression motivated heuristic and systematic processing. *Journal of Personality and Social Psychology, 71*, 262–275.

Cialdini, R. B. (1993). *Influence: Science and practice* (3rd ed.). New York: HarperCollins.

Coleman, J. F., Blake, R. R., & Mouton, J. S. (1958). Task difficulty and conformity pressures. *Journal of Abnormal and Social Psychology, 57*, 120–122.

Cook, T. D., & Campbell, D. T. (1979). *Quasi-experimentation: Design and analysis issues for field settings*. Chicago: Rand McNally.

Cook, T. D., & Flay, B. R. (1978). The persistence of experimentally induced attitude change. In L. Berkowitz (Ed.), *Advances in experimental social psychology* (Vol. 11, pp. 1–57). New York: Academic Press.

Cooper, J., & Fazio, R. H. (1984). A new look at dissonance theory. In L. Berkowitz, (Ed.), *Advances in experimental social psychology*, (Vol. 17, pp. 229–266). San Diego, CA: Academic Press.

Cooper, J., & Scher, S. J. (1994). When do our actions affect our attitudes? In S. Shavitt and T. Brock (Eds.), *Persuasion: Psychological insights and perspectives* (pp. 95–111). Boston: Allyn & Bacon.

Craik, F. I. M., & Lockhart, R. S. (1972). Levels of processing: A framework for memory research. *Journal of Verbal Learning and Verbal Behavior, 11*, 671–684.

Crowne, D. P., & Marlowe, D. (1964). *The approval motive: Studies in evaluative dependence*. New York: Wiley.

Crutchfield, R. S. (1955). Conformity and character. *American Psychologist, 10*, 191–198.

Darke, P. R., Chaiken, S., Bohner, G., Einwiller, S., Erb, H. P., & Hazlewood, J. D. (1998). Accuracy motivation, consensus information, and the law of large numbers: Effects on attitude judgment in the absence of argumentation. *Personality and Social Psychology Bulletin, 24*, 1205–1215.

Das, E. H. H. J., de Wit, J. B. F., & Stroebe, W. (2003). Fear appeals motivate acceptance of action recommendations: Evidence for a positive bias in the processing of persuasive messages. *Personality and Social Psychology Bulletin, 29*, 650–664.

DeBono, K. (2000). Attitude functions and consumer psychology: Understanding perceptions of product quality. In G. R. Maio and J. M. Olson (Eds.), *Why we evaluate: Functions of attitudes* (pp. 195–221). Mahwah, NJ: Lawrence Erlbaum Associates.

DePaulo, B. M. (1994). Spotting lies: Can humans learn to do better? *Current Directions in Psychological Science, 3*, 83–86.

DePaulo, B. M., & Friedman, H. S. (1999). Nonverbal communication. In D. T. Gilbert, S. T. Fiske, & G. Lindzey (Eds), *The handbook of social psychology* (4th ed., Vol. II, pp. 3–40). Oxford, UK: Oxford University Press.

DePaulo, B. M., Stone, J. I., & Lassiter, G. D. (1985). Deceiving and detecting deceit. In B. R. Schlenker (Ed.), *The self and social life* (pp. 323–370). New York: McGraw-Hill.

Deutsch, M., & Gerard, H. B. (1955). A study of normative and informational social influences upon individual judgment. *Journal of Abnormal and Social Psychology, 51*, 629–636.

Devos-Comby, L., & Salovey, P. (2002). Applying persuasion strategies to alter HIV-relevant thoughts and behavior. *Review of General Psychology, 6*, 287–304.

Dijksterhuis, A., Spears, R., Postmes, T., Stapel, D., Koomen, W., Knippenberg, A. V., & Scheepers, D. (1998). Seeing one thing and doing another: Contrast effects in automatic behavior. *Journal of Personality and Social Psychology, 75*, 862–871.

Dovidio, J.F., Kawakami, K., Johnson, C., Johnson, B., & Howard, A. (1997). On the nature of prejudice: Automatic and controlled processes. *Journal of Experimental Social Psychology, 33*, 510–540.

Eagly, A. H. (1974). Comprehensibility of persuasive arguments as a determinant of opinion change. *Journal of Personality and Social Psychology, 29*, 758–773.

Eagly, A. H., & Chaiken, S. (1984). Cognitive theories of persuasion. In L. Berkowitz (Ed.), *Advances in experimental social psychology* (Vol. 17, pp. 267–359). Orlando, FL: Academic Press.

Eagly, A. H., & Chaiken, S. (1993). *The psychology of attitudes.* Orlando, FL: Harcourt Brace.

Eagly, A. H., & Chaiken, S. (1995). Attitude strength, attitude structure, and resistance to change. In R. E. Petty & J. A. Krosnick (Eds), *Attitude strength: Antecedents and consequences* (pp. 413–432). Hillsdale, NJ: Lawrence Erlbaum Associates.

Eagly, A. H., & Telaak, K. (1972). Width of the latitude of acceptance as a determinant of attitude change. *Journal of Personality and Social Psychology, 23*, 388–397.

Edwards, K. (1990). The interplay of affect and cognition in attitude formation and change. *Journal of Personality and Social Psychology, 59*, 202–216.

Edwards, K., & Smith, E. E. (1996). A disconfirmation bias in the evaluation of arguments. *Journal of Personality and Social Psychology, 71*, 5–24.

Ekman, P., & O'Sullivan, M. (1991). Who can catch a liar? *American Psychologist, 46*, 913–920.

Ekman, P., O'Sullivan, M., & Frank, M. G. (1999). A few can catch a liar. *Psychological Science, 10*, 263–266.

Elliot, A. J., & Devine, P. G. (1994). On the motivational nature of cognitive dissonance: Dissonance as psychological discomfort. *Journal of Personality and Social Psychology, 67*, 382–394.

Elms, A. C. (1966). Influence of fantasy ability on attitude change through role playing. *Journal of Personality and Social Psychology, 4*, 36–43.

Erb, H., Bohner, G., Rank, S., & Einwiller, S. (2002). Processing minority and majority communications: The role of conflict with prior attitudes. *Personality and Social Psychology Bulletin, 28*, 1172–1182.

Erb, H., Bohner, G., Schmälzle, K., & Rank, S. (1998). Beyond conflict and discrepancy: Cognitive bias in minority and majority influence. *Personality and Social Psychology Bulletin, 24*, 620–633.

Esses, V. M., & Maio, G. R. (2002). Expanding the assessment of attitude components and structure: The benefits of open-ended measures. In W. Stroebe & M. Hewstone (Eds.), *European review of social psychology* (Vol. 12, pp. 71–102). Chichester, UK: John Wiley & Sons.

Evans, L. M., & Petty, R. E. (2003). Self-guide framing and persuasion: Responsibly increasing message processing to ideal levels. *Personality and Social Psychology Bulletin, 29*, 313–324.

Eysenck, M. W. (1979). Anxiety, learning, and memory: A reconceptualization. *Journal of Research in Personality, 13*, 363–385.

Eysenck, M. W. (1982). *Attention and arousal, cognition and performance.* Berlin, Germany: Springer-Verlag.

Fabrigar, L. R., & Petty, R. E. (1999). The role of affective and cognitive bases of attitudes in susceptibility to affectively and cognitively based persuasion. *Personality and Social Psychology Bulletin, 25*, 363–381.

Fazio, R. H. (1993). Variability in the likelihood of automatic attitude activation: Data re-analysis and commentary on Bargh, Chaiken, Govender, and Pratto (1992). *Journal of Personality and Social Psychology, 64*, 753–758.

Fazio, R. H. (1995). Attitudes as object-evaluation associations: Determinants, consequences, and correlates of attitude accessibility. In R. E. Petty & J. A. Krosnick (Eds.), *Attitude strength: Antecedents and consequences* (pp. 247–282). Hillsdale, NJ: Lawrence Erlbaum Associates.

Fazio, R. H. (2000). Accessible attitudes as tools for object appraisal: Their costs and benefits. In G. R. Maio & J. M. Olson (Eds.), *Why we evaluate: Functions of attitudes* (pp. 1–36). Mahwah, NJ: Lawrence Erlbaum Associates.

Fazio, R. H., Blascovich, J., & Driscoll, D. M. (1992). On the functional value of attitudes: The influence of accessible attitudes upon the ease and quality of decision making. *Personality and Social Psychology Bulletin, 18*, 388–401.

Fazio, R.H., & Olson, M.A. (2003). Implicit measures in social cognition research: Their meaning and use. *Annual Review of Psychology, 54*, 297–327.

Fazio, R. H., Sanbonmatsu, D. M., Powell, M. C., & Kardes, F. R. (1986). On the automatic activation of attitudes. *Journal of Personality and Social Psychology, 50*, 229–238.

Fazio, R. H., Zanna, M. P., & Cooper, J. (1977). Dissonance and self-perception: An integrative view of each theory's proper domain of application. *Journal of Experimental Social Psychology, 13*, 464–479.

Festinger, L. (1957). *A theory of cognitive dissonance.* Stanford, CA: Stanford University Press.

Festinger, L., & Carlsmith, J. M. (1959). Cognitive consequences of forced compliance. *Journal of Abnormal and Social Psychology, 58*, 203–210.

Festinger, L., Gerard, H. B., Hymovitch, B., Kelley, H. H., & Raven, B. (1952). The influence process in the presence of extreme deviants. *Human Relations, 5*, 327–346.

Fishbein, M. (1963). An investigation of the relationships between beliefs about an object and the attitude toward that object. *Human Relations, 16*, 233–240.

Fishbein, M., & Ajzen, I. (1975). *Belief, attitude, intention, and behavior: An introduction to theory and research.* Reading, MA: Addison-Wesley.

Fishbein, M., & Ajzen, I. (1981). Acceptance, yielding, and impact: Cognitive processes in persuasion. In R. E. Petty, T. M. Ostrom, & T. C. Brock (Eds.), *Cognitive responses in persuasion* (pp. 339–359). Hillsdale, NJ: Lawrence Erlbaum Associates.

Fisher, J. D., & Fisher, W. A. (1992). Changing AIDS-risk behavior. *Psychological Bulletin, 111*, 455–474.

Fisher, J. D., Fisher, W. A., Bryan, A. D., & Misovich, S. J. (2002). Information-motivation-behavioral skills model-based HIV risk behavior change intervention for inner-city high school youth. *Health Psychology, 21*, 177–186.

Fiske, S. T., Morling, B., & Stevens, L. E. (1996). Controlling self and others: A theory of anxiety, mental control, and social control. *Personality and Social Psychology Bulletin, 22*, 115–123.

Florack, A., Piontkowski, U., Knocks, I., Rottmann, J., & Thiemann, P. (2002). Attitude change: The case of attitudes towards the "green card" in Germany. *Current Research in Social Psychology, 8*, 39–50.

Freedman, J. L., & Sears, D. O. (1965). Warning, distraction and resistance to influence. *Journal of Personality and Social Psychology, 1*, 262–266.

French, J. R. P., Jr., & Raven, B. H. (1959). The bases of social power. In D. Cartwright (Ed.), *Studies in social power* (pp. 150–167). Ann Arbor, MI: University of Michigan.

Friedrich, J., Fetherstonhaugh, D., Casey, S., & Gallagher, D. (1996). Argument integration and attitude change: Suppression effects in the integration of one-sided arguments that vary in persuasiveness. *Personality and Social Psychology Bulletin, 22*, 179–191.

Garcia-Marques, T., & Mackie, D. M. (2001). The feeling of familiarity as a regulator of persuasive processing. *Social Cognition, 18*, 9–34.

Geers, A. L., Handley, I. M., & McLarney, A. R. (2003). Discerning the role of optimism in persuasion: The valence-enhancement hypothesis. *Journal of Personality and Social Psychology, 85*, 554–565.

Geers, A. L., & Lassiter, G. D. (1999). Affective expectations and information gain: Evidence for assimilation and contrast effects in affective experience. *Journal of Experimental Social Psychology, 35*, 394–413.

Gilbert, D. T. (1991). How mental systems believe. *American Psychologist, 46*, 107–119.

Giner-Sorolla, R., & Chaiken, S. (1997). Selective use of heuristic and systematic processing under defense motivation. *Personality and Social Psychology Bulletin, 23*, 84–97.

Glasman, L. R., & Albarracín, D. (2003). *How do people form attitudes that predict future behavior: A meta-analysis of the attitude-behavior relation following attitude formation.* Manuscript submitted for publication.

Gleicher, F., & Petty, R. E. (1992). Expectations of reassurance influence the nature of fear-stimulated attitude change. *Journal of Experimental Social Psychology, 28*, 86–100.

Gorn, G. J., & Goldberg, M. E. (1980). Children's responses to repetitive television commercials. *Journal of Consumer Research, 6*, 421–424.

Greenwald, A. G. (1968). Cognitive learning, cognitive response to persuasion, and attitude change. In A. G. Greenwald, T. C. Brock, & T. M. Ostrom (Eds.), *Psychological foundations of attitudes* (pp. 147–170). New York: Academic Press.

Gregory, S. W., & Webster, S. (1996). A nonverbal signal in voices of interview partners effectively predicts communication accommodation and social status perceptions. *Journal of Personality and Social Psychology, 70*, 1231–1240.

Grewal, D., Kavanoor, S., Fern, E.F., Costley, C., & Barnes, J. (1997). Comparative versus noncomparative advertising: A meta-analysis. *Journal of Marketing, 61*, 1–15.

Griffin, D., & Buehler, R. (1993). Role of construal processes in conformity and dissent. *Journal of Personality and Social Psychology, 65*, 657–669.

Gruder, C. L., Cook, T. D., Hennigan, K. M., Flay, B. R., Alessis, C., & Halamaj, J. (1978). Empirical tests of the absolute sleeper effect predicted from the discounting cue hypothesis. *Journal of Personality and Social Psychology, 36*, 1061–1074.

Haddock, G., & Huskinson, T. L. H. (2004). Individual differences in attitude structure. In G. Haddock & G. R. Maio (Eds.), *Contemporary perspectives on the psychology of attitudes* (pp. 35–56). London, UK: Psychology Press.

Hafer, C. L., Reynolds, K., & Obertynski, M. A. (1996). Message comprehensibility and persuasion: Effects of complex language in counterattitudinal appeals to laypeople. *Social Cognition, 14*, 317–337.

Hale, J. L., Lemieux, R., & Mongeau, P. A. (1995). Cognitive processing of fear-arousing message content. *Communications Research, 22*, 459–474.

Harkins, S. G., & Petty, R. E. (1981). The multiple source effect in persuasion: The effects of distraction. *Personality and Social Psychology Bulletin, 7*, 627–635.

Harkins, S. G., & Petty, R. E. (1987). Information utility and the multiple source effect. *Journal of Personality and Social Psychology, 52*, 260–268.

Harman, J. J., & Johnson, B. T. (2003). Not all psychologists are classist [Comment]. *American Psychologist, 58*, 144–145.

Harmon-Jones, E. (2000). Cognitive dissonance and experienced negative affect: Evidence that dissonance increases experienced negative affect even in the absence of aversive consequences. *Personality and Social Psychology Bulletin, 26*, 1490–1501.

Harmon-Jones, E., Brehm, J. W., Greenberg, J., Simon, L., & Nelson, D. E. (1996). Evidence that the production of aversive consequences is not necessary to create cognitive dissonance. *Journal of Personality and Social Psychology, 70*, 5–16.

Harmon-Jones, E., & Mills, J. (1999). (Eds.). *Cognitive dissonance: Progress on a pivotal theory in social psychology.* Washington, DC: American Psychological Association.

Hass, R. G., & Grady, K. (1975). Temporal delay, type of forewarning, and resistance to influence. *Journal of Experimental Social Psychology, 11*, 459–469.

Haugtvedt, C. P., & Petty, R. E. (1992). Personality and persuasion: Need for cognition moderates the persistence and resistance of attitude changes. *Journal of Personality and Social Psychology, 63*, 308–319.

Heesacker, M., Petty, R. E., & Cacioppo, J. T. (1983). Field dependence and attitude change: Source credibility can alter persuasion by affecting message-relevant thinking. *Journal of Personality and Social Psychology, 51*, 653–666.

Heine, S. J., & Lehman, D. (1997). Culture, dissonance, and self-affirmation. *Personality and Social Psychology Bulletin, 23*, 389–400.

Hochbaum, G. M. (1954). The relation between group members' self-confidence and their reactions to group pressure to conformity. *American Sociological Review, 19*, 678–687.

Hoshino-Browne, E., Zanna, A. S., Spencer, S. J., & Zanna, M. P. (2004). Investigating attitudes cross-culturally: A case of cognitive dissonance among East Asians and North Americans. In G. Haddock & G. R. Maio (Eds.), *Contemporary perspectives on the psychology of attitudes* (375–398). London, UK: Psychology Press.

Hovland, C. I. (1954). Effects of the mass media of communication. In Lindzey, G. (Ed.), *Handbook of social psychology* (Vol. II, pp. 1062–1103). Cambridge, MA: Addison-Wesley.

Hovland, C. I. (1959). Reconciling conflicting results derived from experimental and survey studies of attitude change. *American Psychologist, 14*, 8–17.

Hovland, C. I., Harvey, O. J., & Sherif, M. (1957). Assimilation and contrast effects in reactions to communication and attitude change. *Journal of Abnormal and Social Psychology, 55*, 244–252.

Hovland, C. I., & Janis, I. L. (Eds.). (1959). *Personality and persuasibility.* New Haven, CT: Yale University Press.

Hovland, C. I., Janis, I. L., & Kelley, H. H. (1953). *Communication and persuasion: Psychological studies of opinion change.* New Haven, CT: Yale University Press.

Hovland, C. I., Lumsdaine, A. A., & Sheffield, F. D. (1949). *Experiments on mass communication.* Princeton, NJ: Princeton University Press.

Hull, C. L. (1943). *Principles of behavior: An introduction to behavior theory.* New York: Appleton-Century-Crofts.

Hurwitz, S. D., Miron, M. S., & Johnson, B. T. (1992). Source credibility and the language of expert testimony. *Journal of Applied Social Psychology, 22*, 1909–1939.

Huskinson, T. L. H., & Haddock, G. (2004). Individual differences in attitude structure: Variance in the chronic reliance on affective and cognitive information. *Journal of Experimental Social Psychology, 40*, 82–90.

Insko, C. A. (1964). Primacy versus recency in persuasion as a function of the timing of arguments and measures. *Journal of Abnormal and Social Psychology, 69*, 381–391.

Insko, C. A., Smith, R. H., Alicke, M. D., Wade, J., & Taylor, S. (1985). Conformity and group size: The concern with being right and the concern with being liked. *Personality and Social Psychology Bulletin, 11*, 41–50.

Ito, K. (2002). Additivity of heuristic and systematic processing in persuasion: Effects of source credibility, argument quality, and issue involvement. *Japanese Journal of Experimental Social Psychology, 41*, 137–146.

Jacks, J. Z., & Devine, P. G. (2000). Attitude importance, forewarning of message content, and resistance to persuasion. *Basic and Applied Social Psychology, 22*, 19–29.

Janis, I. L. (1967). Effects of fear arousal on attitude change: Recent developments in theory and experimental research. In L. Berkowitz (Ed.), *Advances in experimental social psychology.* (Vol. 3, pp. 166–224). San Diego, CA: Academic Press.

Janis, I. L., & King, B. T. (1954). The influence of role playing on opinion change. *Journal of Abnormal and Social Psychology, 49*, 211–218.

Johar, G. V., & Sengupta, J. (2002). The effects of dissimulation on the accessibility and predictive power of weakly held attitudes. *Social Cognition, 20*, 257–293.

Johnson, B. T. (1991). Insights about attitudes: Meta-analytic perspectives. *Personality and Social Psychology Bulletin, 17*, 289–299.

Johnson, B. T., & Eagly, A. H. (1989). Effects of involvement on persuasion: A meta-analysis. *Psychological Bulletin, 106*, 290–314.

Johnson, B. T., & Eagly, A. H. (1990). Involvement and persuasion: Types, traditions, and the evidence. *Psychological Bulletin, 107*, 375–384.

Johnson, B. T., Lin, H., Symons, C. S., Campbell, L. A., & Ekstein, G. (1995). Initial beliefs and attitudinal latitudes as factors in persuasion. *Personality and Social Psychology Bulletin, 21*, 502–511.

Johnson, B. T., & Nichols, D. R. (1998). Social psychologists' expertise in the public interest: Civilian morale research during World War II. *Journal of Social Issues, 54*, 53–77.

Johnson, B. T., Smith-McLallen, A., Killeya, L. A., & Levin, K. D. (2004). Truth or consequences: Overcoming resistance to persuasion with positive thinking. In E. S. Knowles & J. Linn (Eds.), *Resistance and persuasion* (pp. 215–233). Mahwah, NJ: Lawrence Erlbaum Associates.

Johnson, H. H., & Watkins, T. A. (1971). The effects of message repetitions on immediate and delayed attitude change. *Psychonomic Science, 22*, 101–103.

Johnson, R. W., Kelly, R. J., & LeBlanc, B. A. (1995). Motivational basis of dissonance: Aversive consequences or inconsistency. *Personality and Social Psychology Bulletin, 21*, 850–855.

Jonas, K., Diehl, M., & Brömer, P. (1997). Effects of attitude ambivalence on information processing and attitude-intention consistency. *Journal of Experimental Social Psychology, 33*, 190–210.

Judd, C. M., Kenny, D. A., & Krosnick, J. A. (1983). Judging the positions of political candidates: Models of assimilation and contrast. *Journal of Personality and Social Psychology, 44*, 952–963.

Katz, D. (1960). The functional approach to the study of attitudes. *Public Opinion Quarterly, 24*, 163–204.

Kelman, H. C. (1958). Compliance, identification, and internalization: Three processes of attitude change. *Journal of Conflict Resolution, 2*, 51–60.

Kelman, H. C. (1974). Further thoughts on the processes of compliance, identification, and internalization. In J. T. Tedeschi (Ed.), *Perspectives on social power* (pp. 125–171). Chicago: Aldine.

Kelman, H. C. (1992). Informal mediation by the scholar/practitioner. In J. Bercovitch & J. Z. Rubin (Eds.), *Mediation in international relations: Multiple approaches to conflict management* (pp. 64–96). New York: St. Martin's Press.

Kelman, H. C., & Eagly, A. H. (1965). Attitude toward the communicator, perception of communication content, and attitude change. *Journal of Personality and Social Psychology, 1*, 63–78.

Kerr, N. (2002). When is a minority a minority? Active versus passive minority advocacy and social influence. *European Journal of Social Psychology, 32*, 471–484.

Kiesler, S. B., & Mathog, R. (1968). The distraction hypothesis in attitude change. *Psychological Reports, 23*, 1123–1133.

Killeya, L. A., & Johnson, B. T. (1998). Experimental induction of biased systematic processing: The directed thought technique. *Personality and Social Psychology Bulletin, 24*, 17–33.

Knower, F. H. (1936). Experimental studies of changes in attitude. II. A study of the effect of printed argument on changes in attitude. *Journal of Abnormal and Social Psychology, 30*, 522–532.

Krosnick, J. A., Boninger, D. S., Chuang, Y. C., Berent, M. K., & Carnot, C. G. (1993). Attitude strength: One construct or many related constructs? *Journal of Personality and Social Psychology, 65*, 1132–1151.

Kruglanski, A. W. (1989). The psychology of being "right": The problem of accuracy in social perception and cognition. *Psychological Bulletin, 106*, 395–409.

Kruglanski, A., & Thompson, E. (1999). Persuasion by a single route: A view from the unimodel. *Psychological Inquiry, 10*, 83–109.

Kruglanski, A. W., Thompson, E. P., & Spiegel, S. (1999). Separate or equal? Bimodal notions of persuasion and a single-process "Unimodel." In S. Chaiken & Y. Trope (Eds.), *Dual-process theories in social psychology* (pp. 293–313). New York: Guilford.

Kruglanski, A. W., & Webster, D. M. (1996). Motivated closing of the mind: "Seizing" and "freezing." *Psychological Review, 103*, 263–283.

Kumkale, G. T., & Albarracín, D. (2004). The sleeper effect in persuasion: A meta-analytic review. *Psychological Bulletin, 130*, 143–172.

Kunda, Z. (1990). The case for motivated reasoning. *Psychological Bulletin, 108*, 480–498.

Lampron, S. F., Krosnick, J. A., Shaeffer, E., Petty, R. E., & See, M. (2003). *Different types of involvement moderate persuasion (somewhat) differently: Contrasting outcome-based and value-based involvement.* Unpublished manuscript.

LaPiere, R. T. (1934). Attitudes vs. actions. *Social Forces, 13*, 230–237.

Lasswell, H. D. (1948). The structure and function of communication in society. In L. Bryson (Ed.), *The communication of ideas: Religion and civilization series* (pp. 37–51). New York: Harper & Row.

Latané, B. (1981). The psychology of social impact. *American Psychologist, 36*, 343–356.

Latané, B., & Wolf, S. (1981). The social impact of majorities and minorities. *Psychological Review, 88*, 438–453.

Lee, A. Y., & Aaker, J. L. (2004). Bringing the frame into focus: The influence of regulatory fit on processing fluency and persuasion. *Journal of Personality and Social Psychology, 86*, 205–218.

Leventhal, H. (1970). Findings and theory in the study of fear communications. In L. Berkowitz (Ed.), *Advances in experimental social psychology* (Vol. 5, pp. 119–187). New York: Academic Press.

Liberman, N., & Chaiken, S. (1992). Defensive processing of personally relevant health messages. *Personality and Social Psychology Bulletin, 18*, 669–679.

Livingston, R. W. (2001). What you see is what you get: Systematic variability in perceptual-based social judgment. *Personality and Social Psychology Bulletin, 27*, 1086–1097.

Lord, C. G., Ross, L., & Lepper, M. R. (1979). Biased assimilation and attitude polarization: The effects of prior theories on subsequently considered evidence. *Journal of Personality and Social Psychology, 37*, 2098–2109.

Lowenthal, D., & Lowenstein, G. (2001). Can voters predict changes in their own attitudes? *Political Psychology, 22*, 65–87.

Maass, A., & Clark, R. D. (1984). Hidden impact of minorities: Fifteen years of minority influence research. *Psychological Bulletin, 95*, 428–450.

Maass, A., Clark, R. D., & Haberkorn, G. (1982). The effects of differential ascribed category membership and norms on minority influence. *European Journal of Social Psychology, 12*, 89–104.

MacDonald, T. K., & Zanna, M. P. (1998). Cross-dimension ambivalence toward social groups: Can ambivalence affect intentions to hire feminists? *Personality and Social Psychology Bulletin, 24*, 427–441.

Mackie, D. M. (1987). Systematic and nonsystematic processing of majority and minority persuasive communications. *Journal of Personality and Social Psychology, 53*, 41–52.

Maheswaran, D., & Meyers-Levy, J. (1990). The influence of message framing and issue involvement. *Journal of Marketing Research, 27*, 361–367.

Maio, G. R., Bell, D. W., & Esses, V. M. (1996). Ambivalence and persuasion: The processing of messages about immigrant groups. *Journal of Experimental Social Psychology, 32*, 513–536.

Maio, G. R., Esses, V. M., & Bell, D. W. (2000). Ambivalence and inconsistency are distinct constructs. *Canadian Journal of Behavioral Science, 32*, 71–83.

Maio, G. R., & Olson, J. M. (1995a). Involvement and persuasion: Evidence for different types of involvement. *Canadian Journal of Behavioural Science, 27*, 64–78.

Maio, G. R., & Olson, J. M. (1995b). The effect of attitude dissimulation on attitude accessibility. *Social Cognition, 13*, 127–144.

Maio, G. R., & Olson, J. M. (1998). Attitude dissimulation and persuasion. *Journal of Experimental Social Psychology, 34*, 182–201.

Maio, G. R., & Olson J. M. (Eds.). (2000). *Why we evaluate: Functions of attitudes*. Mahwah, NJ: Lawrence Erlbaum Associates.

Maio, G. R., Watt, S. E., & Hewstone, M. (2004). *Effects of anti-racism messages on explicit and implicit intergroup attitudes: The moderating role of attitudinal ambivalence*. Manuscript submitted for publication.

Martin, R., & Hewstone, M. (2001). Determinants and consequences of cognitive processes in minority and majority influence. In J. P. Forgas & K. D. Willimas (Eds.), *Social influence: Direct and indirect processes. The Sydney symposium of social psychology* (pp. 315–330). Philadelphia: Psychology Press.

McConnell, A. R., & Leibold, J. M. (2001). Relations among the implicit association test, discriminatory behavior, and explicit measures of racial attitudes. *Journal of Experimental Social Psychology, 37*, 435–442.

McGuire, W. J. (1960). A syllogistic analysis of cognitive relationships. In M. J. Rosenberg, C. I. Hovland, W. J. McGuire, R. P. Abelson, & J. W. Brehm, *Attitude organization and change: An analysis of consistency among attitude components* (pp. 65–111). New Haven, CT: Yale University Press.

McGuire, W. J. (1964). Inducing resistance to persuasion: Some contemporary approaches. In L. Berkowitz (Ed.), *Advances in experimental social psychology* (Vol. 1, pp. 191–229). New York: Academic Press.

McGuire, W. J. (1968a). Personality and attitude change: An information-processing theory. In A. G. Greenwald, T. C. Brock, & T. M. Ostrom (Eds.), *Psychological foundations of attitudes* (pp. 171–196). San Diego, CA: Academic Press.

McGuire, W. J. (1968b). Personality and susceptibility to social influence. In E. Borgatta & W. Lambert (Eds.), *Handbook of personality theory and research*. Chicago: Rand McNally.

McGuire, W. J. (1969). The nature of attitudes and attitude change. In G. Lindzey & E. Aronson (Eds.), *Handbook of social psychology* (2nd ed., Vol. 3, pp. 136–314). Reading, MA: Addison-Wesley.

McGuire, W. J. (1985). Attitudes and attitude change. In G. Lindzey & E. Aronson (Eds.), *Handbook of social psychology* (3rd ed., Vol. 2, pp. 233–346). New York: Random House.

McGuire, W. J. (1989). Theoretical foundations of campaigns. In R. E. Rice & C. K. Atkin (Eds.), *Public communication campaigns* (pp. 43–66). Newbury Park, CA: Sage.

McGuire, W. J. (1996). The Yale communication and attitude-change program in the 1950s. In E. E. Dennis & E. Wartella (Eds.), *American communication research—The remembered history. LEA's communication series* (pp. 39–59). Mahwah, NJ: Lawrence Erlbaum Associates.

McGuire, W. J. (2000). Standing on the shoulders of ancients: Consumer research, persuasion, and rhetorical language. *Journal of Consumer Research, 27*, 109–114.

McGuire, W. J., & McGuire, C. V. (1991). The content, structure, and operation of thought systems. In R. S. Wyer, Jr., & Srull, T. K. (Eds.), *The content, structure, and operation of thought systems.* (*Advances in social cognition*, Vol. 4., pp. 1–78). Hillsdale, NJ: Lawrence Erlbaum Associates.

Meyerowitz, B. E., & Chaiken, S. (1987). The effect of message framing on breast self-examination attitudes, intentions, and behavior. *Journal of Personality and Social Psychology, 52*, 500–510.

Millar, M. G., & Millar, K. U. (1990). Attitude change as a function of attitude type and argument type. *Journal of Personality and Social Psychology, 59*, 217–228.

Miller, N., Maruyama, G., Beaber, R. J., & Valone, K. (1976). Speed of speech and persuasion. *Journal of Personality and Social Psychology, 34*, 615–624.

Misra, S., & Beatty, S. E. (1990). Celebrity spokesperson and brand congruence: An assessment of recall and affect. *Journal of Business Research, 21*, 159–173.

Moscovici, S. (1980). Toward a theory of conversion behavior. In L. Berkowitz (Ed.), *Advances in experimental social psychology* (Vol. 13, pp. 209–239). New York: Academic Press.

Moscovici, S., Lage, E., & Naffrechoux, M. (1969). Influence of a consistent minority on the responses of a majority in a color perception task. *Sociometry, 32*, 365–379.

Moskowitz, G. B., Skurnik, I., & Galinsky, A. D. (1999). The history of dual-process notions, and the future of preconscious control. In S. Chaiken & Y. Trope (Eds.), *Dual-process theories in social psychology* (pp. 12–36). New York: Guilford.

Mouton, J. S., Blake, R. R., & Olmstead, J. A. (1956). The relationship between frequency of yielding and the disclosure of personal identity. *Journal of Personality, 24*, 339–347.

Murray, S. L., Haddock, G., & Zanna, M. P. (1996). On creating value-expressive attitudes: An experimental approach. In C. Seligman & J. M. Olson (Eds.), *The psychology of values: The Ontario symposium* (pp. 107–133). Mahwah, NJ: Lawrence Erlbaum Associates.

Nail, P. R. (1986). Toward an integration of some models and theories of social response. *Psychological Bulletin, 100*, 190–206.

Nail, P. R., MacDonald, G., & Levy, D. A. (2000). Proposal of a four-dimensional model of social response. *Psychological Bulletin, 126*, 454–470.

Neimeyer, G. J., & Metzler, A. E., & Dongarra, T. (1990). Changing attitudes regarding the effectiveness of cognitive restructuring for treating depression. *Social Behavior and Personality, 18*, 181–188.

Nemeth, C. J. (1986). Differential contributions of majority and minority influence. *Psychological Review, 93*, 23–32.

Nemeth, C. J., & Kwan, J. (1987). Minority influence, divergent thinking and detection of correct solutions. *Journal of Applied Social Psychology, 17*, 788–799.

Newcomb, T. L. (1943). *Personality and social change: Attitude formation in a student community.* New York: Dryden Press.

Nottleman, E. D., & Hill, K. T. (1977). Test anxiety and off-task behaviour in evaluative situations. *Child Development, 48*, 225–231.

O'Barr, W. M. (1982). *Linguistic evidence: Language, power, and strategy in the courtroom.* New York: Academic Press.

Oriña, M. M., Wood, W., & Simpson, J. A. (2002). Strategies of influence in close relationships. *Journal of Experimental Social Psychology, 38*, 459–472.

Osterhouse, R. A., & Brock, T. C. (1970). Distraction increases yielding to propaganda by inhibiting counterarguing. *Journal of Personality and Social Psychology, 15*, 344–358.

Ostrom, T. M. (1989). Interdependence of attitude theory and measurement. In A. R. Pratkanis, S. J. Breckler, & A. G. Greenwald (Eds.), *Attitude structure and function* (pp. 11–36). Hillsdale, NJ: Lawrence Erlbaum Associates.

Ostrom, T. M., Steele, C. M., & Smilansky, J. (1974). Perceived discrepancy and attitude change: An unsubstantiated relationship. *Representative Research in Social Psychology, 5*, 7–15.

Papageorgis, D. (1968). Warning and persuasion. *Psychological Bulletin, 70*, 271–282.

Park, H. S., & Levine, T. R. (1999). The Theory of Reasoned Action and self-construal: Evidence from three cultures. *Communication Monographs, 66*, 199–218.

Perloff, R. M. (2003). *The dynamics of persuasion: Communication and attitudes in the 21st century* (2nd ed.). Mahwah, NJ: Lawrence Erlbaum Associates.

Peterson, R. S., & Nemeth, C. J. (1996). Focus versus flexibility: Majority and minority influence can both improve performance. *Personality and Social Psychology Bulletin, 22*, 14–23.

Petty, R. E. (1994). Two routes to persuasion: State of the art. In G. d'Ydewalle, P. Bertelson, & P. Eelen (Eds.), *International perspectives on psychological science, Vol. 2: The state of the art* (pp. 229–247). Hillsdale, NJ, England: Lawrence Erlbaum Associates.

Petty, R. E., Briñol, P., & Tormala, Z. L. (2002). Thought confidence as a determinant of persuasion: The self-validation hypothesis. *Journal of Personality and Social Psychology, 82,* 722–741.

Petty, R. E., & Cacioppo, J. T. (1977). Forewarning, cognitive responding, and resistance to persuasion. *Journal of Personality and Social Psychology, 35,* 645–655.

Petty, R. E., & Cacioppo, J. T. (1979a). Effects of forewarning of persuasive intent and involvement on cognitive responses and persuasion. *Personality and Social Psychology Bulletin, 5,* 173–176.

Petty, R. E., & Cacioppo, J. T. (1979b). Effects of message repetition and position on cognitive response, recall, and persuasion. *Journal of Personality and Social Psychology, 37,* 1915–1926.

Petty, R. E., & Cacioppo, J. T. (1981). *Attitudes and persuasion: Classic and contemporary approaches.* Dubuque, IA: Brown.

Petty, R. E., & Cacioppo, J. T. (1984). The effects of involvement on responses to argument quantity and quality: Central and peripheral routes to persuasion. *Journal of Personality and Social Psychology, 46,* 69–81.

Petty, R. E., & Cacioppo, J. T. (1986). The elaboration likelihood model of persuasion. In L. Berkowitz (Ed.), *Advances in experimental social psychology* (Vol. 19, pp. 123–205). San Diego, CA: Academic Press.

Petty, R. E., Cacioppo, J. T., & Goldman, R. (1981). Personal involvement as a determinant of argument-based persuasion. *Journal of Personality and Social Psychology, 41,* 847–855.

Petty, R. E., Cacioppo, J. T., & Heesacker, M. (1981). Effects of rhetorical questions on persuasion: A cognitive response analysis. *Journal of Personality and Social Psychology, 40,* 432–440.

Petty, R. E., Fleming, M. A., & White, P. H. (1999). Stigmatized sources and persuasion: Prejudice as a determinant of argument scrutiny. *Journal of Personality and Social Psychology, 76,* 19–34.

Petty, R. E., Harkins, S. G., & Williams, K. D. (1980). The effects of group diffusion of cognitive effort on attitudes: An information processing view. *Journal of Personality and Social Psychology, 38,* 81–92.

Petty, R. E., Haugtvedt, C. P., & Smith, S. M. (1995). Elaboration as a determinant of attitude strength: Creating attitudes that are persistant, resistant, and predictive of behavior. In R. E. Petty & J. A. Krosnick (Eds.), *Attitude strength: Antecedents and consequences* (pp. 93–130). Hillsdale, NJ: Lawrence Erlbaum Associates.

Petty, R. E., Ostrom, T. M., & Brock, T. C. (1981). Historical foundations of the cognitive response approach to attitudes and persuasion. In R. E. Petty, T. M. Ostrom, & T. C. Brock (Eds.), *Cognitive responses in persuasion* (pp. 5–29). Hillsdale, NJ: Lawrence Erlbaum Associates.

Petty, R. E., Priester, J. R., & Wegener. D. T. (1994). Cognitive processes in attitude change. In R. S. Wyer, Jr., & T. K. Srull (Eds.), *Handbook of social cognition, Vol. 2: Applications* (2nd ed., pp. 69–142). Hillsdale, NJ: Lawrence Erlbaum Associates.

Petty, R. E., & Wegener, D. T. (1998a). Attitude change: Multiple roles for persuasion variables. In D. T. Gilbert, S. T. Fiske, & G. Lindzey (Eds.), *The handbook of social psychology* (Vol. 1, 4th ed., pp. 323–390). New York: McGraw-Hill.

Petty, R. E., & Wegener, D. T. (1998b). Matching versus mismatching attitude functions: Implications for scrutiny of persuasive messages. *Personality and Social Psychology Bulletin, 24,* 227–240.

Petty, R. E., & Wegener, D. T. (1999). The elaboration likelihood model: Current status and controversies. In S. Chaiken & Y. Trope (Eds.), *Dual-process theories in social psychology* (pp. 41–72). London: Guilford.

Petty, R. E., Wegener, D. T., & Fabrigar, L.R. (1997). Attitudes and attitude change. *Annual Review of Psychology, 48,* 609–647.

Petty, R. E., Wells, G. L., & Brock, T. C. (1976). Distraction can enhance or reduce yielding to propaganda: Thought disruption versus effort justification. *Journal of Personality and Social Psychology, 34,* 874–884.

Petty, R. E., Wells, G. L., Heesacker, M., Brock, T. C., & Cacioppo, J. C. (1983). The effects of recipient posture on persuasion: A cognitive response analysis. *Personality and Social Psychology Bulletin, 9,* 209–222.

Petty, R. E., Wheeler, S. C., & Bizer, G. Y. (1999). Is there one persuasion process or more? Lumping versus splitting in attitude change theories. *Psychological Inquiry, 10,* 156–163.

Petty, R. E., Wheeler, S. C., & Bizer, G. Y. (2000). Attitude functions and persuasion: An elaboration likelihood approach to matched versus mismatched messages. In G. R. Maio & J. M. Olson (Eds.), *Why we evaluate: Functions of attitudes* (pp. 133–162). Mahwah, NJ: Lawrence Erlbaum Associates.

Petty, R. E., Wheeler, S. C., & Tormala, Z. L. (2003). Persuasion and attitude change. In T. Millon & M. J. Lerner (Eds.), *Handbook of psychology: Vol. 5. Personality and social psychology* (pp. 353–382). New York: Wiley.

Piero, A., Mannetti, L., Kruglanski, A. W., & Sleeth-Keppler, D. (2004). Relevance override: On the reduced impact of "cues" under high-motivation conditions of persuasion studies. *Journal of Personality and Social Psychology, 86,* 251–264.

Pomerantz, E. M., Chaiken, S., & Tordesillas, R. S. (1995). Attitude strength and resistance processes. *Journal of Personality and Social Psychology, 69,* 408–419.

Pratkanis, A. R., Greenwald, A. G., Leippe, M. R., & Baumgardner, M. H. (1988). In search of reliable persuasion effects III. The Sleeper effect is dead. Long live the sleeper effect. *Journal of Personality and Social Psychology, 54,* 203–218.

Prentice, D. A. (1987). Psychological correspondence of possessions, attitudes, and values. *Journal of Personality and Social Psychology, 53*, 993–1003.

Priester, J. R., & Petty, R. E. (1996). The gradual threshold model of ambivalence: Relating the positive and negative bases of attitudes to subjective ambivalence. *Journal of Personality and Social Psychology, 71*, 431–449.

Priester, J. R., Wegener, D. T., Petty, R. E., & Fabrigar, L. R. (1999). Examining the psychological process underlying the sleeper effect: The elaboration likelihood model explanation. *Media Psychology, 1*, 27–48.

Prislin, R. (1996). Attitude stability and attitude strength: One is enough to make it stable. *European Journal of Social Psychology, 26*, 447–477.

Prislin, R., & Ouellette, J. (1996). When it is embedded, it is potent: Effects of general attitude embeddedness on formation of specific attitudes and behavioral intentions. *Personality and Social Psychology Bulletin, 22*, 845–861.

Prislin, R., & Pool, G. J. (1996). Behavior, consequences, and the self: Is all well that ends well? *Personality and Social Psychology Bulletin, 22*, 933–948.

Puckett, J., Petty, R. E., Cacioppo, J. T., & Fisher, D. (1983). The relative impact of age and attractiveness stereotypes on persuasion. *Journal of Gerontology, 38*, 340–343.

Raghunathan, R., & Trope, Y. (2002). Walking the tightrope between feeling good and being accurate: Mood as a resource in processing persuasive messages. *Journal of Personality and Social Psychology, 83*, 510–525.

Raven, B. H. (1992). A power/interaction model of interpersonal influence: French and Raven thirty years later. *Journal of Social Behavior and Personality, 7*, 217–244.

Remmers, H. H., & Morgan, C. L. (1936). Changing attitudes toward a racial group. *Purdue University Studies in Higher Education, 31*, 109–114.

Reynolds, D. J., Jr., & Gifford, R. (2001). The sounds and sights of intelligence: A lens model channel analysis. *Personality and Social Psychology Bulletin, 27*, 187–200.

Rhodes, N., & Wood, W. (1992). Self-esteem and intelligence affect influenceability: The mediating role of message perception. *Psychological Bulletin, 111*, 156–171.

Rogers, R. W. (1983). Cognitive and physiological processes in fear appeals and attitude change: A revised theory of protection motivation. In J. T. Cacioppo and R. E. Petty (Eds.), *Social psychophysiology: A sourcebook* (pp. 153–176). New York: Guilford.

Rogers, R. W., & Prentice-Dunn, S. (1997). Protection motivation theory. In D. S. Gochman (Ed.), *Handbook of health behavior research I: Personal and social determinants* (Vol. 1, pp. 113–132). New York: Plenum.

Romero, A. A., Agnew, C. R., & Insko, C. A. (1996). The cognitive mediation hypothesis revisited: An empirical response to methodological and theoretical criticism. *Personality and Social Psychology Bulletin, 22*, 651–665.

Ronis, D. L., Baumgardner, M. H., Leippe, M. R., Cacioppo, J. T., & Greenwald, A. G. (1977). In search of reliable persuasion effects: I. A computer-controlled procedure for studying persuasion. *Journal of Personality and Social Psychology, 35*, 548–569.

Roskos-Ewoldsen, D. R., Bichsel, J., & Hoffman, K. (2002). The influence of accessibility of source likeability on persuasion. *Journal of Experimental Social Psychology, 38*, 137–143.

Roskos-Ewoldsen, D. R., & Fazio, R. H. (1992). The accessibility of source likability as a determinant of persuasion. *Personality and Social Psychology Bulletin, 18*, 19–25.

Ross, L., Bierbrauer, G., & Hoffman, S. (1976). The role of attribution processes in conformity and dissent: Revisiting the Asch situation. *American Psychologist, 31*, 148–157.

Ross, M., & McFarland, C. (1988). Constructing the past: Biases in personal memories. In D. Bar-Tal & A. W. Kruglanski (Eds.), *The social psychology of knowledge* (pp. 299–314). Cambridge, UK: Cambridge University Press.

Ross, M., McFarland, C., Conway, M., & Zanna, M. P. (1983). Reciprocal relation between attitudes and behavior recall: Committing people to newly formed attitudes. *Journal of Personality and Social Psychology, 45*, 257–267.

Rothman, A. J., & Salovey, P. (1997). Shaping perceptions to motivate healthy behavior: The role of message framing. *Psychological Bulletin, 121*, 3–19.

Rucker, D. D., & Petty, R. E. (2004). When resistance is futile: Consequences of failed counterarguing for attitude certainty. *Journal of Personality and Social Psychology, 86*, 219–235.

Ruiter, R. A., Abraham, C., & Kok, G. (2001). Scary warnings and rational precautions: A review of the psychology of fear appeals. *Psychology & Health, 16*, 613–630.

Saegert, S. C., Swap, W. C., & Zajonc, R. B. (1973). Exposure, context, and interpersonal attraction. *Journal of Personality and Social Psychology, 25*, 234–242.

Sagarin, B. J., Cialdini, R. B., Rice, W. E., & Serna, S. B. (2002). Dispelling the illusion of invulnerability: The motivations and mechanisms of resistance to persuasion. *Journal of Personality and Social Psychology, 83*, 526–541.

Sanbonmatsu, D. M., & Kardes, F. R. (1988). The effects of physiological arousal on information processing and persuasion. *Journal of Consumer Research, 15*, 379–385.

Sarnoff, I., & Katz, D. (1954). The motivational bases of attitude change. *Journal of Abnormal and Social Psychology, 49*, 115–124.

Saucier, D. A., & Miller, C. T. (2003). The persuasiveness of racial arguments as a subtle measure of racism. *Personality and Social Psychology Bulletin, 29,* 1303–1315.

Sayers, S. L., Baucom, D. H., & Tierney, A. M. (1993). Sex roles, interpersonal control, and depression: Who can get their way? *Journal of Research in Personality, 27,* 377–395.

Sengupta, J., & Johar, G. V. (2001). Contingent effects of anxiety on message elaboration and persuasion. *Personality and Social Psychology Bulletin, 27,* 139–150.

Shavitt, S. (1990). The role of attitude objects in attitude functions. *Journal of Experimental Social Psychology, 26,* 124–148.

Sherif, C. W. (1980). Social values, attitudes, and the involvement of the self. In H. E. Howe, Jr. & M. M. Page (Eds.), *Nebraska Symposium on Motivation, 1979* (Vol. 27, pp. 1–64). Lincoln, NE: University of Nebraska Press.

Sherif, C. W., & Sherif, M. (Eds.). (1967). *Attitude, ego-involvement, and change.* New York: Wiley.

Sherif, C. W., Sherif, M., & Nebergall, R. E. (1965). *Attitude and attitude change.* Philadelphia: Saunders.

Sherif, M. (1935). A study of some social factors in perception. *Archives of Psychology, 27,* 1–60.

Sherif, M., & Cantril, H. (1947). *The psychology of ego-involvements: Social attitudes and identifications.* New York: Wiley.

Sherif, M., & Hovland, C. I. (1961). *Social judgment: Assimilation and contrast effects in communication and attitude change.* New Haven, CT: Yale University Press.

Slusher, M. P., & Anderson, C. A. (1996). Using causal persuasive arguments to change beliefs and teach new information: The mediating role of explanation availability and evaluation bias in the acceptance of knowledge. *Journal of Educational Psychology, 88,* 110–122.

Smith, M. B., Bruner, J. S., & White, R. W. (1956). *Opinions and personality.* New York: Wiley.

Smith, S. M., & Shaffer, D. R. (1995). Speed of speech and persuasion: Evidence for multiple effects. *Personality and Social Psychology Bulletin, 21,* 1051–1060.

Snyder, M. (1987). *Public appearances/private realities: The psychology of self-monitoring.* San Francisco: Freeman.

Srull, T. K., & Wyer, R. S. (1989). Person memory and judgment. *Psychological Review, 96,* 58–83.

Stapel, D. A., Koomen, W., & Velthuijsen, A. S. (1998). Assimilation or contrast? Comparison relevance, distinctness, and the impact of accessible information on consumer judgments. *Journal of Consumer Psychology, 7,* 1–24.

Steele, C. M. (1988). The psychology of self-affirmation: Sustaining the integrity of the self. In L. Berkowitz (Ed.), *Advances in experimental social psychology* (Vol. 21, pp. 261–302). San Diego, CA: Academic Press.

Steele, C. M., Spencer, S. J., & Lynch, M. (1993). Self-image resilience and dissonance: The role of affirmational resources. *Journal of Personality and Social Psychology, 64,* 885–896.

Sternberg, R. J. (2003). A duplex theory of hate: Development and application to terrorism, massacres, and genocide. *Review of General Psychology, 7,* 299–328.

Stiff, J. (1986). Cognitive processing of persuasive message cues: A meta-analytic review of the effects of supporting information on attitudes. *Communication Monographs, 53,* 75–89.

Stiff, J. B., & Boster, F. J. (1987). Cognitive processing: Additional thoughts and a reply to Petty, Kasmer, Haugtvedt, and Cacioppo. *Communication Monographs, 54,* 250–256.

Sutton, S. R. (1982). Fear-arousing communications: A critical examination of theory and research. In J. R. Eisner (Ed.), *Social psychology and behavioral medicine* (pp. 307–337). New York: John Wiley & Sons.

Symons, C. S., & Johnson, B. T. (1997). The self-reference effect in memory: A meta-analysis. *Psychological Bulletin, 121,* 371–394.

Tanford, S., & Penrod, S. (1984). Social influence model: A formal integration of research on majority and minority influence processes. *Psychological Bulletin, 95,* 189–225.

Terry, D., & Hogg, M. (1996). Group norms and the attitude-behavior relationship: A role for group identification. *Personality and Social Psychology Bulletin, 22,* 776–793.

Tetlock, P. E. (1983). Accountability and complexity of thought. *Journal of Personality and Social Psychology, 45,* 74–83.

Thomas, W. I., & Znaniecki, F. (1918). *The Polish peasant in Europe and America.* Chicago: University of Chicago Press.

Thompson, E. P., Kruglanski, A. W., & Spiegel, S. (2000). Attitudes as knowledge structures and persuasion as a specific case of subjective knowledge acquisition. In G. R. Maio & J. M. Olson (Eds.), *Why we evaluate: Functions of attitudes* (pp. 59–95). Mahwah, NJ: Lawrence Erlbaum Associates.

Thompson, M. M., Zanna, M. P., & Griffin, D. W. (1995). Let's not be indifferent about (attitudinal) ambivalence. In R. E. Petty & J. A. Krosnick (Eds.), *Attitude strength: Antecedents and consequences* (pp. 361–386). Hillsdale, NJ: Lawrence Erlbaum Associates.

Thurstone, L. L. (1928). Attitudes can be measured. *American Journal of Sociology, 33,* 529–554.

Thurstone, L. L. (1931). The measurement of change in social attitude. *Journal of Social Psychology, 2,* 230–235.

Tormala, Z. L., & Petty, R. E. (2002). What doesn't kill me makes me stronger: The effects of resisting persuasion on attitude certainty. *Journal of Personality and Social Psychology, 83,* 1298–1313.

Triandis, H. C. (1977). *Interpersonal behavior.* Monterey, CA: Brooks/Cole.

Triandis, H. C. (1980). Values, attitudes, and interpersonal behavior. In H. E. Howe, Jr. & M. M. Page (Eds.), *Nebraska Symposium on Motivation, 1979* (Vol. 27, pp. 195–259). Lincoln: University of Nebraska Press.

Trost, M. R., Maass, A., & Kenrick, D. T. (1992). Minority influence: Personal relevance biases cognitive processes and reverses private acceptance. *Journal of Experimental Social Psychology, 28*, 234–254.

Tversky, A., & Kahneman, D. (1974). Judgments under uncertainty: Heuristics and biases. *Science, 185*, 1124–1131.

van Schie, E. C. M., Martijn, C., & van der Pligt, J. (1994). Evaluative language, cognitive effort and attitude change. *European Journal of Social Psychology, 24*, 707–712.

Vinokur, A., & Burnstein, E. (1978). Novel argumentation and attitude change: The case of polarization following group discussion. *European Journal of Social Psychology, 8*, 335–348.

Visser, P. S., Krosnick, J. A., & Simmons, J. P. (2003). Distinguishing the cognitive and behavioral consequences of attitude and certainty: A new approach to testing the common-factor hypothesis. *Journal of Experimental Social Psychology, 39*, 118–141.

Vuokko, P. (1997). The determinants of advertising repetition effects. In W. D. Wells (Ed.), *Measuring advertising effectiveness. Advertising and consumer psychology* (pp. 239–260). Mahwah, NJ: Lawrence Erlbaum Associates.

Watts, W. A., & Holt, L. E. (1979). Persistence of opinion change induced under conditions of forewarning and distraction. *Journal of Personality and Social Psychology, 37*, 778–789.

Wegener, D. T., & Petty, R. E. (1994). Mood management across affective states: The hedonic contingency hypothesis. *Journal of Personality and Social Psychology, 66*, 1034–1048.

Wegener, D. T., Petty, R. E., & Smith, S. M. (1995). Positive mood can increase or decrease message scrutiny: The hedonic contingency view of mood and message processing. *Journal of Personality and Social Psychology, 69*, 5–15.

White, P. H., & Harkins, S. G. (1994). Race of source effects in the elaboration likelihood model. *Journal of Personality and Social Psychology, 67*, 790–807.

Wilder, D. A. (1977). Perception of groups, size of opposition, and social influence. *Journal of Experimental Social Psychology, 13*, 253–268.

Wilson, T. D., Lindsey, S., & Schooler, T. Y. (2000). A model of dual attitudes. *Psychological Review, 107*, 101–126.

Wilson, T. D., & Schooler, J. W. (1991). Thinking too much: Introspection can reduce the quality of preferences and decisions. *Journal of Personality and Social Psychology, 60*, 181–192.

Witte, K., & Allen, M. (2000). A meta-analysis of fear appeals: Implications for effective public health campaigns. *Health Education and Behavior, 27*, 591–615.

Wolf, S. (1987). Majority and minority influence: A social impact analysis. In M. P. Zanna, J. M. Olson, & C. P. Herman (Eds.), *Social influence: The Ontario symposium* (Vol. 5, pp. 207–235). Hillsdale, NJ: Lawrence Erlbaum Associates.

Wood, W. (2000). Attitude change: persuasion and social influence. *Annual Review of Psychology, 51*, 539–570.

Wood, W., Kallgren, C. A., & Priesler, R. M. (1985). Access to attitude-relevant information in memory as a determinant of persuasion: The role of message attributes. *Journal of Experimental Social Psychology, 21*, 73–85.

Wood, W., Lundgren, S., Ouellette, J. A., Busceme, S., & Blackstone, T. (1994). Minority influence: A meta-analytic review of social influence processes. *Psychological Bulletin, 115*, 323–345.

Wood, W., & Quinn, J. M. (2003). Forewarned and forearmed? Two meta-analysis syntheses of forewarnings of influence appeals. *Psychological Bulletin, 129*, 119–138.

Wood, W., Rhodes, N., & Biek, M. (1995). Working knowledge and attitude strength: An information-processing analysis. In R. E. Petty and J. A. Krosnick (Eds.), *Attitude strength: Antecedents and consequences* (pp. 283–313). Hillsdale, NJ: Lawrence Erlbaum Associates.

Worchel, S., & Brehm, J. W. (1970). Effect of threats to attitudinal freedom as a function of agreement with a communicator. *Journal of Personality and Social Psychology, 14*, 18–22.

Word, C. O., Zanna, M. P., & Cooper, J. (1974). The nonverbal mediation of self-fulfilling prophecies in interracial interaction. *Journal of Experimental Social Psychology, 10*, 109–120.

Wyer, R. S., Jr. (1974). *Cognitive organization and change: An information-processing approach*. Potomac, MD: Lawrence Erlbaum Associates.

Zanna, M. P. (1994). Message receptivity: A new look at the old problem of open- versus closed-mindedness. In A. A. Mitchell (Ed.), *Advertising exposure, memory, and choice* (pp. 141–162). Hillsdale, NJ: Lawrence Erlbaum Associates.

Zanna, M. P., & Cooper, J. (1974). Dissonance and the pill: An attribution approach to studying the arousal properties of dissonance. *Journal of Personality and Social Psychology, 29*, 703–709.

Zanna, M. P., Higgins, E. T., & Taves, P. A. (1976). Is dissonance phenomenologically aversive? *Journal of Experimental Social Psychology, 12*, 530–538.

Zanna, M. P., & Rempel, J. K. (1988). Attitudes: A new look at an old concept. In D. Bar-Tal & A. W. Kruglanski (Eds.), *The social psychology of knowledge* (pp. 315–334). Cambridge, UK: Cambridge University Press.

Ziegler, R., Diehl, M., & Ruther, A. (2002). Multiple source characteristics and persuasion: Source inconsistency as a determinant of message scrutiny. *Personality and Social Psychology Bulletin, 28*, 496–508.

Zuckerman, M., DePaulo, B. M., & Rosenthal, R. (1981). Verbal and nonverbal communication of deception. In L. Berkowitz (Ed.), *Advances in experimental social psychology* (Vol. 14, pp. 1–59). New York: Academic Press.

Zuckerman, M., & Driver, R. E. (1985). Telling lies: Verbal and nonverbal correlates of deception. In A. W. Siegman & J. S. Feldstein (Eds.), *Multichannel integrations of nonverbal behavior* (pp. 129–147). Hillsdale, NJ: Lawrence Erlbaum Associates.

16

Social Influence in Attitudes and Attitude Change

Radmila Prislin
San Diego State University

Wendy Wood
Duke University

SOCIAL INFLUENCE: THE ROLE OF SOCIAL CONSENSUS IN ATTITUDES AND ATTITUDE CHANGE

"For the individual, his actions and the beliefs guiding them are either an endorsement of his group, and therefore a bond of social unity, or an expression of conflict with it. This conclusion . . . stands in contrast to those formulations that deal with attitudes in individualistic terms, in terms of their persistence or intensity or stereotypy. Attitudes are not only causally connected with group-conditions, they are also part of the mutually shared field. Therefore the investigation of attitudes brings us to the center of the person's social relations and to the heart of the dynamics of group processes."

—Solomon Asch (1952a, p. 577)

In 1935, Theodore Newcomb, a young social psychologist at the newly founded Bennington College for women, assessed the attitudes of the entering class and other students toward a number of social issues. His research findings would hardly surprise anyone familiar with his students: These daughters from economically-privileged families in the 1930s arrived at college endowed not only with their families' means to pay for higher education but also with their families' political conservatism. Undeterred by the obviousness of these results, Newcomb continued his research, assessing the attitudes of each class just before they graduated.

Reasoning that attitudes form and change with social context, Newcomb hypothesized that his students' attitudes might shift with their adjustment to a new social milieu. Indeed, Bennington College provided a much different social environment than the ones his students left behind. The Bennington College faculty subscribed to John Dewey's then-revolutionary ideas about education as experimentation and discovery. The unconventional curriculum rejected many entrenched traditions of academia, and social issues as well as the classics contributed to the educational discourse. Liberal was the College norm. After four years of intense social interaction in this environment, the majority of baccalaureates left not only with their diplomas but also with substantially less conservative attitudes (Newcomb, 1943). Moreover, true to their alma mater's motto that students should *transform not conform*, the Bennington graduates retained these attitudes, espousing a liberal orientation throughout their lives (Alwin, Cohen, & Newcomb, 1991; Newcomb, Koenig, Flacks, & Warwick, 1967).

The Bennington College study is a classic demonstration of how changes in people's social environments, especially the pattern and content of their social interactions, effect changes in social attitudes. The attitude changes were so profound that they were evident in the social networks that students created later in their lives. These networks tended to support the former students' liberal attitudes (Asch, 1952a; Guimond, 1999). In general, the Bennington study articulates the organizing theme of social influence research, which is that social relations create and are created by attitudes. From this perspective, all attitudes are social in the sense that they develop, function, and change in a reciprocal relation with a social context.

In this chapter, we consider the social nature of attitudes. Our focus differs from the other chapters in this book, which instead emphasize intraindividual attitudinal processes in settings that involve only limited social interaction. In social influence paradigms, attitudes typically are studied in relatively rich social settings that implicate interaction with others. When influence is social, people not only are interested in understanding reality—the prominent motive studied in message-based persuasion research, but also are oriented to relate to others and to adopt a favored self-view. People also might be concerned about the consistency of their attitudes with others, and we briefly consider this motive after discussing how people strive to understand, relate, and be themselves in influence settings. In conducting the present review, we were struck by how much people's responses to social influence appear to be goal directed and how closely these goals fit a small set of motives.

A recurring theme throughout the chapter is the ways in which people use information provided by others, especially information from a consensus of others, in order to achieve social and informational goals. Social consensus refers to the agreed-upon judgments, feelings, and actions of a significant group, typically a majority of others. The chapter is structured so that, after reviewing the motives in influence settings that orient people to consider consensus views, we then evaluate the information-processing mechanisms that underlie social influence. Then, as examples of how people respond to consensus, we consider research on group polarization and minority influence. We also consider the dynamics of influence processes, especially the determinants and consequences of changing consensual views within a group. A dynamic account of the give and take that occurs as group members exert influence on each other raises issues of larger-scale societal and cultural factors in social influence. Our discussion of these societal factors concludes with a critical analysis of contemporary research on social influence and its historical roots.

Early Theorizing and Research on Motives for Influence: The Surveillance Paradigm

According to Deutsch and Gerard's (1955) classic theorizing, people agree with others for normative or informational reasons. Normative influence occurs when people conform to the positive expectations of another, who could represent "another person, a group, or one's self" (Deutsch & Gerard, 1955, p. 629). Informational influence involves accepting the information obtained from others as evidence about reality.

To demonstrate these motives, Deutsch and Gerard (1955) adapted Asch's (1952a, 1952b) widely known line-judging paradigm. In this research setting, participants give judgments of the length of lines after hearing the judgments of experimental confederates who have been trained to give an incorrect answer on some trials. Participants have been found to respond to these incorrect judgments by agreeing with the others on about a third of the trials and giving the incorrect judgment themselves. Perhaps because of the simplicity of the judgment task, this study is often interpreted in social psychology textbooks as an illustration of normative influence. What could be simpler than comparing, as participants did in one of the trials, a 7-inch long line, a 9-inch long line, and an 11-inch long line to the 9-inch standard and deciding which of the former three lines matches the standard in length? When performed individually, the task was boringly easy–as indicated by participants' virtually perfectly correct answers in individual judgment settings. However, when performed in the company of experimental confederates who consensually gave incorrect answers, the task became loaded with difficulty. Naïve participants confronted with consensual dissent not only made errors, they took longer to make their decisions and appeared less certain about their answers (Asch, 1952a).

Deutsch and Gerard (1955) cleverly recognized that, with minor variations in procedure, the line-judging paradigm could establish informational as well as normative motives for agreeing. Normative reasons for agreement emerge because participants express their judgments to others who might form positive or negative impressions of them. Informational reasons arise because the task is to identify the correct solution. Deutsch and Gerard demonstrated normative pressures in their finding that participants agreed more with others' judgments when these others were group members in face-to-face interaction than when these others were anonymous individuals judging in private. Also, suggesting the impact of informational pressures, participants agreed with others more when the lines to be judged were displayed only for a few seconds and were removed before anyone gave their judgments than when the lines were displayed throughout the judgment process. Presumably, removing the lines increased participants' informational dependence on others. Thus, Deutsch and Gerard's (1955) study provided important experimental evidence of their dual-motive scheme.

If the popularity of a concept can be taken as an indicator of its value, then the distinction between normative and informational motives is an important one. For the past 50 years, researchers have used this and related distinctions to explain why people are influenced in social settings (see, e.g., effect dependence vs. information dependence, Jones & Gerard, 1967; normative vs. comparative functions of reference groups, Kelly, 1952; promotion of group locomotion to a goal vs. evaluation of social reality, Festinger, 1950). Yet, the specific meaning of these and related constructs has narrowed somewhat over the years–at least when compared with the initially rich theorizing about how group members' normative motives channeled judgments toward uniformity and their informational motives enabled achievement of group goals (Festinger, 1950; Kelley, 1952). That is, normative motives are now sometimes limited to concern with the outcomes provided by others (e.g., social acceptance and rejection). This narrow definition of normative motives excludes self-related aspects of social pressure, especially the motive to align one's attitudes with valued reference groups (Abrams & Hogg, 1990; Turner, 1991).

In addition to narrowing the definition of normative motives, Deutsch and Gerard's dual-motive scheme has been further simplified in some treatments so that each motive is linked to a particular type of attitude change and processing mechanism. The idea that motives are linked to unique attitude outcomes was presaged by Deutsch and Gerard's (1955) use of the label, "conforming," to refer to normatively-based change and "agreeing" to refer to informationally-based change. Social psychology textbooks in particular have promoted a narrow interpretation of normatively-based conformity as a temporary judgment bolstered by limited issue-relevant information in memory. Supposedly, normative influence is evident only in public settings and is not maintained in private settings in which judgments do not have social consequences.[1] In contrast, informationally-based agreement supposedly instigates thoughtful processing of message content and other relevant information and thus yields enduring change in judgments. Such agreement is presumed to be evident when attitude change holds in private and in public settings. Thus, in this simplified interpretation of Deutsch and Gerard's scheme, motives for attitude change can be diagnosed from the continuity of recipients' judgments across public and private settings.

In summary, over the years, convention has narrowed the meanings of informational and normative motives so that normative motives are now equated with concerns about others' surveillance. Furthermore, normative agreement typically is thought to involve minimal thought about the issue in the appeal and endures only as long as others have surveillance over judgments. In contrast, informational agreement supposedly does not depend on surveillance and is thoughtful and enduring. These simplifications of the dual-motive scheme have been widely promoted in undergraduate textbooks in social psychology, although similar ideas also can be found in some otherwise more advanced treatments of social influence.

Empirical findings, however, have posed a strong challenge to the idea that surveillance heightens normative concerns and thus agreement with others. This point was strikingly demonstrated in a meta-analytic synthesis by Bond and Smith (1996) of 97 studies using Asch's (1952a, 1952b) line-judging paradigm. Contrary to Deutsch and Gerard's (1955) often-cited findings of greater agreement among face-to-face group members than anonymous individuals, the aggregated findings across multiple studies revealed comparable levels of agreement in public and private settings. That is, even though others' surveillance in public settings plausibly enhanced normative pressures to agree, the overall amount of attitude change in public was comparable to that obtained in private. The lack of a systematic difference between public and private expressions of judgment in Bond and Smith's review challenges the notion that normatively-based influence is greatest when people are under public scrutiny.

The failure for surveillance to enhance normative pressures and thus influence is perhaps not surprising. At heart, manipulating social pressure through surveillance suggests an oversimplified view of social impact. Allport's (1985) famous definition of social psychology provided a considerably more differentiated view of social impact, in which the effects of others emerge whether their presence is "actual, imagined, or implied" (p. 3). Because others can be present in these various ways in both public and private contexts, others' effects on attitudes should be found in both contexts. In an inventive study that illustrates how social pressure holds across contexts, Baldwin and Holmes (1987) instructed female participants to think about two of their older relatives or two of their campus peers. Later, when the women were given sexually explicit material to read in a supposedly unrelated context, the ones who had visualized their older relatives reported not liking the material as much as those who had visualized their peers. Presumably, each social group was associated with its own set of moral standards, and these standards continued to exert impact on the women's subsequent experiences. Thus, the normative influence of each group was apparent even when participants gave their judgments privately.

Another reason to anticipate few normatively based differences between public and private settings is that the informational consequences of normative motives can endure even when the motives themselves are no longer potent (Hardin & Higgins, 1996; Ruscher & Duval, 1998; Zajonc, 1960). Especially in influence studies that assess participants' attitudes publicly before they assess them privately, people might retrieve the initial, publicly-influenced judgment or they might retrieve the information on which the judgment was based. When earlier judgments and information are retrieved, the effects of social motives transcend contexts, and positions given in public will be maintained in private.

Finally, normative motives might arise from a variety of features of influence contexts in addition to others' surveillance. Following Deutsch and Gerard's (1955) original theorizing, normative influence can originate in personal expectations about how one should respond. The effects of such personal expectations can be seen in research on forewarning of influence appeals (Quinn & Wood, 2004; Wood & Quinn, 2003). In this research, people are told that they will receive a message that challenges their views on a particular issue. In response, people shift their attitudes toward the impending position—even when their attitudes are assessed privately before the appeal is delivered (Wood & Quinn, 2003). By shifting a little bit initially, people can reduce the apparent impact of the appeal when it is delivered and thereby avoid their own gullibility. Given that these preparatory shifts occurred regardless of whether participants expected to indicate their attitudes after the appeal privately or publicly to the source and others, it appears that this particular normative pressure involved a desire not to be gullible rather than a desire not to seem so to others. Apparently, influence is regulated by normative pressures that include comparisons to personal standards as well as to others' reactions. In general, then, normative influence cannot be diagnosed by evaluating whether attitude change occurs in private as opposed to in public.

There is, however, an exception to the rule that normative pressures cannot be diagnosed from public versus private attitude expressions. One specific type of normative motivation—involving a superficial, strategic attempt to impress others, is likely to be associated with surveillance. Strategic attempts to impress others that involve minimal thought are likely to emerge only in public, to be easily forgotten, and to not maintain into private contexts. For example, despite the overall pattern in forewarning research indicating little effect of surveillance, greater warning impact in public than private has been found in a narrowly circumscribed setting—when people expected an immediate discussion on an uninvolving topic with a person who held opposing views (Wood & Quinn, 2003; see also Cialdini, Levy, Herman, & Evenbeck, 1973; Cialdini, Levy, Herman, Kozlowski, & Petty, 1976). Apparently, the immediacy of the interaction and the low importance of the topic momentarily focused people on the benefits to be gained from a relatively neutral position (i.e., one that is defensible and minimally offensive to the partner). Thus, those expecting to share their attitudes with their partner shifted toward moderation. Attitudes given privately were not subject to these strategic concerns.

In summary, normatively motivated agreement is not simply a product of surveillance but also occurs in private settings. Normatively motivated agreement persists across settings because social motives or their informational consequences carry over into private contexts and because normative motives involve the self as well as other people. Yet, one specific aspect of normative pressure can be diagnosed from comparisons between public and private settings. Relatively thoughtless, strategic statements meant only to impress others are made primarily in public, where they are most likely to accomplish their intended goal. These superficial attempts to impress others yield elastic shifts in judgment that "snap back" when the interaction has ended (Cialdini et al., 1973; Cialdini et al., 1976).

Tripartite Analyses of Motives: Being, Relating, and Understanding

The simplified view of normative and informational motives promoted by social psychology textbooks is slowly giving way to more sophisticated analyses of motives in influence settings. These more fine-grained perspectives recognize distinctions among normative motives, specifically between concerns with the self and concerns with relating to others. The result is a trio of motives that differentiate between normative concerns for (a) *being* oneself as a coherent and favorably evaluated entity and (b) *relating* to others in a way that successfully regulates the rewards and punishments they can provide, and informational concern for (c) *understanding* the entity or issue featured in influence appeals (Chaiken, Giner-Sorolla, & Chen, 1996; Cialdini & Trost, 1998; Johnson & Eagly, 1989; Wood, 1999, 2000). Elements of this framework were evident early on in Kelman's (1961, 1965) processes of social influence and in French and Raven's (1959) theorizing about sources of power. Although each of these more fine-grained analyses possesses unique features, at core they all distinguish between aspects of the need to be, the need to relate to others, and the need to understand.

The additional complexity of postulating three motives instead of two is well justified by the resulting empirical and theoretical gains. Empirical evidence clearly indicates that people respond to influence appeals in unique ways to satisfy each of these motives. In a particularly informative study, Lundgren and Prislin (1998, Study 1) experimentally instigated each motive and examined the effects on information processing and attitudes (see also Chen, Shechter, & Chaiken, 1996; Nienhuis, Manstead, & Spears, 2001). Participants in the study expected to discuss an attitude issue with a partner. Some participants initially were sensitized to their relations with others, and were told that the study focused on agreeableness and rapport skills. When these participants were given a choice of material to read, they selected information that was congruent with the view ostensibly held by their partner, their thoughts about this information tended to support their partner's position, and the attitudes they expressed to their partner were relatively congenial with their partner's views. Other participants were initially informed that the study provided an opportunity to defend their own position on the topic. They selected material to read that supported their own view, generated thoughts supportive of their position, and indicated relatively polarized attitudes. Finally, other participants who initially were told that the study concerned accuracy of understanding about issues selected material to read on both sides of the issue (i.e., pro and con), generated thoughts that were relatively balanced in evaluation of both sides, and indicated relatively neutral attitudes. In summary, participants processed the available information so as to meet whatever goal was salient. When focused on establishing rapport, participants favored information congenial to their partner. When focused on defending their judgments, participants bolstered their own views. Finally, when focused on understanding the issue, participants considered a relatively unbiased sample of information.

In addition to demonstrating the unique effects of the trio of motives, Lundgren and Prislin's findings nicely demonstrate that normative change is *not* always temporary and evident only under surveillance. Instead, regardless of motive, the attitudes participants expressed to their partners persisted when they subsequently indicated their judgments privately. Especially impressive is the persistence of attitudes designed to convey an agreeable impression. That is, attitudes directed by the normative motive of conveying a positive impression were no more "elastic" than were attitudes directed by informational motives. This persistence of normatively-based attitudes makes the glaringly obvious point that people are just as willing to devote extensive thought to themselves and their relations with others as they are to informational concerns of determining the truth about an issue. This persistence also might seem to challenge earlier studies of forewarning in which normative concerns yielded primarily temporary judgment shifts (Cialdini et al., 1973; Cialdini et al., 1976; Hass & Mann, 1979). However, as we argued in the prior section of this chapter, the temporary, public attitude shifts sometimes apparent in early research plausibly reflect a fleeting desire to align with others' views. In contrast, the normative pressures in Lundgren and Prislin's experiment were apparently strong enough to yield enduring attitude shifts that were evident in private.[2]

In summary, it appears that each of the goals to understand reality, relate to others, and be oneself can be addressed through careful thought and analysis and can yield attitude change that endures across settings and time (Chen et al., 1996; Lundgren & Prislin, 1998). However, when these goals are less compelling, people are likely to meet them with more efficient strategies, such as the use of heuristic rules (e.g., people like others who agree with them). Independence between motives and modes of processing is a cornerstone of the dual-mode processing models of persuasion (see chapters 12, 14, & 15 in this volume, by Briñol & Petty; Johnson, Maio, & Smith-McLallen; and Wegener & Carlston, respectively). Research on dual-mode models has demonstrated that motives to understand reality can spur a thoughtful, systematic analysis of the content of persuasive appeals that yields enduring attitude change or a more superficial analysis that yields more temporary judgment shifts (see heuristic-systematic model (HSM),

Chaiken, Liberman, & Eagly, 1989; elaboration likelihood model (ELM), Petty & Cacioppo, 1986). In like manner, concerns about the self and concerns about relations with others can be met through effortful or more efficient processing modes.[3]

In keeping with the chapter's focus on the social context of attitude change, we devote the remainder of our discussion to understanding how a basic facet of this context, the opinions held by a consensus of others, affects people's responses to influence appeals. Consensus is an elementary social variable to which the human mind might be especially tuned (Erb & Bohner, 2001). Given that humans are a group-living species, a number of theorists have speculated that alignment with groups and social acceptance had survival value in our evolutionary past (Barchas, 1986; Caporael & Baron, 1997; Moreland, 1987). The importance of social consensus in guiding attitudes is evident in the tendency for people to project their own attitudes (and other attributes) onto others, thereby rendering each individual a member of a phenomenological majority (Krueger & Clement, 1997).

People often learn about consensus through social norms, defined as shared belief systems about what people typically do or what they ideally should do (Cialdini & Trost, 1998; Cialdini, Kallgren, & Reno, 1991). Descriptive norms, which specify typical responses, can inform attitudes by providing "social proof" about what is likely to be effective. Injunctive norms, which inform about what people should or ideally would do, can inform attitudes by indicating the positions that yield a sense of self-worth and that garner social rewards and avoid sanctions (Cialdini & Trost, 1998; Prentice & Miller, 1996: Wood, Christensen, Hebl, & Rothgerber, 1997). The two types of norms do not always correspond. That is, people's usual responses are not necessarily what they ideally would do. However, typical responses can become ideal ones when, for example, they differentiate a valued ingroup from a rival outgroup (Christensen, Rothgerber, Wood, & Matz, in press). People learn about norms through a variety of means of transmission, ranging from direct appeals from groups of others to indirect, implicit activation of normative standards.

We note that several of the other, more individually oriented chapters in the book also consider social norms. In these other chapters, social norms are often represented as individuals' beliefs about others' expectations regarding typical or desired actions. Norms of valued groups or individuals constitute a building block in many contemporary theories of decision-making (see Ajzen & Fishbein, and Wyer & Albarracín, chapters 5 & 7, respectively, this volume). That is, people do not make decisions in a social vacuum. Instead, as Ajzen and Fishbein (chap. 5, this volume) argue, decisions about behavioral intentions are based on normative beliefs in tandem with attitudes and perceptions of control over a behavior. In other attitude-behavior models, normative beliefs combine with spontaneously activated attitudes to guide behavior (Fazio, 1990). Also, as Wyer and Albarracín (chap. 7, this volume) argue, normative factors influence the structure, acquisition, and change of beliefs. For example, people use normative rules of social communication (e.g., telling the truth) to interpret new information (see Grice, 1975). Information that violates normative principles may be reinterpreted (e.g., as irony) so that it conforms to expectations. Thus, by recognizing that social consensus affects individual decisions, other chapters in this volume address the social context of attitudes and attitude change.

Social consensus plays an especially important role in social influence research. As we explain, whether an attitude position is normative in the sense that it is supported by a consensus of others can determine its validity, social consequences, and personal value.

Understanding Reality Through Social Consensus

The views of other people are important in part because they help to structure the cacophony of stimuli to which we are regularly exposed, and thereby help us to operate among those stimuli. In particular, others' attitudes impose structure and make sense out of the world by indicating whether objects are to be evaluated with some degree of favor or disfavor (Eagly & Chaiken, 1993).

The helpful role of attitudes in structuring the world was recognized in early theorizing (Allport, 1935; James, 1890)[4] and later formalized as attitudes' knowledge function (Katz, 1960) and object appraisal function (Smith, Bruner, & White, 1956). In these early approaches, knowing was one of several important functions an attitude could serve. Some researchers have argued that knowing is *the* central function of attitudes, given that the primary purpose of most attitudes is to understand and orient to the world (Fazio, 1986; Shavitt, 1990; Zanna & Rempel, 1988). Without attitudes, every object and situation, however frequently encountered, would require evaluation anew, making us all lead characters in a perpetual "Groundhog Day" movie.

Attitudes as knowledge can effectively guide people and facilitate their interactions with the environment to the extent that the knowledge is relevant and valid. Social consensus is an important indicator of the apparent validity of information (Asch, 1952a; Dewey, 1922/1930; Festinger, 1954; Sherif, 1936). Judgments acquire truth value through being shared with others (Hardin & Higgins, 1996). As Turner and Oakes (1997) argued, consensual judgments "are rationally more likely to reflect a deeper truth about the world, not because agreement always indicates accuracy, but because they have emerged from, and survived, processes of discussion, argument, and collective testing" (p. 369).

All social consensus, however, is not equivalent in terms of truth value. The positions held by disliked groups or ones with limited ability aren't likely to seem especially valid. Thus, people seeking to understand the correct position to take on an issue are likely to reject the positions of derogated groups (Wood, Pool, Leck, & Purvis, 1996). People who are seen as similar or slightly better (e.g., more competent at some task) are most likely to appear to provide valued information (Festinger, 1954). Also, consensus is likely to have more impact when it represents the positions of greater numbers of people (Darke et al., 1998). That is, people who are motivated to understand an issue appear to be sensitive to the law-of-large-numbers, and they tend to be influenced more by the consensus positions of larger than smaller groups. Furthermore, consensus seems to be more significant for some issues than for others, presumably because ingroup consensus implies subjective validity more strongly for some issues than for others. For example, majority consensus has greater impact on judgments of personal preference than judgments of objective stimuli, presumably because consensus is especially informative about preferences likely to be shared with similar others (Crano & Hannula-Bral, 1994; Wood et al., 1994).

In addition, the way that social consensus develops can affect its apparent validity. Consensus that is established through convergence of independent views and through validation by an individual's own, private cognitive processing should be most effective at establishing the truth about an issue (Mackie & Skelly, 1994; Wilder, 1977). In Asch's (1952a) words, "Consensus is valid only to the extent to which each individual asserts his own relation to facts and retains his individuality... the meaning of consensus collapses when individuals act like mirrors that reflect each other" (pp. 494–495). Consensus therefore conveys validity when it represents agreement among thinking rather than yielding individuals.

Muzafer Sherif's (1935, 1936) pioneering research on norm formation demonstrates how the apparent truth about the environment can emerge as people exchange their independent views. Sherif studied consensus development with a perceptual illusion called the autokinetic effect. This phenomenon has been long known to astronomers who find that, when fixating on a bright stationary star in the dark sky, the star appears to move. Anecdotal evidence that people agree about a star's movement comes from casual observers of the evening sky who lift their heads to admire a star and see—a UFO! The autokinetic effect is easy to create in laboratory. All it requires is a completely dark room and a pinpoint of light. When judging the movement of the light, individual participants in Sherif's research initially gave a range of estimates. When subsequently giving estimates in small groups, each participant gradually converged with the rest of their group toward a consensual estimate of the movement.

Sherif's research with the autokinetic effect demonstrates that, when faced with a new and uncertain task, the result was not chaos. Instead, people imposed structure and made sense out of the situation by developing a common norm. The norm emerged gradually through the exchange of individual judgments as each participant offered his seemingly independent observations of an identical situation. Sherif concluded that this norm formation reflected a rational, accuracy-motivated assessment of the situation (Hood & Sherif, 1962). Interestingly, this consensual response norm endured in new settings, including when participants joined a new group and when they were retested individually–even as much as a year after the initial exposure to others' judgments (Hood & Sherif, 1962; Rohner, Baron, Hoffman, & Swander, 1954).

The idea that people agree in order to understand reality also can account for some of the influence pressure in Asch's (1952a, 1952b) line-judging experiments that we mentioned earlier in our discussion of normative and informational influence. As we noted, this paradigm likely established a variety of reasons for agreeing. Participants' understanding was presumably challenged when other group members consensually gave an obviously incorrect estimate of line length. This challenge turned Asch's laboratory into "Rashomon," with participants trying as desperately as viewers of Kurosawa's movie to understand whose version of reality was correct.

Support for the idea that participants in Asch's research were motivated to understand the task comes from evidence that others' dissent was discounted when it could be attributed to external, situation-irrelevant factors (Ross, Bierbrauer, & Hoffman, 1976). When participants believed that others were being rewarded for making certain judgments, they could explain others' seemingly erroneous answers, and this external attribution stripped away the information value from consensus. Then participants remained independent in their judgments of line length. Although Ross et al. (1976) maintained that others' apparent motives compromised the information value of their judgments, we believe that knowledge of others' motives also can affect normative pressures. If others' responses were tailored to obtain rewards available only to them, then participants would not expect social rejection for disagreeing. In general, attributing others' judgments to external factors plausibly alleviates both informational and social pressures to conform.

Additional evidence that social consensus has information value comes from research that increased motives to understand in an Asch-type line-judging task by providing monetary and psychological incentives for correct answers (Baron, Vandello, & Brunsman, 1996). In this research, strengthening motives for accuracy increased agreement with others' judgments about ambiguous stimuli. In contrast, incentives for accuracy decreased the impact of others' judgments when truth was self-evident because the stimuli were unambiguous. With easy to judge stimuli, participants relied more on their own assessments. It is interesting that this research also suggested that social motives are a component of agreement in this setting, given that accuracy incentives never completely eliminated the impact of others' judgments on easy stimuli.

In summary, research from a variety of influence paradigms suggests that people adopt consensual views in order to understand reality. When so motivated, people are likely to focus on consensus that promises to maximize understanding and to provide the most objective, meaningful interpretation of the attitude issue. As we explain in the next section, social consensus also provides a guide to address social goals in influence settings.

Relating to Others and Social Consensus

Consensual attitudes derive their power in part from people's need to belong and to form relationships with others. The need to relate can take a variety of forms (Bowlby, 1973;

Brewer, 1991; Fromm, 1955; Maslow, 1968). In economic models of human behavior (e.g., social exchange theory, Homans, 1974; Thibaut & Kelley, 1959), people are motivated to form relationships with others in order to achieve goals that they could not accomplish as individuals. An alternative view is that people are intrinsically social creatures and relationships are rewarding in themselves (Baumeister & Leary, 1995). These opposing conceptualizations echo a philosophical discourse on the nature of the human society that underlies relationships. One perspective emphasizes the instrumentality of human relationships. For example, Thomas Hobbes (1651/1957) argued that a social contract is important to protect people from each other. In the opposing view, illustrated by the perspective of Jean-Jacques Rousseau (1762/1978), sociality is inherently rewarding as a vehicle for people to express their innate sympathy for one another.

Reflecting the instrumentality idea, one of the functions of attitudes is to obtain valued rewards and avoid punishments (Katz, 1960). From this perspective, consensus guides attitudinal responses not because of concerns about relationships with others but rather because of concerns about the benefits others can provide. Contrasting with this "relate-for-benefit" conceptualization is the idea of an inherent motivation to relate to others because of the intrinsic value of relationships. This motive is aligned with the social adjustment function of attitudes (Smith et al., 1956). Thus, benefits from relating to others by endorsing consensual views might come from tangible and intangible rewards that others control or from the value of the relationship per se. Of course, these functions need not be mutually exclusive—others can provide material benefits along with social acceptance (see Herek, 1986; Shavitt, 1990).

Classic theories of power and influence also addressed these two relational motives for agreeing with others (French & Raven, 1959; Kelman, 1965).[5] On the one hand, people go along with others in order to obtain rewards and avoid punishments that others control. These incentives are reflected in sources' *reward and coercion power* (French & Raven, 1959) and in their capacity to elicit *compliance* (Kelman, 1965). Compliant attitudinal responses supposedly emerge under a highly circumscribed set of conditions that involve surveillance by the controlling source. In this view, only with surveillance do people receive rewards and avoid punishments for agreeing. On the other hand, people go along with others in order to establish a relationship with them or to identify with them.[6] Relationship incentives are reflected in sources' *referent power* (French & Raven, 1959) and in their capacity to elicit *identification* (Kelman, 1965). Identifying attitude responses supposedly do not depend on surveillance— they are thought to hold as long as the referent other is salient and valued. Kelman (1965) provided some preliminary support for the idea that compliance, but not identification, requires surveillance of the source. Thus, instrumentally motivated attitude change in this paradigm emerged in superficial, strategic shifts when under others' surveillance. However, in general, persistent attitudes are not the province of any particular motive for change (see Chen et al., 1996; Lundgren & Prislin, 1998).

Striking evidence of the instrumental outcomes that regulate attitudes was provided by Schachter's (1951) pioneering study on opinion deviance. In this research, groups of five to seven naïve participants and three confederates discussed an opinion topic. One confederate, the "mode," consistently agreed with the modal group position. Another confederate, the "slider," shifted from an initial extreme opposition to the modal position. The final confederate in each group, the "deviate," consistently advocated an extremely unpopular position. After enduring intense social pressure, the unyielding deviate was rejected by the group of naïve participants, whereas the mode and the slider were rewarded with similar levels of group acceptance. Subsequent research provided ample evidence that ingroup members who opposed group consensus, especially on group-defining issues, are liked less than those who supported consensual positions (Marques, Abrams, & Serodio, 2001; see Levine, 1989, for a review). In general, attitudinal dissent can be met with group disapproval ranging from disliking to derogation to eventual rejection from the group (see Levine & Moreland, 2002, for a review; also Williams, 2001, for research on ostracism).

Impression Motivation.   The idea that influence can be motivated by fear of others' rejection and desire for others' approval is central to research on impression motives (Metts & Grohskopf, 2003; Schlenker, 2003). Impression-motivated recipients are oriented to consider the social consequences of their attitudes. They desire to form or maintain a particular relationship with the source of influence or others who might have surveillance over their responses, and they perceive that their attitudes are instrumental for achieving this goal (Chen et al., 1996; Fiske, Lin, & Neuberg, 1999). The process of impression construction involves choosing the kind of impression to create and finding the most efficient way of creating it (Leary & Kowalski, 1990). Thus, the hallmark of impression motivation is strategic control of attitudinal responses to convey certain impressions to others. Although impression motives are strategic, they are not necessarily intentional and may be activated outside of awareness. Especially when the desired impression can be conveyed with already existing attitudes, people generate strategic responses relatively effortlessly without conscious monitoring (see Pontari & Schlenker, 2000). However, greater deliberation might be required to construct impressions around attitudes that are inconsistent with those in people's existing repertoires.

Often the best response to promote a favorable impression is to agree with others. Greater liking for those who agree than disagree has been demonstrated repeatedly in psychological research (Pilkington & Lydon, 1997; Shaikh & Kanekar, 1994). Additional benefits to agreement emerge with the reciprocity norm. When applied to influence, this norm suggests that people will yield to the influence attempts of others who previously yielded to them. The power of this dictum was evident in a series of studies showing that people changed their attitudes more to align with those who had agreed with them in the past (Cialdini, Green, & Rusch, 1992). Moreover, the tendency to reciprocate social influence in this research appeared to be so fundamental that it was unaffected by idiosyncratic characteristics of the source, the quality of arguments used in the persuasive appeal, or the relevance to the target of the topic under consideration. This process of attitude adjustment through reciprocal yielding is particularly likely in the context of negotiation of social conflict (Pruitt & Carnevale, 1993).

Agreeing with others, however, is not always the best strategy to promote a favorable impression. When uniqueness or independence rather than conformity is the desired impression, attitudes are moved strategically to the appropriate position, even if these reported attitudes differ from those held privately (Schlenker & Weingold, 1990). For example, men have been found to disagree publicly with fellow members of small discussion groups to a greater extent than do women—and to a greater extent than do men who state their attitudes privately (Eagly, Wood, & Fishbaugh, 1981). Presumably, men challenged group consensus in this research in order to establish their independence and their unique stance and potentially to exert influence over others. Thus, impression motives can orient people to disagree with others as well as to agree.

In summary, consensual views can be important in promoting desired relations with others. Although it will often be the case that people agree with others in order to attain the tangible and affective rewards they can provide, sometimes disagreement or independence from consensus positions can best meet people's relational needs.

Being Oneself and Social Consensus

The self is a powerful motivator of attitudes and can drive people's responses to social consensus. People tend to respond defensively to information that doesn't "fit" with their important attitudes and self-views and to react more favorably to information that fits. This selectivity in responding is especially likely with attitudes and beliefs that are closely tied to the self in the sense that they reference important values, implicate gender, religion, race, and other social identities, and involve material self-interests (Chaiken et al., 1996). Self-related motives are represented in functional theories in terms of Katz's (1960) *ego-defensive* function, in which attitudes are formed, held, and changed to preserve existing self-views (see also Smith, Bruner, & White's, 1956, externalizing function). They also are represented in Katz's *value-expressive* function, in which attitudes are oriented to express personal values and core aspects of the self-concept.

What determines whether social consensus and other information fits with important aspects of the self? In some self-theories, "fit" represents consistency with existing self-defining attitudes and other self-views. That is, people strive to hold attitudes that yield a coherent self-view and reduce uncertainty about the world (Heider, 1958; Hogg, 2000; Swann, 1990). The coherence motive is a conservative orientation to maintain and protect existing self-identities and self-views. In other perspectives, "fit" represents self-enhancement. People strive to hold attitudes that promote a favorable self-evaluation and deflect an unfavorable one (Sedikides & Strube, 1997; Tajfel, 1978; Tesser, 2000). With this motivation, people are oriented to maximize the pleasure and minimize the pain of self-evaluation (see also, Brewer's, 1991, needs for assimilation and differentiation).

Motives for coherence and enhancement will often coincide. For example, people with high self-esteem accomplish both goals when a consensus of valued others support their cherished attitudes and self-views. However, for people with lower self-worth, consensual support can generate motivational conflict by enhancing the self but challenging existing negative self-views. The potential to separate these motives has spurred researchers to identify which motive reigns supreme. Despite the efforts of important programs of research, no clear answer has emerged. The research evidence favoring coherence (Swann, 1990; Swann, Rentfrow, & Guinn, 2002) has been criticized for minimizing people's needs to self-enhance by, for example, addressing peripheral aspects of the self-concept and relying on generic assessments of positive or negative self-views instead of participants' own beliefs about what is self-enhancing (see critique by Sedikides & Green, 2004). Yet, research evidence favoring self-enhancement can be faulted for minimizing coherence pressures by including few participants with truly negative self-views whose coherence needs might lead them to self-deprecate instead of enhance (Sedikides & Green, 2004). Thus, no clear conclusion has emerged about the supremacy of one self-motive over another.

In social influence research, the question of whether attitudes are guided by self-coherence versus self-enhancement motives has surfaced in research on intergroup behavior and group influence. Self-enhancement is a key motive in the classic perspective of social identity theory (Tajfel, 1978, 1982; Tajfel & Turner, 1979). In this approach, people meet their needs for a positive identity by comparing their attitudes and other attributes with those held by other individuals or by groups. People can achieve a positive social identity by aligning themselves with positively valued ingroups or social categories and differentiating themselves from negatively valued outgroups or social categories. Thus, people with liberal political attitudes can identify with progressive organizations and feel good about their identity by comparing their own group's positions with those of more conservative, establishment-oriented groups. From a social identity view, then, people identify with groups and adopt group attitudes to the extent that doing so meets their needs for a positive self-concept.

Although research has provided only limited support for the broad claim that self-esteem generally motivates group identification (Hogg, 2001; Rubin & Hewstone, 1998), self-evaluative concerns appear to underlie identification with and influence of important social reference groups. In particular, positions of valued social groups on issues relevant to the group identity can threaten people's sense of self-worth and motivate them to change their attitudes to reduce the threat. In a demonstration of this effect, Pool, Wood, and Leck (1998) informed some participants that a valued majority group (e.g., residents of their state) held attitudes on a relevant issue (e.g., state politics) that differed from participants' own. Other participants learned that a derogated minority group (e.g., a gay and lesbian student organization) held attitudes on an issue (e.g., individual freedom of expression) that were similar to participants' own. Participants who defined themselves as similar to the majority or dissimilar from the minority showed reduced self-esteem on learning the group's position. In contrast, participants who did not define themselves in terms of the group identity were unaffected by the group view. Furthermore, these decreases in self-esteem were alleviated when participants were able to shift their attitudes to align with the valued majority or move away from the derogated minority. Thus, people were influenced by positively- or negatively-evaluated reference groups in ways that promoted a favorable self-view.

Group influence also can originate in people's needs to hold attitudes consistent with their social identities. According to Turner's (1982, 1991) idea of *referent informational influence*, people categorize themselves as group members in part to maximize their own positive distinctiveness, and then they adopt in-group positions in order to reduce subjective uncertainty. That is, agreement with others categorized as similar to the self enhances people's subjective certainty and conveys coherence by suggesting that the shared attitudes reflect external reality and the objective truth of the issue. Disagreement from similarly categorized others yields subjective uncertainty and motivates people to address the discrepancy through, for example, mutual social influence or attributional reasoning to explain the disagreement.

Empirical support for the idea that people are motivated by uncertainty to accept ingroup influence comes from research demonstrating that agreement from others on a judgment task increases people's confidence in their own judgments, whereas disagreement decreases their confidence (McGarty, Turner, Oakes, & Haslam, 1993).[7] By locating the determinants of attitude change primarily in people's construction of group identity and only secondarily in their understanding of attitude issues, self-categorization approaches emphasize normative over informational reasons for agreement. That is, people supposedly adopt the positions of ingroups independent of their understanding of how or why the positions are correct.

Some support for the self-categorization idea that influence stems from construction of group identity is provided by findings that influence varies with the perceived group membership. For example, Haslam, Oakes, McGarty, Turner, and Onorato (1995) reported that, when group membership was salient, outgroup members holding extreme attitudes not only were considered more representative (prototypic) of the outgroup than were moderate outgroup members, but also generated less agreement than moderate outgroup members. Furthermore, when group membership was less salient, extreme and moderate outgroup members were viewed more similarly, and they both generated modest levels of agreement. Thus, influence varied with the apparent position of the source group.

Another source of evidence that has been cited in support of self-categorization predictions is the finding that ingroup influence does not depend on recipients learning the content of the influence appeal (see McGarty, Haslam, Hutchinson, & Turner, 1994; presented also in Haslam, McGarty, & Turner, 1996). Haslam et al. (1996) argued that such learning can occur independently of influence, as people try to understand the group view in order to be an effective group member. That is, as part of categorizing self as a group member, people change their attitudes to align with or differentiate from valued groups, and then they adopt the message reasoning. However, empirical tests do not support the idea that ingroup influence necessarily emerges through a self-categorization process that is separate from thought about the appeal or use of heuristic cues (see van Knippenberg, 1999). For example, research that has used regression designs to test whether the impact of group identity on attitudes is mediated through thought about the appeal has found evidence of such mediation when the identity of the source group is relevant to recipients' own self-definitions (Wood et al., 1996) and when the issue in the appeal is relevant to recipients' membership groups (Mackie, Worth, & Asuncion, 1990). In general, these mediation analyses indicate that the social identity of important reference groups motivates careful scrutiny of the group position and, ultimately, adoption or rejection of the group views.

In summary, the consensus opinions of important reference groups can be influential as people strive to meet self-enhancement and self-coherence goals. These motives generate influence through careful scrutiny of reference group positions as well as through less thoughtful reactions involving self-categorization processes and heuristic rules (van Knippenberg, 1999). The next challenge for theories of group influence will be to identify the circumstances under which enhancement versus coherence motives direct social influence outcomes.

Consistency Motives in Social Influence

The careful reader will notice that our trimotive scheme involves a more limited set of motives than proposed in the other chapters in this book (see Briñol & Petty, chap. 14, this volume; Wyer & Albarracín, chap. 7, this volume). Unlike these other chapters, we have not separated the motive to achieve and maintain cognitive consistency from the three motives we consider. Yet, the idea that people seek to establish and maintain a psychologically consistent world-view has spurred considerable attitude research. The majority of this work builds on the perspective of cognitive dissonance theory (see Harmon-Jones & Mills, 1999; Olson & Stone, chap. 6, this volume).

Cognitive dissonance is thought to be a negative tension state similar to hunger that occurs when one cognition (i.e., belief, attitude, behavior) does not follow from another (Festinger, 1957). Thus, people experience dissonance when, for example, their actions do not reflect their attitudes. Although researchers have focused primarily on such intrapersonal sources of cognitive consistency, Festinger (1957) argued that dissonance also arises from interpersonal factors, especially disagreement from others in a group. Specifically, "the open expression of disagreement in a group leads to the existence of cognitive dissonance in the members. The knowledge that some other person, generally like oneself, holds one opinion is dissonant with holding a contrary opinion" (Festinger, 1957, pp. 261–262). As Cooper and Stone (2000) point out, the first published study on dissonance addressed the reactions of members of a doomsday group when their group's predictions of the apocalypse failed (Festinger, Riecken, & Schachter, 1956).

Evidence that group disagreement generates dissonance was provided in a series of studies by Matz and Wood (in press). In this research, participants in a discussion group reported heightened discomfort on a self-report measure of dissonance when other group members supposedly held opposing positions. In addition, this dissonance caused by group disagreement functioned much like the dissonance that arises from inconsistency in individual cognitions (see Olson & Stone, chap. 6, this volume). That is, participants reported minimal dissonance discomfort when they had little choice about what position to take and the experimenter assigned them to a position that opposed others in the group. Dissonance also was reduced when participants were given the opportunity to "self-affirm" and to reduce the threat to their self-concept by focusing on positive self-attributes. In addition, the research indicated that the motive to establish and maintain consistency in groups guides influence processes in social interaction. Participants' discomfort in disagreeing groups was alleviated when they were able to resolve the inconsistency by changing their own attitudes to align with the rest of their group, by influencing others to agree with them, or by joining a new, more attitudinally-congenial group.

On the one hand, Matz and Wood's research could suggest that it is appropriate to treat consistency as a "master" motive guiding social influence, much like the motives to understand, to relate to others, and to be oneself. The idea that people are purely motivated to achieve and maintain cognitive consistency would be congenial with Festinger's (1957) initial theorizing about cognitive dissonance. On the other hand, cognitive inconsistency could be motivating for other reasons, perhaps because it challenges understanding, relating, or being oneself. For example, people might become concerned about maintaining a consistent understanding of the world when their attitudes are opposed by a consensus of others who presumably hold valid positions. This inconsistency would then be motivating to the extent that people wished to understand the issue. In this latter interpretation, the need for a coherent, consistent world-view arises from other motives. Congenial with this latter view, a number of consistency theories have proposed reasons why dissonant experiences such as disagreement from others generate inconsistency, including that they are associated with social sanctions, threaten judgment validity, and threaten a favored self-view (see Harmon-Jones & Mills, 1999; Olson & Stone, chap. 6, this volume).

Regardless of whether consistency motives are considered to be independent of the three motives we cover in this chapter, cognitive dissonance provides useful insight into social influence processes. Cognitive dissonance theory exemplifies the "hot" motivational mechanisms that underlie much influence. It also provides a common framework to encompass the seemingly disparate strategies that people use to meet their attitudinal goals, including influencing others and joining attitudinally-congenial groups. However, compared with other influence theories we consider in this chapter, consistency theories have not addressed to any great extent the informational mechanisms through which influence occurs. In the next section of the chapter, we discuss these various mechanisms in more detail.

Motives Direct Processing of Consensual Views

People can process information about social consensus in a variety of ways. Serious cognitive weight lifting to evaluate the merits of consensual views can be spurred by any of the motives that we discussed so far. In general, people who are highly motivated to understand, to relate to others, or to be themselves will have a heightened need to be confident about their attitudes (Chaiken et al., 1989). To achieve sufficient confidence, people are likely to carefully scrutinize information relevant to their goals (Albarracín, 2002; Chen et al., 1996; Lundgren & Prislin, 1998), and they may fail to respond evaluatively to information unrelated to these goals (Brendl, Markman, & Messner, 2003). Thus, people keenly concerned about understanding should carefully evaluate the merits of consensus positions along with other information that appears to be objectively valid. People concerned about relating to others or conveying a particular impression should carefully consider consensus views along with other information about what is socially normative and desirable. People oriented to ensuring a favorable or coherent self-view should carefully consider social consensus along with other information that is relevant to their desired self-views.

Investigations of influence processing have not been tailored to the variety of goals in influence settings but instead have examined primarily scrutiny of message-relevant information. Such measures are useful in studies of message-based persuasion, given that recipients' primary goal in this setting is understanding of an issue and that this goal can be met through evaluation of message content. However, motives to relate to others and to be oneself sensitize people to aspects of influence settings in addition to message content. Thus, measures of message processing may not be successful at capturing recipients' thinking when it is instigated by motives other than understanding.

In one of the few exceptions to the predominant focus on message-based processing, Chen et al. (1996, Study 2) examined impression-relevant thinking with respect to social influence. Impression concerns were made salient for some participants in this research by having them imagine themselves in contexts that would require social sensitivity. Subsequently, when expecting to discuss an issue with a partner, participants primed in this way with impression goals expressed marginally more thoughts about their partner and the impending discussion than did participants with accuracy goals (i.e., who had been primed with accuracy motives by imagining themselves thinking and behaving objectively). Thus, measures of thought about interpersonal issues can capture the interpersonal processing that emerges with impression goals. In addition, even though Chen et al. found that accuracy versus impression goals had little effect on how extensively participants thought about the message topic, the direction of their thought varied with specific interpersonal goals. Impression-motivated participants with partners favorable to the issue expressed a predominance of favorable thoughts to the issue and those with unfavorable partners expressed more unfavorable issue thoughts. In general, measures of thinking in influence paradigms could be broadened to capture more effectively the variety of information relevant to participants' goals.

Measures in social influence paradigms also could be broadened to address the specific kinds of thinking found in complex social settings. Asch (1940) argued early on that the primary process in influence is not change in attitudes toward an object but rather change in the definition and meaning of the object. Specifically, social consensus can affect people's interpretation or framing of an issue. For example, in one of Asch's (1940) experiments, participants exposed to others' favorable evaluations of the attitude object, "politicians," apparently assumed that this word referred to statesmen. Presumably because of this interpretation, participants reported relatively favorable views toward politicians themselves. In contrast, participants exposed to others' unfavorable judgments apparently inferred that "politician" referred to the "more offensive forms" of the political animal, and they expressed relatively negative evaluations. Apparently, the positions "imputed to congenial groups produced changes in the meaning of the objects of judgment" (Asch, 1940, p. 462). Although such motivated interpretations are consistent with a number of theoretical perspectives (e.g., Tajfel's, 1982, social identity theory), few studies have directly assessed the interpretations that mediate influence.

Allen and Wilder (1980) provided direct evidence for Asch's change-of-meaning hypothesis through detailed measures of people's construal of attitude issues in conformity contexts. These researchers documented a multistage process of meaning change, in which (a) recipients modify their interpretation of an issue in light of the position advocated by a majority group; (b) this new interpretation makes the source's position seem reasonable and acceptable; and (c) recipients then agree with their (new) interpretation of the advocated position. These changes also can occur in different orders. For example, subjective changes in meaning have been found to emerge following recipients' decisions to conform, presumably to justify that conformity (Buehler & Griffin, 1994; Griffin & Buehler, 1993).

Changes in meaning in social influence settings potentially emerge as people try to understand, relate to others, and be themselves. Wood et al. (1996) demonstrated that meaning construals can be spurred by self-evaluative motives, especially the desire to align with valued reference groups and differentiate from devalued ones. That is, college students who defined themselves as different from the Ku Klux Klan, upon learning that their attitudes on an issue of discrimination coincided with Klan positions, reinterpreted the issue so that they could shift away from the group's position. Students whose self-definition was not tied to the Klan did not undertake this reinterpretation. Because the changed meaning occurred only when participants were appropriately cued by the questionnaire and only when they were highly motivated to differentiate from the Klan, this kind of reinterpretation appears to require considerable capacity and motivation (Wood et al., 1996). Additional research might profitably examine the effects of understanding and being motives on interpretations of influence appeals.

Despite the evidence that people sometimes closely examine the merits of others' attitudes and interpret them in motivated ways, they do not always do so. When motives are not especially powerful, recipients will not have a strong desire to be confident in the attitudes that they are about to express to satisfy those motives (Chaiken et al., 1989). As a result, they might not travel the cognitive highway exploring positions to determine the best one to take but instead stop at whatever position is indicated by various low-effort processes. For example, they might use a simple, motive-relevant heuristic rule-of-thumb. When motivated by a need to understand, people might reason, "consensus is correct." When motivated by relationships, people might think, "go along to get along." When motivated by self-concerns, they might decide, "safety in numbers." Using these heuristics, people can meet their goals by accepting or rejecting others' positions in a relatively effortless manner. In a demonstration of this process, participants in Maheswaran and Chaiken's (1991) study who were not highly motivated to consider a consumer product readily accepted a consensually supported evaluation of the product. In contrast, highly motivated participants who could not reach their desired judgmental confidence by relying solely on consensual information engaged in a more elaborate processing of information about the product.

Although the present chapter considers how people use consensus information to meet their processing goals, consensus is similar to other features of the persuasion context in that it can serve a variety of functions (Petty & Wegener, 1998). In particular, when the position taken by a consensus of others is unexpected, the surprise can itself instigate information processing (Baker & Petty, 1994). That is, when a majority of others advocate an unpopular position that is not held by recipients of the appeal, social consensus violates recipients' expectancies. Such positions can spur a thoughtful, systematic analysis of the relevant issue or object to assess the validity of the discrepant views. In a mirror image of this effect, minority sources can engender surprise and thoughtful message processing when they advocate popular positions that recipients also endorse (Baker & Petty, 1994; De Vries, De Dreu, Gordijn, & Schuurman, 1996). In summary, when people are motivated to understand, their information processing will likely address the validity of consensual information. When they are motivated to belong, information processing will likely address the implications for social relations. Finally, when they are motivated to be themselves, processing will likely address implications for the desired self-view. When these various motives for influence are strong, they instigate thorough, careful processing of the relevant information, as evident in cognitive responses and subjective construals. Less intense desires will likely be met through more efficient processing strategies, including following heuristic rules.

Group Polarization

The tendency for social consensus to engender influence gives credence to John Stuart Mill's (1859/1956) admonition to fear a "tyranny of the majority" (p. 7). We have argued that a pattern of seeming tyranny can arise for multiple reasons, as people strive to understand, relate to others, and be themselves. For these various reasons, people may adopt others' attitudes and join group consensus. Interestingly, when people share their judgments with like-minded others, not only does social consensus become stronger in number but also it changes to "radicalize" itself (Moscovici & Zavalloni, 1969), so that judgments become more polarized and consensus more extreme (Isenberg, 1986; Stoner's study, as cited in Marguis, 1960).

There are several reasons why people's attitudes polarize during discussion with others who agree with them. In one account, often referred to as *persuasive arguments* theory, people who agree have an evaluatively consistent set of arguments to share on the judgment topic (Burnstein & Vinokur, 1977; Hinsz & Davis, 1984). If they discuss the issue and exchange arguments, each individual is likely to learn novel reasons for holding the consensus view, and each individual's attitude then becomes more extreme. Additionally contributing to polarization, discussion gives each person an opportunity to repeat their own views, and simple repetition

688   PRISLIN AND WOOD

can shift people's judgments to be more extreme (Brauer, Judd, & Gliner, 1995). The result of this information sharing is not just polarization in individual positions but also in the overall position that characterizes a discussion group.

Another reason for polarization is that people try to achieve favorable self-views as they exchange opinions with others. According to this normative, *social comparison* explanation for group polarization, people self-enhance by espousing judgments that are more extreme than the consensual view. In so doing, they polarize the consensual position (Goethals & Zanna, 1979; Myers & Lamm, 1976). As Brown (1974) opined, "to be virtuous . . . is to be different from the mean—in the right direction and to the right degree" (p. 469).

Hundreds of studies over several decades have produced impressive evidence in support of persuasive arguments and social comparison explanations but no critical experimental test that would lead an impartial reader to prefer one over the other (see Isenberg, 1986). Failure to find decisive evidence supporting one explanation over another reflects the multifaceted nature of the motives behind group polarization. In spite of solid evidence for the conceptual independence of argument exchange and comparison processes, they appear to work in tandem in producing group polarization (Isenberg, 1986; Kaplan & Miller, 1987). As demonstrated in Asch's (1952a, 1952b) early conformity studies, people are influenced by others' judgments in group contexts because these judgments help them not only to understand reality but also to meet normative needs, such as ensuring a favorable self-view. In summary, the motivational bases of group polarization appear to be a complex combination of understanding issues via exchange of persuasive arguments and achievement of a favorable self-view via social comparison.

Minority Influence

Despite the apparent power of social consensus, history provides many examples of opinion minorities that wielded considerable influence, including the civil rights movement and the women's movement in the United States. These groups eventually swayed majority views so that many of their central tenets became commonplace, mainstream positions.

The idea that opinion minorities have a uniquely powerful impact formed the core of Moscovici's (1980, 1985) theory of minority influence. In his view, minorities who consistently and unanimously express their dissenting views instigate a *validation* process in which recipients experience the minority position as a challenge to their understanding of the issue and respond by carefully reevaluating their own views. The result is presumed to be enduring, private change. However, because of the negative social consequences of aligning the self with a deviant minority, attitude change might not be apparent on the exact issue in the appeal but instead emerge on related issues. In contrast, opposition from a majority is thought to create social conflict and to instigate a *conversion* process in which people are oriented to go along in order to belong. As a result, recipients supposedly respond to majority appeals with immediate, public yielding on the issue under consideration.

The innovative postulates of minority influence theory had an invigorating effect on the field of social influence (De Vries & De Dreu, 2001; Kruglanski & Mackie, 1990; Maas, West, & Cialdini, 1987; Mugny & Perez, 1991), but they received only partial support in empirical tests. A meta-analytic synthesis by Wood et al. (1994) evaluated studies in which minority sources attempted to influence recipients holding majority, consensual positions. Many of these studies compared minority impact with that of a majority source, and the modal finding was greater influence of majorities on both public and private measures of agreement. In addition, minority sources did not exert greater impact in private than in public. In fact, the characteristic effect of minorities evident in the review was to diminish influence: Recipients evidenced little agreement with minorities when their attitudes were assessed directly on the issue in the appeal and it was apparent that their (public or private) judgments could align them with the source's position. However, minority impact was greater when attitudes were assessed indirectly on, for example, issues tangentially related to the appeal, and it was less apparent to recipients that their judgments could align them with the source. Yet, even this indirect effect of minority sources was no greater than the indirect influence of opinion majorities. In general, then, minority influence was inhibited on direct public and private measures of agreement, presumably by recipients' concerns about linking themselves with a deviant minority source.

It is perhaps not surprising that existing research has provided minimal support for the presumed minority-inspired validation process. The minority influence literature has used a wide range of operations of minority and majority source status and has used an equally heterogeneous set of measures to assess influence. Minorities with different identities have different effects, and understanding minority influence requires understanding recipients' motives with respect to a minority source (Wood et al., 1994; Wood, 2000). Unless the minority is positively valued in some way (e.g., as an innovator or an advocate of choices reflective of the Zeitgeist, see Erb, Bohner, & Hilton, 2003), the minority identity likely provides simple decision rules that hinder influence (e.g., deviant social identity, low-consensus position; see De Vries et al., 1996). Even when minorities advocate a strong, cogent position, the deviant identity is not likely to encourage careful attention to and evaluation of their appeals. Instead, careful processing of minority appeals occurs primarily when other factors are present to instigate scrutiny (De Vries et al., 1996; De Vries & De Dreu, 2001). For example, repetition and consistency in minority appeals may be necessary to attract recipients' attention (Wood et al., 1994). In addition, recipients tend to think carefully about minority appeals that advocate proattitudinal positions and thereby imply, somewhat surprisingly, that the recipient is in the minority (Baker & Petty, 1994). However, even when people attend to and process minority appeals, the low consensus, deviant position can lead them to adopt a negatively biased processing orientation that inhibits appreciation of the minority view (De Vries & De Dreu, 2001).

Minority deviancy, however, does not inevitably impede influence. Crano and his colleagues (Alvaro & Crano, 1996, 1997; Crano, 2001; Crano & Alvaro, 1998; Crano & Chen, 1998) have demonstrated the beneficial effects of an ingroup minority identity (see also David & Turner, 1996). Ingroup minorities can exert influence because of (a) the lenient, open-minded evaluation that is accorded to ingroup members who advocate minority, counterattitudinal positions, and (b) the distinctiveness of the minority position that serves to attract attention and instigate systematic analysis. Although the dissimilarity of the minority view attenuates acceptance on direct attitude measures, the relatively open-minded message elaboration creates pressure for change on related attitudes and beliefs. As a result, group members change their attitudes toward the minority view on measures indirectly related to the appeal. Over time, consistency pressures serve to change attitudes on the original issue. Thus, Moscovici's original notion that minorities wield greater indirect than direct influence appears to hold only for certain types of minority sources—those who are members of an ingroup.

Mixed evidence also has been found for Moscovici's idea that agreement with a minority emerges from thought about the issue in the appeal, whereas agreement with a majority emerges from recipients' concern with interpersonal outcomes. Instead, it appears that majorities and minorities both can exert influence by affecting how recipients think about the issue in the appeal. However, the focus of thought varies according to source identity (Nemeth, 1986). Because majorities generally are assumed to be correct, disagreement with them is stressful. Recipients' focus of attention is limited to the majority view, and thought is convergent on the position in the appeal. In contrast, because minorities are initially believed to be incorrect, disagreement with them evokes minimal stress. When minorities advocate their positions with consistency and certainty, recipients experience conflict, which motivates them to carefully evaluate the issue. Recipients think about the issue in a divergent manner and consider novel ideas and solution strategies (Nemeth & Rogers, 1996, Peterson & Nemeth, 1996). Although this kind of open-minded processing orientation may seem unlikely given the typically negative, rejecting orientation toward deviant minority sources found in social influence research (Wood et al., 1994), such an orientation is plausibly more likely in problem-solving contexts. When attempting to solve a problem, challenging, minority viewpoints might appear innovative and creative rather than threatening and deviant. To the extent that recipients are motivated to adopt an innovative minority identity, they should be motivated to generate novel ideas and solution strategies themselves.

In summary, the generally limited influence of opinion minorities can be understood in terms of the motivational and processing principles that we have outlined in this chapter. Overall, such sources are unlikely to meet recipients' motives to understand, relate to others, or be themselves. Thus, recipients typically will not be highly motivated to process minority positions and when they do, they are likely to possess a negative bias to reject the minority identity. However, minorities can exert influence when they argue an especially cogent position that recipients are motivated to evaluate in an open-minded manner—perhaps because the minority is an ingroup member or because the appeal is presented in a problem-solving context. In general, a challenge for theories of minority influence is the variety of ways that researchers have defined minority sources. Research findings are unlikely to cumulate until minorities are defined systematically in ways that establish clear motives for recipients.

Dynamic Changes in Social Consensus

In everyday life, social influence occurs as a dynamic process that changes systematically across social interactions and periods of time. For example, as minority and majority sources influence each other, social consensus changes and minority positions can become majority ones and vice versa. However, the influence theories and experimental paradigms that we have discussed to this point are not configured to capture such dynamic features of influence (with notable exceptions, such as Cialdini et al.'s, 1992, research on reciprocal influence). Instead, they are tailored to predict and explain single appeals given at discrete places and times.

Dynamic models of changing consensus have addressed the determinants and consequences of changing distributions of minority and majority positions in groups. Dynamic social impact theory is one of the best-known models of the determinants of opinion distributions (Latané, 1996; Latané & Nowak, 1997). In this analysis, attitude change among group members proceeds according to the following principles: (a) sources and recipients are close in proximity, (b) sources hold and convey views with greater strength than do recipients, and (c) sources' positions are supported by people in communication proximity to the recipients.

To test the dynamic implications of the model, Latané and Nowak (1997) conducted mathematical simulations, typically beginning with systems in which a group of people's attitudes were assumed to be distributed relatively randomly (see also Latané & Bourgeois, 2001). Attitudes then were allowed to change according to the dynamic social influence principles, and the results indicated that the system ultimately settled into a stable pattern of overall convergence in judgment in conjunction with some clustering of subgroups of people holding minority positions (see also Axelrod's, 1997, cultural dissemination model). Experimental tests also have been conducted of dynamic influence patterns among small groups of participants who interacted via computerized messaging (Latané & Bourgeois, 1996; Latané & L'Herrou, 1996). In these tests, each participant was allowed to communicate with only a small number of others in a given spatial structure (i.e., following the proximity principle). As a result, "local majorities" were created of clusters of people all sharing the same views, and these clusters remained unchanged even with repeated information exchange.

Dynamic systems models address a seeming paradox that exists between individual- and group-level influence outcomes: How can influence processes that yield local convergence in judgments among interacting individuals not lead to convergence at a macrosocietal level? The rather surprising evidence of continuing diversity stems from the tendency for influence in dynamic systems to follow nonlinear change rules and to occur primarily among people close in social space. According to Latané (1996), people's responses, at least on important issues, change in catastrophic-like shifts, which render change unlikely until some threshold value of opposition is experienced. In clusters of minority opinions, people resist the influence of the surrounding majority because the proximity of other minority views reduces the likelihood of any single member of the minority reaching his or her own threshold for change.

Dynamic social impact theory is broadly conceived and has successfully modeled a number of attitudinal phenomena, including group polarization (Liu & Latané, 1998) and the development and structure of public opinion (Lavine & Latané, 1996). However, the lack of specificity in the model's content and process makes it difficult to map the findings of model simulations onto the psychological mechanisms that presumably account for the effects. For example, Liu and Latané's (1998) attempt to track influence as it emerged in the transfer of information between group members revealed instead that attitude shifts occurred when members thought and wrote about their positions with the intent of conveying them to others. This finding is reminiscent of explanations for group polarization as a product of individuals' repetition of their own positions (Brauer, Judd, & Gliner, 1995). However, these attitude change mechanisms differ from the acceptance of influence mechanisms typically invoked to explain the simulation effects. Also making it difficult to link model outcomes with real-world influence phenomena, the simulation outcomes appear to vary according to important extramodel assumptions, including people's motivations (e.g., to imitate others, to deviate from others) and the type of issue being discussed (Latané & Bourgeois, 2001). A challenge for these kinds of predictive models is to provide sufficient specificity to identify the motives that spur influence and the psychological mechanisms through which influence occurs.

Along with addressing the determinants of opinion distributions, dynamic theories have examined the consequences of changing consensus in groups, especially the effects of changing opinion majority and minority status. According to Prislin and her colleagues' dynamic gain-loss asymmetry model (Prislin, Limbert, & Bauer, 2000; Prislin, Brewer, & Wilson, 2002; Prislin & Christensen, 2002), decreases in numerical status that change a positively-valued majority into a minority are experienced as losses and increases in numerical status that change a negatively-valued minority into a majority are experienced as gains. These changes have implications for influence because people's responses to losses and gains are not symmetrical. The former are generally more intense than the latter, reflecting the loss-aversion effect whereby losses loom larger than gains (Kahneman & Tversky, 1979). Thus, people's negative reactions to the loss of a majority position should be stronger than their positive reactions to the gain of a majority position.[8]

Tests of this dynamic model of change have used an experimental paradigm in which members of a small group supposedly exchange views on important social issues in face-to-face interactions (Prislin et al., 2000; Prislin et al., 2002). During the interaction, other group members (actually experimental confederates) apparently change their positions so that participants who initially believed they were in the majority are transformed into minorities and participants who believed they were in the minority are transformed into majorities. Asymmetry in reactions to loss and gain have been apparent in that participants who became a minority dramatically decreased their perceptions of group-self similarity, group attraction, and expectations for positive group interaction. In contrast, participants who became a majority have failed to appreciate the gains and continued to perceive the group as dissimilar from themselves and to evaluate it relatively negatively.

Prislin and her colleagues also found that attitudes varied as a function of the shifts in status. The new minorities tended to agree with the newly emerging attitudinal consensus (Prislin et al., 2000, Study 1) and to interpret the attitudinal differences among group members as diversity rather than deviance (Prislin et al., 2002). These perceptions likely justified their new minority position. In contrast, new majorities strengthened their attitudes by enhancing attitudinal importance, broadening the scope of the positions they considered unacceptable, and expressing less tolerance of opposing views. If these findings can be generalized to a societal level, it seems that immediately following a rise to majority status, the new majority is in need of regulatory mechanisms to channel social influence processes away from destructive norms involving intolerance and toward more constructive ones (e.g., interpreting attitudinal differences as diversity rather than deviance).

Dynamic changes in minority size also can affect influence power. In particular, minorities are more successful at influencing the majority when other majority members are seen to defect to the minority position than when the minority does not gain converts (Clark, 1998). As might be anticipated, defectors from the consensual majority are not well liked by the majority whose position they abandoned (e.g., Kerr, 1981; Levine, Sroka, & Snyder, 1977; Marques, Yzerbyt, & Leyens, 1988). Yet, these minority converts appear to be highly influential. They seem to be more influential at winning over others to their newly endorsed minority views than are members of the original minority (Clark, 2001). Thus, once minorities succeed at converting a few members of the majority to their side, they are likely to further grow in size if they let converts exert social influence by advocating their newly adopted (minority) position.

The increased power of minorities to exert social influence as they expand in size could be due to targets responding based on a "let's join the bandwagon" heuristic. Alternately, minorities growing in size might motivate elaboration of their appeal as targets try to understand what draws others to the minority position. Support for the increased elaboration explanation was obtained in a series of studies showing that expanding minorities elicited more issue-relevant thought than shrinking minorities (Gordijn, De Vries, & De Dreu, 2002). If the minority appeal consists of sound, cogent arguments, this increased systematic processing apparently leads to more attitude change, although not on the issue in the appeal but on indirectly related issues.

Thus, the greatest challenge for a minority initially might be to win over a few highly conspicuous members of the majority. Once the minority gains in size, the likelihood of it being influential further increases. Interestingly, this rule of success (in influence) breeding further success (in influence) does not seem to apply to expanding majorities. If anything, the expanding majority seems to lose its ability to influence, apparently triggering reactance in targets who resist the majority in an attempt to maintain or restore freedom of thought (Gordijn et al., 2002). This research nicely illustrates the dynamic nature of social influence, with minorities becoming more influential and majorities becoming less influential as they grow in size.

In summary, the complexity of dynamic models corresponds to the complexity of influence processes in real life. People assume minority or majority positions in groups and the broader society in part due to exposure to others holding particular viewpoints. As a result, people have histories of being a majority or a minority, and they respond to current influence attempts from the perspective of this historical background. A challenge for dynamic models will be to understand the motives for agreeing or disagreeing that are imposed with these histories and the ways in which information-processing mediators of influence are channeled over time.

An Historical Analysis of Motives in Social Influence and Persuasion

The research we reviewed in this chapter illustrates how the traditions of group-focused social influence research and individual-focused persuasion research can inform and enrich each other. Although these two traditions are often treated as European (group) and North American (individual) approaches to the study of attitudes, the developments on each continent have been affected as much by trans-Atlantic exchanges as by local circumstances (Collier, Minton, & Reynolds, 1991; Farr, 1996; Graumann, 1998). The founders of the individual-focused orientation currently prevalent in North America were European immigrants or were mentored by Europeans. Once stewed in the American melting pot, these influences returned back to Europe after World War II (WWII) to help fill the intellectual and academic void caused by fascism. Moreover, the beginnings of social psychology in the United States were marked by a focus on social groups (Greenwood, 2000). The collectivistic perspectives of Peirce (1903/1997), Dewey (1922/1930), Mead (1934), and other American pragmatists were evident in early research on attitudes, which were almost invariably conceptualized in reference to group-shared norms (Faris, 1925; Herskovits, 1936; Young, 1931).

The location of attitudes within groups sharply contrasted with Gordon Allport's (1935) individualistic definition of an attitude as "a mental and neural state of readiness to respond, organized through experience, exerting a directive and/or dynamic influence upon the individual's response to all objects and situations with which it is related" (p. 810). Gordon Allport's individualistic conceptualization reflected efforts, led by his older brother Floyd Allport (1919), to establish social psychology as a science that, by definition, could not include such vague, non-testable concepts as "group-mind" and "social instincts" (see McDougal, 1920). Social psychology was to become science using the individual as a unit of analysis, behaviorism as a theoretical orientation, and experimentation as a method of inquiry. This orientation resonated well with the Zeitgeist in American society (Collier et al., 1991), and the pendulum swung toward individualism and away from group-focused social influence research. The Yale communication and persuasion program exemplified this individual approach (Hovland, Janis, & Kelley, 1953).

An individual orientation and experimental methodology have persisted as hallmarks of American social psychology in general and the study of attitudes in particular, despite the fact that behaviorism proved to be short-lived. Largely because of the Gestalt orientation of an influential group of Europeans, the study of individual behavior was replaced with the study of the social mind. This orientation paved the way for the social psychologists who immigrated to the United States to flee Nazism, including Lewin, Ischheiser, Koffka, and Wertheimer. Their students' legacy, the study of social cognition, soon became a dominant orientation in American social psychology. The continued focus on the individual as the object of study stems from a variety of factors that range from abstract, metaphysical ones to more mundane—but nonetheless consequential, ones of avoiding commonplace or "obvious" findings (Kelley, 1992), securing resources from granting agencies impressed with reductionistic approaches, and increasing publishing productivity (Berkowitz, 1999).

The group-oriented social influence orientation that prevails in Europe developed in part as a backlash against the post-WWII dominance of American ideas. What "originally (was) much needed and gratefully received reconstruction and reinternalization of science with American aid" (Graumann, 1998; p. 16), later came to be perceived as the "Americanization" of European social psychology. The turbulent 1960s, when American social psychology faced a serious crisis of confidence, proved ripe times to claim a European identity to social psychology (Israel & Tajfel, 1972; Jaspars, Moscovici, Schönbach, & Tajfel, 1974). Although Western Europe in that period had few social psychologists, it had a rich intellectual heritage on which to draw. For example, Moscovici (1980) derived his concept of social representations from Durkheim's (1895-1914/1972) collectivistic approach to social behavior, which, in turn, was influenced by Wundt's Völkerpsychologie (see Danzinger, 1983). In addition, Tajfel (1978) based his theory of social identity on a combination of Gestalt principles of perception and sociological conceptions of identity (see Hogg & Williams, 2000).

A defining characteristic of the European orientation became an emphasis on the social dimension of human psychological functioning (Tajfel, 1978). This emphasis likely was driven not only by the social conflict in the 1960s but also by the fact that Europe more than the United States has historically been socially and geopolitically complex. It is interesting that the European emphasis on social forces did not imply any less an individualistic orientation than found in North American social psychology (Farr, 1996). Instead, the unique European contribution was to identify the social and cultural context for individual responses. As Scherer (1993) noted, "whereas the individual and its functioning is ... the paramount object of study in North American social psychology, with the "social" being part of the information to be processed, much of European social psychology, while studying individuals, is more interested in the social and cultural determinants of cognition and behavior" (p. 250; see also Hogg & Williams, 2000).

The single most important contribution of the (European) social influence paradigm was a more complete insight into the motivational complexities that drive attitudinal reactions. Theories of minority influence and social identity place central focus on the social meaning and patterning of attitude judgments. This emphasis is an important counterpoint to the more individually oriented message-based persuasion research that dominated the field during the 1980s and 1990s (Eagly & Chaiken, 1998; Petty & Wegner, 1998). Yet, persuasion research also has much to offer the study of social influence. Persuasion paradigms offer an elaborated measurement apparatus to document the motivation to understand reality and to track the effects of this motive on processing of persuasive information (Eagly & Chaiken, 1993; Petty & Cacioppo, 1986). In contrast, beyond the manipulations of surveillance that we discussed at the beginning of the chapter, the reviewed research rarely distinguished among the various motives for agreeing or disagreeing with others.

We believe that this failure to document the range of motives established in social influence paradigms has hindered cumulative integration of knowledge in this area. Our interpretation of social influence findings as reflecting particular motivational orientations necessarily remained speculative given the lack of documentation in the original research. The benefits of examining the motives for social agreement and disagreement are readily apparent. For example, influence studies that measured identification with a group in order to test the predictions of social identity theory (Tajfel, 1982) not only were able to provide support for the theoretical rationale but also were able to rule out possible alternative motives (Gagnon & Bourhis, 1996). Research measures of motives also forge new areas for investigation. For example, Tajfel (1982) postulated two components of identification with groups, involving the knowledge of group membership and the value or emotional significance of that membership. Thus, self-related normative concerns could affect reactions to social influence through two processes. Only recently has it been demonstrated that both processes function as mediators of the effects of social influence. For example, Prislin and Christensen (in press) demonstrated that minority influence that successfully reversed the majority and minority positions within a group also changed people's preferences to exit versus remain in a group by affecting both categorization and evaluation processes.

The lack of direct measures of recipients' motives in social influence settings is perhaps understandable given the limited systematic procedures available to assess them. Generally, three types of assessment tools are possible, although all three are not equally useful to assess the trio of motives. First, researchers could use standard self-report measures. For example, a number of measures have been developed to assess self-related normative motives (see Haslam, 2001, for a review of self-report measures of social identification). Of course, self-reports are useful only to the extent that people are aware of their motives and are willing to report on them. Furthermore, even when people are able and willing to report accurately about their motives and current concerns, they rarely will be able to report accurately on the consequences of these motives for attitude judgments (see Chaiken, Giner-Sorolla, & Chen, 1996). Most people will claim that they hold a particular position because it is valid. This belief in the accuracy of one's judgments is likely to be a functional response. Motives of relating to others and being oneself can most effectively be served by the belief that the position that meets these needs also is the most valid one. Thus, even when people report accurately on their motives, their abiding belief that their judgments reflect the truth will typically render reports of motive effects unreliable.

Self-report measures of motives can be supplemented by less-controllable, implicit measures (Coats, Smith, Claypool, & Banner's, 2000, implicit measure of identification). Implicit measures are useful when participants are unaware of their motives or reluctant to report on them accurately. Additionally, more "objective" behavior-based measures of motives can be useful, such as indexing identification from participation in group-defining activities (Phinney, 1990). Similar measures could be devised to assess understanding and relating. For example, based on the logic behind implicit measures, when people are motivated to relate to others, stimuli concerning others' impressions might trigger faster reactions than nondiagnostic stimuli. Also, behavior-based measures could be devised to tap motives of understanding and relating. For example, behavioral indicators of the motives to understand and to relate could be fashioned using effort and time spent analyzing the information relevant to the issue and to others' positions, respectively.

In summary, the focus on social influence in the present chapter is most closely aligned with the European approach to the study of attitudes. Although this approach, like its American cousin, is highly individualistic, European theories of influence tend to ground individuals in social and cultural contexts. As a result, such theories tend to consider a wider range of motivations than the standard American message-based persuasion research. However, social influence research—as it is executed anywhere, has generally not assessed motives for influence. Measures of motives provide insight into why experimental manipulations have the effects that they do, and thereby facilitate cumulation of knowledge across individual social influence studies.

Culture and Social Influence

Our analysis of social and group influences on attitudes inevitably raises the issue of larger-scale societal and cultural effects. Of course, researchers work within cultures themselves, and as members of those cultures they hold assumptions about the relationship between individuals and their social environment. One pervading assumption is the principle of individualism that underlies contemporary social influence theorizing and research within European and American traditions. In psychological theorizing, this principle means that each human constructs a sense of self that is separate and independent from others. As axiomatic as individualism might sound to the Euro-American ear, it does not represent the prevailing, much less uniformly shared, notion of the self in world cultures (Fiske, Kitayama, Markus, & Nisbett, 1998). An alternative to the construal of the self as independent, unique, and separate from others is the construal of the self as interdependent, shared, and related to others.

Understanding the self-concepts of people of different cultures has been an organizing theme for most social psychological investigations of culture (Hofstede, 1980; Kitayama & Markus, 1994; Markus & Kitayama, 1991). In general, an independent sense of self is thought to be typical of individualistic cultures, defined as ones in which people are oriented to develop a positive, unique sense of self, express emotions and attain personal goals, reason socially about individuals rather than situations, and engage in impermanent, nonintensive social relationships (Oyserman, Coon, & Kemmelmeier, 2002). In contrast, an interdependent sense of self is thought to be typical of collectivist cultures, defined as ones in which people are oriented to develop their identity as group members, achieve satisfaction in carrying out social roles and obligations, restrain emotional expression, reason socially about contexts rather than individuals, and engage in fixed, stable group memberships. Much psychological research on culture has followed the logic that, because selves develop differently in individualistic and collectivistic societies, a useful way to examine cultural differences is to study relevant aspects of the self. Thus, crosscultural research in psychology has often equated the cultural dimensions of individualism-collectivism with individual differences in the self-concept related to independence-interdependence (although see Bond, 2002; Miller, 2002).

The extent to which people within a culture tend to be individualistic or collectivistic is of considerable interest for social influence researchers because these clusters of attributes have important implications for influence. Specifically, accepting the attitudes of valued others is more likely to be congenial for people with a collectivistic, rather than individualistic, orientation. In support of this idea, Bond and Smith's (1996) meta-analytic synthesis of research using Asch's line-judging paradigm revealed greater acceptance of others' judgments in collectivistic than in individualistic cultures. Moreover, the impact of culture was substantially greater than that of any other moderator of group influence, including the size of the majority. Similarly, consensus that serves as "social proof" and thus validates understanding has been found to be more impactful in collectivistic than individualistic cultures (Cialdini, Wosinska, Barrett, Butner, & Górnik-Durose, 2001). Suggesting that this effect of culture was mediated through individual differences in social interdependence, Cialdini and colleagues found that the effect of culture, operationalized as country, disappeared once individual interdependence scores were entered into analysis.

Although the dimension of individualism-collectivism appears to be a highly generative framework to understand social influence across cultures, the framework may prove to be a shaky one. Research on individualism-collectivism has been criticized for its overly broad conceptual definition as well as for its measurement operations of poor validity (Oyserman, Coon, & Kemmelmeier, 2002). More troubling is a tendency for researchers to define individualism-collectivism in terms of its consequences and then to examine the same consequences—a practice that yields conclusions bordering on tautology (Oyserman et al., 2002). Social influence research is especially open to this latter criticism. Poorly designed studies risk finding that people from collectivistic cultures, defined in terms of sensitivity to social influence, are more likely than those from individualistic cultures to rely on social consensus.

In keeping with the orientation of the present chapter, we suggest that cultural research on social influence could profitably extend beyond individualism-collectivism and other trait-like measures to examine the cultural foundations of the motives for influence and the informational mechanisms through which these motives guide reactions. As Bond and Smith (1996) suggested, differences among cultures in reactions to group influence may well be qualitative as well as quantitative. That is, stronger alignment with group consensus might not be a result of the same-but-more-intense motive in collectivistic than in individualistic cultures. Instead, cultural differences in core ideas about what is good, moral, and the essence of the self might incite different sets of motives in seemingly identical influence situations (see Kitayama & Markus, 1994). Thus, motives may best be understood in a cultural context.

Cultural influences also might emerge in information processing, given that "systems of thought exist in homeostasis with the social practices that surround them" (Nisbett, Peng, Incheol, & Norenzayan, 2001, p. 304). In general, Western thought is considered to be analytic, categorical, focused on the object, and regulated by the rules of formal logic (see Nisbett et al., 2001; Peng & Nisbett, 1999, for details). In contrast, Eastern/Asian thought is holistic, non-categorical, focused on the entire field, and regulated by the rules of dialectics. These culture-specific styles of thought might affect reactions to influence through the aspects of the environment that are salient and the way that information is interpreted (see Norenzayan, Smith, Kim, & Nisbett, 2002). Ceteris paribus, holistic thinkers should attend to greater amounts of information than analytic thinkers. The holistic belief that "everything is related to every-thing," should increase the likelihood that any specific piece of information is considered relevant when examining an issue (Choi, Dalal, Kim-Prieto, & Park, 2003). Also, to the extent that holistic thinking is intuitive, it might be less accessible to consciousness than analytic, more formal thinking. Finally, holistic and analytic styles of thought might dispose people to polarize or moderate attitude judgments. The holistic principle of contradiction, according to which opposites coexist in everything, implies acceptance of the co-existence of consensual and non-consensual information via an additive processing strategy (see Aaker & Sengupta, 2000). As a result, holistic thinkers might be oriented toward attitude shifts to moderation over polarization. In contrast, analytic thinkers might follow formal logic rules, such as the rule of noncontradiction, according to which only one of the two opposites is valid. If analytic thinkers search for the correct position between consensual and non-consensual views, they might be predisposed to polarization over moderation.

Conceptualizing culture in terms of the interdependence of processes and contents holds promise for better understanding of social influence not only in comparisons between Western and Eastern/Asian cultures, but also across a broad range of other cultures. Although specific motives and components of holistic and analytic thought may not be applicable to other cultures, the general principle of culture affecting reactions to social influence by evoking culture-specific motives and cognition should apply. We guess that progress in understanding the variety of culturally embedded motives and information processing styles will be achieved when the field of social influence itself is characterized by researchers who possess a broad set of cultural backgrounds and experiences.

Summary and Conclusion

In summary, the study of social influence provides a much-needed balance to the research addressed in the other chapters in this book by promoting the central theme that social relations create and are created by attitudes. All attitudes are social in the sense that they develop, function, and change in reciprocal relation with the social context. When influence is social, people not only are interested in understanding reality—the prominent motive addressed in most of the other chapters in this book, but also are oriented to relate to others and to promote their sense of self.

A recurring theme throughout the chapter is the ways in which people use information provided by others, especially information from a consensus of others, in order to achieve their social and informational goals. We argued that social goals are complex in that they involve self and others, and they influence responses in public as well as private. Specifically, people evaluate consensus views in order to understand reality, relate to others and convey desired impressions, and achieve a favorable and coherent self-concept. These motives direct responses to social consensus through a variety of information-processing mechanisms. For example, highly motivated individuals might carefully scrutinize and interpret consensual views and other relevant information. Less strongly motivated people might rely on less effortful heuristic rules ("go along to get along").

In the chapter, we considered how the trio of motives could account for findings in studies on polarization of group attitudes and the influence of opinion minorities. We also consid-ered dynamic models of social influence that identify the determinants and consequences of changing opinion distributions in groups. Dynamic features are intrinsic to social influence in everyday life but until recently have not been a central focus of most attitude theories. We then provided a historical analysis of the development of social influence research over time, espe-cially highlighting the contribution of European social psychologists to our understanding of the social motives that yield influence. Finally, we considered how influence processes depend on culture, especially cultural variation in social and informational motives for influence and in characteristic styles of information processing.

In general, we found a thriving, flourishing research literature addressing a multitude of aspects of social influence. Despite this vigor, social influence research is somewhat disappointing in that it has not yielded a stronger set of cumulative findings. We believe that researchers can promote cumulation with more systematic study paradigms, especially ones that directly assess the motives that drive message recipients to accept or reject an influence appeal.

ACKNOWLEDGMENTS

The writing of this chapter was supported by grants from the National Science Foundation (BSC -0236469) to Radmila Prislin and the National Institutes of Health (1R01MH619000-01) to Wendy Wood.

ENDNOTES

[1] Although not always adequately recognized, early theorizing about social influence also allowed for more enduring attitude change motivated by concerns about one's relationship with the influencing agent. For example, Kelman (1961) discussed identification and French and Raven (1959) discussed expertise and authority as bases for attitude change that would persist as long as the relationship with the influencing agent remained salient.

[2] Our idea that strong normative pressures yield enduring change whereas more superficial, fleeting concerns yield only temporary shifts in attitude judgments requires testing in future research that directly measures the strength and nature of normative motives. Because past research on impression motives has rarely obtained direct measures of the strength of the relevant motive, the possibility that weak and strong motives yield different effects cannot be evaluated directly.

[3] Our analysis of motives differs from the elaboration likelihood model (Petty & Cacioppo, 1986; Petty & Wegener, 1998), which treats self- and other-related motives as biasing factors that direct processing in service of the relevant goal. The objective processing that occurs in the absence of bias and is considered an open-minded, accuracy-oriented motive. In contrast, following the multiple motive heuristic-systematic model (Chaiken, Liberman, & Eagly, 1989; Eagly & Chaiken, 1998), we postulate three overarching goals, each of which guides the extent and the direction of information processing. Thus, a concern with understanding would orient people preferentially to the most valid information.

[4] Although Allport's (1935) multidimensional conception of attitudes differs from our own by including reactions other than evaluations, he recognized that strictly evaluative reactions are useful in structuring the world.

[5] In addition to these socially-oriented motives, Kelman (1961) hypothesized that people wishing to understand reality and to adopt positions congenial with their own values experience *internalization*, in which they integrate a source's position into their existing value system.

[6] Not everyone recognizes the distinction between affective and instrumental reasons for agreeing with others. For example, Hogg and Turner (1987) argued that the outcomes from identification-based relationships are just as instrumental as the tangible outcomes from reward-and-coercion-based relationships. From this perspective, approval and acceptance from valued groups function as a reward in much the same way as any tangible outcome from the relationship.

[7] Additional evidence of the importance of certainty motives comes from Hogg's (2000, 2001) demonstrations that people who are unfamiliar with a task, and thus presumably subjectively uncertain how to respond, appear especially likely to categorize themselves using available social categories. To the extent that this uncertainty also leads people to adopt ingroup attitudes, then this perspective contributes to the idea that coherence motives underlie group influence. However, in our tripartite analysis of motives, this analysis addresses people's need for understanding and not a self-oriented need to be consistent with existing self-defining attitudes and self-views.

[8] An asymmetry in reactions to changes in social status also is consistent with the postulates of social identity and self-categorization theories (Tajfel, 1981; Turner, Hogg, Oakes, Reicher, & Watherell, 1987). That is, perceived similarity with others provides a basis for a shared ingroup category. Individuals (i.e., majority members) who find their opinion supported by others should assimilate with and positively value the ingroup category. Because people expect to agree with and be supported by ingroup members (Turner & Oakes, 1989), disagreements are negatively valued. When disagreements accrue to an extent that changes one's position from majority to minority, the result

should be a decrease in valuation and ultimately decategorization from the group. By the same token, individuals (i.e., minority members) whose opinions are initially rejected by others should be less likely to adopt the group as a social identity. As a result, initial minorities should consider others' reactions, including others' subsequent conversion to supporters, less consequential than if they had originally identified with them.

REFERENCES

Aaker, J. L., & Sengupta, J. (2000). Additivity versus attenuation: The role of culture in the resolution of information incongruity. *Journal of Consumer Psychology, 9*, 67–82.

Abrams, D., & Hogg, M. (1990). Comments on the motivational status of self-esteem in social identity and intergroup discrimination. *European Journal of Social Psychology, 18*, 317–334.

Albarracín, D. (2002). Cognition in persuasion: An analysis of information processing in response to persuasive communication. In M. P. Zanna (Ed.), *Advances in experimental social psychology* (Vol. 34, pp. 61–130). San Diego: Academic Press.

Allen, V., & Wilder, J. (1980). Impact of group consensus and social support on stimulus meaning: Mediation of conformity by cognitive restructuring. *Journal of Personality and Social Psychology, 39*, 1116–1124.

Allport, F. (1919). Behavior and experiment in social psychology. *Journal of Abnormal and Social Psychology, 14*, 297–306.

Allport, G. W. (1935). Attitudes. In C. Murchison (Ed.), *Handbook of social psychology* (pp. 798–844). Worcester, MA: Clark University Press.

Allport, G. W. (1985). The historical background of social psychology. In G. Lindzey & E. Aronson (Eds.), *Handbook of social psychology* (3rd ed., Vol. 1, pp. 1–46). NY: Random House.

Alvaro, E. M., & Crano, W. D. (1996). Cognitive responses to minority- or majority-based communications: Factors that underlie minority influence. *British Journal of Social Psychology, 35*, 105–121.

Alvaro, E. M., & Crano, W. D. (1997). Indirect minority influence: Evidence for leniency in source evaluation and counterargumentation. *Journal of Personality and Social Psychology, 72*, 949–964.

Alwin, D. R., Cohen, R. L., & Newcomb, T. M. (1991). *Political attitudes over the life span: the Bennington women after fifty years.* Madison, WI: University of Wisconsin Press.

Asch, S. E. (1940). Studies in the principles of judgments and attitudes: II. Determination of judgments by group and by ego standards. *Journal of Social Psychology, 12*, 433–465.

Asch, S. E. (1952a). *Social psychology.* Englewood Cliffs, NJ: Prentice-Hall.

Asch, S. E. (1952b). Effects of group pressure on the modification and distortion of judgments. In G. E. Swanson, T. M. Newcomb, & E. L. Hartley (Eds.), *Readings in social psychology* (2nd ed., pp. 2–11). New York: Holt.

Axelrod, R. (1997). The dissemination of culture: A model with local convergence and global polarization. *Journal of Conflict Resolution, 41*, 203–226.

Baker, S. M., & Petty, R. E. (1994). Majority and minority influence: Source position imbalance as a determinant of message scrutiny. *Journal of Personality and Social Psychology, 67*, 5–19.

Baldwin, M. W., & Holmes, J. G. (1987). Salient private audiences and awareness of the self. *Journal of Personality and Social Psychology, 52*, 1087–1098.

Barchas, P. (1986). A sociophysiological orientation to small groups. In E. Lawler (Ed.), *Advances in group processes* (Vol. 3, pp. 209–246). Greenwich, CT: JAI.

Baron, R. S., Vandello, J. A., & Brunsman, B. (1996). The forgotten variable in conformity research: Impact of task importance on social influence. *Journal of Personality and Social Psychology, 71*, 915–927.

Baumeister, R., & Leary, M. (1995). The need to belong: Desire for interpersonal attachments as a fundamental human motivation. *Psychological Bulletin, 117*, 497–529.

Berkowitz, L. (1999). On the changes in U.S. social psychology: Some speculations. In A. Rodrigues & R. V. Levine (Eds.), *Reflections on 100 years of experimental social psychology* (pp. 158–169). New York: Basic Books.

Bond, M. H. (2002). Reclaiming the individual from Hofsede's ecological analysis—A 20-year odyssey: Comment on Oyserman et al. (2002). *Psychological Bulletin, 128*, 73–77.

Bond, R., & Smith, P. B. (1996). Culture and conformity: A meta-analysis of studies using Asch's (1952, 1956) line-judging task. *Psychological Bulletin, 119*, 111–137.

Bowlby, J. (1973). *Attachment and loss: Vol. 2. Separation anxiety and anger.* New York: Basic Books.

Brauer, M., Judd, C. M., & Gliner, M. D. (1995). The effects of repeated attitude expressions on attitude polarization during group discussion. *Journal of Personality and Social Psychology, 68*, 1014–1029.

Brendl, M. C., Markman, A. B., & Messner, C. (2003). The devaluation effect: Activating a need devalues unrelated objects. *Journal of Consumer Research, 29*, 463–473.

Brewer, M. B. (1991). The social self: On being the same and different at the same time. *Personality and Social Psychology Bulletin, 17*, 475–482.

Brown, R. (1974). Further comment on the risky shift. *American Psychologist, 29*, 468–470.

Buehler, R., & Griffin, D. (1994). Change-of-meaning effects in conformity and dissent: Observing construal processes over time. *Journal of Personality and Social Psychology, 67*, 984–996.

Burnstein, E., & Vinokur, A. (1977). Interpersonal comparison versus persuasive argumentation: A more direct test of alternative explanations for group-induced shifts in individual choice. *Journal of Experimental Social Psychology, 9*, 236–245.

Caporael, L. R., & Baron, R. M. (1997). Groups as the mind's natural environment. In J. A. Simpson & D. T. Kendrick: *Evolutionary social psychology* (pp. 317–343). Mahwah, NJ: Lawrence Erlbaum Associates.

Chaiken, S., Giner-Sorolla, R., & Chen, S. (1996). Beyond accuracy: Defense and impression motives in heuristic and systematic information processing. In P. M. Gollwitzer & J. A. Bargh (Eds.), *The psychology of action: Linking cognition and motivation to behavior* (pp. 553–578). New York: Guilford.

Chaiken, S., Liberman, A., & Eagly, A. H. (1989). Heuristic and systematic processing within and beyond the persuasion context. In J. S. Uleman & J. A. Bargh (Eds.), *Unintended thought* (pp. 212–252). New York: Guilford.

Chen, S., Shechter, D., & Chaiken, S. (1996). Getting at the truth or getting along: Accuracy- versus impression-motivated heuristic and systematic processing. *Journal of Personality and Social Psychology, 71*, 262–275.

Choi, I., Dalal, R., Kim-Prieto, C., & Park, H. (2003). Culture and judgment of causal relevance. *Journal of Personality and Social Psychology, 84*, 46–59.

Christensen, P. N., Rothgerber, H., Wood, W., & Matz, D. C. (2004). Social norms and identity relevance: A motivational approach to normative behavior. *Personality and Social Psychology Bulletin, 30*, 1295–1309.

Cialdini, R. B., Green, B. L., & Rusch, A. J. (1992). When tactical pronouncements of change become real change: The case of reciprocal persuasion. *Journal of Personality and Social Psychology, 63*, 30–40.

Cialdini, R. B., Kallgren, C. A., & Reno, R. R. (1991). A focus theory of normative conduct: A theoretical refinement and reevaluation of the role of norms in human behavior. In M. P. Zanna (Ed.), *Advances in experimental social psychology* (Vol. 21, pp. 201–234). San Diego, CA: Academic Press.

Cialdini, R. B., Levy, A., Herman, C. P., & Evenbeck, S. (1973). Attitudinal politics: The strategy of moderation. *Journal of Personality and Social Psychology, 25*, 100–108.

Cialdini, R. B., Levy, A., Herman, C. P., Kozlowski, L. T., & Petty, R. E. (1976). Elastic shifts of opinion: Determinants of direction and durability. *Journal of Personality and Social Psychology, 34*, 663–672.

Cialdini, R. B., & Trost, M. (1998). Social influence: Social norms, conformity, and compliance. In D. T. Gilbert, S. T. Fiske, & G. Lindzey (Eds.), *The handbook of social psychology* (Vol. 2, 4th ed., pp. 151–192). Boston: McGraw-Hill.

Cialdini, R. B., Wosinska, W., Barrett, D. W., Butner, J., & Górnik-Durose, M. (2001). The differential impact of two social influence principles on individualists and collectivists in Poland and the United States. In W. Wosinska & R. B. Cialdini (Eds.), *The practice of social influence in multiple cultures. Applied social research* (pp. 33–50). Mahwah, NJ: Lawrence Erlbaum Associates.

Clark, R. D., III (1998). Minority influence: The role of the rate of majority defection and persuasive arguments. *European Journal of Social Psychology, 28*, 787–796.

Clark, R. D., III (2001). Effects of majority defection and multiple minority sources on minority influence. *Group Dynamics, 5*, 57–62.

Coats, S., Smith, E. R., Claypool, H. M., & Banner, M. J. (2000). Overlapping mental representations of self and in-group: Reaction time evidence and its relationship with explicit measures of group identification. *Journal of Experimental Social Psychology, 36*, 304–315.

Collier, G., Minton, H. L., & Reynolds, G. (1991). *Currents of thought in American social psychology*. London: Oxford University Press.

Cooper, J. T., & Stone, J. (2000). Cognitive dissonance and the social group. In D. J. Terry & M. A. Hogg (Eds.), *Attitudes, behavior, and social context: The role of norms and group membership. Applied social research* (pp. 227–244). Mahwah, NJ: Lawrence Erlbaum Associates.

Crano, W. D. (2001). Social influence, social identity, and ingroup leniency. In C. K. W. De Dreu & N. K. De Vries (Eds.), *Group consensus and minority influence: Implications for innovation* (pp. 122–143). Oxford, UK: Blackwell.

Crano, W. D., & Alvaro, W. M. (1998). The context/comparison model of social influence: Mechanisms, structure, and linkages that underlie indirect attitude change. *European Review of Social Psychology, 8*, 175–202.

Crano, W. D., & Chen, X. (1998). The leniency contract and persistence of majority and minority influence. *Journal of Personality and Social Psychology, 74*, 1437–1450.

Crano, W. D., & Hannula-Bral, K. A. (1994). Context/categorization model of social influence: Minority and majority influence in the formation of a novel response norm. *Journal of Experimental Social Psychology, 30*, 247–276.

Danzinger, K. (1983). Origins and principles of Wundt's Völkerpsychologie. *British Journal of Social Psychology, 22*, 303–313.

Darke, P. R., Chaiken, S., Bohner, G., Einwiller, S., Erb, H.-P., & Hazelwood, J. D. (1998). Accuracy motivation, consensus information, and the law of large numbers: Effects on attitudinal judgment in the absence of argumentation. *Personality and Social Psychology Bulletin, 24*, 1205–1215.

David, B., & Turner, J. C. (1996). Studies in self-categorization and minority conversion: Is being a member of the out-group an advantage? *British Journal of Social Psychology, 35,* 179–199.

Deutsch, M., & Gerard, H. B. (1955). A study of normative and informational influences upon individual judgment. *Journal of Abnormal and Social Psychology, 51,* 629–636.

De Vries, N. K., & De Dreu, C. K. W. (2001). Group consensus and minority influence: Introduction and overview. In C. K. W. De Dreu & N. K. De Vries (Eds.), *Group consensus and minority influence: Implications for innovation* (pp. 1–14). Oxford, UK: Blackwell.

De Vries, N. K., De Dreu, C. K. W., Gordijn, E., & Schuurman, M. (1996). Majority and minority influence: A dual role interpretation. In W. Stroebe & M. Hewstone (Eds.), *European review of social psychology* (Vol. 7, pp. 145–172). Chichester, UK: Wiley.

Dewey, J. (1922/1930). *Human nature and conduct: An introduction to social psychology.* New York: The Modern Library.

Durkheim, E. (1972). *Selected writings.* (A. Giddens, Ed.). Cambridge, UK: Cambridge University Press. (Original work published 1895–1914)

Eagly, A. H., & Chaiken, S. (1993). *The psychology of attitudes.* Fort Worth, TX: Harcourt.

Eagly, A. H., & Chaiken, S. (1998). Attitude structure and function. In D. T. Gilbert, S. T. Fiske, & G. Lindsey (Eds.): *The handbook of social psychology* (pp. 269–322). Boston, HA: McGraw-Hill.

Eagly, A. H., Wood, W., & Fishbaugh, L. (1981). Sex differences in conformity: Surveillance by the group as a determinant of male nonconformity. *Journal of Personality and Social Psychology, 40,* 384–394.

Erb, H.-P., & Bohner, G. (2001). Mere consensus effects in minority and majority influence. In C. K. W. De Dreu & N. K. De Vries (Eds.), *Group consensus and minority influence: Implications for innovation* (pp. 40–59). Malden, MA: Blackwell.

Erb, H.-P., & Bohner, G., & Hilton, D. J. (2003, September). *Conditions of minority influence: The risky option.* Paper presented at the small group meeting of the European Association of Social Psychologists on Minority Influence Processes, Oxford, UK.

Faris, E. (1925). The concept of social attitudes. *Journal of Applied Sociology, 9,* 404–409.

Farr, R. M. (1996). *The roots of modern social psychology 1872–1954.* Oxford, UK: Blackwell.

Fazio, R. H. (1986). How do attitudes guide behavior? In R. M. Sorrentino & E. T. Higgins (Eds.), *Handbook of motivation and cognition: Foundations of social behavior* (pp. 129–150). Hillsdale, NJ: Lawrence Erlbaum Associates.

Fazio, R. H. (1990). Multiple processes by which attitudes guide behavior: The MODE model as an integrative framework. In M.P. Zanna (Ed.), *Advances in experimental social psychology* (Vol. 23, pp. 75–109). San Diego, CA: Academic Press.

Festinger, L. (1950). Informal social communication. *Psychological Review, 57,* 271–282.

Festinger, L. (1954). A theory of social comparison processes. *Human Relations, 7,* 114–140.

Festinger, L. (1957). *A theory of cognitive dissonance.* Evanston, IL: Row, Peterson.

Festinger, L., Riecken, H. W., & Schachter, S. (1956). *When prophecy fails: A social and psychological study of a modern group that predicted the destruction of the world.* Minneapolis, MN: University of Minnesota Press.

Fiske, A. P., Kitayama, S., Markus, H. R., & Nisbett, R. E. (1998). The cultural matrix of social psychology. In D. T. Gilbert, S. T. Fiske, & G. Lindzey (Eds.), *The handbook of social psychology* (4th ed., Vol. 2, pp. 915–981). Boston: McGraw-Hill.

Fiske, S. T., Lin, M. T., & Neuberg, S. L. (1999). The continuum model: Ten years later. In S. Chaiken and Y. Trope (Eds.), *Dual process theories in social psychology* (pp. 231–254). New York: Guilford.

French, J. R. P., Jr., and Raven, B. H. (1959). The bases of social power. In D. Cartwright (Ed.), *Studies in social power* (pp. 150–167). Ann Arbor, MI: University of Michigan, Institute for Social Research.

Fromm, E. (1955). *The sane society.* New York: Holt, Rinehart & Winston.

Gagnon, A., & Bourhis, R. Y. (1996). Discrimination in the minimal group paradigm: Social identity or self-interest? *Personality and Social Psychology Bulletin, 22,* 1289–1301.

Goethals, G. R., & Zanna, M. P. (1979). The role of social comparison in choice shifts. *Journal of Personality and Social Psychology, 37,* 1469–1476.

Gordijn, E. H., De Vries, N. K., & De Dreu, C. K. W. (2002). Minority influence on focal and related attitudes: Change in size, attributions, and information processing. *Personality and Social Psychology Bulletin, 28,* 1315–1326.

Graumann, C. F. (1998). Verbal discrimination: A neglected chapter in the social psychology of aggression. *Journal for the Theory of Social Behavior, 28,* 41–61.

Greenwood, J. D. (2000). Individualism and the social in early American social psychology. *Journal of the History of the Behavioral Sciences, 36,* 443–455.

Grice, H. P. (1975). Logic and conversation. In P. Cole & J. L. Morgan (Eds.), *Syntax and semantics: Speech acts* (pp. 41–58). New York: Academic Press.

Griffin, D., & Buehler, R. (1993). Role of construal processes in conformity and dissent. *Journal of Personality and Social Psychology, 65,* 657–669.

Guimond, S. (1999). Attitude change during college: Normative or informational social influence? *Social Psychology of Education, 2,* 237–261.

Hardin, C. D., & Higgins, E. T. (1996). Shared reality: How social verification makes the subjective objective. In R. M. Sorentino & E. T. Higgins (Eds.), *Handbook of motivation and cognition* (Vol. 3, pp. 28–84). New York: Guilford.

Harmon-Jones, E., & Mills, J. (Eds.). (1999). *Cognitive dissonance: Progress on a pivotal theory in social psychology. Science conference series.* Washington, DC: American Psychological Association.

Haslam, S. A. (2001). *Psychology in organizations: The social identity approach.* London: Sage.

Haslam, S. A., McGarty, C., & Turner, J. C. (1996). Salient group memberships and persuasion: The role of social identity in the validation of beliefs. In J. L. Nye & A. M. Brower (Eds.), *What's social about social cognition? Research on socially-shared cognition in small groups* (pp. 29–56). Thousand Oaks, CA: Sage.

Haslam, S. A., Oakes, P. J., McGarty, C., Turner, J. C., & Onorato, R. S. (1995). Contextual changes in the prototypicality of extreme and moderate outgroup members. *European Journal of Social Psychology, 25,* 509–530.

Hass, R. G., & Mann, W. (1979). Anticipatory belief change: Persuasion or impression management? *Journal of Personality and Social Psychology, 34,* 105–111.

Heider, F. (1958). *The psychology of interpersonal relations.* New York: Wiley.

Herek, G. M. (1986). The instrumentality of attitudes: Toward a neofunctional theory. *Journal of Social Issues, 42,* 99–114.

Herskovits, E. L. (1936). Development of attitudes toward Negroes. *Archives of Psychology, 194.*

Hinsz, V. B., & Davis, J. A. (1984). Persuasive arguments theory, group polarization, and choice shifts. *Personality and Social Psychology Bulletin, 10,* 260–268.

Hobbes, T. (1957). Leviathan or the matter, forme and power of a commonwealth ecclesiasticall and civil. (M. Oakeshott, Ed.). Oxford, UK: Blackwell (Original published 1651).

Hofstede, G. (1980). *Culture's consequences: International differences in work-related values.* Beverly Hills, CA: Sage.

Hogg, M. A. (2000). Subjective uncertainty reduction through self-categorization: A motivational theory of social identity processes. In W. Stroebe & M. Hewstone (Eds.), *European review of social psychology* (Vol. 11, pp. 223–255). Chichester, UK: John Wiley & Sons.

Hogg, M. A. (2001). Self-categorization and subjective uncertainty resolution: Cognitive and motivational facets of social identity and group membership. In J. P. Forgas & K. D. Williams (Eds.), *The social mind: Cognitive and motivational aspects of interpersonal behavior. The 4th annual Sydney Symposium on Social Psychology* (pp. 323–349). New York: Cambridge University Press.

Hogg, M. A., & Turner, J. C. (1987). Social identity and conformity: A theory of referent information influence. In W. Doisa & S. Moscovici (Eds.), *Current issues in European social psychology* (Vol. 2, pp. 139–182). New York, NY: Cambridge University Press.

Hogg, M. A., & Williams, K. D. (2000). From I to we: Social identity and the collective self. *Group Dynamics. Special issue: One hundred years of group research, 4,* 81–97.

Homans, G. C. (1974). *Social behavior: Its elementary forms* (Rev. ed.), xi, 386. Oxford, UK: Harcourt Brace Jovanovich.

Hood, W. R., & Sherif, M. (1962). Verbal report and judgment of an unstructured stimulus. *Journal of Psychology, 54,* 121–130.

Hovland, C. I., Janis, I. L, & Kelley, H. H. (1953). *Communication and persuasion: Psychological studies of opinion change.* New Haven, CT: Yale University Press.

Isenberg, D. J. (1986). Group polarization: A critical review and meta-analysis. *Journal of Personality and Social Psychology, 50,* 1141–1151.

Israel, J., & Tajfel, H. (1972). *The context of social psychology: A critical assessment.* Oxford, UK: Academic Press.

James, W. (1890). *Principles of Psychology* (2 vols). Oxford, UK: Henry Holt.

Jaspars, J. M., Moscovici, S., Schönbach, P., & Tajfel, H. (Eds.). (1974). *European Journal of Social Psychology, 4*(4).

Johnson, B. T., & Eagly, A. H. (1989). Effects of involvement on persuasion: A meta-analysis. *Psychological Bulletin, 106,* 290–314.

Jones, E. E., & Gerard, H. B. (1967). *Foundations of social psychology.* New York: Wiley.

Kahneman, D., & Tversky, A. (1979). Prospect theory: An analysis of decision under risk. *Econometrica, 47,* 263–291.

Kaplan, M. F., & Miller, C. E. (1987). Group decision making and normative versus informational influence: Effects of type of issue and assigned decision rule. *Journal of Personality and Social Psychology, 53,* 306–313.

Katz, D. (1960). The functional approach to the study of attitudes. *Public Opinion Quarterly, 24,* 163–204.

Kelley, H. H. (1992). Common-sense psychology and scientific psychology. *Annual Review of Psychology, 43,* 1–23.

Kelley, H. H. (1952). Two functions of reference groups. In G. E. Swanson, T. M. Newcomb, & E. L. Hartley (Eds.), *Readings in social psychology* (2nd ed., pp. 410–414). New York: Holt.

Kelman, H. C. (1961). Processes of attitude change. *Public Opinion Quarterly, 25,* 57–78.

Kelman, H. C. (1965). *International behavior: A sociopsychological analysis.* New York: Holt, Rinehart, Winston.

Kerr, N. L. (1981). Social transition schemes: Charting the group's road to agreement. *Journal of Personality and Social Psychology, 41*, 684–702.

Kitayama, S., & Markus, H. (1994). A collective fear of the collective: Implications for selves and theories of selves. *Personality and Social Psychology Bulletin. Special issue: The self and the collective, 20*, 568–569.

Krueger, J., & Clement, R.W. (1997). Estimates of social consensus by majorities and minorities: The case for social projection. *Personality and Social Psychology Review, 1*, 299–313.

Kruglanski, A. W., & Mackie, D. M. (1990). Majority and minority influence: A judgment process analysis. In W. Stroebe & M. Hewstone (Eds.), *European review of social psychology* (Vol. 1, pp. 229–261). Chichester, UK: Wiley.

Latané, B. (1996). Dynamic social impact: The creation of culture through communication. *Journal of Communication, 46*, 13–25.

Latané, B., & Bourgeois, M. J. (1996). Experimental evidence for dynamic social impact: The emergence of subcultures in electronic groups? *Journal of Communication, 46*, 35–47.

Latané, B., & Bourgeois, M. J. (2001). Successfully simulating dynamic social impact: Three levels of prediction. In J. P. Forgas & K. D. Williams (Eds.), *Social influence: Direct and indirect processes: The Sydney symposium of social psychology* (pp. 61–76). Philadelphia: Psychology Press.

Latané, B., & L'Herrou, T. (1996). Spatial clustering in the conformity game: Dynamic social impact in electronic groups. *Journal of Personality and Social Psychology, 70*, 1218–1230.

Latané, B., & Nowak, A. (1997). Self-organizing social systems: Necessary and sufficient conditions for the emergence of consolidation, clustering, and continuing diversity. *Progress in Communication Science, 13*, 43–74.

Lavine, H., & Latané, B. (1996). A cognitive-social theory of public opinion: Dynamic social impact and cognitive structure. *Journal of Communication, 46*, 48–56.

Leary, M., & Kowalski, R. (1990). Strategic self-presentation and the avoidance of aversive events: Antecedents and consequences of self-enhancement and self-deprecation. *Journal of Experimental Social Psychology, 26*, 322–336.

Levine, J. M. (1989). Reaction to opinion deviance in small groups. In P. B. Paulus (Ed.), *Psychology of group influence* (2nd ed., pp. 187–231). Hillsdale, NJ: Lawrence Erlbaum Associates.

Levine, J. M., & Moreland, R. (2002). Group reactions to loyalty and disloyalty. In E. Lawler & S. Thye (Eds.), *Group cohesion, trust, and solidarity: Advances in group processes* (Vol: 19, pp. 203–228). Oxford, UK: Elsevier.

Levine, J. M., Sroka, K. R. & Snyder, H.N. (1977). Group support and reaction to stable and shifting agreement/disagreement. *Social Psychology Quarterly, 40*, 214–224.

Liu, J. H., & Latané, B. (1998). Extremitization of attitudes: Does thought- and discussion-induced polarization cumulate? *Basic and Applied Social Psychology, 20*, 103–110.

Lundgren, S., & Prislin, R. (1998). Motivated cognitive processing and attitude change. *Personality and Social Psychology Bulletin, 24*, 715–726.

Maas, A., West, S. G., & Cialdini, R. B. (1987). Minority influence and conversion. In C. Hendrick (Ed.), *Review of personality and social psychology* (Vol. 8, pp. 55–79). Newbury Park, CA: Sage.

Mackie, D. M. (1987). Systematic and nonsystematic processing of majority and minority persuasive communications. *Journal of Personality and Social Psychology, 53*, 41–52.

Mackie, D. M., & Skelly, J. J. (1994). The social cognition analysis of social influence: Contributions to the understanding of persuasion and conformity. In P. G. Devine, D. L. Hamilton, & E. Smith (Eds.) *Social cognition: Impact on social psychology* (pp. 259–289). San Diego, CA: Academic Press.

Mackie, D. M., Worth, L. T., & Asuncion, A. G. (1990). Processing of persuasive ingroup messages. *Journal of Personality and Social Psychology, 58*, 812–822.

Maheswaran, D., & Chaiken, S. (1991). Promoting systematic processing in low motivation settings: Effects of incongruent information on processing and judgment. *Journal of Personality and Social Psychology, 61*, 13–25.

Markus, H., & Kitayama, S. (1991). Culture and the self: Implications for cognition, emotion, and motivation. *Psychological Review, 98*, 224–253.

Marques, J., Abrams, D., & Serodio, R. G. (2001). Being better by being right: Subjective group dynamics and derogation of in-group deviants when generic norms are undermined. *Journal of Personality and Social Psychology, 81*, 436–447.

Marques, J., Yzerbyt, V. Y., & Leyens, J. B. (1988). The "Black Sheep Effect:" Extremity of judgments towards ingroup members as a function of group identification. *European Journal of Social Psychology, 18*, 1–16.

Marquis, D. G. (1960). Individual responsibility and group decisions involving risk. *Industrial Management Review, 3*, 8–23.

Maslow, A. H. (1968). *Toward a psychology of being*. New York: Van Nostrand Reinhold.

Matz, D. C., & Wood, W. (In press). *Cognitive dissonance in groups: The consequences of disagreement. Journal of Personality and Social Psychology*.

McDougal, W. (1920). The group mind. New York: Putnam.

McGarty, C., Haslam, S. A., Hutchinson, K. J., & Turner, J. C. (1994). The effects of salient group memberships on persuasion. *Small Group Research, 25,* 267–293.

McGarty, C., Turner, J. C., Oakes, P. J., & Haslam, S. A. (1993). The creation of uncertainty in the influence process: The roles of stimulus information and disagreement with similar others. *European Journal of Social Psychology, 23,* 17–38.

Mead, G. H. (1934). *Mind, self, and society: From the standpoint of a social behaviorist.* Chicago: University of Chicago Press.

Metts, S., & Grohskopf, E. (2003). Impression management: Goals, strategies, and skills. In J. O. Greene & B. R. Burleson (Eds.), *Handbook of communication and social interaction skills* (pp. 357–399). Mahwah, NJ: Lawrence Erlbaum Associates.

Mill, J. S. (1956). *On liberty.* C. V. Shields (Ed.). Indianapolis & New York: The Library of Liberal Arts. (Original work published 1859)

Miller, J. G. (2002). Bringing culture to basic psychological theory – Beyond individualism and collectivism: Comment on Oyserman et al. (2002). *Psychological Bulletin, 128,* 97–109.

Moreland, R. (1987). The formation of small groups. In C. Hendrick (Ed.), *Group processes. Review of personality and social psychology* (pp. 80–110). Thousand Oaks, CA: Sage.

Moscovici, S. (1976). *Social influence and social change.* London: Academic Press.

Moscovici, S. (1980). Toward a theory of conversion behavior. In L. Berkowitz (Ed.), *Advances of experimental social psychology* (Vol. 13, pp. 209–239). San Diego, CA: Academic Press.

Moscovici, S. (1985). Innovation and minority influence. In S. Moscovici, G. Mugny, & E. Van Avermaet (Eds.), *Perspectives on minority influence* (pp. 9–51). Cambridge, UK: Cambridge University Press.

Moscovici, S., & Zavalloni, M. (1969). The group as a polarizer of attitudes. *Journal of Personality and Social Psychology, 12,* 125–135.

Mugny, G., & Perez, J. A. (1991). *The social psychology of minority influence.* Cambridge, UK: Cambridge University Press.

Myers, D. G., & Lamm, H. (1976). The group polarization phenomenon. *Psychological Bulletin, 83,* 602–627.

Nemeth, C. J. (1986). Differential contributions of majority and minority influence. *Psychological Review, 93,* 23–32.

Nemeth, C. J., & Rogers, J. (1996). Dissent and the search for information. *British Journal of Social Psychology, 35,* 67–76.

Newcomb, T. M. (1943). *Personality and social change: Attitude formation in a student community.* New York: Dryden.

Newcomb, T. M., Koenig, K., Flacks, R., & Warwick, D. (1967). *Persistence and change: Bennington College and its students after 25 years.* New York: Wiley.

Nienhuis, A. E., Manstead, A. S. R., & Spears, R. (2001). Multiple motives and persuasive communication: Creative elaboration as a result of impression motivation and accuracy motivation. *Personality and Social Psychology Bulletin, 27,* 118–132.

Nisbett, R. E., Peng, K., Incheol, C., & Norenzayan, A. (2001). Culture and systems of thought: Holistic versus analytical cognition. *Psychological Review, 108,* 291–301.

Norenzayan, A., Smith, E. E., Kim, B. J., & Nisbett, R. E. (2002). Cultural preferences for formal versus intuitive reasoning. *Cognitive Science, 26,* 653–684.

Oyserman, D., Coon, H. M., Kemmelmeier, M. (2002). Rethinking individualism and collectivism: Evaluation of theoretical assumptions and meta-analysis. *Psychological Bulletin, 128,* 3–72.

Peirce, C. S. (1997). Pragmatism as a principle and method of right thinking: The 1903 Harvard lectures on pragmatism. (P. A. Turrisi, Ed.). Albany, NY: State University of New York Press. (Original work published 1903)

Peng, K., & Nisbett, R. E. (1999). Culture, dialectics, and reasoning about contradiction. *American Psychologist, 54,* 741–754.

Peterson, R. S., & Nemeth, C. J. (1996). Focus versus flexibility: Majority and minority influence can both improve performance. *Personality and Social Psychology Bulletin, 22,* 14–23.

Petty, R. E., & Cacioppo, J. T. (1986). The elaboration likelihood model of persuasion. In L. Berkowitz (Ed.), *Advances in experimental social psychology* (Vol. 19, pp. 123–205). Orlando, FL: Academic Press.

Petty, R. E., & Wegener, D. (1998). Attitude change: Multiple roles for persuasion variables. In D.T. Gilbert, S. T. Fiske, & G. Lindzey (Eds.), *Handbook of Social Psychology* (4th ed., Vol. 1, pp. 323–390). New York: McGraw-Hill.

Phinney, J. S. (1990). Ethnic identity in adolescents and adults: Review of research. *Psychological Bulletin, 108,* 499–514.

Pilkington, N. W., & Lydon, J. E. (1997). The relative effect of attitude similarity and attitude dissimilarity on interpersonal attraction: Investigating the moderating roles of prejudice and group membership. *Personality and Social Psychology Bulletin, 23,* 107–122.

Pontari, B. A., & Schlenker, B. R. (2000). The influence of cognitive load on self-presentation: Can cognitive busyness help as well as harm social performance. *Journal of Personality and Social Psychology, 78,* 1092–1108.

Pool, G. J., Wood, W., & Leck, K. (1998). The self-esteem motive in social influence: Agreement with valued majorities and disagreement with derogated minorities. *Journal of Personality and Social Psychology, 75*, 967–975.

Prentice, D. A., & Miller, D. T. (1996). Pluralistic ignorance and the perpetuation of social norms by unwitting actors. In M. P. Zanna (Ed.), *Advances in experimental social psychology* (Vol. 28, pp. 161–209). San Diego, CA: Academic Press.

Prislin, R., Brewer, M., & Wilson, D. J. (2002). Changing majority and minority positions within a group versus an aggregate. *Personality and Social Psychology Bulletin, 28*, 504–511.

Prislin, R., & Christensen, P. N. (2002). Group conversion versus group expansion as modes of change in majority and minority positions: All losses hurt but only some gains gratify. *Journal of Personality and Social Psychology, 83*, 1095–1102.

Prislin, R., & Christensen, P. N. (in press). The effects of social change and group membership: To leave or not to leave. *Personality and Social Psychology Bulletin.*

Prislin, R., Limbert, W., & Bauer, E. (2000). From majority to minority and vice versa: The asymmetrical effects of gaining and losing majority position within a group. *Journal of Personality and Social Psychology, 79*, 385–392.

Pruitt, D., & Carnevale, P. (1993). *Negotiation in social conflict. Mapping social psychology series.* Belmont, CA: Brooks/Cole.

Quinn, J. M., & Wood, W. (2004). Forewarnings of influence appeals: Inducing resistance and acceptance. In E. S. Knowles & J. A. Linn (Eds.), *Persuasion and resistance* (pp. 193–214). Mahwah, NJ: Lawrence Erlbaum Associates.

Rohner, J. H., Baron, S. H., Hoffman, E. L., & Swander, D. V. (1954). The stability of autokinetic judgments. *Journal of Abnormal and Social Psychology, 49*, 595–597.

Ross, L., Bierbrauer, G., & Hoffman, S. (1976). The role of attribution processes in conformity and dissent: Revisiting the Asch situation. *American Psychologist, 31*, 148–157.

Rousseau, J.-J. (1978). On the social contract. (R. D. Masters, Ed.). New York: St. Martin's Press. (Original published in 1762)

Rubin, M., & Hewstone, M. (1998). Social identity theory's self-esteem hypothesis: A review and some suggestions for clarification. *Personality and Social Psychology Review, 2*, 40–62.

Ruscher, J. B., & Duval, L. L. (1998). Multiple communicators with unique target information transmit less stereotypical impressions. *Journal of Personality and Social Psychology, 74*, 329–344.

Schachter, S. (1951). Deviation, rejection, and communication. *Journal of Abnormal and Social Psychology, 46*, 190–207.

Scherer, K. R. (1993). Two faces of social psychology: European and North American perspectives. *Social Science Information, 32*, 515–552.

Schlenker, B. R. (2003). Self-presentation. In M. R. Leary & J. P. Tangney (Eds.), *Handbook of self and identity* (pp. 492–518). New York: Guilford.

Schlenker, B. R., & Weingold, M. F. (1990). Self-consciousness and self-presentation: Being autonomous versus appearing autonomous. *Journal of Personality and Social Psychology, 59*, 820–828.

Sechrist, G. B., & Stangor, C. (2001). Changing racial beliefs by providing consensus information. *Personality and Social Psychology Bulletin, 27*, 486–496.

Sedikides, C., & Green, J. D. (2004). What I don't recall can't hurt me: Information negativity versus information inconsistency as determinants of memorial self-defense. *Social Cognition, 22*, 4–29.

Sedikides, C., & Strube, M. J. (1997). Self-evaluation: To thine own self be good, to thine own self be sure, to thine own self be true, and to thine own self be better. In M. P. Zanna (Ed.), *Advances in experimental social psychology* (Vol. 29, pp. 209–269). San Diego, CA: Academic Press.

Shaikh, T., & Kanekar, S. (1994). Attitudinal similarity and affiliation need as determinants of interpersonal attraction. *Journal of Social Psychology, 134*, 257–259.

Shavitt, S. (1990). The role of attitude objects in attitude functions. *Journal of Experimental Social Psychology, 26*, 124–148.

Sherif, M. (1935). A study of some social factors in perception. *Archives of Psychology, 27*, 1–60.

Sherif, M. (1936). *The psychology of social norms.* New York: Harper & Bros.

Smith, M. B., Bruner, J. S., & White, R. W. (1956). *Opinions and personality.* New York: Wiley.

Swann, W. B., Jr. (1990). To be adored or to be known? The interplay of self-enhancement and self-verification. In E. T. Higgins & R. M. Sorrentino (Eds.), *Handbook of motivation and cognition: Foundations of social behavior* (Vol. 2, pp. 408–448). New York: Guilford.

Swann, W. B., Jr., Rentfrow, P. J., & Guinn, J. S. (2002). Self-verification: The search for coherence. In M. R. Leary & J. P. Tangney (Eds.), *Handbook of self and identity* (pp. 367–383). New York: Guilford.

Tajfel, H. (1978). Interindividual behaviour and intergroup behavior. In H. Tajfel (Ed.), *Differentiation between social groups: Studies in the social psychology of intergroup relations* (pp. 27–60). London: Academic Press.

Tajfel, H. (1981). *Human groups and social categories.* New York, NY: Cambridge University Press.

Tajfel, H. (1982). Social psychology of intergroup relations. *Annual Review of Psychology, 33*, 1–39.

Tajfel, H., & Turner, J. C. (1979). An integrative theory of intergroup conflict. In W. A. Austin & S. Worchel (Eds.), *The social psychology of intergroup relations* (pp. 33–48). Monterey, CA: Brooks/Cole.

Tesser, A. (2000). On the confluence of self-esteem maintenance mechanisms. *Personality and Social Psychology Review, 4*, 290–299.

Thibaut, J. W., & Kelley, H. H. (1959). *The social psychology of groups.* New York: Wiley.

Turner, J. C. (1982). Towards a cognitive redefinition of the social group. In H. Tajfel (Ed.), *Social identity and intergroup relations* (pp. 15–40). Cambridge, UK: Cambridge University Press.

Turner, J. C. (1991). *Social influence.* Pacific Grove, CA: Brooks/Cole.

Turner, J. C., Hogg, M. A., Oakes, P. J., Reicher, S. D., & Watherell, M. S. (1987). *Rediscovering the social group: A Self-categorization theory.* Oxford and New York: Basil Blackwell.

Turner, J. C., & Oakes, P. J. (1989). Self-categorization theory and social influence. In P. B. Paulus (Ed.), *The psychology of group influence* (2nd ed., pp. 233–275). Hillsdale, NJ: Lawrence Erlbaum Associates.

Turner, J. C., & Oakes, P. J. (1997). The socially structured mind. In C. McGarty & A. S. Haslam (Eds.), *The message of social psychology: Perspectives on mind in society* (pp. 355–373). Malden, MA: Blackwell.

van Knippenberg, D. (1999). Social identity and persuasion: Reconsidering the role of group membership. In D. Abrams & M. A. Hogg (Eds.), *Social identity and social cognition* (pp. 315–331). Oxford, UK: Blackwell.

Wilder, D. A. (1977). Perception of groups, size of opposition, and social influence. *Journal of Experimental Social Psychology, 13*, 253–268.

Williams, K. D. (2001). *Ostracism: The power of silence.* New York: Guilford.

Wood, W. (1999). Motives and modes of processing in the social influence of groups. In S. Chaiken & Y. Trope (Eds.), *Dual process theories in social psychology* (pp. 547–570). New York: Guilford.

Wood, W. (2000). Attitude change: Persuasion and social influence. *Annual Review of Psychology, 51*, 539–570.

Wood, W., Christensen, N. P., Hebl, M. R., & Rothgerber, H. (1997). Conformity to sex-typed norms, affect, and the self-concept. *Journal of Personality and Social Psychology, 73*, 523–535.

Wood, W., Lundgren, S., Ouellette, J. A., Busceme, S., & Blackstone, T. (1994). Minority influence: A meta-analytical review of social influence processes. *Psychological Bulletin, 115*, 323–345.

Wood, W., Pool, G. J., Leck, K., & Purvis, D. (1996). Self-definition, defensive processing, and influence: The normative impact of majority and minority groups. *Journal of Personality and Social Psychology, 71*, 1181–1193.

Wood, W., & Quinn, J. M. (2003). Forewarned and forearmed? Two meta-analytic syntheses of forewarnings of influence appeals. *Psychological Bulletin, 129*, 119–138.

Young, K. (1931). *Social attitudes.* New York: Henry Holt.

Zajonc, R. B. (1960). The process of cognitive tuning in communication. *Journal of Abnormal and Social Psychology, 61*, 159–167.

Zanna, M. P., & Rempel, J. K. (1988). Attitudes: A new look at an old concept. In D. Bar-Tal & A. W. Kruglanski (Eds.), *The social psychology of knowledge* (pp. 315–334). Cambridge, UK: Cambridge University Press.

17

Attitude Theory and Research: Intradisciplinary and Interdisciplinary Connections

Victor Ottati
John Edwards
Nathaniel D. Krumdick
Loyola University, Chicago

INTRODUCTION

Attitudes, according to Allport (1935) in his landmark chapter in the *Handbook of Social Psychology*, are "...probably the most distinctive and indispensable concept in contemporary American social psychology" (p. 798). Even a casual survey of current textbooks, handbooks, conference proceedings and journals reveals that the study of attitudes is a predominant theme of contemporary social psychology. The attitude concept affords linkages with a wide range of topics that interest social psychological theorists, researchers, and practitioners. The present chapter attempts to illuminate how these topics are infused with and connected to fundamental attitudinal concepts and processes. Two distinguishable approaches can be taken when illuminating linkages between the attitude literature and related disciplines: the interdisciplinary approach that addresses social problems by combining the social psychology of attitudes with perspectives from disciplines outside of social psychology (e.g., health care, education, politics, law); and the intradisciplinary approach that focuses on linkages between attitude research and other fundamental topics within the field of social psychology (e.g., impression formation, interpersonal attraction, close relationships, group performance, group decision making).

Interdisciplinary Connections

An obvious approach to forging connections between attitudes and related disciplines involves interdisciplinary applications that are designed to understand and solve social problems. Indeed, the emphasis upon understanding and solving social problems is what, according to some, distinguishes "applied" from "basic" research (Oskamp & Schulz, 1998). Certainly it is easy to identify social problems to which principles about the nature, origin, and consequences of attitudes are intrinsically relevant. All one needs to do is consult the daily news sources to learn about the latest episodes of prejudice, crime, war, failing schools, corruption, poverty, environmental degradation, disease, substance abuse, mental illness, and other forms of human tragedy. People's attitudes inarguably affect and are affected by these issues and problems. Out of practical necessity, those who are directly involved in dealing with human problems do so from groundings in political, economic, educational, health care, criminal justice, religious, and other institutions of society. Each institution possesses its unique body of knowledge, conventional wisdom, language, and culture. Moreover, each social institution is populated by workers with different forms of expertise and training.

Applied interdisciplinary attitude research directly applies attitude theory and research to practical social problems addressed by these social institutions. Applied interdisciplinary attitude research can be divided into subdisciplines, each of which is associated with a different social institution or problem (e.g., political behavior, mental health, consumer behavior). In each case, attitude theory and research is directly applied to a field of study that falls outside of the traditional boundaries of social psychology. A prominent example of this approach is found in current research in consumer psychology. Much of this research involves applying models of attitude formation and change to advertising and consumer behavior. Thus, consumer psychology includes the application of classical conditioning (Shimp, Stuart, & Engle, 1991), cognitive response (Olson, Toy, Dover, 1982), and elaboration likelihood (Petty, Cacioppo, & Schuman, 1983) models of attitude formation and change, just to name a few.

Although the applied interdisciplinary approach is certainly a viable one, the present chapter adopts a broader and more flexible perspective when investigating connections between the attitude literature and related disciplines. From this broader perspective, the connection between the attitude literature and related disciplines is best described as one that involves cross-fertilization, reciprocal influence, or theoretical commonality. This broader approach differs from the applied interdisciplinary approach, an approach that focuses on a unidirectional flow of application from the attitudes literature to related disciplines. This broader perspective does not limit itself to what has been traditionally labeled "applied" research. In a number of cases, purely theoretical connections are forged between the attitude literature and some other basic research area (e.g., impression formation). Here the emphasis is on theoretical commonality and mediating psychological process, an emphasis that is most commonly associated with "basic" research (Oskamp & Schulz, 1998).

Perhaps most importantly, the present approach does not restrict its attention to interdisciplinary connections. To the contrary, it also examines thematic linkages that exist between the attitude literature and other areas within social psychology. Indeed, intradisciplinary connections of this nature are emphasized at the onset, and once established, provide a platform for discussing interdisciplinary connections to areas falling outside of social psychology. Figure 17.1 provides a visual depiction of this approach. We adopt this strategy for two main reasons. First, by initially focusing on intradisciplinary connections, the attitude literature provides an integrative theme that unifies the diverse areas of social psychology. Second, this strategy provides an over-arching scheme for organizing our discussion of interdisciplinary attitude research. That is, it is possible to divide up the field of social psychology into meaningful domains (i.e., intrapersonal, interpersonal, intragroup, and intergroup processes) and to view interdisciplinary attitude research that falls outside of social psychology as extensions of these fundamental domains.

Intradisciplinary Connections

If as Allport (and others) claimed, attitude is probably the most distinctive and indispensable psychological concept, then attitudes would be expected to pervade all aspects of social psychology as a discipline. The intradisciplinary approach, then, considers how attitude research can be explicitly linked to other topics within social psychology. In taking this approach, an initial matter to resolve is how to define the subdivisions and boundaries of the sprawling field of social psychology. The typological scheme adopted in this chapter derives from two

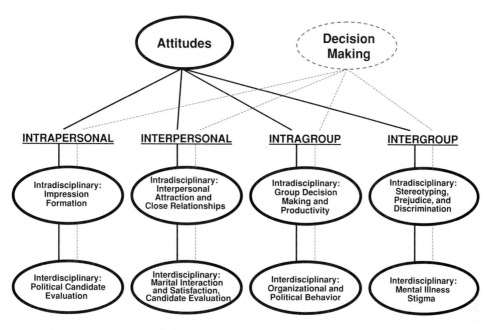

FIG 17.1. A Framework for Connecting Attitude Research to Related Domains.

fundamental units of study in social psychology, individuals and groups, the inner nature of these units and the relations between those units. That is, the contents of social psychology can be divided into four broad domains:

Intrapersonal, i.e., the structures and processes within individuals.
Interpersonal, i.e., forms of interaction between individuals.
Intragroup, i.e., the structures and processes within groups of people.
Intergroup, i.e., forms of interaction between groups.

These four domains will constitute the main body of this chapter as we discuss how attitude theory and research serve as a kind of connective matter that can hold these domains together. Of course, a comprehensive discussion of all attitude-relevant research falling within these domains is beyond the scope of a single chapter. Thus, within each domain, we focus on a limited number of representative intradisciplinary and interdisciplinary linkages with the attitudes literature. Our selection of topics is based upon prominence, social relevance, and personal expertise. That is, we have selected topics that are prominent within social psychology, relevant to social problems, and about which we are most knowledgeable. For example, within the "intrapersonal processes" section, we focus on the connection between attitude research and impression formation research (intradisciplinary connection) and further extensions of that work to the study of political candidate evaluation (interdisciplinary connection).

Figure 17.1 provides a visual diagram of this approach. Solid lines depict the attitude-relevant connections that are emphasized in the present chapter. It is explicitly acknowledged that other research areas (e.g., decision making, learning) can serve a similar, integrative function. As an example, Figure 17.1 includes linkages (using dotted lines) with the decision-making literature. The focus of the present chapter, however, is on illuminating connections with the attitude literature. Before embarking upon this task, we briefly identify some key attitudinal concepts and processes that are of particular relevance to this endeavor.

ATTITUDE CONCEPTS AND PROCESSES

This chapter considers fundamental concepts and processes identified by attitude researchers and illuminates how they can be extended to other domains. An initial order of business involves identifying the attitudinal concepts and processes that are of particular relevance to this endeavor. In the present chapter, our usage and definition of many attitudinal terms is compatible with that adopted by Fishbein and Ajzen (1975). Thus, the term "attitude" is used to describe an individual's overall, bipolar evaluation of an object or behavior (bad versus good). A "belief" is defined as a cognitive association between an object and a descriptive attribute (e.g., "Nader is liberal"). A "behavioral belief" is defined as a cognitive association between a behavior and a consequence (e.g., "My buying a Porsche will put me into debt"). A "subjective norm" prescribes whether an individual should or should not perform a behavior. A "behavior intention" is a likelihood belief that links the self to some behavior.

Additional attitudinal constructs and properties are gleaned from other sources. For example, in accordance with Fazio's (1986) model, we assume that attitudes are stored in memory and can be retrieved (or automatically activated) for purposes of reporting a judgment or enacting a behavior. We also distinguish attitudes from "episodic affective responses" (e.g., emotional reactions, mood states). Unlike attitudes, we view episodic affective reactions as experiential states that occur during a circumscribed interval of time (see Ottati & Wyer, 1993). Moreover, whereas episodic affective reactions are often differentiated (anger, sadness, fear, happiness; Bodenhausen, Sheppard, & Kramer, 1994; Lerner & Keltner, 2001), attitudes are often assumed to vary along a simple bipolar (bad versus good) continuum (Fishbein & Ajzen, 1975). Episodic affect can be attributed to a specific source (e.g., "That man is making me nervous") or occur in an unattributed form (e.g., "I feel nervous, but I'm not sure why"). When attributed to a specific source, an affective state is typically labeled an "emotional reaction;" when unattributed, affect is often labeled a "mood." By defining episodic affective reactions and attitudes as distinct constructs, it is possible to consider episodic affective reactions as a causal determinant of attitudes (e.g., "Mary made me feel happy during our last four dates, therefore I evaluate Mary positive overall").

Many approaches to understanding the antecedents of attitudes are relevant to the present chapter. These include Katz's (1960; Sarnoff & Katz, 1954) suggestion that attitudes are formed in the service of utilitarian, ego-defensive, value expressive, or knowledge-based needs. When considering other antecedent processes, we often make a distinction between those that entail minimal cognitive deliberation or elaboration and those that entail a great deal of thought and elaboration. The former mode of processing is labeled "peripheral" or "heuristic" processing, whereas the latter mode of processing is labeled "central" or "systematic" processing (Petty & Cacioppo, 1986; Chaiken, 1980; Chaiken, Liberman, & Eagly, 1989). Peripheral models include the classical conditioning (Razran, 1938; Staats & Staats, 1958; Krosnick et al., 1992), operant conditioning (Greenspoon, 1955; Insko, 1965), mood misattribution (Schwarz & Clore, 1983; 1996), and self-perception (Bem, 1965, 1967) approaches to attitude formation and change. Approaches that accommodate a more systematic style of processing include the combinatorial (Fishbein & Ajzen, 1981), cognitive response (Greenwald, 1968), and information processing (McGuire, 1968; 1985) models of attitude formation and change.

Attitude models that focus on the cognitive consequences of previously formed attitudes are also relevant to the present chapter. The suggestion that attitudes elicit attitude-congruent processing of subsequently encountered information appeared quite early in the literature (Allport, 1935; Bartlett, 1932; Edwards, 1941; Proshansky, 1943; Seeleman, 1940; Watson & Hartmann, 1939), but received more attention with the advent of balance (Abelson & Rosenberg, 1958; Heider, 1946; 1958; see also Marsh & Wallace, chap. 9, this volume) and dissonance theory (Festinger, 1957; see also Olson & Stone, chap. 6, this volume). These approaches suggest that attitude-consistent or balanced information is selectively attended to, more easily learned, more likely to be inferred, more likely to be thought about, more likely to be viewed as important, and more likely to be retrieved than attitude-inconsistent information (Abelson, 1959; Beckmann & Gollwitzer, 1987; Festinger, 1957; Frey, 1986; Heider, 1958; Olson & Zanna, 1979; Osgood & Tannenbaum, 1955; Rosenberg, 1960; Sweeney & Gruber, 1984; Zajonc & Burnstein, 1965; but see Cacioppo & Petty, 1979; Eagly et al., 2001; Jones & Aneshansel, 1956; Johnson & Judd, 1983; Sears & Freedman, 1965; for a recent review, see Wyer & Albarracin, chap. 7, this volume). Most of these cognitive mechanisms involve a tendency for attitudes to produce balanced beliefs. It should be recognized, however, that balance theory also accommodates the finding that evaluation-relevant beliefs can function as bona fide determinants of attitudes toward an object (Fishbein & Ajzen, 1975).

Two approaches that focus on the behavioral consequences of attitudes (see Ajzen & Fishbein, chap. 5, this volume) are relevant to our present concerns. The first suggests that attitude-relevant constructs (e.g., attitude toward the object, attitude toward the behavior, subjective norm) produce an effect on behavior that is mediated by behavior intention (e.g., Fishbein & Ajzen, 1975; Triandis, 1980). The second suggests that chronically accessible attitudes can be automatically activated by the mere presentation or mention of an attitude object, and that such attitudes can impact behavior in a relatively direct manner (Fazio, 1986).

Having identified fundamental concepts and processes that are of relevance to the present chapter, we now illuminate how these concepts and processes can be extended to each of the four domains of study (intrapersonal, interpersonal, intragroup, intergroup processes).

INTRAPERSONAL PROCESSES

A considerable amount of work, both within and outside social psychology, focuses on intrapersonal processes that underlie social judgment and behavior. In these cases, intrapsychic processes are viewed in relative isolation and reciprocal interaction with other persons or groups is deemphasized. Social psychological approaches that fall in this category include research on the self, as well as models of impression formation that deemphasize reciprocal interaction. The present section focuses on connections between the attitude literature and this latter type of impression formation research. Before embarking upon this discussion, however, it is briefly worth noting that attitudinal connections to the self literature are also extremely pervasive.

Research regarding the self indicates that self-esteem is associated with a variety of cognitive and behavioral outcomes. Self-esteem, of course, can be conceptualized as ones' attitude toward the self (Coopersmith, 1967). Sedikides (1993) has argued that self-esteem serves three identifiable functions: self-assessment, self-enhancement, and self-verification (Sedikides, 1993). Two of these functions overlap considerably with functions served by attitudes more generally (Katz, 1960; for a review, see Kruglanski & Stroebe, chap. 8, this volume). Namely, the self-assessment and self-enhancement functions correspond closely to the knowledge and ego-defensive functions of attitudes, respectively. Other research suggests that an individual's "working self-concept" varies across situations depending on which aspects of the self happen to be currently most accessible (Markus & Nurius, 1986). Thus, in the same way that construal and evaluation of an attitude object can vary across situations (Bem, 1967; Schwarz & Bless, 1992), construal and evaluation of the self can vary across situations. These and other connections with the self literature could easily fill the pages of an entire volume.

As we have noted, however, the present section will focus on attitudinal connections with the impression formation literature. This literature delineates the cognitive processes that unfold "inside a perceiver's head" en route to forming an impression of a target person. In this literature, the target person functions primarily as a "stimulus," and reciprocal interaction between the perceiver and target person is deemphasized. Impression formation research commonly involves presenting a perceiver with a description of a target person. After receiving this description, the perceiver is asked to judge the target person or recall the presented information. Effects of processing objective (e.g., impression set, memory set), prior expectancy (e.g., favorable trait, unfavorable trait), and nature of the description (e.g., expectancy consistent, expectancy inconsistent, ambiguous) are investigated by systematically manipulating these criteria and examining their effect on judgment or recall.

The impression formation paradigm serves as an analogue to many real-world circumstances. For example, an employer might hear someone describe a job applicant, and use that information to judge the applicant's suitability for a job. Alternatively, a bachelor might read a description of a woman in the personal ads, and use that information to evaluate the woman's suitability as a mate. Perceivers are faced with an analogous task when they read about a political candidate in the newspaper, and must assess the candidate's suitability for office. In the discussion that follows, we begin by illuminating attitudinal connections with impression formation research in social psychology, and then move on to explore interdisciplinary connections with the candidate evaluation literature.

Intradisciplinary Connections to Impression Formation

Thematic commonalities are abundant when considering linkages between attitude research and the impression formation literature. One example of this tendency can be found within Wyer's social information-processing model of impression formation (Wyer, 1974, 1981; Wyer & Carlston, 1979; Wyer & Srull, 1989). This model includes comprehension, encoding and interpretation, organization, representation, retrieval, integration, and response generation stages of information processing. Many of the stages contained in this model resemble those contained in McGuire's information processing model of attitude formation and change (McGuire, 1968, 1976, 1985). For example, McGuire's model (1968, 1972, 1985) similarly includes comprehension, retention (analogous to representation and retrieval), and integration stages of processing. Information processing en route to impression formation, then, is not unlike information processing elicited by a persuasive communication. These two models may share a common foundation in basic cognitive models of information processing (Miller, Galanter, Pribram, 1960; Simon & Newell, 1964) and were probably mutually influential in terms of historical and thematic development.

Self-perception theory (Bem, 1965, 1967), a classic model of attitude formation and change, shares an interesting linkage with impression formation research. Self-perception theory posits that individuals are sometimes unable to access a previously stored attitude toward the object (Wood, 1982). As a consequence, individuals infer their own attitude on the basis of their recent behavior toward the attitude object (Bem, 1965, 1967). This inference presumably occurs because the recent behavior is highly accessible. Thus, cognitive accessibility plays a pivotal role in self-perception theory. Cognitive accessibility plays an analogous, pivotal role in theories of impression formation. Namely, it is often assumed that behaviors performed by a target person are encoded and interpreted in terms of the most accessible concept, or that accessible information is more easily retrieved and used as a basis for judging a target person (e.g., Higgins, Rholes, & Jones, 1977; Wyer & Srull, 1989; Schwarz & Bless, 1992). Thus, by emphasizing the role of accessibility, self-perception theory shares a linkage with impression formation models that emphasize the role of cognitive accessibility at a variety of stages of information processing (Wyer & Srull, 1989).

Information processing models of impression formation typically include an information integration stage wherein multiple pieces of information (e.g., behaviors, attributes, traits) are combined to arrive at a summary judgment of the target person. Although the nature of this combinatorial rule is somewhat controversial (Fishbein & Ajzen, 1975; Anderson, 1981), combinatorial models of attitude formation are often used to describe how this process operates to arrive at a global evaluative impression of the target person. Some researchers have assumed, either implicitly or explicitly, that this combinatorial process can be modeled in terms of an equally weighted algebraic rule that involves simply summing up the number of positive attributes and subtracting the number of negative attributes (Kelley & Mirer, 1974; see also Greenwald, 1968; Petty & Cacioppo, 1979 for a similar approach in a persuasion context). In other attitude formation models, the subjective valence of each attribute is permitted to vary along a continuum (Fishbein & Ajzen, 1981). In addition, the weight ascribed to each attribute is often assumed to vary as a function of the subjective certainty that the object possesses the attribute, the accessibility of the attribute, or the importance of the attribute (Fishbein & Ajzen, 1975; Krosnick, Berent, & Boninger, 1994).

Cognitive response theory (Greenwald, 1968), a model of persuasion and attitude change, also shares important linkages with the impression formation literature. Cognitive response theory emphasizes that individuals are not passive recipients of communications pertaining to an attitude object. When receiving a communication, individuals generate cognitive responses that assess the merits of the presented arguments and relate the communication to their prior knowledge (Chaiken, Liberman, & Eagly, 1989; Greenwald, 1968; Petty & Cacioppo, 1986). According to the cognitive response model, the message recipient's attitude toward the communication topic is not determined by the evaluative tone of the communicated (i.e., presented) arguments. To the contrary, it is determined by the evaluative tone of these cognitive elaborations (but see Albarracín & Wyer, 2001; Eagly & Chaiken, 1993; Johnson, Maio, & Smith-McLallen, chap. 15, this volume, for alternative causal interpretations). Cognitive response theory possesses a theoretical "cousin" residing in the impression formation literature, namely, the online model of impression formation (Hastie & Park, 1986).

Both cognitive response theory and the online model of impression formation departed from previous models that emphasized the individual's ability to recall objectively presented information pertaining to the object. For example, early persuasion models assumed that attitude change would persist only if the recipient was able to remember the originally presented communication arguments. This emphasis is because recall (and integration) of the presented arguments was assumed to mediate the effect of the communication on delayed attitude judgments. In contrast, cognitive response theory posited that attitudes toward the communication topic are primarily determined by the message recipient's cognitive responses to the message, not the presented message itself (Greenwald, 1968; Petty, Ostrom, & Brock, 1981). It is the evaluative tone of these self-generated elaborations, not the originally presented arguments, that determines the message recipient's attitude toward the topic. Persistence of attitude change simply requires that the recipient remember the cognitive elaborations (Petty, 1977a, 1977b) and is often unrelated to the recipient's ability to recall the presented message arguments (Cacioppo & Petty, 1979).

An analogous development occurred within the impression formation literature. Early impression formation models often assumed that the effect of the encoded behaviors on delayed judgment was mediated by the perceiver's recall (and integration) of the behaviors. According to this "memory based" model of impression formation, the evaluative tone of recalled behaviors should determine (and therefore predict) delayed likeability ratings (Hastie & Park, 1986). In reality, the correlation between recall of the presented behaviors and delayed judgments of the target person is often low. This finding laid the foundation for the online model of impression formation. In the "online" model, the perceiver evaluates each behavior as it is encountered, and immediately integrates these valences into a running tally as each behavior is encoded (Hastie & Park, 1986). This summary tally is stored in memory. When a judgment is later required, this tally is retrieved from memory rather than the specific behaviors that contributed to it (Hastie & Park, 1986). This model can account for the finding that recall of the presented behaviors is unrelated to the perceiver's summary evaluation of the target person, presumably because memory for the summary tally can persist long after the specific behaviors have been forgotten.

The correspondence between the cognitive response approach and the online model of impression formation is clear. In both models, recall of the presented information has little to do with the reported judgment. In both models, the individual performs a cognitive operation on the presented information as it is acquired (i.e., online). In both cases, it is the outcome of this cognitive operation (cognitive responses, running tally) that is stored in memory and later retrieved for purposes of reporting a judgment, not the presented information (message arguments, behaviors). The primary difference between these two models is that the online model of impression formation involves storage and retrieval of a single, integrated knowledge structure (i.e., the tally), whereas the cognitive response model involves the storage and retrieval of multiple knowledge structures (i.e., multiple cognitive responses). Yet, even this distinction is reduced when one considers an alternative version of the online model that actually appeared earlier (Wyer & Carlston, 1979).

In this alternative version of the online model, the perceiver forms multiple trait inferences when acquiring the behavioral information (e.g., intelligent, generous, humorous), and stores these trait inferences in memory. When an evaluative judgment is later required, these traits are retrieved (and integrated) rather than the specific behaviors they were derived from (Hastie & Park, 1986; Wyer & Carlston, 1979). Just as the cognitive response approach involves the storage and retrieval of multiple cognitive responses, this alternate online model of impression formation involves the storage and retrieval of multiple traits.

Up to this point, we have focused on attitude models that delineate the causal determinants of attitude judgments, and highlighted their connection to the impression formation literature. However, research regarding the cognitive consequences of attitudes also shares important linkages with impression formation research. Both balance theory (Heider, 1946, 1958; Abelson & Rosenberg, 1958; see also Marsh & Wallace and Wyer & Albarracín, chap. 9 and chap. 7, respectively, this volume) and dissonance theory (Festinger, 1957; see also Olson & Stone, chap. 6, this volume) suggest that a previously established attitude can impact subsequent cognitive reactions to an attitude object. As previously noted, these approaches suggest that attitude consistent information is selectively attended to, more easily learned, more likely to be inferred, more likely to be thought about, more likely to be viewed as important, and more likely to be retrieved than attitude-inconsistent information.

A related tenet of impression formation research involves the claim that cognitive expectancies influence subsequent information processing. An example of this tendency occurs when interpretation of an ambiguous behavior is assimilated toward the perceiver's prior impression (see Higgins, Rholes, & Jones, 1977; Srull & Wyer, 1979 for related evidence). For example, if Jesse Jackson were to make a remark indicating that the Ku Klux Klan should be permitted to speak in public, few would interpret such a remark as "racist." To the contrary, most would interpret such a remark as "civil libertarian." An analogous process has been emphasized by attitude researchers based on the assumption that an attitude toward a target person can be regarded as an evaluative expectancy that produces evaluatively consistent interpretations of subsequently encountered information. An example of this tendency occurs when individuals are asked to assess the strength of political candidates' arguments during a debate. Assessments of who won the debate are biased in favor of the candidate who was preferred prior to the debate (Bothwell & Brigham, 1983). Effects such as these, which involve the impact of attitudes on the interpretation of subsequently encountered ambiguous information, were identified long ago (Proshansky, 1943; Seeleman, 1940). Given that early research gave a prominent role to attitudes as determinants of interpretation, it is ironic that modern theories of social perception often ignore the role of attitudes.

Attitudes can also function as expectancies that influence the recall of subsequently encountered information. Early research suggested that individuals are more likely to remember attitude-consistent information than attitude discrepant information (Edwards, 1941; Watson & Hartmann, 1939). However, later research (Jones and Aneshansel, 1956) demonstrated that this effect could be reversed under certain conditions, presumably because participants engage in extensive counterarguing when they encounter uncongenial information (see also Cacioppo & Petty, 1979; Eagly et al., 2000; Johnson & Judd, 1983; Zanna & Olson, 1982; see Eagly et al., 1999; Eagly et al., 2001 for reviews). A recent meta-analysis suggests that, when pooling across past research studies, the overall magnitude of the attitude congeniality effect is quite small (.23 effect size, Eagly et al., 1999; Eagly et al., 2001). Moreover, a variety of factors impact the direction and magnitude of this effect. For example, experimental procedures that control for methodological artifacts (e.g., guessing in a recognition task) yield smaller congeniality effects than experiments that fail to control for such factors (Eagly et al., 1999, Eagly et al., 2001). In addition, congeniality effects are stronger for less controversial attitude objects than for highly controversial attitude objects (Eagly et al., 1999; Eagly et al., 2000), presumably because controversial topics increase motivation to actively refute and elaborate upon uncongenial information. It is also important to distinguish selective processing that occurs at encoding from selective processing that occurs at retrieval. Recent work that focuses on selective retrieval processes has tended to yield congeniality effects (Conway & Ross, 1984; Lydon, Zanna, & Ross, 1988; but see Ross, 1989 for problems in distinguishing retrieval from reconstructive memory effects).

Research on the attitude congeniality effect bears resemblance to impression formation research that examines the recall of behavioral information pertaining to a target person. When provided with a trait expectancy regarding the target person (e.g., intelligent), individuals are least likely to recall trait-irrelevant behaviors (e.g., helped the elderly woman cross the street). Although research suggests that expectancy consistent behaviors (e.g., wrote the best class paper) are most easily associated with the trait expectancy (Wyer & Srull, 1989), many studies reveal that expectancy inconsistent information (e.g., failed the exam) possesses the highest recall advantage (Hastie & Kumar, 1979; Hastie, 1980; Srull, 1981; see Rojahn & Pettigrew, 1992; Stangor & McMillan, 1992 for meta-analyses). This effect presumably emerges because inconsistent behaviors are more surprising, and therefore trigger more elaboration geared toward resolving their inconsistency with other behaviors. This increase in elaboration leads to the formation of interbehavioral linkages in memory that associate the inconsistent behavior with other behaviors performed by the target person (Srull, 1981). When perceivers are later asked to recall the behaviors, inconsistent behaviors are more easily recalled because more associative retrieval paths are linked to them (Srull, 1981). However, expectancy consistent behaviors are most likely to be recalled when participants are unable or unmotivated to elaborate upon the inconsistent behaviors, or alternatively, when they are subsequently provided with an opportunity to bolster their originally formed trait impression (Srull, 1981; Wyer & Srull, 1989; but see Rojahn & Pettigrew, 1992).

The assumption that trait consistent information is more easily associated with the trait expectancy bears resemblance to passive accounts of attitude congeniality effects. When unmotivated to actively refute uncongenial information, individuals may simply ignore or "screen out" uncongenial information (Eagly et al., 2000). Also, in both the attitude and impression formation literature, consistency effects are reduced (or reversed) when the individual expends considerable effort in actively refuting or "explaining away" the inconsistent information. Thus, in both literatures, cognitive motivation plays an important role in determining the relative likelihood of recalling consistent and inconsistent information.

Interdisciplinary Connections to Political Candidate Evaluation

Much of the impression formation research discussed in the prior section is relevant to under-standing the process whereby voters evaluate a political candidate and form a voting preference. For example, the information processing approach, which has linkages with McGuire's model, has been explicitly adopted by a variety of researchers who study candidate evaluation (Ottati, 2001; Ottati, Wyer, Deiger, & Houston, 2002; Lodge, McGraw, & Stroh, 1989; Sullivan, Aldrich, Borgida, & Rahn, 1990). That is, the process of candidate evaluation is often described as one that includes exposure, comprehension, encoding and interpretation, representation, re-trieval, integration, and output generation stages (Ottati, 2001; Ottati et al., 2002).

A variety of information integration models have been applied, either implicitly or explicitly, to the candidate evaluation process. Kelley and Mirer (1974) predicted attitude toward the candidate using the number of likes minus the number of dislikes associated with the candidate. In this case, attribute valences take on a scale value of either $+1$ (positive attribute) or -1 (negative attribute) and are summed to arrive at a combined score. Fishbein and Ajzen (1981) have used their attitude formation model to predict attitudes toward a political candidate. In this case, the subjective valence of each attribute is permitted to vary along a continuum and each attribute is weighted by the voter's certainty that the candidate possesses the attribute. Krosnick and associates (Krosnick et al., 1994; Krosnick & Kinder, 1990) have argued that each attribute is weighted by subjective importance.

In accordance with attitude approaches that emphasize the role of cognitive accessibility (Bem, 1965, 1967), candidate evaluation research suggests that accessible information is given more weight than inaccessible information when voters form a voting preference. It has been shown, for example, that the serial position of information presented about a candidate impacts the weight ascribed to information when voters evaluate a candidate (Lodge & Stroh, 1993; McGraw et al., 1990). When candidate evaluation judgments are arrived at via a memory-based process, this effect is presumably mediated by the cognitive accessibility of the acquired information. Because the Fishbein and Ajzen (1981) model focuses exclusively on beliefs that are "salient" to the voter, it can also accommodate findings of this nature.

Issues given recent and frequent news coverage are highly accessible in the mind of the public (Iyengar & Kinder, 1987; Rogers & Dearing, 1988), and are given greater weight when individuals evaluate a political candidate (Iyengar & Kinder, 1987; for related evidence see Wyer & Albarracín, chap. 7, this volume). In one study, exposure to news coverage of the economy produced a three-fold increase in the weight ascribed to this issue when participants evaluated a congressional candidate (Iyengar & Kinder, 1987). Analogous effects emerge when voters are exposed to news coverage that emphasizes the personal trait characteristics of the candidate. Recent research, however, questions whether effects of this nature are indeed me-diated by cognitive accessibility. In particular, Miller and Krosnick (2000) contend that media coverage serves to convey that an issue is important and consequential. From this perspective, the effect of media coverage on issue weighting is mediated by subjective importance instead of cognitive accessibility.

We previously noted that the distinction between online and memory-based processing shares important linkages with the attitude literature. This distinction has also been emphasized in candidate evaluation research (Lodge, McGraw, & Stroh, 1989; Lodge, Steenbergen, & Brau, 1995). In accordance with the online model of candidate evaluation, memory for specific candidate information decays rapidly, whereas memory for the summary evaluation remains relatively stable and persistent across a long period of time (Lodge et al., 1995). Thus, several weeks after acquiring information about a candidate's issue positions, voters are able to evaluate the candidate even when they are unable to recollect a single issue position. Lodge and Taber

(2001) have recently demonstrated that the online tally is automatically activated by the mere presence or mention of a political candidate. Consistent with basic attitude research on the automatic evaluation effect (Fazio, 1986; Fazio et al., 1995), they demonstrate that evaluation of a candidate can spontaneously be activated even if the individual is not intending to evaluate the candidate.

Research regarding the effects of prior attitudes on subsequent information processing also appears in the candidate evaluation literature. One example of this tendency occurs at the initial, information selection stage of processing (Ottati, 2001; McGuire, 1985). Sweeney and Gruber (1984) investigated this effect as it operated during the Watergate Hearings. They found that McGovern supporters devoted more attention to the Watergate hearings than undecided voters, whereas Nixon supporters devoted less attention than undecided voters. Prior attitudes toward a candidate have also been shown to bias the interpretation of ambiguous information. When assessing the debate performance of two competing candidates, perceptions of who won are biased in favor of the candidate who was preferred prior to the debate (Bothwell & Brigham, 1983).

Work that examines the effect of attitude toward a candidate on subsequent cognitive processing also suggests that balance effects impact a voter's perception of the candidate's stands on the issues. When this occurs, perceptions of the candidate's stands on the issues do not determine attitudes toward the candidate. To the contrary, the direction of causality flows in the opposite direction. That is, perceptions of a candidate's stands on the issues are the rationalized consequence of attitudes that were formed on the basis of other considerations (e.g., image characteristics, partisanship; for a review of related research, see Marsh & Wallace, chap. 9, this volume). In this case, the voter may assume that a liked candidate holds an agreeable position, whereas a disliked candidate holds a disagreeable one (Brent & Granberg, 1982; Granberg & Brent, 1974; Kinder, 1978). Use of this balance heuristic presumably leads voters to assimilate a liked candidate's position toward their own position and to contrast a disliked candidate's position away from their own (Brent & Granberg, 1982; Granberg & Brent, 1974, 1980; Kinder, 1978). Stated another way, voters project their own position onto a liked candidate, and the opposite of their own position onto a disliked candidate.

More recent work, however, suggests that this effect is not so pervasive as originally assumed. According to Ottati and associates (Ottati, Fishbein, & Middlestadt, 1988; Ottati & Wyer, 1993), this is true because perceptions of a candidate's stands on the issues are, to a large degree, constrained by the candidate's objectively expressed position. They report that, when describing their perception of a candidate's issue stances, respondents are more likely to agree with balanced propositions than imbalanced propositions (Ottati et al., 1988). However, respondents also rated objectively true statements (e.g., "Reagan favors an increase in defense spending") as more true than objectively false statements (e.g., "Reagan favors a decrease in defense spending"). Moreover, this later effect was considerably larger than the balance effect. Ottati et al. (1988) concluded that perceptions of the candidates' stands on the issues are constrained by reality and that this tendency is stronger than the tendency to distort a candidate's position to restore balance. Other, more recent research continues to suggest that balance effects may be limited or even completely nonexistent in this context (Krosnick, 2002).

INTERPERSONAL PROCESSES

The present section considers linkages of attitude theory and research with two interrelated areas of social psychology, interpersonal attraction, and close relationships. Whereas the interpersonal attraction literature typically focuses on feelings of attraction that emerge during early stages of an interaction, the close relationships literature focuses on more long term relationships. The interpersonal attraction and close relationships literatures differ from the previously described impression formation literature in two important respects. First, whereas the previously described impression formation research emphasizes the cognitive determinants of person perception, the interpersonal attraction and close relationships literature places greater emphasis on noncognitive factors. These include physical proximity, physical appearance, and episodic affective states. Second, in the previously described impression formation research, the target person functions merely as a presented "stimulus." In contrast, the interpersonal attraction and close relationships literature places greater emphasis on mutual and reciprocal influence that occurs within the context of a developing or ongoing relationship.

Research on interpersonal attraction and close relationships is relevant to the social life of every human being. Consider, for example, the interpersonal experiences of a college student who develops a new circle of friends. Freshman students commonly form attachments with other students who reside in close proximity (Newcomb, 1956) and may be attracted to other students on the basis of their physical demeanor or appearance (Dion, Bersheid, & Walster, 1972). As these relationships continue to develop, compatibility along other dimensions (e.g., attitude similarity) plays an increasingly important role (Newcomb, 1956) and relationship dynamics become increasingly characterized by mutual interpersonal influence (Davis & Rusbult, 2001).

Intradisciplinary Connections to Interpersonal Attraction and Close Relationships

As we have noted, physical appearance is an important determinant of interpersonal attraction, particularly during the initial phases of a relationship. Although some may argue that physical attractiveness is a superficial cue that should be ignored, people respond more favorably to physically attractive individuals than physically unattractive individuals (Berscheid, 1981; Dion et al., 1972; Collins & Zebrowitz, 1995). In a hallmark study, Dion, Berscheid, and Walster (1972) asserted that physical attractiveness activates a "physical attractiveness stereotype" from which other attributes of the person are inferred. Although the attributes that compose this stereotype can vary across cultures (Dion, Pak, & Dion, 1990), research suggests that physically attractive individuals are seen as more poised, interesting, sociable, independent, dominant, exciting, sexy, well-adjusted, social skilled, and successful than unattractive individuals (Dion & Dion, 1987; Moore, Graziano, & Miller, 1987). The tendency for physical attractiveness to elicit halo effects of this nature is consistent with balance theory. Because physical attractiveness triggers a positive impression of the target person, inferences that link the target person to other positive attributes (e.g., successful, poised) are balanced inferences.

There are limits to the physical attractiveness effect, however. Eagly and associates (Eagly, Ashmore, Makhijani, & Longo, 1991) performed an extensive meta-analysis of this literature and concluded that the overall strength of the physical attractiveness effect is only moderate. Furthermore, the magnitude of the physical attractiveness effect varies considerably depending upon the specific judgment assessed and the degree to which other individuating information is present. The attractiveness effect is largest for ratings of social competence; intermediate for potency, adjustment, and intellectual competence, and virtually nonexistent for integrity and concern for others. Moreover, when individuals are provided with other individuating information about the target person, the effect of physical attractiveness is reduced (Eagly et al., 1991).

In addition to physical attractiveness, episodic affect occupies a central role within the interpersonal attraction literature. Positive feelings lead to positive attitudes toward others, whereas negative feelings lead to negative attitudes (Dovidio et al., 1995). These feelings can be elicited by behaviors, verbal statements, or other characteristics of the target person (Downey & Damhave, 1991; Shapiro, Baumeister, Kessler, 1991). For example, a flattering remark might elicit a positive affective reaction whereas an insult might elicit a feeling of irritation or anger. In some cases, however, the affective state that impacts interpersonal attraction is elicited by a contextual cue. For example, one might consistently encounter another person in an aversive situation (e.g., an unpleasant work environment) and thereby develop a negative attitude toward that person. The classical conditioning model might account for this phenomenon. From this perspective, the contextual cue (e.g., unpleasant work environment) functions as an unconditioned stimulus that elicits a state of discomfort or irritation (unconditioned response). Due to repeated pairing of this context with the target person (conditioned stimulus), the individual might eventually form a negative attitude toward the target person. The mood misattribution approach can also account for this phenomenon, but in terms of a different mediating mechanism. In this later approach, affect elicited by the unpleasant work environment is misattributed to the target, resulting in the formation of a negative attitude toward that person (Ottati & Isbell, 1996). Both of these models suggest that interpersonal attraction can be significantly influenced by the situation in which we happen to encounter another person.

Research also suggests that interpersonal attraction is associated with attitude similarity. Research by Newcomb (1956) implies that the direction of causality underlying this association runs from attitude similarity to attraction. Specifically, attitude similarity of individuals before they meet predicts interpersonal attraction months later (Newcomb, 1956). Experimental evidence that manipulates the attitude similarity of a previously unknown target person provides further evidence of this causal effect (Byrne, 1961). The relation between attitude similarity and interpersonal attraction is consistent with balance theory (Hummert, Crockett, & Kemper, 1990). When two individuals (P and O) agree in their attitude toward some issue (X), a tendency for these individuals to view each other favorably constitutes a balanced state of affairs.

The close relationships literature is permeated with attitudinal constructs and core attitudinal principles. Although close relationships can be divided into distinct categories (e.g., close friendship, romantic relationship), definitions of these various relationship categories almost invariably include the assumption that interpersonal attitudes are positive (Kenny & Kashy, 1994; Laurenceau, Barrett, & Pietromonaco, 1998; Shaffer & Bazzini, 1997; Whitbeck & Hoyt, 1994). Romantic relationships are not built on sexual passion alone, but require positive interpersonal liking that resembles that found in close friendships (Hatfield, 1988; Sternberg, 1986; 1988). "Companionate love", which is marked by this form of mutual liking, is critical to the maintenance of marital satisfaction (Sternberg, 1986, 1988). The tripartite view of attitudes has also been applied when defining core constructs within the close relationships literature. For example, it has been suggested that "relationship commitment" is a state that contains an affective (psychological attachment), cognitive (long-term orientation), and conative (intention to persist) component (Arriaga & Agnew, 2001). Relationship commitment is an important predictor of relationship longevity (Arriaga & Agnew, 2001; Etcheverry & Agnew, 2004).

When predicting relationship patterns throughout the life cycle, many theorists have focused on individual differences in attachment style (Bartholomew, 1990; Bowlby, 1982; Griffin & Bartholomew, 1994; McGowan, Daniels, & Byrne, 1999a; Shulman, Elicker, & Sroufe, 1994). In this work, four distinct attachment styles are identified by "crossing" two different attitudes, attitude toward the self and attitude toward others (Bartholomew, 1990; Griffin & Bartholomew, 1994; McGowan, Daniels, & Byrne, 1999b). Those who possess a "secure attachment style" harbor a positive attitude toward the self and others, whereas those who possess a "fearful-avoidant attachment" style are negative both about the self and others. People with a "preoccupied attachment style" harbor a negative view of the self that is accompanied by a positive view of others, whereas people who possess a "dismissing attachment style" like themselves while disliking others. Attachment style, which is often developed early in life (Ainsworth et al., 1978; Bowlby, 1982), presumably impacts relationship patterns all the way into adulthood (Klohnen & Bera, 1998; but see Brennan & Bosson, 1998; Shaver & Hazan,

1994 for the malleability of attachment style). Attachment style is predictive of a variety of relationship outcomes. For example, individuals with a preoccupied attachment style are more likely to interpret events in a relationship in a negative fashion and to expect more relationship conflict (Collins, 1996). On the other hand, individuals with a secure attachment style are most likely to achieve satisfaction and commitment in their marriage (Radecki-Bush, Farrell, & Bush, 1993).

Attitude researchers have emphasized that global attitudes toward an object are determined, at least in part, by episodic affective experiences. Applications of this general notion are plentiful in the relationship satisfaction literature, where it is noted that expressions of positive affect are positively associated with marital satisfaction (Bruess & Pearson, 1993; Levenson, Carstensen, & Gottman, 1994). It has also been suggested that negative emotions aroused in the workplace can negatively impact relationship satisfaction (Chan & Margolin, 1994; Geller & Hobfoll, 1994). Although this later finding may arise for a number of reasons, one possible mediating mechanism involves the misattribution effect (Schwarz & Clore, 1983). Namely, negative affect elicited in the workplace might be misattributed to one's spouse, resulting in an erosion of the relationship.

Balance effects are alive and well in the close relationships literature, and figure as an important determinant of attitudes and interpersonal perceptions in such relationships. It was previously noted that, in accordance with balance theory, attitude similarity elicits interpersonal attraction. In establishing the causal direction of this effect, many have attempted to downplay, eliminate, or control for the reverse possibility, namely that relationships cause people to adopt similar attitudes over time (Caspi, Herbener, & Ozer, 1992; Newcomb, 1956). However, recent research confirms that interacting partners modify their attitudes over time so as to achieve attitudinal balance (Davis & Rusbult, 2001). This "attitude alignment" effect is moderated by a number of factors. For example, it is greater when attitude discrepancies are made salient, and in relationships that are characterized by high levels of closeness (Davis & Rusbult, 2001). Consistent with balance theory, it has also been found that relationship partners exaggerate the extent to which they agree on various issues (Byrne & Blaylock, 1963). Indeed, if relationship partners discover that they actually differ on these issues, they can experience considerable disappointment (Sillars et al., 1994).

Recent research has also applied the theory of reasoned action (Fishbein & Ajzen, 1975) to the study of romantic relationships. When predicting relationship longevity or persistence, it has been suggested that "relationship commitment" functions much like the "behavioral intention" term in the theory of reasoned action (Etcheverry & Agnew, in press). In addition, it has been shown that relationship commitment is determined by the subjective norm. The subjective norm reflects perceptions that significant others believe one should continue in a relationship, weighted by the individual's motivation to comply with the significant other. In this work, subjective norms predicted relationship commitment even after controlling for relationship satisfaction, the quality of alternative relationships available, and the amount of prior investment in the current relationship (Etcheverry & Agnew, in press). This recent emphasis upon the role of normative considerations is, of course, entirely consistent with the theory of reasoned action (Fishbein & Ajzen, 1975).

Interdisciplinary Connections to Political Candidate Evaluation and Marital Interaction

Connections of the attitude literature to interpersonal attraction and close relationships can be extended even further to address core problems in a number of areas falling outside of social psychology. Interdisciplinary applications within the areas of political psychology and marital interaction are prominent examples. Within political psychology, a considerable amount of research has investigated the role of physical attractiveness in determining attitudes toward a political candidate (Ottati, 1990; Rosenberg, Bohan, McCafferty, & Harris, 1984; Rosenberg, Kahn, & Tran, 1991; Rosenberg & McCafferty, 1986). This work confirms that, when presented with a photograph alone, physically attractive candidates are rated higher in competence, leadership ability, integrity, and overall likeableness. Rosenberg and associates found a similar advantage for physically attractive candidates even when voters were provided with party and issue information pertaining to two competing candidates (Rosenberg, Bohan, McCafferty, & Harris, 1986; Rosenberg, Kahn, & Tran, 1991; Rosenberg & McCafferty, 1987).

Ottati and associates (Ottati, 1990; see also Riggle, Ottati, Wyer, Kuklinski, & Schwarz, 1992) found that, when a photograph was accompanied by other politically relevant information (i.e., party, issues), effects differed when comparing a singular candidate evaluation task to a comparative task involving two competing candidates. Within the singular candidate judgment task, attitude toward the candidate was determined solely by the voters' agreement with the candidate's issues. In the comparative judgment task, however, physical attractiveness impacted attitudes toward the candidate, but only when the party and issue information conveyed conflicting evaluative implications (Ottati, 1990; Ottati & Deiger, 2002). Comparative judgment tasks are presumably quite complex and demanding, leading participants to rely more heavily upon the physical attractiveness stereotype as a simplifying or heuristic device (Ottati, 1990). Other evidence suggests that, even within a comparative judgment task, physical attractiveness exerts an effect only if the photograph is salient at the time of judgment (Riggle et al., 1992). Moreover, recent findings suggest that physical attractiveness can produce more *negative* attitudes toward a candidate among expert voters (Hart & Ottati, 2004). This reversal of the physical attractiveness effect presumably emerges because these voters attempt to correct for the biasing influence of physical attractiveness, but inadvertently engage in over-correction.

Within political psychology, research has also investigated the role of episodic affective reactions as determinants of global attitudes toward a political candidate (Abelson, Kinder, Peters, & Fiske, 1982; Marcus & MacKuen, 1993; Ottati, 1997; Ottati & Isbell, 1996; Ottati, Steenbergen & Riggle, 1992; Ottati & Wyer, 1993). Early approaches to this question focused on the degree to which emotional reactions to a political candidate predict attitudes toward the candidate independently of beliefs about the candidate (Abelson et al., 1982; Ottati et al., 1992). When using closed-ended measures in which a common set of belief items is administered to all respondents, emotions predict global attitudes toward a candidate independently of these beliefs (Abelson et al., 1982; Ottati et al., 1992). However, when using an open-ended measure that enables the researcher to specifically assess "emotionally relevant beliefs", beliefs about a candidate are found to fully account for the predictive role of emotions (Ottati, 1997). These conflicting findings suggest that correlational approaches are not well suited for isolating the unique causal role of episodic affect (see Ottati, 1997, 2001; Isbell & Ottati, 2002).

To more clearly isolate the effect of episodic affect on global attitudes toward a candidate, researchers have manipulated participants' mood independently from their beliefs about the candidate (Ottati & Isbell, 1996). In these experiments, the individual's affective state is elicited by a contextual cue (e.g., happy versus sad music), not a feature of the candidate. This ensures that the affective state was not originally elicited by the participant's prior cognitive appraisal of the candidate, thereby isolating the independent effect of affect. In addition to serving this methodological function, this procedure mimics "feel good" campaign techniques that involve surrounding the candidate with contextual cues that elicit positive affect in the electorate (e.g., balloons, American Flag). In these experiments, participants are told they will be completing two ostensibly unrelated tasks. In fact, the first task is the mood induction phase and the second task is the candidate evaluation phase of the experiment (Ottati & Isbell, 1996). Participants are first put in either a positive or negative mood (e.g., by listening to happy or sad nonpolitical music). Immediately following this mood induction procedure, participants receive information about a political candidate. Then (following a brief distracter task or a one week delay), participants are asked to report their attitude toward the candidate.

Among political novices, this procedure elicits an *assimilation effect* (Ottati & Isbell, 1996). That is, independent of the participant's beliefs about the candidate, positive mood participants report a more positive attitude toward the candidate than negative mood participants. Analysis of cognitive measures indicates that this effect is not mediated by mood-congruent processing of the information presented about the candidate (Ottati & Isbell, 1996). Thus, Ottati and Isbell (1996) have concluded that this effect is mediated by mood misattribution. That is, affect elicited by a contextual cue (e.g., happy or sad music) is misattributed to the candidate, resulting in mood-congruent attitudes toward the candidate. Interestingly, Ottati and Isbell (1996) found that political experts rated the candidate more negatively when in a happy mood than when in a sad mood. This *contrast effect* presumably emerged because the experts attempted to correct for the mood induced bias, but inadvertently overcorrected for this bias. Ottati and Isbell (1996) argue that this correction process requires awareness that the original assimilation tendency exists, and the capacity to correct for it. Because experts were able to process the political description of the candidate in a more efficient manner, they were presumably more likely to possess the resources needed to engage in correction. Isbell and Wyer (1999) have demonstrated that this correction process also requires adequate levels of cognitive motivation (see Albarracín & Kumkale, 2003 for further qualification of this effect in a persuasion context).

Connections of the attitude literature to interpersonal attraction and close relationships can also be extended to examine core issues within the marital interaction literature. Marital interaction research often focuses on marital satisfaction as a critical outcome variable. Indeed, almost all of marital counseling is performed with the objective of increasing marital satisfaction and decreasing marital discord. Marital satisfaction, of course, is an attitude. The attitude object in this case is simply one's own marriage.

A considerable amount of research has focused on the relation between marital satisfaction and attribution. A robust finding within this literature is that marital satisfaction is associated with a relationship-enhancing pattern of attribution (Bradbury & Fincham, 1990; Bradbury, Fincham, & Beach, 2000; Fincham, 2001; Thompson & Snyder, 1986). This pattern of attribution is marked by internal, stable, global, and intentional attributions for positive partner behaviors; as well as external, unstable, specific, and unintentional attributions for negative partner behaviors (Fincham, 2001). Marital dissatisfaction is associated with an opposite (conflict promoting) pattern of attribution. Because marital satisfaction and dissatisfaction are positive and negative attitudes, respectively, this pattern is entirely consistent with balance theory (Bradbury & Fincham, 1990).

According to balance theory, attributions and beliefs pertaining to one's own marriage might be balanced for two reasons. First, it is possible that attributions and beliefs causally determine marital satisfaction. This causal assumption was implicit in original interpretations of the association between marital satisfaction and attribution (Bagarozzi & Giddings, 1983). Recent empirical investigations support this causal interpretation. The correlation between attribution and marital satisfaction persists even when controlling for depression, anger, neuroticism, demographics, and so on (Bradbury, Beach, Fincham, & Nelson, 1996; Karney, Bradbury, Fincham, & Sullivan, 1994; Senchak & Leonard, 1993). Moreover, longitudinal studies confirm that causality flows from attributions to marital satisfaction (Fincham & Bradbury, 1987), and that effects of this nature translate into behavior (e.g., marital violence; Holtzworth-Munroe, Jacobson, Fehrenbach, & Fruzzetti, 1992). These findings suggest that therapeutic interventions that promote relationship-enhancing patterns of attribution might significantly improve marital satisfaction. Unfortunately, the impact of attributions on therapeutic outcome has yet to be directly evaluated (Fincham, 2001).

According to balance theory, the association between marital satisfaction and relationship-relevant cognitions might also reflect a reverse causal effect. That is, individuals who are satisfied with their marriage might justify, maintain, or bolster this view by developing positive beliefs about their marital partner, whereas the reverse might be the case for individuals who are dissatisfied with their marriage (Weiss & Heyman, 1990). In this case, attributions and beliefs serve as the consequence of marital satisfaction, not the cause. Consistent with this second possibility, a longitudinal analysis suggested that the causal relation between marital satisfaction and attribution is bidirectional (Fincham & Bradbury, 1993). In addition, other research confirms that marital satisfaction elicits distorted (but balanced) perceptions of a marital partner. In satisfying marriages, individuals perceive more virtue in their partners than is actually the case (Murray, Holmes, Dolderman, & Griffin, 2000). Dissatisfied marriages produce an opposite form of cognitive distortion. These later effects, of course, are consistent with basic attitudinal research regarding the effects of attitudes on cognitive processing.

INTRAGROUP PROCESSES

Perhaps more than any other area of psychology, social psychology emphasizes that a complete understanding of human behavior should include an analysis of group behavior. A comprehensive understanding of the college life experience, for example, must consider the implications of student membership in academic, athletic, religious, or political organizations. What attracts individuals to these groups? How does membership in these groups influence task-oriented performance (e.g., academic performance)? How do groups influence the opinions of individual group members? How do group members combine their individual preferences to arrive at a group decision? These questions focus on intragroup processes, and attitudinal concepts pervade social psychological approaches to answering these questions. After considering intradisciplinary connections of this nature, we explore interdisciplinary connections to research in the areas of organizational behavior and political decision-making.

Intradisciplinary Connections: Group Formation, Performance, Influence, and Decision Making

A logical starting point to understanding intragroup processes involves identifying those forces that motivate individuals to join groups. Generally speaking, groups are seen as providing a means through which specific needs can be met. For instance, group membership has historically been associated with addressing certain *security needs*. The concept of "safety in numbers" exemplifies this notion. Next, groups can be seen as aiding in meeting *objective and informational needs*. That is, groups can enable group members to achieve goals and obtain information that would be difficult, if not impossible, to obtain alone. Furthermore, groups can help the individual to address various *affective needs*. The need to belong and receive attention from others are examples of such needs (Bettencourt, Charlton, Eubanks, Kernahan, & Fuller, 1999; Brewer et al., 1993). Finally, groups aid in satisfying the need for a *positive self-identity*. Membership in a group can become an important trait that characterizes how the individual group member is viewed by others, as well as how an individual views him or herself (Paulus, 1989; Tajfel & Turner, 1986).

Many of these needs resemble the needs included in Katz's (1960) functional analysis of attitudes (utilitarian, knowledge, value-expressive, ego-defensive). For example, when individuals join a group to satisfy security and objective needs, attraction to the group serves a utilitarian function. When individuals join a group to satisfy informational needs, group membership helps to foster attitudes that serve a knowledge function. When individuals join a group to satisfy self-identity needs, membership and attraction to the group serves a value-expressive and ego-defensive function.

Once formed, groups often face the challenge of performing some task or arriving at a group decision. A key factor influencing group performance and decision-making is group cohesiveness. Cohesiveness is often indexed by simply assessing the average attitude toward the group among group members. However, a careful scrutiny of the cohesiveness literature reveals that group cohesiveness is a multidimensional attitudinal construct that includes a variety of forces that cause members to remain in a group. According to Festinger (1950; Festinger, Schacter, & Back, 1950), cohesiveness contains three components. These are interpersonal attraction, liking for or commitment to the group task (or goal), and group prestige or pride. From the perspective of attitude theory, these reflect attitudes toward individual group members, attitudes toward the group task, and attitudes toward the group taken as a whole, respectively. Each of these components is partially unique from the other, and different components can exert differing (even opposite) effects on performance (Mullen, Anthony, Salas, Driskell, 1994). For example, Hogg (Hogg & Hains, 1996) has noted that the "interpersonal attraction" and "depersonalized attraction" components of cohesiveness exert unique effects. Interpersonal attraction reflects liking between individual group members that is based upon their respective, individuating characteristics. Depersonalized attraction to group members occurs because they simply belong to or represent the group.

In many cases, cohesiveness increases motivation among group members, thereby facilitating task persistence and task performance. Cohesiveness has been shown to decrease social loafing, and this effect may be linked to a cooperative interaction style. In comparison to competitive or individualistic working styles, cooperative efforts are more likely to promote liking among group members (Johnson & Johnson, 1989, 1998). Positive interpersonal relationships that result from cooperation produce a number of positive outcomes. Among students, these include decreased absenteeism, lower dropout rates, increased commitment to educational goals, and increased persistence toward educational goal achievement (Johnson & Johnson, 1994). Even attendance at a fitness class increases as a function of cohesiveness (Spink & Carron, 1994). It is important to note, however, that effects of this nature do not necessarily generalize to all of the components of cohesiveness. For example, Mullen and Copper (1994) report that the commitment to task component of cohesiveness is what primarily serves to increase the quantity of group performance. Other work, however, suggests that task oriented cohesion increases performance under some conditions, whereas social cohesion increases performance under other conditions (Spink & Carron, 1994).

Groups function not only to perform tasks, but also as a context in which individuals share their opinions, influence one another, and combine their opinions to arrive at a group decision. All of these processes share important linkages with the attitude literature. Research on group influence, for example, has traditionally made a distinction between "normative social influence" and "informational social influence" (Deutsch & Gerard, 1955). Normative social influence occurs when a group member simply adopts the group preference in order to be liked and accepted by group members. In contrast, informational social influence occurs when a group member considers specific arguments mentioned by other group members, and on the basis of this information, is persuaded to adopt the group opinion. The distinction between normative and informational social influence shares linkages with dual-process models of attitude change. The normative social influence process, which involves a minimal amount of cognitive deliberation, exemplifies the peripheral or heuristic route to attitude change. Informational social influence, which involves a more extensive consideration of communicated arguments, exemplifies the central or systematic route to attitude change (Petty & Cacioppo, 1986; Chaiken, 1980; Chaiken, Liberman, & Eagly, 1989).

Linkages with the attitude literature are just as clearly apparent when considering the group decision-making process. Attitudes of individual group members are often the "substance" entered into group decision-making calculations, and a group preference or attitude is often the result of this calculation. Also, the process whereby groups combine individual attitudes to arrive at a group preference (Davis, 1973; Vinokur & Burnstein, 1974) is analogous to the process whereby individuals combine specific pieces of information to arrive at a global attitude toward an object (Fishbein & Ajzen, 1975). Moreover, the tendency for communicated information to influence group decisions more than unmentioned information (Gigone & Hastie, 1993) is analogous to the notion that accessible information carries more weight than inaccessible information when individuals combine information to arrive at a global attitude judgment (Bem, 1965, 1967).

Another question addressed by group decision-making researchers involves factors that influence the quality of group decisions. In this case, it is often suggested that group cohesiveness can reduce the quality of group decisions. According to some analysts, this has led cohesive groups to make a number of disastrous decisions throughout world history (e.g., Bay of Pigs, Watergate). According to Janis (1972; see also Kameda & Sugimori, 1993), cohesiveness is a central cause of "groupthink." Groupthink is "a mode of thinking that people engage in when they are deeply involved in a cohesive ingroup, when members' striving for unanimity overrides their motivation to realistically appraise alternative courses of action" (Janis, 1972, p. 9). When groupthink occurs, there is a strong tendency for group members to assume the group cannot be wrong and to reject any information that might contradict the group's conclusion. To some degree, these tendencies are compatible with balance theory. Insofar as cohesiveness reflects a positive attitude toward the group among group members, the belief that the group is accurate and correct constitutes a balanced state of affairs. Groupthink is often contrasted from "vigilant decision-making", a style of thinking that involves careful consideration and deliberation regarding a variety of decision alternatives (Janis, 1972). The distinction between groupthink and vigilant decision making shares linkages with the previously mentioned dual-process models of attitude change. That is, groupthink may involve a tendency for individuals to engage in peripheral or biased forms of central processing, whereas vigilant decision making may exemplify an unbiased form of systematic processing (Petty & Cacioppo, 1986; Chaiken, 1980; Chaiken, Liberman, & Eagly, 1989).

More recently, some researchers have suggested that there is little empirical support for the notion that group cohesiveness reduces decision-making quality (Park, 1990; Hogg, 1992; Fuller & Aldag, 1998). This lack of support might be because much of the research on groupthink has failed to consider important qualifications regarding the linkage between cohesiveness and groupthink. For example, some researchers have failed to recognize that not all components of cohesiveness were originally predicted to produce the same effect on group decision-making quality. Janis (1972) originally hypothesized that the interpersonal attraction and pride components would be associated with a decrease in decision-making quality, whereas the commitment (to task) component would be associated with an increase in decision-making quality. A meta-analysis performed by Mullen and associates (Mullen, Anthony, Salas, & Driskell, 1994) yielded at least partial support for these predictions. In studies where the cohesion index taps interpersonal attraction, cohesion is associated with a reduction in decision-making quality. However, in studies where the cohesion index reflects task commitment, cohesion is associated with an increase in decision-making quality (Mullen et al., 1994). From the perspective of attitude research, this finding is not surprising. Given that the interpersonal attraction and commitment components focus on distinct attitude objects, it is only natural that they are differentially predictive of behavior.

It should also be noted that Janis (1972) originally suggested that cohesion would elicit groupthink only if other antecedent conditions are present. These additional antecedent conditions include a lack of norms for methodical decision making, a highly directive group leader, and so on (Janis, 1972; Mullen et al., 1994). When these other antecedent conditions are absent (e.g., the group relies on methodical decision-making procedures, the group leader is nondirective), cohesiveness should be associated with an increase in decision-making quality (Mullen et al., 1994). A meta-analysis has revealed that the relation between cohesiveness and decision making quality is in fact moderated by the presence of these other antecedent conditions (Mullen et al., 1994).

Interdisciplinary Connections to Organizational Behavior and Political Decision-Making

Few individuals work alone. To the contrary, most people work within some sort of group or organizational setting. Thus, the study of industrial and organizational behavior reflects an important interdisciplinary extension of groups research. The concept of "organizational commitment" is closely linked to group cohesiveness. Organizational commitment, which is often assessed by simply measuring employee attitudes toward the company (Brown, 1996; Keller, 1997), has been shown to promote prosocial behavior in organizations. Individuals who harbor a positive attitude toward their company are more likely to help other employees, attend voluntary meetings, tolerate unfavorable conditions without complaining, and so on, even when these behaviors are not explicitly rewarded (Randall, Fedor, & Longenecker, 1990). Researchers have been less successful, however, when trying to demonstrate that organizational commitment increases actual job productivity. This lack of success could be true for a variety of reasons. In many cases, variability in job performance is minimal because the job leaves little room for variation in speed or quality of performance (e.g., a production line job). A variety of job characteristics impact job performance independent of organizational commitment (e.g., availability of resources, amount of task structure). Thus, whereas organizational commitment appears to facilitate altruistic forms of behavior within work organizations, the effect of organizational commitment on actual job productivity appears to be overshadowed by other factors (see Mathieu & Zajac, 1990 for a meta-analysis).

Discussions regarding the effects of group cohesiveness in a political context paint a more dismal picture. In particular, it has been frequently suggested that group cohesiveness erodes the effectiveness of political decision making and thereby has contributed to a number of catastrophic political decisions made throughout history. Examples of this groupthink phenomenon, as it occurs in the political domain, are purported to be numerous. These include the decision by President Kennedy and his advisors to authorize the invasion of Cuba at the Bay of Pigs, decisions by President Johnson and his advisors to escalate the Vietnam War in the middle 1960s, the decision by President Nixon and his advisors to cover up the Watergate break in, and so on.

To identify the antecedents and symptoms of groupthink, Janis (1972) compared four catastrophic political decisions to two successful decisions. The catastrophic decision scenarios included the decisions to invade Cuba and escalate the Vietnam War, the 1941 decision to ignore the need for increasing the defensive capability of Pearl Harbor, and the 1950 decision by Truman and his advisors to escalate the Korean War by entering North Korea. The two successful scenarios were the decision to develop the Marshall Plan in order to avoid economic deterioration in post-war Europe, and the decision regarding how to handle the Cuban missile crisis in 1962. Later, Janis (1972) performed a systematic case history analysis of the Watergate scandal to test the generality of the theory. He considered the Watergate cover-up to be the quintessential example of groupthink. Taken together, this work led Janis (1972, 1982) to identify a number of antecedent conditions that promote groupthink. These included cohesiveness, insulation, lack of impartial leadership, lack of methodical decision-making procedures, member homogeneity, and high stress.

Tetlock and associates (Tetlock et al., 1992) adopted a more empirical approach by using a Q-sort methodology to analyze historical writings pertaining to 10 historical cases. Their analysis tended to support Janis's prior classifications of the various cases. However, when using LISREL to investigate the causal determinants of groupthink, Tetlock failed to obtain evidence to support the claim that group cohesiveness increases groupthink (see also McCauley, 1989). These findings may be consistent with Mullen et al.'s (1994) meta-analysis of laboratory experiments. Mullen et al. (1994) found no overall relationship between cohesiveness and decision quality. To the contrary, they found that the effect of cohesiveness on decision quality differed depending upon what component of cohesiveness was manipulated (interpersonal attraction versus task commitment) and depending on whether other antecedent conditions were present or absent.

INTERGROUP PROCESSES

Having discussed the implications of attitude theory and research for intragroup processes, we now consider attitudinal phenomena as they operate at the intergroup level. Intergroup processes impact human relations in a variety of social arenas (e.g., competitive sports, politics, interracial relations). Difficulties in intergroup relations often result in intergroup conflict, and intergroup cooperation can be difficult to achieve (Insko et al., 2001; Schopler et al., 2001). One need only consult the daily newspaper to find evidence of intergroup conflict, violence, and war.

Intergroup conflict is often rooted in intergroup stereotyping, prejudice and discrimination, which are key domains of study within social psychology. In accordance with the tripartite view of attitudes, these three domains reflect the cognitive, affective, and behavioral component of intergroup psychology, respectively. A "stereotype" can be defined as a cognitive representation of a social group that is stored in memory. This cognitive representation associates the social group with certain traits (e.g., "lazy") or behaviors (e.g., "sleep all day"). In contrast, "prejudice" refers to a negative affective reaction, evaluation, or attitude toward a group. "Discrimination," the last component of the trinity, refers to negative behaviors or actions that are directed toward group members (e.g., refusing to rent an apartment to a group member). These three components are often causally interrelated. For example, an employer who believes Mexicans are lazy (stereotype) might consequently evaluate a Mexican individual negatively (prejudice), and therefore refuse to hire that person for a job (discrimination). From the perspective of attitude theory, this association simply means that beliefs can determine attitudes, which in turn can determine behavior.

We begin by considering intradisciplinary connections to the stereotyping, prejudice, and discrimination literature within social psychology. We then move on to consider interdisciplinary extensions to the mental health arena, specifically focusing on mental illness stigma.

Intradisciplinary Connections to Stereotyping, Prejudice, and Discrimination

Many of the previously described attitude models can be used to understand the antecedents of intergroup prejudice. According to the operant conditioning model, reinforcement of behavior that implies a negative attitude or punishment of behavior that implies a positive attitude toward an object will engender negative attitudes toward the object (Greenspoon, 1955; Insko, 1965). This effect presumably occurs even when the individual is unaware of the behavior-reinforcement contingency (but see Dulany, 1962; Fishbein & Ajzen, 1975; Uleman, 1971).

Operant conditioning can foster prejudice. For example, parental reinforcement of a child's racist remarks might foster racial prejudice in the child. Alternatively, parental disapproval of a child's relationship with a minority group member might foster prejudice. In these instances, the reinforcer or punisher might be a subtle one (e.g., the parent softly chuckles, the parent exhibits a tense nonverbal demeanor) and parents may not be fully aware that they are fostering prejudice in this manner. Operant conditioning also provides a mechanism for reducing intergroup prejudice, namely, punish prejudicial remarks or reward remarks that convey tolerance.

According to the classical conditioning model of attitude formation (Razran, 1938; Staats & Staats, 1958), an attitude toward an object is acquired by learning experiences that repeatedly pair a pleasant or unpleasant unconditioned stimulus with the attitude object (conditioned stimulus). For example, a child might observe its mother frown whenever policemen are present. The mother's frown is an aversive unconditioned stimulus that elicits discomfort in the child. Repeated pairing of this unconditioned stimulus with policemen (conditioned stimulus) results in a classically conditioned negative attitude toward policemen. Some research suggests this process does not require conscious cognitive mediation (see Krosnick et al., 1992; Olson & Fazio, 2002 for related evidence; for reviews see Clore & Schnall, chap. 11, this volume; Kruglanski & Stroebe, chap. 8, this volume). An analogous process can operate to produce prejudicial attitudes. For example, a white child might observe that its father behaves fearfully (e.g., locks the car door, avoids eye contact) whenever African Americans are present. The father's fearful behavior is an aversive unconditioned stimulus that elicits a negative affective reaction in the child (e.g., fear). Repeated pairing of this unconditioned stimulus with African Americans might eventually foster a classically conditioned form of prejudice in the child. Effects of this nature may be difficult to consciously control, even among individuals who reject prejudice and discrimination at a conscious level (see Fazio et al., 1995 for related evidence).

The mood misattribution approach (Schwarz & Clore, 1983; 1996) offers an alternative explanation for the effect described above. This model emphasizes that individuals are often unaware of the actual source of their affective state. As a consequence, affect elicited by a contextual stimulus can be misattributed to the attitude object and produce an assimilation effect on attitudes toward that object (Ottati & Isbell, 1996; Schwarz & Clore, 1983, 1996). In this formulation, the father's fearful behavior serves as a contextual stimulus that is the actual source of the child's fear. If the child incorrectly attributes the feeling of fear to African Americans, the child will develop a prejudicial attitude toward African Americans. An analogous process might operate when movies and television programs present minority group members within a seedy or unpleasant context (e.g., burned out basements, dirty alleys). Negative reactions to these situational cues might be misattributed to the minority group member and thereby foster a negative attitude toward the minority group (Ottati, Bodenhausen, & Newman, in press). Reduction of prejudice, according to this model, might entail presenting minority group members in a more favorable context or simply reminding the individual that the actual source of their discomfort is the context, not the minority group member.

Cognitive approaches to understanding the determinants of prejudice often emphasize the role of categorization (Allport, 1954; Tajfel, 1969). Categorization of objects and events (e.g., "chair","military invasion") occurs in a relatively automatic fashion, and is necessary for survival in a complex and varied stimulus environment. It allows individuals to group together multiple stimuli into a common category (e.g.,"automobiles"), and to form reasonable expectations about objects and events that fall in the same category (e.g.,"Automobiles can be used for transportation, racing"). For similar reasons, categorization occurs in the social world. By categorizing the multitude of people into groups (e.g., African Americans, females, homosexuals), the individual acquires a sense of predictability and control over situations. In addition to containing trait expectations (e.g., lazy, violent, unintelligent), social category representations include the perceiver's attitude toward the group (e.g., bad). These representations provide the perceiver with a predictable view of the group, and an ability to generate appropriate behavioral reactions to group members. Thus, if a parent teaches their child that "Nazi's are bad", the child immediately knows that this social group is to be avoided (as is the case with other "bad" things). From this perspective, prejudicial evaluations of a social group are a natural outgrowth of a basic categorization process that is required for survival in a complex and varied environment.

Even when stereotypes are derived on the basis of fundamental categorization processes, it does not mean that such stereotypes are accurate. Although there are undoubtedly multiple determinants of stereotype inaccuracy, one cause of inaccuracy shares linkages with the attitude literature. As noted previously, an important aspect of self-perception theory was that it emphasized the role of concept accessibility. Accessibility also plays an important role in the illusory correlation model, a model of stereotype formation that can account for negatively biased stereotypes of minority groups. Many studies have shown that people tend to over-estimate the association (i.e., correlation) between negative characteristics and minority group membership (Fiedler, 2000; Hamilton & Gifford, 1976). One explanation for this phenomenon involves the tendency for distinctive information to be highly accessible (Hamilton & Gifford, 1976; but see Fiedler, 1991). Because minority group members are by definition uncommon, it is relatively more noteworthy when we encounter them. In addition, negative behavior is more distinctive than positive behavior (Fiske, 1980). Thus, a minority group member performing a socially undesirable behavior constitutes a doubly distinctive event that is especially memorable. This memory effect engenders an illusory correlation between minority group membership and the performance of negative behaviors, even when there are no preconceptions about the minority group at all (Hamilton & Gifford, 1976; see Fiedler, 1991 for an alternative interpretation). Thus, a natural outgrowth of the cognitive accessibility effect is that it leads to a negative and prejudicial view of minority group members.

Stereotypes and attitudes toward a social group also function as expectancies that bias the processing of subsequently encountered information. Effects of this nature often resemble those obtained when examining more basic research regarding the effects of attitudes on information processing (e.g., the balance effect, the attitudinal congeniality effect). Researchers have demonstrated that social group expectations influence attention, interpretation, and retrieval of information pertaining to group members. Often times, these biases preserve an evaluatively consistent or balanced view of social groups. Bodenhausen (1988) provided evidence of this tendency within the context of a criminal trial. He found that stereotypic expectations led participants to attend to and use incriminating evidence more frequently when the defendant was Hispanic than when the defendant was a mainstream white individual.

Other research confirms that an ambiguous behavior is more likely to be interpreted in a negative fashion when enacted by a negatively evaluated group member than when enacted by a positively evaluated group member. For example, research has demonstrated that the act of poking someone with a pencil is perceived as hostile when performed by an African-American actor but is perceived as playful when performed by a European actor (Sagar & Schofield, 1980). Analogous effects emerge when examining intergroup attributional inferences. When observing outgroup members, perceivers tend to attribute positive behaviors to situational factors and negative behaviors to dispositional factors (Hewstone, Bond, Wan, 1983). This pattern of attribution, which is consistent with balance theory, is presumably triggered by the perceiver's negative evaluation of the outgroup.

Intergroup stereotyping research also suggests that prior expectations regarding a social group are used to "fill in" missing information that is unavailable (for a review, see Wyer & Albarracín, chap. 7, this volume). For example, if a perceiver's stereotype of a social group includes the trait "stingy," the perceiver might "remember" that the target person provided the waitperson with a poor tip at the end of a meal, even if the perceiver left the restaurant too early to witness such an event. Effects of this nature may also arise when the perceiver's expectancy is purely evaluative. Indeed, some of the earliest claims regarding the reconstructive nature of memory emphasized this possibility. Long ago, Bartlett (1932) noted that attitudes (like any other stored knowledge) are used to reconstruct past events. Thus, it would appear that stereotyping research regarding reconstructive memory possesses a historical linkage with the attitude literature.

Stereotypes and prejudicial attitudes often culminate in discriminatory behavior directed toward outgroup members. Prejudicial attitudes that are conscious and explicit (e.g., "old-fashioned racism") might determine behavior in an intentional manner (e.g., explicit refusal to hire an African American). In other cases, however, automatically activated prejudice may elicit discriminatory behavior in a relatively unconscious and automatic manner (see Ajzen & Fishbein, chap. 5, this volume; Bassili & Brown, chap. 13, this volume). In some of these instances, attitude research suggests that automatically activated prejudice influences behavior independent of more explicit and conscious attitudes toward a social group (Fazio et al., 1995; Song Hing, Chung-Yan, Grunfeld, Robichaud, Zanna, in press).

Interdisciplinary Connections to Mental Illness Stigma

In western culture, stereotypes of people with mental illness suggest that they are dangerous, incompetent, unable to care for themselves, and childlike (Corrigan, Watson, & Ottati, 2003; Phelan, Link, Stueve, Pescosolido, 2000). These beliefs are commonly associated with an overall prejudicial attitude toward people with mental illness, as well as more specific emotional reactions to members of this social group (e.g., fear, anger). Discrimination against people with mental illness occurs in a variety of social contexts, including failing to hire a person with mental illness (Bordieri & Drehmer, 1986; Link, 1987), refusing to rent an apartment to a person with mental illness (Page, 1995), or pressing false criminal charges against a person with mental illness. Some researchers have concluded that many of the problems associated with mental illness are due to the public's reaction to this social group rather than inherent shortcomings associated with this segment of the population.

The previously described models of prejudice, each of which possesses connections to the attitude literature, can be applied to understand mental illness stigma. For example, classical conditioning effects might play a role in determining this form of prejudice. Parents might grimace, frown, or otherwise convey discomfort when they encounter persons with mental illness. A child's negative reactions to these cues might become classically conditioned to persons with mental illness (Ottati et al., in press). The operant conditioning approach can also be applied. Parents might reinforce the child (e.g., smile, chuckle) for making derogatory remarks about persons with mental illness (e.g., "That kid is completely nuts"). Observation that a sibling is reinforced in this manner would presumably elicit an analogous, vicarious operant conditioning effect.

Many of the other more cognitively oriented models can also be applied to understand the antecedents of mental illness stigma. As previously noted, categorization is a fundamental and necessary psychological process and social stereotyping and prejudice can be regarded as specific forms of categorization. The process of categorization is quite explicit when psychologists and psychiatrists diagnose an individual (Ottati et al., in press). When clinicians place a client into a diagnostic category (e.g., bipolar disorder), they are focusing on the similarity between the client and the category prototype. This process resembles stereotyping. Subsequent treatment of the client may be based upon the symptom profile that characterizes the general diagnostic category, rather than the individuating characteristics of the specific client. This reliance on a diagnostic category can produce insensitivity to the unique characteristics of the client. Analogous problems emerge when the lay public categorizes or labels individuals as "mental ill."

Two cognitively oriented approaches, both of which possess linkages to the attitude literature, can account for the finding that people with mental illness are often viewed in an unrealistically negative manner. These involve the selective exposure (Frey, 1986) and accessibility effect (Higgins, Rholes, & Jones, 1977), respectively. With regard to the former, it is important to recognize that clinicians are in the business of helping individuals who have a problem. Once the client has improved significantly, the services of the clinician are less frequently sought. Thus, on a daily basis, clinicians are rarely exposed to cases that demonstrate significant improvement. As a consequence, psychiatrists commonly characterize individuals with schizophrenia as showing ever-worsening and residual impairment (Harding, Brooks, Ashikaga, Strauss, & Breier, 1987). Although this characterization describes schizophrenic patients who remain under psychiatric treatment, it is not an accurate portrayal of this group of patients taken as a whole (Corrigan, Watson, & Ottati, in press). In fact, a significant number of people with schizophrenia improve and achieve rehabilitation. Thus, clinical observation of people with mental illness contains a selective exposure bias that produces an overly pessimistic view of mental illness, a view that has been coined the "clinician's illusion" (Harding et al., 1992; Harding & Zahniser, 1994).

As noted previously, the illusory correlation model emphasizes the role of cognitive accessibility, an emphasis that shares linkages with self-perception theory. The illusory correlation model has relatively obvious implications when applied to the problem of mental illness stigma. Because people with serious mental illness constitute a minority of the population, it is notable when we encounter them. In addition, negative behavior is more distinctive and notable than positive behavior (Fiske, 1980). Thus, when a person with mental illness behaves in a negative fashion (e.g., violent behavior), it is a doubly distinctive event that is especially memorable. Even if there were no actual association between a specific disorder (e.g., schizophrenia) and the tendency to perform a negative behavior (e.g., physical assault), and even if there were no preconceptions about the disorder, people would nevertheless associate this group with the negative behavior, given the distinctiveness of the conjunction.

As is the case with attitudes more generally, prejudicial attitudes toward people with mental illness can trigger expectancy-confirming cognitive biases that serve to maintain the prejudicial attitude. In a study performed by Langer and Abelson (1974), traditional (analytically oriented) therapists were shown a videotape of a man being interviewed. Half of the therapists were told the man was a "job applicant," whereas the other half were told that he was a "patient." All therapists saw the same videotape. When subsequently asked to rate the man's level of psychological adjustment, the therapists rated the "patient" as more disturbed than the "job candidate." This effect may have been mediated by biased interpretation of ambiguous behavior performed by the man being interviewed. For example, whereas bodily fidgeting may have been interpreted as "excitement about the job" when the man was described as a job applicant, it may have been interpreted as "neurotic anxiety" when the man was described as a patient. Other work, however, suggests that biased interpretation effects can arise even when people observe psychiatric patients perform relatively commonplace and benign behaviors. Rosenhan (1973) provided a vivid demonstration of this possibility by having himself and a number of his colleagues admitted to a psychiatric ward under the bogus diagnosis of schizophrenia. Although these individuals attempted to act as they would normally, members of the hospital staff perceived them as disturbed.

CONCLUSION

The present chapter demonstrates that many areas of study, both within and outside of social psychology, are infused with and connected to attitudinal processes. In this sense, attitude theory and research serves as an integrative theme that permeates a variety of approaches to understanding human behavior. The present chapter does not provide a comprehensive analysis of all possible connections with the attitude literature. To the contrary, it simply provides a sampling of such connections that exist within four broad domains of study (i.e., intrapersonal, interpersonal, intragroup, and intergroup processes). Additional connections can be found within each of these domains.

With regard to the study of intrapersonal processes, we have already suggested that additional connections can be forged with social psychological research regarding the self, and related work that falls outside social psychology. Clinical or psychiatric research that further articulates the antecedents and consequences of self-esteem is an obvious candidate for such an endeavor, as is research and intervention geared toward alleviating depression. Within the domain of interpersonal processes, social psychological research on aggression stands out as an additional area that offers promising linkages with the attitude literature. Examples include social learning accounts of aggression that overlap with conditioning models of attitude formation, as well as cognitive accounts of aggression that overlap with cognitive models of attitude formation. Connections of this nature can be extended to interdisciplinary research regarding the effects of televised violence and violent video games, among other things.

Additional connections can also be forged when considering intragroup processes. One involves the effect of group norms on individual behavior and its connection to attitude models that emphasize the role of internalized social norms. This includes the effect of general group norms (e.g., politeness norms), role specific norms (e.g., children should obey their parents), and norms involving social justice (e.g., reciprocity, equity). Connections can also be forged when considering attitude-relevant processes as they relate to intergroup relations. These include attitude-relevant processes that emerge during instances of intergroup conflict, intergroup cooperation, and intergroup negotiation.

In concluding, it is important to emphasize that we do not regard attitude research as the sole starting point for those who wish to explore integrative themes that underlie the study of human behavior. Undoubtedly, other areas of research can serve a similar integrative function. For example, one might start with the premise that many areas of study are infused with and connected to fundamental concepts and processes identified in the decision making literature. The integrative perspective adopted by any given researcher is undoubtedly related to that individual's unique area of expertise and training. However, we do believe it is important that each researcher adopt some sort of integrative vision of the various approaches to studying human behavior. An over-arching, integrative perspective serves as an invaluable guide when researchers formulate and select the questions they wish to answer. It enables researchers to focus on important and impactful questions, and potentially, to discover answers that reverberate across disciplines.

REFERENCES

Abelson, R. P. (1959). Modes of resolution of belief dilemmas. *Journal of Conflict Resolution, 3,* 343–352.

Abelson, R. P., Kinder, D. R., Peters, M. D., & Fiske, S. T. (1982). Affective and semantic components in political person perception. *Journal of Personality and Social Psychology, 42,* 619–630.

Abelson, R. P., & Rosenberg, M. J. (1958). Symbolic psychologic: A model of attitudinal cognition. *Behavioral Science, 3,* 1–13.

Ainsworth, M. D. S., Blehar, M. C., Waters, E., & Wall, S. (1978). *Patterns of attachment.* Hillsdale, NJ: Lawrence Erlbaum Associates.

Ajzen, I. (1991). The theory of planned behavior. *Organizational Behavior and Human Decision Processes, 50,* 179–211.

Albarracín, D., & Kumkale, G. T. (2003). Affect as information in persuasion: A model of affect identification and discounting. *Journal of Personality and Social Psychology, 84,* 453–469.

Albarracín, D., & Wyer, R. S. (2001). Elaborative and non-elaborative processing of a behavior-related communication. *Personality and Social Psychology Bulletin, 26*, 691–705.

Allport, G. W. (1935). Attitudes. In C. Murchison (Ed.), *Handbook of social psychology* (Vol. 2, pp. 798–844). New York: Russell and Russell.

Allport, G. W. (1954). *The nature of prejudice*. Oxford, England: Addison-Wesley.

Allport, G. W. (1979). *The nature of prejudice*. New York: Doubleday Anchor Books. (Original work published 1954)

Allport, G. W. (1985). The historical background of social psychology. In G. Lindzey & E. Aronson (Eds.), *The handbook of social psychology* (Vol. 1, pp. 1–46). Reading, MA: Addison-Wesley.

Anderson, N. H. (1981). Integration theory applied to cognitive responses and attitudes. In R. E. Petty, T. M. Ostrom, & T. C. Brock (Eds.), *Cognitive responses in persuasion* (pp. 361–397). Hillsdale, NJ: Lawrence Erlbaum Associates.

Arriaga, X. B., & Agnew, C. R. (2001). Being committed: Affective, cognitive, and conative components of relationship commitment. *Personality and Social Psychology Bulletin, 27*, 1190–1203.

Bagarozzi, D. A., & Giddings, C. W. (1983). The role of cognitive constructs and attributional processes in family therapy. In L. R. Wolberg & M. L. Aronson (Eds.), *Group and family therapy*. New York: Brunner/Mazel.

Bargh, J. A. (1997). The automaticity of everyday life. In R. S. Wyer (Ed.), *Advances in social cognition* (Vol. 10, pp. 1–62). Mahwah, NJ: Lawrence Erlbaum Associates.

Bartholomew, K. (1990). Avoidance of intimacy: An attachment perspective. *Journal of Social and Personal Relationships, 7*, 147–178.

Bartlett, F. C. (1932). *Remembering: A study in experimental and social psychology*. Cambridge, UK: Cambridge University Press.

Beckmann, J., & Gollwitzer, P. M. (1987). Deliberative versus implemental states of mind: The issue of impartiality in predecisional and postdecisional information processing. *Social Cognition, 5*, 259–279.

Bem, D. J. (1965). An experimental analysis of self-persuasion. *Journal of Experimental Social Psychology, 1*, 199–218.

Bem, D. J. (1967). Self-perception: An alternative interpretation of cognitive dissonance phenomena. *Psychological Review, 74*, 183–200.

Berscheid, E. (1981). A review of the psychological effects of physical attractiveness. In G. W. Lucker, K. A. Ribbens, & J. A. McNamara (Eds.), *Psychological aspects of facial form* (pp. 1–23). Ann Arbor, MI: Center for Human Growth.

Bettencourt, B. A., Charlton, K., Eubanks, J., Kernahan, C., & Fuller, B. (1999). Development of collective self-esteem among students: Predicting adjustment to college. *Basic and Applied Social Psychology, 21*, 213–222.

Bettencourt, B. A., & Hume, D. (1999). The cognitive contents of social-group identity: Values, emotions, and relationships. *European Journal of Social Psychology, 29*, 113–121.

Bless, H., Bohner, G., Schwarz, N., & Strack, F. (1990). Mood and persuasion: A cognitive response analysis. *Personality and Social Psychology Bulletin, 16*, 331–345.

Bless, H., Mackie, D. M., & Schwarz, N. (in press). Mood effects on encoding and judgmental processes in persuasion. *Journal of Personality and Social Psychology.*

Bodenhausen, G. V. (1988). Stereotypic biases in social decision making and memory: Testing process models of stereotype use. *Journal of Personality and Social Psychology, 55*, 726–737.

Bodenhausen, G. V., Kramer, G. P., & Susser, K. (1994). Happiness and stereotypic thinking in social judgment. *Journal of Psychology and Social Psychology, 66*, 621–632.

Bodenhausen, G. V., Sheppard, L. A., & Kramer, G. P. (1994). Negative affect and social judgment: The differential impact of anger and sadness. *European Journal of Social Psychology, 24*(1), 45–62.

Boller, G. W., Swasy, J. L., & Munch, J. M. (1990). Conceptualizing argument quality via argument structure. *Advances in Consumer Research, 17*, 321–328.

Bordieri, J., & Drehmer, D. (1986). Hiring decisions for disabled workers: Looking at the cause. *Journal of Applied Social Psychology, 16*, 197–208.

Bothwell, R. K., & Brigham, J. C. (1983). Selective evaluation and recall during the 1980 Reagan-Carter debate. *Journal of Applied Social Psychology, 13*, 427–442.

Bowlby, J. (1982). *Attachment and loss: Vol. 1. Attachment* (2nd ed.). New York: Basic Books.

Bradbury, T. B., Beach, S. R. H., Fincham, F. D., & Nelson, G. M. (1996). Attributions and behavior in functional and dysfunctional marriages. *Journal of Consulting and Clinical Psychology, 64*, 569–576.

Bradbury, T. N., & Fincham, F. D. (1990). Attributions in marriage: Review and critique. *Psychological Bulletin, 107*, 3–33.

Brehm, J. W., & Cohen, A. R. (1962). *Explorations in cognitive dissonance*. New York: Wiley.

Brennan, K. A., & Bosson, J. K. (1998). Attachment-style differences in attitudes toward and reactions to feedback from romantic partners: An exploration of the relational bases of self-esteem. *Personality and Social Psychology Bulletin, 24*, 699–714.

Brent, E., & Granberg, D. (1982). Subjective agreement with the presidential candidates of 1976 and 1980. *Journal of Personality and Social Psychology, 42*, 393–403.

Brewer, M. B., & Gardner, W. (1996). Who is this "We"? Levels of collective identity and self representations. *Journal of Personality and Social Psychology, 71*, 83–93.

Brewer, M. B., Manzi, J. M., & Shaw, J. S. (1993). In-group identification as a function of depersonalization, distinctiveness, and status. *Psychological Science, 4*, 88–92.

Brock, T. C. (1962). Cognitive restructuring and attitude change. *Journal of Abnormal and Social Psychology, 64*, 264–271.

Brown, S. P. (1996). A meta-analysis and review of organizational research on job involvement. *Psychological Bulletin, 120*, 235–255.

Bruess, C. J. S., & Pearson, J. C. (1993). "Sweat pea" and "pussy cat": An examination of idiom use and marital satisfaction over the life cycle. *Journal of Social and Personal Relationships, 10*, 609–615.

Burnstein, E., & Vinokur, A. (1973). Testing two classes of theories about group-induced shifts in individual choice. *Journal of Experimental Social Psychology, 9*, 123–137.

Burnstein, E., Vinokur, A., & Trope, Y. (1973). Interpersonal comparison versus persuasive argumentation: A more direct test of alternative explanations for group-induced shifts in individual choice. *Journal of Experimental Social Psychology, 9*, 236–245.

Byrne, D. (1961). Interpersonal attraction and attitude similarity. *Journal of Abnormal and Social Psychology, 62*, 713–715.

Byrne, D., & Blaylock, B. (1963). Similarity and assumed similarity of attitudes between husbands and wives. *Journal of Abnormal and Social Psychology, 67*, 636–640.

Cacioppo, J. T., & Petty, R. E. (1979). Effects of message repetition and position on cognitive response, recall, and persuasion. *Journal of Personality and Social Psychology, 37*, 97–109.

Campbell, D. T. (1963). Social attitudes and other acquired behavioral dispositions. In S. Koch (Ed.), *Psychology: A study of a science* (Vol. 6, pp. 94–172). New York: McGraw-Hill.

Caspi, A., Herbener, E. S., & Ozer, D. J. (1992). Shared experiences and the similarity of personalities: A longitudinal study of married couples. *Journal of Personality and Social Psychology, 62*, 281–291.

Chaiken, S. (1980). Heuristic versus systematic information processing and the use of source versus message cues in persuasion. *Journal of Personality and Social Psychology, 39*, 752–766.

Chaiken, S., & Eagly, A. H. (1983). Communication modality as a determinant of persuasion: The role of communicator salience. *Journal of Personality and Social Psychology, 45*, 241–256.

Chaiken, S., Liberman, A., & Eagly, A. H. (1989). Heuristic and systematic information processing within and beyond the persuasion context. In J. S. Uleman & J. A. Bargh (Eds.), *Unintended thought* (pp. 212–252). New York: Guilford.

Chan, C. -J., & Margolin, G. (1994). The relationship between dual-earner couples' daily work mood and home affect. *Journal of Social and Personal Relationships, 11*, 573–586.

Clore, G. L. (1992). Cognitive phenomenology: Feelings and the construction of judgment. In L. L. Martin & A. Tesser (Eds.), *The construction of social judgments* (pp. 133–163). Hillsdale, NJ: Lawrence Erlbaum Associates.

Collins, M. A., & Zebrowitz, L. A. (1995). The contributions of appearance to occupational outcomes in civilian and military settings. *Journal of Applied Social Psychology, 25*, 129–163.

Collins, N. L. (1996). Working models of attachment: Implications for explanation, emotion, and behavior. *Journal of Personality and Social Psychology, 71*, 810–832.

Conway, M., & Ross, M. (1984). Getting what you want by revising what you had. *Journal of Personality and Social Psychology, 47*, 738–748.

Cooper, J., & Worchel, S. (1970). Role of undesired consequences in arousing cognitive dissonance. *Journal of Personality and Social Psychology, 16*, 199–206.

Coopersmith, S. (1967). The antecedents of self-esteem. San Francisco: Freeman.

Corrigan, P., Ottati, V., & Watson, A. (in press). Some social causes of mental illness stigma. In P. Corrigan (Ed.), *A comprehensive review of the stigma of mental illness: Implications for research and social change*. Washington, DC: American Psychological Association.

Corrigan, P. W., Watson, A. C., & Ottati, V. (2003). From whence comes mental illness stigma? *International Journal of Social Psychiatry, 49*(2), 142–157.

Davis, J. H. (1973). Group decision and social interaction: A theory of social decision schemes. *Psychological Review, 80*, 97–125.

Davis, J. L., & Rusbult, C. E. (2001). Attitude alignment in close relationships. *Journal of Personality and Social Psychology, 81*, 65–84.

Deutsch, M., & Gerard, H. B. (1955). A study of normative and informational social influences upon individual judgment. *Journal of Abnormal and Social Psychology, 51*, 629–636.

Dion, K. K., Berscheid, E., & Walster, E. (1972). What is beautiful is good. *Journal of Personality and Social Psychology, 24*, 285–290.

Dion, K. K., Pak, A. W. -P., & Dion, K. I. (1990). Stereotyping physical attractiveness: A sociocultural perspective. *Journal of Cross-Cultural Psychology, 21*, 158–179.

Dion, K. L., & Dion, K. K. (1987). Belief in a just world and physical attractiveness stereotyping. *Journal of Personality and Social Psychology, 52*, 775–780.

Dovidio, J. F., Gaertner, S. L., Isen, A. M., & Lowrance, R. (1995). Group representations and intergroup bias: Positive affect, similarity, and group size. *Personality and Social Psychology Bulletin, 21*, 856–865.

Downey, J. L., & Damhave, K. W. (1991). The effects of place, type of comment, and effort expended on the perception of flirtation. *Journal of Social Behavior and Personality, 6*, 35–43.

Dulany, D. E. (1962). The place of hypotheses and intentions: An analysis of verbal control in verbal conditioning. *Journal of Personality, 30*, 102–129.

Eagly, A. H., Ashmore, R. D., Makhijani, M. G., & Longo, L. C. (1991). What is beautiful is good, but . . . : A meta-analytic review of research on the physical attractiveness stereotype. *Psychological Bulletin, 110*, 109–128.

Eagly, A. H., & Chaiken, S. (1993). *The psychology of attitudes.* Fort Worth, TX: Harcourt Brace Jovanovich College Publishers.

Eagly, A. H., Chen, S., Chaiken, S., Shaw-Barnes, K. (1999). The impact of attitudes on memory: An affair to remember. *Psychological Bulletin, 125*, 64–89.

Eagly, A. H., Chen, S., Kulesa, P., & Chaiken, S. (2001). Do attitudes affect memory? Tests of the congeniality hypothesis. *Current Directions in Psychological Science, 10*, 5–9.

Eagly, A. H., Kulesa, P., Brannon, L. A., Shaw-Barnes, K., Hutson-Comeaux, S. (2000). Why counterattitudinal messages are as memorable as proattitudinal messages: The impact of active defense against attack. *Personality and Social Psychology Bulletin, 26*, 1392–1408.

Edwards, A. L. (1941). Rationalization in recognition as a result of a political frame of reference. *Journal of Abnormal and Social Psychology, 36*, 224–235.

Etcheverry, P. E., & Agnew, C. R. (2004). Subjective norms and romantic relationship state and fate. *Personal Relationship, 11*, 409–428.

Fazio, R. H. (1986). How do attitudes guide behavior? In R. M. Sorrentino & E. T. Higgins (Eds.), *Handbook of motivation and cognition: Foundations of social behavior* (pp. 204–243). New York: Guilford.

Fazio, R. H., Chen, J., McDonel, E. C., & Sherman, S. J. (1982). Attitude accessibility, attitude-behavior consistency, and the strength of the object-evaluation association. *Journal of Experimental Social Psychology, 18*, 339–357.

Fazio, R. H., Jackson, J. R., Dunton, B. C., & Williams, C. J. (1995). Variability in automatic activation as an unobtrusive measure of racial attitudes: A bona fide pipeline? *Journal of Personality and Social Psychology, 69*, 1013–1027.

Fazio, R. H., & Zanna, M. P. (1981). Direct experience and attitude-behavior consistency. In L. Berkowitz (Ed.), *Advances in experimental social psychology* (Vol. 14, pp. 161–202). San Diego, CA: Academic Press.

Festinger, L. (1950). Informal social communication. *Psychological Review, 57*, 271–282.

Festinger, L. (1954). A theory of social comparison processes. *Human Relations, 7*, 117–140.

Festinger, L. (1957). *A theory of cognitive dissonance.* Evanston, IL: Row, Peterson.

Festinger, L., & Carlsmith, J. M. (1959). Cognitive consequences of forced compliance. *Journal of Abnormal and Social Psychology, 58*, 203–210.

Festinger, L., Schachter, S., & Back, K. W. (1950). *Social pressures in informal groups.* New York: Harper.

Fiedler, K. (1991). The tricky nature of skewed frequency tables: An information loss account of distinctiveness-based illusory correlations. *Journal of Personality and Social Psychology, 60*, 24–36.

Fiedler, K. (2000). Illusory correlations: A simple associative algorithm provides a convergent account of seemingly divergent paradigms. *Review of General Psychology, 4*, 25–58.

Fincham, F. D. (2001). Attributions in close relationships: From Balkanization to integration. In G. J. Fletcher & M. Clark (Eds.), *Blackwell Handbook of Social Psychology* (pp. 3–31).

Fincham, F. D., & Bradbury, T. N. (1987). The impact of attributions in marriage: A longitudinal analysis. *Journal of Personality and Social Psychology, 53*, 481–489.

Fincham, F. D., & Bradbury, T. N. (1993). Marital satisfaction, depression, and attributions: A longitudinal analysis. *Journal of Personality and Social Psychology, 64*, 442–452.

Fishbein, M., & Ajzen, I. (1975). *Belief, attitude, intention, and behavior: An introduction to theory and research.* Reading, MA: Addison-Wesley.

Fishbein, M., & Ajzen, I. (1981). Attitudes and voting behavior: An application of the theory of reasoned action. In G. M. Stephenson & J. M. Davis (Eds.), *Progress in applied social psychology* (pp. 253–313). Chichester, UK: Wiley.

Fishbein, M., & Ajzen, I. (1981). Acceptance, yielding and impact: Cognitive processes in persuasion. In R. E. Petty, T. M. Ostrom, & T. C. Brock (Eds.), *Cognitive responses in persuasion* (pp. 339–359). Hillsdale, NJ: Lawrence Erlbaum Associates.

Fiske, S. T. (1980). Attention and weight in person perception: The impact of negative and extreme behavior. *Journal of Personality and Social Psychology, 38*, 889–906.

Fiske, S. T. (1998). Stereotypes, prejudice, and discrimination. In D. Gilbert, S. Fiske, & G. Lindzey (Eds.), *Handbook of social psychology* (4th ed., pp. 357–411). Oxford, UK: Oxford University Press.

Frey, D. (1986). Recent research on selective exposure to information. In L. Berkowitz (Ed.), *Advances in experimental social psychology* (Vol. 19, pp. 41–80). San Diego, CA: Academic Press.

Fuller, S. R., & Aldag, R. J. (1998). Organizational tonypandy: Lessons from a quarter century of the groupthink phenomenon. *Organizational Behavior and Human Decision Processes, 73*, 163–184. San Diego, CA: Academic Press.

Geller, P. A., & Hobfoll, S. E. (1994). Gender differences in job stress, tedium and social support in the workplace. *Journal of Social and Personal Relationships, 11*, 555–572.

Gigone, D., & Hastie, R. (1993). The common knowledge effect: Information sharing and group judgment. *Journal of Personality & Social Psychology, 65*(5), 959–974.

Gigone, D., & Hastie, R. (1997). The impact of information on small group choice. *Journal of Personality and Social Psychology, 72*, 132–140.

Goethals, G. R., Cooper, J., & Naficy, A. (1979). Role of foreseen, foreseeable, and unforseeable behavioral consequences in the arousal of cognitive dissonance. *Journal of Personality and Social Psychology, 37*, 1179–1185.

Granberg, D., & Brent, E. E. (1974). Dove-hawk placements in the 1968 election: Application of social judgment and balance theories. *Journal of Personality and Social Psychology, 29*, 687–695.

Granberg, D., & Brent, E. E. (1980). Perceptions of issue positions of presidential candidates. *American Scientist, 68*(6), 617–646.

Greenspoon, J. (1955). The reinforcing effect of two spoken sounds on the frequency of two responses. *American Journal of Psychology, 68*, 409–416.

Greenwald, A. G. (1968). Cognitive learning, cognitive response to persuasion, and attitude change. In A. G. Greenwald, T. C. Brock, & T. M. Ostrom (Eds.), *Psychological foundations of attitudes* (pp. 147–170). San Diego, CA: Academic Press.

Griffin, D., & Bartholomew, K. (1994). Models of the self and other: Fundamental dimensions underlying measures of adult attachment. *Journal of Personality and Social Psychology, 67*, 430–445.

Hamilton, D. L., & Gifford, R. K. (1976). Illusory correlation in interpersonal perception: A cognitive basis for stereotypic judgments. *Journal of Experimental Social Psychology, 12*, 392–407.

Harding, C., Brooks, G., Ashikaga, T., Strauss, J., & Breier, A. (1987). The Vermont longitudinal study of persons with severe mental illness: Long-term outcome of subjects who retrospectively met DSM-III criteria for Schizophrenia. *American Journal of Psychiatry, 144*, 727–735.

Harding, C., & Zahniser, J. (1994). Empirical correction of seven myths about schizophrenia with implications for treatment. *Acta Psychiatrica Scandinavica, Supplementum, 90*, 140–146.

Harding, C., Zubin, J., & Strauss, J. (1992). Chronicity in schizophrenia: Revisited. *British Journal of Psychiatry, 161*, 27–37.

Hart, W., & Ottati, V. (2004). [Physical attractiveness and candidate evaluation]. Unpublished raw data.

Hastie, R. (1980). Memory for behavioral information that confirms or contradicts a personality impression. In R. Hastie, T. M. Ostrom, E. B. Ebbesen, R. S. Wyer, Jr., D. L. Hamilton, & D. E Carlston (Eds.), *Person memory: The cognitive basis of social perception* (pp. 155–177). Hillsdale, NJ: Lawrence Erlbaum Associates.

Hastie, R., & Kumar, P. Q. (1979). Person memory: Personality traits as organizing principles in memory for behavior. *Journal of Personality and Social Psychology, 37*, 25–38.

Hastie, R., & Park, B. (1986). The relationship between memory and judgment depends on whether the judgment task is memory-based or on-line. *Psychological Review, 93*, 258–268.

Hatfield, E. (1988). Passionate and companionate love. In R. J. Sternberg & M. I. Barnes (Eds.), *The psychology of love* (pp. 191–217). New Haven, CT: Yale University Press.

Heider, F. (1946). Attitudes and cognitive organization. *Journal of Psychology, 21*, 107–112.

Heider, F. (1958). *The psychology of interpersonal relations.* New York: Wiley.

Hewstone, E. M., Bond, M. H., Wan, K. C. (1983). Social factors and social attributions: The explanation of intergroup differences in Hong Kong. *Social Cognition, 2*, 142–157.

Higgins, E. T., Rholes, W. S., & Jones, C. R. (1977). Category accessibility and impression formation. *Journal of Experimental Social Psychology, 13*, 141–154.

Hogg, M. A. (1992). *The social psychology of group cohesiveness: From attraction to social identity.* New York: New York University Press.

Hogg, M. A., & Abrams, D. (1988). *Social identifications.* London: Routledge.

Hogg, M. A., & Hains, S. C. (1996). Intergroup relations and group solidarity: Effects of group identification and social beliefs on depersonalized attraction. *Journal of Personality and Social Psychology, 70*, 25–309.

Holtzworth-Munroe, A., Jacobson, N. S., Fehrenbach, P. A., & Fruzzetti, A. (1992). Violent married couples' attributions for violent and nonviolent self and partner behaviors. *Behavioral Assessment, 14*, 53–64.

Hummert, M. L., Crockett, W. H., & Kemper, S. (1990). Processing mechanisms underlying use of the balance schema. *Journal of Personality and Social Psychology, 58*, 5–21.

Insko, C. A. (1965). Verbal reinforcement of attitude. *Journal of Personality and Social Psychology, 2*, 621–623.

Insko, C. A., Schopler, H. J., Gaertner, G., Wildschutt, T., Kozar, R., Pinter, B., Finkel, E. J., Brazil, D. M., Cecil, C. L., & Montoya, M. R. (2001). Interindividual-intergroup discontinuity reduction through the anticipation of future interaction. *Journal of Personality and Social Psychology, 80*, 95–111.

Isbell, L., & Ottati, V. (2002). The emotional voter: Effects of episodic affective reactions on candidate evaluation. In V. Ottati, R. S. Tindale, J. Edwards, F. B. Bryant, L. Heath, D. C. O'Connell, Y. Suarez-Balcazar, & E. J. Posavac (Eds.), *The social psychology of politics: Vol. 5. Social psychological application to social issues* (pp. 55–74). New York: Kluwer Academic-Plenum Publishers.

Isbell, L. M., & Wyer, R. S. (1999). Correcting for mood-induced bias in the evaluation of political candidates: The roles of intrinsic and extrinsic motivation. *Personality and Social Psychology Bulletin, 25*, 237–249.

Iyengar, S., & Kinder, D. R. (1987). *News that matters: Television and American opinion.* Chicago: University of Chicago Press.

Janis, I. L. (1972). *Victims of groupthink: A psychological study of foreign-policy decisions and fiascoes.* Boston: Houghton Mifflin.

Jetten, J., Branscombe, N. R., & Spears, R. (2002). On being peripheral: Effects of identity insecurity on personal and collective self-esteem. *European Journal of Social Psychology, 32*, 105–123.

Johnson, D. W., & Johnson, R. T. (1989). *Cooperation and competition: Theory and research.* Edina, MN: International Book Company.

Johnson, D. W., & Johnson, F. (1994). *Joining together: Group theory and group skills* (5th ed.). Englewood Cliffs, NJ: Prentice-Hall.

Johnson, D. W., & Johnson, R. T. (1998). Cooperative learning and social interdependence theory. In R. S. Tindale, L. Heath, J. Edwards, E. J. Posavac, F. B. Bryant, Y. Suarez-Balcazar, E. Henderson-King, & J. Myers (Eds.), *Theory and research on small groups: Vol. 4. Social psychological applications to social issues* (pp. 9–36). New York: Plenum.

Johnson, J. T., & Judd, C. M. (1983). Overlooking the incongruent: Categorization biases in the identification of political statements. *Journal of Personality and Social Psychology, 45*, 978–996.

Jones, E. E., & Aneshansel, J. (1956). The learning and utilization of contravaluant material. *Journal of Abnormal and Social Psychology, 53*, 27–33.

Kahneman, D., & Tversky, A. (1971). Subjective probability: A judgment of representativeness. *Cognitive Psychology, 3*, 430–454.

Kahneman, D., & Tversky, A. (1982). The psychology of preferences. *Science, 246*, 136–142.

Kameda, T., & Sugimori, S. (1993). Psychological entrapment in group decision making: An assigned decision rule and a groupthink phenomenon. *Journal of Personality and Social Psychology, 65*, 282–292.

Karney, B. R., Bradbury, T. N., Fincham, F. D., & Sullivan, K. T. (1994). The role of negative affectivity in the association between attributions and marital satisfaction. *Journal of Personality and Social Psychology, 66*, 413–424.

Katz, D. (1960). The functional approach to the study of attitudes. *Public Opinion Quarterly, 24*, 163–204.

Keller, R. T. (1997). Job involvement and organizational commitment as longitudinal predictors of job performance: A study of scientists and engineers. *Journal of Applied Psychology, 82*, 539–545.

Kelley, H. H., & Thibaut, J. W. (1978). *Interpersonal relations: A theory of interdependence.* New York: Wiley.

Kelley, S., & Mirer, T. (1974). The simple act of voting. *American Political Science Review, 61*, 572–591.

Kenny, D. A., Albright, L., Malloy, T. E., & Kashy, D. A. (1994). Consensus in interpersonal perception: Acquaintance and the big five. *Journal of Personality and Social Psychology, 116*, 245–258.

Kenny, D. A., & Kashy, D. A. (1994). Enhanced coorientation in the perception of friends: A social relations analysis. *Journal of Personality and Social Psychology, 67*, 1024–1033.

Kessler, T., Mummendey, A., & Leisse, U-K. (2000). The personal-group discrepancy: Is there a common information base for personal and group judgment? *Journal of Personality and Social Psychology, 79*, 95–109.

Kinder, D. R. (1978). Political person perception: The asymmetrical influence of sentiment and choice on perceptions of presidential candidates. *Journal of Personality and Social Psychology, 36*, 859–871.

Kinder, D. R., & Kiewlet, R. D. (1979). Economic discontent and political behavior: The role of personal grievances and collective judgments in congressional voting. *American Journal of Political Science, 23*, 495–527.

Klohnen, E. C., & Bera, S. (1998). Behavioral and experiential patterns of avoidantly and securely attached women across adulthood: A 31-year longitudinal perspective. *Journal of Personality and Social Psychology, 74*, 211–223.

Krosnick, J. A. (1988). Attitude importance and attitude change. *Journal of Experimental Social Psychology, 24*, 240–255.

Krosnick, J. A. (2002). The challenges of political psychology: A review of research on the projection hypothesis. In J. Kuklinski (Ed.), *Thinking about political psychology*. New York: Cambridge University Press.

Krosnick, J. A., Berent, M. K., & Boninger, D. S. (1994). Pockets of responsibility in the American electorate: Findings of a research program on attitude importance. *Political Communication, 11*, 391–411.

Krosnick, J. A., Betz, A. L., Jussim, L. J., & Lynn, A. R. (1992). Subliminal conditioning of attitudes. *Personality and Social Psychology Bulletin, 18*, 152–162.

Krosnick, J. A., & Kinder, D. R. (1990). Altering the foundations of popular support for the president through priming. *American Political Science Review, 84*, 497–512.

Langer, E. J., & Abelson, R. P. (1974). A patient by any other name. . . : Clinician group differences in labeling bias. *Journal of Consulting and Clinical Psychology, 42*, 4–9.

LaPiere, R. T. (1934). Attitudes vs. actions. *Social Forces, 13*, 230–237.

Laurenceau, J. -P., Barrett, L. F., & Pietromonaco, P. R. (1998). Intimacy as an interpersonal process: The importance of self-disclosure, partner disclosure, and perceived partner responsiveness in interpersonal exchanges. *Journal of Personality and Social Psychology, 74*, 1238–1251.

Lerner, J. S., & Keltner, D. (2000). Beyond valence: Toward a model of emotion-specific influences on judgment and choice. *Cognition and Emotion, 14*, 473–493.

Lerner, J. S., & Keltner, D. (2001). Fear, anger, and risk. *Journal of Personality & Social Psychology, 81*(1), 45–62.

Levenson, R. W., Carstensen, L. L., & Gottman, J. M. (1994). The influence of age and gender on affect, physiology, and their interrelations: A study of long-term marriages. *Journal of Personality and Social Psychology, 67*, 56–68.

Link, B. (1987). Understanding labeling effects in the area of mental disorders: An assessment of the effects of expectations of rejection. *American Sociological Review, 52*, 96–112.

Lodge, M., McGraw, K., & Stroh, P. (1989). An impression-driven model of candidate evaluation. *American Political Science Review, 83*, 399–419.

Lodge, M., Steenbergen, M. R., & Brau, S. (1995). The responsive voter: Campaign information and the dynamics of candidate evaluation. *American Political Science Review, 89*, 309–326.

Lodge, M., & Stroh, P. (1993). Inside the mental voting booth: An impression-driven process model of candidate evaluation. In S. Iyengar & W. McGuire (Eds.), *Explorations in political psychology. Duke studies in political psychology* (pp. 225–263). Durham, NC: Duke University Press.

Lodge, M., Taber, C. (2001). Automatic affect for political candidates, parties, and symbols. Paper presented at the Annual Meeting of the Midwest Political Science Association, Chicago, IL.

Lydon, J., Zanna, M. P., & Ross, M. (1988). Bolstering attitudes by autobiographical recall: Attitude persistence and selective memory. *Personality and Social Psychology Bulletin, 14*, 78–86.

Marcus, G. E., & MacKuen, M. (1993). Anxiety, enthusiasm, and the vote: The emotional underpinnings of learning and involvement during presidential campaigns. *American Political Science Review, 87*, 672–685.

Markus, H., & Nurius, P. (1986). Possible selves. *American Psychologist, 41*, 954–969.

Mathieu, J. E., Zajac, D. M. (1990). A review and meta-analysis of the antecedents, correlates, and consequences of organizational commitment. *Psychological Bulletin, 108*, 171–194.

McCauley, C. (1989). The nature of social influence in groupthink: Compliance and internalization. *Journal of Personality and Social Psychology, 57*, 250–260.

McGowan, S., Daniels, L. K., & Byrne, D. (1999a). Self-esteem and interpersonal trust: Evidence consistent with Bartholomew's conceptualization of attachment. Manuscript submitted for publication.

McGowan, S., Daniels, L. K., & Byrne, D. (1999b). The Albany Measure of Attachment Style: A multi-item measure of Bartholomew's four-factor model. Manuscript submitted for publication.

McGraw, K., Lodge, M., & Stroh, P. (1990). On-line processing in candidate evaluation: The effects of issue order, issue importance, and sophistication. *Political Behavior, 12*, 41–58.

McGuire, W. J. (1968). Personality and attitude change: An information-processing theory. In A. G. Greenwald, T. C. Brock, & T. M. Ostrom (Eds.), *Psychological foundations of attitudes* (pp. 171–196). San Diego, CA: Academic Press.

McGuire, W. J. (1972). Attitude change: The information-processing paradigm. In C. G. McClintock (Ed.), *Experimental social psychology* (pp. 108–141). New York: Holt, Rinehart & Winston.

McGuire, W. J. (1985). Attitudes and attitude change. In G. Lindzey & E. Aronson (Eds.), *Handbook of social psychology* (3rd ed., Vol. 2, pp. 233–346). New York: Random House.

Miller, G. A., Galanter, E., Pribram, K. H. (1960). *Plans and the structure of behavior*. New York: Henry Holt & Co., Inc.

Miller, J. M., & Krosnick, J. A. (2000). New media impact on the ingredients of presidential evaluations: Politically knowledgeable citizens are guided by a trusted source. *American Journal of Political Science, 44*, 301–315.

Moore, J. S., Graziano, W. G., & Miller, M. G. (1987). Physical attractiveness, sex role orientation, and the evaluation of adults and children. *Personality and Social Psychology Bulletin, 13*, 95–102.

Mullen, B., Anthony, T., Salas, E., & Driskell, J. E. (1994). Group cohesiveness and quality of decision making: An integration of tests of the groupthink hypothesis. *Small Group Research, 25,* 189–204.

Mullen, B., & Copper, C. (1994). The relation between group cohesiveness and performance: An integration. *Psychological Bulletin, 115*(2), 210–227.

Murray, S. L., Holmes, J. G., Dolderman, D., & Griffin, D. W. (2000). What the motivated mind sees: Comparing friends' perspectives to married partners' views of each other. *Journal of Experimental Social Psychology, 36,* 600-620.

Newall, A., Shaw, J. C., Simon, H. A. (1958). Elements of a theory of human problem solving. *Psychological Review, 65,* 151–166.

Newcomb, T. M. (1956). The prediction of interpersonal attraction. *Psychological Review, 60,* 393–404.

Olson, J. C., Toy, D. R., Dover, P. A. (1982). Do cognitive responses mediate the effects of advertising content on cognitive structure? *Journal of Consumer Research, 9,* 245–262.

Olson, J. M., & Zanna, M. P. (1979). A new look at selective exposure. *Journal of Experimental Social Psychology, 15,* 1–15.

Olson, M. A., & Fazio, R. H. (2002). Implicit acquisition and manifestation of classically conditioned attitudes. *Social Cognition, 20,* 89–103.

Osgood, C. E., & Tannenbaum, P. H. (1955). The principle of congruity in the prediction of attitude change. *Psychological Review, 62,* 42–55.

Oskamp, S., Schulz, P. W. (1998). *Applied social psychology.* Saddle River, NJ: Prentice-Hall.

Ottati, V. (1990). Determinants of political judgments: The joint influence of normative and heuristic rules of inference. *Political Behavior, 12,* 159–179.

Ottati, V. (1996). When the survey question directs retrieval: Implications for assessing the cognitive and affective predictors of global evaluation. *European Journal of Social Psychology, 26,* 1–21.

Ottati, V. C. (1997). When the survey question directs retrieval: Implications for assessing the cognitive and affective predictors of global evaluation. *European Journal of Social Psychology, 27*(1), 1–21.

Ottati, V. (2001). The psychological determinants of political judgment. In A. Tesser & N. Schwarz (Eds.), *Blackwell Handbook of Social Psychology: Intraindividual Processes* (pp. 615–634). Oxford: Blackwell.

Ottati, V., Bodenhausen, G., & Newman, L. (in press). Social psychological models of mental illness stigma. Chapter to appear in P. Corrigan (Ed.), *A comprehensive review of the stigma of mental illness: Implications for research and social change.* Washington, DC: American Psychological Association.

Ottati, V., & Deiger, M. (2002). Visual cues and the candidate evaluation process. In V. Ottati, R. S. Tindale, J. Edwards, F. B. Bryant, L. Heath, D. C. O'Connell, Y. Suarez-Balcazar, & E. J. Posavac (Eds.), *The social psychology of politics: Vol. 5. Social psychological applications to social issues* (pp. 75–87). New York: Kluwer Academic-Plenum Publishers.

Ottati, V., Fishbein, M., & Middlestadt, S. E. (1988). Determinants of voters' beliefs about the candidates' stands on issues: The role of evaluative bias heuristics and the candidates' expressed message. *Journal of Personality and Social Psychology, 55,* 517–529.

Ottati, V., & Isbell, L. (1996). Effects of mood during exposure to target information on subsequently reported judgments: An on-line model of misattribution and correction. *Journal of Personality and Social Psychology, 71,* 39–53.

Ottati, V., Steenbergen, M., & Riggle, E. (1992). The cognitive and affective components of political attitudes: Measuring the determinants of candidate evaluations. *Political Behavior, 14,* 423–442.

Ottati, V., & Wyer, R. S., Jr. (1993). Affect and political judgment. In S. Iyengar & J. McGuire (Eds.), *Explorations in Political Psychology* (pp. 296–320). Durham, NC: Duke University Press.

Ottati, V., Wyer, R. S., Deiger, M., & Houston, D. (2002). The psychological determinants of candidate evaluation and voting preference. In V. Ottati, R. S. Tindale, J. Edwards, F. B. Bryant, L. Heath, D. C. O'Connell, Y. Suarez-Balcazar, & E. J. Posavac (Eds.), *The social psychology of politics: Vol. 5. Social psychological applications to social issues* (pp. 3–28). New York: Kluwer Academic-Plenum Publishers.

Page, B. I. (1976). A theory of political ambiguity. *American Political Science Review, 70,* 742–752.

Page, S. (1995). Effects of the mental illness label in 1993: Acceptance and rejection in the community. *Journal of Health and Social Policy, 7,* 61–68.

Park, W. (1990). A review of research on groupthink. *Journal of Behavioral Decision Making, 3,* 229–245.

Paulus, P. B. (Ed.). (1989). *Psychology of group influence* (2nd ed.). Hillsdale, NJ: Lawrence Erlbaum Associates.

Petty, R. E. (1977a). The importance of cognitive responses in persuasion. *Advances in Consumer Research, 4,* 357–362.

Petty, R. E. (1977b). A cognitive response analysis of the temporal persistence of attitude changes induced by persuasive communications. Unpublished doctoral dissertation, Ohio State University.

Petty, R. E., & Cacioppo, J. T. (1979). Issue involvement can increase or decrease persuasion by enhancing message-relevant cognitive responses. *Journal of Personality and Social Psychology, 37,* 1915–1926.

Petty, R. E., & Cacioppo, J. T. (1986). *Communication and persuasion: Central and peripheral routes to attitude change.* New York: Springer-Verlag.

Petty, R. E., Cacioppo, J. T., & Schuman, D. (1983). Central and peripheral routes to advertising effectiveness: The moderating role of involvement. *Journal of Consumer Research, 10,* 135–146.

Petty, R. E., Ostrom, T. M., & Brock, T. C. (1981). Historical foundations of the cognitive response approach to attitudes and persuasion. In R. E. Petty, T. M. Ostrom, & T. C. Brock (Eds.), *Cognitive responses in persuasion* (pp. 5–29). Hillsdale, NJ: Lawrence Erlbaum Associates.

Phelan, J., Link, B., Stueve, A., & Pescosolido, B. (2000). Public conceptions of mental illness in 1950 and 1996: What is mental illness and is it to be feared? *Journal of Health and Social Behavior, 41,* 188–207.

Proshansky, H. M. (1943). A projective method for the study of attitudes. *Journal of Abnormal and Social Psychology, 38,* 393–395.

Radecki-Bush, C., Farrell, A. D., & Bush, J. P. (1993). Predicting jealous responses: The influence of adult attachment and depression on threat appraisal. *Journal of Social and Personal Relationships, 10,* 569–588.

Randall, D. M., Fedor, D. P., & Longenecker, C. O. (1990). The behavioral expression of organizational commitment. *Journal of Vocational Behavior, 36,* 210–224.

Razran, G. H. S. (1938). Conditioning away social bias by the luncheon technique. *Psychological Bulletin, 35,* 693.

Regan, D. T., & Fazio, R. H. (1977). On the consistency between attitudes and behavior: Look to the method of attitude formation. *Journal of Experimental Social Psychology, 13,* 28–45.

Riggle, E. D., Ottati, V., Wyer, R. S., Kuklinski, J., & Schwarz, N. (1992). Bases of political judgments: The role of stereotypic and nonstereotypic information. *Political Behavior, 14,* 67–87.

Rogers, E. M., & Dearing, J. W. (1988). Agenda-setting research: Where has it been and where is it going? In J. A. Anderson (Ed.), *Communication yearbook* (Vol. 11, pp. 555–594). Beverly Hills, CA: Sage.

Rojahn, K., & Pettigrew, T. F. (1992). Memory for schema-relevant information: A meta-analytic review. *British Journal of Social Psychology, 31,* 81–109.

Rosenberg, M. J. (1960). An analysis of affective-cognitive consistency. In C. I. Hovland & M. J. Rosenberg (Eds.), *Attitude organization and change: An analysis of consistency among attitude components* (pp. 15–64). New Haven, CT: Yale University Press.

Rosenberg, S. W., Bohan, L., McCafferty, P., & Harris, K. (1986). The image and the vote: The effect of candidate presentation on voter preference. *American Journal of Political Science, 30*(1), 109–126.

Rosenberg, S. W., Kahn, S., & Tran, T. (1991). Creating a political image: Shaping appearance and manipulating the vote. *Political Behavior, 13,* 345–367.

Rosenberg, S. W., & McCafferty, P. (1987). The image and the vote: Manipulating voters' preferences. *Public Opinion Quarterly, 51*(1), 31–47.

Rosenhan, D. L. (1973). On being sane in insane places. *Science, 179,* 250–258.

Ross, M. (1989). Relation of implicit theories to the construction of personal histories. *Psychological Review, 96,* 341–357.

Rusbult, C. E. (1980). Commitment and satisfaction in romantic associations: A test of the Investment Model. *Journal of Experimental Social Psychology, 16,* 172–186.

Sagar, H. A., & Schofield, J. W. (1980). Racial and behavioral cues in black and white children's perceptions of ambiguously aggressive acts. *Journal of Personality and Social Psychology, 39,* 590–598.

Sarnoff, I. (1960). Psychoanalytic theory and social attitudes. *Public Opinion Quarterly, 24,* 251–279.

Sarnoff, I., & Katz, D. (1954). The motivational basis of attitude change. *Journal of Abnormal and Social Psychology, 49,* 115–124.

Schopler, J., Insko, C. A., Wieslquist, J., Pemberton, M., Withcher, B., Kozar, R., Roddenberry, C., Wildschut, T. (2001). *Journal of Personality and Social Psychology, 80,* 632–644.

Schwarz, N. (1990). Feelings as information: Informational and motivational functions of affective states. In E. T. Higgins & R. M. Sorrentino (Eds.), *Handbook of motivation and cognition: Foundations of social behavior* (Vol. 2, pp. 527–561). New York: Guilford.

Schwarz, N., & Bless, H. (1992). Constructing reality and its alternatives: An inclusion/exclusion model of assimilation and contrast effects in social judgment. In L. Martin & A. Tesser (Eds.), *Construction of social judgments* (pp. 217–245). Hillsdale, NJ: Lawrence Erlbaum Associates.

Schwarz, N., & Clore, G. L. (1983). Mood, misattribution, and judgments of well-being: Informative and directive functions of affective states. *Journal of Personality and Social Psychology, 45,* 513–523.

Schwarz, N., & Clore, G. L. (1996). Feelings and phenomenal experiences. In E. T. Higgins & A. W. Kruglanski (Eds.), *Social psychology handbook of principles* (pp. 433–465). New York: Guilford.

Sears, D. O., & Freedman, J. L. (1965). Effects of expected familiarity with arguments upon opinion change and selective exposure. *Journal of Personality and Social Psychology, 2,* 420–426.

Sedikides, C. (1993). Assessment, enhancement, and verification determinants of the self-evaluation process. *Journal of Personality and Social Psychology, 65,* 317–338.

Seeleman, V. (1940). The influence of attitudes upon the remembering of pictorial material. *Archives of Psychology*, (monograph No. 258).

Senchak, M., & Leonard, K. E. (1993). The role of spouses' depression and anger in the attribution-marital satisfaction relation. *Cognitive Therapy and Research, 17*, 397–409.

Shaffer, D. R., & Bazzini, D. G. (1997). What do you look for in a prospective date? Reexamining the preferences of men and women who differ in self-monitoring propensities. *Personality and Social Psychology Bulletin, 23*, 605–616.

Shapiro, J. P., Baumeister, R. F., & Kessler, J. W. (1991). A three-component model of children's teasing: Aggression, humor, and ambiguity. *Journal of Social and Clinical Psychology, 10*, 459–472.

Shaver, P. R., & Hazan, C. (1994). Attachment. In A. L. Weber & J. H. Harvey (Eds.), *Perspectives on close relationships* (pp. 110–130). Boston: Allyn & Bacon.

Shimp, T. A., Stuart, E. W., Engle, R. W. (1991). A Program of Classical Conditioning Experiments Testing Variations in the Conditioned Stimulus and Context. *Journal of Consumer Research, 18*, 1–12.

Shulman, S., Elicker, J., & Sroufe, L. A. (1994). Stages of friendship growth in preadolescence as related to attachment history. *Journal of Social and Personal Relationships, 11*, 341–361.

Sillars, A. L., Folwell, A. L., Hill, K. C., Maki, B. K., Hurst, A. P., & Casano, R. A. (1994). *Journal of Social and Personal Relationships, 11*, 611-617.

Simon, H. A., Newell, A. (1964). Information processing in computer and man. *American Scientist, 53*, 281–300.

Song Hing, L. S., Chung-Yan, G. A., Grunfeld, R., Robichaud, L. K., Zanna, M. P. (in press). Exploring the discrepancy between implicit and explicit prejudice. A test of aversive racism. In J. P. Forgas, K. William, B. Von Hippel (Eds.), *Social motivation: conscious and unconscious processes* . New York: Psychology Press.

Spink, K. S., & Carron, A. V. (1994). Group cohesion in exercise classes. *Small Group Research, 25*, 26–42.

Srull, T. K. (1981). Person memory: Some tests of associative storage and retrieval models. *Journal of Experimental Psychology: Human Learning and Memory, 7*, 440–462.

Srull, T. K., & Wyer, R. S., Jr. (1979). The role of category accessibility in the interpretation of information about persons: Some determinants and implications. *Journal of Personality and Social Psychology, 37*, 1660–1672.

Staats, A. W., & Staats, C. K. (1958). Attitudes established by classical conditioning. *Journal of Abnormal and Social Psychology, 57*, 37–40.

Stangor, C., & McMillan, D. (1992). Memory for expectancy-congruent and expectancy-incongruent information: A review of the social developmental literatures. *Psychological Bulletin, 111*(1), 42–61.

Sternberg, R. J. (1986). A triangular theory of love. *Psychological Review, 93*, 119–135.

Sternberg, R. J. (1988a). *The triangle of love.* New York: Basic Books.

Sternberg, R. J. (1988b). Triangulating love. In R. J. Sternberg & M. J. Barnes (Eds.), *The psychology of love* (pp. 119–138). New Haven, CT: Yale University Press.

Sullivan, J. L., Aldrich, J. H., Borgida, E., & Rahn, W. (1990). Candidate appraisal and human nature: man and superman in the 1984 election. *Ploitical Psychology, 11*(3), 495–484.

Sweeney, P. D., & Gruber, K. L. (1984). Selective exposure: Voter information preferences and the Watergate affair. *Journal of Personality and Social Psychology, 46*, 1208–1221.

Tajfel, H. (1969). Cognitive aspects of prejudice. *Journal of Social Issues, 25*, 79–97.

Tajfel, H. (1981). *Human groups and social categories: Studies in social psychology.* Cambridge, UK: Cambridge University Press.

Tajfel, H., & Turner, J. C. (1979). An integrative theory of intergroup conflict. In W. G. Austin & S. Worchel (Eds.), *The social psychology of intergroup relations* (pp. 33–47). Monterey, CA: Brooks/Cole.

Tajfel, H., & Turner, J. C. (1986). The social identity theory of intergroup behavior. In S. Worchel & W. Austin (Eds.), *Psychology of intergroup relations.* Chicago: Nelson-Hall.

Tetlock, P. E., Peterson, R. S., McGuire, C., Chang, S., & Feld, P. (1992). Assessing political group dynamics: A test of the groupthink model. *Journal of Personality and Social Psychology, 63*, 403–425.

Thompson, J. S., & Snyder, D. K. (1986). Attribution theory in intimate relationships: A methodological review. *American Journal of Family Therapy, 14*, 123–138.

Trafimow, D., Triandis, H. S., & Goto, S. G. (1991). Some tests of the distinction between the private self and the collective self. *Journal of Personality and Social Psychology, 60*, 649–655.

Triandis, H. C. (1980). Values, attitudes, and interpersonal behavior. In H. E. Howe, Jr., & M. M. Page (Eds.), *Nebraska Symposium on Motivation, 1979* (Vol. 27, pp. 195–259). Lincoln, NE: University of Nebraska Press.

Turner, J. C. (1987). *Rediscovering the social group: A self-categorization theory.* Oxford, UK: Blackwell.

Tversky, A., & Kahneman, D. (1974). Judgment under uncertainty: Heuristics and biases. *Science, 185*, 1124–1131.

Uleman, J. S. (1971). Awareness and motivation in generalized verbal conditioning. *Journal of Experimental Research in Personality, 5*, 257–267.

Vinokur, A., & Burnstein, E. (1974). Effects of partially shared persuasive arguments on group-induced shifts: A group problem-solving approach. *Journal of Personality and Social Psychology, 29*, 305–315.

Watson, W. S., & Hartmann, G. W. (1939). The rigidity of a basic attitudinal frame. *Journal of Abnormal and Social Psychology, 34*, 314–335.

Weiss, R. L., & Heyman, R. E. (1990). Observation of marital interaction. In F. D. Fincham & T. N. Bradbury (Eds.), *The psychology of marriage* (pp. 87–117). New York: Guilford.

Whitbeck, L. B., & Hoyt, D. R. (1994). Social prestige and assortive mating: A comparison of students from 1956 and 1988. *Journal of Social and Personal Relationships, 11*, 137–145.

Wood, W. (1982). Retrieval of attitude-relevant information from memory: Effects on susceptibility to persuasion and on intrinsic motivation. *Journal of Personality and Social Psychology, 42*, 798–810.

Wyer, R. S., Jr. (1974). *Cognitive organization and change: An information processing approach.* Potomac, MD: Erlbaum.

Wyer, R. S., Jr. (1981). *Cognitive organization and change: An information-processing approach.* Hillsdale, NJ: Lawrence Erlbaum Associates.

Wyer, R. S., Jr., & Carlston, D. E. (1979). *Social cognition, inference and attribution.* Hillsdale, NJ: Lawrence Erlbaum Associates.

Wyer, R. S., Jr., & Ottati, V. (1993). Political information processing. In S. Iyengar & J. McGuire (Eds.), *Explorations in Political Psychology* (pp. 264–295). Durham, NC: Duke University Press.

Wyer, R. S., Jr., & Srull, T. K. (1989). *Memory and cognition in its social context.* Hillsdale, NJ: Lawrence Erlbaum Associates.

Zajonc, R. B., & Burnstein, E. (1965). The learning of balanced and unbalanced social structures. *Journal of Personality, 33*, 153–163.

Zanna, M. P., & Olson, J. M. (1982). Individual differences in attitudinal relations. In M. P. Zanna, E. T. Higgins, & C. P. Herman (Eds.), *Consistency in social behavior: The Ontario Symposium* (Vol. 2, pp. 75-103). Hillsdale, NJ: Lawrence Erlbaum Associates.

Zanna, M. P., & Sande, G. N. (1987). The effects of collective actions on the attitudes of individual group members: A dissonance analysis. In M. P. Zanna, J. M. Olson, & C. P. Herman (Eds.), *Social influence: The Ontario Symposium* (Vol. 5, pp. 151–163). Hillsdale, NJ: Lawrence Erlbaum Associates.

18

Attitude Research in the 21st Century: The Current State of Knowledge

Alice H. Eagly
Northwestern University

Shelly Chaiken
New York University

It is both an honor and a burden to be invited by the editors of this handbook to write a final chapter that comments on the progress of the current generation of attitude researchers and that suggests directions for the future. As we read through the chapters, our foreboding at the magnitude of the task of studying such a large number of rather long chapters changed to pleasure and excitement about the growth and deepening of attitude theory and research that the authors of these chapters have so ably described. Each chapter represents a formidable scholarly effort by authors who analyze a particular area of attitude research in a way that both celebrates achievements and charts issues needing new research.

For us, much of the appeal of research on attitudes lies in the breadth and inclusiveness of the set of issues that fit within this domain. Because attitudes were classically defined as encompassing cognition, affect, and behavior (Katz & Stotland, 1959; Rosenberg & Hovland, 1960), the area has long had the potential to serve as an integrative force within psychology. Attitude theory and research thus were cognitive long before psychology's cognitive revolution but also emphasized motivation and emotion even in the height of the field's shift toward cognition. Moreover, the prediction of behavior has always been a core issue in the study of attitudes.

Most psychological research is somewhat specialized insofar as it addresses single response classes such as perception, cognition, or emotion. In contrast, attitude research encompasses all response classes even though it focuses on evaluation in the sense of the goodness versus badness of entities. In addition, because the entities that are evaluated can be anything that is discriminated by individuals, the study of attitudes encompasses all classes of stimuli. In contrast, most other research areas within social psychology are confined to a single stimulus class, such as the study of interpersonal attraction, which pertains to people as stimuli, or the study of prejudice, which pertains mainly to social groups as stimuli.

In the relatively long history of attitude theory and research, the potential breadth of the field seemed not to be fully realized by the scope of the research undertaken. Two reasons for this limitation stand out. First, many problems are inherently attitudinal, such as the study of prejudice or interpersonal attraction, proceeded with limited input from mainstream attitude theory, despite its obvious relevance. Second, most attitude researchers concentrated on a particular set of issues that remained encapsulated mainly within social psychology. For example, during the early history of attitude research, there was much interest in whether and how attitudes could be measured (see Himmelfarb, 1993; Krosnick, Judd, & Wittenbrink, chap. 2, this volume). Although attention to assessment constituted a healthy beginning, helping attitude research to gain scientific credibility, these assessment advances did not consistently prove their worth in studies of attitudinal functioning, whose practitioners often adopted relatively casual measurement practices. Subsequent attitude research, stimulated by World War II, came to focus on persuasion and attitude change, to the neglect of other attitudinal topics (Hovland, Janis, & Kelley, 1953; see Johnson, Maio, & Smith-McLallen, chap. 15, this volume). These efforts were widely admired by many social psychologists but did not hold center stage within psychology as a whole. Somewhat later, after attitude researchers were challenged by an apparent deficit in attitudes' ability to predict behavior, many moved forward to the critical psychological issue of how behavior can be predicted and what processes mediate between attitudes and behavior (Ajzen & Fishbein, chap. 5, this volume). Although the achievements of attitude-behavior research are formidable, its scientific profile within psychology as a whole has been modest.

To many psychologists, the study of attitudes has seemed to be just one of many relatively small research areas, pursued by a subgroup of social psychologists. Yet the potential exists for attitude research to provide a broadly inclusive psychological framework. In this chapter, we consider whether in the contemporary period the potential inclusiveness of attitude theory is being realized to a greater extent than in the past. The chapters of this handbook provide an ideal opportunity for addressing this question. The set of issues considered in the chapters encompasses nearly all of those pursued by attitude researchers who find their disciplinary home within psychology departments. We consider the extent to which attitude theory and research now include concerns and questions that lie within its conceptual boundaries but beyond the traditional research topics pursued by earlier attitude researchers. In analyzing whether attitude researchers have in fact achieved integrative frameworks, we focus on several issues in this chapter.

We first address the central issue of the nature of attitudes themselves, including the perennially challenging question of how attitudes should be defined. This issue links to contemporary efforts to understand attitudes that are assessed by explicit and implicit measures and that can sometimes appear as dual or multiple attitudes. Also in this section, we consider whether attitudes should be regarded as stable and enduring or contextual and repeatedly constructed and reconstructed. We then consider the increase in attention to affective processes, involving emotions and moods, and relate affective phenomena to central issues in attitude theory. Our chapter then turns to issues of motivation and recognizes the power of motivational analyses to organize and elucidate many attitudinal phenomena, including the processes that mediate attitude formation and change. Our chapter then analyzes perspectives that emphasize the interpersonal and social context of attitudes, an area of increasing sophistication and integrative power. Finally, we recognize continued growth in research on other attitudinal topics and suggest directions for additional development of the field.

THE NATURE OF ATTITUDES

Attitudes as Tendencies to Evaluate

Definitions of attitude have varied over the years, although they have centered on evaluation that is associated with, or directed toward, a particular entity or *attitude object*. Most definitions have been consistent with Campbell's (1963) discussion of *acquired behavioral dispositions*, that is, states of the person that come into being on the basis of some transaction with the environment. Consistent with Campbell's treatment, attitudes do not exist until an individual distinguishes an attitude object as a discriminable entity, sometimes without conscious awareness, and responds to this object on an explicit or implicit basis. That initial response may be shaped in part by hard-wired predispositions, as in the case of a fearful response to snakes or spiders (Oehman & Mineka, 2001), or, more generally, by heritable precursors (Tesser, 1993). Nonetheless, an attitude toward an entity such as snakes does not come into being until an individual first encounters an instance of the entity. The initial response, presumably negative in the case of a snake, then leaves a mental residue in the person that predisposes him or her to an unfavorable or avoidant response on subsequent encounters. This evaluative residue of past experience is a hypothetical construct—that is, an intervening state that hypothetically accounts for the covariation between stimuli relevant to the attitude object and the evaluative responses elicited by these stimuli.

In *The Psychology of Attitudes* (Eagly & Chaiken, 1993), our general review and integration of attitude theory and research, we referred to this residue as a *tendency* to evaluate. The term tendency reflected a careful choice, intended to avoid restricting attitudes in a temporal sense by implying either that they must be enduring or that they are necessarily short-term and temporary. Because in psychology the word *state* implies temporariness and the word *disposition* implies greater permanence, neither term seemed appropriate to refer to attitude as an acquired behavioral disposition. Moreover, an appropriate term would not imply that attitudes are necessarily accessible to consciousness. In order that the definition of attitude could serve as a broad umbrella for attitude research, we therefore settled on attitude as *a psychological tendency that is expressed by evaluating a particular entity with some degree of favor or disfavor*.

In concert with many other theorists (Zanna & Rempel, 1988), we argued that attitudes can be formed through cognitive, affective, and behavioral processes and expressed through cognitive, affective, and behavioral responses. Attitudes thus can have varied antecedents on the input side and varied consequences on the output side. Yet, we parted company with some of these theorists by objecting to the definition of attitude as being a response per se—for example, the categorization of the attitude object on the evaluative continuum (Zanna & Rempel, 1988). Similarly, we part company with Kruglanski and Stroebe's (chap. 8, this volume; see also Wyer & Albarracín, chap. 7, this volume) definition of attitudes as *evaluative judgments*. Categorizations, evaluative judgments, and, more generally, overt or covert evaluative responses are best regarded as *expressions* of the tendency that constitutes attitude. Although evaluative judgments and categorizations of instantiations of an attitude object are of course attitudinal in the sense that they express attitudes, they are not synonymous with attitude itself. Attitude is a tendency or latent property of the person that gives rise to judgments and categorizations, as well as many other types of responses such as emotions and overt behaviors. The separation in attitude theory between the inner state that constitutes attitude and the responses that express this inner state is crucial to understanding the relation between these tendencies, which are residues of past experience, and current responding, which reflects a variety of influences in addition to those that emanate from the inner state. This separation between the tendency that constitutes attitude and its expression in attitudinal responding facilitates theory development concerning attitude change, the attitude–behavior relation, and other attitudinal phenomena.

Regarding attitudes as latent properties of the person challenges psychologists to specify the nature of that inner state. By providing a minimalist definition of attitudes merely as psychological tendencies to evaluate in *The Psychology of Attitudes*, we welcomed continuing debate on the description of the psychological and physiological events that constitute that state and thus underlie attitudes. Theorists of attitudes define these constituents of attitudes in varying ways, depending on their particular theoretical preferences (Wegener & Carlston, chap. 12, this volume). For example, Fazio (1989) defined attitudes as an association in memory between an attitude object and an evaluation. This way of thinking about the latent property that constitutes attitude follows from associative learning models, such as associative network models of memory (Anderson, 1983). Also reflecting an associative learning approach, Fabrigar, MacDonald, and Wegener (chap. 3, this volume) defined attitude as "a type of knowledge structure stored in memory or created at the time of judgment" (p. 80).

A recent effort to specify the nature of the psychological tendency that constitutes attitude is Bassili and Brown's (chap. 13, this volume, p. 552) proposal that attitudes are "emergent properties of the activity of microconceptual networks that are potentiated by contextually situated objects, goals, and task demands." This definition thus links the attitude concept to connectionist models in which attitudes are represented by a pattern of activation of units within a module (Smith, 1996; Smith & DeCoster, 1998). The microconcepts that populate this inner state contain evaluative information and thus are consistent with the consensual definition of attitudes as evaluative. Borrowing a term from Rosenberg (1968), Bassili and Brown named this inner state an *attitudinal cognitorium*.

Psychologists should neither expect nor desire a consensus about the precise definition of the inner state known as attitude. We instead welcome the various insights that flow from particular specifications of this state. Such specifications are metaphoric because they do not have an inherent reality in terms of a psychological tendency or state that can be directly verified. In other words, researchers cannot directly observe object-evaluation associations, knowledge structures, or microconcepts. Instead, thinking about attitudes in terms of one of these specifications of the tendency to evaluate enables and guides theorizing about attitudes. Each treatment favors certain types of hypotheses about attitudinal functioning. For example, Doob (1947) defined the inner state that constitutes attitude as a learned, implicit anticipatory response, a treatment that borrowed language from the then-popular framework of Hullian learning theory. Although attitude researchers no longer are guided by this particular metaphor, it enhanced understanding within one theoretical tradition.

Attitude researchers should welcome these specific, distinctive instantiations of the latent tendencies that constitute attitudes because each of them serves as a metaphor for a particular theoretical perspective. Each promotes certain insights about attitudes, and its proponents have the challenge of proving its ability to inspire testable hypotheses that are subsequently confirmed. All of these metaphors are consistent with the essential definition of attitude as an evaluative tendency. This broad definition of attitude thus transcends particular theoretical preferences and embraces psychologists' shifting metaphors for understanding the inner state that constitutes attitude.

Attitudes as Enduring or Temporary Constructions

Our minimalist definition of attitudes as evaluative tendencies allowed it to encompass the variability of attitudes along a temporal dimension. Some attitudes are relatively enduring, in some cases formed in early childhood and carried through one's lifetime. Other attitudes are formed but then are changed. Still other attitudes are formed but not subsequently elicited and thus they recede or, in effect, disappear from the psyche. Understanding the determinants of attitudinal persistence remains an underdeveloped agenda in attitude research, but surely elementary observations of social life suggest that attitudes may vary from ephemeral to enduring.

The main reason why some investigators have concluded that most, if not all, attitudes are unstable, constantly emerging anew in specific situations, is that they have equated variability in the expression of attitudes with variability in the evaluative tendency that constitutes attitude. This attitudes-as-constructions position (Schwarz & Bohner, 2001; Wilson & Hodges, 1992) conflates variability in attitudinal responses with variability in attitude itself. Constructionist theorists are entirely correct to argue that attitudinal judgments are constructed anew on each occasion of encountering an attitude object because such judgments are influenced by the specific context in which they take place as well as by the particular aspect of the attitudinal tendency to evaluate that is activated. These context effects should be and are pervasive, as Schwarz and Bohner (2001) argued, because attitudinal judgments are not pure expressions of attitude but outputs that reflect both attitude and the information in the contemporaneous setting (see Wegener & Carlston, chap. 12, this volume). This setting contains cues that elicit the attitude, information that provides new inputs to the attitude, and contextual stimuli that provide standards against which to judge the current instantiation of the attitude object. The observed attitudinal judgments or other responses such as overt behaviors reflect this composite of influences. Whereas attitudinal responses, such as judgments, are therefore labile depending on the judgment context, the inner state or latent construct that constitutes attitude can be relatively stable. Therefore, judgments often vary around an average value that is defined by the tendency that constitutes the attitude. We thus agree with Krosnick et al. (chap. 2, this volume) that to understand this variability, psychologists must model the psychological processes that mediate between the person's evaluative tendency and the particular attitudinal responses that are elicited in varied circumstances.

Attitudes as Implicit or Explicit

An important development in contemporary research on the nature of attitudes is the proposal that attitudinal responses can be implicit as well as explicit. Researchers have devoted considerable attention to understanding attitude expressions that are implicit in the sense that they are not consciously recognized by the individual who holds the attitude (Greenwald & Banaji, 1995). Several chapters provided thoughtful discussions of these developments (Ajzen & Fishbein, chap. 5, this volume; Bassili & Brown, chap. 13, this volume; Krosnick et al., chap. 2, this volume).

Researchers have theorized that, even when a person does not have conscious access to an attitude, it may be automatically activated by the attitude object or cues associated with the object. Attitudes that are implicit in this sense can direct responding, especially more spontaneous behaviors (Dovidio, Brigham, Johnson, & Gaertner, 1996). In contrast, explicit attitudes to which one has conscious access may be activated in a more deliberative manner that requires cognitive effort. Such attitudes may under some circumstances override implicit attitudes, and they better predict behaviors that are under volitional control (see review by Ajzen & Fishbein, chap. 5, this volume).

Much attention has been directed to innovative implicit measures, which seek to assess attitudes without asking respondents for direct reports of these attitudes (Fazio & Olson, 2003; Krosnick et al., chap. 2, this volume). These methods continue a long history of *indirect measurement* in attitude research, which includes disguising attitude measures as tests of knowledge (Hammond, 1948) and assessing physiological responses (e.g., pupillary responses, Hess, 1965; eletromyographic activity in facial musculature, Schwartz, Ahern, & Brown, 1979). Although such measures succeed in assessing attitudes without asking for a verbal report, there is, as Fazio and Olson (2003) indicated, no assurance that respondents are unaware of implicitly assessed attitudes or that these attitudes are in some sense unconscious.

The question of exactly what implicit measures assess is the focus of considerable contemporary research. Clouding understanding are the generally low correlations between attitude assessments that use different implicit measures as well as the variable magnitude of correlations between implicit and explicit measures (Ajzen & Fishbein, chap. 5, this volume; Fazio & Olson, 2003). The issues raised concern the validity of the instruments as well as the nature of the processes that underlie these measurements. The Implicit Association Test (IAT), for example, the most popular implicit measure of attitudes (Greenwald & Nosek, 2001), likely reflects, at least in part, associations that are common in one's environment and thus may be culturally determined and not necessarily endorsed by the individual respondent. Olson and Fazio (2004) frame this issue in terms of *extrapersonal associations* that do not contribute to an individual's evaluation of an attitude object and propose a variant *personalized IAT* that reduces the influence of such associations. Others argue that IAT responses reflect a mix of controlled and automatic processes (Conrey, Sherman, Gawronski, Hugenberg, & Groom, 2004), whereas ideally the measure would assess only the automatic processes inherent in the notion of attitudes that are not necessarily accessible to introspection.

Given the imperfections and ambiguities of current implicit measures of attitudes, researchers would be well advised to use caution in claiming that the IAT or other indirect or implicit measures assess attitudes that are implicit in the sense that the attitudes are unconscious or not accessible to introspection. These measures may sometimes assess implicit attitudes, but the jury is still out on this matter. Moreover, dissociations between implicitly and explicitly measured attitudes can reflect a variety of factors other than lack of awareness of implicitly measured attitudes, including discordance in the specific content of explicit and implicit measures and social desirability constraints that make people reluctant to admit to certain attitudes on explicit measures.

Dual and Multiple Attitudes

The idea that people can hold more than one attitude simultaneously has arisen in several guises in attitude research. One manifestation of this idea is the concept of attitudinal ambivalence, whereby an individual may be described as holding two attitudes, one positive and one negative, in relation to the same attitude object (Eagly & Chaiken, 1998; Fabrigar, MacDonald, & Wegener, chap. 3, this volume). Ambivalence can arise from various sources and challenges the traditional idea of attitudes as located on a single bipolar continuum. The gains from separating positive from negative attitudes are several (Cacioppo, Gardner, & Berntson, 1997). For example, this separation coordinates with findings indicating that positive and negative responding have different physiological correlates and that negative aspects of people's attitudes often exert stronger effects on behavior and judgments than positive aspects. It is therefore often useful to regard attitudes as consisting of coexisting positive and negative tendencies.

Another manifestation of the multiple attitude idea is Wilson, Lindsey, and Schooler's (2000) conception of dual attitudes, by which people have an implicit attitude and an explicit attitude toward the same attitude object. Implicit attitudes can be automatically activated, whereas explicit attitudes require motivation and capacity to be retrieved from memory. Whereas the construct of ambivalence implies that positive and negative evaluations can both be activated, producing a subjective state of conflict, Wilson and colleagues assumed that generally only one of the dual attitudes is active. Such bipartite attitudes can arise, for example, when new information changes an attitude, creating a new explicit attitude. Yet the old attitude may continue to be present, but often in implicit form.

In agreement with Bassili and Brown (chap. 13, this volume), we believe that attitudes can be not merely dual, but multiple. If the inner tendency of evaluation has been laid down by many encounters with the attitude object at various points in time, different aspects of that residue of past experience may form the basis of attitudinal responding under differing circumstances. Consider, for example, people's attitudes toward their mothers. An affect-laden attitude is ordinarily formed by the young child, and this attitude is elaborated and changed by numerous inputs as the child matures. For example, a rebellious teenager may form a negative attitude in response to a mother's restrictions. The attitude of the mature son or daughter becomes more complex with more knowledge of the mother's functioning in a wider range of settings.

However, the adult child may sometimes revert to a childish or adolescent attitude, perhaps without awareness of the activation of such attitudes, when returning to the family home and engaging in some of the social interactions that resemble those of earlier periods. The residue of past experience that constitutes the attitude is thus multifaceted and can be crystallized in various forms, depending on situational cues. The attitude active at any point in time may be more implicit or more explicit. A tentative, working hypothesis is that attitudes exist on an implicit-explicit continuum, depending on the degree to which the individual has conscious access to them. Awareness of one's own attitude may sometimes be ambiguous, sometimes vague and imperfect, and sometimes absent.

Once More, the Nature of Attitudes

Given these complexities of implicit and explicit attitudes and attitudes that may be dual or multiple in other senses, does it make sense to define attitude as *a psychological tendency that is expressed by evaluating a particular entity with some degree of favor or disfavor* (Eagly & Chaiken, 1993)? We believe that this definition remains appropriate. The more recent proposals of ambivalent, dual, or multiple attitudes are compatible with the idea of attitudes as acquired dispositions that take the form of evaluative tendencies. But are these more complex formulations consistent with the "some degree of favor or disfavor" aspect of the definition? They are consistent if theorists allow for multiple tendencies—positive attitudes and negative attitudes, old attitudes and new attitudes, and implicit attitudes and explicit attitudes. The evaluative content of such attitudes may be quite discrepant, and therefore the evaluative responses that are influenced by these attitudes may be discordant. People may thus have multiple attitudes toward the same attitude object. Yet, in many circumstances, attitudes are not multiple but can be quite simply represented by a single point along a pro-con dimension. For example, attitudes toward everyday products such as shampoos and breakfast cereals may generally be unitary, whereas attitudes toward more richly experienced attitude objects such as family members may commonly be multiple. Mapping these complexities should be high on the agenda of attitude research.

UNDERSTANDING THE CONTRIBUTION OF AFFECT TO ATTITUDES

Zajonc's (1980, 1984) arguments for the primacy of affect stimulated a growth of interest in affective processes among attitude researchers. This growth is well represented in this handbook. Schimmack and Crites (chap. 10, this volume) document the enormous increase in attention to affective issues since 1980. Basic to these advances is identification of this domain as an aspect of attitudes. Specifically, fewer psychologists now use the terms *affect* and *affective* synonymously with *evaluation* and *evaluative*. In contemporary terminology, evaluation is viewed as integrative of all response classes, including affects in the sense of emotions and moods. Nonetheless, terminology remains problematic. Sometimes the terms affect and affective processes seem to refer quite loosely to all processes that cannot be identified as cognitive and therefore to a wide range of emotional and motivational constructs and mechanisms that do not fit easily under the rubric of cognitive structures and processes.

   More constructive for scientific progress are less generic terms that do not lump together all affective and motivational phenomena. Affect thus refers to the feelings, moods, emotions, and sympathetic nervous-system activity that people experience. Like behaviors and cognitive responses, these affective responses express positive or negative evaluation of greater or lesser extremity. Affects are ordinarily understood as a momentary or short-lived pleasant or unpleasant states of one's feelings or emotions (Clore & Schnall, chap. 11, this volume; Schimmack & Crites, chap. 10, this volume). Consequential for the study of attitudes are affects that are experienced as caused by an attitude object and those that are merely associated with an attitude object.

Much of the attention that psychologists have devoted to understanding and classifying affective processes has not been carried out by attitude researchers but has been independently developed (Schimmack & Crites, chap. 10, this volume). For example, emotion researchers developed and refined theories that disentangle the cognitive, affective, and physiological processes that underlie emotions. Similarly, there is progress in understanding how endogenous bodily states interact with exogenous events to create moods. Developing the implications of this new knowledge for attitude research remains a future agenda.

Attitude Formation by Affective Processes

One reason that research on affect is important is that it has special relevance to the question of how attitudes are formed. This issue has received less attention over the years than the question of how attitudes are changed. So-called simple, elementary, or primitive learning mechanisms, such as classical conditioning, may constitute a major set of processes by which attitudes are formed (see Wegener & Carlston, chap. 12, this volume), although attitudes are of course also formed through the presentation of complex verbal information. Redressing the balance in attitude research to give greater consideration to attitude formation is a welcome shift, regardless of whether researchers concentrate on simple affective and cognitive processes or more complex information processing. Yet, elementary learning mechanisms have not turned out to be simple as detailed knowledge has developed concerning how they work. In particular, debates continue about whether these simple learning mechanisms are primarily affective rather than more generally evaluative and whether people have conscious access to the processes underlying these mechanisms.

Attention to elementary learning processes in attitude formation is not a new theme. Conditioning and mere exposure have long attracted attention (see Eagly & Chaiken, 1993), and these phenomena are the focus of considerable recent research. Emerging from these efforts is a consensus that some of these processes are affective at least in the basic sense that they are not mediated by conscious thinking about the nature of the associations that are learned.

Classical Conditioning.   In the classical Pavlovian conditioning model, when a stimulus comes to signal a positive or negative experience, the stimulus acquires positive or negative affect. With respect to the processes that mediate classical conditioning, recent reviews of research (Boakes, 1989; Lovibond & Shanks, 2002) have continued to reiterate Brewer's (1974) early conclusion that existing evidence does not support the conclusion that classical conditioning occurs in humans without their awareness of the contingencies that are produced (see Clore & Schnall, chap. 11, this volume; Schimmack & Crites, chap. 10, this volume). Instead, the individual acquires an expectancy as the conditioned stimulus comes to function as a signal of the later event. Because people generally have conscious access to such expectancies, the promise that classical conditioning might provide unambiguous evidence of noncognitive evaluative processes has faded.

Evaluative Conditioning.   The promise that learning without awareness could be demonstrated in humans has met with greater success within the evaluative conditioning paradigm. Thus, important in understanding simple learning mechanisms is the distinction between classical conditioning and evaluative conditioning (Baeyens, Eelen, Crombez, & Van den Berg, 1992). In classical conditioning a first event (e.g., the sounding of a bell) comes to signal a second event (e.g., food powder in the mouth), so that the participant prepares for the later event. In contrast, evaluative conditioning follows from the association of stimuli or from the mere fact that the meanings of two stimuli are processed together, ordinarily because of their spaciotemporal contiguity. In view of this distinction, most of the demonstrations of attitude conditioning that were labeled classical conditioning would now be classified as evaluative conditioning. For example, Staats and Staats (1957) showed that pairing nonsense syllables with positive or negative words changed evaluative responses to the syllables and considered this research to demonstrate classical conditioning.

Conditioning that associates stimuli in the manner of the Staats and Staats (1957) experiment is aptly described as occurring in an evaluative association paradigm. Such conditioning is resistant to extinction through presentation of the stimulus in the absence of the stimuli earlier associated with it, whereas classical conditioning does show extinction. Also, a reasonably strong case has been made that evaluative conditioning can occur without awareness (De Houwer, Thomas, & Baeyens, 2001), as the target stimulus (conditioned stimulus, or CS) merely takes on the affective tone of the associated stimuli (unconditioned stimulus, or UCS) without signaling that the UCS will follow. The mediation of such effects deserves attention and apparently does not consist of the formation of expectancies. Clore and Schnall (chap. 11, this volume) raise the issue of whether such effects occur because (a) the UCS makes salient features of the CS that are consistent with the UCS or (b) the CS makes the participant think, consciously or unconsciously, of the UCS, without the expectation that it will occur. These proposals of elementary cognitive mechanisms raise questions about the extent to which the associative paradigm should be described as solely affective rather than a broader mix of both affective and cognitive processes.

Whatever the detailed mediation of evaluative conditioning may turn out to be, the recent attention to this mechanism promises to shed light on phenomena such as the persistence of many prejudices and stereotypes even in the face of disconfirming information. Moreover, the effects of evaluative conditioning can spread from one attitude object to another—that is, the affect transferred to the target stimulus then spreads to stimuli associated with the target stimulus through an associative chain (Walther, 2002). This spreading affect appears to be resistant to extinction and is not the product of conscious deliberation. This phenomenon has provocative implications for prejudice: Bad feelings about a single member of a social group may spread to induce negative attitudes toward other members of the group.

Mere Exposure.   The mere exposure paradigm whereby repeated presentations of a neutral stimulus produce a pleasant response continues to attract research attention, in part because of ambiguity concerning the correct explanation of the phenomenon. Mere exposure effects are no doubt ubiquitous in daily life and constitute an important mechanism of attitude formation. The automaticity of the phenomenon rests on demonstrations that mere exposure effects are weaker when stimuli are consciously perceived compared with subliminally presented (Bornstein & D'Agostino, 1992). When people are aware of the stimulus presentations, cognitive processes intervene, perhaps in the form of new associations about the stimuli or knowledge that the true source of one's positive affect is the repeated exposures. Such processes apparently lessen the mere exposure effect.

Many hypotheses have competed to provide explanations of mere exposure effects. Perceptual fluency explanations appear to be strong candidates. These explanations have been refined, with increasing consensus that fluency does carry positive affective value. Yet, it is also possible that fluency intensifies emotions or that the absence of negative consequences following a stimulus serves as a positive unconditioned stimulus (see Clore & Schnall, chap. 11, this volume; Schimmack & Crites, chap. 10, this volume). Regardless of the continuing lack of clarity about causation, some earlier candidates for explaining mere exposure have been abandoned (e.g., deliberative inference processes, response competition; see Eagly &

Chaiken, 1993), and current candidates feature a range of relatively automatic processes. The robust quality of the mere exposure effect continues to attest to its likely importance in daily life as a prominent mechanism through which attitudes are formed.

Affective Priming

One of the signature phenomena on which claims of the primacy of affect are staked is affective priming, which examines the influence of an attitude object prime on responses to a subsequently presented target object. It is unclear whether this paradigm implicates affect in the sense we have defined it, or more general evaluation. At any rate, so-called affective priming was initially demonstrated by Fazio, Sanbonmatsu, Powell, and Kardes (1986), who exposed participants to positive or negative adjectives preceded by positive or negative attitude object primes (e.g., music, guns). When the interval between the prime word and target word was short (about 0.3 second), the response of classifying the target word as positive or negative was quicker if the prime and target word had the same valence compared with opposite valence. For example, exposure to a positive noun as a prime (e.g., music) facilitated categorizing a positive adjective (e.g., appealing) as positive relative to categorizing a negative adjective (e.g., repulsive) as negative (see Klauer, 1998).

Although Fazio and his colleagues initially argued that these effects occur only for more accessible attitudes, later research showed that these effects can occur for more or less accessible attitudes (Bargh, Chaiken, Govender, & Pratto, 1992) and even for completely novel attitude objects (Duckworth, Bargh, Garcia, & Chaiken, 2002). Moreover, affective priming has been demonstrated with subliminal prime stimuli (see Klauer & Musch's, 2003, review). In a related paradigm, participants make good-bad ratings of neutral stimuli, which tend to be assimilated to the valence of the subliminal primes that preceded them (Murphy & Zajonc, 1993).

Research on affective priming is consistent with the position that all attitude objects can elicit automatic evaluation. However, questions have been raised about Bargh's (1997) claim that attitude objects are processed evaluatively before they are processed semantically, or descriptively (Clore & Schnall, chap. 11, this volume). In experiments independently varying the semantic and evaluative similarity of stimulus words to target words, Storbeck and Robinson (2004) demonstrated semantic priming but not affective priming at the short prime-target latencies that produced affective priming in other experiments. Their procedures established semantic congruence and incongruence by having the positive and negative primes and targets come from the same general category (e.g., butterfly and skunk from the category animal) or from different categories (e.g., butterfly and skunk from the category animal; angel and devil from the category religion). This research suggests that semantic categorization precedes evaluative categorization and that declarative memory is generally organized semantically rather than evaluatively. Although affective priming is readily demonstrable in laboratory experiments in which primes and targets have distinctively different semantic meaning, this research raises questions about the priority of affective categorization in natural settings in which stimuli may often be amenable to semantic categorization. We expect that this set of issues will produce considerable debate because of its challenge to claims of the primacy of affect.

Types of Affects

Research on affect has continued to emphasize the development of taxonomies of affects (see Schimmack & Crites, chap. 10, this volume). Critical to attitude research is the distinction that many researchers make between emotions and moods. Emotions generally have a known cause, which attitude researchers treat as the attitude object. For example, a wife becomes angry at her husband, and this negative feeling influences her attitude toward him. Similarly, sensory affects, triggered by sensory experiences such as tastes and smells, provide information about the attitude objects from which they emanate. In contrast, moods more often are free-floating affective states that are not necessarily associated with a cause yet can have implications for attitudes.

Attitude researchers have explored how moods affect attitudes, with interest in memory-based models, heuristic models, and affect-as-information models (Clore & Schnall, chap. 11, this volume). According to Clore and Colcombe (2003), mood may be just one of many affectively meaningful cues that convey evaluative information; other such cues could include unconsciously primed evaluative concepts, visceral feelings, and feedback from facial musculature. This view seems plausible. Insofar as such experiences do not produce beliefs and are not accessible to consciousness, they challenge earlier views that cognitions or beliefs are necessarily the crucial precursors of attitudes (Fishbein & Ajzen, 1975).

Moods also exert indirect effects on information processing and thus affect the types of information that are used and the amount of scrutiny given to evaluative information contained in persuasive communications. Basic findings in these areas have been known for some time—for example, the tendency for positive moods to reduce systematic processing of arguments—and researchers continue to refine their understanding of the processes by which such effects occur (Clore & Schnall, chap. 11, this volume).

Despite this continuing interest in the effects of moods, understanding of the effects of specific emotions on attitudes or of emotions in general is not very well developed. This situation is surprising, given the early interest of attitude researchers in fear-arousing appeals and the development of sophisticated theories of the influence of such appeals on attitudes (Janis, 1967). Research on fear appeals has continued, primarily in relation to health communications (Das, deWit, & Stroebe, 2003), and there is a growing interest in political communication (Marcus, 2002). However, relatively little research has considered the full array of emotions that may affect the persuasiveness of messages.

An exciting focus of future research could be the role of positive emotions, such as joy, contentment, and love, in relation to attitudinal phenomena. According to Fredrickson (2001), positive emotions enlarge people's momentary thought-action repertoires and build personal resources that foster effective coping. This theory could be specified with respect to attitudinal effects—for example, positive emotions might enhance the correspondence between positive attitudes and relevant behaviors. In addition, it would be informative to compare the persuasiveness of communications arousing positive emotions with that of communications not arousing emotions or arousing negative emotions such as fear.

Psychologists also should devote more effort to understanding how affective experiences contribute to the formation of attitudes, especially experiences associated with specific emotions such as fear, pain, joy, and excitement. People thus experience positive and negative emotions on a moment-to-moment basis, often in relation to a particular attitude object. These experiences contribute to the global evaluation that constitutes attitude. Research suggests specific principles that govern the relation between affective experiences and global evaluations. In particular, global evaluations appear to be predictable from a peak-and-end rule whereby the affect at the moment of peak affective intensity and the affect at the end of the episode predict global evaluation, with little impact of the duration of affective episodes (Fredrickson, 2000; Fredrickson & Kahneman, 1993). The generality of these principles with respect to a wide range of attitude objects deserves exploration.

MOTIVATION AS AN ENDURING THEME
IN ATTITUDE RESEARCH

Motives refer to the goals or end-states toward which people strive, and motivation refers to the power of motives to energize and direct thoughts and behavior. As Marsh and Wallace (chap. 9, this volume) point out, motives can be conceptualized at varying levels of abstraction. The term *need* generally refers to a general end state (e.g., high self-regard) that is served by attaining various more specific goals (e.g., holding a good job, being invited to parties). In the study of social influence and persuasion, most interest centers on motives that are formulated as broad needs, and many attitudinal phenomena are thought to reflect these needs.

Invoking motives connects attitudinal phenomena to broader themes of psychological functioning, and therefore motivational themes lend breadth and scope to attitude theory. Motivation was a major theme in most early attitude theories and was prominent in incentive and drive-reductions theories, cognitive consistency theories (particularly dissonance), and functional theories of attitudes (see Eagly & Chaiken, 1993). Because motives associate attitudes with wide-ranging concerns of individuals, these early attitude theories were big-picture theories. With the cognitive revolution of the 1970s, attention turned, at the expense of motivation, toward detailed issues of cognitive processing. As abundantly demonstrated in many of the chapters in this handbook, motivational issues have once again taken center stage in attitude theory and research.

Types of Motives

Functions of Attitudes.   Older motivational traditions in attitude research were often framed in terms of attitudes' functions (see Johnson et al., chap. 15, this volume), and functional analyses have continued to invigorate attitude research, especially in the 1990s (see Maio & Olson, 2000). Investigators of attitudes developed functional analyses to answer the question of why people hold attitudes. Functions, as invoked by attitude theorists, signify the individual's broad goals or needs that direct attitudinal processes.

Attitude theorists generally agree that the fundamental and overarching function of attitudes is to produce knowledge of objects' favorable or unfavorable implications (Kruglanski & Stroebe, chap. 8, this volume). Smith, Bruner, and White (1956) named this function *object appraisal*. It encompasses the cognitive aspects of appraising attitude objects (Katz's, 1960, *knowledge* function) as well as the assessment of attitude objects' potential to provide rewards and punishments (Katz's, 1960, *instrumental* or *utilitarian* function). Because the object-appraisal function essentially restates, in abstract motivational language, the definitional proposition that attitude is a tendency to evaluate an object, theorists have also proposed less abstract functions, which acknowledge less broad but still very personal goals. Attitudes' facilitation of rewarding outcomes has thus been broken down into less abstract descriptions of several different types of rewarding outcomes. In this manner, theorists have specified additional functions of attitudes such as value expression, social adjustment, and ego defense (see review by Eagly & Chaiken, 1998).

Attitudes can be regarded as serving a wide array of even more specific goals such as anxiety reduction that do not necessarily fit easily within the taxonomies of functions proposed by early attitude theorists. Also, Kruglanski and Stroebe (chap. 8, this volume) argued that some functional analyses might be better regarded as specifying functions served by attitude objects rather than functions of holding the attitude—for example, Prentice and Carlsmith's (1999) analysis of attitudes toward possessions and Shavitt's (1990) analysis of attitudes toward products.

Other Typologies of Motives.   Motivational concepts have arisen in the context of theories of social influence and persuasion. Demonstrating the power of a motivational scheme to organize social influence findings, Prislin and Wood (chap. 16, this volume) framed their chapter on social influence in terms of three fundamental social motives: the needs (a) to understand reality, (b) to achieve a positive and coherent self-concept, and (c) to relate to other people and convey an appropriate impression to them. The first two of these motives were prominent in classic theorizing about informational and normative motives that govern conformity in group settings (Deutsch & Gerard, 1955). This classification is similar to the earlier tripartite proposal by Chaiken and her colleagues (Chen & Chaiken, 1999; Chaiken, Liberman, & Eagly, 1989). Focusing on persuasion settings, they classified message recipients' motivations in terms of three motives: *accuracy motivation*, the desire to align attitudes with objective reality; *defense motivation*, the desire to form, maintain, or defend particular attitudinal positions, and *impression motivation*, the desire to express attitudes that facilitate positive self-presentation. Although Prislin and Wood's self-concept motive is framed more broadly than Chaiken's defense motivation, the two schemes are quite similar.

A related triad of motives reflects an older tradition in persuasion research that understood message recipients' motivations in terms of the psychological state of *involvement*, which consisted of arousal induced by an association between an attitude and the self-concept. Johnson and Eagly (1989) proposed that this broad involvement term had been used in three distinct ways by attitude theorists: *outcome-relevant involvement*, induced by an association between an activated attitude and an individual's ability to attain desirable outcomes; *value-relevant involvement*, induced by an association between an activated attitude and the individual's important values; and *impression-relevant involvement*, induced by an association between an activated attitude and the public self. The impression-relevant component of this scheme is virtually identical to the impression components of the Prislin and Wood (chap. 16, this volume) and the Chaiken et al. (1989) classification. If understanding outcomes is regarded as a critical aspect of understanding reality and values are regarded as crucial to the self-concept, the other two components of this treatment of involvement are at least partially overlapping with the other tripartite schemes.

Concentrating on persuasion settings, Briñol and Petty (chap. 14, this volume) provided a motivational frame for research on individual differences in attitude change. They organized individual difference variables that have been important in attitude research in terms of four motives that they argued govern thinking and action: the needs (a) to know, (b) to achieve consistency or internal coherence of one's explanatory system, (c) to develop and maintain a positive self-concept, and (d) to obtain social inclusion and approval. This organization raises the question of whether individual difference variables that are similar in terms of representing one of these broad motives have similar effects on persuasion and social influence. With respect to the agreement of this classification of motives with the other lists of motives we have noted, it is largely concordant, except for the addition of the consistency and internal coherence motive, which could be regarded as part of the first, or knowing, motive.

A Definitive List of Motives?

It is not surprising that there is considerable overlap between the motivational taxonomies that are popular in attitude research. Even though researchers have identified motives based on research traditions in somewhat different areas of investigation (e.g., persuasion, social influence, individual differences), the schemes are quite similar. It is especially clear that an accuracy or appraisal motive appears in all of the formulations, whether as a need for objective appraisal or accuracy or understanding outcomes in one's environment. Reflecting on these motivational themes in research in attitudes and social cognition, Kunda (1990) contrasted a motive to arrive at accurate beliefs with motives to arrive at particular, directional conclusions (see also Kruglanski, 1980). The directional conclusions could include positive self-regard, cognitive consistency, social approval, value affirmation, and other positive states.

These motives that foster directional conclusions are more variable across the various motivational taxonomies and have been identified at somewhat differing levels of abstraction. For example, the need to develop and maintain a positive self-concept is commonly included in lists of motives and may underlie more specific motives such as value-relevant involvement and the value-expressive function because values are intimately associated with positive self-regard. For that matter, the need to relate to other people and convey an appropriate impression could also reflect the need for positive self-regard.

With types of motives conceptualized sometimes more broadly and sometimes more narrowly, there appears to be no definitive list of motives in attitude theory. Theorists strive to strike a balance between very general abstractions about motivation—for example, the idea that people seek to maximize perceived utilities—and more concrete descriptions of motives—for example, the idea that people seek to make a positive impression on others. Whereas very general abstractions have an elegant simplicity, more concrete renditions of motives can be more obviously useful to explain behavior in particular circumstances.

Motives and Information Processing

In general, motives to achieve accurate beliefs and to arrive at directional conclusions can be somewhat in conflict, with accuracy motives restraining directional motives. Despite this restraint by reality, a wide range of preferences for directional conclusions bias exposure to information, processing and thinking about information, and memory (Kunda, 1990; Wyer & Albarracín, chap. 7, this volume). Consistent with Marsh and Wallace's (chap. 9, this volume) review, an especially common theme in attitude research is that attitudes themselves are a source of motivational and cognitive bias by fostering attitude-consistent beliefs through biased processing of information.

Development of the insight that motivation affects cognition requires understanding of the circumstances under which these varied effects occur and the mechanisms through which bias exerts its effects. One common sequence is that motivation triggers cognitive processes by which people reach desired conclusions (Chaiken et al., 1989; Kunda, 1990). These cognitive processes may involve counterarguing threatening information, bolstering prior attitudes, and many other specific mechanisms (Abelson, 1959). In a persuasion context, motives may affect attitudes through a variety of processes discussed in the context of dual process theories of persuasion. The heuristic-systematic model (HSM) has thus pointed to the influence of motives on heuristic and systematic processing (Chaiken et al., 1989), and the elaboration likelihood model (ELM) has implicated these and other processes (Briñol & Petty, chap. 14, this volume).

Prediction from motives to attitudinal processes can be less than straightforward because there is no necessary relation between the motives that are activated and the manner in which messages are processed. Motives may be served by a wide range of specific processes. For example, within the dual-process tradition of persuasion theories, a motive may be served by a thoughtful, systematic analysis of the message content or by a more superficial analysis (Chen & Chaiken, 1999).

Despite these complexities, the authors of the chapters have suggested several overarching principles that may link motives with attitudinal processes. In general, people appear to prefer and select information that satisfies their goals. One specification of this principle assumes that to the extent that people desire to defend their existing attitudes (i.e., defense motivation; Chaiken et al., 1989), they are biased in favor of attitudinally agreeable information and against attitudinally disagreeable information. This bias has often been named the *congeniality bias* or *hypothesis* (Eagly & Chaiken, 1993, 1998). For example, people who anticipate defending their own view choose to read information that supports their own view, whereas those who focus on accuracy of understanding choose to read a less biased sample of the available information (Prislin & Wood, chap. 16, this volume).

Another principle is that matching motives to persuasive information can enhance its persuasiveness (Katz, 1960). Such *matching effects* are common in persuasion research. For example, matching persuasive messages to attitude functions increases persuasion (Lavine & Snyder, 1996; Johnson et al., chap. 15, this volume). A recent example of a quite subtle matching effect pertained to regulatory fit and persuasion (Cesario, Grant, & Higgins, 2004). In these studies, a state of fit was induced by matching message recipients' promotion or prevention focus to descriptions of an eager or vigilant means of attaining goals. Messages that fit message recipients' self-regulatory orientation—that is, eager means with promotion focus and vigilant means with prevention focus—were more persuasive than those that did not fit. Regulatory fit evidently makes people feel "right" because their personal orientation is congruent with their strategic manner of pursuing goals, and the subjective experience of feeling right transfers to the persuasive message.

Another useful principle, discussed by Prislin and Wood (chap. 16, this volume), is that stronger motives tend to favor more thoughtful processing. This generalization follows from the well accepted proposition that systematic or elaborative processes require both the motivation to process information and the capacity to process it (Chaiken et al., 1989; Petty & Cacioppo, 1986). Given adequate capacity, motivation is crucial to thoughtful processing.

These ideas about the effects of motives are also consistent with Chaiken's (1987; Chen & Chaiken, 1999) argument that processing strategies that demand less cognitive effort are applied before those that require more effort. If we assume that people desire both to minimize effort and to achieve adequate judgmental confidence, they may first process messages more simply or heuristically and, if this approach does not yield adequate confidence, then invoke systematic processing. In the more formal terms of Chaiken's *sufficiency principle*, perceivers' actual level of confidence is often lower than their desired level of confidence. High levels of motivation deriving from variables such as task importance generally increase the gap between actual and desired levels of confidence because they raise the desired level of confidence. When confidence is less than desired, people will attempt to bring their confidence to the desired level. If low-effort processes do not close the confidence gap, high-effort, systematic processing is more likely to occur.

Motives and Memory for Attitude-Relevant Information

Some of the reasons that psychologists have developed complexity in their understanding of motivational effects are well illustrated by research on memory for attitude-relevant infor-mation. Researchers' traditional expectation was for a congeniality bias whereby people have better memory for attitudinally congenial than uncongenial information. The usual assumption was that people are motivated to defend their attitudes against challenging material. People were presumed to accomplish this defense by screening out uncongenial information at var-ious stages of information processing: Individuals might thus avoid exposure to uncongenial information; if exposed to it, they might not pay attention to it or distort its meaning; and subsequently not store or retrieve it effectively.

Despite some early confirmations of the congeniality hypothesis in attitude memory experi-ments, much of the early research suffered from methodological weaknesses, and congeniality effects have been inconsistently obtained over the years (see meta-analysis by Eagly, Chen, Chaiken, & Shaw Barnes, 1999). The flaw in the reasoning of early theorists is their assump-tion that motivation to defend attitudes necessarily proceeds through passive processes that allow message receipts to avoid the challenging implications of the information. Instead, given sufficient motivation and capability, people are likely to mount an active defense, which en-hances memory for counterattitudinal information. This explanation of the common absence of congeniality effects on memory was confirmed by Eagly, Kulesa, Brannon, Shaw, and Hutson-Comeaux (2000), who showed that congenial and uncongenial messages were equally memorable. More important, the processes by which the messages became memorable differed.

Agreeable information appeared to be remembered by a fairly superficial process by which message recipients matched the information to their existing attitudes, whereas disagreeable information was remembered by active and skeptical scrutiny of its content. This research thus illustrates the inadequacy of the simple congeniality bias hypothesis for understanding memory effects and shows that memory for persuasive information can be achieved through differing processes.

Motivated Reasoning and Biased Processing

In summary, the effects of motives and goals on information processing and persuasion are an important contemporary theme of attitude research. Research has provided many illustrations of the biasing effects of attitudes, and, as Marsh and Wallace's (chap. 9, this volume) review ably summarizes, there is also considerable evidence that variables such as stimulus ambiguity moderate the biasing effects of attitudes (Chaiken & Maheswaran, 1994). The classic theme that attitudes themselves bias information-processing and reasoning has broadened so that researchers have explored the effects of a range of motives on attitudinal processes. Bringing these varied phenomena together into a coherent theoretical structure should be high on the agenda of attitude researchers.

THE SOCIAL CONTEXT OF ATTITUDES

In *The Psychology of Attitudes*, we argued that researchers had given insufficient attention to the social context of attitudes. Although we noted some important exceptions to the neglect of social context, we argued that then-popular attitude theories had seldom taken into account the structure of social settings within which attitude change occurs in natural environments. Because of this neglect, most theory had remained narrowly psychological, even though some pioneers in the study of attitudes had given considerable attention to social context. For example, some had delineated forms of social power or of role relationships that bind influencing agents and targets (French & Raven, 1959; Kelman, 1961). Although such models had pointed the way toward treatments of attitude change that connect social and the psychological influences within a common framework, at least by the early 1990s these approaches had not inspired as much further development as some social psychologists had anticipated. Instead, theory had developed mainly as strictly psychological although, as we have already noted, some researchers acknowledged distinctively social motivation in the form of motives for social inclusion and making a positive impression on other people.

We acted on our advocacy of increased attention to the social context of attitude formation and change by including a chapter on this topic in *The Psychology of Attitudes*. In this chapter, we recognized research and theory on social influence that retained considerable focus on psychological processes while taking social context into account. Our chapter therefore reviewed classic work on normative and informational influence as well as on the role of relationships within which influence takes place. We discussed research on conformity and minority influence in considerable detail because some of these investigations had incorporated some of the theoretical advances of modern theories of persuasion, especially dual-process theories (see Johnson et al., chap. 15, this volume), and joined these insights with analyses that recognized the importance of social context.

The integrative analyses of conformity and minority influence that we discussed were the vanguard of renewed attention to social influence. The newer developments in this general area are ably reviewed by Prislin and Wood (chap. 16, this volume). Important in these developments is the meta-analysis of minority influence research by Wood, Lundgren, Ouellette,

Busceme, and Blackstone (1994), which greatly clarified typical research findings pertaining to minority and majority influence. Wood and her colleagues thus showed that minorities can have quite variable effects, depending on the motives that they arouse, and that understanding how minorities are portrayed is crucial to understanding these effects.

Recent and notable efforts to understand the social context of attitude change include dynamic models of social influence that are designed to elucidate changes in influence processes that occur over time (Prislin & Wood, chap. 16, this volume). These efforts include dynamic social impact theory, which models opinion distributions in groups (Latané & Nowak, 1997). In addition, Prislin and her colleagues (Prislin, Limbert, & Bauer, 2000) have applied a dynamic gain-loss asymmetry model built on the principle that the decreasing size that changes a majority into a minority is experienced as a loss whereas the increasing size that changes a minority into a majority is experienced as a gain. Because people react more strongly to losses than gains, having one's subgroup change from majority to minority status has negative effects that are larger than the positive effects of having one's subgroup change from minority to majority status. These and other effects of changes in minority and majority status have begun to capture some of the complexities of influence in long-term groups.

Many challenges remain in studying attitudes under conditions that take into account some of the complex embedding of change in dyadic and group processes that extend over time. To build on psychological theories of attitudes and social influence, researchers must relate these social phenomena to the psychological processes that govern changes in attitudes and to the motives that organize and direct these changes. Although progress in these directions has not been rapid, researchers have made important advances in recent years.

THE INTERACTIVE RELATIONS BETWEEN ATTITUDES AND BEHAVIOR

The Influence of Attitudes on Behaviors

One of the greatest successes of attitude research is the substantial progress made in predicting behavior from attitudes subsequent to the low point of Wicker's (1969) claim that attitudes are very poor predictors of behavior. Wicker's challenge inspired research on the attitude-behavior relation from several theoretical perspectives. In our earlier reviews of this research (Eagly & Chaiken, 1993, 1998), we acknowledged the important principle, first articulated by Fishbein and Ajzen (1974; Ajzen & Fishbein, 1977), that relatively good prediction can be readily achieved if researchers design their measures of attitudes and behaviors at the same level of generality. This principle received major emphasis in this handbook (see Ajzen & Fishbein, chap. 5, this volume; Jaccard & Blanton, chap. 4, this volume) and still remains valid.

A number of points in Ajzen and Fishbein's (chap. 5, this volume) excellent discussion of the current status of attitude–behavior research should serve as invitations to additional research on attitude-behavior relations. One useful idea that deserves to be pursued is that attitudes toward objects influence behavior through their effects on attitudes toward behaviors, regardless of the extent to which individuals engage in deliberative processes. Also suggesting new directions is Ajzen and Fishbein's discussion of the *literal inconsistencies* that occur when people fail to carry out their intentions. As they note, the formation of implementation intentions pertaining to when, where, and how people will carry out their intentions can reduce intention–behavior discrepancies (Gollwitzer, 1999). An important direction of research is the elaboration of the mechanisms whereby implementation intentions induce behavior consistent with intentions. These mechanisms may include more automatic links whereby environmental cues elicit goals or motives without people being aware of this activation. These unconscious goals or motives, along with more conscious ones, may then affect information processing and behavior, as Bargh (1990, 1997) has maintained in the context of his auto-motive model.

Ajzen and Fishbein (this volume) also ably evaluate the current status of the theories of reasoned action and planned behavior, which they and others have developed over many years. This popular perspective has survived numerous challenges to its validity, despite considerable debate about the extent to which its various formulations provide a sufficient causal explanation of people's intentions and actions. Ajzen and Fishbein acknowledge that other investigators have added various predictors not included in their original models but argue that these predictors are efficacious mainly in particular behavioral domains–for example, moral norms account for additional variability for predicting behaviors that have a clear moral aspect (e.g., cheating, community volunteering). They recognize that such additions can improve the prediction of behavior beyond that yielded by the predictors included in the standard reasoned action and planned behavior models. However, they maintain that, because these gains in predictability are small, the rule of parsimony suggests caution in adding additional predictors. They also argue that emotions and other noncognitive determinants of behavior are important but act indirectly though affecting the attitudes and intentions that are accessible during behavioral performance. These conclusions invite careful evaluation in new research.

Departing from the reasoned action and planned behavior theories are approaches that give a major role to automatic processes in inducing behavior. Some researchers have examined the role of habit in controlling behavior (Ouellette & Wood, 1998). Proponents of habit as a determinant of behavior have reasoned that with repeated performance in stable contexts, behavior habituates because the processing that initiates and controls the performance becomes automatic. In contrast, conscious decision making by means of processes such as those specified by reasoned action and planned behavior theories predominate when behaviors are not well learned or when they are performed in unstable or difficult contexts. Under these conditions, past behavior nonetheless affects behavior, but by contributing to intentions, which subsequently guide behavior.

Despite the impressive evidence for these views offered by Wood and her colleagues (Ouellette & Wood, 1998; Wood, Quinn, & Kashy, 2002), Ajzen and Fishbein (chap. 5, this volume) remain skeptical that past behavior affects later behavior through its impact on habit. They argue that frequent performance is no guarantee that a behavior has habituated and point out that researchers have not so far produced a valid independent measure of habit strength. Another of their arguments is that the tendency for people to revert to an earlier response in the face of difficulty in implementing a new response may create the illusion that behavior is habitual. Jaccard and Blanton (chap. 4, this volume) weigh in with the view that the processes through which past behavior affects future behavior can be difficult to demonstrate directly and unambiguously. They describe several processes, including habit, by which past behavior can influence future behavior. Jaccard and Blanton also give excellent advice on measurement and statistical analyses appropriate for predictions of behavior (e.g., how to scale behaviors and statistically analyze behavioral counts vs. continuous behavioral variables). Investigators should thus proceed to clarify the role of habit compared with other mechanisms in accounting for the effects of prior behavior on future behaviors.

Attitude-behavior relations have also been interpreted in terms of automatic linkages that do not depend on habit. The best known contender in this tradition is Fazio's (1990) MODE (motivation and opportunity as determinants of behavior) model, which features an automatic link between attitudes and behaviors as well as a more deliberative route involving cost-benefit analysis of the utility of behaviors (see also Fazio & Towles-Schwen, 1999). According to this approach, attitudes can be automatically accessed without active attention or conscious thought and then, by biasing perceptions in the immediate situation, these attitudes may cause behavior to follow without any conscious reasoning process. Increasing the plausibility of relatively automatic attitude–behavior links is research suggesting that implicit but not explicit measures of attitudes can predict a variety of more spontaneous and subtle behaviors, such as nonverbal behaviors, that are for the most part not consciously controlled (Ajzen & Fishbein, chap. 5, this volume). The details of the relatively automatic route from attitudes to behavior remain to be more fully understood. One possibility is that, as Marsh and Wallace (chap. 9, this volume) suggest, attitudes can be primed or activated in such a way that they activate goals or motives that then affect behavior. For example, subliminally priming a liked significant other increased commitment to a goal that the significant other had for participants and improved goal performance (Kruglanski, Shah, Fishbach, Friedman, Chun, & Sleeth Keppler, 2002). This mediational route as well as the mediation by biased information processing postulated by Fazio are just two possibilities for explaining the automatic links between attitudes and behaviors. No doubt researchers will continue to investigate the details of more automatic attitude–behavior relations.

The Influence of Behaviors on Attitudes

At an early point, social psychologists came to appreciate that attitude change is sometimes a consequence of engaging in behavior. Seminal experimental evidence suggested that people were often persuaded by the messages that they themselves had delivered (Janis & King, 1954), and later studies frequently confirmed this finding.

This handbook contains a fine review of behavior-attitude relations (Olson & Stone, chap. 6, this volume) that reveals a great deal of forward progress since our earlier reviews of this area (Eagly & Chaiken, 1993; Chaiken, Wood, & Eagly, 1996). Ever since the provocative research by Janis and King (1954) on role-playing and by Festinger and Carlsmith (1959) on counterattitudinal advocacy, researchers have attempted to delineate the processes through which behavior affects attitudes. Many candidates vie for a piece of the causal territory, and Olson and Stone consider a full range of explanatory theories and possible mechanisms.

This updating of the status of debates on the processes by which counterattitudinal behavior affects attitudes underscores once again the enormous generativity of cognitive dissonance theory in this domain. Olson and Stone (chap. 6, this volume) recount the history of Festinger's version of dissonance theory and the subsequent generations of experimentation that first demonstrated dissonance effects and then set the parameters that defined the conditions under which these effects occur.

Especially important is Olson and Stone's (chap. 6, this volume) review of new models that have extended the dissonance model and taken into account the numerous boundary conditions that research has established. The self-standards model proposed by Stone and Cooper (2001) argues that people can interpret their behavior in relation to varying standards. Their behavior may violate normative standards if it departs from what is regarded as appropriate in their culture, or it may violate personal standards if it departs from what an individual regards as appropriate according to his or her personal self-concept. Only if personal standards are violated should self-concept variables moderate the arousal that constitutes cognitive dissonance. Attitude change would ordinarily follow from violation of self-standards, but self-affirmation could reduce arousal through having people think about positive aspects of themselves that are unrelated to the source of the dissonance. This new model is integrative of several earlier dissonance models and has proven to be quite successful in accounting for the varied effects of counterattitudinal behavior on attitudes. This approach also resonates with aspects of the motivational taxonomies that we have noted in this chapter, especially in its recognition of people's concern with appropriateness, which pertains to the impression they make on others, as well as their concern with personal standards, which are crucial to a positive self-concept.

Additional possibilities have also emerged as contenders for accounting for dissonance effects, including an action-orientation model and constraint satisfaction connectionist models (Olson & Stone, chap. 6, this volume). The cognitive dissonance tradition is thus alive, well, and generating new theory and experimentation as we near the 50th birthday of the first publication of the theory (Festinger, 1957).

THE ENDURING IMPORTANCE OF THEORY AND RESEARCH ON PERSUASION

Persuasion research remains an important focus of contemporary attitude research. As Johnson et al. (chap. 15, this volume) explain, the issue of how attitudes are formed and modified as people gain information about attitude objects was an early focus of attitude research in the 1950s. The research area gained momentum in the 1970s with more sophisticated attention to the cognitive processes that underlie persuasion. Theories of persuasion made major advances in the 1980s, with the introduction of dual-process models. The elaboration likelihood model (Petty & Cacioppo, 1986; Petty & Wegener, 1999) and the heuristic-systematic model (Chaiken et al., 1989; Chen & Chaiken, 1999) then took center stage in persuasion research. These models both assume qualitatively different dual modes of processing and thus contrast more effortful modes of processing with less effortful modes. Johnson et al. (chap. 15, this volume) provide an effective discussion of these two models, appropriately noting their differences and similarities.

The elaboration likelihood and heuristic-systematic models have been enlarged over the years. The elaboration likelihood model has provided an organizational scheme for several of the reviews contained in this handbook (Briñol & Petty, chap. 14, this volume; Wegener & Carlston, chap. 12, this volume; Fabrigar et al., chap. 3, this volume). As this theory has expanded, encompassing a wide range of psychological processes, its practitioners often find coherence among complex and contingent empirical findings. However, with many persuasion variables serving multiple roles, depending on message recipients' level of elaboration, the theory has a flexibility that some attitude researchers believe makes the theory difficult to disconfirm.

Newer entrants as persuasion models include Kruglanski's (Thompson, Kruglanski, & Spiegel, 2000) unimodel, which posits that a single process accounts for the range of findings that dual-process theories explain in terms of qualitatively different processes. The initial statement of this theory proved to be controversial when it was published with commentaries in *Psychological Inquiry* (Kruglanski & Thompson, 1999), and attitude researchers remain divided on the merits of the approach. Kruglanski's claim that all persuasive information represents a type of evidence from which conclusions may be drawn surely is a truism. However, the processes by which conclusions are drawn are amenable to classification in terms of qualitatively different types of processes. The gains from postulating distinct processes are evident in the large body of research inspired by the elaboration likelihood model and the heuristic-systematic model. Although many of these findings can be reinterpreted in terms of the unimodel, the gains from this reinterpretation remain a subject of debate. It is unlikely that most of these phenomena would have been discovered without the metaphor of dual processes, and the gains from an arguably more parsimonious interpretation are not yet clear.

Another newer entrant is Albarracín's (2002) cognition in persuasion model (CPM), which posits that a sequence of processes occur when responding to a persuasive message. According to this model, the cognitive processes involved in forming attitudinal judgments are relatively invariant but the order and type of information that enter via these processing steps can vary. Like McGuire's (1972) information-processing model and Wyer's (Wyer & Srull, 1989) social information-processing model of impression formation, Albarracín's approach gives a major role to message reception processes and introduces contemporary social cognitive theory in considering the various steps of the model.

CONCLUSION

In the introduction to this chapter, we asked whether the wide territory set forth in the traditional conceptualizations of attitude as encompassing cognition, affect, and behavior has in fact been effectively occupied by attitude theory and research. We are encouraged by the chapters of this handbook and give a tentative affirmative response to our question.

There are several especially heartening themes in the chapters of this book. One trend is that most authors invoke evidence that is not necessarily confined within the purview of social psychology; they link their attitudinal analyses to research in other areas within cognitive and personality psychology and neuroscience. One clear trend is a rapprochement of attitude research with research on social cognition. Sophisticated cognitive models are increasingly incorporated into attitude theory (Wegener & Carlston, chap. 12, this volume; Wyer & Albarracín, chap. 7, this volume). In addition, as we explained earlier in this chapter, the understanding of affective processes has greatly enlarged, with renewed attention to elementary processes of attitude formation and change. Also, emotion research, especially pertaining to moods, has had considerable impact on the study of attitudes. Finally, consideration of motives has become more routine in attitude research, with attention to the effects of varied motives on multiple aspects of attitudinal processes. This motivational theme links attitude research to basic research on motivation in psychology.

The chapter by Ottati, Edwards, and Krumdick (chap. 17, this volume) speaks more directly than other chapters to the issue we raised about the scope of attitude research. These authors demonstrate that attitude research and theory are in fact serving as an integrative function both within and beyond social psychology. For example, Ottati and colleagues identify many parallels between research on impression formation, ordinarily considered to be in the domain of social cognition, and research on attitude formation and change. These two streams of research have influenced research on the evaluation of political candidates, among other topics. Research on interpersonal attraction has also moved in parallel with many themes in attitude research, with the development of increasingly explicit links between the research areas. As we discussed earlier in this chapter, theory and research on social influence have incorporated important themes from the study of persuasion. Finally, the study of ideology, traditionally within the domain of political science, is profiting substantially from insights emanating from research on attitudes and social cognition (Jost, Glaser, Kruglanski, & Sulloway, 2003; see review by Eagly & Chaiken, 1998).

The most obvious opportunity for attitude theory and research to prove their worth is in understanding of prejudice and discrimination. Because prejudice is generally given an attitudinal definition, as a negative attitude toward a group, and discrimination consists of negative behavior toward group members, the principles of attitude formation and change and attitude-behavior prediction should be front-and-center in the study of prejudice and discrimination. However, social cognitive research on stereotyping and stigma has been more important to the study of prejudice research than has attitude research. Therefore, we urge attitude researchers to take a more active interest in the study of prejudice. The content of several chapters shows that some investigators have already moved in this direction (e.g., Briñol & Petty, chap. 14, this volume; Ajzen & Fishbein, chap. 5, this volume; Ottati et al., chap. 17, this volume)

The study of attitudes by psychologists is familiar territory for us, and this domain is now far richer and more elaborated that it was when we wrote our 1993 book. That endeavor was a labor of love for a field of scientific and intellectual activity that has powerfully attracted us for all of the years of our careers in social psychology. This handbook only deepens our fascination with the study of attitudes.

REFERENCES

Abelson, R. P. (1959). Modes of resolution of belief dilemmas. *Journal of Conflict Resolution, 3,* 343–352.

Ajzen, I., & Fishbein, M. (1977). Attitude-behavior relations: A theoretical analysis and review of empirical research. *Psychological Bulletin, 84,* 888–918.

Albarracín, D. (2002). Cognition in persuasion: An analysis of information processing in response to persuasive communications. In M. P. Zanna (Ed.), *Advances in experimental social psychology* (Vol. 34, pp. 61–130). San Diego, CA: Academic Press.

Anderson, J. R. (1983). *The architecture of cognition.* Cambridge, MA: Harvard University Press.

Baeyens, F., Eelen, P., Crombez, G., & Van den Bergh, O. (1992). Human evaluative conditioning: Acquisition trials, presentation schedule, evaluative style and contingency awareness. *Behaviour Research and Therapy, 30,* 133–142.

Bargh, J. A. (1990). Auto-motives: Preconscious determinants of social interaction. In E. T. Higgins & R. M. Sorrentino (Eds.), *Handbook of motivation and cognition* (Vol. 2, pp. 93–130). New York: Guilford.

Bargh, J. A. (1997). The automaticity of everyday life. In R. S. Wyer, Jr. (Ed.) *The automaticity of everyday life: Advances in social cognition* (Vol. 10, pp. 1–61). Mahwah, NJ: Lawrence Erlbaum Associates.

Bargh, J. A., Chaiken, S., Govender, R., & Pratto, F. (1992). The generality of the automatic attitude activation effect. *Journal of Personality and Social Psychology, 62,* 893–912.

Boakes, R. A. (1989). How one might find evidence for conditioning in adult humans. In T. Archer & L.-G. Nilsson (Eds.), *Aversion, avoidance and anxiety: Perspectives on learning and memory* (pp. 381–402). Hillsdale, NJ: Lawrence Erlbaum Associates.

Bornstein, R. F., & D'Agostino, P. R. (1992). Stimulus recognition and the mere exposure effect. *Journal of Personality and Social Psychology, 63,* 545–552.

Brewer, W. F. (1974). There is no convincing evidence for operant or classical conditioning in adult humans. In W. B. Weimer & D. S. Palermo (Eds.), *Cognition and the symbolic processes* (pp. 1–42). Hillsdale, NJ: Lawrence Erlbaum Associates.

Cacioppo, J. T., Gardner, W. L., & Berntson, G. G. (1997). Beyond bipolar conceptualizations and measures: The case of attitudes and evaluative space. *Personality and Social Psychology Review, 1,* 3–25.

Campbell, D. T. (1963). Social attitudes and other acquired behavioral dispositions. In S. Koch (Ed.), *Psychology: A study of a science* (Vol. 6, pp. 94–172). New York: McGraw-Hill.

Cesario, J., Grant, H., & Higgins, E. T. (2004). Regulatory fit and persuasion: Transfer from "feeling right." *Journal of Personality and Social Psychology, 86,* 388–404.

Chaiken, S. (1987). The heuristic model of persuasion. In M. P. Zanna, J. M. Olson, & C. P. Herman (Eds.), *The Ontario Symposium: Social influence* (Vol. 5, pp. 3–39). Hillsdale, NJ: Lawrence Erlbaum Associates.

Chaiken, S., Liberman, A., & Eagly, A. H. (1989). Heuristic and systematic processing within and beyond the persuasion context. In J. S. Uleman & J. A. Bargh (Eds.), *Unintended thought* (pp. 212–252). New York: Guilford.

Chaiken, S., & Maheswaran, D. (1994). Heuristic processing can bias systematic processing: Effects of source credibility, argument ambiguity, and task importance on attitude judgment. *Journal of Personality and Social Psychology, 66,* 460–473.

Chaiken, S., Wood, W. L., & Eagly, A. H. (1996). Principles of persuasion. In E. T. Higgins & A. Kruglanski (Eds.), *Social psychology: Handbook of basic principles* (pp. 702–742). New York: Guilford.

Chen, S., & Chaiken, S. (1999). The heuristic-systematic model in its broader context. In S. Chaiken & Y. Trope (Eds.), *Dual-process theories in social psychology* (pp. 73–96). New York: Guilford.

Clore, G. L., & Colcombe, S. (2003). The parallel worlds of affective concepts and feelings. In J. Musch & K. C. Klauer (Eds.), *The psychology of evaluation: Affective processes in cognition and emotion* (pp. 335–369). Mahwah, NJ: Lawrence Erlbaum Associates.

Conrey, F., Sherman, J. W., Gawronski, B., Hugenberg, K., & Groom, C. (2004). *Beyond automaticity and control: The quad-model of behavioral response.* Unpublished manuscript, Northwestern University, Evanston, IL.

Das, E. H. H. J., de Wit, J. B. F., & Stroebe, W. (2003). Fear appeals motivate acceptance of action recommendations: Evidence for a positive bias in the processing of persuasive messages. *Personality and Social Psychology Bulletin, 29,* 650–664.

De Houwer, J., Thomas, S., & Baeyens, F. (2001). Associative learning of likes and dislikes: A review of 25 years of research on human evaluative conditioning. *Psychological Bulletin, 127,* 853–869.

Deutsch, M., & Gerard, H. B. (1955). A study of normative and informational social influences upon individual judgment. *Journal of Abnormal and Social Psychology, 51,* 629–636.

Doob, L. W. (1947). The behavior of attitudes. *Psychological Review, 54,* 135–156.

Dovidio, J. F., Brigham, J. C., Johnson, B. T., & Gaertner, S. L. (1996). Stereotyping, prejudice, and discrimination: Another look. In N. Macrae, C. Stangor, & M. Hewstone (Eds.), *Stereotypes and stereotyping* (pp. 276–319). New York: Guilford.

Duckworth, K. L., Bargh, J. A., Garcia, M., & Chaiken, S. (2002). The automatic evaluation of novel stimuli. *Psychological Science, 13,* 513–519.

Eagly, A. H., & Chaiken, S. (1993). *The psychology of attitudes.* Fort Worth, TX: Harcourt, Brace, Jovanovich.

Eagly, A. H., & Chaiken, S. (1998). Attitude structure and function. In D. Gilbert, S. Fiske, & G. Lindzey (Eds.), *The handbook of social psychology* (4th ed., pp. 269–322). New York: McGraw-Hill.

Eagly, A. H., Chen, S., Chaiken, S., & Shaw-Barnes, K. (1999). The impact of attitudes on memory: An affair to remember. *Psychological Bulletin, 125,* 64–89.

Eagly, A. H., Kulesa, P., Brannon, L. A., Shaw, K., & Hutson-Comeaux, S. (2000). Why counterattitudinal messages are as memorable as proattitudinal messages: The importance of active defense against attack. *Personality and Social Psychology Bulletin, 26,* 1392–1408.

Fazio, R. H. (1989). On the power and functionality of attitudes: The role of attitude accessibility. In A. R. Pratkanis, S. J. Breckler, & A. G. Greenwald (Eds.), *Attitude structure and function* (pp. 153–179). Hillsdale, NJ: Lawrence Erlbaum Associates.

Fazio, R. H. (1990). Multiple processes by which attitudes guide behavior: The MODE model as an integrative framework. In M. P. Zanna (Ed.), *Advances in experimental social psychology* (Vol. 23, pp. 75–109). San Diego, CA: Academic Press.

Fazio, R. H., & Olson, M. A. (2003). Implicit measures in social cognition research: Their meaning and uses. *Annual Review of Psychology,* 54, 297–327.

Fazio, R. H., Sanbonmatsu, D. M., Powell, M. C., & Kardes, F. R. (1986). On the automatic activation of attitudes. *Journal of Personality and Social Psychology, 50,* 229–238.

Fazio, R. H., & Towles-Schwen, T. (1999). The MODE model of attitude-behavior processes. In S. Chaiken & Y. Trope (Eds.), *Dual-process theories in social psychology* (pp. 97–116). New York: Guilford.

Festinger, L. (1957). *A theory of cognitive dissonance.* Evanston, IL: Row, Peterson.

Festinger, L., & Carlsmith, J. M. (1959). Cognitive consequences of forced compliance. *Journal of Abnormal and Social Psychology, 58,* 203–210.

Fishbein, M., & Ajzen, I. (1974). Attitudes toward objects as predictors of single and multiple behavioral criteria. *Psychological Review, 81,* 59–74.

Fishbein, M., & Ajzen, I. (1975). *Belief, attitude, intention, and behavior: An introduction to theory and research.* Reading, MA: Addison-Wesley.

Fredrickson, B. L. (2000). Extracting meaning from past affective experiences: the importance of peaks, ends, and specific emotions. *Cognition and Emotion, 14,* 577–606.

Fredrickson, B. L. (2001). The role of positive emotions in positive psychology: The broaden-and-build theory of positive emotions. *American Psychologist, 56,* 218–226.

Fredrickson, B. L., & Kahneman, D.(1993). Duration neglect in retrospective evaluations of affective episodes. *Journal of Personality and Social Psychology, 65,* 44–55.

French, J. R. P., Jr., & Raven, B. (1959). The bases of social power. In D. Cartwright (Ed.), *Studies in social power* (pp. 150–167). Ann Arbor: University of Michigan.

Gollwitzer, P. M. (1999). Implementation intentions: Strong effects of simple plans. *American Psychologist, 54,* 493–503.

Greenwald, A. G., & Banaji, M. R. (1995). Implicit social cognition: Attitudes, self-esteem, and stereotypes. *Psychological Review, 102,* 4–27.

Greenwald, A. G., & Nosek, B. A. (2001). Health of the Implicit Association Test at age 3. *Zeitschrift für Experimentelle Psychologie, 48,* 85–93.

Hammond, K. R. (1948). Measuring attitudes by error-choice: An indirect method. *Journal of Abnormal and Social Psychology, 43,* 38–48.

Hess, E. H. (1965). Attitude and pupil size. *Scientific American, 212,* 46–54.

Himmelfarb, S. (1993). The measurement of attitudes. In A. H. Eagly & S. Chaiken *The psychology of attitudes* (pp. 23–87). Fort Worth, TX: Harcourt Brace Jovanovich.

Hovland, C. I., Janis, I. L., & Kelley, H. H. (1953). *Communication and persuasion: Psychological studies of opinion change.* New Haven, CT: Yale University Press.

Janis, I. L. (1967). Effects of fear arousal on attitude change: Recent developments in theory and experimental research. In L. Berkowitz (Ed.), *Advances in experimental social psychology* (Vol. 3, pp. 122–224). New York: Academic Press.

Janis, I. L., & King, B. T. (1954). The influence of role playing on opinion change. *Journal of Abnormal and Social Psychology, 49*, 211–218.

Johnson, B. T., & Eagly, A. H. (1989). The effects of involvement on persuasion: A meta-analysis. *Psychological Bulletin, 106*, 290–314.

Jost, J. T., Glaser, J., Kruglanski, A. W., & Sulloway, F. J. (2003). Political conservatism as motivated social cognition. *Psychological Bulletin, 129*, 339–375.

Katz, D. (1960). The functional approach to the study of attitudes. *Public Opinion Quarterly, 24*, 163–204.

Katz, D., & Stotland, E. (1959). A preliminary statement to a theory of attitude structure and change. In S. Koch (Ed.), *Psychology: A study of a science* (Vol. 3, pp. 423–475). New York: McGraw-Hill.

Kelman, H. C. (1961). Processes of opinion change. *Public Opinion Quarterly, 25*, 57–78.

Klauer, K. (1998). Affective priming. In W. Stroebe and M. Hewstone (Eds.), *European review of social psychology* (Vol. 8, pp. 67–103). New York: Wiley.

Klauer, K. C., & Musch, J. (2003). Affective priming: Findings and theories. In J. Musch & K. C. Klauer (Eds.), *The psychology of evaluation: Affective processes in cognition and emotion* (pp. 7–49). Mahwah, NJ: Lawrence Erlbaum Associates.

Kruglanski, A. W. (1980). Lay epistemology process and contents. *Psychological Review, 87*, 70–87.

Kruglanski, A. W., Shah, J. Y., Fishbach, A., Friedman, R., Chun, W. Y., & Sleeth Keppler, D. (2002). A theory of goal systems. In M. P. Zanna (Ed.), *Advances in experimental social psychology* (Vol. 34, pp. 331–378). San Diego, CA: Academic Press.

Kruglanski, A. W., & Thompson, E. P. (1999). Persuasion by a single route: A view from the unimodel. *Psychological Inquiry, 10*, 83–109.

Kunda, Z. (1990). The case for motivated reasoning. *Psychological Bulletin, 108*, 480–498.

Latané, B., & Nowak, A. (1997). Self-organizing social systems: Necessary and sufficient conditions for the emergence of consolidation, clustering, and continuing diversity. *Progress in Communication Science, 13*, 43–74.

Lavine, H., & Snyder, M. (1996). Cognitive processing and the functional matching effect in persuasion: The mediating role of subjective perceptions of message quality. *Journal of Experimental Social Psychology, 32*, 580–604.

Lovibond, P. F., & Shanks, D. P. (2002). The role of awareness in Pavlovian conditioning: Empirical evidence and theoretical implications. *Journal of Experimental Psychology: Animal Behavior Processes, 28*, 3–26.

Maio, G. R., & Olson, J. M. (2000). *Why we evaluative: Functions of attitudes*. Mahwah, NJ: Lawrence Erlbaum Associates.

Marcus, G. F. (2002). *The sentimental citizen: Emotion in democratic politics*. Universiy Park, PA: Pennsylvania State University Press.

McGuire, W. J. (1972). Attitude change: The information-processing paradigm. In C. G. McClintock (Ed.), *Experimental social psychology* (pp. 108–141). New York: Holt, Rinehart, & Winston.

Murphy, S. T., & Zajonc, R. B. (1993). Affect, cognition, and awareness: Affective priming with optimal and suboptimal stimulus exposures. *Journal of Personality and Social Psychology, 64*, 723–739.

Oehman, A., & Mineka, S. (2001). Fears, phobias, and preparedness: Toward an evolved module of fear and fear learning. *Psychological Review, 108*, 483–522.

Olson, M. A., & Fazio, R. H. (2004). Reducing the influence of extrapersonal associations on the Implicit Association Test: Personalizing the IAT. *Journal of Personality and Social Psychology, 86*, 653–667.

Ouellette, J. A., & Wood, W. (1998). Habit and intention in everyday life: The multiple processes by which past behavior predicts future behavior. *Psychological Bulletin, 124*, 54–74.

Petty, R. E., & Cacioppo, J. T. (1986). The elaboration likelihood model of persuasion. In L. Berkowitz (Ed.), *Advances in experimental social psychology* (Vol. 19, pp. 123–205). San Diego, CA: Academic Press.

Petty, R. E., & Wegener, D. T. (1999). The elaboration likelihood model: Current status and controversies. In S. Chaiken & Y. Trope (Eds.), *Dual-process theories in social psychology* (pp. 41–72). New York: Guilford.

Prentice, D. A., & Carlsmith, K. M. (1999). Opinions and personality: On the psychological functions of attitudes and other valued possessions. In J. M. Olson & G. R. Maio (Eds.), *Why do we evaluate? Functions of attitudes* (pp. 223–248). Mahwah, NJ: Lawrence Erlbaum Associates.

Prislin, R., Limbert, W., & Bauer, E. (2000). From majority to minority and vice versa: The asymmetrical effects of gaining and losing majority position within a group. *Journal of Personality and Social Psychology, 79*, 385–392.

Rosenberg, M. J. (1968). Hedonism, inauthenticity, and other goads toward expansion of a consistency theory. In R. P. Abelson, E. Aronson, W. J. McGuire, T. M. Newcomb, M. J. Rosenberg, & P. H. Tannenbaum (Eds.), *Theories of cognitive consistency: A sourcebook* (pp. 73–111). Chicago: Rand McNally.

Rosenberg, M. J., & Hovland, C. I. (1960). Cognitive, affective, and behavioral components of attitudes. In C. I. Hovland & M. J. Rosenberg (Eds.), *Attitude organization and change: An analysis of consistency among attitude components* (pp. 1–14). New Haven, CT: Yale University Press.

Schwartz, G. E., Ahern, G. L., & Brown, S. L. (1979). Lateralized facial muscle response to positive and negative emotional stimuli. *Psychophysiology, 16*, 561–571.

Schwarz, N., & Bohner, G. (2001). The construction of attitudes. In A. Tesser & N. Schwarz (Eds.), *Blackwell handbook of social psychology: Intraindividual processes* (pp. 436–457). Malden, MA: Blackwell.

Shavitt, S. (1990). The role of attitude objects in attitude functions. *Journal of Experimental Social Psychology, 26,* 124–148.

Smith, E. R. (1996). What do connectionism and social psychology offer each other? *Journal of Personality and Social Psychology, 70,* 893–912.

Smith, E. R., & DeCoster, J. (1998). Knowledge acquisition, accessibility, and use in person perception and stereotyping: Simulation with a recurrent connectionist network. *Journal of Personality and Social Psychology, 74,* 21–35.

Smith, M. B., Bruner, J. S., & White, R. W. (1956). *Opinions and personality.* New York: Wiley.

Staats, C. K., & Staats, A. W. (1957). Meaning established by classical conditioning. *Journal of Experimental Psychology, 54,* 74–80.

Stone, J., & Cooper, J. (2001). A self-standards model of cognitive dissonance. *Journal of Experimental Social Psychology, 37,* 228–243.

Storbeck, J., & Robinson, M. D. (2004). Preferences and inferences in encoding visual objects: A systematic comparison of semantic and affective priming. *Personality and Social Psychology Bulletin, 30,* 81–93.

Tesser, A. (1993). The importance of heritability in psychological research: The case of attitudes. *Psychological Review, 100,* 129–142.

Thompson, E. P., Kruglanski, A. W., & Spiegel, S. (2000). Attitudes as knowledge structures and persuasion as a specific case of subjective knowledge acquisition. In G. R. Maio & J. M. Olson (Eds.), *Why we evaluate: Functions of attitudes* (pp. 59–95). Mahwah, NJ: Lawrence Erlbaum Associates.

Walther, E. (2002). Guilty by mere association: Evaluation conditioning and the spreading attitude effect. *Journal of Personality and Social Psychology, 82,* 919–934.

Wicker, A. W. (1969). Attitudes versus actions: The relationship of verbal and overt behavioral responses to attitude objects. *Journal of Social Issues, 25,* 41–78.

Wilson, T. D., & Hodges, S. D. (1992). Attitudes as temporary constructions. In L. L. Martin & A. Tesser (Eds.), *The construction of social judgments* (pp. 37–65). Hillsdale, NJ: Lawrence Erlbaum Associates.

Wilson, T. D., Lindsey, S., & Schooler, T. Y. (2000). A model of dual attitudes. *Psychological Review, 107,* 101–126.

Wood, W., Lundgren, S., Ouellette, J. A., Busceme, S., & Blackstone, T. (1994). Minority influence: A meta-analytical review of social influence processes. *Psychological Bulletin, 115,* 323–345.

Wood, W., Quinn, J. M., & Kashy, D. A. (2002). Habits in everyday life: Thought, emotion, and action. *Journal of Personality and Social Psychology, 83,* 1281–1297.

Wyer, R. S., & Srull, T. K. (1989). *Memory and cognition in its social context.* Hillsdale, NJ: Lawrence Erlbaum Associates.

Zanna, M. P., & Rempel, J. K. (1988). Attitudes: A new look at an old concept. In D. Bar-Tal & A. W. Kruglanski (Eds.), *The social psychology of knowledge* (pp. 315–334). Cambridge, UK: Cambridge University Press.

Zajonc, R. B. (1980). Feeling and thinking: Preferences need no inferences. *American Psychologist, 35,* 151–175.

Zajonc, R. B. (1984). On the primacy of affect. *American Psychologist, 39,* 117–123.

Author Index

Note: Numbers in *italics* indicate pages with complete bibliographic information.

A

Aaker, J. L., 312, *314,* 416, *435,* 603, 604, *610,* 640, *663,* 697, *699*
Aarts, H., 130, 145, *165, 170,* 191, 202, *210,* 333, *365,* 399, *428*
Abbey, J., 551, *572*
Abdi, H., 164, *165*
Abele, A. E., 621, *656*
Abelson, R. P., 10, 11, *16, 18,* 79, 85, 115, *116, 123,* 232, 240, *264,* 286, 287, 288, 290, 307, 311, *314, 319,* 330, 335, *360,* 370, 377, 385, 387, *390, 394,* 516, *529,* 586, 600, *604,* 710, 711, 714, 721, 731, *732, 738,* 756, *764*
Aberbuch, S., 524, *541*
Abin, R., 334, 336, 345, 346, 351, *366*
Abraham, C., 648, *666*
Abrahamsen, A., 551, *569*
Abrams, D., 673, 680, *699, 703, 736*
Abramson, P. R., 52, *64*
Ackbar, S., 90, 91, 92, 95, 97, *121*
Adams, C. M., 425, *430*
Adaval, R., 276, 290, *314, 321,* 464, 465, 472, 473, *481*
Adler, N., 161, *165*
Adolph, K. E., 407, *426*
Adolphs, R., 60, *64,* 419, 424, *426, 427*
Adorno, T. W., 586, *604*
Agnew, C. R., *666,* 719, 720, *733, 735*
Agostinelli, G., 143, *170*
Agustsdottir, S., 235, *269*
Aharon, I., 425, *426*
Ahee, J. W., 467, 469, *486*
Ahern, G. L., 747, *766*
Ahern, R. K., 198, *214*
Ahlering, R. R., 582, *604*
Ahlm, K., 274, *320*

Ahn, M. N., 373, *393*
Aiken, M., 324, *365*
Ainsworth, M. D. S., 719, *732*
Ajzen, I., 3, 4, 10, 11, 13, *16, 17,* 21, *64, 67,* 80, 96, 97, 106, 108, *116, 118, 120,* 126, 130, 131, 132, 133, 139, 141, 142, 144, 145, 158, 160, 161, 165, *165, 166, 167, 170,* 178, 179, 181, 182, 183, 187, 188, 190, 191, 192, 193, 194, 195, 196, 198, 199, 200, 201, 202, 203, 208, *210, 211, 212, 213, 214, 217, 314, 316,* 324, 326, 329, 336, 337, *360, 363,* 384, *390,* 453, 456, 477, *483,* 503, 504, 507, 528, *529, 533,* 548, 569, *570, 571,* 620, 622, 623, 624, 639, 651, 652, *656, 660,* 710, 711, 713, 716, 720, 725, 727, *732, 735,* 753, 759, *764, 765*
Alba, J. W., 522, *531*
Albarracín, D., 11, 14, *16,* 82, 98, 115, *117,* 144, 145, 146, *165,* 188, 196, 201, 204, *211,* 225, 250, 253, 259, 263, *264,* 276, 283, 284, 297, 306, 313, *314,* 351, 359, *360,* 372, 373, 378, 385, 387, *390,* 406, *426,* 468, 469, 471, *481,* 511, 512, 513, 518, 527, 528, *529, 535,* 578, 583, 589, *604,* 622, 623, 624, 626, 629, 630, 631, 635, 650, 651, 652, *656, 660, 662,* 685, *699,* 713, 722, *732, 733,* 762, *764*
Albert, R. D., 224, *267,* 514, *533*
Albright, L., *737*
Alcaraz, R., 204, *217*
Aldag, R. J., 725, *736*
Aldrich, J. H., 716, *741*
Alessis, C., 635, *660*
Alexander, C. J., 403, *434*
Alfert, E., 403, *430*
Alicke, M. D., 590, *604, 636, 661*
Alkire, M. T., 458, *482*
Allen, A., 586, *605*
Allen, B. P., 51, *64, 68*

Allen, J. J. B., 451, 452, *484*, 509, *534*
Allen, M., 640, *656, 668*
Allen, V., 686, *699*
Allison, P. D., 33, *64*
Allison, S. T., 253, *265*, 373, 380, *390, 393*
Allport, F. H., 618, *656*, 693, *699*
Allport, G. W., 10, *16*, 22, *64*, 125, *166*, 175, 177, 208, 211, 323, *361*, 462, *481*, 545, *569*, 576, *604*, 618, *656*, 674, 678, 693, 698, *699*, 707, 710, 728, *733*
Allyn, J., 638, *656*
Altemeyer, B., 578, 586, 587, *604*
Altom, M. W., 520, *536*
Alvarez, J. M., 62, *65*
Alvaro, E. M., 689, *699*
Alvaro, W. M., 689, *700*
Alwin, D. F., 36, 44, 45, 47, 63, *64, 69, 71*, 324, *361*, 601, *604*, 649, *656*
Alwin, D. R., 672, *699*
Ambady, N., 563, *573*
Ames, S., 595, *606*
Amodio, D. M., 210, *213*, 564, *570*
Anderson, A. K., 424, 425, 426, *426*
Anderson, B. A., 52, *64*
Anderson, C., 163, *166*
Anderson, C. A., 514, *529*, 639, *667*
Anderson, J. R., 86, *117*, 144, *166*, 279, *314*, 453, *481*, 553, 561, *569*, 746, *764*
Anderson, N., 504, *529*
Anderson, N. H., 12, 13, *16, 17*, 96, 97, *117*, 126, 127, 132, 153, *166*, 296. *314*, 330, *361*, 453, 454, *481*, 504, *529*, 622, *656*, 713, *733*
Andow, K., 249, *269*
Andreoli, V. A., *265*
Andrews, C., 425, *431*
Andrews, F. M., 63, *64*
Aneshansel, J., 711, 715, *737*
Anhalt, R. L., 376, *393*
Ansay, C., 516, *531*
Anthony, T., 724, 725, 726, 727, *739*
Apple, K. J., 582, *610*
Arcuri, L., 61, *70*, 520, *531*
Areni, C. S., 512, *529*, 639, *656*
Argyle, M., 636, *656*
Ariely, D., 420, 421, 425, *426, 427*
Aristotle, 556, *569*
Arkes, H. R., 388, *392*, 453, *481*
Arkin, R. M., 309, *314*, 578, 590, *611*
Armitage, C. J., 101, 109, *117, 118*, 188, 192, 196, 199, 200, 201, 203, *211, 212*
Armony, J. L., 422, 424, *427*
Armor, D., 383, *395*
Arnold, T. J., 603, *605*
Aron, A. P., 411, *428*
Aronson, E., 85, *116*, 143, *166*, 226, 227, 230, 231, 232, 234, 235, 237, 239, 240, 241, 242, 244, 256, 258, 260, *264, 265, 266, 267, 270, 271*, 311, *314*, 330, 345, 356, *360, 361*, 370, *390*, 516, *529*, 586, 600, *604*
Aronson, J., 146, *170*, 238, 262, *265*, 590, *606*

Arriaga, X. B., 719, *733*
Asakawa, K., 309, *315*
Asch, S. E., 11, *16*, 342, 354, 355, *361*, 587, *604*, 635, 636, *656*, 671, 672, 673, 674, 678, 679, 686, 688, *699*
Ascuncion, A. G., 466, *486*
Ashbrook, P. W., 467, *483*
Asher, T., 587, *608*
Ashikaga, T., 731, *736*
Ashmore, R. D., 561, *573*, 718, *735*
Astington, J. W., 448, *481, 489*
Asuncion, A. G., 372, 373, *393*, 506, 523, *536*, 595, 610, 684, *703*
Ataoev, T., 175, *215*
Atash, M. N., 339, 356, *364*, 582, *610*
Atkin, C. K., 52, *64*
Atkinson, R. C., 45, *64*
Audrain, P. C., 452, 459, *485*
Austin, J. T., 130, *166*
Averill, J. R., 327, *361*
Avtgis, T. A., *604*
Axelrod, R., 690, *699*
Axsom, D., 230, 255, *265*, 346, 350, *361*, 581, *604*
Ayabe-Kanamura, S., 406, *427*
Ayidiya, S. A., 42, 45, *64*
Azam, O., 596, *613*
Aziza, C., 260, *271*

B

Babad, E., 373, 374, 380, 381, *390*
Bachorowski, J., 130, *166*
Back, K. W., 724, *735*
Baddeley, A., 501, *529*
Baddeley, A. D., 45, *64*
Baeyens, F., 343, *361*, 408, 409, *427, 428*, 441, 444, 445, 460, *481, 483, 484*, 507, 508, *532*, 558, *569, 570*, 750, 751, *764*
Bagarozzi, D. A., 722, *733*
Bagozzi, R. P., 191, 193, 201, *211*, 652, *657*
Baillargeon, R., 449, *486*
Bakeman, R., 128, *166*
Baker, S. M., 358, *361, 529*, 529, 637, *657*, 687, 689, *699*
Baker, W. E., 450, *481*
Baker-Brown, G., 84, *117*
Baldwin, J. M., 126, *166*
Baldwin, M. W., 101, *118*, 252, 255, *265*, 330, *361*, 381, *390*, 511, *531*, 674, *699*
Ballachey, E. L., 177, *217*
Ballard, E. J., 84, *117*
Balloun, J. L., 514, *530*
Baltes, M. M., 418, *430*
Bamberg, S., 145, *166*, 198, 201, *211*
Banaji, M. R., 14, *17*, 26, 57, 58, 62, *66, 68, 72*, 86, *120*, 161, *168*, 206, 207, *213, 215*, 338, *363*, 523, *533*, 544, 549, 550, 555, 559, 565, 566, *570, 571, 572*, 596, 599, *605, 608*, 747, *765*

Bancroft, J., 160, *166*

Bandura, A., 191, 193, 196, 199, 200, *211,* 375, *390,* 516, *529, 530*

Banner, M. J., 695, *700*

Banse, R., *433*

Barch, D. M., 399, *434*

Barchas, P., 677, *699*

Barclay, J. R., 280, 290, *315*

Barden, J., 579, 596, *605, 610*

Bargh, J. A., 10, 11, *16,* 25, 26, 61, 62, *64, 65, 67,* 90, 91, 93, 94, 97, 108, 110, *117,* 128, 130, 142, 161, *166, 171,* 186, 191, 206, *211, 212,* 259, *265,* 281, *314,* 326, 327, 332, 339, *361, 363, 367,* 474, *481,* 495, 520, 525, *530, 534, 541,* 544, *569,* 582, *605,* 624, 628, 638, 642, *657, 658, 733,* 752, 760, *764, 765*

Barker, T. R., 500, *540*

Barkmeier, J., 598, *611*

Barmada, C., 188, *216*

Barnes, J., 651, *660*

Baron, R., 648, *657*

Baron, R. M., 235, 236, 245, *268,* 677, *700*

Baron, R. S., 245, *270,* 679, *699*

Baron, S. H., 679, *705*

Baron-Cohen, S., 449, *481*

Barquissau, M., 242, *265*

Barrett, A. M., 402, *430*

Barrett, D. W., 593, *606,* 696, *700*

Barrett, L. F., 404, 412, 413, *427, 432,* 719, *738*

Barrett, P., 602, *607*

Barsalou, L. W., 478, *481*

Bar-Tal, D., 334, 336, 345, 346, 351, *361, 366,* 509, *535*

Barter, J., 39, *75*

Bartholomew, K., 719, *733, 736*

Bartlett, F. C., 458, *481,* 710, 730, *733*

Bartlett, M. Y., 457, 461, *483*

Bartoshuk, L. M., *427*

Baskin, R., 188, *216*

Bassett, J. F., 64, *66*

Bassett, R., 146, *167,* 586, *606*

Bassili, J. N., 61, *64,* 88, 100, 106, 108, *117,* 332, 344, *361,* 519, *530,* 544, 547, 557, *569,* 636, 641, 642, *657*

Basu, A. K., 38, *74*

Bathe, S., 603, *605*

Batts, V., 204, *217,* 595, *611*

Baucom, D. H., 644, *667*

Bauer, E., 691, 692, *705,* 759, *766*

Baum, A., 130, *166*

Baumann, C., 405, *430*

Baumeister, R., 680, *699*

Baumeister, R. F., 128, *169,* 306, *314,* 411, *427,* 576, 585, 586, 590, 592, *605, 609,* 624, *657,* 718, *741*

Baumgardner, M. H., 518, *538,* 635, 650, *665, 666*

Baumgartner, H., 652, *657*

Bayens, F., 343, *363*

Bazzini, D. G., 719, *741*

Beaber, R. J., 635, *664*

Beach, K. R., 564, 565, *570*

Beach, R., 586, *608*

Beach, S. R., 450, *486*

Beach, S. R. H., 722, *733*

Bear, G., 286, *314*

Bearden, R. G., *605*

Bearden, W. O., 590, 593, *605, 614*

Beattie, A. E., 294, *321*

Beatty, S. E., 645, *664*

Beauchamp, G. K., *427*

Beaudoin, G., 425, 426, *430*

Beauregard, M., 425, 426, *430*

Beauvois, J. L., 245, 246, 256, 258, 262, *265,* 511, 516, *530*

Bechara, A., 389, *390*

Bechtal, W., 551, *569*

Beck, L., 200, *212*

Becker, M., 137, 165, *168,* 193, *214*

Becker, M. H., 193, *212, 218*

Becker, S. L., 45, *64,* 100, *117*

Beckmann, J., 711, *733*

Beebe-Center, J. G., 406, 416, *427*

Beggan, J. K., 380, *390*

Bekerian, D. A., 413, *428*

Bell, D. E., 600, *610*

Bell, D. W., 104, 110, *117, 121,* 331, 332, *365,* 642, *663*

Belson, W. A., 46, *72*

Bem, D. J., 11, 13, *16,* 80, 82, *117,* 126, 143, 161, *166,* 249, 250, 251, 252, 253, 257, *265,* 278, 289, 292, *314,* 325, 334, *361,* 501, 511, 516, *530,* 586, *605,* 633, 636, 653, *657,* 710, 711, 712, 716, 725, *733*

Bendig, A. W., 38, *64*

Bennett, S. E., 47, *65*

Benson, P. L., 53, *64*

Bentler, P. M., 201, *212,* 651, *657*

Bera, S., 719, *737*

Berent, M. K., 40, 47, 49, *69, 70,* 83, 88, 89, 90, 91, 92, 93, 94, 95, 96, 97, 98, 110, 115, *117, 120,* 381, *390,* 621, 642, *662,* 713, 716, *738*

Berg, I. A., 41, 45, *65*

Berger, I. E., 186, *212*

Berglas, S., 594, *610*

Berglund, B., 416, *427*

Berglund, U., 416, *427*

Berkhof, J., 406, *431*

Berkowitz, L., 3, 12, *16,* 237, *265,* 475, *481,* 508, 517, *530,* 591, *605,* 693, *699*

Berman, L., 274, *320*

Bernard, M., 650, *657*

Bernard, M. M., 263, *268*

Bernatzky, G., 406, *431*

Bernberg, R. E., 175, *212*

Bernreuter, R., 176, *212*

Bernston, G. G., 159, *166*

Berntson, G. G., 60, 61, *65, 66,* 159, *166,* 410, 416, 417, 418, 422, *427,* 507, 528, *530, 531,* 748, *764*

Berridge, K. C., 398, 400, 407, 422, 423, 424, *427, 434*

Berscheid, E., 5, *16,* 515, *530,* 718, *733, 735*

Bessenoff, G. R., 544, *569*

Bettencourt, B. A., 723, *733*

Betz, A. L., 443, *485,* 528, *535,* 558, *571,* 710, 728, *738*

Bevard, L., 150, *170*

Bichsel, J., 634, *666*

Biddle, S. J. H., 196, 197, *215*

Biek, M., 83, 94, 96, 99, 102, 104, *117, 124,* 641, 644, *668*

Bierbrauer, G., *666,* 679, *705*

Biller, B., 299, *321,* 519, *541*

Binder, N., 409, *434,* 452, *488*

Bird, C., 174, *212*

Birkett, N. J., 38, *65*

Birnbaum, M. H., 296, *314,* 504, *530*

Bishop, G. D., 90, 96, *117*

Bishop, G. F., 40, 45, 47, *65*

Bizer, G., 582, *612*

Bizer, G. Y., 90, 91, 94, 95, 101, 104, *117, 122,* 352, *366,* 526, *538,* 582, 583, *605, 615,* 627, 647, *665*

Black, J. B., 275, *314, 315*

Black, K., 200, *212*

Blackstone, T., 357, *368, 668,* 678, 688, 689, 690, *706,* 759, *767*

Blair, E., 149, 150, *166*

Blair, I., 543, 551, 561, 562, 564, 565, *569*

Blair, I. V., 596, *605*

Blake, R. R., 635, 636, *658, 664*

Blankenship, V., 602, *605*

Blanton, H., 161, *166,* 193, 201, 203, 210, *212, 215,* 238, 242, 256, 260, 262, *265*

Blascovich, J., 339, *361, 362, 435,* 478, *481,* 642, *657, 659*

Blatt, S. J., 576, *608*

Blaylock, B., 720, *734*

Blehar, M. C., 719, *732*

Bless, H., 26, 27, *65, 73,* 299, 309, *315, 319, 321,* 335, 344, *366,* 462, 463, 466, 467, 468, 471, *481, 487,* 519, *541,* 546, 549, 557, *573, 574,* 645, *657,* 711, 712, *733, 740*

Blessum, K. A., 326, *367,* 549, *573*

Bloch, P. H., 603, *605*

Bloom, P., 448, 460, *481*

Bluck, S., 84, *117*

Blumer, H., 175, *212*

Boakes, R. A., 408, *434,* 444, *481,* 750, *764*

Bobo, L., 204, *219*

Bobocel, D. R., 128, *166,* 598, *614*

Bobrow, D. G., 280, *315*

Bochner, S., 520, *530,* 640, *657*

Bodenhausen, G., 728, 730, *739*

Bodenhausen, G. V., 26, *65,* 289, 290, 309, 311, *315, 321,* 462, 463, 465, *481,* 520, *536,* 559, 561, 562, *572,* 710, 729, *733*

Böeckenholt, U., 416, *433*

Boettger, R., 383, *395*

Bogardus, E. S., 4, *16,* 22, *65,* 126, *166,* 618, *657*

Bogart, K., 595, *605*

Bogart, L., 47, *65*

Bohan, L., 721, *740*

Bohner, G., 4, *18,* 27, *75,* 80, *123,* 274, 284, 309, *315, 320,* 323, 325, 326, 329, 342, *361, 366,* 466, 467, 468, *481, 487,* 496, 526, *531, 539,* 543, 545, 546, 547, 566, *573,* 628, 634, 637, 645, *657, 658, 659,* 677, 678, 689, *700, 701, 733,* 746, 747, 766

Bolan, G. A., 198, *214*

Boller, G. W., *733*

Bonanno, G. A., 420, *433*

Bond, M. H., 556, *574,* 696, *699,* 729, *736*

Bond, R., 674, 696, *699*

Boninger, D. S., 50, *70,* 83, 88, 89, 90, 91, 92, 93, 94, 95, 96, 97, 98, 110, 115, *117, 120,* 381, *390,* 603, *614,* 621, 642, 650, *657, 662,* 713, 716, *738*

Bonnel, A.-M., 450, *487*

Bonoma, T. V., 239, 240, *271,* 516, *540*

Boote, A. S., *65*

Bordieri, J., 730, *733*

Borg, M. J., 52, *67*

Borgida, E., 10, *18,* 91, 95, 107, *117, 121,* 335, 365, 381, 382, *392, 395,* 418, *430,* 716, *741*

Bornstein, R. F., 25, *65,* 342, *361,* 409, *427,* 450, 451, 461, *481, 482,* 509, *530,* 556, 557, *569,* 653, *657,* 751, *764*

Borsari, B., 161, *166*

Bosson, J. K., 719, *733*

Boster, F. J., 470, *482,* 627, 640, *657, 667*

Bothwell, R. K., 377, 378, *390,* 714, 717, *733*

Bourgeois, M. J., 690, 691, *703*

Bourgouin, P., 425, 426, *430*

Bourhis, R. Y., 694, *701*

Bower, G. H., 203, *215,* 275, 279, *314, 315, 319,* 384, *391,* 452, 453, 455, 461, *481, 482, 484*

Bowlby, J., 679, *699,* 719, *733*

Boyes-Braem, P., 413, *432*

Boysen, S. T., 422, *427*

Bradburn, N., 25, *75,* 84, 91, *124*

Bradburn, N. M., 25, 48, *73, 74,* 149, *166,* 546, *574*

Bradbury, T. B., 722, *733*

Bradbury, T. N., 722, 723, *733, 735, 737*

Bradley, G. W., 377, *390*

Bradley, M. M., 60, *65, 66, 70,* 402, 415, 419, *427, 430*

Brajkovich, G., 407, *432*

Brandstätter, V., 190, 191, *215*

Brannon, L. A., 83, *119,* 373, 382, 383, *391,* 521, *532,* 715, *735, 757, 765*

Branscombe, N. R., *737*

Bransford, J. D., 280, 290, *315*

Brau, S., 716, *738*

Brauer, M., 90, 91, 92, 93, 94, *117, 118, 120,* 207, *212,* 564, 565, *569,* 688, 691, *699*

Braun, K.A., 409, *430*

Braver, S., 191, *212*

Braverman, J., 512, 514, *532*

Brazil, D. M., 727, *737*

Breckler, S. J., 80, 82, 98, 105, *117, 122,* 209, *212,* 276, *315,* 327, *361,* 371, *390, 427*

Bregman, A. S., 478, *482*

Brehm, J. W., 11, *16,* 227, 229, 231, 232, 236, 237, 238, 239, 247, 251, 256, 260, 262, *265, 267, 268, 270, 271,* 311, *321,* 328, 370, 375, 385, *394, 395,* 514, 516, *530, 534, 539,* 575, *605,* 632, 646, *657, 661, 668, 733*

Brehm, S. S., 646, *657*

Breier, A., 731, *736*

Breiter, H. C., 425, *426*

Brekke, N., 517, *541,* 579, *615*

Brendl, M. C., 685, *699*

Brennan, K. A., 719, *733*

Brennan, M., 648, *657*

Brent, E. E., 337, *363,* 374, 375, 380, 382, *391,* 717, *734, 736*

Bressler, S. L., 552, *569*

Brewer, M., 691, 692, *705*

Brewer, M. B., 56, 58, *65, 70,* 462, *482,* 555, *572,* 579, 596, *605, 610,* 680, 682, *699,* 723, *734*

Brewer, W. F., 443, *482,* 750, *764*

Brewer, W. H., 279, 280, *315*

Bridges, M. W., 578, 592, *613*

Brigham, J., 206, 207, *213*

Brigham, J. C., 377, 378, *390,* 595, *605,* 714, 717, *733,* 747, *765*

Briley, D. A., 312, 313, *315*

Briner, R. B., 418, *431*

Briñol, P., 14, *18,* 472, 473, *482,* 508, 517, 519, *530, 537, 538, 540,* 577, 578, 579, 581, 587, 588, 589, 590, 591, 595, 599, 600, *605, 611, 612, 614, 615,* 642, *665*

Brirnacombe, C., 154, *171*

Broadbent, D. E., 498, *530*

Brock, T. C., 296, 297, *318,* 512, 513, 514, 521, 529, *530, 537, 538,* 591, *611,* 623, 638, 643, 650, *657, 664, 665,* 713, *734, 740*

Brock, T. D., 512, 522, *538*

Brockner, J., 235, *265*

Broemer, P., 326, 331, 332, *364*

Bromer, P., 95, 98, 109, 110, *120*

Brömer, P., 642, *662*

Bromley, S., 204, 205, *213,* 564, *570*

Bronfenbrenner, U., 162, *166*

Brook, L., 46, *69*

Brooks, G., 731, *736*

Brooksbank, L., 99, *119*

Brosh, M., 351, *361*

Brown, A., 34, *72*

Brown, D. R., 602, *605*

Brown, J., 303, *317,* 509, *534*

Brown, J. D., 514, *530,* 576, 590, *614*

Brown, L. B., 448, *482*

Brown, R., *361,* 399, *430,* 688, *700*

Brown, R. D., 557, *569*

Brown, R. W., 13, *17,* 508, *534*

Brown, S. D., 196, *217*

Brown, S. L., 747, *766*

Brown, S. P., 726, *734*

Brown, T. C., 190, *211*

Browne, M., 499, *541*

Brownridge, G., 39, *75*

Brubaker, R. G., 198, *212*

Bruck, M., 601, *606*

Bruess, C. J. S., 720, *734*

Brunel, F. F., 603, *605*

Bruner, J. S., 79, 82, *123,* 338, 360, *367,* 519, *530,* 627, 629, 642, 643, 646, *667,* 678, 680, 682, *705,* 754, *767*

Brunsman, B., 679, *699*

Bryan, A. D., 649, *660*

Bryk, A., 140, 162, *166*

Buchanan, T. W., 419, *427*

Bucy, P. C., 424, *430*

Budd, E. C., 42, *74*

Budesheim, T. L., 294, *321*

Buehler, R., 636, *657, 660,* 686, *700, 701*

Bungert, M., 511, *530*

Burger, J. M., 253, *265*

Burgess, D., 102, *121*

Burgess, S. L., 420, *430*

Burgoon, M., 163, *167,* 595, *605*

Burnkrant, R. E., 512, *530*

Burns, L. R., 415, *428*

Burnstein, E., 288, *320,* 609, 639, *668,* 687, *700,* 711, 725, *734, 741, 742*

Burrows, L., 128, *166,* 281, *314*

Burt, D. M., 425, *431*

Burton, S., 149, 150, *166,* 196, *218*

Busceme, S., 357, *368, 668,* 678, 688, 689, 690, *706,* 759, *767*

Bush, J. P., 720, *740*

Bush, M., 253, *270*

Bushman, B. J., 163, *166,* 411, *427*

Bushway, S. D., 204, *212*

Buss, A. H., 585, *607*

Buss, D. M., 575, *605*

Butler, D., 207, *212*

Butner, J., 593, *606,* 696, *700*

Button, C. M., 108, *120*

Buttram, R. T., 518, 525, *540*

Butzine, K. W., 508, *534*

Bybee, J. A., 381, 385, 386, 387, 388, *395*

Byrne, D., 453, *482,* 719, 720, *734, 738*

Byrnes, D., 408, *432*

C

Cabanac, M., 422, *427*

Cacioppo, J. T., 4, 12, 14, *16, 18,* 21, 24, 26, 34, 59, 60, 61, *65, 66, 68, 72,* 82, 92, 98, 99, 101, 104, 106, 107, *118, 122,* 128, 146, 159, *166, 167, 170,* 176, 198, *218,* 234, 259, *268, 269,* 296, 309, *315, 319,* 323, 332, 347, 348, 349, 352, 353, 355, 356, 359, *361, 366,* 372, 382, 385, *393,* 410, 415, 416, 417, 418, 422, *427, 429, 430, 435,* 451, 452, 461, 465, 466, 467, 471, *485, 487, 489,* 504, 505, 506, 507, 508, 509, 510, 511, 512, 513, 514, 515, 516, 518, 519, 522, 523, 524, 528, 529, *530, 531, 536, 537,*

538, 542, 577, 578, 579, 581, 582, 584, 586, 594, 598, 599, 600, 602, *606, 608, 611, 612,* 620, 623, 624, 626, 627, 634, 638, 639, 640, 643, 644, 646, 647, 650, *657, 661, 665, 666,* 677, 694, 698, *704,* 708, 710, 711, 713, 715, 725, *734, 739, 740,* 748, 757, 762, *764, 766*

Cadell, D., 188, *216*

Cahill, L., 419, 424, *427,* 439, 458, 459, 461, *482*

Cairns, K. J., 590, *605*

Cajdric, A., 457, 461, *483*

Calder, B. J., 516, *531*

Calsyn, D. S., 42, *65*

Calsyn, R. J., 42, *65*

Cameron, J. A., 62, *65*

Campbell, B., 107, *117*

Campbell, B. A., 52, *65*

Campbell, D. T., 30, 44, 45, 59, *65, 71, 72,* 127, 148, 164, *166, 170, 171,* 175, 176, 177, 189, 190, 207, *212, 216,* 324, 343, *361,* 499, 522, 524, *531, 535, 537,* 565, *569,* 618, 619, *658, 734,* 744, *764*

Campbell, J. D., 590, *606*

Campbell, L. A., 370, *392,* 621, 644, *662*

Campbell, W. K., 602, *613*

Campbell, W. K., 398, 411, *429, 435*

Campos, J. J., 407, *427*

Cantor, N., 389, *393, 611*

Cantril, H., *73, 367,* 373, 374, 377, 378, 380, 389, *390, 392,* 620, *667*

Capitanio, J. P., 210, *216*

Caporael, L. R., 677, *700*

Cappella, J., 198, *214*

Carey, K. B., 161, *166*

Carey, M. P., 152, 153, 165, *170*

Carli, L. L., 600, *607*

Carlsmith, J. M., 226, 229, 230, 231, 232, 234, 235, 236, 239, 242, 246, 250, *265, 266,* 516, *529, 533,* 568, *571,* 632, *659, 735,* 761, *765*

Carlsmith, K. M., 340, *366,* 754, *766*

Carlson, E. R., 11, 12, *17*

Carlson, M., 411, *431*

Carlston, D. E., 13, *17,* 274, 278, 279, 280, 286, 296, *315, 321,* 327, 336, 353, *361, 368,* 453, *489,* 494, 498, 507, 524, 528, *531, 534, 539,* 568, *569,* 712, 714, *742*

Carnevale, P., 681, *705*

Carnot, C. G., 50, *70,* 83, 88, 89, 90, 91, 92, 93, 94, 95, 96, 97, 98, 110, 115, *120,* 586, *608,* 621, 642, *662*

Carp, F. M., 46, *65*

Carrasco, M., 416, *427*

Carroll, J. M., 416, *433*

Carron, A. V., 188, *215,* 724, *741*

Carson, R. T., 47, 49, *70*

Carstensen, L. L., 720, *738*

Cartwright, D., 85, *118,* 288, *315*

Carvajal, F., 190, *211*

Carver, C. S., 179, *212,* 239, *269,* 578, 585, 592, *606, 613*

Casano, R. A., 720, *741*

Casey, R. L., 128, *166*

Casey, S., 639, *660*

Caspi, A., 720, *734*

Castelli, J., 62, *74*

Castelli, L., 520, *531*

Castillo, S., 154, *168*

Ceci, S. J., 601, *606*

Cecil, C. L., 727, *737*

Cejka, M. A., 59, *74,* 81, 91, 94, 106, 110, 115, *123,* 520, *540,* 547, *573*

Centerbar, D. B., 477, *489*

Cesario, J., 757, *764*

Chabris, C. F., 425, *426*

Chaffee, S. H., 52, *64*

Chaiken, S., 4, 5, 10, 14, 15, *17,* 22, 24, 25, 26, *64, 65, 66, 67,* 80, 83, 85, 90, 91, 92, 93, 94, 97, 98, 99, 101, 102, 103, 106, 107, 108, 109, 110, 115, 116, *117, 118, 122,* 126, *167,* 184, 186, 187, 198, 202, *211, 212, 213,* 226, 252, 255, 259, 264, *265, 266,* 273, 281, 288, 292, 306, 308, *315, 316,* 323, 324, 325, 326, 330, 332, 334, 335, 339, 346, 348, 349, 350, 351, 352, 355, 358, 359, *361, 362, 365, 367,* 370, 372, 377, 378, 379, 380, 381, 382, 383, 385, 386, 387, 388, *390, 391, 392, 393,* 402, 410, 419, *427, 428,* 438, 465, 466, 468, 469, 470, *482, 483,* 494, 503, 504, 505, 506, 510, 511, 512, 513, 514, 518, 521, 524, 525, 526, 529, *530, 531, 532, 533, 536,* 544, 558, 566, *569, 570,* 577, 579, 580, 581, 582, 586, 603, *604, 605, 606, 607, 612, 614,* 618, 620, 621, 622, 623, 624, 626, 627, 628, 633, 634, 638, 639, 640, 641, 642, 643, 648, *657, 658, 659, 660, 663, 664, 665,* 675, 676, 677, 678, 680, 681, 682, 685, 687, 694, 695, 698, *700, 701, 703,* 710, 711, 713, 715, 725, *734, 735,* 745, 748, 749, 750, 752, 754, 755, 756, 757, 758, 759, 761, 762, 763, *764, 765*

Chamberlain, A. G., 405, 415, *431*

Champion, V. L., 193, *219*

Champney, H., 39, *65*

Chan, C.-J., 720, *734*

Chan, D. K.-S., 192, 196, *212,* 503, *536*

Chan, J. C., 46, *65*

Chan, T., 204, *217*

Chang, C., 602, *606*

Chang, E. C., 309, *315*

Chang, S., 727, *741*

Chapanis, A., 232, *265*

Chapanis, N. P., 232, *265*

Chapman, I., 34, *72*

Charlton, K., 723, *733*

Chartrand, T. L., 130, 142, 161, *166,* 206, *212*

Chassein, B., 153, *170*

Chassin, L., 143, *170,* 382, *394*

Chasteen, A. L., 501, *535*

Chattopadhyay, A., 522, *531*

Chatzisarantis, N. L. D., 196, 197, *215*

Chave, E. J., 126, *167,* 174, *220*

Checkley, S. A., 405, *430*

Chen, H. C., 638, *658*

Chen, J., 81, 108, *119,* 186, *214,* 381, *391, 735*

Chen, M., 61, *65,* 128, *166,* 281, *314,* 642, *658*

Chen, S., 26, *66, 118,* 370, 372, 377, 382, 383, 385, 387, *390, 391,* 419, *428,* 521, *532,* 580, *606,* 624, 626, 628, 638, 643, *658,* 675, 676, 680, 681, 682, 685, 695, *700,* 711, 715, *735,* 755, 756, 757, 762, *764, 765*

Chen, X., 689, *700*

Cheng, D. T., 425, *428*

Cheng, J., 297, *319*

Cheng, S., 52, *66*

Cherulnik, P. D., 595, *606*

Cheung, S.-F., 192, 196, *212*

Chiu, C., 578, 589, 602, *607, 609*

Choi, I., 285, *315,* 697, *700*

Chomsky, N., 448, *482*

Christensen, N. P., 677, *706*

Christensen, P. N., 677, 691, 692, 694, *700, 705*

Christie, C., 161, *166*

Christie, R., 578, 595, *606*

Christoff, K., 426, *426*

Chuang, Y. C., 50, *70,* 83, 88, 89, 90, 91, 92, 93, 94, 95, 96, 97, 98, 110, 115, *120,* 621, 642, *662*

Chun, W. Y., 332, 337, 351, *362, 364,* 505, *531, 535,* 761, *766*

Chun, Y. W., 351, *362*

Chung-Yan, G. A., 730, *741*

Chwalisz, K., 403, *428*

Cialdini, R. B., 126, 146, 161, *167,* 191, 199, 203, *212, 219,* 245, *265,* 331, *362,* 386, *390, 391,* 508, 514, *534, 539,* 578, 586, 587, 593, *606, 608,* 632, 633, 636, 650, *658, 666,* 675, 676, 677, 681, 688, 690, 696, *700, 703*

Cinotti, L., 426, *432*

Cioffi, D., 165, *167*

Clancy, K. J., 42, *66*

Clark, A., 442, 478, *482*

Clark, J. K., 95, 103, *118*

Clark, L. A., 405, 414, 415, *428, 435*

Clark, M., 453, 461, *485*

Clark, R. D., 636, *663*

Clark, R. D., III, 357, *365,* 692, *700*

Clary, E. G., 386, *391*

Claypool, H. M., 526, *541,* 695, *700*

Clement, R. W., 677, *703*

Clevenger, T., Jr., 100, *120*

Cliff, N., 28, *66*

Clore, G., 439, *484*

Clore, G. L., 13, *18, 73,* 276, 305, 306, *316, 320, 321,* 327, 334, *366,* 397, 398, 400, 404, 406, 409, 411, 412, 414, 416, 419, *428, 429, 431, 432, 434,* 438, 439, 446, 452, 453, 454, 455, 456, 458, 461, 462, 463, 464, 465, 466, 467, 468, 471, 472, 473, 475, 477, *481, 482, 483, 484, 485, 486, 487, 488, 489,* 528, *539,* 710, 720, 728, *734, 740,* 753, *764*

Close, S., 201, *212*

Coats, S., 496, *531,* 695, *700*

Cobos, P., 403, *428*

Codispoti, M., 402, *427*

Cohen, A. R., 231, 232, 236, 256, 261, *265, 733*

Cohen, D. J., 449, *481*

Cohen, G., 590, *606*

Cohen, G. L., 239, *270*

Cohen, J., 52, *66*

Cohen, J. B., 250, *264*

Cohen, J. D., 422, 424, *427,* 500, *531*

Cohen, R. E., 649, *656*

Cohen, R. L., 324, *361,* 601, *604,* 672, *699*

Colarelli, S. M., 164, *167*

Colcombe, S., 417, 418, *433,* 438, 452, 456, *482,* 753, *764*

Colcombe, S. J., 290, 291, *315, 321*

Colder, C. R., 405, *435*

Coleman, J. F., 635, *658*

Coles, M. G., 60, *65*

Collier, G., 693, *700*

Collins, A., 397, 400, 404, 409, 412, 414, 416, *431,* 477, *487*

Collins, A. M., 279, *315*

Collins, B. E., 558, *571*

Collins, M., 46, *69*

Collins, M. A., 718, *734*

Collins, N. L., 720, *734*

Colman, D. E., 513, *537*

Colombo, A., 126, *169*

Comer, R., 234, *269,* 472, *487*

Conaway, M., 47, 49, *70*

Condry, J., 254, *265*

Conlee, M. C., 386, *394*

Conner, M., 97, 101, 109, *117, 118,* 144, *169,* 183, 188, 192, 196, 197, 199, 200, 201, 203, *211, 212, 217*

Conrey, F., 748, *764*

Converse, J. M., 47, 49, 52, *66, 73*

Converse, P. E., 47, *66,* 79, 80, 85, 86, 90, 96, *118,* 263, *266,* 380, *391,* 545, *570*

Conway, M., 25, *73,* 150, *170,* 292, *315,* 376, 383, *394,* 455, 467, *482,* 649, *666,* 715, *734*

Conway, M. A., 413, *428*

Cook, M., 447, *486*

Cook, S. W., 176, 177, *212,* 220, 221

Cook, T. D., 148, *170,* 300, *315,* 549, *574,* 618, 619, 635, 649, 650, *657, 658,* 660

Coombs, C. H., 48, *66*

Coombs, L. C., 48, *66*

Coon, H., 593, *611*

Coon, H. M., 695, 696, *704*

Cooney, J. W., 442, *482*

Cooper, E., 601, *606*

Cooper, H. M., 600, *606*

Cooper, J., 11, *19,* 54, *76,* 143, 146, *167,* 207, *221,* 230, 233, 234, 235, 236, 237, 238, 239, 240, 242, 243, 244, 245, 246, 247, 251, 255, 256, 257, 258, 260, 261, 262, *265, 266, 267, 268, 269, 270, 271,* 311, 312, *315,* 322, 356, *362,* 384, *391,* 471, 472, *482,* 489, 502, 511, 516, *531, 533, 540, 542,* 632, 633, 652, *658, 659, 668, 734, 736,* 761, *767*

Cooper, J. T., 684, *700*
Coopersmith, S., 711, *734*
Copper, C., 724, *739*
Corby, N. H., 200, *212, 216*
Corey, S. M., 174, 175, *212*
Cornell, D. P., 239, 260, *271,* 516, *540*
Correll, J., 379, *391,* 590, *606*
Correll, J. S., 587, *611*
Corrigan, P., 731, *734*
Corrigan, P. W., 143, *167,* 730, *734*
Corty, E., 298, *320*
Costa, 575, 602, *606*
Costa, P. T., Jr., 160, *167, 611*
Costermans, J., 516, *531*
Costes, N., 426, *432*
Costley, C., 651, *660*
Cotter, P., 52, *66*
Cotter, P. A., 405, *430*
Couch, A., 42, *66*
Coulter, P. B., 52, *66*
Courneya, K. S., 192, 202, *213*
Cowan, C. L., 386, 387, *394*
Craik, F. I. M., 282, 284, 300, 310, *315,* 529, *531,* 627, *658*
Crain, A. L., 241, 242, 256, *270*
Crandall, C. S., 448, 450, *482*
Crano, W., 163, *167*
Crano, W. D., 94, *118,* 179, *219,* 382, *391,* 678, 689, *699, 700*
Crary, R. W., 590, *606*
Crawford, C. C., 42, *75*
Crawford, M. T., 387, 389, 390, *391,* 507, *539*
Crelia, R. A., 107, *121,* 517, 518, 528, *536*
Critchley, H., 425, *431*
Critchlow, B., 234, 261, *270,* 516, *540*
Crites, S., 417, *433*
Crites, S. L., Jr., 60, 61, *65, 66,* 82, 97, 100, 109, 113, *118, 119,* 199, *213*
Crockett, W. H., 719, *737*
Crombez, G., 343, *361,* 409, *427,* 444, 445, 460, *481,* 750, *764*
Cronbach, L. J., 28, 31, 45, 49, *66*
Crosby, F., 204, 205, *213,* 564, *570*
Crow, T., 378, *392*
Crowne, D. P., 636, *658*
Croyle, R. T., 312, *315*
Crucian, G. P., 402, *430*
Crutchfield, R. S., 177, *217,* 276, *317,* 324, *364,* 587, 601, *606,* 636, *658*
Cruz, M. G., 602, *607*
Culbertson, F. M., 514, *531*
Culpepper, I. J., 49, *66*
Cunningham, M. R., 253, *270*
Cunningham, W. A., 60, 62, *66, 72,* 206, 207, *213,* 565, *570*
Curtin, M. F., 45, 47, *75*
Cuthbert, B. N., 60, *65, 66, 70,* 402, *427*
Cutler, B. D., *609*
Czasch, C., 191, *211*

D

Dabbs, J. M., Jr., 64, *66*
D'Agostino, P. R., 25, *65,* 342, *361,* 409. *427,* 450, 451, 461, *481,* 509, *530,* 653, *657,* 751, *764*
Dalal, R., 697, *700*
Damasio, A. R., 60, *64,* 389, *390, 391,* 424, *426,* 455, 461, 474, *482,* 556, *570*
Damasio, H., 389, *390*
Damhave, K. W., 718, *735*
Damrad-Frye, R., 253, 259, *266*
D'Andrade, R., 25, *75,* 84, 91, 95, *124*
D'Anello, S., 448, *482*
Daniels, L. A., 204, *213*
Daniels, L. K., 719, *738*
Danzinger, K., 693, *700*
Darke, P., 352, *362,* 512, 526, *531,* 627, *658*
Darke, P. R., 526, *531,* 634, *658,* 678, *700*
Das, B., 188, *216*
Das, E. H. H. J., 346, *362,* 640, *658,* 753, *764*
Dasgupta, N., 457, 461, *483,* 562, *570*
Davey, G. C. L., 444, 445, *482*
Davey, L. M., 128, *166*
David, B., 689, *701*
David, J. P., 406, *428*
Davidson, A. R., 83, 92, 94, 106, 109, *118,* 548, *570*
Davidson, M., 447, *486*
Davidson, R. J., 161, *167,* 404, 406, 422, *428,* 476, *483*
Davies, M. F., 587, *607*
Davis, F. D., 201, *220*
Davis, J. A., 687, *702*
Davis, J. H., 725, *734*
Davis, J. L., 718, 720, *734*
Davis, K. E., 494, *535*
Davis, K. J., 289, *317*
Dawes, R. M., 23, 28, *66,* 324, *362*
Dean, J.B., 590, *611*
Dean, L. R., 175, *213*
Dearing, J. W., 716, *740*
Deary, I. J., 405, *429, 431*
Deaux, K., 345, *362*
DeBono, K., 646, *658*
DeBono, K. G., 100, 104, *118, 123,* 340, *362, 367,* 579, 597, 603, *607, 613, 614*
Deci, E. L., 197, *213,* 254, *266,* 511, *532,* 576, *607*
DeCoster, J., 81, *123,* 494, 499, *539,* 599, *613,* 746, *767*
De Dreu, C. K. W., 687, 688, 689, 692, *701*
DeFleur, M. L., 175, 178, 181, *213, 220*
De Grada, E., *610*
DeGraff, M. H., 43, *73*
De Houwer, J., 25, 57, 58, *66,* 408, 409, *427, 428,* 441, 444, 445, 460, 475, *483,* 507, 508, *532,* 544, 555, 558, *570,* 583, *609,* 751, *764*
Deiger, M., 716, 721, *739*
De Jong, P., 399, *435*
DeJong, W., 253, *266*
Delespaul, P., 406, *431*
Demaine, L. J., 587, *608*

DeMaio, T. J., 546, *570*
Dember, W., 592, *607*
Demerath, N. J., 324, *365*
Denburg, N. L., 419, *427*
Denes-Raj, V., 584, 599, *607*
DePaulo, B. M., 50, *66,* 632, *658, 669*
Derman, D., 594, *607*
Dermer, M., 515, *530*
Desharnais, R., 183, 192, *215*
Desor, J. A., 406, *429*
DeSteno, D., 457, 461, 467, 470, 471, *483, 487,* 512, 514, 518, *532*
Deutsch, B., 154, *170*
Deutsch, M., 12, *17,* 355, 356, 357, *362,* 635, 636, *658,* 672, 673, 674, *701,* 724, *734, 755, 765*
Deutscher, I., 175, *213*
Devine, P. G., 25, *66,* 204, 210, *213, 218,* 237, 240, 241, 243, 260, *265, 266,* 333, *362,* 399, *428,* 462, 471, *483,* 502, 516, *532,* 543, 563, 564, *570, 572,* 578, 596, *607, 612,* 633, 638, *659, 661*
Devos, T., 457, 461, *486*
Devos-Comby, L., 640, *659*
de Vries, B., 84, *117*
de Vries, M., 406, *431*
de Vries, N., 200, *218*
de Vries, N. K., 203, *220,* 687, 688, 689, 692, *701*
Dewey, J., 678, 693, *701*
de Wit, J. B. F., 346, *362,* 640, *658,* 753, *764*
Dickerson, C., 241, 256, *266*
Dickinson, J. R., 49, *66*
Dickinson, T. L., 40, *66*
DiClemente, C. C., 148, *170*
Diehl, M., 95, 98, 109, 110, *120,* 326, 331, 332, *364,* 529, *542,* 634, 642, *662, 669*
Diener, E., 398, 400, 403, 411, 414, 415, 416, 417, 418, 419, 421, *428, 430, 433, 434*
Dienes, B., 439, 446, 463, 465, 472, *482*
Dietz, M., 47, *72*
Digman, J. M., 575, 602, *607*
Dijksterhuis, A., 130, *165,* 191, *210,* 399, *428,* 508, *532,* 544, *571,* 621, *659*
Dillard, J. P., 253, *266,* 602, *607*
Dillehay, R. C., 176, *213,* 285, *316,* 374, *391,* 505, *532*
Dimberg, U., 399, *428*
Dinerman, H., 601, *606*
Dion, K. I., 718, *735*
Dion, K. K., 718, *735*
Dion, K. L., 718, *735*
Distel, H., 406, *427*
Dittmar, K., 446, *487*
Ditto, P. H., 377, 378, 379, 382, 383, *391,* 511, *532*
Dittus, P., 126, 137, 150, 151, *168*
Dodson, C. S., 500, *532*
Dolan, K. A., 374, 375, 381, *391*
Dolan, P. O., 500, *536*
Dolan, R., 476, *483*
Dolan, R. J., 424, 425, *431*
Dolderman, D., 723, *739*

Doll, J., 106, 108, *118, 213,* 548, *570*
Dollard, J., 462, *483*
Donahoe, J. W., 508, *532*
Donchin, E., 61, *67*
Dongarra, T., 644, *664*
Donnelly, J. M., 399, *434*
Donnerstein, E., 53, *66*
Donnerstein, M., 53, *66*
Donohew, L., 577, *609*
Donovan, J., 130, *167*
Doob, L. W., 746, *765*
Doogan, S., 446, *483*
Dossett, D. L., 201, *215*
Doty, R. M., *611*
Dover, P. A., 708, *739*
Dovidio, J. F., 53, 54, 61, *66, 67,* 204, 206, 207, *213, 215, 216,* 333, *363,* 544, 560, 564, 565, *570, 571,* 596, *607,* 652, *659,* 718, *735,* 747, *765*
Downey, J. L., 718, *735*
Downing, J., 89, 115, *124,* 513, *541*
Downing, J. W., 80, 85, 86, 90, 91, 94, 96, *118, 120*
Downing, L. L., 386, *391*
Downs, D. L., 576, *610*
Drake, C. E., 587, *611*
Drake, R. A., 80, 85, 86, 91, 94, *120*
Drapalski, A. L., 420, *433*
Drehmer, D., 730, *733*
Driscoll, D. M., 339, *362,* 517, *539,* 642, *659*
Driskell, J. E., 724, 725, 726, 727, *739*
Driver, B. L., 199, *211*
Driver, M. J., 284, *319*
Driver, R. E., 632, *669*
Droba, D. D., 126, *167*
Duckworth, K. L., 352, *362,* 512, 526, *531,* 627, *658,* 752, *765*
Duclaux, R., 422, *427*
Dulany, D. E., 10, *17,* 523, *532,* 727, *735*
Dunbar, K., 500, *531*
Duncan, B. L., 235, *266*
Duncan, L. E., 586, *607*
Duncan, S. C., 162, *167*
Duncan, T. E., 162, *167*
Dunn, D. S., 12, *19,* 83, 106, 108, 109, *124,* 325, 327, *368,* 381, 385, 386, 387, 388, 389, 390, *395,* 514, *541*
Dunn, E. W., 528, *541*
Dunn, J. C., 501, *532*
Dunn, L. W., 464, 465, *483*
Dunn, M., 518, 528, *541*
Dunn, M. A., 562, *574*
Dunning, D., 335, 345, 355, *362,* 498, *532,* 576, *607*
Dunton, B. C., 27, *67,* 93, 106, 107, *118, 119,* 161, *167,* 205, 206, 207, 210, *213, 214,* 524, 525, *532,* 547, 564, *570,* 596, *607,* 717, 728, 730, *735*
Durkheim, E., 693, *701*
Dutton, D. G., 411, *428*
Duval, L. L., 674, *705*
Duval, S., 240, *266*
Dweck, C. S., 578, 589, 602, *607, 609, 610*

Dyomina, N. V., 64, *66*
Dywan, J., 451, *485*

E

Eagly, A. H., 4, 5, 10, 14, 15, *17*, 22, *67*, 80, 85, 92, 98,
    103, 106, 109, *118*, 126, 161, *167*, 184, 186, 187,
    198, 202, *213*, 226, 264, *266*, 273, 288, *316*, 324,
    325, 326, 334, 335, 346, 347, 348, 349, 350, 351,
    353, 355, 356, 359, *362*, *363*, 370, 372, 373, 382,
    383, 385, 386, 387, *390*, *391*, *392*, 402, 410, 418,
    419, *427*, *428*, 438, 465, 466, 468, 469, 470, *482*,
    483, 494, 504, 505, 506, 510, 511, 512, 513, 518,
    520, 521, 524, 529, *531*, *532*, *542*, 558, *570*, 577,
    579, 600, *606*, *607*, 618, 620, 621, 622, 623, 624,
    626, 627, 628, 634, 638, 639, 640, 641, 642, 643,
    658, *659*, *662*, 675, 677, 678, 681, 687, 694, 698,
    700, *701*, *702*, 710, 711, 713, 715, 718, 725, *734*,
    735, 745, 748, 749, 750, 751, 754, 755, 756, 757,
    759, 761, 762, 763, *764*, *765*, *766*
Earleywine, M., 58, *69*, 411, *431*
Ebbesen, E. B., 251, *270*
Ebel, R. L., 43, *67*
Ebert, J. E. J., 387, 390, *391*
Edelman, B., 164, *165*
Edwards, A., 132, 133, *167*
Edwards, A. L., 276, *316*, 710, 715, *735*
Edwards, C. S., 603, *614*
Edwards, J. A., 578, 584, *607*, *615*
Edwards, K., 91, 99, 100, *118*, *119*, 469, 470, 471, *483*,
    511, *532*, 622, 647, *659*
Edwards, M., 143, *167*
Edwards, R. E., 515, *535*
Eelen, P., 25, *66*, 343, *361*, *363*, 407, 408, 409, 410,
    427, *429*, 441, 444, 445, 460, *481*, *484*, 508, *532*,
    544, 558, *569*, *570*, 583, *609*, 750, *764*
Effrein, E. A., 253, *266*, 443, *483*
Egloff, B., 415, *428*
Ehrlichman, H., 406, *428*
Eichler, A., 193, *214*
Eid, M., 415, *434*
Eifermann, R. R., 43, *67*
Einstein, G. O., 528, *534*
Einwiller, S., 526, *531*, 634, 637, *658*, *659*, 678, *700*
Eiser, J. R., 115, *119*, 325, *362*, 528, 532, *532*, 568,
    570
Ekman, G., 416, *427*
Ekman, P., 161, *167*, 402, 404, 406, 412, *428*, *430*, 632,
    659
Ekstein, G., 621, 644, *662*
Ekstrom, R. B., 594, *607*
Elicker, J., 719, *741*
Elkin, R. A., 234, *266*, 502, 516, *532*
Ellen, P. S., 192, 196, *217*
Elliot, A. J., 204, *213*, 240, 241, 243, 260, *266*, 502,
    516, *532*, 633, *659*
Elliott, A. J., 471, *483*
Ellis, A., 151, *170*
Ellis, A. L., 210, *213*

Ellis, A. W., 495, *532*
Ellis, H. C., 467, *483*
Ellis, S., 334, 336, 351, *362*
Ellsworth, P. C., 403, 404, *434*, 553, *570*
Elmehed, K., 399, *428*
Elms, A. C., 224, 225, 232, *266*, 514, *532*, 650, *659*
Ely, T. D., 419, 425, *429*
Emmons, R. A., *428*
Engen, T., 416, *427*
England, L. R., 34, *67*
Engle, R. W., 409, *434*, 508, 528, *539*, *540*, 708, *741*
Ensley, E., 582, *610*
Epley, N., 473, *483*
Epstein, G. F., 245, *266*
Epstein, J. A., 50, *66*
Epstein, S., 139, *167*, 576, 584, 599, 599, *607*, *611*,
    613
Erb, H., 637, *659*
Erb, H. P., 351, 352, *362*, 505, 526, *531*, *535*, 628, 634,
    657, *658*, 677, 678, 689, *700*, *701*
Erber, M. W., 88, 90, 91, 92, 93, 94, 95, 96, 97, 110,
    119, 325, 326, *362*
Erber, R., 562, *574*
Ernst, J. M., 339, *361*, *435*, 642, *657*
Espinoza, P., 206, *219*
Esses, V. M., 104, 110, *117*, *121*, 128, *168*, 331, 332,
    365, 452, 464, *483*, 583, 600, *610*, 641, 642, *659*,
    663
Estrada, M., 521, *540*
Etcheverry, P. E., 719, 720, *735*
Etcoff, N., 425, *426*
Etcoff, N. L., 399, *435*
Eubanks, J., 723, *733*
Eurich, A. C., 42, *67*
Evans, L. M., 603, *607*, 647, *659*
Evans, N., 206, 207, *213*
Evans, R. I., 51, *67*
Evenbeck, S., 675, 676, *700*
Eysenck, H. J., 51, *71*, 602, *607*
Eysenck, M., 470, *483*
Eysenck, M. W., 495, *532*, 648, *659*
Eysenck, S. B. G., 602, *607*

F

Faber, R. J., 299, 300, 301, *320*
Fabiani, M., 61, *67*
Fabrigar, L. R., 34, 41, 46, 50, *70*, 82, 83, 88, 90, 91,
    92, 94, 95, 96, 97, 98, 99, 100, 102, 103, 104,
    107, 109, 111, 112, 113, 115, 116, *117*, *118*,
    119, *121*, *123*, *124*, 199, *213*, 469, 470, *483*,
    499, 513, 518, 519, 520, 521, 524, 528, 529,
    532, *538*, *539*, *540*, *541*, 582, *613*, 635, 647,
    653, *659*, *665*, *666*
Facheux, C., 354, 356, *365*
Faes, S., 190, *220*
Falender, V. J., 253, *266*
Fallon, A. E., 406, 407, *432*
Fallon, J., 458, *482*

Faris, E., 693, *701*

Farnham, S. D., 549, 550, *571*

Farr, R. M., 693, 694, *701*

Farrell, A. D., 720, *740*

Fathi, D. C., 149, 151, 152, *169*

Faulkenberry, G. D., 48, *67*

Fazandeiro, T., 342, *368*

Fazendeiro, T. A., 451, 461, *489, 557, 574*

Fazio, R. H., 4, 10, 11, 13, 14, *17,* 24, 25, 26, 27, 55, 57, 59, 62, *67, 72, 73, 74,* 80, 81, 87, 89, 90, 91, 92, 93, 94, 99, 100, 101, 103, 105, 106, 107, 108, 109, 110, 114, 115, 116, *118, 119, 120, 122, 123, 124,* 130, 143, 146, 161, *167,* 178, 179, 180, 184, 185, 186, 187, 203, 205, 206, 207, 208, 210, *213, 214, 218, 219, 221,* 236, 244, 246, 251, 253, 255, 256, 258, 259, 260, 264, *266, 270, 271,* 311, 312, *315,* 324, 326, 328, 329, 336, 338, 339, 343, 356, *362, 363, 365,* 372, 373, 377, 378, 379, 381, 382, 384, *391, 392, 394,* 408, *431,* 443, 460, 471, 474, 477, *482, 483, 486,* 493, 496, 502, 508, 510, 511, 516, 517, 519, 520, 524, 525, 528, *531, 532, 533, 534, 537, 539, 540, 542,* 543, 544, 546, 547, 558, 559, 560, 564, 565, 566, 567, 568, *570, 571, 572, 573,* 583, 585, 596, 597, *607, 613, 615,* 632, 633, 634, 642, 643, 652, *657, 658, 659, 666,* 677, 678, *701,* 710, 711, 717, 728, 730, *735, 739, 740,* 746, 747, 748, 752, 760, *765, 766*

Feaganes, J. R., 98, *121*

Feather, N. T., 448, *482*

Fedaku, Z., 201, *214*

Fedor, D. P., 726, *740*

Fehrenbach, P. A., 722, *737*

Fein, S., 562, *574*

Feinglos, M. N., 405, *435*

Feinstein, A. H., 528, *538*

Feinstein, J. A., 14, *16,* 581, 602, *606,* 644, *657*

Feld, P., 727, *741*

Feldman, S., 47, *76,* 389, *393*

Feldman Barrett, L., 414, *428*

Fenigstein, A., 585, *607*

Ferber, R., 49, *67*

Ferguson, M. J., 624, 628, *657*

Fern, E. F., 651, *660*

Fernandez, J. K., 309, *320*

Feshbach, S., 469, 471, *485*

Festinger, L., 11, 13, *17, 21, 67,* 85, 95, *120,* 126, *167,* 175, *214,* 226, 227, 228, 229, 230, 231, 232, 234, 236, 238, 239, 242, 246, 249, 250, 255, 258, 261, *266,* 297, 306, 311, *316,* 355, 356, *363,* 370, *391,* 471, *483,* 501, 515, 516, *533,* 568, *571,* 577, 585, 586, 587, *607,* 632, 633, 636, 638, 651, *656, 659, 660,* 673, 678, 684, 685, *701,* 710, 711, 714, 724, *735,* 761, 762, *765*

Fetherstonhaugh, D., 639, *660*

Fiedler, K., 461, 463, *481, 483,* 729, *735*

Field, N. P., 420, *433*

Field, P. B., 600, *609*

Fincham, F. D., 722, 723, *733, 735, 737*

Findley-Klein, C., 375, *394*

Fine, B. J., 346, *363*

Fink, E. L., 600, *607*

Finkel, E. J., 727, *737*

Finkel, S. E., 52, *67*

Finlay, K. A., 197, *214, 220*

Finucane, M., 455, 461, *488*

Fischer, G. H., 594, *608*

Fischer, H., 60, *68*

Fischoff, B., 44, *69, 305, 316,* 346, *367*

Fishbach, A., 332, 337, *364, 761, 766*

Fishbaugh, L., 681, *701*

Fishbein, M., 3, 4, 10, 11, 13, *16, 17,* 21, *67,* 80, 96, 97, *120,* 126, 130, 131, 132, 133, 138, 139, 141, 144, 145, 158, 161, 163, *165, 167,* 178, 181, 182, 183, 187, 188, 191, 193, 194, 195, 196, 198, 200, 201, 204, 208. *211,* 210, *211, 214, 216, 217, 220, 221,* 263, *264,* 273, 274, 276, 278, 284, 296, 297, *316,* 324, 329, 336, 337, *363,* 384, *390,* 453, 456, 477, *483,* 495, 498, 503, 504, 528, *533, 536, 537,* 548, 558, *569, 571,* 620, 622, 623, 624, 639, 651, 652, *656, 660,* 710, 711, 713, 716, 717, 720, 725, 727, *735, 739,* 753, 759, *764, 765*

Fisher, D., 634, *666*

Fisher, D. L., 349, *366*

Fisher, J. D., 188, 193, *215,* 622, 649, *660*

Fisher, W. A., 188, 193, *215,* 622, 649, *660*

Fiske, A. P., 695, *701*

Fiske, D., 565, *569*

Fiske, D. W., 30, *65,* 177, *212,* 499, *531*

Fiske, S. T., 154, *167,* 204, *215,* 280, 281, 289, 301, 306, *316, 320,* 335, *360,* 449, 460, 462, 464, 465, *483, 484,* 498, 519, 521, 522, *533, 537, 540,* 576, 595, 597, *608,* 635, *660,* 681, *701,* 721, 729, 731, 732, *736*

Fitzpatrick, A. R., 386, *391*

Flacks, R., 672, *704*

Flaste, R., 254, *266*

Flay, B. R., 193, 197, 198, *218,* 300, *315,* 635, 649, *658, 660*

Fleiss, J. L., 31, *74*

Fleming, M. A., 81, *123,* 497, 528, *538,* 595, 596, *608, 612,* 629, 635, *665*

Flesch, D., 197, *212*

Fletcher, G. J. O., 310, *319*

Fletcher, J., 100, *117*

Fletcher, J. F., 519, *530*

Flood, M. G., 191, *211*

Florack, A., 650, *660*

Flores, E. T., 600, *607*

Floyd, J., 345, *361*

Flugstad, A. R., 275, *321*

Flynn, L. R., 590, *608*

Folger, R., 265

Folsom, J. K., 22, *67*

Folwell, A. L., 720, *741*

Fonda, C. P., 48, 49, *67*

Fong, C., 562, *574*

Fong, G. T., 198, 204, *216, 217,* 310, *319*

Fong, G. W., 425, *430*

Ford, T. E., 339, *363*

Forehand, G. A., 42, *67*

Forgas, J. P., 13, *17,* 203, *215, 363,* 384, *391,* 452, 455, 461, *484,* 498, *533*
Förster, J., 61, *67,* 476, *486,* 516, *540*
Foss, M. A., 398, *428*
Fossum, T., 413, *427*
Foster, C. A., 398, *429*
Fowler, C., 198, *212*
Fowler, S. C., 59, *67*
Franc, R., 179, *215*
Frank, M. G., 632, *659*
Franks, J. J., 280, 290, *315*
Franzoi, S. L., 354, *363*
Fraser, S. C., 253, *266,* 586, 587, *608*
Frederiksen, N., 42, *71*
Fredricks, A. J., 201, *215*
Fredrickson, B. L., 420, 421, *429,* 753, *765*
Freedman, J. L., 231, 253, *266,* 586, 587, *608, 660,* 711, *740*
Freeman, L. C., 175, *215*
Frei, E., 405, *429*
French, J. R. P., 346, *365,* 758, *765*
French, J. R. P., Jr., 634, 635, *660,* 675, 680, 698, *701*
French, J. W., 594, *607*
Frenkel, Y., 524, *541*
Frenkel-Brunswik, E., 586, *604*
Freud, S., 333, *363*
Freund, T., 26, *70,* 179, *217,* 352, *364,* 509, *535*
Frey, D., 10, *17,* 231, *267,* 310, *321,* 376, *391,* 515, *533,* 711, 731, *736*
Freyd, J. J., 386, *391*
Fridlund, A. J., 59, *67*
Fried, C. B., 241, 242, 256, *265, 267,* 270
Friedman, H. S., 632, *658*
Friedman, R., 332, 337, *364,* 761, *766*
Friedrich, J., 639, *660*
Frier, B. M., 405, *429, 431*
Frijda, N., 439, *484*
Frijda, N. H., 400, 401, 402, 403, 404, 408, *429, 435*
Froming, W. J., 585, *608*
Fromkin, H. L., 578, 593, *613*
Fromm, E., 680, *701*
Frost, S., 476, *485*
Fruzzetti, A., 722, *737*
Fulero, S., 154, *171*
Fuller, B., 723, *733*
Fuller, S. R., 725, *736*
Funayama, E., 60, 62, *72*

G

Gabrieli, J. D. E., 426, *426*
Gaertner, G., 727, *737*
Gaertner, L., 603, *608*
Gaertner, S. L., 53, 54, 56, *66, 67,* 204, 206, 207, *213, 215,* 333, *363,* 544, 564, 565, *570, 571,* 718, *735,* 747, *765*
Gaes, G. G., 239, *267*
Gage, N. L., 42, *67*

Gagnon, A., 694, *701*
Galanter, E., 712, *738*
Galinsky, A. D., 239, 240, 262, *267,* 561, *571,* 627, *664*
Gallagher, D., 403, *428,* 639, *660*
Gallardo, I., 590, *605*
Galley, D. J., 450, *482*
Gallois, C., 199, 200, *216, 218*
Gamma, A., 405, *429, 430*
Gangestad, S., 179, *215*
Gannon, K. M., 35, *72*
Garcia, A. W., 196, *215*
Garcia, C., 403, *428*
Garcia, J., 447, 460, *484*
Garcia, M., 752, *765*
Garcia, M. T., 25, *67*
Garcia-Marques, T., 639, *660*
Gardner, C. W., 384, *394*
Gardner, W., *734*
Gardner, W. L., 34, 60, 61, *65, 66, 68,* 603, *610,* 748, *764*
Garnham, A., 275, *316*
Gary, M. L., 561, *573*
Garza, A. A., 501, *542*
Gasper, K., 306, *316,* 406, *429,* 439, 446, 452, 463, 465, 468, 472, *482, 484*
Gatenby, J., 60, 62, *72*
Gaudreau, D., 450, *487*
Gaunt, R., 335, *367*
Gawronski, B., 748, *764*
Gazzaniga, M. S., 442, *482*
Geen, T. R., 82, *118*
Geer, J. G., 34, *67*
Geerken, M. R., 42, *68*
Geers, A. L., 592, *608,* 621, 640, *660*
Geis, F. L., 207, *212,* 578, 595, *605, 606*
Geiselman, R. E., 39, *75*
Gelfand, M., 593, *614*
Gelfand, M. J., 593, *608*
Geller, P. A., 720, *736*
Gendolla, G. H. E., 621, *656*
Gentry, W. D., 144, *168*
Gerard, H. B., 12, *17,* 229, *267,* 355, 356, 357, *362,* 635, 636, *658, 660,* 672, 673, 674, *701, 702,* 724, *734,* 755, *765*
Gerbner, G., 300, *316*
Gerrard, M., 143, 161, *167,* 193, 201, 203, *215*
Gervais, R., 426, *432*
Ghahremani, D. G., 426, *426*
Gibbons, F., 161, *167*
Gibbons, F. X., 143, *167,* 193, 201, 203, *215,* 585, *608, 613*
Giddings, C. W., 722, *733*
Gifford, R., 199, *216,* 632, *666*
Gifford, R. K., 300, 301, *316,* 729, *736*
Gigerenzer, G., 149, *167*
Gigone, D., 725, *736*
Gilbert, D. T., 26, *67,* 243, 260, *268,* 293, 298, *316,* 387, 390, *391,* 477, *489,* 510, *533,* 563, *571,* 622, *660*
Gilligan, S. G., 453, 461, *482*
Gilljam, M., 47, *67*

Gillund, G., 303, *316*
Gilmore, J. B., 224, 232, 255, 259, *268*
Gilovich, T., 473, *483*
Giner-Sorolla, R., 25, *67,* 85, 89, 90, 101, 110, *118, 120,* 324, 330, 332, *362,* 377, 379, *391,* 397, *429,* 529, *533,* 641, 643, *658, 660,* 675, 682, 685, 695, *700*
Gips, C. J., 49, *69*
Gitta, M. Z., 598, *614*
Givon, M. M., 38, *67*
Glaser, D., 407, *434*
Glaser, J., 577, 586, *609,* 763, *766*
Glasman, L. R., 14, *16,* 115, *117,* 284, 313, *314,* 359, *360,* 583, *604,* 650, 651, *656, 660*
Glass, D., 235, *267*
Gleason, J. M., 309, *314*
Gleicher, F., 603, *614,* 648, *660*
Glenberg, A. M., 275, *316,* 478, *484*
Glendenning, K., 476, *485*
Glenn, N. O., 601, *608*
Glenn, S. B., 587, *611*
Gleser, G. C., 31, *66*
Glick, P., 595, *608*
Gliner, M. D., 90, 94, *117,* 688, 691, *699*
Glisson, C., 162, *167*
Glover, G., 426, *426*
Glucksberg, S., 48, *67,* 497, *536*
Godek, J., 81, *123,* 497, *538*
Godin, G., 183, 188, 192, 196, 201, *215, 220*
Goethals, G. R., 292, *316,* 688, *701, 736*
Goffman, E., 50, *67*
Gohm, C. L., 439, 446, 463, 465, 468, 472, *482, 484*
Gold, A. E., 405, *429*
Gold, R. S., 203, *215*
Goldberg, L., 160, *167,* 278, 284, 285, 295, *321,* 336, 353, *368*
Goldberg, M. E., 644, *660*
Goldman, R., 128, *170,* 510, *538,* 598, *612,* 643, *665*
Goldman, S. L., 416, *429*
Goldsmith, R. E., 42, *67,* 590, 603, *608*
Goldstein, D., 278, 303, *317*
Goleman, D., 475, *484*
Golisano, V., 462, 467, 471, *481*
Gollob, H. F., 288, *316*
Gollwitzer, P. M., 188, 190, 191, 203, *215, 363,* 464, *486,* 518, *537,* 596, *611,* 711, *733,* 759, *765*
Gonzales, B., 162, *168*
Gonzales, M. H., 85, 86, 90, 96, *121*
Gonzales, P. M., 210, *212*
Goodie, A. G., 602, *613*
Gorassini, D. R., 253, *267*
Gordijn, E., 687, 689, *701*
Gordijn, E. H., 692, *701*
Gordon, R. A., 52, *67*
Gordon, S. E., 280, 291, *316*
Gore, J. C., 60, 62, *72*
Gorman, T. F., 311, *321*
Gorn, G. J., 643, *660*
Górnik-Durose, M., 593, *606,* 696, *700*
Gorsuch, R. L., 200, *215,* 602, *614*

Gotlib, I. H., 402, *432*
Goto, S. G., *741*
Gottman, J. M., 720, *738*
Gouaux, C., 453, 461, *484*
Gove, W. R., 42, *68*
Govender, R., 25, *64,* 90, 91, 93, 94, 97, 108, 110, *117,* 186, *211,* 326, 332, *361,* 582, *605,* 642, *657,* 752, *764*
Grady, K., 638, *661*
Graesser, A. C., 280, 291, 293, *316*
Graf, P., 501, *535*
Grafton, S. T., 419, *429*
Graham, W. K., 38, *69*
Granberg, D., 47, *67,* 337, *363,* 374, 375, 380, 382, *391, 392,* 717, *734, 736*
Grant, H., 757, *764*
Grant, M. J., 108, *120*
Grant, N., 110, *121*
Gratton, G., 61, *67*
Graumann, C. F., 693, *701*
Gray, J. A., 402, 405, *429, 430*
Gray, N. S., 57, *68*
Gray, W. D., 413, *432*
Graziano, W. G., 515, *530,* 718, *738*
Greblo, P., 590, *611*
Green, B. F., 132, *168*
Green, B. L., 681, 690, *700*
Green, D., 251, *267*
Green, D. M., 500, *533*
Green, D. P., 416, *429*
Green, G. M., 293, *316*
Green, J. D., 97, *121,* 398, *429,* 682, *705*
Green, M. C., 42, 47, 49, *68, 70*
Green, P. E., 39, *68*
Green, P. J., 406, *428*
Green, S. B., 38, 39, *70*
Greenberg, J., 51, *68,* 236, 237, 238, 239, 241, 256, 260, 262, *267, 269, 270,* 309, *319,* 516, *534, 539,* 576, *613,* 632, *661*
Greenberg, M. A., 415, *430*
Greene, D., 11, *18,* 143, 165, *169, 170,* 254, *268,* 358, *366,* 511, *535*
Greene, L. S., 406, *429*
Greenspoon, J., 710, 727, *736*
Greenwald, A. G., 12, 14, *17,* 25, 26, 56, 57, 58, *68, 72,* 80, 86, 98, 105, *120, 122,* 161, *168,* 206, *215,* 224, 225, 251, *267,* 296, *316,* 338, *363,* 371, 377, *392, 394,* 445, 450, *484, 485,* 502, 509, 511, 513, 518, 523, 524, *533, 535, 538,* 544, 549, 550, 559, 562, 564, 566, *570, 571, 572,* 582, 586, 599, *608,* 623, 630, 631, 635, 650, *660, 665, 666,* 710, 713, *736,* 747, 748, *765*
Greenwald, M. K., 402, 415, 419, *427, 430*
Greenwell, M. T., 46, *71*
Greenwood, J. D., 693, *701*
Gregg, A., 80, *124*
Gregoire, M., 426, *432*
Gregory, S. W., 635, *660*
Greiling, H., 575, *605*

Gresham, L. G., 507, *533*
Grewal, D., 651, *660*
Grice, H. P., 293, *316*, 677, *701*
Griffin, D., 636, *657, 660*, 686, *700, 701*, 719, *736*
Griffin, D. W., 84, 85, 89, 95, 98, *124*, 331, *367*, 586, *614*, 642, *667*, 723, *739*
Griffitt, W., 453, 461, *484*
Griffitt, W. B., 507, *533*
Grigorenko, E. L., 601, *614*
Grigoriadis, S., 344, *367*
Grill, H. J., 423, 424, *429*
Grob, A., 405, 415, *433*
Grohskopf, E., 681, *704*
Groom, C., 748, *764*
Gross, J. J., 402, *432*
Gross, L., 300, *316*
Gross, S. R., 94, 95, 97, 98, *120*, 586, *608*
Grossman, A. H., 189, *216*
Grossman, R. P., 408, *429*
Groswasser, Z., 524, *541*
Group, P. R. S., 198, *214*
Groves, R. M., 39, *68*
Gruber, K. L., 376, *394*, 515, *540*, 711, 717, *741*
Gruder, C. L., 300, *315*, 635, 650, *657, 660*
Gruenfeld, D. H., 284, 294, *316, 322*
Grunfeld, R., 730, *741*
Gschneidinger, E., 454, *488*
Guadagno, R. E., 587, *608*
Guialamo-Ramos, V., 126, 131, 150, 162, *168*
Guilford, J. P., 176, *215*
Guimond, S., 672, *702*
Guinn, J. S., 682, *705*
Guisinger, S., 576, *608*
Gunnthorsdottir, A., 595, *608*
Guterbock, T. M., 52, *67*
Guthrie, C. A., 196, 199, 201, *219*

H

Ha, Y., 44, *69*
Haberkorn, G., 636, *663*
Hacker, A., 204, *215*
Haddock, G., 100, *122*, 128, *168*, 323, *363*, 470, *485*, 519, *533*, 583, *609*, 641, 646, *660, 661, 664*
Hadley, J. M., 49, *69*
Haemmerlie, F. M., 253, 267
Hafer, C. L., 644, *660*
Hagger, M. S., 196, 197, *215*
Haidt, J., 457, *484*
Haier, R. J., 458, *482*
Hains, S. C., 724, *736*
Hakala, P., 406, *432*
Halamaj, J., 635, *660*
Halberstadt, J., 407, *432*
Hale, J. L., 648, *660*
Hall, V. C., 254, *270*
Halpern, J. N., 406, *428*
Hamann, S., 150, *170*, 425, *429*

Hamann, S. B., 419, 425, *429*
Hamilton, D. L., 62, *74*, 90, 96, *117*, 289, 300, 301, *316*, 343, *363*, 464, *484*, 729, *736*
Hamm, A. O., 402, 415, *430*
Hammond, K. R., 176, *215*, 453, *481*, 523, 524, *533*, 747, 765
Han, S., 593, 598, *608, 613*
Hanamann, W. M., 47, 49, *70*
Handley, I. M., 592, *608*, 640, *660*
Handlin, A., 163, *169*
Haney, B., 102, *121*
Hanley, C., 42, *68*
Hannula-Bral, K. A., 678, *700*
Hansen, J. M., 39, *73*
Hansen, W. B., 51, *67*
Harary, F., 85, *118*, 288, *315*
Hardee, B. B., 204, *217*, 595, *611*
Hardesty, D., 590, *605*
Hardin, C., 445, 448, *486, 488*
Hardin, C. D., 561, 563, *572*, 674, 678, *702*
Harding, C., 731, *736*
Harkins, S. G., 374, *393*, 512, *534*, 579, *606*, 635, 636, 644, *660, 661, 665, 668*
Harkins, S. J., 506, 514, *538*
Harman, H. H., 594, *607*
Harman, J. L., 655, *661*
Harmon-Jones, C., 246, 247, 256, 262, *267*, 516, *534*
Harmon-Jones, E., 210, *213*, 236, 237, 239, 240, 242, 246, 247, 256, 261, 262, *267*, 451, 452, 471, 475, *481, 484*, 509, 516, *534*, 565, *570*, 632, *661*, 684, 685, *702*
Harnish, R. J., 597, *607*
Harris, B., 442, *484*
Harris, J., 160, *169*, 593, *610*
Harris, K., 721, *740*
Harrison, A. A., 450, *484*, 556, *571*
Harrison, D. A., 200, 201, *215*
Hart, A. J., 60, *68*
Hart, W., 721, *736*
Harter, S., 53, *71*
Hartman, D. A., 618, *656*
Hartmann, G. W., 710, 715, *742*
Hartmann, K., 418, 419, *433*
Hartwick, J., 188, 196, 201, *219*, 282, 283, 284, 286, 294, 295, 298, 300, *322*
Harvey, O. J., 306, *316*, 621, *661*
Hasher, L., 278, 303, *317*
Haslam, S. A., 683, 694, *702, 704*
Hass, G., 345, *363*
Hass, R. G., 333, *364*, 595, 596, *609*, 638, *661*, 676, *702*
Hastie, R., 304, 305, *317, 318, 319*, 372, 383, 385, *392*, 498, 522, 523, *534*, 583, *608*, 713, 714, 715, 725, *736*
Hastorf, A. H., 373, 377, 378, 389, *392*
Hatfield, E., 719, *736*
Haugtvedt, C., 578, 581, *612*
Haugtvedt, C. P., 94, *122*, 382, *393*, 513, 517, 519, 522, 523, *534, 538*, 581, 582, *608, 613*, 624, 650, *661*, 665

Hausenblas, H. A., 188, *215*
Hawilo, M. E., 407, *434*
Hawkins, C., 513, *538,* 582, *612*
Hawkins, S. A., 305, *317*
Hazan, C., 719, *741*
Hazelwood, J. D., 526, *531,* 634, *658,* 678, *700*
Heath, Y., 199, *216*
Heaton, A. W., *363*
Hebl, M. R., 677, *706*
Hedderley, D., 109, *123, 219*
Hedges, S. M., 415, *434*
Heesacker, M., 594, *608,* 634, 640, 643, *661, 665*
Heider, F., 11, *17,* 85, *120,* 226, 247, *267,* 287, 306, 311, *317,* 370, 383, *392,* 446, *484,* 510, 515, 528, *534,* 549, *571,* 586, *608,* 682, *702,* 710, 711, 714, *736*
Heier, H., 584, 599, *607*
Heilman, K. M., 402, *430*
Heine, S. H., 590, *608*
Heine, S. J., 248, *267,* 309, *317,* 633, *661*
Heise, D., 147, *168,* 412, 414, *431*
Heise, D. R., 478, *484*
Helic, A., 40, *72*
Hell, D., 405, *429*
Helmstetter, F. J., 425, *428*
Hemenover, S. H., 406, 417, *429*
Hemsley, D. R., 405, *430*
Hendersen, R., 459, *484*
Hendrickx, H., 558, *570*
Hennessy, M., 198, 210, *214, 217, 221*
Hennigan, K. M., 300, *315,* 635, *660*
Henninger, M., 285, *317*
Herbener, E. S., 720, *734*
Herbst, K. C., 603, *608*
Herek, G. M., 210, *216,* 680, *702*
Hergovich, A., 594, *609*
Herman, C. P., 332, *363,* 675, 676, *700*
Hermans, D., 25, *66,* 343, *363,* 407, 408, 410, *429,* 441, 445, *484,* 583, *609*
Hermsen, S., 560, *571*
Herr, P. M., 253, *266,* 528, *534,* 547, *571*
Herskovits, E. L., 693, *702*
Hertzman, M., 578, 594, *615*
Hervitz, E. F., 304, *320*
Herzog, T. R., 450, *484*
Heslin, R., 592, *613*
Hess, E. H., 59, *68,* 747, *765*
Hess, T. G., 602, *605*
Heuer, F., 419, *432*
Hewitt, E. C., 598, *614*
Hewstone, E. M., 729, *736*
Hewstone, M., 161, *169,* 354, *363, 365,* 627, 653, *663,* 682, *705*
Heyman, R. E., 723, *742*
Higgins, E. T., 5, *17,* 61, *67,* 234, 261, *267,* 271, 274, 281, 283, 293, 294, 300, 312, 313, *317,* 326, 339, 345, 346, 356, 357, 359, *363, 364,* 471, *484,* 519, 520, *534,* 555, 559, *571,* 582, 586, 603, *609, 610, 614,* 633, *668,* 674, 678, *702,* 712, 714, 731, *736,* 757, *764*

Hildum, D. C., 13, *17,* 508, *534*
Hill, A. J., 450, *487*
Hill, K. C., 720, *741*
Hill, K. T., 648, *664*
Hills, M., 380, 381, *390*
Hilton, D. J., 689, *701*
Hilton, J. L., 57, *69,* 206, 207, *216,* 561, 564, 569, *571*
Himelstein, P., 175, 178, 181, *216*
Himmelfarb, S., *17,* 51, 59, *68,* 744, *765*
Hinsz, V. B., 687, *702*
Hintzman, D. L., 278, 279, *317*
Hippler, H. J., 45, 49, *65, 68, 73,* 154, *170*
Hirt, E. R., 373, 374, *393*
Hitch, G. J., 45, *64*
Hittner, J. B., 143, *170*
Hixon, G., 563, *571*
Hmel, B. A., 593, *609*
Hnat, S. M., 602, *605*
Ho, K., 456, 461, *486*
Ho, R. M., 651, 652, *656*
Hobbes, T., 680, *702*
Hobfoll, S. E., 720, *736*
Hoch, S. J., 376, *392*
Hochbaum, G. M., 635, *661*
Hock, M., 415, *428*
Hodges, S. D., 12, *19,* 25, *75,* 80, 88, 90, 91, 92, 93, 94, 95, 96, 97, 108, 110, *119, 124,* 128, *171,* 325, 326, *362,* 388, *390, 392, 395,* 496, 514, *534, 542,* 746, *767*
Hodgkins, S., 190, 191, *218*
Hodun, A., 286, *314*
Hoffman, E. L., 679, *705*
Hoffman, J. M., 425, *429*
Hoffman, K., 634, *666*
Hoffman, M. L., 401, *429*
Hoffman, P. J., 42, *68,* 295, 296, *321*
Hoffman, S., 595, *610, 666,* 679, *705*
Hoffmann, J. P., 162, *168*
Hofstede, G., 695, *702*
Hogg, M. A., 243, *269,* 354, *363,* 652, *667,* 673, 682, 693, 694, 698, 699, *702, 706,* 724, 725, *736*
Holbrook, A. L., 34, 42, 47, 49, *68, 70,* 583, *605*
Holbrook, T. M., 374, 375, 381, *391*
Holland, R. W., 236, 264, *267*
Hollander, E. P., 49, *73*
Holmberg, S., 374, *392*
Holmes, C., 46, *68*
Holmes, J. G., 306, 311, *317,* 674, *699,* 723, *739*
Holmvall, C. M., *166*
Holt, D., 40, *69*
Holt, L. E., 285, *317, 321,* 638, 650, *668*
Holtz, R., 94, 95, 97, 98, *120,* 586, *608*
Holtzworth-Munroe, A., 722, *737*
Homans, G. C., 680, *702*
Hommer, D., 425, *430*
Hong, Y., 578, 589, 602, *607, 609*
Hood, R., 585, *613*
Hood, W. R., 679, *702*
Hooker, K. A., 584, *607*

Horcajo, J., 581, 590, *605, 612*
Hornak, J., 425, *431*
Hornik, R., 188, 198, *214, 216*
Horton, K. D., 501, *541*
Hosch, H. M., 154, *168*
Hoshino-Browne, E., 249, *267,* 633, *661*
Houde, S. J. R. J., 521, *540*
Hough, K. S., 51, *68*
House, P., 11, *18,* 143, *170,* 358, *366*
Houston, D., 716, *739*
Houston, D. A., 90, 94, 99, 100, 101, 116, *120,* 377, 378, 381, *392,* 517, 519, 520, *534*
Houston, M. J., 49, *68*
Hovland, C. I., 4, 10, 13, *17, 18,* 21, 45, *68, 74,* 79, 82, *123,* 175, 177, *216, 218,* 224, 229, *267,* 297, 300, *317,* 344, *363,* 370, 385, *394,* 470, *484,* 494, 518, 520, *534, 539,* 600, *609,* 619, 620, 621, 623, 640, 646, 648, 653, *661, 667,* 693, *702,* 743, 744, *765, 766*
Howard, A., 61, *66,* 206, 207, *213,* 544, 565, *570,* 596, *607,* 652, *659*
Howard, D. J., 512, *530*
Howe, S., 592, *607*
Hoxworth, T., 198, *214*
Hoyle, R. H., 577, *609*
Hoyt, D. R., 719, *742*
Hoyt, W. T., 154, *168*
Hsee, C. K., 389, *392,* 456, 461, *485*
Hubbard, M., 304, *319*
Huddy, L., 210, *216*
Hudson, R., 406, *427*
Huff, J. W., 106, *121*
Hugenberg, K., 748, *764*
Hui, C. H., 578, 593, *614*
Hulbert, J., 39, *70*
Hull, C. L., 620, *661*
Hume, D., *733*
Hummer, M., 592, *607*
Hummert, M. L., 719, *737*
Humphreys, M. S., 551, *574*
Hunt, D., 306, *316*
Hunt, E. B., 495, *532*
Hunt, R. R., 528, *534*
Hunt, W. A., 144, *168*
Hunter, G. L., 593, *614*
Hunter, P. G., 417, *429*
Huntsinger, J., 448, *488*
Hurd, A. W., 34, *68*
Hurst, A. P., 720, *741*
Hurwitz, S. D., 635, *661*
Husain, G., 405, *429*
Huskinson, T. L. H., 470, *485,* 583, *609,* 641, *660, 661*
Huston, T. L., 345, *363*
Hutchinson, J. W., 300, *318*
Hutchinson, K. J., 683, *704*
Hutson-Comeaux, S., 373, 382, 383, *391,* 521, *532,* 715, *735, 757, 765*
Hutto, D. B., 595, *606*
Hutton, D. G., 585, 590, *605, 609*
Hyman, D. B., 381, 385, 386, 387, 388, *395*

Hyman, H., 39, 40, *74*
Hyman, H. H., 546, *571*
Hymes, C., 93, *117,* 186, *212,* 525, *530,* 544, *569*
Hymovitch, B., 636, *660*

I

Iatesta, M., 198, *214*
Idson, L. C., 61, *67*
Incheol, C., 696, *704*
Infante, D. A., 578, 589, *609*
Ingham, R., 203, *216*
Inman, M., 648, *657*
Insko, C. A., 13, *17,* 285, *316,* 374, *391,* 505, 508, 516, 520, 522, *530, 531, 532, 534,* 603, *608,* 623, 636, 640, *657, 661, 666,* 710, 727, *727, 737, 740*
Iran-Nejad, A., 416, 417, 418, *428*
Irwin, W., 422, *428,* 476, *483*
Isard, E. S., 42, *68*
Isbell, L., 406, *429,* 439, 446, 452, 455, 458, 461, 463, 465, 468, 472, *482, 485, 487, 489,* 719, 721, 722, 728, *737, 739*
Isbell, L. M., 276, 305, *321,* 455, 463, 465, *485,* 517, *537*
Isen, A. 1987, 466, 467, *485*
Isen, A. M., 453, 461, *485,* 718, *735*
Isenberg, D. J., 592, *609,* 687, 688, *702*
Israel, G. D., 45, *68*
Israel, J., 693, *702*
Issanchou, S., 416, *434*
Ito, K., 628, *661*
Ito, T. A., 60, *75,* 410, 415, *429*
Iyengar, S., 716, *737*
Izard, C. E., 49, *73,* 402, 412, *429*

J

Jaccard, J. J., 126, 131, 137, 141, 150, 151, 158, 162, 165, *167, 168,* 183, 210, *212, 214,* 295, *317,* 548, *570*
Jackman, M. R., *68*
Jacks, J. Z., 638, *661*
Jackson, D. C., 476, *483*
Jackson, D. N., 42, *68, 75*
Jackson, J. R., 27, *67,* 93, *119,* 161, *167,* 206, 207, *214,* 524, 525, *532,* 547, 564, *570,* 717, 728, 730, *735*
Jacobs, W. J., 459, *485*
Jacobsohn, L., 188, *216*
Jacobson, J. A., 584, *615*
Jacobson, N. S., 722, *737*
Jacoby, J., 38, 39, 40, *68, 71*
Jacoby, L. L., 303, *317,* 451, *485,* 499, 500, 501, 509, *534, 535, 536, 540*
Jaffee, S., 517, *530*
Jajodia, A., 58, *69*
Jako, R. A., 376, *393*

James, R., 109, *118*
James, W., 401, *429,* 458, *485,* 576, *609,* 678, *702*
Jamieson, D. W., 51, *73,* 84, *120,* 179, *216*
Jamieson, K., 163, *167*
Jamner, M. S., 200, *212, 216*
Janda, L. H., 446, *487*
Jang, K. L., 160, *169,* 334, *366*
Janis, I., 344, 346, *363*
Janis, I. L., 4, 11, 13, *17,* 21, *68,* 175, *216,* 224, 225,
    229, 232, 255, 259, *266, 267, 268, 363,* 469, 470,
    471, *484, 485,* 494, 513, 514, 520, *534, 535, 536,*
    586, 591, 600, *609,* 620, 623, 646, 648, *661,* 693,
    702, 725, 726, *737,* 744, 753, 761, *765, 766*
Janiszewski, C., 450, *485*
Jarvis, B. G., 582, *612*
Jarvis, W. B. G., 14, *16, 17,* 508, *537,* 578, 581, 583,
    602, *606, 609, 612,* 644, *657*
Jasechko, J., 303, *317,* 509, *534*
Jaspars, J. M., 693, *702*
Javalgi, R. G., *609*
Jemmott, J. B. I., 198, *216, 219*
Jemmott, L. S., 198, *216*
Jenike, M. A., 399, *435*
Jenkins, G. D., 38, *69*
Jepson, C., 11, *18*
Jessor, R., 130, *167*
Jetten, J., 561, 562, *572, 737*
Jiang, T., 407, *434*
Jo, E., 517, *530*
Johannesen-Schmidt, M., 161, *167*
Johanson, G. A., 49, *69*
Johar, G. V., 110, *123,* 470, *488,* 628, 633, 648, *661, 667*
John, O. P., 59, *72*
Johnson, B., 61, *66,* 206, 207, *213,* 544, 565, *570,* 596,
    607, 652, *659*
Johnson, B. T., 58, 62, *70,* 144, 145, *165,* 188, 196, 201,
    204, 206, 207, *211, 213,* 344, 349, 353, 355, *363,*
    370, 374, 375, 379, 382, 388, *392,* 512, 513, *535,*
    545, *572,* 619, 620, 621, 622, 623, 635, 638, 639,
    643, 644, 650, 655, *656, 661, 662, 667,* 675, *702,*
    747, 755, *765, 766*
Johnson, C., 61, *66,* 206, 207, *213,* 544, 565, *570,* 596,
    607, 652, *659*
Johnson, D. J., 229, *268*
Johnson, D. M., 413, *432*
Johnson, D. W., 724, *737*
Johnson, E. J., 203, *216,* 305, *317*
Johnson, F., 724, *737*
Johnson, H. H., 650, *662*
Johnson, J. D., 46, *69*
Johnson, J. T., 711, 715, *737*
Johnson, K. W., 600, *607*
Johnson, M., 478, *485*
Johnson, M. K., 500, *532*
Johnson, M. P., 178, *219*
Johnson, R. T., 724, *737*
Johnson, R. W., 632, *662*
Johnson-Laird, P. N., 404, 412, *431,* 495, *532*
Johnston, M., 196, *218*
Johnston, S., 309, *314*

Johnstone, 404, *433*
Johnstone, T., 553, *573*
Jonas, K., 95, 98, 109, 110, *120,* 326, 331, 332, *364,*
    642, *662*
Jones, C. R., 559, *571,* 712, 714, 731, *736*
Jones, D. M., 405, 415, *431*
Jones, E. E., 91, 96, *121,* 176, *216,* 233, 239, 247, 257,
    259, *268,* 289, *317,* 494, *535,* 673, *702,* 711, 715,
    737
Jones, R. A., 251, *268*
Jones, S. C. 1973, 235, *268*
Jones, S. K., 388, *392*
Jordan, N., 510, *535*
Jordens, K., *170,* 248, *271,* 471, *488, 541*
Josephs, R. A., 204, *219*
Jost, J. T., 360, *364,* 516, *535,* 577, 586, *609,* 763, *766*
Joubert, S., 425, 426, *430*
Joule, R. V., 245, 246, 256, 258, 262, *265,* 516, *530*
Judd, C. M., 10, *17,* 23, 25, 26, 27, 28, 31, 55, 56, 62,
    69, 75, 80, 84, 85, 86, 90, 91, 92, 93, 94, 96, 97, 98,
    117, 118, 120, 206, 220, 399, *435,* 514, *535,* 556,
    562, *574,* 621, *662,* 688, 691, *699,* 711, 715, *737*
Judice, T. N., 584, *611*
Judkins, D., 188, *216*
Jurkowitsch, A., 27, *75*
Jussim, L., 154, *168*
Jussim, L. J., 443, *485,* 528, *535,* 558, *571,* 710, 728,
    738

K

Kahn, D. F., 49, *69*
Kahn, S., 721, *740*
Kahneman, D., 11, *19,* 290, 296, 298, 304, *317, 321,*
    416, 420, 421, *427, 429, 430, 434,* 519, *535, 540,*
    567, *571,* 591, *609,* 622, *668,* 691, *702, 737, 741,*
    753, *765*
Kaiser, C. F., 143, *170*
Kalakanis, L., 407, *432*
Kalin, N. H., 408, *431, 476, 483*
Kalle, R. J., 239, *267*
Kallgren, C. A., 92, 101, 104, 109, 115, *120, 124,* 370,
    395, 510, *542,* 639, 643, *668,* 677, *700*
Kalton, G., 40, 46, *69*
Kamb, M., 198, *214*
Kameda, T., 725, *737*
Kamenetzky, J., 346, *367*
Kanekar, S., 681, *705*
Kanfer, F. H., 193, *214*
Kanouse, D. E., *75*
Kao, C. F., 14, *16,* 518, *531*
Kao, C. G., 581, *606*
Kaplan, K. J., 84, 97, *120,* 327, 331, 332, *364,* 586, *609*
Kaplan, M. F., 13, *17,* 688, *702*
Kaplan, R., 450, *484*
Kaplan, S., 450, *484*
Karabecnick, S. A., 347, *364*
Karabenick, S. A., 53, *64*
Karama, S., 425, 426, *430*

Kardes, F. R., 24, 25, 55, *67*, 81, 91, 93, 94, 108, *119*, 185, *214*, 474, *483*, 512, *535*, 544, 547, 565, *571*, 583, *607*, 642, 643, *659*, *666*, 752, *765*
Karis, D., 61, *67*
Karney, B. R., 722, *737*
Karp, L., 453, 461, *485*
Karp, S., 594, *615*
Karpinski, A., 57, *69*, 206, 207, *216*, 561, 564, 569, *571*
Kasch, K. L., 402, *432*
Kashima, Y., 199, 200, *216*, *218*, 494, *535*
Kashy, D. A., 31, 50, *66*, *69*, 719, *737*, 760, *767*
Kaspryzk, D., 204, *220*
Kassin, S., 154, *168*
Kassin, S. M., 582, *609*
Katkin, E. S., 403, *431*
Katz, D., 4, 5, *17*, 79, 82, *120*, 177, *216*, 276, *317*, 324, 338, 360, *364*, 627, 629, 642, 643, 646, 651, *662*, *666*, 678, 680, 682, *702*, 710, 711, 723, *737*, *740*, 743, 754, 756, *766*
Katz, I., 333, *364*, 595, 596, *609*
Katz, Y., 373, 374, 380, *390*
Kavanoor, S., 651, *660*
Kawakami, K., 54, 61, *66*, 206, 207, *213*, *216*, 544, 560, 564, 565, *570*, *571*, 596, *607*, 652, *659*
Keator, D., 458, *482*
Kehr, H. M., 600, *609*
Keillor, J. M., 402, *430*
Keir, R., 447, *486*
Keisler, C., 558, *571*
Keith, B. R., 143, *169*
Keller, R. T., 726, *737*
Kellerman, J., 253, *268*
Kelley, C. M., 303, *317*, 451, *485*, 509, *534*
Kelley, H. H., 4, 11, 13, *17*, 175, *216*, 224, 229, 250, *267*, *268*, 323, 335, 344, *363*, *364*, 470, *484*, 494, 520, *534*, *535*, 620, 636, 646, 648, *660*, *661*, 673, 680, 693, *702*, *706*, *737*, 744, *765*
Kelley, J. J., 21, *68*
Kelley, S., 713, 716, *737*
Kellogg, C. E., 416, 418, *430*
Kelly, G. A., 452, *485*
Kelly, R. J., 632, *662*
Kelman, H. C., 11, *17*, 82, *120*, 176, *216*, 224, 225, 235, 236, 245, 264, *268*, 355, 356, *364*, 629, 634, 635, *662*, 675, 680, 698, *702*, 758, *766*
Kelsey, R. M., 642, *657*
Keltner, D., 452, 459, *485*, 710, *738*
Kemmelmeier, M., 593, *609*, *611*, 695, 696, *704*
Kemper, S., 719, *737*
Kendzierski, D., 107, *123*, 179, 180, *219*, 597, *609*
Keniston, K., 42, *66*
Kennedy-Moore, E., 415, *430*
Kenny, D. A., 31, *69*, 147, *168*, 621, *662*, 719, *737*
Kenrick, D. T., 668
Kerekes, A. R. Z., 494, *535*
Kerker, R. M., 294, *321*
Kerlinger, F. N., 10, *17*
Kernahan, C., 723, *733*

Kerner, M. S., 189, *216*
Kerr, N., 637, *662*
Kerr, N. L., 239, *270*, 692, *703*
Kessler, J. W., 718, *741*
Kessler, T., *737*
Ketelaar, T., 461, *485*
Khan, S. R., 501, *535*
Kibler, J., *435*
Kidder, L. H., 176, 207, *216*, 524, *535*
Kiesler, C. A., 191, 198, *216*, 232, 251, 253, *268*, 407, *435*, 443, *489*, 508, *542*
Kiesler, S. B., 510, *535*, 628, *662*
Kiewlet, R. D., *737*
Killeya, L. A., 370, 379, 388, *392*, 512, 513, *535*, 619, 622, 623, 639, 644, 650, *662*
Kilts, C. D., 419, 425, *429*
Kim, B., 285, *318*
Kim, B. J., 696, *704*
Kim, H. S., 59, 60, *65*
Kim, J. L., 84, *124*
Kim-Prieto, C., 697, *700*
Kinder, D. R., 26, 39, *69*, *73*, 333, 335, *360*, *364*, 545, *571*, 716, 717, 721, *732*, *737*, 738
Kindt, M., 399, *435*
King, A. C., 196, *215*
King, B. T., 11, *17*, 224, *268*, 513, 514, *535*, 586, *609*, 623, *661*, 761, *766*
King, G. A., 519, *534*, 559, *571*
King, G. W., 131, *168*, 295, *317*
Kinney, T. A., 602, *607*
Kipnis, D., 253, *269*
Kirby, L. D., 399, *434*
Kirsch, I., 384, *392*
Kirsch, K., 253, *270*
Kirsch, M. P., 376, *392*
Kirscht, J. P., 144, *170*
Kirsner, K., 501, *532*
Kirson, D., 412, 413, *434*
Kirzner, E., 49, *66*
Kitayama, S., 248, 249, *268*, 590, 592, 593, *608*, *609*, *610*, 695, 696, *701*, *703*
Klaaren, K . J., 128, *171*
Klare, G. R., 49, *69*
Klauer, K., 474, *485*, 752, *766*
Klauer, K. C., 25, 56, 57, 62, 64, *69*, *71*
Klayman, J., 44, *69*
Klein, C., 584, *609*
Klein, C. T. F., 651, 652, *656*
Klein, D. J., 422, *427*, 512, *541*
Klein, M., 143, *169*
Klein, W. M., 153, *168*, *169*
Kleinhesselink, R. R., 515, *535*
Kleinke, C. L., 402, *430*
Klem, A., 584, *610*
Kline, R. B., 31, *69*
Kline, S. L., 179, *216*
Klinger, M. R., 25, 26, *68*, 450, *485*, 509, *535*
Klockars, A. J., 41, *69*

Klohnen, E. C., 719, *737*
Klonoff, E. A., 204, *217*
Klopfer, F. J., 48, *69*
Klumb, P. L., 418, *430*
Klumpp, G., 299, *319*
Klüver, H., 424, *430*
Kmett, C. M., 388, *392*
Knepprath, E., 100, *120*
Knetsch, J., 591, *609*
Knight, D. C., 425, *428*
Knippenberg, A. V., 621, *659*
Knobloch, S., 405, *430*
Knocks, I., 650, *660*
Knower, F. H., 619, *662*
Knurek, K. A., 508, *530*
Knutson, B., 425, *430*
Kobayakawa, T., 406, *427*
Koelling, R. A., 447, 460, *484*
Koenig, K., 672, *704*
Koenig, O., 426, *432*
Koestner, R., 599, 600, *610*
Kohlberg, L., 457, *485*
Kohlmann, C., 415, *428*
Kok, G., 188, 196, *215*, 648, *666*
Kokkinaki, F., 108, *120, 186, 216*
Komatsu, S., 501, *535*
Kommana, S., 143, *167*
Komorita, S. S., 38, *69*
Koole, S. L., 544, *571*
Koomen, W., 621, *659, 667*
Kopp, R. J., 47, 49, *70*
Koriat, A., 44, *69*
Kortenkamp. S., 402, *430*
Koskenvuo, M., 406, *432*
Köster, E. P., 416, *434*
Kothandapani, V., 82, *120,* 177, 183, *216*
Kowalski, R., 681, *703*
Kozar, R., 727, *737, 740*
Kozlowski, L. T., 675, 676, *700*
Kozlowski, S. W., 376, *392*
Kraft, D., 12, *19,* 83, 106, 108, 109, *124,* 325, 327, *368,* 386, 388, 389, 390, *395,* 514, *541*
Kraft, P., 201, *214*
Kramer, G. P., 462, 463, 465, *481,* 710, *733*
Krantz, D. H., 11, *18,* 28, *70*
Krantz, S. E., 203, *215,* 384, *391,* 452, *484*
Kraus, S. J., 105, *120,* 183, *216*
Krech, D., 177, *217,* 276, *317,* 324, *364*
Kringelbach, M. L., 425, *431*
Krohne, H. W., 415, *428*
Krosnick, J. A., 25, 34, 35, 37, 38, 40, 41, 42, 43, 44, 45, 46, 47, 48, 49, 50, 63, *64, 66, 68, 69, 70, 71, 72, 73, 75,* 80, 83, 85, 86, 88, 89, 90, 91, 92, 93, 94, 95, 96, 97, 98, 105, 106, 110, 115, *117, 120, 121, 122, 124,* 179, 185, *217, 218,* 284, *317, 366,* 373, 375, 381, 382, *390, 392, 393, 395,* 443, *485,* 494, 513, 518, 528, *535, 538, 541,* 545, 547, 558, *569, 571,* 583, 586, 601, *605, 612, 615,* 621, 642, *662, 668,* 710, 713, 716, 717, 728, *737, 738*

Krowitz, A., 407, *427*
Krueger, E. T., 126, *169*
Krueger, J., 677, *703*
Kruglanski, A. W., 14, *18, 19,* 26, *70,* 98, *121,* 179, *217,* 286, 306, 308, 309, *317, 321,* 323, 327, 331, 332, 334, 336, 337, 339, 351, 352, 355, 356, 357, 359, 360, *362, 363, 364, 366, 368,* 372, 378, *392,* 498, 503, 505, 509, 516, 526, *531, 535, 538,* 576, 577, 578, 579, 582, 583, 584, 586, *609, 610, 612, 615,* 622, 624, 626, 628, 629, 634, 644, *662, 665, 667,* 688, *703,* 755, 761, 762, 763, *766, 767*
Krull, D. S., 293, *316*
Krysan, M., 204, *219*
Kudo, M., 476, *485*
Kuebler, A., 557, *574*
Kühnen, U., 517, *539*
Kuipers, P., 404, *429*
Kuklinski, J., 302, *318,* 721, *740*
Kulesa, P., 370, 373, 382, 383, 385, 387, *391,* 521, *532,* 711, 715, *735, 757, 765*
Kulik, J. A., 10, *17*
Kumar, A. P., 522, *534*
Kumar, P. Q., 715, *736*
Kumari, V., 405, *430*
Kumkale, G. T., 115, *117,* 250, *264,* 306, *314,* 351, *360,* 406, *426,* 468, 469, 471, *481,* 518, *535,* 626, 630, 631, 635, 650, 651, 652, *656, 662,* 722, *732*
Kuncel, R. B., 36, *70*
Kunda, Z., 11, *18,* 99, *121,* 306, 307, 308, 310, 312, *317, 319, 320,* 335, 345, 355, 356, *364,* 377, *392,* 563, 568, *572, 573,* 590, *610,* 627, *662,* 755, 756, *766*
Kunst-Wilson, W., 450, 460, *485*
Kunst-Wilson, W. R., 24, *70,* 509, *535,* 556, *572*
Kutner, B., 176, *217*
Kwan, J., *664*
Kwavnick, K. D., 375, *394*

L

Lafay, M. R., 210, *216*
LaFleur, S. J., 128, *171*
Lage, E., *664*
Laird, J. D., 25, *70,* 253, 259, *266, 268,* 594, *610*
Lakoff, G., 478, *485*
Lambert, A. J., 294, *321,* 501, *535*
Lamm, H., 688, *704*
Lampron, S. F., 621, *662*
Lancaster, D. W., 446, *487*
Lance, C. E., 376, *392, 394*
Landrine, H., 204, *217*
Lane, D. J., 161, *167*
Lane, J. D., 405, *435*
Lane, M., 39, *75*
Lang, P. J., 60, *65, 66, 70,* 402, 410, 415, 419, *427, 429, 430*
Langer, A., 407, *427*
Langer, E. J., 206, *217,* 731, *738*
Langleben-Cohen, D., 524, *541*

Langlois, J. H., 407, *432*
Lanning, L., 584, *607*
Lanzetta, J. T., 60, *71*
LaPiere, R. T., 10, *18,* 174, 175, 176, 178, 189, *217,* 651, *662, 738*
LaPointe, J. A., 376, *392*
Larkins, A. G., 42, *70*
Larsen, J. T., 414, 417, 418, *430*
Larsen, K. S., 595, *610*
Larsen, R. J., *430*
Laska, M., 406, *427*
Lassiter, G. D., 582, *610,* 621, 632, *658, 660*
Lasswell, H. D., 619, *662*
Latané, B., 636, *662,* 690, 691, *703,* 759, *766*
Laulhere, T. M., 420, *430*
Laurenceau, J.-P., 719, *738*
Lautrup, C., 161, *167*
Lavenne, F., 426, *432*
Lavine, H., 85, 86, 90, 91, 95, 96, 100, 101, 102, 104, 106, *121,* 335, 340, *365,* 381, 382, *392, 395,* 418, *430,* 597, *610,* 691, *703,* 757, *766*
Lavoro, S. A., 415, *431*
Law, S., 409, *430*
Lazarus, E., 448, *482*
Lazarus, R., 399, 403, 404, *430*
Lazarus, R. S., 403, *430*
Leach, M., 210, *217*
Leary, M., 680, 681, *699, 703*
Leary, M. R., 576, 592, *605, 610*
Leavitt, G. S, 42, *67*
Le Bars, D., 426, *432*
LeBlanc, B. A., 632, *662*
Le Bon, G., 556, *572*
Leck, K., 678, 683, 684, 686, *705, 706*
Lecky, P., 247, *268*
Lecours, A. R., 425, 426, *430*
Ledbetter, J. E., 91, 94, 106, 110, *119,* 339, *362*
LeDoux, J., 459, 475, 476, *485*
LeDoux, J. E., 60, *70,* 422, 424, *427, 430,* 558, *572*
Lee, A. Y., 312, *314,* 603, 604, *610,* 640, *663*
Lee, M. B., 399, *435*
Leech, G. N., 41, *70*
Leggett, J. C., 41, 42, *70,* 176, *217*
Lehman, D., 633, *661*
Lehman, D. R., 248, *267,* 309, *317,* 590, *608*
Lehmann, D., 405, *429*
Lehmann, D. R., 39, *70*
Leibold, J. M., 54, 57, *71,* 652, *663*
Leippe, M. R., 234, *266,* 502, 516, 518, *532, 538,* 635, 650, *665, 666*
Leisse, U.-K., *737*
Lemieux, R., 648, *660*
Lenn, T. M., 443, *483*
Lenski, G. E., 41, 42, *70,* 176, *217*
Lent, R. W., 196, *217*
Lenton, A., 551, 561, 562, *569*
Leonard, K. E., 722, *741*
Leone, C., 12, *18,* 91, 96, *123,* 387, *394,* 514, *540,* 582, *610*

Leone, D. R., 450, *482*
Lepage, L., 192, *215*
Lepore, L., 399, *430*
Lepper, M. R., 21, 26, *395, 70,* 99, 101, 107, 116, *121,* 165, *169,* 247, 248, 254, 262, *268, 270,* 304, *319,* 323, 326, *365, 367,* 373, *375,* 377, 378, 380, 385, *392,* 496, 511, 514, 515, 517, *529, 535, 536, 539,* 549, *572, 573, 663*
Lepper, M. R., 304, *319*
Lerner, J. S., 383, *395,* 457, 461, *485,* 710, *738*
Lerner, M. J., 287, 306, 311, *317, 318*
Lerner, R. M., 53, *64*
Leroux, J.-M., 425, 426, *430*
Leslie, A. M., 448, *485*
Levenson, R. W., 402, *430,* 720, *738*
Leventhal, H., 346, *365,* 648, *663*
Levin, K. D., 370, *392,* 512, 513, *535,* 619, 639, 644, *662*
Levine, J. M., 680, 681, 692, *703*
Levine, L. J., 420, *430, 433*
Levine, T. R., 652, *664*
Levinson, D. J., 586, *604, 610*
Levy, A., 675, 676, *700*
Levy, D. A., 634, *664*
Levy, M., 595, *605*
Levy, P., 151, *170*
Levy, S., 589, *610*
Lewan, P. C., 101, *121*
Lewis, A. C., 387, 389, 390, *391*
Lewis, C., 448, *485*
Lewis, H. G., 578, 594, *615*
Lewis, J., 253, *268*
Lewis-Beck, M. S., 374, *392*
Leyens, J., 44, *76*
Leyens, J. B., 692, *703*
L'Herrou, T., 690, *703*
Li, W., 128, *170,* 242, *270*
Liberman, A., 14, *17,* 92, 98, *118,* 334, 346, 348, 349, 350, 351, 355, 359, *361, 362,* 372, 377, 378, 380, 382, 385, 386, *390, 392,* 436, 465, *482,* 505, 514, 529, *531, 536,* 577, *606,* 624, 626, 643, *658,* 677, 687, 698, *700,* 710, 713, 725, *734, 755,* 756, 757, 762, *764*
Liberman, N., 648, *663*
Lichtenstein, E. H., 280, *315*
Lichtenstein, M., 290, *315*
Lichtenstein, S., 44, *69,* 278, 295, *320,* 346, *367*
Lickteig, C., 51, *68*
Lieberman, M. D., 243, 260, *268*
Liebold, J. M., 544, *572*
Liechti, M. E., 405, *430*
Likert, R., 21, 32, 35, *70*
Lilly, J., 648, *657*
Limbert, W., 691, 692, *705,* 759, *766*
Lin, H., 621, 644, *662*
Lin, H. Y., 370, *392*
Lin, M. T., 681, *701*
Lindem, K., 275, *316*
Linder, D. E., 233, 239, 247, 251, 257, *268*

Lindsey, S., 11, 14, *19*, 24, *75*, 85, 86, 87, *124*, 205, 206, *220*, 323, 327, 333, 338, *368*, 386, 388, *395*, 524, *542*, 543, 544, 550, 559, 564, 566, *574*, 599, *615*, 655, *668*, 748, *767*
Lingle, J. H., 274, *318*, 494, 517, 520, 527, *536*
Link, B., 730, *738, 740*
Linn, L. S., 175, 181, 189, *217*
Linton, S., 463, 465, *488*
Linville, P. W., 84, 91, 96, *121*, 284, *318*
Lipkus, I. M., 97, *121*
Lisle, D. J., 12, *19*, 108, 109, *124*, 128, *171*, 386, 388, 389, 390, *395*, 514, *541*
Lissitz, R. W., 38, 39, *70*
Lissner, L., 406, *432*
Litardo, H., 131, *168*
Liu, J. H., 691, *703*
Liu, T. J., 25, 26, *68*, 312, *320*
Livingston, R. W., 56, *70*, 555, *572*, 633, *663*
Loach, J., 199, *211*
Lock, T. G., 384, *393*
Locke, K. D., 452, 459, *485*
Lockhart, R. S., 282, 284, 300, 310, *315*, 529, *531*, 627, *658*
Lodge, M., 455, *485*, 716, *738*
Loewenstein, G., 420, 421, *427*, 457, 458, 461, *485*
Loewenstein, G. F., 389, *392*, 456, 461, *485*
Loftus, E. F., 149, 151, 152, *169*, 279, 291, *315*, *318*, 420, *430*
Logan, H., 648, *657*
Loken, B. A., 280, *318*
Lombardi, W. J., 520, *534*
Long, S., 155, 156, 165, *169*
Longenecker, C. O., 726, *740*
Longo, D. A., 196, *217*
Longo, L. C., 718, *735*
Lopez, D. F., 377, 378, 379, 382, 383, *391*, 511, *532*
Lopyan, K. J., 585, *608*
Lorch, E. P., 577, *609*
Lord, C. G., 21, 26, *70*, 99, 101, 107, 116, *121*, 323, 326, *365*, *367*, 373, 377, 378, 380, 385, *392*, 496, 515, 517, *536*, 549, *572*, 573, *663*
Lories, G., 516, *531*
Lorig, T. S., 159, *166*, 528, *530*
Losch, M. E., 59, 60, *65*, 234, *268*, 471, *485*, 516, *536*
Lott, A. J., 378, *392*
Lott, B. E., 378, *392*
Lovibond, P. F., 441, 444, *485*, 507, *536*, 750, *766*
Lowenstein, G., 653, *663*
Lowenthal, D., 653, *663*
Lowery, B., 445, *486*
Lowery, B. S., 561, 563, *572*
Lowin, A., 231, *268*
Lowrance, R., 718, *735*
Lowrey, T. M., 598, *613*
Lubin, B., 397, *435*
Luce, R. D., 28, *70*
Ludwig, J., 35, *73*
Lui, T. J., 237, 260, *270*
Luke, M. A., 263, *268*

Lumsdaine, A. A., 175, *216*, 300, *317*, 344, *363*, 518, *534*, 619, 620, 623, 640, *661*
Lundgren, S., 357, *368*, *668*, 676, 678, 680, 685, 688, 689, 690, *703*, *706*, 758, *767*
Lundy, R. M., 591, *605*
Lunt, P., 108, *120*, 186, *216*
Lurie, L., 274, *317*
Lushene, R. E., 602, *614*
Lusk, C. M., 84, 91, 96, 97, *120*, 514, *535*
Lutz, R. J., 512, *529*, *536*, 639, *656*
Lydon, J., 383, *393*, 715, *738*
Lydon, J. E., 681, *704*
Lynch, M., 238, 244, 245, *270*, 633, *667*
Lynch, M. E., 578, 590, *611*
Lynn, A. R., 443, *485*, 528, *535*, 558, *571*, 710, 728, *738*
Lynn, M., 593, *610*
Lynn, S., 274, *320*
Lynn, S. J., 384, *392*, 393
Lyon, J. D., 288, *322*

M

Ma, J., 551, 561, 562, *569*
Maas, A., 688, *703*
Maass, A., 61, *70*, 126, *169*, 357, *365*, 592, *611*, 636, *663*, *668*
MacCallum, R. C., 88, *119*
Maccoby, E., 297, *316*
MacCulloch, M. J., 57, *68*
MacDonald, G., 634, *664*
MacDonald, T. K., 110, *121*, 204, *217*, 642, *663*
MacDougall, B. L., 90, 91, 92, 95, 96, 97, 98, *121*, *123*
MacGregor, D. G., 455, 461, *488*
Machover, K., 578, 594, *615*
Mack, D. E., 188, *215*
Mack, K., 188, *216*
MacKenzie, S. B., 512, *536*
Mackie, D., 107, *121*, 357, *364*
Mackie, D. M., 13, *19*, 335, 349, 358, *365*, 372, 373, *393*, 452, 457, 461, 462, 464, 466, 468, 469, 471, 479, *481*, *484*, 486, *487*, *488*, 489, 506, 512, 517, 521, 523, *536*, *539*, 595, *610*, 636, 639, 650, *660*, *663*, 678, 684, 688, *703*, 733
MacKuen, M., 721, *738*
MacKuen, M. B., 465, *486*
MacLeod, C. M., 59, *70*
MacLeod, K. M., 405, *429*
Macrae, C. N., 520, *536*, 559, 561, 562, *572*
Madden, T. J., 192, 196, *217*
Madden, T. M., 48, *69*
Maddux, W. W., 579, 596, *610*
Mae, L., 507, *539*
Maguelone, G. F., 426, *432*
Maheswaran, D., 107, 116, *118*, 352, 358, *362*, *365*, 513, 514, *531*, 581, *606*, 628, 640, *658*, *663*, 687, *703*, 758, *764*
Maier, S. F., 405, *430*

Maio, G. R., 104, *121,* 263, *268,* 323, 331, 332, 338, 341, 344, 349, *363, 365, 366,* 582, 583, 600, *610,* 621, 627, 633, 639, 641, 642, 650, 653, *657, 659, 663,* 754, *766*
Makhijani, M. G., 718, *735*
Maki, B. K., 720, *741*
Maklin, D., 188, *216*
Malhotra, N. K., *609*
Malle, B. F., 578, 595, *612*
Maller, O., 406, *429*
Malloy, T. E., *737*
Malone, P. S., 293, *316*
Malpass, R., 154, *171*
Mandler, G., 409, *431,* 451, 452, *486,* 509, *536*
Mandler, J., 280, *318*
Mann, L., 53, *71,* 514, *536*
Mann, W., 676, *702*
Mannetti, L., 351, 351. 352, 352, *362, 366,* 505, 526, *535, 538,* 579, *610, 612,* 629, *665*
Mannheim, K., 601, *610*
Manstead, A. S. R., 183, 199, 200, 201, *217, 218,* 676, *704*
Manzi, J. M., 723, *734*
Mao, H., 425, *429*
Maracek, J., 235, *268*
Marburger, W., 152, *169*
Marcus, G. E., 465, *486,* 721, *738*
Marcus, G. F., 753, *766*
Marcus-Newhall, A., 411, *431,* 568, *573*
Margolin, G., 720, *734*
Mariette, P., 511, *530*
Mark, M. M., 466, 467, 468, 471, *488*
Markman, A. B., 685, *699*
Markman, K. D., 373, 374, *393*
Markus, H., 494, *536,* 695, 696, *703,* 711, *738*
Markus, H. R., 248, 249, *268,* 590, 592, 593, *608, 609, 610,* 695, *701*
Marlier, L., 406, 407, *433, 434*
Marlowe, D., 636, *658*
Marques, J., 680, 692, *703*
Marquette, J. F., 45, 47, *75*
Marquis, D. G., 687, *703*
Marrow, A. J., 346, *365*
Marschat, L. E., 34, *72*
Marsh, K. L., 58, 62, *70,* 375, *393,* 545, *572*
Marshall, H., 39, *65*
Marshall-Goodell, B. S., 508, *530,* 579, *606*
Martijn, C., 650, *668*
Martin, L., 21, 24, 27, *74,* 84, 96, *123,* 507, 514, *540*
Martin, L. L., 25, 27, 38, 39, *70, 74,* 107, *121,* 301, *320,* 456, 467, 469, *486, 488,* 517, 518, 528, *536,* 557, 559, *572*
Martin, P., 161, *169*
Martin, R., 161, *169,* 275, *321,* 354, *365,* 406, *428,* 627, *663*
Martin, S., 592, *607*
Martin, W. S., 39, *71*
Maruyama, G., 635, *664*
Marwell, G., 324, *365*

Maslow, A. H., 575, 576, *610, 703*
Mason, R., 48, *67*
Masson, M. E. J., 551, *572*
Masters, J. R., 38, *71*
Masterson, R., 476, *485*
Matarazzo, J. D., 144, *168*
Matell, M. S., 38, 39, 40, *68, 71*
Mathews, C. O., 45, *71*
Mathieu, J. E., 726, *738*
Mathiowetz, N. A., 149, *169*
Mathog, R., 510, *535,* 628, *662*
Matsumoto, D., 402, *431*
Matsumoto, H., 592, *609*
Matthews, G., 160, *169,* 405, 415, *431*
Mattlar, C., 406, *432*
Matz, D. C., 677, 684, *700, 703*
Mavin, G. H., 559, *571*
Mayer, J. D., 455, 461, 474, *486, 487*
McAdams, D. P., *610*
McArdle, J., 198, *214*
McAuley, E., 192, 202, *213*
McCabe, K., 595, *608*
McCafferty, P., 721, *740*
McCaffree, K., 198, *216*
McCallum, D. M., 143, *169*
McCaskill, C. C., 405, *435*
McCauley, C., 727, *738*
McCaulley, M. H., 584, *611*
McCleary, R. A., 399, *430*
McClelland, D. C., 599, 600, *610*
McClelland, G. H., 23, 28, 31, *69*
McClelland, J. L., 500, *531,* 551, 568, *572*
McClendon, M. J., 42, 45, 47, *64, 71*
McCloskey, M., 48, *67,* 497, *536*
McConahay, J. B., 90, 96, *117,* 204, *217,* 595, *611*
McConnell, A. R., 54, 57, *71,* 387, 389, 390, *391,* 544, *572,* 589, *611,* 652, *663*
McConnell, H. K., 251, *265,* 292, *314,* 653, *657*
McCracken, S. G., 143, *167*
McCrae, 575, 602, *606*
McCrae, R. R., 160, *167, 611*
McCrimmon, R. J., 405, *431*
McCullogh, M. L., 154, *169*
McCusker, C., 578, 593, *614*
McDavid, J. W., 600, *613*
McDermott, J. B., 603, *607*
McDermott, R., 475, *486*
McDonald, R., 150, 151, *168*
McDonel, E. C., 81, 108, *119,* 186, *214,* 381, *391,* 735
McDougal, W., 693, *703*
McElree, B., 500, *536*
McFarland, C., 150, *170,* 310, *319,* 383, *394,* 649, 653, *666*
McGarty, C., 683, *702, 704*
McGaugh, J. L., 419, 424, *427,* 439, 458, 459, 461, *482*
McGhee, D. E., 56, 58, *68,* 206, *215,* 445, *484,* 524, *533, 544, 571,* 582, 599, *608*
McGowan, S., 719, *738*
McGraw, A. P., 417, 418, *430*

McGraw, K., 716, *738*

McGregor, D., 374, 380, *393*

McGregor, I., 85, *122,* 242, 243, 256, 261, *268,* 332, *365,* 587, *611*

McGuire, C., 727, *741*

McGuire, C. V., 14, *18,* 177, 195, *217,* 282, 283, 284, 309, 310, *318,* 371, 374, 375, 382, 384, 387, *393,* 512, 526, *536,* 622, *664*

McGuire, W. J., 11, 12, 14, *18,* 80, 85, 101, *116, 121,* 126, 161, 163, *169,* 195, *217,* 232, 263, *264, 268,* 278, 282, 283, 284, 285, 286, 294, 295, 296, 297, 306, 309, 310, 311, 313, *314, 318,* 324, 327, 330, 336, 337, 345, 346, 347, 348, 353, 359, 360, *360, 365,* 370, 371, 373, 374, 375, 378, 382, 383, 384, 385, 387, *390, 393, 394,* 495, 504, 505, 512, 521, 522, 526, *536, 541,* 548, *572,* 586, 588, 589, 591, 600, 601, *604, 611,* 618, 619, 620, 622, 625, 630, 631, 639, 644, 648, 650, *663, 664,* 710, 712, 717, *738,* 762, *766*

McHugo, G., 60, *71*

McInerney, S. C., 60, *68,* 399, *435*

McIntosh, A. R., 552, *572*

McKelvie, S. J., 40, *71*

McKenna, P. A., 409, *434, 452, 488*

McKenzie, J., 160, *169*

McLarney, A. R., 592, *608, 640, 660*

McLaughlin, J., 47, *72*

McLaughlin, J. P., 56, *67*

McLean, J., 419, *432*

McLemee, S., 474, *486*

McMillan, B., 183, *217*

McMillan, D., 715, *741*

McNatt, P. S., 650, 651, 652, *656*

McNaught-David, A. K., 500, *540*

Mead, G. H., 693, *704*

Means, B., 149, *169*

Meddis, R., 416, *431*

Medin, D. L., 520, *536*

Meekers, D., 143, *169*

Meertens, R. M., 236, *267*

Mehl, E., 47, *72*

Meier, B. P., 475, *486*

Meissner, P. B., 578, 594, *615*

Mellers, B. A., 417, *430,* 456, 461, *486*

Mellot, D. S., 549, 550, *571*

Melton, R., 592, *607*

Memon, A., 154, *168*

Mendolia, M., 84, 96, *123,* 514, *540*

Menon, G., 149, *169,* 299, *318*

Mensink, W., 333, *365*

Menzies, R. G., 407, 408, *431*

Menzies, R. N., 419, *431*

Mervis, C. B., 413, *432*

Messé, L. A., 239, *270*

Messick, D. M., 253, *265*

Messick, S., 28, 42, *71*

Messner, C., 685, *699*

Metcalfe, J., 27, *71*

Mettee, D., 235, *268*

Metts, S., 681, *704*

Metzler, A. E., 644, *664*

Mewborn, C. R., 346, *366*

Meyer, D., 346, *365*

Meyer, D. E., 54, *71*

Meyer, M., 275, *316*

Meyerowitz, B. E., 640, *664*

Meyers-Levy, J., 640, *663*

Mezei, L., 178, 181, *218*

Mezzacappa, E. S., 403, *431*

Michaelis, W., 51, *71*

Midden, C., 191, *210*

Middlestadt, S., 558, *571*

Middlestadt, S. E., 193, *214,* 498, 503, 504, 528, *533, 536, 537,* 717, *739*

Midgley, E. H., 380, *390*

Mierke, J., 57, *71*

Mikkulainen, R., 551, *572*

Milburn, M. A., 90, 96, *120*

Milgram, S., 53, *71,* 125, *169,* 587, *611*

Mill, J. S., 687, *704*

Millar, K. U., 100, 101, 102, *121,* 470, *486,* 647, *664*

Millar, M., 91, 96, 97, 109, 116, *121, 122*

Millar, M. G., 100, 101, 102, *121,* 203, *217,* 381, 386, 388, *393,* 470, *486,* 514, *536,* 647, *664*

Miller, C. E., 510, *537,* 688, *702*

Miller, C. T., 176, *219,* 655, *666*

Miller, D., 241, 256, *266*

Miller, D. T., 287, 306, 311, *317,* 677, *705*

Miller, G. A., 548, *572,* 712, *738*

Miller, G. R., 595, *605*

Miller, J. A., 146, *167,* 586, *606*

Miller, J. G., 696, *704*

Miller, J. M., 716, *738*

Miller, L. C., 247, *269,* 568, *573*

Miller, M. G., 718, *738*

Miller, N., 44, 60, *71, 75,* 94, 95, 97, 98, *120,* 411, *431,* 499, 513, 522, *537,* 558, *571,* 586, *608,* 635, *664*

Miller, N. E., 462, *483*

Miller, R. R., 595, *615*

Miller, T. Q., 193, 197, 198, *218*

Miller, W. E., 35, *71*

Millman, L., 406, 407, *432*

Mills, J., 226, 230, 231, 251, 261, *265, 267, 268, 269,* 502, *539,* 632, *661,* 684, 685, *702*

Milne, A. B., 520, *536,* 561, 562, *572*

Mineka, S., 447, *486,* 745, *766*

Mingay, D. J., 46, *71,* 149, *169*

Minton, H. L., 693, *700*

Mintun, M. A., 399, *434*

Mirels, H. L., 590, *611*

Mirer, T., 713, 716, *737*

Miron, M. S., 635, *661*

Mirowsky, J., 43, *71*

Mischel, W., 389, *393,* 494, *537*

Misovich, S. J., 649, *660*

Misra, S., 645, *664*

Mitchell, A. A., 186, *212*

Mitchell, A. L., 578, 589, *604,* 651, 652, *656*
Mitchell, J. P., 555, *572*
Mitchell, P., 448, *485*
Mitchell, R. C., 47, 49, *70*
Mittal, B., 202, *217*
Mittlemark, M. B., 51, *67*
Mladinic, A., 418, *428*
Mohr, P. J., 45, *65*
Molenaar, I. W., 594, *608*
Moll, J., 560, *571*
Moll, M., 551, *572*
Monahan, J. L., 450, 451, *486,* 509, 528, *537*
Mongeau, P., 470, *482,* 640, *657*
Mongeau, P. A., 648, *660*
Monin, B., 243, *269*
Monson, T., 515, *530*
Montano, D., 204, *220*
Montano, D. E., 83, 92, 106, 109, *118*
Monteiro, K. P., 453, 461, *482*
Monteith, M. J., 204, *213,* 596, *611*
Montgomery, R. L., 253, *267*
Montieth, M. J., 462, *483*
Montoya, M. R., 727, *737*
Moody, W. R., 47, 49, *70*
Moon, Y., 602, *611*
Moore, D. J., 638, *658*
Moore, D. L., 300, *318*
Moore, J., 175, 178, 181, *216*
Moore, J. S., 718, *738*
Moore, M., 109, *122*
Moore, S. E., 471, 472, 473, *486*
Moreland, R., 677, 681, *703, 704*
Moreland, R. L., 450, *486*
Morgan, C. L., 619, *666*
Morgan, J. J., 126, *169*
Morgan, M., 300, *316*
Morgan, R. L., 412, 414, *431*
Morin, C., 188, *216*
Morin, R., 35, *71*
Morling, B., 635, *660*
Moroi, E., 197, *214*
Morojele, N.K., 203, *217*
Morris, J. S., 424, *431*
Morris, K. J., 581, *606*
Morris, M., 57, *68,* 312, *315*
Morris, P., 151, *170*
Morton, D. R., 600, *607*
Moscovici, S., 335, 342, 354, 356, 357, 358, *365,* 592, *611,* 636, *664,* 687, 688, 693, *702, 704*
Moscowitz, G. B., 339, 344, *367*
Moskowitz, G. B., 464, *486,* 518, *537,* 596, *611,* 627, *664*
Moskowitz, G. D., 561, *571*
Mouton, J. S., 635, 636, *658, 664*
Mowen, J. C., 593, *615*
Moylan, S., 452, *484*
Mucchi-Faina, A., 592, *611*
Muellerleile, P. A., 144, 145, *165,* 188, 196, 201, 204, *211,* 622, *656*

Mugny, G., 505, *537,* 688, *704*
Mullen, B., 724, 725, 726, 727, *739*
Müller, G., 153, *170*
Mummendey, A., *737*
Munch, J. M., *733*
Muraven, M., 128, *169,* 624, *657*
Murphy, K. R., 376, *393*
Murphy, S. T., 25, *71,* 450, 451, *486,* 509, 528, *537,* 556, 557, *572,* 752, *766*
Murray, D. M., 51, *71*
Murray, H. A., 575, *611*
Murray, S. L., 100, *122,* 646, *664,* 723, *739*
Musch, J., 25, 56, 62, 64, *69,* 752, *766*
Mussweiler, T., 302, *318*
Myers, B., 384, *393*
Myers, D. G., 354, *365,* 688, *704*
Myers, I. B., 584, *611*
Myers, J., 133, *169*
Myers, S. L., 204, *217*

N

Nadel, L., 459, *485*
Naffrechoux, M., *664*
Naficy, A., *736*
Nagengast, B., 343, *367*
Nahl, M., 446, *487*
Nail, P. R., 11, *18,* 587, *611,* 634, *664*
Nakamura, G. V., 279, *315*
Nakamura, Y., 409, *431,* 451, 452, *486,* 509, *536*
Nanda, H., 31, *66*
Narayan, S., 40, 42, 45, *70, 71*
Nasco, S. A., 375, *393*
Nayakankuppum, D., 497, *538*
Nayakankuppum, D. J., 81, *123*
Neale, J. M., 415, *434*
Near, D., 595, *615*
Nebergall, R. E., 45, *74,* 370, 383, *394,* 620, 621, *667*
Neely, F., 210, *216*
Neely, J. H., 55, *71*
Neimeyer, G. J., 644, *664*
Nelson, D. E., 236, 237, 239, 256, *267,* 516, *534,* 632, *661*
Nelson, E. E., 408, *431*
Nelson, G. M., 722, *733*
Nelson, L., 590, *613*
Nelson, M. R., 339, *366,* 598, *611*
Nelson, T. O., 360, *364,* 516, *535*
Nemeth, C. J., 636, *664,* 689, 690, *704*
Nerb, J., 477, *488*
Nerentz, D., 346, *365*
Netemeyer, M. F., *605*
Netemeyer, R. G., 196, *218*
Neter, J., 152, *169*
Neuberg, S. L., 462, *484,* 521, *537,* 584, *611,* 681, *701*
Neuman, W. R., 465, *486*
Neumann, R., 476, *486*
Nevin, J. R., 49, *68*

Newall, A., *739*

Newby-Clark, I. R., 85, *122,* 242, 243, 256, 261, *268,* 332, *365, 587, 611*

Newcomb, T. M., 42, *71,* 85, *116,* 226, 232, *264, 269,* 311, *314,* 324, 330, *360, 361,* 370, *390,* 586, 600, 601, *604, 611,* 649, *656, 664,* 671, 672, *699, 704,* 718, 719, 720, *739*

Newell, A., 712, *741*

Newman, J. P., 130, *166*

Newman, L., 728, 730, *739*

Newman, L. S., 181, *220,* 344, *367*

Newman, M. G., 415, *430*

Newsom, J. T., 245, *265,* 331, *362,* 578, 587, *606*

Nichols, D. R., 619, 620, *662*

Nicolson, N. A., 406, *431*

Niedenthal, P., 207, *212,* 564, 565, *569*

Niedenthal, P. M., *537,* 558, *572*

Nielsen, A. C., 299, *318*

Nielson, K., 459, *486*

Nienhuis, A. E., 676, *704*

Nigam, A., 149, *169*

Nisbett, R. E., 10, 11, *18,* 165, *169,* 253, 254, *268,* 285, *315,* 376, 386, 389, *393,* 511, 514, 525, *535, 537,* 695, 696, *701, 704*

Noelle-Neumann, E., 45, *73*

Norasakkunkit, V., 592, *609*

Norcross, J. C., 148, *170*

Norem, J. K., *611*

Norenzayan, A., 285, *315, 318,* 696, *704*

Norgren, R., 423, 424, *429*

Norman, D. A., 48, *72,* 280, *315*

Norman, P., 109, *122,* 144, *169,* 188, 201, 203, *211, 212, 218*

Norman, R., 109, 110, *122,* 179, *218,* 330, *365*

Norman, R. M. G., 510, *537*

Norris, C. J., 159, *166,* 528, *530*

Norton, M. I., 243, *269*

Norwood, M., 83, 92, 106, 109, *118*

Nosek, B. A., 57, 58, *68, 72,* 544, 549, 550, 555, 564, 566, *571, 572,* 748, *765*

Noseworthy, J., 108, *120*

Notani, A. S., 188, *218*

Nottleman, E. D., 648, *664*

Notz, P., 415, *434*

Nowak, A., 690, *703,* 759, *766*

Nowlis, V., 405, 416, *431*

Nucifora, J., 200, *218*

Nurius, P., 711, *738*

Nusbaum, H., 159, *166,* 528, *530*

O

Oakes, P. J., 678, 683, 698, *702, 704, 706*

Oatley, K., 404, 412, *431*

O'Barr, W. M., 635, *664*

Obertynski, M. A., 644, *660*

Ochsner, K. N., 243, 260, *268,* 419, *431*

O'Connor, C., 412, 413, *434*

O'Connor, E., 425, *426*

O'Connor, K. J., 60, 62, *72*

Oddy, K., 160, *169*

O'Doherty, J., 425, *431*

O'Driscoll, M., 380, 381, *390*

Oehman, A., 745, *766*

O'Guinn, T. C., 299, 300, 301, *318, 320*

Öhman, A., 447, *486*

Oishi, S., 398, 400, 411, 415, 418, 419, 421, *431, 433*

Okut, H., 162, *167*

Oldendick, R. W., 47, *65*

O'Leary, J. E., 183, 199, *220*

Oleson, K. C., 578, 590, *611*

Ollinger, J. M., 399, *434*

Olmstead, J. A., 636, *664*

Olson, D. R., 448, *489*

Olson, J., 582, *610*

Olson, J. C., 708, *739*

Olson, J. M., 91, 94, 95, *123,* 160, *169,* 179, 180, *221,* 229, 231, 239, 245, 253, 259, 260, 263, *267, 268, 269, 271,* 274, *318,* 323, 324, 325, 334, 338, 341, *366,* 597, 598, *614, 615,* 621, 627, 633, 639, 650, *657, 663,* 711, 715, *739, 742,* 754, *766*

Olson, M. A., 57, 62, *72, 73,* 81, 87, *119, 122,* 206, 207, *214,* 343, *365,* 408, *431,* 443, 460, *486,* 493, 496, 508, 519, 524, *533, 537,* 558, 559, 560, 564, *570, 572,* 652, *659,* 728, *739,* 747, 748, *765, 766*

Oltman, P., 594, *615*

O'Muircheartaigh, C., 40, *72*

Onishi, K., 449, *486*

Onorato, R. S., 683, *702*

Orbell, S., 145, *171,* 188, 190, 191, 200, 201, 202, *218, 219, 220*

Oriña, M. M., 634, *664*

Orne, M. T., 549, *572*

Ortberg, J., 200, *215*

Ortony, A., 397, 398, 400, 404, 409, 412, 414, 416, *428, 431,* 438, 439, 477, *482, 484, 487*

Osgood, C. E., 4, *18,* 32, 33, 35, *72,* 93, *122,* 210, *218, 366,* 370, 383, *393,* 475, *487,* 510, 515, *537,* 711, *739*

Osgood, D. W., 284, *320*

Osgood, E. E., 226, *269*

O'Shaughnessy, M., 419, *432*

Oskamp. S., 707, 708, *739*

Oster, H., 407, *432*

Osterhouse, R. A., 296, 297, *318,* 513, *537,* 623, *664*

Ostrom, T. M., 10, *18,* 35, *72,* 82, *122,* 177, *218,* 274, *318,* 324, *366,* 494, 512, 517, 522, 527, *536, 538,* 618, 623, 640, *664, 665,* 713, *740*

O'Sullivan, M., 632, *659*

Ottati, V., 302, *318,* 452, 455, *487,* 503, 517, *537,* 710, 716, 717, 719, 721, 722, 728, 730, 731, *734, 736, 737, 739, 740, 742*

Ottati, V. C. 1997, 721, *739*

Otto, S., 418, *428*

Ouellette, J., 641, *666*

Ouellette, J. A., 14, *18,* 144, 148, *169,* 201, 202, *218,* 309, *320,* 357, *368, 668,* 678, 688, 689, 690, *706,* 758, 760, *766, 767*
Oyserman, D., 593, *611,* 695, 696, *704*
Ozer, D. J., 720, *734*

P

Pacini, R., 584, 599, *607, 611*
Packer, M., *118*
Page, B. I., *739*
Page, M. M., *537,* 558, *572*
Page, R., 51, *74,* 564, *573*
Page, S., *169,* 730, *739*
Pak, A. W.-P., 718, *735*
Pallak, M. S., 233, 251, *269*
Pallak, S. R., 510, *537*
Palmer, J., 291, *318*
Palmer, S. N., 403, *431*
Palmgreen, P., 577, *609*
Panitz, D., 426, *426*
Panksepp, J., 402, 406, *431*
Papageorgis, D., 638, *664*
Parducci, A., 39, *75*
Park, B., 25, 26, 27, 55, 56, 62, *75,* 206, *220,* 372, 383, 385, *392,* 399, *435,* 523, *534,* 556, 562, *574,* 583, *608,* 713, 714, *736*
Park, H., 697, *700*
Park, H. S., 652, *664*
Park, W., 725, *739*
Parker, D., 200, 201, *218*
Parker, L. D., 582, *604*
Parkinson, B., 418, *431*
Pascual-Marqui, R., 405, *429*
Patrick, C. J., 415, *431*
Patterson, J. R., 586, *615*
Paul, B. Y., 60, *75*
Paul, D., 163, *169*
Paulhus, D. L., 43, 51, 52, *72,* 152, *169*
Paulus, P. B., 723, *739*
Pavelchek, M. A., 449, 464, 465, *484*
Pavlos, A. J., 51, *72*
Pavlov, I. P., 407, *431*
Pavot, W., 421, *428*
Payne, B. K., 501, *535*
Payne, D. G., 384, *393*
Payne, J. D. 1971, 46, *72*
Payne, S. L., 45, 47, *72,* 547, *572*
Peak, H., 11, *18,* 276, *318,* 329, *366*
Pearl, J., 147, *170*
Pearson, H., 459, *487*
Pearson, J. C., 720, *734*
Pedersen, W. C., 411, *431*
Pederson, W. C., 499, *537*
Peeters, F., 406, *431*
Peirce, C. S., 693, *704*
Pemberton, M., 727, *740*
Peng, K., *609,* 696, *704*
Pennington, N., 304, *318, 319*

Penrod, S., 154, *171,* 636, *667*
Peretz, I., 450, *487*
Perez, J. A., 505, *537,* 688, *704*
Perez, S., 375, *394*
Peri, N., *610*
Perloff, R. M., 591, *611,* 624, 627, 628, *664*
Perrett, D., 425, *431*
Perry, C. L., 51, *71*
Pescosolido, B., 730, *740*
Peters, E., 455, 461, *488*
Peters, M. D., 335, *360,* 721, *732*
Peterson, B. E., 586, *607, 611*
Peterson, B. L., 39, *74*
Peterson, C., 284, *320*
Peterson, H., 242, 247, *267*
Peterson, R. C., 493, *537*
Peterson, R. S., 383, *395,* 636, *664,* 690, *704,* 727, *741*
Peterson, T. R., 402, *430*
Petraitis, J., 193, 197, 198, *218*
Petry, M. C., 419, *427*
Pettigrew, T. F., 715, *740*
Petty, R. E., 4, 12, 14, *16, 17, 18,* 21, 24, 25, 26, 27, 49, 50, 59, 60, *65, 70, 72, 75,* 80, 82, 84, 85, 86, 87, 89, 91, 92, 94, 95, 97, 98, 99, 100, 101, 103, 104, 105, 106, 107, 109, 113, 115, 116, *118, 119, 122, 123, 124,* 128, *170,* 176, 185, 198, 199, *213, 217, 218,* 259, *269,* 284, 296, 309, *315, 317, 319,* 323, 332, 341, 347, 348, 349, 352, 353, 355, 356, 358, 359, *361, 366,* 372, 374, 377, 378, 379, 381, 382, 385, 386, *391, 393, 395,* 400, 426, *431, 435,* 465, 466, 467, 468, 469, 470, 471, 472, 473, *482, 483, 487, 488,* 494, 504, 505, 506, 508, 510, 511, 512, 513, 514, 515, 517, 518, 519, 520, 521, 522, 523, 524, 526, 528, 529, *529, 530, 531, 532, 534, 535, 537, 538, 540, 541,* 557, *574,* 577, 578, 579, 581, 582, 583, 584, 586, 587, 588, 589, 590, 591, 594, 595, 596, 597, 598, 599, 600, 601, 602, 603, *605, 606, 607, 608, 609, 610, 611, 612, 613, 614, 615,* 620, 621, 623, 624, 625, 626, 627, 628, 629, 634, 635, 636, 637, 638, 639, 640, 642, 643, 644, 645, 646, 647, 648, 650, 653, *657, 659, 660, 661, 662, 664, 665,* 666, 667, 668, 675, 676, 677, 687, 689, 694, 698, 699, *700, 704,* 708, 710, 711, 713, 715, 725, *734, 739, 740,* 757, 762, *766*
Pham, L. B., 203, *219*
Pham, M. T., 276, *319*
Phelan, J., 730, *740*
Phelps, E. A., 60, 62, *72,* 424, 425, *426*
Phinney, J. S., 695, *704*
Picek, J. S., 287, *319*
Piehl, A. M., 204, *212*
Piero, A., 629, *665*
Pierro, A., 339, 351, 351. 352, 352, 356, *362, 364, 366,* 505, 526, *535, 538,* 579, 582, *610, 612*
Pietromonaco, P., 281, *314*
Pietromonaco, P. R., 719, *738*
Pilkington, N. W., 681, *704*
Pilkonis, P. A., 407, *435,* 443, *489,* 508, *542*
Pincus, A. L., 593, *609*
Pinter, B., 727, *737*

Piontkowski, U., 650, *660*
Pittman, R. K., 459, *487*
Pittman, T. S., 233, 251, *269*
Plant, E. A., 210, *213, 218,* 564, *570, 572,* 578, 596, *612*
Plata-Salaman, C. R., 423, *434*
Plaut, D. C., 501, *538*
Pliner, P., 410, *434*
Pliner, P. L., 450, *487*
Poe, G. S., 47, *72*
Poehlmann, K. M., 578, 590, *611*
Polivy, J., 333, *363*
Pollock, V. E., 411, *431*
Pomazal, R. J., 175, *220*
Pomazal, R. P., 131, *168*
Pomerantz, E. M., 85, 101, 110, 115, *118, 122,* 324,
    330, 332, *362,* 377, 378, 382, *393,* 586, *612,* 641,
    642, *658, 665*
Pomery, E., 161, *167*
Pontari, B. A., 681, *704*
Pool, G. J., 632, *666,* 678, 683, 684, 686, *705, 706*
Posavac, S. S., 108, *122*
Posner, M. I., 55, *72*
Postmes, T., 621, *659*
Potter, J., 325, *366*
Poulton, R., 407, 408, *431*
Povey, R., 109, *118*
Powell, D. M., 521, *540*
Powell, M. C., 24, 25, 55, *67,* 81, 90, 91, 92, 93, 94,
    108, *119, 122,* 185, 186, *214,* 474, 477, *483,* 544,
    547, 565, *571,* 583, *607,* 642, *659,* 752, *765*
Prado, A., 188, *216*
Pratkanis, A. R., 80, 98, 105, *122,* 371, 376, *393, 394,*
    518, *538,* 586, *612,* 635, 650, *665*
Pratto, F., 25, 59, *64, 72,* 90, 91, 93, 94, 97, 108, 110,
    117, 186, *211,* 326, 332, *361,* 578, 583, 595, *605,*
    612, 642, *657,* 752, *764*
Preacher, K. J., 62, *66,* 206, 207, *213,* 565, *570*
Preisler, R. M., 101, 104, *124,* 510, *542*
Premack, D., *487*
Prentice, D. A., 340, *366,* 646, *665,* 677, *705,* 754, *766*
Prentice-Dunn, S., 648, *666*
Prescott, T. J., 115, *119,* 528, *532,* 568, *570*
Presser, A., 47, 49, *70*
Presser, S., 39, 40, 45, 47, *66, 73,* 115, *123,* 545, 546,
    556, *573*
Presson, C. C., 143, *170,* 382, *394*
Preston, E., 26, *70*
Pribram, K. H., 712, *738*
Priesler, R. M., 639, 643, *668*
Priester, J. M., 581, 586, *612*
Priester, J. R., 81, 84, 85, 89, 91, 94, 95, 97, 98, 99, 103,
    104, 105, 109, *119, 123,* 426, *431,* 497, 507, 508,
    510, 511, 513, 518, 519, 528, *531, 532, 538,* 577,
    612, 635, 642, *665, 666*
Prislin, R., 632, 641, *666,* 676, 680, 685, 691, 692, 694,
    703, 705, 759, *766*
Pritzker, H. A., 297, *317*
Prochaska, J. O., 148, *170*
Proffitt, C., 183, *217*
Prohaska, V., 420, *430*

Proshansky, H. M., 377, 378, *394,* 599, *613,* 710, 714,
    740
Prosser, M. A., 521, *540*
Provencal, A., 636, *657*
Pruitt, D., 681, *705*
Pryor, J. B., 585, *613*
Puckett, J. M., 349, *366,* 634, *666*
Pujol, J.-F., 426, *432*
Purvis, D., 678, 684, 686, *706*
Pyszczynski, T., 51, *68,* 241, 260, *269,* 576, *613*
Pyszczynski, T. A., 309, *319*

Q

Queller, S., 568, *572*
Quigley-Fernandez, B., 51, *72*
Quinlan, S., 150, 151, *168*
Quinn, J. M., 345, *368,* 638, 639, *668,* 674, 675, *705,*
    706, 760, *767*
Quinn, S. B., 46, *72*

R

Rabe, C., 462, 467, 471, *481*
Radecki, C., 137, *168*
Radecki-Bush, C., 720, *740*
Raden, D., 105, *123,* 185, *218*
Radvansky, G. A., 11, *19,* 275, 290, 291, 293, 298, 306,
    322
Raghubir, P., 149, *169,* 299, *318*
Raghunathan, R., 644, *666*
Rahn, W., 716, *741*
Rajaratnam, N., 31, *66*
Ramsay, J. O., 39, *72*
Rancer, A. S., 578, 589, *609*
Randall, D. M., 188, *218,* 726, *740*
Randell, R., 475, *483*
Rank, S., 637, *659*
Rankin, R. E., 59, *72*
Rao, V. R., 39, *68*
Rapaport, G. M., 41, 45, *65*
Rasinski, K. A., 24, 25, *75,* 84, 91, 95, 108, *124,* 325,
    367, 496, *540*
Raskas, D. F., 235, *265*
Raskin, E., 594, *615*
Ratcliff, C. D., 549, *573*
Ratcliff, D. D., 326, *367*
Rauch, S. L., 60, *68,* 399, *435*
Raudenbush, S., 140, 162, *166*
Raven, B., 636, *660,* 758, *765*
Raven, B. H., 634, 635, *660, 666,* 675, 680, 698, *701*
Raviv, A., 334, 336, 345, 346, 351, *361, 366*
Raymark, P., 150, *170*
Raymond, P., 186, *212,* 525, *530,* 544, *569*
Raynor, R., 442, 460, *488*
Razran, G. H. S., 441, 442, 460, 467, *487,* 507, *538,*
    557, *573,* 710, 728, *740*
Rea, C., 638, *658*

Read, S. J., 247, *269,* 568, *573*
Reardon, R., 638, *658*
Reber, R., 25, *72,* 342, *368,* 409, *432,* 451, 452, *487, 489,* 557, *574*
Reckless, W., 126, *169*
Reckman, R. F., 292, *316*
Reddy, M. E., 582, *609*
Redoute, J., 426, *432*
Reed, M., 595, *610*
Reed, T., 378, *392*
Regan, D., 297, *319*
Regan, D. T., 179, 180, *218, 740*
Reich, C. M., 286, 287, *314*
Reicher, S. D., 698, *706*
Reinecke, J., 165, *170*
Reingold, E. M., 501, *540*
Reinisch, J., 160, *166*
Reis, H. T., 179, 200, 201, *221*
Reisberg, D., 419, *432*
Reis-Bergan, M., 143, *167*
Reisenzein, R., 398, 403, 404, 405, 406, 412, 413, 414, 415, 416, 418, 419, *432, 433, 434*
Remmers, H. H., 34, *72,* 619, *666*
Rempel, J. K., 4, 5, *19,* 80, 82, *124,* 276, *322,* 324, 334, 335, 336, 337, 359, 360, *368,* 470, *489,* 618, 641, *669,* 678, *706,* 745, *767*
Reno, R. R., 677, *700*
Rentfrow, P. J., 682, *705*
Revenson, T. A., 130, *166*
Rey, L. D., 600, *607*
Reyes, R. M., 275, *319*
Reynolds, D. J., Jr., 632, *666*
Reynolds, G., 693, *700*
Reynolds, K., 644, *660*
Reynolds, K. D., 514, *539*
Reynolds, S., 418, *431*
Rhodes, F., 198, *214*
Rhodes, G., 407, *432*
Rhodes, N., 83, 94, 96, 102, 104, *124,* 348, *366,* 521, *538,* 591, 601, *613,* 622, 641, 644, *666, 668*
Rhodewalt, F., 234, 235, *267, 269,* 471, 472, *484, 487,* 516, *531*
Rholes, W. S., 559, *571,* 712, 714, 731, *736*
Rice, J. A., 420, *430*
Rice, W. E., 632, 650, *666*
Rich, C. E., 49, *69*
Richard, R., 200, *218*
Richeson, J. A., 563, *573*
Richman, S. A., 467, 471, *487,* 513, 517, 528, *538,* 581, *612*
Richter, L., *368*
Rickett, E., 159, *166,* 528, *530*
Ridgeway, C. L., 210, *218*
Ridout, J. B., 416, *427*
Riecken, H., 227, *266*
Riecken, H. W., 684, *701*
Rigby, S., 154, *168*
Riggle, E., 302, *318,* 721, *739*
Riggle, E. D., 721, *740*
Riggle, E. D. B., 210, *213*

Rimm, D. C., 446, *487*
Rind, B., 253, *269*
Rips, L. J., 149, *166*
Rissanen, A., 406, *432*
Ritov, I., 456, 461, *486*
Rittenauer-Schatka, H., 299, *319*
Rittle, R. H., 253, *269*
Roades, L. A., 42, *65*
Roberts, J., 40, *69*
Robertson, I. T., 196, *218*
Robichaud, L. K., 730, *741*
Robin, N., 163, *167*
Robinson, J. P., 35, *73*
Robinson, M., 474, *488*
Robinson, M. D., 419, *432,* 473, 475, *486, 488,* 752, *767*
Robinson, T. E., 424, *427*
Roddenberry, C., 727, *740*
Rodriguez, R., 518, *531*
Rodriquez, R., 14, *16*
Roediger, H. L., 523, 524, *538*
Roennemaa, T., 406, *432*
Roese, N. J., 51, *73,* 91, 94, 95, *123,* 274, *318*
Rogers, E. M., 716, *740*
Rogers, J., 690, *704*
Rogers, P. J., 450, *487*
Rogers, R. W., 346, *366,* 470, *487,* 648, *666*
Rohner, J. H., 679, *705*
Rojahn, K., 715, *740*
Rokeach, M., 14, *18,* 178, 181, *218,* 263, *269,* 284, *319,* 578, *613*
Rolls, E. T., 406, 423, 425, *431, 432, 435,* 474, *487*
Roman, R. J., 339, *367*
Romanski, L., 475, *485*
Romer, D., 650, *657*
Romero, A. A., *666*
Roney, C. J. R., 306, *319,* 598, *614*
Ronis, D. L., 144, *170,* 650, *666*
Rosch, E., 413, *432,* 478, *488*
Rose, R. L., 590, *605*
Roseman, I. J., 403, 404, *432*
Rosen, N. A., 285, 309, *319*
Rosen, R., 403, *434*
Rosenberg, M., 578, 591, *613*
Rosenberg, M. J., 12, *18,* 79, 82, 85, *116, 123,* 177, *218,* 232, 233, 239, *264, 269,* 288, 311, *314,* 327, 329, 330, 331, 332, 339, *360, 366,* 370, 371, 373, 383, 384, 385, 387, *390, 394,* 397, *432,* 549, 552, *573,* 586, 600, *604,* 710, 711, 714, *732, 740,* 743, 746, *766*
Rosenberg, N., 49, *73*
Rosenberg, S. W., 721, *740*
Rosenhan, D. L., 731, *740*
Rosenstein, D., 407, *432*
Rosenstock, I. M., 193, *218, 219*
Rosenstone, S. J., 39, *73*
Rosenthal, L., 599, *613*
Rosenthal, R., 632, *669*
Roskos-Ewoldsen, D. R., 25, *73,* 91, 94, 103, 114, *123,* 510, *539,* 547, *573,* 583, *613,* 634, *666*
Ross, C. E., 43, *71*

Ross, L., 11, *18,* 21, *70,* 99, 101, *121,* 143, *170,* 304, *319,* 358, *366,* 373, 375, 377, 378, 380, 385, *392, 395,* 514, 515, 517, *529, 536, 663, 666,* 679, *705*
Ross, M., 149, 150, *170,* 251, 259, *269, 271,* 291, 292, 310, *315, 319,* 376, 383, *393, 394,* 516, 519, *531, 542,* 649, 653, *666,* 715, *734, 738, 740*
Rosselli, F., 466, 469, *486, 487*
Rossnagel, C., 25, *69*
Rothenberg, B. B., 42, *73*
Rothermund, K., 64, *75*
Rothgerber, H., 677, *700, 706*
Rothman, A. J., 519, 520, *539,* 640, 655, *666*
Rotondo, J. A., 381, 385, 386, 387, 388, *395*
Rottenberg, J., 402, *432*
Rottmann, J., 650, *660*
Rousseau, J.-J., 680, *705*
Royet, J., 426, *432*
Royzman, E. B., 409, *432*
Rozin, P., 406, 407, 408, 409, *432*
Rubenstein, A. J., 407, *432*
Rubin, H. K., 45, *73*
Rubin, M., 682, *705*
Ruch, G. M., 43, *73*
Rucker, D. D., 103, *122,* 467, 470, 471, *487,* 512, 514, 518, *532,* 583, 586, 587, 588, 589, *605, 612, 613,* 628, *666*
Ruder, M., 628, *657*
Rudman, L. A., 549, 550, 561, *571, 573*
Ruechelle, R. C., 100, *123*
Rugg, D., *73,* 545, 546, *573*
Ruiter, R. A., 648, *666*
Rumelhart, D. E., 279, *319,* 499, *539,* 551, 568, *572*
Rundquist, E. A., 40, *73*
Rusbult, C. E., 229, *268,* 718, 720, *734, 740*
Rusch, A. J., 681, 690, *700*
Ruscher, J. B., 674, *705*
Russell, D. W., 143, *167,* 193, 201, 203, *215*
Russell, J. A., 404, 412, 414, 416, *428, 432, 433,* 439, *487*
Russin, A., 560, *571*
Ruther, A., 529, *542,* 634, *669*
Rutledge, T. R., 402, *430*
Ruud, P. A., 47, 49, *70*
Ryan, R. M., 197, *213*
Ryle, G., 359, *366*

S

Sacks, O., 446, *487*
Sacks, R., 589, *609*
Sadler, O., 385, 389, *394,* 514, *539*
Sadri, G., 196, *218*
Saegert, S., 410, *433*
Saegert, S. C., 618, *666*
Safer, M. A., 420, *430, 433*
Sagar, H. A., 729, *740*
Sagarin, B. J., 632, 650, *666*
Saito, S., 406, *427*
Sakai, H., 242, 249, *269*

Sakall, N., 448, *482*
Salancik, G. R., 25, *73*
Salas, E., 724, 725, 726, 727, *739*
Salomon, K. L., 642, *657*
Salovey, P., 416, *429,* 455, 461, 474, *486, 487,* 640, 655, *659, 666*
Salvi, D., 61, *70*
Sample, J., 179, *219*
Sanbonmatsu, D. M., 24, 25, 26, 55, *67, 73,* 81, 91, 93, 94, 99, 107, 108, *119, 122, 123,* 185, *214,* 372, *394,* 474, *483,* 544, 547, 564, 565, 566, *571,* 583, *607,* 642, 643, *659, 666,* 752, *765*
Sanchez, M., 403, *428*
Sande, G. N., 229, 242, *271, 742*
Sander, K., 425, *433*
Sanders, J. D., 501, *542*
Sanders, L. M., 26, *69*
Sanderson, C. A., 198, *219*
Sandman, C. A., 59, *65*
Sandvik, E., 421, *428*
Sandvold, K. D., 235, *271*
Sanford, R. N., 586, *604, 610*
Sanitioso, R., 310, *319*
Sanna, L. J., 305, 309, *315, 319*
Saris, W., 43, *73*
Sarnoff, I., 651, *666,* 710, *740*
Satin, M. S., 415, *434*
Sattler, D. N., 143, *170*
Saucier, D. A., 176, *219,* 655, *666*
Sawyer, J. D., 280, 291, *316*
Saxe, L., 204, 205, *213,* 564, *570*
Sayeed, S., 198, *214*
Sayers, S. L., 644, *667*
Schaal, B., 191, *215,* 406, 407, *433, 434,* 464, *486,* 518, *537,* 596, *611*
Schachter, S., 227, 233, 260, *266, 269,* 403, *433,* 680, 684, *701, 705,* 724, *735*
Schacter, D. L., 61, *75,* 243, 260, *268,* 544, *573*
Schaefer, P. S., 602, *613*
Schaeffer, N. C., 48, *73*
Schaller, M., 203, *219*
Schank, R., 10, *18*
Schank, R. C., 280, 290, *319*
Scheepers, D., 621, *659*
Scheich, H., 425, *433*
Scheier, M. F., 239, *269,* 578, 585, 592, *606, 607, 613*
Schellenberg, E. G., 405, 410, 417, *429, 434*
Schennum, A., 598, *611*
Scher, S. J., 237, 258, *269,* 632, *658*
Scherer, K. R., 403, 404, 405, *433,* 553, *573,* 694, *705*
Scherpenzeel, A., 63, 64, *73*
Schicker, I., 406, *427*
Schimmack, U., 398, 399, 400, 401, 405, 409, 410, 411, 413, 414, 415, 416, 417, 418, 419, 421, *429, 430, 431, 432, 433, 434*
Schlenker, B. R., 50, *73,* 226, 239, 240, *269, 271,* 516, 540, 681, *704, 705*
Schmälzle, K., 637, *659*
Schmidt, P., 145, 165, *166, 170,* 198, 201, *211*
Schmukle, S. C., 415, *428*

Schnall, S., 456, 478, *487*
Schneider, W., 25, *74*
Schofield, J. W., 729, *740*
Schönbach, P., 693, *702*
Schönpflug, W., 403, 406, *432*
Schooler, J. W., 128, *171*, 390, *395*, 650, *668*
Schooler, T. Y., 11, 12, 14, *19*, 24, *75*, 85, 86, 87, *124*, 205, 206, *220*, 323, 327, 333, 338, *368*, 386, 388, *395*, 524, *542*, 543, 544, 550, 559, 564, 566, *574*, 599, *615*, 655, *668*, 748, *767*
Schopler, J., 727, *737*, *740*
Schorr, 404, *433*
Schorr, A., 553, *573*
Schreiber, C. A., 420, 421, *434*
Schroder, H., 306, *316*
Schroder, K. E, 152, 153, 165, *170*
Schroeder, H. M., 284, *319*
Schuette, R. A., 101, 107, 116, *123*, 187, *219*, 381, 382, *394*, 519, *539*
Schulz, P. W., 707, 708, *739*
Schuman, D., 708, *740*
Schuman, H., 35, 39, 40, 45, 47, 52, *70*, *73*, 115, *123*, 178, 204, *219*, 545, 546, 547, 556, *571*, *573*
Schumann, D. W., 467, 471, *487*, 513, 517, 528, *538*, 581, *612*
Schure, E., 404, *429*
Schut, H., 333, *365*
Schuurman, M., 687, 689, *701*
Schvaneveldt, R. W., 54, *71*
Schwartz, A., 456, 461, *486*
Schwartz, G. E., 59, *67*, 747, *766*
Schwartz, J., 412, 413, *434*
Schwartz, J. C., 412, *434*
Schwartz, J. L. K., 56, 58, *68*, 206, *215*, 445, *484*, 524, *533*, 582, 599, *608*
Schwartz, L. K., 544, *571*
Schwartz, N., 557, *574*
Schwartz, R., 127, *171*
Schwartz, S. H., 263, *269*
Schwartzman, D., 514, *539*
Schwarz, H., 309, *315*
Schwarz, N., 4, 13, *18*, 24, 25, 26, 27, 39, 45, 49, *65*, *68*, *72*, *73*, *74*, 80, *123*, 149, 153, 154, *169*, *170*, 274, 276, 284, 294, 299, 301, 302, 305, *318*, *319*, *320*, 323, 325, 326, 327, 329, 334, 335, 342, 344, *366*, *367*, *368*, 398, 406, 409, 411, *432*, *434*, *435*, 439, 444, 451, 452, 453, 454, 455, 461, 462, 466, 467, 468, 471, 477, *481*, *482*, *487*, *488*, *489*, 496, 519, 520, 528, *539*, *540*, 543, 545, 546, 547, 549, 566, *573*, *574*, 645, *657*, 710, 711, 712, 720, 721, 728, *733*, *740*, 746, 747, *766*
Schwenkmezger, P., 415, *434*
Scott, C. A., *367*, 511, *539*
Scott, G. M., 587, *611*
Scott, R., 437, *487*
Scott, S. K., 424, *431*
Scott, T. R., 423, *434*, *435*
Scott, W. A., 83, 84, *123*, 284, *320*
Scott-Sheldon, L. A. J., 58, 62, *70*, 545, *572*
Sczesny, S., 517, *539*

Seamon, J. G., 409, *434*, 452, *488*
Sears, D. O., *219*, 231, *266*, 333, *364*, 545, *571*, 601, *613*, *660*, 711, *740*
Sechrest, L., 127, *171*
Sechrist, G. B., *705*
Sedikides, C., 51, *73*, 98, *121*, 559, *573*, 576, *613*, 682, *705*, 711, *740*
See, M., 621, *662*
Seeleman, V., 710, 714, *741*
Seeman, I., 47, *72*
Seger, C. A., *573*
Seidlitz, I., 419, *434*
Sekaquaptewa, D., 61, *75*, 206, *219*
Seligman, C., 253, *270*
Seligman, M. E. P., 442, 446, 460, *488*
Selltiz, C., 176, *212*
Semenik, R. J., 299, 300, 301, *320*
Semin, G. R., 62, *70*
Senchak, M., 722, *741*
Sengupta, J., 110, *123*, 470, *488*, 628, 633, 648, *661*, 667, 697, *699*
Sentis, K. P., 288, *320*
Serna, S. B., 632, 650, *666*
Serodio, R. G., 680, *703*
Servan-Schreiber, D., 422, 424, *427*
Seta, J. J., 107, *121*, 517, 518, 528, *536*
Sexton, J., *64*, 203, *211*
Shadish, W. R., 148, *170*
Shaeffer, E., 621, *662*
Shaffer, D. R., 635, 643, *667*, 719, *741*
Shaffer, J. W., 42, *73*
Shaffer, L. M., 501, *535*
Shaffer, S. D., 375, *394*
Shah, J. Y., 332, 337, 339, 356, *364*, 582, *610*, 761, *766*
Shaikh, T., 681, *705*
Shalker, T. E., 453, 461, *485*
Shallice, T., 501, *539*
Shanks, D. P., 441, 444, *485*, 750, *766*
Shanks, D. R., 507, *536*
Shao, L., 593, *608*
Shapira, Z. B., 38, *67*
Shapiro, J. P., 718, *741*
Shavelson, R., 31, *73*
Shaver, J. P., 42, *70*
Shaver, P., 412, 413, *434*
Shaver, P. R., 35, *73*, 719, *741*
Shavitt, S., 82, 100, *123*, 203, *219*, 339, *366*, 593, 598, *608*, *611*, *613*, 646, *667*, 678, 680, *705*, 754, *767*
Shaw, J. C., *739*
Shaw, J. S., 723, *734*
Shaw, K., 373, 382, 383, *391*, 521, *532*, 757, *765*
Shaw-Barnes, K., 370, 382, 383, *391*, 419, *428*, 521, *532*, 715, *735*, 757, *765*
Sheatsley, P. B., 546, *571*
Shebo Van Zandt, B. J., 509, *536*
Shechter, D., 26, *66*, 638, 643, *658*, 676, 680, 681, 685, *700*
Sheeran, P., 188, 189, 190, 191, 196, 200, 201, *212*, *218*, *219*

Sheffield, F. D., 175, *216,* 300, *317,* 344, *363,* 518, *534,* 619, 620, 623, 640, *661*

Sheline, Y. I., 399, *434*

Shelton, S. E., 408, *431*

Shephard, R. J., 183, *215*

Shepherd, B. H., 188, 196, 201, *219*

Shepherd, R., 109, *118, 123,* 196, 199, *219*

Sheppard, L. A., 462, 463, 465, *481,* 710, *733*

Shepperd, J. A., 309, *320,* 375, *394*

Sherif, C. W., 45, *74,* 370, 383, *394,* 520, *539,* 620, 621, 635, 653, *667*

Sherif, M., 4, 10, 11, *18,* 45, *74,* 354, *367,* 370, 383, *394,* 520, *539, 613,* 620, 621, *661, 667,* 678, 679, *702, 705*

Sherman, B. R., 310, *320*

Sherman, D., 590, *613*

Sherman, D. K., 239, *270*

Sherman, J. W., 289, *316,* 544, *569,* 596, *613,* 748, *764*

Sherman, S. J., 62, *74,* 81, 108, *119,* 126, 143, *169, 170,* 178, 186, *214, 219,* 253, *266,* 274, 287, 298, 304, *319, 320,* 343, *363,* 371, 378, 381, 382, 387, 389, 390, *391, 394,* 514, 516, 517, 521, 527, *539, 735*

Shestowsky, D., 518, *539,* 582, *613*

Shevell, S. K., 149, *166*

Shiffrin, R. M., 25, 45, *64, 74,* 287, 303, *316, 319*

Shimamura, A. P., 27, *71*

Shimp, T. A., 409, *434,* 507, 508, 528, *533, 539, 540,* 708, *741*

Shin, L. M., 60, *68*

Short, J. C., 578, 596, 598, *614*

Shraugher, J. S., 235, *270*

Shrout, P. E., 31, *74*

Shrum, L. J., 299, 300, 301, *318, 320*

Shulman, R. F., 251, *269*

Shulman, S., 719, *741*

Shultz, J. S., 595, *613*

Shultz, T. R., 247, 248, 262, *270,* 515, *539*

Sia, T. L., 326, *367,* 549, *573*

Sidanius, J., 578, 595, *612*

Sidera, J., 101, *118,* 647, *657*

Sideris, J., 241, 260, *269*

Siemer, M., 400, 401, 405, 414, *434*

Sienkiewicz, Z. J., 423, *435*

Sigall, H., 51, *74,* 176, *216,* 502, *539,* 564, *573*

Sigelman, C. K., 42, *74*

Signorielli, N., 300, *316*

Sillars, A. L., 720, *741*

Silver, B. D., 52, *64*

Simmons, H. C., 287, 311, *318*

Simmons, J. P., 382, *395,* 642, *668*

Simon, H. A., 308, *320,* 337, *367,* 439, *488,* 712, *739, 741*

Simon, J., 58, *74*

Simon, L., 236, 237, 238, 256, 260, 262, *267, 270,* 329, 516, *534, 539,* 632, *661*

Simons, A., 299, *319*

Simonson, I., 312, *315*

Simpatico, T., 143, *167*

Simpson, J. A., 634, *664*

Sinclair, L., 335, 345, 355, *364,* 563, *573*

Sinclair, R. A., 466, 467, 468, 471, *488*

Sinclair, R. C., 456, *488*

Sinclair, S., 445, 448, *486, 488,* 561, 563, *572*

Singer, J., 403, *433*

Singer, J. E., 130, *166,* 233, 260, *269,* 380, *394*

Singer, M., 280, 293, *316*

Sipski, M. L., 403, *434*

Sistrunk, F., 600, *613*

Sivacek, J., 179, *219*

Sjöberg, L., 337, *367*

Skalaban, A., 374, *392*

Skelly, J. J., 469, *487,* 678, *703*

Skinner, B. F., 229, *270, 539*

Skolnick, P., 592, *613*

Skorinko, J., 448, *488*

Skov, R. B., 304, *320*

Skowronski, J. J., 150, *170,* 507, 524, *531, 539,* 559, *573*

Skurnik, I., 238, 262, *265,* 627, *664*

Slaw, R. D., 582, *610*

Sleeth-Keppler, D., 332, 337, 351, 352, *364, 366,* 526, *538,* 579, *612,* 629, *665,* 761, *766*

Sletto, R. F., 40, *73*

Slovic, P., 278, 295, 298, *317, 320,* 346, *367,* 455, 461, *488*

Slusher, M. P., 639, *667*

Small, D. A., 457, 461, *485*

Small, E. M., *319*

Small, H., 162, *167*

Small, M., 154, *171*

Smart, J., 183, *217*

Smilansky, J., 640, *664*

Smith, 465, *486*

Smith, C. A., 399, 403, 404, *432, 434*

Smith, C. N., 425, *428*

Smith, E. E., 99, *119,* 511, *532,* 622, *659,* 696, *704*

Smith, E. R., 13, *17, 18,* 59, *74,* 81, 91, 94, 106, 110, 115, *123,* 278, 280, *315, 320,* 327, *361,* 452, 457, 461, 479, *486,* 494, 496, 499, 518, 520, 525, 528, *531, 539, 540,* 547, 548, 551, 561, 568, *569, 572, 573, 574,* 599, *613,* 695, *700,* 746, *767*

Smith, H. N., 174, *219*

Smith, J., 57, *68*

Smith, L., 109, *122,* 201, *218*

Smith, M. B., 79, 82, *123,* 338, 360, *367,* 374, *391,* 505, *532,* 627, 629, 642, 643, 646, *667,* 678, 680, 682, *705,* 754, *767*

Smith, M. C., 61, *64,* 344, *361*

Smith, M. M., 285, *316*

Smith, P. B., 556, *574,* 674, 696, *699*

Smith, R. H., 636, *661*

Smith, S. M., 83, 90, 91, 92, 94, 95, 96, 97, 98, 109, 113, *119, 121, 122, 123, 488,* 513, 517, 519, 521, 522, *538, 540,* 578, 581, *612, 613,* 624, 635, 643, 644, *665, 667, 668*

Smith, T. L., 23, 28, *66,* 324, *362*

Smith, T. W., 39, *74*

Smith, V., 595, *608*

Smith, V. K., 47, 49, *70*

Smith, W. R., 42, 45, 49, *66, 70*

Smith-McLallen, A., 344, 349, *363,* 370, *392,* 512, 513, *535,* 619, 622, 639, 644, *662*

Smoak, N. D., 99, 100, 103, *124,* 520, 529, *541*

Smolensky, P., 551, *574*

Smyth, M., 151, *170*

Snibbe, A. C., 161, *165,* 249, *268*

Sniezek, J., 593, *608*

Snowden, R. J., 57, *68*

Snyder, A., 603, *607*

Snyder, A. Z., 399, *434*

Snyder, C. R., 578, 593, 597, *613*

Snyder, C. R. R., 55, *72*

Snyder, D. K., 722, *741*

Snyder, H. N., 692, *703*

Snyder, M., 26, *74,* 100, 101, 102, 104, 107, *121, 123,* 179, 180, *215, 219,* 245, 251, 253, *270,* 340, *365, 367,* 378, *394,* 514, *540,* 578, 579, 596, 597, *610, 613, 614,* 638, *667,* 757, *766*

Snyder, M. L., *270*

Soares, J. J. F., 447, *486*

Sobel, N., 426, *426*

Solarz, A. K., 61, *74*

Soldat, A. S., 456, *488*

Solomon, S., 51, *68,* 241, 260, *269,* 576, *613*

Solomonson, A. L., 376, *394*

Song-Hing, L. S., 730, *741*

Son Hing, L. S., 128, *166, 170,* 242, *270*

Sonnemons, J., 439, *484*

Sorrentino, R. M., 306, *319,* 578, 596, 598, *614*

Soussignan, R., 402, 406, 407, *433, 434*

Southwell, B., 188, *216*

Southwick, L., 516, *540*

Southwick, L. L., 234, 261, *270*

Sparks, P., 97, 109, *118, 123,* 196, 199, 201, *212, 219*

Spears, R., 621, *659,* 676, *704, 737*

Speckart, G., 201, *212,* 651, *657*

Spector, N. H., 422, *427*

Speigel, S., 339, 351, *364,* 505, *535*

Spencer, S. J., 238, 244, 245, 249, *267, 270,* 379, *391, 398, 434,* 562, *574,* 590, *606,* 633, *661, 667*

Spenner, K., 600, *607*

Sperber, D., 293, *320*

Spiegel, S., 351, 352, *362,* 372, *392,* 505, *531, 535,* 582, *610,* 624, 626, 628, 634, *662, 667,* 762, *767*

Spielberger, C. D., 602, *614*

Spielhofer, C., 404, *432*

Spink, K. S., 724, *741*

Spiro, R. J., 280, 291, *320*

Spruyt, A., 407, 408, 410, *429*

Spurlock, D., 593, *608*

Srinivasan, V., 38, *74*

Sroka, K. R., 692, *703*

Sroufe, L. A., 719, *741*

Srull, T. K., 5, 13, *19,* 274, 280, 281, 300, *320, 322,* 325, *368,* 463, *489,* 522, 529, *540, 542,* 553, 559, *574,* 629, *667,* 712, 714, 715, *741, 742,* 762, *767*

Staats, A. W., 343, 359, *367,* 408, *434,* 441, 442, 448, 460, *488,* 507, *540,* 557, *574,* 710, 728, *741,* 751, *767*

Staats, C. K., 343, 359, *367,* 408, *434,* 441, 442, 448, 460, *488,* 507, *540,* 557, *574,* 710, 728, *741,* 751, *767*

Stafford, T., 115, *119,* 528, 532, *532,* 568, *570*

Stagner, R., 174, *219*

Stalder, D. R., 245, *270*

Stallworth, L. M., 578, 595, *612*

Stang, D. J., 450, *488*

Stanger, R., 586, *614*

Stangor, C., *705,* 715, *741*

Stanley, D. J., 128, *166*

Stanton, A. D., 163, *169*

Stapel, D., 621, *659*

Stapel, D. A., 496, *540,* 546, 549, *574,* 621, *667*

Stappen, I., 426, *426*

Stark, H. A., 61, *75*

Steeh, C., 204, *219*

Steele, C. M., 143, 146, *170,* 204, *219,* 234, 237, 238, 244, 245, 246, 256, 260, 261, *270,* 312, *320, 367,* 515, 516, *540,* 576, 590, *606, 613, 614,* 633, 640, *664, 667*

Steele, D., 188, *216*

Steenbergen, M. R., 716, 721, *738, 739*

Stegner, S., 296, *314*

Stein, E. A., 425, *428*

Steiner, J. E., 407, *434*

Steinmetz, J., 304, *319*

Stember, H., 39, 40, *74*

Stephens, L., 558, *571*

Stephenson, G. M., 203, *217*

Stephenson, M. T., 577, *609*

Stepper, S., 25, *74,* 456, *488,* 507, *540*

Stern, L. D., 500, *540*

Sternberg, R. J., 601, *614,* 618, *667,* 719, *741*

Stevens, L. E., 635, *660*

Stevenson, R. J., 408, *434*

Stewart, P., 127, *170*

Stewart, A. M., 376, *392*

Stewart, T. L., 518, 525, *540*

Steyer, R., 415, *434*

Stice, E., 241, *270*

Stiff, J. B., 627, 639, *667*

Stock, C. B., 304, *320*

Stocker, S. L., 305, *319*

Stoleru, S., 426, *432*

Stone, A. A., 415, *430, 434*

Stone, G. C., 42, *67*

Stone, J., 229, 239, 240, 241, 242, 244, 245, 256, 258, 260, 261, 262, *265, 266, 267, 270,* 516, *540,* 684, *700,* 761, *767*

Stone, J. I., 632, *658*

Storbeck, J., 474, 475, *488,* 752, *767*

Storm, C., *434*

Storm, T., *434*

Stotland, E., 5, *17,* 79, 82, 101, *120, 121,* 177, *216,* 276, *317,* 743, *766*

Strack, F., 24, 25, 27, 45, *65, 73, 74,* 153, 154, *170,* 294, 299, 301, 302, 304, 309, *315, 318, 319, 320,* 325, *366, 367,* 454, 456, 466, 467, 468, 476, *481, 486,*

488, 507, 516, 517, *540,* 545, 546, 557, 566, *573, 574,* 645, *657, 733*

Stradling, S. G., 200, 201, *218*

Strahan, E. J., 88, *119,* 398, *434*

Strathman, A., 513, *534*

Strathman, A. J., 467, 471, *487,* 513, 517, 528, *538,* 581, *612*

Strathman, D., 603, *614*

Stratton, P., 200, *212*

Stratton, V. N., 405, *434*

Strauss, J., 731, *736*

Strecher, V. J., 193, *218, 219*

Streufert, S., 284, *319*

Stroebe, W., 325, 332, 333, 337, 346, 354, *362, 363, 365, 367,* 640, *658,* 753, *764*

Stroessner, S. J., 464, *484, 488,* 589, 596, *610, 613*

Stroh, P., 716, *738*

Strube, G., 149, *170*

Strube, M. J., 51, *73,* 682, *705*

Strycker, A. H., 162, *167*

Stuart, E. W., 409, *434,* 508, 528, *539, 540,* 708, *741*

Stubing, M. J., 241, 260, *269*

Stuckey, C., 587, *611*

Stueve, A., 730, *740*

Stukat, K. G., 345, *367*

Stults, D. M., 239, *270*

Suci, G. E., *366*

Suci, G. J., 4, *18,* 32, 33, 35, *72, 93, 122,* 210, *218,* 475, *487*

Sudman, S., 25, *74,* 546, *574*

Suedfeld, P., 84, *117, 124*

Sugimori, S., 725, *737*

Suh, E., 400, 418, *433*

Sullivan, J. L., 91, 95, 102, *121,* 381, *392,* 716, *741*

Sullivan, K. T., 722, *737*

Sulloway, F. J., 575, 577, 586, 602, *609, 614,* 763, *766*

Sulmont, C., 416, *434*

Suls, J., 406, *428*

Suppes, P., 28, *70*

Surwit, R. S., 405, *435*

Susser, K., *733*

Sussman, B., 35, *74*

Sutton, J., 441, 460, *488*

Sutton, S., 144, *170*

Sutton, S. R., 640, *667*

Suzuki, T., 249, *268*

Swan, S., 294, *321*

Swander, D. V., 679, *705*

Swann, W. B., Jr., 378, *394,* 682, *705*

Swap, W., 410, *433*

Swap, W. C., 618, *666*

Swasy, J. L., *733*

Sweeney, D., 106, *121*

Sweeney, P. D., 376, *394,* 515, *540,* 711, 717, *741*

Swets, J. A., 500, *533*

Symons, C. S., 370, *392,* 621, 644, *662, 667*

Szpunar, K. K., 410, *434*

T

Taber, C., 716, *738*

Taber, C. S., 455, *485*

Taber, T., 295, *321*

Taber, T. D., 38, *69*

Tager-Flusberg, H., 449, *481*

Tajfel, H., 682, 686, 693, 694, 698, *702, 705, 706,* 723, 728, *741*

Tambor, E. S., 576, *610*

Tamir, M., 473, *488*

Tamulonis, V., *74*

Tanford, S., 636, *667*

Tang, C., 458, *482*

Tang, S., 254, *270*

Tanke, E. D., 245, *270,* 597, *614*

Tannenbaum, P. H., 4, *18,* 32, 33, 35, *72,* 85, 93, *116, 122,* 210, *218,* 226, 232, *264, 269,* 311, *314,* 330, *360, 366,* 370, 383, *390, 393,* 475, *487,* 510, 515, *537,* 586, 600, *604,* 711, *739*

Tassinary, L. G., 508, *530,* 579, *606*

Tausch, A., 415, *428*

Taves, P. A., 234, *266, 271,* 633, *668*

Taylor, C. L., 45, *68*

Taylor, S., 196, *219,* 636, *661*

Taylor, S. E., 154, *167,* 203, *219,* 252, *270,* 280, 281, 301, 306, *316, 320,* 498, 511, 519, 522, *533, 540,* 576, 590, *614*

Tedeschi, J. T., 51, *72,* 239, 240, *267, 271,* 516, *540*

Teel, J. E., *605*

Telaak, K., 520, *532,* 621, 642, *659*

Tellegen, A., 13, *19,* 414, 415, *435,* 439, *488*

Terdal, S. K., 576, *610*

Terry, D., 652, *667*

Terry, D. J., 183, 199, 200, 201, *220*

Tesser, A., 6, 12, *18,* 21, 25, *74,* 84, 91, 96, 97, 109, 116, *121, 122, 123,* 203, *217,* 238, 239, 241, 260, 262, *271,* 325, 334, *367,* 381, 385, 386, 387, 388, 389, *391, 393, 394,* 514, 516, *536, 539, 540,* 576, 581, 590, *614,* 682, *706,* 745, *767*

Tetlock, P. E., 26, *74,* 83, 84, *117, 124, 320,* 383, 386, 388, *394, 395,* 638, 644, *667,* 727, *741*

Thagard, P., 389, *395,* 477, *488,* 568, *572*

Thaler, R., 591, *609*

Thayer, R. E., 405, *434*

Thibaut, J. W., 680, *706, 737*

Thibodeau, R., 235, 237, 241, 256, *266, 271*

Thiemann, P., 650, *660*

Thistlewaite, D. L., 346, *367*

Thomas, D. L., 418, 419, *434*

Thomas, G. V., 446, *483*

Thomas, K., 183, *214*

Thomas, S., 408, *428,* 441, 444, 445, 460, *483,* 507, *532,* 751, *764*

Thomas, W. I., 22, *74,* 174, *220,* 618, *667*

Thompsen, C. J., *365,* 335

Thompson, E. P., 14, *18*, 98, *121*, 323, 339, 351, 352, 356, 359, *364, 367*, 372, *392*, 478, *488*, 498, 503, 505, 526, *535*, 582, *610*, 622, 624, 626, 628, 634, *662, 667*, 762, *766, 767*

Thompson, J. S., 722, *741*

Thompson, M., 206, *219*

Thompson, M. M., 84, 85, 89, 95, 98, *124*, 331, 332, *367*, 584, 586, *611, 614*, 642, *667*

Thompson, W. C., 275, *319*

Thompson, W. F., 405, *429*

Thomsen, C. J., 85, 86, 90, 91, 95, 96, *121*, 382, *392*, *395*, 418, *430*

Thunberg, M., 399, *428*

Thurstone, L. L., 4, *19*, 21, 23, 28, 32, 35, *74*, 79, *124*, 174, 177, 180, *220*, 276, *320*, 324, 331, *367*, 397, *435*, 493, *537, 540*, 618, 619, *667*

Tian, K. T., 593, *614*

Tice, D. M., 590, *605*, 624, *657*

Tiedens, L. Z., 463, 465, *488*

Tierney, A. M., 644, *667*

Till, B. D., 408, *429*

Tobin, S. J., 584, *614, 615*

Todorov, T., 290, *320*

Tokusato, D., 518, 528, *541*

Tomaka, J., 339, *361, 435*, 642, *657*

Tomkins, S. S., 397, *435*

Toppin, T., 278, 303, *317*

Tordesillas, R. S., 115, *122*, 377, 378, 382, *393*, 586, *612*, 641, 642, *665*

Tormala, Z. L., 14, *18*, 86, 87, 103, *122*, 506, 508, 513, 517, 519, *530, 537, 538, 540*, 578, 579, 581, 582, 583, 586, 587, 588, 589, 590, 591, *605, 612, 614*, 628, 642, 653, *665, 667*

Toth, J. P., 501, *540*

Totterdell, P., 418, *431*

Tourangeau, R., 24, 25, *75*, 84, 91, 95, 108, *124*, 325, *367*, 496, *540*

Towles-Schwen, T., 91, 94, 106, 107, 110, *119, 124*, 130, *167*, 184, 205, 208, 210, *214*, 339, *362*, 372, *391*, 564, *571*, 760, *765*

Toy, D. R., 708, *739*

Trabasso, T., 280, 293, *316*

Trafimow, D., 188, 197, *214, 219*, 220, 221, *741*

Tran, T., 721, *740*

Tranel, D., 60, *64*, 389, *390*, 419, 424, *426, 427*

Transue, J., 102, *121*

Trapp, R., 589, *614*

Trasselli, G., 343, *367*

Triandis, H. C., 126, 131, 144, *170*, 177, 188, 193, 200, 202, *214, 220*, 578, 593, *614*, 651, *667, 668*, 711, *741*

Troccoli, B., 517, *530*

Trope, Y., 184, *212*, 323, 335, *362, 367*, 503, *531*, 567, *569*, 624, 644, *658, 666, 734*

Trost, M. R., 245, *265*, 331, *362*, 578, 587, 593, *606, 668*, 675, 677, *700*

Trott, D. M., 42, *75*

Trudeau, J. V., 226, *269*

Tubb, V. A., 154, *168*

Tubbs, S. L., 595, *605*

Tuchfarber, A. J., 47, *65*

Tucker, L., 140, *170*

Tulloch, W. F., 582, *609*

Tulving, E., 61, *75*, 149, *170*

Turner, J. C., 673, 678, 682, 683, 689, 698, *701, 702, 704, 706*, 723, *741*

Turner, T., 275, *314*

Turner, T. J., *315*, 414, *431*

Turrisi, R., 162, *168*

Tversky, A., 11, *19*, 28, 58, *70, 75*, 203, *216*, 290, 296, 298, 304, 305, *317, 321*, 519, *540*, 622, *668*, 691, *702, 737, 741*

Twenge, J. M., 411, *435*

Tybout, A. M., *367*

Tykocinski, O., 603, *614*

Tyler, R. B., 206, 207, *213*

U

Uleman, J. S., 344, *367*, 523, *541*, 727, *741*

Uttl, B., 501, *535*

V

Vaidya, J., 415, *435*

Vaillancourt, P. M., 47, *75*

Vakil, E., 524, *541*

Valentin, D., 164, *165*

Valins, S., *614*

Vallacher, R. R., 10, *19*, 244, *271*

Vallerand, R. J., 254, *271*

Vallone, R. P., 375, 377, *395*

Valois, P., 183, 192, *215*

Valone, K., 635, *664*

Vanable, P., 152, 153, 165, *170*

Vance, S. L., 210, *213*, 565, *570*

Vancouver, J. B., 130, *166*

Vandello, J. A., 679, *699*

van den Berg, H., 408, *435*

Van den Bergh, O., 343, *361*, 444, 460, *481*, 558, *569*, 750, *764*

van den Putte, B., 188, 196, *220*

van der Pligt, J., 200, 203, *218, 220*, 650, *668*

van Eekelen, S. A. M., 199, *217*

van Engen, M., 161, *167*

van Knippenberg, A., 145, *170*, 202, *210*, 264, *267*, 544, *571*

van Knippenberg, C., 145, *170*

van Knippenberg, D., 683, 684, *706*

Vanman, E. J., 60, *75*, 568, *573*

Van Overwalle, F., *170*, 248, *271*, 471, *488, 541*

van Reekum, C. M., 408, *435*

Van Ryn, M., 198, *220*

van Schie, E. C. M., 650, *668*

Van Vugt, M., 236, *267*

Van Zandt, B. J., 409, *431*, 451, 452, *486*

Varela, F. J., 478, *488*

Vargas, P., 61, *75*, 206, *219*

Varner, J. L., 425, *430*
Vaughan, G. A., 354, *363*
Vaughn, K., 242, 247, *267*
Vaughn, L. A., 519, *539*, 585, *615*
Vegas, R., 508, *532*
Veitch, R., 453, 461, *484*
Velthuijsen, A. S., 621, *667*
Ven den Hout, M. A., 399, *435*
Vera, M. N., 403, *428*
Vermette, L., 201, *220*
Vernon, P. E., 176, *220*
Vernon, P. A., 160, *169*, 334, *366*
Verplanken, B., 145, *170, 171*, 190, 202, *210, 220*, 264, *267*
Vila, J., 403, *428*
Vinokur, A., 639, *668*, 687, *700*, 725, *734, 741*
Vinokur, A. D., 198, *220*
Visser, P. S., 34, 45, 47, *68, 75*, 382, *395*, 499, *541*, 601, *615*, 642, *668*
Vollenweider, F. X., 405, *429, 430*
von Haeften, I., 163, *167*, 204, *220*
Von Hendy, H. M., 597, *608*
von Hippel, W., 61, *75*, 91, 100, *119*, 206, *219*, 469, 470, *483*
Vroom, V. H., 175, *220*
Vrugt, A., *271*
Vuokko, P., 653, *668*

W

Wachsler, R. A., 42, *66*
Wade, J., 636, *661*
Wagar, B. M., 389, *395*
Wagenaar, W. A., 151, *171*
Wagner, S. H., 102, 106, *121*
Waksberg, J., 152, *169*
Walker, D., 375, *394*
Walker, G. R., 585, *608*
Wall, S., 719, *732*
Wallace, H. M., 14, *16*, 115, *117*, 284, 313, *314*, 359, *360*, 583, *604*, 650, *656*
Wallace, K. A., 380, *390*
Wallbott, H. G., *433*
Walster, E., 5, *16*, 229, *271*, 287, *321*, 718, *735*
Walther, E., 87, *124*, 343, 344, *367*, 407, *435*, 444, *488*, 507, *541*, 751, *767*
Waly, P., 176, *220*
Wan, C., 141, 150, 151, *168*
Wan, K. C., 729, *736*
Wang, C. L., 593, *615*
Wänke, M., 26, 27, *65, 75*, 299, *321*, 325, 342, *361, 367*, 519, *541*
Wanner, J., 589, *614*
Wapner, S., 578, *615*
Warburton, J., 200, 201, *220*
Ward, D., 21, *74*
Ward, D. W., 467, 469, *486*
Ward, W. D., 235, *271*
Ware, J. E., *75*

Warland, R., 179, *219*
Warner, L. G., 178, *220*
Warner, S. L., 51, *75*
Warr, P., 39, *75*
Warren, R., 201, *212*
Warshaw, P. R., 188, 191, 193, 196, 201, *211, 219, 220*
Warwick, D., 672, *704*
Wasel, W., 207, *212*, 464, *486*, 518, *537*, 564, 565, *569*, 596, *611*
Wason, P. C., 43, *75*
Waterman, C. K., 233, *271*
Waters, E., 719, *732*
Watherell, M. S., 698, *706*
Watkins, L. R., 405, *430*
Watkins, T. A., 650, *662*
Watson, A., 731, *734*
Watson, A. C., 730, *734*
Watson, D., 12, *19*, 39, *75*, 405, 414, 415, *428, 435*, 439, *488*
Watson, D. R., 42, *75*
Watson, J. B., 174, *220*, 442, 460, *488*
Watson, W. S., 710, 715, *742*
Watt, S. E., 653, *663*
Watts, W., 224, *271*
Watts, W. A., 285, *321*, 514, 522, *541*, 638, 650, *668*
Way, J. H., 595, *606*
Weary, G., 578, 584, 585, *615*
Webb, E. J., 127, *171*
Webb, N., 31, *73*
Weber, E. U., 389, *392*, 456, 461, *485*
Weber, S. J., 549, *574*
Webster, D. M., 14, *19*, 309, *321*, 331, *364, 368*, 577, 578, 582, 583, 584, *609, 610, 615*, 644, *662*
Webster, S., 635, *660*
Wedell, D. H., 39, *75*
Wegener, D. T., 4, *18*, 24, 27, 50, *75*, 80, 88, 89, 91, 94, 95, 98, 99, 100, 101, 103, 104, 106, 107, 115, *118, 119, 122, 124*, 341, 349, *366*, 372, 377, 378, 379, *393, 395*, 468, 469, *487, 488*, 499, 506, 510, 512, 513, 514, 515, 517, 518, 519, 520, 523, 524, 526, 528, 529, *532, 534, 538, 539, 541*, 557, *574*, 577, 579, 581, 582, 591, 597, 598, 600, 601, *608, 612, 613, 615*, 624, 626, 635, 643, 644, 645, 647, 653, *665, 666, 668*, 687, 694, 698, 762, *704, 766*
Wegner, D. M., 10, *19*, 142, *171*, 206, *220*, 244, *271*, 294, *321*, 359, *368, 488*, 495, *541*, 562, *574*
Weick, K., 154, *171*
Weigel, R. H., 181, *220*
Weinberger, J., 599, 600, *610*
Weiner, B., 403, *435*
Weingold, M. F., 50, *73*, 681, *705*
Weinstein, N. D., 153, *169*, 309, *321*
Weiskrantz, L., 424, *435*
Weiss, R. L., 723, *742*
Weiss, S. M., 144, *168*
Weitz, S., 207, *220*
Weitzenhoffer, A. M., 600, *615*
Weitzenhoffer, G. B., 600, *615*
Welch, N., 389, *392*, 456, 461, *485*

Well, A. D., 133, *169*
Wellman, H. M., 448, *488*
Wells, G. L., 153, 154, *171*, 512, 514, 521, 529, *538*, 623, 638, 643, *665*
Wentura, D., 64, *75*
Wenzlaff, R. M., 294, *321*, 359, *368*
Werner, P. D., 181, *220*
Wesman, A. G., 43, *75*
West, S. G., 584, *611*, 688, *703*
Westie, F. R., 53, *75*, 175, 178, 181, *213*
Whalen, P. J., 60, *68*, 399, *435*
Wheatley, T., 206, *220*
Wheeler, S. C., 86, 87, 101, 104, *122*, 352, *366*, 400, *435*, 526, *538*, 578, 582, 583, 599, 600, *605, 612, 615*, 627, 647, *665*
Whitaker, D., 21, *74*
Whitbeck, L. B., 719, *742*
White, G. L., 229, *267*
White, P. H., 518, 528, *538*, 591, 596, *608, 612*, 629, 635, *665, 668*
White, R. W., 79, 82, *123*, 338, 360, *367*, 627, 629, 642, 643, 646, *667, 678*, 680, 682, *705*, 754, *767*
Wicker, A. W., 10, *19*, 175, 177, 178, 181, 187, *220*, 759, *767*
Wicklund, R. A., 179, *220*, 227, 231, 240, *266, 270, 271*, 311, *321*, 515, *533*, 585, *613*
Widaman, K. F., 177, *220*
Wiebe, D. J., 143, *169*
Wieczorkowska, G., 448, *482*
Wiegand, A. W., 242, 256, 260, *270*
Wierzbicka, A., 404, 412, *435*
Wiese, D., 415, *435*
Wiesenfeld, B. M., 235, *265*
Wiesenthal, N. L., 90, 91, 96, 97, 98, *123*
Wieslquist, J., 727, *740*
Wiggins, E. C., *427*
Wiggins, J. S., 154, *171*
Wiggins, N., 295, 296, *321*
Wilcox, R. R., 155, 156, *171*
Wilder, D. A., *668*, 678, *706*
Wilder, J., 686, *699*
Wildschutt, T., 727, *737, 740*
Wiles, J., 551, *574*
Wilkins, C., 176, *217*
Willerman, B., 345, *361*
Willetts, D., 199, *211*
William, J., *488*
Williams, C., 161, *167*
Williams, C. C., 602, *613*
Williams, C. J., 27, *67*, 90, *93*, 94, 101, 108, 116, *119*, 185, 186, 206, 207, *214*, 324, *362*, 381, *391*, 524, 525, *532*, 547, 564, 566, *570, 571*, 717, 728, 730, *735*
Williams, K. D., 374, *393*, 514, *538*, 644, *665*, 681, 693, 694, *702, 706*
Williams, P., 416, *435*
Williams, P. G., 405, *435*
Willingham, D. T., 528, *541*
Wilson, D., 293, *320*, 346, 350, *361*
Wilson, D. E., 501, *541*

Wilson, D. J., 691, 692, *705*
Wilson, D. S., 595, *615*
Wilson, G. D., 586, *615*
Wilson, J. P., 408, *434*
Wilson, T., 137, *168*
Wilson, T. D., 11, 12, 14, *19*, 24, 25, *75*, 80, 83, 85, 86, 87, 88, 90, 91, 92, 93, 94, 95, 96, 97, 106, 108, 109, 110, *119, 124*, 128, *171*, 205, 206, *220*, 323, 325, 326, 327, 333, 338, *362, 368*, 376, 381, 385, 386, 387, 388, 389, 390, *391, 392, 393, 395*, 477, *489*, 496, 514, 517, 524, 525, *534, 537, 541, 542*, 543, 544, 550, 559, 564, 566, *574*, 579, 599, *615*, 650, 655, *668*, 746, 748, *767*
Windschitl, P. D., 153, *171*, 275, *321*
Winkielman, P., 25, *72*, 342, *368*, 398, 400, 409, *427, 432, 435*, 444, 451, 452, 461, *487, 489*, 509, *542*, 557, *574*
Winkler, J. D., *75*
Winslow, M. P., 241, 242, 256, *270*
Winston, J., 425, *431*
Winter, D. G., 586, *607, 611*
Wiseman, F., 52, *75*
Witcher, B. S., 398, *429*
Withcher, B., 727, *740*
Witkin, H. A., 578, 594, *615*
Witte, K., 640, *668*
Wittenbrink, B., 25, 26, 27, 55, 56, 62, *75*, 206, *220*, 399, *435*, 556, 562, *574*
Wohlgemuth, A., 416, *435*
Wolf, S., 636, *662, 668*
Wolfe, C. T., 562, *574*
Wolff, J. A., 188, *218*
Wolitski, R. J., 200, *212, 216*
Wölk, M., 462, 467, 471, *481*
Wolpe, J., 442, *489*
Wong, L. K., 504, *530*
Wong, R., 504, *530*
Wood, E., 162, *168*
Wood, G., 141, *168*
Wood, W., 14, *18*, 83, 92, 94, 96, 97, 99, 101, 102, 104, 109, 115, *117, 120, 124*, 144, 148, *169*, 201, 202, *218*, 273, *321*, 335, 345, 348, 357, *362, 366, 368*, 370, *395*, 510, 511, 521, *532, 538, 542*, 591, 593, 600, 601, *607, 613, 615*, 622, 634, 638, 639, 641, 643, 644, 653, *664, 666, 668*, 674, 675, 677, 678, 681, 683, 684, 686, 688, 689, 690, *700, 701, 703, 705, 706*, 712, *742*, 758, 760, *766, 767*
Wood, W. L., 761, *764*
Woodmansee, J. J., 177, *221*
Woodruff, G., *487*
Worchel, S., 236, *265, 266*, 646, *668, 734*
Word, C. O., 54, *76*, 207, *221*, 652, *668*
Worth, L. T., 13, *19*, 335, *365*, 462, 466, 468, 471, *486, 489*, 512, 521, *536*, 595, *610*, 684, *703*
Wortman, C. B., 375, *395*
Wosinska, W., 593, *606*, 696, *700*
Wright, R. A., 585, *608*
Wrightsman, L. S., 35, *73*
Wrzesniewski, A., 408, *432*
Wu, J., 458, *482*

Wu, S., 412, *434*

Wundt, W., 412, 416, *435*

Wyer, M. M., 50, *66*

Wyer, R. S., 4, 5, 11, 13, *19,* 39, *73, 126, 171,* 274, 275, 276, 278, 279, 280, 281, 282, 283, 284, 285, 286, 288, 289, 290, 291, 293, 294, 295, 296, 297, 298, 299, 300, 301, 302, 305, 306, 309, 310, 311, 313, *314, 315, 316, 317, 318, 319, 320, 321, 322,* 439, 446, 453, 455, 458, 461, 463, 465, 467, 468, 469, 472, *482, 485, 486, 489,* 512, 513, 528, *529,* 548, 559, *574,* 622, 623, 626, 629, 630, *656, 667,* 713, 716, 721, *733, 737, 739, 740,* 762, *767*

Wyer, R. S., Jr., 11, *16,* 82, *117,* 146, *165,* 225, 253, 263, *264,* 325, 336, 337, 353, 359, *368,* 373, 385, 387, *390,* 406, *429,* 495, 504, 505, 522, *542,* 622, 625, *668,* 710, 712, 714, 715, 717, 721, *739, 741, 742*

X

Xagoraris, A., 475, *485*

Y

Yacobos, E., 374, *390*

Yalch, R. J., 511, *539*

Yamagishi, M., 41, *69*

Yanevitzky, I., 188, *216*

Yantis, S., 83, 92, 106, 109, *118*

Yarrow, P. R., 176, *217*

Yates, J. F., 144, *170*

Yates, S., 381, 388, *390*

Yates, S. M., 103, *118, 581, 604*

Yaxley, S., 423, *435*

Ybarra, O., 197, *221*

Yeung, C. W. M., 276, *322*

Yi, Y., 652, *657*

Ying, Y., 49, *76*

Yingling, J., 589, *614*

Yoshida, M., 416, *435*

Yost, J. H., 578, 590, *611*

Young, B., 586, *608*

Young, K., 693, *706*

Yzer, M., 198, *214*

Yzer, M. C., 210, *221*

Yzerbyt, V. Y., 44, *76,* 692, *703*

Z

Zador, P., 188, *216*

Zahniser, J., 731, *736*

Zajac, D. M., 726, *738*

Zajonc, R., 450, 460, *485*

Zajonc, R., 13, *19,* 24, *70*

Zajonc, R. B., 21, 25, 26, *71, 76,* 342, *368,* 398, 406, 409, 410, 424, *433, 435,* 444, 450, 451, 452, 460, 475, *486, 489,* 494, 498, 509, 510, 528, *535, 536, 537, 542,* 556, 557, *572, 574,* 618, *666,* 674, *706,* 711, *742,* 749, 752, *766, 767*

Zakai, D., *610*

Zalanowski, A. H., 405, *434*

Zald, D., 426, *432*

Zald, D. H., 423, 424, *435*

Zaller, J., 47, *76*

Zanna, A. S., 249, *267,* 633, *661*

Zanna, M. P., 4, 5, 11, *19,* 54, *76,* 80, 82, 84, 85, 89, 95, 98, 100, 109, 110, *120, 121, 122, 124,* 128, 143, 150, *166, 167, 168, 170,* 179, 180, 204, 207, *214, 216, 217, 221,* 229, 231, 233, 234, 239, 242, 243, 245, 249, 251, 253, 256, 258, 259, 260, 261, 264, *266, 267, 268, 269, 270, 271,* 274, 276, 311, *318, 322,* 324, 331, 332, 334, 335, 336, 337, 359, 360, *363, 365, 366, 367, 368,* 379, 383, *391, 393, 394,* 398, 407, 418, *430, 434, 435,* 443, 452, 464, 470, 471, 472, *483, 484, 489,* 502, 508, 511, 516, 519, *533, 542,* 586, 587, 590, 597, *606, 611, 614, 615,* 618, 633, 641, 642, 646, 649, 652, 655, *659, 661, 663, 664, 666, 667, 668, 669,* 678, 688, *701, 706,* 711, 715, 730, *735, 738, 739, 741, 742,* 745, *767*

Zanutto, E., 188, *216*

Zárate, M. A., 501, *542,* 548, *574*

Zarrow, M., 149, *169*

Zavalloni, M., 687, *704*

Zebrowitz, L. A., 718, *734*

Zeelenberg, M., 403, 404, *429*

Zelazo, P. D., 448, *489*

Zellinger, P. M., 40, *66*

Zenilman, J. M., 198, *214*

Zentner, M. R., 405, *433*

Zevon, M. A., 414, *435*

Zhao, K., 449, *489*

Ziegler, R., 529, *542,* 634, *669*

Zillmann, D., 405, *430*

Zimbardo, P., 595, *605*

Zimmer, E., 163, *167*

Znaniecki, F., 174, *220,* 618, *667*

Znaniecki, R., 22, *74*

Zogmeister, C., 520, *531*

Zubin, J., 731, *736*

Zuckerman, M., 179, 200, 201, *221,* 397, *435,* 590, *615,* 632, *669*

Zuwerink, J. R., 204, *213*

Subject Index

Note: *n* denotes a note

A

Ability
  bias correction and, 517–518
  as determinant of elaboration, 506
  of message recipient, 643–645
  as source of bias, 515
Absolute judgments, 302
Abstract memory representations, 279
Accuracy, 356, 643
  explicit attitudes and, 560
  incentives for, 679
  of perception of self and environment, 308–309
Accuracy motivation, 355, 755
Acquiescence, 41–42
  controlling for, 42–43
Acquired behavioral dispositions, 744–745
Action
  affect in attitude toward, 456–457
  attitude toward, 126, 461
  behavior and, 131, 141
  intention *vs.*, 178, 189–190
Action-based model, 516
Action focus, 440
Action identification, 244
Action-orientation model, 246–247, 762
Activation, of attitudes, 544
Act rationalization, 246
Adaptive-connectionist program, 248
Adaptors, 603
Additivity hypothesis, 350, 628
Adrenaline, 459
Advertising, 651–652

Affect, 397–426
  arousal and, 439, 440, 458
  aspects of affective experiences, 418–426
  attitudes *vs.*, 5, 397
  behavior and, 160–161
  category-triggered, 449, 464
  conscious and unconscious, 397–400
  defined, 3, 397, 749–750
  duration of affective experiences, 420–421
  emotions. *See* Emotion(s)
  episodic, 718–719, 720, 721–722
  evaluation and, 324
  as evidence, 472–474
  frequency of affective experiences, 418–420, 421
  implication of types for attitude research, 410–412
  influence on attitude. *See* Affect-attitude relation
  influence on beliefs, 305–306
  intensity of affective experiences, 420
  moods. *See* Mood(s)
  multiple kinds of, 476–477
  need for, 583
  origins of, 400–412
  pleasure and displeasure, 416–418
  qualities of affective experiences, 412–418
  self-affirmation and positive, 239
  sensory affects, 406–410, 415–416
  stereotyping and, 462–465
  structure of, 9, 12–13
  types of, 752–753

  types of affective experiences, 400–412
  valence and, 439, 440
Affect-as-evidence hypothesis, 480
Affect-as-information model, 13, 439, 453–455
Affect-attitude relation, 3, 7–9, 13, 327, 437–480, 748–753
  affect as evidence, 472–474
  affect decision theory, 456–457
  affective priming, 752
  affective value, 439
  alternative affective representations, 455–456
  amygdala and, 475–476
  anger and, 457
  arousal as importance, 458–460, 461
  associationism, 441–442
  attitude formation and, 749–752
  attitude object and, 439–440
  attitudes as evaluative conditions, 438–439
  automatic evaluation effect, 474–475
  awareness, 443–444
  category-triggered affect, 449
  classical conditioning of attitude, 442–443, 460
  cognitive dissonance and, 471–472
  conditioning explanations, 445–449, 460
  direct effects of affect on attitude, 528*n*6
  direct influences, 441–461
  embodied evaluation, 477–478
  evaluative association *vs.* classical conditioning, 444–445
  evaluative constancy and, 478–479
  indirect influence, 461–474

807

mere exposure, 450–452, 460–461
mood and evaluative judgment, 452–455, 461
mood effects, 445–446
multiple kinds of affect and, 476–477
persuasion and, 465–471
priming, 445–446
stereotyping and, 462–465
types of affects and, 752–753
Affect confirmation hypothesis, 472–473
Affect decision theory, 456–457, 461, 479
Affect heuristic, 455
Affect infusion model, 455
Affective certainty, 473
Affective forecasting, 387
Affective immediacy principle, 446, 472
Affective information, attitude accessibility and, 89, 90, 92
Affective learning, 424
Affective measures, 177–178
Affective needs, group membership and, 723
Affective neuroscience, 421–426
Affective primacy, 556, 749
Affective priming, 474, 752
Affective states, 710, 718–719
persuasion and, 466–469
unawareness of, 728
Age, persuasion and, 601
Aggregation, principle of, 180–182, 208
Aggression, 411, 732
Agreeableness, 602
Agree/disagree questions, 43
Allegiance bias, 374
Alogical functioning, 337
Alternation vs. co-occurrence, 417
Alternatives, spreading of, 229
Ambivalence, 84–85, 327, 331–334, 494, 748–749
antecedents of, 332
attitude accessibility and, 90, 92–93
attitude-behavior consistency and, 109–110, 111, 113–114
attitude change and, 101, 103, 104–105
attitude extremity and, 97
between-dimension, 85, 93
cross-dimension, 103, 105, 113
dual-attitude structure vs., 87
index of, 331
intra- and inter-component, 641–642
measuring, 331
no opinion responses and, 48
no responses and, 49
preference for consistency and, 587
strength-related beliefs and, 97–98
types of, 85
within-dimension, 85, 93, 103, 105, 113
working knowledge and, 95

Ambivalent sexism inventory, 595
American Journal of Community Psychology, 162
American social psychology orientation, 693–695
Amygdala
affective neural processing and, 423, 424–425
attitude measurement and, 60
emotion and, 475–476
memory formation and, 458, 459
Anger, 461
attitude and, 457
reliance on stereotypes and, 463, 465
selective thought and, 515
Anxiety
affective messages and, 470
estimating likelihood of negative event on, 305–306
message effects and, 648
persuasion and proneness to, 602–603
Approach, latency and intensity of, 61
Approach motivation, 425
Aptitude, behavior and, 160
Argumentativeness, 589
Arguments
attitude change and use of, 579
defining quality of, 655
quality and quantity of, 638–640
validity and strength of, 374
Arousal
affective experience and, 439, 440
attitude formation and, 479
aversive, 633
energetic, 405
as importance, 458–460
influence on attraction, 411
irrelevant, 459
memory and, 458–460, 480
memory formation and, 461
message effects and, 648–649
role in dissonance theory, 233–234, 502
role in self-perception theory, 251
sexual, 426
Arousal-calmness, 412
Asch paradigm, 354–355
Assimilation effects, 549, 559, 722
Associationism, 441–442, 460
Associations, 447
Associative learning, 406
Associative network principles of spreading activation, 86
Associative network theories, 279, 493–494, 546
Associative theories of belief organization and change, 282–284
Attachment style, 719–720
Attention, 521
memory and, 520–523
persuasion and, 622
Attenuation hypothesis, 350

Attitude accessibility, 81
ambivalence and, 90, 92–93
attitude-behavior consistency and, 108, 110–111, 114
attitude change and, 100, 101, 103–104
attitude extremity and, 90, 91, 93–94
defined, 559
dissonance reduction and, 256
influence on attitude-judgment relations, 116n16
mental illness stigma and, 731
simultaneous, 243–244
strength-related beliefs and, 94–95
type of attitude-relevant information and, 89, 90, 92
working knowledge and, 90, 92
Attitude-as-construction models, 325–326, 328
Attitude-behavior consistency, 256
accessibility and, 108, 110–111, 114
ambivalence and, 109–110, 111, 113–114
attitude measure and, 106
attitude stability and, 106
deliberative and nondeliberative influences of attitude, 106–107
distinguishing between prediction and influence, 105
literature on, 105
types of attitude-relevant information, 109, 111–112, 114
working knowledge/complexity and, 109, 111, 112, 114
Attitude-behavior relation, 8, 10, 173–210, 759–762
components of attitude toward behavior, 199
explicit vs. implicit attitudes and, 204–207
historical overview of research on, 174–178
inconsistency of attitudes' effect on behavior, 175–178
meaningfulness of attitude's effect on behavior, 198–199
MODE model, 184–187
predicting intentions, 193–204
predicting single behaviors, 182–192
predictive validity of general attitudes, 178–182
principle of aggregation and, 180–182
principle of compatibility and, 182–183
Attitude-belief congruence, 369
moderators of, 379–383
Attitude-belief relation, 3, 7–9, 11–12, 14, 297–298, 369–390
biased perceptions and, 370
changing beliefs by changing attitudes, 383–389
effects on belief retrieval, 370–373
moderators of, 379–383
motivated inferences, 373–379

Attitude certainty, working knowledge
    and, 97
Attitude change, 341–358, 359, 360
    accessibility and, 100, 101, 103–104
    affect and, 439–440
    ambivalence and, 101, 103,
        104–105
    attitude activation and, 519–520
    attitude formation vs., 254–255
    awareness of, 653–654
    belief change and, 384–389
    causal uncertainty and, 584–585
    cognition in persuasion model
        (CPM), 625–626, 629–630, 762
    cognitive processes and, 503–506
    complexity and, 101, 102–103, 104
    cultural differences in
        dissonance-induced, 249
    dual process models, 348–351
    elaboration likelihood model and.
        See Elaboration likelihood
        model
    evaluative conditioning, 342–344
    field dependence and, 594
    heuristic-systematic model and. See
        Heuristic-systematic model
    implicit attitudes and, 652–653
    majority and minority influence and,
        354–358
    mere exposure effects and, 342
    metacognition and, 516
    need for closure and, 583–584
    need for uniqueness and, 593
    persistence of, 649–651
    persuasion and. See Persuasion
    postdecisional, 229
    role of choice following induced
        compliance, 247–248
    role playing and, 224–226
    sad moods and, 471–472
    self-awareness and, 585
    self-reported emotion and, 241
    self-standards model and, 245
    social influence on. See Social
        influence on attitudes/attitude
        change
    strategic impression management
        and, 239
    strong attitudes and, 185
    thoughtfulness and, 98–100
    types of attitude-relevant
        information and, 100–101,
        101–102, 104
    unimodel. See Unimodel
    unpleasant arousal and, 233–234
    working knowledge and, 101,
        102–103, 104
    See also Attitude formation;
        Dissonance theory; Elaboration
        Persuasion
Attitude change, communication and,
    617–655
    arousal and message effects,
        648–649

attitude function and message
    effects, 646–647
attitude structure and message
    effects, 647–648
attitude valence and message effects,
    645–646
awareness of attitude change and,
    653–654
behavioral effects of, 651–652
cognitive response model of
    persuasion, 623
combinatorial models of persuasion,
    622–623
contemporary process models of
    persuasion, 623–630
implicit attitudes and, 652–653
information processing theory,
    621–622
messages, 638–640
nature of message communicator,
    631–637
nature of message recipient,
    640–645
persistence of attitude change,
    649–651
persuasive communication and,
    344–348
social judgment model, 620–621
Yale program, 344–348, 619–620
Attitude change, individual differences
    in, 14, 575–604
    adaptors vs. innovators, 603
    age and, 601
    anxiety proneness and, 602–603
    gender and, 600–601
    implicit/explicit motives and,
        599–600
    intelligence and, 601–602
    motives/processes leading to,
        577–580
    need for consistency and,
        585–590
    need for knowledge and, 580–585
    need for self-worth and, 590–592
    need for social inclusion and,
        592–596, 755
    personality traits and, 602
    preferences between motives,
        596–599
    self-guides and, 603
Attitude congeniality effects, 521, 522,
    715
Attitude-congruent behavior,
    attitude-incongruent behavior
    vs., 251–252, 258, 263
Attitude-consistent memory, 419
Attitude dynamics. See Attitude
    change
Attitude extremity
    ambivalence and, 97
    attitude accessibility and, 90, 91,
        93–94
    complexity and, 96–97
    working knowledge and, 96

Attitude formation, 710
    activation of attitudes/knowledge,
        519–520
    affect and, 439–440
    bounded process descriptions, 506
    classical conditioning and, 750
    cognitive processes and, 503–506
    cognitive responses, 513–515
    combination/integrative processes
        and, 512–513
    component process descriptions,
        518–519
    dissonance theory and, 515–516
    effect of prior attitude on, 717
    elaboration consequences and, 518
    evaluative conditioning and,
        750–751
    expectancy-value approach to,
        503–504
    implicit processes and, 523–525
    inferential approaches to, 509–511
    information integration and, 504
    level of process description and,
        525–527
    low to moderate elaboration
        processes and, 507–511
    memory and, 520–523, 583
    mere association and, 507–509
    mere exposure and, 751–752
    metacognition and, 516–518
    moderate to high elaboration
        processes and, 511–518
    online, 6, 80–81, 325–326, 328,
        372, 583, 716–717, 746–747
    probabilogical/syllogistic/if-then
        reasoning, 504–505
    universal process descriptions, 503
    using elaboration continuum to
        organize, 506–523
    See also Attitude change
Attitude functions, 338–341, 359, 360,
    642–643
    functions of attitudes or of attitude
        objects, 339–340
    goal magnitudes and processing
        extent, 340–341
    history of, 338–339
    message effects and, 646–647
    primacy of knowledge function and,
        339
Attitude measurement
    attitude construct and, 23
    attitude reports, 24–28
    behavioral observation, 53–54
    behavior as means of, 127
    criteria for, 28–31
    direct self-report methods. See
        Self-report methods (direct)
    explicit, 565
    implicit, 52–63, 544–545, 565,
        747–748
    limitations of implicit techniques,
        62–63
    meta-attitudinal measures, 88

operative measures, 88
physiological measures, 59–61
principle of compatibility and, 183
response bias and, 176
response latency measures, 54–59
techniques, 21
use of, 21
verbal, 176
word-fragment completion task, 61
Attitude objects, 22, 328–329, 438,
    744–745
    association with mood, 467–468
    context and, 555–556
    function of, 339–340
    See also Objects
Attitude polarization, 385–386
    moderators of, 387–388
Attitude reports, 24–28
    automatic activation phase, 24–25
    deliberation phase, 25–26
    response phase, 26–27
Attitude representation theory, 326
Attitude research, 15, 743–764
    affect-attitude relation, 749–753
    attitude-behavior relation, 759–761
    attitude formation, 750–752
    behavior-attitude relation, 761–762
    dual and multiple attitudes, 748–749
    implications of types of affect for,
        410–412
    motivation, 753–758
    nature of attitudes, 744–748
    persuasion, 762–763
    social context of attitudes, 758–759
Attitude(s)
    accessibility of, 81, 186
    activation of, 519–520, 544
    affect *vs.*, 5, 397
    attitude-object relation, 327
    automatic activation of, 544
    bases of, 334–336
    as beliefs, 327–328, 334
    beliefs *vs.*, 276–278
    classical conditioning of, 442–443
    complexity of, 83–84
    concepts, 710–711
    context and, 23–24
    defining, 4–5, 22–24, 126, 324,
        493–494, 744–748
    dispositional *vs.* episodic, 324–326
    dual, 85, 748–749
    effect of social group membership
        on, 161
    effect on accuracy of behavioral
        self-report, 150
    as enduring *vs.* temporary
        constructions, 746–747
    epistemic authority and, 334–335
    evaluative aspects, 23
    as evaluative judgments, 324, 326,
        328, 438
    evaluative tendencies and, 4, 5
    as expectancies, 715

explicit. *See* Explicit attitudes
    as expression of liking, 277
    formation of. *See* Attitude formation
    functional nature of, 82–83
    function of, 754
    general, toward objects, groups,
        policies, 173–174
    global, 721
    group-based, 655
    heritability of, 6, 325, 328, 334
    impact of persuasive communication
        on, 15
    implicit. *See* Implicit attitudes
    influence of affect on. *See*
        Affect-attitude relation
    influence of behavior on. *See*
        Behavior-attitude relation
    influence of beliefs on, 9, 11–12,
        297–298
    influence of goals on, 9, 11–12
    influence on behavior. *See*
        Attitude-behavior relation
    influence on beliefs. *See*
        Attitude-belief relation
    instrumental, 329
    learning, 342–344
    multi-dimensionality of, 176–178
    multiple, 748–749
    nature of, 254–256
    as object-evaluation associations,
        80–81
    predicting behavior and, 131–132,
        133
    prediction of intention and, 196–197
    as predictors of single behaviors,
        208
    preexisting, 252–253, 255–256
    related constructs, 327–328
    social context of, 758–759
    social influence on. *See* Social
        influence on attitudes/attitude
        change
    stability of, 5–6, 545–546
    as stored knowledge structure,
        80–81
    as tendencies to evaluate, 744–746
    toward a behavior, 174
    tripartite theory of, 79, 82, 277, 324,
        327
    true, 380, 546
    types of, 173–174
    valence and, 79
    validation of, 4–5
Attitude scaling technique, 180
Attitude stability, 116n12
    attitude-behavior consistency and,
        106, 108
Attitude strength
    attitude-belief congruence and,
        381–383
    measuring, 46–50
    need for cognition and, 581
    need for knowledge and, 580–585

Attitude structure, 8, 10, 79–116,
    328–338, 359–360
    affective/cognitive/behavioral bases,
        82
    associations with ambivalence,
        84–85, 97–98, 331–334
    associations with attitude
        accessibility, 81, 89–95
    associations with complexity, 95–97
    associations with working
        knowledge, 95–97
    attitude systems, 85–86
    bases of attitudes, 334–336
    complexity of, 83–84
    constructionist view, 80–81
    defined, 80
    dual-attitude structure, 86–87
    expectancy-value models, 328–329
    functional nature of attitudes, 82–83
    information integration *vs.*
        consistency, 330–331
    message effects and, 647–648
    probabilogical models, 336–337
    role in attitude-behavior consistency,
        105–114
    role in attitude change, 98–105
    taxonomies of, 87–89
    variability in, 641–642
    working knowledge, 83
Attitude systems, 85–86
Attitude valence, message effects and,
    645–646
Attitudinal affect, 397. *See also* Affect
Attitudinal ambivalence. *See*
    Ambivalence
Attitudinal cognitorium, 552–553, 558,
    563, 566, 567, 746
Attitudinal congeniality effect, 729
Attitudinal congruence effect, 729
Attitudinal features, of attitude-belief
    congruence, 380–383
Attitudinal position, 340
Attitudinal primitives
    beliefs as, 547–548
    connectionist networks as, 550–552
    exemplars as, 548–549
    multiple attitudes as, 550
    object-evaluation associations as,
        546–547
    schemas as, 549–550
Attribution, 463, 510–511
    marital satisfaction and, 722–723
Attributional complexity, 245
Attributional perspective on
    dissonance, 236
Attribution manipulations, 454
Audience effects, 347–348
Augmentation, 335
Authentic beliefs, 355
Authoritarianism, 586–587
Authority, 698n1
Autokinetic effect, 678–679
Automatic activation phase, of attitude
    report, 24–25

Automatic behaviors, 142–143
Automatic categorization effect, 475
Automatic evaluation
    of attitude objects, 474–475,
        751–752
    behavior and, 760–761
    measuring, 59
Automatic evaluation hypothesis, 480
Automatic factors, influence on
        behavior, 161
Automatic processes, 259–261
Automatic processing. *See* Explicit
        attitudes; Implicit attitudes
Automatic social information
        processing, 449
Availability heuristic, 298–303
Aversive arousal, 633
Aversive consequences theory,
        236–237, 255, 516
Avoidance motor movements, 61
Awareness
    conditioning and, 443–444
    implicit processes and, 523, 525

B

Background factors, role in predicting
        intention, 197–198
Backward conditioning, 528*n*7
Balance effects, 720
    stereotypes and, 729
Balance formulations, 226
Balance theory, 507, 510
    attitude formation and, 714
    groupthink and, 725
    marital satisfaction and, 722–723
    relation between attractiveness and
        attitude similarity, 718, 719
Bandwagon effect, 375
Behavior
    affect and, 160–161
    attitude-incongruent *vs.*
        attitude-congruent, 251–252
    attitude measurement and, 127
    attitude toward, 174
    automatic, 142–143, 161
    behavioral groupings, 129–131
    biological and physiological
        influences on, 159–160
    as causal factor, 143–144
    causal frameworks for, 156–159
    constrained, 257
    construct of, 125–127
    continuous, 136–137
    data-analytical perspectives on
        behavioral criteria, 154–156
    defined, 3, 128
    defining attitude with relation to,
        126
    demographic variables, 161–162
    developmental perspectives on, 163
    dichotomous, 136–137

dissonance reduction and change in,
        227
    elements of, 131–132
    emotions and, 160–161
    end-state, 141–142
    environmental contexts of, 162
    explicit responses, 127–128
    goal-directed, 130
    goals *vs.*, 191–192
    habit, 144–146, 201–203, 760
    health, 130
    hypocrisy and change in, 242
    implicit measure of attitudes and
        spontaneous, 544–545, 747
    implicit responses to, 127–128
    impulsive, 130
    influenced mediators and, 143–144
    influence of attitudes on. *See*
        Attitude-behavior relation
    influence of past on present and
        future, 142–146
    influence on attitudes. *See*
        Behavior-attitude relation
    intentions as predictor of, 187–192
    interpersonal/social, 130, 131
    knowledge and, 160
    meaningful *vs.* trivial, 128–129
    media influences, 163
    metrics for measuring, 152–154
    multivariate bases of, 163–164
    nature of, 257–258
    observer reports of, 154
    origins and structure of, 8, 10
    outcomes of, 141–142
    parenting, 130
    perceived control of, 199–200
    perceived *vs.* actual, 148–154
    personality and aptitudes and, 160
    predicting single, 182–192
    predicting *vs.* postdicting, 146–148
    as a proxy, 142–143
    relation to attitudes, 3, 7–9. *See also*
        Attitude–behavior consistency
    scaling, 132–136
    single-act *vs.* multiple act criteria,
        138–141
    social influences on, 161
    taxonomy of, 128, 129–131
    theory of planned, 142–143
    typologies for, 127
    unconscious/automated, 130
    volitional, 130, 191–192, 257
Behavioral alternatives, 137–138
Behavioral basis of attitudes, 82
Behavioral beliefs, 193–195, 197, 710
Behavioral counts, 136–137
Behavioral events, 128
Behavioral generalization, 150
Behavioral intentions, 158
Behavioral observation, unobtrusive,
        53–54
Behavioral scale values, 141
Behavioral traces, 127

Behavioral units, 128
Behavior-attitude relation, 8, 11,
        223–264, 761–762
    action-orientation model, 246–247
    aversive consequences model,
        236–237
    biased scanning, 224–226
    computational models of dissonance
        theory, 247–248
    counterattitudinal essay writing,
        231–232
    cultural models of dissonance
        processes, 248–249
    decisions and free-choice paradigm,
        228–229
    dissonance theory and, 226–249
    dissonance thermometer, 240–241
    effort justification paradigm, 230
    forced compliance paradigm,
        229–230
    future research on, 261–264
    group level dissonance processes,
        242–243
    hypocrisy paradigm, 241–242
    insufficient punishment, 230–231
    mechanisms underlying, 262–263
    moral *vs.* hedonic dissonance,
        235–236
    nature of attitude and, 254–256
    nature of behavior and, 256–258
    nature of underlying processes,
        258–261
    radical model of dissonance,
        245–246
    role of arousal, 233–234
    role of choice, 232–233
    role of commitment, 232
    role of simultaneous
        accessibility/explicit memory,
        243–244
    selective exposure hypothesis, 231
    self-affirmation theory, 237–239
    self-consistency theory, 234–235
    self-perception theory, 249–254
    self-standards model, 244–245
    strategic impression management
        motives, 239–240
Behavior-behavior relationships,
        142–146
Behavior intention, 710
    See also Habit
Behaviorism, 620, 693
Behavior repertory, 227
Being oneself, 675
    social consensus and, 681–684
Belief-discrepant behavior, self-esteem
        and, 312
Belief formation and change
    belief-attitude relations, 297–298
    conditional inference processes,
        294–295
    formal models of, 294–298
    heuristic bases of, 298–306

information processing models,
   296–297
linear models of belief formation,
   295–296
role of implicit theories in,
   290–292
Belief in just world, 311
Belief(s), 273–278
   about causality, 289
   accessibility of, 370–373
   affective influences on, 305–306
   ambivalence and strength-related,
      97–98
   associative theories of belief
      organization and change,
      282–284
   attitude accessibility and, 94–95
   attitude-behavior consistency and
      ambivalence in, 109
   attitude change and change in,
      384–389, 622
   attitudes as, 4, 334
   attitudes vs., 276–278
   as attitudinal primitives, 547–548
   authentic, 355
   based on plausibility of antecedent
      condition, 303–304
   behavioral, 158, 160, 193–195, 197,
      710
   belief salience, 284
   consistency in, 311–312
   control, 193–195, 197, 199
   defensive confidence in, 589
   defined, 3, 710
   distinguishing from other concepts,
      276–278
   formation of, 9, 11
   inconsistency in, 285
   inferences vs., 276
   influence of attitudes on. See
      Attitude-belief relation
   influence on attitudes, 9, 11–12,
      297–298
   inter-attitudinal structure and
      strength-related, 98
   judgments vs., 276
   knowledge and, 274–276
   knowledge belief organization and,
      278–286
   motivational bases for, 306–313
   normative, 158, 193–195, 197
   opinions vs., 276–278
   perceptions vs., 276
   predictions regarding, 371
   probabilogical models of belief
      organization and change,
      284–286
   responses to belief dilemmas,
      307–308
   role in dual process models of
      attitude change, 350–351
   self-efficacy, 199
   in something vs. about something,
      274

spontaneous vs. deliberative
   processes of formation of,
   292–294
from unimodel perspective, 353
working knowledge, complexity and
   strength-related, 97
Belief systems, 80
Bennington College study, 671–672
Between-dimension ambivalence, 93
Bias, 514–515
   affective, 455
   allegiance, 374
   attitude-belief relation and, 370
   attitudes and, 756
   attitudes as biasing factor on
      behavior, 107
   congeniality, 756, 757–758
   correction of, 515
   directional motivation and, 345
   existing attitudes and, 195
   in frequency judgments of affective
      experiences, 418–419
   hindsight, 305
   MODE model and, 184
   mood and processing, 644–645
   mood-induced, 722
   motivated, 529n12
   motivated reasoning and bias
      processing, 758
   motivational, 335
   in processing new information,
      376–379
   response, 176, 379
   self-esteem and, 591
   social desirability response, 50–52
   in use of heuristics, 379
Bias correction, 517–518, 585
Biased elaboration, 116n13
Biased hypothesis testing, 378
Biased information seeking, 378
Biased processing, 116n13, 758
Biased scanning theory, 224–226
   attitude change and, 255–256
   constrained behavior and, 257
   deliberative processing and, 259
   joint effects of incentives and,
      224–225
Bias hypothesis, 350
Bi-directional causal relationship, 156,
   157
Big Five personality traits, 602
Binge drinking studies, 163–164
Biological factors
   affective influence and, 446–447
   in behavior, 159–160
   in moods, 405
Blackwell Dictionary of Cognitive
   Psychology, 495
Bogus pipeline technique, 51
Bolster-counterargue scale, 588
Bolstering, 307, 310, 588–589, 756
Boomerang effect, 621, 639
Bounded process descriptions, 495,
   506, 526–527

Bounded processes, 499, 527
   attitude activation and, 519
   elaboration and, 518
   quantitative and qualitative
      distinctions among, 506–507
Bounded rationality, 337
Bounded theories, 505
Brain, affect and areas of activity in,
   423–426
Brain activity assessment, 60
Brainwashing, 126
Brand names, 464–465

C

Categorical representations, 280
Categorization, 520
   mental illness stigma and, 730
   prejudice and, 728–729
Category-triggered affect, 449
Causal analysis, of behavior, 156–159
Causality
   beliefs about, 289
   reasoned action model and, 198
Causal relationship
   bi-directional, 156, 157
   direct, 156, 157
   moderated, 157
   reciprocal, 156, 157
   spurious, 156, 157
   unanalyzed, 156–157
Causal uncertainty, attitude change
   and, 584–585
Ceiling effects, 115n8
Central route, processing via, 14, 259,
   348–349, 624, 627, 710
   affect and, 465–466, 468
   groupthink and, 725
   See also Elaboration likelihood
      model
Certainty, ambivalence and perceptions
   of, 98
Certainty motives, 698n7
CEST. See Cognitive-experiential
   self-theory
CFA. See Confirmatory factor analysis
Change-of-meaning hypothesis, 686
Cheating, attitudes toward, 174
Choice, role in dissonance theory,
   232–233
Classical conditioning, 343–344, 407,
   440, 460, 507–508, 710, 719
   affective association and, 441–444
   attitude formation and, 442–443, 750
   evaluative association vs., 444–445
   evaluative conditioning vs., 408
   implicit attitudes and, 557–559
   mental illness stigma and, 730
   prejudice and, 728
   sensory affects and, 407
Clinician's illusion, 731
Closed questions, 34–35
Close relationship research, 717–720

Closure, attitude change and need for, 583–584
Coding scheme, 34
Coefficient alpha values, 29
Coercion, persuasion and, 634, 646
Coercion-based relationships, 698n6
Cogency, of argument, 639
Cognition
  affect vs., 556, 557
  attitude change and need for, 581–582
  behavior and, 160
  embodied, 478
  need for, 581–582, 644
  role for emotions, 403
  role in persuasion, 372–373
Cognition in persuasion model (CPM), 625–626, 629–630, 762
Cognitive accessibility, self-perception theory and, 712
Cognitive attitudes, instrumental behavior and, 109
Cognitive balance theory, 287–288
Cognitive basis
  of attitudes, 82
  of mere exposure, 450–451, 452
Cognitive capacity, attitude activation and, 185, 187
Cognitive capacity hypothesis, 466–467
Cognitive consistency theories, 85, 311–312, 370–371, 510
  belief change and, 383–385
Cognitive dissonance. See Dissonance
Cognitive effort, responses to belief dilemmas, 307
Cognitive elements, dissonance and, 227–228
Cognitive-experiential self-theory (CEST), 599
Cognitive fluency, mere exposure effects and, 479
Cognitive measures, 177–178
Cognitive preparedness, affective influence and, 447
Cognitive processes, 493, 494–495
  attitude change and, 503–506
  attitude formation and, 503–506
  bounded processes, organizing, 506–523
  cognitive approaches to distinguishing, 499–501
  cognitive content vs., 497
  combination/integrative processes, 512–513
  defining, 495–502
  identifying, 496–498
  implicit vs. explicit, 523–525
  level of process description, 525–527
  process identification in social psychology, 501–502
  qualitative vs. quantitative differences in, 497–498

Cognitive processing principles, 371–373
Cognitive resources, deliberation and, 26
Cognitive response approach to behavior-attitude relation, 226
Cognitive response model of persuasion, 623
Cognitive responses, 513–515
  biased, 379
  objectivity and bias in thinking, 514–515
  in response to messages, 513
  when there is no message, 513–514
Cognitive response theory, 710, 713–714
Cognitive skills, primacy effect and, 46
Cognitive theories of emotions, 403–404
Collectivism/collectivist cultures, 593–594
  affective influence and, 448
  behavior effects of attitude change and, 652
  response to cognitive dissonance, 248
  sense of self in, 695–696
Combination/integrative processes, 512–513
Combinatorial models of attitude formation, 710, 713
Combinatorial models of persuasion, 622–623
Commitment
  organizational, 726
  role in dissonance theory, 232
Communication
  anticipated, 638–640
  attitude change and. See Attitude change, communication and
Communication norms, 293–294
Communicator, 631–637
  credibility of, 620
  interaction with message recipients, 645–649
Companionate love, 719
Comparative judgments, 302
Comparison process, conflict theory of influence and, 356–357
Compartmentalization, 307
Compatibility, principle of, 182–183, 199, 208
Competitiveness molecules, 288
Completion principle, 287, 290
Complexity
  assessment of, 84
  attitude-behavior consistency and, 109, 111, 112, 114
  attitude change and, 101, 102–103, 104
  attitude extremity and, 96–97
  attitudes and knowledge, 83–84
  integrative, 84

working, 92
  working knowledge and, 84, 97
Compliance, 356, 634, 680
Component process descriptions, 518–519, 526–527, 527
Component processes, 495, 499, 503
Comprehension, 347–348, 521
  memory processes and, 290–291
  persuasion and, 622
Computational models of dissonance theory, 247–248
Conative measures, 177–178
Concept learning task, 444
Concept priming, 55–56
Conceptual categorization, 445
Conceptual fluency, 451
Conceptualization of recognition memory, 303
Concurrent validity, 39
Conditional inference processes, 294–295
Conditional probability judgments, 419
Conditioned aversion, 442
Conditioned reflex, 441
Conditioned stimuli-unconditioned stimuli contingency, 507–508, 558
Conditioning
  backward, 528n7
  classical. See Classical conditioning
  evaluative, 342–344, 408–409, 750–751
  fear, 558–559
  operant, 508, 710, 727–728, 730
  priming and, 445–446
  reverse, 407–408
Condom use studies, 131–132, 188, 197, 204, 241, 242, 652
Confidence, 517
Confidence interval, 40
Confirmatory factor analysis (CFA), 31
Conflict theory of majority and minority influence, 356–357
Conflict within attitude, ambivalence and, 332
Conforming, 673
Conformity, 354–356, 593, 636
  Asch paradigm, 354–355
  theories of, 355–356
Congeniality bias, 756, 757–758
Congruent origins, 283
Congruity theory, 226, 510
Connectionism, 568n1
Connectionist models, 528n2
Connectionist networks, 115n1, 494
  attitudinal primitives as, 550–552
Connotative meaning, 475
Conscientiousness, 602
Conscious affect, 397–400
Conscious control of attitudes, 205
Consensual judgments, 678
Consensus, 677, 678
  being oneself and, 681–684
  culture and, 696

dynamic changes in, 690–692
motives direct processing of
    consensual views, 685–687
relating to others and, 679–681
understanding reality through,
    677–679
Consensus cue, 350
Consensus heuristic, 334, 355, 358
Conservatism, 577
Consistency
attitude change and, 578, 585–590
in beliefs and opinions, 311–312
explicit attitudes and, 560
need for, 575–576
preference for, 245, 587
social influence and, 684–685
Consistency motive, information
    integration *vs.*, 330–331
Consistency perspective, 226
Consonance model, 247–248
Constrained behavior, 257
Constraints, on evaluative meanings,
    438–439, 441
Constraint satisfaction connectionist
    model, 762
Constraint-satisfaction methods,
    247–248
Constructionist view of attitudes,
    80–81
Construction model, 496–497
Construct validity, 28, 30
Consummatory behavior, affective
    attitudes and, 109
Consumer self-doubt scale, 590
Context effects, 545–546, 556
attitude and, 23–24, 325, 747
implicit/explicit attitudes and,
    555–556
of inconsistency, 227
Continuous behavior, 136–137
Contrast effects, 39, 549, 559, 722
Control, prediction of intention and,
    196–197
Control beliefs, 193–195, 197, 199
Convergent validity, 29–31
Conversion process, 688
Co-occurrence *vs.* alternation, 417
Cooperative interaction style, 724
Coping, wishful thinking and, 375
Correspondent inference theory, 289
Costs and benefits, of behaviors, 193
Counterarguing, 296–297, 307,
    588–589, 715, 756
intelligence and, 601
Counterattitudinal advocacy, 502
Counterattitudinal essay writing,
    231–232, 233, 239, 245,
    250–251, 471
Counterbalancing rating scales, 46
CPM. *See* Cognition in persuasion
    model
Credibility, persuasion and, 635
Cross-dimension ambivalence, 103,
    105, 113

Cross-sectionary studies, 147–148
Cued recall, 151–152
Cues, 350, 352
attitude change and use of, 579–580
correcting for prejudice and, 596
facial, 632, 637
field dependence and, 594
peripheral, 624, 627, 644
persuasion, 379
retrieval, 279
stereotyping and affective, 462
Cultivation effect, 300
Cultural models of dissonance
    processes, 248–249
Cultural preparedness, affective
    influence and, 447–448
Culture
collectivist. *See* Collectivism/
    collectivist cultures
differences in promotion and
    prevention focus and, 312–313
individualistic. *See* Individualism/
    individualistic cultures
positive self-views and, 590
social influence and, 695–697
Socratic effect and, 285–286

D

Decision making
affect and, 456–457
attitude research and, 709
conscious, 760
free-choice paradigm and, 228–229
group, 724–726
political, 726–727
vigilant, 725
Declarative memory, 474–475
Defense motivation, 378, 755, 756
Defensive confidence, in beliefs, 589
Deliberation phase, of attitude report,
    25–26
Deliberative behaviors, attitudes and,
    106–107
Deliberative processing, 184–185,
    259–261, 291, 292–294
Demographic variables
effect on behavior, 161–162
reasoned action and planned
    behavior models and, 200
Dependability, 602
Dependent variable, 159
Depersonalized attraction, 724
Depression, 732
peripheral cues and, 644
Descriptive norms, 161, 199, 677
Descriptive priming, 474, 480
Desirability, wishful thinking and,
    309–310
Developmental perspectives, on
    behavior, 163
Deviance regulation theory, 161
Dichotomous behavior, 136–137

Dichotomous outcomes, logistic
    regression and, 155, 156
Dichotomous scales, 36–37, 39, 46
Direct causal relationship, 156, 157
Direct cue, attitude as, 106
Direct effects, of affect on attitudes,
    528*n*6
Direct experience
of attitude object, predicting
    behavior on basis of, 179, 180
attitudes based on, 336
knowledge and, 275
Directional motivations, 345, 353
Discounting, 335
Discriminant construct validity, 499
Discriminant validity, 29–31
Discrimination, 204–207, 208–209,
    727–730, 763
authoritarianism and, 586
implicit attitudes and, 652
Discriminative process validity, 499
Dismissing attachment style, 719
Disposition, 745
Dissimulation
effects of, 632–633
signs of, 632
Dissociation model, 205
Dissociative method, in neuroscience,
    501
Dissonance
affect and, 471–472
defined, 226
future research on, 262
moral *vs.* hedonistic, 235–236
reduction of, 515–516
self-monitoring and, 597
vicarious, 243
Dissonance arousal, 260
Dissonance ratio, 245–246
Dissonance theory, 126, 143, 226–249,
    515–516
action-orientation model, 246–247
attitude change and, 356
attitude formation and, 714
automatic *vs.* deliberative
    processing and, 259–260
aversive consequences model,
    236–237
avoidance of dissonance and, 228
behavior-attitude relation and, 761
cognitive consistency and, 311
computational models of, 247–248
counterattitudinal essay writing and,
    231–232
cultural models of dissonance
    processes, 248–249
dissonance reduction and, 227–228
effects of dissimulation and, 633
effort justification paradigm, 230
experience of psychological
    discomfort and, 240–241
first generation, 228–232
forced compliance paradigm,
    229–230

free-choice paradigm, 228–229
group level dissonance processes, 242–243
hypocrisy paradigm, 241–242
insufficient punishment and, 230–231
motivational processes and, 261
original version, 226–228
radical model of dissonance, 245–246
role of arousal, 233–234
role of choice, 232–233
role of commitment, 232
role of simultaneous accessibility and explicit memory, 243–244
second generation, 232–240
selective exposure hypothesis, 231
self-affirmation theory, 237–239
self-consistency theory, 234–235
self-perception and, 501–502
self-perception theory as alternative interpretation of, 250
self-standards model, 244–245
social influence and, 684–685
strategic impression management motives, 239–240
third generation, 240–249
Dissonance thermometer, 240–241
Distraction, 521
attitude and belief change and, 385
effect on persuasive message, 514–515
elaboration and, 466
Distributed connectionist model, 568nl
Distributive justice, hedonic dissonance and, 236
Dogmatism, 14, 586–587
Domain expertise, 96, 115n9
Dominance, 602
Dominant reactions, 104
Dopamine, 405, 423
Double dissociation, 501
Double-forced compliance procedure, 246
Dual attitudes, 85, 327, 748–749
incompatible attitudes and, 333–334
Dual-attitude structure, 86–87
ambivalence vs., 87
Dual process analyses of minority and majority influence, 357–358
Dual process models of attitude change, 348–350
role of goals and beliefs in, 350–351
Duration, of affective experiences, 420–421
Duration neglect, 420, 421
Dynamic social impact theory, 690–691, 759

E

Ease-of-generation heuristic, 519–520
Ease-of-retrieval heuristic, 298–303

EAST. See Extrinsic Affective Simon Task
Ecological model, 162
Effect dependence, 673
Efficacy feedback, 461, 463, 465
Efficiency, affective certainty and, 473
Effort justification paradigm, 230
Egalitarian goals, 464
Ego defense, 356
Ego-defensive function, 82, 83, 338, 682, 711, 724
Ego-defensive motives, 562–563
Ego involvement, social judgment and, 621
See also Involvement
Elaboration
consequences of, 518
correcting for prejudice and, 596
effects on persuasion, 588
motivation and ability as determinants of, 506
self-esteem and, 591
Elaboration continuum, to organize bounded processes, 506–523
Elaboration likelihood model (ELM), 14, 98–100, 348–349, 372, 467–468, 505, 624–627, 677, 756, 762
attitude change and, 577–578, 579
cognitive response and, 513
high elaboration, 99, 101–103, 511–518
low elaboration, 99, 100–101, 507–511
moderate elaboration, 100, 103–105, 507–518
motivation and, 698n3
persistence of attitude change and, 650
source characteristics and, 634
Embedded Figures Test, 594
Embeddedness, 382, 641
Embodied cognition, 478
Embodied evaluation, 477–478
Embodied nature of affect, 480
Emergent properties, affect and cognition and, 478
Emotional gestalts, 477
Emotional intelligence, 455
Emotional reaction, 710
Emotional stability, 602
Emotional states, 438
Emotion(s), 400, 401–404, 412–414, 438
amygdala and, 475–476
behavior and, 160–161
behavior prediction and, 200
cognitive theories of, 403–404
examples of, 401
facial feedback theory, 402–403
hierarchical structure of, 412–414
James-Lange theory of, 401–402
moods vs., 752–753
positive, 753

reasoned action and planned behavior models and, 203
structural theories, 404
two-factor theory of, 260, 403
See also Affect
EMS. See External motivation to respond without prejudice scale
Endorphins, 423
End-state behavior, 141–142
Energetic arousal, 405
Entitativity, 343
Entity theory, 589
Environment, perception of, 306, 308–309
Environmental context, of behavior, 162
Episode models, 290
Episodic affect, 718–719, 720, 721–722
Episodic affective responses, attitudes vs., 710
Episodic memory, 149, 150
Epistemic authority, 351
as basis for attitudes, 334–335
persuasion and, 346–347, 360
Epistemic motivation, 335, 338, 344
Equal-appearing intervals method, 32
Equity, hedonic dissonance and, 236
ERP. See Event-related brain potentials
Error-choice technique, 176
European social psychology orientation, 693–695
Evaluation
affect and, 324
affect vs., 749
attitude change and need for, 582–583
attitudes and, 4, 5, 23
automatic, 546
based on feelings, 277
based on nonaffective criteria, 277
embodied, 477–478
as process vs. structure, 496–497
types of, 477
Evaluation apprehension, 232–233
Evaluative association, 751
classical conditioning vs., 444–445
Evaluative conditioning, 342–344, 408–409
attitude formation and, 750–751
Evaluative constancy, 480
attitudes and, 478–479
Evaluative inconsistency, 178–182
empirical evidence for, 179–180
moderating variables explanation for, 178–179
Thurstone's explanation for, 180–182
Evaluative judgment
attitudes as, 324, 326, 328, 744–746
mood and, 452–455
Evaluative priming, 55, 56, 474, 480
Evaluative tendency, 369
Event-related brain potentials (ERP), 60–61

Evidence
  affect as, 472–474
  credibility of, 335–336
  goals as, 338
Evolutionary perspectives, on
    behavior, 164
Excuses, 239
Exemplars, as attitudinal primitives,
    548–549
Exosystems, 162
Expectancies
  attitudes as, 715
  cognitive, 714–715
  outcome, 193, 456–457
  stereotypes and, 729
Expectancy-value models, 12, 185,
    328–329, 384, 503–504, 505,
    512, 548
Expectations, 274
Expertise, persuasion and, 344–345,
    634, 698n1
Expertise cue, 350
Expertise heuristic, 351
Explanations
  effect of generating explanation on
      predictions, 304–305
  generating on hindsight bias, 305
Explanatory parsimony, 526
Explicit attitudes, 86–87, 204–207,
    543–545, 747–748
  awareness in, 559–560
  context and, 546–552, 555–556
  existing concurrently with implicit,
      550
  implicit affect and mere exposure
      and, 556–557
  implicit attitudes vs., 204–207
  potentiated recruitment framework
      and, 552–567
  predicting behavior from, 206–207,
      209
  prejudice and, 564–565
  as response mode, 560
  social desirability and, 563–565,
      566
  working memory and, 564, 566
Explicit conclusions, 346–347
Explicit measure, 524
Explicit memory, role in dissonance
    processes, 243–244
Explicit motives, 600
Explicit processes, 524
Explicit responses, 127–128
Exposure effects, 509
Exposure frequency, effects of, 300,
    301
External cues, self-perception and,
    252
Externalization function, of attitudes,
    338
External motivation to respond without
    prejudice scale (EMS),
    564–565

Extinction
  classical conditioning and, 343–344
  sensory affects and, 407–408
Extrapersonal associations, 748
Extraversion, 602
Extrinsic Affective Simon Task
    (EAST), 58–59
Eyeblink reflexes, measuring, 60
Eyewitness testimony, 291

F

Facets of affective experience,
    420–426
Facial cues, 632, 637
Facial EMG measures, 59–60, 400
Facial feedback theory, 402–403
Facial muscles, response to persuasive
    message and, 645–646
Factual accuracy, working knowledge
    and, 83
False memory paradigm, 562
False statements, spontaneous
    identification of, 293
Familiarity, ease of retrieval and,
    302–303
Fast response measure, 145
Fear, 461
  amygdala and, 424
  attitude and, 457
  compliance and, 469–470
  conditioning and extinction and,
      408
Fear appeals, 620, 640, 648–649, 753
Fear arousal, 648
Fear conditioning, 558–559
Fearful-avoidant attachment style, 719
Fear learning, 447
Field dependence, 594
Fixed parameters, 247
Fluency, 461
  conceptual, 451
  mere exposure and, 509, 751–752
  mere exposure effect and, 451–452
  perceptual, 451
  repetition and, 409–410
Foot-in-the door effect, 253
Forbidden toy paradigm, 231, 248, 516
Force choice task, 398
Forced compliance paradigm,
    229–230, 232
Forewarnings, 638, 675, 676
Form-resistant correlation hypothesis,
    46
Frames of reference, 324
Free-choice paradigm, 228–229, 232,
    248
Free speech belief study, 302
Frequency
  of affective experiences, 418–420,
      421
  of knowledge retrieval, 281

Frequency-based rating scales,
    152–154
F tests, 31
Functional matching, 100, 597–598,
    647

G

Gain frames, 640
Galvanic skin response (GSR), 59,
    176
Gambling paradigm, 417
Gender
  audience effects and, 347
  persuasion and, 600–601
General behavioral principle, 150
Generalizability theory, 31
Gestalt basis of conditioning,
    445–446
Gestalt principle, 460, 479
Global attitudes, 721
Global evaluations, 753
GNAT. See Go/No-go Association
    Task
Goal magnitudes, 340–341
Goals
  attitude ambivalence and, 332–333
  attitudes and, 327
  behavior and, 130, 160
  behaviors vs., 191–192
  classical conditioning and, 344
  classification of, 356
  egalitarian, 464
  as evidence vs. epistemic
      motivation, 338
  group locomotion and, 355
  influence on attitudes, 9, 11–12
  of persuasive communication,
      345–346
  role in dual process models of
      attitude change, 350–351
  social, 697
  from unimodel perspective, 353
Go/No-go Association Task (GNAT),
    58, 544, 561, 562
Greenpeace, attitudes toward, 264
Group-based attitudes, 655
Group cohesiveness, 724
  organizational commitment and, 726
Group decision making, 724–726
Group identification, 680
  self-esteem and, 682–683
Group identity, 595
Group level dissonance processes,
    242–243
Group locomotion, 355
Group membership, 723–724
Group norms, 732
Group polarization, 687–688, 691
Groupthink, 725–726, 726–727
GSR. See Galvanic skin response
Guttman's scaling, 133, 135, 177

H

Habit, 144–146, 760
 attributes of, 145
 reasoned action and planned
  behavior models and, 201–203
Halo effects, 376, 718
HAM model. *See* Human associative
  memory model
Handbook of Social Psychology, vii,
  707
Happy mood, 480
 contrast effect and, 722
 effect on persuasion, 466–467, 471
 selective thought and, 515
 stereotyping and, 462–463, 465
 See also Mood(s)
HCM. *See* Hedonic contingency model
Health behaviors, 130, 198
Health belief model, 193
Health interventions, 651
Hedonic consequences, accessible
  attitudes and, 94
Hedonic contingency model
  (HCM), 469
Hedonic dissonance, moral dissonance
  vs., 235–236
Hedonic fluency model (HFM), 509
Hedonic tone, 416
Helpfulness, 253
Heritability of attitudes, 6, 325, 328, 334
Heterosexual attitudes toward
  homosexuality scale, 595
Heuristic bases of belief formation and
  change, 298–306
 affective influences on belief,
  305–306
 ease of retrieval, 298–303
 simulation, 303–305
Heuristic cues, 352
Heuristic processing, 259, 627–628
 affect and, 465–466, 468
 emotions and, 463
 See also Heuristic-systematic model
Heuristics, 350, 510, 676
 affect, 455
 biased use of, 379
 consensus, 355, 358
 correcting for prejudice and, 596
 ease-of-generation, 519–520
 ease-of-retrieval, 298–303
 reliance on, 580
 salience of, 528n9
Heuristic-systematic model (HSM),
  14, 98–100, 348, 349–350, 372,
  377, 505, 625–626, 627–628,
  676, 756, 762
 attitude change and, 577–578, 580
 motives in, 698n3
HFM. *See* Hedonic fluency model
Hierarchical Cluster Analysis, 412
Hindsight, generating explanations on,
  305

Historical analysis of motives in social
  influence, 692–695
Holistic belief, 696–697
Horizontal structure, 101
Hostile media phenomenon, 377
HSM. *See* Heuristic-systematic model
Human associative memory (HAM)
  model, 453
Humanitarianism-egalitarianism scale,
  596
Hypocrisy paradigm, 241–242, 256,
  258

I

IAPS. *See* International Affective
  Picture System
IAT. *See* Implicit Association Test
Identification
 group, 680
 persuasion and, 634
Identification-based relationships,
  698n6
Identification process, 356
Identify and count strategy, 149
Identity-analytic model, 239
Ideological reasoning, value pluralism
  model of, 383
Ideological theory of prejudice, 448
Ideology, 763
 attitude-belief congruence and, 383
 attitudes and, 86
 effect of behavior on, 263
 political, 577, 649, 671–672
If-then reasoning, 504–505
Illusory correlation model, 729
 mental illness stigma and, 731
Immediacy principle, 480
Impact effects, 263
Implementation intentions, 190–191,
  759–760
Implicational molecules, 286–290
 stereotypes as, 289–290
Implicit affect, implicit/explicit
  attitudes and, 556–557
Implicit Association Test (IAT), 54,
  56–58, 64n3, 443, 445, 508,
  524, 544, 549, 599, 747–748
 personalized, 748
 race, 555, 561, 562, 652
Implicit attitudes, 86–87, 204–207,
  524–525, 543–545, 747–748,
  748
 attitude change and, 652–653
 awareness in, 559–560
 classical conditioning and, 557–559
 context and, 546–552, 555–556
 existing concurrently with explicit,
  550
 explicit attitudes *vs.,* 204–207
 implicit affect and mere exposure
  and, 556–557

influence on behavior, 161
 malleability of, 560, 567
 potentiated recruitment framework
  of, 552–567
 predicting behavior from, 206–207,
  209
 prejudice and, 560–562, 564–565
 priming and, 559
 as response mode, 560
 social desirability and, 563–565, 566
 social-regulatory motives, 563, 566
 spontaneous behavior and, 544–545
Implicit conclusions, 346–347
Implicit learning paradigm, 558
Implicit measures, 524, 525, 747–748
Implicit memory, 524
Implicit motives, 599, 600
Implicit processes, 523–525
Implicit responses, 127–128
Implicit social cognition, 559
Implicit theories of change
 individual differences in, 589–590
 role in belief formation, 290–292
Importance-accessibility association,
  91, 94–95
Impression formation, 503, 763
 intradisciplinary connections to,
  712–715
Impression formation task, 444
Impression management, 356, 516
Impression motivation, 681, 755
Impression-relevant involvement, 639,
  755
Impression-relevant thinking, 685–686
Impulsive behavior, 130
IMS. *See* Internal motivation to
  respond without prejudice scale
Incentives, 521
 forced compliance paradigm and, 229
 joint effects of biased scanning and,
  224–225
 referent power and, 680
 social consensus and, 679
Inclusion-exclusion model, 500, 549
Incongruity, 529n14
 resolution of, 522, 529n13
Inconsistency
 evaluative, 178–182
 evaluative-cognitive, 332
 literal, 178, 189–190
 pseudo-inconsistency, 189–190
 uncertainty orientation and, 598
Incremental theory, 589
Independent-trace theories, 278–279
Independent variable, 159
Indirect cue, 106, 116n13
Individual, as focus of social
  psychology, 693
Individual differences, 575
 in evaluation of minority groups,
  595–596
 in implicit theories of change,
  589–590

in motivation to control for
    prejudice, 596
in preferences between motives,
    596–599
    See also Attitude change, individual
    differences in
Individualism/individualistic cultures,
    593–594, 695–696
    affective influence and, 448
    response to cognitive dissonance,
    248
Induced compliance paradigm, 236
Inducements, wishful thinking and,
    380. *See also* Rewards
Infallibility, 334
Infant feeding practices, predicting,
    183
Inference rules, 347
Inferences, 276, 344
    motivated, 373–379
Inferential approaches, 509–511
    attribution, 510–511
    balance, 510
    use of heuristics, 510
Influence
    informational, 672–673
    normative, 672–673
Influenced mediators, 143–144
Information
    accessibility of belief-relevant,
        301–302
    affect used as, 455
    attitude accessibility and type of
        relevant, 89, 90, 92
    attitude-behavior consistency and
        attitude relevant, 109, 111–112,
        114
    attitude change and types of attitude
        relevant, 100–101, 101–102,
        104
    biased analysis and evaluation of,
        378
    biased information seeking, 378
    biased processing of ambiguous,
        377–378
    biased processing of new, 376–379
    effect of persuasion and ordinal
        position of, 352
    effects on belief formation, 304
    memory for attitude-relevant,
        757–758
    persuasion and, 634
    recall of, 715
    selection exposure to, 231
    sensory affects and survival, 407
    somatically marked, 389
    trait consistent, 715
Informational influence, 356, 357,
    635–636, 672–673
Informational motives, 592–593,
    673
Informational needs, group
    membership and, 723, 724

Informational social influence, 355,
    724–725
Information dependence, 673
Information integration, 504, 512,
    712–713
    consistency motive *vs.,* 330–331
Information-motivation-behavioral
    skills model, 193
Information processing, 498–499
    belief change and, 383–385
    cognitive expectancies and, 714–715
    cultural influences on, 696–697
    moods and, 753
    motives and, 756–757
Information-processing models,
    296–297, 621–622, 710, 762
    Fishbein and Ajzen, 297
    McGuire, 296–297
Informed consent forms, 152
Ingroup influence, 683–684
Ingroup minorities, 689
Ingroups, 457
Injunctive norms, 161, 199, 677
Innate sensory affects, 407
Innovators, 603
Inoculation research, 650
Instrumental attitude, 329
Instrumental behavior, 109
Instrumental function, 754
Instrumental learning, 440
Insufficient punishment, effect on
    behavior and attitudes,
    230–231
Integration, persuasion and, 634
Integrative complexity, 84
Intelligence
    persuasion and, 601–602
    reception and, 521
    relation to yielding and
        comprehension, 347
Intensity, of affective experiences,
    420
Intentions
    behavior and, 160
    contradiction with action, 178
    implementation, 190–191, 759–760
    predicting, 193–204
    as predictors of behavior, 187–192
    in reasoned action model, 194
    stability of, 188
Inter-attitudinal structure, 80, 85–87
    complexity of knowledge and,
        95–96
    strength-related beliefs and, 98
Intercomponent ambivalence, 641–642
Interdisciplinary attitude research,
    707–708
Interdisciplinary connections
    to marital interaction, 720–723
    to mental illness stigma, 730–731
    to political candidate evaluation,
        716–717, 720–723
Intergroup conflict, 727

Intergroup processes, 727–731
    interdisciplinary connections to
        mental illness stigma, 730–731
    intradisciplinary connections to
        stereotyping, prejudice, and
        discrimination, 727–730
Intergroup stereotyping research,
    729–730
Internal cues, self-perception and, 252
Internalization, 356, 698n5
Internal motivation to respond without
    prejudice scale (IMS), 564–565
International Affective Picture System
    (IAPS), 415
Interpersonal attraction, 717–720, 724
Interpersonal behavior, 130, 131
Interpersonal influence, need for
    cognition and, 582
Interpersonal processes, 717–723
    interdisciplinary connections to
        political candidate evaluation
        and marital interaction,
        720–723
    intradisciplinary connections to
        interpersonal attraction and
        close relationships, 718–720
Interpersonal replication studies,
    250–251
Interrater agreement, 39
Interval properties, of reported counts,
    153
Interviewer effects, 52
Interviewer opinions, effect on
    responses, 39
Intra-attitudinal structure, 80
Intracomponent ambivalence, 641–642
Intradisciplinary attitude research, 707,
    708–709
Intradisciplinary connections
    to impression formation, 712–715
    to stereotyping, prejudice, and
        discrimination, 727–730
Intragroup processes, 723–727
    group formation, performance,
        influence, and decision making,
        723–726
Intrapersonal processes, 711–717
    interdisciplinary connections to
        political candidate evaluation,
        716–717
    intradisciplinary connections to
        impression formation, 712–715
Intrinsic motivation, 253–254
Involvement, 621, 638, 639, 755
    affective, 49, 407, 475
    and attitude-behavior, 179, 186
    and attitude change, 529n15, 621,
        627–628, 639
    and controlled or deliberate
        processes, 553, 560
    and subjective conviction, 642
    and memory, 564–566
    ego, 621

emotional, 595
    impression-relevant, 755
    outcome-relevant, 755
    value-relevant, 755, 756
Issue framing, social consensus and,
    686
Item operating characteristic (IOC),
    132–136
Item reversals, 42–43
Item-total correlations, 29

J

James-Lange theory of emotions,
    401–402
Jealousy molecules, 288
*Journal of Personality and Social
    Psychology,* 527
Judgment, 276
    affect and, 479
    attitudes and, 4, 5, 6
    attitudes as evaluative, 745
    consensual, 678
    effect of prior judgments on
        subsequent ones, 301–302
    effects of comparative judgments on
        absolute ones, 302
    fluency and, 451
    mood and, 461
    mood and evaluative, 452–455
    social, 578
Judgmental self-doubt scale, 590
Just desserts processing molecule, 287
Justifications, 239
Just world, belief in, 311

K

Knowledge, 115n2
    activation of, 519–520
    attitude change and, 578, 580–585
    attitudes as, 678
    behavior and, 160
    beliefs and, 274–276
    gender and need for, 600
    inter-attitudinal structure and
        complexity of, 95–96
    as moderator of attitude-belief
        congruence, 381
    need for, 580–585
    need to know, 575, 577, 755
    persuasion and prior, 350–351
    procedural, 440
    referents of, 274–275
    semantic, 440
    sources of, 275
    specificity of, 275–276
    statistical, 275
    subjective, 115n3, 628
    working. *See* Working knowledge
Knowledge accessibility, 339, 519–520

Knowledge belief organization,
    278–286
    associative network theories, 279
    associative theories, 282–284
    content and structure of thought
        systems, 282–283
    independent-trace theories, 278–279
    probabilogical models of belief
        organization and change,
        284–286
    schema theories, 279–280
    storage bin models, 280–281
Knowledge function, 82, 338, 339,
    678, 724, 754
Knowledge-listing technique, 83
Knowledge organization, chematic
    theories of, 286–294

L

Late positive potential (LPP), 61
Latitudes, 45, 236, 251–252, 258, 370,
    511, 620–621, 631, 642
Learning
    affective, 424
    of attitudes, 342–344
    effect on sensory affects, 406
    fear, 447
    implicit, 558
    instrumental, 440
    reward, 440
    of word meanings, 448–449
Legitimate authority, persuasion and,
    634
LEI. *See* Life Event Inventory
Lexical decision task, 56
Liberal political ideology, 649,
    671–672
Life Event Inventory (LEI), 453–454
Life-satisfaction judgments, 421, 454
Likert scales, 32–33, 177
Liking
    attitude as expression of, 277
    positive affect and, 461, 465
    social consensus and, 681
    of stimulus, 450, 451
    wanting *vs.,* 424
Linear models of belief formation,
    295–296
Line-judging paradigm, 672–673, 674,
    679, 696
Literal inconsistency, 178, 189–190,
    759
Localist connectionist model, 568n1
Localization procedures, 528n4
Logistic regression, 155
Longitudinal studies, to analyze
    behavior, 147–148
Long-term memory, 45, 458
Loss frames, 640
Lost-letter technique, 53
LPP. *See* Late positive potential

Lumping, 526–527
Lying, social desirability response bias
    and, 50–52

M

Machiavellianism, 245, 594–595
Macrosystems, 162
Majority, influence of minorities on,
    636
Majority influence, 635–637,
    689–692
Malleability
    of implicit attitudes, 560, 567
    of intelligence, 602
Marital interaction research, 720–723
Marital satisfaction, 722–723
Marketing, 651–652
Marlow-Crowne scale, 152
Masking, 443
Matching effects, 599–600, 756–757
Matching postulate, 326
MBTI. *See* Myers-Briggs Type
    Indicator
MDS. *See* Multidimensional Scaling
Means-goals framework, 327, 334
Measurement
    of attitudes. *See* Attitude
        measurement
    of behavior, 152–154, 183
Media effects, 299–301
    hostile media phenomenon, 377
    influence on behavior, 163
    persuasion and, 619–620
Memory
    arousal and, 461, 480
    attention and, 520–523
    attitude-consistent, 419
    attitude evaluation and activation
        of, 25
    attitude formation and, 583, 716–717
    for attitude-relevant information,
        757–758
    attitudes and, 4
    attitudes and accessibility of, 25–26
    attitudes represented in, 5–6, 494
    comprehension and, 290–291
    conceptualization of recognition,
        303
    context-sensitivity of past emotional
        experiences, 419–420
    declarative, 474–475
    emotion and, 458–460
    episodic, 149, 150
    explicit, 243–244
    implementation intentions and, 191
    implicit, 524
    influence of valence on, 419
    for messages, 522–523
    moods and, 753
    order of response alternatives and,
        44–45

reconstructive, 291–292
semantic, 149–150
spreading activation model of, 279
Memory-based models of judgment,
    453, 454–455
Memory organization packet, 280
Mental illness stigma, 730–731
Mere association, 507–509, 579
Mere exposure, 342, 409–410,
    460–461, 509
    affective influence and, 450–452
    affective vs. cognitive basis of,
        450–451
    attitude and, 479
    attitude formation and, 751–752
    implicit/explicit attitudes and,
        556–557
    sensory affects, 406
    unconscious affect and, 398
Mesosystems, 162
Message arguments, 351, 352, 379
Message communicator, 631–637
    effects on deceivers' attitudes,
        632–633
    interaction with recipient, 645–649
    signs of dissimulation, 632
    source numeracy, 635–637
    source reinforcers, 633–635
Message effects
    arousal and, 648–649
    attitude function and, 646–647
    attitude structure and, 647–648
    attitude valence and, 645–646
Message framing, 640, 655
Message recipient, 640–645
    ability of, 643–645
    attitude function, 642–643
    interaction with communicator,
        645–649
    motivation of, 643–645
    subjective conviction of, 642
    variability in attitude structure and,
        641–642
Messages
    functional matching and, 598
    memory for, 522–523
    persuasive, 598, 638–640
    self-generated, 513–514
    strong vs. weak, 512
    two-sided, 640
    uncertainty orientation and, 598
Message variables effects, 345–346
Meta-analysis, 63n1
Meta-attitudinal measures, 88
Metabeliefs, 387, 587–588, 602
Metacognition, 360, 388, 516
    attitude change and, 578
    attitude reports and, 27
    bias correction, 517–518
    self-validation hypothesis, 517
Metrics, 152–154
Microconcepts, 569n3
    defining attitudes and, 746
    potentiated recruitment of, 552–555

Microsystems, 162
Midpoints, rating scale, 37, 40
Minority groups, individual differences
    in evaluation of, 595–596. See
    also Discrimination; Prejudice
Minority influence, 687, 688–692
Misattribution, 260, 410, 454, 502,
    516, 720
Mise en scene, 446
Mixed feelings, structural models of
    affect and, 416–418
Model of judgment survival, 650–651
MODE (motivation and opportunity as
    determinants of behavior)
    model, 106, 116n13, 130,
    184–187, 208, 372, 381, 564,
    567, 760–761
    applied to prejudice/discrimination
        relation, 205
    empirical support for, 186
    issues related to, 186–187
Moderated causal relationship, 157
Moderating variables explanation, of
    evaluative inconsistency,
    178–179
Moderator-like hypotheses, 158
Modern racism scale, 595
Montage, 445–446
Mood-as-information model, 398
Mood disorders, 405
Mood effects, conditioning and,
    445–446
Mood misattribution approach, 728
Mood(s), 400, 404–406, 414–415,
    438, 710
    effect on accuracy of behavioral
        self-report, 150
    emotions vs., 752–753
    evaluative judgment and, 452–455
    examples of, 401
    functions of, 405
    induction in laboratory settings, 406,
        453
    influence on attitude object, 411–412
    influence on information processing,
        335, 753
    judgment and, 461, 630
    message processing bias and,
        644–645
    need for cognition and, 581
    reasoned action and planned
        behavior models and, 203
    selective thought and, 515
    stereotyping and angry, 463
    stereotyping and happy, 462–463,
        465
    See also Affect
Moral dissonance, hedonic dissonance
    vs., 235–236
Moral dumbfounding, 457
Moral norm, 200–201
Motivated bias, 529n12
Motivated inconsistency reduction-
    dissonance theory, 370

Motivated inferences, 373–379
    biased predictions based on current
        attitudes, 375–376
    biased processing of new
        information, 376–379
    breadth and mechanisms of effects,
        376
    wishful thinking, 373–375
Motivation, 753–758
    accuracy and, 355, 755
    approach, 425
    attitude activation and, 185, 187
    attitude bases and, 112, 113
    attitude change and, 577–580
    attitude formation and, 82
    attitude strength and, 580–599
    bias correction and, 517–518
    central route processing and, 349
    defense, 378, 755, 756
    defined, 753
    as determinant of elaboration, 506
    directional, 345, 353
    dissonance and, 226–227
    epistemic, 335, 338, 344
    expression of prejudice and, 564
    group cohesiveness and, 724
    heuristic processing and, 350
    impression, 681, 755
    information processing and, 629
    intrinsic, 253–254
    mere exposure and, 509
    of message recipient, 643–645
    normative, 673–676
    prevention focus, 312–313
    processing, 353
    processing of consensual views and,
        685–687
    promotion focus, 312–313
    to reflect on attitude, 26
    as source of bias, 515
    use of heuristics and, 510
Motivational bias, 335
Motivational distortion
    empirical evidence for, 377–378
    mechanisms of, 378–379
Motivational processes, 261
Motivation to control prejudiced
    reactions scale, 596
Motives
    certainty, 698n7
    defined, 753
    explicit, 600
    implicit, 599, 600
    individual differences in preferences
        for, 596–599
    informational, 592–593, 673
    information processing and, 756–757
    memory for attitude-relevant
        information and, 757–758
    normative, 592–593, 673–677
    types of, 306–307, 754–755
Motor functions, affect and, 422
Multi-dimensionality of attitudes,
    176–178

Multidimensional Scaling (MDS), 412
Multi-operationalization, 30–31
Multiple-act, repeated-observation
 criterion, 139–141
Multiple-act, single-observation
 criterion, 139–141
Multiple attitudes, 748–749
Multiple regression analysis, 155–156
 identifying individual differences in
  weight given to cues, 295–296
Multitrait-multimethod matrix, 30, 31
Music, influence on moods, 405–406
Myers-Briggs Type Indicator (MBTI),
 584

N

Name letter preference tasks, 544
Narrative, sense making and, 445–446,
 460
Need, defined, 754
Need for closure, 577, 583–584
Need for cognition, 581–582, 644
Need for consistency, 585–590
Need for evaluation, 582–583
Need for knowledge, 580–585
Need for self-worth, 590–592
Need for social inclusion, 592–596,
 755
Need for uniqueness, 593
Need to know, 575, 577, 755
Negative affect, 414–415
 effect on beliefs, 306
Negative binomial regression, 156
Negative mood
 effect on message processing, 645
 effect on persuasion, 466–467, 468,
  471
 See also Mood(s)
Neural network models of behavior,
 164
Neuroscience, 763
 affective, 421–426
 social, 501
Neuroticism, 602
Nodes, 279
Non-attitude thesis, 545
Nondeliberative behavior, attitudes
 and, 106–107
Nonspecific activation model, 451
Nonverbal behavior, prediction of
 social interactions and, 653
Nonverbal communication measures,
 54
No-opinion filters, 46–50
No responses, attitude measurement
 and, 49
Normative beliefs, 158, 193–195, 197
Normative expectations, semantic
 memory and, 149
Normative influences, 143, 161, 356,
 357, 635–636, 672–673, 698n2
Normative motives, 592–593, 673–677

Normative social influence, 355,
 724–725
Normative standards, 244
Norms
 communication, 293–294
 descriptive, 161, 199, 677
 group, 732
 injunctive, 161, 199, 677
 moral, 200–201
 partner, 200–201
 personal, 201
 prediction of intention and, 196–197
 reciprocity, 681
 role specific, 732
 social, 592, 677
 social justice, 732
 subjective, 199–200, 710, 720
Novelty, effects of, 300–301
Nucleus accumbens, 425
Null effects, 529n14

O

Obedience and Authority (Milgram),
 125, 164
Object-appraisal function, 338,
 642–643, 678, 754
Object-evaluation associations, as
 attitudinal primitives, 546–547
Object focus, 440
Objective judges, 132
Objective needs, group membership
 and, 723
Objectivity, 514–515
Objects
 of behavior, 131, 141
 of emotions, 438–439
 expectancy-value approach to
  evaluating, 503–504
 See also Attitude objects
Observer reports, of behavior, 154
Odor judgment, 416, 426
Online construction of attitudes, 6,
 80–81, 325–326, 328, 372,
 583, 716–717, 746–747
Online model of impression formation,
 713–714
Openness to experience, 602
Open questions, 34–35
Operant conditioning, 508, 710
 mental illness stigma and, 730
 prejudice and, 727–728
Operative measures, 88
Opinion deviance, 680–681
Opinions
 beliefs vs., 276–278
 consistency in, 311–312
 See also Attitudes; Beliefs
Opportunity structure, 137
Optimism, 592, 640, 644
Optimism-pessimism questionnaire,
 592
Optimizing, 48–49

Oral presentation, recency effects,
 45–46
Orbitofrontal cortex, 425–426
Order effects, 620
Ordinal properties, of reported counts,
 153
Ordinal regression, 165n3
Ordinary least squares regression, 155,
 156
Organizational behavior, 726–727
Organizational commitment, 726
Others, constancy of attitudes toward,
 478–479
Outcome expectancies, 193, 456–457
Outcome-relevant involvement, 639,
 755
Outgroups, 457, 479–480, 730
 authoritarianism and hostility
  towards, 586–587
 group identification and, 683–684
Overjustification effect, 253–254

P

Paired-picture paradigm, 418
PANAS. See Positive Affect and
  Negative Affect Schedule
Paper-and-pencil measures, 61
Parallel distributed processing, 13
Parallel effects
 for mood, 456
 of task instructions, 56
Parallel evaluative neural systems,
 423–424
Parallel forms, 28–29
Parenting behavior, 130
Parsimony
 benefits of, 525–526
 unimodel and, 505
Partner norms, 200–201
Past, reconstructing, 291–292
Past attitudes still there (PAST) model,
 86–87
Pathways, 279
Peak-end rule, 420–421, 753
Perceptions, 276
 attitudes as, 478
Perceptions of self, 306
Perceptions of world, 306
Perceptual consistency-balance theory,
 370
Perceptual contrast effects, 45
Perceptual distortions, 520
Perceptual fluency, 342
Perceptual fluency/attributional model,
 451–452
Peripheral cues, 352, 578, 584, 624,
 627, 644
Peripheral route, processing via, 14,
 259, 348–349, 624, 627, 710
 affect and, 465–466, 468
 See also Elaboration likelihood
  model

Personality
   behavior and, 160
   Big Five traits, 602
   dissonance arousal and, 260
   persuasion and, 347–348
   reasoned action and planned
      behavior models and, 200
Personalized IAT, 748
Personal norms, 201
Personal relevance, attitude-belief
      congruence and, 382
Personal standards, 244
Persuasion, 259, 342, 344–351, 762–763
   affect and, 465–471
   affective immediacy principle, 472
   affective messages and, 469–471
   affect regulation and, 469
   age and, 601
   audience effects and, 347–348
   cognition in persuasion model
      (CPM), 625–626, 629–630, 762
   cognitive response model of, 623
   combinatorial models of, 622–623
   communication and, 617–618
   communication discrepancy and,
      655
   contemporary process models of,
      623–630
   dual process models and, 348–350
   effects of positive mood on,
      466–467, 471
   experiments in, 618–619
   extent of elaboration in processing
      and, 511–512
   gender and, 600–601
   implicit vs. explicit conclusions and,
      346–347
   information processing theory and,
      621–622
   intelligence and, 601–602
   Machiavellianism and, 594–595
   need for closure and, 584
   need for consistency and, 585–590
   need for self-worth and, 590–592
   need for social inclusion and,
      592–596
   rational-experiential inventory and,
      599
   resistance to, 587–588
   social-cognitive models of, 372
   social judgment model of, 620–621
   unimodel of, 351–354
   Yale program, 344–348, 619–620
   See also Attitude change
Persuasion paradigms, 694
Persuasive arguments theory, 687–688
Persuasive messages, 15, 638–640
Pessimism, 644
Phobias, conditioning and extinction
      and, 408
Physical attractiveness stereotype, 718
   role in political candidate
      evaluation, 721

Physical exercise
   attitude-behavior relation and, 183
   prediction of, 202
Physiological influences on behavior,
      159–160
Physiological measures, 59–61
Physiological responses
   to emotions, 401–402
   to persuasive message, 645–646
Planned behavior, theory of, 142–143,
      193–204, 760
Plausibility technique, 176
Pleasant experiences
   approach motivation and, 425
   orbitofrontal cortex and, 426
Pleasure-displeasure, as core of
      emotional experience, 412,
      414, 416–418
Poisson regression, 156
Polarization, 697
Political attitude studies, 374
Political candidate evaluation, 717,
      720–723
Political decision making, 726–727
Political ideologies, 577, 671–672
Positive affect, 306, 414–415
Positive Affect and Negative Affect
      Schedule (PANAS), 414–415
Positive emotions, 753
Positive mood
   dissonance reduction and, 472
   effect on message processing,
      644–645
   effect on persuasion, 466–467, 471
   See also Mood(s)
Positive self-attributes, self-affirmation
      and, 238
Postdicting behavior, 146–148
Prediction
   attitude-behavior consistency and,
      105
   biased, 375–376
   effect of generating an explanation
      on, 304–305
   of intentions, 196–198
   predictive validity of general
      attitudes, 178–182
Prediction of behavior, 131–132, 133,
      146–148
   implicit and explicit attitudes and,
      206–207, 209
   intentions and, 187–192
   of single behaviors, 182–192
Predictive validity, 39
Preexisting attitudes, 252–253,
      255–256
Prefrontal cortex, 423
Prejudice, 204–209, 727–730, 763
   authoritarianism and, 586
   explicit attitudes and, 564
   ideological theory of, 448
   implicit attitudes and, 560–562,
      564–565, 652

   individual differences in, 595–596
   individual differences in motivation
      to control for, 596
   role of motivation in expression of,
      564
   training to suppress, 560–562
Pre-message attitude, influence on
      attitude change, 99–100, 101
Preoccupied attachment style, 719
Prevention focus, 312–313
Prevention motives, 356
Primacy effects, 43, 44–45
   in judgment formation, 352
   need for cognition and, 582
   visual presentation and, 45–46
Priming, 346, 445–446
   affective, 474, 752
   concept, 55–56
   descriptive, 474, 480
   evaluative, 55, 56, 474, 480
   implicit attitudes and, 559
   sequential, 54–55
   subliminal, 27, 556–557
Priming measures, 54–56, 64n2
Prince, The (Machiavelli), 619
Principle of aggregation, 180–182,
      208
Principle of compatibility, 182–183,
      199, 208
Prisoner's dilemma game, 196
Probabilogical conceptualization,
      294
Probabilogical models, 284–286,
      336–337, 353, 371, 504–505,
      512, 548
Problem behavior theory, 130–131
Procedural knowledge, 440
Process, defining, 495–502
Process description parsimony, 526
Process-dissociation, 500, 501
Processing extent, 340–341
Processing fluency, repetition and,
      409–410
Processing motivation, 353
Projection, 375, 376
Promotion focus, 312–313
Promotion motives, 356
Propaganda, 617–618
Propositions, knowledge and, 275
Protestant ethic scale, 596
Prototype/willingness model, 193
Pseudo-inconsistency, 189–190
Psychological discomfort, dissonance
      and experience of, 240–241
Psychological Inquiry, 762
Psychology, attitude research's profile
      within, 744. See also Social
      psychology
Psychology of Attitudes, The (Eagly &
      Chaiken), vii, 745, 758
Public expressions, 355
Public opinion, dynamic social impact
      theory and, 691

Punishment
   attitudes and avoiding, 680
   insufficient, 230–231
   operant conditioning and, 508
   orbitofrontal cortex and, 425–426
Pupillary responses, 59

Q

Questionnaire satisficing. See
   Satisficing
Questions
   agree/disagree, 41, 43
   context effects of answering, 546
   ensuring comprehension of, 151
   open vs. closed, 34–35
   order effects, 39
   rhetorical, 640
   true/false, 42, 43
   yes/no, 42, 43

R

Racism scales, 595
Racism studies, 174. See also
   Discrimination; Prejudice
Radical model of dissonance,
   245–246, 256, 262, 516
Random error, 28
Randomized response technique,
   51–52
Rasch model, 594
Rating scales
   clarity of scale point meanings,
     36–37
   dichotomous, 36
   discerning natural scale
     differentiation, 39–40
   frequency-based, 152–154
   labeling points, 40–43
   middle alternatives, 40
   number of points on, 35, 36, 38–40,
     63n1
   order of response alternatives, 43–46
   7-point, 35, 36, 37, 38, 40
   reliability of, 38–39
   satisficing and, 37–38, 40
   theoretical issues, 35–36
   translation ease, 36
   trichotomous, 36
   uniformity of scale point meaning,
     37
   validity of, 39
   verbal labeling, 37
Rational-experiential inventory (REI),
   599
Rationality
   bounded, 337
   emotion and adaptive, 474
Rationalization, 283, 373

Reality, understanding through social
   consensus, 677–679, 754
Reasoned action, theory of, 136, 158,
   165n1, 720, 760
Reasoned action and planned behavior
   models, 193–204, 208
   assumption that action is reasoned,
     203–204
   empirical evidence for, 195–196
   past behavior and, 201–203
   questions regarding causal model,
     198–200
   sufficiency of, 200–201
Reasoning, biased processing and
   motivated, 758
Reasons analysis, 514
Recall, cued, 151–152
Recency effects, 43, 44–45
   of knowledge retrieval, 281
   need for cognition and, 582
   oral presentation and, 45–46
Reception processes, 347–348, 521,
   591, 630
Reception-yielding model, 347–348,
   591, 630
Reciprocal activation, of affect,
   417–418
Reciprocal relationship, 156, 157
Reciprocity norm, 681
Reconstructive memories, 291–292
Recycling study, 241–242
Referent bin, 280
Referent informational influence,
   683
Referent power, 680
   persuasion and, 634
Regression analysis, 155–156
REI. See Rational-experiential
   inventory
Reinforcement theory, 620
Reinterpretation, 307
Relating to others, 675, 754
   social consensus and, 679–681
Relational processing, 528–529n11
Relationship commitment, 719, 720
Relationship satisfaction research,
   720
Relevance override, 629
Reliability
   attitude measurement and, 28–29
   closed-ended questions and, 34
   defined, 28
   of rating scales, 38–39
   split-half, 29
   test-retest, 29
Religiosity studies, 181
Religious conversion, 649
Reported counts, 153–154, 155–156,
   165n3
Representation postulate, 326
Representativeness heuristic, 290
Representative period, 149
Repression-sensitization, 245

Repressors, 260
Resistance
   to attitude change, 345
   to persuasion, 587–588
Responding, socially desirable, 152
Response biases, 176
Response competition measures,
   56–59, 64n2
Response latency measures, 54–59
   priming measures, 54–56, 64n2
   response competition measures,
     56–59, 64n2
Response phase, of attitude report,
   26–27
Retention, 521
Retrieval cues, 279
Reverse conditioning, 407–408
Reverse incentive effect, 232–233
Revised life orientation test, 592
Reward-based relationships, 698n6
Reward learning, 440
Rewards, 528n8
   attitudes and obtaining, 680
   orbitofrontal cortex and, 425–426
   persuasion and, 634
Rhetorical questions, 640
Rhetoric (Aristotle), 619
Risk-as-fear, 479
Risk-as-feeling, 456, 461
Role playing, effect on attitudes,
   224–226, 623, 761
Role specific norms, 732

S

Sad moods, 480
   attitude change and, 471–472
   contrast effect and, 722
   effect on processing, 466, 468, 471
   See also Mood(s)
Salient cues, 26
Satisficing, 37–38, 40, 308
   no opinion responses and, 48–49
   response order and weak, 44
Schemas, 280
   as attitudinal primitives, 549–550
   implicational molecules as,
     286–287
Schemata, 324
Schema theory, 279–280, 449
Schematic processing, of knowledge,
   281
Schematic representations, 280
Schematic theories of knowledge
   organization, 286–294
Scripts, 290
Seating task, 53
Secure attachment style, 719
Security needs, group membership
   and, 723
Selective exposure, 231, 516, 731
Selective thought, 515

Self
  accuracy of perception of, 308–309
  motivation to think well of, 309–310
  perceptions of, 306
Self-administered questionnaires,
    socially desirable responses
    and, 52
Self-affirmation theory, 237–239, 255,
    256, 516, 590
Self-assessment, 711
Self-awareness, attitude change and,
    585
Self-categorization theory, 698n8
Self-censorship, 546
Self-coherence, 682
Self-concept
  attitude and, 755
  dissimulation and, 633
  effect of self-presentation on, 226
  moral dissonance and, 236
  self-consistency theory and,
    234–235
Self-consciousness, evaluative
    inconsistency and, 179
Self-consistency theory, 234–235, 516
Self-deception, 52
Self-defense motivation, 643
Self-doubt scale, 590–591
Self-efficacy beliefs, 199
Self-enhancement, 682, 711
Self-esteem, 591–592, 711
  antecedents and consequences of,
    732
  attitudes and, 82
  belief-discrepant behavior and, 312
  dissonance processes and, 244–245
  group identification and, 682–683
  of message recipient, 644
  reception and, 521
  schemas and, 549
  tactics, 590
Self-esteem scale, 591
Self-expression, attitudes as, 338
Self-generation studies, 513–514
Self-guides, ideal vs. ought, 603
Self-identity
  identification with behavior and, 201
  need for positive, 723
Self-image
  ego-defensive motives and,
    562–563
  need to maintain, 576
Self-knowledge, selective retrieval of,
    304–305
Self-monitoring, 245, 596–598, 646
  evaluative inconsistency and, 179
Self-perception, 13, 82, 126, 249–254,
    292, 507, 511, 516, 710, 731
  as alternative interpretation of
    dissonance theory, 250–252
  of attitude-behavior consistency, 143
  attitude-congruent behavior and,
    251–252, 258

attitude domains amenable to
    self-perception effects,
    253–254
attitude-incongruent behavior and,
    251–252, 258
automatic processing and, 259
of behavioral consistency, 165n2
conditions under which
    self-perception processes
    occur, 252–253
deliberative processing and, 259
dissonance and, 501–502
effects of dissimulation and, 633
helpfulness, 253
impression formation and, 712
interpersonal replication studies,
    250–251
intrinsic motivation, 253–254
role of arousal, 251
social perception vs., 249–250
voluntary behavior and, 257
Self-presentation, explicit attitudes
    and, 560
Self-report methods (direct), 31–50
  alternatives to direct, 50–63
  classic, 32–33
  designing, 33–50
  equal-appearing intervals method,
    32
  implicit measurement techniques,
    52–63
  labeling rating scale points, 40–43
  no-opinion filters and attitude
    strength, 46–50
  open vs. closed questions, 34–35
  order of response alternatives, 43–46
  rating scales, 35–43
  reliability, 38–39
  satisficing, 37–38, 40
  semantic differential, 33
  social desirability response bias,
    50–52
  summated ratings method, 32–33
  theoretical issues, 35–36
  validity, 39
Self-reports, 695
  of attitudes, 14
  of intention-behavior gap, 190–191
Self-reports, of past behavior, 149–150
  accuracy of, 150–151
  improving accuracy of, 151–152
Self-standards model, 244–245, 262,
    516, 761
  automatic and deliberative
    processing and, 260–261
Self-threat, 382
Self-validation, 473, 517, 579
Self-verification, 711
Self-worth, 576
  attitude change and, 578
  persuasion and need for, 590–592
Semantic analysis, 475
Semantic differential method, 33

Semantic knowledge, 440
Semantic memory, 149–150
Sensory affects, 406–410, 415–416,
    420, 421
  classical conditioning and, 407
  evaluative conditioning and,
    408–409
  extinction and, 407–408
  innate, 407
  mere exposure and, 409–410
Sensory functions, affect and, 422
September 2001 terrorist attacks,
    impact on attitudes/beliefs, 173
Sequential priming, 54–55
Serotonin, 405
Setting/situation
  of behavior, 131, 141
  effect on accuracy of behavioral
    self-report, 150
  effects on belief formation, 304
Short-term memory, 458
  coherence and, 446
  order of response alternatives and,
    45
Signal detection, 500
Signal learning, 343
Simon paradigm, 59
Simulations, 39, 303–305
Simultaneous accessibility, role in
    dissonance processes, 243–244
Single-act, repeated-observation
    criterion, 138–141
Single-act, single-observation
    criterion, 138–141
Situational constraints, on
    attitude-belief congruence, 380
Situational cues, 26
Situational factors, motivational
    orientations and, 313
Skin conductance response, 425
Sleeper effect, 635, 650
Social-adjustment function, 82–83,
    338, 643, 646
Social approval, 596–597
  attitude change and, 578
Social attribution, 287
Social behavior, 130
  predicting, 651
Social cognition, 693, 763
  implicit, 559
Social-cognitive models of persuasion,
    372
Social cognitive theory, 193, 196
Social communication, normative
    principles and, 293–294
Social comparison, group polarization
    and, 688
Social context of attitudes, 758–759
Social desirability, implicit/explicit
    attitudes and, 563–565, 566
Social desirability response bias,
    50–52
  documenting, 51–52

Social dominance orientation scale, 595
Social exchange theory, 680
Social goals, 697
Social group membership, effect on attitudes, 161
Social group stereotyping, 729–730
Social identity theory, 682, 686, 698n8
vicarious dissonance and shared, 243
Social-impression management, 643
Social inclusion, 576, 596–597, 755
persuasion and need for, 592–596
Social influence, 758–759
on behavior, 161
consistency motives in, 684–685
culture and, 695–697
Social influence on attitudes/attitude change, 15, 671–698
analyses of motives, 675–685
being oneself and social consensus, 681–684
changes in social consensus, 690–692
culture and social influence, 695–697
group polarization, 687–688
historical analysis of motives in, 692–695
minority influence, 688–690
motives direct processing of consensual views, 685–687
relating to others and social consensus, 679–681
surveillance paradigm, 672–675, 676
understanding reality through social consensus, 677–679
Social influence paradigms, 694
Social information processing, automatic, 449
Social information-processing model of impression formation, 712, 762–763
Socialization
attitude formation and, 6
behavior and, 163
Social judgment theory, 370, 520, 578, 620–621, 631, 653
Social justice norms, 732
Socially desirable responses, 152, 176
Social mind, 693
Social neuroscience, 501
Social norms, 592
consensus and, 677
Social perception, 249–250
Social power, persuasion and, 634–635
Social psychology
defined, vii, 22, 174
domains of, 709
historical development of, 693–695
process identification in, 501–502
Social reality, 299–301, 355

Social-regulatory motives, 563
Social representations, 324
Social status
acquiescence and, 42
attitude change and shifts in, 692
changes in, 698n8
Social tuning, 563
Society for Experimental Social Psychology, vii
Socratic effect, 285–286, 337, 382
Somatically marked information, 389
Source attractiveness, persuasion and, 655
Source numeracy, 635–636
Source power, 345
Source reinforcers, 633–635
Spearman-Brown Prophecy formula, 29
Split-half reliability, 29
Split semantic differential method, 331
Spontaneous behavior, implicit attitudes and, 747
Spontaneous evaluations, attitude report and, 24–25
Spontaneous identification of true and false statements, 293
Spontaneous processes of belief formation, 292–294
Spontaneous processing, strong attitudes and, 184–185, 187
Spontaneous validation processes, implications of, 293–294
Spreading activation model of memory, 279
Spreading of alternatives, 229
Spurious causal relationship, 156, 157
Stability
of attitudes, 324–325, 328, 545–546
of intentions, 188
Standards
normative, 244
personal, 244
States, 438, 745
State-Trait Anxiety Inventory, 602–603
Status quo effect, 377
Stereotypes/stereotyping, 449, 461, 568n1, 727–730, 763
affect and, 462–465
brand names, 464–465
category-triggered affect, 464
egalitarian goals and, 464
formation of, 729
as implicational molecules, 289–290
physical attractiveness, 718
promotion of counterstereotyping, 562
schemas and, 549
training to suppress, 560–562
Stimulus, consciously perceived vs. subliminally presented, 450
Storage bin models, 280–281

Story-order conditions, 304
Story skeletons, 290
Strategic impression management motives, 239–240
Strength of association, of knowledge units, 281
Stress hormones, memory formation and, 458, 459
Strong attitudes, effect on behavior, 264
Stroop task, 59
Structural consistency, 115n4
Structural equation modeling, 156
Structural theories of emotions, 404
Subjective beliefs, persuasion and, 345
Subjective conviction, 642
Subjective experience, beliefs and, 273
Subjective knowledge, 115n3, 628
Subjective knowledge scale, 590
Subjective norm, 199–200, 710, 720
Subjective relevance parameter, 353, 354
Subliminal primes, 556–557
Submissiveness, 602
Subsymbolic connectionist model, 568–569n1
Sufficiency principle, 757
Sufficient reason, 371
Summated ratings method, 32–33
Surveillance paradigm, 672–675, 676
Syllogisms, 371
triads of, 384
Syllogistic inference processes, conditional inference processes and, 295
Syllogistic reasoning, 512
Syllogistic theory, 504–505
Sympathy, of communicators, 345
Systematic processing, 259, 627, 637, 710
affect and, 465–466, 468
emotions and, 463
See also Heuristic-systematic model

T

Task difficulty, rating scale and, 37–38
Taxonomy of attitude structure, 87–88
limitations of research on, 88–89
Television, effect on beliefs and opinions, 299–301
Temperaments, 438
Templates, 324
Temporal consistency theory, 292
Tension-relaxation, 412
Terror management theory, 576
Test of Field Dependence, 594
Test-retest reliability, 29
Thalamus, 424, 476
Thematic Apperception Test, 599

Theories of reasoned action and planned behavior, 193–204, 384, 760

Theory of Cognitive Dissonance, A (Festinger), 226

Theory of mind, 448–449

Theory of planned behavior (TPB), 142–143, 651

Theory of reasoned action (TRA), 13, 136, 158, 165n1, 651, 720

Theory of trying, 193

Theory testing, 130

Think-backward strategy, 149

Think-forward strategy, 149

Thinking
    attitude change and amount of, 578
    attitude change and direction of, 578, 579
    bias in, 514–515
    objectivity in, 514–515
    wishful, 283, 309–310, 337, 360, 373–375, 380–381

Thoughtfulness, attitude change and, 98–100

Thought introspection, 386–387

Thought systems, structural features, 282–283, 579

Thurstone's explanation of evaluative inconsistency, 180–182

Thurstone's scaling, 132, 134, 177, 277

Time
    behavior and, 131, 141
    causal models of behavior and, 158
    effect on accuracy of behavioral self-report, 151

Tolerance threshold, 308

TPB. *See* Theory of planned behavior

TRA. *See* Theory of reasoned action

Training, to suppress stereotypes and prejudice, 560–562

Trait consistent information, 715

Transcendence, 307

Trichotomous scale, 36, 37

Tripartite theory of attitude, 79, 82, 277, 324, 327

Trivialization, dissonance reduction and, 516

True attitudes, 380, 546

True/false questions, 42, 43

True score, 28

True statements, spontaneous identification of, 293

Trustworthiness, 636
    persuasive communication and, 344–345

Truth, social consensus and, 678

Trying, theory of, 193

Two-factor theory of emotions, 260, 403

Two-sided messages, 640

U

Unanalyzed causal relationship, 156–157

Uncertainty orientation, 598–599

Unconscious
    affect, 397–400
    behavior, 130
    conditioning, 443–444
    factors, influence on behavior, 161

Uncoupled activation, of affect, 417

Understanding entity, 675

Unimodel, 14, 351–354, 505, 622, 625–626, 628–629, 762
    beliefs and goals and, 353
    prior attitude-change formulations and, 353–354

Uniqueness, need for, 593

Universal process descriptions, 495, 503, 527

Utilitarian function, 82, 643, 754

Utility maximization, 282, 283

V

Valence
    affective experience and, 426, 439, 440
    argument, 639
    attitude formation and, 479
    attitudes and, 79
    influence on memory, 419
    perceptual fluency and, 452

Validation process, 357

Validity
    closed-ended questions and, 34
    concurrent, 39
    construct, 28, 30
    convergent, 29–31
    discriminant, 29–31
    discriminant construct, 499
    discriminative process, 499
    ELM and, 627
    predictive, 39
    of rating scales, 39
    social consensus and, 678

Value-expression, 86

Value-expressive function, 82, 83, 643, 682, 724

Value pluralism model of ideological reasoning, 383

Value-relevant involvement, 621, 755, 756

Values
    ambivalence and conflicting, 333
    behavior and, 160, 263
    sources of, 477

Variables
    dependent, 159
    independent, 159

Vested interest
    attitude-belief congruence and, 382
    predicting behavior on basis of, 180

Vicarious dissonance, 243

Vigilant decision making, 725

Visual presentation, primacy effects and, 45–46

Volitional behavior, 130, 191–192, 257

Voting study, 340

W

Wanting, liking *vs.*, 424

Weak attitudes, effect on behavior, 264

Weekday *vs.* weekend, pleasant experiences and, 415

Wishful thinking, 283, 309–310, 337, 360, 373–375, 380, 381

Within-dimension ambivalence, 93, 103, 105, 113

Witness-order conditions, 304

Word-fragment completion task, 61, 544

Words
    activating affective response, 399
    automatic inferences about meaning, 475
    conditioning and negative/positive, 442
    emotion, 412
    methods of learning meaning of, 448–449
    typical mood, 401

Working complexity, 92

Working knowledge
    activation of, 519–520
    ambivalence and, 95
    attitude accessibility and, 90, 92
    attitude-behavior consistency and, 109, 111, 112, 114
    attitude change and, 101, 102–103, 104
    attitude extremity and, 96
    attitudes and, 83–84
    complexity and, 84, 97

Working memory
    explicit attitudes and, 553, 557, 564, 566, 567
    implicit attitudes and, 553, 557

Y

Yale communication and attitude change program, 344–348, 619–620

Yes/no questions, bias towards yes, 42, 43

Yielding, 347–348, 622